INSIDE

3D STUDIO MAX® 2

VOLUME ONE

STEVEN ELLIOTT
PHILLIP MILLER

JEFFREY ABOUAF

DAVE ESPINOSA-AGUILAR

STEVEN ALEXANDER

DOUG BARNARD

PAUL KAKERT

DAVE KALWICK

KEVIN KELM

MICHAEL KOCH

MARK WILLIAMSON

COVER ART BY STEVE BURKE

New Riders Publishing, Indianapolis, Indiana

Inside 3D Studio MAX 2 Volume I

By Steven Elliot, Phillip Miller, Jeffrey Abouaf, Dave Espinosa-Aguilar, Steve Alexander, Doug Barnard, Paul Kakert, Dave Kalwick, Kevin Kelm, Michael Koch, and Mark Williamson

Published by:
New Riders Publishing
201 West 103rd Street
Indianapolis, IN 46290 USA

© 1998 New Riders Publishing

Printed in the United States of America 1 2 3 4 5 6 7 8 9 0

Library of Congress Cataloging-in-Publication Data: 97-80887

ISBN: 1-56205-857-6

Warning and Disclaimer

PUBLISHER	Jordan Gold
EXECUTIVE EDITOR	Alicia Buckley
MANAGING EDITOR	Brice Gosnell

DEVELOPMENT EDITORS
Laura Frey
Naomi Goldman

PROJECT EDITOR
Katie Purdum

COPY EDITORS
Michael Brumitt
San Dee Phillips

TECHNICAL EDITORS
Mark Gerhard
Larry Minton

SOFTWARE PRODUCT DEVELOPER
Patty Brooks

TEAM COORDINATOR
Michelle Newcomb

BOOK DESIGNERS
Dan Armstrong
Glenn Larsen
Louisa Klucznik

COVER DESIGNER
Dan Armstrong

COVER ILLUSTRATION
Steve Burke

GRAPHICS IMAGE SPECIALISTS
Wil Cruz
Steve Adams
Sadie Crawford
Tammy Graham
Oliver Jackson

PRODUCTION TEAM
Carol Bowers
Mona Brown
Julie Geeting
Ayanna Lacey
Gene Redding
Elizabeth San Miguel

INDEXERS
CJ East
Becky Hornyak

Trademark Acknowledgments

All terms mentioned in this book that are known to be trademarks or service marks have been appropriately capitalized. New Riders Publishing cannot attest to the accuracy of this information. Use of a term in this book should not be regarded as affecting the validity of any trademark or service mark. Studio MAX 2 is a registered trademark of KINETIX.

Dedications

Doug Barnard - To Oakie and Dooley, the faithful Render Dogs.

Dave Espinosa-Aguilar - I would like to dedicate my chapters to Jeremy Hubbell and Andy Murdock. My revisionary work with this edition was entirely based on their previous efforts, and both did a fantastic job with the previous edition's content.

Paul Kakert - To infinity, or damn close.

Acknowledgements

Jeffrey Abouaf - I would like to extend special thanks to those individuals and and companies who graciously contributed product and support to me for this project, in particular, LaVina Larkey and Digimation, Inc., David Schmidt and Animation Science, Inc., Dan Ambrosi and Lightscape Technologies, Inc., Dolores at REM Infographica, and Kinetix. Thank you for your fine contributions to 3DS MAX R2 and to this industry.

David Kalwick - I would like to thank my wonderful wife and best friend, Marilyn, and the two most beautiful daughters this world has ever seen, Nicole and Megan, for their support and patience through this project. I would also like to thank New Riders and Kinetix for their expediency in making this project possible. (No polygons were harmed in the making of this product.)

About the Authors

Jeffrey Abouaf is a fine artist and designer, working in 3D graphics/animation for online and television projects. He reports on events and products for various industry publications, including *CyberEdge, Information Services*, and the *Spectrum*. He teaches 2D and 3D graphics applications, and he is currently teaching 3DS MAX at the San Francisco State University Multimedia Studies Program. He recently completed online tutorials for Kinetix for 3D Studio MAX Release 2.0, and is a contributing author on the upcoming revision to the Inside 3DS MAX series. He can be reached at **Ogle cg/fa**, mail to: **jabouaf@ogle.com**; **http://www.ogle.com**.

Dave Espinosa-Aguilar is a project manager, programmer, and animator for Toxic Frog Multimedia, Inc. A graduate in electrical engineering and physics of Gonzaga University, Dave has been training architects and engineers for 13 years on 3D modeling and visualization. Dave served as President of Autodesk User Group International in 1996 and has been a regular faculty member of AutoCAD, Animator, and 3D Studio courses offered at Autodesk University, A/E/C Systems, MechanCAD, and other Multimedia/CAD conferences. In his spare time, Dave also does product support for Autodesk on CompuServe's AMMEDIA, KINETIX, and ACAD forums.

Steven Alexander is an instructor at several universities in the New York City area. He is an Assistant Professor at The Pratt Institute in Brooklyn, New York, and teaches at the Pratt Manhattan campus. He can also be found teaching at the College of Aeronautics in Queens, New York. Steve teaches animation using 3D Studio MAX, and he is co-author of the *XtraActive MAX Tutorials*. Steve has also beta-tested RadioRay and MAX 2.0. When he is not preparing for classes, he can be found in his living room in Long Island, playing jazz guitar to his wife and two daughters.

Doug Barnard has been a freelance modeler/animator for the past ten years, and is a contributing editor for *DV* magazine. His studio, Virtual Acreage, supplies visuals for the game, architecture, and entertainment industries of the greater Los Angeles area. Current projects include an architectural flythru for a major record label and cut scene animation for a fantasy strategy game.

When not hammering away at the keyboard, Doug's idea of a good time is to paddle off to some hot springs in his homemade sea kayak with his wife. His project for next summer is to use MAX to design a sea kayak based on the art of HR Giger. He spends most weeknights training in the martial art of aikido, in which he holds the rank of shodan (1st degree black belt). He can be reached at **dbarnard@ virtualacreage.com**, or his Web site: **http://virtualacreage.com**.

Paul Kakert is founder and president of Fresh Look Design, Inc., a multimedia-3D animation company based in Davenport, Iowa. His company does business as Forensic Media, offering visualization services for litigation. Primarily an animator, he is also a contributing writer for *3D Artist* magazine, he wrote a chapter on forensic animation for *Inside 3D Studio MAX Volume III: Animation*, and he teaches 3D Studio MAX at Maycrest University in Davenport, Iowa. To find out more about Paul and his company, visit their Web site at **www.forensicmedia.com**.

David Kalwick is the Director of 3D Animation for Pacific Multimedia Productions in sunny San Diego, California. David's focus has been on producing animation for the medical and pharmaceutical marketplace. David has produced broadcast animation, most recently for the Emmy '97 Nominations Reel for the 23rd Annual Southwestern Area Emmy Awards broadcast. David is also author of *3D Graphics Tips, Tricks, and Techniques*, published by AP Professional. David can be reached via email at **dkalwick@worldnet.att.net**.

Kevin Kelm is a freelance animator currently located in Calgary, Alberta. Kevin went to school at the University of Calgary and Applied Multimedia Training Centers. He started out as a traditional artist and moved on to computer art several years ago, starting with 3D Studio R3 and Photoshop. He has produced sales and training videos for various companies and currently does some architectural rendering of interiors and exteriors. He mainly uses 3D Studio MAX as well as Rhino 3D and SoftImage. You can view his Web site at **http://www.nucleus.com/~kckelm**.

Michael Koch is a longtime 3D Studio MAX user and has worked as a freelancer for several game projects in Germany, where he currently lives. He is writing articles for both *digitalproduction* and *3D Artist* magazines. Today he is nearing completion of a BS in physics in Mainz, Germany.

Mark Williamson is a freelance 3D Studio instructor who has been teaching the program since R1 for DOS. He is responsible for the design and maintenance of the 3D Studio KTC program at San Francisco State University's downtown Multimedia center. He has been one of five Kinetix Training Specialists for the last two years, teaching dealers and in-house employees for Kinetix. He has trained worldwide, bringing the power of MAX to advertising agencies, game producers, architects, lawyers, doctors, and corporate clients. He currently runs Animatix of Tiburon, CA, managing contract projects and acting as tech support for subcontractors on those projects. He also runs the San Francisco 3D Studio Users Group (**http://www.sf3dsug.com**) as a resource for skills enhancement and job location.

Contents at a Glance

Table of Contents

Part V: Lighting and Cameras

17 Lighting in MAX

Introduction

INTRODUCTION

Inside 3D Studio MAX 2 Volume I is a companion to the excellent User's Guide and Tutorials that ship with 3DS MAX. This book adds greater detail to the new and sophisticated concepts that you must master. Inside 3D Studio MAX 2 also demonstrates techniques and strategies for accomplishing effects that will help you to produce more and better results.

Inside 3D Studio MAX 2 will help you get more out of the program, regardless of your current experience level. If you are new to using 3DS MAX, you will find this book to be a valuable next step on the learning curve after you work through the documentation included with the software.

If you are an intermediate or advanced user of 3DS MAX, you will find that this book provides many fresh insights and tips that you can add to your professional toolkit.

Getting the Most from *Inside 3D Studio MAX 2 Volume I*

As previously stated, *Inside 3D Studio MAX 2 Volume I* is a companion to the documentation that ships with the 3DS MAX program, not a replacement. The best approach to getting the most out of 3DS MAX is to make sure that you have at least lightly read the User's Guide volumes and performed the tutorials. The 3DS MAX documentation provides the foundation on which *Inside 3D Studio MAX 2* is built.

Two approaches are available for using *Inside 3D Studio MAX 2*. One is to just sit down and read it. Several figures are included to illustrate techniques and discussions in the book. In addition, you will find figures for the major steps in the examples so that you can simply read the examples and pick up the important concepts.

A better method for using *Inside 3D Studio MAX 2*, however, is to try working through the examples at your computer. To expect you to sit at your computer while reading the sections between the examples is unrealistic. Therefore, here is one possible strategy. Read one or two chapters at your leisure away from the computer. While reading, mark the examples or techniques that you have trouble visualizing. After completing one or two chapters, go to your computer and try the examples for those chapters. Refer to the marks you made while reading and manually work through those techniques. By using this method, you can maximize your comfort while reading in your favorite chair and maximize your productivity at the computer.

Using the 3D Studio MAX Documentation with This Book

To save time and maximize the value you receive from this book, a strong effort has been made to avoid repeating information that you could get from the 3DS MAX documentation. Although it is not possible to avoid repetition completely, you will find that the majority of the information *Inside 3D*

Studio MAX 2 Volume I presents is either a completely new strategy for using 3DS MAX or information that builds upon concepts and functions that were only introduced or lightly covered in the documentation.

This approach assumes you are partially familiar with the information in the 3D Studio MAX documentation. Sometimes you will encounter a reference to a description or tutorial in the 3D Studio MAX documentation while reading this book. You need not be familiar with the referenced information to proceed, but it will help. You can use references from *Inside 3D Studio MAX 2 Volume I* to help identify portions of the documentation that you missed or forgot about and then return to the 3DS MAX documentation and review the appropriate sections.

Organization of the Book

Inside 3D Studio MAX 2 Volume I is organized in seven parts:

Part 1   Core Concepts of 3DS MAX R2, Chapters 1 and 2

Part 2   Design Theory for Animators, Chapters 3 through 6

Part 3   Modeling, Chapters 7 through 13

Part 4   Materials and Maps, Chapters 14 through 16

Part 5   Lighting and Cameras, Chapters 17 through 19

Part 6   Animation, Chapters 20 through 26

Part 7   Rendering and Compositing, Chapters 27 through 30

Part 1 covers issues of setting up and configuring 3D Studio MAX 2 and file management techniques. The chapters in this section provide a framework for using 3DS MAX. By the end of this section, you will have arranged all of your tools and prepared them for use.

Part 2 delves into the concepts of perspective, color, motion, and some universal techniques that are common to most tasks that you perform with 3DS MAX. The chapters in this section cover the design basics you will need to know before you get started working in MAX.

Part 3 contains the details for creating and modifying models. It covers all the modeling methods including modeling with patches, meshes, and the new modeling tool, NURBS.

Part 4 concentrates on defining the materials for surfaces. It covers Map types, Material types, Map channels, and mapping for materials. The part also covers the additional flexibility of the Material editor.

Part 5 gets into the all-important topic of lighting and cameras in your scenes. These chapters cover the major aspects of lighting your scenes, placing and animating cameras, and setting up the environment.

Part 6 relates specifically to animation. Rather than describe what can be animated, this section explores how to control animation. It contains coverage of particles, space warps, animation utilities, and MAXScript.

Part 7 concludes by detailing the methods for getting the incredible images created in 3DS MAX to print, video, or film.

How to Read the Examples

Unlike most tutorials that you read, the *Inside 3D Studio MAX 2* examples do not rigidly dictate every step you perform to achieve the desired result. These examples are designed to be flexible and to work with a wide range of situations. The benefits you receive from this approach include

- A better understanding of the concepts because you must think through the example rather than blindly follow the minutiae of many steps.

- A stronger capability to apply the examples to your own work.

Most exercises begin with some explanatory text as shown in the following sample exercise. The text tells you what the exercise should accomplish and sets the context for the exercise.

You may encounter text such as this at the beginning of or in the middle of an exercise when one or more actions require an extended explanation.

SAMPLE EXAMPLE FORMAT

1. Numbered steps identify your actions to complete the exercise.

Additional text adds extra explanation about the previous step when it is needed.

Because this book is designed for people who already have some experience with 3D Studio, some exercise steps are implied rather than explicitly stated. You may, for example, find yourself instructed to "Create a smooth, 20-segment sphere with a radius of 100 units," rather than reading all the steps required to create the sphere.

Exercises and the CD-ROM

Some of the examples and exercises use files that are included on the *Inside 3D Studio MAX 2 Volume I* CD-ROM. Example files are located in the projects folder and are organized by chapter on the CD-ROM. Instructions on how to use the CD-ROM files or how to install them on your hard drive are described in the following section.

Using the *Inside 3D Studio MAX 2 Volume I* CD-ROM

Inside 3D Studio MAX 2 Volume I comes with a CD-ROM packed with many megabytes of texture maps, demos, plug-ins, and other sample software. The files can be used directly from the *Inside 3D Studio MAX 2 Volume I* CD-ROM or you may want to copy files from the CD-ROM to your hard drive or another storage device. In that case, you can use the CD-ROM install routine or copy the files directly to a directory on your hard disk. A number of sample scenes and several megabytes of texture maps are provided on the CD-ROM for your use. These scenes and texture maps are licensed free for use in your animations. You cannot, however, resell or otherwise distribute the files.

Installing the Example Files

Example files not included with 3D Studio MAX are contained in a single subdirectory on the *Inside 3D Studio MAX 2 Volume I* CD-ROM: projects. You can access these files directly from the CD-ROM when you execute the examples or you can run the install routine by double-clicking setup.exe. Some of the example files require maps from the CD-ROM that ships with 3D Studio MAX. You will need to copy these files to a subdirectory that is referenced in the 3DS MAX Map-Paths parameter. See Chapter 6, "Planning Your Projects," for details on setting your map paths.

3DS MAX automatically looks for map files in the directory from which a scene file is loaded. If you copy the example files to your hard drive, make sure you keep the mesh files and map files together or at least put the map files in a directory where 3D Studio can find them at rendering time. Details about organizing and managing map files are also presented in Chapter 5.

Using CompuServe and the Web

The CompuServe Information Service is an online, interactive network that you can access with a modem and special access software. The most important feature of this service (at least as far as this book is concerned) is the KINETIX forum.

The KINETIX forum is an area of CompuServe that is maintained by Kinetix for the direct support of 3D Studio MAX and other Kinetix software. Hundreds of people from all over the world visit this forum daily to share ideas, ask and answer questions, and generally promote the use of 3D Studio MAX. If you ask a question on the forum, you are as likely to receive an answer from one of the original programmers as you are to receive an answer from any number of other 3D Studio MAX artists. And every question, from the most basic to the most mind-bending puzzler, receives the same quick and courteous treatment.

Kinetix also maintains a site on the World Wide Web where you can get the latest information about 3DS MAX, future software releases, and plug-in development. You can also send questions and feedback direct to Kinetix and download software. The Kinetix web site is www.ktx.com.

New Riders Publishing

The staff of New Riders Publishing is committed to bringing you the very best in computer reference material. Each New Riders book is the result of months of work by authors and staff who research and refine the information contained within its covers.

As part of this commitment to you, the reader, New Riders invites your input. Please let us know if you enjoy this book, if you have trouble with the information and examples presented, or if you have a suggestion for the next edition.

Please note, however, that New Riders staff cannot serve as a technical resource for 3D Studio MAX or for questions about software- or hardware-related problems. Please refer to the documentation that accompanies 3D Studio MAX or to the application's Help systems.

If you have a question or comment about any New Riders book, there are several ways to contact New Riders Publishing. We will respond to as many readers as we can. Your name, address, or phone number will never become part of a mailing list or be used for any purpose other than to help us continue to bring you the best books possible. You can write us at the following address:

New Riders Publishing
Attn: Alicia Buckley
201 W. 103rd Street
Indianapolis, IN 46290

If you prefer, you can fax New Riders Publishing at 317-817-7070.

The Three Volume Set

Inside 3D Studio MAX 2 Volume I is actually the first of a three volume set. Due to the robust nature of 3DS MAX, New Riders is dedicated to bringing users detailed, top-quality information on all the features and functions of the software. Although *Inside 3D Studio MAX 2 Volume I* is a complete tutorial and reference, we are publishing two more volumes to provide in-depth, advanced information on modeling, Material editor, and animation not available anywhere else. These volumes will be presented in the favorite *Inside* style, packed full of detailed tutorials and valuable tips and techniques from industry experts to take you to the next level after mastering *Inside 3D Studio MAX 2 Volume I*. *Volume II: Modeling and Material Editor* and *Volume III: Animation* will be published in early 1998.

Part I

CORE CONCEPTS OF 3D STUDIO MAX R2

Chapter 1

Basic Concepts of 3D Studio MAX

3D Studio MAX is a radically new approach to 3D modeling and rendering. The underlying concepts and methods of how 3D Studio MAX manages objects and data in your scene are expanded beyond earlier versions of 3D Studio and other 3D modeling programs. These concepts and methods also must be understood if you are to be fully productive with 3DS MAX.

In Release 2 of Max, the core has been changed only to make it more intuitive and powerful for the new user, while these same core concepts will enable the Max 1.0 user to evolve to the next level of proficiency.

Concepts covered in this chapter include the following:

- Object-oriented behavior and the basic 3D Studio MAX object types

- Definition of sub-objects and how to access them

- Object dataflow and how it affects your modeling process

- Using transforms and modifiers, and how they differ

- Copies, instances, and references, and how they behave

- How 3D Studio MAX uses hierarchical organization

- How 3D Studio MAX defines and controls animation

- How 3D Studio MAX defines and uses materials

- MAXScript and its applications

- Description of plug-ins and how to organize them

Concepts of 3DS MAX Objects

The term object is used repeatedly throughout 3DS MAX; it is an object-oriented program. Looking at 3DS MAX in programming terms, everything you create is an object. The geometry, cameras, and lights in your scene are objects. Modifiers are also objects, as are animation controllers, bitmaps, and material definitions. You can manipulate many objects, such as meshes, splines, and modifiers, at a sub-object level.

For the purposes of this book, the term "object" refers to anything you can select and manipulate in 3DS MAX. When extra clarity is needed, the term "scene object" is used to differentiate geometry and anything created using the Create panel from other object types. Scene objects include lights, cameras, space warps, and helper objects. Other objects are referred to by specific type, such as modifiers, maps, keys, and controllers. The following sections explain object-oriented behavior in 3DS MAX.

Object-Oriented Behavior

What is meant when it is said that 3DS MAX is an object-oriented program? Object-Oriented Programming (OOP) is a sophisticated approach to writing software and is currently becoming widely adopted in the design of commercial software. From your point of view as a 3DS MAX user, the most important aspect of object-oriented programming is how it affects the user interface.

When you create objects in 3DS MAX, they carry information about which functions can be performed on them and what is considered valid behavior for each object. This information affects what you see in the 3DS MAX interface. Only operations that are valid for the selected object are active; other operations become inactive and are grayed out or hidden in the interface.

Consider the following examples of object-oriented behavior:

■ Create a sphere and click the Modify panel to apply a modifier to the sphere. Notice that the Extrude and Lathe modifiers are inactive. This occurs because Extrude and Lathe are invalid operations for a sphere. Only Shape objects can use the Extrude or Lathe modifiers. Figure 1.1 shows how the Modify panel changes when a sphere primitive is selected as compared to when a shape is selected.

FIGURE 1.1

The Modify panel for a selected sphere primitive and for a circle shape.

■ Let's say you are creating a loft object and want to select a loft shape. After you click the Get Shape button, the cursor changes as you move over objects in your scene to indicate which objects are valid choices for the loft shape. Only shape objects meeting certain requirements are valid choices for the Get Shape operation. Figure 1.2 shows the appearance of the Get Shape cursor when it is over a valid path shape.

In both of the previous examples, 3DS MAX queries the objects to determine which choices and operations are valid based on the current program state. 3DS MAX then presents only those valid choices.

FIGURE 1.2
The Get Shape cursor as it appears when placed over a valid path shape.

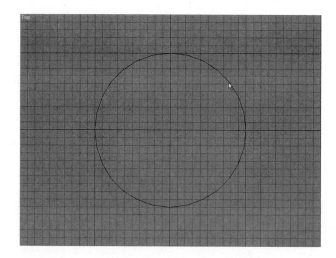

This seemingly simple concept enhances productivity and saves a considerable amount of time. Compare this capability of 3DS MAX to older programs in which after selecting objects or executing commands, you are confronted by an error message stating that the selected object or operation is invalid.

The downside of this method is that if you're the sort of person who learns software by just poking around and seeing what happens, you may never find certain tools because the buttons will only appear when certain objects are selected.

Parametric Objects

Most objects in 3DS MAX are a form of parametric object. A parametric object is defined by a collection of settings, or parameters, rather than by an explicit description of its form. For example, let's examine two methods to define a sphere—one non-parametric and the other parametric.

- **Parametric sphere:** This preserves the parameters of the radius, and the number of segments, and displays a representation of the sphere based on the current value of the parameters. The parametric definition of the sphere is stored as the radius and number of segments. You can change and even animate these parameters at any time.

■ **Non-parametric sphere (Editable mesh):** This takes a radius and a number of segments and uses that information to create an explicit surface out of vertices and faces. The definition of the sphere only exists as a collection of faces. The radius and segment information are not retained. If you want to change the radius, you must scale the sphere. If you want to change the number of segments, you must delete the sphere and create a new one.

Figure 1.3 shows the base parameters for a parametric sphere and for a sphere imported as an explicit editable mesh.

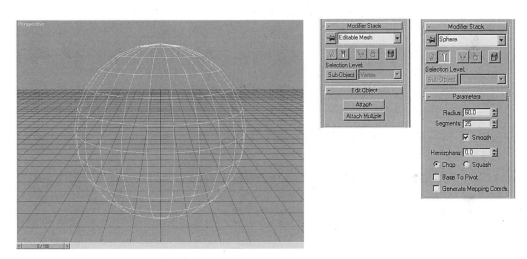

FIGURE 1.3

Base parameters for a parametric sphere and an editable mesh sphere.

Parametric objects provide considerable modeling and animation options. In the best of all worlds, you would want to preserve the parametric definition of an object as long as possible. Some 3DS MAX operations convert parametric objects to non-parametric, which is sometimes called explicit objects or editable meshes. If your modeling techniques are based on face extrusion and vertex manipulation, you're probably going to be working on non-parametric objects.

Fortunately, many operations do not discard an object's parametric properties. Examples of operations that discard parameters include the following:

- Attaching objects to each other using one of the Edit modifiers.

- Collapsing an object's Modifier Stack.

- Converting an object to a NURBS surface.

- Exporting objects to a different file format. In this case, only objects in the exported file lose their parametric properties. The original objects in the 3DS MAX scene are unaffected.

Perform these operations only when reasonably sure that you no longer need to adjust the parameters of the affected objects.

TIP

If you save a version of the object using Save Selected with the objects uncollapsed and the parameters intact, you can merge in the parametric objects if needed later.

Compound Objects

In the Create panel, you can combine two or more objects to create a new parametric object, called a compound object. The important concept to keep in mind about compound objects is that you can still modify and change the parameters of the objects that make up the compound object. A compound object is a type of parametric object in which the parameters include the objects being combined and the description of how the objects are combined.

Examine a Boolean operation, for example, in which you subtract a sphere from the corner of a box (see Figure 1.4). When using many 3D programs, the result of this operation is an explicit mesh that represents the Boolean solution. If you want to change the position of the box or the radius of the sphere, you must create a new box and sphere, and perform the Boolean operation again.

TIP

Although you can create objects with many Boolean objects, it's more stable to collapse these to an editable mesh.

FIGURE 1.4

A box and sphere, and the result of a simple Boolean subtraction.

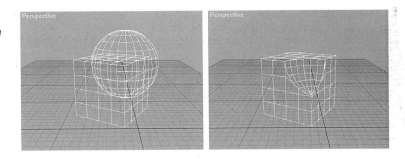

The box and the sphere are preserved as part of the parametric compound Boolean object. You can still access and animate the parameters of the box and the sphere, as well as animate their relative positions. Figure 1.5 shows the result of changing the length of the box and the radius of the sphere for the compound Boolean object, shown earlier in Figure 1.4.

FIGURE 1.5

The result of changing the length of the box and the radius of the sphere of a compound Boolean object.

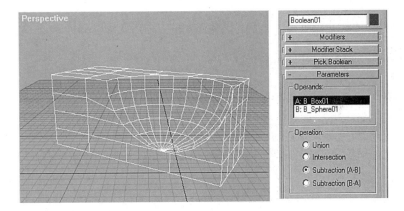

3DS MAX ships with seven standard compound objects:

- Boolean objects
- Morph objects
- Conform objects
- Scatter objects
- Connect objects
- ShapeMerge objects
- Loft objects

Sub-Objects

The term sub-object refers to any component of something that can be selected and manipulated. A common example of a sub-object is one of the faces that make up a mesh. In an editable mesh, you can select a sub-object, such as a face, and then move, rotate, collapse, or delete it. In a parametric object, you can apply an Edit Mesh modifier to do the same.

It is easy to think of sub-objects as vertices or faces, but the concept extends to many other things beyond scene objects. Examples of sub-objects you can manipulate in 3DS MAX include the following:

- Vertices, segments, and splines of shape objects

- Vertices, edges, and faces of mesh objects

- Vertices, edges, and patches of patch objects

- Shapes and paths of loft objects

- Operands of Boolean objects

- Targets of morph objects

- Gizmos, centers, control points, lattices, of modifiers

- Keys of motion trajectories

- Control vertices, control points, surfaces, curves, and imports of NURBS objects

In turn, many of the preceding sub-objects have their own sub-objects, thus creating situations in which multiple layers of sub-object editing can be performed. Imagine animating the parameters of a modifier applied to a sub-object selection of vertices from a mesh object, which itself is a sub-object operand of a Boolean object. The depth of 3DS MAX is limited only by your imagination.

In all of the previous examples, you access sub-objects by clicking a Sub-Object button in a command panel. Clicking this button puts you into a sub-object mode, restricted to working with a specific type of sub-object until you turn off the mode. Figure 1.6 shows two examples of sub-object selections and the corresponding sub-object button in the related command panel.

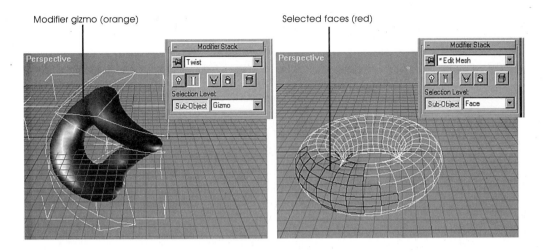

FIGURE 1.6

Sub-object selections of a modifier gizmo and selected mesh faces.

With the addition of NURBS Modeling in Max R2, you have several fundamentally different ways of approaching geometry creation and manipulation at your disposal. NURBS surfaces, Parametric objects, Editable Meshes, and patches each have unique qualities and advantages that you will discover as you work with each. Of course, you can still loft objects as in the original 3D Studio. In the next section, we'll look at the fundamentals of scene object creation.

Concepts of Scene Object Creation

Your first actions with 3D Studio MAX are the creation of scene objects that you later animate and render. When you create a scene object, you are creating a process that defines how the parameters of a basic object are modified, transformed, warped, assigned properties, and finally displayed in your scene. This process is called the dataflow and understanding the dataflow is critical to understanding how 3DS MAX behaves.

The following sections describe each of the components of the dataflow individually—master object, modifiers, transforms, space warps, and properties—with the "Object Dataflow" section explaining how all of the components come together to place an object in your scene.

Master Object

Master object is the term that refers to the parameters of an original object you create, using functions from the Create panel. This master object can be thought of as an abstract definition of an object that does not exist in your scene until the entire dataflow has been evaluated. The master object is just the first step.

The master object provides the following information about an object:

- The object type, such as a sphere, camera, loft, or patch. The object type is what you see at the bottom of the Modifier Stack or next to the Object container in Track View.

- The object parameters, such as the length, width, and height of a box. The object parameters are visible when the master object is selected in the Modifier Stack and when you expand the object container in Track View.

- The origin and orientation of the object's local coordinate system. The local coordinate system defines the origin of the object, the orientation of the object, and the coordinate space used to locate the sub-objects within the object. This definition of origin, orientation, and space is referred to as the object space.

Figure 1.7 shows an object with its master object properties identified. As you will learn in the section "Creating Instances," later in this chapter, more than one object in your scene can use the same master object.

Object Modifiers

After you create a master object, you can apply any number of Object Modifiers, such as Bend or Stretch. Modifiers manipulate sub-objects, such as vertices, with respect to the object's local origin and coordinate system. In other words, modifiers change the structure of an object in object space.

Because modifiers operate on sub-objects in object space, they have the following characteristics:

- Modifiers are independent of the object's location and orientation in the scene. The top pair of objects in Figure 1.8 show that a Bend is not affected if the object is moved or rotated. Both objects have the same form and same amount of bend regardless of where they are in the scene.

■ Modifiers are dependent on the order of other modifiers and the structure of the object at the time they are applied. The middle pair of
objects in Figure 1.8 show the result of changing modifier order. Both
objects have Bend and Stretch modifiers applied, but the order of
application is reversed.

FIGURE 1.7
*Identifying master
object properties.*

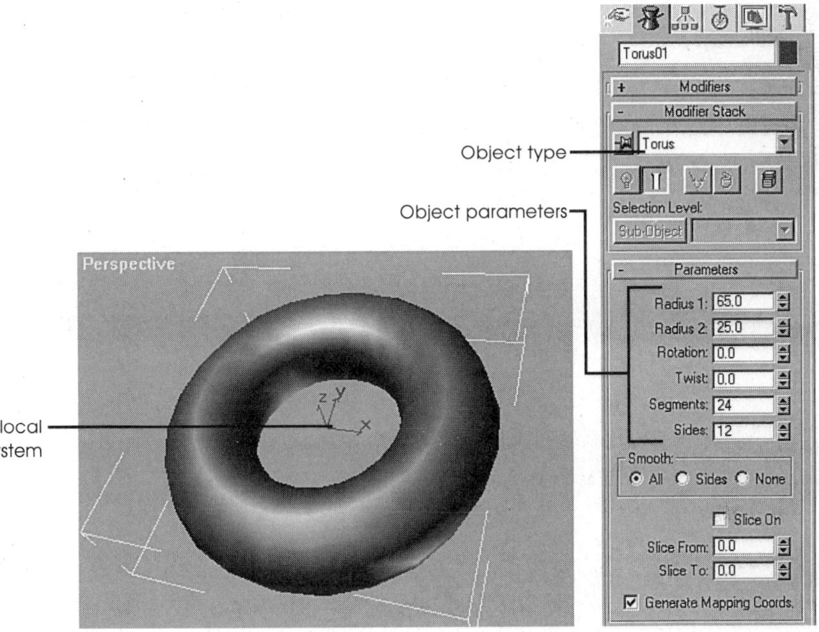

Object type

Object parameters

Object's local
coordinate system

NEW TO R2

3D Studio MAX 2 enables you cut and paste the modifiers both within the stack and to other
objects.

■ Modifiers can be applied to the entire object or to a partial selection of
sub-objects. The bottom pair of objects in Figure 1.8 show a Twist
applied to the full object on the left and to a sub-object selection of only
the upper-half of the object on the right.

Think of modifiers as your primary modeling tool because you have control
over the order in which modifiers are applied. Also, the effect of a modifier
on an object is consistent regardless of where the object is located.

FIGURE 1.8

*Characteristics of
Object Modifiers.*

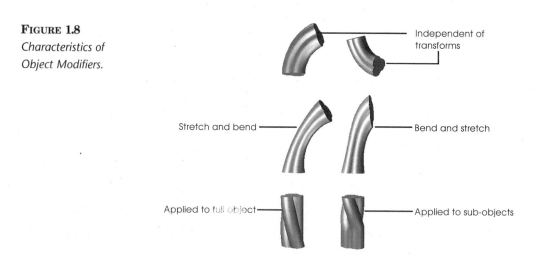

Independent of
transforms

Stretch and bend

Bend and stretch

Applied to full object

Applied to sub-objects

Object Transforms

You can position and orient objects using transforms. When you transform an object, you are changing its position, orientation, and size with respect to the scene. The coordinate system that describes the entire scene is called world space. The world space coordinate system defines the global origin of the scene and a set of global coordinate axes that never change.

Object Transforms define the following information:

- Position defines the distance of an object's local origin from the world space origin. Position might define, for example, that an object's origin is 40 units to the right (X=40), 25 units above (Z=25), and 15 units behind (Y=15) the world origin.

- Rotation defines the orientation between an object's local coordinate axes and the world coordinate axes. Rotation can define, for instance, that an object's local coordinate axes are rotated 45 degrees about the world y-axis, 0 degrees about the world x-axis, and 15 degrees about the world z-axis.

- Scale defines the relative size between an object's local axes and the world axes. For example, scale might define an object's local space measurements, which are scaled by 200 percent in world space. Therefore, a cube might have parameters that specify a size of 40 units to a side, but because the cube was scaled 200 percent, it measures 80 units to a side in the scene.

The combination of position, rotation, and scale is called the object's transformation matrix. Notice that it is this matrix that you are changing when you transform a complete object. Figure 1.9 shows how transforms define an object's location in world space. The teapot in Figure 1.9 has been moved, rotated, and non-uniformly scaled 25 percent along the objects local y-axis.

FIGURE 1.9

Transforms define an object's location in world space.

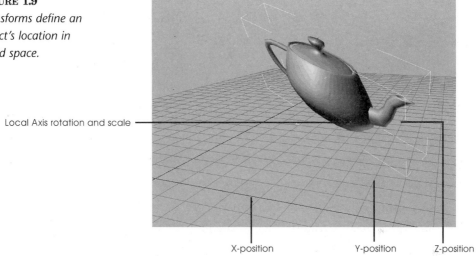

Local Axis rotation and scale

X-position   Y-position   Z-position

Object transforms have the following characteristics:

- They define an object's location and orientation in the scene.

- They affect the entire object.

- They are calculated after all modifiers have been calculated.

This last point is particularly important. It does not matter whether you apply modifiers first and then transform the object, or transform the object first and then apply modifiers. The transforms are always calculated after the modifiers.

TIP

If you want the transforms to calculate before the modifiers use a XForm (transform) modifier, which is the preferred method. 3D studio MAX 2 gives you a warning message each time you apply a non-uniform scale transform just to teach you this. (You can turn this message off in Preferences, General, UI Display).

Space Warps

A space warp is an object that can affect other objects based on their location in world space. You might think of space warps as combining the effects of modifiers and transforms. Like modifiers, space warps can change the internal structure of an object, but the effect of a space warp is determined by how you transform the affected object around the scene.

Quite often you will find identical effects implemented as both modifiers and as space warps. For example, look at the Ripple modifier compared to the Ripple space warp. Figure 1.10 shows a Ripple modifier and a Ripple space warp applied to identical objects. The parameters for both the modifier version and the space warp version are similar. The main difference is the way in which the two versions of Ripple act on an object. The Ripple modifier is directly applied to the object on the left and does not change as the object moves around the scene. The Ripple space warp exists as an independent object and the object on the right is bound to it. The effect of the Ripple space warp changes as the bound object moves through the scene. Notice that moving the object has no effect on the Ripple modifier, but moving the object bound to the Ripple space warp has a great effect.

Use a modifier when you want to apply an effect that is local to an object and the effect is dependent on other modifiers in the dataflow. You usually use modifiers for modeling operations. Use a space warp when you want to use an effect that can be global to many objects and the effect is dependent on the objects' locations in the scene. Use space warps to simulate environmental effects and external forces.

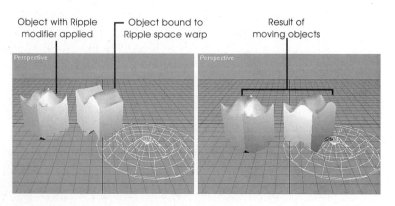

Object with Ripple modifier applied

Object bound to Ripple space warp

Result of moving objects

FIGURE 1.10
Comparing modifiers to space warps.

Object Properties

All objects have unique properties that are neither base object parameters nor the result of modifiers or transforms. These properties include such things as the object's name, wireframe color, assigned material, and shadow casting capability. Most of an object's properties can be displayed or set using the Object Properties dialog (see Figure 1.11). To display the Object Properties dialog, select an object and then right-click it.

FIGURE 1.11

The Object Properties dialog box.

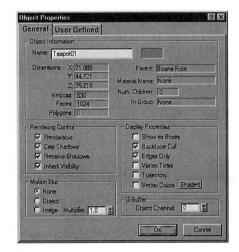

The Object Dataflow

Modifiers, transforms, space warps, and object properties come together in the object dataflow to define and display an object in your scene. The object dataflow works like a set of assembly instructions. Each step is completed in the proper order before the next step is begun. The object dataflow steps are as follows:

1. The master object defines the object type and holds the values you set in the object parameters.

2. Modifiers alter the object in Object Space and are evaluated according to the order in which you applied them.

3. Transforms locate the object in the scene.

4. Space warps alter the object based on the result of the transforms.

5. Object properties identify the object name and other characteristics.

6. The object appears in your scene.

Figure 1.12 illustrates this sequence of object dataflow steps and its effect on a sphere.

FIGURE 1.12

The object dataflow.

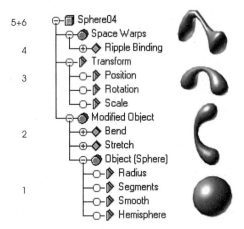

The object appears in the viewport, displayed by the interactive renderer. The object appearance in the finished image or animation is created with a combination of lighting, cameras, materials, and composite effects that go beyond the geometric definitions. Many of these are also displayed in the viewport, but some are not.

The power of 3D Studio MAX lies in the number of choices available to you to animate and create. Animating the parameters and the gizmo of the modifiers, space warps, or the objects themselves offers countless options to achieve any animation you want.

Concepts of Changing Objects

As you've read in the previous sections, a well-defined progression exists from the object parameters, through the modifiers, to the transforms, and finally ends with the space warp and object properties. Often you can achieve similar results by changing an object's parameters, applying modifiers, transforming the object, or even by using a space warp. Which method should you choose? Does it matter?

The answer is, "Yes, it does matter." The appropriate method for changing an object depends on the object dataflow, how the object is built, and what you plan to do with the object later. The knowledge to successfully make such a choice comes with practice and experience. The following sections provide general guidelines for determining the optimal method of changing your objects.

Changing Base Parameters versus Transforming

The earlier you make a change to an object in the dataflow, the greater the influence that change will have on the final appearance of the object. The very first information in the object dataflow is the set of object parameters; and if you want to change the basic size, shape, or surface characteristics of an object, you should look at those object parameters.

Consider the difference between changing the height parameter for a cylinder, for example, and applying a non-uniform scale along the cylinder's local z-axis. Imagine you have a cylinder that is 40 units tall and you want it to be 80 units tall. If you're not familiar with parametric modeling, you first might think of using non-uniform scale.

If you scale the cylinder 200 percent along its length, you get a cylinder that is 80 units tall, right? Well, not quite. If you examine the object parameters for the scaled cylinder, you see that the reported height is 40 units. What you really have is a cylinder that is 40 units tall with a 200 percent local z-axis scale. If you want a cylinder that is 80 units tall, you should change the height parameter rather than scaling the cylinder.

This change might seem like a subtle distinction, but it has a profound effect when you begin applying modifiers to the cylinder. Remember: In the object dataflow, transforms, such as scale, are calculated after the modifiers. Figure 1.13 illustrates the difference. The cylinder on the left had its height parameter changed from 40 units to 80 units and was then bent along the z-axis 180 degrees. The cylinder on the right was scaled 200 percent to reach a height of 80 units and then bent along the z-axis 180 degrees. Note that even though the scaling was performed before applying the bend, it is calculated in the dataflow after the bend, causing a non-uniform scale of the bent cylinder.

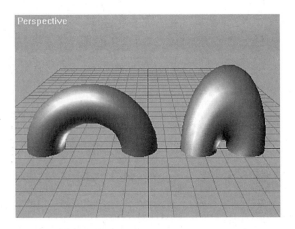

When changing an object parameter produces results similar to the results of transforming an object, use the following guides to determine which method to use:

- Change object parameters whenever you want to make a modeling change or a change that will be picked up by any modifiers.

- Transform an object when the transform effect is the last change you want to apply, or when the change is being used to affect the location of the object in your scene.

Modifying Objects

Use modifiers when you want to explicitly change the structure of an object and have the maximum amount of control over that change. Much of the modeling and animation capability of 3DS MAX is accessed through modifiers and their organization in the modifier stack.

Object parameters and object transforms affect the entire object only at the beginning or end of the dataflow. You can use modifiers to affect any portion of an object and apply changes that are dependent on their relationship to other modifiers in the stack.

For example, compare two arrangements for applying Bend and Twist modifiers to a box, as shown in Figure 1.14. If you bend the box first and then apply a twist, as for the object on the left, you get a much different result than if you twist the cylinder first and then apply a bend, as for the object on the right.

FIGURE 1.14

Comparing differences in modifier order.

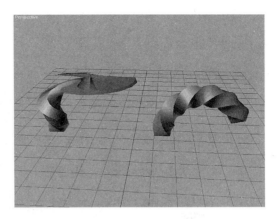

Because modifiers are so dependent on order, it is important that you plan your modeling strategy. Think about how you will approach a modeling job and the best way to combine modifiers. Your modeling plan does not need to be perfect, because 3DS MAX makes it easy to go back and change things if you change your mind. Developing a plan, however, can save you considerable time by avoiding the need to frequently backtrack as a result of trial and error.

Applying Transforms with Modifiers

At times you may need to apply a transform at a specific point in the modifier stack. You may need to scale a non-parametric object along a single axis before applying a Bend, for example. Other times you may need to move or rotate just a part of an object.

You can apply a transform at a specific point in the modifier stack, or to just a portion of an object, by using an XForm modifier to apply the transform. The following are three ways to apply transforms with modifiers:

■ Use one of the Edit modifiers to transform sub-objects. Edit modifiers provide access to the vertices, edges, and faces that make up various object types. Transforms that are applied with an Edit modifier cannot be animated. Figure 1.15 shows the result of scaling faces selected with an Edit Mesh modifier.

FIGURE 1.15

Transforms: scaling sub-objects with an Edit Mesh modifier.

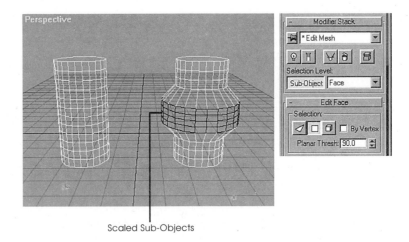

Scaled Sub-Objects

■ Transform the Gizmo or Center of a modifier. Modifiers contain their own sub-objects, called gizmos, and a center that can also be transformed. You can transform modifier sub-objects to rotate the orientation of a twist or move the center of a bend. Figure 1.16 shows the result of moving the center of a Bend modifier.

FIGURE 1.16

Transforms: moving the center of a Bend.

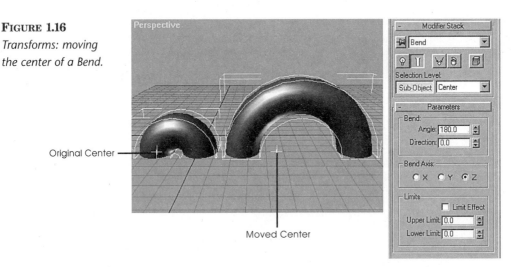

Original Center

Moved Center

■ Use a special XForm modifier. This modifier has no effect other than to supply a gizmo that you can use to transform objects and sub-objects within the modifier stack. Use an XForm modifier whenever you want a transform to occur at a specific point in the stack or when you want to animate the transforms of sub-objects selected with an Edit modifier. Figure 1.17 shows the result of moving the vertices of a spline with an XForm modifier.

FIGURE 1.17

Transforms: moving vertices with an XForm modifier.

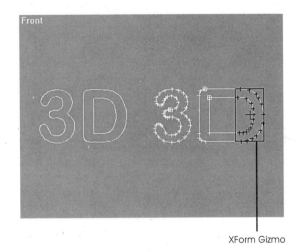

XForm Gizmo

NEW TO R2

In MAX 2, a slight change in concept around Edit Mesh and Editable mesh has been implemented. All non-parameterized meshes are Editable meshes, which have all the properties of Edit Mesh with the addition of all sub-objects having animation capabilites. If you intend to use an Edit Mesh modifier on an object, you will probably not go back down the stack to change anything because you will create unpredictable results. It is suggested then that you either convert to or collapse the stack to an Editable Mesh. Because the sub-objects of an Editable Mesh can be animated there is also less need for the XForm modifier

Cloning Objects

You can clone just about everything in 3DS MAX. Clone is a general purpose term used to describe the action of creating a copy, instance, or reference. Most objects, such as geometry, modifiers, and controllers, can be copied and instanced. Scene objects such as cameras, lights, and geometry also can be referenced.

The following list defines copies, instances, and references:

- **Copies.** Everything that defines an object is duplicated elsewhere in 3DS MAX. Once you copy something, the original object and its copy are independent.

- **Instances.** These describe the technique of using a single object definition in more than one place. Almost anything can be instanced in 3DS MAX. A single object, modifier, or controller can be used for many purposes in your scene.

- **References.** Available only for scene objects. A reference looks at the parameters of a master object and a selected number of modifiers before the dataflow splits, forming two objects that each contain its own set of unique modifiers. You can use references to build a family of similar objects that share the same basic definition, but each has its own unique characteristics.

You can choose from several methods to make clones. The method you choose to use will vary according to the type of object with which you are working. These methods include the following:

- Press the Shift key while transforming an object. Depending on the object, either a copy is made or a dialog appears where you choose to make a copy, instance, or reference. For example, pressing Shift while moving animation keys copies the keys. Pressing Shift while scaling a sphere displays the Clone Options dialog, where you can copy, instance, or reference the sphere.

- Choose Clone from the Edit menu. Use this method to clone scene objects without transforming them.

- Use Copy and Paste in Track View. When you paste a controller in Track View, you can choose to make a copy or instance of that controller.

- Use Drag and Drop. You can drag material and map definitions from one slot to another in the Material Editor. When you drop the material or map into a slot, the map is copied. You also can choose to make a copy or instance of the map.

Creating Copies

Create copies whenever you want to duplicate an object of which the duplicates are unique and have no relationship to the source object. Some examples of useful copy techniques include the following:

- Copy keys when you want to duplicate an action from one time of the animation to another time.

  For example, you might animate an object that quickly bends over and back again. To repeat that action at irregular times throughout an animation, you copy the original keys to different times.

- Copy controllers when you want the animated behavior of one object duplicated by another.

  For example, you may want many objects to follow the same path, but you plan to adjust each path controller so each object is in a slightly different location. To accomplish this, assign and set up a path controller for one object and then copy the controller to all of the remaining objects. You can then change the location of each object on the path, having saved yourself the task of assigning and setting up the controller for each object.

- Copy scene objects when you want to begin with a group of similar objects and then individually modify each one.

  You create a single flower, for example, and copy it repeatedly as part of a bouquet. You then change and modify the copies to give them each a unique "personality." When you copy a scene object, an entirely new dataflow is created for the copied object (see Figure 1.18).

- Copy and paste modifiers between different objects. You can also cut and paste modifiers to rearrange their order within the modifier stack.

FIGURE 1.18

Dataflow after copying a scene object.

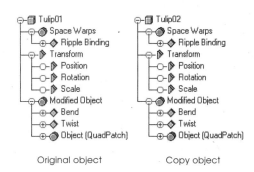

Original object   Copy object

Creating Instances

Create instances when you want to use a single object in more than one place. Because all of the instances are really the same object, changing one instance causes all of the instances to change. Instances can save considerable effort when used properly. Some examples of useful instance techniques include the following:

- You should instance modifiers when you want to apply the same effect to a selection of different objects.

  You could, for instance, create a scene in which a selection of objects stretches in unison. Begin by selecting all the objects and click Stretch in the Modify panel to apply an instance of the same modifier to all the objects. Changing the Stretch parameters for any object changes them all. Figure 1.19 shows the result of an instanced stretch modifier.

Normal   Stretched

FIGURE 1.19

Using an instanced Stretch modifier.

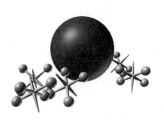

- You can instance controllers when you want a selection of objects to behave in exactly the same way.

  For example, you might model a set of window blinds and want to animate them tilting shut. You first animate the rotation of one slat and use Copy and Paste in Track View to assign an instance of the slat's rotation controller to all the other slats. Then, when you rotate one slat, all the others rotate the same amount. Figure 1.20 shows the result of using an instanced Rotation controller to open and close blinds.

- You can instance maps in the Material Editor when you want to use the same map in multiple map slots and maintain a precise registration.

  Let's say you want to design a ceramic tile material. You can use instances of a map to control the diffuse texture, bump, and shininess of the material. Changing the parameters for any instance of the map changes the parameters of all the maps and maintains registration. Figure 1.21 shows the result of using an instanced map to build a material.

FIGURE 1.20

Results of using an instanced Rotation controller.

Original image map   Diffuse mask

FIGURE 1.21

Using instanced maps.

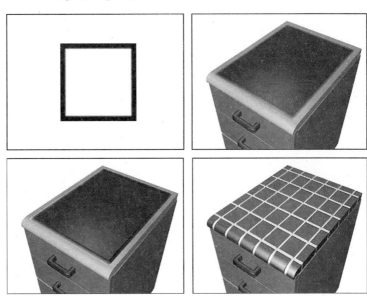

Bump map   Shininess map and tiling changed

First, the map is applied as a diffuse mask and then an instance of the map is applied as a bump map. Finally, another instance of the map is applied as a shininess map, and its tiling parameters are changed to create smaller tiles. Because diffuse, bump, and shininess are all instances of the same map, changing tiling for shininess also changes tiling for the other two.

■ You can instance scene objects when you want to place the same object in multiple locations in your scene. Modifying or changing the parameters of any instance changes all of the instances.

Here we'll work with a row of bottles on a grocery shelf. Model one bottle and fill the shelf with instances. When you change the design of one bottle, the other bottles also change. Figure 1.22 shows the result of using instance objects.

FIGURE 1.22

Using instanced scene objects.

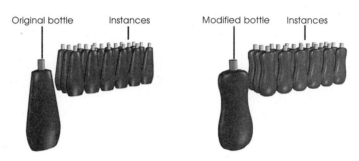

When you instance a scene object, all instances share the same dataflow from the master object through all of the modifiers. The dataflow branches after the modifiers, so each instance has its own set of transforms, space warps, and object properties. Figure 1.23 shows the dataflow for multiple instances.

FIGURE 1.23

Dataflow after instancing an object.

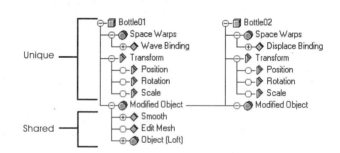

Creating References

Only scene objects can have references. Create references when you want multiple objects to share the same root parameters and modifiers, but also maintain the capability to further modify each object independently. Think of references as being a cross between copies and instances.

Let's say you want to animate a line of chess pawns. Each pawn must share the same root design but also must bend or stretch on its own. First, model the basic pawn and then make references. You can then modify each pawn independently or return to the basic model to change all the references. Figure 1.24 shows the result of using references.

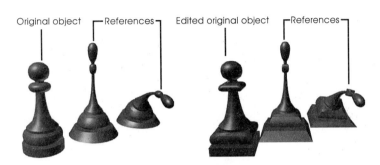

FIGURE 1.24

Using referenced scene objects.

When you reference a scene object, all references share the same master object and an initial set of modifiers. When the reference is made, the dataflow branches after the last modifier, but you can still apply new modifiers that are unique to each branch. Each reference has its own set of transforms, space warps, and object properties. Whether a modifier affects one reference, some references, or all references depends on where in the dataflow the modifier is applied. A modifier affects all references that branch from the dataflow after the point in the modifier stack where the modifier is applied. Figure 1.25 shows the dataflow for multiple references.

FIGURE 1.25

Dataflow after referencing an object.

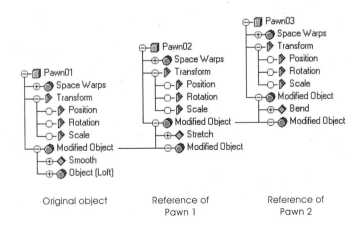

Making Instances and References Unique

Anytime you are cloning an object, carefully consider whether the best choice is a copy, instance, or reference. If you are not sure, you should err on the side of instances or references. If you decide to make something an instance and later decide that you want independent copies, you can make the instances unique. Making an instance unique duplicates all the information shared with other instances and converts the selected instance to an independent copy.

Unfortunately, 3DS MAX isn't very consistent in its methods for making instances unique. Different instances use different methods:

- Map instances are made unique by pasting a copy of the instance back into the map slot.

- Modifier instances are made unique by clicking the Make Unique button in the Modify panel.

- Scene objects and controllers are made unique by clicking the Make Unique button in Track View.

Concepts of Scene Hierarchy

Almost everything in 3DS MAX is organized into a hierarchy which makes it easy to understand. If you've ever written a report using an outline to organize your thoughts, you've used a hierarchy.

All hierarchies in 3DS MAX follow the same principles. Higher levels in the hierarchy represent general information, or levels of greatest influence. Lower levels represent detailed information, or levels of lesser influence. Track View displays the hierarchy of your entire scene, as seen in Figure 1.26:

- The top level is the World. You can make certain global changes to everything in your scene by changing the World track in Track View.

- The level just below the world holds five categories that organize all of the objects in your scene. These categories are Sound, Environment, Material Editor, Scene Materials, and Objects.

- The many levels below the five categories contain the details for everything else in your scene.

FIGURE 1.26

Displaying the scene hierarchy in Track View.

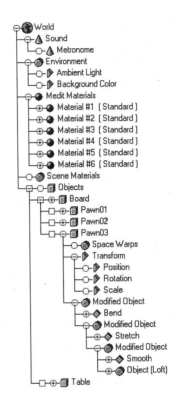

Material and Map Hierarchies

Material and map definitions are also organized in a multilevel hierarchy. Simpler programs use single materials and might allow only a single map as a texture. Others might enable one map for each channel, such as bumpiness or opacity. Using 3DS MAX, you can build hierarchical material and map definitions.

Material definitions can be multilevel hierarchies:

■ The top level holds the basic material name and material type.

■ Depending on the material type, you can have multiple levels of submaterials. These submaterials can also consist of multiple submaterials.

■ A material type of Standard is the lowest level of a material hierarchy. It contains material details, such as color and mapping channels.

The mapping channels for a standard material can also be multilevel hierarchies:

- Depending on the map type, such as Mask or Checker, you can have multiple levels of submaps. These submaps can also consist of multiple submaps.

- A simple bitmap is the lowest level of a map hierarchy and provides details for map output and coordinates.

Figure 1.27 shows a Top/Bottom material with its hierarchy displayed. The material shows a map hierarchy where maps are used in the bump slots of each submaterial, as well as a diffuse map in the Top material.

FIGURE 1.27

Displaying material and map hierarchies in the Material Editor.

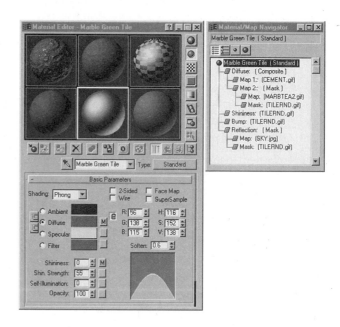

NEW TO R2

Notice that in Release 2, only values related to the current material are displayed in the Material/Map Navigator. The red map icon next to diffuse map #2 indicates that the map displays in the viewport.

Object Hierarchies

Object hierarchies are probably the most familiar to anyone who has used a computer animation program. By using tools to link objects, you can build a hierarchy where transforms applied to one object are inherited by the objects linked below it. You can link objects and build object hierarchies to model and animate jointed structures. Figure 1.28 shows an example of an object hierarchy.

The terminology used for object hierarchies is as follows:

■ The top level of the hierarchy is called the root. Technically, the root is always the World, but most people refer to the root as the highest level object in the hierarchy.

■ An object that has other objects linked below it is called a parent object. All of the objects below a parent are its descendants.

■ An object that is linked to an object above it is called a child object. All of the objects that can be traced from the child object back to the root are called ancestors.

FIGURE 1.28

Displaying object hier-
archies.

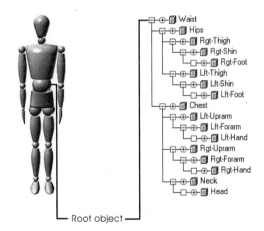

Video Post Hierarchies

Video post can be used to composite multiple camera views, animation segments, and images into a single animation. The way you build up the source material for Video Post is also organized as a special kind of hierarchy.

The Video Post hierarchy is organized as follows:

- Components of the Video Post hierarchy are called events.

- The top level of the Video Post hierarchy is called the queue. Unlike the other hierarchies, the queue can have multiple events at the top level. Each event is processed sequentially according to its order in the queue.

- Each event in the queue can represent a hierarchy of layering, filter, image, and scene events.

- The lowest level in a Video Post event hierarchy is the Image Input or Scene event.

- The last event in the queue is usually an Image Output event.

Figure 1.29 shows an example of a Video Post hierarchy and identifies its components.

FIGURE 1.29

Displaying a Video Post hierarchy.

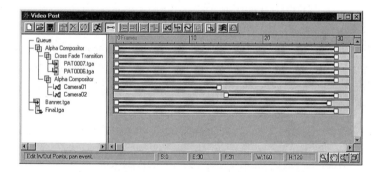

These are the basics for the scene organization inside of 3D Studio Max. Objects are created and duplicated into copies/instances and references. Hierarchies are used to organize and order materials, object linkages, track view, and video post effects.

Concepts of Animation

The traditional definition of animation is the process of producing many images showing an object in motion and then playing back those images so rapidly that we see movement. Oddly, even live action footage falls under this definition of animation. A movie or video camera captures images of live action at high speed for playback at high speed. The phenomenon called persistence of vision fools our eye into seeing motion where there is really only sequential still images.

What differentiates animation from live action is the process of how the image is produced. Live action uses cameras to capture the images for playback. Traditional animation requires that each image is drawn and then photographed as a single frame for playback.

This difference in process is why discussions of animation time are so heavily frame based. Each image, or frame of film, has to be drawn, inked, and colored by hand. This process led animators to think in frames: "This action takes this number of frames and this should happen during that frame."

Imagine the response a director would get from an actor if the director said, "Now run to the porch in about 90 frames, pause for 20 frames, and fling open the door." Thinking in frames is an unnatural skill, forced by the limitations of animation technology. It would be so much easier if you could animate in real-time: "I want this to last for four seconds and then half a second later I want that to happen."

At the heart of 3DS MAX, your animation actually occurs in real-time. It is not until you get ready to render that you must decide how you want time divided into frames.

Defining Time

3DS MAX is based on a time measurement system of ticks. Each tick is 1/4800th of a second. Everything you animate in 3DS MAX is stored in real-time at a precision of 1/4800th of a second. As the animator, you choose how you want time displayed while you work and how you want it divided into frames when you render.

Specify the time display method and the rendering frame rate using the Time Configuration dialog. Using the Time Configuration dialog shown in Figure 1.30, choose time display methods conforming to traditional animation and video standards, or choose to work in real minutes and seconds. You can also set frame rates based on various standards or specify any custom rate that fits your needs.

FIGURE 1.30

*Defining time in the
Time Configuration
dialog box.*

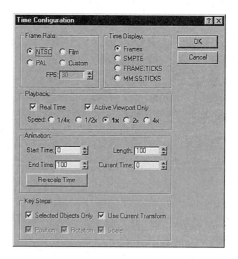

FIGURE 1.30

*Defining time in the
Time Configuration
dialog box.*

Defining Keys

Traditional animation relies heavily on a technique called keyframing. Keyframing is what a master animator is doing when he draws the most important frames of an animated sequence, the keys, and then passes on the work to an assistant animator to finish the frames between the keys. Depending on how difficult the animation is, the master animator might have to draw many closely spaced keys, or maybe just a few.

3DS MAX works in much the same way since you are the master animator. You specify exactly what you want to happen and when it should happen by creating animation keys at specific times. 3DS MAX is your assistant animator and takes care of the animation that occurs in the time between the keys. The following short exercise shows you how to create animation keys.

CREATING ANIMATION KEYS

1. Turn on the Animate button in the lower-right corner of the 3DS MAX window (see Figure 1.31).

2. Drag the Time Slider, at the bottom of the 3DS MAX window, to the time when you want something to happen (see Figure 1.31).

FIGURE 1.31

Setting animation keys with the Animate button and Time Slider.

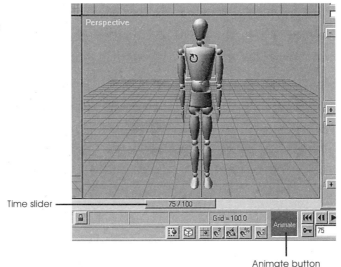

Time slider

Animate button

3. Move, rotate, scale an object, or change virtually any parameter for anything in your scene. You can animate the vast majority of parameters in 3DS MAX. Only a few parameters cannot be animated.

4. Drag the Time Slider all the way to the right.

5. Move rotate or scale the object again.

6. Return to Frame 1 by dragging the Time slider all the way to the left.

7. Hit the Play button and watch the animation play in the viewport.

MAX uses this paradigm to create animation. Turn the Animate button on and then whatever you do at a frame creates a key. Turn the Animate button off and whatever you do at a frame is reflected in the first frame of the animation segment. You can also create keys directly by clicking the time slider, or by copying keys in track view. In MAX 2, you can also create keys with a Shift+right-click over parameters spinners in the right hand command panel. You also can animate by applying various animation controllers through the motion panel or via trackview.

Real-time animation is even possible using the new Float Motion Capture controller. This enables you to do digital puppeteering using your mouse, keyboard, joystick, or MIDI device.

Animation Controllers

All animation in 3DS MAX, whether key-based animation or parametric animation, is managed by animation controllers. How an animation is stored, whether it uses keys or parameters, and how animation values are interpolated from one time to the next are all handled by an animation controller (or just controller for short).

3DS MAX automatically assigns a controller to any parameter that you animate using the Animate button and Time Slider technique mentioned previously. If you want to use a parametric controller, such as Noise, you must assign it yourself by using tools in Track View or the Motion panel. You can tell whether a parameter can be animated, or whether it has already been assigned an animation controller, by looking for the parameter in Track View, which is explained in the following list:

■ Any item in Track View with a green triangle icon can be animated. Figure 1.32 shows cylinder parameters displayed in Track View that can be animated.

FIGURE 1.32

Animated parameters and controllers in Track View.

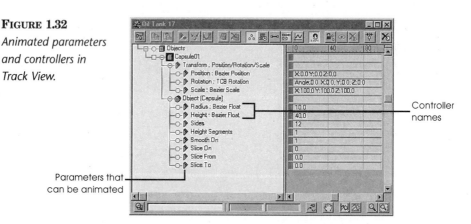

Parameters that can be animated

Controller names

■ Parameters that cannot be animated do not appear in Track View. Figure 1.32 also compares cylinder parameters that can be animated with all of the cylinder's parameters in the Create panel. Note that only the Generate Mapping Coordinates check box cannot be animated.

■ Use filters in Track View to display the name of any controllers assigned to parameters. Controller names are appended after the name of the parameter. If a parameter does not have a controller name next to it, the parameter has not yet been animated. In Figure 1.32, only the radius and height of the cylinder have been animated.

Animation Controllers define nearly everything about the animation of an object; the movement of them can be linear or Bézier, with crisp discontinuous changes, or smooth flowing ones. A Path controller will not display any keyframes, because is it not keyframe-based, and list controllers enable you to mix controllers together. Thus, each controller offers unique advantages and disadvantages, best learned through exploration.

Several new controllers have been added to MAX 2 included position controllers for independent x,y,z keyframing and the float motion capture controller for real-time animation. Bezier controllers have been added to visibility keys to give gradual fades via track view.

Concepts of Materials and Mapping

To give mesh objects the look and feel of reality, materials can be defined, applied, and mapped. The interface for materials, although extensive, is laid out in a logical format making it easy to define and refine a vast array of material possibilities. If the material definition contains bitmaps (GIFs, AVIs), how that material is arranged on objects is determined by assigning mapping coordinates to the faces of those objects.

MAX 2 automatically generates mapping coordinates on objects that can generate them. Also new is the Unwrap UVW Map Modifier, which facilitates exact placement of textures on objects.

Material Components

Material definitions are stored either in a material library on the hard disk in a .mat file, or in the .max file you are working in. Only materials saved to a material library are available to other .max files, unless you merge a .max file into the current one. Material libraries enable you keep separate definitions for different projects. The 3dsmax.mat file is the default library and is in the maps subdirectory.

A Material definition starts with one of the material types, such as Standard, MultiSub-object, or Raytracing. Depending on its type, the definition hierarchy can be composed of more material types as in double-sided or basic parameters, extended parameters, maps, and dynamics properties as in the Standard material. You can display your material's hierarchy through the Material/Map Navigator, which creates a graphical representation, as you define your material or through Track View while animating material parameters (see Figure 1.33).

FIGURE 1.33

The material map navigator displaying a material's hierarchy and Track View showing its animatable parameters.

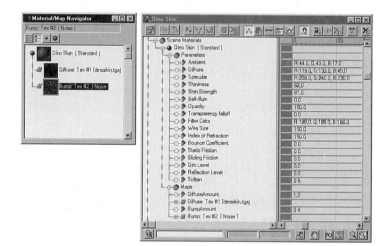

Basic parameters are components with variable values like color, shininess, and transparency, or On/Off values like two-sided, face map, and wire. The variable value components can be defined by a single value or by assigning maps to them. Another basic parameter is the material shading method, which determines the quality of rendering, such as whether the object is smoothed or not, or whether it looks metallic.

Maps used in materials are simply pictures in an electronic format either scanned in, created in a paint package, or generated procedurally. The slot you assign your map to, such as diffuse, bump, or opacity, determines what values of that map are used. In the diffuse slot, the map's colors are used to give an object the look of something like brick or carpet, although in the bump slot, only the grayscale values are used to make the object look as if it has a textured surface, like gravel or grooves. Where the picture is lighter, the object will appear raised; where darker, the object will appear recessed.

Procedural maps are simply pictures generated according to mathematical parameters. Some are designed to work mostly on their own in a definition and include things like Wood, Smoke, Stucco, Planet, Marble, and Water. Others are used to refine and enhance like Flat mirror, Thinwall refraction, RGB tint, Composite, and Raytrace. You can even use third-party Adobe Photoshop and Premier plug-ins as procedural maps.

You can use any of the 31 stock map types in any of the 14 or so map slots with varying intensities in each slot. It is enough to say that just about any real world material is definable through the Materials editor.

Dynamics properties, found at the bottom of the Standard and Raytracing materials, are for defining solid material attributes for use with the Dynamics utility. They are only applicable if an object is used in a Dynamics simulation definition.

Mapping Materials

When assigning a material with a bitmap to an object, 3D Studio MAX no longer has to be told how to arrange that map on the object if the object can automatically create a mapping coordinate. Max now automatically turns on the mapping coordinates to any object with a texture mapped materials. On other objects (imported objects and editable meshes), you can apply your own using UVW Mapping modifiers applied at the object or sub-object level. If you want to apply UVW to sub-object selection sets of faces, you'll need to create Multi materials and use Material ID #'s. These can be assigned directly to Editable meshes or applied as Modifiers.

Taking the time to master the use of materials is critical to success with MAX. Geometric flaws are often disguised by clever material usage, and getting the right look in your renderings is often a function of how much you know about material definitions. The new raytracing material offers a quantum leap of possibilities to building better looking images.

One new addition to MAX 2 adds unlimited functionality to the software. In the next section, you'll take a peek at the concepts of the new scripting utility, MAXScript.

Concepts of MAXScript

Those of you who used Release 4 of 3D Studio remember that a scripting language for the keyframer made doing more complex animation tasks much easier. MAXScript gives the user access to about 85 percent of 3D

Studio MAX's functionality through a command line interface. The question the user always comes to when deciding whether to learn a new programming language or not is "How hard will it be to get what I want?" If you've ever written a batch file in DOS or created a macro in a word processor, you will have no problem creating scripts to speed up and ease your everyday use of MAX. If you are able to use higher level programming languages such as C++, you will find MAXScript capable of extremely sophisticated programming tasks.

MAXScript Components

MAXScript is accessed through the Utilities panel and is composed of an editor for creating and editing scripts. It also includes a listener, which acts as a runtime command line, recording your input and returning results and errors. You may load and run scripts (files with extension .ms) or immediately start entering commands. A drop-down menu displays scripts called utilities, which have a command panel interface written into them.

Most MAXScript commands have the same name as the buttons used in the GUI to access them like scale, hide, align, select, zoom, and undo. Its syntax has almost no punctuation making it easy for nonprogrammers to learn. The following simple exercise steps you through doing a simple command line entry.

CREATING WITH MAXSCRIPT

1. Go to the Utilities panel and click the MAXScript button.

2. Click the Open Listener button.

3. Type in the following: **box length:20**. Then press the Enter key on the number pad (see Figure 1.34). Note that pressing the Enter key on the keyboard brings you to the next line, which allows you to choose between editing and execution.

4. Notice the box in the editor is at 0,0,0. Now type in **move $Box01 [20,20,20]**. Press Enter on the number pad and the box moves.

FIGURE 1.34

The MAXScript Utility, the modeless Listener and Editor dialog boxes.

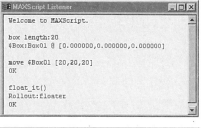

While it may seem simple and unimportant at first, the scripter provides the ability to bottle the sequences of complex techniques that advanced animators develop, just through this command line interface to MAX 2.

With MAXScript you can also do the following:

- Import data from programs like Excel for scene creation based on external data, such as the placement of trees on a landscape.

- Run DOS or Windows programs like a data retrieval utility hooked up to a weather measuring device.

- Create utilities with command panels interfaces and floating modeless dialog boxes with all the buttons and spinners you would find in any command panel.

- Create a start-up script (startup.ms) that autoloads any series of utilities upon the startup of MAXScript.

Scripting is only one of the thousand new features of MAX 2, but it is the one feature that could potentially create an additional thousand features through its power to automate MAX. 3D Studio's power is also extended through its plug-in architecture, which allows for anyone with a programming skill in Visual C++ to create their own tools for MAX.

Concepts of Plug-In Extensibility

Many programs support the concept of plug-ins to extend the functionality of the core application. The ease of use and value of plug-ins vary depending on the design of the core application and how well plug-in development is supported. Fortunately, 3DS MAX has a tightly integrated, robust plug-in architecture.

3DS MAX as a Plug-In System

The 3DS MAX plug-in architecture is so central to the overall design of the application, you could consider 3DS MAX to be a graphics plug-in operating system, rather than a graphics application. In fact, most of the features that ship in the box with 3DS MAX are implemented as plug-ins. The following benefits are included in the 3DS MAX plug-in architecture:

- The core functionality of the program can be upgraded quickly and easily with new plug-ins.

- Plug-ins load automatically and are ready for use when you start 3DS MAX.

- 3DS MAX can be customized and extended as easily as dropping new plug-ins into the 3dsmax\plugins directory.

- Developers can integrate their new plug-ins so well that you may be hard pressed to tell where 3DS MAX leaves off and a plug-in begins.

Using Plug-Ins

If plug-ins are so well-integrated, why have a topic about using them? Yes, you can just drop a plug-in into a directory and start using it, but there are a few techniques that you might find helpful.

Installing Plug-Ins

If you install all your plug-ins into the default \plug-ins directory, you could quickly end up with a mess of cryptic files lumped together in one place. Most major plug-in developers write setup programs that place their plug-ins in special custom directories and register those directories with 3DS

MAX. You might want to consider setting up specialized directories for other plug-ins that you collect as well.

3DS MAX makes identifying alternate plug-in directories quite easy. The Configure Paths dialog box contains a panel in which you can identify as many plug-in directories as you need, as shown in Figure 1.35. Any plug-ins in a directory identified in the Configure Paths dialog load whenever you start 3DS MAX.

FIGURE 1.35

The Plug-ins panel of the Configure Paths dialog.

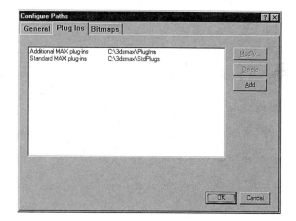

To configuring alternate plug-in directories, complete the following steps:

1. Create any new directories and place your plug-ins there.

2. Start 3DS MAX.

3. Choose Configure Paths from the File menu.

4. Click the Plug-ins tab in the Configure Paths dialog.

5. Click Add.

6. Choose one of your new directories from the directory browser, type a description in the Description field, and click OK.

Repeat steps 5 and 6 for each new plug-in directory created.

Finding Plug-Ins

After you install a new plug-in, where do you find it? That depends on what type of plug-in it is. In general, use the following six methods to access plug-ins:

- Use the file extension as an indicator of the type of plug-in you're installing: .dlo (object creation); .dle, (export); .dli, (import); .flt, (video post filter); .dlm, (modifier); .dlu, (utility); .dlt, (procedural material); .dlf, (font controller), .dlc, (animation controller), .bmi, (bitmap controller), .dlr, (renderer); .dls, (shapes).

- Object creators usually show up as a new sub-category under one of the seven creation categories of the Create panel.

- It is also possible for creation plug-ins to show up as a new button in the Object Type rollout of one of the existing sub-categories.

- Modifiers show up in the Modifiers dialog after you click the More button in the Modify panel.

- Utilities show up in the Utilities dialog after you click the More button in the Utilities panel.

- Most other plug-ins appear in option lists. Examples of these types of plug-ins include material and map plug-ins in the Material/Map Browser, controller plug-ins in the Replace Controller dialog, renderers in the Choose Renderer dialog under the Rendering tab of Preferences, and atmosphere plug-ins in the Add Atmospheric Effect dialog.

Working with Missing Plug-ins

One of the most important aspects of the 3DS MAX plug-in architecture is what happens when you load a file that uses a plug-in that is not installed on your system. It would not be too surprising if the file simply failed to load.

When 3DS MAX detects that a required plug-in is missing, it displays the Missing DLLs dialog, as shown in Figure 1.36. This dialog lists the missing DLLs, provides information about their file names and usage, and provides the option to proceed loading the file or cancel.

If you proceed, placeholders are created for the missing DLLs, the DLL data is saved, and everything else in the file is displayed. A simple cube replaces geometry generated by an object creation plug-in, for example. You can work with the file as you normally would, with the exception that you cannot make any changes to parts of the scene controlled by the missing DLL. Later, if you install the missing plug-in and reload the file, all of the information displays properly.

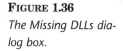

FIGURE 1.36

The Missing DLLs dialog box.

In Practice: Using 3D Studio MAX's Basic Concepts

- **Object-oriented behavior:** As a result of 3DS MAX being an object-oriented program, only operations that are valid for the selected object are active. Other operations become inactive or are hidden in the interface.

- **Parametric objects:** Because parametric objects provide considerable modeling and animation options, you'll want to preserve an object's parametric definition as long as possible (except for polygonal modelers). Operations that discard parameters include attaching objects using one of the Edit modifiers, collapsing an object's Modifier Stack, and exporting objects to a different file format.

- **Modifiers versus space warps:** Identical effects can be implemented as both modifiers and space warps. Remember, however, that modifiers are directly applied to the object and do not change as the object moves around the scene. Space warps, on the other hand, exist as independent objects to which other objects are bound. The effect of a space warp changes as a bound object moves through a scene. Use modifiers to apply an effect directly to an object. Use space warps to simulate environmental effects or external forces.

- **Changing object parameters versus transforming objects:** Change object parameters whenever you want to make a modeling change or a change that will be picked up by any modifiers. Transform an object when the transform effect is the last change you want to apply, or when the change is being used to affect the location of the object in your scene.

- **Material Mapping:** When assigning a material with maps as part of its definition, mapping coordinates must be applied. MAX objects with a Generate Mapping Coords parameter will automatically turn on at rendering time if they are off. All other objects must have a UVW Map modifier applied.

- **Installing plug-ins:** To reduce the number of plug-in files loaded into the default plug-ins directory, you can set up specialized directories for plug-ins by using the Configure Paths dialog. Any plug-ins in a directory identified in the Configure Paths dialog load whenever you start 3DS MAX.

- **MAXScript:** The scripter enables you to control Max through a script. You can design buttons and boxes in the command panel as well as floaters. You can use the scripter to tie Max to outside programs, such as text files or Excel spreadsheets. Any of your favorite techniques can be wrapped up into a utility that the scripter can launch for you.

Chapter 2

GETTING ORIENTED IN 3D SPACE

In any project, one must get the lay of the land before build-
ing anything on it and then take stock of the tools and
resources so that planning can happen and intended results
can be achieved. 3D Studio MAX has a lot of features that
make maneuvering in its editor both complex and powerful.
It also has a strong set of tools for managing the creative
process. This chapter will cover those tools that are
designed to manage objects and keep their relationships
organized, and then to control those objects in accurate and
intuitive ways.

Specifically, this chapter covers:

- The basics of creating objects

- Using selections

- Using groups

- Using grids and helpers

- Using transforms and coordinate systems

- Choosing Snap options

The Basics of Creating Objects

Creating objects in MAX, at its foundation, is based on coordinate geometry and uses all the components common to that system. The world coordinate system, composed of the origin (0,0,0) and the X/Y/Z axes, are the foundation that all other MAX components use as a reference for defining their existence. Most objects in MAX are first defined by vertices in that system and then secondly defined by either splines connecting or influenced by those vertices, or faces using the vertices as their corner points.

Most of the object-creating tools in MAX decide for you how those vertices, splines, and faces (all sub-objects) are initially and automatically arranged. You can have access to most of these sub-objects for creation at any time when the object has been reduced to an editable mesh, but many of the MAX object-creating tools are designed to allow parametric adjustments to make object creation (and the arrangement of its sub-objects) quick, easy, and intuitive. This section explains, by example, the basic guidelines for creating parametric objects. You can then use the objects you create for experimentation through the rest of this chapter.

Although objects in 3D Studio MAX may seem quite complex, creating them is a fast and easy process. Every object you create is parametric in nature, meaning that its form is defined by a series of parameters. The act of creating objects usually involves three basic steps:

- Choosing the plane which you want the object to rest upon (most often this just means activating a particular viewport).

- Choosing the point on the plane for the beginning point of the object (this is just a click in the viewport at the desired spot).

- Dragging your mouse to define the remaining parameters for the object.

Creating Interactively

One of the features that stands out in MAX is that when creating an object, the numeric values representing the object's definition are continually being updated while they are created. After initial creation of the object, you can also adjust those values while interactively observing changes to the objects in the viewports.

The following example shows this by taking you through the creation of a box. It covers all the components involved in its creation. See how some of those components can be seen in the viewports and some in the Command panel. The procedure for creating a box is as follows:

CREATING A BOX

1. Click the Box button in the Create panel and choose which viewport to start in. Doing this also selects which construction you are working on.

2. Click and hold the left mouse button.

3. Drag the mouse to create a rectangular shape and then release the left mouse button.

4. Drag the mouse to adjust the height and click once more to accept that height.

The second step actually begins creation, the third determines length and width, and the fourth, height.

The rest of the objects found in the Standard and Extended Primitive panels are created using the same or similar steps with their respective buttons chosen first. Other objects found throughout the Create panel have methods of execution different than primitives, but the interactivity will be as intuitive.

More than just a box has been created in the previous example, however; a number of additional components were created automatically in relation to the object, such as color, object name, and bounding box. It is important to understand these components, as they are common to every object created in MAX.

In the Command panel, you'll notice the Name field has been filled in automatically and a color assigned. At this point, you may rename the object and change the color to something that pertains to the organization of objects in your scene (see Figure 2.1). In the viewport, a transform or pivot tripod has been created on the bottom center of the box, displaying the X/Y/Z axes of the current coordinate system. Also, if your object is shaded and selected, you will see the object's bounding box. The bounding box is always a box regardless of the object's shape.

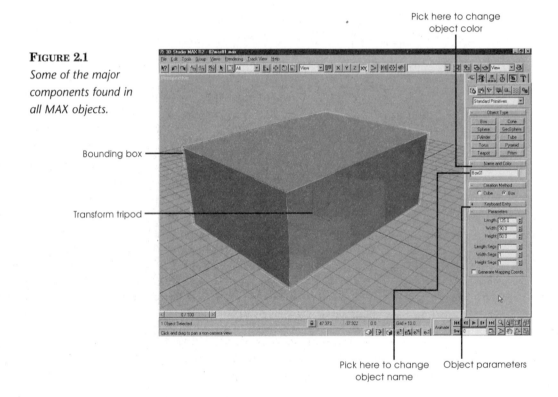

FIGURE 2.1

Some of the major components found in all MAX objects.

Pick here to change object color

Bounding box

Transform tripod

Pick here to change object name

Object parameters

There are more components associated with an object and these can be accessed by right-clicking a selected object to bring up the Object Properties dialog box. These properties, such as whether the object casts shadows or how the object displays in the viewport, are discussed in more detail throughout this book.

The next components that will be discussed are parametric primitives, which are present in almost every MAX object in one form or another.

Using Parametric Primitives

As you create an object, you are interactively adjusting its parameters; you can observe them changing as you create. The following brings you again through creating a box but goes a little deeper into the relationship between what's onscreen and what's in the Command panel:

ADJUSTING PARAMETRIC PRIMITIVES

1. Start the Box command by clicking its button.

2. Click the left mouse button and hold it down in the Perspective viewport. Notice that a name has been entered in the Object Name field and an axis tripod is present.

3. Drag out to create the length and width, and notice the fields for those parameters in the Command panel updating to reflect the movements of the cursor.

4. Let go of the mouse button, drag the mouse, and notice the height parameter updating.

5. Click the left mouse button to complete the command.

6. In the Command panel, adjust the parameters by clicking and holding the spinners while dragging the mouse. Notice the box in the viewport updating to reflect the changes.

The parameters are adjustable for as long as the box remains a primitive. They can only be adjusted in the Create panel during the object's creation. Once you have started any other process in MAX, you must go to the Modify panel while the object is selected to make changes to its parameters.

Now that you have gone through creating some objects and learned how creation works in MAX, the next section will show the different kinds of objects that can be created.

Types of MAX Objects

In computer modeling, there are many different types of objects and MAX makes available the most popular modeling methods for creating them. The following is a list of basic geometric objects, which can be created in MAX:

- **Editable Mesh**: The least common denominator that all objects can be reduced to.

- **Standard and Extended Primitives**: Objects that are the foundation for creating more complex objects by combination and conversion.

- **Compound Objects**: These use multiple objects to define themselves through various combination techniques.

- **Shapes and Editable Splines**: Objects composed of splines combined to define 3D objects through various methods.

- **Lofts**: Composed of shapes allowing complex 3D extruded objects.

- **NURBS**: A class of objects composed of splines and surfaces using sophisticated mathematics to create organic-looking shapes.

- **Patch Grids**: A popular method for creating organic models until NURBS came along.

- **Particle Systems**: For rain, smoke, water, and so on.

- **Architectural:** Highly parameterized objects for easy creation of Doors and Windows (see Figure 2.2).

Non-geometric objects include:

- Lights and Cameras

- Helper objects

- Space Warps

- Systems

Any of the Standard Primitives are useable for experimentation in this chapter, but the reader is encouraged to go through the new 3DS MAX Online Help for each of the above listed objects. Besides providing reference information, the Online Help provides quick tutorials to give a basic understanding of how each process works.

FIGURE 2.2

An example of architectural doors and windows complete with frames. Many parameterized options are adjustable, such as sill width or the number of glass panels.

T IP

Be sure to update your online help files every so often by clicking Connect to Support and Information under the Help pulldown menu. This takes you to the Kinetix Web site and enables you to download updates and tutorials. The main online Help file is updated in total every three months, but more often there will be tutorials made available as they are developed.

The next tools covered help you select which objects you will make changes to, apply materials to, delete, and so on.

Using Selections

Because selections are so important, you will find Selection tools throughout the 3D Studio MAX interface. The basic 3DS MAX selection techniques should be familiar to anyone who has used a Windows-based CAD or modeling program, but it might take a while for you to become proficient at identifying and using the many 3DS MAX-specific selection methods.

To help you become familiar with the fundamentals of selections, this section explains 3DS MAX selection basics and then covers sub-object selection, selecting objects by property, and building named selection sets.

Selection Basics

Before you can perform any action, you must select the objects that will be affected by that action. 3D Studio MAX uses a strategy called noun-verb selection. This means that you select your objects first and then choose an action to apply to the selection. This wouldn't be such a good idea if you were forced to use a single selection tool before you could use any other tool. 3D Studio MAX has a selection-only tool, but it also includes selection as a function of all of its transform tools—Select and Move, Select and Rotate, and Select and Scale. The tool used in creating hierarchies also applies—Select and Link.

The only exception is the Unlink Selection tool, which does not select, but operates on the existing selection.

Using Selection Tools

Figure 2.3 shows the basic selection tool along with the Transform tool buttons, the Link tool button, and the Bind to Spacewarp button in the 3D Studio MAX toolbar. You can select objects whenever the selection, Link, Bind to Spacewarp, or any of the transform buttons are active. You will find that you select most often with the Transform buttons though you will use the Selection tool to select individual items and keep from applying an unintentional transform.

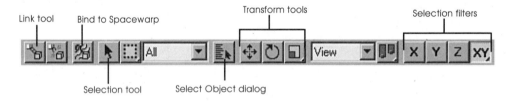

FIGURE 2.3

Selection and transform tools.

Whenever the selection tool or one of the transforms is active, you can tell what effect clicking or dragging will have by looking at the screen cursor. The appearance of the screen cursor, its meaning, and its effect, are as follows:

- **System cursor (arrow):** The cursor is over empty space or over an object that is not valid for the current selection mode. Clicking deselects any currently selected objects; dragging performs a region selection.

- **Select cursor (white cross):** The cursor is over an unselected object that is valid for the current selection mode. Clicking selects the object and deselects any other selected objects; dragging selects and transforms the object while deselecting any other selected objects.

- **Transform cursor (black cross with arrows):** The cursor is over a selected object. Clicking keeps the object selected while deselecting any other selected objects; dragging transforms the object and all other selected objects.

TIP

If a selected object is in front of another object, you can deselect the front object and select the back object by clicking in an area where the objects overlap. Clicking in an area where objects overlap begins by selecting the front object. Every successive click deselects the current object and selects the objects deeper in the scene. This works for any number of overlapping objects.

Because of the ambiguities associated with selecting overlapping objects, however, if you have the logical organizational skills needed to navigate a verbal interface, it's always a good habit to select by name from the toolbar list, or using the H key shortcut, rather than selecting by clicking in the viewport.

Figure 2.4 shows all three cursors displayed with the Move transform. The left viewport shows the system cursor because the cursor is over empty space. The middle viewport displays the select cursor because the cursor is over a valid, unselected object. The right viewport displays the Move transform cursor because the cursor is over a selected object.

You also have all the convenient global selection techniques available in the Edit menu. Select All selects all objects in the scene, Select None is the same as selecting in empty space, and Select Invert inverts the current selection so that all unselected objects are now selected and all selected objects are now unselected.

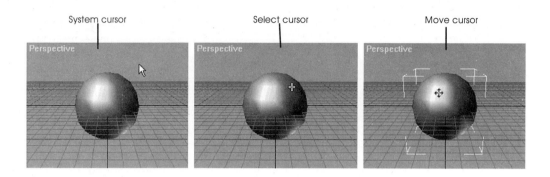

FIGURE 2.4
The system arrow, selection, and transform cursors for the Move transform.

Using Region Selection

As mentioned previously, you can select objects by clicking them or by dragging a region that selects all the objects contained by the region. Use the Region Select controls on the toolbar, Prompt Line, and Edit menu to set the shape and behavior of region selections.

The shape of a region selection is set by the region flyout on the toolbar (see Figure 2.5). The three types of region selection are:

- **Quad Dragging** defines a rectangular region in which one corner is located where you press the mouse and the opposite corner is located where you release it.

- **Circle Dragging** defines a circular region in which the center is located where you press the mouse and the radius is set where you release it.

- **Fence Dragging** defines the first segment of the fence boundary. Click to define more segments. Double-click or click on the start point to close the fence and complete the selection. A cross displays to indicate you are over the start point.

Region behavior is set by the region toggle in the prompt line or by choosing Region from the Edit menu (refer to Figure 2.5). The two types of region behavior are Window, which selects only objects that are completely within the region, and Crossing, which selects any object that touches the region boundary or is completely within the region.

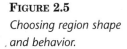

FIGURE 2.5

Choosing region shape and behavior.

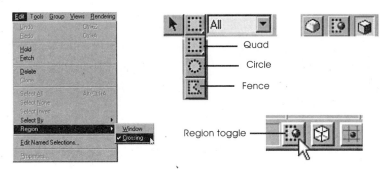

Adding and Removing Objects from a Selection

You can also use standard Windows modifier keys to add and remove objects from a current selection. You can use the Ctrl or Alt key while selecting objects as follows:

- **Ctrl:** To toggle the selection state of objects, press the Ctrl key while clicking. Clicking unselected objects or dragging a region around them adds them to the selection; clicking selected objects or dragging a region around them removes them from the selection.

- **Alt:** To remove objects from the selection set, press the Alt key while clicking objects or dragging regions.

T IP

Although the Alt option may seem redundant, it is better used than Ctrl when performing a region select for removal to avoid toggling the select state of objects already unselected.

Filtering a Selection

What do you do when you are working in a very complex scene and you want to select objects of only a certain type? Imagine you are lighting the interior of a convention center made of hundreds of objects, for example. You want to select only lights so you can adjust their parameters and position them properly, but you keep accidentally selecting walls and furniture instead.

FIGURE 2.6

The Selection Filter pulldown menu and Filter Combinations dialog box.

You could hide everything except the lights, but then you wouldn't know where to place the lights. Or you could freeze everything except the lights, but then your shaded viewports would not show how the lighting changes affect the frozen objects. Your best choice is to filter the selection using the Selection filters on the toolbar (see Figure 2.6).

You can filter to select any combination of categories using the Filter Combination dialog box, which adds entries to the Selection Filter pulldown list.

TIP

If you use the Filters, be sure to turn them off after use, or the next time you go to select some geometry you won't be able to.

Locking a Selection

When you are working with a very complex selection or want to use the same selection for a sequence of commands, it is a good idea to lock the selection. Locking a selection prevents you from accidentally releasing the selection. It also enables you to perform operations on the selected objects without the cursor resting directly on the selection.

You can toggle a selection between being locked and unlocked by doing either of the following actions:

- Clicking the Lock Selection Set button in the status line at the bottom of the 3DS MAX window (see Figure 2.7).

- Pressing the spacebar.

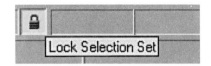

TIP

It's a good idea to train yourself to always select by name and then press the spacebar to lock your selection. That way you never have to touch the object with the cursor. The Locked Selection Set tool lets you touch anywhere in the viewport to transform the object. If you allow this method of selection to become your default method of selecting, you will avoid many selection problems. Note, however, that certain operations using snap won't work well in conjunction with Lock Selection Set.

Sub-Object Selection

Many situations exist in which you can select just a few components of an object, or in other words, define a sub-object selection. All sub-object selection begins by first selecting an object and then clicking a Sub-Object button to enter Sub-Object Selection mode. This is an important point; you first select an object and then turn on Sub-Object mode to go deeper into that object. As long as Sub-Object mode is active, you can select only components within the original selected object.

The Sub-Object button highlights in yellow to indicate that you are in Sub-Object Selection mode. If you find yourself trying to select objects and nothing happens, look at the Command panel to see whether or not you are in this mode. If so, click the Sub-Object button to turn off Sub-Object mode and return to normal selection methods.

TIP

Trying to select something but you can't? It's probably one of three things:

■ You're in Sub-Object Selection mode.

■ You've got the selection set locked.

■ You've left your Filters on to something other than All.

NOTE

Sub-Object Selection mode is almost always accessed from the Modify panel either as part of a modifier or as the base parameters of an object. The exceptions (as of release 2) are Trajectories, which display a Sub-Object button in the Motion panel, systems plug-ins that are also modified under the Motion panel, and any custom dialogs that may be written through the Scripting utility.

Selecting Objects by Property

Selecting single objects, or dragging a region to select multiple objects, becomes quite limiting when you have more than a handful of objects in your scene. You quickly realize that what you really need is the ability to select objects by property, such as selecting all the objects using a certain material or all the objects starting with the letter B. 3DS MAX has many tools for selecting both objects and sub-objects by their properties.

Selecting Objects by Name

Naming strategies play an important role in organizing any project. Whether you are organizing manila folders in a file drawer, word processing files on your hard disk, or objects in 3DS MAX, naming imposes a certain organizational strategy. If you are careful about how you name your objects, you can later quickly select groups of related objects using their names.

You select objects by name using the Select Objects dialog box or the Selection Floater (a new R2 feature, shown in Figure 2.8). You can display the Select Objects dialog box by using any of the following actions:

- Press H.
- Click the Select by Name button on the toolbar.
- Choose Select By, Name from the Edit menu.

You can open the Selection Floater under the Tools pulldown. It has all the same functionality that the Select Objects dialog has with the added benefit of being modeless. This capability enables you to see objects being selected in the viewports while choosing them in the dialog list box without having to close the dialog. You may want to reassign the H key to bring up the Selection Floater instead of the Select Objects dialog as there is no reason to continue using the Select Objects dialog over the Selection Floater. That can be done under File, Preferences, Keyboard.

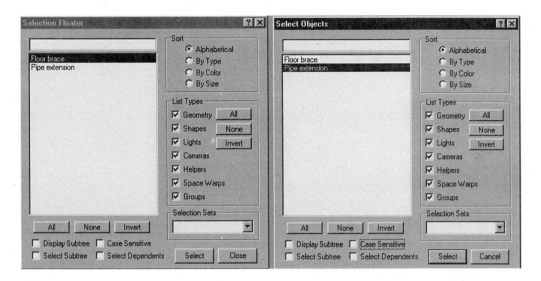

FIGURE 2.8

To select objects by name, use the Selection Floater or Select Objects dialog box. Notice the Selection Floater has a Close button instead of Cancel.

In either dialog box, you can select an object by clicking its name in the selection list or by entering a selection pattern in the Edit field above the selection list as shown in Figure 2.9.

Selection patterns can use the following wild cards to expand the search:

- **?** accepts any single character at that point in the search string. For example, B?x selects Box and Bix, but not Ball or even Box01.

- ***** accepts any number of characters at that point in the search string. For example, B*x* selects Box, Blox, Boxes, and Box01.

Another technique for selecting objects by name is to use the hierarchy list of the Track View window. The Track View hierarchy window displays the names of all the objects in your scene under the Objects branch. Clicking the yellow cube icon to the left of an object's name also selects the object in the scene, as seen in Figure 2.10.

FIGURE 2.9

*Selecting objects by
name using a selection
pattern.*

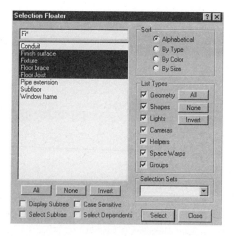

FIGURE 2.10

*Selecting objects in the
Track View hierarchy
list is another good
way of selecting
objects by name.*

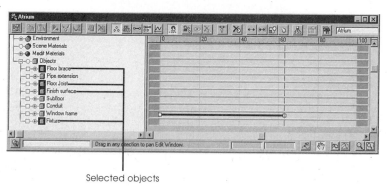

Selected objects

NOTE

Don't confuse picking the name of the object with the object icon in front of the name in the
Track View Hierarchy window.

Selection Using Sort, Subtree, and Dependency Options

Additional organizational strategies for selecting groups of objects can be
based on the sorting, subtree, or dependency options, all found in the Select
Objects and Selection Floater dialog boxes.

The Display subtree in the Selection by Name section gives you a quick way
to see the Hierarchy in a scene. Otherwise, you need to use Track View to
check on the links.

In the Sort section of the dialog box, you can choose to sort by any of the following methods:

- Alphabetically

- By type

- By color

- By size

Selection by Color in the Sort option of the Selection dialog boxes provides a total of 336 total colors to sort through, found in both palettes of the Object Color dialog box. To open that dialog box, you simply click the color swatch next to the Object Name field in the Command panel (see Figure 2.11). You must turn off Assign Random Colors in the Object color dialog box to control what color your objects will be at creation. Using this option, you can sort objects by their object color.

FIGURE 2.11

Displaying the Object Color dialog.

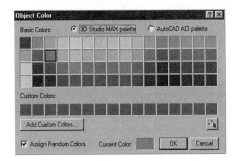

The Size sort option in the Selection dialog boxes is based on the face count of an object. If you sort by size, you can easily select the largest objects in your scene for face optimization.

By using Select Subtree, you can select all the objects in the hierarchy of, say, a mechanical arm. If you select an object with Select Dependents on, all of that object's instances and references will also be selected.

Selecting Objects by Material

The Select By Material button in the Material editor enables you to select all objects to which that material is assigned. You can tell at a glance whether the material is assigned to objects in the scene by looking at the Material editor. Material that is assigned to an object in the scene is called a hot material, which is indicated by a white triangle in the corner of the sample slot. If the material is not hot, it is not assigned to any object and the Select By Material button is inactive.

You pick in a hot material slot in the Material editor and then click the Select By Material button. The Select Entities dialog appears with all objects assigned the current material highlighted in the selection list (see Figure 2.12).

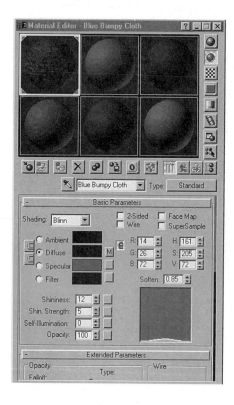 

FIGURE 2.12

Selecting objects by material.

Building Named Selection Sets

3D Studio MAX enables you to recall selection sets by storing them in Named Selection sets.

To name a selection set, do the following:

1. Define a selection set of objects using any selection methods discussed previously.

2. Click the Named Selection Set field in the toolbar.

3. Enter a name for the selection. Press Enter.

Make sure that you press Enter after typing the name of the selection. If you fail to press Enter, the selection name is not recorded and is discarded the next time you click anywhere in the 3DS MAX window.

To access a saved selection set, pick the Named Selection Set option pull-down arrow and select a name in the list (see Figure 2.13). You may also select sets in the Select Objects dialog and Selection Floater under the Selection Set option pulldown.

FIGURE 2.13

Choosing a named selection set.

Editing Named Selection Sets

Now in release 2, you can add and subtract objects through the Edit Named Selections dialog found under the Edit pulldown (see Figure 2.14). You can also use Boolean operations to combine, subtract, and create intersections of selection sets.

Named selections simply identify a group of objects. If you delete one of the objects in a named selection set, the selection set still exists and contains the remaining objects in the selection. New in release 2, empty selection sets remove themselves from the Selection Set list.

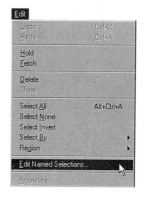

FIGURE 2.14

Editing named selection sets.

Naming Sub-Object Selections

You can also name selection sets of sub-objects, such as a selection of faces, vertices, or the keys of a trajectory. A named Sub-Object Selection is saved with the Edit modifier, or animation controller that is used to create the selection. You cannot share named Sub-Object Selections among Edit modifiers (or editable meshes/NURBS), but you can share between controllers. Also, named Sub-Object Sets in a modifier (or editable meshes/NURBS) are not copied to the new object(s) when cloning but are copied for controllers.

Using Groups

Somewhere between named selection sets and permanently attaching multiple objects to form a single object is where groups lie. Groups are sort of hybrids of a combined object, a semi-permanent selection set, and a special linked hierarchy. A group is an object itself that contains other objects as members of the group. Groups can be animated, modified, and linked to other objects. Anything that you do to the group also affects the member objects inside the group. What makes groups unique is that you can open a group and individually animate and modify the objects inside.

Use groups whenever you want a collection of objects to behave as a single object yet preserve the ability to edit objects in the group individually.

Everything you need to build, edit, and disassemble groups begins with the choices in the Group menu on the toolbar.

T IP _____

Groups were originally implemented in MAX to accommodate the importation of AutoCAD files, allowing Blocks to be converted to groups. In release 1 of MAX, some instability existed in the groups code, and though it has been improved in release 2, it is suggested the user save often when working with groups.

Building Groups

Two commands are used to build groups: Group and Attach. Use the Group command to define any selection as a new group. Use Attach to add any selection to an existing group.

To create a new group from a selection of objects, complete the following steps:

1. Select one or more objects.

2. Choose Group from the Group menu.

3. Enter a name in the Group dialog (see Figure 2.15).

FIGURE 2.15

Creating a new group object.

All objects are valid choices for membership within a group. You can mix geometry, lights, space warps, and even other groups within the same group. When you place a group inside another group, you have what is called a nested group.

T IP _____

Usually you don't want to nest groups more than one or two layers deep. Nesting any further makes it tedious to get to an object in the deepest group.

When you create a group, a special Dummy object called the group node is created. This Dummy object is normally invisible, but when you open the group, the Dummy object appears as a pink colored box that surrounds the objects in the group. When viewing objects in Track View or any other display of hierarchy, the group node is represented as the parent of the member objects.

To add objects to an existing group, do the following:

1. Select one or more objects.

2. Choose Attach from the Group menu.

3. Click any object that is part of an existing group.

To remove an object from a group, do the following

1. Select the group.

2. In the Group pulldown, choose Open.

3. Select the object to be removed and choose detach from the Group pulldown.

NEW TO R2

A new feature in release 2 enables you to see the name of an object simply by holding the cursor over anything unselected. In a group, the group name is in brackets before the name of the object under the cursor.

Transforming and Modifying Groups

You can transform and modify groups in two ways. One way is to transform and modify the full group just as you would with any other object. A second way is to open the group and transform and modify individual objects inside the group.

Transforms and modifiers behave differently when applied to a group as compared to when applied to a single object:

- Transforms applied to a group are carried by the group node. Objects inside the group follow as children of the group node. When you detach an object from a group, it is also detached from the transforms applied to the group. This is especially noticeable when the group transforms are animated. Detaching an object from an animated group drops the object at its current place in the scene and the object no longer inherits any transform animation from the group.

■ Modifiers applied to a group are applied to the selection of all member objects. Each object receives an instance of the modifier. An object retains its instanced modifier even after you detach it from the group.

You can transform or modify individual objects inside a group by first opening the group and then selecting one or more of the member objects. After the group is open, you can work with the member objects the same as you would with any other object in the scene. Any animated effect that you apply to an object inside a group is preserved even after the group is closed.

To open a group in order to transform and modify group members, follow these steps:

1. Select any member object of the group you want to open.

2. Choose Open from the Group menu. When you do, you will see the pink box around the group members. As mentioned earlier, this box is the group node (see Figure 2.16).

FIGURE 2.16
The group node of an open group.

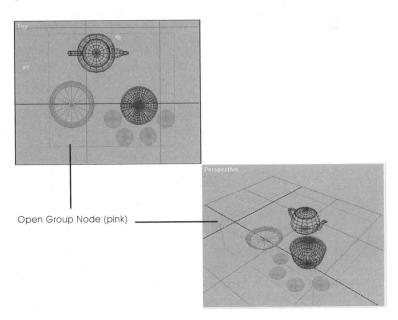

Open Group Node (pink) _____

3. Transform and modify individual members of the group.

For example, imagine that you have modeled an insect inside a glass jar. You then select the insect, jar, and lid and place them inside a group named Bug_Zoo. You can open the group and animate the insect flying around inside the jar. After you close the group, you can animate the entire group moving around the scene while the insect continues to fly around (staying inside the jar).

When a group is open, you have access to the members of the group, but you can also transform with the full group. Transforming the pink group node transforms all the members of the group in the same way as when the group is closed. You cannot, however, apply modifiers to the group while it is open. Either close the group or manually select all members of the group to apply a modifier.

TIP

A quick way to select all the members of an open group is to double-click the group node.

If the open group contains any nested groups, you can open the nested groups by using the same procedure. When you are finished working with the members of an open group, select any member of the open group and choose the Close command. Then the selected group and any open nested groups inside the selected group are closed.

Taking Groups Apart

After you create a group, you may decide that you want to remove some objects from the group or even completely dissolve the group. Take groups apart using three commands from the Group menu: Detach, Ungroup, and Explode.

Use Detach to remove one or more selected objects from an open group.

To detach an object from a group:

1. Open the group containing the objects you want to detach.

2. Select one or more objects to detach.

3. Choose Detach from the group menu.

4. Close the group.

Use Ungroup and Explode to quickly dissolve an entire group. You first select a group and then choose Ungroup or Explode from the Group menu.

The Ungroup command dissolves the selected group, thereby returning the group members to individual object status. Nested groups become separate groups. Any transform animation applied to the group node is lost.

The Explode command dissolves the selected group and all groups nested inside it. All members of the group become individual objects—no nested groups remain. All transform animation applied to group nodes is lost.

Grouping Strategies

Now you know what groups are, as well as how to create, modify, and dissolve them. The only question left is when to use groups. Like everything else in life, groups have benefits and trade-offs. Use the following guidelines to help decide when to use groups.

Use a group to combine objects when:

- You want to transform, modify, and animate the combined objects as a single object. Groups are more convenient than linking all the objects to a Dummy object because you can easily select all the members (children) of a group by selecting any one member.

- You want to animate the individual objects but also have the objects inherit the group animation.

- You want the combined objects to behave as a single object but still want access to the Modifier Stack and Base Parameters of each member of the group. If you combine objects using the Attach command of the Edit Mesh modifier, each attached object becomes a plain mesh and loses its Modifier Stack and Base Parameters.

Do not use a group to combine objects when:

- You will be animating individual objects more than you will be animating the group. Frequently opening and closing groups can become tedious and defeat the benefits of using groups.

- You are organizing related objects for selection purposes. Use named selection sets to organize collections of related objects. Named selection sets are much more flexible for most organizational purposes. For example, one object can belong to multiply named selection sets. If an object is a member of a group, it can be a member of only one group, and any named selection sets it belongs to must include all the members of its group.

■ You need to weld vertices or smooth between the combined objects. The Attach command of the Edit Mesh modifier is the only way to combine objects so that you can weld and smooth between them.

Using Grids and Helpers

The first steps for building precision models involve setting up your reference grids and snap system. While you work in your scene, you can choose from three fixed grids, any number of custom grids, and two distinct snap systems. You also have a number of helper objects that you can create to locate points in space and measure distances.

The use of grids is an important modeling tool that, when used properly, can greatly increase your productivity. The following items are important points to remember about grids:

■ The active grid defines where new objects are created in space. It is also referred to as the Construction plane because everything you construct is placed and aligned with the active grid.

■ Grids define the default snap spacing.

■ Grids and helpers define coordinate systems for transforming objects.

■ Grids and helpers provide a visual reference for defining space and measuring distance.

Setting Up the Home Grid

3DS MAX displays three permanent grids, called the Home grids, for construction and visual reference. These three grids align with the world coordinate system and intersect at the World Coordinate origin. The three Home Grids and their relationship to the World Coordinate system are identified as follows:

- The Top/Bottom grid is aligned with the world X,Y axes. Because this grid is horizontal and often defines the floor of your scene, it is referred to as the Ground plane. It is viewable in the Top, Bottom, User, Perspective, Camera, and Spotlight views.

- The Left/Right grid is aligned with the world Y,Z axes and is viewable in the Left and Right viewports.

- The Front/Back grid is aligned with the world X,Z axes and is viewable in the Front and Back viewports.

The visible grid in a viewport also defines the Construction plane for that view.

You can control the display of the Home grid in the active viewport by any of the following methods:

- Choose Show Grid from the viewport pop-up menu.

- Choose Grids, Show Home Grid from the Views menu.

- Press Shift+G.

Setting Home Grid Spacing

You set the grid spacing for the Home grids by using the Home Grid panel of the Grid and Snap Settings dialog (see Figure 2.17). You display the dialog by choosing Grid and Snap Settings from the Views menu, or by right-clicking the 3D/2.5D/2DSnap Toggle, the Angle Snap Toggle, or the Percent Snap button.

FIGURE 2.17

Home grid settings in the Grid and Snap Settings dialog box.

The Grid Spacing option sets the initial distance between grid lines and sets the Grid Snap value. When you set the Grid Spacing option, keep in mind that you cannot snap to increments smaller than the Grid Spacing. The actual grid spacing varies for each viewport as you zoom in and out of a view. Look at the status line just to the left of the Animate button to see the current grid spacing for the active viewport.

TIP

If you want to snap to increments smaller than Grid Spacing, turn off Inhibit Grid Subdivision below Grid Spacing in the Home Grid tab of the Grid and Snaps Settings dialog.

The Major Lines every Nth option determines which grid lines are emphasized for visual reference. If you set Major Lines every Nth to 10, for example, every tenth line on the grid is emphasized, as shown in Figure 2.18. You need to choose this setting carefully because it also serves as a multiplier for the adaptive grid display used by 3DS MAX.

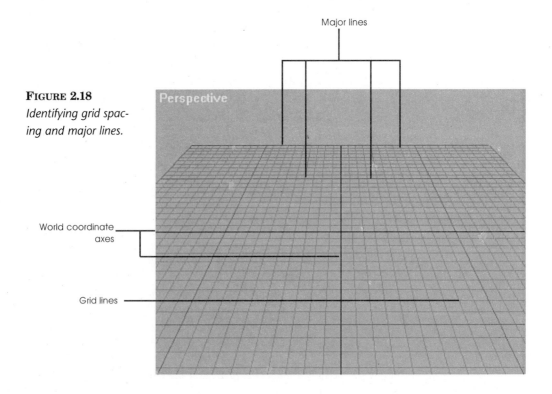

FIGURE 2.18
Identifying grid spacing and major lines.

The adaptive grid display adjusts grid spacing on-the-fly, so that viewports always display a usable grid regardless of their zoom magnification.

To see this, do the following:

1. Choose the Zoom tool, and click and hold it in the Top viewport.

2. As you move your mouse down the screen, watch the Grid Display adapt to the zoom factor changing.

Adaptive Grid Display works exceptionally well for metric units of measure, but it is rather problematical for U.S. standard units. Imagine you are working with a Grid Spacing of 1.0 inch and a Major Lines value of 12 (1.0 foot). When you zoom out, Grid Spacing is resized times 12 (1.0 foot) and Major Lines are at every 12 feet—not a very common measuring scale. If you think carefully about your project, you can probably come up with Grid Spacing and Major Lines values that will even work well with U.S. standard units.

Setting Background and Grid Colors

To change the Viewport Background settings, choose Preferences from the File menu, click the Colors tab, and then change the settings in the Main UI area under Viewport Background (see Figure 2.19). The grid color may be set either as a darker or lighter intensity of grey, or a specific color using the Color Selector dialog.

FIGURE 2.19

Viewport Background and grid color settings.

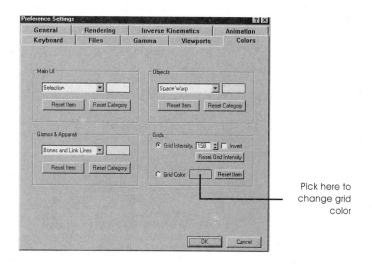

Pick here to change grid color

WARNING

Do not set your background color to pure white unless you change the Selection color to other than white. Otherwise, you will not see your objects selected. Selection color is the first option in the Main UI area of Preferences. You may also want to avoid other colors, such as the pink of groups, the orange of modifiers, and the yellow, red, or green of sub-objects unless you change those also.

Working with Grid Objects

Using the Home Grid is fine for most operations, but what if you want to construct something on top of a table or on the sloping side of a roof? That is when you need to use Grid Objects. Grids are helper objects that can take the place of the Home Grid for construction and transformation commands.

Uses for grids include the following:

- **As an alternative construction plane.** You can align a Grid Object with the surface of another object and then create new objects sitting on the grid.

- **As an alternative Transform Coordinate System.** You can place a Grid Object anywhere in space, such as on a slope and then use the grid's Local Coordinate system for transforming other objects.

- **As a spatial reference.** You can use Grid Objects to define planes and volumes in space. Because Grid Objects do not render, they are very convenient for defining Reference planes in your scene.

Creating a Grid Object

Create a Grid Object by clicking the Helpers category button in the Create panel and then clicking Grid in the Object Type rollout (see Figure 2.20). Dragging in any viewport defines the length and width of the Grid Object. You can adjust the Grid Spacing by following the steps in the exercise below.

NOTE

You will only see the results after the grid is active.

FIGURE 2.20

*Creating a Grid
Object.*

ADJUSTING GRID SPACING

1. Create a Grid Object in the Perspective viewport.

2. Pick the Rotate button in the toolbar, and select and rotate the grid out of alignment with the World Coordinate system.

3. Right-click the Grid Object and choose Activate grid.

4. Pick the Modify tab in the Command panel, adjust the Spacing parameter, and then observe the change. If you do something to a grid but don't see any results, you probably forgot to activate it.

Grid Objects can be used in place of the Home Grid, but they follow a few different rules:

■ When a Grid Object is active, everything you create is placed on the active grid regardless of which view is active (when using non-Grid Display option viewports).

- Grid Objects do not use adaptive grid display. The Grid Spacing and Grid Size are fixed. The Grid Size only controls the visible boundaries of the grid. This grid itself is infinite and you can create objects outside the edges of the grid.

- New in release 2, you can choose the active color to be standard grey, the object color, the Home Grid color, or the Home Grid intensity setting under the Colors tab of Preferences.

Creating with Grid Helpers

Grid Objects are available when you need to construct on planes other than the Home Grid or wish to use the same plane in all viewports. You may find the default Home Grids sufficient when using 3DS MAX to create independent, isolated models. You will, however, find Grid Objects very useful when your models grow in complexity and you need to coordinate with other assemblies, possibly from other programs. Grids prove invaluable for defining Construction planes that are aligned to views, faces, and objects.

New to R2

The option to choose the XY, YZ, and XZ for use and display of a grid has been added in release 2, making it easy to work in a Construction plane perpendicular to a Grid Object not parallel to the World Coordinate system. In addition, you may have a viewport assigned to displaying any of the views of a Grid Object you would normally find available to the Home Grid, such as Top or Right.

Grid Objects are manipulated like any other object, so you can move, rotate, and align them quite easily. The Normal Align function is particularly valuable when building in relation to models.

Using a Grid Object

To use a Grid Object, you must first activate it by selecting a Grid Object and either right-clicking (as shown in Figure 2.21) or by choosing Grids/Activate Grid Object from the Views menu. Once activated, the Home Grids disappear and the grid lines of the Grid Object are displayed. For discussion purposes in this book, the currently active grid refers to either an activated Grid Object or the visible Home plane grid in the current viewport.

FIGURE 2.21

Activating a Grid Object by right-clicking the Grid Object.

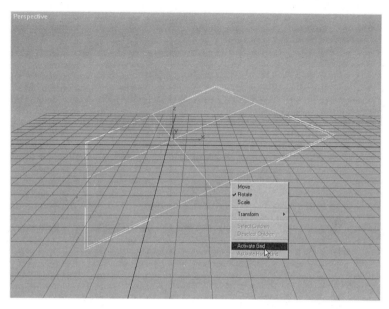

WARNING

It is not advisable to scale Grid Objects. When you scale a Grid Object, its Grid Spacing remains unscaled. The relationship between the visual grid and the snap grid is now disconnected. If you want a larger grid, you should *always* change its creation parameters. If you have accidentally scaled a grid, you can reset the scale to 100 percent with Transform Type-In.

Grid Viewport Options

A viewport can be assigned to be a grid viewport and displays the chosen XY/YZ/XZ-plane view of the currently active Grid Object. When the Home Grids are active, grid viewports display the XY-plane Home Grid (ground plane). Grid views dynamically update as you position and rotate the active Grid Object. Grid views are particularly useful when creating splines at angles to the world axes. In this sense, grid views can be thought of as picture planes upon which to draw in the traditional perspective sense.

Grid Objects are not limited to aiding only in creation. Referencing the active Grid Object as the current coordinate system for transforms, alignment, arrays, and mirroring is often very useful and is especially common for objects that are created on or aligned to the grid.

A good use of a Grid Object is in concert with the Align to View capability found in the Align flyout on the toolbar (covered later in this chapter). A common use of Grid Objects is to draw masks in Video. Let's say, for instance, you want to draw in the Camera view to create a mask (matte object) to cover up geometry with the background. You first create a grid, align it to the Camera view, and then position it between the camera and the first object. Then you can draw in the Camera view to create the mask.

NOTE

Importing models from other programs sometimes places the models extremely far from the world origin because they were modeled in the other program. This location can have the undesirable effect of causing round-off errors in 3DS MAX. One solution is to move the entire scene closer to the origin. This solution, though, is equally undesirable if you plan to continue coordination with the external database. In this case, you need to increase the System Unit Scale under General Preferences.

Using Other Helper Objects

Other types of helper objects are as useful as are Grid Objects. You use these helpers to measure and define points in space and to establish alternate coordinate systems for transforms. Some examples of other types of Helper Objects, discussed in the following sections, are:

- Tape measures

- Points

- Dummy Objects

Using Tape Measures

A tape measure is a handy graphical device used to measure distances. To create a tape, click Tape in the Create panel and drag in any viewport. The triangular head of the tape is placed where you begin dragging, and the tape target is placed where you release the drag. After you create the tape, you can move either the head or the target to place the tape between points that you want to measure. The length of the tape is displayed in the length field of the tape's base parameters, as shown in Figure 2.22.

Figure 2.22

Reading a tape mea-sure's length.

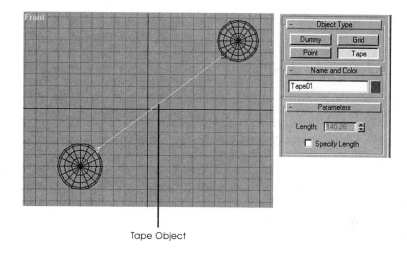

Tape Object

WARNING

Never scale a tape object. Just as with Grid Objects, scaling a tape causes it to display false length values.

Keep in mind that the displayed length of the tape is a three-dimensional distance that can lead to inaccurate results if you concentrate on placing the tape in only a single viewport. Figure 2.23 shows an example of the wrong way to measure the width of an object.

If you concentrate on only the Front viewport, you may think that you are properly measuring the object's width without realizing that the tape also runs back along the length of the object, as evident in the Perspective viewport. In this case, you are not measuring the width of the object, but rather the diagonal distance across the top. You should always check the placement of the tape in at least two viewports to ensure you are measuring the correct distance.

Use Vertex or Edge snap to be sure your tape measure point meets your geometry.

You can also use the tape to mark off a preset distance by checking the Specify Length check box in the tape's Parameters rollout. When you select Specify Length, the Length field jumps to a default value of 100 units. Set the length you want and the tape grows or shrinks to that distance. It may look weird that the tape target does not move with the end of the tape, but just think of the target as an aiming handle—you move the target to aim the tape in the direction you want to measure.

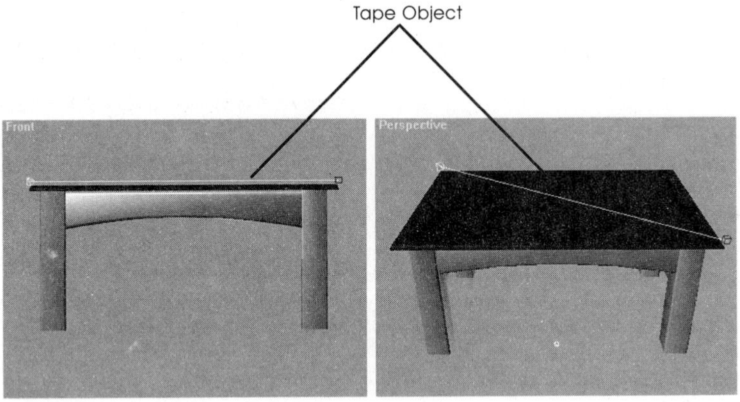

Tape Object

FIGURE 2.23

Incorrectly measuring the width of an object.

Using a tape to mark off a preset distance is particularly useful when you want to position objects a known distance from a given base point. Place the head of the tape at the base point, check Specify Length, and aim the tape in the direction you want to measure. After setting the tape length, you can use 3DS MAX Snaps to position objects at the end of the tape.

Another good use for tape objects is to set up an alternate Transform Coordinate system. The local Z axis of the tape head is aligned with the length of the tape. You can create a tape object between any two points and then slide an object along the length of the tape by picking the tape head as the Transform Coordinate system and constraining movement to the Z axis. Details about choosing Transform Coordinate systems are presented later in this chapter.

Using Points

You use point helpers to define a point and coordinate axis orientation in space. You create a point by clicking Point in the Create panel and then clicking in any viewport. The Point object appears as a yellow X with its local axis tripod displayed (see Figure 2.24). Use the point's base parameters to control the display and length of the axis tripod. The axes are aligned with the active grid axes for the viewport in which the point is created.

One very useful application for Point objects is as Object Snap handles. If you find that none of the new 3D Snaps give you a handle on your object where you want it, you can add a point and define it and the object as a group.

FIGURE 2.24

Creating a Point object.

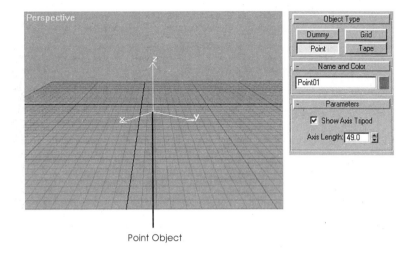

Point Object

Using Dummy Objects

Traditionally, Dummy objects are used as Invisible Link objects when building linked hierarchies (see Chapter 21, "Building and Animating Hierarchies," for more information about linking). Dummies can also be used as placeholders for animation, which can be replaced later with a mesh that may have been in production at the same time.

Dummies also enable the use of more than one kind of animation controller to be applied to an object. An example would be having a noise controller applied to a truck to make it randomly bump up and down, assigning a Dummy to a path controller to follow the road, and then linking the truck to the Dummy.

Basically you can use a Dummy anywhere you need an object without faces and vertices. You can create one by clicking Dummy in the Create panel and then dragging out the radius of a Dummy cube in any viewport. Dummy objects have no parameters, are transformable, and cannot be modified.

Now that you have a feel for where you're working in space, the following section explains how to maneuver objects around in it.

The term "transform" refers to the basic operations of Move, Rotate, and Scale. The design of MAX incorporates both a powerful and intuitive interface for using transforms by allowing the user to choose different Transform Coordinate systems, Transform centers, and Transform Axis constraints. These functions are called Transform Managers. The Transform buttons and Transform Managers are located near the middle of the toolbar (see Figure 2.25).

FIGURE 2.25
*Transform Managers
on the toolbar.*

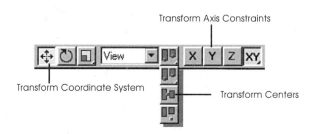

As mentioned in Chapter 1, "Basic Concepts," transforms are always applied toward the end of the dataflow, after all the modifiers in the modifier stack. Also, some objects give up their transforms when used for some purposes. Shape objects, for example, give up their transforms when used as a path or cross-section shape in a Loft object. Mesh objects also give up their transforms when used as targets in a Morph object.

Another way of looking at this is to realize that modifiers change the geometry within an object whereas transforms change only the location of the object in space. Technically speaking, a scale transform does not change geometry within the object. Scale changes the location of the object by varying its size, even if it varies size non-uniformly along each of the three local axes.

The following sections describe how to apply transforms to objects and how to use the various transform managers.

Using the Transform Managers

The Transform Managers are used to control the behavior of the Transform commands. These managers control three properties of transforms:

- **Reference Coordinate system:** Controls how your Construction plane is oriented.

- **Transform center:** Determines the center for the rotation and scale transforms.

- **Restrict to X/Y/Z, XY/YZ/XZ:** Constrains the transform to a single axis or any pair of axes.

3DS MAX remembers the Transform Manager settings you choose for each of the Move, Rotate, and Scale transforms. For example, when you click Move, the settings used the last time you moved are restored to the Transform Managers. Likewise, when you click Rotate, the last rotation settings are restored.

T IP

The fact that your last Transform Manager settings are saved can be a productivity boost after you get used to it, but at first it isn't obvious. You should develop the habit of looking at the Transform Managers every time you use a transform.

Choosing a Transform Coordinate System

You cannot move, rotate, or scale an object in any arbitrary direction. All transforms in 3DS MAX are applied along the X,Y,Z coordinate axes. This would be incredibly restrictive if it were not for the fact that you can choose any arbitrary X,Y,Z coordinate system.

If you have a CAD background, you may be accustomed to specifying an arbitrary rotation axis or arbitrary mirror axis as part of a Transform command. 3DS MAX includes this same functionality, but you set up the axis first by choosing your coordinate system. Then you proceed with the transform.

Keep in mind, the active grid (either the Home Grid or a Grid Object) only affects where objects are created and where Snap points are projected. Transform Coordinate systems affect how you place an object in your scene after the object is created. The Transform Coordinate system can use the active grid, but it doesn't have to.

You can choose from the seven Transform Coordinate systems on the drop-down list in the 3DS MAX toolbar (see Figure 2.26). (For some odd reason the tool tip for this list calls it the Reference Coordinate system even though it works only for transforms.) The View, Screen, and World systems are permanently fixed and unchanging. The Local, Parent, Grid, and Pick systems vary according to the objects you select and your active grid choice. All these systems are described in detail in the Online Reference of MAX under the Transformation Axis Coordinate System List.

Of all these coordinate systems, Pick is probably the most fascinating. By using Pick, you can use the Local Coordinate system of any object in your scene as the Transform Coordinate system for any other object. At first, this might seem to be just an amusing oddity, but consider what you can do using the Pick Coordinate system with a Helper object.

FIGURE 2.26

The Reference (Transform) Coordinate System list.

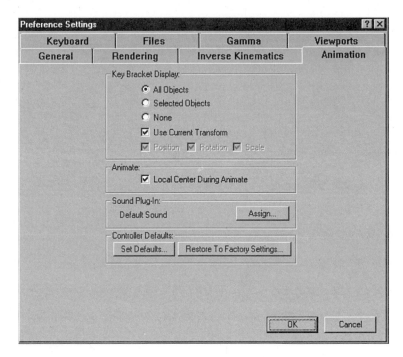

You can use a tape object to define a plumb line between any two points. By using the Pick Coordinate system, you can move or rotate objects about that plumb line. For example, you might pick a tape object placed between two electrodes as your coordinate system. You could then move electrons along the tape by constraining movement to the tape's Z axis.

Choosing a Transform Center

Use the three-button flyout to the right of the coordinate system list to define the transform center (see Figure 2.27). The center comes into play only for rotation and scale transforms. When you move an object, it really doesn't matter what center you use; the object just moves.

FIGURE 2.27

Transform center flyout.

The three transform center choices are as follows:

- **Pivot Point Center** uses each selected object's local Pivot point as the center of rotation and scale. Each object rotates or scales an equal amount about its own Pivot point.

- **Selection Center** uses the geometric center of a bounding box surrounding all selected objects as the center of rotation and scale. The selected objects rotate and scale as a single unit, much the same as if you place the objects in a group.

- **Coordinate System Center** uses the center of the Transform Coordinate system as the center of rotation and scale. This choice is quite useful when using the Parent or Pick Coordinate systems. In those situations, the center of rotation and scale is either the pivot point of the selected object's parents or the Pivot point of the Pick object.

Pivot Point Center is the only valid choice if you want to animate a pure rotation or scale transform. The other two choices combine a move with the rotation and scale. That's why the transform center flyout is gray and cannot be changed when the Animate button is on.

T IP

You can activate the Transform Center buttons when the Animate button is on by unselecting the Local Center During Animate in the Preferences dialog under the Animation tab. Be sure you have experimented with this feature before becoming dependent on it, however. Your results may not always be what you expect.

Object Pivot

Though the next control is not on the toolbar with the rest of the Transform tools, it is still highly integral to the transforming of objects and is most logically spoken of here.

Where an object's Pivot point lies in that object is dependent on the way the object was created. If it is a Standard Primitive, then the programmer of that plug-in determined what its default pivot position is upon creation. If it is an import from another program, and one wasn't assigned in the original program, then the pivot is assigned to the center of the object's bounding box. The pivot of a compound object is defined by the first operand's pivot. The same is true for a Loft object.

The Affect Pivot Only button under the Hierarchy tab of the command panel is used to move or rotate an object's pivot (you cannot scale the pivot). When activated, a Red/Green/Blue 3D tripod superimposes the normal axis tripod (see Figure 2.28). '

TIP

As in the Affect Pivot Only tripod display, you will find that in many places in MAX, Red/Green/Blue is used to represent X/Y/Z, providing a quick graphical tool to help sort out a complicated display of information.

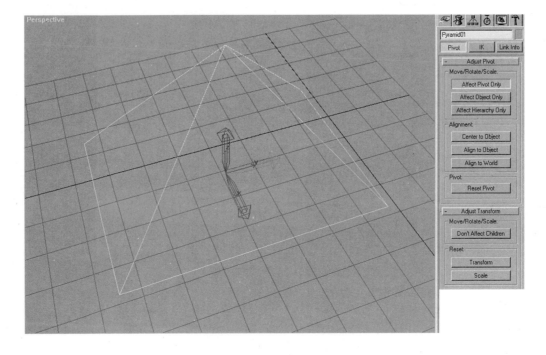

FIGURE 2.28
The Affects Pivot Only button and the 3D pivot displayed.

The following will take you through adjusting the position of the pivot of an object:

1. Make a pyramid in the perspective viewport and observe the position of the axis tripod.

2. Rotate the object to observe how it rotates and then Undo.

3. In the Hierarchy command panel, pick the Affect Pivot Only button and move or rotate the pivot away from its original position.

4. Pick the Affect Pivot Only button again to deselect it.

5. Now rotate the object and observe the change.

NOTE

Object snaps can override the tendency to rotate or scale around an object's pivot. Use that option carefully if you intend to animate your transforms. See the section on using Snap options later in this chapter.

Constraining Transforms

Axis constraints are the final set of Transform Managers. You can choose from the three single axis constraints or from a flyout of three dual axis (planar) constraints. The active transform axis constraint locks the transform effect to that axis or plane. For example, if the X axis constraint is active, you can move along only the X axis.

The default keyboard shortcuts for choosing axis constraints are as follows:

■ **'(grave)** cycles through choosing the four constraint buttons—X, Y, Z, and current dual axis.

■ **~ (tilde)** cycles through the dual axis options without choosing the button.

■ **F5** chooses the X axis constraint.

■ **F6** chooses the Y axis constraint.

■ **F7** chooses the Z axis constraint.

■ **F8** chooses the dual axis constraint. If the dual axis is already chosen, F8 cycles through the dual axis options.

Using the Keyboard to Transform with Precision

If you need real precision for Move, Rotate, and Scale operations, you can use the keyboard to perform the transform. You can use the arrow keys for accuracy using pixels or the Transform Type-In dialogs for accuracy using mathematically precise values.

Using Arrow Keys to Transform

You can Move, Rotate, and Scale objects by using the arrow keys in much the same way you zoom and rotate views. Simply place the cursor over the selected object you want to transform, with a Transform button selected, and use the arrow keys.

The type of transform you use determines which arrow keys you can use:

- Move and Rotate uses both horizontal and vertical arrow keys. If a Transform Axis constraint limits horizontal or vertical movement, the arrow keys still move the cursor, but the selection does not move along the constrained axis.

- Scale Uses only the vertical arrow keys. Up equals increasing scale and down equals decreasing scale.

The arrow keys are actually moving the cursor on the screen—the same as if you were dragging the cursor—and 3DS MAX is translating that movement into transform values. Each key press is read as one pixel of cursor movement. If snaps are on, your object won't transform until your cursor is coincident with a snap position.

Using the Transform Type-In Dialog

You can use the Transform Type-In dialog to enter very precise values for Move, Rotate, and Scale transforms. This dialog floats above the 3DS MAX window and you can use it any time you are transforming an object. To use the Transform Type-In dialog box, choose Transform Type-In from the Edit menu (see Figure 2.29) or right-click an Active Transform button.

The Transform Type-In dialog has two parts. The fields on the left side of the screen always show the absolute values for Move or Rotate in the World Coordinate system and absolute Scale values in the Local Coordinate system for the selected objects. As an example, when using the dialog box for Move, you use the fields on the left to either position an object at a specific coordinate point or to find out what that object's current position is. The right side fields always show a value of 0.0 and are where you enter a relative transform. This means that when you enter a value in a relative field, the object transforms that value relative to the current values in the left or absolute fields.

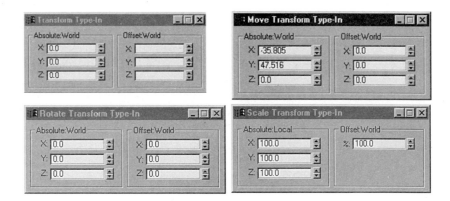

FIGURE 2.29

The Transform Type-In dialog for Move, Rotate, and Scale.

The following example gives you hands-on practice using the Transform dialog to move a box you have created:

MOVING A SELECTED BOX USING THE TRANSFORM TYPE-IN DIALOG BOX

1. Create a box in the perspective viewport away from 0,0,0.

2. Pick to activate and then right-click the Move transform button.

3. In the Transform Type-in dialog, right-click each of the Absolute World spinners to zero them out and watch the movement of the box for each click.

4. Type in 20 in the X Offset World field and observe that the field immediately zeros out after hitting Enter and the Absolute World field for X increments to 20.

As you can see in Figure 2.30, you can Move, Rotate, or Scale selected objects by entering values on either side of the dialog.

FIGURE 2.30

Controlling the position of an object using the Move Transform Type-In dialog box. You call it up by picking and then right-clicking the Select and Move button.

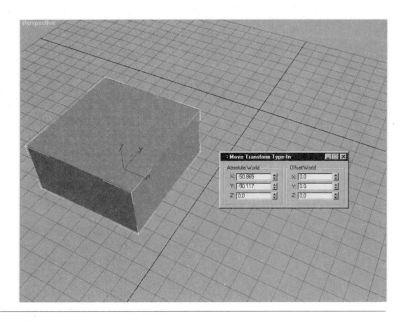

TIP

When you import geometry from other programs or merge in geometry that is positioned in some far off location, select the objects by name and then use Type-In Transforms to move it back to the origin.

NOTE

Notice that the Transform Type-In dialog for Uniform Scale has only one field for Offset World, whereas Non-Uniform Scale and Squash have fields for all three axes.

The Transform Type-In dialog has the secondary benefit of revealing the current transform values of a selected object. Because the dialog always displays absolute world values, you can examine the exact position, rotation, and scale values of an object at any time.

Mirror, Array/Snapshot, and Align

3D Studio MAX combines Move, Rotate, and Scale to create the special transform techniques of Mirror, Array, and Align. Their buttons are to the right of the Transform Managers, as shown in Figure 2.31.

FIGURE 2.31

Mirror,
Array/Snapshot, and
Align buttons on the
toolbar.

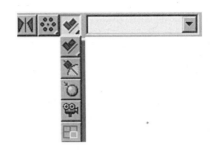

Mirroring Objects

Mirroring an object is a scale transform with a value of –100 percent. You can easily create mirrored objects by using the options in the Mirror dialog (see Figure 2.32). You interactively set options for Mirror Axis, Mirror Offset, and Clone method.

FIGURE 2.32

The Mirror dialog pro-
vides the options for
which axis to use, how
far to move or offset it
from its original posi-
tion, and whether to
clone it.

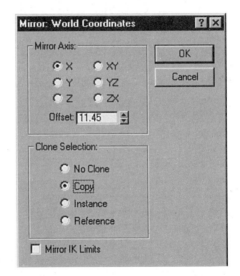

The Mirror dialog reports the current Transform Coordinate system as part of the dialog title. Make sure you set the Transform Coordinate system you want before you click Mirror. If you click Mirror and then realize that you want to change coordinate systems, you must cancel the Mirror dialog, change the coordinate system, and then click Mirror again.

You have three decisions to make when mirroring an object:

- **Mirror Axis:** Choose one of the six options for either single-axis or dual-axis mirroring from the Mirror Axis area of the dialog. The Mirror Axis passes through the current transform center point and the axis orientation is set by the current coordinate system.

- **Mirror Offset:** If you don't want the mirrored object to stay in its default location, you can specify an offset distance in the Mirror Axis area of the dialog. The offset moves the object an additional distance along the Mirror Axis from the default location. You can type the distance into the field or drag the spinner to watch the mirrored object move away from its original location.

- **Clone Method:** Usually you mirror an object because you want a mirrored clone of the original object. This is useful when you model objects with symmetry. You model one-half of the symmetrical object and then mirror it to get the other half, placing it using Offset. Choose Copy, Instance, or Reference from the Clone Selection area to create a new mirrored object from the original. Choosing No Clone mirrors the original object.

T IP

Even if you do not want to clone the mirrored object, you may find it handy to choose Copy while you experiment with various Mirror axes and offsets. With Copy selected you always see the original object and the Mirror result; this gives you a base reference to judge the effect of your choices. When you decide on the Mirror axis and offset you want, choose No Clone before clicking OK.

Arraying Objects

Arrays are made by cloning objects with multiply repeated transforms. You can create arrays by using one of these two methods:

- Press shift while dragging a transform and enter the number of copies you want in the Clone Options dialog (see Figure 2.33). This technique is handy for simple, quick, linear, radial, and scale arrays.

- Click the Array button on the toolbar to enter values in the Array dialog.

Pressing Shift while dragging causes the Clone Options dialog to appear (see Figure 2.33). Choose the Clone Method of Copy, Instance, or Reference and set the number of clone objects you want to create in the simple array.

FIGURE 2.33

Clone Options dialog.

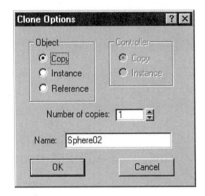

You can quickly build up complex geometry by using the Array dialog as shown in Figure 2.34. As in the Mirror process, make sure you set the coordinate system and center you want before clicking Array.

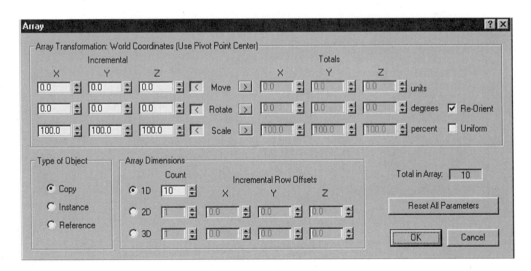

FIGURE 2.34

The Array dialog box revised in R2.

Although the new release 2's revised Array dialog looks somewhat daunt-ing, it is easy to use once you understand the reasons for its layout. The following paragraphs begin by explaining how to create linear, grid, and volume arrays, followed by radial arrays.

Working in the Array Transformation Area

The Array Transformation area is simply used to determine how much movement, rotation, and scale you want in each copy of the original object. For example, if you enter 50 in the X parameter of the Incremental Move row, you create copies 50 units apart in the X direction. If you enter 20 in the Z parameter of the Incremental Rotate row, each copy rotates around its own axis 20 degrees more than the last copy.

The Array Dimensions area determines how many copies in each of three directions you want. Think direction instead of dimension in this area of the dialog to more easily follow what is happening.

The 1D field is used to create a linear array, which just means an array in a single direction. Using only the Move portion of the above example, 10 in the 1D Count field gives you 10 copies along the X axis 50 units apart.

The 2D fields are used to array the 1D values to create a grid array—in other words, an array of rows and columns in a plane. Ten in the 2D Count field with 50 in the Y parameter field gives you 10 copies of the previous 10, incremented 50 units between each copy in the Y direction.

The 3D fields are used to array the 2D values to create a volume array. Ten in the 3D Count field with 50 in the Z parameter field gives you 10 copies of the previous 100, incremented 50 units in the Z direction.

The following example walks you through the steps in creating and experi-menting with the various types of arrays described above.

CREATING LINEAR, GRID, AND VOLUME ARRAYS

1. Using the standard primitive Prism, create a prism in the perspective view with 10 units for each side and also for the height.

2. Start the Array command, using Figure 2.35 as a guide to enter the incremental X Move value and the 1D value in the Array Dimensions area and hit OK.

6. If you'd like to experiment by creating a spiral staircase (also known as a helix array), press Undo and start the Array command again.

7. In the Z field of the Move row of the Incremental section, enter 20 and press OK.

Again, with a little experimentation, you'll find it easy to predict what values will give you desired results.

The Reorient button at the end of the rotate row determines whether or not objects are rotated around their local axis when being rotated around the Coordinate Axis or Selection center. The difference can be seen in Figure 2.36.

FIGURE 2.36
Affect of using Reorient with radial arrays

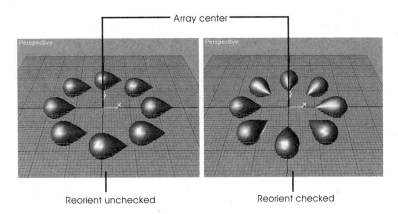

Array center

Reorient unchecked   Reorient checked

Snapshot Arrays

One last type of array uses the Snapshot button in the Array flyout (see Figure 2.37). A snapshot is a type of temporal array that creates clones based on an object's changes over time. Snapshot is the only array technique that can also capture and freeze animated modifier changes.

For Snapshot to be of any use, you must first animate an object's transforms or modifiers. You then use options in the Snapshot dialog to specify how many clones you want to create over time. Snapshot then creates clones at regular time intervals.

The options in the Snapshot dialog fall into two groups: Snapshot and Clone Method. With the Snapshot option, you choose the time parameters for creating the snapshots. Select Single to create a single clone at the time set by the Time Slider; choose Range to specify a time range and the number of clones to create over that range. With the Clone Method option, you can choose one of the three standard options of Copy, Instance, or Reference, or you can choose the special option Mesh.

FIGURE 2.37

*Use the options in the
Snapshot dialog to
determine how many
clones you want to
create over time.*

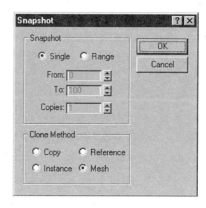

The Mesh option collapses the modifier stack to freeze the modified form of
the object at each time interval. This process wipes out all modifiers and
base parameters, converting the object to a simple mesh. See Chapter 7,
"Modifier Basics" for information about collapsing the Modifier stack.

It is possible to create a helix array with snapshot. To do so, you first create
a helix shape and animate an object following the helix as a motion path.
Once the object is animated, you can use snapshot to place copies of the
object around the helix (see Figure 2.38).

FIGURE 2.38

*You can create a heli-
cal array using
Snapshot.*

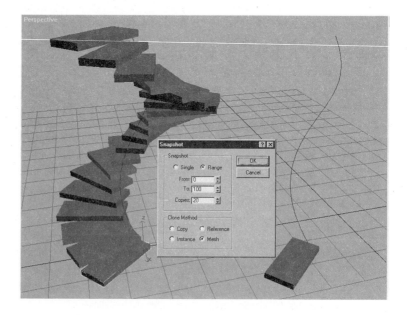

TIP

The biggest annoyance in creating arrays is that they are not parametric objects. If you create an array of 10 windows and later decide you really wanted 20 windows, there is no Array parameter to go and change. To create parametric arrays, use the new Scatter object (see Chapter 10). You can use one parametric object as the distribution object, which you can change at anytime to update your array.

Working with Alignment Tools

Alignment, like Array, is just a transform technique for positioning objects according to specified relationships. Align forms no special connection to objects and as soon as you complete the command, you can use another transform to move the objects out of alignment.

If you want aligned objects to remain aligned, you must group or link them. Use the buttons in the Align flyout to move and rotate objects to align with other objects automatically (see Figure 2.39). With release 2 of MAX you now can align selected sub-objects with other objects. You can also use the new Link Controller to align objects over time.

FIGURE 2.39
Buttons in the Align flyout.

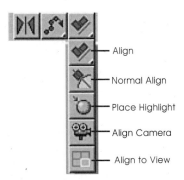

Align

Normal Align

Place Highlight

Align Camera

Align to View

Align

Align moves an object to occupy the same X,Y or Z coordinates as another object. It also allows rotation alignment relative to the local axis as well as match the scale of the aligned to object. The Align command is most useful for the following alignment tasks:

- Aligning objects by geometric extents. This works best with regular, straight-edged geometry, such as boxes and cylinders.

- Aligning objects by pivot point. This is useful when setting up hierarchies and IK joints.

- Aligning helper objects to other objects.

Align uses three techniques:

- **Align positions (move)** is based on the objects' bounding box in the current reference coordinate system.

- **Align orientation (rotate)** is based on the object's Local Coordinate system.

- **Match scale** is new in release 2 and matches scale based on the object's Local Coordinate system.

To perform an align, you need to select the source objects, click Align, and then click a target object to display the Align Selection dialog (see Figure 2.40).

FIGURE 2.40

Align Selection dialog.

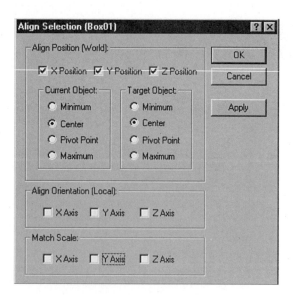

The following exercise walks you through the steps to perform an align.

ALIGNING OBJECTS USING THE ALIGN COMMAND

1. Reset if necessary and create two boxes in the Perspective viewport. The first 30 × 30 × 30 units and the other 100 × 15 × 15.

2. With the second box selected, click the Align command to bring up the Align Selection dialog.

3. Although the dialog is not modeless, you may still see the effects of changes in the viewports. Move the dialog so you can observe the Perspective viewport.

4. Turn on the X, Y, and Z position buttons one at a time and observe the changes.

5. Try different combinations of Current and Target Object options.

Aligning by Face Normals

Use the Normal Align button to align objects surface to surface. This is especially useful when you are working with very irregular geometry or need to place objects so that they are tangent to each other. After the objects are aligned, you can Rotate or Move the source objects about the aligned normal axis.

The following exercise reviews Align by aligning a window with a Boolean created hole and then shows how to use Normal Align by placing a handle on the window frame.

ALIGNING OBJECTS BY FACE NORMALS USING NORMAL ALIGN

1. Open Normal Align.max from the accompanying CD.

2. In the upper viewport, select the window, start the Align command, and pick the wall.

3. Pick X, Y, and Z Position, Center for Current Object, Pivot Point for Target Object, X for Align Orientation, and hit OK.

4. Pick the Move Transform button, constrain to Y, and move the window to sit properly in the wall.

5. Select the handle in the right viewport, pick and hold down on the Align button to open the flyout and choose Normal Align.

6. Click the surface of the handle that will mate with the window frame. Notice a blue arrowed line displays to help determine the center of alignment (see Figure 2.41).

FIGURE 2.41

Placement of the normals for aligning the handle to the window frame.

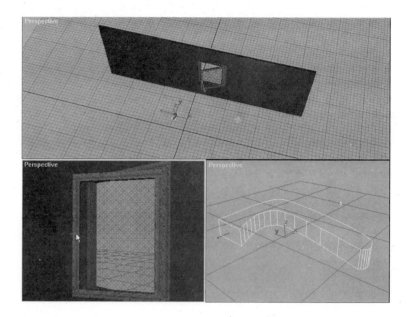

7. In the left viewport, pick the window frame as in the figure. Notice the green arrowed line defining where you want the normal and the handle to sit.

8. Set the Rotation Offset to 90 and render. Notice that if the placement of the current or target normal is a little off, you can adjust the current objects Position Offset.

NEW TO R2

New to release 2, Normal Align now respects the smoothing groups of an object rather than being limited to only face normals. You can test this by aligning to a standard sphere and then comparing the results to aligning with Smooth turned off for the sphere in the Modify panel.

Figure 2.43 shows the procedure for selecting source and target normals, and the Normal Align dialog.

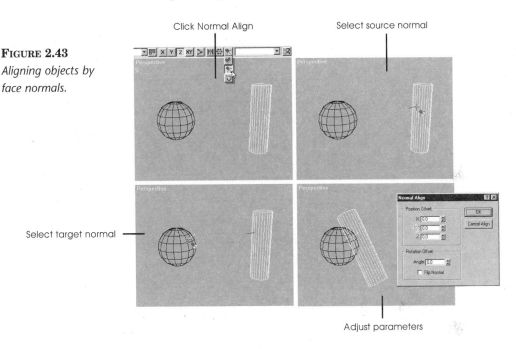

FIGURE 2.43

Aligning objects by face normals.

TIP

An extremely useful technique is to align a Grid Object to another object using Normal Align. Doing this creates a Construction plane aligned with the surface of an object. You can the use the grid as a reference coordinate system to Transform objects aligned with the surface or as the active grid to create new objects aligned with the surface.

Aligning with Place Highlight

You use Place Highlight to align source objects' negative Z axes with the reflected line of sight off a face of the target object. The result produced by Place Highlight is dependent upon the view in which you select the target face.

The original purpose for Place Highlight was to help place lights to create specular highlights at specific locations on an object's surface. It was later found that it was excellent for locating objects to get them to reflect at a specific point on a reflective surface, such as the moon on a lake. The following exercise illustrates how you would use Place Highlight to create such a scene.

CREATING THE MOON'S REFLECTION USING PLACE HIGHLIGHT

1. Open Align Highlite.max from the book's CD.

2. Select the Moon object (Sphere01).

3. Pick Place Highlight from the Align flyout.

4. Pick, hold down, and drag on the water in the Camera viewport, releasing when you have the Blue Normal icon about where you want the majority of the moon to reflect.

5. Render in Draft mode. Repeat steps 3 and 4 until satisfied with the result. Then render in Production mode.

Be aware that some solutions for the angle of the moon relative to the surface of the water require more precision than can be calculated with MAX—specifically those solutions that bring the moon closer to the horizon. This is why sometimes nothing seems to happen as you move the normal around.

Align Camera

The Align Camera command (new to R2) is very similar to the Normal Align, except that it only works with cameras and does not allow for adjustment after the alignment. Any adjustments you may need to do can be done using normal Camera Display buttons. It works with both camera types. For a target camera, it places the target on the face you are aligning the camera to. For a free camera, it places the center of the view plane on the face normal you are aligning to.

Match Camera to View

Another alignment tool (new to R2) for cameras not found in the Align flyout is the Match Camera to View option found in the Views pulldown. Simply select a camera, right-click the viewport you want it matched to in order to make that viewport current, and choose Match Camera to View. This is a long awaited for wishlist item—good for when you have that perfect Perspective view you want to save or use to animate.

Align to View

This feature (new to R2) simply aligns an object to the viewing plane of the current viewport. When you start the command, a dialog comes up enabling you to align one of the three local axes of the object in either the negative or positive direction of the axis using Flip (see Figure 2.44).

FIGURE 2.44

Accessing the Align to View dialog.

Working with Snap Options

To give more accuracy to the placement and creation of objects, a feature found common to CAD programs called Snap is also found in MAX. Snap is fundamentally a tool that uses specific grid and object features to attract the cursor. This means if you have Snap set to grid points, whenever your cursor comes close to a grid intersection the cursor snaps to occupy that point with eight decimal point accuracy. Snap can also be used to limit a transform to specific increments, such as rotating an object such that the rotation only rests at five degree increments.

3DS MAX has a fairly complex Snap system. You may find the Snap system a little confusing at first, but in time you will find it to be quite useful. Position Snaps are based on parts of the grid, such as the grid lines or grid intersections, and parts of objects, such as vertex, edge, or bounding box. Snap values also control Rotation Angle and Scale Percentage snaps when the Angle Snap Toggle and Percent Snap Toggle buttons.

Which Snap method is active at any given time is a function of the Command mode you are in and your choice of Snap modes from the prompt line. Figure 2.45 identifies the various Snap controls in 3DS MAX.

FIGURE 2.45

Snap controls in 3DS MAX.

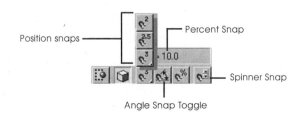

In 3D Studio VIZ (an Architectural version of R1), the Position Snap function was overhauled to accommodate the requests of architects made since the first release of 3D Studio. The code was so successful it has been included in release 2 of MAX. Priority over what gets snapped to has been removed, but object snaps have been added, allowing the user to snap to more parts of an object than just its vertices and edges.

NOTE

For the purposes of this book, the term "Object Snaps" refers to the options in the Snaps tab of the new Grid and Snaps Settings dialog. Object Snap is a term used in AutoCAD and is used here to create consistency for the user base this feature was targeted at.

Setting Up Grid and Spatial Snaps

If you have read the previous sections of this chapter on using grids and creating Grid Objects, then you already know that the Grid Spacing value also sets the Grid Snap. You set grid spacing for the Home Grid using the Grid and Snap Settings dialog; you set grid spacing for Grid Objects using their parameters spinner.

You can set Spatial Snap options by using the Snaps tab of the Grid and Snap Settings dialog (see Figure 2.46).

Snap Strength sets the radius of a snap field around the cursor; geometry must be within the snap strength radius before the cursor snaps to that location. High values make the cursor very sensitive, jumping from snap point to snap point. Low values make the cursor less sensitive, so that you must move the cursor very close to a snap point before it "snaps."

FIGURE 2.46

Snaps panel in the Grid and Snap Settings dialog.

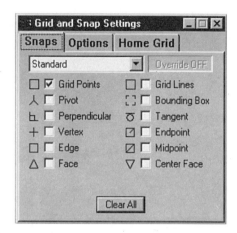

Using Snap for Creation

When you use snap to create objects, you are using a mixture of spatial snaps and grid snap. Spatial snaps control the location of points on the Construction plane and Grid Snap controls height values along the Z axis of the Construction plane.

Your options for creating object snaps vary, depending on the settings you have chosen. Keep the following points in mind when using snap for creation:

- When the Spatial Snap button is set to 2D or 2.5D, you can only snap to vertices and edges that lie directly on the Construction plane.

- When the Spatial Snap button is set to 3D, the selected Snap options in the Snaps tab of the Grid and Snap Settings dialog determine where your objects start their creation and are always created parallel to the current construction plane.

- Height values such as Cylinder, Box, and Cone height snap to the grid spacing of the active grid.

TIP

In addition to the new Third Object Snaps, an Object Snap overrides function can be used to temporarily choose an object snap other than those selected in the Snaps tab of the Grid and Snaps Settings dialog. You can invoke that function at any time by holding down Shift while right-clicking in a viewport.

Using Snap for Moving Objects

If you are looking for the Absolute/Relative options found in R1 of MAX, you will see that the button on the status bar and in the Grid and Snaps Settings dialog for toggling that feature has been removed. Now whether an object is moved to rest on the current grid or moved in snap increments relative to its initial position is determined by how you use Object Snaps.

The following exercise shows you how to use snap for moving objects first relative to its original position and then relative to the grid:

USING SNAP TO MOVE AN OBJECT

1. Create a box in the Perspective viewport with snap toggled off, making sure that the corners do not rest on the grid.

2. Make sure the 3D Snap Option is visible and on, and right-click it to bring up the Grid and Snaps Settings dialog box.

3. In the Snaps tab of the dialog box, check only the Grid Points option. You may leave the dialog open, as it is now modeless in R2.

4. Select and move the box. Notice that it moves in snap increments relative to its original position.

5. Now make it so that both Grid Points and Vertex are checked in the settings dialog.

6. Move your cursor so that it rests over one of the lower corners of the box, until a Blue Cross icon shows on that vertex.

7. Click and drag the box and notice that the corner now snaps to the grid intersections, behaving as an absolute snap.

The rest of the object snaps found in the Grid and Snaps Settings dialog box will enable you to snap to different parts and aspects of objects. You are encouraged to read the short descriptions of each object snap in the Online Reference under help and to experiment with each option.

Using Angle Snap

The Angle Snap setting is useful for object and view rotation. Enter a value in the Angle field of the Grid and Snap Settings dialog under the Options tab to specify a constraint angle for interactive rotations. The default setting is 5.0 degrees, but if you are, for example, an architect, you might consider 15.0 degrees a more useful value. An Angle Snap of 15 degrees enables you to easily specify the major angles common to architecture and manufacturing: 15, 30, 45, 60, and 90 degrees.

Angle Snap applies only to interactive rotations where you drag in a viewport. Angle Snap has no effect on angle fields, such as a bend angle.

Using Percent Snap

Enter a value in the Percent field under the Options tab of the Grid and Snap Settings dialog box to specify a percentage increment for interactive scale operations.

TIP

The default keyboard shortcuts for the different snap functions are S to toggle on/off position snaps (2D/2.5D/3D), A to toggle on/off angle snap, and Shift-Ctrl-P to toggle on/off scale percent snap.

Using Spinner Snap

This snap controls how much a numeric field changes when you click the Up or Down spinner arrows. You use it to control the increments that all spinner fields step through. Spinner Snap is set in the General panel of the Preference Settings dialog. You can quickly display the General panel of the Preference Settings dialog by right-clicking the Spinner Snap button.

Spinner Snap affects only the result of clicking the Up and Down spinner arrows. It does not constrain the values you type into a field, nor does it affect dragging a spinner arrow.

Click the Spinner Snap button on the Prompt line to toggle Spinner Snap on and off.

In Practice: Getting Oriented in 3D Space

- **Selecting Objects:** The Transform tools can also be used for selection. Press Ctrl to add to a selection and press Alt to remove from a selection.

- **Named Selection Sets:** Use named selection sets as a way to manage and organize the objects in your scene.

- **Select by Property:** Use selection filters and options in the Select Objects dialog to efficiently select objects based on common properties such as color, object type, and name.

- **Grouping Objects:** Use groups to combine objects so that they can be manipulated as a single object. Groups are more permanent than named selection sets but more flexible than attaching objects with an Edit modifier.

- **Using Helpers:** Use Helper objects to build connections between objects (through linking) and to define alternative coordinate systems and snap points.

- **Transforms:** Use Transform Managers to work with alternative coordinate systems, alternative center points, and to constrain transforms to selected axes.

- **Work Precisely:** Set Grid and Snap options to work to regular spacings. Use numeric fields and Transform Type-In to set precise values.

Part II

DESIGN THEORY FOR ANIMATORS

Chapter 3

MIXING COLOR AND LIGHT

As a 3D animator, you may be the ultimate jack of all trades. When you plan your animation, you assume the tasks of creative direction, scene design, scene lighting, and choreography. What starts out as a creative idea quickly turns into a major undertaking, and 3DS MAX R2 provides you with most of the tools you need to complete most projects. Think of the program as your virtual Swiss army knife. Before you can effectively use 3DS MAX R2, however, you should understand some key concepts related to the many tasks in any project. One of the most important concepts is using color and light.

Look around you. Why are stop signs red? Why are baby nurseries blue and pink? The decision of which color to use in certain situations is crucial. Color has the effect of creating mood, and suggesting emotional and physical actions. With animation, as in any visual medium, you are primarily telling a story with pictures. The use of colors and lighting affects should be a conscious part of your design process. Your understanding of the concept of mixing color and light can dramatically enhance your work.

In this chapter, you explore various concepts of color and light and how they relate to computer graphics and 3D Studio MAX. In particular, this chapter discusses the following topics:

- Pigment color models

- Color as reflected light

- Mixing color in 3D Studio MAX

- Color composition

- Influences of natural light color

- Influences of artificial light color

- Influence of colored lamps

Color is usually the most referred to characteristic of a surface. When a stop sign appears red to your eye, you make the conclusion that the stop sign is "red," or that it is painted red. In reality, it is not the surface that is red, but the light reflected from it. The pigment with which the sign is painted absorbs all the light spectrum except for red, so it is the red part of the spectrum that reflects back to your eye. Your eye senses the reflected red light, and your brain concludes that the sign is indeed red. Figure 3.1 diagrams how white light reflects off such a sign.

In daily life, you do not interact with colors of light. You don't specify them, you rarely mix or play with them, and you are in only a few situations where the majority of the spectrum is not present. You are accustomed to the effects of white, or near-white, light during most of your life. For the most part, you interact with color by dealing with substances that reflect light predictably, which are called pigments. Even if you do not use traditional artistic pigments, such as paints or ink, you experience the color mixing of pigments whenever you cook, mix drinks, spill liquids, or even have laundry disasters. Color is an important component of your life—you coordinate and match colors whenever you design, decorate, or dress.

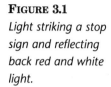

FIGURE 3.1
Light striking a stop sign and reflecting back red and white light.

Colors in computer graphics are quite different from colors in daily life. You use a computer, and a program such as 3DS MAX R2, to create, mix, and manipulate light. The color of light you create in 3DS MAX R2, which pigments reflect, is actually the "color" that your eyes see. Manipulating the lighting in your animation affects the perception of different colors in your scene and can be confusing at first. By first understanding the colors of pigment, learning about the intricacies and effects of light becomes much easier.

Pigment Color Models

The color model you learned as a child is based on pigment; yellow paint mixed with blue paint forms green paint. These are the color rules that pigments, paints, and even crayons follow, and the three primary colors are red, yellow, and blue. As primaries, these colors are pure—they are not mixed from any others and are used to mix all other colors. When these primary colors are mixed in equal strength, the secondary colors—orange, green, and purple—are formed. The infinite number of gradations possible between these primary and secondary colors is often referred to as being harmonious, or analogous. Because color models are based on their primaries, this model is often referred to as the Red-Yellow-Blue (RYB) color model. Although intuitive, this model is not completely correct because every color cannot be mixed from the three primaries.

The RYB Color Model

The color wheel is the traditional tool for demonstrating the RYB model, as shown in Figure 3.2. The primaries are placed on an equilateral triangle that has the secondary colors forming an inverse triangle. Colors proceed around the circle in the order of the light spectrum, or rainbow. Many artists organize their palettes as a color wheel so that color mixing is quick and predictable. (It is somewhat ironic that although the palette is organized according to the light spectrum, it is primarily used to discuss the mixing of pigments.)

FIGURE 3.2
The RYB Color Wheel and overlapping paint circles. This figure refers to color plate 1.

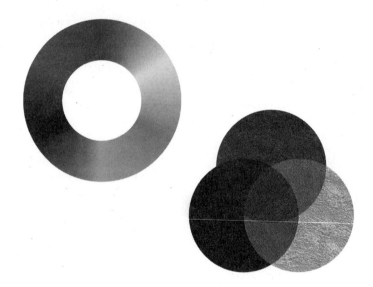

Blending Pigment Color

Three overlapping circles of primary colored "paint" serve to show the basics of pigment blending (see the first color plate). In the plate, the three circles mix to form the secondaries. Brown is formed as the three blend together in the middle, which is also the result of mixing complementary colors. Because these are across from each other on the RYB color wheel, they contain all three primaries. White is represented by the absence of color because it's actually the canvas or paper on which pigment is applied.

The color missing from the color wheel is black. As a child, you were taught to create black by mixing all the other colors, but that usually results in creating "mud," not black. Because of this difficulty, many people regard black as a primary and purchase it as a separate pigment. As the properties of color are further understood, however, it is apparent that the absence of black is actually a weakness in the RYB color model. Although the RYB model is intuitive in relation to the world's common colors, it is actually incomplete.

The CYM Color Model

Although the RYB model is extremely old and was used by most of the masters, it is not an accurate color model. Obtaining the true, intense colors of violet, magenta, and cyan by mixing the RYB primaries is as impossible as mixing a true black. Confronted with this dilemma, many art students are told that these colors are simply difficult to mix and that it is best to purchase them in tube form. This is actually a misunderstanding of color because the colors mentioned previously can never be mixed from red, yellow, and blue—they are *true* primaries. This is not to say that traditional artists do not know what they are doing; they are using a color model that they can relate to the world around them.

Pigment Primaries

The three pigment primaries of cyan, yellow, and magenta are actually the complementary colors of white light, whose primaries are red, green, and blue. Both of these models are shown in Figure 3.3. All pigments (or subtractive substances) are formed from these three colors. The use of these primary colors make this the CYM color model. In the CYM model, red is a mixture of magenta and yellow, blue is a blend of cyan and magenta, and what most people regard as yellow tends to be yellow with a tint of magenta. One reason the CYM color model is not extensively taught is that these intense, primary colors are unnatural and difficult to find and relate to in the real world. A true primary in nature is rare, as is its day-to-day use

FIGURE 3.3

Three intersecting cir-cles of RGB light and CYM ink (refer also to color plate 1).

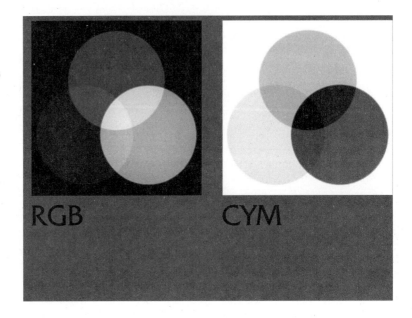

NOTE

If nature abhors a vacuum, it at least hates a pigment primary. This difficulty of creating true cyan, magenta, and yellow pigments is one strong reason why the RYB model has been used for so long and persists today. Pure yellows weren't actually available until the 1800s and a true magenta wasn't developed until the 1850s. Artists through the ages have been forced to use pigments whose colors have already been subtracted, or mixed. A good example is to look at old color plates that use RYB as their mixing model. They often look flat and muddy because they rely heavily on black for darkening. This lack of intense primaries also is one reason that the old masters' paintings have a certain mood and color theme common to them; the intense primaries simply weren't available. You should consider this a testament to the skill and observations of earlier artists, rather than a reflection of their unfamiliarity with the CYM or RGB model.

Four-Color Printing and CYMK

An important difference with CYM is that mixing the primaries together results in black and not the familiar brown result of mixing red, yellow, and blue.

NOTE

When you create colors with the CYM model, and thus mix pigments, the ingredients often are expressed in terms of percentages of the mix (for example, 50 percent yellow, 45 percent cyan, and five percent magenta make a certain shade of green). These form the recipes for a painter's sundries. Using ratios to describe color is quite analogous to the color amounts you specify in 3DS MAX R2.

Color printing is a pigment-based media that requires black and uses the CYM model globally. Because of this, CYM often is referred to as an *ink color model*, in which cyan, yellow, and magenta are the primaries, and black is created by mixing them. Three overlapping circles of "ink" serve to show this basic model. In reality, the mixed black is a very deep and intense blue or purple, but is perceived as black. Although you can mix all printed black after this fashion, the printing industry uses black ink in addition to CYM to prevent the alignment nightmare of requiring all three primaries to produce the black you see in most text and graphics. Printing is referred to as a four-color process, in which black is an added color, the K in CYMK.

Color as Reflected Light

Pigment color actually is the light reflected from an object. Colored light, the light reflected off objects, is what makes up our visible world. An object is red because it absorbs the blue and green spectrum and reflects the remaining red light. Figure 3.4 demonstrates this process by showing the illumination of two red stop signs with white lettering. The first sign is illuminated with white light, which reflects red off the field, and red, green, and blue off the lettering. The second sign is illuminated with only cyan light. Because there is no red to reflect back, the field remains black and absorbs all the green and blue light. The white lettering reflects back the green and blue light and now reads as being cyan.

Each pigment absorbs a particular portion of the spectrum and reflects the light with which it is associated. Mixed pigments actually subtract the various colors of the spectrum from the blend to form the new "color." Blue (which does not reflect red or yellow) mixed with yellow (which does not reflect red or blue) forms green by completely subtracting the capability of the blend to reflect red. Pigments are subtractive and are what 3DS MAX R2 refers to when it talks about a transparent material in the Materials Editor being "subtractive."

The RGB Model

When white light refracts through a prism, its color components separate to create a rainbow. This rainbow is the spectrum particular to white light and the color range that the human eye can perceive. The colors proceed across the spectrum in the order red, orange, yellow, green, blue, indigo, and violet to form the acronym ROYGBIV (indigo is included primarily to make the abbreviation pronounceable). Of these spectral colors, the primaries are red, green, and blue, and the color model for light is referred to as the RGB model.

NOTE

Non-white lights refract their own spectrum because part of the total (white) spectrum must be missing for them to be "colored."

Whereas white is the absence of pigment in the CYM model (represented by the white of the canvas), black is the absence of light in the RGB model (and can be thought of as true darkness). The three primaries of light blend to form white light. As they blend with each other, they form the secondaries of cyan, yellow, and magenta, the primaries of the CYM pigment model.

The dichotomy between light and pigment is an important concept to grasp to fully understand how materials appear in varying lighting conditions. Light and pigment are opposites yet are also complements to one another. One model's primaries are the other model's complements. RGB emits light; CYM reflects it. An object's pigment cannot be seen without light striking it, whereas colored light needs an opaque surface to strike to be seen. Combining all light colors results in white, whereas combining all pigment colors results in black. RGB mixes its colors by adding them, and CYM by subtracting them.

Mixing Colors of Light

Three overlapping "spotlights" of light demonstrate this basic model (refer once again to the first color plate). Here, black is represented by the absence of color, and white is created by the mixing of the three primaries red, green, and blue. As the pools of light mix, they form the secondaries cyan, magenta, and yellow. Viewing the two models side-by-side, it is suddenly obvious that the RGB model is truly the inverse of the CYM model, as each one's primaries are the other's secondaries.

The example model lightrgb.max uses three spotlights to demonstrate the additive RGB light color model. The model is made up of three spotlights shining down on a matte white square. The spotlights represent pure colored light on a white surface with no other light or pigment affecting them.

The scene in Figure 3.5 shows three primary colored spotlights of red, green, and blue in two shaded viewports. These circles represent the light primaries. Where only two of the circles overlap, you see the pigment primaries of yellow, cyan, and magenta. Where all three circles overlap, you see the mixture of all light (white), which is equal to the absence of all pigment.

N OTE

The circles of light appear "jagged" around their edges in the shaded viewports because the 3DS MAX interactive renderer uses Gouraud shading for its display. This method calculates lighting effects by shading the vertices in the model. The effect of lighting will appear only as accurate as the displayed mesh is dense. To see the true effect of the light, you will need to perform a production rendering.

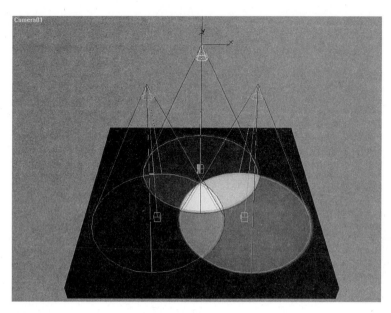

FIGURE 3.5

The three spotlights of primary color in lightrgb.max.

The following exercise demonstrates the additive RGB color model.

USING SPOTLIGHTS TO EXAMINE RGB COLOR

1. Load the lightrgb.max scene from the accompanying CD.

2. Activate the Top viewport and press the Quick Render button. The pools of light render as perfectly round circles.

3. Select the red spotlight, Spot-Red, and click the Modify panel to see the light's current settings.

4. Spot-Red has the RGB amounts 255,0,0—meaning that it is pure red light without green or blue components. The other spotlights are similarly saturated.

5. You can experiment with the effect of light by adjusting the color of the spotlights and repositioning them.

What you have to get used to is that light color is additive and pigments are subtractive. With additive colors, the more color you add, the whiter the hue; with pigments, the more color you add, the darker the hue. This concept is understandably foreign because most people outside the theater or lighting industry have little to no experience (or even the opportunity) mixing colors of light. In reality, however, you are in the presence of the RGB model every day because every color television and computer monitor displays color through separate red, green, and blue channels.

A thorough understanding of the RGB model is worth mastering because nearly all computer-based color applications are based on the model. Happily, 3DS MAX's Color Selector (see Figure 3.6) provides an excellent method for mastering the concept of mixing RGB color amounts.

FIGURE 3.6

The Material Editor and 3DS MAX Color Selector.

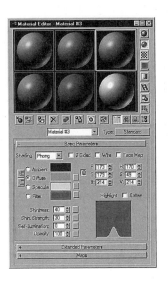

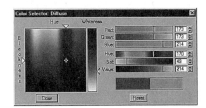

EXPLORING RGB COLOR

1. Enter the Materials Editor by clicking the Toolbar's Materials Editor button.

2. Double-click the Diffuse color swatch to bring up the Color Selector (it does not matter what material is active because you will be changing the color). The Color Selector simultaneously adjusts the color in its sliders and color swatch as well as the Materials Editor amounts, colors, and rendered sample sphere.

3. Click a color in the Hue gradient or Hue slider and make sure that the Whiteness slider is not at the bottom of its range.

4. Move the Sat (Saturation) slider to 255 (all the way to the right) and ensure that the Value slider is not at an extreme. This creates a fully saturated color with at least one of the RGB amounts maximized to the current level of the Value slider, while at least one of the others is minimized to zero.

5. Move the Hue slider back and forth while watching the RGB sliders. As you move the slider across the Hue spectrum you notice that only one channel of the RGB sliders moves at a time. As you cycle through the spectrum, you are exploring the maximums and minimums of each red, green, and blue light component.

6. Drag the Saturation slider to 0 (all the way to the left). As you decrease the color's saturation, notice that the RGB components slide toward one another until they align. Because the RGB amounts now are in balance, the light has no color and the swatch is gray. Remember this as a shortcut to create gray. Notice that the hue and luminance amounts are still intact, and if you increase the saturation, the original color is restored.

7. Manipulate all three RGB sliders so that they are not aligned and are not at either end of the slider, and then drag any one of the RGB sliders to 0. The Saturation slider moves to the right and the color swatch becomes fully saturated.

8. Drag the same RGB slider back to the right and you notice the Saturation slider moves to the right and the color swatch "grays."

   Any color that has one or two of the RGB sliders at 0 is always a fully saturated color. This is evident as you drag one of the RGB sliders to the left. As you do this, the saturation slider moves to the right and reaches full saturation at the same time that the color slider reaches 0.

9. Set the Saturation amount to 255 and then drag the Value slider to the right and then back to the left.

All three RGB sliders move to the right and then back to the left simultaneously. As you increase the color's value, all three of the RGB channels increase to the right until the pure spectrum color (hue) is created. Decreasing the value moves the RGB sliders to the left until black is formed, and no light is reflected. You can create the same effect by sliding the RGB channels all the way to the right or left, with one important difference. The hue amount is constantly changing and is effectively eliminated at the extremes because there is no color.

An interesting exercise that illustrates the CYM model can be done with light sources in 3DS MAX. Unlike the world around us, spotlights in 3DS MAX can be given negative multipliers to subtract light from the scene rather than adding it. Figure 3.7 illustrates how negative lights act much like pigments, as they strike surfaces and subtract the illumination of other (positive) light sources.

FIGURE 3.7

The three negative spotlights of primary "ink."

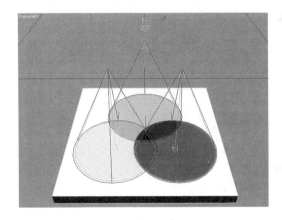

USING LIGHT TO EXPLAIN CYM PIGMENT

1. Load the lightrgb.max scene from the accompanying CD.

2. Click the Create tab to view the Create Command panel and click the Lights button at the top of the Create Command Panel.

3. Click the Directional button and place the new directional light in the center of the Top viewport.

4. Move the Directional light up to about the same height as the existing three spotlights.

5. Click the Modifier tab and increase the V: setting to 255 to create a pure white light. You will probably notice light is restricted to a central area.

6. Check the light's overshoot box. This unrestricts the extents of the light source and allows it to illuminate all areas with the same intensity. The illumination of the other lights should be completely washed out because the surface is reflecting the white light back; there is nothing more for the red, green, and blue lights to contribute. The box surface should now be bright white.

7. Press the H Key and select Spot-Red and change its multiplier amount from 1.0 to –1.0. The once-red spotlight is now subtracting red from the white directional light and appears to be cyan.

8. Adjust the multiplier amounts for the remaining two spotlights to –1.0 as well.

The result is three circles of "ink," light—cyan, yellow, and magenta, that overlap to form the primaries of light—red, green, and blue. As all three circles overlap in the center, they form black because they are removing all positive light from the scene.

9. The resulting file can be found as lightcym.max on the accompanying CD.

T IP

Lights can be used to correct or adjust how individual objects look in a scene by using the include/exclude feature.

Mixing Color in 3D Studio MAX

3D Studio MAX provides a unique color selector that gives you an intuitive method to select and manipulate color. Although all colors are stored within the system as raw RGB (Red, Green, Blue) values, the Color Selector enables you to pick and explore colors with a variety of methods (see Figure 3.8).

FIGURE 3.8

The standard 3DS MAX Color Selector.

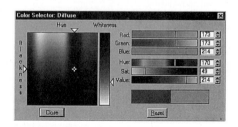

Describing Color with HSV

Color can be elusive. "What type of green was that green awning?" "It was a deep, teal-green, but I'm not sure how blue of a teal, or really how dark it was." Recalling colors from memory accurately is difficult for anyone. Even when you concentrate on understanding an object's color, it changes as the character of the light that illuminates it shifts position and tone. "Oh, but that awning looked greener later in the day." For clarity, the color of a pigment is often described by three of its properties. Although most agree on the basis for these descriptions, there are several schools of thought as to what these terms are actually called.

The part of the color wheel that a color is based upon is known as *hue*. If you were to take the Color Selector's Hue Slider and bend it into a circle, you'd have the color wheel. When people refer to the color of an object, they are actually referring to its hue. The term hue has fairly universal acceptance among color description systems and in the case of the awning described previously, the hue is blue-green.

The purity of a color is referred to as its chroma, intensity, strength, or *saturation* (as in 3DS MAX). You also can think of saturation as the degree to which a color has been mixed with other colors. A pure color is fully saturated because it has not been mixed with any other, in contrast to a gray color that has been mixed substantially and thus has a low or zero saturation. To continue using the awning reference, the color is teal, so it could not have been mixed with much red; it has fairly high saturation.

Each hue can range from very dark to very light and is often referred to as the color's luminance, depth, or as in 3DS MAX, its *value*. As a color deepens and approaches black, it has a low value; as it brightens its amount increases. A monochrome painting is a good example of one hue being used through all of its values. To finish with the awning, the fabric was deep in color, and so had a lower value.

Together, these descriptions of color are known as the HSV model (hue, saturation, and value) and can be used together to describe all colors. For traditional artists, these correspond directly to the Munsell System's hue, chroma, and value scales. 3DS MAX provides HSV color sliders as an option whenever you choose colors with its standard Color Selector.

Adjusting Color with Whiteness and Blackness

3DS MAX gives further control over color with the Color Selector's Whiteness and Blackness sliders. A color whitens and blackens by manipulating its saturation and amount simultaneously. The effect is similar to adding black or white pigment to an existing paint color and is quite easy to identify with.

In practice, sliding the Whiteness slider from top to bottom adjusts Saturation from 255 to 0, while adjusting the Value from a starting amount to 255. Sliding the Blackness slider from top to bottom adjusts Saturation from a starting point to 0, while adjusting the Value from 255 to an ending amount. The Whiteness and Blackness controls do not influence each other or the Hue. Their effect is to manipulate only the Saturation and Value amounts.

3DS MAX's Color Selector is a great environment to learn color mixing. The following exercise helps you explore the meaning of the HSV color sliders and how they affect each other. Figure 3.9 shows how the Color Selector is also available from the Object Color dialog box.

FIGURE 3.9

The 3DS MAX Color Selector from the Object Color dialog boxes.

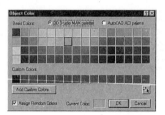 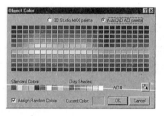

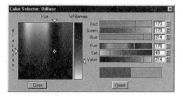

EXPLORING THE COLOR SELECTOR

1. Click the Object Color swatch in the Command Panel to access the Object Color dialog box and then double-click the Active Color: color swatch to bring up the Color Selector (this Color Selector is identical to that of the Materials Editor).

2. Click any color in the Hue slider and increase the Saturation and Value sliders to 255.

    You now have a pure spectral, or color-wheel-based, color hue displayed in the sample color swatch.

3. Drag the Hue slider left and right and notice the color changes in the color swatch.

    As you increase and decrease the Hue amount with the slider, the color shifts smoothly across the spectrum within the swatch. You are traversing the entire spectrum for pure color.

4. Drag the Whiteness slider down to the bottom and the sample swatch increases in brightness until it is pure white.

    As you increase the Whiteness, the Saturation amount decreases because additional RGB must be added to achieve whiter colors. Thus the original color is desaturated, and the Value must increase to lighten the color.

5. Drag the Blackness slider down to the bottom and the sample swatch decreases in brightness until it is a gray (the lower your Whiteness slider, the brighter the gray).

    As you increase the Blackness, the Saturation amount decreases because additional RGB must be subtracted to achieve grayer colors, and the Value must decrease to darken the color.

6. Drag the Saturation slider to the right and both the Whiteness and Blackness sliders rise.

7. Drag the Value slider left and right and you will notice that as the Value increases, the Blackness rises and the Whiteness lowers; the reverse is true when the Value is decreased.

This exercise points out an important concept when mixing color in 3DS MAX. When you adjust either the Saturation or Value slider, or adjust both with Whiteness and Blackness, you are exploring the range of a given hue. Although there are similarities in creating color ramps between the two methods, the results of each are quite different. If you are creating a range of colors intended to share a chromatic range, you should stick to one method. Ramps of adjacent colors should be made by either adjusting the Value or Saturation independently or by only adjusting the Whiteness and Blackness controls. If the methods are mixed, the resulting colors will not be part of a consistent ramp.

The other fact to remember is that all color values in 3DS MAX are stored in RGB values only. This means that while HSV is displayed, it is the corresponding RGB values that are stored. Whiteness and Blackness never display values because they manipulate Saturation and Value simultaneously and are color mixing assistants only. Although you can refer to and record a given HSV value, the Whiteness and Blackness values are merely visual indicators.

Color Composition

Color is individual and personal—you have your favorite colors and preferences for combining them, yet there are rules or guidelines by which colors are coordinated, matched, and mixed. An understanding of these considerations is important even when you are creating entirely imaginative worlds. Color composition influences us significantly whether you are painting textures with pigment or illuminating our world with light. Good color choices can set a mood and lend a sense of unity to a scene, while bad color choices make a scene look unrealistic, garish, dull, or cartoonish. This section discusses various subjective properties of color and how to use them.

You are simulating pigment in 3DS MAX when you define materials, backgrounds, and atmospheres. In all cases, these are or represent surfaces. A surface reflects light and the light it reflects back to your viewpoint is its color. The color of this reflected light is influenced by what colors the surface absorbs (which is the surface's color) and the color of light that is illuminating it. When discussing pigment colors, it is assumed that the majority of the spectrum is present with near white light.

Many terms are used to describe color, and the art world has standardized many of these terms and descriptions. Although you may not consider yourself an artist at this time, it is important to develop an understanding of these concepts because your work with 3DS MAX will undoubtedly bring you into contact with artists and their writings. These terms will be used throughout the rest of this book when describing color.

Complementary Colors

Colors opposite one another on the color wheel represent each other's complementary color. For the basic RYB model, the primary color complements are red and green, yellow and purple, and blue and orange. Complementary colors can be derived from any location on the wheel, as a reddish-orange would complement a greenish-blue.

Complementary colors have several important features. Used side-by-side, a complementary color brings out the intensity in its associated color and creates the maximum visual contrast to it. This also creates the most visual strain because the complements compete for one another's color, that which is missing from themselves. This can create an undesirable "jumping" or "buzzing" effect when stared at by the human eye. Blended together, complements create shades of brown and gray, acting to neutralize the intensity of the parent's hue and are usually avoided in traditional color mixing. When a colored object casts a shadow, it is shifted toward the object's complementary color. This effect extends to colored light sources that have the effect of casting shadows with a complementary color shift.

Warm versus Cool Colors

The type and extent of hue present is commonly referred to as the color's temperature. Warm colors contain more red, orange, and yellow, whereas cool colors contain more blue. Warm violets are red-based and cool greens are blue-based. Neutral browns and grays also are distinguished by temperature.

Temperature is an important concept when assigning colors to share across an object or a scene. You should decide if an object is "cool" or "warm," then maintain consistency with your color assignments. Animals, for example, tend to share families of warm colors, whereas plants tend to be cool. A forbidding scene would tend to be quite cool in nature, whereas a pleasant scene would usually have a warm palette.

Advancing and Receding Colors

Warm and cool colors have the psychological effect of advancing or receding, an effect of the human eye's interpretation of the spectrum order (where red is first and violet last). Warm colors, especially red, appear to advance and come closer, whereas cool colors appear to recede and move away; this is one reason the majority of store signage is red.

Your experience with distance serves to reinforce this perception because the atmosphere cools colors by reflecting blue onto them as they extend into the horizon. Distant objects lose their color intensity and approach gray while their hues shift toward the blue spectrum. Keep this in mind when you create and edit background images.

As the scene recedes into the horizon, it should lose intensity and become cooler. Doing this manually by using a paint program, or in 3DS MAX with a Mix or RGB Tint material, should be regarded as a subtle but essential step in creating realistic backgrounds. An appropriately colored fog environment can be used to obtain the same result for both the background and the entire scene.

Restrictions on the Use of Black and Gray

Many artists never use true black but prefer to mix their own very dark, deep color blends. When mixed in full saturation, some adjacent colors on the RYB color wheel (Indigo and Crimson or Ultramarine and Hooker's Green are common combinations) can produce deep colors that approach black. The reason for this mixing choice is that black pigment ("out-of-the-tube") gives a flat, unnatural appearance. The dark, rich colors created from mixing are preferred because they appear to the eye to have more depth, and actually appear darker than colors mixed with pure black. Artists have learned to reserve black for creating burnt and stained effects because it tends to neutralize hues and create "dirty" colors.

Black also is reserved for mixing extremely cold and unnatural true grays. Very little in the real world is actually absent of color or truly gray, let alone black. Nearly all the colors that you see around you have some red, yellow, or blue. Because this reflects human perception, it is an important concept to remember when you assign and mix colors in 3DS MAX. Although true gray is easily attained by sliding the Saturation to zero, it isn't in the world around you.

Because it is very rare for a gray to be absent of color, you should use true grays carefully. Objects based on true grays and lit with "gray" lights look unnatural and computer-generated. The reason is simple—creating this effect in the real world is very difficult. In general, a slight warm or cool color shift in lights, as well as materials, appears to be much more realistic.

The Impact of Lighting's Color

A scene can be full of surfaces with vibrant and well-designed materials but still look incredibly flat and pale. This is quite possible because a surface is merely a reflection of the scene's lighting. The color, placement, and intensity of your scene's lighting has the greatest impact on the resulting images. The following sections discuss color considerations for light. Chapter 16, "Lighting and Atmosphere" explores techniques for placement and intensity.

A perceived correlation exists between the color of a light source and the level of illumination. Bright illumination usually is associated with a bright blue sky and cool colors, whereas low illumination is associated with candlelight, fire, dimmed lights, and warm colors. Keep this in mind when you select the color of a primary light source.

Influences of Natural Light Color

The light that nature provides during the day is primarily white. Experience teaches you that bright sunlight is true white light, and it is natural to believe that the colors of an object are truest when viewed under direct sunlight. In actuality, the color of sunlight varies considerably in relation to the time, season, and weather.

You might be most aware of sunlight's color rendering capabilities when it is absent. Think of the number of times you have been in a store and been unconvinced of a material's color. The man-made light that illuminates the store doesn't provide the entire visible spectrum to correctly see the color. Your eye knows it and is trying to compensate for the lost color. You might even have taken the item near a window, or out the door, to view it in natural light and confirm the "true" color.

Sunlight

Sunlight is not easy to quantify because it expresses itself in many tones and hues. Early morning sun can be a warm gray light on a clear day or a cool gray light on a foggy day. Late afternoon sun can produce a very warm, yellow tone, whereas a sunset can range from brilliant red to a mauve-purple. High-noon sun can easily be near white, while the ambient light casting through a north facing skylight at the same time might just as easily be cool. There are no formulas to calculate all the qualities of sunlight, so you must learn to observe the world around you and apply your observations to the scene you create. Learn to look deeply into a photograph or a horizon and analyze the quality of light. When animating the sun, perhaps for a shadow study, you should also take into account how the sun changes color during the course of the day.

Atmosphere

The earth's atmosphere has much to do with the quality and color of sunlight. The more atmosphere there is, the more color effect, which is why you have spectacular sunrises and sunsets. When the sun is perpendicular at midday, it penetrates the smallest amount of atmosphere and is at its whitest. Sunlight also has varying properties according to longitude and time of year. The sun is directly overhead at the equator, low in the sky at the poles, high in the summer, and low in the winter. The sunlight found in the equatorial desert is some of the whitest that strikes the earth.

The atmosphere also has a magnifying effect on the sun and moon when they are close to the horizon. The bodies are visually larger during this time and their color influence is magnified as well. You need to consider the condition of the atmosphere because it also affects the light quality. An industrial, polluted sky creates a warm brown light, and the water-laden air of fog, rain, or snow creates a cool light. An overcast sky causes most light to be of a reflective nature and notably grayer.

Light in Outer Space

If you observe a scene that has no atmosphere, there is no filtering of the light, and there is very little, if any, reflected or ambient light to illuminate other portions of the environment. Scenes on the moon or in space should have extremely white light and nearly no ambient light, resulting in very crisp, black shadows characteristic of NASA photographs. Only areas of an object that can trace a line of sight to the sun are visible. The rest of the object is as black as the surrounding void. The shadow the earth casts on the moon is such an example. The dim outline of the new moon is all that can be seen from the ambient light of space.

Moonlight

Moonlight is nature's other contribution that illuminates the world. Most of us tend to think of it as a yellow-based "light," but doing so is too simple. The moon is just reflecting light from the sun. As the sun's light filters through the atmosphere, so does the moon's. The moon changes color as it moves in the night sky, much as the sun does. The moon's light is a characteristically warm yellow as it sits low in the sky and becomes whiter as it climbs higher. Because the moon is such a weak light source, the illumination available is low and the amount of light reflected off surfaces is minimized. The ambient light of a scene that portrays moonlight should be quite low and have a strong color shift to the moon's complementary color.

Influences of Artificial Light Color

Much of your time is spent indoors within environments illuminated primarily by artificial light. If you are to render and animate interior scenes correctly, you must understand the various colors of artificial light and how your eye perceives them. The lighting industry has many terms for its trade and this book tries to respect standard terminology when appropriate. When describing real-world lighting, a lamp is a light source (most often referred to as a "bulb"); a fixture or luminaire is the housing for the lamp; light is the energy from the light source before it strikes a surface; and illumination is light reflecting off surfaces. Thus, a lighting fixture contains a lamp that emits light and illuminates the scene. With 3DS MAX, a light object is equivalent to a lamp and fixtures are strictly optional, so it is appropriate to say a spotlight illuminates the scene with warm colored light.

Lamp Temperature

Man has created many forms of light. Their color characteristics are often described in terms of Kelvin temperature (not to be confused with warm and cool colors). This term is analogous to a piece of metal being heated; it begins with a deep red glow, warms to a brilliant red, heats to orange, then yellow, and on through the spectrum until it becomes "white hot." As a guideline, a sunrise is about 2,000 degrees Kelvin, the noon sun 5,000 degrees, an overcast sky 7,000 degrees, and a blue sky 10,000 degrees.

This book does not go into the specifics of each light source temperature. They are presented here primarily as a comparative tool and as a bit of background information for readers new to the subject.

Kelvin temperature is somewhat equivalent to the hue and saturation, while the brightness or intensity of a light is really a function of the light color's value. Light fixtures that are intended to be of the same type in a scene can be given different intensities, but should share close to the same hue and saturation values. In such a case, the light's color value acts much like a "dimming switch."

Incandescent Lamps

The oldest and most common artificial lamp is the incandescent light bulb. Incandescent lamps are point sources and their intensity is limited only to how many watts you provide at that point. The color cast from an incandescent lamp is warm and orange-based with a color temperatures close to that of a sunrise. The extent to which incandescent lamps vary by wattage is evident with dimmer switches where at very low levels the light is quite orange. Halogen lamps also are of the incandescent family but have a much higher temperature. They produce significantly brighter illumination and cast a far whiter, yet warm light. Halogen lamps still turn orange when dimmed.

Fluorescent Lamps

Fluorescent lamps cast a much whiter, blue-to-green-based colored light than incandescent lamps. The higher-temperature fluorescent lamps are probably at fault if you can't tell the color of an item in a store. Even though these lamps are "whiter," their light causes many colors, especially the complementary colors of red, orange, and skin tones, to wash out. The amount of light a fluorescent lamp produces is a fixed quantity. If you need more illumination, you increase the linear footage of the lamp. Although fluorescent lamps are linear light sources, they are most commonly grouped together or are folded back onto themselves to create sufficient illumination levels. In daily use, they act more as a "point" source than a linear one. This observation is important because 3DS MAX does not yet support true linear light sources.

Influence of Colored Lamps

Some artificial lamps are worse at color rendition than fluorescent ones. Sodium-based lamps often are found in use as street lights and in factories. These lamps are some of the brightest and most energy efficient available, but they cast a very saturated orange-to-yellow light. Mercury lamps are an older lamp type, common to street lamps, that cast a saturated blue-green light.

Light fixtures sometimes add color to that of their lamps. Incandescent lamps are available with a wide range of tinted coatings, and translucent colored lenses can be added to cast any imaginable color. Stoplights are an example of colored lenses that you see every day. 3DS MAX's spotlights and directional lights reproduce the effects of colored lenses when they are casting ray-traced shadows and the lens material is using Filter opacity with an appropriate color.

The most dramatic colored lights you experience daily are neon. These emit very saturated colors and can illuminate a scene in a fascinating way. Re-creating their effects in 3DS MAX can be tricky but are well worth the effort. Chapter 16 explores creating neon effects in-depth.

Although the color quality of artificial lamps varies greatly, you should be aware that this variation is not generally considered favorable. Lighting manufacturers do their best to produce lamps that come the closest to creating white light. Understanding how artificial light affects the overall quality of a scene is important when you analyze the world around you. As an artist and animator, your goal is to portray moods, not to perfectly simulate a lighting condition.

Using Colored Light

Having read about artificial light, you probably don't need to use much of it directly. Your primary goal in 3DS MAX is to create a believable scene, an artistic expression, or simply a pleasing image. The way you manipulate light to achieve your results is completely up to you. You are probably best off using the information about particular lamps as a mental reference while you analyze the world around you.

What you see in your 3DS MAX world depends upon how you illuminate it; what you see is entirely dependent upon your light objects' color and position. The colors you choose for light sources have a dramatic effect on the scene's mood and the color rendition of your objects.

Highly saturated lights should be used with caution when you illuminate entire scenes because they can completely skew the perception of your world. Reproducing the characteristics of yellow/orange sodium lamps, for instance, does not illuminate blue-to-purple-based objects and makes white objects appear the same as orange objects. An example is searching for a bright blue car in a parking lot illuminated with such lights. Because there is no blue in the orange light to reflect, the car appears pure black.

Re-creating the color of poor, man-made lights can portray your scene as sterile or color-washed, which might be exactly what you want if you are demonstrating the effects of different lighting choices. For the most part, however, you want to make a scene as alive with color as possible.

NOTE

Photographers who are forced to take pictures under poor artificial lighting conditions commonly use colored filters to correct, or at least minimize, the effect that colored lights have on the scene.

Intensely colored lights can have fantastic effects if they are used with care. If you look at theater lighting from the stage's point of view, you don't see white light but entire batteries of vibrant, colored light. Theaters commonly use pure red, green, blue, yellow, magenta, and cyan lights in various combinations. These pure colors of light mix on stage, giving some areas and many shadows more richness and vibrancy than could ever be achieved from even, white illumination. Colored lights can have impressive effects when used on completely white objects as well as monochromatic scenes. The white surfaces reflect the entire light spectrum and display the mixing hues and intensity of the various lights cast on them.

Complementary Colors in Light

If you are in an environment illuminated with colored light, your eye adapts to the environment by becoming very sensitive to the complementary color of the light source—the color required to restore white light. This phenomenon is known as *color constancy* and has the effect of placing the complementary color in the non-illuminated or shadowed areas in the mind's eye. The most common day-to-day example of this is the purple-to-blue based shadows evident in a scene lit by the yellow-to-orange based light of an incandescent light. The more color-intense the light source, the more shift is perceived in the shadows.

Artists, scene painters, and set designers recognize this effect and maximize the perceived depth of their shadows by color-shifting them toward the complementary color of the light. Examine a theater's stage set under house lights and you will probably find an abundance of purple and deep blue being used in many of the painted shadows. Most light, whether natural or man-made, has at least a slight yellow-to-orange hue that produces complements of violet to deep blue. Because this is closer to human perception of light than actual pigment, "helping" 3DS MAX make this slight color shift is important because viewers look at an image rather than participate in the scene.

3DS MAX uses Ambient Light (located in the Environment dialog) to simulate the total accumulated reflected light present in a scene. It contributes light to all objects uniformly, regardless of additional light sources, and is the light present in non-illuminated objects and shadows. For added realism, a color shift in the ambient light to the complement of the dominant light source produces the effect of color constancy and deeper, richer darks and shadows throughout the scene.

Reflected Light and Radiosity

Light that strikes an object is absorbed or reflected. Red objects, for example, absorb green and blue light, reflecting the red light back to our eyes. Besides reflecting to our eyes, the reflected light affects nearby objects with bounced light. Placing a matte red object against a matte white wall and illuminating the scene with a white light source creates a red tint on areas of the "white" wall. The wall is said to have inherited the bounced color. A more common example is a typical room illuminated by recessed lighting fixtures. The room is being illuminated entirely from above, yet the details and color of the ceiling are distinguishable. This is because the ceiling is being illuminated from light reflected off the floor, walls, and furnishings. This effect of bounced, inherited, and reflected light is known in computer graphics as *radiosity*.

NEW TO R2

Max 2 adds radiosity and raytracing to its rendering capabilities to add another level of realism to your scenes.

Ray-traced rendering traces rays from a source to a surface, continually reflecting off surfaces and striking others until they are no longer within the scene. The traditional use of raytracing is for calculating reflections from shiny, specular surfaces.

The 3DS MAX default scan-line renderer uses raytracing techniques to calculate ray-traced shadows. New in Max R2 is the use of ray-traced material type that enables you to assign a ray-traced effect to selected objects in your scene. Full ray-traced renderers trace vectors from your viewing position to every surface. If the surface is specular, an additional ray is reflected to capture what is visible in the reflection. If another shiny surface is encountered by the ray, it is reflected again until the ray bounces out of the scene or lands on a non-specular surface. This is how the recursive reflections typical of ray-traced imagery are created and is also the reason why ray-traced rendering is slow. With the selective raytracing material, MAX gives you the advantages of a raytraced look and enables you to assign it only to those objects that will benefit from the affect. The result is faster rendering times than full raytracing.

Radiosity renderers differ from ray-traced renderers by calculating diffuse rather than specular reflections. The light energy from each light source is traced to each surface, calculating the absorption and then reflecting the remaining energy to other surfaces in the scene. This energy bounces in relation to diffuse surface color, rather than shine or specularity. In doing so, radiosity renders the effect of reflected light but not specular reflections. The lighting is perfect, but everything in the scene is flat.

The rendered effects of radiosity rendering are stunning, but the calculations and computer time are extremely intense. While ray-traced rendering takes an order of magnitude longer than scan-line rendering, radiosity adds yet another order of magnitude to the equation. This is because ray-traced reflections pertain to just one viewing position and the reflected rays eventually find a conclusion, while the rays of reflected energy in the radiosity model bounce within the scene forever constantly becoming weaker. Radiosity renderings are termed solutions because they have been stopped at a certain point to produce the given image. Radiosity renderings that exhibit specular reflections are actually a combination, the radiosity solution being combined with the reflections of a ray-traced rendering.

Rendering times are significantly longer with radiosity and ray-tracing and using the effects may not be supported by your deadline. This does not mean that you should disregard or give up on this effect because you can simulate much of its effects within 3DS MAX by the careful placement of lights and material definitions. Radiosity is a perceivable, real-world phenomenon and, if your goal involves photo-realism, some effort should be expended to approximate its effects. This is especially true if the final product is to be a still image where the eye has time to evaluate the scene. If rendering time is a factor, try some tests using the new materials versus simulating the affects by other, speedier, means.

Kinetix has recently shipped a radiosity renderer called Radioray. This radiosity renderer works with 3D Studio VIZ and 3D Studio MAX 1.2, but is not yet available to work with 3D Studio MAX 2.

In Practice: Mixing Color and Light

- **Primary Colors:** The primary colors of pigment are cyan, yellow, and magenta. These are complements to light's primary colors of red, green, and blue.

- **Mixing colors:** Mixing light color is additive, where mixing more approaches white. Mixing pigment color is subtractive, where mixing more approaches black.

- **Blacks and grays:** True blacks and grays should be used with caution because nearly every light source or pigment surface is either warm or cool by nature. Although true grays are all too easy to define within computer graphics, they rarely exist in daily life.

- **Colored surfaces:** Surface color is actually reflected light. For a colored surface to be seen, there must be corresponding color components within the light source to be reflected. This is important to remember as you define the colors of your light sources.

Chapter 4

COMPOSITION AND PERSPECTIVE

Understanding basic elements of setting up your scene in MAX is essential in creating a quality image or animation. As with color and light, many methods of composition and perspective relate directly to art and photography. Based on that relationship, think of MAX as the artist's palette or the photographer's stock of different lenses and tripods. This chapter focuses on how to bring proven methods of traditional composition into the digital world. Topics covered include:

- Methods of 3D viewing, both traditionally and in 3DS MAX.

- Orthographic projections and axonometrics.

- Traditional perspective terminology as compared to 3D Studio MAX and the standard classifications of perspective.

- Comparing human vision to 3D Studio MAX usage of cameras.

- Parallax and perspective correction.

- Elements that define your composition.

- Figure-ground relationships.

Understanding 3D Viewing Methods

Everything in our world occupies three dimensions, yet we usually need to represent them in two dimensions. Whether the medium is a canvas, a photograph, or a computer screen, three dimensions are being abstracted onto a two-dimensional plane.

In computer modeling, you are performing the same analysis that draftsmen, designers, and artists have performed for centuries. On the computer, however, the information within a three-dimensional model can be viewed from any vantage point at any time. In this way, computer modeling is most similar to sculpture, yet you have to abstract the sculpture to the screen's two dimensions when constructing it. As a result, you will tend to use traditional and perspective views both interchangeably and simultaneously as you change from drafting methods to sculptural ones.

Most everything that is manufactured begins as a drawing in some detail. Whether a simple gear or a highly complex aircraft, somewhere a drawing or series of drawings exists to define its construction. Much of what you create in 3DS MAX will come directly or indirectly from drawings. Sketches from an art director may need to be interpreted, blueprints and measured drawings may need to be translated, or drawings from other CAD programs may be provided. These become templates for creating 3D models in 3DS MAX. Therefore, an understanding of drawing terms and how they are used is valuable. The majority of standard drawing conventions can be related to working in 3DS MAX viewports, which enables you to use established methods of construction while viewing the whole in a more natural perspective. This section explains the following types of views and related terminology:

- Orthographic viewing
- Axonometric viewing
- Perspective viewing

Orthographic Viewing

The vast majority of drawings of items to be made are orthogonal; they are drawings that represent views at exact 90-degree angles to the subject without any perspective. Orthographic views are important because they show the exact relationships of height and width. All portions of the subject are displayed parallel to the viewing plane and are free of the distortion and foreshortening found when viewing in perspective. Everything in an orthogonal view is at the same scale, unlike in a perspective view where closer subjects are larger and distant ones are smaller. The perpendicular views that characterize orthogonal viewing form a "cube" around the subject in a manner similar to Figure 4.1.

FIGURE 4.1

Mechanical termin-ology for orthographic projections (of the orthocar.max scene).

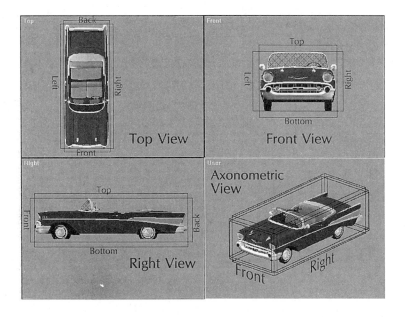

Many professions, such as manufacturing, draw their parts with three views and perhaps an additional axonometric or non-perpendicular view. Axonometric views are explained in more detail later in this section. Other professions (architecture, for example) tend to show all views—even if they are redundant—and include sectional views. They also include views showing relationships and structural details.

Orthographic Projections

3D Studio MAX has six orthographic projection views: Top, Bottom, Front, Back, Right, and Left (with standard keyboard shortcuts of T, B, F, K, R, L) that relate orthogonally to the World X,Y,Z axes. These terms are similar to those used in manufacturing where it makes the most sense to describe views in relation to the object. The architectural industry uses different terms for similar views because buildings have a universal frame of reference. In architectural terms, the Top and Bottom views are called plans and the Front, Back, Left, and Right side views are called elevations. This terminology is shown in Figure 4.2 in relationship to 3D Studio MAX views. The term plan is usually accompanied by what it is a plan of (floor plan, ceiling plan, site plan, roof plan, and so on), whereas elevation names are paired with the direction they face on the compass (North, South, Southwest, and so on).

FIGURE 4.2

Architectural terminology for orthographic projections (of the orthouse.max scene).

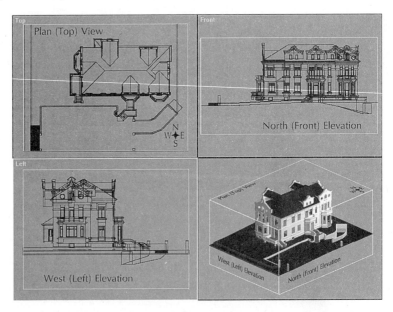

When a side view, or elevation, is taken within the space of the subject it is called an interior elevation and shows only what you would see if you were to stand inside the space. If the view also shows the width (and perhaps structure) of the surrounding walls, it's termed a section. A section is basically an elevation at a given slice of the subject, as shown later in this chapter. Sections are used extensively to describe structure and interior relationships. Although often difficult to conceptualize, sectional drawings are valuable to the 3D Studio MAX modeler because they are the perfect shapes to use when modeling 3D objects by lofting. Lofting uses a series of shapes, like those created in sectional drawings, as paths to create the framework for objects. (see Chapter 9, "Building Loft Objects," for more information on modeling lofted objects). You can create a dynamic sectional view of your model in 3DS MAX by adjusting a camera's clipping planes.

NEW TO R2

You also can use the new Section tool to automatically create the 2D drawing.

Axonometric Views

When views depart from being perpendicular, they begin to display more than one side at the same time, and the view becomes skewed. Views of this type are termed axonometric and are what 3DS MAX terms "User views."

NOTE

Many users refer to User views as being isometric or oblique. Isometric actually refers to a very specific type of axonometric where the angles of rotation are all the same (typically 30 degrees). Oblique drawings keep one plane undistorted (either the plan or elevation) and angle the corresponding projections. This type of projection cannot be represented in 3DS MAX with its User view.

User axonometric views are valuable references because they maintain the relationship of parallel lines. Lines do not diminish to vanishing points as they do in our daily vision; they remain parallel. Relationships are easy to identify because the location of any detail can be projected back to any other area of the view. The scale of the subject is consistent for details that lie on any given angle. In examining Figure 4.3, notice that the features of each cube remain parallel, whereas the relative scale of the features changes according to the rotation.

FIGURE 4.3

User axonometric views of toyblock.max maintain the relationship of parallel lines.

You may find User views preferable to Perspective views because the elements in the scene are in proportion to one another, relationships can be easily identified, and the viewing controls are the same as orthogonal views. Although working in perspective can be quite natural at times, distance is often difficult to estimate and the Zoom Window Option is not available.

Relating Perspective Views to the 3DS MAX Camera

In an everyday sense, perspective refers to the appearance of objects in depth as perceived by normal human vision. We view everything around us in perspective. Cameras, television, and film display the world they capture on the 2D planes of film, glass, or screen. While these devices place their images automatically, artists have traditionally needed to construct their perspectives by hand, translating the three-dimensional world they see to the two-dimensional plane of paper or canvas. The manner in which artists have come to represent perspective is important to learn so that its compositional impact is understood and terminology can be exchanged with those not in computer graphics.

Within the context of drawing, perspective refers to the various techniques that artists have developed for representing three-dimensional objects and depth relationships on a two-dimensional surface. Several empirical, mechanical, and construction-based methods for drawing perspectives are in use daily. These methods employ specific steps and procedures for creating a hand-drawn perspective. Luckily, 3DS MAX does all this for you within its Camera viewport, and with greater accuracy than most delineators even come close to achieving. The following discussion relates the perspective terms that artists traditionally use to 3DS MAX's camera analogy.

Traditional perspective theory places the observer's eye at a station point and looks at a point in the distance, termed the center of vision. This is equivalent to the placement of the camera and the camera's target in 3DS MAX. A correlation between the two models can be seen in Figure 4.4.

FIGURE 4.4

Traditional perspective terminology in comparison to 3DS MAX's camera analogy.

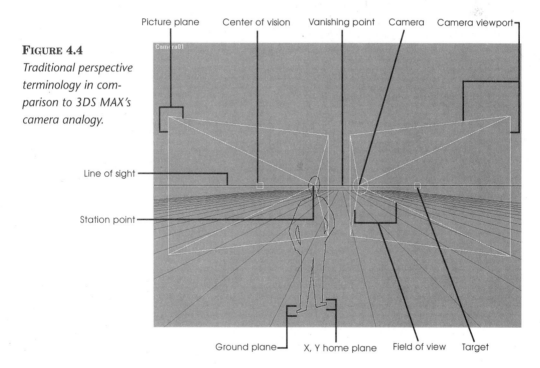

Lines of Sight

A line struck between your eye and your center of vision is often termed the line of sight. 3DS MAX draws this line visually to connect the camera and target. This vector traces your eye's center of vision and in so doing shows what your eye is capable of seeing. If an object is blocking this line, you cannot see past it. You can use this line of sight for reference when viewing the scene from above to position your cameras and targets with the knowledge of what can be seen.

Lines of sight can be traced between your eye and each object in the scene. These lines are plotted on a theoretical plane suspended between you and the scene; this plane is termed the picture plane. For an artist, this is equivalent to the piece of paper on which a scene is drawn. For 3DS MAX, it's the frame of the final image and so is actually the Camera viewport.

NOTE

The concept of a picture plane is actually how perspective technique was first formalized. A sheet of glass was used to frame a scene with the lines of sight between the artist and objects "traced" onto the glass.

The plane upon which the observer stands while regarding a scene is described as the ground plane—the floor or land on which the majority of objects in the scene are resting. The ground plane is located at your eye height's distance below you, that is, the height of the horizon between five and six feet for most people. In 3DS MAX, the ground plane is the plane of the X,Y home grid displayed in User and Perspective views.

Working With the Horizon Line

The height of your eye (station point), or camera location, is also the height of the scene's horizon. The horizon line is drawn through the station point, or camera, parallel to the ground plane. All lines parallel to the ground converge to points on the horizon. You can think of the horizon as an infinitely large plane extending into the distance that always maintains a constant height from the ground plane. As items recede into the distance, they come closer to appearing to lie on the horizon.

Because most people are within a foot of being the same height, their eyes share the same horizon as yours if they stand on the same ground plane as you. The eyes of a crowd are thus co-linear and align with the horizon, as illustrated in Figure 4.5. If you see a head above the horizon, you know the person is taller than you are or is standing on higher ground. If a head is below the horizon, the person is either shorter than you or on lower ground.

FIGURE 4.5

The eyes of a crowd aligning on the horizon.

Horizon above eye level

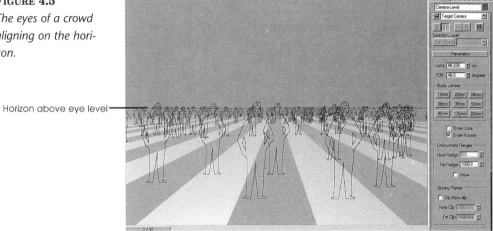

When your eye level is parallel to the ground plane, the horizon is perfectly centered in the view. As you tilt your head and move your center of vision or camera target, the horizon moves up and down in the view. Whereas the horizon moves in the composition, its height from the ground does not change; it is always at the same height as your eye.

Obviously, a horizon line exists in the computer scene only if sufficient objects exist in the distance to define it. Most models do not have geometry extensive enough to diminish to a natural horizon. An exterior scene commonly uses a background to create depth and establish a horizon. Pay careful attention to the true horizon line (the height of your camera) and the background's illustrated horizon line. If the horizons are not close, the corresponding scene looks as if it has either been sunk in a valley or perched on a hill. If neither of these effects is desirable, you should move your camera to the background's horizon level or adjust the background image. Figure 4.6 demonstrates how tilting the head up and down moves the horizon but does not change its relationship to the ground plane, as opposed to moving the camera up to higher ground.

It is all too easy to place a stock image as a background only to find that it does not align with the height of the camera, the true definition of where a horizon line is. Objects and lines in the scene diminish in perspective correctly, but the vanishing points do not fall on the horizon. This may seem somewhat trivial, and sometimes subtle, but most people will realize that something is not quite right with the image.

FIGURE 4.6

The horizon positions resulting from tilting the camera and moving the camera vertically.

High horizon line
Low horizon

Camera—low
Camera—high ground

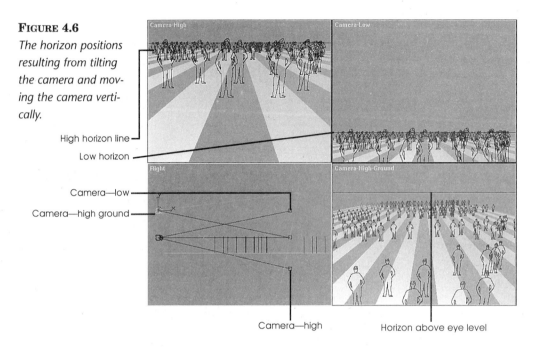

Camera—high   Horizon above eye level

TIP

You can display the horizon line of 3DS MAX cameras to guide compositions and properly position camera views to match displayed background images.

Vanishing Points

The horizon is important because all horizontal lines (lines that lie on planes parallel to the ground plane) visually converge to vanishing points located on it. Lines on planes below your eye converge upward to the line of the horizon, whereas lines above your eye converge downward. Lines in the scene directly at eye level are coincidental with the horizon and read as one "line." 3DS MAX has no term for vanishing points because it doesn't require their use. By understanding the existence of vanishing points, you can better place objects within a scene and determine the best point from which to view them. Vanishing points also have a tendency to pull the observer's eye and become a natural point of interest. The location(s) have an impact on your composition's strength.

Field of View

An angle you can view from side to side is termed the cone of vision or angle of view, equivalent to 3DS MAX's Field of View (FOV), as shown in Figure 4.7. When constructing traditional perspectives, the angle of view is often considered to be 30 degrees to either side of the line of sight. This is actually more from the convenience of using a 30 to 60 degree triangle than physical truth. The angle upon which the human eye can focus is closer to 45 degrees, the Field of View provided by 3DS MAX's default 51.944mm lens.

FIGURE 4.7

The default Field of View from default 3DS MAX cameras.

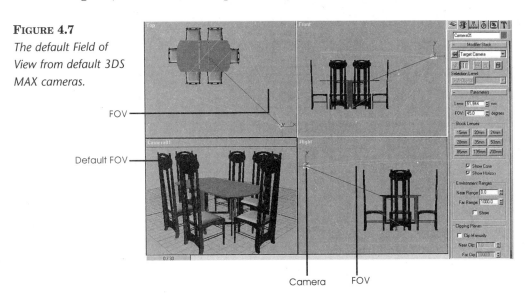

Defining One-Point Perspective

Perspective is conventionally described according to the number of primary vanishing points occurring in the scene. The world is based primarily on right angles. You write on rectangular paper, create objects composed of square corners, and build most buildings perpendicular to the ground and place them "square to the world" on an orthogonal grid of streets and blocks. Perspective has the most impact on parallel lines and right angles. As a result, it is common to talk of perspective in relation to a simple cube (see Figure 4.8).

FIGURE 4.8

The toy block model viewed in one-point perspective.

Parallel lines—

Horizon line —

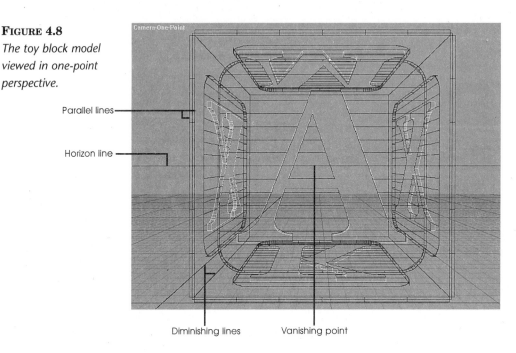

Diminishing lines   Vanishing point

The example in this section and the ones to follow refer to figures of a toy block that demonstrate various principles of perspective. You can load the toyblock.max scene from the accompanying CD-ROM into 3DS MAX if you want to experiment with the views yourself.

EXPLORING PERSPECTIVE

1. Choose File, Open, and then choose toyblock.max from the accompanying CD-ROM.

    When you are "square" to the side of the cube, only the lines perpendicular to you converge on the horizon. You can see the effect in the Camera01 viewport, as shown in Figure 4.8. The vanishing point of the cube's sides lies on the horizon line and coincides with the center of vision. The block's other lines have a vanishing point of infinite distance to either side. Thus, there is effectively no vanishing point at all. These lines do not converge and are parallel to you and your horizon. Such a view is termed a one-point perspective because there is only one vanishing point.

2. Minimize the current view by pressing W or clicking the Min/Max icon in the lower-right corner.

3. Click the Move icon and then select both the camera and its target in the Top view.

4. While in the Top view, move the camera in the X,Y plane and notice the results in the Camera01 viewport.

   The camera view remains in one-point perspective as you move the camera because the camera and target are level and the line of sight remains perpendicular to the face of the cube. A one-point perspective is maintained as long as these conditions are met.

5. Press the spacebar to lock your selection and then move the camera and target about in the Front view.

   The camera's line of sight is still perpendicular to the cube so the resulting view remains in one-point perspective.

Two-Point Perspective

If you are not square to the block, there is a vanishing point for each of the two visible sides. These vanishing points are located off-camera, on the horizon line, to the left and right. You can see the result in the two-point camera viewport shown in Figure 4.9. Such a view is called a two-point perspective because there are now two vanishing points. Where a one-point view must be perpendicular to one of the block's faces, a two-point view can be from anywhere. Keep in mind that you must maintain a level line of sight (the target and camera must be level with the ground plane) to ensure that vertical lines remain vertical. It is quite easy for delineators to determine distances using two-point perspective because these vertical planes remain constant, one reason two-point perspective is the most common hand-drawn perspective model.

The effect of two-point perspective can be seen by adjusting the camera in the scene from the preceding exercise.

1. Unlock your selection by pressing the spacebar; select only the camera in the Top viewport (Right-click and deselect the target).

2. Move just the camera in the X,Y plane of the Top view and examine the results in the Camera01 viewport.

   The sides of the block that were parallel are now diminishing in perspective. Two vanishing points for the scene can now be seen, one for each side of the block. Also, notice that the vertical sides of the block remain parallel because the camera and target remain level as you move the camera.

FIGURE 4.9

The Toy Block model viewed in two-point perspective.

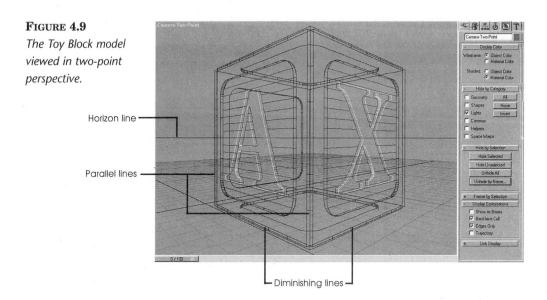

Horizon line

Parallel lines

Diminishing lines

Three-Point Perspective

When you are no longer looking at the block along a level line of sight, that is, you are looking up or down, vertical lines also converge to a vanishing point. You can see this result in the three-point camera viewport, as shown in Figure 4.10. All three of the block's planes now have vanishing points and such a view is predictably termed a three-point perspective. The cube's vertical lines visually converge to a vanishing point on a line drawn vertically from the center of vision. If you are looking down at a point below the horizon, the block's vertical lines converge downward. These lines converge upward if you're looking at a point above the horizon. If you are looking level with the horizon, you have a two-point perspective.

A three-point perspective is easily viewed in the current scene, as follows:

With just the camera selected, move the camera vertically in the Front viewport. The sides of the block that were previously parallel now begin to slant and converge to a vanishing point. A three-point perspective has been created because the camera no longer has a level line of sight to its target.

In one point, as in three point perspective, all lines have vanishing points. In a scene that you construct, the geometry may be at numerous angles and there may be hundreds of vanishing points. When drawing such complex scenes, delineators and artists are usually concerned with the basic three and make approximations as to the rest. Each line that is parallel with the ground plane, or resting evenly on the floor, has a vanishing point on the horizon. If lines are vertically skewed, slanted, or leaning from the ground plane, they converge to vanishing points located directly above or below the horizon. As you can see, a full three-point perspective can be a complex ordeal. This complexity is one reason that artists prefer to avoid using full three-point perspectives. 3DS Max makes this process easier, however, by taking care of the calculations and enabling you to spend your time in composition.

FIGURE 4.10

The Toy Block model viewed in three-point perspective.

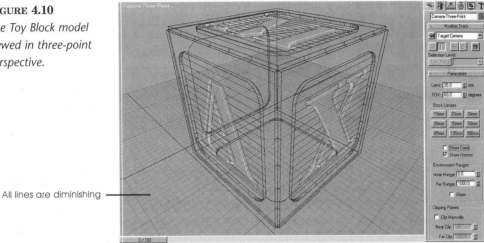

All lines are diminishing

Understanding Human Vision versus Camera Perspectives

You are probably familiar with the example of straight railroad tracks extending on flat ground to the horizon. The tracks appear to converge in the distance at a single point (see Figure 4.11). The convergence of these lines is a basic trait of perspective. The tracks are an extreme example because few observations are so distinct and separable. This example does not reflect the true complexity of the visual data you experience at almost any given moment.

Your eye takes in many images—very rapidly—that your mind then composes to form an overall picture of the scene from which it makes conclusions. The brain organizes shapes and forms according to spatial relationships. If you analyze a snapshot of a scene, you see that all lines are "slanting" or converging. But the mind's eye tends to correct the real-world view and understands these lines as being parallel rather than converging. This is an interpretation of reality. After all, the objects really are parallel. It is also much easier to navigate through a world that your mind spatially understands. Imagine a world where you would need to constantly judge the effects of perspective before walking across the room to pick up a glass! The ability to not see the world in perspective is quite useful and by far the norm. Your mind does this spatial transformation automatically.

FIGURE 4.11

Train tracks converging to a vanishing point on the horizon.

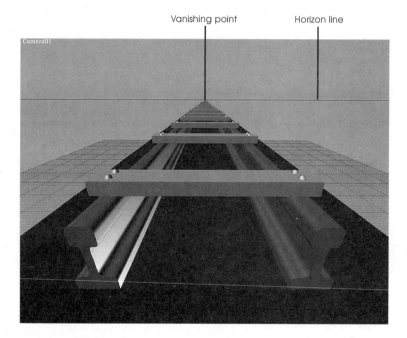

To truly understand perspective, you must learn how to see the world not as it appears in your mind's spatially transformed images, but rather as it appears in the snapshots taken by a camera. Perspective is learned; it is not readily apparent. Artists learn to find converging lines and vanishing points when they draw a scene and keep these rules in the back of their minds when they sketch objects. It was not until the Renaissance that a full understanding of perspective was achieved, so don't worry if it isn't immediately obvious to you.

Although your mind may not interpret what it sees according to the rules of perspective, it does know them. A drawing or illustration that has perspective flaws looks "off" to anyone. You may not be able to identify what is wrong, but you know intuitively that something is not right.

Perspective also has a great influence on the perceived mood and action of an image. A scene portrayed with flat perspective appears to be stable and at a distance. By contrast, an extremely flared perspective makes the scene appear in motion, very close, and possibly unstable. Perspective is an important contribution to composition. Learning the basic rules of perspective helps you compose scenes to get the desired effects. Figure 4.12 shows two similar views of a city, one with a flat perspective and one with a flared perspective. Both views are along the same line of sight (through different sized lenses and at different distances) but deliver very different impressions of the same scene.

FIGURE 4.12

Different views of a city with very different perspective.

Camera—telephoto

Camera—wide angle

You can much more readily understand the rules and effects of perspective by analyzing photographs. These frozen images, made from a stationary vantage point, prevent you from assembling a mind's eye view of them. Each perspective view that 3DS MAX gives you is, in essence, such a photograph.

The 3D Studio MAX Camera Analogy

Excellent perspective capabilities are built into the 3D Studio MAX environment through its cameras, Perspective viewport, and even Spotlight viewports. You can use these to learn quite a bit about how perspective affects the perception and drama of a view as you experiment with them in your scenes.

3D Studio MAX relates the rules of perspective in photographic terms. The basis for descriptions is the 35mm single-lens-reflex (SLR) camera, by far the most common camera available with interchangeable lenses. All the lens terminology that 3DS MAX uses corresponds directly to the 35 mm camera

NOTE

The 35mm designation refers to the size of the film and not the size of the lens.

The camera is a good analogy because you can pick up any 35mm camera and reproduce the compositional effects that 3DS MAX creates. If you can view it through a 35mm camera, you can recreate it in a camera viewport.

35mm Camera Lens Types

You should become familiar with how the lens sizes of a 35mm camera affect vision, because it is the analogy 3DS MAX uses to describe field of view in its camera viewports (see Figure 4.13). Note that this relationship is valid only for as long as you are referring to the same camera type. Other film dimension standards (for example, 4"×5" or 70mm motion picture) have different ranges of lens sizes to associate with field of view. 3DS MAX's default lens is 43.456mm, which delivers a field of view equivalent to your natural eyesight, 45 degrees.

Changing Lens Sizes

The smaller your camera's lens size, the wider the field of view and the more pronounced the perspective becomes. Try this yourself by adjusting one of the cameras in the Toy Block model. As you select smaller lens sizes, the field of view increases. Manipulating the lens size makes this relationship obvious, as shown in the following exercise:

FIGURE 4.13

The stock lenses for 3D Studio MAX cameras.

EFFECTING PERSPECTIVE AND FIELD OF VIEW WITH LENS SIZES

1. Load toyblck3.max from the accompanying CD-ROM.

2. Press H to access the Select Objects dialog. Choose Camera-Three-Point and then click Select to select the camera.

3. Click the Modify panel to view the parameters for Camera-Three-Point.

   The camera is currently a moderately wide, 35mm lens.

4. Click the 15mm button.

   The camera view seems to "zoom out" while the camera itself does not move (as seen in the Top viewport). The camera's FOV has grown substantially and the perspective of the cube in the camera view is extremely flared.

5. Now try larger lenses, such as 85mm and 135mm.

   The camera does not move but the FOV indication continues to shrink as the camera view "zooms in" and the perspective flare lessens.

6. Click 35mm to restore the original FOV and activate the Camera-Three-Point viewport.

7. Click the Perspective icon and drag the mouse up and down.

This performs a simultaneous dolly and FOV change that demonstrates exactly how much the perspective flare is changing as the lens size changes (see Figure 4.14). (This effect is described further in Chapter 19, "Cameras and Setting the Shot.")

FIGURE 4.14

Adjusting the perspective of the camera viewport automatically adjusts the camera's field of view and lens size.

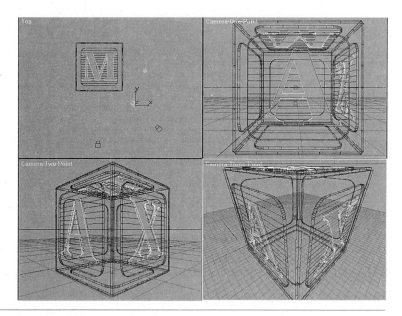

Wide-Angle Lenses

Lens sizes below 50mm (or more appropriately, below 48.24mm) take in more of a field of view than is normally possible by the human cone of vision. These lenses are considered to be wide-angle lenses and produce wide-angle views. The effects of perspective viewed through such lenses are exaggerated. The stock lenses provided by Camera/Adjust correspond to stock lenses in a camera store.

Selecting a lens below the standard 35mm and 28mm wide-angle lenses can cause excessive perspective distortion, which can produce dramatic or confusing effects, depending on how you compose the final scene. Very small lenses, 10 to 15mm, are often called fish-eye lenses because the actual lens begins to appear spherical. Geometry viewed through a fish-eye lense's corners appear "bent" as you look from side to side. 3D Studio MAX's smallest lens, a 9.8mm fish-eye, delivers a 178 degree field of view, which has the effect of almost seeing behind yourself! You should reserve such lenses for extremely special effects.

An important human perception concerning three-point perspective is that the more an object flares, the larger the object (or the smaller the observer) appears to be. This effect stems from daily observations. If a building is quite tall and you are near, it is obvious that the building's vertical lines converge upward and away from you. The closer you are, the more the building fills the scene. As you strain your neck to see it, the more distorted the view becomes. The flaring of a three-point perspective (see Figure 4.15) can reinforce these effects; a simple block appears quite large.

FIGURE 4.15

Flaring perspective with a wide-angle lens.

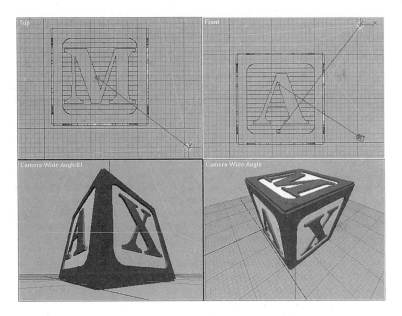

Telephoto Lenses

Camera lenses that are more than 50mm in length are known as telephoto lenses. These lenses can zoom in to the scene closer than your eye can, similar to a telescope. Large telephoto lenses actually are the size of small telescopes. The amount of the scene these lenses can take in is proportionally smaller, and their effect is to flatten perspective. The perspective flare is minimized because only a small angle of the scene is viewed. You can simulate this effect on a photograph by cropping a small region and analyzing the lack of converging lines—the larger the lens, the smaller this cropped view becomes and the flatter the perspective appears.

The 85mm lens is nicknamed a portrait lens because it slightly flattens the features of the subject and results in a more flattering image. If you use a wide-angle lens for a portrait, it distorts your subject's features, and you might lose your commission.

You should never run out of the high range in camera lens selections. 3DS MAX has an unbelievably high 100,000mm lens limit (with a corresponding FOV of 0.025). Such a lens is the equivalent of a large observatory telescope or highly powerful electron microscope. A lens of this size effectively eliminates perspective and makes the view appear as a planer projection or a true elevation. With such a setting, MAX performs much like a 2D CAD program, although your objects are in 3D, they appear flat. This might be used if you're creating architectural drawings.

Understanding Parallax

Many artists and delineators prefer to confine their illustrations to a two-point perspective because of human perception and ease of use. Human perception tends to "correct" the splaying of a scene's vertical lines. Seeing an image in three-point perspective makes many people question its correctness, which is typical in interior views where wide-angle lenses are required to get enough of the view. The vertical lines near the edge of the view begin to splay in a way that makes the viewer uncomfortable; everyone knows that walls are normally straight up and down.

The convergence of vertical lines in photography is termed parallax. Whenever you aim your camera up or down so that it is not level with the ground plane, your view becomes a three-point perspective and begins to show signs of parallax. These effects are most apparent at the edges of a view, and they exaggerate more and more as the field of view widens. Figure 4.16 shows an interior view with parallax.

Perspective Correction

In traditional illustration, especially architectural and interior photography, parallax should be avoided and photographers go to great lengths to correct it. You can avoid this effect completely by always keeping your camera level to the ground. This can lead to less than exciting compositions, however, and is likely to force you to crop a scene or move your camera to an unreasonable height.

View finder cameras, also known as large format, variable plane, or 45s, enable a photographer to correct the effects of parallax by manipulating the internal mirrors. The same capability is available with 35mm cameras that have special perspective control (PC) lenses. 3DS MAX provides much of the same capability with the Renderer's Blowup option (see Figure 4.16).

FIGURE 4.16
Interior exhibiting parallax due to a tilted camera.

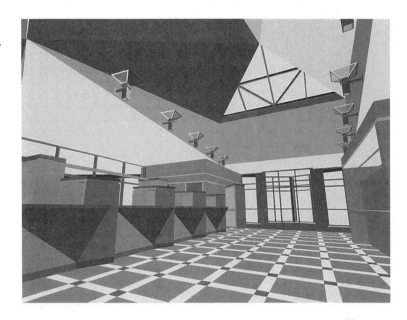

FIGURE 4.17
Same interior from identical vantage point perspective correction.

NOTE

See Chapter 19, "Cameras and Setting the Shot," for more details on perspective correction using the Renderer's Blowup option.

Understanding Compositional Elements

An understanding of perspective helps you stage and view your scenes, but do the objects that make up your scenes truly define your composition? Your composition, as a work of art, contains two main elements: form and content. Here are some brief definitions:

■ **Form:** Think of form as the way in which you portray the theme, or content, of your scene. In the most basic sense, form describes the objects and shapes you create. However, form can more accurately be defined as the result of your design and planning. It's literally how your ideas become reality.

■ **Content:** Disregard any style or technique used to create form, and you have content. Think of content as the collective sum of your ideas and how they are represented in the scene. Content can be thought of as the theme of your composition. It's how you represent your ideas in the objects you create.

■ **Composition:** The arrangement of objects in a scene, the relationship to their surroundings, and the way they are viewed. Form and content are aspects of your composition.

You are the master of your own creation. Thus, your idea of successful composition may differ from those who view your scene or animation. Since the objective behind most of your work is to convey a message, however, being aware at least of traditional compositional elements will help you complete successful works of art.

Few artists agree on one definition of composition, yet the majority agree on whether a particular piece of art has or lacks good composition. Recognizing effective composition is a feel, or intuition, developed over time and based in part on some objective guidelines.

Underlying principles exist that many people regard as rules of thumb, or at least items for consideration, when organizing a composition. Consider the following principles when you create compositions, but remember they are just guidelines and not hard and fast rules. Employing one principle effectively often diminishes the importance of the others. With experience you develop a sense of when to follow these rules and when to ignore them in the interest of good composition:

1. **Center of Interest** Scenes should be organized around a center of interest. The center does not have to be the geographic center of the images, but rather the thematic focus of the scene. Scenes that lack a center of interest look cluttered, noneventful, or just plain boring. A center of interest need not be an object; it could be a vanishing point in a one-point perspective, for example. In Figure 4.18, the mouse character is clearly our center of interest.

FIGURE 4.18

As shown here, a center of interest is not necessarily in the center of your scene.

2. **Symmetry** Scenes should not be perfectly symmetrical about either axis. Scenes that are perfectly centered on a symmetrical axis look stagnant, pat, and extremely formal. When the horizon is centered, the scene appears to be split and it can be difficult to create a center of interest (see Figure 4.19).

3. **Balance** Scenes should have balance. Balance refers to the overall visual "weight" that compositional pieces have. This can refer to the color, darkness, or visual complexity, as well as the size of the objects (see Figure 4.19).

4. Without some overlap of form, elements within compositions may appear to float and may not seem firmly rooted to the scene. Overlapping objects within a scene provide a greater definition of depth (see Figure 4.19).

5. Nongeometrical issues Compositional issues are not limited to an object's geometry. Textures assigned to objects, the shadows they cast, reflections of other objects, and the use of background images are all compositional elements to be considered.

FIGURE 4.19

This scene displays many of the aspects of good composition you should be aware of, including balance, symmetry and overlap.

As with all rules, these are made to be broken. It's possible to create a good composition that betrays the basic "rules." It is not uncommon for artists to see another's work, scratch their heads, and say, "I can't believe it works!"

Figure Ground

Artists sometimes reduce a scene's components to their silhouettes as an aid to develop and confirm their compositions. This technique makes all the objects in a scene entirely black against a white background, which has the effect of viewing the scene with a powerful white light cast from behind. Only the total, overall form is present. The internal edges and overlaps of objects are obscured. The scene reads as one quick gesture and this technique is referred to as figure ground.

You can use this technique to get a feel for spatial relationships in your composition; quickly identifying clutter and unbalanced scenes. You can analyze your image's figure ground in 3DS MAX with each rendering you do. Figure 4.20 shows how the Display Alpha Channel button displays the alpha channel for every rendering you perform in MAX. This is not an option you need to set because 3DS MAX always renders the alpha channel and you can always view it whether you intend to save it or not.

FIGURE 4.20

Comparing the RGB rendering with the alpha channel to analyze figure ground.

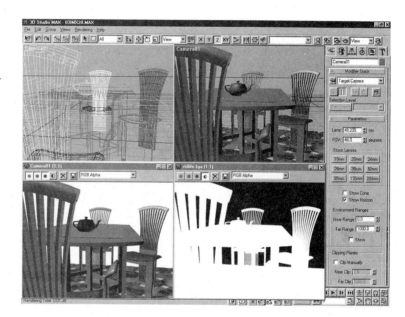

Thumbnail Sketches

Artists and filmmakers often use small, quick thumbnail sketches to develop and refine compositions. These sketches do not need to be detailed or even very accurate since the term thumbnail refers to size. A sketch of this type should only be big enough to capture the overall composition of a scene: a figure ground study, stick figures, overlapping box "stand-ins," or whatever best represents the elements in the composition. Many who use thumbnail sketches do them quickly and often. It is not uncommon to do five or six sketches per minute, trying different combinations. The advantage is that these thumbnail sketches give you a reference of what you've tried and where you are going.

Cloning Cameras

3DS MAX's cameras are extremely powerful compositional tools. They enable you to analyze unlimited viewing angles and proportions from any point. Specifically, one useful technique for experimenting with composition is to clone the working camera by pressing Shift as you move it, or use the Edit\Clone command. Change one of the viewports to show this new, cloned, camera view. Keep the original Camera viewport active for comparison and experiment with the new clone. After you arrive at a satisfactory view, clone again and again until you are convinced of your final composition. You may want to save some of your preliminary ideas, especially if they entail the complexity of animation. So at this point, you can keep the other cameras for reference, save them to their own MAX file for future use, or keep the original and inherit the tracks of the keeper in the Keyframer. If you're sure you won't need the ideas again, you can delete the cloned cameras.

In Practice: Viewing, Perspective, and Composition

- **Viewport options:** The 3D Studio MAX viewport options relate directly to traditional methods of creating orthogonal construction documents, explanatory axonometric views, and illustrative perspectives.

- **One- and two-point perspectives:** These perspectives rely on keeping the camera level to the ground plane. When level, all vertical lines perpendicular to the ground plane are parallel in the resulting view.

- **Three-point perspective:** Three-point perspectives are formed when the camera is tilted from the ground plane. The convergence to the third vanishing point produces an effect termed parallax, which is undesirable for many applications. Parallax can be overcome by keeping the camera level and using the Renderer's Blowup feature.

- **Horizon line:** The horizon line is always equal to your eye level with the horizon's location in the composition being dependent on your viewing angle. If you look up, the horizon lowers, and if you tilt/roll the camera, the horizon rotates.

- **35 mm camera analogy:** 3D Studio MAX's camera analogy places normal human vision at a lens size of approximately 50mm. Lenses below this allow in more of the scene, flare the perspective, and are often called wide-angle lenses. Lenses above 50mm zoom in on the scene, flatten the perspective, and are commonly termed telephoto lenses.

- **Scene Composition:** Your scene is made up of form and content. There are various rules of thumb you can use as a guide to produce effective images, but you should also use your creativity to guide you. The figure ground technique, use of quick thumbnail sketches, and camera cloning can also be used to develop and experiment with your composition.

Chapter 5

ANIMATION AND STORYBOARDING

There's a creative hazard that comes with the development of software, such as MAX, that lends itself so well to intuitive design. It's tempting to start a project by firing up the software and playing around until you create something wonderful. It's a trap many animators fall victim to, and it's a habit you should never develop. Good designs start as good ideas, and only become reality with proper execution. Successful animation depends heavily on a process that allows you to follow through with the execution of strong ideas. In short, good animation starts with good storyboards.

Storyboards benefit the animator, as well as the client, in many ways. The most basic of which is to tell your story and share your good idea with those involved with production, and those paying the bill. Only after you successfully tell a story through storyboards should you start to develop the elements of your design.

This chapter discusses how to plan and lay out an animation project by using storyboards and introduces some of the basic concepts behind effective animation, including:

- The use of storyboards to plan your animation.

- Motion design for animation.

- Use of traditional animation techniques, such as squash and stretch.

- Studies of natural motion for character animation.

Using Storyboards

Storyboards are an important part of designing any presentation. They were developed in the 1930s as directors and animators realized the traditional written script did not effectively work for describing how to shoot an animated film. Live-action drama relies heavily on dialog, but animation, on the other hand, tries to minimize dialog and tell the story through the action.

Originally, story writers sketched each major scene or important action and tacked these images to a board for review. The sketches contained a minimum amount of text to describe dialog or camera effects. If the scene didn't work graphically, it was discarded. This technique proved so beneficial that today nearly all films and professional presentations rely on storyboards during the design phase.

NOTE

One important benefit of using storyboards involves their use as a contract document. You should create the storyboard for an animation and get the client to approve it before any work on building models and scenes begins. Both you and the client should sign the storyboard or a letter confirming its approval. Then if a dispute arises over changes to the animation, you can refer to the storyboard as the original source of the agreement.

The Process

Before you can create a storyboard, you must have a story to tell. Too many animators jump into the program and expect the story and sequence of actions to reveal themselves as the animation develops. Nothing could be further from reality. You must have three things in hand before you sit down in front of your computer:

- A story to tell.

- A storyboard of the important scenes.

- A script for the action and any sound effects.

Your storyboards may combine all elements mentioned in the previous list in one document. Regardless of the form that the elements take, the most important thing is you must fully plan and develop all three before you begin animating.

Storytelling

What story are you going to tell with this animation? How will you hold the audience's attention? How will the story start? How will it end? How much time will the story take to tell? You must consider all of these details. Sometimes you have the complete story handed to you for animation; more often you receive the seed of a story idea and a requirement for a certain amount of running time.

A client may say, "Produce an animation of our proposed new building to help attract tenants." That is a story idea, but it is not detailed enough to move into the storyboard phase. You need to consider questions such as, "What are the main selling features of the building?" or "Is proximity to transportation hubs being promoted?" If transportation access is important, maybe you should consider a bird's-eye view that points out major transportation centers.

How do you show the entry sequence leading to the lobby and public reception area? How do you show the office suites? How do you get to the office suites? As the animator, your job is to come up with an interesting way to tell the story and do it within the time constraints set by the client.

Storyboard

Now that you have a story to tell, read it a few times. Has your good idea developed into a good story? Read it again. Let your client read it. Make sure the story is what you had in mind with your good idea. Just imagine what Disney's *Toy Story* would have been like if the toys had just sat in Andy's bedroom and played checkers all day. The animation was incredible, but the story made it a great movie. Once you are happy with your story, use storyboards to determine how it will translate to animation.

Take the story and break it down into the major scenes, important sequences of action, and transitions between scenes. If you are not sure a scene or action is important enough, include it anyway. You'll find it easier to weed out and discard scenes than to begin animation and discover you left an important issue unresolved.

Draw quick, conceptual sketches of each scene or action. Even stick figures can set up shots and enable you to see how your story flows. If you spend any time trying to make the storyboard sketches look good, you'll lose the flow of the action and miss the purpose of creating the storyboard. Figure 5.1 shows four roughly sketched frames from a project that leads the viewer through a client's new office.

FIGURE 5.1

Samples from an actual storyboard using rough sketches to describe the scene.

With all the sketches complete, tack them on a board or spread them out on a table and review the story. Does the action flow from one scene to the next? Is there any awkwardness in the way the story unfolds? Does anything seem to be missing? Can all of these scenes be animated in the allotted time frame? Ideas that are over-ambitious become apparent in the storyboard. Analyze the storyboard. If you have to read the notes next to a sketch to figure out what is happening at that point of the story, you have a problem. The scene or action in question is too weak. Give the scene more emphasis or discard it. The text next to a sketch exists only for detail information and to describe how the scene is put together.

Here is where you apply one of the fundamental principles of animation: staging. Any action you create needs to be inframe and readable. In the storyboard stage, you can play with how the action relates to the frame, and see that it is easily conveyed to the viewer. Action in profile allows the animation to be quickly taken in by the eye, and you should check your storyboards for this.

At some point in the storyboarding process, you need to get the client involved and get their approval. You might want to develop the initial storyboard, making sure it conveys your story the way you intended, and then bring in the client. If all goes well, have them sign an approval form, or the storyboards themselves, before proceeding. With that taken care of, use the storyboards as guides for your production, and also as a future reference if the client questions how things are progressing.

Script

With the storyboard approved, it's time to write the script. Your script will focus on identifying animation keys and defining what happens at those keys. If you plan to include sound effects, you must indicate when sounds occur and how they relate to the animation keys as well.

One useful approach to the script is to take a copy of the storyboard and begin adding time references or frame numbers next to the sketches. This also provides a convenient place to note what sound effects belong with each scene. At this point, your assumptions about timing and the overall length of the animation will be put to the test. Anticipate working through the storyboard and script many times until you find the right timing for the animation.

It is extremely useful to get a stopwatch and time imaginary action as you imagine it in your head, or act it out. These times can be placed on the storyboard or translated into frame numbers.

Types of Storyboards

You can use any type of storyboard you want. A typical type of storyboard follows closely what was described earlier—a quick, rough sketch of the relevant scenes with notations to the side for timing, camera effects, and sound.

Other types of storyboards are used as presentation devices. Remember the advice that both the animator and the client sign off on the final storyboard as part of the contract requirements? Many times you may not be comfortable presenting the rough, working version of the storyboard for client signature. In that case, you can buy commercially available storyboard forms that include small blank screens with lined blocks for your notes. A sample storyboard sheet is shown in Figure 5.2. Redraw the storyboard cleanly on these forms for presentation and client approval. You might also use a word processor to combine cleaned up sketches or even preliminary images into one document for approval (see Figure 5.3).

FIGURE 5.2

A typical preprinted storyboard sheet.

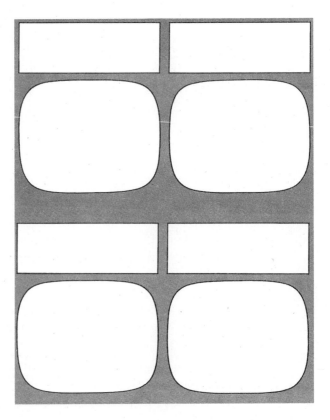

FIGURE 5.3

A cleaned up story-board with added narration and transition notes for client approval.

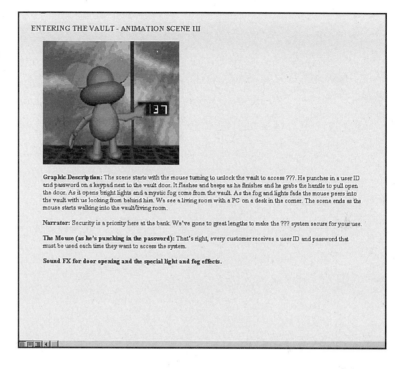

You should create this type of storyboard (Figure 5.3) only after you have completed the working storyboard and are satisfied with its contents. Trying to draw a presentation storyboard and working out the animation at the same time just doesn't work.

Drawing a Storyboard

The drawing technique used should be fast and rough—anything that slows the flow of ideas kills the creative process. Using preprinted storyboard forms that contain multiple scenes on a single large sheet tends to inhibit the drawing process; you try too hard to keep things in the lines, and the sharp edges of the frames are not compatible with a fast drawing technique. Also, if multiple frames are on a single sheet, it is difficult to discard or replace frames as you make changes. Every scene should be on a separate sheet of paper, so if that scene does not work out, you can simply discard it.

The drawings of each scene should be kept small to promote fast, conceptual drawing. Don't fill in unnecessary detail and background to make the drawing more "finished." The small, gummed-back sketch pads or even cheap notepads make great storyboard sheets.

After the client has signed off on the storyboard and you begin the animation, everyone involved in production should continue referring to the storyboard to guide their work. You should not sit in front of the workstation without having the storyboard close at hand.

Creating the Big Bounce Storyboard

The following example gives you a chance to create a quick storyboard for a simple animation. Remember, the sketches for a storyboard should be very loose and rough, and each scene or action should be on a separate page.

The Story

You will create a storyboard for the story titled "The Big Bounce." The final animation runs about 20 seconds.

You are looking at a beautiful landscape at the edge of a cliff when a red ball rolls up to the edge of the cliff and stops. The ball seems to look over the edge, and then after a brief pause, it bounces twice and jumps over the edge.

You follow the ball down, gaining speed as you go—just inches away from the face of the cliff. Suddenly, the ball strikes the ground with great force and rebounds out of view.

You are left standing at the base of the cliff, wondering what just happened, when you notice three more balls in the background. Slowly, the balls rotate, one by one, revealing scores of 9.5, 9.6, and 9.4. A near-perfect bounce.

Drawing the Storyboard

The first step is to divide the story into its major scenes and action sequences. Consider the following scenes:

1. Opening shot. Cliff with landscape.

2. Ball rolls out to edge of the cliff.

3. Ball looks over edge.

4. Ball bounces.

5. Ball goes over the edge.

6. Falling.

7. Ball hits the ground.

8. Ball bounces out of view.

9. Shot of balls in the background.

10. Balls roll over revealing numbers.

11. Zoom in on middle ball.

12. Ball fades to black with just numbers on the screen.

You may have ideas for a slightly different division of scenes. If so, feel free to draw them. Figure 5.4 shows an example of what part of the storyboard might look like.

FIGURE 5.4

Sample storyboard frames.

Adding Frame Numbers

Consider when each action occurs. Add time references and camera descriptions to each storyboard sketch. The following list shows a suggestion of how the timing could work out, assuming you have set a frame rate of 15 frames per second in the Time Configuration dialog:

1. Opening shot. Pause on scene of the cliff. (From 0.0 to 3.0 seconds, frames 1–45.)

2. Ball rolls out to edge of the cliff. (From 3.0 to 5.0 seconds, frames 46–75.)

3. Ball pauses and looks over edge. (From 5.0 to 7.0 seconds, frames 76–105.)

4. Ball bounces two times, quickly, in place. (From 7.0 to 10.0 seconds, frames 106–150.)

5. Ball goes over the edge. (From 10.0 to 10.5 seconds, frames 151–158.)

6. Falling. See cliff flashing by. Ball stretches during fall. (From 10.5 to 13.0 seconds, frames 159–195.)

7. Ball hits the ground. Squashes flat. Ground shakes. (From 13.0 to 13.5 seconds, frames 196–203.)

8. Ball bounces out of view. (From 13.5 to 14.0 seconds, frames 204–210.)

9. Shot of balls in the background. Pan and zoom in on balls. (From 14.0 to 15.0 seconds, frames 211–225.)

10. Balls roll over, one at a time, revealing numbers. Pause. (15.0 to 18.0 seconds, frames 226–270.)

11. Zoom in on middle ball. (18.0 to 19.0 seconds, frame 271–285.)

12. Ball fades to black with just numbers on the screen. (From 19.0 to 20.0 seconds, frames 286–300.)

You have just worked through the process of devising a story, drawing a storyboard, and producing a script for a simple animation. Even for a simple animation such as this, working out the timing and the key frames for all the scenes is quite involved. Imagine trying to create a sophisticated animation without first working out the storyboard and the script.

Animation Concepts

Many people approach computer animation solely from the standpoint of building the model. They assume that if you build a sufficiently good-looking model, it will come to life by itself. Unfortunately, they assume wrong. You can avoid this trap by realizing that in any animation, motion is an important part of the overall product. You must design your motion with as much care as you give to building the model and applying materials. In fact, motion is such an integral part of 3DS MAX that it is difficult to properly design materials, or model an object, without considering how they will be animated.

Understanding how objects move and how to simulate their movement in computer animation requires becoming familiar with the concepts of motion theory.

Design of Motion

Effective motion is as important to the success of your animation as any other element of the design. You readily accept animation of unreal or fantastic objects, such as talking animals and battling spacecraft, because those objects move in a lifelike manner. You also have seen animation where the subject is modeled in great detail and painstakingly rendered, but for some reason it just does not hold your attention. An analysis of unsuccessful animation usually reveals too little motion or motion that is not lifelike. In other words, your imagination often quietly fills in the missing detail in a model, but it does not forgive crude and unrealistic motion, which has long been the downfall of 3D character animation. Even if the model looks and talks just like a real person, it's just not believable if it moves like a robot.

Planning for motion begins even before you build the model. Examine your storyboard. How are objects moving, and where are they going? A brief look at the physics of motion will help you design the motion in your animation.

The Physics of Motion

How does the theory, "Every action causes an equal and opposite reaction" translate into believable motion?

Imagine a standing figure about to perform a broad jump. The figure does not suddenly pop across space. First, it crouches down as the hips move back, and the torso leans forward to maintain balance. As the crouch begins, the arms swing backward until everything comes to a stop with the body in a full crouch, leaning forward, and arms extended fully back. After the most brief pause, the figure raises up on its toes, and the arms begin to swing forward. Next, the legs drive the body forward as the arms swing out, and the figure leaves the ground. Finally, as the figure flies across space, the arms reach fully forward, and the legs start to swing forward to prepare to land. Figure 5.5 illustrates this sequence.

FIGURE 5.5
The motion of a broad jump.

The previous jumping sequence uses nearly all the important elements of animating believable motion:

- Anticipation
- Squash and stretch
- Overlapping action
- Follow-through
- Exaggeration
- Secondary action

Try to imagine the landing sequence of the jumping figure. Sketch the actions of a broad jump as a storyboard, and then play the animation jump.avi from the CD-ROM to compare it with your sequence.

Anticipation

Anticipation is a preliminary action that sets up a primary action. One use of anticipation is to simulate real motion. If an object is at rest, some preliminary action must occur that transfers energy to the object to execute the primary action. Use the previous broad jump sequence as an example. Before the figure can jump, it has to crouch down and swing its arms for counterbalance. (Just try to jump without bending your knees or swinging your arms.) Figure 5.6 identifies the anticipation portion of the broad jump motion.

Essentially anticipation is used to give the viewer time to recognize that something is going to happen but hasn't yet. The event usually goes by very fast, so the viewer must be expecting it to happen or they might not ever see it.

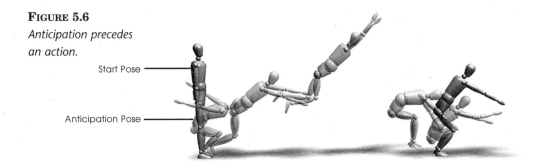

Start Pose ──

Anticipation Pose ──

Anticipation is used to prepare the audience for what is about to happen or directs audience attention to where the action is going to happen. Imagine a rope snapping under a heavy load. You have experienced this when a shoelace breaks or an overloaded clothesline snaps. The action is abrupt and without warning. If you animated such a sequence true to life, the audience would miss the actual breaking of the rope and would probably miss other important points of the animation while trying to figure out what had happened. The traditional solution to this scenario uses an extreme case of anticipation to prepare for the primary action. A close-up of the rope shows it stretching; a few strands snap; and then suddenly, POW! The rope breaks, and you accept that the heavy safe is about to land on Porky's head. The anticipation of the close-up prepares you for the breaking of the rope. You have seen this sequence a hundred times, and yet you probably never stopped to think, "Gee, ropes really don't break that way!"

You can use anticipation to direct audience attention with camera movement. Imagine an architectural walkthrough of a house. Employ anticipation by panning the family room and finish with the camera facing an open passage into the kitchen. A brief pause on the still image of the kitchen, before switching to a camera view in the kitchen, anticipates the cut. The audience makes the mental jump to the kitchen before the animation actually cuts to that scene.

Squash and Stretch

Many objects in your animation are soft and deform under the stress of motion. Think of the last time you watched the slow-motion replay of a hard-hitting football tackle. The body of the ball carrier probably deformed in ways that didn't seem humanly possible. This is an example of squash and stretch. All objects, unless they are very dense and very hard, exhibit some form of squash and stretch.

Remember the storyboard of the bouncing ball? The elongation of the ball as it fell and the flattening of the ball when it hit the ground also demonstrated the principle of squash and stretch. Imagine how a bowling ball and a rubber ball bounce. The bowling ball bounces very little and does not deform when it hits the ground, as shown in Figure 5.7—you might even consider making the ground deform when the bowling ball lands. A rubber ball, however, deforms more than the bowling ball and bounces higher, as shown in Figure 5.8.

FIGURE 5.7

A bowling ball bouncing on the ground.

FIGURE 5.8

A rubber ball bouncing on the ground.

Another approach to squash and stretch applies to jointed figures. Rather than deforming the geometry of the figure, you indicate squash and stretch in the positioning of the figure's joints. You can see this by looking again at the broad jump. Anticipation often involves a squash or stretch. Quick motion almost always employs a stretch, and a sudden stop always employs a squash (sometimes a violent squash). Figure 5.9 identifies these effects in the broad jump sequence.

As a general rule, do not violate the law that states, "no matter how much an object deforms, it must always maintain the same apparent volume." Consider a water balloon that deforms as you handle it. You aren't adding or removing any water as it deforms, so the volume remains constant. The exception to the rule occurs in stylized cartoon animation, where squashing and stretching may be highly exaggerated. You may still want to preserve a sense of constant volume. In 3D Studio MAX, the Squash scale transformer and the Stretch modifier both employ this technique. When an object squashes along one axis, it automatically expands along the other two.

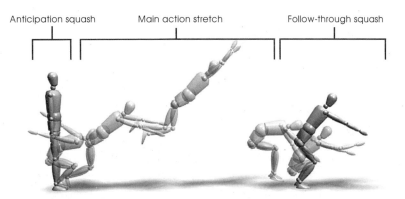

Anticipation squash   Main action stretch   Follow-through squash

FIGURE 5.9
Squash and stretch in a broad jump.

For simple geometry, maintaining a constant volume while squashing and stretching is fairly easy, and the tools in MAX do the work for you. With more sophisticated meshes, however, it is harder to accomplish. You may need to deform human models or other complex objects such as vehicles. An easy way to create such deformations is with the HyperMatter plug-in from Second Nature Industries. The plug-in enables you to deform any object in any way imaginable. You assign such properties as elasticity and density for objects in your scene. Presets, (see Figure 5.10) such as *bowling ball* and *water bomb*, contain settings that make objects react as the names imply. You can also define custom settings for objects. As you can see in Figure 5.11, this plug-in makes it easy to create 3D animation equivalents of traditional cell animation techniques.

Squash and Stretch is an example of using exaggeration to visually convey your message. Cartoon physics at work in the service of art.

Overlapping Action

Another important element of believable motion is the concept of overlapping action. Not everything happens at the same time. Overlapping action is seen in safety films that show crash dummies in a car that slams into a wall. A novice animator might position the car model at the point of impact and start adjusting the positions of all the objects in the car. When you look closely at the film, you see what really happens. In the first few frames after impact, the front of the car crumples and crushes all the way back to the front wheels, but the car's interior and the dummies haven't moved. They have yet to experience the impact. The situation rapidly changes in the next few frames as the dummies lunge forward against their safety belts, the windshield explodes, and so on. All this action is the result of a single event—the crash—yet each action begins at a different time. If you watch the rest of the crash, you notice that everything stops at different times as well.

FIGURE 5.10

HyperMatter includes a library of preset object properties, each with an animated preview (using a ball) to show the effects the settings will have on your objects.

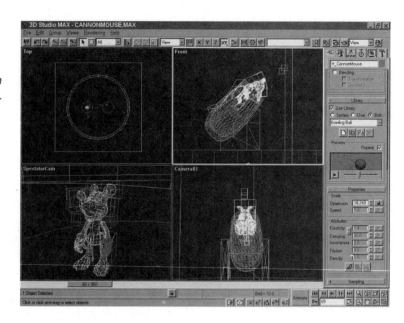

FIGURE 5.11

Squash and stretch effects, common to traditional cell animation, are easy to produce with HyperMatter. Consider this mouse who is deformed as he is shot from a cannon.

You employ this technique in animation, for example, when moving a figure's arm from a position of rest to pick up a glass on a table. The proper sequence requires that the upper arm begins to rise first, and then the forearm pivots out, followed by the wrist bending back. Finally, the fingers curl around the glass. Each of these motions begins before the preceding motion is complete, providing the realistic overlap that your audience subconsciously expects. Traditional animators often refer to this technique as "the successive breaking of joints," because the motion is visualized by the joints breaking free from the at-rest position in a successive order. The motion begins at the shoulder and works its way down to the knuckles in the fingers.

Follow-Through

Follow-through is a companion to overlapping action and it means the same thing for animation as it does for throwing a ball or swinging a bat. An action almost never comes to a complete and sudden stop. Instead, inertia carries the object beyond the termination point, often causing the object to slowly reverse direction and settle back to the intended stop location.

3D Studio MAX includes Bézier and tension, continuity, and bias (TCB) animation controllers to help you create natural motion and follow-through. Although these controllers are useful, you must not rely on them too much. Most of the time, you need to manually specify the appropriate follow-through, and then fine-tune the motion in Track View.

Staging

The idea behind staging is that objects in motion should be positioned in a way so that the motion is quickly detected and clearly understood. If your audience cannot detect an action, why use it?

Visualize the primary objects in your scene as silhouettes. If an action occurs within the silhouette of another object, that action is hard to detect. If you move the action to one side, where it is not masked by another object, the action stands out. As an example, look at Figure 5.12. The rendered view of the robot arm shows it picking up a box. When you view the scene in silhouette, you cannot easily discern what is happening. Compare Figure 5.12 with Figure 5.13. The scene in the second figure is easier to understand in both the rendered and silhouette views. The only difference is that the action is staged to the side of the robot arm.

FIGURE 5.12

View of a robot arm with poor staging.

FIGURE 5.13

View of a robot arm with better staging.

TIP

To test for proper staging, turn off all the lights in the scene and hide any unimportant or distant background objects; keep only the primary object in the scene, along with any nearby secondary or background objects. Set your background color to something other than black and render a preview. The result is an .avi of the main objects in your scene, rendered as black silhouettes against your viewport background color. If the motion that you want to convey is visible in silhouette, then it is easy to recognize in the final animation.

Exaggerated Motion

You must often exaggerate a motion or effect, to ensure that the audience catches it. In no way does the proper use of exaggeration invalidate or harm the believability of an animation. The possible exception is technical animations produced for courtroom presentations or used for mechanical or architectural prototyping, in which strict adherence to precise motion is more important than good presentation.

Exaggeration works in conjunction with anticipation and staging to direct the audience's attention to the action that you want the audience to see. Anticipation sets up the action, staging ensures that the action occurs where it can be seen, and exaggeration makes sure that the action is not so subtle that the audience fails to notice.

You can see good examples of exaggeration while watching a TV sitcom and then a drama show. Sitcoms are full of gross exaggeration—the double takes, stumbles, and sweeping motions used to accomplish mundane tasks. Those exaggerations are employed for comedic effect. Now watch a drama with the same critical eye. The exaggeration is still there, just toned down. Notice the extra flourishes that occur when an actor reaches for the phone or pulls out some keys. Notice how facial expressions are more pronounced than in real life. Such exaggeration does not detract from the reality of the scene; rather, it enhances reality by making sure the audience catches what is happening. Employ these same techniques in your animation.

Secondary Action

Secondary action happens as a result of another action. It is easy to forget about secondary action, because in real life you take such side effects for granted. Even though you might not consciously notice secondary action in real life, you need to include it if your animation is to be interesting and realistic.

Consider an animation that shows a basketball bouncing off the rim of the basket. The deflection of the rim from the force of the bounce is a secondary motion, and its absence makes the animation look fake and mechanical. Figure 5.14 shows the sequence of a rim deflecting from the bounce of a ball.

FIGURE 5.14
Rim deflection as a secondary action.

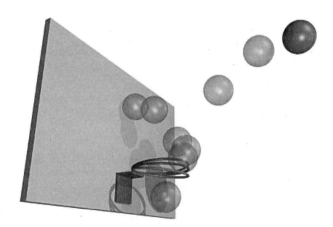

Load and play the file rim.avi from the accompanying CD-ROM to see the result of applying secondary action to the rim of a basketball hoop. Notice that the rim of the basket deflects downward as the ball strikes, and springs up when the ball leaves.

Studies of Animal Motion

The recognized reference on both animal and human motion is the collected work of Eadweard Muybridge, a photographer who took high-speed photographs of animals and people while they were performing various tasks. His book, *Complete Human and Animal Motion*, is a required reference for anyone who wants to animate living creatures.

Understanding and using correct human and animal motion is critical, but alone, it is not enough to bring your subjects to life. You must also give the creature a personality. Use anticipation and exaggeration to add an extra bounce to the walk of a puppy, or to add frantic scrambling to the legs of a running mouse. Take a look at some classic animated characters like Bugs Bunny and Wile E. Coyote. You'll discover much of their personality stems from how they move.

Studies of Human Motion

Your audience is much more aware of how the human body moves, as opposed to animal motion, and are less forgiving of exaggeration or movement that goes too far beyond what is really possible. The best way to get a feel for what is possible is to observe how the people around you move.

TIP

A useful plug-in to help you animate human and animal forms is Character Studio. For creatures that walk on two legs, the plug-in will automatically set footsteps and keyframes to make your figure walk, run, or jump. Character Studio takes much of the work out of creating correct bipedal motion, but much of the fine-tuning that makes your character appear life-like is still adjusted by the animator.

You need to concentrate on two properties of human motion that often are overlooked: balance and curved motion.

Balance

With the exception of falling, the body is always balanced. If you extend your right arm, your left arm, shoulder, and torso, all pivot and move back. This action balances the extended mass of your right arm. Likewise, few people stand perfectly ramrod straight. Instead, they shift their weight to one leg, causing the hips and torso to twist as they shift to balance. The other leg carries little weight and acts as an outrigger to compensate for small changes in balance.

NOTE

Walking and running are special cases of falling. When you walk, you are constantly cycling through the process of falling forward, restoring balance, and falling forward again. Running works the same way except that you are spending most of your time falling forward.

Figure 5.15 demonstrates the difference between an unnatural straight pose and a realistic-looking balanced pose. Remember that every motion of one part the body is offset by a balancing motion in another part of the body.

FIGURE 5.15

A stiff, unnatural pose versus a natural pose.

Stiff pose

Natural pose

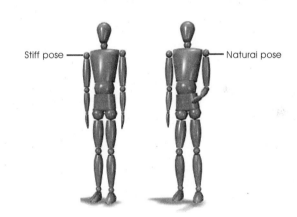

Curved Motion

No straight lines exist in nature. This statement also applies to natural motion. The default animation controllers in 3DS MAX are set up to deliver curved motion, but remember that you use these to fine-tune a motion that you design manually. Two examples where curved motion often is missed are arm swings and head turns.

Watch someone swing their arm up for a handshake. The arm not only swings up, but also swings out from the side and back in again. This subtle motion makes all the difference between an unnatural, robotic move and a move that appears lifelike.

See Figures 5.16 and 5.17 for examples of two head turns. Many people may make the mistake of animating the head turn as it appears in Figure 5.16. The features of the face follow a straight line as the head turns from side to side. The result is an unnatural, robotic head turn in which the features seem to slide across the face.

FIGURE 5.16

An unnatural head turn.

Unnatural straight motion

FIGURE 5.17

A natural head turn.

Natural curved motion

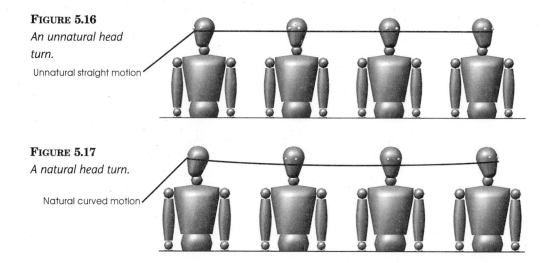

Figure 5.17 demonstrates a more realistic head motion. Notice that the head dips down and back up as it turns. The features of the face now follow a curved path from one side to the other. The greater the amount of dip, the more emotion conveyed by the turn.

In Practice: Employing Good Animation Techniques

- **Use storyboards:** A storyboard aids planning your animation and leads to better results and less wasted time. Added benefits of storyboards include helping explain proposals to clients, and saving a record of what type of animation a client approved.

- **Make motion believable:** Use traditional animation techniques such as anticipation, squash and stretch, follow-through, and overlapping action to make even the wildest animation more believable.

- **Make motion visible:** Use the concepts of staging and exaggeration to ensure your audience doesn't miss the action you worked so hard to create.

- **Duplicate natural patterns of motion:** Animals and people maintain balance in their motion and move in arcs rather than straight lines. If you ignore these traits your animation will appear mechanical and lifeless.

Chapter 6

PLANNING YOUR PROJECTS

An important time in any project is the period just before you start production. If you have planned for the important issues, and decided what is not so important, you are likely to succeed. If, instead, you just jump in and start building a scene, you will likely experience extra errors and wasted time and will probably need to redo a greater portion of your work. This chapter looks at the issues you need to consider when beginning a project and shows you how to set up your scene to get started.

This chapter covers issues that will help you plan your projects and avoid wasted effort. These issues include the following:

- Modeling decisions

- Working with files

- Preventing disaster

You have an idea for an animation. You have worked out the story and drawn the story boards. Now you have an empty scene waiting to be filled with animated objects. Your next step is to model those objects.

Modeling Decisions

Think about the objects you need to create. Do they need to be dimensionally accurate or can they just look good? Are they highly detailed or rough and schematic? How important is quick rendering time, and how much modeling can you replace with texture maps? When you can answer these questions, you have an idea about the levels of accuracy, detail, and complexity you need in your scene.

Accuracy

How accurate your models need to be depends on the subject and use of your animation. For courtroom or technical uses, accuracy is adhered to slavishly. In other, more creative applications, you can take advantage of 3D Studio MAX and be looser and more flexible in your accuracy. For creative uses, a good rule of thumb is, "If it looks right, it is right." 3D Studio MAX is a visualization tool capable of accommodating any level of accuracy your project demands.

For non-technical projects, you can achieve appropriate accuracy by trusting your sensibilities. What makes a model appear accurate often has little to do with exact dimensions. The human visual system excels at comparing proportions and relationships. If you are comfortable with the proportions and relationships between the objects in your scene, your audience will be comfortable, too.

Sometimes, you must give extra attention to dimensional accuracy. Good examples are scientific animation, courtroom (forensic) presentations, and architectural or engineering presentations. However, even for projects that demand extreme accuracy, thresholds exist beyond which any extra precision is wasted. The two main thresholds you need to concern yourself with are:

- Image output threshold

- 3DS MAX numeric thresholds

Image Output Threshold

One way to evaluate your threshold for precision is to examine your intended output media. Determine the visible width and height of your scene and divide those values by the width and height of your output resolution. The result is the model dimension covered by one pixel. You can waste a lot of effort by modeling to a precision that is less than one-half of a single pixel's dimension.

NOTE

In an animation, the visible width and height of your scene varies depending on camera position and field-of-view (FOV). Calculate your precision requirements from the most critical scene in the animation.

The following example measures the image output precision threshold in a scene. Imagine that you plan to create a rendering of a low-rise office building to display onscreen at a resolution of 800×600 pixels. You want to know how precise to make the model.

The example makes use of two types of helper objects called Grids and Tape Measures. The example also measures the size of the view Safe Frame.

Figure 6.1 shows a scene—Precise.max—that you can load from the accompanying CD-ROM to follow along with this example. The scene contains a stand-in for an office building 180' wide, 130' deep, and 34' tall.

Study the camera view in the lower-right viewport. Notice the concentric rectangles around the edge of the view. These rectangles are the View Safe Frame. The outer rectangle at the edge of the viewport is called the Safe Frame. It indicates the exact size of the final rendered image.

To properly determine your precision threshold, you need to know the width and height of the Safe Frame in camera view, measured at the building. You take these measurements by creating a grid object aligned to the camera, and then creating tape measures on the grid.

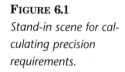

FIGURE 6.1

Stand-in scene for calculating precision requirements.

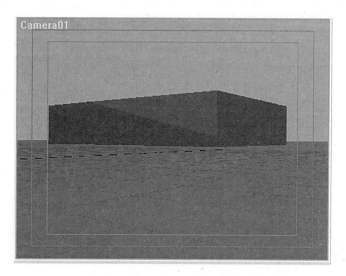

MEASURING PRECISION THRESHOLD IN A SCENE

1. Load Precise.max from the accompanying CD-ROM.

2. Click Grid from the Helpers Standard category of the Create panel.

3. Drag the cursor in the center of the camera viewport to create a grid.

   In Figure 6.2, a 50-unit square grid is created in the Camera01 viewport.

4. Choose Views, Grids, Activate Grid Object to make the grid object you just created your active construction plane.

5. With the Camera01 viewport active, choose Views, Grids, Align To View to align the grid with the Camera01 viewport.

   Figure 6.2 shows the results of the previous four steps. After using the Align To View command, the grid moves and rotates so it is aligned with the camera and centered on the camera's location.

You now need to move the grid along the camera's line of sight until the grid is located at the center of the subject (the building). You do this by moving the grid along its local Z axis .

6. Click Move and set the Reference Coordinate System to Local coordinates and Z-axis constraint.

7. Move the grid so it is centered on the building as shown in Figure 6.3. You can move the grid in any convenient viewport.

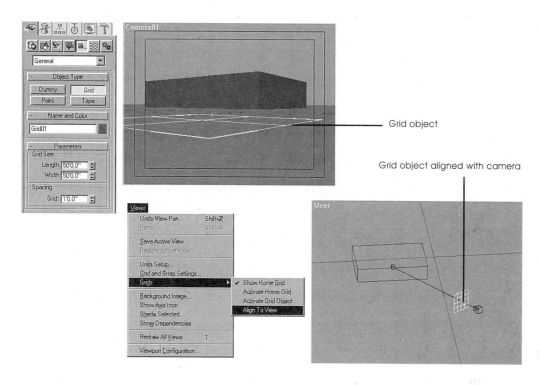

Grid object

Grid object aligned with camera

FIGURE 6.2

Creating and aligning the grid object.

FIGURE 6.3

Moving the grid to center it on the subject of the scene.

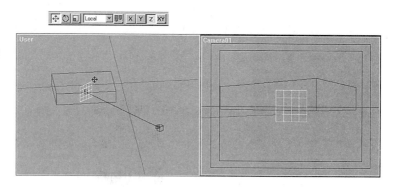

Finally, you are ready to create two Tape helpers to measure the height and width of the Safe Frame in the camera view.

8. Click in the Camera01 view to make it active.

9. Click Tape from the Helpers Standard category of the Create panel.

10. Create one tape that measures the width of the Safe Frame and a second tape that measures the height, as seen in Figure 6.4.

FIGURE 6.4

Creating Tape objects on the aligned grid.

Tape objects ——

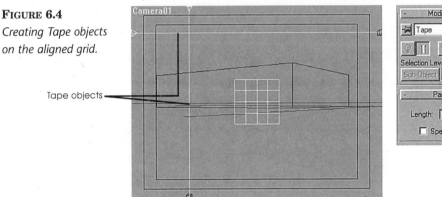

11. From the Modify panel, select each tape one at a time. Note their lengths in the Length field.

12. Divide the measured width and height by the configured render width and render height. The results should be close to the following:

Width: 284'/800=0.36
Height: 213'/600=0.36

The result of 0.36', or just over 4", means that each pixel in the image covers a little more than 4" in the scene. If you assume that an object is centered on a pixel, then that object can move about 2" to either side and will still be within the same pixel. This model and camera view have an image output precision threshold of plus or minus 2".

Using the information from the previous example, you can determine that for the given camera angle and output resolution, modeling any detail less than 2" wide is a waste of effort. Also, you want to carefully consider whether any details less than 4" wide are really needed in the shot.

NOTE

In the preceding exercise, you calculated the same value of 0.36' for both the height and the width of the image. These values are equal only when the aspect ratio for your rendering device is set to 1.0.

When you specify rendering output resolutions, the aspect ratio reported in the Render Scene dialog is not always 1.0. The configuration for a video resolution of 512 × 486 yields an aspect ratio of 1.25. When this occurs, the result is two different values for the distance covered by one pixel—one result for when you measure horizontally and one for when you measure vertically. You must decide which value governs the most critical details in your scene.

You can employ a similar technique for projects in which precision is not that critical. Make some rough estimates about the size of primary views, and divide those sizes by the output resolution. These calculations provide an estimate of the precision threshold suitable for many projects.

T IP

The previous example uses a technique of aligning a grid object with a camera view to create objects on the perspective picture plane. You can use this same technique whenever you need to trace objects or create objects aligned with a perspective view.

3DS MAX Numeric Thresholds

3D Studio MAX uses single precision floating point numbers (floats) to store numeric values. This choice improves 3D Studio MAX performance at a slight cost of some precision when working with very large or very small models. Floats can represent incredibly large and incredibly small numbers, but they are limited to seven significant digits, meaning that 3D Studio MAX can accurately track numbers over a range of seven digits, but after that range is exceeded, round-off errors occur.

How likely are you to be affected by numeric round-off? It depends upon the subjects you model, your modeling style, and the number of calculations needed to represent your object in the scene. The following are a few examples about where round-off occurs.

If your system unit is set to the default of 1.0", some approximate ranges of accuracy include:

- Accurate to 1" over a range of 60.8 miles.

- Accurate to 1/8" over a range of 7.8 miles.

- Accurate to one centimeter over a range of 6.12 kilometers.

- Accurate to one millimeter over a range of 765 meters.

Notice that you can easily work with metric (SI) units even though the system unit is set to 1.0". Details about setting your working units are presented in the section "Setting a Unit of Measure" later in this chapter.

Because of the way floats are calculated, it is difficult to exactly determine where round-off occurs for any given model. The following list includes general guidelines to help avoid round-off:

■ Model at an appropriate level of detail for the scale of the scene. If your scene covers an entire city the size of Manhattan, for example, it makes no sense to model your door knobs.

■ Keep your model near the world origin. When you import models from CAD systems with much higher precision, it is not uncommon for objects to be located millions of units away from the world origin. Move these objects back to the world origin, either in the CAD system before you export or in 3D Studio MAX immediately after you import. Use Typein Transform to achieve this.

■ Change the System Unit Scale in the Preference Settings dialog only when absolutely necessary. For example, if you plan to model extremely small objects, such as at a molecular scale, you might consider changing the System Unit to millimeters. If you plan to model extremely large objects, such as at an astronomical scale, you might consider setting the system unit to miles or kilometers. You should, however, rarely need to change the scale. More details are presented in the section "Setting the System Unit Scale" later in this chapter.

Modeling Detail

The issue of appropriate detail is closely related to precision. In the previous example scene, one pixel equals a distance of about 4". Detail smaller than 4" loses definition in the final rendering.

You also want to consider appropriate visual detail for your scenes. If small details aren't important in the scene, you might want to leave them out. For instance, take the example of the office building described previously. You might want to add some people and cars in the foreground. You calculate the precision threshold for the cars and realize that details, such as windshield wipers and hood ornaments, would be visible. Do not model them. The details on the cars detract from the main subject of your rendering, the building.

You also can consider employing an artist's technique in your models. Often, an artist represents a detail with just a suggestion of a shape or a shadow where something belongs. The viewer then subconsciously fills in the details.

Another situation in which you might leave out detail is when you create animation for a courtroom presentation. Realistic-looking human figures that resemble victims or defendants can prejudice the jury and are often rejected as evidence. Certain subject matter, however, such as product liability work, requires high detail. You must work closely with your client to determine the appropriate level of detail for such a project.

Model Complexity

Model complexity refers to the number of faces used to build models. Use as few faces as possible to achieve the required level of realism. The more faces in a scene, the longer that scene takes to render.

You can summarize the many different techniques for reducing model complexity into the following strategies:

- Control the creation of faces through the various object parameters, such as segments and sides for primitives, path and shape steps for loft objects, and tessellation controls for some modifiers. These settings directly control the number of faces used to display an object and many of these parameters can be animated to add and reduce complexity as needed over the course of an animation.

- Use the Optimize modifier to reduce the complexity of a model. The Optimize modifier uses multiple parameters to analyze an object and reduce the number of vertices and faces used. The Optimize parameters can also be animated to change the amount of optimization over time.

- Use maps instead of actual geometry. You can represent many details in a model by applying a map, or picture, of the detail, rather than actually modeling the detail with faces. Figure 6.5 shows an example of this technique by using a model of a calculator. The extremely simple geometry produces a complex rendering through the careful use of maps. The rule here is to "Never model in geometry what can be represented with a map."

- Consider NURBS (Non-Uniform Rational B-Splines) to create your models. NURBS in 3D Studio MAX R2 have View Dependent Tesselation, because the polygon creation only happens at render time, and the model complexity is in part based on the distance from the camera. Since Nurbs are a non-polygonal structure, this is one way around the polygon detail problem.

FIGURE 6.5

The wireframe model with mapped and rendered versions of a calculator.

Setting Up Units

Two places exist where you control how 3D Studio MAX defines and measures units in your scene: the Units Setup dialog and the System Unit Scale in the Preference Settings dialog.

Your primary method for defining your working units is through the Units Setup dialog, which enables you to specify how units are measured and displayed.

The System Unit Scale sets the internal value for what a generic unit represents. This value should rarely, if ever, change.

Setting a Unit of Measure

Use the Units Setup dialog, from the Views menu, to define how you want to measure and display distances in your scene. The Units Setup dialog has four options, as shown in Figure 6.6.

The first two options are Metric (SI) and US Standard (feet and inches) methods of measurement. These choices are pretty straightforward and they offer sub-options within their specific methods. For example, two of the US Standard options are Decimal Feet (a civil engineering standard) and Feet with Fractional Inches (an architectural standard). The Metric method can measure in Millimeters, Centimeters, Meters, or Kilometers.

FIGURE 6.6

*The Units Setup dia-
log.*

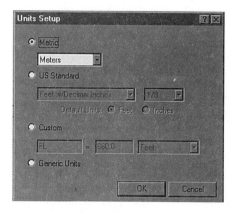

Use the third option, Custom, to define any custom unit of measurement that you want to use. The only restriction is that you must be able to describe the unit of measure using units that 3DS MAX already understands. Specify the suffix for the unit you want to define, followed by the amount of known units the custom unit equals.

The 3D Studio MAX User's Guide uses an example of defining an ancient unit of measure know as a cubit, but custom units are handy for other modern measuring methods as well. Suppose, for example, that you wanted to model very small objects. A US Standard method expresses small measures in mils, which equals 0.001 inches. If you wanted to work in mils, you might define the following custom unit:

  Mil = 0.001 Inches

The last option is to use Generic Units. 3D Studio MAX doesn't assign any particular meaning to generic units, and the size of your objects is governed by the current setting for the System Unit Scale.

Working in generic units is not a very good idea. Every time you create an object, you have in mind some particular unit of measure. People do not naturally think in terms of generic units. Look at the following statement:

  "My desk is 30 by 60 units."

This statement is vague and implies some very odd spatial relationships—until you assign the correct unit of measure:

  "My desk is 30 by 60 inches."

The same confusion occurs when you model in generic units. This confusion is made worse when you arbitrarily decide that one generic unit represents something other than 1.0 inch (the system unit default). Working in generic units almost guarantees that you will have difficulty sharing files with other 3DS MAX users because no one will know for sure what a unit is supposed to represent. Always define the unit of measure you want to use.

Rescale World Units is a new utility in MAX R2 that is useful if you're importing a file that was created in MAX or a CAD program, using a different unit of measure than the project you're importing into MAX. This simple utility, located in the Utility panel, enables you to rescale selected objects or the entire scene by any factor you enter.

Setting the System Unit Scale

The setting for the System Unit Scale is buried on the General panel of the Preference Settings dialog for good reason. You should not change a setting as a matter of habit. 3D Studio MAX internally stores distances in generic units that have no particular meaning. The System Unit Scale is applied as the base scale when 3D Studio MAX displays measurements in various parameter fields. Changing the meaning of the System Unit Scale changes the meaning of all measurements in your scene.

The System Unit Scale is stored in the 3dsmax.ini file and not in individual .max scene files. All measurements in a scene file are stored in generic units and those units are multiplied by the current System Unit Scale when you open or merge a scene file. For example, create a cube with 10-inch sides by using the default System Unit Scale of 1.0". When you save the scene, the box is stored as having sides 10 units long. If you then change the System Unit Scale to one foot, and open the scene containing the box, it now reports that the box is 10 feet to a side. The box never changed. It is still 10 units to a side; it's just that the meaning of the unit changed.

It is difficult to merge and share files between workstations using different System Unit Scales. You should try to leave the System Unit Scale at its default of 1.0" and only change the System Unit Scale after carefully considering its effect on the overall project and how the file might be used in the future.

The only reason you change the System Unit Scale is to avoid round-off problems when modeling extremely large or extremely small scenes. (See the discussion of numeric thresholds and single precision floating point numbers earlier in this chapter.) Round-off affects not just the precision of your scene but also the capability to transform objects and zoom magnification levels.

Let's say you are modeling the entire Earth, for example. Using a System Unit Scale of 1.0, the Earth's 24,900 mile circumference is more than 1.5 billion inches. Setting the unit of measure to miles helps you work with such numbers, but 3D Studio MAX is still working in inches. Single precision round-off occurs at about 40 feet and you will encounter many problems working with such large numbers—the most obvious problem being that the maximum view is limited to a width of just less than four million units; you won't be able to view the extents of your scene.

If you change the System Unit Scale to 1.0 Mile, the numbers become much more manageable. The Earth's circumference is 24,900 system units; you have plenty of room to zoom the view and your precision is still good to 40 feet.

Working with Files

The final issue when setting up a project concerns strategies for finding, managing, and storing the many files that go into making a successful project. Issues such as saving files, merging files, backing up files, archiving files, and managing file structures are covered in the following sections.

Combining Multiple Scene Files

The first file management technique involves the construction of the scene and all its supporting models. If your subject is simple, you can model the whole scene in a single .MAX scene file. It is more likely, however, that your scene consists of many objects and that modeling these objects separately is an easier approach. Assuming that you have decided to model each object independently, you must decide how you want all of the objects to come together for the final rendering.

Scene File Strategies

Modeling strategies fall into two basic techniques.

With one technique, you model each object separately and independently from the other. After all of the objects are modeled, you bring them together into a single file and arrange them as necessary. Such a technique works extremely well in the following two situations:

- The scene is relatively simple and composed of common, well-known objects. You know what a coffee mug or a light bulb looks like, for example, so it is easy to start a new file and create them from scratch.

- You already have an appropriate model on file. The model was used in an earlier project, was included on the 3D Studio MAX CD-ROM, or was purchased from a third-party vendor. If you need a detailed mesh model of a coffee maker, for example, you could use a model from one of the many providers of pre-built models, rather than build one yourself (see Figure 6.7). In this case, make a copy of the file, edit it as needed, and merge it into your main scene.

NOTE

In your search for pre-built models, keep in mind that MAX can import DXF, DWG, AI, PRJ, and 3DS files, as well as its native MAX files. This will greatly increase the number of models available to you.

FIGURE 6.7

A mesh model of a coffee maker from Kinetix Residential 3D Props.

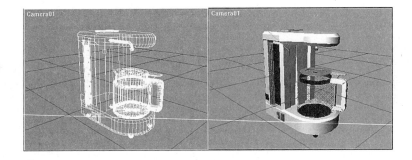

The other modeling technique requires you to set up the main scene first. You represent the objects in the scene by using simplified geometry or stand-in objects. The stand-in objects are copied out of the scene to serve as guides for the creation of detailed models, which eventually replace the stand-ins in the main scene. This approach offers the advantage of determining the basic shape, volume, and position of each object before you spend much time on modeling. A common mistake is to model an object in great detail only to have it end up far away in the background or, worse yet, completely obscured by a foreground object. This second approach is a necessity for almost any type of large, complicated scene.

As you may have guessed, most projects require a blending of these two techniques. Starting with a simplified stand-in scene, and then modeling detail only where needed, usually results in a better, more efficient model.

Merging and Replacing Objects in Your Scene

You can now browse your MAX files from the asset Manager and then merge them into the scene by dragging them directly from the AM to the viewport. You also can drag scenes directly from the Windows Explorer into the viewport, but that opens the file, instead of merging.

After you have built your various models in separate files, you need to merge the files together into a scene. If you modeled a stand-in scene, you also need to replace the stand-in objects with the detailed objects. You perform both of these actions using the Merge command from the File menu.

Choose Merge command from the File pulldown menu to combine objects from one .MAX scene file with the current scene. After you select the file to Merge, a second Merge dialog appears; you select which objects you want to merge (see Figure 6.8). You can choose to merge all objects from the selected file or any number of objects you select from the list.

It is possible to have multiple objects with the same name in a 3D Studio MAX scene, so there is no problem if the objects you merge use the same names as objects already in the scene.

FIGURE 6.8

Selecting objects to merge.

If you are using the stand-in method to build up the scene, you might want to automatically delete the stand-in objects when the same-named detail model is merged. To replace objects in the current scene with merged objects using the same name, check the Same Name check box near the lower-right corner of the Merge dialog. When Same Name is checked, only objects in the merge file that have names matching objects in the current scene appear in the selection list. Selecting objects from the list replaces the same-named objects in the current scene.

One of the drawbacks to this method is that the Same Name option requires that the merged objects have the exact same name as objects already in the scene. If there is not a perfect name match, the unmatched objects are ignored.

You might frequently create a single stand-in object that will be replaced by a detail model made up of multiple objects. The Same Name option only merges the single object that has the same name as the stand-in object; all other objects with different names are ignored. The best way to get around this restriction is to avoid using the Same Name option and manually delete the stand-in objects after merging the detail models. Leaving the stand-in object in the scene provides a benefit in that the stand-in can be used as a size and position check against the merged object.

Coordination with Other Modeling Programs

Although 3D Studio MAX is one of the most powerful modeling tools around, you sometimes must resort to another program to get a job done.

You can open models written with other formats using the Import command from the File menu. The files types supported include the following:

- **3DS**: The standard 3D scene and animation file from 3D Studio R4 for DOS.

- **SHP**: The 2D Shaper file from 3D Studio R4 for DOS. This file contains 2D splines that are converted to shape objects in the 3D Studio MAX scene.

- **PRJ**: The standard project file from 3D Studio R4 for DOS. This file combines both the 3D and 2D information from 3D Studio. Only splines from the 2D Shaper, meshes, and animation from the 3D Editor and Keyframer are imported into 3D Studio MAX. All other PRJ information, including the 3D Lofter, is ignored.

- **DWG**: AutoCAD R13 and earlier 2D and 3D drawing files.

- **DXF**: Autodesk Drawing Exchange Format. This file type is supported by AutoCAD and many other CAD and 3D modeling programs. It supports both 2D and 3D data.

- **AI**: Adobe Illustrator 88 file format. Many spline based 2D illustration programs support this file type. The splines in an AI file are converted to 3D Studio MAX shapes.

- **STL**: Stereolithography format. Stereolithography is a process that creates physical models from 3D data. This format works great to import Mechanical files from Pro Engineer, and AEC files from Form-Z.

Another useful option is the InterChange program by Syndesis Corporation. This program directly reads the file formats of many 3D design and CAD programs and translates them into the formats of other programs, including 3DS MAX.

A new feature in MAX R2 is the Asset Manager. Located in the Utilities panel, this utility brings up a window that enables you to view thumbnails of most graphic formats, including native .MAX files. You can import entire MAX files into your existing scene by dragging and dropping from the Asset Manager window to the active viewport in your scene (see Figure 6.9).

FIGURE 6.9

The Asset Manager allows you to browse .MAX and most image format files for easy drag and drop importing.

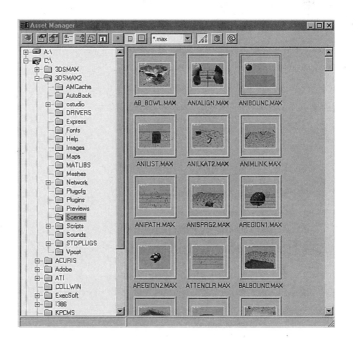

File Conversions

After choosing a modeling strategy—either creating all objects in one file or multiple files of individual objects—you must convert the file from its native format into the 3D Studio MAX scene format.

Because most CAD and modeling programs write DXF files, you can use 3D Studio MAX's built-in DXF reader to handle the conversion. Select Import from the File menu, and choose .DXF from the Files of Type list.

At this point, 3D Studio MAX displays the Import DXF File dialog, which has options you can choose from to control how the DXF file is converted (see Figure 6.10).

FIGURE 6.10

Import DXF File dialog.

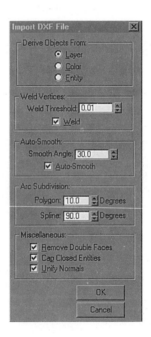

Maintaining File Coordination

A primary concern when using external modelers with 3D Studio MAX is how to maintain coordination between the modeling program and the 3D Studio MAX scene file. If all the design work in the external modeler is complete, this is a non-issue. Simply treat the converted files as your master models and begin building the scene. If, however, the models are part of an ongoing design process, you must take steps to ensure that your 3D Studio MAX model stays in synchronization with the design model in the other program.

The solution lies in always making design changes in the master file of the external modeler. Using the external modeler, you first identify discreet components of the overall project and write them out as independent DXF files. These DXF files are then converted to 3D Studio MAX files and are maintained as separate models.

When design changes occur, you first change the master design file in the external modeler. After the change is complete, you write out only those components that were affected as DXF files and convert them to replace the corresponding 3D Studio MAX models. The key lies with the component models. If you converted the entire design model every time a change occurred, you would spend all of your time converting models and no time rendering and animating. Maintaining the component models enables you to convert only those components that have changed and thus preserve the work that you have completed on the rest of the model.

Managing Maps and Materials

Another organizational issue concerns where to store all the bitmaps and libraries of materials that you apply to the surfaces of your model. The definitions of the materials are stored in both in the 3D Studio MAX scene file and in a library file that uses the MAT extension. The material definitions contain the settings of all of the attributes that control color, shininess, transparency, and so on, as well as references to image files assigned as maps.

When 3D Studio MAX renders a model, it reads the reference to the image file and searches specific directories on your hard disk to find the requested image. If the image is not found, a warning dialog appears, as shown in Figure 6.11. You must either cancel the rendering or proceed without properly rendering that material.

You can load image files from any directory or drive to which your computer is connected. 3DS MAX stores the full path to every image file that you use. You can also specify any number of alternate directories for 3D Studio MAX to search should it fail to find the image in the stored path. You specify these alternate search directories by adding paths to the Bitmaps panel of the Configure Paths dialog. Choose Configure Paths from the File menu to display the Configure Paths dialog.

FIGURE 6.11

Missing Map Files warning dialog.

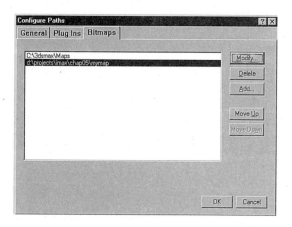

Depending upon your opinion, all this flexibility is either a blessing or a curse. In one sense, you might never suffer the frustration of 3D Studio MAX failing to find a needed image file. On the other hand, it is now possible to create an incredible mess of directories where your scenes pull image files from all over your hard disk and network. The following paragraphs describe techniques on how to make sense of these options.

Global Libraries

One technique is to create global libraries accessed by any project or scene. These libraries might consist of a global materials library directory where the master MAT files are stored, and a series of master image directories where all of the image files are stored.

The default location for MAT libraries is the 3dsmax\maps directory that is automatically created when you install 3D Studio MAX. Separate MAT files can be stored in this or any other directory, with each file addressing a certain type of material. For example, some library files you might consider creating include the following:

■ METALS.MAT for metal materials.

■ FOLIAGE.MAT for grasses, leaves, and vines.

■ BLOCKS.MAT for bricks, blocks, and tiles.

The preferred strategy for organizing global image directories is to organize images by subject. This results in directories named WOOD, MARBLE, SKIES, BACKGRND, and so on. Such an organization makes it easy for you find images of a specific subject.

Because 3D Studio MAX stores the path to any image and can alternately search many directories, you can also organize your images into precise topics. A good example of this strategy can be seen in the arrangement of the map directories provided on the 3D Studio MAX CD-ROM (see Figure 6.12).

NEW TO R2

Release 2 of MAX now ships with the WorldCreating Toolkit, with all the original 3DS maps and directories.

FIGURE 6.12

Map directories on the 3D Studio MAX CD-ROM.

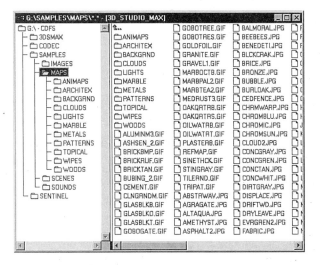

Project Libraries

Global libraries are great when you first put together a project, but what about later? It is terribly frustrating to restore an old project from backups, load it into 3D Studio MAX, and find out at render time that needed map files for critical materials are missing or have been altered. This is particularly troublesome when custom maps are created for a specific project.

The solution is to create separate libraries for each project. Each project should have its own directory for related scenes and image files. Right from the start, you can create a MAT file unique to that project and save it in the project directory. As materials are created and applied to the model, you can store their definitions in the project MAT file.

When you create an image file as a custom map for the project, store it in the project directory and not in one of the global directories. Later, if you feel that a custom map might be useful to other projects, copy the image file into the appropriate global directory. Also, after the final material definitions are set, copy all image files used by those materials from the global directory into the project directory. This might sound like a terrible waste of disk space, but this technique ensures that the global directory images your materials rely on won't be deleted or altered. And unless you place no value on your time, the cost of disk space is always cheaper than the cost to rebuild lost map files.

Managing Output

After you have built your scene, set up the cameras, lights, and applied materials, you are ready to render an image or an animation. The question now becomes an issue of what file format to use and where to place the files. One location for your output files is the project directory. Another, possibly better, solution is to create an output subdirectory below the project directory, on a separate removable drive, or on a large network drive.

Two concerns drive the decision to create a separate output subdirectory. First, rendering still images and animation creates several large files. Handling all of these files is easier if they are separate from everything else. The second reason is closely related in that you want to avoid mixing rendered images in the same directory as your map images and scene files. Unless your file-naming strategies are very well planned, you might find it difficult to tell the difference between renderings and maps by looking at the file name alone.

Preventing Disaster

No matter how fast you can build models or how many productivity techniques you know, they are all worthless if you lose your work. A program as powerful as 3DS MAX gives you an almost unlimited opportunity to mess up. The following sections describe some strategies for protecting yourself from disaster.

Saving Files

As with any program, you should save your files often. 3DS MAX is unique in the number and flexibility of its various file-saving strategies. Several commands exist for saving your work, including an option for saving incrementally numbered files. Figure 6.13 shows a standard Save dialog that identifies the File name field, the file format list, and the file increment button.

FIGURE 6.13

A 3D Studio MAX standard Save dialog.

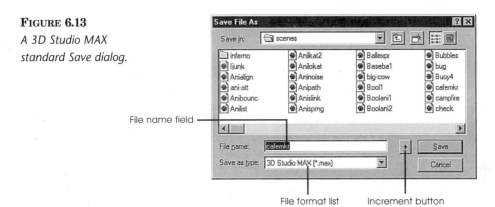

File name field

File format list   Increment button

You can enter any valid file name in the File name field. 3D Studio MAX uses the current file name in the field as a default for convenience. If you click on the file increment button, 3D Studio MAX appends a two-digit number to the name in the File name field. This is a fast way to create incrementally numbered files as a history of your progress.

Backup Files

You can use two automated methods for creating backup files in 3D Studio MAX. One method creates backup files whenever you save a scene file to an existing file name. The other method saves backup files at regularly timed intervals.

When you save a scene to the same name as an existing file, 3D Studio MAX can create a backup file as well. Check the Backup File option in the File panel of the Preference Settings dialog to enable the writing of backup files. The backup file is a copy of the original file that uses the name MaxBack.bak. If you check the Increment on Save option in the File Preferences dialog, 3D Studio MAX creates sequentially numbered backup files rather than continually overwriting the same MaxBack.bak file. The MaxBack.bak file is always placed in the 3dsmax\scenes directory regardless of what directory your scene file is loaded from.

If you check the Auto Backup Enable option in the Preference Settings dialog, 3D Studio MAX saves backup files at regularly timed intervals. The files are named Autobak1.mx through a maximum of Autobak9.mx and are placed in the 3dsmax\scenes directory. Once the maximum number of automatic backup files is reached, 3DS MAX starts over again at autobak1.mx. You can limit the number of Autobak files to create and specify the time interval in minutes between saves. The time interval field goes all the way down to 0.01 minutes, so if you're really worried about losing any work you can have 3D Studio MAX save backup files every 0.6 seconds!

Obviously, backup files certainly are not appropriate for long-term storage, and they were never intended for that purpose. The purpose for the backup files is to provide you with an escape route if you accidentally save a file to an existing name. If you realize the mistake soon enough, you can Alt+tab to the Window NT Explorer or File Manager and rename the backup file back to an appropriate 3D Studio MAX file.

Undoing a Mistake

The single most important development in the history of computing is the Undo command—or so it would seem. Most software users have come to rely heavily on the use of the Undo command, even to the extent of using Undo instead of regularly saving their work. If you have fallen into this trap, be warned. Relying on the Undo command can be an extremely painful mistake.

3DS MAX provides multiple Undo methods, as seen in the following list:

- Undo or redo screen changes.

- Undo or redo scene changes.

- Hold or fetch temporary files.

Using Undo/Redo

3D Studio MAX supports five undo/redo buffers: one buffer for the scene and one buffer for each of four viewports. You can use these undo/redo buffers to back your way out of most problems.

Use Undo/Redo from the Edit menu, or the Undo/Redo buttons on the toolbar, to reverse changes you make to your scene. Almost anything you do in the scene can be undone. If you want to be sure about what effect Undo will have on your scene, use Edit, Undo rather than the Undo button. The Undo menu item usually includes the name of the action to be undone.

You can set how many commands to store in the scene undo buffer by changing the Undo Levels value in the General panel of the Preference Settings dialog.

A right click on the Undo/Redo Icons in the Toolbar reveals the new Undo/Redo List in MAX 2. Now you can see all the steps you have taken and decide how far back you want to undo or redo.

WARNING

You can now undo the application or deletion of modifiers as well as collapse the stack. You usually can't undo numerical values entered in the command panel, as well as certain Material Editor actions. The Collapse Utility is another example of something that can't be undone. When you find an operation that can't be undone, train yourself to use Hold and Fetch to avoid ugly screw-ups.

Use Undo/Redo from the Views menu to reverse viewport changes, such as pan and zoom. Each viewport carries its own independent undo buffer. The viewport undo buffers are fixed at 20 levels of undo each.

Note that changes to Camera and Spotlight viewports are really scene changes because you are changing camera and spotlight objects in the scene. Use the Edit, Undo command to reverse changes to Camera and Spotlight viewports.

In MAX 2, you can now save all the viewports and retrieve them later. Simply activate the viewport and then choose Views/Save Active Viewport. You can save a total of eight different views.

Using Hold and Fetch

Another method for reversing the effects of multiple commands is to use Hold and Fetch from the Edit menu. Choosing Edit, Hold saves the state of the current scene in a temporary file. You can then perform any number of commands and still return to the held state by choosing Edit, Fetch.

Hold and Fetch are much more convenient for reversing a sequence of commands as opposed to clicking the Undo button multiple times. Get in the habit of choosing Hold whenever you are about to try a complex technique. Then, if the technique doesn't work out, you can use Fetch to quickly return to your starting point.

Also, if your system should crash, preventing you from exiting 3D Studio as you normally would, you can still retrieve the contents of the temporary Hold file. The temporary Hold file is named maxhold.mx and is located in the 3dsmax\scenes directory. You can directly load this file into 3D Studio MAX or rename it as a normal scene file.

Archiving and Backing Up Your Files

Back up your data files! If you want to kill your chances as a professional animator, try explaining to a client that their presentation is not ready because you lost all of the files when your disk drive failed.

Invest in a good, high-capacity backup device and use it regularly. The most important feature of a good backup device is that it is removable. It does no good to have your backup on a second internal hard drive when your office catches fire and the whole system melts. Remove your backup media and store it someplace far away from your office.

3DS Archive Command

3D Studio MAX includes a convenient menu pick to combine a scene file with all of the referenced image maps into one compressed archive. 3DS MAX uses the PKZIP program for creating archives. You specify the location of your registered PKZIP program using the File panel of the Preference Settings dialog.

A drawback to the built-in Archive command is that it only saves a single 3D Studio MAX scene with all of its related image maps. Unfortunately, many projects use multiple scenes, external program files, and video post queues; these are left behind by the Archive command. Also, any special plug-ins used by the scene are not included in the archive. Every plug-in used to create a scene must be in place to effectively reload the scene. If you archive a file and then delete a needed plug-in, that part of the scene is lost. The best use of the Archive command is as a fast and convenient way to pack up your current work while you are still in 3DS MAX. Do not rely on it as a complete archive of your whole project.

WARNING

The current version of PKZIP (version 2.50 for Windows 3.1, 95 and NT) supports long file names, but older versions, such as 2.04g, do not. Also, if you intend to use WinZip, don't use password encrypted files. WinZip is unable to open them without PKZIP installed as well. For guaranteed compatibility with all versions of PKZIP and WinZip, use standard 8.3 file naming for your 3DS MAX scene and map files.

Manual Archiving

If you want to archive all the various files associated with a project, you still must do it manually. Use your favorite archiving program to compress all the files in your project directory into a single file. If you have created separate map or output subdirectories under the project directory, be sure to tell the archive program to recurse subdirectories and store the path names. This enables you to restore the project files back into the same directory structure later on. If you are archiving a completed project for long term storage, it is not a bad idea to archive 3D Studio MAX along with all its plug-ins with the project.

TIP

A handy trick is to use 3DS MAX's built-in Archive command as a map collector. It quickly pulls copies of all the referenced image maps into your project directory. Unzip the 3D-Studio-MAX-created archive to restore the maps. You can then archive the whole directory into one big file.

In Practice: Planning, Organizing, and Getting Started

- **Modeling Decisions:** Determine your requirements for accuracy and detail to avoid unnecessary modeling work or creating overly complex scenes.

- **System Unit Scale:** Avoid changing the system unit scale unless absolutely necessary. Understand how the system unit scale affects numeric round off and how to avoid round off errors.

- **Unit of Measure:** Set up logical units of measurement that fit your scene. Setting the right unit of measurement makes numeric entry easier and helps you avoid the trap of modeling unnecessary detail.

- **Viewport Layout:** Set up a comfortable viewport arrangement and change view orientation as needed.

- **Saving Files:** Save your files often and take advantage of the many 3DS MAX methods for backing up and protecting your data.

- **Organize Files:** Plan well-organized global and project file directories. They save time and prevent lost files.

Part III

MODELING

Chapter 7

MODIFIER BASICS

MAX 2 modeling starts with a base object, which is then modified in a series of steps. All of these steps are contained in the Modifier Stack, and can be accessed and manipulated at any time. This is a powerful system; edits can be made early in the Stack and the subsequent modifiers ripple the changes through the model. This flexible approach differs markedly from other 3D modeling systems, which see their edits as permanent changes. This chapter covers the basic concepts of editing and modifying the edit history with the Modifier Stack. The discussion will serve as the basis for more advanced topics later in this book. Specifically, this chapter covers the following points:

- Basics of applying modifiers

- Using the Modifier Stack

- The difference between transforms and modifications

- Editing at the sub-object level

- Basics of sub-object modeling

- Sub-object modeling and animation

Basics of Applying Modifiers

Modifying single objects is accomplished by selecting the object and clicking the appropriate modifier. The modifier is assigned at the current level in the object's Modifier Stack and is ready for receiving values. Once applied, you can adjust the parameters of modifiers from their dialogs in the Command Panel (screen interaction is rarely required). Additional modifiers for an object accumulate sequentially on top of previous modifiers in the Modifier Stack. Figure 7.1 shows steps in an accruement of modifiers on a tube primitive.

FIGURE 7.1

Three modifiers applied to a tube primitive.

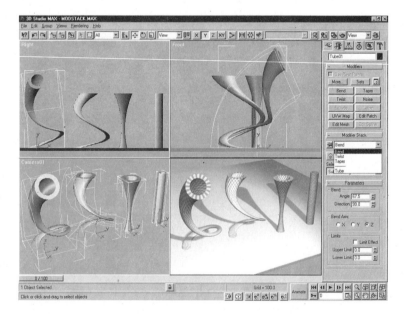

Modifiers are easy to apply to objects. It's good to experiment with simple objects to get the hang of what the particular modifier does before moving on to more complex objects. The following exercise, for example, walks you through applying some basic modifiers to a simple box object.

APPLYING MODIFIERS TO A SIMPLE OBJECT

1. Create a Box primitive, approximately 20 units long, 20 units wide, and 100 units in height.

2. Set the Length and Width segments to 2, and the Height segments to 8.

3. Shift+Move the Box along the X-axis to create three additional copies.

4. Click on Box01, shift over to the Modify panel, and apply the Bend modifier. Experiment with the settings to see what happens to the box.

5. Repeat on the other boxes with Taper, Twist, and Noise. The results should look something like Figure 7.2, but feel free to alter the settings.

FIGURE 7.2

Experimenting with modifiers on a Box primitive.

While every modifier is unique, most share some basic characteristics. The first is a list of parameters. These values define and control the modifier's effect. Modifiers can be applied in either Object Space (OSMs), or in World

Space (WSMs). OSMs operate in the local coordinate system of the object, and are influenced by the object's pivot point. WSMs are globally applied, and directly influence an object's position in World Space.

As an example, the WSM Path Deform leaves the path in place while moving the object to the path, and the OSM Path Deform modifier leaves the object in place while moving the path to the object (see Figure 7.3). A WSM can be likened to a Space Warp; it's sort of a modifier hanging in space that has a local sphere of influence. Relative changes in position between the WSM and the bound object cause changes in the object's mesh. OSMs, on the other hand, always stay with their bound object, no matter where it goes.

FIGURE 7.3

This example shows the difference between an Object Space modifier and its World Space counterpart. The snake and the text have a WSM Path Deform applied to them, while the snake's tongue is locked to a spline with an OSM Path Deform.

Selections of multiple modifiers, even noncontiguous selections, can be cut, copied, and pasted within an object's Stack. These modifier selections can also be applied to completely different objects. When pasting, a copy of all the modifiers in the clipboard is inserted above each selected modifier (if more than one modifier is selected, then more copies are inserted).

World Space modifiers and Object Space modifiers can be copied and pasted, but they can't be mixed together. Also, Object Space modifiers can't be pasted above the double line in the Edit Modifier Stack dialog (see Figure 7.4).

In the Stack, the single line, one up from the bottom, signifies base geometry that can't be moved. The double line is the demarcation between WSMs on top and OSMs below. If a mixed selection set containing both modifier types is pasted below the double line, the process completes, but the WSMs jump to a position above the double line.

FIGURE 7.4

In this illustration, the Path Deform modifier is above the double line, while the Skew and Taper modifiers are below it.

As Part I, "Core Concepts of 3D Studio MAX," described, Object Space modifiers should be applied immediately after the object's creation definition and before transforms and space warps. Because modifiers are applied in object space, they pay particular attention to the location of the object's pivot point and the orientation of the object when it was created.

Modifying Single Objects

Modifiers can be applied to a single object, a selection of objects, or a sub-object selection within an object. Most modifiers that affect topology (for example, Smooth, Normal, and Optimize) do not have sub-object components and the sub-object button is grayed out. The edit class of modifiers (EditMesh, EditPatch, and EditSpline) work with selection sets in their sub-object mode. All other modifiers have a graphical representation, called a gizmo, which can be manipulated just like an object to gain finer control over the modifier's effect. Gizmos, in turn, have a center that is very similar to a pivot point. The center controls the point from which the modifier's effect is generated.

When applied to a single object, modifiers usually configure their gizmos to the extents of the object and locate their centers at the object's pivot point. The gizmo always reaches to the geometric extents as they are seen at that point in the edit history. The gizmo's shape is primarily a visual aid and does not directly impact the modifier's effect. What generates the effect is the location of the gizmo's center and the modifier's parameters.

When applied to selection sets, modifiers configure their gizmos to the extents of the set and place their Centers at the geometric center of the selection's bounding box as shown in the left of Figure 7.5. The result is as if objects were combined into one large object with a single modifier applied.

FIGURE 7.5

The same modifier applied to a selection of objects without and with the Use Pivot Point option.

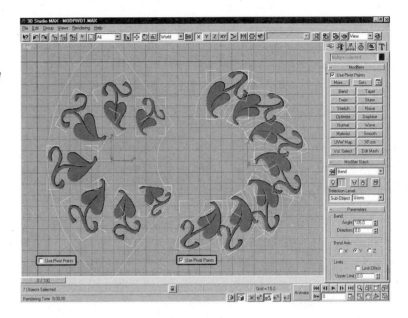

Modifying Selections of Objects

When a selection of objects is modified, it shares a single, instanced modifier. Selecting one of the modified objects and adjusting the shared modifier affects all the other object's modifiers as well because the modifiers are all instances. The stack's history can be edited to convert instances to references, or to copies, by using the proper buttons in Edit Stack.

TIP

Identifying which objects an instanced modifier affects can be difficult because their gizmos occupy the same space. The Views, Show Dependencies option makes these relationships clear by highlighting objects having instanced modifiers in green.

When the Use Pivot Points box is checked, this option makes the modifier perform as if it were affecting the selected objects individually. As the right side of Figure 7.6 shows, each object is given a gizmo that reflects its geometry with the gizmo's center located at the pivot point. Although these appear as individual modifiers, they are instances—adjusting one's parameters affects them all. The gizmos for every object of the original selection are displayed when instanced modifiers are being affected.

Applying a modifier to a set of objects and then later having to adjust one of them differently from the rest is common. Making instanced modifiers unique is the purpose of the Modifier Stack's Make Unique button. Figure 7.6 shows a horse whose legs have one Bend modifier applied to the front, and one to the rear sets of legs. During an animation the legs needed to walk, so the Bend modifiers for each of the legs were made unique and adjusted for the walk.

FIGURE 7.6

Making common modifiers unique to allow for individual animation.

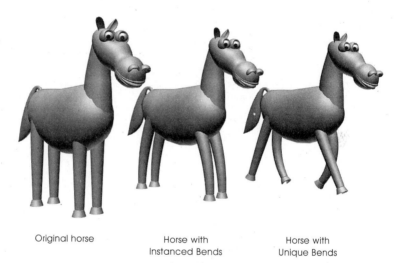

Original horse   Horse with   Horse with
                      Instanced Bends   Unique Bends

The following exercise puts Modifiers to work in a practical situation. In this exercise, you'll put a bend in the horse's legs to finish the model for posing, then alter it to make it ready for animation.

APPLYING THE BEND MODIFIER AND USING MAKE UNIQUE

1. Open horsey.max from the accompanying CD-ROM.

2. Select both front legs and apply a Bend modifier.

3. Select the sub-object center, and move it up to the top of the legs. This enables the legs to bend from the shoulders.

4. In the Parameters rollout, set the Bend Angle to about 25 and the Direction to 90. The bend should be along the Z-axis.

5. Repeat the operation with the rear legs, except make the Direction −90. Return to Object mode (A shortcut to get you out of sub-object mode is Ctrl+B). The results should resemble the second horse in Figure 7.6.

Applying the Bend modifier like this is fine for a static shot, but this horse has places to be. To get him walking, you have to make the legs so that they can move independently.

6. Select the left front leg. Notice how the Gizmo surrounds both legs.

7. In the Modifier Stack rollout, click Make Unique. The button grays out, but the Gizmo stays the same size. Try adjusting the Bend angle and notice how only the left leg is affected.

8. Repeat step 7 on one of the rear legs, and the model should now be similar to the third horse in Figure 7.6.

If you had any problems with the last exercise, open up horsey3.max from the CD to check your work. It is set up with a number of modifiers for you to experiment with.

Applying a modifier to a selection set is a quick and accurate method for locating a common gizmo center for a given modifier. The chair slats in Figure 7.7 were assigned a Bend modifier as a selection and then, while a selection, were made unique. Each slat then had the exact same center location for their concentric bends.

When multiple objects are selected with the Modify panel open, 3DS MAX examines the selection to determine if any common modifiers exist. If found, the common modifiers are presented in the stack. If none are found, or there's an additional modifier on one of the objects, the drop-down list is blank. All the objects of the shared modification do not have to be selected to adjust an instanced modifier. If, for example, 10 objects were tapered, the Taper modifier would be shown if 1 to 10 of the objects were selected. But if an object other than the 10 were included in the selection, commonality would not occur and the stack list would be blank.

FIGURE 7.7

A selection bent without Use Pivot Points to ensure common gizmo centers and then made unique to make concentric bends.

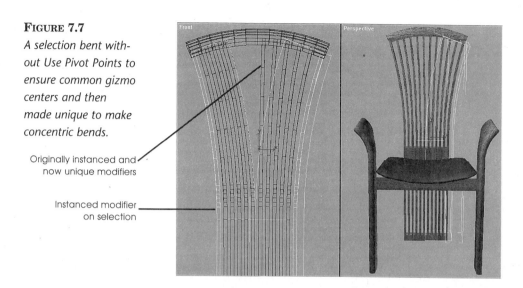

Originally instanced and now unique modifiers

Instanced modifier on selection

Using the Modifier Stack

Of all the areas in 3DS MAX's interface, the Modifier Stack is by far the most powerful. The Modifier Stack contains a small section of seven buttons and two drop-down lists (see Figure 7.8). Proficiency in using the modifier Stack and its toolbar is of paramount importance in mastering 3DS MAX. The modifier Stack provides access to an object's modeling history. Every modeling operation performed on the object is stored there for adjustment or removal. Operations in the Stack are stored with the scene until explicitly removed, enabling a fluid approach to modeling.

FIGURE 7.8

The modifier Stack roll-out.

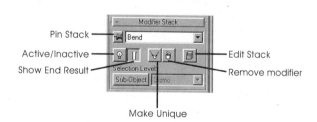

The Modifier Stack itself is housed in a drop-down list. When an object is selected, the last modifier added to the object is displayed at the top of the Stack and next to the drop-down arrow. The first modifier added to the object—the earliest information 3DS MAX has on the object—is shown at the bottom of the Stack. In the case of geometric primitives, their parameters are always at the bottom of the Stack. Models imported from other programs (such as 3DS files) usually have Mesh, Editable Mesh, Patch or Bézier Spline as their first (bottom) Stack entry. Because this is the beginning state of an object, a modifier can never be placed below it in the Stack.

The buttons surrounding the Stack drop-down have distinct roles to play in managing the Stack. Each entry in the Stack can be worked on and displayed individually:

- **Pin Stack (state):** Freezes the modifier's current state, enabling the transformation of other objects in the scene while the pinned modifier for the original selection is still active. Pin Stack provides an exception to the way 3DS MAX normally works because the Modify panel is not reflecting what is currently selected. This exception can be useful for coordinating a modifier's result with the position and orientation of another object. Many modelers use Pin Stack as a method to maneuver "template" objects as guidelines for modifier operations.

NOTE

The Pin Stack state will not enable the transformation of another object if the current modifier is in sub-object mode.

- **Active/Inactive (toggle):** Determines whether the result of the current modifier is passed along the modifier pipeline. The modifier still displays its gizmo but no longer has an effect on the geometry. This attribute can be very useful when assigning an intensive modifier (such as Displace or MeshSmooth) and you want to manipulate the object in a simpler form later in the Stack.

- **Show End Result (toggle):** Determines whether the remaining modifiers in the Stack display their results. This allows for direct viewing of a modifier's effect, without being distracted by any additional modifiers. Modelers often turn off Show End Result when adjusting a modifier and toggle it back on to check its relevance. Turning off Show End Result can save time when the remainder of the Stack is RAM-intensive and interactivity is impeded.

- **Make Unique (action):** Makes an instanced modifier unique to that object. Make Unique is used to eliminate the dependency of other objects sharing the same modifier. It breaks the connection to the rest of the objects.

- **Remove modifier (action):** Deletes the selected modifier from the Stack. The result is as if the modifier had never been applied to the object. Modifiers applied afterwards are unaffected.

- **Edit Stack (dialog):** Brings up the Edit Modifier Stack dialog shown in Figure 7.9, enabling the capability to make unique, remove, or collapse selections of modifiers and rename individual ones. Modifiers can be cut, copied and pasted, both in the same Stack and between discreet objects. Objects can also have their copy type (Copy, Instance, or Reference) changed.

FIGURE 7.9

The Edit Modifier Stack dialog.

To rename a modifier, simply select the modifier and enter a new name at the bottom of the dialog. That name is now present in the Stack and in Track View. Making a modifier unique resets the modifier's name as it breaks the connection to other dependent modifiers. If the modifier is already independent, the Make Unique option is still active and can be used as a method for quick renaming. Removing and making modifiers unique work the same with selections as with individual modifiers.

The first (bottom) entry in the Stack cannot be affected within the Edit Stack dialog and cannot be renamed. This entry is its geometric class and renaming the base object type would cause considerable confusion. Geometric classes include the parametric objects, Editable Mesh, Patch, Bézier Spline, Loft, Boolean, NURBS Surface, and Morph. The first entry cannot be collapsed or removed because nothing is below it to collapse. The first entry will often be modified, however, as the result of a Stack collapse.

Collapsing the Stack

Although an object's Modifier Stack is quite valuable, it does come with a costly RAM and file size penalty. Every step in the Stack takes a bit of RAM, with Edit modifiers costing the most because they contain actual copies of the object as modified to that point. The Edit modifiers record every action done within them. This is not a mere undo list, but an actual progression of every decision that is made. Although only what is in the current 3DS MAX session can be undone, the Edit modifier preserves all of the edits in the MAX scene file.

To have objects consume less RAM, their Stack can be collapsed. This operation causes an evaluation of the geometry pipeline and reduces the object to its highest geometric class. The effect of each modifier is maintained, but its effect is now explicit and frozen in time. What is seen in the viewport is the result from the collapse.

This does not mean that collapsing always saves disk space. Primitives, for example, require the same disk space regardless of their segmentation and resulting face count because the primitives are only storing parameters in the file. When fully collapsed, objects become explicit meshes or patches (or in the case of Extrudes and Lathes, NURBS Surfaces) and the entire mesh must be saved to disk.

After one or more modifiers have been selected (above the bottom one), the Collapse To button is available. Clicking Collapse To collapses the Stack from the point of the selection to the bottom of the Stack. Collapsing the Stack can be confusing when there is a selection of modifiers. At first glance, it would seem that the Stack would collapse only within the selection. Figure 7.10 shows that when collapsing a selection, the last (top) modifier in the selection determines from which point the Stack is collapsed, while the bottom of the collapse is always the bottom of the Stack.

There are three ways to collapse a primitive to base geometry. The standard method is to press the Edit Stack button. If the object has no modifiers attached to it, a Convert To list pops up. Select your choice of base geometry, and you're done. If modifiers have been added, the Edit Mesh dialog comes up and offers Collapse as a choice. A flexible way to get base geometry is to use the Collapse utility. The resultant object can be either an editable mesh or the result of the Modifier Stack. This procedure is also a good method for converting a number of separate objects into a single object. Boolean operations can be done at the same time, but without the flexibility of the Compound Object, Boolean command.

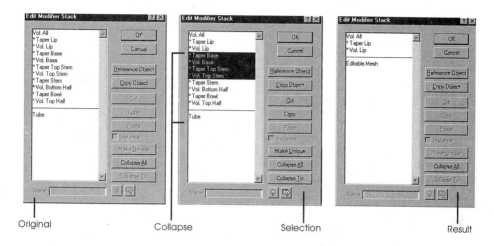

Original   Collapse   Selection   Result

FIGURE 7.10

The result of using Collapse To on a selection of modifiers.

The collapse of the Stack is the usual indication that modeling has been completed on that particular object. After the Collapse, RAM usage is less, file size is smaller, and screen update is faster. Even though Undo is an option, collapsing should not be undertaken lightly. Cloning the object in various intermediate stages of work is a good idea. Collapsing the Stack always eliminates a primitive's base parameters, for example, and returning to them is often quite useful. Using Save Selected or saving the entire file as a backup insures the ability to re-edit an otherwise "finished" object. The Merge command provides an easy method for this replacement if the originals are available for reference.

Navigating the Modifier Stack

After a modifier has been added to an object's Stack, you need to consider where in the Stack, or more properly, where in that object's history the next modifier should go. Mapping, for example, is often easier and more appropriate to apply early in an object's history, before the geometry is deformed. An understanding of how modifiers are saved, their order is evaluated, and their sub-object elements are used is essential to making proper use of this powerful capability. The first two are covered in the following sections, while sub-object modeling is covered later in the chapter.

How Modifiers Are Saved

Everything in a 3DS MAX scene is actually the result of a series of operations. What is seen on the screen or, in some cases, a rendering, is the result of those operations at that point in time. When the scene is saved to a file, the beginning state of the objects is saved and then a "script" of every modification that has been applied to them is added. The resulting geometry is never saved in a MAX file directly. Instead, the original object and all the steps to create that geometry are saved, allowing you to change your mind at any time in the future while modeling.

The calculation of the Stack is performed only when necessary. The result is a *validity mesh*, and the period of time that result is valid is termed the *validity interval*. When a scene is first loaded, each object's Modifier Stack is evaluated and the result is displayed. This state is cached and will not be reevaluated unless the object is modified—by adding a new modifier, adjusting a parameter in the Stack, or moving to a point in time when a parameter changes. Performing transforms on an object does not require a reevaluation of the Stack; just one reason why the moving, rotating, and scaling of objects is so fast in 3DS MAX.

Modifier Order

The order in which modifiers are applied has paramount impact on the results and requires careful planning. Figure 7.11 shows the dramatic differences between two identical modifiers placed in a different Stack order.

The Modifier Stack is the way to go back to any point in time and place a new modifier at any location. Stack entries can be re-ordered through the Edit Modifier Stack dialog. If a modifier is applied in the wrong order, the incorrectly placed one can be cut and placed at the appropriate place in the Stack. The original settings will be maintained. The interactive viewports telegraph any errors when a modifier is placed at the wrong point in the edit history.

Manipulating Gizmos

In general, a gizmo should be moved only to establish a new visual reference but not to control its effect. Instead, move the sub-object center. Moving the gizmo's center is nearly always the same as moving the gizmo except that the gizmo's extents remain intact with the modified object.

Moving the gizmo creates a visual departure that can be confusing during the life of the model. Figure 7.12 shows the same model with equal Bend modifier values. The right Bend modifier's center was moved to the object's top while the gizmo was moved up on the left. The center is in the same location after both operations, but, as can be seen when the gizmo is moved, its boundary no longer matches what is being deformed. When the Center is moved, the gizmo boundary respects the deformed object.

FIGURE 7.11

The effects of reversing modifier orders in the Stack.

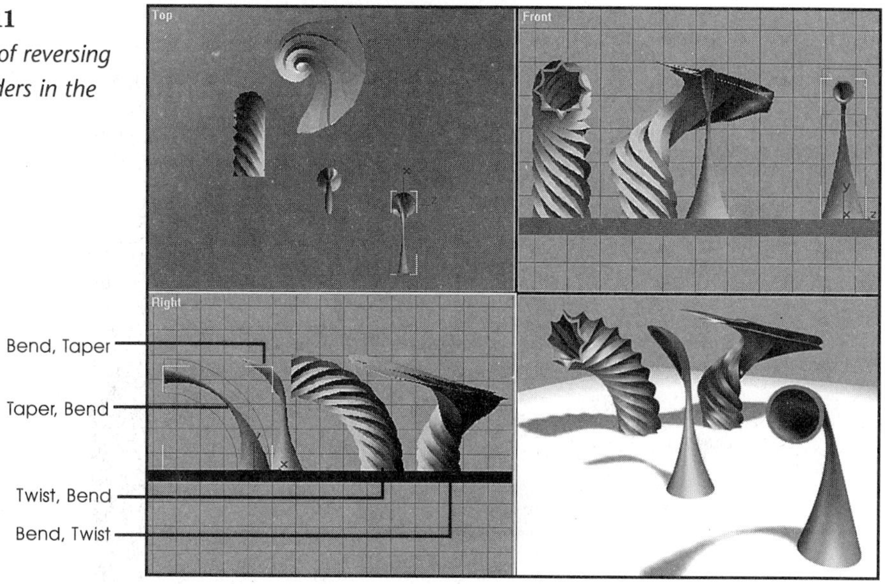

The location of an object's pivot point determines the initial location of the modifier's center and orientation of the gizmo's own local coordinate system. Many modifiers provide the parameters necessary to rotate their effect. If available, such as with Bend and Skew, they should be used because they keep the gizmo's boundary in better relation to the modified object. Figure 7.13 shows the effect of using a Bend's Direction parameter and rotating the gizmo.

When using the modifiers that do not have a directional component, such as Taper, Stretch, and Twist, the only choice is to rotate the gizmo. Many times a model's orientation is not conducive to the direction the modifier needs to be applied. Figure 7.14 shows such a model. The cannon is orientated to the world, but the barrel is tilted. The middle cannon shows the effect of applying the modifier according to the default axis, while the near cannon has its Taper gizmo rotated to match the barrel's incline.

FIGURE 7.12

The difference between moving the Center and moving the gizmo on the gizmo's boundary.

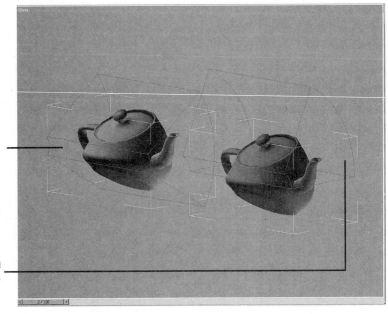

Center has been moved. Gizmo is still in place.

Gizmo has been moved and now looks out of alignment.

Gizmo rotated 90 degrees

FIGURE 7.13

The difference between using a Direction parameter and rotating a gizmo on the gizmo's boundary.

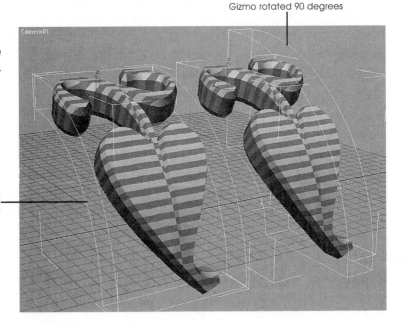

Modifier with a direction of 90 degrees

FIGURE 7.14

Rotating a modifier's gizmo to align with geometry.

Default modifier orientation

Rotated gizmo to align with geometry

Bounding boxes of object and initial modifier

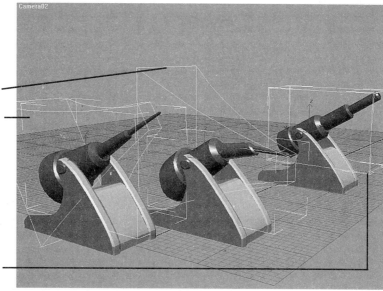

The following exercise puts together some of the concepts that were discussed up to this point. You will create the beak for an Ostrich using the latching technique, adding modifiers, and applying one of the most powerful modifiers, Free Form Deformations.

FINISHING THE OSTRICH'S BEAK

1. Open the file ostrich.max from the accompanying CD. You can see in Figure 7.15 the nearly complete bird, along with a Line that profiles his beak.

2. Select the Line and click Lathe from the Modify panel. Set Degrees to 180, Direction to Y (the default) and Align to Min.

3. Click Angle Snap to turn it on and rotate the Lathe –90 degrees. Move the Lathe into the approximate final position, as shown in Figure 7.16.

Now you are going to apply a Non-Uniform Scale to the beak that you want to affect the mesh as a modifier, not a transform. (This concept is discussed later in the chapter.)

4. Click the More button under modifiers, and Choose XForm.

FIGURE 7.15

The ostrich in need of a beak.

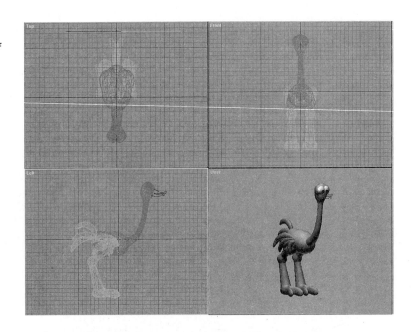

FIGURE 7.16

The Lathe in approximate position.

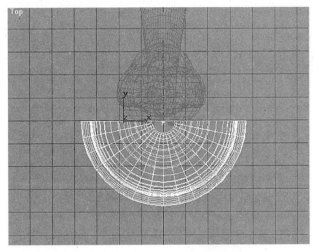

5. Notice that you are already in sub-object mode. Click the NU-Scale button (you may have to drop down the Scale icon to get to it), and select the X dimension restrictor from the tool bar. Rescale the beak in the top view so that it is the width of the head.

6. Whoops! The scaling is off-center. Move the Center of the XForm effect to make it happen properly. Under the sub-object drop down, select Center, and use the Move tool to place the Center in the axis of the Lathe.

Now when you NU-Scale the beak, it goes to the proper location (see Figure 7.17).

FIGURE 7.17

The beak non-uniform scaled with the XForm center in proper position.

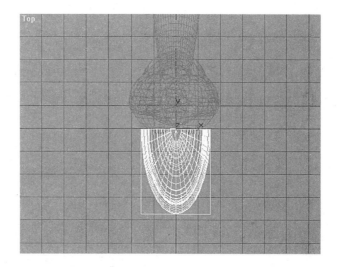

At this point, the beak looks pretty bad. Adding a Free Form Deformation will not only finish out the beak nicely, it will set the beak up for animation.

7. Click More again. Select FFD 3 × 3 × 3.

8. Click Sub-Object, and select Control Points. Using the Move and NU-Scale, push and pull the control points to resemble Figure 7.18. If you're having trouble, you can always open up ostrich2.max from the CD.

The beak looks good. In order to get a feel for how Free Form Deformations work, the following steps take you behind the scenes to look at the modifier and gizmo.

9. Go to the Sub-Object Lattice, and try moving the lattice around. See how the effect acts like a Space Warp? Lattice (and Gizmo) location is crucial to having a reliable effect (see Figure 7.19). Be sure to Undo after you've finished.

FIGURE 7.18

The finished beak, with NU-Scaled XForm and a Free Form Deformation.

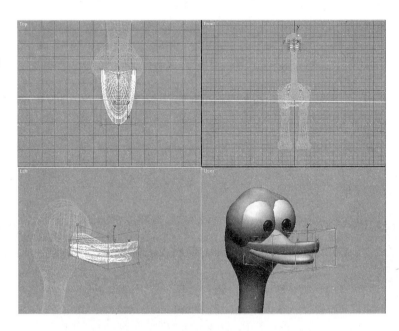

FIGURE 7.19

Gizmo location controls how the effect works. In this sense, modifiers closely resemble Space Warps.

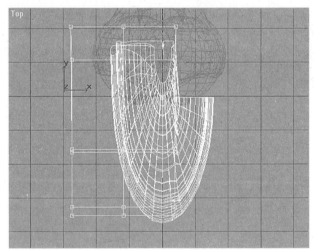

10. Select the Edit Stack button. Select the XForm modifier, and Cut it. Notice the changes to the model. Try pasting it in twice. Notice how the beak is now twice as narrow. Try pasting it in under Lathe. The beak is now too short. Modifier order directly affects the outcome of the edits, so care should be taken to order them properly.

In this exercise, you've used modifiers to radically alter an object's geometry. Modifiers should be thought of as integral to the modeling process, not as an effect to be placed in at the end.

Scaling Gizmos

Scaling a gizmo magnifies the modifier's effect. Performing a Uniform Scale is identical to increasing the modifier's strength. The top two objects in Figure 7.20 show the same end result—the first from scaling the gizmo and the second from increasing the modifier's strength.

FIGURE 7.20
Scaling a modifier's gizmo.

Scaled gizmo

Modifier with increased angle

Gizmos with non-uniform scale

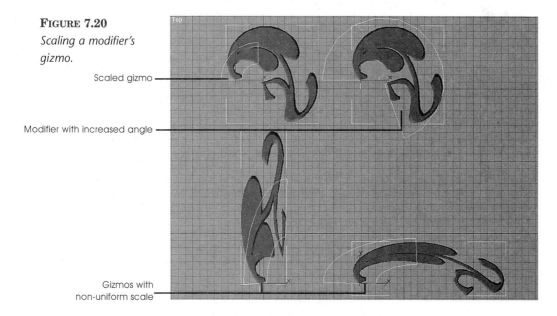

Performing a Non-Uniform scale to the gizmo, however, produces different results. The bottom two objects in Figure 7.20 show the results of Non-Uniform scales on the gizmos. Either adjusting the strength or placing the center cannot duplicate this effect.

TIP

When using modifier limits, the maximum or minimum effect of a modifier may not be strong or subtle enough. To amplify the modifier's effect, perform a Uniform Scale on the gizmo about its center.

After scaling gizmos, determining exactly how much they have been scaled and along what axes can be difficult. This process can be frustrating when comparing similar modifiers. Transform Type-In does not display the current location of gizmos as it does for objects. The only option is to use the Track View. The Track View gives an interactive readout of all parameters associated with an object, including information on modifiers assigned to it. A fast way to get the information is to select the object, open the Track View, then use the Selected Objects filter.

Placement and transformation of gizmos are crucial to their proper use. Use of the gizmo's center can keep the behind the scenes modeling information more easily understood, by having gizmos in their proper place.

Using Modifier Limits

Many modifiers include the capability to limit the location of their effect with parameters called *limits*. They are controlled by Upper and Lower (sometimes referred to as From and To) parameter limits and the location of the gizmo's center. Limits differ from sub-object modification because they influence the entire object but place their deformation only within a given range.

A bent drinking straw is a good example of when to use limits. Figure 7.21 shows several attempts to bend a straight straw (a tube primitive). Starting from the left, the first bend affects the entire straw, which was not the intent. The second bends just the top half of the tube (using a Volume Select modifier), but doesn't allow for a straight section after the bend. The third tries to bend a middle section of the straw (again with Volume Select) and meets with bad results. The fourth bend is applied to the entire straw (just like the first straw), but the effect is localized with limits to produce the classic bent straw.

Modifier Limits are based on the gizmo's center. The Upper and Lower Limit parameters indicate the distance from the center the modifier is affecting. The location of the center then determines where along the axis the limited effect takes place. The next exercise shows how Modifier Limits can come in handy by keeping an effect from making unwanted distortions to an object.

FIGURE 7.21

Attempts at bending a straw.

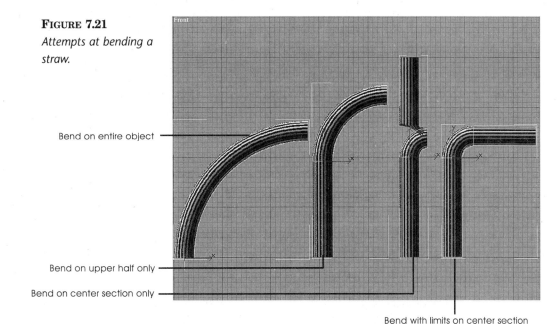

Bend on entire object

Bend on upper half only

Bend on center section only

Bend with limits on center section

USING ATTACH AND BENDING THE OSTRICH'S NECK

1. If your ostrich file is still open, use that. Otherwise, open ostrich2.max from the CD.

2. Select the head object, and in the Edit Object rollout, attach the beak using the Do Not Modify Materials option. Right–click in the active window to get out of Attach mode.

3. Go to the Sub-Object Face Selection Level. The beak is an unsightly shade of white, which we can begin to fix by selecting it using the Element Selection method (the little cube).

4. Scroll down the pane, and in the Edit Surface section, increase the Material ID to 4. The beak turns yellow. A Multi-Sub-Object material was applied to the ostrich beforehand, and the beak's yellow was in the fourth slot. For more in-depth coverage of sub-object materials and their use, see Part IV, "Materials and Maps."

5. Use Ctrl+B to get out of sub-object mode and apply a Bend modifier to the head. Make sure that the Bend Axis is Z, then set the Angle and Direction to 90 (see Figure 7.22).

FIGURE 7.22

The ostrich's head and neck with a Bend modifier applied.

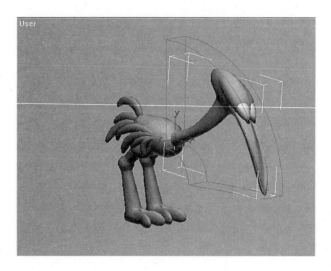

6. The effect is interesting, but not what you want to do for this exercise. Turn on Limit Effect and set the Lower Limit spinner to –15.

7. The effect now works properly. Play with the Angle spinner to watch the ostrich bend his neck (see Figure 7.23).

FIGURE 7.23

The ostrich's head and neck with the Limit Effect box checked in the Bend modifier parameters.

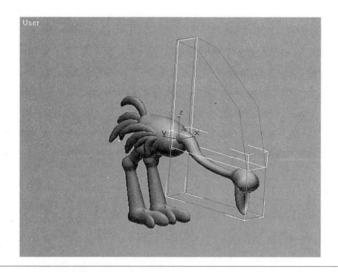

Modifiers with limits typically affect the entire object. The influence of one limited modifier can adversely impact that of another because they may overlap. The order in which modifiers are applied have an effect as well. In general, limited modifiers should be "stacked" along the object's length in order to avoid conflicts. When applying multiple, limited modifiers, applying the modifier farthest from the Center first and working backwards is always best. If the object's pivot point is in the center, there are conceivably two "stacks" to work with: Upper Limit modifiers above the pivot and Lower Limit modifiers below the pivot.

Although simple in concept, modifier limits provide a capability that is not possible in most other programs. Although useful, they are also extremely efficient. In terms of modeling, only one modifier needs to be adjusted for the effect—not a modifier and a previous sub-object selection modifier. In terms of memory, they require no more than a single modifier (which is quite small) and far less RAM than an Edit modifier. Finally, in terms of file size, modifiers are just a list of a few parameters and require little storage. On the other hand, each Edit modifier significantly increases the size of the file.

The Differences Between Transforms and Modifiers

As described in Chapter 1, the geometry pipeline evaluates objects by first processing their creation parameters, applying any modifiers in Stack order, accumulating transforms (as assigned from the toolbar), and finally applying any space warps bindings. This process means that transforms are always processed after all modifiers have been applied. It doesn't matter when the transform is applied in regards to the object's edit history; the transform is always applied last. The result is not a problem with translation, rotation, and uniform scale but can be a problem with Non-Uniform scale or Squash.

Non-Uniform Scale

When an object is scaled about only one or two of its axes, the operation is termed a Non-Uniform scale (or NU-scale for short) because all three axes are not consistently scaled. The object is said to "stretch" or "shrink" in one or two directions, while the third direction stays constant.

Care should be practiced when applying a Non-Uniform scale. Figure 7.24 shows the vast difference between performing a NU-scale as a modifier and as a transform. In both cases, the Z-axis scaling occurs before the bend. The surprising distortion is because transforms are always applied at the end of the pipeline, after all modifiers. The order that transforms are applied in regard to modifiers doesn't matter. Transforms are always applied after the entire Stack of modifiers.

FIGURE 7.24
Non-Uniform scale XForm versus non-uniform scale transform.

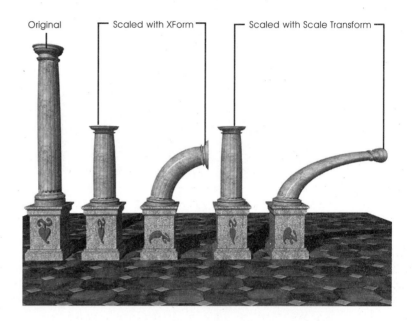

Mistaking this transform operation as a modification is easy. After all, the object did appear to permanently distort. In reality, it did not. Applying an opposite transformation can reverse the effect. Modifiers usually distort the object and can even alter topology. Performing a second operation can rarely reverse the previous one. 3DS MAX blurs the distinction between these two types of operations by enabling the adjustment of the parameters of a given operation after it is applied, and even its removal from the Stack. Most modeling programs are not so lenient. Once applied, a modifier usually has a significant effect on the object's future, whereas a transformation can easily be altered.

Using XForm Instead of Transforms

The XForm modifier is used to apply the effect of a transform (move, rotation, or scale) as a modifier—meaning that Non-Uniform scaling is treated as a modifier and not a transform at the object level. Chapter 8, "Shape Modeling," shows this modifier also used as the primary method for animating sub-object geometry.

The XForm modifier produces a gizmo that encompasses the selection set and immediately places you into sub-object mode. Simply transforming the gizmo does all adjustments to the XForm modifier. It is "the better half" of Mesh Select, in that Mesh Select chooses sub-object selections, but can do no transformations on them.

XForm is an interesting modifier in that it doesn't appear to do anything. The sub-object drop-down contains the gizmo and the gizmo's center. No other parameters are found because XForm relies entirely on the transform tools in the toolbar for control. After all, XForm is just taking transforms and making them part of the data history.

As with all modifiers, XForm has an effect on the objects to which it is applied when it is current in the modifier panel. If sub-object mode is active, the transforms are being recorded on the gizmo and they behave like a modifier. If sub-object mode is inactive, transforms are performed as normal and are applied after all the modifiers. When an XForm is first applied, it immediately enters sub-object mode because it assumes that the adjustments are to be recorded in the Stack.

The effect is occurring as a modifier in object space, and subsequent transforms do not affect it—a key concept. If the object is to be made part of a hierarchical chain and animated, not using XForm causes bizarre scaling problems when the object rotates, as illustrated in Figure 7.25. Essentially, if the transform is to have a permanent effect on the model, it should be used in conjunction with XForm.

Though a great deal of modeling can be done by using various modifiers on objects, many times the editing has to be taken to a finer level, or only certain parts of the object need work. This is where you enter the realm of the sub-object.

FIGURE 7.25
Non-Uniform scale XForm versus Non-Uniform scale transform in a hierarchy. This is an all-too-common error made in many animations.

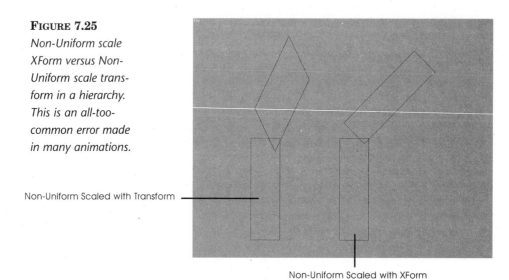

Non-Uniform Scaled with Transform

Non-Uniform Scaled with XForm

Sub-Object Modeling

Although many objects can be modeled from primitives or defined by a loft, many more can be created by manipulating the fundamental parts of the geometry: vertices, faces, edges, and patches. This is where computer modeling becomes more like sculpting. Modelers adept at these techniques are often called vertex sculptors, or polygon pushers.

By definition, when anything less then the entire object is affected, you are sub-object modeling in 3D Studio MAX. There are essentially two forms of sub-object modeling: manipulating the sub-object entities themselves, and restricting modifiers to sub-object selections. In the first form, you are actively pulling, scaling, and rotating sets of vertices, and possibly changing the topology by adding or deleting sections. In the second form, you define a selection of vertices with one modifier and pass that selection along up the Stack for subsequent modifiers to affect.

Editing at the Sub-Object Level

Sub-Object modeling takes place whenever you are manipulating discrete entities or regions within an object. To model at the vertex, face, edge, spline, segment, or patch level, a modifier must be added that gives access to the desired sub-object level, or the object must be collapsed to its base object type. The sub-entities an object has and the modifier used to edit those sub-entities will vary, depending upon the geometry of the object (see Figure 7.26):

■ Bézier Spline shapes contain vertices (with tangent handles), segments, and splines and are edited with the EditSpline modifier.

■ Loft objects contain shapes and paths (made of Bézier splines), which are edited within the Loft object definition.

■ Mesh objects contain vertices, faces, edges, and elements and are edited with the EditMesh modifier.

■ Bézier Patch objects contain vertices (with tangent handles) and lattices with edges and patches, and are edited with the EditPatch modifier.

■ Boolean compound objects contain operands made of other objects, which in turn are edited within the Boolean object definition.

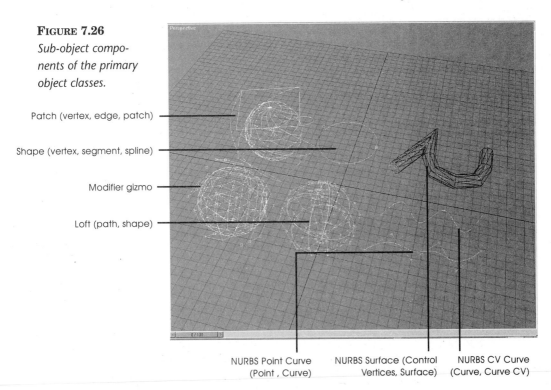

FIGURE 7.26
Sub-object components of the primary object classes.

Patch (vertex, edge, patch)

Shape (vertex, segment, spline)

Modifier gizmo

Loft (path, shape)

NURBS Point Curve (Point , Curve)   NURBS Surface (Control Vertices, Surface)   NURBS CV Curve (Curve, Curve CV)

When working in most modeling programs, editing sub-object sections of a model is nearly always a permanent decision, but in 3D Studio MAX, permanence is only there when desired. Modeling with the Editable Mesh object is explicit and final, whereas modeling done within EditMesh and with selection modifiers is reversible.

Using Selection Modifiers

Modifiers in 3D Studio MAX are available in two types, those that define selections and those that act upon selections handed to them. This book refers to these as Selection modifiers and Modeling modifiers respectively. Understanding this basic difference enables the planning of the sequence of the Edit Modifier Stack quite well.

Examples of 3DS MAX Selection modifiers are the Edit modifiers (EditMesh, EditSpline, and EditPatch), Mesh Select and Volume Select. These modifiers select specific portions of the model to pass along for manipulation by the remaining modifiers. The exception to this is the Editable Mesh object, which enables the definition of a single sub-object selection without adding a modifier. For discussion purposes, Editable Mesh can be considered a selection modifier, even though it's an object class.

The Stack's Active Selection

The Modifier Stack passes along what is termed the active selection. This is the geometry that subsequent modifiers "see" and to which they apply their effect. The contents of the active selection can change throughout the Stack by adding other select modifiers, with the other modifiers applying their effect to whatever selection is passed to them. This fact may not be apparent when modeling at the object level because the active selection is the entire object, and the fact that a selection is being passed along is not obvious. The power of this concept is that adding or adjusting a selection modifier defines what is being modified at any point in the Stack.

N OTE

Sub-object selections are active only when the Edit modifier's sub-object button is depressed and yellow (yellow always alerts the user to being in sub-object mode). In contrast, Volume Select modifiers are always active because their sub-object mode is for gizmo manipulation and not selection levels.

The Stack's active selection can change from modifier to modifier. The goblet shown in Figure 7.27 illustrates this concept. The Stack began as a Tube primitive and was the result of five tapers following five different volume selections. Each selection replaced the previous one and defined a new active selection for the Stack. An EditMesh was added at the end to finalize the smoothing and perform the bulged grip. The Stack allows for the return to any previous selection and the subsequent change of the active selection. Subsequent modifiers operating on that selection affect the new selection immediately, as the change ripples up the Stack.

FIGURE 7.27

Multiple active selections within the same Stack.

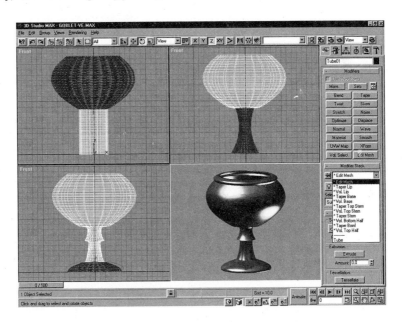

The following is an exercise that demonstrates how sub-object selections can be modified. When the snake's head and body were put together with the Connect Compound Object, it left the junction a bit rough. You will fix it with Mesh Smooth, and not affect the rest of the model.

SMOOTHING THE SNAKE'S NECK

1. Open the file snake.max from the CD. You can see in Figure 7.28 that the neck junction needs some work.

Area to be smoothed

FIGURE 7.28

The snake, before Mesh Smooth is applied to neck area.

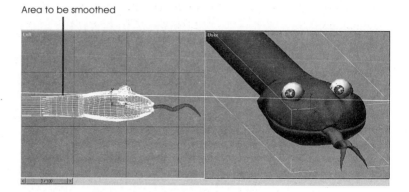

2. Select the snake's body, and in the Modify panel go to the Face level of sub-object mode. Select the faces shown in Figure 7.29.

FIGURE 7.29

Faces selected for smoothing.

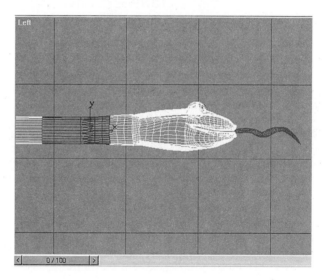

3. Making sure NOT to go out of sub-object mode, click More in the modifiers section, and select Mesh Smooth.

4. Set Strength and Relax Value to 1, and check Quad Output. As you can see in Figure 7.30, the snake's neck flows into the body.

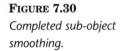

FIGURE 7.30

Completed sub-object smoothing.

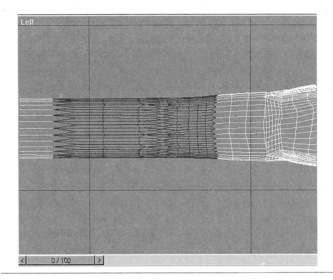

As you can see from the snake's neck, sub-object selections can pinpoint modifier effects to exact areas.

The Edit Modifiers

Although innocent in appearance, the simple buttons preceded by the word Edit arguably contain the most power in modifier panel. All three Edit modifiers (EditMesh, EditSpline, and EditPatch) serve two roles in 3D Studio MAX: they enable sub-object editing of their respective geometry, and they define sub-object selections for future modifiers in the Stack to act upon.

NOTE

The EditMesh modifier actually does triple duty by containing face-level surface property tools.

Defining Selections with Volume Select

When created, the Volume Select modifier establishes its gizmo at the extents of the active selection. This is a one-time-only adjustment; unlike other modifiers, Volume Select does not adjust the extents of its gizmo as the active selection below it changes. Unfortunately, the Volume Select gizmo does not have an adjustable center. Its pivot point is always its centroid. Because of this, using another object (most likely a dummy helper) as the Pick Coordinate System when the selection volume is being adjusted can alter the position of the effect's center. Because the modifier does not have size parameters, the only way to adjust its defined volume is with the scale transform. Using a Pick Coordinate center to scale about is often critical to making accurate and quick adjustments of the volume.

T IP

When working with a sub-object selection, the subsequent modifier's center can be located at the object's pivot point by first assigning a Volume Select modifier, leaving it at the object select level, and then assigning the modifier. The Volume Select modifier can then be used for sub-object selection, or delete it and use the original Edit modifier. The newly added modifier will adjust its gizmo to the new selection while leaving its center at the object's pivot point.

Modifiers that are previous in the Stack do not deform Volume Select modifiers. Although this is a trait shared by all modifier gizmos, it has incredible impact with Volume Select. An example is tapers made with a Volume Selection at the top of a cylinder. If the entire cylinder is Bent from the base of the Stack, the Volume Select gizmo remains stationary and the vertices of the cylinder bend through the selection volume. The selection set for the subsequent tapers then changes as the bend increases. In this case, another Volume Select modifier at the end of the Stack should have been added to return the selection to the entire object. The bend should have been applied after that to ensure that the selection volume remained consistent as the entire object was bent. This trait is not unique to the Volume Select modifier but actually occurs with all modifier gizmos.

Edit Modifier Mechanics

Every Edit modifier added to the Stack adds overhead in RAM, so that all edits are interactive and changeable. Thus, applying a dozen Edit modifiers to the same object increases the RAM requirements of that object by more than a factor of 12, although it may have the same number of faces throughout its history and even far less at the end. Because of this overhead, Edit modifiers should be used with extreme discretion and perhaps for limited periods of time. The Mesh Select modifier is always the preferred choice for passing irregularly shaped selections up the Stack.

Each Edit modifier records its actions a bit differently. EditMesh records a delta for every vertex that is affected, so the size of the modified object can double in size *only* if all of the vertices are transformed. EditSpline and EditPatch are quite different in that they record every single edit operation performed, and keep it in the order applied. Thanks to this record keeping, the important curve and tangency relationships of spline geometry are properly adjusted when items earlier in the Stack are modified. Such extensive record keeping also has implications for memory overhead. When using EditSpline, the Stack should be Collapsed often to reduce RAM consumption and file size.

Within each Edit modifier is a DeleteObject that records all the destruction that has been done to the object. This is why the entire model can be found at an earlier stage in the Stack, or modifiers can be removed and the "deleted" portions reappear. This characteristic of keeping a record of deleted geometry also allows for the detaching and exploding of portions into new objects and then the restoration of the original object by removing the Edit modifier.

Notice in snake.max that the snake is smiling. He was eyeing a rodent that has since the last exercise become his dinner. In the following exercise, you will make a bulge that can be animated traveling down the snake's body.

ANIMATING A SUB-OBJECT BULGE

1. Open the file snake2.max from the CD. You can see in Figure 7.31 that a PathDeform has been applied and the snake has been unified into a single mesh.

2. Under More in the Modify panel, choose Volume Select. Set Stack Selection Level to Vertex and Selection Volume type to Sphere.

3. Reduce the size of the volume by selecting the Sub-Object Gizmo, and performing a NU-Scale in the XY dimensions in the Top View. The result should look somewhat like Figure 7.32.

4. Going once again to the More section of the Modifiers menu, this time select Spherify. Turn down the Percent spinner to 50 Percent.

5. Click the Stack drop-down list, and select the Volume Select modifier. Making sure that the Show End Result toggle is on, go to the Sub-Object Gizmo and move the Gizmo along the snake's body with the Move tool.

FIGURE 7.31
Modified snake ready for bulging.

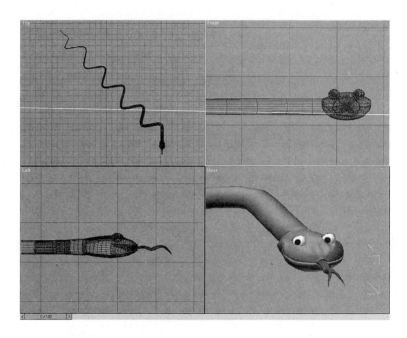

FIGURE 7.32
Volume Select Gizmo resized properly.

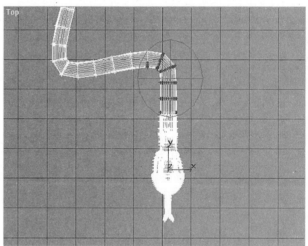

6. Notice how the bulge effect follows the Gizmo as you move it down the snake's body (see Figure 7.33).

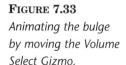

FIGURE 7.33

Animating the bulge by moving the Volume Select Gizmo.

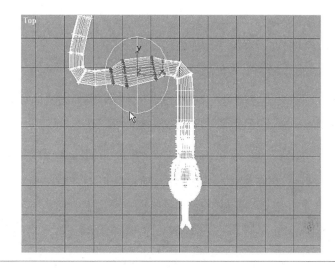

Selection Levels Within Edit Modifiers

Edit modifiers each contain separate and distinct sub-object selection levels for their entities. Each selection level acts as a separate selection set and does not influence other selection levels (with the exception of hidden faces and vertices). Sub-Object selection sets can be named using the Named Selections List on the main Toolbar. These sets can be copied from one modifier to another within the same object, or copied to another object of the same variety, by using the Copy and Paste commands from within the Edit Stack dialog.

As it happens, each of the Edit modifiers maintains three selection levels:

- EditMesh: Vertices, Faces, and Edges.

- EditSpline: Vertices, Segments, and Splines.

- EditPatch: Vertices, Edges, and Patches.

Because an Edit modifier determines the active selection at a given time, it is of paramount influence on subsequent modifiers. The selection level (Vertex, Face, or Edge for EditMesh, for example) defines both the content and type of geometry the next modifier in the Stack "sees." This can be important because some modifiers work only with certain types of geometry. A Normal modifier, for example, acts upon only an active selection of faces and ignores selections of vertices or edges.

Defining Sub-Object Selections for Other Modifiers

As previously described, modifiers act upon the Stack's active selection. There is actually a bit of an art to defining the correct selection at the appropriate point in edit time. The definition of the selections for modifiers when modifying sub-object portions should be made using the following priorities:

1. Use modifier Limits when the influence is over the entire object but affecting only a portion of it (a bent straw, for example).

2. If a sub-object selection needs to be the entire object, add a Volume Select modifier (at the object level) before the modeling modifier.

3. Use Volume Select when modifying selections definable by one or more rectangular, cylindrical, or spherical volumes. This enables previously defined topology to change but does not work if the previous geometry changes dimensions.

4. Use Mesh Select selections when modifying selections that are irregular or noncontiguous. This enables previously defined dimensions to change but does not work if the previous topology changes.

5. Use Edit Mesh or Editable Mesh selections only when the modifiers themselves are necessary. These two should be reserved as Modeling modifiers for most needs.

Basics of Sub-Object Modeling

Previously, the discussion has been on how the sub-object selections defined by EditMesh, Editable Mesh, and the other Edit modifiers are passed to other modifiers. Passing selections is just a by-product of what the modifiers were intended to do: sub-object modeling. EditMesh and Editable Mesh were designed for direct mesh editing, where the raw mesh is being manipulated by its vertices, faces, and edges. New mesh parts are constructed and others are refined or deleted. Finally, the surface characteristics of what is seen, how light is reflected, and what material is present are all assigned through mesh editing. All of this editing is performed at the sub-object level.

Many subtleties of realistic and efficient modeling are at the vertex and face level. After an object is created, you may need to stretch vertices, turn or align faces, and build additional faces. Smoothing groups are perfected and face normals are best analyzed at the sub-object level as well. Many modelers spend the majority of their time working at sub-object level, using mesh editing tools and perfecting their surface properties. The rest of this chapter analyzes the functions that manipulate these finite entities and give specific character to models. The next chapter builds on these basic principles as it explores the details and techniques of using each of the sub-object modeling tools.

Concepts Common to Edit Modifiers

The Edit modifiers have many things in common because each manipulate sub-object geometry and work in a manner that is usually thought to be explicit (when performed in other modeling programs). Because of this, numerous procedures are the same between the Edit modifiers. These include attaching objects in order to work with them, the way pivot point centers work with different selection types, the use of angle thresholds, and principles of animating sub-object selections. Several efficiency techniques are also commonly used by modelers to make working with the Edit modifiers convenient. These include the use of grid objects, point helpers, and numerous keyboard shortcuts. EditMesh and Editable Mesh have many more capabilities than EditSpline and EditPatch.

Object Level Attaching

Attach is the one function the Edit modifiers contain that does not involve sub-object selections. The Attach function joins two objects, with the result that one becomes the active object and one becomes the attached object, an element of the active object. This action of joining objects together is required for actions that "stitch" sub-object geometry together, with the most common needs being for vertex welding between separate objects. If you haven't done so already, completing the "Using Attach, and Bending the Ostrich's Neck" exercise can illustrate this concept.

Common Terms and Concepts for Meshes

The sophistication of models possible in 3D Studio MAX is staggering and it's easy to be taken aback by their apparent complexity. Even the most intricate models are comprised of simple, discreet elements. In fact, 3D

Studio MAX uses only a few very basic geometric types to define the many worlds created within it (see Figure 7.34). EditMesh, Editable Mesh, Mesh Select, and Volume Select all use the same geometric terminology when making selections.

FIGURE 7.34

The geometric compo-nents of 3D Studio MAX meshes.

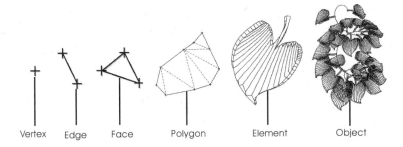

Vertex   Edge   Face   Polygon   Element   Object

Mesh editing relies on the capabilities contained within the EditMesh modifier. The same capabilities, with a few exceptions, are also present in the Editable Mesh object definition.

A mesh generically refers to a mesh object or a collection of its faces. The term mesh is used when referring generically to geometry and is not a specific entity type. Meshes are composed of triangular faces that in turn define any combination of flat, curved, or bent surfaces.

Vertices define points in three-dimensional space and are the most basic of entities. A vertex defines no geometry except the location of a point in space. It has no surface or properties of its own, and so cannot be seen in a rendering. The sole purpose of vertices is to build faces. A vertex that is not connected to other vertices by faces to form a mesh is known as an isolated vertex. 3DS MAX stores mapping coordinates with vertex locations so that when vertices move, the associated mapping moves with them.

Faces are what "skin" a model, give it form, and enable it to have materials and reflect light. As faces are assembled, they define surfaces and identifiable forms. Faces are triangular surfaces formed by connecting three vertices. Because each face has only three points, each defines a geometric plane, and each is flat by definition.

Each face defines a Normal, a direction that is perpendicular to the face's surface and that points away from the face's visible side. Normal direction is an important consideration, in that faces are invisible when the Normal is facing away from the camera. Of course, a two-sided material can always be used as a quick fix but is no substitute for good modeling practice.

Edges are the lines that connect two vertices and form a face's border. Each face, therefore, has three edges. Adjacent faces that share two vertices are also said to share an edge. Edges are not created directly, but rather are the result of creating faces. Edges are used to manipulate faces or serve as the basis for creating new faces. A face always possesses three edges, and these edges can be either visible or invisible. Edge visibility influences redraw speed, clarity, and the boundaries of polygon selections. Visible edges are used primarily for clarity and influence only the mesh's rendering when given a wireframe material. Many gaming engines ignore invisible edges, so they can be "fooled" into thinking that a object is composed primarily of quad faces by making strategic shared edges between two faces invisible.

Polygons are coplanar sets of welded faces that make up the facets, sides, and ends of meshes. 3DS MAX uses the term polygon to define coplanar sets for faces within a mesh for the purpose of face selection. A polygon's definition stops at visible edges or at a planar threshold. In 3DS MAX, polygons are a tool only for selecting faces—they are not entities with special manipulation capabilities. When polygons are selected and transformed, it is in reality a selection of faces.

Elements are 3D Studio MAX's term for a discrete sub-object mesh. When adjacent faces build off of the same vertices, they are said to be "welded" together. Vertices used by more than one face are said to be shared or welded vertices. An element extends as far as the mesh has welded faces. Often, elements within the same object appear to be continuous, when in fact they use a duplicate set of vertices along the common edges. Such vertices are known as coincidental vertices and are required when a distinct break in the mesh is wanted, but still is continuous. Gaming engines typically find these coincidental vertices unpalatable, so care should be used if the model is to be exported. An element can be quite large or as small as a single, isolated face, and any number of elements may occupy the same object. Although separate meshes, elements cannot be animated themselves without a modifier.

Mesh objects contain one or more elements and can be thought of as an organization of elements. Unlike an element, an object does not need to be a continuous mesh. An object is commonly composed of widely separated elements, and it may contain isolated vertices (which are, in turn, individual elements). Objects are named and colored, and only objects have transforms, pivot points, data history stacks, and animation tracks.

Therefore, a geometrical hierarchy for mesh objects exists within 3D Studio MAX. This hierarchy is shown the following order (from lowest to highest):

1. Vertex (can be isolated)

2. Face (built upon three vertices)

3. Edge (result of a face, and connects two vertices)

4. Polygon (contains coplanar, welded faces)

5. Element (contains continuously welded faces)

6. Object (contains elements of continuous faces and possibly isolated vertices)

Animating with Sub-Object Components

A new feature with 3D Studio MAX 2 is the ability to directly animate the faces, edges, and vertices within an Editable Mesh object. Selected vertices can be named and saved in Selection Sets. This can still make for a tedious, non-intuitive process when dealing a complex task like facial animation.

Linked XForms work much the same way that the standard XForm modifier does, in that a selected set or single vertex is passed up the Stack and then acted upon. Linked XForms enable the use of an additional object, typically a Dummy Object, that directly controls the vertices in question. A "control panel" of Dummy Objects can be used to adjust sets of vertices that can blink an eye, or cause a face to smile, all without using Morph Targets and their significant overhead. Linked XForms can also control the vertices of Patch Objects and NURBS. When this methodology is used with a Reference Copy, a static face can be used for facial control, while the Reference face, mounted to a figure that is being controlled by skeletal animation is moving around the scene. This powerful system is beyond the scope of this volume but is covered in *Inside 3D Studio MAX 2, Volume 3: Animation*.

Overview of Modifiers

Modifiers work according to their entity type. While the majority of the modifiers are primarily for meshes and patches, a few deal with splines and NURBS. The NURBS modifiers will be discussed in Chapter 13, "NURBS Modeling." The following table quickly reviews the different types of modifiers.

TABLE 7.1

Modifier Overview

Modifier	Definition
World-Space Modifiers	
Camera Map	Applies UVW mapping coordinates that are generated from a designated camera. Mapping will change to match the background when the object is moved.
MapScaler	Maintains the scale of a map applied to an object, even when that object's scale is changed. A wall mapped with bricks maintains the brick size when the wall is scaled.
PatchDeform	Deforms objects based on the shape of a patch. Objects will move to target patch.
PathDeform	Deforms objects based on the shape of a path. Objects will move to target path.
SurfDeform	Deforms objects based on the shape of a NURBS Point or CV surface. Objects will move to target surface.
Object-Space Modifiers	
Affect Region	Allows for a bubble-shaped animatable area on a mesh.
Bend	Flexes objects and sub-objects around a single axis in one or two dimensions.
Camera Map	Applies UVW mapping coordinates that are generated from a designated camera. Mapping won't change to match background when object is moved.
Cap Holes	Finds connecting edges that have only one face and builds a face between them.
DeleteMesh	Parametric deletion of an object selection passed up the Stack.
Displace	An object's geometry is reshaped by Displace with either its Gizmo or a bitmap.

continues

TABLE 7.1, CONTINUED

Modifier Overview

Modifier	Definition
Edit Mesh	Mesh modifier that enables access to sub-objects and can pass sub-object selections up the Stack. A holdover from version 1.2.
Edit Patch	Patch modifier that enables access to sub-objects and can pass sub-object selections up the Stack.
FFD modifiers (Free Form Deformation) (2X2X2, 3X3X3, 4X4X4, box and cyl)	Surrounds a mesh with an animatable, deformable lattice.
Face Extrude	Animatable modifier that takes the faces passed up the Stack and extrudes them along their normal, building sides as it goes.
Lattice	Converts all segments of a mesh into cylindrical struts and places user-definable geometry at the junctions.
Linked XForm	Transform modifier that takes a sub-object selection passed up the Stack and links it to a user-defined control object.
Material	Allows for the animation of sub-object materials.
MeshSmooth	Adds faces at corners and edges of a mesh, to ease the edges.
Mesh Select	Primary method for passing sub-object selections up the Stack.
Mirror	Animatable mirror effect for objects and sub-objects.
Noise	Modulates an object's vertices along any of three axes.
Normal	Allows the way that the surface points to be flipped or unified on a mesh.
Optimize	Reduces the number of faces and vertices in an object.
PatchDeform	Deforms objects based on the shape of a patch. Objects remain stationary and the target patch moves to them.

Modifier	Definition
PathDeform	Deforms objects based on the shape of a path. Objects remain stationary and the target patch moves to them.
Preserve	Keeps the edges, face angles, and volume close to the original when working on a copy of the object.
Relax	Averages an object by moving vertices closer to their neighbors about a definable center point. The object gets smoother and a little smaller.
Ripple	Produces an animatable concentric wave deformation in an object's geometry.
STL-Check	Checks geometry for export to a stereo lithography file. Also good for gaming engine validation.
Skew	Offsets object or sub-object geometry in three axes and is fully animatable.
Smooth	Animatable smoothing functions.
Spherify	Animatable distortion of a base object into a spherical object.
Stretch	Animatable "squash and stretch" modifier. Maintains approximate volume as one axis decreases while the other axis increases.
SurfDeform	Deforms objects based on the shape of a NURBS Point or CV surface. Objects remain in place.
Taper	Simultaneously scales two axes on one end of an object.
Tessellate	Increases the number of faces on a selection being passed up the Stack. Allows for animation of tension.
Twist	A single axis corkscrew affect on objects and sub-objects.
UVW Map	Places mapping coordinates onto an object.
UVW XForm	Provides adjustment for existing coordinates. Useful when altering a base object that has been built with "Generate Mapping Coordinates" option checked.
Unwrap UVW	Allows for direct editing in UV mapping space.

continues

TABLE 7.1, CONTINUED

Modifier Overview

Modifier	Definition
Vol. Select	Uses a Gizmo to define a selection to be passed up the Stack.
Wave	Applies an undulating effect to an object.
XForm	Applies transformations (Move, Scale, and Rotate) to objects and sub-objects.
Spline Modifiers	
Bevel	Extrudes splines with up to three flat or rounded bevels in profile. Useful for 3D text.
Bevel Profile	Extends the functionality of Bevel by enabling a user-defined shape or NURBS curve to be used as the profile.
DeleteSpline	Parametric deletion of a spline selection passed up the Stack.
Edit Spline	Spline modifier that allows access to sub-objects and can pass sub-object selections up the Stack.
Extrude	Adds depth to a 2D shape.
Fillet/Chamfer	Allows for rounding and beveling of straight segments.
Lathe	Revolves a shape around an axis.
Spline Select	Passes sub-object selections of shapes up the Stack.
Trim/Extend	Cuts apart or lengthens splines to allow them to meet at a single point.
NURBS Modifiers	
NCurve Sel	Enables the selection to pass up the Stack of all NURBS sub-objects, excluding surfaces and imports.
NSurf Sel	Enables the selection to pass up the Stack of all NURBS objects, excluding imports.

In Practice: Modifier Basics

- **Editing objects:** An object's Modifier Stack contains the modifiers that are applied to the object, enabling the adjustment of any modeling decisions at a later date. Each modifier entry is an entity with its own effect and animation capabilities.

- **Collapsing the Stack:** Collapsing the Stack flattens every modifier that has been applied into one static model. The resulting geometry of the collapse depends on the modifiers collapsed. A partial collapse always collapses every modifier from the selected one down to the bottom of the Stack.

- **Sub-object Gizmos:** Many modifiers contain sub-object gizmos that enable the refinement and animation of the modifier's effect as if it were an object with standard transforms.

- **Modifier Limits:** Modifier limits enable the control of the extents that a modifier's effect has on an object. This gives the control that would otherwise require sub-object selections and numerous edits.

- **Modifier Order:** The order modifiers are applied is paramount to the resulting effect. An object's creation parameters are evaluated first, the Modifier Stack is evaluated from bottom to top, then the cumulative transform is applied, and finally Space Warp bindings are added.

- **Non-Uniform Scale Transform:** A Non-Uniform scale transform appears to be a modification and can have surprising results because the scale transform is applied after the Modifier Stack. In practice, it is mandatory to use an XForm when performing Non-Uniform scaling to make the scale part of the Modifier Stack.

- **Defining Selections:** The Modifier Stack enables different selections to be defined at any point in the edit history, with each modifier affecting the active selection at its point in the Stack. The selection can be the entire object, or one of a variety of sub-object selection types (vertices, faces, edges, and so on). The Stack enables the contents of the selection to be changed at later times.

- **Edit Modifiers:** The Edit modifiers combine powerful modeling with sub-object selection capabilities, with an overhead in RAM being required for their flexibility.

- **Defining Selections with Volume Select:** Whenever possible, use the Volume Select or Mesh Select modifier to define a selection instead of EditMesh to minimize RAM requirements. A selection defined by EditMesh can often be assumed by a subsequent Volume Select modifier, allowing the costly EditMesh modifier to be removed.

- **Choosing Selection Methods:** Volume Select is ideal when you want to adjust the topology and density of your underlying model but do not need to change its size (such as changing the segmentation of the original cylinder, for example). Mesh Select becomes the preferred selection method when the underlying topology is fixed, but its dimensions change (such as changing the radius of the original cylinder, for example).

Chapter 8

MODELING WITH SHAPES

Shape tools in 3D Studio MAX inhabit the two-dimensional world and include objects such as Lines, Circles, and Rectangles. These familiar entities bridge the gap between a drawing or CAD program and a three-dimensional modeling and animation product.

Shape objects are put to use in 3DS MAX as source geometry for creating other objects and trajectories for animation. Shapes form the foundation of other objects in much the same way that a painter stretches a canvas over a frame or a sculptor builds a wire armature to hold the clay.

This chapter looks at the general issues behind creating shapes and introduces some shape-based 3D modeling techniques. These issues include:

■ Understanding what spline shapes are and the terms used to describe them

■ Exploring how decisions you make when creating shapes can affect the complexity and performance of your scene

■ How to create and edit shape objects

■ Applying modifiers to shape objects

■ Special techniques for employing shape objects as precision tools

Of course, the place to start is with the creation of shape objects.

Creating Shape Objects

You create shape objects by clicking the Shapes tab in the Create panel and then clicking one of the shape buttons in the Object Type rollout such as Line, Circle, Ellipse, and so on (see Figure 8.1). Drag in a viewport and set shape parameters in the Create panel to complete the shape.

FIGURE 8.1

Splines section of the Shape button in the Create panel.

From the General rollout in the Edit panel, from Rendering, check Renderable. The shape renders even though it is 2D. Adjusting the Thickness spinner adds line thickness. Mapping coordinates are an option, and application is as simple as checking a box. The result is a three-dimensional sketch of the geometry, as shown in Figure 8.2.

FIGURE 8.2

The Rendering section of the Edit panel and the results of the settings.

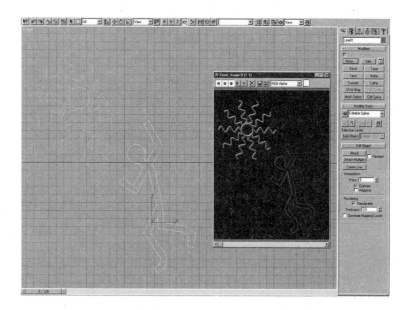

Recognizing Spline Terminology

Before creating and editing shapes, you need a basic understanding of spline-based shape terminology. NURBS curves can also be used as shapes, for modifiers such as Extrude, Lathe, and Bevel. Refer to Chapter 13, "NURBS Modeling," for a complete discussion of this topic.

The following list defines spline shape terminology used in 3DS MAX and Figure 8.3 illustrates these terms.

- **Vertices**   The points at either end of spline segments. Vertex properties are defined as a corner, smooth, or Bézier type. Vertices are shape Sub-Objects.

- **Tangent**   Handles Shape vertices set to the Bézier vertex type display tangent handles. Drag tangent handles to control the curvature of the spline segment as it enters and leaves the vertex. Tangent handles are properties of a vertex.

FIGURE 8.3
*Identifying spline-
based shape terms.*

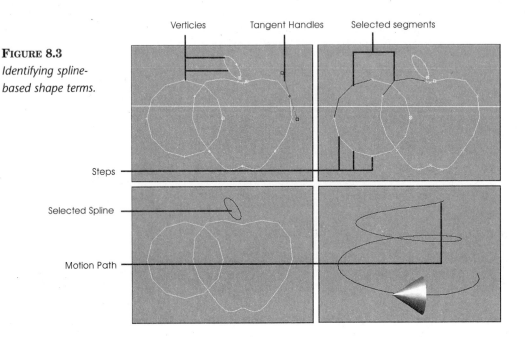

- **Segment**   The part of the spline between two vertices. The spline segment's curvature is controlled by changing the properties of the vertices at either end of the segment or by changing the properties of the segment itself. Set the segment properties to define whether the segment is a line or a curve. Line segments ignore vertex properties. Segments are shape Sub-Objects.

- **Steps**   The number of segment divisions used to represent a curve. When creating geometry with shapes, the curves in the shape must be converted into triangular faces. The step setting controls how many face edges, or facets, are generated by the shape. High step values create smooth curves that generate many faces. Steps are a shape parameter.

- **Splines**   A collection of connected segments. Splines are a type of a smooth adjustable curve, but 3DS MAX includes options for inserting corners and defining linear segments. Splines are shape Sub-Objects.

- **Shapes**   A collection of splines defines a shape object. Restrictions on the number and type of splines in a shape vary with the intended use of the shape. Shapes can be chosen with Select by Name, as they are named objects.

- **Paths** A term used to describe a shape. A path describes a shape containing a single spline used as a vector for another entity. Examples include Loft paths, Path Controller paths, and Path Deform paths. Remember that whenever 3DS MAX refers to a path, it is simply a single spline shape.

Creating Lines

Click the Line button in the Create panel to create the most basic type of shape. Creating lines involves more than picking points on the screen. The following considerations apply to all line creation:

- All the segments created in a single Line command are part of the same spline and same shape. If you want to create separated line segments, you must right-click to complete the first Line command and click in a viewport to begin another line.

- You create flat lines on the construction plane by clicking in a viewport or in full three-dimensional space. If you use 3D Snap or Keyboard Entry, you can also vary the Z value of spline vertices.

- Lines are either straight or curved depending on the Creation Method choices. Dragging as you create also can alter vertex type.

Line Creation Methods

The choices made in the Creation Method rollout are critical to controlling the initial properties of Lines. You have two Creation Method types to choose from, as follows:

- **Initial Type** These options should be called Click Type because they set the type of vertex created when you click the left mouse button to start creating a line. The default is Corner. Corner vertices produce segments that are linear as they enter and leave the vertex.

  Smooth vertices produce a curve through the vertex in which the amount of curvature on either side of the vertex is equal. The tangent of a smooth vertex is always parallel to a line drawn between the two vertices to either side of the smooth vertex.

- **Drag Type** These options set the type of vertex created when you drag the mouse as you create a line. The choices include Corner and Smooth, just like Initial Type and Bézier. In all cases, you place the vertex at the location with the first mouse click. Dragging the mouse activates the chosen drag type for the vertex. The direction and distance that you drag before releasing the mouse only matters if the drag type is Bézier.

Drag direction sets the tangent direction of the curve as it passes through the vertex. Drag distance sets the magnitude of the curve at the vertex.

Figure 8.4 shows the two Creation Method types and the supported line vertex types.

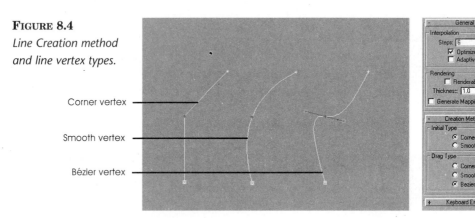

FIGURE 8.4
Line Creation method and line vertex types.

Corner vertex

Smooth vertex

Bézier vertex

Interactive Line Creation

The most common method for creating Lines is interactively clicking in a viewport. Lines can also have their coordinates manually entered in the Keyboard Entry section of the rollout. The following rules govern interactive line creation:

- Line creation can only occur in a single viewport. You cannot switch viewports after starting to create a line. You must right-click to complete the command before you can switch to another viewport.

- Vertex type is set in the Creation Method rollout. Be careful when using the Bézier drag type. Dragging the first vertex of a line can lead to inappropriate results. Some users find it easier to create all vertices and then use Edit Spline to convert them to adjustable Bézier vertices.

- Lines lie flat on the current construction plane unless 3D Snap is active. If 3D Snap is active, Line vertices lock on to specified options in the Snap dialog box, as signified by the changing cursor.

■ The Local coordinate system is placed on, and aligned with, the current construction place, regardless of line creation parameters.

A frequent use of 3D software is to model the infamous "flying logo," as seen on TV. You use a logo project in the following exercise and throughout this chapter to demonstrate shape modeling in a production environment.

It's important to be able to import even the worst of sketches as a starting point for your modeling. For this exercise, you use MAX much in the same way that you use a 2D drawing package such as CorelDRAW! or Adobe Illustrator.

USING THE LINE TOOL TO TRACE AN IMAGE

1. Open a new file in MAX. You might need to use File/Reset to return to the default settings.

2. Select the Front View, and go to Views/Background Image. Select elven.jpg from the CD-ROM, and set the Aspect Ratio to Bitmap. Zoom out in the Front viewport so that you can see all the logo; then click Lock Zoom/Pan to set the scaling. Right-click the title in the Front View and turn off the Show Grid option. Figure 8.5 shows the settings and the template in place.

FIGURE 8.5

The background template in place with its proper settings.

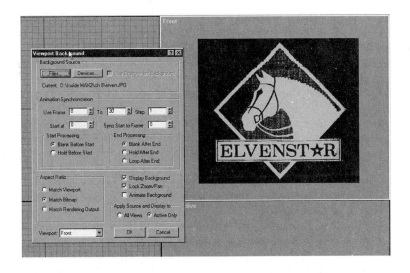

NOTE

This fax image was modified in Adobe Photoshop to make it more suitable as a template. After scaling and cropping to 782 × 680, the image was converted to RGB Color, had its Map Inverted, and its Hue/Saturation changed by using the Colorize option. Settings were Hue −175, Saturation 100, and Lightness −45. Colorizing the template blue makes it easier to see the selected splines when they turn white.

3. Maximize the view and select Line from the Create/Shapes panel. Remove the check mark from Start New Shape and then trace around the horse's head, beginning with the lower-right corner. Drag as you set points to get a curve or just click to get a corner. Don't worry if the line doesn't match the head well; you'll fix that in a later tutorial. Trace the outer edge, including the reins and then the areas inside the reins. Allow MAX to close the splines. The result looks somewhat like Figure 8.6. (The splines have been enhanced to make them easier to see.)

FIGURE 8.6
The first pass at tracing the horse's head.

4. Save the file as elven.max. You will use it throughout this chapter.

You can zoom in to make it easier to see the outline of the horse, but close zooming uses vast amounts of RAM.

Creating Parametric Shapes

The remaining shapes are parametric objects, with vertex locations and types set by parameters in the Create panel. The creation technique gives further distinguishing characteristics. With two exceptions, defining either a radius or a rectangle creates the shapes. The exceptions are arcs and text.

Create most shapes by first selecting the type and then dragging out a radius. The shapes that use this technique are:

- Donut
- Circle
- Helix
- NGon
- Star

The following steps walk you through the process for creating any of the these shapes:

1. Choose a Creation Method. Choose Edge to define by diameter or Center to define by radius.

2. Drag in a viewport to define shape location and Radius 1.

3. If necessary, click in the viewport to set remaining parameters, as follows:

   Donut and star: Click to set Radius 2.

   Helix: Click to set Height. Click again to set Radius 2.

4. Set any remaining parameters in the Parameters rollout.

Dragging the diagonal of a rectangle creates Rectangles and Ellipses. The creation technique for these shapes is as follows:

1. Choose a Creation Method. Choose Edge to define by corner to corner or Center to define by center to corner.

2. Drag in a viewport to define shape location and the diagonal of a rectangle that defines Length and Width.

3. Set any remaining parameters in the Parameters rollout.

Creating Arcs

Your creation method choice determines the arc's parameters. Define an arc by using one of two methods:

- **Center-End-End**   This is the most familiar method and is useful when you want to hit an exact center and starting point. You can't precisely predict the location of the second endpoint because it is a function of the arc radius.

   To create a Center-End-End arc, left-click to define the arc center and drag to define the radius and start point. Click to define the second endpoint.

- **End-End-Middle**   Use this method when you want the arc to exactly hit two endpoints. The method for creating an End-End-Middle arc is as follows:

   To create an End-End-Middle arc, click to define the first endpoint and drag to define the second endpoint. Click to define the radius of the arc.

Whichever technique you use, the arc parameters are stored as a radius, a From angle, and a To angle. Only the center point of the arc is fixed. Changing any of the three parameters causes the endpoints of the arc to move.

The following exercise continues with the logo started earlier in this chapter. This exercise provides you with hands-on experience creating a parametric shape—in this case, a rectangle.

ADDING THE RECTANGULAR FRAME

1. You can continue with your file from the last exercise or open elven.max from the CD-ROM.

2. This time, select Rectangle from the Create/Shapes panel. Control-Drag out a square that is 232 units to a side. Click the Angle Snap toggle to On and rotate the square 45 degrees. Move it into position on the outside of the frame.

3. Next, Shift-Scale the Rectangle to form a new shape that matches the inside of the frame.

4. Select Star from the Object Type area. Drag out a 5-point Star that has Radius 1 equal to 20, and Radius 2 equal to 8. Click off the angle snap and rotate the Star into position.

5. Shift-Scale the Star to form the inner line of the text star template. Save your work as elven2.max. The results resemble Figure 8.7.

FIGURE 8.7

Adding the frame and the star to the logo.

Creating Text

Text is the easiest shape to create as the interface is straightforward (see Figure 8.8). The current construction plane can receive the text object by clicking in any viewport. You can also drag to see the text as you move the cursor around the viewport; wherever you release the mouse specifies text placement.

FIGURE 8.8

The Text Shape tool.

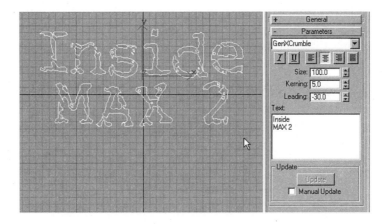

3DS MAX can use any True Type font installed in the Windows NT system and any Adobe Type 1 PostScript font that you place in the directory that the max.ini or Configure Paths specifies. Click in the font list to choose any available font. Clicking the two buttons below the font list toggles the use of italic style and underlined text. Multiline text alignment is set in one of four modes: Left, Right, Centered, and Justify. Kerning (which font experts recognize as *tracking*) and leading work quite similarly to a page layout program: The first controls spacing between all letters in the entire text object and the latter controls the spacing between lines.

TIP

Some poorly made fonts come with shapes that aren't closed. Because of this, the top and bottom surfaces of the letters won't form when Extruded or Beveled. Using the Cap Holes modifier after collapsing down to an Editable Mesh can fix this problem.

You can paste text in directly from the Windows Clipboard with the following restrictions:

- The font, size, and style of the text from the Clipboard are ignored. 3DS MAX uses the current font, style, and size in the Parameters rollout.

- Only "hard" returns are read from the Clipboard; 3DS MAX ignores soft line breaks from word wrapping in text processors.

WARNING

Text created with a null string (no text in the text field) forms an invisible pivot point. Selection is possible only by region selection or as a named selection set. Always make sure you have something in the text field before you click in a viewport.

Text in 3DS MAX has an interesting split personality. The text is parametric, so you can go back and edit the text as text. Because the text is also a spline, you can edit text as geometry. This dual nature of text objects gives you the best of both worlds.

In the following exercise, you practice your text creation skills by adding creating text and adding it to the logo you worked on in previous examples.

ADDING THE TEXT TO THE LOGO

1. Continue with the file from the last exercise or open elven2.max from the CD-ROM.

2. Select Text from the Splines Create panel and replace the Text with the word ELVENSTAR. In this case, Gilgamesh Regular was the font used, but you can use any font on your system that is similar to the template.

3. Drag in the window to place the text. Adjust the size to match the template. You can use kerning to space the letters out, and you might want to apply an Xform modifier to Non-Uniform scale the text horizontally to get a better fit. See the previous chapter for a discussion on Xforms if this is unfamiliar to you.

4. The text still needs some work, but you'll have a chance to edit it in a later exercise. Save your file as elven3.max if it looks similar to Figure 8.9.

FIGURE 8.9

The unedited text in place on the logo.

Creating Sections

The Section shape is unique; it isn't a shape itself. The Section shape's purpose is to create shapes. Use Section when you want to generate a cross-section shape based on a slice through a mesh object. Simply positioning the object and hitting the Create Shape button gives you a separate spline, as shown in Figure 8.10.

FIGURE 8.10

Using Section to gen-
erate two ellipses from
the torus. The cursor
points to one of the
new shapes.

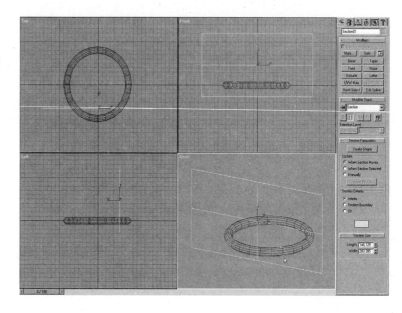

Creating Multiple Splines in the Same Shape

Compound shapes, such as donuts and text, contain multiple splines in the same shape. A donut shape contains two circular splines; a text shape contains at least one spline for each letter, and many letters require multiple splines.

Create compound shapes by removing the check mark from the check box next to the Start New Shape button (see Figure 8.11).

- When you check the box, the Start New Shape button is always on, and everything you create becomes a separate shape object.

- When the box is clear, the Start New Shape button pops out, and everything created becomes a spline in one big compound shape.

- You can manually start a new shape by clicking the Start New Shape button.

You can always go back to any shape and add to it, using one of the following three techniques:

- Select a shape object and then clear the Start New Shape check box. Any shapes you create after that are added as splines to the selected shape.

- Apply an Edit Spline modifier to a shape and use Attach to add other shapes to the selected shape. Edit Spline is discussed in the section "Using Edit Spline" later in this chapter.

- Collapse the shape and use Attach or Attach Multiple.

The Start New Shape button is fast and convenient, but Edit Spline provides greater control over how the splines are located. Also, using the Start New Shape button prevents you from going back and accessing any shape parameters after you finish creating the shape. By using Edit Spline, you can preserve parameters for at least one of the splines in the compound shape.

Understanding Shape Interpolation

All the basic shape objects contain a parameter rollout labeled *Interpolation* (see Figure 8.11). This rollout contains three parameters that control the number of steps in each spline segment. Understanding and properly using the interpolation parameters is critical to the efficient use of shapes.

FIGURE 8.11

Shape interpolation parameters.

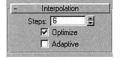

As mentioned earlier in this chapter, steps are divisions along a spline segment. Steps control two properties of a shape: smoothness of the shape curves and the number of faces generated by the shape. With the smoothness of the shape curves, higher step settings produce a smoother curve; with the number of faces generated by the shape, higher step settings generate more faces. This is in contrast to NURBS curves, which always produce a smooth edge, whatever the setting.

The interpolation parameters, listed next, control the number of steps in a shape:

- **Steps**   Enter a value in this field to manually specify the number of steps used for all spline segments in the shape. Use the Steps parameter to gain exact control over the number of faces generated when the shape is used to create 3D geometry. The Adaptive check box must be clear to use the Steps field.

- **Optimize**   When checked, steps are reduced to 0 for all linear spline segments in the shape. Because steps are used to represent curves, they are not needed to accurately represent linear segments and can be removed. Optimize remains as the default setting.

  However, you might want to turn off Optimize if you plan to deform the spline along the linear segments. The segments might be linear now, but if you plan to bend or twist them, you need the extra segments removed by optimizing. You might also want to turn off Optimize if you plan to generate Morph targets from the shape. All Morph targets must have the same number of vertices. Optimization removes shape segments that generate mesh vertices for a Morph target, making it difficult to generate Morph targets from shapes containing flat sides and other shapes containing curved sides.

  The Adaptive check box must be clear to use the Optimize check box.

- **Adaptive**   Automatically calculates steps for each spline segment in the shape. The steps are set so that a change in angle from one step to the next is no more than 2 degrees. Linear segments receive no steps.

  Use Adaptive when smooth, accurate splines are to be used as motion paths or loft components. Adaptive is not a good choice for splines used to generate 3D geometry with modifiers such as Extrude or EditMesh. The smoothness of an adaptive spline generates an inefficient number of faces.

  Checking Adaptive disables the Steps and Optimize Parameters.

Figure 8.12 shows three text shapes using the letter D that have been converted to a mesh by applying an EditMesh modifier. All three shapes are identical except for the interpolation settings. The displaying of the edges emphasizes the difference in curve resolution.

The letter on the left side of Figure 8.12 uses Adaptive interpolation. You can barely tell that the letter is smoother than the others. Applying EditMesh creates a mesh object using 141 faces.

The letter in the middle of Figure 8.12 also uses a Steps setting of 1 and Optimize is not checked. Applying EditMesh creates a mesh object using 38 faces. The middle letter has 73 percent fewer faces than the letter on the left.

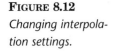

FIGURE 8.12

Changing interpolation settings.

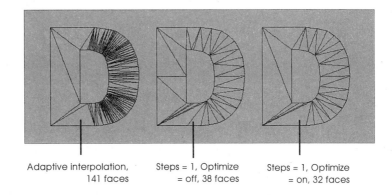

Adaptive interpolation,   Steps = 1, Optimize   Steps = 1, Optimize
141 faces   = off, 38 faces   = on, 32 faces

The letter on the right of Figure 8.12 uses a Steps setting of 1 with Optimize checked. Applying EditMesh creates a mesh object using 32 faces. The letter on the right has 16 percent fewer faces than the middle letter and 77 percent fewer faces than the letter on the left.

More faces consume more disk space, more memory, and, most importantly, more rendering time. It is always better to use the fewest faces necessary to produce a given image quality. In the preceding example, the Adaptive setting might be appropriate if you plan to fly a camera in and around the letter. For most situations, however, using the Steps setting and Optimize is the best choice. An alternative in MAX R2 is to use a NURBS Object that creates faces based on camera distance, tesselating on-the-fly. Simply attach your spline to a NURBS curve to convert it to NURBS.

One word of caution about 3D Studio and Text. It is extremely easy to bog down your system when using a lot of text. Before you make the entire credits 3D, consider the geometry you will generate versus your hardware. It pays to Optimize and then Collapse to an Editable Mesh and lose the memory overhead from the Text.

Using Edit Spline and the Editable Spline Object

Use the Edit Spline modifier to edit and transform the Sub-Objects of shapes. (Despite its name, it's really an Edit Shape modifier.) The following information about Edit Spline focuses on basic shape modeling techniques. As covered in Chapter 7, "Modifier Basics," Edit Spline is memory-intensive and typically used in limited circumstances. The Editable Spline object has all the functionality of Edit Spline (except the capability to return to the base parametric object) and has the added bonus of sub-object animation.

Working with Shape Sub-Objects

Shape terminology and definitions of shape Sub-Objects were presented at the beginning of this chapter. By using the Edit Spline modifier, or collapsing down to a base Editable Spline Object, the following shape Sub-Objects are available for editing:

- **Vertices**   The lowest level of shape Sub-Objects. Vertices carry Bézier curve information. Working with vertices is the only way to exercise full control over shape curves.

- **Segments**   The middle level of shape Sub-Objects. Few segment editing tools are available, and many segment editing techniques are simply a convenient way of working with vertices.

- **Splines**   The top level of shape Sub-Objects. Many shapes contain a single spline, so editing at the spline Sub-Object level might seem to be the same as editing the object, which is not the case. All Sub-Object editing occurs in object space and has no effect on the Local coordinate system or object transformations.

Select these shape Sub-Objects by clicking the Sub-Object button and choosing the Sub-Object level appropriate for editing. Then select a Sub-Object by using the standard selection tools.

Detaching Sub-Objects

Segments and splines can be detached from a shape to create new shape objects. The location and orientation of the pivot point of the original shape is copied for the new shape. Figure 8.13 compares pivot point locations between an original shape and a new shape created by detaching some of its segments.

Both the Edit Segment and Edit Spline rollouts contain a Detach button with two options: Copy and Reorient.

When the Copy option is checked, the selected segment or spline is left undisturbed and copied to a new shape object. This technique is useful when duplicating parts of a shape as a starting point for another shape.

When not checked, the selected segment or spline becomes a new shape. Even after detaching a segment or spline, the Edit Spline modifier keeps a record of the detached Sub-Objects. Deleting the Edit Spline modifier from the Modifier Stack restores the spline to its original form, without affecting the new shape.

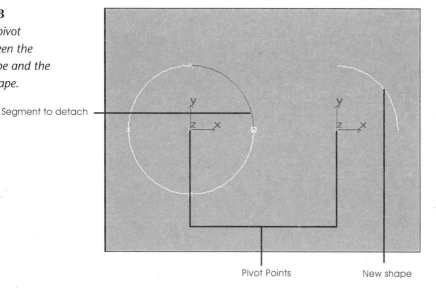

Segment to detach

Pivot Points   New shape

When the Reorient option is checked, the detached objects align with the current construction plane or active grid by rotating and translating. The pivot point of the new object moves to the origin of the construction plane and aligns with the construction plane axes (see Figure 8.14). The new object's pivot point is copied from the creation pivot point of the original shape.

Perspective

Original shape

Reoriented new shape

When Reorient is not checked, the new shape remains in its original location. The new shape has changed color and cannot be selected as long as the Sub-Object mode of Edit Spline is active. Telling the difference between the new shape with the detached Sub-Objects and the original shape when Reorient is not checked can be difficult, so using Select by Name can expedite this process.

TIP

Keep in mind that the new shape object created by a detach operation has no base parameters. The new object is a simple Editable Spline, not a parametric shape. Make sure that the interpolation parameters for the original shape are set correctly before detaching any Sub-Objects.

Deleting Sub-Objects

It is possible to delete any shape Sub-Objects by selecting the Sub-Objects and then clicking the Delete button or pressing Del. The Edit Vertex, Edit Segment, and Edit Spline rollouts all contain a Delete button.

Similar to detaching Sub-Objects, the Edit Spline modifier keeps a record of all Sub-Objects deleted. You can resurrect the shape by deleting the Edit Spline modifier from the Modifier Stack.

Transforming Sub-Objects

Use the transform tools of Move, Rotate, Scale and Align with shape Sub-Objects the same as you use an Xform modifier with full objects. The special transforms of Mirror and Array work only on full objects.

Follow the same rules as for transforming objects when you choose a Sub-Object transform center and transform coordinate system. The exceptions are using the Pivot Point center or the Local coordinate system. The behavior of Sub-Objects using these transform managers is as follows:

- **Pivot Point Center** Ignored for all Sub-Object coordinate system choices, except when transforming vertices with the Local coordinate system. In all other situations, Pivot Point center is the same as Selection center.

- **Local Coordinate System** Uses the World coordinate system and the World origin as the transform center, except when transforming vertices. For this reason, avoid using the Local coordinate system when you transform Sub-Object segments and splines.

Minimizing Edit Spline System Overhead

Edit Spline keeps a record of all Sub-Objects that are detached or deleted. Edit Spline also records every change made to every Sub-Object. This recording technique is what enables Edit Spline modifiers to exist anywhere in the Modifier Stack. This arrangement allows for an Edit Spline to be deleted from the stack and the object revert to its previous form. The price paid for this flexibility is increased memory and file space usage.

General techniques for the use of Edit Spline include the following:

- Use Edit Spline only if other methods do not work. If you are contemplating changes at the spline Sub-Object level, you can often achieve the same result by applying an Xform or other modifier to the entire shape. This usually uses less memory than using Edit Spline.

- Use Edit Spline modifiers only for modeling, not to pass Sub-Object selections up the stack. The Select Spline modifier is a better choice to pass selections up the stack, uses little memory, and is useful for animating shapes.

- Place Edit Spline modifiers used for modeling near the bottom of the Modifier Stack and collapse them when modeling is complete. You cannot animate the modeling changes you make with Edit Spline. After you finish modeling the static form of the shape, collapse the Edit Spline modifiers to save memory.

Edit Spline is a powerful tool that you must use with care. Collapse the modifier when you finish modeling. Using this one technique can save a considerable amount of memory and improve the overall performance of 3DS MAX. Remember that most of the functionality of Edit Spline exists in the Editable Spline type of object, so the discussion of the features for Edit Spline applies to Editable Spline, as well.

Editing at the Object Level

Turning off Sub-Object mode makes three useful features accessible: Attach, Attach Multiple, and Create Line. You can find these features in the Edit Object rollout as shown in Figure 8.15.

FIGURE 8.15

*Buttons in the Edit
Object rollout of Edit
Spline.*

Using Attach and Attach Multiple

Use Attach to add other shapes to the selected shape with the Edit Spline modifier. Keep the following important points in mind when you use Attach:

- The attached shape gives up its identity as a separate object. This means that the attached shape is collapsed into a simple Bézier Spline.

- The attached shape's base parameters or any of the modifiers that were on the attached shape's Modifier Stack are no longer accessible.

- If the Reorient check box is not checked, the attached shape stays where it is but becomes part of the selected shape.

- If Reorient is checked, the attached shape moves and rotates so that its former pivot point and Local coordinate system match the position and orientation of the selected shape's pivot point.

Attach Multiple brings up the Select By Name dialog box and enables for many objects to be selected at the same time. If you haven't done so already, you might perform the exercise "Using Attach and Bending the Ostrich's Neck" in the previous chapter to gain greater understanding.

The shapes from the previous exercises are in need of some editing. The following exercise walks you through the necessary steps for uniting some shapes and detaching others, using the skills discussed in this section. Later exercises build on this work, using the united and detached shapes to make objects.

EDITING THE ATTACHMENTS OF SHAPES

1. Continue with the file from the last exercise, or open elven3.max from the CD-ROM.

2. Select the outer rectangle of the large frame and click on the Edit Stack icon. Collapse the rectangle to an Editable Spline, as shown in Figure 8.16.

FIGURE 8.16

Collapsing to an Editable Spline.

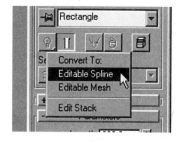

3. Select Attach and click on the interior rectangle. The two splines now form one shape.

4. Right-click to get out of Attach mode and select the Text Shape. Collapse this as well and go to the Sub-Object Spline pulldown.

5. Select the "A" that lies over the Star shape, and either click the Delete button or press Del. Don't be afraid of selecting the underlying star, as you are in Sub-Object mode and can only access pieces of the selected text object. Only the outer portion of the "A" is gone; the shape lost its identity as a letter when it was collapsed. Select the remaining triangle from the "A" and delete it, as well.

6. Select each of the letters one by one to scale and move them to more closely match the template. Xform is unneeded here, as you are in Sub-Object mode. When completed, the logo resembles Figure 8.17. Save the file as elven4.max.

FIGURE 8.17

The logo as it appears once the shapes have been edited.

Using Create Line

Click the Create Line button to begin drawing lines on the current construction plane. Any new lines created are considered to be part of the selected spline. This method is a convenient shortcut to creating a line and then attaching it to the shape. The 3D Snaps are quite useful when adding on to a shape with Create Line.

The main difference between the regular Line tool and Create Line in Edit Shape is that you have no control over the creation vertex type when using Create Line. Dragging always produces a Bézier vertex, and clicking produces a Corner type. The vertex type can be changed with the standard right-click when the drawing process is over (see the following section).

Editing at the Vertex Level

The first Sub-Object level in the Edit Spline Sub-Object list is Vertex. Choosing the Vertex Sub-Object level displays the Edit Vertex rollout of Edit Spline (see Figure 8.19).

Working with Vertex Properties

Setting vertex properties controls the curvature of shapes. Select some vertices and right-click the selection to see the Vertex properties menu. The curve type for a vertex can be set to Corner, Smooth, Bézier, and Bézier Corner. The four choices are described in the following list and are illustrated in Figure 8.19.

FIGURE 8.18

Buttons in the Edit Vertex rollout of Edit Spline.

FIGURE 8.19

Shape vertex properties.

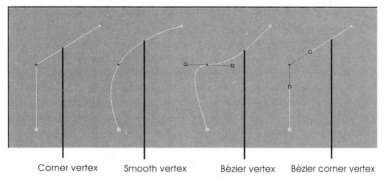

Corner vertex   Smooth vertex   Bézier vertex   Bézier corner vertex

- ◼ **Corner** Produces linear segments as they enter and leave the vertex.

- ◼ **Smooth** Produces a curve through the vertex where the amount of curvature on either side of the vertex is equal. The tangent of a smooth vertex is always parallel to a line drawn between the two vertices to either side of the smooth vertex.

- **Bézier** Produces a curve through the vertex with an adjustable tangent. Changes made to the direction and length of the handles are applied equally to both sides of the vertex.

- **Bézier Corner** Produces an adjustable curve through the vertex that can have a sharp corner. Both the tangent direction and magnitude of the curve can be set independently for each side of the vertex.

T IP

When converting from a Bézier Corner vertex to a Bézier vertex, one handle moves to align with the other stationary handle. It is more useful for both handles to move to an average between the vertices on either side and resemble a Smooth vertex. To accomplish this, first convert to Smooth and then to Bézier.

Making a Vertex the First Vertex

Each spline within a shape contains a first vertex. The first vertex is used for many purposes and can be critically important in some situations. Use the first vertex as follows:

- The starting point for splines that are used as paths. Features that use shape splines as paths include Loft paths, Path controllers, Motion Trajectories, and Path Deform space warps. The first vertex sets the initial condition or starting point for these features.

- The vertex ordering point for geometry. This is especially important for geometry generated from multiple shapes or shapes with multiple splines. The first vertex of each spline is the starting point for constructing the mesh. By aligning the first points, the spacing and regularity of the generated mesh is improved.

If the spline is closed, select any vertex on the spline; if the spline is open, select one of the endpoints. Click Make First. Using Reverse in the Spline sub-object area accomplishes the same function.

The first vertex can be identified by the small box drawn around it, as shown in Figure 8.20.

Connecting Vertices

Use the Connect button to drag from one vertex to another to connect them with a straight segment. Both of the vertices must be located at the end of an open spline. The new segment responds to commands as any segment does; you can right-click to change the vertex type.

FIGURE 8.20

Identifying the first vertex of a spline.

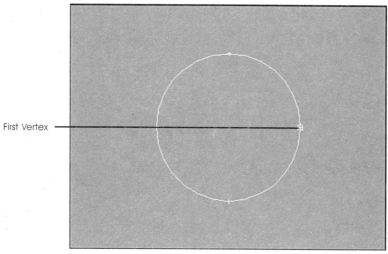

First Vertex

Adding Vertices

The three different methods for adding vertices to a spline are:

- **Insert** Use Insert to build details or extensions off an existing spline. Click Insert and then click anywhere on a spline segment to insert a vertex into that segment. When you click, the new vertex remains attached to the cursor, and you can move it into position. At this point, you have three options:

  The first option is to click to drop a corner vertex at its current location and insert another vertex following the new vertex. To perform the second option, drag to drop a Bézier vertex at the current location and insert another vertex following the new vertex. The remaining option is to right-click (or press Esc) to cancel the current vertex insert and exit the insert operation.

  Unlike other modes in 3DS MAX, you must right-click or press Esc to exit Insert.

- **Refine** Use Refine to add extra vertices to a spline without changing its form. Click Refine and click anywhere on a spline segment to insert a Bézier vertex at that location. Automatic adjustment of the Bézier handles preserves the original shape of the curve.

- **Break**   Use break to split spline segments by replacing a single vertex with two unconnected vertices in the same location. Select the vertices and then click Break. Two unconnected vertices of the same type replace each selected vertex.

Welding Vertices

Making one vertex out of two vertices is called *welding*. Although the Edit Vertex rollout contains only one Weld button, you have two methods for welding vertices.

- Click Move and drag one end vertex to within approximately five pixels of another end vertex. When you release the drag, a dialog box pops up asking if you want to weld the coincident vertices. This technique only works when dragging end vertices to other end vertices. The resulting vertex is always a Bézier Corner vertex except when both vertices were originally smooth vertices; then, the result is another smooth vertex.

- Select a group of vertices, set the Weld Threshold distance in the Edit Vertex rollout of Edit Spline, and click Weld. Selected vertices within the weld threshold that meet the other restrictions weld at a single averaged point.

However, the following restrictions to welding vertices apply:

- End vertices can weld only to other end vertices.

- Vertices in the middle of a spline can weld only to other vertices on the same spline.

- Welded vertices in the middle of a spline cannot "skip over" a vertex. For example, you can never weld every other vertex of a spline.

- Welds can only take place with vertices of the same spline.

Transforming Vertices

Vertices and their tangent handles can be transformed by using the standard transform tools on the toolbar. This transformation is fully animatable.

As mentioned previously in this chapter, Pivot Point centers do not work when transforming vertices about any coordinate system other than Local.

With other transform coordinate centers, Pivot Point centers behave the same as Selection center. When you choose the Local coordinate system, you are locked to using only Pivot Point centers. (You can choose another center type, but the type always behaves as a Pivot Point center.) Transforming vertices by using the Local transform coordinate center is convenient when you work with Bézier vertex tangent handles.

NOTE

Spline vertices cannot exist by themselves. They must always be part of a spline with at least one other vertex. Because of this restriction, you cannot use the Shift-Clone technique to copy vertices.

Transforming Bézier Vertex Handles

Selecting the Bézier and Bézier Corner type of vertices causes their tangent handles to become visible. These components allow for complete control over the direction and curvature of a segment by manipulating the tangent handles:

- **Tangent direction** Each segment is tangent to its handle at the vertex location. If both handles are parallel, forming a straight line, the curve passes smoothly through the vertex. If the handles don't form a straight line, the curve contains a kink, or sharp point, at the vertex location. Figure 8.21 shows tangent handles for both a smooth curve and a kinked curve.

  Bézier vertices are always smooth, with the tangent handles locked to form a straight line. Vertices in which the tangent handles form a kink are always Bézier Corner vertices.

- **Magnitude** The length of a tangent handle sets the magnitude (degree of curvature) for its corresponding segment. The longer the handle, the greater the curvature of the segment. Figure 8.21 shows segments demonstrating both long and short tangent handles.

  Although technically incorrect, you might find it helpful to think of the length of the tangent handle similar to the radius of the arc of the curve. A long tangent handle creates an arc with a large radius as the segment leaves the vertex. An extreme amount of curvature is necessary to bend the segment back around to the direction of the next vertex.

FIGURE 8.21

Comparing tangent handle direction and length.

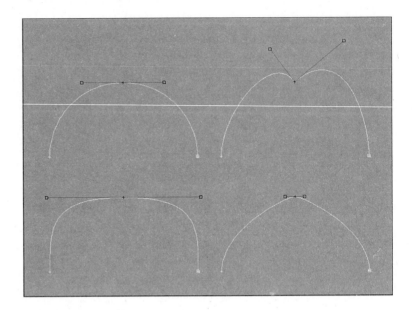

The most common way to transform vertex handles is to use the Move tool. To transform a tangent handle, drag on the green box at the end of the handle rather than on the vertex itself. Even if you have multiple vertices selected, you can drag only one tangent handle at a time. Dragging a tangent handle works in the following way:

- A Bézier type of vertex keeps the handles symmetrical and always produces smooth curves.

- A Bézier Corner type of vertex allows for independent editing of the handles, and can produce sharp curves or corners.

- Dragging the handle out from the vertex makes the curve bigger.

- Rotating the handle rotates the curve around the vertex.

- Pressing Shift while dragging converts a Bézier vertex to a Bézier Corner vertex so that you can drag a single handle.

You can also drag the handles of a selection of vertices or lock Bézier Corner handles together by using the Lock Handles options (see Figure 8.22). The Lock Handles options rely on the concept of vertex order. Each spline stores its vertices in order, starting with the designated first vertex and progressing to the last vertex. The tangent handle is then identified as the incoming handle for the one pointing back to the previous vertex and the outgoing handle for the one pointing forward to the next vertex. You can't tell the difference by looking at them, but it makes a difference when using the Lock Handles Alike option.

FIGURE 8.22

The Lock Handles options in the Edit Vertex rollout.

The lock options of Alike and All behave differently depending on whether working with a selection of one or multiple vertices.

- Lock Handles All for a single vertex causes both handles of a Bézier Corner vertex to be affected by dragging either handle.

- Lock Handles All for multiple vertices causes all handles of all selected vertices to be affected by dragging a single handle.

- Lock Handles Alike for a single vertex has no effect because a single vertex has two handles, one incoming and the other outgoing, both different.

- Lock Handles Alike for multiple vertices causes the matching handle of all selected vertices to be affected by dragging an incoming or outgoing handle. This difference is noticeable only if the selected vertices are Bézier Corner vertices. For Bézier vertices, dragging either handle affects both.

- Press Shift while dragging with Lock Handles Alike to convert all selected vertices to Bézier Corner vertices.

A drawback of dragging tangent handles is that it is difficult to control the drag when you want to change only one property, such as direction. A handy solution is to rotate or scale a selection of vertices using the Local transform coordinate system.

- Rotating a vertex using the Local coordinate system rotates the tangent handles without affecting the magnitude of the curve.

- Scaling a vertex using the Local coordinate system changes the magnitude of the curve without changing the tangent direction.

Animating Vertex Transformations

None of the features of the Edit Spline modifier allow for animation. Convert the spline to an Editable Spline for animation of the vertices or tangent handles. Once accomplished, the process is simple: go to the desired frame, press the Animate button, and move the vertex or handle.

Groups of selected vertices can be animated by passing the selections (preferably with SplineSelect) up the Modifier Stack to an Xform or Linked Xform modifier, by following these steps:

1. Select vertices with Edit Spline or SplineSelect.

2. Leave Sub-Object Vertex active and click the More button in the Modify panel.

3. Choose Xform from the Modifiers dialog box.

   A yellow rectangle appears around the selected vertices. This is the Xform gizmo.

4. With Sub-Object Gizmo activated for the Xform modifier, turn on the Animate button and move, rotate, or scale the Xform gizmo.

   When you animate the Xform gizmo, it carries the selected vertices with it.

At last, it is time to clean up the vertex placement from the first exercise. The following exercise gives you hands-on experience with editing vertices. It focuses on the vertices in the horse's head in the logo you've been working with.

CLEANING UP THE VERTEX PLACEMENT ON THE HORSE'S HEAD

1. You can use the file from the last exercise or open elven4.max from the CD-ROM.

2. Select the head spline and go to the Sub-Object Vertex mode. Remember how you started drawing the spline from the lower-right corner? The First Vertex is there, as it is outlined by a small box. Right-click it and convert it to a Bézier Corner type.

3. Drag the lower handle so that the curve lies inside the area of the two rectangles that make up the frame. Refer to Figure 8.23 for exact placement.

4. Go through the rest of the vertices, changing the vertex type so that they more closely follow the contour of the template. A shortcut is to hold down the Shift key to convert a Bézier handle to a Bézier Corner.

5. You might have to Refine the spline to get better detail in some of the curved area. Try to keep this to a minimum, as having too many vertices makes a model unwieldy and consumes memory. When you have completed your edits, the model looks like Figure 8.23. Save the file as **elven5.max**.

You can right-click on the window label to temporarily turn the template off. It's always wise to check your work without the background distractions to make sure that it will look good. When you're done, turn the template back on.

Editing at the Segment Level

The next Sub-Object editing level in the Edit Spline modifier is Segment. Choosing the Segment Sub-Object level displays the Edit Segment rollout of Edit Spline (see Figure 8.24). The Edit Segment rollout has far fewer options than the Edit Vertex rollout.

Detach and Delete have already been described for all Sub-Object levels at the beginning of the Edit Spline discussion. The remaining options are described in the following sections.

FIGURE 8.24

Buttons in the Edit
Segment rollout of Edit
Spline.

Breaking Segments

The Break button has an effect similar to Break in the Edit Vertex rollout, although it is applied somewhat differently. Instead of splitting two segments apart at a selected vertex, you can now split a segment into two pieces anywhere along the segment. After clicking Break, click anywhere on a segment to insert two unconnected vertices at the point you click.

Refining Segments

The Refine button is moonlighting from the Edit Vertex rollout and works exactly the same. Click Refine and then click a segment to insert a single vertex.

Dividing Segments

When a segment must be divided into a specific number of segments, use the Divide button to set the number of segments.

Inserting Segments

If a vertex is to be added and moved to another location, Insert does the same job as Refine and the Move tool.

Working with Segment Properties

Setting segment properties can control the curvature of segments. Select some segments and right-click the selection to see the Segment properties menu. The following two choices for segment properties are available:

- **Curve** Choosing Curve doesn't necessarily cause the segment to curve. Rather, this property causes the segment to follow the properties set for the vertices at either end of the segment. If the vertices are corner vertices, the segment appears linear; if the vertices are Smooth or Bézier, the segment appears curved.

- **Line** Choosing Line causes the segment to ignore the vertex properties and create a straight line. It is readily apparent when a segment is using the Line property because tangent handles for Bézier vertices at either end show an X rather than a box. The X indicates that the segment, as shown in Figure 8.25, ignores the tangent handle.

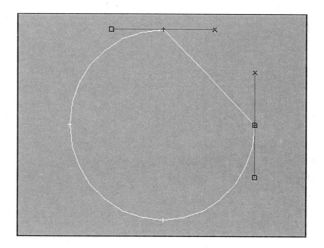

Using the Line segment property is a convenient way to flatten a segment without affecting the curvature of the segments to either side of it. You can get the same result by converting the vertices to Bézier corner vertices and then adjusting the tangent handles to make the segment linear, but this process requires a lot of work.

Transforming Segments

Transform the segments by using the standard selection and transform tools on the toolbar, including the Shift-Clone technique to make copies of segments. These types of transforms are animated in the standard fashion.

If the effect of transforming more than one segment needs to be animated, use the Xform technique described previously for vertices.

As mentioned earlier in this chapter, Pivot Point centers do not work when transforming segments about any coordinate system. Also, choosing the Local coordinate system locks you into the World coordinate system with a World Origin center.

Editing at the Spline Level

Choosing the Spline Sub-Object level displays the Edit Spline rollout of Edit Spline (see Figure 8.27).

FIGURE 8.26

Buttons in the Edit Spline rollout of Edit Spline.

Detach and Delete have already been described for all Sub-Object levels at the beginning of the Edit Spline discussion. The remaining objects in the Edit Spline rollout are described in the following sections.

Closing Splines

This simple command draws a segment from the last vertex of an open spline back to the first. Select a spline and click Close.

Outlining Splines

Outlining a spline is a fast and convenient way to produce multiple, concentric copies of a closed spline or to produce a double-line version of an open spline. These copies are handy when you want to create outline text, hollow logos, or similar shapes. The Outline feature can be tricky at first but has a lot of flexibility.

Clicking the Outline button puts you into Outline mode. As long as the button is active, you can continue to select and outline any spline in the selected shape. To exit Outline mode, click another button or right-click in the active viewport.

The Center check box determines generation of the outline from the outline distance.

- When not checked, the original spline remains, and the new spline is placed the Outline Width's distance away from the original.

- When checked, the original spline is deleted, and two outlines are placed one-half the Outline Width's distance to either side of the original.

After selecting a spline to outline, proceed with one of the following techniques:

- Drag the selected spline to define the outline location. As you drag, the outline appears. When you release the drag, the outline drops into place. When you drag a spline, you can define only a positive outline width—the outline can go in one direction determined by the vertex order of the spline. Outlines for clockwise splines always drag out, away from the spline center; outlines for counterclockwise splines always drag in, toward the spline center. If the direction the outline takes is not the one you want, cancel the operation by right-clicking and use one of the other techniques.

- Drag the spinner next to the Outline Width field. You can drag the spinner to define both positive or negative outline widths. When you release the spinner, the outline drops into place, and the spinner value resets to 0.0. Do not click the spinner. Each click creates a new outlined spline.

- Type a value in the Outline Width field. When you press Enter, the outline is created, and the spinner is reset to 0.0.

The type-in method is convenient for setting precision outlines and for generating repetitive multiple outlines. Each time Enter is pressed, an outline is created, and the Outline width field is reset. These steps create multiple outlines with a spacing of 5 units between each copy (see Figure 8.27).

FIGURE 8.27

Creating concentric outlines.

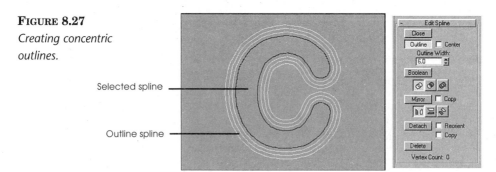

Selected spline

Outline spline

Boolean Operations

The Boolean command combines two source splines and always deletes both sources in the process of creating the Boolean spline.

Performance of Boolean operations on splines must meet the following requirements:

- Splines must be part of the same shape. Be sure to attach one shape to another before attempting the Boolean.

- Splines must be closed.

- Splines cannot intersect themselves.

- Splines must overlap. A spline completely enclosed within another is not considered an overlapping spline.

Beyond these restrictions, the Boolean command is a very easy and stable tool. Figure 8.28 shows examples of invalid and valid splines for Boolean operations.

To perform a Boolean operation between two splines, complete the following steps:

1. Select a single spline.

2. Click Boolean.

3. Click the Boolean operation type Union, Subtraction, or Intersection.

4. Click a second spline.

FIGURE 8.28

Valid and invalid splines for Boolean operations.

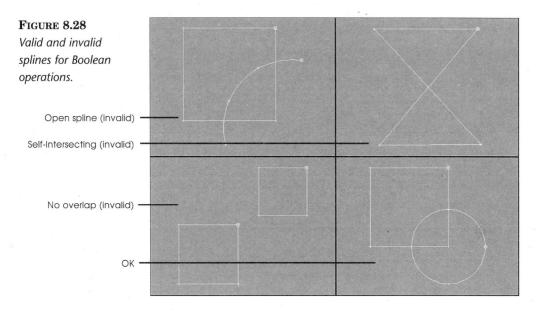

Open spline (invalid)

Self-Intersecting (invalid)

No overlap (invalid)

OK

If the chosen operation is Subtraction, the second spline is always subtracted from the first.

The following exercise shows you how to complete the bridle and prepare the splines to receive the geometric modifiers, using Spline Booleans and outlines.

USING SPLINE BOOLEANS AND OUTLINES

1. Continue with the file from the last exercise, or open elven5.max from the CD-ROM.

2. Create a 52 × 312 spline rectangle that surrounds the box holding the text, and collapse it to an Editable Spline. Access the Sub-Object Spline area and click on Outline. Drag outward, and watch the outline spline form the inside of the frame.

3. Right-click to get out of Outline mode and access the Line tool from the Create panel. Draw around the marking on the horse's forehead. Next, draw lines down the center of each of the bridle components, as shown in Figure 8.29.

4. One by one, select each of the bridle splines, and perform a Sub-Object Spline Outline function. This time, use the Center check box and interactively set the outline distance in accord with the template.

FIGURE 8.29

*Adding the bridle com-
ponents by drawing
centerlines.*

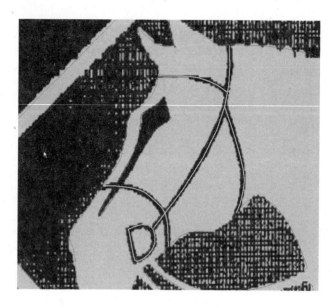

5. Select one of the bridle components, and Attach the rest of the components to it. The result is one shape consisting of the five components.

6. Under Sub-Object Spline, make sure that Union is selected, click on the
   outer part of the "D" shape, and click Boolean. Click on the long component that intersects the "D" shape. The splines are united.

7. Continue clicking on the rest of the parts to make one entire bridle.

8. Finally, Attach the horse's head to the frame, and Boolean the two parts
   together. The procedure is the same, expect that you want to click on
   the inner frame, then select Subtraction, and then select Boolean. The
   results are similar to Figure 8.30. Save the file as elven6.max.

This completes the drawing of all the shapes necessary to finish the
logo. In the last two exercises, you give the shapes depth.

FIGURE 8.30

The completed splines, ready to go to the third dimension.

Mirroring Splines

Mirroring splines produces results similar to those produced by using the Mirror object command on the toolbar. In both cases, an object is being flipped over one or two axes with a concurrent option to copy.

Two important differences between mirroring splines and mirroring objects are as follows:

- Splines always mirror about the local centers regardless of the transform center option.

- Splines always mirror about the shape's local axes regardless of the transform coordinate system chosen.

To mirror a spline, complete the following steps:

1. Select a spline.

2. Set the Copy check box for whether you want to make a copy.

3. Click a Mirror axis button for the direction of the Mirror.

4. Click Mirror.

Transforming Splines

Splines are no different from vertices and segments when it comes to transformation and animation. Pivot Point centers do not work when transforming splines about any coordinate system. Choosing the Local coordinate system locks you into the World coordinate system with a World Origin center.

Using Shape Modifiers

The modifiers that ship with 3DS MAX do one of two things when applied to a shape object. They enable the modification of the shape geometry leaving the shape still a shape, or they convert the shape to a mesh and modify the mesh geometry.

Applying Geometric Modifiers to Splines

Applying and animating modifiers to shape objects opens many modeling possibilities and is basically the same as modifying an object. Imagine the possibilities of animating a shape used to create a surface of revolution or animating a Loft path. Figure 8.31 shows examples of applying modifiers to shapes.

FIGURE 8.31
Bending a helix and skewing text.

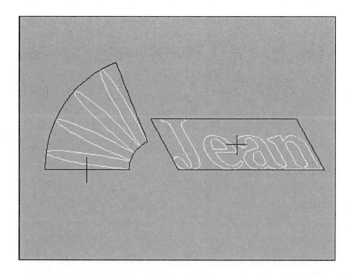

One important point to remember about applying modifiers to shapes is that most shapes are flat (or at least they start out flat); the shape has no dimension along its local z-axis. By coincidence, most modifiers default to acting on the local z-axis of the object.

If you don't see an effect when you apply a modifier, check the modifier's active axis. If the shape is a flat shape, set the active axis to x or y.

Converting Shapes to Flat Meshes

When a texture map won't do, like for signage in a scene, a shape must be pressed into service by converting it to a flat mesh. Many modifiers convert a shape to a mesh object—the most obvious one being the EditMesh modifier. Merely clicking on the stack editor and collapsing to an Editable Mesh causes the shape to disappear. The preferable methods to convert shapes to meshes include any of the surface modifiers, such as Normal, Smooth, or Material. The surface modifiers are simple and don't carry the potential for memory overhead that the Edit Mesh does.

Extruding Splines

Use the Extrude modifier whenever you need to extrude along a straight line. The next chapter describes how to create Loft objects that can extrude any number of shapes along almost any kind of spline. Except for a single shape along a straight line, Extrude is the best choice.

Virtually any shape can be extruded, including shapes with open splines that form sheets or ribbon-like surfaces. Some shapes, however, work better than others do. For example, shapes with overlapping splines or splines that intersect can produce odd results when capping is turned on. Figure 8.32 shows examples of extruded shapes.

The two primary concerns when extruding shapes are the Extrusion amount and the number of segments:

- **Amount** Set the length of the extrusion as measured along the shape's local z-axis. Most shapes lie flat on the local XY plane, creating flat-topped extrusions. If you extrude shapes containing splines rotated off the local xy plane, you can create skewed or diagonal cut extrusions. Figure 8.33 shows the result of extruding a shape when you use Edit Spline to rotate one of the splines off the XY plane.

FIGURE 8.32
Examples of extruded shapes.

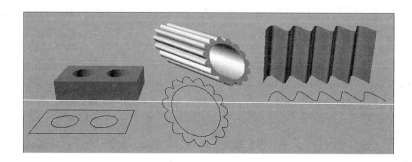

FIGURE 8.33
Extruding non-flat shapes.

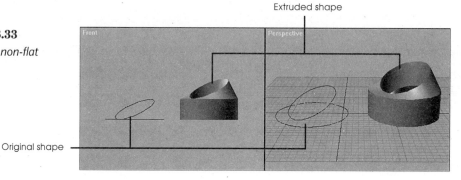

- **Segment**   Set the number of divisions along the length of the extrusion. Increase segments if you plan to bend or otherwise deform the extrusion with another modifier.

You can choose from the following options when extruding a shape:

- **Capping**   You can choose to cap either or both ends of the extrusion and choose between Morph or Grid capping methods. Morph capping uses fewer faces but does not deform as well as Grid capping. Morph capping is necessary if you plan to use variations of the extruded object as Morph targets.

- **Generation of Mapping Coordinates**   Checking this option applies mapping coordinates to the extruded sides for use with mapped materials. You need to manually apply mapping coordinates to the caps of the object.

- **Output**   Chooses whether the result of the extrusion is a mesh, patch, or NURBS object. The proper choice is highly dependent on what you plan to do with the object. The default choice of Mesh is appropriate for most purposes.

Lathing Splines

Apply Lathe to a shape object to generate a surface of revolution. Surfaces of revolution are also something that you can create as a Loft, but as with Extrude, if you are revolving a single shape around an arc, Lathe is a better choice.

Also (as with Extrude), you can lathe virtually any shape. Figure 8.34 shows examples of lathed shapes.

FIGURE 8.34
Examples of lathed shapes.

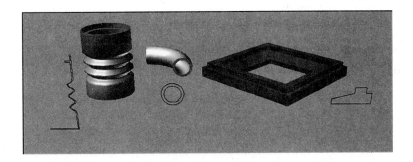

Your most important decisions when lathing shapes are setting the Lathe axis options and setting surface of revolution options.

Setting the Lathe Axis

The default location for the Lathe axis runs through the shape's creation center and aligns with the shape's local y-axis. The creation center is the default location of the pivot point.

WARNING

Because of a bug in 3DS MAX, the Lathe axis appears to run through the pivot point of the shape, but the actual Lathe center is located at the original creation center of the shape. The placement of the Lathe axis is correct only if you haven't manually moved the pivot point before applying the Lathe. Do not move the pivot point of a shape object if you plan to apply a Lathe modifier later. Otherwise, the Lathe axis will appear in the wrong place.

If you need to change the position of a spline with respect to a shape's pivot point, you are better off using Edit Spline to move the spline rather than using Adjust Pivot to move the pivot.

If you want to use something other than the default axis location, you have four choices:

- **Min**   Click to locate the axis at the negative x-axis boundary of the shape.

- **Center**   Click to locate the axis at the geometric center of the shape. Depending on which type of editing you performed on the shape, the geometric center might or might not be the same as the default creation center.

- **Max**   Click Max to locate the axis at the maximum x-axis boundary of the shape.

- **Sub-Object**   Click and manually move or rotate the axis to any place you want. You can also non-uniform scale the Lathe axis to produce elliptical surfaces of revolution (see Figure 8.35). Usually you want to scale along the active axis of the lathe.

FIGURE 8.35

Result of scaling a Lathe axis.

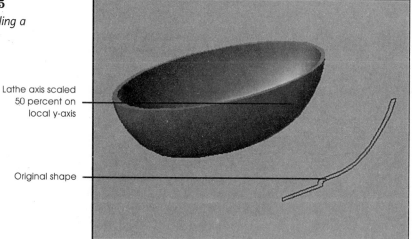

Lathe axis scaled 50 percent on local y-axis

Original shape

You have no guaranteed way to reset the axis to its default location after the axis has been moved. You must delete the Lathe modifier and reapply it if you want to return to the default axis location.

You can set the orientation of the Lathe axis by using the three orientation buttons. Click the X, Y, or Z button to align the Lathe axis with the Local axis of the selected shape. You need to consider the following issues when selecting the Lathe axis:

- The default orientation of the Lathe axis is aligned with the shape's local y-axis.

- If you choose to align the Lathe axis with the shape's local x-axis, you cannot use the Min, Center, or Max buttons. You must manually move the Lathe axis if you align with the local x-axis.

- Most shapes that you lathe are flat, making the y-axis and x-axis your primary choices. Lathing about the z-axis is useful only if the shape does not lie flat on its local XY plane.

Controlling the Surface of Revolution

Three surface of revolution options control the degree of revolution and the complexity of the mesh generated:

- **Degrees**   Sets the number of degrees of revolution. If you use values less than 360 degrees, you will probably want to check capping for both the start and the end of the lathe.

- **Segments**   Sets the number of intermediate copies of the shape you want to create around the lathe. High segment values produce a smoother round lathe, whereas lower values produce rougher surfaces or even geometric frames.

  If you want a round shape, you usually need 16 segments or higher for 360 degrees of revolution. Lower values (between 4 and 8) are useful for creating regular geometric frames, as shown in Figure 8.36.

FIGURE 8.36

Using different seg-ment settings.

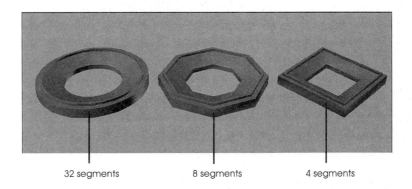

| 32 segments | 8 segments | 4 segments |

- **Weld Core**   Core vertices are vertices of the shape that lie on the Lathe axis. Each core vertex of the shape is duplicated for each segment of the lathe, causing many vertices to "stack up" at the center of the lathed object and leading to rendering errors. Check Weld Core whenever a shape vertex lies on the Lathe axis.

You might want to remove the check mark from Weld Core when you create Morph targets and you need to preserve a predictable vertex count.

Capping options and the choice between Mesh, Patch, and NURBS output is the same as for Extrude.

Lathe also includes the Generate UV Coordinates check box to apply mapping coordinates to the sides to the Lathed object. If you do not use a full 360 degrees, you need to manually apply mapping coordinates to the caps of the object.

Here's your chance to practice extruding splines. In this exercise, you learn to give the logo some depth by extruding the splines along the local z-axis.

EXTRUDING SPLINES IN THE LOGO TO ADD DEPTH

1. Continue with the file from the last exercise, or open elven6.max from the CD-ROM.

2. You can turn off the Background template, as you won't be needing it anymore. Either access the dialog box from the Views menu, or right-click on the title of the window and remove the check mark the Show Background option.

3. Minimize the window. Select the horse and frame, and use Extrude from the Modify panel to set a depth of –10.

4. Select the bridle and extrude it +5.

5. Select the forehead mark and extrude it +2. At the end of these tasks, your logo resembles Figure 8.37. Save the file as elven7.max.

Beveling Splines

Use this modifier to simultaneously extrude and bevel a shape. The most popular use for this modifier is the creation of classic beveled text and logo treatments, as shown in Figure 8.38.

FIGURE 8.37
The logo extruded.

FIGURE 8.38
Beveled text and logos.

Just as with Extrude and Lathe, you can create beveled objects as lofts. For most classic bevel situations, the Bevel modifier is your best choice.

Your main considerations when beveling a shape include:

- Setting Bevel values

- Choosing edge treatment

- Cleaning up edge intersections

Setting Bevel Values

Create the beveled object by setting the following bevel values:

- All beveled objects require a minimum of two levels: a start, and an end. The Start Outline field is the only parameter for the start level.

Think of the start level as being Level 0. Level 1 is the default end level for a two-level object. You can optionally enable two more levels for a total of four levels. The highest numbered level used is always considered the end level.

The classic bevel treatment uses all four levels. Figure 8.39 shows a classic bevel and identifies one possible level arrangement.

FIGURE 8.39

Four levels for a classic bevel.

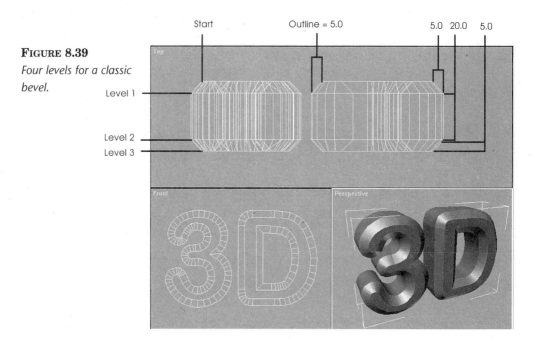

The last operation to perform of the logo is to give some depth to the text and its frame. This exercise uses a fancier approach by adding bevels.

FINISHING THE LOGO BY BEVELING THE TEXT AND FRAME

1. You can use the file from the last exercise, or open elven7.max from the CD-ROM.

2. Select the text and the frame (but not the star), and apply a Bevel modifier by hitting the More button and choosing it from the list.

3. Select Keep Lines From Crossing, and set the Bevel Values to the following:

Start Outline: 0.0 (no change from original shape)
Level 1 Height: 1.0 (come up 1 unit)
Level 1 Outline: 1.0 (bevel out 1 unit)
Level 2 Height: 4.0 (the body of the letter is 4 units)
Level 2 Outline: 0.0 (hold the same size out as Level 1)
Level 3 Height: 1.0 (come up 1 more unit)
Level 3 Outline: –1.0 (bevel back to the original shape)

4. Select the outer star, and give it an Edit Spline modifier. Get out of Sub-Object mode and then Attach the inner star.

5. Set the Bevel Values to:

Start Outline: 0.0 (no change from original shape)
Level 1 Height: 4.0 (come up 4 units)
Level 1 Outline: 0.0 (no bevel)
Level 2 Height: 0.0
Level 2 Outline: –1.5 (creates a flat top 1.5 units wide)
Level 3 Height: –2.0
Level 3 Outline: 0.0 (sinks down in 2 units and forms a flat bottom)

6. A close-up shot illustrates how your bevels look if you followed these steps accurately (see Figure 8.40).

FIGURE 8.40

Close-up of the edge bevel treatments.

7. Go to the Top View and select the text, the star, and their frame. Move them forward (down) in the view, and the logo is complete. Your efforts resembles Figure 8.41.

FIGURE 8.41

The completed logo.

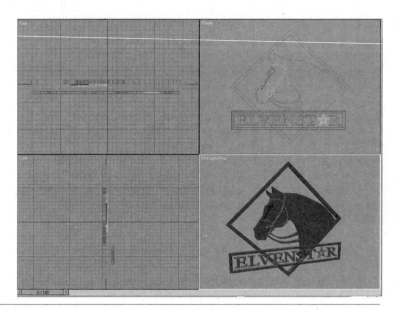

This series of exercises has taken the original fax image to a fully finished 3D logo, ready for an industrial video. Even if your specialty isn't logo treatments, the lessons learned are valuable for all types of modeling chores.

Looking at the preceding exercise, you see the basic rules for creating classic four-level bevels:

- The Start Outline sets the base size of the bevel.

- Levels 1 and 3 are the same value but have opposite signs.

- If you want a 45-degree bevel, the Height for Level 1 and Level 3 is positive and equal to the Outline value.

- Level 2 outline is always zero.

- Recognizing that the Start Outline sets the base size of an object, you can set up the bevel conditions for levels 1, 2, and 3 and then experiment with the overall size of the object by changing the Start Outline.

- The height parameter sets the distance from the previous level to the current level as measured along the shape's local z-axis. For classic bevels, the Height values are always positive and usually equal. You can create interesting bevel variations by combining positive and negative height values.

Choosing Edge Treatment

The options in the Surface area of the Parameters rollout set how the edge surfaces are treated. The options primarily control whether the sides are flat, chamfered sides or smooth, rounded sides:

- **Linear or Curved Sides**   Choose the option for the type of side interpolation you want. Curved Sides uses a spline curve to interpolate from one level to the next. You must set Segments greater than 1 to see the effect of choosing Curved Sides.

- **Segments**   Increase the segments if you are using Curved Sides or plan to deform the object with another modifier.

- **Smooth Across Levels**   Applies smoothing groups to smooth the side faces of the object. Bevel never tries to smooth from the sides into the face of the object. Check this option if you use Curved Sides or multiple segments.

The options for UV (Mapping) coordinates and capping are typical for all objects, with a small exception for the meaning of Top and Bottom capping. Most capped objects are labeled Start and End. The objects don't care about the spatial relationship of the caps. Bevel checks the local z-axis heights of the start level and the end level. Checking Top caps the level with the greatest local z-axis value, whereas checking Bottom caps the level with the least local z-axis value. The Generate UV Coordinates check box must be checked to apply mapping coordinates to the sides of the beveled object. Mapping coordinates need to be manually applied to the caps of the object.

Check the Keep Lines from Crossing check box to turn on intersection checking. Enter a value in the Separation field to set the minimum distance to be maintained between edges. You can set this value as small as 0.01 units, creating a bevel that appears to come to a point. Figure 8.42 shows the result of checking Keep Lines from Crossing for the previous beveled object with crossing intersections.

NOTE

The Keep Lines from Crossing option can take considerable time to calculate all the intersection constraints, especially with complex serif letters. After you have the bevel set the way you want, you might want to consider collapsing the Modifier Stack to convert the bevel to an Editable Mesh and prevent the need to recalculate.

FIGURE 8.42

Using the Keep Lines from Crossing option.

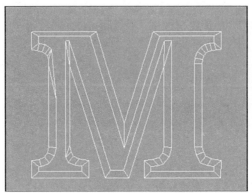

In Practice: Modeling with Shapes

- Shapes are used as components for other objects. Shapes render as visible surfaces only when the Renderable box is checked. A shape is typically modified or used as a Sub-Object to define a visible 3D surface. Shapes can also be used to define animation paths.

- Text shapes have the capability to be edited as text or geometry. You can change the parameters of a text shape to edit spelling and change fonts. You can also apply modifiers to text shapes to deform them like geometry.

- Attached shapes are nonparametric. If you attach shapes, or use the Start New Shapes button, to build shapes containing multiple splines, the attached shapes give up the parametric properties.

- Shape interpolation settings affect object complexity. Your choices for shape interpolation have a great impact on the face density of objects generated from the shape. Carefully consider your choices for shape steps setting and other interpolation parameters.

- Collapse Edit Spline modifiers. Edit Spline modifiers can generate enormous memory overhead. Once you are certain that you want your Edit Spline Sub-Object changes to be permanent, collapse the Edit Spline modifier. Collapsing the modifier saves memory and improves system performance.

- Animate shape Sub-Objects using the base Editable Spline object. For Selection Sets of Sub-Objects, use an Xform or Linked Xform modifier. Use SplineSelect modifier to define a Sub-Object selection and then apply an Xform modifier to the selection. You can then animate the Xform gizmo.

Chapter 9

BUILDING LOFT OBJECTS

*Loft objects can be some of the most complex and interest-
ing types of objects built in 3D Studio MAX. A loft object is
created by combining cross-section shapes with a single
path shape. Because creating loft objects is completely
dependent on the source shapes that are used, it would be
helpful to read Chapter 8, "Modeling with Shapes," if you
haven't already done so.*

This chapter presents the following discussions about creating loft objects:

■ Strategies for creating source shapes

■ Two ways to create the initial loft object

■ How to build the loft by adding additional shapes

■ Controlling loft parameters for detail and appearance

■ Using special loft deformation tools

■ Editing the loft

■ Animating the loft

■ Using Fit Deformation

Understanding the Basics of Creating Loft Objects

A common analogy for lofting is the building of a ship's hull. The loft path is analogous to the keel (or the boat's "spine") and the loft shapes as the ribs of the hull, arranged along the keel. You'll see this analogy come to life in the second exercise in this chapter, which shows you how to build a kayak.

Another way of looking at the lofting process is to examine the way industrial designers or sculptors build up study models. These professionals use a form of spatial sketching to build three-dimensional models by arranging lines in space. The lines usually take the form of cross sections of the object and are held in place by a central core. As the design progresses, a surface is formed by filling the spaces between the cross sections with a sculpting material (like clay) or by stretching a skin over the cross sections (as if it were plaster-soaked cloth). In the final exercise in this chapter, a shampoo bottle makes use of the 3D sketch methodology.

Creating loft objects in 3D Studio MAX involves creating a central core (the path), which can support any number of cross sections (the shapes). As editing progresses on the path and the shapes, the loft surface parameters are used to interactively display the surface in both wireframe and shaded form.

Loft Terminology

Loft objects employ special terminology along with the basic terms used to describe Shape objects. The following definitions review shape terminology as applied to loft objects and introduce new, loft-specific terms. Detailed definitions for shape terms are presented in Chapter 8.

- **Steps**: The number of segment divisions used to represent a curve. The number of steps used defines the smoothness and mesh density of the loft surface. Lofts use their own step settings for the path and cross section shapes, ignoring the interpolation settings of the shapes themselves.

- **Shapes**: A collection of splines defines a shape object. A path shape can contain only a single spline. Cross section shapes can contain any number of splines as long as all cross section shapes on the path contain the same number of splines. In a loft, shapes become sub-objects.

- **Paths**: Describes the one shape that defines the central core of the loft.

- **Level**: Intermediate positions along the loft path. At the very least, each vertex on the path defines a level. Shape locations and deformation curve control points can also define additional levels.

- **Deformation Curve**: Defines the basic form of a loft by percentage change along the curve. These curves allow for the further modification of the loft to adjust scale, angle, and size of the shapes. A good way to think of Deformation Curves is to visualize them as a graph, not an actual profile.

- **Control Point**: Vertices on the deformation curves. Control points appear and behave like shape vertices with a few added restrictions on their use.

- **First Vertex**: All shapes have a first vertex. 3DS MAX builds the loft surface by matching the first vertices of each shape on the path and stretching the skin from the first vertex to the last vertex and constructing the faces between shapes starting from the first vertices on each shape. Without the first vertices aligned, the loft object pinches and twists in an unacceptable manner.

Creating Source Shapes for Cross Sections and Paths

Virtually any shape can be used as a source for cross sections or paths, and observing a few restrictions will help to increase the chances for successful creation of shapes for lofts.

Path shapes have only one restriction—they can contain only a single spline. 3DS MAX refuses to accept any shape containing more than one spline as a path (such as a donut). All vertices must be welded into a unified shape, if it has been assembled from components.

Two restrictions apply to cross section shapes. First, all the shapes on the path must contain the same number of splines, which is not as restrictive as you might think. You can easily make what appears to be a single shape split into multiple shapes by building the "single shape" out of a series of unconnected splines. Figure 9.1 shows a fork that uses this technique. The shapes that make up the handle of the fork are made of two splines. One spline each for the left and right side enables the loft to split when it reaches the tines of the fork.

FIGURE 9.1

Splitting a single shape into multiple shapes.

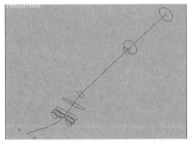 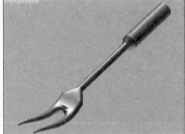

Loft object with split shapes   Loft object with nested shapes

The second restriction is that all shapes on the path must have the same nesting order. If the first shape on the path contains two splines inside another spline, then all shapes on the path must contain two splines. You can get around this restriction by opening the outer spline. Open splines, even if their endpoints are touching, do not nest. The odd object in Figure 9.2 shows the use of this technique. Breaking a corner vertex using the Edit Spline modifier has opened the outer rectangle of the loft shape.

FIGURE 9.2

Changing nesting order.

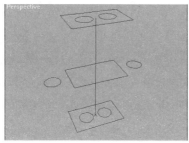 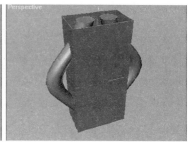

Loft object with nested shapes   Rendered loft skin

Both methods mentioned for avoiding restrictions on the spline number and the nesting order involve using shapes containing open splines. The main drawback to using open splines is that they cannot be capped using the loft capping parameters. If loft objects need to be capped with open splines, consider using the following techniques:

- Create other objects to serve as caps and then group, link, or attach the objects to the loft.

- Apply an Edit Mesh modifier to the loft and manually build faces to create a cap. Use of the Edit Mesh modifier is discussed in Chapter 7, "Modifier Basics."

- Use Edit Mesh to weld the vertices together, then use the new Cap Holes modifier.

- Use loft scale deformation to abruptly scale the loft shape down to zero percent at the ends of the loft. Loft scale deformation is discussed in the section "Using Scale Deformation" later in this chapter.

The following sections introduce other techniques to make loft modeling more successful.

Transforming Shapes

A great source of confusion when creating loft objects concerns the effects of transforms applied to the source shapes. Transforms applied to shapes at the object level are ignored when the shape is added to a loft object.

With the exception of moving or rotating the first shape used to create a loft, shape transforms are generally not part of the loft. Chapter 1, "Basic Concepts," discusses the object dataflow and how information about the object progresses from the base parameters through the modifiers, on to transforms, and finally to space warps. When a shape is used in a loft, the dataflow for that shape splits off after shape modifiers and before the shape transforms. Transforms such as Move, Rotate, and Scale do not travel with the shape into the loft.

Use the following two rules when applying transformations to shape objects that are used as loft shapes:

■ Use Move and Rotate to place shapes in convenient locations in your scene. Keep in mind that moving or rotating a shape has no effect on how the shape behaves in a loft.

■ Never Transform scale a shape! This is good advice for just about any object, but it is especially important for shapes used in lofts. The transform scale factor is not carried into the loft. The shape appears in the loft using its original non-scaled size.

If you need to Move, Rotate, or Scale a shape as part of the loft design, you have several options, summarized in the following list.

■ **Change base parameters**: Many scale functions can be handled by changes to a shape's parameters. Change the radius of a circle or the height of a helix rather than using a Transform scale.

■ **Apply XForm modifiers**: Any time you want to Move, Rotate, or Scale an object as part of a modeling operation use an XForm modifier. Because an XForm is a modifier, it carries the effect of a Move, Rotate, or Scale operation into the loft.

■ **Use Loft Sub-Object mode**: You can Move, Rotate, or Scale a shape as a sub-object operation within the loft. Click the Sub-Object button and transform shapes on the loft path. These transforms are carried within the loft.

■ **Apply an Edit Spline modifier**: Using Edit Spline Sub-Object mode you can Move, Rotate, or Scale sub-objects, such as vertices and splines.

Which techniques are utilized depends on your modeling style and what conveniently fits into the workflow. In any case, do not transform shapes at the object level and expect the transform to show up in the loft.

Creating Shapes In-place

Source shapes for loft objects can be created in any viewport and any orientation. Lofts are assembled using the Local coordinate systems of the source shapes, so it doesn't really matter in which viewport the shapes are created.

The generation of the loft surface begins at the first vertex of the path and progresses to the end vertex. Shapes are placed on the path so that their local Z axis is tangent to the path and pointing in the direction of the path end. What you might consider to be the face or front of the shape is pointing to the end of the path.

The following list presents some techniques to follow in order to lay out loft shapes in a predictable manner.

- Draw the path shape from the base of the loft object to its top. In the case of horizontal objects, draw the path from the back of the object to the front.

- Draw shapes in the viewport that most closely matches the top or front view of the loft object.

TIP

Drawing the path and the cross section shapes all in the same view can make it difficult to predict how the shapes and the path will align. Use different views for creating the shapes and the path.

Changing the Cross Section Shape Pivot Point

When adding a cross section shape to a loft object, it is placed with the path running through the pivot point of the shape. You can preset where the path intersects the shape by moving its pivot point.

Imagine you are lofting a series of stars along a path, for example, and you want the path to pass through the top point of each star. You use the Affect Pivot Only button in the Hierarchy panel to move the pivot of each star before adding it to the loft. When you use Get Shape to add the stars to the loft, the path passes through the star's pivot location. Figure 9.3 shows a loft shape with its original pivot location and what happens if you change the pivot location and get the shape a second time.

FIGURE 9.3

Changing the pivot location for loft shapes.

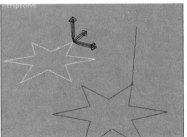

The pivot location is examined only at the time the shape is added to the loft. Changing a shape's pivot point after the shape is added to a loft has no effect.

The loft also ignores the pivot point orientation of a shape. Rotating a shape's pivot point has no effect when the shape is added to a loft. If you want to rotate a shape with respect to its local coordinate system and have that rotation show up in the loft, the shape must be rotated at the sub-object level.

Using Loft Creation Methods

Once the source shapes have been created, you are ready to create the loft object. Access the Loft Creation Methods by clicking the Geometry button in the Create panel and choosing Loft Object from the category list. The Loft button is inactive until a shape is selected. Clicking the Loft button displays the Creation Methods rollout as shown in Figure 9.4.

The first two shapes you use to create the loft must be the path shape and a cross section shape. More cross section shapes can be added, or the path shape replaced. The basic steps involved in creating a loft object are:

1. Create the source shapes.

2. Select an initial shape to start the loft.

NOTE

This first shape is very important because it sets the position and orientation of the loft object.

3. Access the loft object Creation Methods.

4. Get a path or a cross section shape.

FIGURE 9.4

Accessing the Loft Creation methods.

The choices in the Creation rollout set the shape clone method and determine whether the initial shape is a path or a cross section. The rule of thumb here as to which method to use is this: If you want the Path to stay put, select the path and use Get Shape. If you want the Cross Section to remain where it is, select the section and use Get Path.

Using the Cross Section as the Initial Shape

Click Get Path when you want to build the loft using the position and orientation of a selected cross section shape. Clicking Get Path accesses a pick mode in which only a single shape can be selected for the path. The cursor changes to display the Get Path cursor whenever it is positioned over a valid path shape. Clicking a shape when the Get Path cursor is displayed accepts that shape as the Loft path.

The shape picked as the path is moved to the selected shape's pivot point and rotated to align with the selected shape's original local coordinate system. This technique should be used when the base spline has been created or aligned at the point where the bottom of the loft belongs. Get Path then brings the path exactly to the shape.

For example, you might want to loft a docking hatch projecting from the side of a spaceship. To do this, you would create the outline shape of the docking hatch and use Normal Align to align the shape with the surface of the ship. Use Get Path to begin building the loft at the shape's location. Figure 9.5 shows the steps used for this example.

FIGURE 9.5

Lofting with Get Path.

Original 3D surface and shapes

Cross section shape

Loft using Get Path

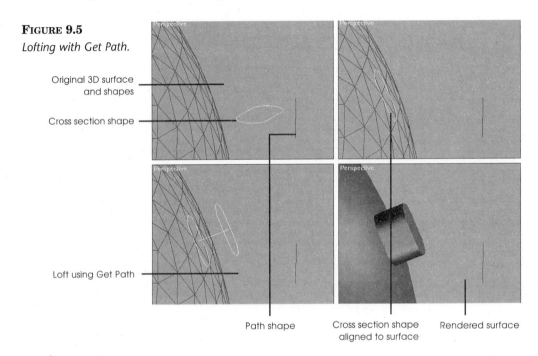

Path shape

Cross section shape aligned to surface

Rendered surface

Using the Path as the Initial Shape

Clicking Get Shape enables you to pick a starting cross section. This is the method used when building the loft using the position and orientation of a selected path shape.

When you click Get Shape, you are put into a pick mode in which you can select only a single shape. The cursor changes to display the Get Shape cursor whenever it is positioned over a valid cross section shape. When a loft object is first created, every shape is a valid cross section shape. Only when more shapes are added to the path do invalid cross section shapes begin to appear (see the section "Adding Shapes to the Path" later in this chapter). Clicking a shape when the Get Shape cursor is displayed accepts that shape as a cross section on the path.

The shape picked as the cross section is moved and rotated to align with the selected path. You might want to loft a spring for a coil-over shock absorber, for example. To do so, you would create a helix as the spring path and position it around the shock absorber cylinder. Use Get Shape to bring a cross section to the path. Figure 9.6 shows the steps used for this example.

FIGURE 9.6

Lofting with Get Shape.

Original 3D object and shapes

Path shape

Cross section shape

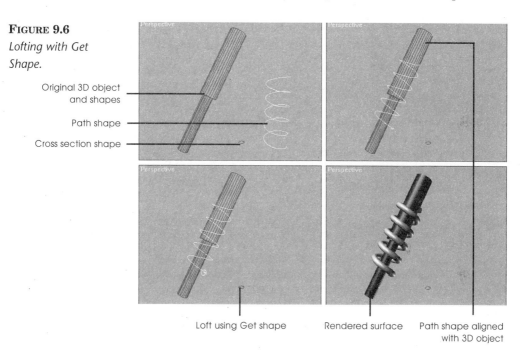

Loft using Get shape   Rendered surface   Path shape aligned with 3D object

NOTE

When using both Get Path and Get Shape, pressing Ctrl while picking a shape can flip the default shape alignment. If the first attempt at getting a path or cross section shape comes in with an undesired orientation, press Ctrl and pick the shape again.

Choosing the Clone Method

When shapes are brought into the loft, you can decide whether the shape is absorbed into the loft, or whether it is cloned as a copy or an instance. The choice you make affects how you edit the loft later on. Don't worry too much about making a wrong choice; 3DS MAX contains plenty of options you can use if you change your mind after you've brought in the shape.

Moving from the Create Panel to the Modify Panel

After the completion the basic loft (a path with a single shape), moving to the Modify panel permits ease of alteration. Using the Modify panel has the following advantages:

- You don't have to worry about dropping out of creation mode if you click a transform or some other button on the toolbar.

- The Modify panel displays the Loft Parameters anytime the loft is selected.

- You can use Sub-Object mode only in the Modify panel.

- You can use Loft deformations only in the Modify panel.

The Modify panel gives you a more stable environment, with more features, in which to finish your loft. Figure 9.7 compares Loft Parameters in both the Create and Modify panels.

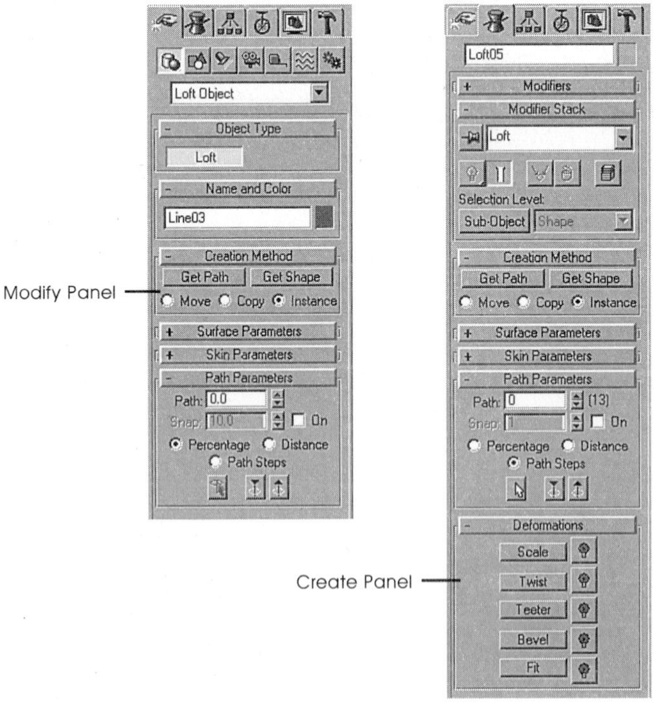

FIGURE 9.7

Comparing Loft parameters in the Create and Modify panels.

Modify Panel

Create Panel

Building Lofts with Multiple Shapes

You can create many loft objects using a single shape on a path, but placing multiple shapes on a path, as shown in Figure 9.8, can create many more interesting and complex objects.

FIGURE 9.8

Objects created by placing multiple shapes on the path.

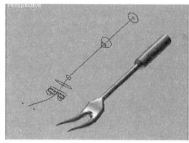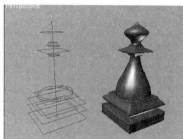

The following sections present the commands and techniques necessary to the successful building of lofts with multiple shapes. The main issues involve adding shapes at specified locations on the path, using shapes of differing forms, and a technique for making one shape appear to split into two shapes.

Adding Shapes to the Path

You can add shapes to a loft while you are still in creation mode, or at a later time by selecting the loft and accessing its parameters in the Modify panel. The basic procedure for adding shapes to the loft path is as follows:

1. Set the current path level in the Path Parameters rollout to specify where on the path the shape will be added.

2. Click Get Shape in the Creation Methods rollout.

3. Set the clone method for Move, Copy, or Instance.

4. Pick a shape.

Setting the Path Level

Set where on the path a shape is added using the options in the Path Parameters rollout (see Figure 9.9). A small X on the path represents the current path level.

FIGURE 9.9

*Options in the Path
Parameters rollout.*

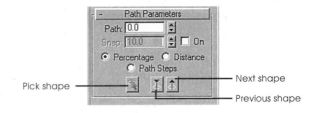

Except when Path Steps is on, entering a value in the Path field sets the current path level. This value can be specified as a percentage of the path length or as an absolute distance along the path. Set which method is used by choosing the Percentage or Distance radio buttons in the Path Parameters rollout. The following guidelines will help you decide which method to use:

- Choose Percentage to enter a value between 0 and 100 percent of the path length.

- Choose Distance to enter a value in current units to specify the distance measured from the first vertex of the path.

- Choose Path Steps to place shapes directly on the path steps and vertices. This is reminiscent of the way that 3DS R4 placed shapes from the 2D Shaper.

Using the Path Steps method may relocate shapes to unwanted locations. Only a single shape can be on a vertex or step, versus the almost unlimited area of the Distance or Percentage method. There is no data loss when shifting between methods. Adaptive Path Steps is disabled when choosing this Path Level method.

In both Distance mode and Percentage mode, you can check the Snap check box to specify a Distance or Percentage snap value.

Using Get Shape

After the path level has been set, click Get Shape to pick a shape to place at that level. Get Shape only allows for the picking of one shape at a time. As described in the previous section, the cursor changes to display the Get Shape cursor whenever it is positioned over a valid cross section shape. Valid shapes are defined as shapes that contain the same number of splines and same nesting order as the first shape used to create the loft.

If Get Shape is used at a level where a shape already exists on the path, the new shape replaces the current shape.

If you change your mind and decide to use shapes with a different number of splines or a different nesting order, you must first delete all the current shapes from the path.

Navigating Path Levels

After some shapes have been placed on the path, the remaining three buttons on the Path Parameters rollout are used to navigate the path levels containing shapes, as follows:

- Next Shape Moves forward along the path to the level of the next shape.

- Previous Shape Moves backward along the path to the level of the previous shape.

- Pick Shape Click any shape on the path to jump to the level of that shape.

The main reason to use these navigation controls is to quickly jump to a shape's level in order to replace that shape with a Get Shape operation.

Now that the basics of lofting methods have been discussed, the following exercise walks you through the steps for lofting a simple column. The column's base and capital use squares and the rest of the column uses a circle. Most columns stand vertically on the ground plane.

EXECUTING A SIMPLE LOFT

1. Open a new file in MAX. You may need to use File, Reset to get back to the default settings.

2. Create the path for the column in the Front view, using the Create/Splines/Line Object Type. Turn on the 3D Snap toggle to get a straight line. Start at the bottom of the viewport and finish near the top.

3. Create the cross section shapes in the Top view. Doing so orients the shapes in the same direction as the top of the column. Make a Circle that's 20 units in diameter, and a square also 40 units per side. The components should resemble Figure 9.10.

FIGURE 9.10

A Perspective view of the shapes and path for the Loft.

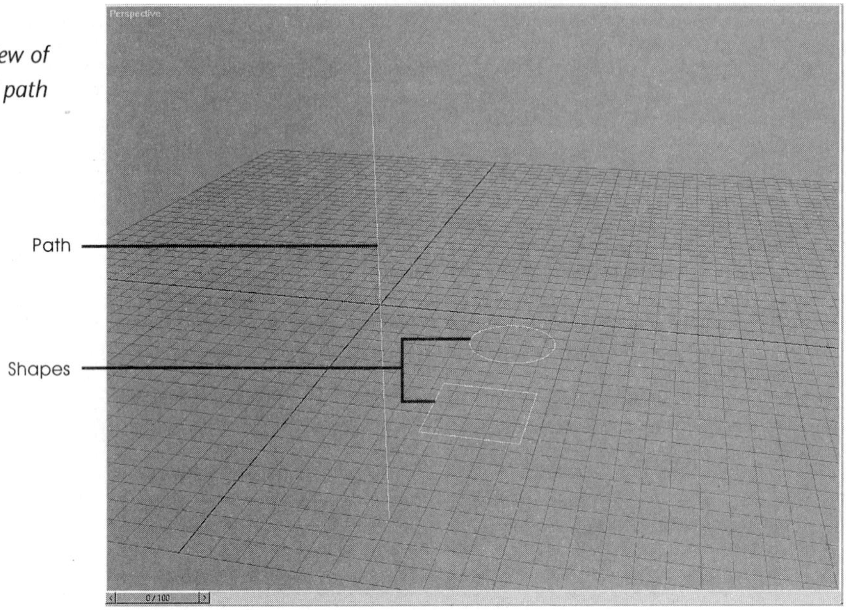

1. Select the path and go to the Loft Object section of the Create Geometry panel, which is accessed by using the down arrow next to "Standard Primitives." Click Loft and Get Shape for the Creation Method. Pick the square.

2. An Instanced copy of the square appears at the bottom of the path. The Path Parameters should have the Percentage method checked. Turn on Snap. Make sure that Snap units are set to 1.0.

3. Click the Up Arrow of Path. The parameter should read "10.0." Click the square again.

4. Change the Path parameter to 11.0. This time, select the circle.

5. Change the Path parameter to 89.0 (100 percent minus 10 plus 1).

6. Select the circle again.

7. Set the Path spinner to 90 and select the square. The result should look like Figure 9.11. If your results don't match, you can use the file column.max from the CD to troubleshoot your work.

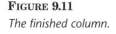

FIGURE 9.11

The finished column.

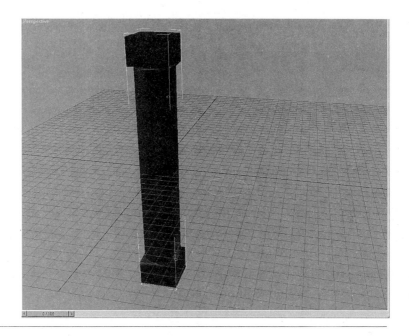

Changing from One Form to Another

Usually, creating a loft object involves placing multiple shapes of varying forms on the path. For example, you might loft a screwdriver using a combination of circles, squares, and custom shapes. You can place shapes of almost any form on the path and 3DS MAX will figure out how to generate a surface between them. The following two techniques will help to exercise control over how the surface is generated.

Matching the First Vertex

3DS MAX builds the loft surface by matching the first vertex of each shape on the path. If the first vertices are not aligned, there is a twist in the surface as the edges shift from vertex to vertex. Figure 9.12 shows two loft objects to compare the difference between misaligned and aligned first vertices.

Two ways of aligning the first vertices of your loft shapes are as follows:

- Apply an Edit Spline to each shape. Use the Make First button in the Edit Vertex rollout to assign a new first vertex that aligns with the other shapes. See Chapter 8, "Shape Modeling," for information about using Edit Spline.

■ Enter the Loft's Shape Sub-Object mode in the Modify panel. Select shapes on the path and rotate them until their vertices align. Transforming shapes at the Sub-Object level is discussed later in this chapter.

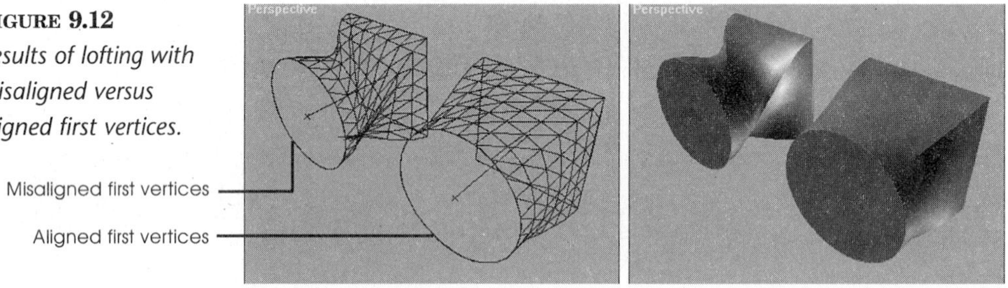

FIGURE 9.12
Results of lofting with misaligned versus aligned first vertices.

Misaligned first vertices ———
Aligned first vertices ———

TIP

Sometimes both of these techniques need to be combined to achieve the desired results.

Matching Vertices

It is unnecessary to have the same number of vertices in each cross section shape used in a loft object. 3DS MAX can interpolate between shapes with varying numbers of vertices. This feature is extremely helpful while building the loft object, but matching vertex counts and vertex positions between shapes maximizes your amount of control over the loft surface.

When shapes on the path are irregular or have widely varying vertex counts, the loft skin can twist and stretch in unpredictable ways. Such twisting of the loft skin can lead to rendering anomalies and difficulty when modifying the loft with other modifiers.

Loft modeling would be weak if limited to regular shapes, or shapes that all share the same vertex count. Post-creation modifications can significantly alter the appearance of the loft. Improving the loft skin involves inserting vertices into the loft shapes to control how the skin is generated.

Figure 9.13 shows a loft object that uses two very irregular shapes. The object on the left uses 3DS MAX defaults to interpolate from the four vertices in the circle to the 12 vertices in the cross. The interpolation creates a slightly irregular surface on the left object. The object on the right uses Edit Spline to add vertices to the circle that match the vertices in the cross. The right object has a more regular surface.

FIGURE 9.13

Matching vertices to control the loft skin.

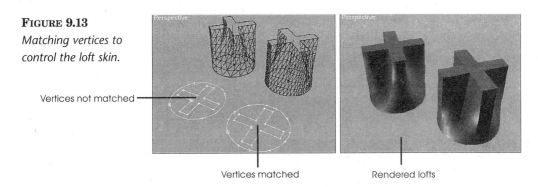

Vertices not matched

Vertices matched

Rendered lofts

Combining Open and Closed Shapes

Loft objects with slits or ruptures in their surfaces are modeled using shapes that transition from open to closed. Keep the following points in mind when combining open and closed shapes in the same loft:

■ All shapes in the loft must contain the same number of splines. A closed shape is a single spline. If the open shape has only one opening, then it is also a single spline.

■ If shapes are used with multiple openings, the closed shape must be divided into an equal number of splines as the open shape. See the following section for details about this technique.

■ The first vertex at one of the ends of the open shape is matched to the first vertex of the closed shapes, increasing the importance of matching first vertex locations when combining open and closed shapes in the same loft.

Figure 9.14 shows an example of combining open and closed shapes in the same loft.

Once you understand these techniques, it's a good time to try a more complicated loft. The following exercise lofts a Greenland-style sea kayak, illustrated in Figure 9.15, from a set of pre-drawn splines.

FIGURE 9.14

Combining open and closed shapes in the same loft.

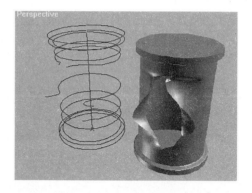

FIGURE 9.15

The finished sea kayak loft. The hull is see-through because the default material is one-sided.

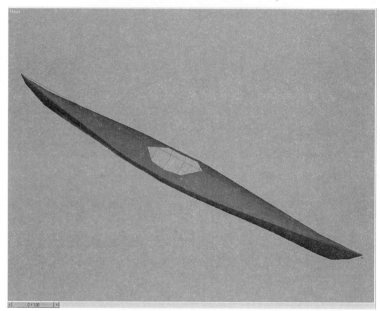

LOFTING THE KAYAK

1. Open kayak.max from the CD. Figure 9.16 shows the cross sections and the path of the kayak. On your screen, the cross sections are in green, and the path is in blue. An outline template has been frozen to aid in section alignment.

2. Select the spline farthest aft (the back of the boat), xc16. It's very small, so that you might want to use Select by Name. Go to Create, Geometry, Loft Object, and click the Loft button.

3. Click Get Path, and then click the blue path. An Instance of the path is now connected to xc16, and is highlighted. Under Skin Parameters, set the path steps to 0.

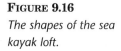

FIGURE 9.16

The shapes of the sea kayak loft.

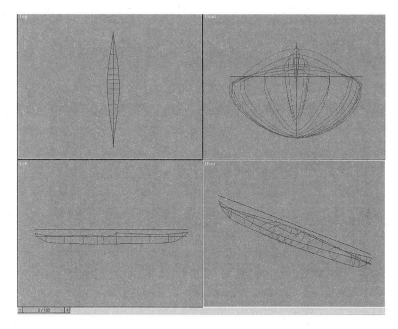

4. Under Path Parameters, select the Path Steps method. Click Yes in the warning dialog.

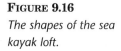

> **NOTE**
>
> Notice that the number 16 is in parentheses next to the Path level. The Path has been Refined so that its vertices align with the cross sections. This is a good method for section placement when precision is needed.

5. Increase the Path Level by clicking the Up Arrow next to Path. The yellow square moves to the next section.

6. Click Get Shape, and select the section under the yellow box.

7. Continue increasing the Path Level one step at a time, and selecting the shape under the yellow box. When completed, the kayak will be pretty lumpy and should look like Figure 9.17. Save the file and keep the file open; you will use it in the next exercise.

The reason for the lumpiness is that the cross sections are placed on the path at their respective pivot points. It is necessary to move the cross sections into position in order for the kayak to look right. The following exercise continues with the kayak and adjusts the cross sections to complete the figure.

FIGURE 9.17

The initial loft of the kayak.

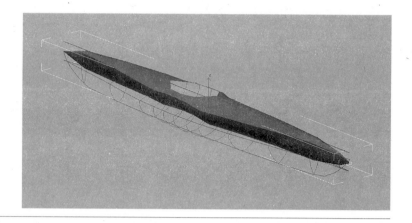

ADJUSTING THE CROSS SECTIONS TO COMPLETE THE KAYAK

1. Maximize the Left view to aid with placement. Go to the Modify panel with the loft still selected.

2. Access the Shape Sub-Object mode. Turn on Restrict to Y and move down the cross sections one at a time so that they lie between the frozen lines of the template (see Figure 9.18). Don't forget the very small section at the end point of the path.

FIGURE 9.18

Adjusting the cross sections in Sub-Object mode.

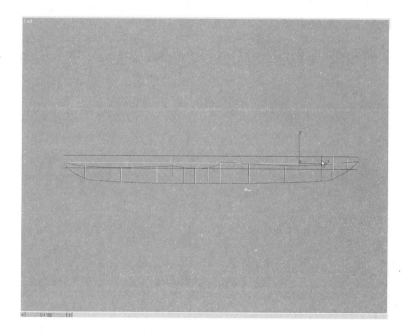

The kayak should look like Figure 9.15. If it doesn't, you can open kayak2.max from the CD to see how it was done.

Splitting from One Spline to Two

Another useful loft technique is to split the loft from what appears to be a single shape into multiple shapes. The rule that requires every shape in the loft to contain the same number of splines still remains inviolate; to work around this, resort to a little sleight of hand. Splitting a loft relies on using Edit Spline to divide what appears to be a single spline into multiple splines. You do this using Break in the Edit Vertex or Edit Segment rollout of the Edit Spline modifier.

Remember that the Break command splits a spline without changing its location or curvature. Break behaves differently depending upon whether you use it from the Edit Vertex or Edit Segment rollout of the Edit Spline modifier:

- In the Edit Vertex rollout, Break inserts a second vertex at the selected vertex and breaks the spline between those two vertices. Use this method when the spline already contains a convenient break point.

- In the Edit Segment rollout, Break inserts two vertices at the point you click and breaks the spline between those two vertices. Use this method when you want to break the spline in the middle of a segment.

Details on using the Break command of Edit Spline are presented in Chapter 8.

To split a loft from one spline into multiple splines, follow these steps:

1. Create all the shapes needed for the loft object.

2. Count the number of splines in the shape containing the greatest number of splines.

3. Apply Edit Spline to the remaining shapes and use Break in the Edit Vertex rollout to divide the shapes into the same number of splines.

4. Select a path and get the shapes to the loft.

The key to how well this technique works lies in the choice of break points and first vertices for all the splines. Because of working with multiple splines in each shape, there is a need to match the first vertices of all the splines in one shape with the matching splines in the next shape on the path. Three issues described in the following bullets drive the decisions made about where to break a spline and where to locate the first vertices:

- Place first vertices in a shape as close as possible to matching first vertices in the next shape.

- Divide splines to eliminate any ambiguity about how the loft skin transitions from one shape to another. This step often requires dividing splines into more pieces than seems necessary.

- Match up the first vertices of all the splines within the shape to avoid twisting.

This technique is tricky and not for the faint of heart, but it can pay off with incredible loft models.

NOTE

You will also need to apply an Edit Mesh modifier to the loft so you can weld the seams created by all of the split shapes and unify normals. See Chapter 11, "Mesh Modeling," for details of using Edit Mesh.

Controlling the Loft Surface

The Skin Parameters rollout contains many options that affect not only the display of the loft skin, but also the mesh density and interpolation methods used. A second rollout named Surface Parameters contains the options to control how the loft surface renders. Figure 9.19 shows both of these rollouts.

Setting Skin Detail

Some of the most important decisions made regarding loft objects concern the density of the surface mesh (or skin). As mentioned in previous chapters, there is a choice between a number of tradeoffs when making decisions about how complex to make a loft object. Consider the following when making your decision:

- Dense meshes show more detail than sparse meshes.

- Dense meshes deform more uniformly than sparse meshes.

- Dense meshes can render a smoother profile than sparse meshes.

- Sparse meshes consume less memory and display faster than dense meshes.

- Sparse meshes are often easier and faster to work with than dense meshes.

- Sparse meshes render faster than dense meshes.

FIGURE 9.19

Surface Parameters and Skin Parameters rollouts for loft objects.

You achieve the best all-around solution by creating the sparsest mesh possible to satisfy the deformation and rendering requirements of your project. You can also use the Optimize modifier to display a low-resolution model for modeling, while storing a high-resolution model for final rendering. See Chapter 15, "Map Channels and Map Types," for information about the Optimize modifier. The Level of Detail utility can help to ease the polygon count dilemma during animation by allowing for the automatic replacement of low-count poly models with their high-count equivalents.

Notice that many of the settings discussed next are similar to definable options in the Shape Interpolation rollout used when creating shapes. Remember that shape interpolation settings are not used when getting shapes into a loft. Instead, the loft object overrides shape interpolation settings with its own settings. For this reason, the Adaptive interpolation setting is used while creating loft shapes, to work with the smoothest shapes possible, and control mesh density using the loft options.

All of the parameters discussed in the following sections are found in the Skin Parameters rollout for loft objects.

Setting Path Steps and Path Level Interpolation

Path Steps set the number of interpolated steps between each level of the loft path. Path levels and path steps combine to define the number of divisions along the length of the path in much the same way Height segments define the number of divisions along the height of a cylinder. The higher the number of steps and levels on the path, the more dense the final mesh is.

The path levels' effect on the skin is determined by using the Adaptive Path Steps option. When Adaptive Path Steps is checked, a level is created along the path at the following locations:

- At every vertex on the path shape.
- At the location of every shape on the path.
- At every control point on a loft deformation curve.

When Adaptive Path Steps is unchecked, path levels are only created at path vertices, making for a more efficient surface. This capability comes with the possible price of a loss of detail, if some of the shapes are not located at a vertex or at an intermediate step setting.

The idea behind the Adaptive Path Steps option is to automatically create path levels wherever they might be needed, but Adaptive Path Steps can sometimes create more path levels than necessary. An example is when vertices on the path do not match up with important shape locations in the loft. In such cases, levels are created at both the vertex locations and the shape locations with the vertex levels possibly being unnecessary. Figure 9.20 shows the same loft comparing the difference between Adaptive Path Steps checked and unchecked. Both lofts use the default Path Steps setting of five.

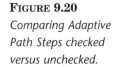

FIGURE 9.20

Comparing Adaptive Path Steps checked versus unchecked.

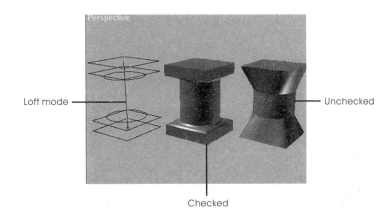

After determining how you want to handle the path levels, use the Path Steps field to specify how many intermediate divisions are wanted between each level. The higher the value, the smoother the path curves are represented in the loft skin. Memory requirements and rendering time go up accordingly. Some useful guidelines for setting path steps and how they are generated are:

- Set path steps lower if the path has few curves.

- Set path steps lower if Adaptive Path Steps is checked. (Usually the added path levels make up for the lower step setting.)

- Set path steps higher if you plan to deform the loft either through deformation curves or with modifiers.

- Set path steps higher if Adaptive Path Steps is unchecked.

One feature missing from the path steps equation is an Optimize option. If you remember from Chapter 8, "Shape Modeling," checking Optimize removes intermediate steps from straight segments. If loft surface efficiency is crucial, one of the following techniques to simulate optimization on the path can be very useful:

- **Edit Spline:** Apply an Edit Spline to the path and use Refine in the Edit Vertex rollout to add extra vertices along curved segments. After adding the vertices the path steps can be reduced to near zero. The extra vertices added to the path provide surface detail at the curves while the reduced path steps optimize the straight portion of the path. Some benefits of this technique are that the extra vertices go exactly where they are needed, and it works regardless of whether Adaptive Path Steps is checked or unchecked. The biggest drawback is that it is difficult to remove an added vertex in later edits.

- **Loft Deformation Curve:** Use a deformation curve to add extra levels when Adaptive Path Steps is checked. Details about using deformation curves are presented later in this chapter. The trick is to employ an otherwise unused deformation curve to insert extra levels. Leave the control points at the default values to prevent the curve from deforming the loft and reduce the Path Steps setting. For example, you could insert control points in the Teeter deformation curve but leave all the control point values at zero degrees of teeter. Teeter is a good choice for this technique because almost no one uses teeter deformation. The main advantages of this technique is that the control points are easily moved or deleted if you change your mind about where you want a level, and the control points can be animated. A relatively minor drawback is that you specify control point locations by percentage along the path, rather than picking exact locations on the path.

Setting Shape Steps and Optimization

The Shape Steps field and Optimize Shapes check box set the number of interpolated steps between each vertex of a cross section shape. These parameters apply to all shapes on the path and override the steps and optimize settings in each shape's base parameters. See the discussions of "Steps and Optimize" in Chapter 8 for more information.

Checking Optimize Shapes when there are both curved and linear shapes on the path can produce interesting results as 3DS MAX attempts to construct a surface between shapes with widely varying numbers of steps. Using Optimize Shapes in such situations reduces surface complexity but might make the mesh more difficult to deform.

Capping

The capping parameters determine whether 3DS MAX covers the ends of your lofted object and how those ends are constructed. Because 3DS MAX is a surface modeler, everything you create is hollow. Capping the ends of objects creates the illusion of solidity. If you want your object to appear open and hollow, uncheck the capping parameters to leave one or both of the ends uncapped.

You can choose between Morph or Grid capping methods. Morph capping uses fewer faces but does not deform as well as Grid capping. If you plan to use variations of the loft object as Morph targets, Morph capping is necessary.

If you do not cap your loft objects, the side walls appear thin and unrealistic. They will be one-sided by default, requiring the use of a two-sided material or a Normal modifier for the object to render properly.

NOTE

If you loft an object on a closed path, 3DS MAX ignores the Cap Start and Cap End check boxes. Examples of closed paths are circles or rectangles. A closed path has no ends, so the settings of the Cap check boxes have no meaning.

Setting Surface Characteristics

Surface characteristics affect the shape of a loft surface without changing the number of faces created. Parameters that affect surface characteristics are found in the Skin Parameters rollout and are discussed in the following sections.

Contouring the Surface

The Contour check box controls whether the shapes on the path turn to follow curves. In many ways, Contour is like the difference between the Skew and Bend modifiers. If Contour is checked, shapes turn as they follow curves in the path. Contour forces the shapes to stay perpendicular to the path, resulting in smooth bends where the path curves. If Contour is unchecked, the shapes remain parallel to the shape at path level 0, regardless of how the path curves, producing an object that is skewed from side to side rather than bent. Figure 9.21 shows the difference between a loft object with Contour checked and with Contour unchecked.

TIP

Usually, if you design a path with a curve, you want your object to bend. In such cases, check Contour.

FIGURE 9.21

A loft object with Contour checked versus unchecked.

Checked ———   ——— Unchecked

Banking the Surface

The Banking check box controls whether cross section shapes spin about the path (bank) as the path turns and climbs along its Z axis. The Banking parameter is used only when Contour is also checked. If Contour is unchecked, Banking is ignored.

When Banking is checked, 3DS MAX twists cross section shapes around the loft path based on the sharpness of the path bend and the rate of the path climb. When Banking is unchecked, cross section shapes hold a constant orientation to the path as defined by the shape at path level 0. Figure 9.22 shows the difference between a loft object with Banking checked and an object with Banking unchecked.

FIGURE 9.22

A loft object with Banking checked versus unchecked.

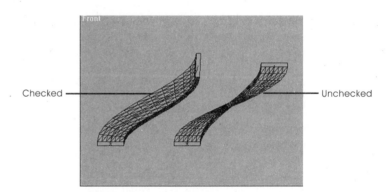

Checked ———   ——— Unchecked

If you want complete control over the bank angle, leave Banking unchecked and apply manual banking using Twist deformation. Loft deformations are described later in this chapter.

Using Constant Cross Section

New to version 2, this handy check box eliminates the need for conversion factors (1/cosine of angle of rotation, or 141 percent wider on a 90 degree angle turn) as a lofted shape goes around a hard corner. As in the previous selection, Contour must be checked for Constant Cross Section to work. Constant Cross Section produces mitered corners automatically, and for the most part, should always be left checked (see Figure 9.23).

FIGURE 9.23

Two loft objects with Constant Cross Section checked versus unchecked.

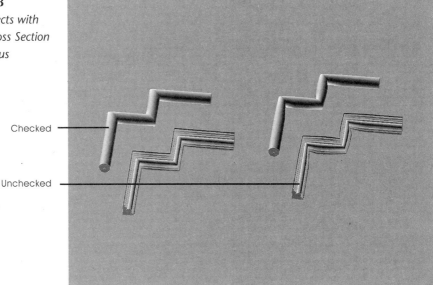

Choosing a Linear or Curved Surface

The Linear Interpolation check box controls how the skin is interpolated between shapes on the path. When Linear Interpolation is checked, the skin is stretched tight between the cross section shapes. When Linear Interpolation is unchecked, the skin appears looser and follows a spline curve through the cross section shapes.

TIP

Consider checking Linear Interpolation when you create machined objects. Uncheck Linear Interpolation when you create organic or sculpted objects.

Figure 9.24 shows the difference between a loft object with Linear Interpolation checked and an object with Linear Interpolation unchecked.

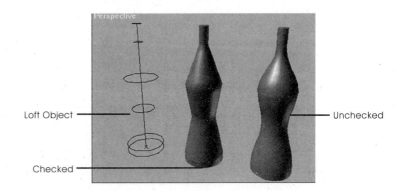

If complete control is needed over skin curvature, leave Linear Interpolation unchecked and apply manual skin curvature using Scale deformation. The description of loft deformations appears later in this chapter. Though we normally think of lofts as smooth, flowing shapes, many times it is necessary to have sharp transitions. Precision control of lofting attributes can make otherwise difficult tasks a breeze.

A typical problem for architectural visualization is putting a crown moulding up at the juncture of the walls and ceiling. The following exercise gives you hands-on practice using your lofting skills and experimenting with the Skin Parameters rollout and its various options.

LOFTING THE CROWN MOULDING

1. Open the file moulding.max from the CD. A room with window and door openings is frozen.

NOTE

Note that the file system units are set to feet, not the default scale of inches. It's important to use real world measurements as often as possible, as modeling tasks are far easier when measurements are consistent with their real-life counterparts.

2. Select the path at the top of the walls, and go to Create, Geometry, Loft Object. Click Loft and then Get Shape, and click the profile.

3. In the Front view, you can see that the moulding has been centered on the path—not what is desired here; the moulding needs to fit exactly into the corner. Go to the Modify panel, and click Sub-Object Shape.

4. Select the profile, and click Bottom and Right. The moulding is now in the proper position. Zoom and Arc Rotate in the User view to see more detail, so that your viewport looks like Figure 9.25. Turn off Sub-Object mode.

FIGURE 9.25

The crown moulding in place.

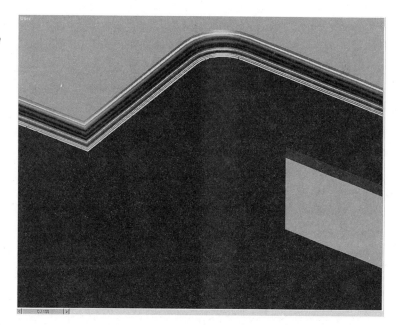

5. Open the Skin parameters rollout, and check Display Skin. Turn on Optimize Shapes, and set the Shape Steps and the Path Steps down to 1. The loft still looks good, but now has far fewer faces.

6. Try turning off Constant Cross Section, and observe what happens to the right angle corners.

Building the crown moulding in the above manner was a real time- and polygon count saver over making individual mouldings and trying to cut them together. You should consider lofting whenever the need arises to have shapes flow along a path.

Setting Surface Rendering Properties

The final set of surface properties affects neither the number of faces nor the shape of the skin. Rather, the parameters in the Surface Parameters rollout control how the surface appears when it is rendered.

Smoothing the Surface

Two smoothing check boxes determine whether the object appears as a smooth or faceted surface. This is similar to checking or unchecking the Smooth check box in a cylinder's base parameters. The difference is the control over whether the length, the width, or both are smoothed.

Checking Smooth Length instructs 3D Studio MAX to smooth the object along the length of the path. This produces smooth bends as the object follows a curved path, but it renders the cross-sectional shape as faceted. Smooth Length is checked for the top left object in Figure 9.26.

FIGURE 9.26

The effects of smoothing.

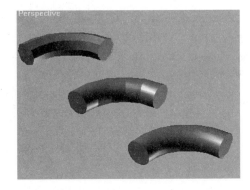

Checking Smooth Width smoothes the perimeter of the object. This setting produces smoothly curved cross sections but renders curves in the path as faceted. Smooth Width is checked for the middle object in Figure 9.26.

Checking both parameters renders a fully smoothed object. Figure 9.26 shows three 90-degree bends rendered as fully smoothed, smooth length only and smooth width only. Both smoothing options are checked for the bottom right object in Figure 9.26.

Mapping the Surface

Many loft objects defy the capabilities of the standard mapping types found in the UVW Mapping modifier. Use a loft object's own mapping parameters to apply mapping coordinates that follow the path and surface deformations of a loft object. Figure 9.27 shows an example of a drinking straw mapped with lofted mapping coordinates. This effect would be nearly impossible to duplicate using other mapping techniques.

FIGURE 9.27

Example of using lofted mapping coordinates.

When Apply Mapping is checked in the Surface Parameters rollout, the following parameters are enabled:

- **Length Repeat**: Sets the number of times the map repeats along the length of the path.

- **Width Repeat**: Sets the number of times the map repeats around shapes on the path.

- **Normalize**: When checked, mapping is scaled evenly along the length of the path and around the perimeter of the cross section shapes. When unchecked, mapping is scaled unevenly based upon the spacing of levels and vertices. For most applications, Normalize should remain checked.

TIP

The UV Tiling fields in the Map Coordinates rollout of the Materials Editor is used to control the number of map repetitions when both repeat fields are set to 1.0 and Normalize is checked. Using this technique, map tiling can be animated, whereas the loft repeat fields cannot be animated.

Editing Loft Shapes

After the cross section shapes are placed on the path, the shapes might require revision. You can edit shapes on the loft path by entering Shape Sub-Object mode in the Modify panel, as shown in Figure 9.28. You can now select shapes in the loft object using standard selection techniques.

FIGURE 9.28

Accessing Sub-Object Shape mode of a loft object.

The next sections describe the various ways to edit loft shapes. Techniques, such as using alignment commands in the Shape Commands rollout and accessing the shape's Modifier Stack to apply modifiers and Edit Spline, are used for the following editing tasks:

- Comparing Shapes

- Positioning Shapes

- Modifying Shapes

- Animating Shapes

Comparing Shapes

If there are multiple shapes on the path, there is often a need to compare the position, orientation, or vertex alignment of one shape to another. If your path is perfectly straight, you can easily compare them by setting up a user view that looks down the path. If the path is curved, Compare in the Shape Commands rollout can be used to display two or more shapes in a window based on their spatial relationship to the path.

The shapes desired for comparison are displayed in the Compare window by clicking the Pick Shape button in the window's toolbar. The Compare window displays each shape on its own local XY plane, ignoring the effects of path curvature, Contour, and Banking. The path is represented as a cross that is common for all displayed shapes. Figure 9.29 shows an example of a loft object with a curved path and how the shapes appear in the Compare window.

FIGURE 9.29

A loft object and shapes in the Compare window.

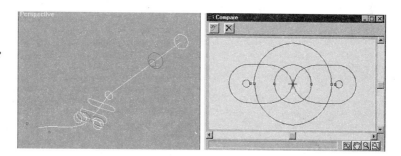

The Compare window's primary use is to examine and compare the first vertex location of shapes on the path. The first vertex of each shape appears as a small box.

Positioning Shapes

There are many ways to change the position of a shape on the path. You face your first shape position decision when you specify the Path Level before getting a shape. After that, shape positions can be changed using techniques in Shape Sub-Object mode.

Remember that a shape is placed on the Loft path with its local X and Y axes perpendicular to the path and its local Z axis tangent to the path. Changing the position of a shape is performed in the shape's Local coordinate system.

Changing Path Level

The path level of a shape can be changed by selecting the shape and changing the Path Level in the Shape Commands rollout, or by moving it along its local Z axis. See the discussion about transforming shapes in a later section.

Using the Alignment Buttons

Select a shape and click one of the buttons in the Align section of the rollout to change the position of the shape with respect to the path. The alignment buttons move a shape in its local XY plane in the following manner:

- **Left**: Moves the shape so that its negative X axis boundary is on the path.

- **Right**: Moves the shape so that its positive X axis boundary is on the path.

- **Center**: Moves the shape so that both its X and Y axis extents are centered on the path.

- **Top**: Moves the shape so that its positive Y axis boundary is on the path.

- **Bottom**: Moves the shape so that its negative Y axis boundary is on the path.

- **Default**: Moves the shape so that its Pivot Point is centered on the path.

Figure 9.30 shows a shape in the Compare window with its original orientation after Get Shape and the results of using each of the alignment functions.

Deleting Shapes

The only way to remove shapes from the path is to delete them in Shape Sub-Object mode. Clicking the Delete button in the Shape Commands rollout or press Del on the keyboard removes the unwanted shapes.

FIGURE 9.30

Using the loft shape alignment buttons.

Shape in original position —

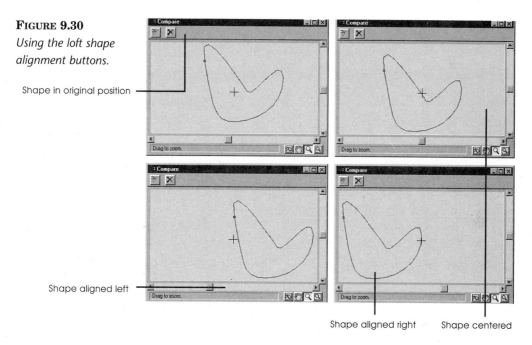

Shape aligned left —

Shape aligned right   Shape centered

Using Transforms

Transforming shapes on the path is similar to transforming any other object. The main difference is that the transform coordinate system is locked to the shape's local coordinate system and the transform center is the point where the path intersects the shape's local XY plane. Transforming loft shapes in Shape Sub-Object mode follows these special conditions:

- Moving shapes along the X or Y axis moves them perpendicular to the path.

- Rotating shapes along the X or Y axis is similar to using teeter deformation.

- Rotating shapes about the Z axis spins the shapes about the path and is similar to using twist deformation.

- Scaling shapes is similar to using scale deformation.

- All Scale and Rotate transforms applied to a loft shape can be removed by clicking Reset in the Shape Commands rollout. Reset does not affect the results of moving or aligning a shape.

- Transforms applied to shapes on the path are internal to the loft object and are not reflected in any instances of the shapes elsewhere in the scene.

This last point is important to remember. Scale and Rotate transforms applied to shapes in the scene are discarded when you use Get Shape to bring them into a loft. If you want to scale or rotate loft shapes, consider using Get Shape first and then scaling or rotating the shapes on the path using Shape Sub-Object mode.

Modifying Shapes

Modifiers such as Bend, Twist, or Edit Spline can be applied to shapes in a loft. Modifiers such as Extrude and Normal that convert a shape to another object type make the loft object invalid and cause the loft to disappear from the screen. The loft object can still be rescued by using the Select Objects dialog, and deleting the offending shape modifier to restore the loft to a valid object.

Apply a modifier to a loft cross section shape using one of the following two techniques:

■ To apply a modifier directly to a loft shape:

1. Select the shape using Shape Sub-Object mode.

2. Choose the Shape object below the loft object in the Modifier Stack. The Shape object appears in the Modifier Stack only after having selected a shape in Shape Sub-Object mode.

3. Apply a modifier to the shape.

   Working directly on shapes in a loft, however, can be confusing because of differences between the shape's and loft's local coordinate systems. Most people find it easier to apply modifiers to an instance of a loft shape somewhere else in the scene, which is the main reason for using the Instance option with Get Shape.

■ To apply a modifier to an instance of a loft shape, complete the following steps:

1. Select an instance of the shape in the loft rather than selecting the loft itself.

2. Apply a modifier to the instance.

   If the Instance option is not used with Get Shape, an instance of the loft shape can be put back to the scene using the Put button in the Shape Commands rollout.

Animating Shapes

Animating the shapes on the loft path can generate a great variety of deformations along the path. Three techniques for animating loft shapes include:

- Animating the base parameters of a parametric loft shape.

- Animating modifiers applied to loft shapes.

- Using XForm modifiers with Edit Spline to animate individual vertices of loft shapes.

Notice that all these methods involve working with a shape's modifier stack. Animating instances of a loft shape is the easiest way to set up this kind of animation.

Editing Loft Paths

Edit loft paths in the same way cross section shapes are manipulated: by entering Sub-Object Path mode in the Modify panel (see Figure 9.31).

FIGURE 9.31

Accessing Sub-Object Path mode of a loft object.

To edit loft paths, complete the following:

1. Select a loft object.

2. Choose Loft from the base of the Modifier Stack in the Modify panel.

3. Click the Sub-Object button and choose Path as the Sub-Object level.

The path is automatically selected when entering Path Sub-Object mode because each loft object has only one path. There is only one button in the Path Commands rollout for putting the path to the scene and all but one transform is inactive in the toolbar. The only transform available is rotation about the local Z axis of the path shape at path level 0.

Applying modifiers to path shapes follows the same procedure described for modifying cross section shapes. As with modifying cross section shapes, the best method is to modify an instance of the path shape somewhere else in the scene and observe the effect on the loft.

The following topics describe a few techniques involving the creation and modification of loft path shapes.

Closed Paths

A closed path is any path in which the first and last vertices are welded together. A path can be created where the first and last vertices are coincident, but unless they are welded together 3DS MAX considers such a path as open.

Closed paths exhibit two important traits, as follows:

- They are not capped because they have no beginning and no end.

- When smoothed along their length, they show no seam where the first and last vertex meet.

Backtracking Paths

An extremely powerful but seldom mentioned modeling technique is the capability of a path to backtrack over itself. The best way to demonstrate this is to examine an object that uses this technique. Figure 9.32 shows a model of a mechanic's socket created using a backtracking path.

FIGURE 9.32

Example of an object using a backtracking path.

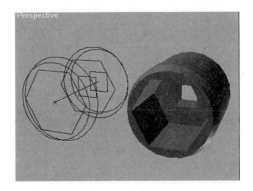

At first glance, this loft seems to use a straight path. Only when the skin of the loft is examined, or the vertices on the path are manipulated, is the truth revealed. What had seemed to be a simple, straight path is actually a three vertex closed path that doubles back on itself. Figure 9.33 is a diagram of the object with the backtracking path pulled apart to show the shape locations. Table 9.1 describes what is happening with this object.

FIGURE 9.33

*Diagram of a back-
tracking path.*

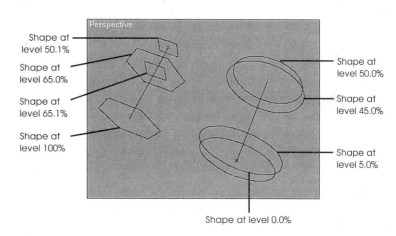

Shape at level 50.1%

Shape at level 65.0%

Shape at level 65.1%

Shape at level 100%

Shape at level 50.0%

Shape at level 45.0%

Shape at level 5.0%

Shape at level 0.0%

TABLE 9.1

Analysis of the Socket Path

Level	Inside Description	Level	Outside Description
0.0%	Circle solid. Forms front face of socket.	50.1%	Square hole. Path changes direction back toward level 0.0%. Shape transitions from circle solid to a square hole.
5.0%	Circle solid. Forms outer surface of socket.	65.0%	Square hole. Continues drive hole of Socket.
45.0%	Circle solid. Continues outer surface of socket.	65.1%	Hexagonal hole. Transitions to socket hole of Socket.
50.0%	Circle solid. Forms back face of socket.	90.0%	Hexagonal hole. Path closes with level 0.0%. Shape transitions from hexagonal hole to circle solid.

A convenient way to visualize this type of path is to think of an athletic tube sock. Stretch the sock out, and the path runs down its center—the fabric represents the surface created by shapes on the path. If the open end of the sock is rolled back on itself, the path doubles back as well; what was once the inside of the sock becomes the outside. Closing the path is like snipping off the toe of the sock and stitching the two ends together.

By examining the Socket path, you can see that at the location where the path doubles back on itself, the shapes on the path become holes drilled back into the object. Many people use Booleans to create such forms, but more efficient and predictable objects can be created using this loft technique.

An interesting side effect of backtracking paths is their effect on smoothing. If you render the Socket, 3DS MAX tries to smooth around the flat end where the path doubles back on itself. When lofting backtracking paths, uncheck the Smooth Length option and manually smooth the object by applying a Smooth modifier.

Animating Loft Paths

Animating the loft path shape can create many popular effects, such as wiggling snakes or growing vines. Three techniques for animating a loft path shape include the following:

- Animating the base parameters of a parametric loft path shape.
- Animating modifiers applied to a loft path shape.
- Using XForm modifiers with Edit Spline to animate individual vertices of a loft path shape.

Notice that all these methods involve working with the shape's modifier stack. Animating instances of a loft path shape is the easiest way to set up this kind of animation.

Using Loft Deformation Curves

Only so much can be accomplished by manipulating the path or by placing different shapes along the path. A vital tool for creating lofts is the use of Deformations. This section looks at the first four deformations of Scale, Twist, Teeter, and Bevel. The last deformation option, Fit, is discussed in its own section later in this chapter.

Before moving on to specific deformation commands, you should be familiar with the general aspects shared by all the deformation grids. Figure 9.34 shows a typical deformation window. In general, the vertical lines represent the levels on the path (solid lines for levels containing shapes, and dotted lines for path vertices and other levels). The horizontal lines represent values on the deformation grid and the curve is a deformation control curve. A deformation window can display up to two curves, a red curve for X axis deformation, and a green curve for Y axis deformation.

FIGURE 9.34

Example of a loft deformation window.

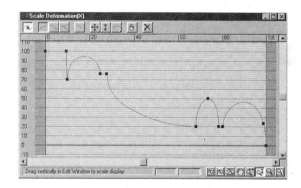

The following list points out a few general rules to keep in mind when working with deformation grids:

- Snap works with the vertical grid values. If the snap spacing is set at 10 units and Snap is on, you are constrained to increments of 10 percent in the Scale grids and increments of 10 degrees in the Twist and Teeter grids. Snap has no effect on horizontal path position in the graph.

- Always check the setting of the Make Symmetrical button. Scale and Teeter both use the Make Symmetrical button in the deformation window toolbar. Always decide whether the adjustments are to be independent or symmetrical about the X and Y axes, and examine the Make Symmetrical button before making adjustments.

- Remember that the deformation curve is not the path, nor is it the profile. The shape and control point spacing of the deformation curve are completely independent of the path. Although the shape of the deformation curve controls the shape of the lofted object, it does not necessarily look like the final lofted object.

- The number of Path Steps and the setting of the Adaptive Path Steps check box control how closely the deformation grid is followed. The value of the deformation curve is applied at each path step and path level. If Adaptive Path Steps is checked, new levels are inserted for every control point added to the deformation curve.

Animating the value and path percent of the deformation curve control points can have fantastic animated effects. An example is animating a bulge moving through an object by animating scale deformation. To animate a deformation control point, follow these steps:

1. Select a control point on a deformation grid.

2. Turn on the Animate button.

3. Drag the time slider to a new frame.

4. Move the control point or enter new path percent and deformation amount values in the fields at the bottom of the deformation window.

Using Scale Deformation

Use the Scale deformation window to alter the X and Y scale factor of the shape. The scale base point is always on the path. A powerful modeling option is to use scale deformation on shapes that are not centered on the path. Figure 9.35 shows an appliance handle lofted by scaling a shape with its edge aligned to the path.

FIGURE 9.35

Scale deformation for an appliance handle.

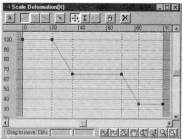 

Using Twist Deformation

The Twist deformation grid controls rotation of the shape about the path. Similar effects are available by placing multiple shapes on the path and rotating the shapes at the Shape Sub-Object level, but most people find the Twist deformation grid easier to use.

Using Teeter Deformation

Teeter enables you to rotate the shape about the X and Y axes perpendicular to the path. Teeter can often be used with a shape offset from the path to generate objects that are difficult to create by any other means. Figure 9.36 shows an arch lofted with an Y axis Teeter.

FIGURE 9.36

Teeter deformation for an arch.

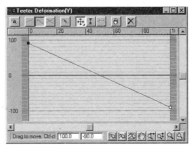 

Using Bevel Deformation

The Bevel deformation window performs a function similar to the manufacturing process of chamfering. Use the deformation curve to specify the exact units to cut back or push out a shape from its original size. Bevel deformation is best used in small increments near the ends of the loft.

Bevels work best with large blocky shapes. Thin shapes or shapes with sharp points are difficult to bevel. For such shapes, consider using the Bevel modifier or other modeling methods.

Sometimes the attempted bevel causes a shape to self-intersect and produces rendering errors or even causes some faces on the object to disappear. Remember that the Bevel deformation curve can be used to add size to a shape, as well as cut it back.

TIP

Often, changing the direction of a bevel enables the operation to succeed. Using one of the other methods of beveling, Adaptive Linear or Adaptive Cubic, can also improve the results.

Figure 9.37 shows the result of a Bevel deformation on the letter "M." Note the very small scale of the deformation, and that the effect is isolated to the extreme ends of the letter. Using the Bevel deformation's Zoom Extents might be necessary to get the scale of the effect down to a manageable size. Bevel deformations are quite similar to Scale deformations; the main difference being that Bevel deformations use an exact number, while Scale deformations use percentage.

FIGURE 9.37

The use of a Bevel deformation to chamfer the ends of a loft.

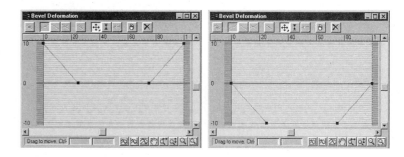

Creating with Fit Deformation

The final deformation is Fit deformation, which is used to create three-dimensional objects by specifying the profile of the top, side, and front view of the object. This command has a few restrictions and can be the most daunting Deformation to use, but it is still an extremely fast and powerful technique for generating complex geometry.

Fit deformation relies on the specification of three shapes that serve as the profiles of the three-dimensional object. 3DS MAX refers to these three shapes as Fit X, Fit Y, and the Loft Shape. Fit X and Fit Y represent the top and side views of the object and actually serve as scaling limits for the Loft shape. The Loft shape can be thought of as the front or cross-sectional view of the object, and it is the shape actually passed along the path.

When these shapes are being created, arrange them the way a draftsman would draw them by hand. That is, draw the top view first, project the side view out to the right or left, then project the front view down. This technique makes it easy to check that the top view and side are the same length. Figure 9.38 shows an example layout of shapes ready for import into the Fit Deformation window.

TIP

An important consideration in modeling is that Fit Deformations align the local X axis of the fit shape with the length of the path. The most predictable results are produced when you draw your fit shapes in the Top view with the X axis aligned with the length of the shape.

FIGURE 9.38

Three shapes ready for fit deformation.

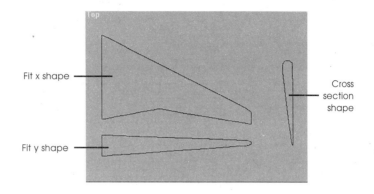

Figure 9.39 shows the Fit Deformation setup and the loft object created from the shapes in Figure 9.38.

FIGURE 9.39

A fit deformed loft object created from the shapes in Figure 9.38.

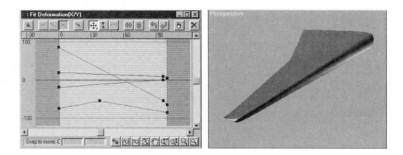

Your chances for a successful Fit deformation can be dramatically improved by adhering to the following rules of thumb:

- The top view shape (Fit X) and the side view shape (Fit Y) should be the same length. This is not an explicit requirement, but if the two shapes are of unequal length, 3DS MAX scales the first Fit Shape that is imported to match the length of the second Fit Shape.

- A level is placed on the path for every vertex in both the top view (Fit X) and side view (Fit Y) shapes. Getting these vertices to line up can reduce the complexity of the final object.

- Multiple front view or cross-sectional shapes can be placed on the path. If the cross section of your object changes along the path, import another shape at that level. Many users overlook this capability. See the example on lofting a shampoo bottle later in this chapter for an example of this technique.

- The path can be edited after clicking Generate Path. In fact, the Generate Path button can be ignored altogether, and the fit shapes can be used on any path that you manually create.

Four basic restrictions for the Fit X and Fit Y shapes are outlined in the 3D Studio MAX User's Guide:

- The fit shapes must be a single spline. No outlines or nested shapes are allowed.

- The fit shape must be closed.

- No curved segment can extend beyond the first or last shape vertex in the X axis.

- The fit shapes cannot contain undercuts. An easy way to check for undercuts is to imagine a line aligned with the shape's local Y axis passing through the shapes. If the line can be placed in a position so that it cuts through the shape in more than two places, there's an undercut. Figure 9.40 shows undercuts revealed by this technique.

FIGURE 9.40

Invalid undercuts in fit shapes.

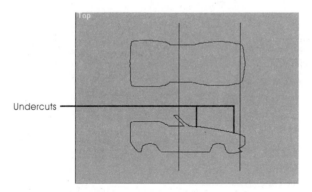

Only the first restriction, shape must contain a single spline, prevents the use of the shape as a fit shape. Shapes with extremely curved segments or undercuts can be selected as fit shapes and 3DS MAX flattens the curves and ignores the undercuts.

The following example shows how to use Fit deformation to loft a shampoo bottle. An important variation is the use of multiple shapes on the path to enable the circular top to flow into the oval bottle shape.

LOFTING A SHAMPOO BOTTLE WITH FIT DEFORMATION

1. Open the file shampoo.max from the CD. The path and shapes, are shown in Figure 9.41.

FIGURE 9.41

Source shapes and path for the shampoo bottle.

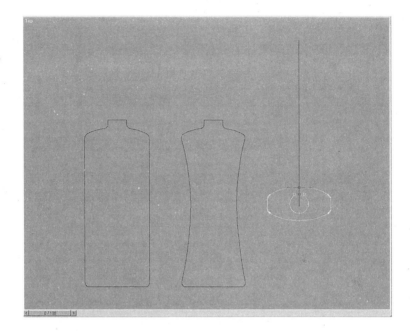

2. Select the path shape and click Loft in the Create panel. Using Get Shape, select the circle. A cylinder appears.

3. Set the Path Parameters Path to 5 and hit the Enter key. Be sure to use the Percentage method for this operation. Select the oval shape. The bottle should now resemble Figure 9.42.

4. With the loft still selected, go over to the Modify panel. Open the Deformations rollout and select Fit. The Fit Deformation window appears, as shown in Figure 9.43. Clear Make Symmetrical and then click Get Shape. Click the left-hand bottle shape.

5. The shape is going across the loft rather than along it, so rotate it 90 degrees with the Rotate 90 CCW button. Next, click the Display Y Axis button and select the concave bottle shape. Rotate it 90 degrees as before.

6. Click off Get Shape, and click the Zoom Extents for the Fit Deformation Window. Click Display XY Axes to see both of the shapes together.

FIGURE 9.42

Preliminary loft of the bottle.

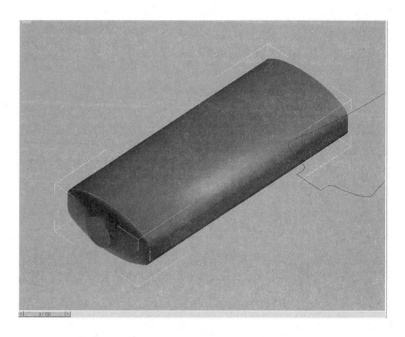

FIGURE 9.43

The Fit Deformation window.

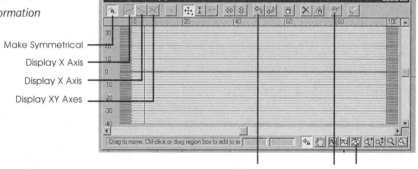

Make Symmetrical

Display X Axis

Display X Axis

Display XY Axes

Rotate 90 Degrees CCW   Get Shape   Zoom Extents

7. The bottle looks pretty good, but it's a bit too fat. Click Display Y Axis and select all of the points on the sides of the bottle, excluding the area around the opening. Using Scale Control Point, bring the sides in so that the window looks like Figure 9.44.

The bottle is now complete and is ready to have a top built and a label texture mapped on so that it may stand proudly on a supermarket shelf. That's beyond the scope of this exercise, but you may want to try those extras on your own. If your bottle doesn't look like Figure 9.45, carefully review the steps in this exercise, or open shampoo2.max from the CD to troubleshoot your model.

FIGURE 9.44

The Fit Y Shope's vertices selected, and moved into position.

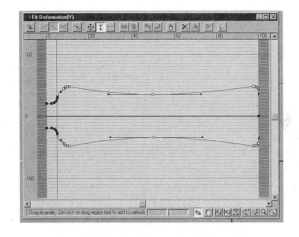

FIGURE 9.45

The finished shampoo bottle.

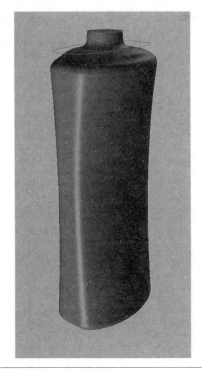

In Practice: Building Loft Objects

■ **Creating Source Shapes**: Almost any shape can be used as a path, cross section, or fit shape with only a few critical shape restrictions. Path shapes must contain a single spline. All cross section shapes on the path must contain the same number of splines and same nesting order. Fit shapes must contain a single closed spline.

■ **Creating a Loft**: Create a loft by starting with the path shape or the first cross section shape. The method chosen sets the original position and orientation of the loft object. You can also choose to add the original shape to a loft or add a copy or instance of a shape. Usually adding instances is the best choice for ease of editing.

■ **Editing Loft Shapes**: Enter Shape or Path Sub-Object mode in the Modify panel to edit shapes in the loft object. If shapes were added as instances, modifiers can be applied to the instanced shape outside the loft and the changes are reflected in the shapes inside the loft.

■ **Using Deformations:** Use the Deformations rollout in the Modify panel to apply changes in scale, rotation, and beveling to the shapes on the path. Fit Deformation can also be used to create complex objects based on top, side, and cross section profiles.

■ **Animating Lofts**: You can animate the Sub-Object object shapes that make up a loft and animate the control points on the deformation curves. The easiest way to animate loft shapes is to animate the modifiers applied to instances of the shape.

Chapter 10

COMPOUND OBJECTS

As you go beyond simple object creation and modification, processes used to model become more varied and difficult to categorize. Compound object creation starts to fall in to an odds and ends category, but with more similarities between the different compound object plug-ins than plug-ins found in the Utilities panel. This chapter goes over those similarities and then moves into how the functions that are different in each compound object works. In this chapter the following topics will be covered:

- Basics of compound objects
- Creating compound objects from compound objects
- Working with Booleans
- Morphing geometry
- Conforming an object to another
- Embedding a shape into the surface of a mesh
- Scattering objects
- Object connecting

Basics of Compound Objects

Through the compound object functions of MAX you can combine different geometric objects to create a single object in a number of variations. Every compound object has at least two operands and each operand is used in different ways depending on the compound object type.

The following is a list and short description of the six compound objects that ship with MAX R2:

- **Boolean:** Uses two objects to create a result that is either a union, intersection, or subtraction of those two objects.

- **Morph:** Uses one seed object and one or more target objects to change the shape of the seed object over time.

- **Connect:** New to MAX R2. Creates geometry between the holes of a base object and one or more target objects.

- **Scatter:** New to MAX R2. Distributes an object either over the surface of a second object or according to transform parameter settings in the command panel.

- **Conform:** New to MAX R2. Projects the faces of one object onto the surface of another. Frequently used to create Morph targets.

- **ShapeMerge:** New to MAX R2. Projects a shape (spline object) into the surface of a mesh object embedding it in the surface.

Compound object plug-ins are found in the command panel under Create, Geometry-Compound objects in the object type drop-down list. In order to access a compound object button, a geometric object must be selected. Particle systems, Space warps, lights, cameras, and helpers are all not eligible for use in compound objects. NURBS are useable in some compound objects but are sometimes auto-converted to a mesh or spline.

Working with Operands

When you create a compound object, the selected object is moved into the compound object as Operand A. If you want to use that object again for another operation you need to clone it before creating the compound object. Cloning it as an instance is a good idea as it allows for easy editing, removing the need to go down the edit stack to get to it.

The remaining operand(s)—some compound object processes allow more than two operands—can be taken as copies, references, or instances of the original object or the objects can be moved into the compound object definition. The default method of handling the remaining operands (copy, move, instance, reference) varies in each compound object, based on what is most likely to be convenient to the user (see Figure 10.1).

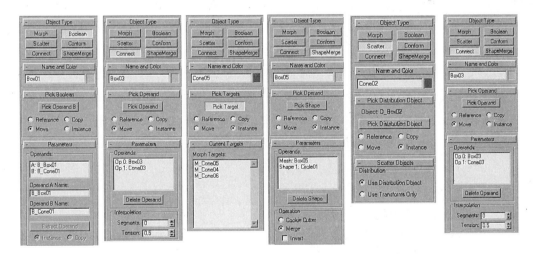

FIGURE 10.1

Different compound object panels showing varying methods of selection of the second or remaining operands. Notice which cloning method is set as the default for the different compound object types.

You can click the Pick Operand B button and pick another Operand B as many times as you want. In Compound objects that have only one Operand B, this can be a problem. If the first time you pick Operand B you had Move chosen and then you pick a new Operand B, the original operand is deleted from the scene. If you pick the wrong object as Operand B, click Undo before picking another Operand B.

Accessing Operands

You can access any of the operands through the Modify panel by clicking their names in the command panel and then going into and down the modifier stack. The fields that hold the operand names are not consistent from plug-in to plug-in, but they usually can be found under the Parameters rollup in the Operands field. Because the operands remain as objects, you can interact with them as you would any other object when editing. Each operand maintains its original modifier stack and can be modified from the Command panel. The operands can be transformed at the sub-object level and you can even animate them, creating amazing effects.

Displaying Operands

Methods for displaying operands are also not consistent in the various compound objects, but you can always view the components used to create any compound object for as long as it remains a compound object.

For some of the plug-ins, you have the ability to control when the changes you make update—either automatically, onscreen, or only in the rendering (see Figure 10.2). This is very useful when just one small change in a parameter takes a while to update on the screen because of high face count.

Creating Compound Objects from Compound Objects

Because compound objects are objects, you can use them to make other compound objects. Two ways exist in MAX R2 to create compound objects from compound objects: collapsing the stack of the compound object and nesting.

4.

The
the
like
pur
sar
Sul
A)
wit
Fig

FIGURE 10.3

The four types
Boolean opera

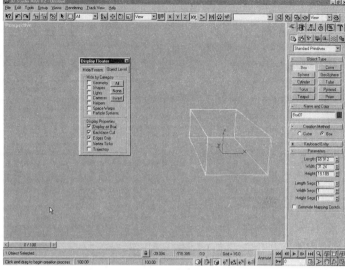

FIGURE 10.2

Use the Update options in the command panel and Display as Box in the Display Floater to increase
the speed of display of compound objects in the viewports.

Collapsing the Compound Object's Stack

The first way is to collapse the stack of the compound object that you want
to use as the Operand A in the new compound object to an editable mesh.
The main advantage of this method is you don't bring along the extra calculation involved with recalculating the compound object's result, lending
speed to rendering and providing more stability to MAX. The main disad-
vantage is that you no longer have access to the original compound object's
operands for later modification.

TIP

If you intend to collapse any object in MAX, consider making a copy of it and hiding it, or use
Save Selected under the File pull down, to save it to a file. This allows for later modification and
replacement simply by unhiding or merging the copy.

Boole

W
th
op
C
le
cr

T
B
o]
B
b

N

W

FIGURE 10.4
A Boolean compound object's Track View listing.

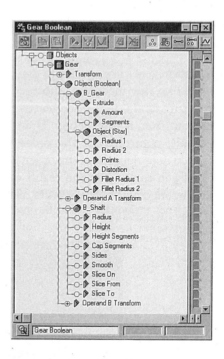

Boolean are now sub-object operands. The remaining options perform the Boolean result with either a copy, instance, or reference of the selected object. In all three cases, the object chosen for Operand B remains unchanged, and the Boolean result is performed with the new operand object. In these cases, it could appear that nothing has happened until you move or hide one of the two objects.

New in R2 if you used the default move option when choosing Operand B you now have the choice to extract an instance or copy of it or Operand A using the Extract Operand button when in the Modify panel. Another way to make an instance from an object that is already an operand is through Track View. Copy the operand's object definition (indicated by a blue circle in the hierarchy) to the clipboard and paste it into another object's definition as an instance. You can use this technique in reverse as well, completely redefining the geometry of the defining operands—changing all the square holes to round ones, for example.

NEW TO R2

Animation contained in an object used for Operand B is no longer discarded. Operand B's transforms, however, are added to Operand A's transforms if Operand A's transforms are animated. To see this, open Boolean Operand Animation.max on the CD and play the animation.

After a Boolean object has been created, you can change the choice of Operand B from within the Boolean object's Modify panel with the same choices that were present at creation. Choosing another operand is the same as replacing the operand's object definition in Track View, except that you have the option to make a reference, which is not present in Track View.

After you create a Boolean object, you can return to each operand's modifier stack in the Modifier panel (see Figure 10.5). The first time you enter a Boolean object's Modify panel neither of the operands is selected, so the Modifier Stack shows only itself in the stack. To modify a particular operand's stack, you need to choose it from the Operand's list. The operand you select now displays its stack. You can adjust any modifier in the stack and add new ones that affect the operand object before the Boolean. There are no additional restrictions on what parameters can be animated.

To transform an operand, you must activate the sub-object mode for the Boolean object. In this way, you can think of the operands as being similar to gizmos, with the exception that, unlike gizmos, operands have their own modifier stacks.

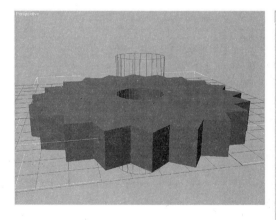
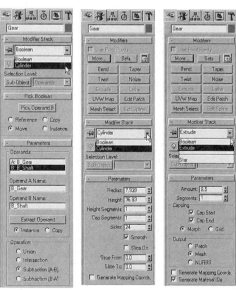

FIGURE 10.5

Using the Boolean's Modify panel to manipulate the operands.

Update Options

The Boolean Update options control how the Boolean calculations are actually performed. For complex objects, the Boolean calculations can be time-consuming. These calculations also slow the editing of other objects, if these objects are instances or references of Boolean operands. If you are experiencing a pause in your modeling, change the Update method from automatic to one of the other options. The Manual option is the most conservative method, and it provides you with the most control over when the operations are evaluated. This mode is recommended for complex models. The When Rendering method does not evaluate the operation until a production rendering is performed and then returns the updated result to the scene. The When Selected method is somewhat unreliable when it actually updates the result and should not be your first choice.

To speed modeling operations, keep the operands simple. When you complete your Boolean operations and modifications, return to the operand's earlier definitions and increase their density. If both operands are instances, increase all their complexity and then manually update the result all at once.

T IP ——————————————————————————————————

You can terminate a lengthy Boolean calculation by using the Escape key while the wait cursor is being displayed. When you terminate the calculation, the Update mode is automatically changed to Manual so you can now control the exact time an update should be calculated. Also, Display is changed to Operands from Result.

Interactive Booleans

When you enter a Boolean's sub-object mode, you can transform the operands independently of one another. Whichever operand has its name selected is the one eligible for movement, rotation, or scale. When the operand is manipulated at the sub-object level, you are literally performing an interactive Boolean because as you move one operand the other remains stationary, and the display updates the Boolean result as you move the operand. For small models or fast machines, this is often in real time.

Understanding the Boolean Display options is the key to making interactive changes. The default option, Result, shows the result of the Boolean operation. If you change to the Operands option, both A and B operands are displayed as if no Boolean occurred. Although easy to see, the fully displayed operand obscures the Boolean result, which makes you work blind to some extent. In practice, the best combination is usually to choose Result with the Show Hidden Ops option enabled. This displays the missing operands as wireframes (but only in shaded viewports) and provides you with the information of exactly where the operand is and its current influence to the Boolean operation.

NOTE

You can assign another object's controller to an operand or a unique Path, Look At, or Expression controller for effects such as animated drill holes or Bugs Bunny's rabbit hole swimming through the ground.

Nested Boolean Objects

You are not limited to one Boolean operation per object. You can perform as many as you like, with each operation creating its own set of operands, one nested inside the other. The only "limit" is the practical number you wish to navigate.

After creating a Boolean object, you can perform additional Boolean operations to the same geometry by selecting the object as Operand A for a new Boolean compound object. Each time you perform a Boolean operation on an object, you are actually making the original an operand of a new Boolean object. You are thus creating a "Boolean tree" composed of single branches—a very linear progression of steps. Every Boolean operation you conduct can be accessed at a later time, although the method for doing so takes a bit of practice because it all occurs in the Modify panel. Figure 10.6 shows the results of making three successive Boolean operations. A Box subtracts a Sphere, then subtracts a Cylinder, and finally subtracts a Cone.

TIP

To advance deeper into a Boolean tree, continue to choose the Operand A and then go to the next Boolean in the stack. You can use Operand B's stack to go forward, but you can use only Operand A's stack to go backward in the edit history. You can also navigate an object's modifier stack via Track View. If you click the blue ball next to an object, or diamond next to a modifier, you are taken to that level in the modifier stack.

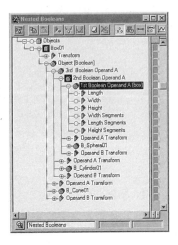

You need to be careful when performing several Boolean operations, one after the other—a common situation when you are chamfering or filleting all the corners of an object and have the pieces all arranged. After you complete an operation and so complete the Boolean compound object, you must end the Boolean process or your subsequent pick will replace the operation you just performed and delete that object from the scene. To end the Boolean process, just right-click in the active viewport and then click the Boolean button to define the next Boolean object.

Boolean Characteristics

When creating a Boolean object, the smoothing groups and material IDs of the separate objects are preserved. Mapping, unfortunately, is totally removed and needs to be applied after the final Boolean result. If your object's mapping was assigned with UVW modifiers, you can restore it. If you make a copy—not an instance—of your original object or modifier, assign a new UVW Map after the Boolean, and use the modifier's Acquire function to restore it. Note that this operation does not work for procedural mapping assignments.

Mapping coordinates are removed because the vertices of the Boolean result are always welded. Having unique Material IDs for each operand before the

Boolean operation assists greatly in making the face-level selection for mapping coordinate assignment. You can then use Mesh Select to choose faces by Material ID.

Warning

Adding an EditMesh modifier to the stack of a Boolean, especially if it's nested, can add another degree of instability to the operation.

Material IDs are probably your most valuable tool in controlling the final surface results of a Boolean object, especially for nested Booleans. Giving each operand a Material modifier with a separate ID means you have a guaranteed method of selecting the faces after the Boolean operations are complete.

Sometimes a Boolean result appears to have kinked or warped imperfections. These imperfections are often caused by similar smoothing groups acting with each other in ways they shouldn't, or vertices not being welded so smoothing cannot occur. If you see these imperfections, apply an EditMesh modifier, select all the vertices, and perform a Weld Selected. If the imperfections persist, you need to analyze your smoothing group assignments (before or after the Boolean operation).

In most cases, it is far easier to select critical regions before they become part of a Boolean operation. If you know a portion of the model requires unique smoothing (for example, the chamfer in figure 10.7), assign those faces a unique smoothing group or material ID so that after the Boolean operation they have the proper smoothing.

FIGURE 10.7

Assigning surface characteristics before Boolean operations occur.

This discussion may make it seem as if you must put in a considerable amount of forethought and planning before you can even perform a Boolean operation, when in fact, the Modifier Stack enables the process to be much less structured. It is common practice to create the Boolean objects quickly and then return to earlier in the operand's history to make smoothing and material assignments as necessary. Again, note that this is much easier to do if you have instanced the objects before they became operands.

Carving with Boolean Subtraction

Boolean subtractions tend to be the most commonly used of the operation types and is, therefore, the default. These subtractions can be thought of as "taking a bite from," "sculpting," "carving," "removing from," "drilling," "punching," or whatever analogy makes the most sense to you.

Successful sculpting with Boolean subtractions begins with an understanding of what shape you want the eventual subtraction to be. This form leads you to think of what geometry is required to accomplish that pattern. Many times the object being subtracted bares little resemblance to the finished result; the object simply provides the shape of the carving knife that slices the surface. The second operand can be thought of as a "chisel" or "router bit" that creates a particular "groove" in the first object. A Boolean subtraction is also a good—if not the primary—method for creating chamfers and fillets on existing objects.

NOTE

You may find it useful to maintain a selection of "carving tools" as Bézier shapes that you can extrude, loft, or lathe for Boolean subtractions. More complex Boolean cutting forms can be saved as meshes and merged when needed.

Scooping New Objects with Boolean Intersection

A Boolean intersection creates the object that would have otherwise been "carved out" with a Boolean subtraction. The result is sometimes difficult to visualize, but it can create geometry that would have otherwise been very difficult to model (see Figure 10.8). In this situation, the second operand is acting like a six-directional cut.

FIGURE 10.8

*Complicated geometry
formed from a Boolean
intersection.*

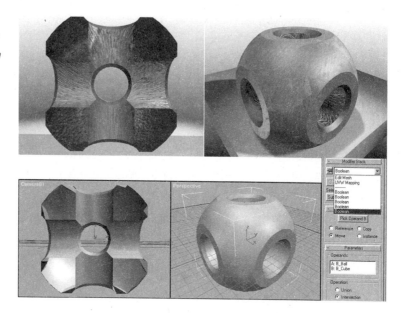

One of the primary uses for a Boolean intersection is to retrieve what would be taken "out" in a Boolean subtraction. Often, you'll find it necessary to use the piece that "fell on the floor" in an animation. You may want to show the piece that is punched out from a metal die, for example. To do this, copy the original objects and perform two Boolean operations, thereby creating the "cut" object and what was "cut out."

Modeling with Boolean Union

A Boolean union operation combines the two operands and removes any overlapping geometry. Before performing a union, you should consider carefully whether the union is even necessary. If the underlying intersection can be seen, then using the union is the correct choice. If the intersection of the two is hidden, you may be better off allowing the objects to simply intersect. A common use of union is when you need smoothing groups to continue across the joint. In this case, the Boolean union is probably just the first step in a more complex modeling sequence.

A Boolean union is most commonly used with objects that appear to be "solid." The surface is closed, and there is no need for an interior structure, so the object is only one face thick.

You also can use a Boolean union to create two elements that could be separated for other uses with Detach after collapsing it to an editable mesh. When you use a Boolean union operation to edit objects, no mesh is formed where the geometry once overlapped. As the resulting elements are separated, there is a hole in each mesh element where they were joined. To use this technique effectively, it is best to assign each operand a unique Material ID# so you can select the faces easily (by Material ID#), after collapsing the Boolean to an editable mash when performing the detachment. This technique is especially useful for creating same shaped holes between the two objects on which you intend to use the Connect compound object command.

Creating Booleans with the Collapse Utility

What this chapter has covered on Booleans until now has been, to a large part, to accommodate animators that want to use the animatable nature of the operands in the Boolean compound object. To save steps when intending to collapse your Boolean to an editable mesh anyway, use the Collapse Utility in the Utility panel (see Figure 10.9). Not only does it bypass the complexity of editable operands, it also enables you to Boolean more than one object at a time. In the case of Union and Intersection, the result of such an operation is obvious, but what about subtraction? Whichever object is selected first is the operand from which all other objects are subtracted.

The following exercise shows the steps for doing a multiple object Boolean subtraction to create holes in a house frame for the placement of doors and windows.

MULTIPLE OBJECT BOOLEAN USING THE COLLAPSE UTILITY

1. Open a copy of Collapse Boolean.max from the accompanying CD. In the Top view, select the house frame.

2. Hold the Ctrl key down and select each of the blue boxes that make the holes for the doors and windows (they are a selection set labeled Holes).

3. Under the Utility tab in the command panel, choose the Collapse button.

4. In the Collapse To area, choose Single Object, check the Boolean option, and choose Subtraction.

5. Pick the Collapse Selected button to complete the operation.

Notice there is a cancel button while the operation is being performed. Note also that this function does not undo in MAX R2.

FIGURE 10.9

The Collapse utility under the Utility tab of the command panel.

Considerations for Better Booleans

The Boolean code in 3DS MAX is extremely general, enabling it to work between arbitrary surfaces. This generality means, however, that not every object forms a valid Boolean and that some "valid" results may have artifacts (such as long splinter faces) or undesirable results. The following checklist should assist you in troubleshooting and building models that are Boolean-friendly:

- The normals for the entire surface must be unified without any rogue faces pointing the wrong direction. Face normals are used in determining the direction of the surface and the resulting Boolean.

- The mesh must be properly built, meaning that faces that share an edge must share two vertices, and that an edge can be shared only by two faces. (The inner vertex core faces from a lathe is a typical nightmare situation for the latter rule.)

- Ensure that all vertices are welded. Welding all the vertices manually with EditMesh may be necessary, even between consecutive Boolean operations.

- Coplanar faces, especially those within the same operand, are troublesome to deal with and should be avoided. One of the worst cases is back-to-back coplanar faces (easily created by making a primitive with a zero height).

- Booleans work reliably only between single elements. If either operand is composed of multiple elements (such as the Teapot or Hedra), only one element can be successfully acted upon at a time.

- If the operation is not successful, turn off the Optimize Result option at the bottom of the rollout so the final pass that checks for coplanar faces is not calculated. This can sometimes make an invalid result valid.

- If the operation is still not successful or is producing splintered faces, try a slight move transform adjustment between the two operands.

- Increase the operand's level of detail, especially at the area local to the actual Boolean operation.

Do not let this checklist scare you into avoiding Boolean operations. Most of these options work on the first try, especially if your geometry adheres to the first three rules, which it probably will if it was built within 3DS MAX.

When animating Boolean operations, you may encounter a sudden "flash" or surface "twitch" on a frame or two, most likely the result of the Boolean operation failing or creating odd faces on that one frame. Considering the drama and impact of an animated Boolean, it is worth the time to advance the animation frame by frame to examine the Boolean result. If a condition arises that causes a rendering error, simply adjust the geometry slightly on that frame to get a better result and continue. If numerous adjustments are needed, you may be better off assigning a Linear controller to the operand's position track and adjusting nearly every frame.

Booleans offer a more geometric and mechanical method of animating the shape of your object but if you want a more organic method Morphing is one way.

Morphing Geometry

Morphing, which is short for Polymorphic Inbetweening, is an attractive method of animating surfaces because of its relative ease of use compared to its result. The modifier tools of MAX go a long way to allowing anim atable object modification, and now, with the animatability of individual vertices in R2, that ability is even further extended. Morphing offers results that can't be created any other way, particularly with the new barycentric morphing controller. You can now specify weighted mixes of any number of morph targets at any key. This means that you can create a target to represent the movement of an eye blink and can schedule that blink any number of times over an animation. You can then create another target that represents the smile of a mouth on that same object and schedule it also at any time in the animation.

This section starts with the basics of morphing and then moves into the more complex processes.

Morphing Basics

Before you begin morphing, you must create a seed object and target objects. These objects should be geometric—either mesh, shape, or NURBS—and both the seed and the target objects must be of the same geometric type. Likewise, the seed and target objects need to have the same number of vertices, control vertices, or control points in order to produce a morph.

The following exercise will take you through using the Morph command to make a bird fly.

MORPHING A BIRD FLYING

1. Open a copy of Bird Morph.max from the accompanying CD-ROM. Select the left-most bird object labeled Seed in the scene.

2. Make a copy of Seed by holding the Shift key down and dragging it below the original. Rename it to **Seed Copy**.

3. Click the Morph button in the Compound Objects command panel to start the morph command.

4. Slide the animation slider to frame 25, click the Pick Target button and select the second bird labeled 1st Target object.

5. Slide the animation slider to frame 50 and select the third bird marked 2nd Target.

6. Slide the animation slider to frame 75 and select the fourth bird labeled 3rd Target.

7. Slide the animation slider to frame 100 and select the second bird labeled 1st target.

8. Slide the animation slider to frame 125 and select the Seed Copy.

9. Play the animation. Figure 10.10 illustrates part of this exercise.

FIGURE 10.10

Using the Morph compound object to create the animation of a bird flying.

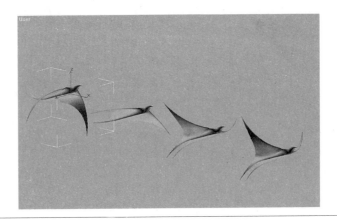

The Morph Compound Object command is quite stable and works with large number of faces if you are willing to be patient during a morph's construction. Although the limitation of the need for the same number of vertices in all operands is present, this can be overcome by the use of the Conform Compound Object, which enables you to shrink wrap an object around another. This is covered in detail in the Conforming an Object to Another section of this chapter.

TIP

When you animate vertices, they show up in Track View and are labeled by number. As of R2, there is no utility for changing the assigned number of a given vertex, but this is still a good way to compare objects and their vertex numbers to aid in predicting results. You can temporarily select and animate the vertices you are concerned with, view them in Track View, and then undo to remove the animation.

As mentioned before, you can animate the individual vertices of any geometric object lessening the need to morph between geometric objects—except in two cases. In the first, you may want to flip back and forth between multiple versions of an object, particularly when working with a face. Dealing with a large number of vertices of a particular object in track view is possible but may be more cumbersome than morphing. The second would be if you wanted to combine the changes of two or more already morphed objects.

NOTE

It is possible to nest a morph object in another morph where the new seed is also a target in the nested morph. The results create a kind of feedback effect with unpredictable results, but it doesn't create any instabilities in the program if you happen to do it by accident.

With the new Barycentric Morph controller (now the default), you can now assign percentage weights to each of the targets at any frame, allowing you to fine-tune minor changes. It also makes it easy to move back and forth between targets over the animation. This enables you to set keys for individual movements of, say, a face part like a blink or to do combinations of movements in concert to create, for instance, a surprised expression. The use of the new Barycentric Morph controller is covered in more detail in Chapter 25, "Using Controllers and Expressions."

TIP

Some third party plug-ins also give you weighted morphing, their advantage being ease of use because of their well-designed interfaces. Check out MorphMagic at www.3Dcafe.com, and Smirk at www.lambsoft.com.

Morph Object Materials

The material for a morph object is determined by the material assigned to the seed object. Materials of the targets are disregarded.

There are two basic methods in MAX R2 for working with materials for morphs. One is to use a blend material, animating the shift from one sub-material to the other (see Figure 10.11). You will also need the Unwrap Object Texture utility (found on the accompanying CD) and a paint program like Photoshop. The Unwrap utility takes the mapping coordinates of your 3D mesh and flattens them out to create a 2D plan map representing your wire frame. This is usually for morphing from one distinct object to another, such as from a bird to an airplane. The second method has to do with mapping and involves the use of the new Unwrap UVW modifier.

FIGURE 10.11

Using the Blend material for morphing.

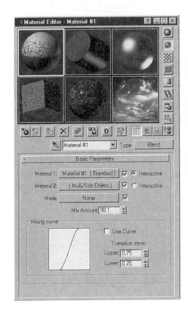

The following steps are a guideline to give you a direction that can be gone in to deal with morph materials.

1. You must create a material for the morph from and to operands. Using the Unwrap Object Texture utility, create a plan map to use as a foundation for building the final map for each object (see Figure 10.12).

FIGURE 10.12

An object and its mapping coordinates unwrapped using the Unwrap Object Texture utility.

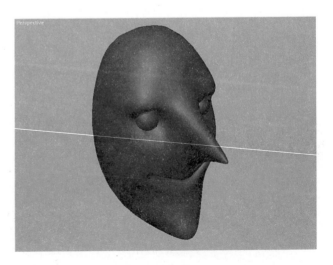

2. In a paint program, cut and paste the different components of your material to match their position on the object. If your original object has many material IDs, Unwrap allows you to render out each set of ID's assigned faces separately.

3. In the Material Editor create a blend material and assign the maps to the diffuse map slot in each sub-material.

4. After creating the morph object, assign the blend material and animate the Blend parameter from one sub-material to the other over the time of the morph.

The second method for dealing with materials for morphs applies to objects that are simply changing topologically and only need one standard material. The Unwrap UVW modifier lets you edit the relationship of the UVW mapping used in the mesh's material, to vertices on the mesh. That process is animatable allowing subtle adjustments over the length of the morph animation.

The limitation of same vertex operands for morphing has been essentially overcome with a new compound object called Conform.

Conforming an Object to Another

The main purpose of the Conform Compound Object is to allow morphing between two mesh objects with different numbers of vertices. This is called a radial Conform and will "shrink-wrap" a mesh around another (see Figure 10.13). This enables you to create, say, a couple of spheres with the same number of vertices, place each one around a separate template object (where each template object has different numbers of vertices), and conform each sphere to each template. You can then use the spheres as operands in a morph because they now have the same number of vertices.

The secondary purpose is to conform an object to match the variations of a surface. This is used more in a linear fashion where all vertices project in a parallel direction. An example would be a magic carpet floating over the surface of a landscape conforming to the contours.

Conform Basics

The faces of the wrapper object are projected to the surface of the wrap-to object according to seven possible choices in the command panel. Vertex Projection Direction options are as follows:

■ **Use Active Viewport:** Projects vertices of Operand A to the surface of Operand B parallel to the Z axis of the current viewport. This is one way to allow an object to glide over the surface of another taking on the shape of whatever portion of the wrap-to object the glider object is over. You can adjust the view and recalculate the projection until satisfied with the results.

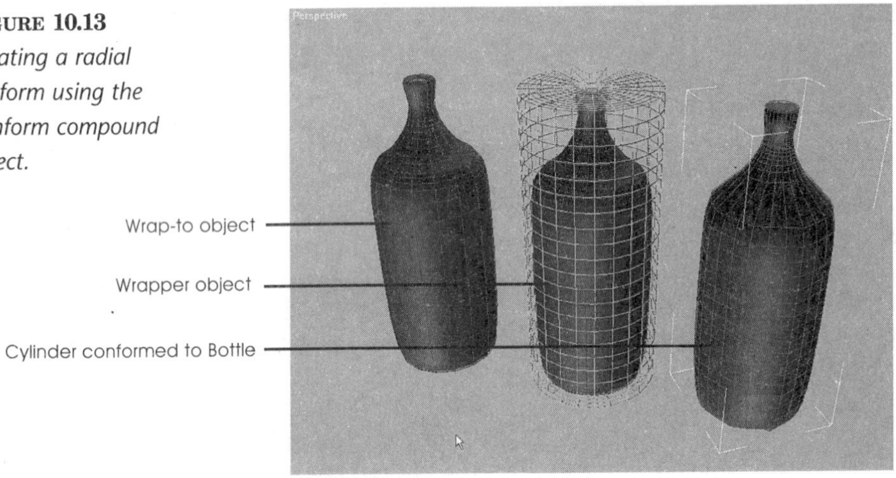

FIGURE 10.13

Creating a radial conform using the Conform compound object.

Wrap-to object

Wrapper object

Cylinder conformed to Bottle

■ **Use Any Object's Z Axis:** Much the same as Use Active Viewport but uses a selected object's local Z axis to determine projection direction.

■ **Along Vertex Normals:** This projects the vertices of the wrapper object along its own vertex normals anywhere those vertices will intersect the wrap-to object. Those vertices that don't intersect the wrap-to object will project the distance set in the Default Projection Distance field.

■ **Towards Wrapper/Wrap-to Center/Pivot:** These options allow a radial projection of the vertices of the wrapper object towards a point defined by the pivot or center of an operand. The center of an operand is the same as that object's bounding box's center. When using the pivot option of the Wrap-To object, if you want to change the pivot placement you can do it to the wrap-to object using Affect Pivot Only under the Hierarchy panel (see Figure 10.14). You must then re-pick the Wrap-To object.

Radial Conform

A radial conform shrinks an object around another where the faces of the Wrap-to object collapse towards some common point determined by the option chosen in Vertex Projection Direction area of the command panel. Deciding what wrapper object is best for a pair of potential operand templates is decided by the average shape of both. The common shape you choose sometimes requires trial and error, but your choice will almost always require a high number of vertices whatever the shape. You can sometimes use a copy of Operand A to wrap over Operand B's template by carefully considering its orientation.

FIGURE 10.14

Clicking the Affect Pivot Only button in the Hierarchy panel enables you to set the position of a Wrapper or Wrap-to Pivot for use in a Conform.

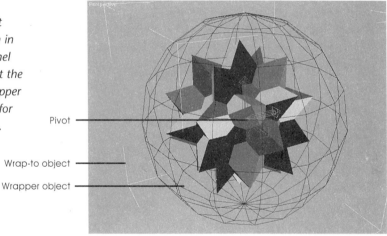

Pivot

Wrap-to object

Wrapper object

NOTE

Finding the balance between number of vertices in a wrapper object (or any object) and how fast your workstation calculates your choices is always a juggling act. Always start with a lower number of vertices for your wrapper object increasing that number until you reach an acceptable result. Also to speed your work you can set your Update option to When Rendering or Manually.

The following exercise will take you through the process, but be warned that due to the high number of vertices and faces, wait times could be high depending on the power of your machine. Be sure to turn on Manual update where possible.

USING CONFORM TO MORPH FROM A HEAD TO A MONITOR

1. Open a copy of Morph.max from the CD and observe that the intended wrapper objects are 50x50x50 boxes changed to Display as Box in the Display command panel.

2. Select the box (box01) surrounding the head, start the Conform command from the Compound Objects panel, and under Display set Update to When Rendering.

3. Choose Towards Wrap-To Center as the Vertex Projection direction, set stand off distance to 0, and click Hide Wrap-To Object under Update.

4. Pick the head as the Wrap-to object. This may take some time to calculate so be patient.

5. Repeat steps 3 and 4 for the monitor.

6. Select Box01, which has now been calculated to wrap around the head, and in the Compound Objects panel click Morph.

7. Slide the animation slider to frame 100, click the Pick Target button, and pick box02.

8. Render. Figure 10.15 shows the final scene.

FIGURE 10.15

*Morphing a head
to a monitor using
Conform to create the
morph targets.*

The previous example demonstrates the basic conform process. What it doesn't do is point in a definitive direction for creating accuracy because as you can see, Conform doesn't always give the most accurate result.

A new feature in R2 is the changed functionality of the Visibility track in Track View (see Chapter 20). Instead of either being on or off, you can vary visibility at any key by changing the visibility track's controller from on/off to Bezier in Track View.

Working with the beginning of the Morph, you would align the morph object to occupy the same space as the Operand A template. You would then assign a Visibility track to each object and set the morph object's visibility to start with zero percent. Depending on your intended playback speed, you would reduce the visibility of the template from 100 percent to zero over a number of frames and then increase the visibility of the morph object from 0 to 100 percent over the same number of frames. You would then adjust in Track View when you wanted the morph to actually start its morphing. The same process would work in reverse for the end of the morph and Operand B.

This is an advanced technique and you need to have a fair command of Track View, but it works quite well. A completed version of that process is in Morph Completed.max using the previous exercise components. It is best observed rendered and be sure to look at the Visibility settings in Trackview for each object.

Linear Conform

The Linear portion of Conform was developed to enable extruded text to follow the contours of a noise modified surface. With Linear Conform, you also can project a selected set of vertices of an object to the surface of another to create a "hand in glove" fit. The following exercise demonstrates this by taking the flat surface of an extruded object and projecting it towards an uneven surface:

CONFORMING THE GONDOLA TO A BLIMP

1. Open Blimp Exercise.max from the accompanying CD and maximize the Right viewport.

2. Open a Selection Floater from the Tools menu item and select the Gondola object.

3. In the Modify panel click the Sub-object button to enter the vertex editing mode.

4. Select the upper most level of vertices of the Gondola (see Figure 10.16).

FIGURE 10.16

Selecting the upper-
most vertices of the
Gondola.

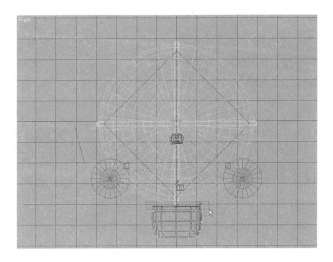

5. Change the view to Bottom (by pressing B on the keyboard), click Use Selected Vertices in the Wrapper Parameters area. Set Standoff Distance to 0 and click Use Active Viewport.

6. Click the Conform button in the Compound Objects panel and select the Balloon object as the Wrap-To object.

7. Change the view to Camera03 by pressing C twice on the keyboard. Observe how the Gondola conforms to the Balloon.

8. You can repeat steps 3 through 6 with the Gondola lattice but remove the lattice modifier from the stack first and then re-add it after the conform. The scene will not render otherwise due to the illegal creation of surfaces.

You can see how difficult it would be to move each vertex up to the Balloon to create the effect that Conform allows. It would also be easy to move the Gondolla forward or back and re-Conform simply by picking Balloon object again as the Wrap-to object in the bottom view. You may choose to save this file for use in exercises that use the Blimp Exercise.max file later.

Conform Space Warp

There is a space warp version of Conform. It's faster than the compound object version and allows more than one object to be affected. It also does linear conforms, but it does not do radial conforms. An advantage of the

Conform compound object over the space warp, however, is that it can be collapsed, making it, like all the compound objects, a modeling tool.

The previous tools have been working exclusively with 3D meshes. These next three will allow the combination of shapes and meshes.

Embedding a Shape in the Surface of a Mesh

Until now, adding faces to a mesh surface, although possible, was tedious and time consuming. It meant adding vertices to the mesh, which were difficult to place without object snaps, and then building the faces one at a time. Now with ShapeMerge, that process is automatic and easy to set up.

The ShapeMerge Compound Object

The ShapeMerge command embeds a shape into the surface of a mesh object. It projects along the –Z axis of the shape onto the surface creating new vertices, faces and edges to accommodate the shape. You can then perform modifications on the newly created sub-objects or make the shape a cookie cutter (see Figure 10.17).

FIGURE 10.17

Different uses of the ShapeMerge command.

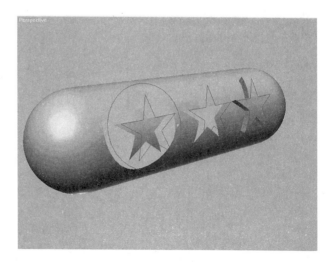

The setup for creating a ShapeMerge requires one mesh object and one or more splines, open or closed. Though you can use open splines, you will get results that won't create a selection set of faces to work with later. You arrange the shape so that its –Z axis points somewhere on the faces of the mesh object. Then with the mesh selected, start the ShapeMerge command, which makes the mesh Operand A, and then pick the shape to merge it. You can pick successive shapes to merge them into the mesh also.

EMBEDDING A SHAPE IN A MESH

1. Open a copy of Daily Planet.max from the CD and select the Planet object.

2. Click the ShapeMerge button in the Compound Objects command panel, click the Pick Shape and select the text.

3. In the Modify panel click the Mesh Select button. This will help you to see the embedded shape.

4. Now the selected faces can be deleted, or a modifier can be applied-like Face Extrude or Material.

How your shapes are oriented relative to the mesh object determines how the shape appears in the mesh. You can experiment with the previous example by clicking Sub-Object in the Modify panel and rotating or moving the text operand embedded in the mesh. This works for the vertex, face, and edge options. Notice that if you rotate the text shape 180 degrees around the Z axis the embedded text ends up on the other side of the sphere. From this you can see that what construction plane you create the shape in—Front or Back, Left or Right—is important for determining the –Z axis of the shape you want to merge (see Figure 10.18).

FIGURE 10.18

How the shape's axis is oriented, which affects its position on the Mesh. Notice the orientation of the local axis tripod in each example.

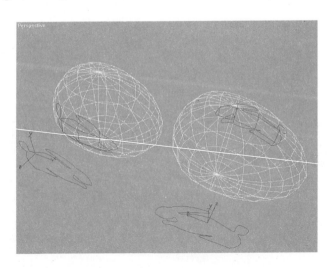

TIP

Because shapes are projected along the −Z axis, bending and then wrapping text halfway around a sphere does not give you the results you may have had in mind. After bending and collapsing the text to an editable spline you would have to detach each letter and pick them as operands one at a time in order to have them project properly. This repetitive process would be a good thing to practice MAXScripting on.

The Mesh Select modifier can be used to pass on face information to be used to extrude a shape on the surface of a mesh using the Face Extrude modifier, or to create a label on a bottle giving the selected faces a different material ID.

The following exercise shows how to embed text in an object and pass the associated faces up the modifier stack to a Material modifier:

CREATING A FLASHING LOGO IN THE SIDE OF A BLIMP

1. Open a copy of the Blimp Exercise.max from the accompanying CD or a saved version from the Conform section of this chapter.

2. Select the Balloon object and pick the ShapeMerge button in the Compound Objects panel.

3. Click the Pick Shape button and select the Eat at Max's text. This embeds the text in the surface of the blimp.

4. In the Modify panel, click Mesh Select and under More pick the Material modifier.

5. Set the Material ID to 2 and press the play button to play the animation. If your computer has difficulty with playback, either render using the Render options or with video post, which applies a glow to the sign.

    You may save this file for later use in the Connect section of this chapter. Figure 10.19 shows the final blimp scene.

You can pick multiple shapes to change the surface of your mesh, but if you want the auto selection of faces through Mesh Select you will have to do the following steps:

1. After picking the first shape, pick Mesh Select and then Material or Smooth under More in the Modify panel.

2. Assign a material ID or a smoothing group to those faces.

FIGURE 10.19
The Blimp with its
flashing sign embed-
ded in the Balloon.

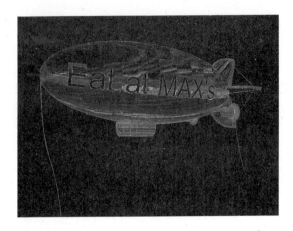

3. Repeat the previous steps for each shape you use as an operand.

Mesh Select with the use of a ShapeMerge object enables the selection of faces, edges, or vertices and as you move between each of the sub-object options you will see the associated sub-objects selected (see Figure 10.20). Mesh Select only passes selection information up the stack for frame zero for ShapeMerge, however, so the Output Sub-Mesh Selection area of ShapeMerge is added to allow animation of the shape to be passed up the stack to the next modifier.

FIGURE 10.20
Mesh Select highlights
each type of sub-
object associated with
the merged shape.

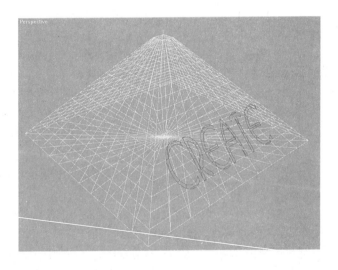

A few modifiers are not sub-object specific, like XForm and Volume select, where you would need to specify which sub-object type you want to work with. You then choose the sub-object type you want to pass up in the Output Sub-Mesh Selection area.

Scattering Objects

The new particle systems of R2 enable the distribution of instanced geometry. Fewer controls exist there, however, over how objects are distributed than with a Scatter compound object. With a Scatter object, you can collapse it, making it a modeling tool-and you don't even need a distribution object to create the scatter.

Using Scatter

Although there are a number of parameters in the command panel for scatter, they are divided into three basic categories: how many scatter objects you want, how they are distributed, and how they are randomly transformed from their default position.

When clicking Scatter, the object that is scattered as instances must be selected. You then choose the distribution object, if you are using one, and decide how you want the scatter objects arranged. You can choose to have them aligned perpendicular to the faces of the mesh object or not. You can choose which faces on the distribution object will be used for distribution by applying a Mesh Select modifier to it and selecting the desired faces. The distribution methods under Distribute Using are very clearly explained in the Online Reference under Help, but by simply trying each option you will grasp quickly what each one does.

CREATING ANIMATED SEA GRASS

1. Open a copy of Sea Grass.max from the accompanying CD.

2. With the cone (labeled Blade) selected, click the Scatter button in the Compound Objects panel, choose the Move option, and Pick the sphere (labeled Lump) as the Distribution Object.

3. Set the duplicates to 120 (or more if your machine will handle it) and set Distribute Using: to Area.

4. In the Modify panel apply a Noise modifier, set Scale to 15, X and Y Strength to 10, click Animate Noise, and set Frequency to 0.05.

5. Right-click the animation play button and set play back to 1/4 Speed and play back the animation.

Though you have animated the compound object as a whole in the previous example, both operands could have been animated separately. Animating the scatter object operand makes all the instances move in sync with one another rather than the semi-randomness you just observed.

NOTE

Using a NURBS surface as a distribution object can give you unpredictable results if it is animated. The Curvature option of the surface approximation routine of NURBS changes its representative mesh as you alter it—both in number of faces, and position of vertices. Because the scatter instances depend on face position information for their own position, they appear and disappear with no discernible uniformity. Therefore it's recommended you use the Parametric option (see Chapter 13).

TIP

Collapsing a Scatter compound object creates an editable mesh composed of separate elements allowing you to detach and edit each of the scattered objects. This is not possible when using particles systems to scatter with, without acquiring a particle snapshot plug-in.

The Transforms rollout areas are for giving each scatter instance a position, rotation, or scale different from its neighbor (see Figure 10.21). The value that any one instance gets from a parameter in these areas is some random percentage of the range between the + and − of the value in the parameter field. If under Rotation, Z is set to 22, then each instance gets some random value between 22 and −22. The Use Maximum Range option simply auto-assigns the highest value of the three axes to all three fields.

FIGURE 10.21

The Transforms rollout of the Scatter compound object.

The translation (position) of each instance can be changed relative to its own initial position in the scatter using Local Translation, or relative to the surface of the distribution mesh using Translation on Face. The Translation on Face option is disabled when there is no distribution object.

The following is an example of a scatter with no distribution object using Transform parameters.

CREATING A SCATTER OBJECT WITHOUT A DISTRIBUTION OBJECT OPERAND

1. In the Perspective view create a sphere with radius of 5 and Segments of 4.

2. Make a copy of the sphere at a distance of 5 or 10 units in any direction and collapse the copy to an editable mesh in the Modify panel.

3. Click Sub-object, choose the face selection level, select all the faces of the sphere, and delete them.

4. Answer No to Delete Faces, click Sub-Object to get out of sub-object selection mode, click on Attach, and attach the other sphere to this invisible one. This gives us an object that has a pivot out side of the visible mesh. Though this could have been done with Affect Pivot Only under Hierarchy, the pivot would have been discarded with the use of Scatter.

5. Click Scatter in the Compound Objects panel and in the Distribution area choose Use Transforms Only.

6. In the Source Object Parameters area, set Duplicates to 40.

7. Right-click the command panel while the cursor is a hand and choose Transforms from the pulldown.

8. Under Rotation set X to 45, Y to 90, and Z to 360. Under Local Translation to 100 for X and click Use Maximum Range.

9. Turn on the Animate button, slide the frames slider to 100 and set each field in Rotation to 360 (don't use maximum range)

10. Play the animation. From a distance this could be a swarm of gnats or with proper coloring, bees.

Scatter has an extended display function that is similar to Particle systems (see Figure 10.22). It enables you to represent the scatter objects with a wedge that approximates their size but with less faces when Proxy is selected under Display Options. If that isn't enough to speed up your display, you can reduce the percentage of scatter objects displayed in the viewport. Neither display option has any effect on rendering. The Uniqueness field acts as the starting value for the randomizing aspect of the Transforms options.

FIGURE 10.22

*The Display and
Load/Save Presets
rollout of the Scatter
compound object.*

You can save the settings for a particular scatter sequence for later use in another scatter compound object. The Load/Save Presets function works exactly the same as that option in MAX's newest particle systems and is covered in detail in Chapter 22, "Using Particle Systems."

TIP

Included in the CD is the freeware Scatter Utility by Peter Watje, which enables you to paint the scatter objects, allowing precise positioning on the distribution surface.

Lastly this chapter discusses a compound object that makes it easy to connect holes between two geometric objects: the Connect Compound object.

Object Connecting

To make it easy for character modelers to connect a head or an arm to a torso, the Connect compound object is created. Its use is simple and has very few options but works great. It creates a bridge between any two holes that are lined up in a way that will logically work. You can connect between any hole in a mesh object or a closed spline, and any other hole or closed spline. A sample result is achieved in Figure 10.23.

FIGURE 10.23

Using the Connect compound object.

NOTE

Because NURBS has its own set of tools for connecting and blending, Connect will not work with NURBS objects without collapsing them to meshes or splines.

Using Connect

When first using Connect, a non-segmented bridge is created. Then the number of segments and the tension governing tangency at the intersection between each object and the bridge can then be adjusted.

The following is a simple example of connecting two meshes with holes in them:

CONNECTING A LAMP TO ITS BASE

1. Open a copy of Lamp Connect.max from the CD.

2. Select the lamp base and click the Connect button in the Compound Objects command panel.

3. Click the Pick Operand button and select the lamp.

4. In the Interpolation area set Tension to .07, set Segments to 4 and render.

The material of the bridge and second operand becomes the same as the first operand unless you're working with a multi-sub-object material that is common to both operands and each has material ID's assigned to them. In the following example when the bridge is first created, a random material ID is assigned to it. When you turn on Smoothing for the ends, the material ID of the first operand is assigned to the bridge.

FINISHING THE BLIMP

1. Open either a saved version from earlier in this chapter or from the accompanying CD, Blimp Exercise.max.

2. In the Camera01 view select the Port Motor. (Remember, you can hold your cursor over objects to determine their name.)

3. Click the Connect button in the Compound Objects section of the Create panel.

4. Click the Pick Operand button and select the Balloon object.

5. Set the Segments to 7, the Tension to 0.3, and turn on smoothing for both Bridge and Ends.

6. Notice the bridge change color when you picked Ends.

7. Change a viewport to Camera02 and do the same with the Starboard Motor.

You can also connect between two splines or between a spline and a mesh (see Figure 10.24). When connecting a single closed non-self-intersecting spline to any other object, it will automatically be capped. Sometimes when you connect using a spline, no bridge displays. This is because a bridge is only created from a spline in the direction of its local -Z axis. When that happens, you just need to flip the spline 180 degrees.

FIGURE 10.24

Connecting some shapes to a mesh.

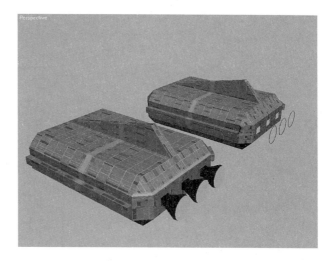

The following example shows how to make a bridge display when it doesn't initially:

MAKING AN INVISIBLE CONNECT BRIDGE VISIBLE

1. Create two circle shapes with a radius of 15 in the Perspective viewport and move one in the Z direction so that it rests above the other about 20 units up.

2. With either circle selected, start the Connect command and pick the other circle as the second operand.

3. Notice they are both capped but there is no bridge.

4. Now flip either circle 180 degrees along the X or Y axis and observe the appearance of the bridge.

If a mesh object has two holes in it and no second operand is chosen, Connect creates a bridge between the holes—even if they are not directly across from each other. You will have to flip the normals of the whole object and apply and a 2-Sided transparent material in order to see the bridge, however.

In Practice: Using Compound Objects

- **Operands** Compound Object operations are comprised of two or more objects that are kept as editable operands. Each operand can be transformed, edited, and animated like any other object.

- **Nested Compound Object operations** Compound Object operations can be nested by creating a compound object that uses another compound object as an operand. Collapsing a compound object before using it as an operand in another compound object increases speed and reduces instability.

- **Calculating Compound Object operations** You can choose when the compound object operation is calculated. This can be important when the operands contain complex geometry, the calculation is intensive, and interaction is impaired. When performance become sluggish, it's best to change the Update mode to Manually or When Rendering when possible.

- **Material ID#s** Assigning some defining material ID#s to each object before they become compound object operands is a useful technique for being able to select the separate pieces after they are combined.

- **Booleans** Combine geometric primitives to model and sculpt new objects. Provide enough faces in each operand to assure valid results.

- **Morphing** Transition from one mesh shape to one or more other shapes with the same number of vertices. Use the Blend material and the Unwrap UVW modifier to work with materials.

- **Conform** Use Conform to "shrink-wrap" copies of one object around other objects with different numbers of vertices to create legal targets for Morphing. Display Wrapper objects as boxes to increase display response.

- **ShapeMerge** Use shapes to embed outlines of those shapes in the surfaces of meshes. Use Mesh Select to pass sub-object information to modifiers like Extrude and Smooth.

- **Scatter** Make instances of one object and distribute them over the surface of another. Use Transforms to randomize their position, rotation, and scale.

- **Connect** Creating a bridge of faces between holes of two objects is made easy using Connect. Flip shapes 180 degrees to create bridges that don't show as expected.

Chapter 11

MESH MODELING

Mesh editing involves modeling at the Sub-Object level with explicit vertex, face, and edge selections. Chapters 7 and 8 discussed these selection levels and this chapter focuses on how to manipulate these discreet pieces with the Editable Mesh object and the now-superfluous EditMesh modifier. Modelers who are working with low polygon count models for game engines should pay particular attention to this chapter, because only by working in Sub-Object mode can excess faces be eliminated and the model optimized for export. Because low polygon modeling techniques scale up well to the more complex, smoother meshes, this chapter will concentrate on modeling with a low polygon count budget in mind.

Major topics for this chapter include:

- Modeling with vertices
- Modeling with faces
- Surface control with faces
- Modeling with edges

Modeling with Vertices

Vertex manipulation is the most basic and often the most appropriate precision control for fine-tuning a mesh. The vast majority of 3DS MAX transformation and modification operations manipulate vertices, with the faces simply being pulled along. Transforming vertices is tantamount to moving, rotating, and scaling faces or edges. The reason for this similarity is that mesh editing always affects vertex locations. Faces and edges that make up the mesh follow along to the new positions dictated by their vertices. Thinking of this when you perform any mesh editing operation, or any modification for that matter, should make the results of edits more comprehensible.

Vertex Level Basics

As soon as you enter the Vertex selection level (see Figure 11.1), all vertices become visible, even if they are on parts of the mesh whose face normals point away from you. Every selection made consists of vertices, with transforms affecting them only.

Isolated and solitary vertices usually exist for only one purpose: as a base upon which to build faces. Vertices never define a mesh by themselves and cannot be independently rendered. When faces are deleted, 3DS MAX prompts whether you want to delete the orphaned vertices at the same time. Unless you plan to build new faces on these vertices in the future, your answer should always be yes. In case there might be a few lurking about, Remove Isolated from the Sub-Object Vertex, Miscellaneous section can be used to get rid of them.

FIGURE 11.1

The Vertex Level common to both Editable Mesh and EditMesh.

Hiding Vertices

Hiding vertices is a method of removing them from accidental editing. Hidden vertices hide their display ticks but do not hide the mesh they define. When hidden, vertices are no longer selectable and are no longer affected by your actions. In this state, vertices are very similar to frozen objects. Hiding vertices is an extremely valuable tool when you want to preserve a certain area of the mesh but want to modify other parts—especially those that are close to the hidden vertices. Hidden vertices can also be used to segregate areas of the mesh from face level operations. They cannot have faces built upon them and are not considered in face selections when using the By-Vertex face selection option.

WARNING

When you hide a selection of vertices, these vertices are still considered the active selection and can be accidentally deleted or, if you press the spacebar lock, transformed. To be safe, it is best to perform a Select None, or click in the viewport to empty the selection after hiding vertices to ensure they are not affected by mistake.

Due to their size, vertices can be difficult to see. Before selecting vertices for an edit, it is good practice to perform a Select None to ensure that your selection is only what you intend. Because selections are passed up the stack, it is easy to forget about an earlier selection that is now active—especially when the selection was established by a much earlier modifier.

Transforming Vertices

The toolbar's Move, Rotate, and Scale transforms are your principle methods for manipulating vertices, and the subtleties described earlier in the "Common Terms and Concepts for Meshes" section of Chapter 7 are of particular importance. One of the primary benefits of Mesh Editing is that transformations are automatically applied as a modification; no need to worry about nonuniform scaling coming back to haunt you. Much of the secret to manipulating vertices effectively is in selecting the correct vertices to be edited and leaving the others alone.

Although you can edit vertices individually, most vertex editing is done with selections. Animation of a single vertex can alter the shape of an object over time; rotating or scaling a single vertex requires the use of the coordinate system center to have any effect. Otherwise, you are rotating and scaling about the vertex itself and nothing occurs.

Many of the exercises in this chapter focus on using mesh modeling skills to build a General Dynamics M1 Main Battle Tank (see Figure 11.2, which shows the finished product). Every polygon matters on the low Level of Detail tank, so it would be suitable for a game, or as a distant model in a more complex scene. The first exercise, which follows, shows how to build the main cannon.

It is very common to take 3D primitives and convert them to entirely different objects through vertex editing. This exercise takes a basic hexagonal cylinder and creates all the indentations with just a few vertex edits.

SCALING A CYLINDER INTO A CANNON

1. Open the Preferences dialog from File, Preferences and in the General tab, set the System Unit Scale to 1 Unit = 1 Meter.

FIGURE 11.2

The finished tank.

You should get into the habit of always modeling objects to a known scale. That way, you build up a library of objects that can be universally used in future scenes. Besides, it's far easier to use a tape measure on common real objects than to guess at their sizes relative to other elements in the scene.

2. Open the file m1.max from the accompanying CD. Figure 11.3 shows a frozen set of shapes, a three-dimensional sketch of the tank. This is a good way to set up a scene for modeling a known object; there is less memory overhead and faster redraws than using three background bitmap templates.

3. Create an NGon with six sides in the Left window, at the location of the base of the cannon. The radius of this cylinder is the maximum radius of the cannon (see Figure 11.4).

4. Toggle the Angle Snap and rotate the shape -90 degrees in the Top view. Extrude it out to a Mesh that is 3.5 units, with 10 segments and only an End Cap. Collapse the extrusion to an Editable Mesh.

5. Maximize the Left view and go to Sub-Object Vertex mode. Select the vertices of the vertical section lines one by one, and center them over the level changes of the cannon, as shown in Figure 11.5.

FIGURE 11.3

A 3D sketch of the tank.

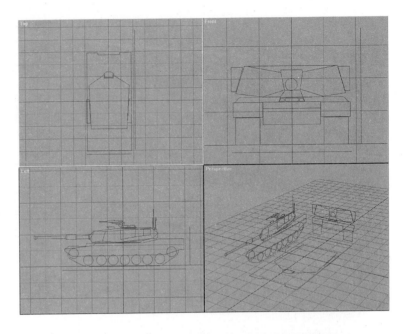

FIGURE 11.4

Placement of the NGon.

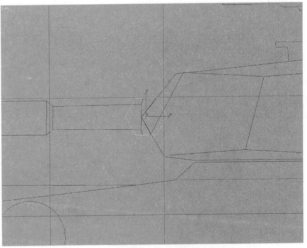

6. Once again, select each set of section vertices and Uniform Scale transform them to match the contour of the cannon. The result looks a little weird (see Figure 11.6), because the smoothing groups have not been set properly, which will be accomplished in a later exercise. Save your model as **m1a.max**.

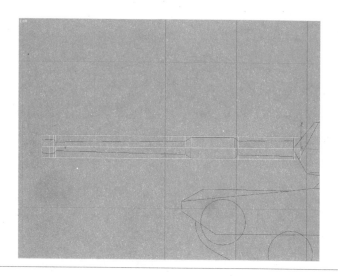

Modeling with Affect Region

The Affect Region function enables you to influence an entire region of vertices with a much smaller selection or, more often, only a single vertex. When you check the Affect Region check box in the Edit Vertex rollout, every transform you perform affects a region of vertices instead of only the ones you selected. Checking this box fundamentally changes the way vertex editing works, because a single vertex now acts like a magnet by pulling others when it changes position by a Move, Rotate, or Scale transform.

Affect Region works in conjunction with its controlling region curve. The region curve is a visualization of the result of moving a single vertex from a flat grid. Clicking Edit Curve brings up the Edit Affect Region Curve dialog (see Figure 11.7). As you can see, the Falloff setting defines the radius of a selection "sphere." Every vertex within this sphere is affected according to the values of the region curve.

There are ways to get around this limitation. The default on position of Ignore Backfaces keeps any faces whose normals face away from the region from being affected. This feature comes in handy when modifying geometry that has two sides close to each other, like a table. If you want your table to blister up, keep Ignore Backfaces on. If you want your table to be dented all the way through, turn it off.

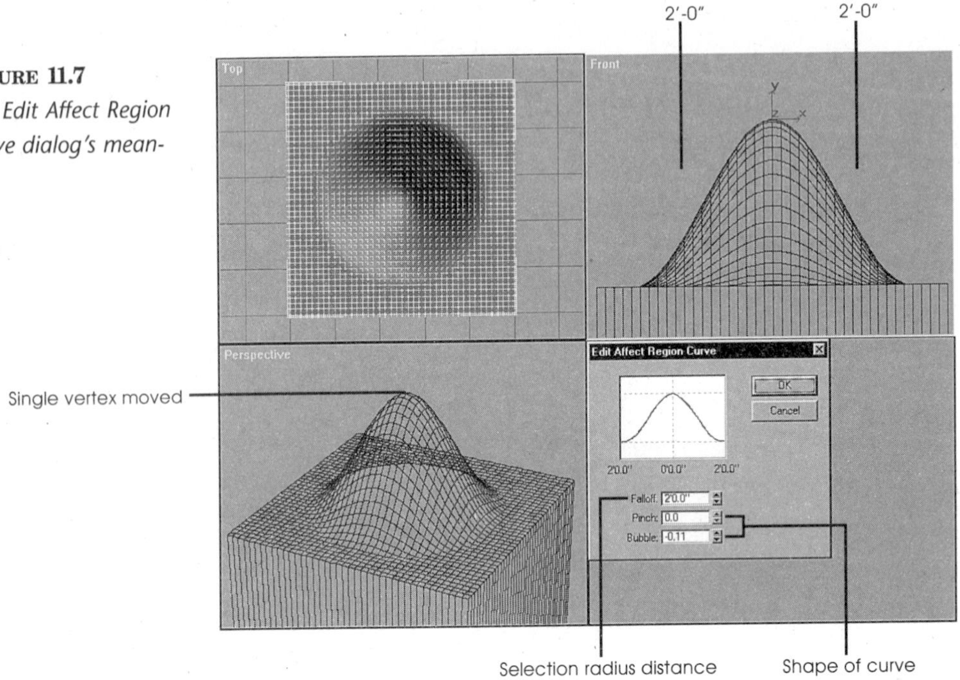

FIGURE 11.7

The Edit Affect Region Curve dialog's meaning.

Single vertex moved

Selection radius distance   Shape of curve

The other way to defeat the Region Curve is to use the Edge Distance option. This limits the distance of the effect by the number of edges that surround the selected point in a concentric radius. Imagine the selected point as a bull's-eye and the iterations as the number of bands surrounding it.

WARNING

The Affect Region Function mode does not respect the status of hidden vertices. Every vertex within the falloff radius is affected.

Creating Vertices

Every time you create or clone a mesh, you also create vertices because the faces are defined by the vertices. Although this method often provides the vertices you need for other modeling, you may need to create other vertices independently, and at exact locations, for creating stitching faces.

Vertices cannot be created in isolation. They must be created from within the Editable Mesh object. Within the object, you can create vertices individually with the Vertex/Create function or you can clone vertex selections as part of the object or as a new object. Cloning vertices of an existing mesh is the only method for creating isolated vertices as objects.

The Vertex/Create function places you in a mode in which every click on the screen creates a new vertex at that location on the active grid. Creating vertices in this manner is especially useful when used with an active Grid object and the nudge keys. This nudging enables you to move the active grid, without leaving your current Sub-Object command, and creates layers of vertices at controllable heights.

Using Vertex Create

Vertex Create is the only method for creating vertices from scratch, other than cloning. The vertices you create are always part of the original object and usually serve as the building points for future faces. When creating vertices, each point you pick defines two coordinates, with the third being supplied by the viewport's active grid. This can be overridden when using vertex and edge snapping.

Vertex Create works well with vertex and edge snapping. Checking your Vertex and Endpoint snap priorities box and unchecking the others (see Figure 11.8) ensures that you are only snapping to vertices. When using 3D Snap, Vertex Create lets you create the framework on which to build bridging faces. When using 2.5D Snap, you create a projected template of vertices onto the viewport's active grid. Although rarely needed, flattened projections of other meshes can be created from these projected templates.

FIGURE 11.8

The Snap settings for
3D Vertex snapping.

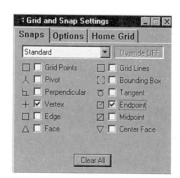

Vertex Topology

With vertices, you work with the defining points of your mesh. It is only natural to affect the topology with them as well. Besides the ever-available Delete, several functions are unique to vertices, with the most often used being Weld.

Welding Vertices

Welding fuses two or more vertices together to form a single vertex, which drags with it any faces built upon the original vertices. Welding is used for knitting together separate faces to form an element, or consolidating faces of an element into a simpler mesh. The Weld function is by far the most commonly used button in the Vertex level and with it you can weld either precisely or generally.

NOTE

Although you can assign a single EditMesh to multiple objects, you can weld only vertices of the same object because welding changes the object definition. If you want to weld between objects, you must attach one to the other first.

Although mapping coordinates can extend over unwelded faces, smoothing groups cannot. Without the capability to properly smooth, a mesh never looks quite right. Edges that meet without having welded and, thus, shared vertices cannot be smoothed over and always form an edge.

Weld's Target method places you in a mode in which you select vertices and drag them over a target vertex as shown in Figure 11.9. Your cursor determines the vertex to which you are welding and changes to crosshairs when it's over a vertex on the same object. What determines a targeted vertex is the proximity of your cursor in screen pixels. This value is set in the Target Threshold field. Your active viewport thus has a great influence over what you are welding. Working in an orthogonal viewport enables you to weld vertices that are a great distance apart (in screen depth), which can be either ideal or unwanted. Working in a User or Perspective view usually gives you a clearer understanding of vertex relationships when welding. An often convenient method is to select vertices in orthogonal views and perform the Target weld in a User or Perspective view.

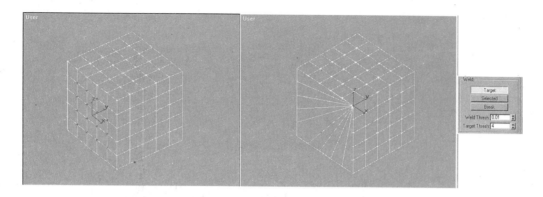

FIGURE 11.9

Welding a selection with Weld Target.

NOTE

Weld Target is commonly combined with Edge Turn and Divide to sculpt defining lines in your mesh.

The Weld Selected method examines your current vertex selection and uses the Weld Threshold value as a range "string" to swing about each of the selected vertices. If any vertices fall within each other's threshold range, they are welded together. If all the vertices are out of each other's threshold range, none are welded and the alert shown in Figure 11.10 appears.

The locations of all vertices that fall within the threshold are averaged to form the new location for the resulting, welded vertex. The resulting vertex remains selected for quick manipulation. Because an averaging of locations occurs, welded vertices move unless they are already coincidental. If you want to weld only coincidental vertices and do not want any chance of the vertices shifting, set your Weld Threshold to zero. With very large thresholds, Weld Selected can be similar in function to performing a Vertex Collapse on the same selection.

FIGURE 11.10

Weld Selected's Weld
Threshold alert.

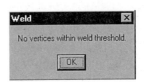

TIP

If you want to weld a selection of vertices about an averaged point, Uniform Scale the selection until the vertices are close and then perform a Weld Selected. This is often faster than adjusting the Weld Threshold and then resetting it.

In practice, Weld Selected is most often used when you are welding portions of a model that are aligned with coincidental vertices or have vertices that are very close to being so. Perhaps these separate elements used to be together, are the result of a Boolean object, or are from another program that did not afford the capability to weld meshes. In these cases, performing a Select All and welding with a low threshold works well. For accurate welding, Weld Target should be your choice, because with it you can be confident of obtaining the desired results.

The final method of welding is Weld Break. This functions similarly to Vertex Break found in the Editable Spline Vertex Sub-Object mode. After using Weld Break, all the selected vertices no longer share multiple faces. Each remaining vertex is used by only one face. Vertices that already use only one face or are isolated are unaffected by the weld.

Collapsing Vertices

The Collapse function is destructive but very useful. When you click Collapse, the current selection of vertices is welded into one common vertex. The location of the new vertex is the average location of the selected vertices. This location is quite predictable when the collapsed vertices are coplanar, as shown in Figure 11.11. When not coplanar, the averaged position of the new welded vertex usually causes a "dent" in the surface. Unlike Edge or Face Collapse, Vertex Collapse does not work on a single vertex because there is nothing with which to average. In actuality, Edge and Face Collapse are supersets of Vertex Collapse, affecting two and three vertices respectively.

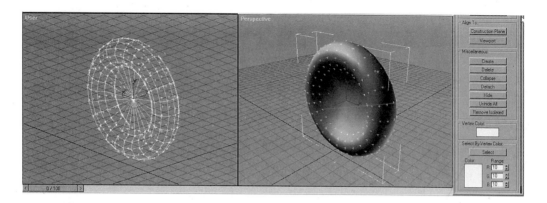

FIGURE 11.11

Collapsing a set of vertices around a central point.

Detaching Vertices

Detaching vertices breaks the vertices and every face they define from the mesh into a new object. Detaching vertices is similar to detaching faces except that when detaching vertices, you are more certain of the mesh's extent. You can easily miss a face and not select one whose normal is facing away from you. With vertices, you can be sure you're defining the entire mesh.

If you want to detach vertices and not faces, you need to clone the selection instead of detaching it. Cloning is done by performing a Transform (most often Move) and pressing your Shift key. This creates a vertex cloud without faces. When cloning, you have the option to make the selection a new object. If the selection of cloned vertices is made into a new object, you are not able to build faces onto it from the original object. If you do not create a new object, the new vertices remain selected for you to manipulate. Unlike detaching, cloning does not automatically prevent the vertices from moving. If you want to ensure the cloned vertices do not move, enable your snap, press Shift, and click once over the selection.

Deleting Vertices

Vertex deletion is a fast way to clear unwanted sections of a mesh, because nothing is left behind, and you aren't slowed down by prompts. When you delete a vertex, you also delete any and all faces that share it. Deleting the central vertex of a cylinder's cap, for example, deletes the entire cap. You may find this surprising, but remember that the criteria for making a crossing selection of faces is to enclose any of their vertices. As always, the Delete key is the keyboard alternate for the Delete function.

In the next exercise, you'll use vertex manipulation to construct the main objects that comprise the tank that you started in the previous exercise. This exercise is the "bread and butter" of low polygon count modeling and the techniques covered can be applied to many types of objects.

BUILDING THE MAIN TANK WITH VERTEX EDITING

1. You can use your model from the last exercise, or open the file m1a.max from the CD.

2. Trace around the perimeter of the turret, excluding the hatches and other detail, as shown in Figure 11.12.

FIGURE 11.12

Tracing around the turret.

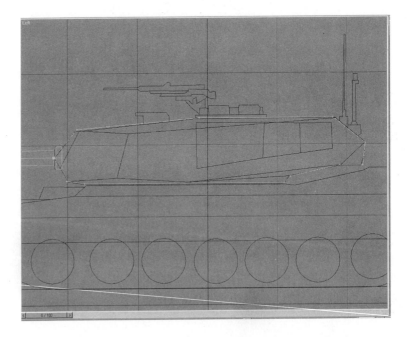

3. Go over to the Modify panel. You may have to adjust some of your vertices to get them in place properly with Sub-Object Vertex transforms. In the Top view, move your profile about 1.7 units to the right, so that

it aligns with the edge of the turret. Extrude the shape about 3.25 units and give it three segments, capping both the Start and the End. Your turret should look like Figure 11.13.

FIGURE 11.13

The extruded turret.

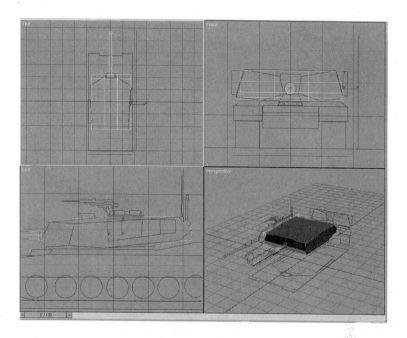

4. Collapse to a mesh and go into Sub-Object Vertex mode. Using the three views, move around the vertices until you get a result that resembles Figure 11.14. Selecting Use Pivot Point Center enables you to make transforms using multiple points.

5. As you can see in Figure 11.14, there are too many vertices. Drag a selection rectangle around the extra vertices, and then drag them so that they lie on top of the vertices below them. Be sure that the Weld Threshold is set to the default of .1 and then hit Selected. The extra vertices are gone and the turret looks like Figure 11.15.

6. Next, trace around the armored skirts in the side view. Move and Extrude the spline as before and set the segments to 1. The skirt should look like Figure 11.16.

FIGURE 11.14

The partially edited turret with its extra vertices.

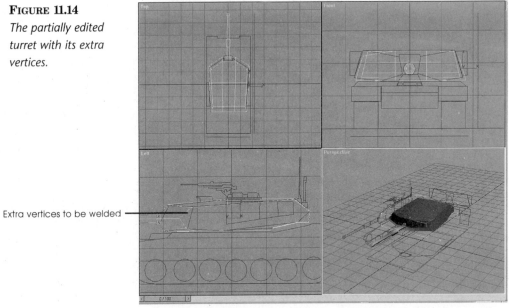

Extra vertices to be welded

FIGURE 11.15

The turret with its extra vertices gone.

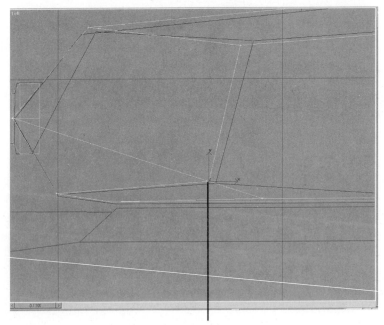

Result of the weld

FIGURE 11.16

The finished skirt.

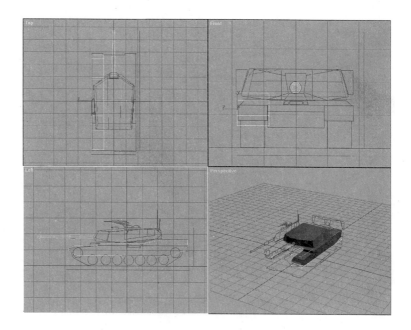

7. Unfreeze the splines named main body and treads. Extrude the main body so that it extends into the treads on both sides. Capping both sides should be on for both the body and the tread, and segments should be set to 1. Then, select treads. Turn down its Interpolation to zero and go to Sub-Object Spline mode. Give the spline an outline of about .1 and then extrude a tread for the left side of the tank. The result is Figure 11.17.

8. Create a six-sided NGon over one of the wheels and extrude it with capping on both sides so that it's inside the tread area. Shift-Move the wheel so that all wheels on the left side have hexagons.

NOTE

Six-sided wheels are used in this case because the wheel will be opacity mapped to make it appear round. This maneuver can save many polygons. For a further discussion of different mapping types, see Part IV, "Materials and Maps."

9. Finally, select the treads, skirt, and wheels and Mirror Clone them to the other side of the tank, which, at this point, should look like Figure 11.18. Save your file as m1b.max.

FIGURE 11.17
The tread and main body in position.

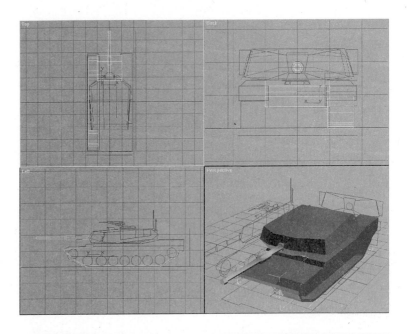

FIGURE 11.18
The tread assembly mirror cloned and moved to the other side.

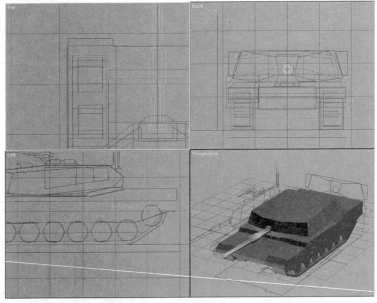

The exercises in this section have given you practice modeling with vertices. If you have followed along in creating the tank, you have seen how to move and delete vertices in order to create the desired shape. The following section discusses the next level of mesh editing.

Modeling with Faces

This section moves from vertices to faces, the second major component of mesh editing. Manipulating face locations is much like working with vertices in sets of three, but faces define much more information than vertices. Vertices define the location of a face's boundary, while faces define a directional normal that specifies a one-sided surface. Faces are the objects that render with material, mapping, and smoothing assignments. When editing vertices, you are modeling the object's form and are concerned only with position. When editing faces, you are also concerned with how the surface reflects light.

T IP

Minimizing the Modifiers rollout provides valuable Command Panel real estate that is useful when working at the Face level. If you make Sub-Object cycle and Sub-Object mode keyboard alternates, you can collapse the Modifier Stack rollout as well.

Face Level Basics

The face level (see Figure 11.19) provides several modes for selecting and manipulating faces. Navigation of the face level rollout—one of 3DS MAX's longest rollouts—can quickly become an art. However, the rollout is long for a reason. Faces have many properties and you cannot edit a face without at least thinking about the ramifications to the rendered surface.

Selecting Faces

You can select faces in a variety of ways: singularly, by region, by mesh extents, by coplanar relationships, or even by material and smoothing assignments. Selecting the quickest, most accurate method from among these alternatives is part of the art of good modeling. As always, selection methods are for controlling the results of the selected item; the current selection mode never affects the result of subsequent functions.

FIGURE 11.19

The Edit Face rollout of Editable Mesh.

Face selection is categorized into three geometric definitions:

- **Face selection:** selects a single, triangular face and is the fastest selection method offered, being much faster than Polygon or Element when working with very large meshes. Face selection displays all edges of selected faces, even if normally invisible.

- **Polygon selection:** selects welded faces that are not separated by visible edges and fall within the Planar Threshold value. Checking Ignore Visible Edges enables the selection to include any welded face that falls within the Planar Threshold value. Often, it is convenient to select by polygon and then switch to Face Select mode to display every edge of the selection.

- **Element Selection:** selects all faces that can trace a path of shared (welded) vertices. Element selection ignores edge visibility and Planar Threshold, concerning itself only with mesh extents. Element selection is always in Crossing mode.

The By Vertex check box changes the manner in which your selection is evaluated. When By Vertex is not checked (the default), clicking anywhere within a face, polygon, or element selects that sub-object. When By Vertex is checked, you must click (or enclose) a vertex of the desired sub-object in order to select it. Activating the By Vertex option is primarily for window selections because there is no longer an initial selection with your first pick. When By Vertex is active, selection is done according to vertices, so the hidden state of vertices is respected.

Every time you click and drag, you begin a region selection. The shape is controlled by the toolbar's Selection flyout. It can be either rectangular, circular, or fence. Changing the region shape is common and makes for a very convenient keyboard alternative. Region selection works hand-in-hand with the window and crossing selection methods. A window selection must enclose the entire geometry of the selection—all three vertices of a face or all the vertices of a polygon. A crossing selection needs to enclose only a single vertex to select every face, polygon, or element that shares that vertex. Crossing mode is most useful for fast selections, whereas window is best for careful ones.

WARNING

The window selection mode is not consistent. Elements always ignore window and always use crossing, whereas irregularly-shaped polygons often do not need to be fully enclosed to be selected. In addition, the By-Vertex option ignores window mode and makes all selections by crossing mode.

Region selections project back into the viewport and select faces that you might not be able to see; there's no filtering of back faces unless you check the Ignore Backfaces box. Even so, it is good practice to always check your selection in various viewports to confirm what has been selected. The axis tripod is a reliable signal of an accidental selection. If the axis is not more or less centered or more than one axis appears, you have probably selected more than you want.

TIP

When using the By Vertex option, the hidden state of vertices is respected and their faces are excluded from selection.

The By Vertex option becomes very important with region selections performed within a mesh. Without it, your first mouse click to define the region selects the face, polygon, or element—a result you rarely want. With By Vertex on, nothing is selected with your first click, so your region selection performs an accurate region selection of the vertices you then enclose.

Hiding Faces

Hiding faces does more than remove them from view. When hidden, faces are no longer selectable and affected by your actions. Hiding faces is an extremely valuable tool when you want to protect certain areas of the mesh from selection or modification, especially when you are selecting or modifying nearby faces. Hidden faces can also be used to segregate areas of the mesh from vertex- and edge-level operations.

NOTE

Although hidden faces are protected within the Edit modifier, they can be affected by modifiers added later in the stack. Volume Select does not ignore them and object level actions always affect them.

After hiding faces, you can Select All the remaining faces and perform an operation without affecting the hidden ones. Hidden faces are unaffected by the deletion of any or all other faces. Hidden faces are affected only when the vertices upon which they are built are modified. If you transform faces that are welded to hidden faces, the welded vertices of the hidden faces are transformed as well. Vertices unique to the hidden faces cannot be influenced while at the face level.

Transforming Faces

The toolbar's Move, Rotate, and Scale transforms are your principle methods for manipulating faces. Transforming faces is very similar to moving, rotating, and scaling the equivalent vertex selections with one enormous difference: faces enable you to transform individual centers.

When you are in Pivot Point Center mode, each selection of faces determines its own coordinate system based on the averaged normals of the selection. This enables you to Move, Rotate, and Scale noncontiguous face selections all at once, as if you were manipulating them one at a time.

TIP

It is often convenient to use the Local Coordinate System when using Pivot Point Center on face selections. This option ensures that the axis orientations of the selections are consistent with one another, with Z always pointing along the normal.

Creating Faces

Faces can be created in numerous ways within the Face level. They can be extruded, tessellated, cloned, and even built one at a time. Of these options, Extrude is the most powerful, Build the most common, and Tessellate the most face count intensive.

Extruding Faces

The Extrude function creates faces by moving the selected faces outward and building sides or "walls" that connect the selection and its perimeter. Clicking Extrude places you in an extrusion mode and takes you out of your current toolbar transform.

TIP

The best way to exit Extrude mode is to click the desired toolbar button. Exiting the mode by clicking Extrude automatically changes your toolbar state to Move, even if you were previously in Pick, Rotate, or Scale.

Extrude is one of the rare 3DS MAX functions that actually enables you to define its result within the viewport, in addition to using the spinner on a selection. In Extrude, your cursor turns into an Extrude icon when it is placed over a selection. You then can define the extrusion by dragging your cursor; the Amount field reports the height of the extrusion.

TIP

The fastest way to use Extrude is to use the Extrusion spinner with a selection, which extrudes the faces but does not affect your toolbar status. You can move between extrusion and transforms without delay.

An extrusion cannot be adjusted. After you make an extrusion, it is set. Trying to "adjust" the extrusion results in an additional extrusion on the same selection. Therefore, you should analyze your extrusion carefully before releasing the spinner arrow or dragging the cursor. Adjusting an existing extrusion is a great timesaver when you want to quickly give successive segments an extrusion. Figure 11.20 shows how to give objects sequential extrusions to add segments.

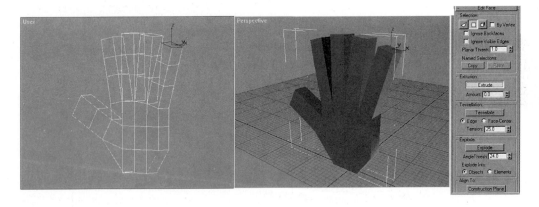

FIGURE 11.20
Using multiple Extrudes to add height segments.

Extrude moves the selection of faces according to its averaged normal. If the selection is flat or coplanar (probably the result of a polygon selection), the extrusion is perpendicular to the plane. If the selection is not coplanar, the normals of the selected faces are averaged and the extrusion follows this vector. Selecting the adjacent sides of a box, for example, extrudes the sides at 45 degrees. For controlled results, Extrude is best used with coplanar selections.

The Extrude function ignores the state of the toolbar's selection center and always treats it as if you were using Pivot Point Center. Each noncontiguous selection of faces has its own normal. You can make noncontiguous selections and extrude them all at once, and they extrude as if you extruded them one by one.

The normals of Extruded faces face outward if the extrusion is positive and face inward if negative. Mapping coordinates are "stretched" along the length of the new sides.

Tessellating Faces

Tessellation is primarily used to increase mesh density; it is used on selected areas to create additional vertices and faces for manipulation or to increase overall detail for future modifiers. A mesh may not have enough segments to bend properly, for example, or a Displace modifier may require a denser mesh to achieve more detail for its displacing bitmap. This functionality can be animated by using the Tessellate Modifier, when applied to a selection that has been passed up the Stack.

Face-Center Tessellation

Tessellation's Face-Center option splits each selected face into three faces. The new edges actually bisect the angles of the original face and the new vertex is the original face's centroid. Faces created with this option are always coplanar with the originally selected faces. This method creates an interesting pattern that can be useful in its own right, as shown in Figure 11.21. Repeated applications of Face-Center continue to add density to the same selected region; the affected area does not grow in the way that Edge tessellation does.

Edge Tessellation

Tessellation's Edge method splits each selected face into four by dividing each edge in half and connecting the new vertices with a central face. If the edge is shared with another face, the addition of the new vertex causes that face to be divided into two faces. This explains how Edge Tessellation propagates its effect to adjacent faces. Such propagation may seem to create more faces than necessary, but you really need the adjacent faces to be created in order to prevent a seam. Smoothing cannot occur between adjacent faces that do not share two vertices. Figure 11.22 illustrates tessellating the top of a vessel so a rounded lip can be modeled there.

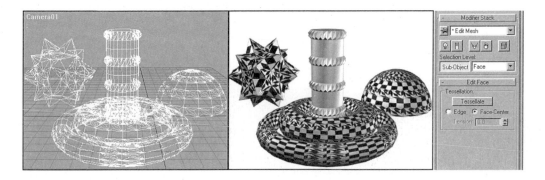

FIGURE 11.21

Patterning geometry with Face-Center tessellation.

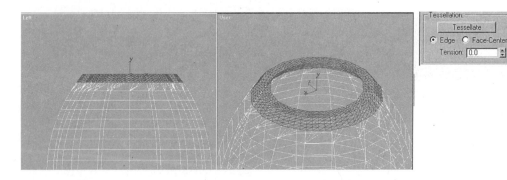

FIGURE 11.22

Edge tessellating specific regions for modeling.

Tension Value

The Edge method also works with the Tension value (grayed out when Face-Center is active), which controls the location of the newly created vertices. The vertices of the original faces are unaffected, while new vertices project outward, or "inflate," with positive tension, and project inward, or "deflate," with negative tension. Tension is a value from −100 to 100, with 0 having no effect. If you want your tessellated faces to remain coplanar (as with Face-Center), use a Tension of zero.

Without Tension, tessellation increases only the mesh density; it does not affect the profile. If your object has curves, you might want the new vertices to conform to the projected curve. The reference (default) value for Tension is +25. This value projects the new vertices to follow a circle or sphere. Edge tessellating an entire sphere with a Tension of 25 has the same effect as doubling its segmentation (see Figure 11.23). The correct choice for the Tension value depends on your geometry's curvature. Performing multiple tessellations, especially with extreme Tension values, is a great method for "crumpling" and roughening a surface.

FIGURE 11.23

Tessellating spheres with a Tension value of 25.

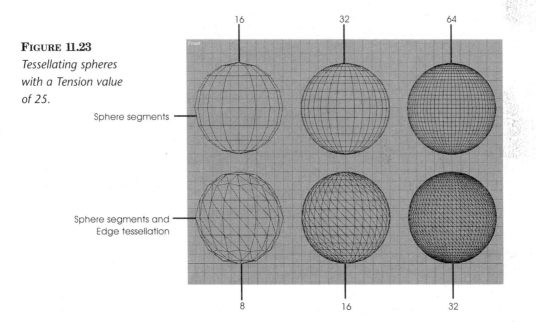

Sphere segments

Sphere segments and Edge tessellation

NOTE

The MeshSmooth modifier provides a superior method for adding mesh density with more accurate curvature than tessellation with tension does.

The following exercise continues with the tank you have been modeling from previous exercises in this chapter. It walks you through the necessary steps using Edge Tesselation and face editing in order to add the stowage boxes to the tank.

USING EDGE TESSELLATION AND FACE EXTRUSION

1. You can use your model from the last exercise or open the file m1b.max from the CD.

2. Select the turret and go to Sub-Object Face mode. Select all the faces on the back two-thirds of the left side, as shown in Figure 11.24. Using the Edge method, set the Tension to 0.0, and hit Tessellate.

FIGURE 11.24

Selecting faces to perform a tessellation.

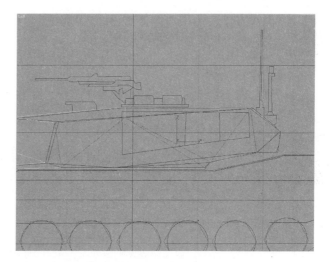

3. The result seems to be quite a mess, but we'll clean it up presently. Go to Sub-Object Vertex mode and move around the vertices until you get something like Figure 11.25. There should be an edge along the perimeter of the stowage box.

4. Select the faces inside the box perimeter and Face Extrude them out to come close to the box in the Back template of the front of the tank. In the Back view, rotate the faces and move them down a bit, improving the match, as shown in Figure 11.26.

FIGURE 11.25

The vertices have been moved to form an edge perimeter on the stowage box.

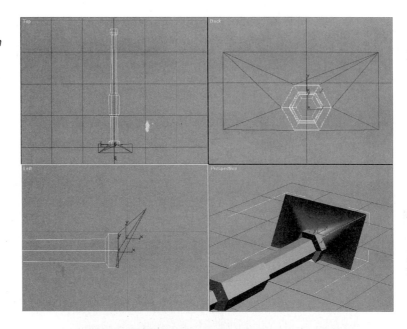

FIGURE 11.26

The box extruded.

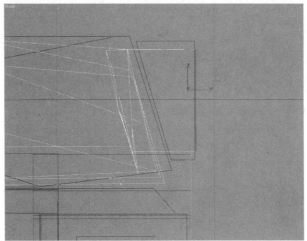

5. There's a problem, however. The faces slant to the rear and they need to be parallel to the treads. You'll need to make a Grid Object to align the faces. Under Create/Helpers, select Grid and place it so that it is in position for the align, parallel to the edge of the tank.

6. Go to the Views menu and select Grids/Activate Grid Object. Cycle the Sub-Objects mode to Vertex and select all the vertices that need to be aligned. Click Align To: Construction Plane and the vertices form a flat plane.

7. The results should look like Figure 11.27. Return to the Home grid by using the command under View/Grids. Save your file as **m1c.max**.

FIGURE 11.27

The turret with its stowage box in place.

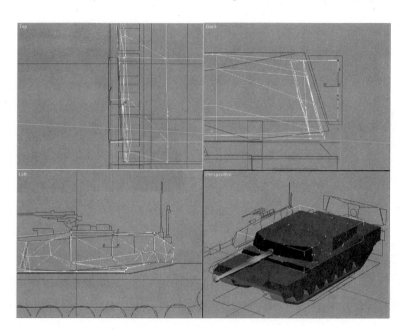

If you feel inclined, repeat the exercise on the other side of the tank.

You've used Tessellation and Face Extrude to construct geometry on an existing object. Because of this approach, not one polygon is added to the scene that doesn't need to be there. The next section further deals with adding faces, this time building them from scratch.

Building Faces

The Build Face enables you to create triangular faces, one by one, upon existing vertices. Clicking Build Face places you in a mode for stitching faces, which is the only method in 3DS MAX for creating faces by hand. This mode switches the vertex display to ticks, so your target vertices are easily seen.

Building faces is a "connect-the-dots" procedure using three vertices that determine the new face. All three vertices must belong to the same object and must be unhidden to be used because only the visible vertices of the selected object display as ticks. Building faces does not create or alter the vertices, so the new faces are automatically welded to faces already sharing the vertices. Your cursor turns into a crosshair whenever it is over a valid vertex.

T IP

Selecting the last vertex of a long, tapering, "splinter" face can be somewhat difficult because the rubber band triangle tapers to such a sharp point. In building such faces, you will find it easier to select the longest sides first, thereby reducing the acuteness of the rubber band triangle. You likely will need to zoom close and pan interactively as you build the face to make sure you hit the correct vertices.

The normal direction of the newly-built face is dictated by the order in which you select the three vertices. Picking the vertices in a counterclockwise manner makes the face visible to you, whereas a clockwise selection order points the face away from you.

N OTE

Sometimes it is more convenient to build faces with Backface off. This way you can see both sides of the mesh and not worry about the face's normal orientation or the order in which you pick vertices. After you finish, switch Backface mode back on and either flip incorrect normals or unify the mesh.

Newly built faces are given the default assignments of Material ID#1, and, if any mapping is assigned to the mesh, box-mapping coordinates. Newly built faces are devoid of smoothing groups and although the Material ID#1 assignment is often correct, the mapping and lack of smoothing are rarely what you want. Usually, you will want to complete your face building and then assign the correct smoothing and mapping coordinates.

For any three vertices, there are two possible faces—one facing in each direction with opposite face normals. If you try to create a face that already exists, the alert shown in Figure 11.28 appears and you cannot proceed with the creation. This prohibition exists because meshes with duplicate faces cause problems, including rendering anomalies and failed Boolean operations.

Creating faces is frequently used to join two pieces of geometry. In the next exercise, you'll develop skills that can be used as a last resort when faced with a seemingly impossible modeling task. The turret and the cannon must be edited so that they meet smoothly.

USING BUILD FACE TO FINISH THE CANNON

1. You can use your model from the last exercise or open the file m1c.max from the CD.

2. Select the turret in the Left view and zoom in to see the faces around the cannon. Go to Sub-Object Vertex mode and move the front vertices so that you have what is shown in Figure 11.29.

FIGURE 11.29

The front vertices of the turret in position.

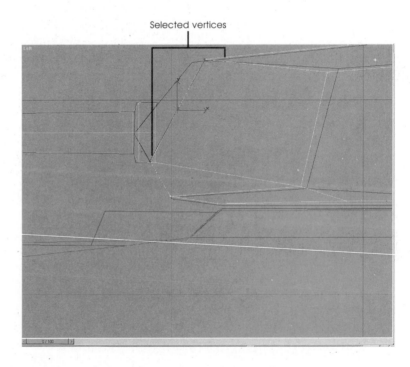

Selected vertices

3. With the front vertices still selected (as seen in Figure 11.29), Shift-Clone them by using Restrict to X and moving them sideways. Say Yes at the "Do you want to create a new object?" prompt. Remember the name that they are given (the Default is Object) because they will disappear as soon as you release the mouse.

4. Exit Sub-Object mode and select the vertices using Select By Name. You still can't see anything (you would have to be in Sub-Object Vertex mode). Attach them to the cannon, accepting the default for material assignment, then go into Vertex Sub-Object mode, and move them back to their previous position.

5. Select and hide all the cannon vertices except for the last hexagon, then do the same for the faces. The result looks like Figure 11.30.

FIGURE 11.30

Hiding the faces and vertices of the cannon.

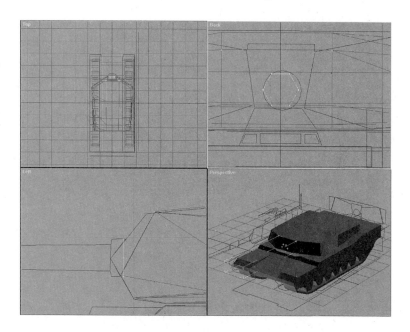

6. Go to the Back view and, using Build Face, construct the polygons that fit between the four lone vertices and the cannon hexagon. Click three adjoining vertices to form a triangle. The process looks like Figure 11.31.

FIGURE 11.31

Building the faces of
the cannon.

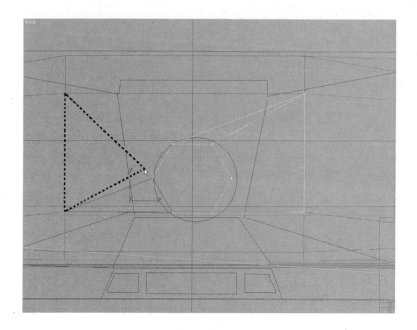

7. Unhide all the vertices and faces. The result is Figure 11.32. Save your
    file as **m1d.max**.

FIGURE 11.32

The finished cannon.

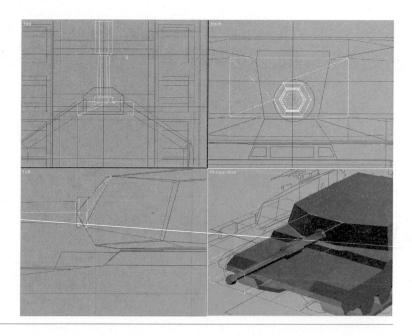

The "brute force" method of adding faces is sometimes the only method available to build the geometry necessary for a scene. Frequently other, more efficient methods are available and they should be tried before resorting to building individual faces.

Changing Face Topology

Several functions enable you to change the surface topology of your mesh through explosion, detachment, collapsing, making planar, and deletion. These functions tend to be destructive and are primarily used when you want to substantially change the surface of your model.

Exploding Faces

Consider Face Explode a tool for breaking apart or dissecting meshes. Explode separates meshes by creating duplicate vertices and "unwelding" the faces. Whether the exploded mesh breaks into faces or elements depends on the accompanying Angle Threshold value.

Faces, whose angular relationship to one another falls below the Angle Threshold, form elements to be exploded into. An angle of 0 degrees explodes all faces, whereas a 180 degree angle breaks objects by elements. When applied to a cube, for example, an angle threshold of 90 degrees leaves the cube intact, whereas 89 degrees separates it into six elements (one for each side), and 0 degrees separates it into individual faces. When you are comfortable with analyzing the angle threshold, use Explode to separate portions of your model for use as pieces elsewhere.

The option to explode into objects or elements is simply that. If you want the exploded pieces to have their own edit history and animation tracks, choose objects. If you want to keep exploded pieces part of the same object, explode the pieces into elements.

TIP

Exploding an object with an angle threshold of 180 degrees splits every element into a new object—a timesaver when you want to give numerous objects sequential names. Simply attach all the objects to one (use Editable Mesh's Attach Multiple option), select all the faces, and explode with 180 degrees into objects. Each object is now named sequentially.

Remember that when using EditMesh, the history of your actions is maintained with the modifier. If you explode an object into other objects, you can later delete the EditMesh modifier. The original object reappears intact, whereas the objects created from the explosion remain. This is one method for splitting portions off a model without harming the original.

Detaching Faces

The Detach function is used to create new objects from pieces of the selected one. The entire selection becomes one object, even if it results in numerous elements. The new object inherits the bounding box orientation of the original object.

T IP

To detach faces to an element without making an object, explode the face selection with an Angle Threshold of 180 degrees. This procedure also enables you to create multiple objects in one step.

Collapsing Faces

The Collapse function simplifies a mesh by using a unique method of deleting faces. The selected faces are deleted and replaced by a centered vertex. Every adjacent face that shares a vertex with a deleted face is stretched (and welded) to the new vertex location. If an adjacent face shares two vertices with a deleted face (an edge), it is deleted. Collapsing a single face can delete a maximum of four faces at one time, the collapsed face and three with shared edges. Collapsing a selection of faces results in very quick model face reduction that preserves a meshed surface, which is especially useful for eliminating coplanar faces. Collapsing faces that are adjacent to corners pulls the faces from the adjacent sides. You can chip away at corners easily, as shown in Figure 11.33.

Making Faces Planar

The Make Planar function examines the normals of the selected face and determines an average based on their face's overall size (for example, faces at a right angle to one another only form a 45 degree angle if they are the same size). The faces are then rotated to align on the same plane. Even noncontiguous face selections are angled to form a common plane. This function is most commonly used to flatten out irregularities in what should be a flat plane. With skill, the Make Planar function can be used to create planar relationships among numerous elements to make critical relationships quickly.

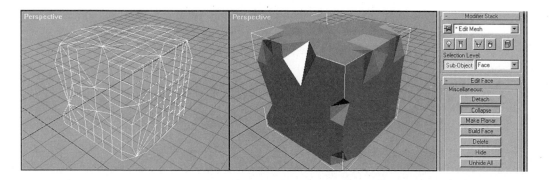

FIGURE 11.33
"Chiseling" a mesh by collapsing selected faces.

TIP

Use Make Planar on an entire mesh to flatten the mesh. This can create an interesting morph target for an animation.

Deleting Faces

The Delete function does exactly what its name says—it performs the exact same function as the keyboard's Delete key. The effect of Delete is obvious except in conjunction with hidden faces.

Immediately after a selection is hidden, its perimeter remains highlighted in red, because the hidden faces are still in a selected state and will be deleted if you press or click Delete. Faces that are hidden but not yet deleted can act as a delete "preview" of sorts. You can hide faces and add to the selection by keeping your Ctrl key depressed. You can continue to select and hide faces, all the while building a "hidden" selection. After you are comfortable with the result in the viewport, press Delete, and what was hidden is removed.

Surface Control with Faces

What faces really define are surfaces that reflect light. The color of the light depends on the material assigned to it and the color of the light illuminating it. If no material is assigned, the object color is used to reflect light. The way the color is shaded across a surface is further controlled by smoothing. If it is not smooth, each face reflects light as an independent plane. If it is smoothed with adjacent faces of the same mesh, the shared edges are smoothed over and the geometry renders much rounder than it really is.

Smoothing Faces

The correct use of smoothing groups can make a simple model appear intricate and a complex model perfect, whereas the incorrect use of smoothing groups causes odd streaks or eliminates detail. By carefully assigning smoothing groups to select faces within a mesh, you can create economical and visually correct models.

NOTE

Remember that smoothing is a rendering illusion that always attempts to approximate the shading of the same form—a sphere. No "degrees" of smoothness exist. Faces are either smoothed or they aren't.

Understanding Face Smoothing

Smoothing can occur only between welded faces and therefore cannot occur between elements or objects. Faces will continue to smooth with one another as long as they can trace a line of welded faces that contain the same smoothing group.

The Smoothing function always tries to approximate the effect of a spherical form. Figure 11.34 shows how smoothing faces that meet at angles more acute than 60 degrees, especially 90 degrees, can result in unrealistic effects because the program attempts to smooth the corners in a spherical fashion. The objects with acute angles in this figure reveal awkward smoothing on their vertical surfaces because the shading is pulled diagonally across the mesh's sides. As a mesh gains more sides and those sides become progressively smaller, the diagonal highlight sharpens in angle and approaches a vertical, revealing more natural-looking smoothing. As a rule, smoothing angles sharper than 120 degrees (which equals an Angle Threshold of 60) produces undesirable results.

FIGURE 11.34

The effect of smoothing the sides of various angled meshes (tops and bottoms have no smoothing assigned).

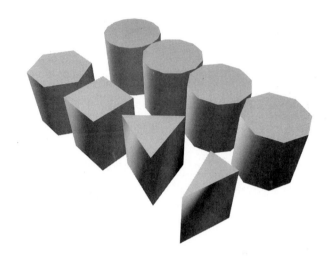

Using AutoSmooth

The AutoSmooth function provides the easiest method for assigning smoothing groups to a selection of faces. AutoSmooth compares its accompanying Threshold value to the angle between selected, welded faces. If the angle between selected welded faces is less than the Angle Threshold, AutoSmooth assigns a common smoothing group to those faces.

NOTE

If smoothing appears incorrect, check the mesh's construction. Coincidental vertices or adjacent faces may cause seams, and redundant faces may cause rendering irregularities such as "flashing."

AutoSmooth works best when the mesh's faces form angles that are consistent with their smoothing needs. A mesh that has many 45-degree chamfers, some of which need to be smoothed and some of which need to stay sharp, is an example of a poor candidate for AutoSmooth.

Identifying Smoothing Groups

The array of 32 Smoothing Group buttons is your first clue in identifying which smoothing groups are assigned to which faces. When you select a face, any smoothing groups assigned to it are shown as depressed buttons. In a selection of faces, the buttons are depressed if the group is shared by all of them, and the button is grayed-out (but not depressed) if the group is assigned to just some of the faces in the selection.

NOTE

Odd streaks and overly darkened edges are often signs of incorrect smoothing assignments. If an object does not seem to be rendering correctly, check to see that its smoothing group assignments are appropriate.

The Select By Smooth Group function presents a dialog (see Figure 11.35) that shows every smoothing group currently assigned to the object. Depressing a numbered button and clicking OK selects every face assigned to that group. The Clear Selection option performs a Select None and then selects by the smoothing groups you have chosen. Leaving this option off adds the selection by smoothing to the current selection of faces.

FIGURE 11.35

The Select By Smooth Groups dialog.

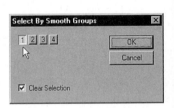

TIP

You can select every face that has no smoothing assignments by selecting every smoothing group and then performing an Invert Selection.

Manual Smoothing Assignments

A selection of faces can be assigned or cleared of smoothing group assignments with the 32 Smoothing Group buttons. This manual assignment gives you complete control over the result, rather than the automatic method afforded by AutoSmooth. To clear a smoothing group, click its button to undepress it. If the button is grayed out and, therefore, not common among the selection, you need to click the button twice—once to assign the group to the entire selection and again to remove it.

When assigning smoothing groups, you need to consider several questions about your model's form. What pieces should render round? Which sections should have crisp edges? Which planes should be faceted? After making these decisions, assigning smoothing groups manually becomes a study in face selection.

When smoothing intricate shapes, such as ornate iron work or beveled fonts, it's common to make multiple selections involving regions, deselection, invert, and face hiding. A common strategy is to identify flat surfaces first. The flat surfaces should be selected, assigned a unique smoothing group, and then hidden to make way for further selections. Making subsequent selections becomes increasingly fast because there are fewer unassigned faces with each pass.

Another common method is to Select All, perform an AutoSmooth, and then correct only the incorrect faces. The smooth shaded viewports report the state of smoothing and give you a clear account of how well the smoothing is assigned. If you spot errant smoothing, select the face and check its group numbers. Select adjacent faces, compare, and decide how to proceed. Often the best route is to clear all the smoothing from these difficult areas and start assigning to a clean slate.

When choosing smoothing group numbers, you have complete freedom; don't be overwhelmed by the choice of 32 groups. That number is provided so you can organize your selections without confusion and it also ensures that even the most complex models have enough groups. There is no significance to choosing low, high, or consecutive numbers. Lower numbers are filled by AutoSmooth first, so you may want to use the higher numbers to avoid a conflict. You will probably find that most meshes need only between two and six smoothing groups. More groups usually means that the mesh is very intricate or that separate groups are being maintained to double as selection sets.

TIP

Some modelers assign the same smoothing group number for a given geometric condition so the groups become convenient selection methods. Consistently assigning group 32 to caps, for example, provides a fast method for selecting caps later on. The same goes for bevels, sides, round areas, fillets, and so on.

Controlling Face Normals

Each face possesses a normal that emanates perpendicular from its center. The normal points away from the visible side of the face. The inability to see the other side of the face is termed a backface cull, a method that is commonly used to speed graphics and is the default mode for 3DS MAX's interactive and production renderers. Face normals are also an important indication of the geometry because consistent normals define a surface's direction and, in doing so, whether it's an interior volume or exterior surface. Because of these reasons, face normals are used by several functions to make both rendering and modeling decisions. A mesh that has consistent normals throughout its surfaces is said to be unified.

NOTE

When an object appears to be "backward" or "inside out," the cause is usually reversed normals. This incorrect facing is common when working with surfaces of revolution. What you may see as "in," the normals make "out." Figure 11.36 shows several objects with reversed normals.

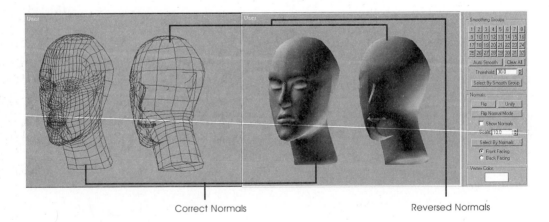

Correct Normals   Reversed Normals

FIGURE 11.36

The visual impact of reversed normals.

Normals determine far too much within 3DS MAX for you to ignore them. With EditMesh, normals define a face's Pivot Point Center, the direction of extrusion, and the angle thresholds used by Explode, AutoSmooth, and AutoEdge. Other modifiers, such as Optimize, Displace, MeshSmooth, and Relax calculate their effects by normals as well. Having unified normals is critical when creating Boolean compound objects. Some materials, including face maps and many procedural textures, base their results on face normals.

Unifying Normals

The Unify function resets a selection of face normals according to the 3DS MAX default, reorienting the normals to face out from the selection's center. This function is a fast method for unifying an entire mess (working well with Select All) and should usually be your first step with an incorrect mesh. For Unify to work correctly, a mesh's faces and vertices must already observe the golden rule of mesh building: every face that shares an edge with an adjacent face must also share two vertices.

NOTE

A misleading situation occurs when adjacent faces have coincidental vertices and only appear to be welded. If an apparently correctly built mesh is having problems with normal unification, make sure its vertices are actually welded and that no duplicate faces exist.

Showing Normals

The Show Normals option displays the normals of every face you select as a blue-to-white vector. This designation makes a misdirected normal easy to spot. Therefore, using Show Normals to identify misdirected faces can be more efficient than examining the faces. The accompanying Scale parameter in Show Normals scales the size of the normal vector and has no impact on the mesh. With some geometries, it can be useful to increase the Scale dramatically to see the intersection of normals (for example, the normals of an interior dome intersect at the dome's center). Normal vectors are for display only and cannot be manipulated directly (you must use the Flip function on selected faces instead).

Flipping Normals

Normal Unify will not work with every mesh. Coplanar, interior, revolved, or imported meshes must have their normals adjusted manually. This task can be quick, as when the normals are simply facing the wrong direction, or quite tedious, as when the mesh is built incorrectly and the normals are haphazard. Using the Edged Faces display mode can be a helpful tool to be able to spot the offendig faces quickly. A common situation is when you want to see inside an object you created. Unifying the normal always faces the normals outward from the selection's center, and you have to manually flip the entire mesh to face them inward.

When the mesh is unified but pointed in the wrong direction, select by element or Select All and click Flip. The normals now face in the opposite direction. This procedure works well for quickly flipping coplanar meshes, surfaces of revolution (such as a lathe), and objects meant to be viewed from the inside.

Two additional methods are available for selecting and flipping normals. If numerous, non-contiguous faces need fixing, use Flip Normal mode. When turned on, any face that is clicked will instantly flip. Right-clicking cancels this mode. Select By Normals uses the active viewport to assist in selecting faces. The Front Facing and Back Facing radio buttons specify how this modality works. Be sure to verify selections in other windows before performing operations on them.

Unifying Normals versus Two-sided Materials

You always have the two-sided option to render both sides of a face and thus skip the time required to correct face normals. This can be done by the property of a material, or the renderer can be forced to treat the entire scene as two-sided. This modeling "shortcut" costs rendering time because each face is calculated in both directions. The memory requirements of the two-sided option have an increasing impact if your rendering is casting shadows or calculating reflections.

N OTE

Making objects two-sided gives them the appearance of having extremely thin shells, something that does not exist and looks odd when rendered. Because nearly everything constructed has thickness, you should consider modeling both the inside and outside of your models unless it is made up of a thin material, such as a dollar bill.

In order to believably convey the natural properties of certain materials, notably glass, a two-sided material is necessary. Meshes visible on both sides and not close enough in the scene to be perceived as infinitely thin, such as leaves, flags, paper, cloth, and bags, are also good candidates for two-sided materials. The backs of objects that reflect into mirrors are often given two-sided materials to make up for their one-sidedness. For specific, troublesome objects that refuse to render correctly, you can assign two-sided materials as an alternative to rendering the entire scene in Force two-sided mode.

It's easy to conclude that a two-sided material takes only twice the resources to render as a one-sided material and is thus not too much of an expense. Reality shows, however, that closer to four times more faces are calculated by the renderer by each shadow casting light and by each reflecting surface within the scene. These extra faces are the result of rendering both sides of what is facing you (2×) and then both sides of what is not facing you (perhaps an additional 2×, but possibly more).

Assigning Material IDs

Each face begins, by default, with Material ID#1 assigned to it. Faces do not keep a record of the actual material name but rather the ID#. If the material is anything except Multi/Sub-Object, the material ID has no impact. Most primitives assign more than one material ID#. For example, in a cylinder, ID#1 is assigned one cap, #2 the other, and #3 the sides. When you assign the object a Multi/Sub-Object material, the material ID corresponds directly to which Sub-Object material in the material definition is assigned.

When deciding how to assign a Sub-Object material to selected faces, you should first consider whether the selected faces should remain part of the larger object. Usually when part of an object requires a different material than the rest of it, a visible break appears in the surface, at least a seam, between the two materials. Careful editing of the texture maps and pinpoint accuracy of the UVW coordinates are the solutions to the problem.

The actual assignment process is an easy one. With a selected set of faces, just bump the ID spinner in the desired direction (see Figure 11.37). If a Multi/Sub-Object material has already been assigned, the Shaded view instantly updates as the definition changes.

FIGURE 11.37

Changing the Material ID on a set of faces.

The Unwrap UVW modifier gives an editable picture of the coordinates and is covered in Chapter 15, "Map Channels and Map Types." Additional utilities can help from the painting side. Peter Watje's free Unwrap Object Texture (available from his web site) gives a pictorial grid that can be ghosted over the texture map. You can find Peter's site at http://www.blarg.net/~peterw/spectral.html.

Human Software's Squizz is a PhotoShop plug-in that can blend different textures together. At $125, it's a bit pricey, but in cases like mapping hair on to a character's head, it can prove invaluable.

A typical situation where you need to smooth and must use Material IDs with a Multi/Sub-Object material is with separate paints or finishes on a continuous surface. A bumpy wall with differing paint colors, a chrome handle with a knurled grip, and a vase with changing glazes are all examples of where you need smoothing to continue but require different materials.

Selecting By ID

The consideration of Material IDs concludes for now by noting that the assignment of IDs still enables face selection and selection set storage. Selecting by Material ID creates a selection of the faces with the chosen ID, enabling you, when you are using multi-materials, to see which part of your mesh is assigned which material. If you are not using a Multi/Sub-Object material, you can safely store selection sets of faces with different ID#s. This is fully animatable using the Material modifier, when a selection set has been passed up the Stack. Storing the selection sets has no impact on the material but creates very convenient face-level selection sets.

Given the discussion of smoothing and controlling face normals, it's time now to set those smoothing groups from the first exercise and fix some of the topology. In the shaded perspective view, the flange attached earlier seems to be missing faces. The faces are there, but their normals are flipped the wrong way.

Modeling with Edges

The third of the three major
by-product of creating faces a
are not a piece of geometry u
them to manipulate the face
which additional faces can be

Edge Level Basics

The Edge rollout shown in
Object levels. Edges obey t
selections as face selection d
play all the edges, it is diffic
cially true when making reg
face selection has a By Vert
ing a region, your first mous
and can easily hit an unwa

FIGURE 11.40

*The Edit Edge rollout
of Editable Mesh.*

FINISHING THE TANK

1. You can use your model from the last exercise or open the file m1d.max from the CD.

2. Hide everything but the cannon. Zoom in close to the flange area and select the cannon. Go to Sub-Object Face mode and scroll down the window to the Normals area. One by one, click the invisible faces and click Flip. The faces then become visible. A faster way is to click Flip Normal Mode, and then it is a one-click process.

3. Next, go up to the Smoothing Groups area. The current groups are incorrect (the cannon doesn't look smooth), so select the faces on the entire cannon and click Clear All, which enables you to start fresh. Select the flange plate and click the group square number 1. The flange is smooth and looks like Figure 11.38.

FIGURE 11.38

*The normals fixed and
the flange smoothed.*

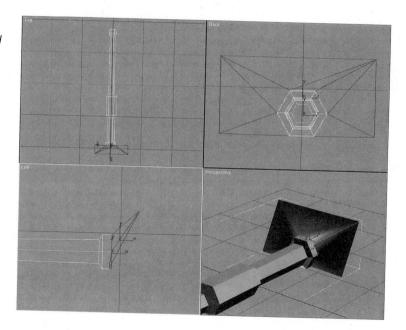

4. Select the next two sections of barrel and then hit square number 2. The flange plate and the barrel are both smooth, but a dividing line exists between them that helps with the detail. Continue on down the cannon barrel, smoothing each of the bulges separately, until you get to something that looks like Figure 11.39.

FIGURE 11.39

*The barrel of the can-
non smoothed.*

5. Unhide the re
   saw at the be
   CD and analy

This ends the exe
further detail, de
modifier, and Boo
game engine or to

WARNING

Be careful when using the Select All option with edges. Unlike hidden faces and vertices, invisible edges are acted upon as if they are selected, and Select All *does* select invisible edges. Any modification you apply after Select All with Edges affects invisible and visible edge selections with likely undesirable consequences.

Transforming Edges

When you transform an edge, you are actually transforming the two vertices that define it. Edges are a way to lock two vertices in a relationship to one another as you manipulate the edge. Think of an edge as a rigid barbell that moves the weights at either end without deforming itself. The way an edge locks two vertices in relationship is similar to how a face locks a selection of three vertices.

With an Editable Mesh, each edge possesses a local axis so you can use the pivot point center. As with faces, each contiguous selection determines a selection center.

Controlling Edge Visibility

Edges are not hidden but rather are made "invisible." Invisible edges behave differently from hidden faces and vertices. On the other hand, hiding faces and vertices "protects" them from further modification; making edges invisible does not. You can select, transform, extrude, divide, turn, collapse, and delete edges without ever seeing them. Although modifying invisible edges can be convenient, it can also be dangerous because you may be affecting far more than you want.

In modeling, visible edges define the boundary for polygon selection. In rendering, only visible edges are rendered when the faces they belong to are given a wireframe material (see Figure 11.41). Also, hidden edges influence the orientation of face mapped materials. For the most part, however, the only differences between visible and invisible edges are organizational and visual clarity. Invisible edges often make your model cleaner and more understandable because only prominent lines are displayed. In addition, invisible edges increase redraw speed because fewer lines need to be drawn.

For those who are modeling for export to a gaming engine optimized for four-sided (quad) faces, many programmers write a filter into their import functions that ignores hidden faces. This enables MAX, a tri-face modeler, to emulate a quad face modeling system.

FIGURE 11.41
The effect of hidden edges on wireframe materials.

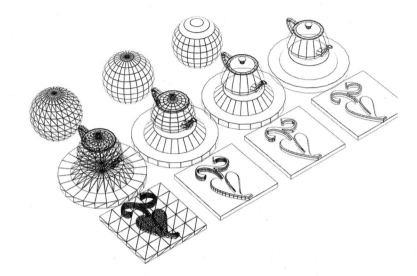

You can display invisible edges with the Edges Only option, found under Display Optimization in the Display panel. If you plan to work with edges, you will want to enter the Display panel and turn off Edges Only before you perform much editing. The Edges Only option has no influence on rendering.

Manual Visibility Assignment

You can control the display of edges precisely with the Visible and Invisible option. Decide which edges should be visible, select them, and click Invisible or Visible to change their status. Although selecting visible edges to make them invisible is straightforward, selecting invisible ones to make them visible may not be so simple. Remember that, unlike hidden faces and vertices, you can select invisible edges even though they are not displayed. To be sure of what you are selecting, turn off the Edges Only option. This can be done from either the Display panel, or in the Object Properties dialog accessed by right-clicking the object.

TIP

To make turning off the Edges Only option easier, you are highly encouraged to make Edges Only a keyboard alternate so you do not have to leave the Modify panel to change it.

Using AutoEdge

Although manual visibility assignment gives you control, it can be tedious. AutoEdge examines your edge selection and compares the normals of faces sharing those edges to the accompanying Angle Threshold value. As with AutoSmooth and Explode, the higher the Angle Threshold value is, the more edges qualify to be made invisible. The higher you make the threshold, the more acute the angle is that falls within its range.

TIP

To use AutoEdge on an entire object, perform a Select All, which selects all visible and invisible edges at once.

By working on a selection, you can control what part of your model is evaluated with the current Angle Threshold value. This evaluation can be important when different parts of your model have different angularity and a general AutoEdge would display too much or too little in a given area.

Creating Faces with Edges

Although edges are not a geometric entity in their own right, 3DS MAX enables you to create faces based on face edges with Extrusion and Dividing.

Extruding Edges

Extruding an edge is similar to extruding a face, except only one side is created. Each extruded edge moves the vertices of the edge and creates two new faces. Extruding individual edges is unpredictable because two vertices cannot define a plane. The function attempts to determine an extrusion direction based on faces adjacent to the edge, but this rarely produces the desired angles. A similar difficulty occurs if you extrude noncontiguous selections of edges.

As with Face Extrude, you can extrude interactively with your mouse or the amount spinner. Every drag and release of the mouse or spinner creates another extrusion, enabling you to quickly create strips of extruded faces.

Tip

The fastest way to use Extrude is to use the Extrusion spinner with a selection. This choice extrudes the faces but does not affect your toolbar status. You can move between extrusion and transforms without any delay.

Dividing Edges

The Edge Divide mode affects a single edge by inserting a new vertex at its midpoint and splitting the original face into two. If the edge is shared between two faces, both are split, resulting in four faces. The newly created edges are always made visible so you can see the results. Edge Divide is similar to EditSpline's Edge/Refine function and may be thought of as "insert vertex at midpoint." Regardless of what it is called, its capability to create a vertex and faces at midpoint locations can be valuable.

Dividing edges is a convenient way to introduce a vertex and add a face at mesh areas that need to be welded. Many models created in other programs are improperly tessellated and may have dissimilar vertex counts at transition points (AutoCAD's 3DS export of ACIS solids is an example of this). For these surfaces to smooth properly, vertices need to be created to balance the vertex counts at joints. Once a similar number is achieved at the transition, the vertices from either side need to be welded to allow smoothing to continue and deny the seam.

Faces that are newly created by Divide inherit the parent's mapping coordinates but do not acquire any smoothing groups. If your model uses smoothing, you need to assign smoothing groups after you finish dividing edges.

Note

When dividing edges on smoothed models, you can select the newly created faces by using Select by Smooth to select every smoothing group and performing a Select Invert.

Edge Topology

Although seemingly a minor function, Edge Turning is one of the most basic mesh editing tools. This tool is often used before and after Edge Divide, Vertex Collapse and Weld, and Face Extrude to produce the correct surface topology for the mesh.

Turning Edges

Edge Turn affects a single, shared edge by redirecting the edge to the other vertices of the two faces. Edge Turn has no effect on isolated faces or perimeter, unshared edges. Because mapping coordinates are actually stored with the vertices, Turning Edges does not affect mapping. You can reverse an edge's turn quickly by turning the same edge again.

NOTE

The direction of an edge changes the way face-mapped materials render and can be a critical tool in adjusting their appearance.

Turning an edge is a subtle modeling tool that is often used to alter a mesh's profile. Turning is a readjustment that does not make the mesh any more complex because it simply reorients what already exists. If a mesh's area needs to be roughed or smoothed a little, turning an edge can help.

If a Boolean operation is not working, turning an edge on coplanar faces may readjust the geometry enough for it to work without otherwise changing the object's position or complexity. The most common uses of edge turning, however, is to establish patterns within a mesh and to orient edges for subsequent modeling operations. Figure 11.42 shows a 12-sided cylinder that has had selected edges turned and every other pair of vertices on the top welded together. Turning edges can also be useful when faces are to be detached into another object that will border the original object, like the hem of a dress.

Collapsing Edges

Edge Collapse acts on the current edge selection. Collapsing an edge is similar to collapsing a vertex or face, but it is much less predictable than the other two. Collapsing an edge eliminates one of the vertices on the edge and "pulls" all edges that previously shared that vertex to the remaining one. The two faces that shared the original edge are removed and covered by the adjacent faces' stretch. Unfortunately, there's no way to determine to which vertex an edge is going to collapse.

Creating geometric patterns by turning and dividing faces.

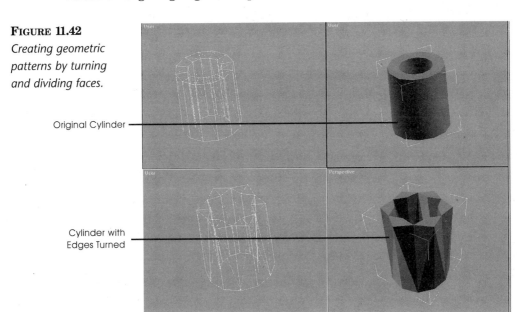

Original Cylinder

Cylinder with Edges Turned

When collapsing a selection of edges, each contiguous selection collapses to a single vertex. This vertex tends to be at an extremity of the selection, but its location cannot be predicted reliably. What constitutes a contiguous selection may be difficult to see as well because every face that shares the selected edge is considered for the collapse.

Deleting Edges

Edge Delete works on the current selection of edges. When you delete an edge, you are actually deleting the faces that share the edge while leaving the vertices intact. This deletion explains why you never receive a "Delete Isolated Vertices" message when deleting edges, in contrast to deleting faces. You can select, and thus delete, invisible edges. As always, be careful after performing a Select All because invisible edges may still be active. You can be confident of your deletion if you perform a Select None before building your edge selection.

Other Edge Tools

Edges can be separated from the parent mesh and converted to a spline by using the Create Shape command. The original edges are unharmed by this operation.

If there is a hole in the mesh, it can easily be found by using Select Open Edges. This is especially useful when used after building faces to check your work.

In Practice: Mesh Modeling

- **Affecting vertices:** Most mesh modeling affects vertices. Face, polygon, element, and edge selections are often just alternative methods for affecting the vertices that comprise them. When you adjust vertices, you adjust all faces that are built upon them.

- **Face level functions and normals:** Many face level functions base their effect on face normals or the averaged normal of the selection. Modifiers, such as Boolean compound objects and MeshSmooth, depend on proper normals for their results as well.

- **Vertex editing:** The vertex level's Affect Region option radically changes the way vertex editing works. When active, vertex selections act as "magnets" that push and pull regions of other vertices as defined by the shape of an adjustable region curve.

- **Preventing accidental editing:** Hiding faces and vertices is a method to segregate them from other selections and "protect" them from accidental editing. This should not be confused with edge level visibility that does not impact the selectability of the edges.

- **Smoothing groups:** Smoothing groups are key to perfecting a surface's quality. AutoSmooth works well for models with distinct transitions, while manual smoothing group assignments are needed when the model is very irregular or subtle in its transitions. Smoothing can occur only between welded faces.

- **Mesh functions:** Although the edges are a by-product of face definitions, functions are often used by serious mesh artists. In practice, Edge Turn and Edge Divide are among the most often used mesh functions besides transforms.

- **Material IDs:** Material IDs must be assigned at the face level for objects to contain more than one material definition (through the use of a Multi/Sub-Object material). Material IDs can also be used as a means of storing face selections when only single material is being used on the object.

- **Storing selections:** Named Sub-Object selections are a convenient method to store selections for a series of actions within a modifier. Named selections cannot, however, be used between modifiers.

Chapter 12

Patch Modeling

Modeling with Bézier patches is a complete alternative to traditional mesh editing. Computer modeling programs tend to be mesh-, patch-, NURBS-, or solids-based in their approach. 3D Studio MAX is somewhat different in that it enables any object class to exist and introduces the basics of patch editing with its Patch class and EditPatch modifier.

Although NURBS modeling is the current media darling, many artists find that patch modeling can be more effective, especially when it comes to character and facial modeling. Modelers who have come up through the ranks learning programs like Adobe Illustrator and CorelDraw can often find a familiar paradigm in patch modeling, which has far less memory overhead. That alone could be the deciding factor between NURBS and patches. Patches also work well for morph targets, because the face count remains the same as the different targets are constructed.

Patch modeling in 3D Studio MAX is capable of creating some impressive work with its tool set. This chapter will explain patch modeling and will cover the following areas:

- Characteristics of patch models and types of patches in 3DS MAX

- Understanding how Bézier curves are defined and how they relate to Bézier patch editing

- Using the patches formed from a variety of creation methods, such as primitives, Extrude, Lathe, and meshes

- Techniques in using the EditPatch modifier for Sub-Object patch modeling and the Vertex, Edge, and Patch levels

- Procedures for keeping your model as patches without converting to meshes until you need to

Understanding Patch Type Basics

There are currently two types of patches in 3DS MAX, QuadPatches and TriPatches, both of which are based on Bézier curves. The QuadPatch and TriPatch primitives (found under Patch Grids in the Create Panel's Geometry drop-down list) create single patches of these types, which you can add additional patches to with the EditPatch modifier.

Modifiers, such as Lathe and Extrude, can export their objects as patches. Meshes can be converted to patch objects as well. The important thing to realize is that the various creation methods can produce either Tri- or QuadPatches and that these two basic patch types produce different results when edited. Figure 12.1 shows two patches and their resulting forms after a few basic edits. The vertices and tangent handles of both patches are positioned in the same manner.

As you can see from the figure, the TriPatch object mesh tends to bend evenly, much like a piece of paper. The QuadPatch object tends to bend more like rubber than paper because QuadPatches affect a "quad" of adjacent control vertices; vertices at a diagonal affect each other's surface. In contrast, TriPatches only influence vertices with which they share an edge and the surfaces from diagonal vertices aren't affected. In more practical terms, TriPatches work well when folds (like the area around the corners of a mouth) are needed and QuadPatches are the best choice for more flowing surfaces where you want to avoid any pinching.

FIGURE 12.1

Differences between TriPatch and QuadPatch deformations.

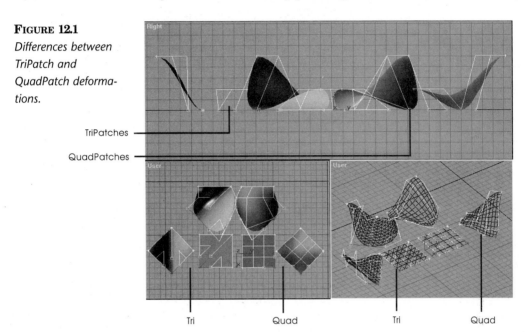

Patch Display Options

A Lattice that produces a surface defines Patch objects. The Lattice is a grid of the control vertices, vector handles, and intermediate vertices (see Figure 12.2). You have the option of displaying either the Lattice or the surface or both. In practice, you will probably want to hide the Lattice when working at the Vertex level and show the Lattice at the Edge or Patch level.

Edges and Patches are only "seen" on the Lattice itself. When working at the Edge or Patch level, all your selections are indicated on the Lattice and no selection indication is made on the surface. If the Lattice isn't present, your selections are still made, but they aren't visible (a sometimes dangerous situation). You cannot select new edges or patches when Lattice is off, however. The controls for the Lattice and surface display are provided at all levels because you will turn them on and off constantly as you work.

FIGURE 12.2

Display elements of patches.

Patch level patches

Edge level edges

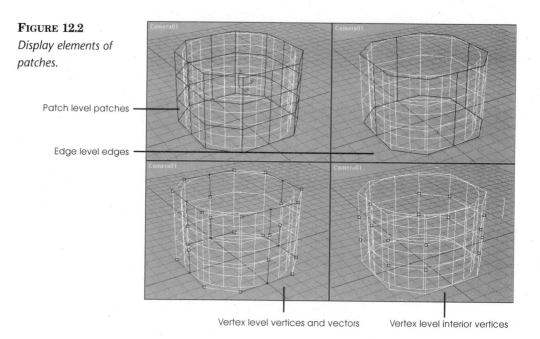

Vertex level vertices and vectors

Vertex level interior vertices

The patch surface is a result of the Lattice and can't be edited directly. This is a great asset, not a limitation, because it enables you to define the density of the patch surface at any time. As a result, you can work with a very simple representation and increase the surface density when editing becomes more subtle or your rendering output requires it.

Understanding Bézier Curves

Bézier patches behave in much the same way that Bézier splines do. The classic Bézier spline uses four points to determine its curve. The curve passes through the first and last points and interpolates between the middle two. Figure 12.3 shows how, with patches, the vertices are the spline's end control points and the patch vector handles are the spline's intermediate control points.

The concept of two intermediate control points is essential to understanding exactly what the patch Lattice is. Patch vertices are the end points through which the Bézier spline passes. These vertices are the easiest to relate to because they're part of the object's surface. The patch vector handles on the Lattice are thus the defining splines' other two control vertices.

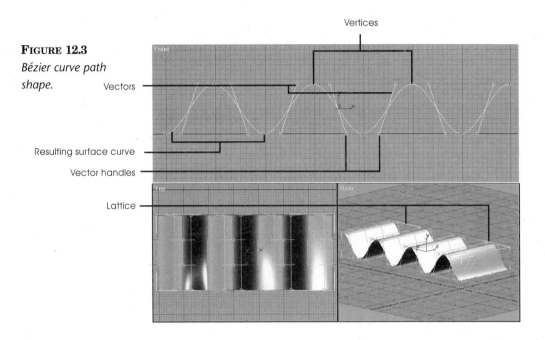

FIGURE 12.3

Bézier curve path shape.

Vertices

Vectors

Resulting surface curve

Vector handles

Lattice

Patch edges comprise the perimeter of a patch, whether Quad or Tri, and have three connected line segments. Although they may look boxy and somewhat odd, they actually connect the four defining points of the Bézier curve. Each edge begins and ends at a vertex with the segments being defined by the vector handle locations. Patches are thus composed of either three or four edges, depending on whether they are a QuadPatch or TriPatch. These edges define the Bézier splines that in turn define the patch.

Vectors are the lines that connect patch handles to vertices. The handles are actually the intermediate control points for the Bézier spline that defines the patch edge, meaning that there are two vector handles between each patch vertex, with a vertex having as many vectors as it has edges intersecting it. Vectors are often referred to in other programs as nodes, knots, or control points. This chapter refers to vectors as the visual line and handles as the control point at the end of the vector.

NOTE

Manipulating behave the vertices with the Lattice turned off can be confusing. The vectors appear to be properties of the vertex with the Lattice turned off, when, in fact, they are the interpolation points for the defining spline edge.

Creating Patches

Patches can be created in many ways. You can create them as raw rectangular patches, change Extrude or Lathe output to be patches, or convert 3D primitives to patches. Finally, 3DS MAX enables you to convert any arbitrary mesh to a patch and any patch to a mesh. This is accomplished through the use of two different types of Bézier patches: rectangular (bicubics) and triangular (quartics). These basic forms enable patches and meshes to change into one another.

Using Patches from Primitives

You may often be forced into working with one type of patch over the other. When meshes are converted to patches (by adding an EditPatch modifier) they are always converted to TriPatches, even if their topology produces quadrilateral polygons. QuadPatches, which are often more preferable, are formed as the result of specifying "Patch" when the object is being created. Most of the standard primitives, as well as splines given an Extrude or Lathe modifier, produce QuadPatches. Figure 12.4 shows the resulting patch geometry immediately after giving primitives an EditPatch modifier.

FIGURE 12.4

The patch equivalents for the standard primitives.

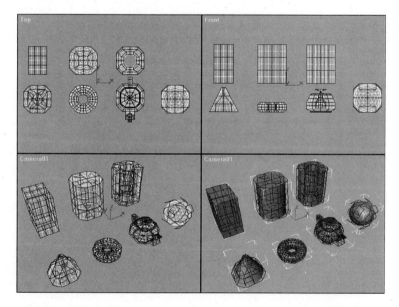

TIP

Creating primitives with negative heights creates patches with reversed normals. This can be a very convenient method for creating patch objects for containers, vessels, and rooms from boxes, cylinders, tubes, and cones.

As Figure 12.4 shows, every primitive except spheres and geoSpheres converts to QuadPatches (prisms, pyramids, and all the extended primitives are also TriPatches). Spheres convert to TriPatches due to a problem of QuadPatches "pinching" at the poles (a condition you can reproduce by lathing a half circle as a patch). The patch density of primitives is fixed. You can increase the density by using EditPatch's Subdivide function with the Propagate option. This shouldn't be an inconvenience because an EditPatch has to be initially added to convert primitives to patches.

Using Patches from Extrude and Lathe

Extrude and Lathe both have the option to output patches rather than meshes. In doing so, they become two of the most convenient methods with which to begin patch modeling. Figure 12.5 shows the patch models, beginning as splines, converted to QuadPatches by Extrude and Lathe.

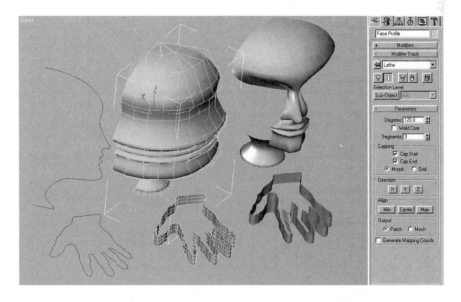

FIGURE 12.5

Using Extrude and Lathe for generating QuadPatches.

Splines are natural starting points for patch models because both splines and patch models base themselves on the same geometric form: the Bézier spline. Splines can be converted into patches by using the Extrude or Lathe modifier. Unfortunately, lofting doesn't produce patches as an option.

TIP

Ironically, you can create patch objects from lofts if you have 3D Studio, release 4. The 3DS models created by the 3DSR4 3D Surfer module are translated into 3DS MAX patches on import, as shown in Figure 12.6.

FIGURE 12.6

A 3D Studio R4 3D Surfer loft brought into MAX by .3ds import and turned into a patch.

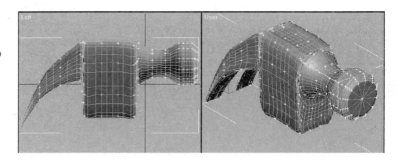

The Lathe modifier is extremely useful for creating basic forms for patch modeling. Lathe can be thought of as a potter's wheel, spinning a spline into soft, malleable patch clay. The tricky thing about using Lathe is directing its normals. Unlike meshes, you can't redirect the normals of a patch. If a patch's normals are facing the wrong way, you either have to change the manner in which the normal was created, reorient the existing patch, or use two-sided material. This last option is one to be avoided because turning Backface Cull off makes anything but the most basic of patch editing difficult.

Capping Patches

Patch objects formed with Extrude and Lathe are not as easily capped as their mesh equivalents. If the end cap is three-sided, it's capped with a TriPatch, and if it's four-sided, it's capped with a QuadPatch. If the cap has more sides, which is most likely, a more elaborate analysis should be done, with the following rules as guidelines:

- Nested shapes can't be capped (an extruded donut, for example).

- A clear line of sight must exist from each vertex to the shape's center.

In practice, it's the second rule that usually prevents capping and can be a bit frustrating. Figure 12.7 shows this situation, where the interior vertices just cross one another and invalidate the cap. To prevent this, you could place the star with the vertices in the left position and then edit with EditPatch to arrive at the position that previously canceled the capping.

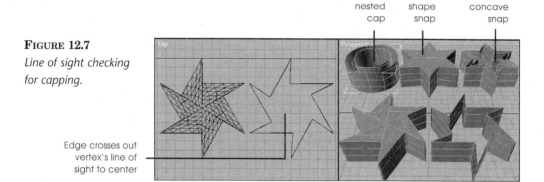

FIGURE 12.7

Line of sight checking for capping.

For more elaborate shapes, such as the hand shown in Figure 12.8, you need to cap the shape yourself. In this case, patches are added to the exposed edges (with EditPatch's Add Quad function) and then their vertices are welded to the vertices across from them. This is actually preferable for organic shapes because you now have control over where the patch lines occur and what type of patch is generated (automatic capping usually produces TriPatches). Most importantly, the patches you add and stitch across the face of the object have continuous smoothing—something that doesn't occur along automatically capped edges. The next section discusses capped edges in detail.

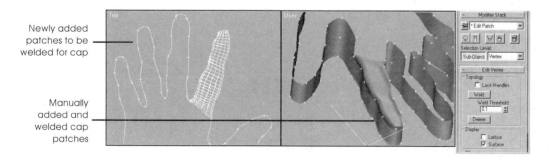

FIGURE 12.8

Manually capping a complex shape by adding patches to edges and welding.

Smoothing Continuity

A spline's vertex type dramatically impacts the resulting surface smoothing of the patch extrusion or lathe. Although Smooth or Bézier vertex types result in smooth patches, Corner or Bézier Corner vertex types result in crisp edges over which surface smoothing cannot continue. This situation is similar to that described below for primitives, although, unlike primitives, you can return to EditSpline to change these vertices to either Smooth or Bézier (see Figure 12.9).

If you collapsed the stack for a patch object created with Extrude or Lathe and now have a patch object, the surface smoothing continuity of the object is fixed and can't be changed. You should, therefore, carefully analyze your models before collapsing them to see if the spline vertices need reclassification.

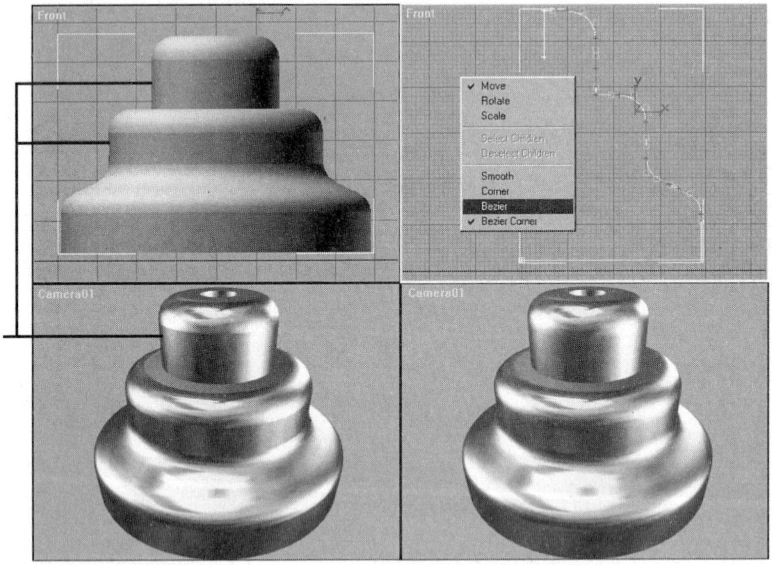

FIGURE 12.9

Vertex type's influence on smoothing continuity.

Smoothing discontinuity

Caps created by Extrude and Lathe modifiers, or defined as part of a parametric object, always exhibit a smoothing discontinuity along their capped edges. This is exactly the same situation previously described for splines with corner vertex types. The only difference is that there is no way to change this for caps; the edge always renders as a ridge.

TIP

If you need a smoothing to continue across the capped edge of an Extrude or Lathe, first remove the cap by either deleting the patches or removing the cap option in the modifier. Then add patches to the edges, stretch the exposed vertices to the opposite edges, and weld.

The patches generated by the standard primitives have a property that can't be duplicated with other patch modeling and unfortunately can't currently be changed. Primitives that begin with caps (crisp, hard edges such as the top of a cylinder or sides of a box, for example) maintain those hard edges for the life of the patch. Unlike Extrude or Lathe cap edges, patches added to primitives along originally capped edges always render as an edge.

Figure 12.10 shows the situation where the top vertex of a cylinder was deleted and the newly exposed edges were given QuadPatches. Because the cylinder's top was originally "hard," an edge exists, even though the patch vertices are later welded and remain tangent. This is a unique situation because this smoothing discontinuity can't be introduced for other patches, nor can it be eliminated for these.

FIGURE 12.10
Smoothing break between "hard" edges unique to caps.

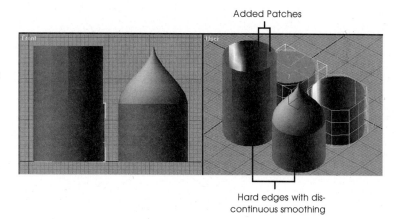

Added Patches

Hard edges with discontinuous smoothing

Using EditPatch

EditPatch is your primary tool for patch editing. It's similar in concept to EditMesh and EditSpline, although admittedly less robust. As with the EditSpline modifier, EditPatch saves every edit you perform in sequence, meaning that the longer you work with the modifier, the larger the file, and the larger your RAM requirements, becomes.

As you arrive at stages where you're comfortable with your model, you're definitely encouraged to collapse the stack. Models with large edit histories might even have their file sizes increase by a factor of 100 or more. As long as you do not include a modifier that converts the model to a mesh, the result of the stack collapse will be a Patch object, upon which you can apply the EditPatch modifier and return to patch modeling.

EditPatch is your only tool for establishing Sub-Object patch selections. Unlike mesh modeling, the Volume Select modifier doesn't work for patches; it unfortunately converts patches to a mesh instead and the Sub-Object animations must have their selections established with EditPatch. Because of its overhead, you are best off defining these selections in EditPatch modifiers that don't perform any editing, only selection. Adding specific EditPatch selection modifiers should be your standard method, whether animating transforms with XForm, modeling with modifiers, or animating that modeling.

Adding EditPatch as the very first entry in a primitive's edit history converts the primitive to a patch object. The primitive remains a patch until you add a modifier that requires it to convert to a mesh (such as Normal or Volume Select). Adding any modifier other than EditPatch as the lowest stack modifier converts a primitive to a mesh and removes any patch editing you may do with subsequent EditPatch modifiers. For example, to add a UVW Map before the first EditPatch, you must add another EditPatch first. You will find that navigating EditPatch is very similar to the other Edit modifiers.

The following exercise gives you hands-on practice working with the EditPatch modifier. In this chapter, the exercises focus on applying patch editing skills in building a cartoon bear's head (shown in Figure 12.11). The process is split up into three exercises that utilize different patch editing skills. The finished bear will be ready to animate, by using either Sub-Object vertex transformation, Linked XForms connected to the vertices (see Chapter 7, "Modifier Basics"), or by altering the patch grid to build morph targets (see Chapter 10, "Compound Objects").

N OTE

The "radial" method is used to build the character for this chapter. It's called that because the patches radiate out concentrically from the mouth, go around the head, and meet at the opening of the neck. This often-used method gives the widest range of facial expressions possible. The radial method of facial modeling works well with NURBS, too.

FIGURE 12.11

The finished bear.

BUILDING THE BEAR'S MUZZLE

1. Start with a fresh scene—you may have to reset MAX to get back to the defaults. In the Left view, draw a spline with six vertices that looks similar to Figure 12.12. Make sure that every vertex except the first is a Bézier type.

FIGURE 12.12

The six vertex splines that initially define the bear's muzzle.

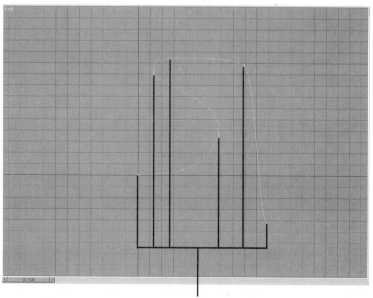

The six vertices

2. Put a Lathe modifier on the spline with a direction of Y and an align of Min. Set segments to 4 and Output to Patch. You may also have to flip the normals as well.

3. Rotate the Lathe -90 degrees about the Z axis in the Left view, change the Perspective view to User, turn off the Grid, and Arc Rotate the User view so that your screen looks like Figure 12.13.

FIGURE 12.13

The Lathe set up for patch editing.

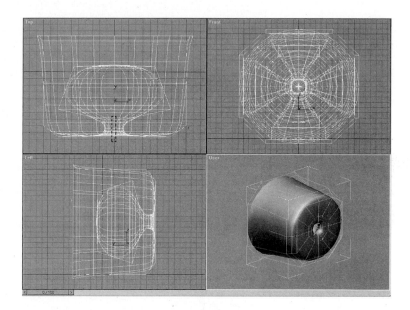

4. Add an Edit Patch modifier and stay in Vertex mode. Select a vertical stripe of vertices in the Top View (as shown by the marquee area in Figure 12.13) and drag them out so that you get something that resembles Figure 12.14. Make sure that, in addition to just getting the outer edge vertices of the front of the face, you get the vertices just behind the lips as well. Turning off the Lattice makes it a bit easier to see.

5. With the front vertices still selected, add all the mouth interior vertices shown in Figure 12.15 to the selection in the Front view. Toggle on Use Selection Center and NU-Scale the vertices in the X dimension in the Front view to square out the muzzle.

6. Next, select the corners of the mouth one at a time. The easiest way is to select them both in the Left view, then Drop out one side from the selection set. Scale the corners down in the X dimension in the Top view so that you get something that looks like Figure 12.16.

FIGURE 12.14

The front vertices selected and pulled out.

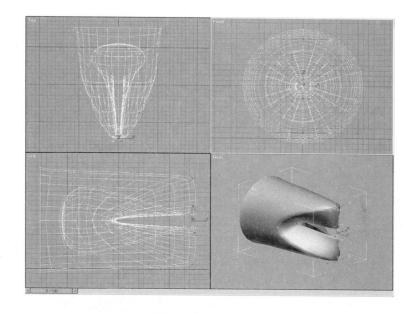

FIGURE 12.15

The exterior of the muzzle squared out.

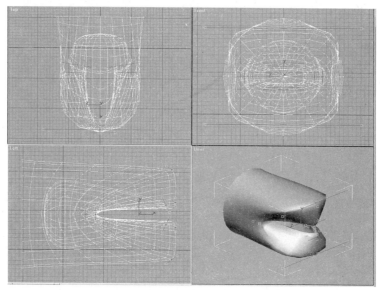

7. Scale out in X the upper and lower vertices for both of the lips. Bring up the jaw vertex and scale it in X in the Front view, so that you wind up with Figure 12.17.

FIGURE 12.16

The corners of the mouth scaled in.

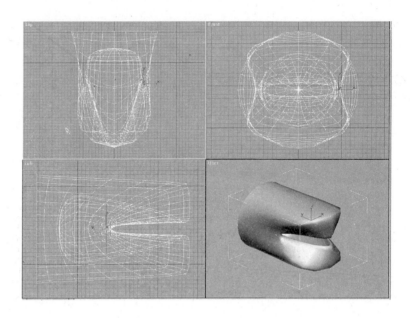

FIGURE 12.17

The lips scaled out and the jaw adjusted.

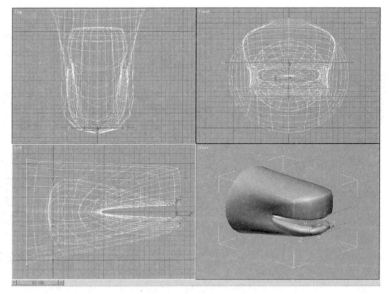

8. Finally, select all the mouth corners, scale them out in X in the Top view, and drag them back and up a bit in the Left view to give the bear a smile. You should have a muzzle that looks like Figure 12.18. If it doesn't, open up bear1.max from the CD to troubleshoot your model. After you're satisfied, save your file as bear1.max.

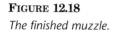

FIGURE 12.18

The finished muzzle.

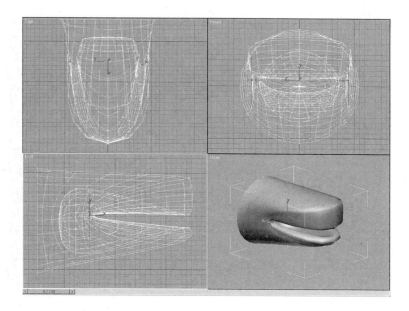

Notice how the muzzle has a mouth that is sealed on the inside. This keeps you from having to use a two-sided material and also gives the mouth better realism. Because we're working with patches, the inside of the mouth always stretches and compresses along with the muzzle.

The next four sections describe adjusting the EditPatch object and using the tools found within the three Sub-Object selection levels of EditPatch:

- Object level
- Patch level
- Edge level
- Vertex level.

Working with Patches at the Object Level

The Object level of EditPatch (see Figure 12.19) enables you to add other patch objects and contains your control for the mesh density of the entire patch object. It's not uncommon to return to the Object level while modeling at other levels to adjust the Steps setting for faster or more accurate vertex modeling.

FIGURE 12.19

The Object level of EditPatch.

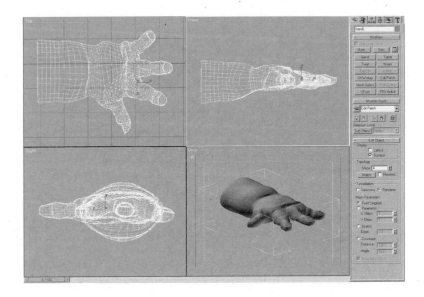

WARNING

Unlike EditSpline or EditMesh, cloning is not supported at any level within EditPatch; you can forget about using your Shift key when patch editing. Your only method for creating something similar to a clone is to detach patches with the Copy option.

Patch Topology

The Steps parameter influences how many subdivisions are made within all the patches of the object. As with everything in 3DS MAX, geometry must be converted to faces for rendering. The Steps parameter dictates how many subdivisions, and thus how many faces, are made within every patch of the object. This is very much like the steps settings for spline primitives, where adjusting the steps makes the spline rounder.

Unlike splines, however, patches always give you control over their steps, even after they have been collapsed. Just add an EditPatch modifier and you can always adjust the patch steps at that point in time (see Figure 12.20). This is one of the most powerful aspects of patch modeling because the model's complexity (and the resulting RAM requirements) can be adjusted as needed. Because this is an animatable value, the density of your patch model can adjust as its prominence in the scene changes.

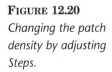

FIGURE 12.20
Changing the patch density by adjusting Steps.

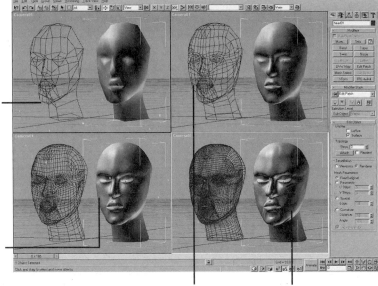

Zero steps: 250 faces

Three steps: 4000 faces

One step: 1000 faces   Seven steps: 16,000 faces

Although the amount of disk space your patch model requires is independent of its Steps setting, the RAM required for displaying and rendering is not. The number of faces generated is $(steps + 1)^2$ for every patch. A high Steps setting can thus bring your system to its knees if you are not careful.

WARNING

The maximum value for Steps is 100, creating more than two million faces for the model. Do not use the Ctrl accelerator key when adjusting the Steps spinner!

Attaching Patches

Attach enables you to bring another patch object into the same patch object definition. This is usually done for the purpose of welding patches together because welding can occur only within the same patch object. Objects attached that are not patch objects are translated into patch objects during the attachment. Figure 12.21 shows how a cylinder primitive is converted to a patch as part of the attach.

WARNING

You should be careful of attaching large mesh objects when your steps setting is high because doing so dramatically inflates the size of the model.

Unlike EditMesh, but similar in action to EditSpline, the Attach function provides a Reorient option. If checked, the selected object is reoriented so its transform matches that of the EditPatch object, as shown in Figure 12.21. The Reorient option centers the selected object according to its creation center onto the creation center of the active object. The rotation and scale values of the active object are simply copied to the attached object. For rotation, this has the effect of aligning the attached object and is usually desirable. The same cannot be said for the scale transforms, which affect your model's geometry. To prevent this scaling, you should use the XForm modifier rather than a transform to perform the scale of the base object.

FIGURE 12.21

Using the Reorient option of Attach to align the target objects' centers.

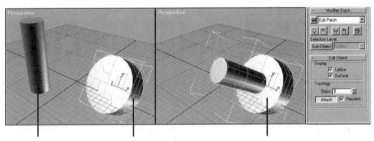

Cylinder Primitive   Local Centers aligned   Primitive converted to patch

NOTE

Because the Reorient option can be a bit surprising, it's advisable to use the Align function to center your objects before attaching to ensure that the reoriented result is desirable.

Tessellation

The tessellation area is where the mesh density is specified. The functionality is very similar to the way that a NURBS surface is defined. Please see Chapter 13, "NURBS Modeling," for a complete discussion on the use of tessellation.

Patch Modeling at the Patch Level

The Patch level (see Figure 12.22) provides the basics of patch control. Here you make broad transforms, change the status of interior vertices, and surgically detach, delete, and subdivide. Ironically, some Patch level operations (such as deletion and subdividing) affect far less than either the vertex or edge levels do. In practice, the Patch level is used primarily for detaching and subdividing patches as well as defining the status of interior vertices.

FIGURE 12.22

The Patch level of the EditPatch modifier.

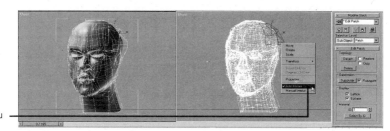

Right-click menu

Interior Vertices

Other lines of the Patch Lattice criss-cross the patch. These interior "edges" end at vector handles and pass through what are termed interior vertices. These vertices are actually secondary control handles that influence the curvature across the patch. (Calling these "vertices" is extremely misleading and you are best off thinking of them as interior handles or interior control points.)

These interior control vertices behave much like vector handles, controlling the Bézier curvature in a more subtle way. Note that, although patch edges form true Bézier splines (passing through the patch vertices), the interior Lattice "splines" don't because their end points are vector handles that don't have to be on the surface.

Interior vertices can be important because they enable you to distort a single patch in a manner that would otherwise require additional vertices and thus more patches. Figure 12.23 shows how adjusting the interior vertices deforms a single patch in a manner that would normally require the vertices of four patches.

FIGURE 12.23

Adjusting interior vertices versus vertices from additional patches.

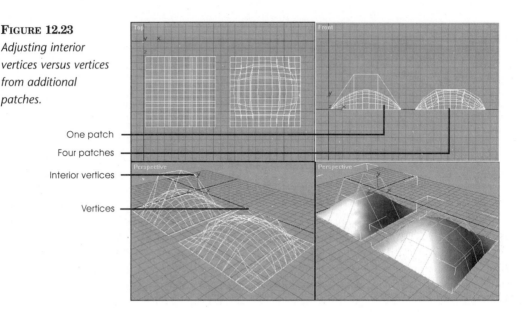

One patch

Four patches

Interior vertices

Vertices

Patch Editing in Auto Interior versus Manual Interior Mode

Although interior vertices may be useful, they are a bit difficult to get at. When first editing a patch, the patch is in Auto Interior mode and the interior vertices are invisible because the interior control points are being moved when you adjust vector handles, edges, and patches. The interior vertices don't appear until you change the patch(es) to Manual Interior mode by right-clicking them while in the Patch Sub-Object selection level.

When you place a patch in Manual Interior mode, nothing happens visually until you return to the Vertex selection level. Then all the interior vertices appear in yellow for every patch currently in Manual Interior mode, four vertices for a QuadPatch and three for a TriPatch (see Figure 12.23). Unlike with vector handles, you don't have to select anything first to manipulate them—they're always available for manipulation.

What may not be obvious is the effect Manual Interior has on edge and patch editing. When you're in the default Auto Interior mode, the interior vertices are moved when you manipulate edges and patches. Manual Interior, on the other hand, effectively freezes the interior vertices to where they are. They can now be edited only, by hand, individually at the Vertex level. The inability to multiple-select can cause difficulty when attempting to keep a model symmetrical. Figure 12.24 shows the moving of an edge in Auto Interior versus Manual Interior.

FIGURE 12.24

Moving an edge with the patch in Auto Interior and Manual Interior modes.

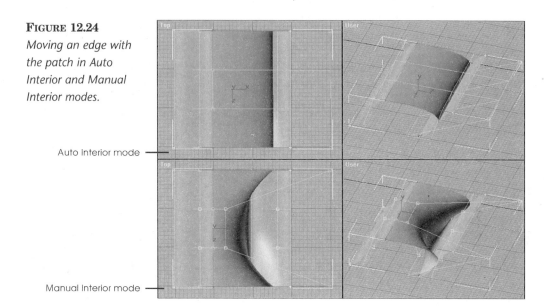

Auto Interior mode

Manual Interior mode

Editing vertices is also different when the patch is in Manual Interior mode because the interior vertices are no longer pulled along. Figure 12.25 shows the same vertex edits in both modes. Moving vertices without their neighboring interior vertices results in sharp-edged surfaces. Of course, editing just the interior vertices results in equally useful surface qualities, as shown in Figure 12.26.

FIGURE 12.25

Moving single vertices with the patch in Auto Interior and Manual Interior modes.

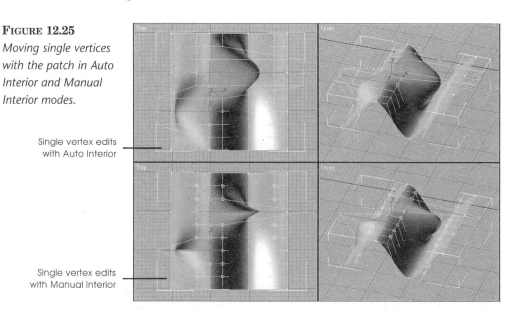

Single vertex edits with Auto Interior

Single vertex edits with Manual Interior

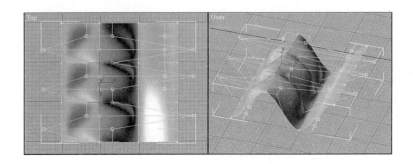

Transforming a patch or edge transforms the vertices and vector handles of
the edge or patch, but this leaves the interior vertices behind. Although
transforming a patch or edge can be useful, it also can be very confusing if
you aren't prepared for it. When you're prepared for the result, Manual
mode can be quite useful.

WARNING

Changing a patch from Manual Interior to Auto Interior cancels any editing you've done to the
interior vertices. If you begin manipulating interior vertices, you must keep the patch in manual mode to maintain your edits.

Subdividing and Propagation

Subdividing a patch divides every selected patch into four patches. The new
patches, whether Quad or Tri, have edges at the midpoints of the original
patch's edges. As Figure 12.27 shows, this doesn't necessarily mean that the
entire object quadruples. Only the patches that border divided edges themselves divide and many divide just once.

The Propagate option divides patches as necessary to maintain consistent
vertices along edges. Unless you want a visual break in the model, you
should always propagate your patch subdivisions. Without propagation,
smoothing can't continue over the edge. The reason is simple—the new vertices have nothing with which to weld. The visual effect is a ridge at the
seam because smoothing cannot continue across the edge. This makes the
area similar to a "flap" that is ready to be peeled away, without affecting
neighboring patches, as shown in the lower-right of Figure 12.28.

FIGURE 12.27

Repeated subdividing with Propagation on.

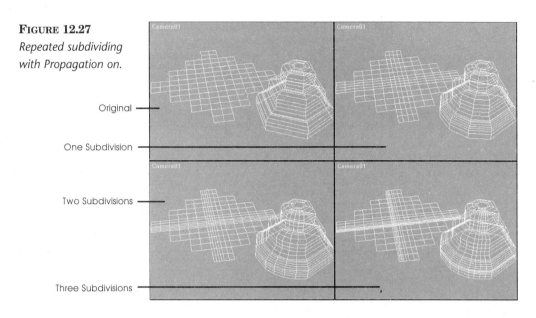

Original

One Subdivision

Two Subdivisions

Three Subdivisions

FIGURE 12.28

Seams caused by subdividing with Propagation off.

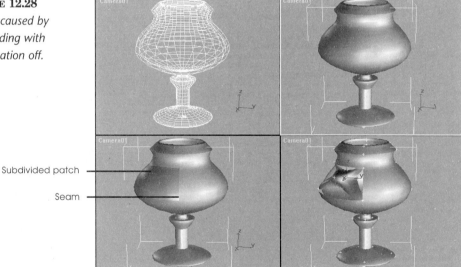

Subdivided patch

Seam

Transforming Patches

When you move, rotate, or scale a patch, you're actually transforming all its vertices as a locked selection. In general, working at the Patch level is limited to initial, broad adjustments. The finer detail is provided at the Edge level, or especially the Vertex level. Deleting at the Patch level is the most controllable method for deleting patches because only what you select gets deleted; patches that share edges are not deleted.

The one thing to be very careful about when transforming patches is the status of interior vertices. When using the default Auto Interior method, the interior vertices always move with the patch. If Manual Interior is active, however, interior vertices are frozen in place and can't be moved. Figure 12.29 shows the effect of scaling patches that have their interior vertices in Manual Interior mode.

FIGURE 12.29

Scaling patches in Manual Interior mode, leaving their interior vertices unaffected.

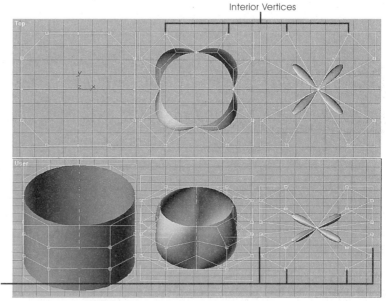

Detaching Patches

Unlike EditMesh, detaching a patch always results in the creation of a new object. In addition, the option to keep the new patch as an element isn't available. If you need the new patch to be part of the same object, you need to use Attach at the Patch Object level.

Like Attach, Detach provides a Reorient option that attempts to move the detached patch object to an aligned position on the active grid. Due to the nature of patches, however, the result of using Reorient usually isn't desirable and you're better off not using this option and using the standard Align function instead.

Sub-Object Materials

As a response to vociferous complaining by MAX 1.x users, Kinetix has added the ability to put more than one material on a patch. Patches now have the same materials features as meshes. For a complete discussion on Sub-Object materials, please refer to Chapter 11, "Mesh Modeling," and Chapter 14, "Materials and Textures."

Patch Modeling at the Edge Level

Working with a patch edge is similar to manipulating two vertices at the same time. Edges can be a bit difficult to identify because you nearly always have to be viewing the Lattice to ensure that you have the correct edge. Figure 12.30 shows the Edge Level rollout of Edit Patch. Notice that there is no Delete function seen in the controls because you aren't able to delete at the Edge level. In practice, you will probably be using the Edge level for adding new patches more than anything else.

 **W**ARNING

Using the Delete key with a selected Edge deletes the *entire* patch object because there isn't a Delete function and the Delete key is being used at the Object level instead.

FIGURE 12.30

The Edge Level con-
trols of EditPatch.

Patch edges of original
lather selection

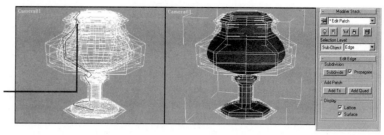

Transforming Patch Edges

You may be surprised by what can be accomplished by transforming edges, especially when you rotate them. Figure 12.31 shows the formation of a wave from a flat strip by simply rotating the edges as individual selections. In this case, not a single vertex is relocated; they still remain on the original flat plane. The interior vertices, however, are displaced by the very nature of Bézier patches.

FIGURE 12.31

Rotating edges to form
a ribbon of waves.

Rotated edges

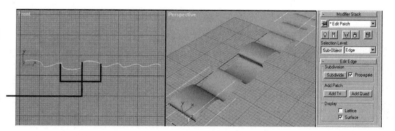

Like patches, edges can't affect interior vertices that are currently in Manual Interior mode. These vertices are "left behind" as you transform the edge. Returning the patch to Auto Interior mode reverts interior vertices to their default locations and edge transforms will now affect them.

WARNING

Patch edges treat the Local coordinate system as the world, and always rotate and scale about the world origin. Using the Local coordinate system is thus discouraged for the Edge level.

Adding Patches

Your primary reason for being at the Edge level is to add patches. Adding edges is the only way to extend a patch object's boundary other than welding. Added edges weld themselves to the selected edge. The remaining vertices of the new patch (two for a Quad or one for a Tri) are then free to be manipulated. In most cases, you weld these to other patches.

Adding edges isn't quite as basic as it might first seem. After selecting an edge, you either click Add Tri or Add Quad to add the appropriate patch type. What may not be obvious is that every selected edge receives a patch. This can be a problem when duplicate patches are created where there appears to be only one. Figure 12.32 shows a typical situation where extra patches are accidentally added because too many edges were selected. As the lower-right viewport shows, the duplicate edges can be peeled from one another to expose the duplicates.

Figure 12.32

Duplicate patch creation resulting from selecting adjacent edges.

Correctly selected edges ⎯

Duplicate edges ⎯

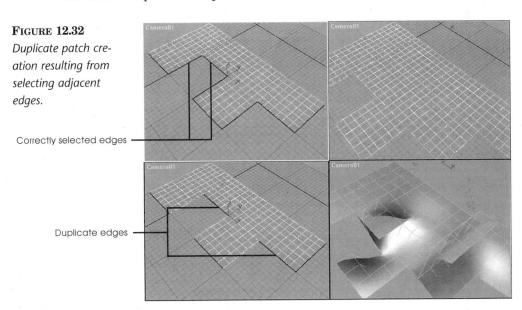

The correct method to add patches in interior corners is to select single edges with an eye as to how far they will extend (see the lower-left viewport of Figure 12.32). After new patches are added, return to the Vertex level, perform a Select All, and weld the entire patch so that the newly added patches share the adjacent edges. You don't have to be this careful when adding patches to exterior edges because it's usually obvious where the new patches will be placed. Figure 12.33 illustrates adding TriPatches to a QuadPatch and then moving the vertices to create the beginnings of a flower.

Patches are added tangent to the patch belonging to the selected edge. When you're adding patches to more organic models, as shown in Figure 12.34, the resulting patches might easily project at odd angles.

FIGURE 12.33

Adding TriPatches to begin a flower.

Original Patch

Four TriPatches added

Eight TriPatches added

Transformed Vertices

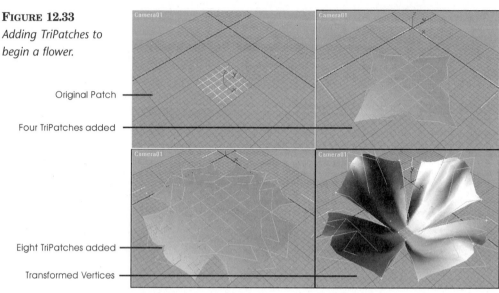

FIGURE 12.34

Tangent patches added to selected edges.

Selected Edges

New QuadPatches

Tangency maintained

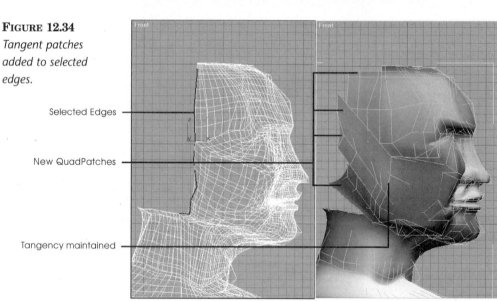

When you're closing holes or knitting between parts, the edge you select to receive the new patch dictates this direction. Happily, it doesn't matter which edge you select because when you weld to the next patch, the new patch assumes its continuity. Your choice of edges to add to should be based on whatever produces the most convenient result. If the patch results at a sharp twisted angle, undo and select another side to which to add. Your aim is usually to create a patch that has vertices that are easily selectable for any subsequent transform or weld operation you may need to perform.

As the beginning of this chapter indicated, the type of patch you add impacts how it deforms and behaves. Although mixing the two patch types is perfectly legal, you should be very cautious about doing so because editing methods differ across your model. When closing an organic object based on QuadPatches, for example, it may appear simpler to use TriPatches at certain junctures. This can result in areas that have challenging edge smoothing conditions because the different patches on either side of the edge bend in fundamentally different ways. Figure 12.35 shows a situation where a TriPatch is added in the midst of QuadPatches. The result is an edge that still needs some vertex vector handle adjustment to smooth out the resulting ridge.

FIGURE 12.35
A TriPatch added in the midst of QuadPatches.

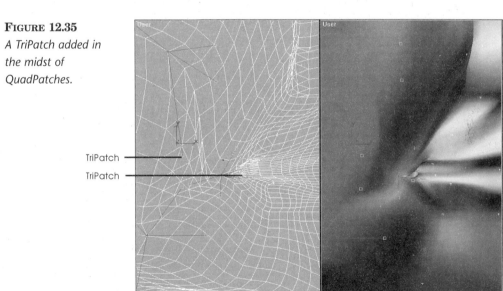

TriPatch
TriPatch

Patch Modeling at the Vertex Level

The Vertex level (see Figure 12.36) is where the vast majority of patch modeling occurs because it is only at this level that the critical tangent vectors are accessible. Unlike mesh vertices, a patch vertex and its vectors have a tremendous impact on the surrounding surface. In fact, adjusting single patch vertices is similar to transforming single mesh vertices with the Affect Region option.

FIGURE 12.36

The Vertex Level roll-out of EditPatch.

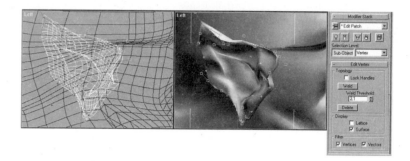

TIP

You are likely to find that when editing vertices you have no need to ever show the patch lattice because all vertices are part of the patch surface, and their influence is quite apparent. When working with vertices, it's usually best to turn off the Lattice.

The density of the patch, controlled at the object level by the Steps setting, has no impact on your vertex edits. Low step levels can betray the effect of your editing because not enough faces are produced to show the resulting curvature. When making final edits to your model, you want to increase the Steps so the shading subtleties, dictated by tangencies, are apparent as you edit. Remember, you can always lower this setting without harm. Higher settings don't impact file sizes, only RAM.

Vertex filters are quite useful, although their check box options can be a bit confusing. There are two options in the Filter area: Vertices and Vectors. When both options are checked (the default), then both the vertices and vector handles can be selected. Clicking Vertices filters out the vertices so that only vector handles can be selected, and clicking Vectors filters the vectors out so that only vertices can be selected. The somewhat odd toggling of these options is to prevent the filtering of both because in that case, nothing can be selected.

Even so, if you filter Vertices before selecting any, you won't be able to affect vectors because they're displayed only when their vertices are selected. To work with just vector handles, you need to perform a Select All and then check Filter Vertices. Filters are primarily used when vector handles are coincidental or close to their vertices, and you need to ensure the selection of one over the other.

Welding Vertices

Welding vertices is your method for joining patches to one another or sealing the open edges of patches newly added to edges. Weld works in conjunction with its Threshold value. This value indicates the maximum distance that vertices can be from one another to be welded. Vertices found to be within each other's threshold have their positions averaged to arrive at a new location for the welded vertex. Welding patch vertices involves a few more rules than welding mesh vertices. The rules for welding patch vertices are as follows:

- Welding can't be done to two vertices on the same patch.

- Patches must belong to the same object.

- Welding can occur only between open edges.

- No weld can take place if the result forms an edge that would be used by more than two patches.

- If you attempt to weld a vertex that isn't on an exposed edge, it is ignored, enforcing the above restrictions.

The positional averaging that occurs between welded vertices can either be exactly what you want, or it can result in a horrible mess. Although EditPatch doesn't have a Weld Target option (as does EditMesh), it gives you control through a somewhat hidden method. You can keep a vertex anchored and force the other vertex to move to it by simply selecting the patch (at the patch level) to which the target vertex belongs. Selected patches can't move their vertices during a weld operation unless the other vertex being welded is also part of a selected patch.

TIP

Selecting patches for vertices you don't want to alter is critical when adding patches to areas of an already finished section of your model.

Welding patches may seem a bit "magical" because of the way the welded patches are adjusted to be tangential and smooth. When welded, the edges that the vector handles and vertices define have new points through which to interpolate. The Bézier curves then produce a naturally smooth surface. Figure 12.37 shows how several added patches, which start out smooth on their attached edges, are given continuity when their corner vertices are adjusted to be close to one another and welded. This is a wonderful property of Bézier curves in that they maintain continuity between adjacent curves and, in this case, patches.

FIGURE 12.37

Continuity created between welded edges.

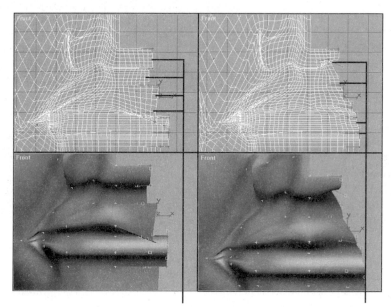

Newly added patches   Vertices welded

When working on symmetrical models, such as noses and faces, it's very convenient to model only half the form. After you're to a point where it becomes necessary to see the other side, mirror the model about the central edge and make the new object an instance or reference. Consequently, when you work on one side, the changes are duplicated on the other. Figure 12.30 shows this technique with a head, where all edits done to one side are dynamically updated on the other as you work. After you're finished, attach the second side to the first and weld the seam shut (as was done in the lower-right view of Figure 12.38).

TIP

If you have begun modeling on an entire model that is symmetrical and wish to use this technique, simply detach or delete half the model and mirror the remainder. Weld's averaging of vertex positions is often an aid in creating a straight mirror seam.

Keeping this mirroring technique in mind, it's now time to continue with the radial construction method discussed in the first exercise. In this exercise, you will be adding patches that radiate out from the muzzle.

FIGURE 12.38

Patch modeling with a mirrored instance.

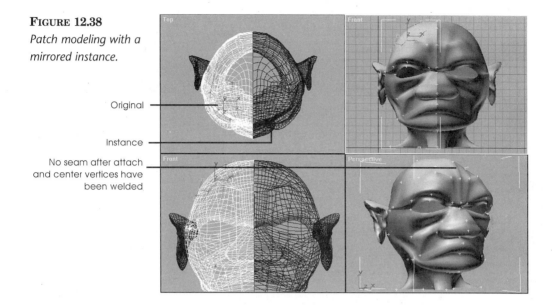

Original ——

Instance ——

No seam after attach
and center vertices have
been welded

ADDING THE HEAD TO THE MUZZLE

1. Continue with your bear from the previous exercise or open bear1.max from the CD.

2. Go to Sub-Object Edge, turn off the Surface display, and turn on the Lattice. Select one of the open edges on the muzzle and click Add Quad (see Figure 12.39). Continue on around the muzzle, adding QuadPatches.

3. Go to Sub-Object Vertex and try moving one of the newly created vertices at the end of the patch. Half of the model moves; it's not a contiguous surface. Region-select both vertices at the joint and bump up the Weld Threshold to 5. Click Weld. Now the vertex moves both surfaces. Continue on around and weld together the new patches.

4. Extend out the upper two edges twice more, welding the upper vertex each time. Your bear should now resemble Figure 12.40.

5. Go to Sub-Object Vertex and begin to move around the vertices and their handles to round out the top of the head. It's not too hard, because there are so few vertices to deal with. Work one view at a time and try to get the upper head as round as possible.

FIGURE 12.39
Extending the model by using Add Quad.

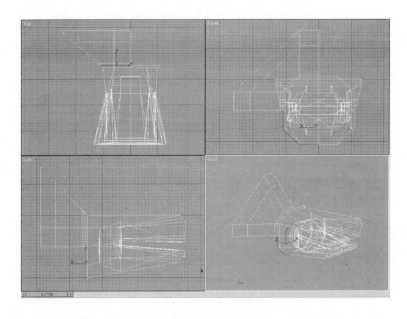

FIGURE 12.40
The upper head ready for editing.

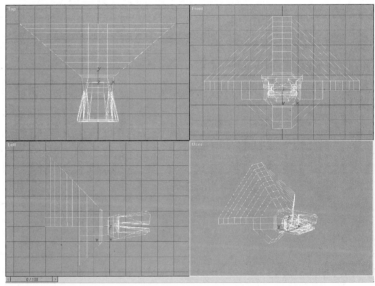

T IP

Some people find it helpful to draw a circular spline as a template to assist with the process, and then delete it after they're done.

6. Be sure to turn on the Surface display to check your work. When your bear looks like Figure 12.41, it's time to move on to the next step.

FIGURE 12.41

The upper head edited.

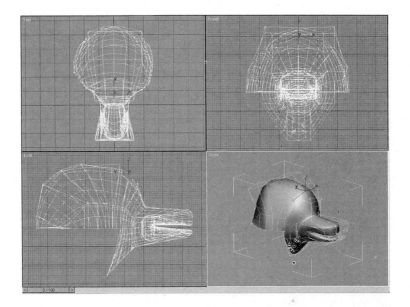

7. One at a time, select the edges on the lower half of the head and extend them out with Quad patches. This time the patches aren't as neat, so carefully bring the vertices together to form the neck opening. Now the push and pull of patch modeling begins. Using all three views, refine the head by adjusting the position of the vertices and their handles. The head gradually takes shape until it begins to look like Figure 12.42. When completed, save your file as bear2.max.

Don't get frustrated if the head doesn't come together right away. This is very much a sculptural process and the head will take some time to get right. You can adjust the vertices to match Figure 12.42 or take off in your own direction if something good starts to form. Patch modeling is an artistic endeavor and should be approached with an eye to esthetics.

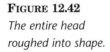

FIGURE 12.42

The entire head roughed into shape.

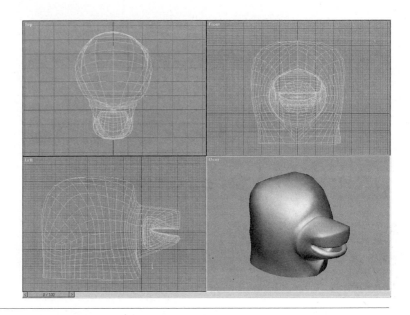

Transforming Vertices and Vector Handles

Nearly all your edits with patches involve transforming vertices and their tangent vectors. Each vertex should really be thought of as a cluster of points, never just one because each vertex has a vector handle for every edge that shares it. When you move, rotate, or scale a patch vertex you're also transforming its handles. Rotations and scale, operations that do nothing for single mesh vertices, can have a significant impact on patch vertices. Vector handles can be adjusted only when their vertex has been selected and it's common to select several vertices and adjust their handles independently.

When adjusting vertex tangent handles, it's important to remember that you can't animate them directly. Patch animation takes place with either the XForm or Linked XForm modifier, and both of these only operate upon vertices. When you're designing your patch model for animation, this needs to be taken into account. You can animate all of a vertex's vector handles in a group by applying an XForm scale or rotation to a single vertex. The vectors then scale and rotate about the vertex in a uniform manner without disturbing the vertex itself.

The FFD (Free Form Deformation) modifiers can animate patch surfaces in a manner that is very similar to adjusting the tangent handles. The FFD modifiers preserve the model as a patch and are extremely valuable tools for manipulating patch models.

Vector handles are interesting and extremely valuable controls because they usually impact the curvature of two patches (those that share the edge to which they initially "point"). The vector is just a "lifeline" of sorts that visually shows you what vertex the handle belongs to. All that matters is the location of the handle. Vector handles concern themselves only with position. When you rotate or scale a vector handle, the handle simply rotates about or scales to the vertex to which it belongs.

To move a single vector handle perfectly along its vector, scale the handle and it moves co-linear to the parent vertex.

Editing Vector Type

Right-clicking a vertex, or selection of vertices, enables you to edit their vector type. This procedure is similar to spline vertices, except there are only two options: Coplanar and Corner. The Corner option enables you to adjust each vector independently, so editing one doesn't impact the others. This does not influence path smoothness or continuity. The Coplanar option adjusts the Vertex handles to be coplanar with one another and then locks the vectors so that they maintain their coplanar relationship. What may be surprising is that this doesn't ensure or enforce tangency of the affected patches; it aligns only the vector handles on a common plane.

After the Coplanar option is applied, all handles adjust when one is manipulated to maintain the coplanar relationship. The only way to move one handle and not affect the other is to scale it. Vertices having only two vectors (those on outside corners) are always treated as Corner because three points are required to define a plane. Although changing a vertex from Corner to Coplanar often changes the curvature a bit, changing from Coplanar to Corner has no initial effect on the patch surface.

T IP

When modeling organic forms, you will probably want to use corner vectors, and perhaps change them to Coplanar after you're nearly finished. You will find that this gives you more freedom for manipulating each vertex as you concentrate on the form.

Transforming Patch Vertices in the Local Coordinate System

Transforming patch vertices is different from transforming patches or edges when using the Local coordinate system. When Local is active, your vertices rotate and scale about a local axis that has the same axes alignment as the object itself. This is regardless of the current pivot point center option. This means that when using the Local coordinate system with vertices, the Use Selection Center option has no effect. Although a bit confusing, this capability enables you to independently rotate and scale vertices; the effect being that the vector handles spin around and move to and from the static vertices. If you need to rotate them about a collective center, you need to choose another Coordinate system type (such as a parent).

Lock Handles

The Lock Handles option locks handles so that adjusting one influences the others. Only when a handle moves along its vector (scaled) are the others not affected. Lock Handles is a global setting for the patch object that is identical in operation to the way handles adjust when their vertices have Coplanar settings. In practice, you probably will not want this setting on. Its primary use is for adjusting Corner vertices that require their handles to maintain the same relationship.

Deleting a Vertex

Deleting a vertex deletes all the patches that share it. In this way, it is very similar to deleting mesh vertices where every face that shares a vertex is deleted. Deleting patches by their vertices is not nearly as surgical as deleting individual patches. Remember that you aren't allowed to delete at the Edge level.

Staying in Patch Mode

When working with patches, the last thing you usually want to do is introduce something in the Modifier Stack that causes the Patch object to convert to a mesh. Certain modifiers do this every single time and should be used only at the very end of the stack, so your patch modeling can continue below it without harm. Modifiers that are designed to work with meshes or faces (nearly anything dealing with a surface) must convert the object to a mesh. The following always convert patches to meshes when applied:

EditMesh	Material
Smooth	Normal
VolumeSelect	MeshSmooth
Relax	Optimize
Mesh Select	

As a result, it's very prudent to create a button set that includes only modifiers that can work with patch objects. Figure 12.43 shows a "Patch Edit" button set that includes such commands, as well as the commands for spline editing because the two go very well together.

FIGURE 12.43

A Patch Edit button set to ensure Patch geometry does not go to mesh.

The only surface-related modifier that you can apply is a UVW Map modifier. Internally, this is because both the Mesh and Patch object classes belong to the "mappable" object class, which enables modifiers to store mapping without affecting topology. The same capability is unfortunately not afforded smoothing, materials, and normals, pointing to a very significant aspect of patch editing. The smoothness of your model is entirely dependent on the tangencies of your model and how it was constructed.

Using Modifiers on Patches

Modifiers can be added in your edit history in much the same way that you add modifiers to meshes. Remember to avoid Optimize, Relax, and MeshSmooth modifiers. Although modifiers operate in the same way for patches and meshes, their effect is usually different. Both meshes and patches are actually modified by their vertices. The difference in applying modifiers to patches is that the vertices are the control points and not the surface. Thus, a modifier is manipulating patch vertices, which obviously has a more dramatic impact on the surface than mesh vertices.

Figure 12.44 shows the moving of a Displace modifier diagonally across a patch surface. In all four frames, the modifier is level and its values constant. The reason for the dramatically different effect is that the control vertices of the patch are displaced and because they define the patch surface through interpolation, the surface is displaced considerably.

FIGURE 12.44

A Displace modifier's effect on patch vertices.

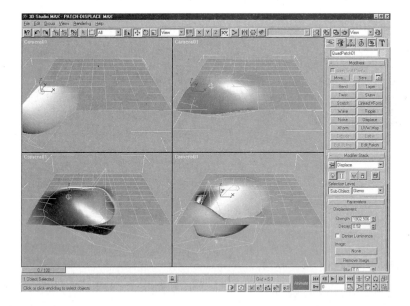

If you have a patch model and need the result to behave like a mesh instead of a patch, place a simple modifier, such as Normal, at the end of the path editing stack to convert the model to a mesh. Figure 12.45 shows the same four frames of the model shown in Figure 12.44, except that a Normal modifier has been placed between EditPatch and Displace to turn the patch into a mesh for the displacement.

FIGURE 12.45

The Displace modifier's effect on the same surface as a mesh.

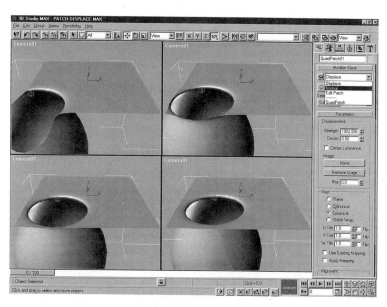

Switching from patch modeling to mesh is fairly painless because your model's surface complexity doesn't change. The surface defined by the EditPatch Steps setting is used to define the resulting mesh. Adding an additional EditPatch modifier after mesh editing increases your model's geometry significantly because every face is turned into a TriPatch. Ideally, you should perform all your mesh editing after your patch editing and return to patch editing by going lower in the Edit History stack.

WARNING

Be careful returning to EditPatch after mesh modeling because its Steps setting affects the vertex and face ordering used by subsequent mesh modifiers.

The bear from the previous exercises needs some more detail in the face area, so in the following exercise you'll increase the number of control points. The first task is to delete half of the head and mirror instance the half back into place so that you won't have to worry about keeping the face symmetrical.

FINISHING THE BEAR

1. Continue with your bear from the previous exercise or open bear2.max from the CD.

2. Click the head and go to Sub-Object Patch. Turn off the Surface display and turn on the Lattice. Select and delete the patches on half of the head, as shown in Figure 12.46.

FIGURE 12.46

Deleting half of the head.

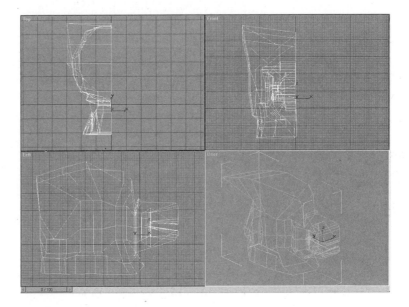

3. Exit Sub-Object mode and mirror instance clone the half-head across the X axis. Now any changes made to the original head are automatically applied to the instanced copy. Don't worry about the seam; it'll disappear when the halves are reattached.

4. Go back into Sub-Object Patch mode and select the patch around the eye of the original head. Make sure that Propagate is checked on and click Subdivide. The head becomes rounder and there is more patch detail around the eye (see Figure 12.47). Select the eye area again and subdivide once more.

T IP

In patch modeling, it's always best to start out with as few control points as possible, then add more points where they're needed. Even on a simple model, it can be very confusing trying to move just the right point.

5. You're back to editing Sub-Object Vertices, pushing and pulling until the face comes into focus. It's best to work with the Lattice off and the Surface on. When you get the eye socket location set, you might want to hide the instanced half to make editing easier.

FIGURE 12.47

Subdividing the face with Propagate on.

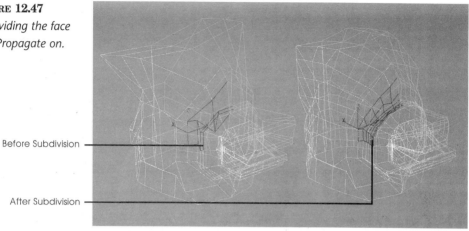

Before Subdivision

After Subdivision

TIP

A good rule of thumb to use is to get the vertices and their handles into place, then right-click the vertex to change it to a Coplanar type. This smoothes out the point, making it flow into the surface better.

When your bear looks like Figure 12.48, it's time to move to the final step.

FIGURE 12.48

The bear, with facial details added.

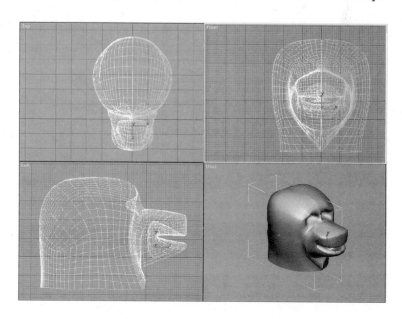

6. Go out to the Object level of Edit Patch and click the original head, click Attach, and click the instanced copy. Right-click to get out of Attach mode.

7. Get into Sub-Object Vertex mode and select the thin stripe of vertices down the center to be welded. Bump up the Weld Threshold to 10 and click Weld. The seam disappears. Your finished bear should look like Figure 12.49.

FIGURE 12.49

The finished bear.

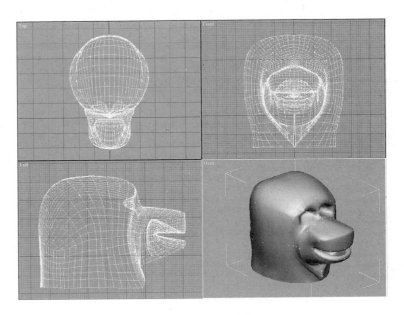

This concludes the bear tutorial, but you can go on your own to model the nose, eyes, and ears as shown in the original figure of the bear (see Figure 12.11). All these components are spheres. Free Form Deformations are used on the nose and ears; open bear3.max from the CD to see how it was accomplished.

Patch Modeling Plug-ins

Digimation markets a plug-in that can make patch modeling a breeze. Surface Tools, written by Peter Watje, takes a spline network and builds patches across the splines. It's the Bézier patch version of building a NURBS surface from Curves. Dummy objects can be attached to the spline's control points with Linked XForm, so that the patch surface is deformed smoothly with the splines for facial animation. Surface Tools is reasonably priced at under $100 and should be in every patch modeler's arsenal.

In Practice: Patch Modeling

- **Patch models:** Patch models are ideally defined from the beginning as patches or derived from Lathe and Extrude modifiers. Deriving patches from meshes should be a secondary choice because the conversion is to Tri instead of Quad patches.

- **Interior vertices in Manual mode:** Switching interior vertices to Manual mode should be viewed as a permanent setting because returning the patches to Auto Interior mode resets manually positioned vertices to their default locations.

- **Adding modifiers to patch models:** Remember that Optimize, MeshSmooth, Relax, Normal, Smooth, Material, and Volume Select converts the model to a mesh.

- **Patch edge smoothness:** Welding patches together at an edge automatically gives the two patches a smooth continuity across the edge. Smoothing can occur only between patches that share edges with one another.

- **Patch surface smoothness:** Vertex positioning and tangent handle adjustment are the only methods to influence the smoothness of a patch surface. The concept of smoothing groups is available only to meshes.

- **FFD modifiers:** The FFD (Free Form Deformation) modifiers work very well for deforming patch models and can overcome the limitations of not being able to animate tangent handles.

Chapter 13

NURBS MODELING

As MAX grows, methods of modeling progress towards ever increasing sophistication. There is a line of measurement where at one end is the simplest of geometric objects and at the other end is organic and particulate objects that are expensive both in calculation and the time it takes to create them. NURBS in MAX reduces that expense for interactively creating organic, smooth surfaces and at the same time gives you real-time shading, a feature not found in even the highest end modeling programs. This chapter will go over the most important tools for working with NURBS in MAX and take you through some of the applications of those tools.

Specifically, this chapter covers the following topics:

- Defining NURBS
- NURBS structure and components
- Creating NURBS objects
- Creating curves, points, and surfaces within NURBS objects
- Modifying and editing NURBS objects and sub-objects
- Animating NURBS
- Materials and NURBS

Like the term "multimedia," NURBS became a popular buzzword among animators who heard it was cool and powerful but didn't know what its applications were. Now that it's in MAX, you will see that it is just another modeling tool that fills a gap that wasn't covered well by any other tools available in MAX. NURBS are powerful, but they're useful only for the kind of modeling they do. You wouldn't use them for mechanical or most architectural modeling, but you would use them to create objects like animals, cars, hands, and faces.

Defining NURBS

NURBS in MAX are a set of tools based on complex mathematics used to create smooth, organic shapes and surface models. They also allow the creation of curved paths—the same kind of paths you would use for lofting or as animation paths for cameras—which are easier to create and adjust than a standard spline. NURBS also enable you to model surfaces by pushing and pulling control points or vertices in a way that is similar to how one might model in clay.

NURBS is an acronym for Non-uniform Rational Basis Spline and is a classification of the mathematics behind NURBS, which are complex and intricate. A book called The NURBS Book has approximately 15,000 equations carefully explained, starting with a circle and ending with the most complex of surfaces 400 pages later. The tools in MAX for creating NURBS have been designed to make it easy for you to create without knowing how NURBS do their magic, but it is suggested that you read the section in the *MAX Users Guide* on NURBS Concepts before continuing with this chapter.

WARNING

The singular form of NURBS is still NURBS and you'll be looked upon as not being in the know by calling an object a NURB. NURB with out the S is a Non-Uniform Rational Bee and is to be avoided at all times.

Because NURBS are a highly integrated set of tools, it is possible to categorize and present them in many different ways, all logical from one point of view or another. Because of this, you are encouraged to jump ahead to topics that are mentioned in the current section to help complete your understanding of how some part of NURBS works in the overall picture. It is also a good idea to read Chapter 10 in the *MAX Users Guide* and all the topics in the Online Reference under the Help pulldown before, during, and after reading this chapter.

NURBS Objects

The terminology for MAX NURBS can be confusing because, depending on the context, each term, such as NURBS curve or NURBS surface, may mean something different. For the discussions in this chapter a *NURBS object* will either be a NURBS curve or NURBS surface. When talking about Sub-Object curves, they will be simply called curves, and likewise for surfaces. Because points can't exist outside a NURBS curve or NURBS surface, no differentiation is needed.

A NURBS curve or NURBS surface is created using one of the buttons found under NURBS Surfaces or NURBS Curves in the Create command panel. They can also be created by converting a Standard Primitive using the Edit Stack button in the Modify command panel (Extended Primitives don't convert). A NURBS curve or NURBS surface can have within them any of the three basic NURBS components—points, curves, and surfaces—as well as imports as sub-objects.

Consider a NURBS curve or a NURBS surface as a basic container for creating NURBS sub-objects within it; when it's created, it automatically contains a sub-object. That sub-object could be deleted, still leaving a NURBS object with nothing in it and nothing displaying onscreen. When you use, say, the Point Curve tool, you are creating a NURBS curve with an Independent Curve Sub-Object, the sub-object being what you see.

Points, curves, and surfaces are further differentiated as dependent or independent, meaning that their definition may or may not depend on the existence and form of another sub-object. For example, a Dependent curve can be created using the cross-section of a surface and would change its shape if the surface it is dependent on is modified. There are many ways to create Dependent points, curves, and surfaces and each will be gone over in its respective section covered later in the chapter.

Surfaces and Curves have two ways of controlling their shape: Point and Control vertices (see Figure 13.1):

- **Point vertices:** Curves/surfaces pass through these vertices and the curve/surface curvature adjusts accordingly.

- **Control vertices or CVs:** These vertices influence or bias the curve/surface towards or away from the CV based on the weight of the CV. They are visually different than Point objects in that the have a Lattice (in yellow) that passes through the CVs.

FIGURE 13.1

Control Vertices (CVs) and Points are used to shape curves and surfaces.

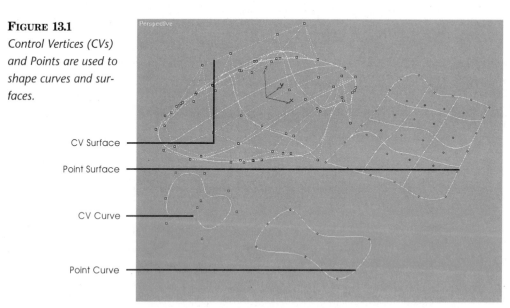

CV Surface

Point Surface

CV Curve

Point Curve

Vertex and point mean nearly the same thing. They are markers for a position in space represented by an XYZ value. It is simply the context in which they are being referenced that determines what they are called. With a Control Vertex (CV) you are leaning a curve or surface towards a position in space, and with a Point you are passing the curve or surface through a position.

The choice to use the Point or CV option is a personal preference in most cases. They can be chosen, however, because of differences in result. Figure 13.2 shows the result of creating a rounded shape using four points or four CVs that are snapped to the grid and closed with a fifth pick.

FIGURE 13.2

Point Curve and CV Curve created by picking four corner points using Snap and closing the curve.

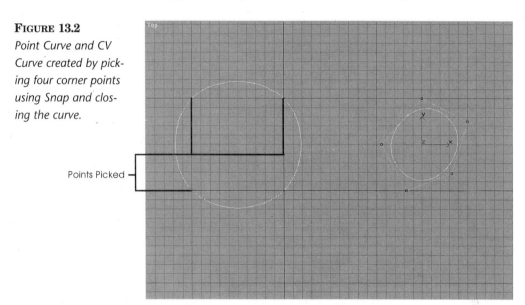

Points Picked —

The Point curve seems to have more symmetry in this example. Not only is the CV curve uneven, but the CVs have rearranged themselves and one edge is against the CV Lattice, which requires some modifying to move it away. In Figure 13.3, five points or CVs are used to create a straight line and the middle point or CV moves up to create a bump in the middle of the line.

Notice the Point curve creates dimples on either side of the bump, which requires moving the two points on either side of the bump or the addition of more points to get rid of the dimples. It does, however, create a more pronounced bump than the CV curve, which would require adjusting the CV's weights to achieve the same effect (see Figure 13.4).

Once a NURBS object is created, you must go to the Modify panel to either add components like points and curves or modify those and other sub-objects. When not in Sub-Object mode, you can open the NURBS Creation Toolbox floater, which enables you to add points, curves, and, if within a NURBS surface, surfaces. Figure 13.5 shows the floaters for curves and surfaces as well as the Modify panel button that invokes them.

FIGURE 13.3

In this case, the Point curve creates dimples and the CV curve is less pointed.

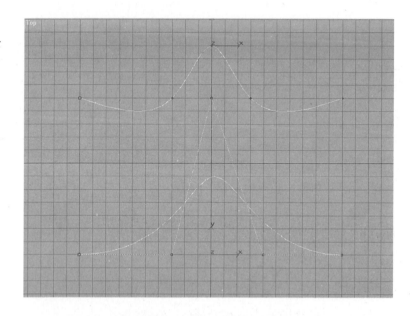

FIGURE 13.4

Points are added to remove the dimples. CVs are moved and their weight is increased to sharpen the bump.

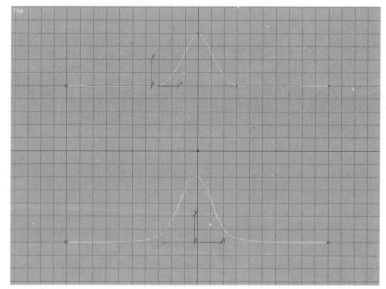

You can convert CV curves to Point curves and back, and Point surfaces can be converted to CV surfaces easily. Converting CV surfaces to Point surfaces can be done, but this requires a number of steps and is better started as a Point surface (the subject of converting is covered in each basic component's section).

FIGURE 13.5

The Curve and Surface version of the NURBS Creation toolbox and the button for invoking them.

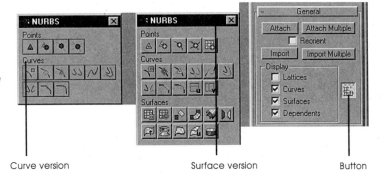

Curve version   Surface version   Button

NURBS Sub-Objects

All the work done in a NURBS object is done by creating or editing one or more of the sub-objects found in the following list:

- **Points:** This includes points used to create a Point curve, Dependent points, and Independent points.

- **Curve CV:** Control vertices used to adjust a CV curve.

- **Surface CV:** Control vertices used to adjust a CV Surface.

- **Curve:** Any of the Dependent or Independent curves including an import.

- **Surface:** Any of the Dependent or Independent surfaces, including an import.

- **Import:** A spline shape or Standard Primitive added to a NURBS curve or NURBS surface with the Import button.

TIP

Because you will be using these sub-objects often, it is good to get in the habit of using the keyboard shortcuts for toggling Sub-Object Selection on and off (default Ctrl+B) and Cycle Selection Level (default Insert). While you're at it, if you assign or re-assign:

Shift+T to Modify Command Mode

Ctrl+B to Sub-object Selection Toggle

Alt+B to Cycle Sub-object Level

Alt+N or V to Plug-in Keyboard Shortcut Toggle

you will find that it nicely works with NURBS Plug-in shortcuts described in the "NURBS Surface and NURBS Curve Main Panel" section of this chapter. You can do the (re)assignments in the Keyboard tab of the Preferences dialog found under the File pulldown.

Sub-objects are accessed for editing by clicking the Sub-Object button in the Modify panel and choosing the level you want to work with. Only sub-objects that actually exist in the selected NURBS curve or NURBS surface are listed in the Selection Level dropdown. The next sections go over the controls used to create each of those three basic components of NURBS objects.

NURBS curves and points are a subset of NURBS surfaces, so the creation of curves and points will be covered first and then surfaces. Editing processes that are common to these objects will then follow.

After you have started using NURBS curves, it will be hard to find reasons to use the standard Line shape for other than straight lines. NURBS splines are so easy to shape and control compared to using the green handled controls on the vertices of a Bezier spline.

T IP

It sometimes happens that a NURBS object is selected, you do not have the Sub-Object button on, and pressing the Delete key does nothing. You can always pick Delete in the Edit pull-down, which will do the job. At this point, it is also a good idea to save your work and restart MAX as this feature is the sign of a memory leak.

NURBS Curves

The NURBS curve object is a subset of a NURBS surface object, which means anything you can do within in a NURBS curve can be done within a NURBS surface. The reason for using a NURBS curve over a NURBS surface is that a NURBS surface cannot be used as a path or a shape in loft and animation path applications.

NURBS curves can be used both for NURBS and non-NURBS applications. Anywhere you can use a spline shape in MAX, you can use a NURBS curve. This includes lofts, compound objects, paths for path animation controllers; they can be modified using modifiers usually only available to splines, like Lathe, Extrude, Bevel, and Bevel Contour. You can also use them as ropes, cables, and so on by making them renderable.

Curves can be divided into dependent, independent, and imports. A Dependent curve derives its definition from its relationship to another sub-object and can only be edited indirectly by editing the sub-objects it is dependent on. An Independent curve is one that can be directly edited either by its Control points or its CVs. An import is a spline that is edited by going down the Modifier stack and editing it the same way you would edit a normal spline.

The following sections cover these types of curves in detail as well as the different ways of creating curves and how they might be used for non-NURBS surface uses. The more complex uses of curves in relation to surfaces will be covered under NURBS surfaces.

Independent Curves

Independent curves are sub-objects of an NURBS curve. They are what you see when creating a NURBS curve from scratch and are directly editable by their control points or CVs. There are three basic ways of generating independent curves:

- Using the Point/CV Buttons in the Create panel to create a NURBS Curve object where the resulting visible curve is a Curve Sub-Object.

- Using the Point/CV buttons in the NURBS Creation toolbox to create Curve Sub-Objects within an existing NURBS curve.

- Selecting an existing Dependent curve and clicking the Make Independent button while in the Curve Sub-Object Selection level of the Modify Command panel.

The following quick exercise takes you through the steps to create a simple NURBS curve.

CREATING A SIMPLE NURBS CURVE

1. Under the Create Tab in the Command panel, under Shapes, pick the Down arrow of the dropdown list and choose NURBS Curves.

2. Click Point Curve and pick points in the top view to create a curve. Right-click after picking the last point to finish the command.

3. Click CV Curve and do the same as in step 2.

4. Click the box next to Start New Shape to uncheck it and pick points to create another curve.

You now have two NURBS curves; one with one curve sub-object adjustable by points and the other with two curve sub-objects, adjustable by CVs.

Either NURBS curve can be used as an Animation path or a path for a loft, but only the first curve created in a multi-curved NURBS curve can be used for those applications.

If you want to have a second curve within the first NURBS curve of the previous exercise, you will have to proceed to the Modify panel and call up the NURBS Creation toolbox. There you can pick either the Point curve or CV curve buttons, which will let you create more independent curves.

Dependent Curves

Dependent curves are dependent on another curve, a set of points, or a surface for its shape in that if the sub-objects they are dependent on change in transform or shape, the Dependent curves match the sub-object's change.

The Dependent curves available are as follows:

- **Fit curve:** Enables you to pass a curve through Control, Dependent, and Independent points, whose positions the curve is dependent upon.

- **Transform curve:** Creates a curve that is similar to referencing except that changes in transform, as well as shape changes made to the original curve, are reflected in this Dependent curve.

- **Blend curve:** Connects two curve endpoints with another curve that is seamless at its connections and always tangent to the other curves.

- **Offset curve:** Creates a curve offset to one side or the other of the curve it is dependent on.

- **Mirror curve:** Creates a mirrored copy of the curve it is dependent on. It mirrors both changes to shape and transform of the original object.

- **Chamfer:** Creates a Beveled corner between two curves. It trims the curves based on parametric distances along them to fit the bevel.

- **Fillet:** Creates an Arc Curve corner between two curves, trimming them based on a parametric radius.

- **U/V Curve:** Uses a cross-section of a surface to create a curve. These two buttons only show up when working within a NURBS surface.

Figure 13.6 shows the different types of Dependent curves.

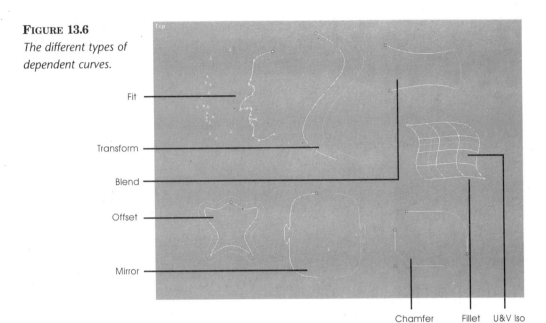

FIGURE 13.6

The different types of dependent curves.

To better understand how to use each of the Dependent curves, the following series of exercises will take you through using each type. You may want to save the results of each exercise to use for experimenting with surfaces when you get to that section. Note that some of the tools for curves are repeated for surfaces and only the differences between them are covered in the "Working with Surfaces" section.

Fit Curves

Creating Fit curves is one of the most commonly used methods for creating curves for connecting appendages to an existing surface, such as an arm to a torso. That process will be covered in full later in the "Attaching a Fin to a Whale" series of exercises. The following simple exercise will take you through using the Fit Curve tool.

CREATING A FIT CURVE

1. Open Fit Curve.max from the accompanying CD.

2. Pick any of the points to select the NURBS curve, and in the Modify panel, turn off Sub-Object mode (if it's on). Then click the NURBS Creation toolbox button and arrange the floater so it doesn't cover the points.

3. Pick Create Fit Curve and select each of the points starting at the top to match the shape next to it.

Notice how smoothly the shape of the curve transitions from point to point. Try turning on the Sub-Object button and adjust the shape by moving the points the curve is dependent on. Note that you can select more than one point at a time to adjust the shape.

Transform Curves

As mentioned previously, Transform curves create a curve in which changes made in transform and in shape to the original curve are reflected. This means if you create a Transform curve and rotate the original, the new Dependent curve will also rotate. The same is true for Move and Scale.

These curves are used for such solutions as creating parallel animation paths or having one Curve object move the same distance as the original but in another direction. The following exercise will take you through simple Transform curve creation and some of its characteristics:

CREATING AND ADJUSTING TRANSFORM CURVES

1. Open Transform Curve.max from the accompanying CD. Select the curve in the top viewport and open the NURBS Creation Toolbox floater.

2. Click the Transform curve button and pick the curve. To the right of the original curve, drag another curve.

3. Click the Sub-Object button and move a point on the original curve and observe a duplicate change on the Dependent curve.

4. In the Perspective viewport, pick any of the curves to select the NURBS curve, click the Sub-Object button, and choose the curve level to work with.

5. Pick and move the White curve and observe how the other curve objects move. Notice that the smaller curves that are scaled by 50 percent move only half as fast as the curves they're dependent on. (Adjust your view using Arc Rotate to see the relationship between the larger and smaller curves.) You can try rotating and scaling the White curve to see what effects they have on the Dependent curves.

In creating this exercise, each Dependent curve on the Construction plane is rotated 90 degrees, so when the Parent curves are moved, each dependent curve also moves but along its own local axis.

It is fairly easy to predict what a Transform curve will do if you just look at it as a reference of the original that reflects Transform changes to the original.

Mirror Curves and Blend Curves

The Mirror tool in NURBS is like the Mirror command in the MAX toolbar in that it behaves similar to the Reference option in the Mirror dialog box. If you make changes to the shape of the original, the changes are reflected in the mirrored clone. The difference is that transforms made to the original curve also reflect in the Dependent Mirrored curve (this is also true for the Mirror Surface tool when working with surfaces).

Blend simply creates a smooth tangent curve between two curves that adjusts to changes made to those curves.

The next exercise will take you through using Mirror and Blend to create a symmetrical and continuous shape.

CREATING A MIRROR CURVE AND CONNECTING IT WITH BLEND CURVES

1. Open Mirror Blend.max from the accompanying CD. Select the NURBS curve and open the NURBS Creation Toolbox floater in the Modify panel.

2. Click Create Mirror curve, pick the original curve, and move the mouse down to bring the Mirror curve closer to the original curve.

3. Scroll down to the Mirror Curve rollout and adjust the offset to bring the Mirror curve just a few units away from the original. Do a Zoom Extents so the curves are large and visible. You can do this also by being in the Curve Sub-Object Selection level, clicking the Move tool, picking the Mirror curve, and then picking the yellow axis and moving it left or right.

4. Click Create Blend Curve and position the cursor over the end of one of the curves so that a blue box appears.

5. Pick and drag the cursor over the corresponding end of the other curve until a blue box appears and release the pick button.

6. Do the same with the other ends of the curves.

7. Right-click to cancel the Blend tool, turn on Curve Sub-Object level, pick the Mirror curve, move or rotate the center axis, and observe that the Blend curves adjust accordingly.

8. Choose the Curve CV Sub-Object Selection level, adjust the original curve by moving the CVs and observe the corresponding changes in the Mirror curve (see Figure 13.7).

You may want to experiment with adjusting the tension of either end of one of the blend curves by choosing one while in Curve Sub-Object level, scrolling to the bottom of the Command panel and adjusting Tension 1 and 2.

FIGURE 13.7

A Blend curve and Mirror curve used to create the outline of a character.

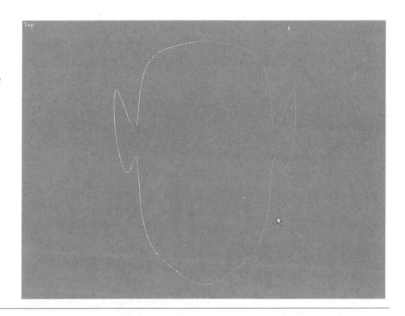

This combination of Mirror and Blend are commonly used in creating symmetrical objects, such as a face or torso. What is nice about blend is that it makes it easy to adjust to get a satisfying result when trying to connect two curves smoothly.

Chamfer Curves and Fillet Curves

As with the Fillet/Chamfer modifier, Chamfer and Fillet are used simply for creating a straight bevel or an arc at the corner of two curves. Creating them in NURBS, however, allows for more flexibility in that they are adjustable for as long as they remain dependent and continue to retain their nature if you chose to move the curves they are filleting or chamfering. Also, the endpoints of the curves do not have to be coincident like they do with the Modifier version. The following exercise will show you how each works.

CREATING CHAMFER AND FILLET CURVES

1. Open Chamfer Fillet.max from the accompanying CD. Click the NURBS curve to select it and open the NURBS Creation toolbox in the Modify panel.

2. Click the Chamfer Curve button, hold the cursor over the uppermost curve (A) until a blue box appears on the right end of it. Click and drag over the right vertical curve (B) and release.

3. Click the Sub-Object button, choose the Curve Selection level, select the Chamfer curve, and scroll the Command panel up to display the Chamfer controls.

4. Adjust the Lengths, turn off and on Trim Curve and Flip Trim, and observe the results.

5. Repeat steps 2, 3, and 4 with Fillet and curves labeled C and D.

6. Try filleting or chamfering the open corners between curves and observe that initially an orange line may appear. This means an invalid sub-object has been created and you'll need to adjust it to make it valid using step 3 as a guideline.

NOTE

As of MAX 2.0, the hit testing for Fillet and Chamfer curves is not completely accurate. This means that not every attempt to create them will work. You will have the best luck if you pick somewhere on the curve away from the end points. This is pretty much true anywhere these blue boxes or blue lines show up for selection reasons.

Also, whenever a sub-object displays as orange, MAX is indicating that an invalid solution is present and needs attention.

You can always change the parameters of a Chamfer or Fillet by selecting the curve when you are in the Curve Sub-Object Selection level and by scrolling to the bottom of the Command panel.

U and V ISO Curves

U and V Iso Curves create a curve based on a cross-section of a surface along its latitudinal (U) or longitudinal (V) direction. Again, you will only see these buttons when working within a NURBS surface.

The following exercise takes you through creating a U Iso curve:

CREATING A U ISO CURVE

1. Open Iso Curve.max from the accompanying CD. Click the NURBS surface to select it and open the NURBS Creation toolbox in the Modify panel.

2. Click the U Iso Curve button, hold the cursor over the surface, and notice that as you drag over it, a blue curve moves to follow the cursor.

3. Pick to create a curve and continue to pick to create as many curves as needed.

You can try making V Iso Curves also—the process is the same. Try turning the viewport shader on and observe that you can still see the blue line creation process.

U and V Iso curves can be used to get cross-sectional curves from a face, for example, allowing you to make them independent. Then you can adjust them before U-lofting them into a surface.

Import Curves

Importing is for bringing spline shapes in without converting them to CV curves. Because the NURBS curve is a subset NURBS surface, the Editing tool panels have redundant options. There is no strong reason for using splines as imports to an NURBS curve. If you intend to use the shape for lofting or as an animation path, it would be best to attach it or leave it as a spline.

You import using the Import or Import Multiple buttons in the General rollup, which displays when the Sub-Object button in the Modify panel is off.

Importing is most useful when bringing in splines you want to use as part of a NURBS surface but want to edit as Bézier splines. This means that in order to edit an import you have to go back through the Modifier stack to edit it as a spline. You can do this by clicking the Sub-Object button, choosing Curve as the Sub-Object Selection level, selecting the import, and going down the Modifier stack to edit it. Imports can be edited either as a curve or an import when at the Curve or Import Sub-Object level.

To create additional curves within a NURBS curve, a number of options are available in the NURBS Creation toolbox, accessed by clicking its button next to the Display area in the General roll-up. If the Plug-in Keyboard Shortcut Toggle button is on, Ctrl+T toggles the toolbox on and off. All the buttons in the toolbox are duplicated in rollup panels at the bottom of the Modify panel when not in Sub-Object mode.

Using a NURBS Curve as a Path

Using a NURBS curve as a path for animation requires some adjustment to the shape as the movement along the curve tends to be uneven in velocity. The procedure for adjustment involves converting the curve to a trajectory, then to a spline shape (which as of 2.0 is the only way to convert a NURBS curve to a spline), and finally applying the freeware Normalize Spline modifier to it, which is found on the accompanying CD-ROM.

The following steps take you through preparing a NURBS curve as a constant velocity path for a Path animation controller. You'll have to put the Normalize.dlm file into the Plug-ins folder and restart MAX if you haven't done that already.

PREPARING A NURBS CURVE FOR USE AS AN ANIMATION PATH

1. Open Normalize path.max from the CD and select the NURBS curve Path. (This curve is created by fitting a curve through some points attached to the NURBS surface Terrain, which is detached and then moved up along the Z axis.)

2. Click the Motion tab in the Command panel and click the Trajectories button.

3. Set Samples under Sample Range to 5 and click Convert From. Click the Curve01 that creates a trajectory for the curve of the same shape and moves the curve to the beginning of the trajectory.

4. Click Convert To to convert the trajectory to a spline.

5. Erase the original curve. With the new shape selected, apply the Normalize modifier and set the segment length to 5.

To make use of the path, you can now assign a path controller to the Flyer and choose the normalized spline as its path.

This process may seem a little involved, but it could be written as a script. Considering the ease and control NURBS curves gives you compared to splines when creating animation paths, the payoff of going through this process is worth it.

The NURBS Curve Main Panel

As mentioned previously, all NURBS objects are used in the Modify panel after their creation. Both CV curves and Point curves have basically the same tools for modifying.

When editing an NURBS curve, what is displayed in the Command panel depends on whether the Sub-Object button is turned on or not, and if so, what level of Sub-Object is being displayed. This section discusses the tools that display with the Sub-Object button off.

The first option to consider under the General rollup is Attach. You may Attach any NURBS curve or spline shape to make it a part of the current NURBS curve.

What kind of curve they become—dependent or independent—when attached is based on what they were before attachment. When attaching an NURBS curve, the curves contained in it transfer over as what they were. When attaching a spline shape, all splines in that shape are converted to Independent CV curves.

One problem with attaching a spline is that it is broken into separate segments, converting each to a separate curve (see Figure 13.8). To connect them you would use the Join tool found in the Curve Common rollup within the Curve Sub-Object selection level. If you have more than four or five curves, this process can be tedious as you can only join one segment at a time and are dealing with the semi-unstable Blue Selection Box process.

You can connect them automatically using a freeware script on the CD called NURBS Spline Join.ms. You will need to copy it to the Scripts folder in your MAX directory to use it in the next exercise, which will take you through how to use it.

FIGURE 13.8

A Star spline shape attached to an NURBS curve. In 2.0, each spline segment is converted to a separate curve.

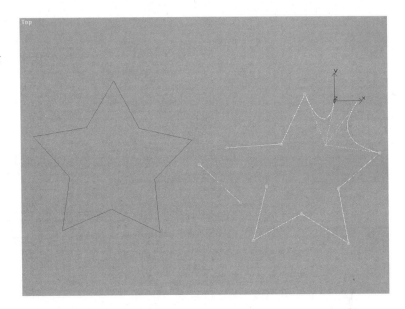

The following exercise takes you through the steps of attaching a spline shape that is created using a Dingbat font. Then using NURBS Spline Join.ms, you create a single curve from the multiple ones that resulted from the attachment.

IMPORTING A SPLINE SHAPE

1. Open Import Spline.max from the accompanying CD. Select the border NURBS curve, click the Attach button, and pick the spline shape.

2. Choose the Curve CV selection level of Sub-Object and try moving some of the CVs of the Neptune symbol and observe the discontinuity. Undo to return the symbol back to its original shape.

3. Click the MAXScript button under the Utility tab in the Command panel, click run script, and double-click NURBS Spline Join.ms.

4. Click in the Utilities drop-down, choose NURBS Sub-Objects, click the Pick NURBS Object, and click anywhere on the NURBS curve.

5. In the NURBS Sub-objects list window, click Text01 for Initial Curve to Join, click Text50 for Final Curve to Join, and click the Join button.

6. Now try moving some of the CVs now and observe that the curve is continuous.

Sometimes every other CV wants to rest on and stay attached to a curve converted in this way. Just delete one of those CVs and the curve resets to work as normal.

The next option in the main panel is Import, which has been covered in the Imports section earlier in the chapter.

Following that are Display options, which are covered in the NURBS surface section of this chapter as well as the NURBS Creation toolbox button (which can be accessed with Ctrl+T).

Notice that, as in the new R2 feature that allows splines to be renderable, curves are also renderable. With that and the Generate Mapping Coordinates button, you can easily create objects like the branches of trees, arteries and veins, tunnel mazes, and rope.

The next option, Curve approximation, works much the same as that option for splines. Its purpose is to determine the resolution (number of segments) of a curve such that there aren't too many segments that increase file size or there aren't too few, which makes the curve look segmented. It's best to leave Adaptive checked, which does well to give you the best balance between too many or too few segments, but if you aren't satisfied with the results, turn off Adaptive and bump up the steps until you have the desired smoothness.

The Create Points and Create Curves roll-ups (as well as the Create Surfaces roll-up in the NURBS surface main panel) are redundant as they have equivalent buttons in the NURBS Creation toolbox.

Since the panels that show up when the Sub-Object button is on are a subset of those found in the NURBS Surface panels, they will be covered later in the chapter under NURBS Command panels. However, the following sections discuss how to use some of those panels for converting curves from one state to another.

Converting Curves

There will be times when you want one kind of curve to be another, such as a Dependent curve to be independent, or a Point curve to be a CV curve. The following are the different conversions you can do and the steps to accomplish them:

- **CV curve to Point curve**: Select the curve, choose the Curve Selection level in Sub-Object, and click Make Fit. A dialog asks you how many points you want to use to define the curve. The more points there are, the closer the new curve will look like the original.

- **Point curve to a CV curve**: Select the curve, choose the Curve Selection level in Sub-Object, and click Make Independent. You do not have direct control over how many CVs are assigned, but if you want more or less, apply Make Fit to the curve first and increase or reduce the number points used to define it. Then click Make Independent.

- **Dependent curve to an Independent curve**: Select the curve, choose the Curve Selection level in Sub-Object, and click Make Independent. This converts it to a CV curve.

- **NURBS curve to a spline shape**: Select the curve, click the Motion tab of the Command panel, click the Trajectories button, click the Convert From button, and pick the curve again. Then click the Convert To button to complete the process. This actually leaves the NURBS curve rather than converting it, but in 2.0 it's the only workaround. If there is more than one Curve Sub-Object in the NURBS curve, only the curve first created in it will convert.

NURBS Points

Along with Curve Sub-Objects, Point Sub-Objects are essential to the creation of NURBS objects. The points you create here are not really any different than the points that are used to define, say, a Point curve. In fact, the Sub-Object Selection level you use to edit the points, which you create in this section, is the same level for editing those in a Point curve or Surface.

Points can only be created when a NURBS curve or NURBS surface already exists. Points are created when editing a NURBS object in the Modify panel. They can Control curves or surfaces, be controlled by (dependent on) curves or surfaces, or both. The points you pick when creating a Point curve or the points that show up when creating a Point surface are Control points. Any of the points you create from the following list can be Control points used to control a Fit curve. Some, however, do that indirectly because they are controlled by another sub-object.

The following is a list of the five kinds of points you can create using the NURBS Creation toolbox:

- **Independent point:** A point that as no direct relationship with any NURBS component except that it can only exist as part of a NURBS object.

- **Point point:** A point that is dependent on and has the same XYZ coordinates as (unless offset) an existing point in a NURBS object, which can be a Control point, an Independent point, or any of the Dependent points.

- **Curve point:** A point that is dependent on and embedded within a Dependent or Independent curve. As the curve changes, the point follows.

- **Curve Curve point:** A point that is dependent on the intersection of two curves. As you move or change either curve, the point tends to remain at their intersection. The curves must be coincident or the point displays in orange and is unusable.

- **Surface point:** A point that is dependent on and embedded within a Dependent or Independent surface. As the surface changes, the point follows.

You can create Control points in two other ways: by clicking Make Fit with a CV curve selected and the Curve Selection Level chosen, or by clicking the Curve button in the Refine area of the Point rollup with the Point Selection Level chosen.

A good use for Independent points is to bring in coordinates of a large number of points (sometimes called a point cloud) either through a device like a 3D digitizer or through a script file that could convert a database of coordinates generated from, for example, a land survey to recreate a landscape. You would then create curves from the points using Fit curve and then use the curves to create surfaces using U-loft.

Point points are good for getting just a few points from a curve or surface for the purpose of creating a new curve from them.

The following exercise will take you through capturing the shape of a portion of a face to use as part of another. You will be creating Point points by which you can make them independent and use them for a Fit curve:

Using Point Points

1. Open Point Point.max, click the NURBS curve to select it, and open the NURBS Creation toolbox in the Modify panel.

2. Click the Sub-Object button, choose Point Selection level, click the Point point button and observe that the Command panel displays offset choices.

3. Starting with the last point of the chin, click it and set the offset value for Z to 5.

4. Repeat that step for each point up to the nose.

5. Right-click to cancel the Point point tool. Select all the points above the original curve in the front view and click Make Independent.

6. In the top viewport, move the still selected points to the right.

7. Start the Fit Curve tool and dot to dot the points to recreate the mouth and chin of the face. You can now edit those points to refine the shape in the same way you can edit any point curve.

It is through the method of making Independent points from the Point point, the Curve point, the Curve Curve point, and Surface point that you can extract curve or surface data from NURBS objects to edit for the creation of new ones.

A Curve Curve point enables you to trim two intersecting curves and keeps the trim dynamic in that if you move the curves, the point remains at their intersection.

The Curve point simply places a point on a curve that can be either offset or used to trim the curve. You can use this tool to extract curve information from a CV curve in the same way that the "Using Point Points" exercise does.

Joining Surfaces with Points

As mentioned previously, you will most often use points to create curves that can then be used to create surfaces. In this way you can also create a surface that interfaces with another surface, so that when the main surface changes topology, the joint between the main surface and the dependent surface remains contiguous. For the purposes of this chapter, a surface created by this method is called a Joined surface.

An example of a Joined surface is the fin of a fish. The joint where a fin would exist on the fish's body could have the Lattice for that area of the body refined with many rows and columns of CVs and then could be pulled out to shape a fin.

Creating a ring of points on the fish body, however, is just as effective and even less tedious. Use the ring of points to create a Dependent curve and then U-loft between this curve and the other curves that define the fin. The result is that as the body bends at the fin, the first curve of the fin stays flush to the body.

The following exercise takes you through the process of creating Surface points in preparation for attaching a fin to a surface that's part of a whale. This is one of four parts:

PART ONE: ATTACHING A FIN TO A WHALE

1. Open Whale Fin.max from the accompanying CD. Click the NURBS surface named Whale to select it and open the NURBS Creation toolbox in the Modify panel. You see a portion the side of a whale, which you will eventually attach a fin to.

2. Click the Create Surf Point button in the NURBS Creation toolbox and use the semi-oblate-shaped cross-section as a guide to create the first set of points on the whale surface (see Figure 13.9).

FIGURE 13.9

Placing Surface points in preparation for Fit curves.

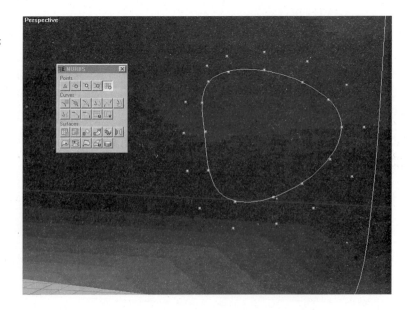

3. Click Sub-Object, choose Point Selection level, select all the points just created, and at the bottom of the Command panel click the Normal radio button and set it to 1 unit. This raises the points off the whale body so that the surface that passes through them and the next set of points creates a smooth transition out to the rest of the fin. The purpose of this will become clearer later in other parts of this exercise.

4. Using Surface Point again, create another set of points in a ring just outside the first as in Figure 13.9. This second set of points ensures a smooth integration of the fin to the body.

5. Choose Curve selection level, pick the semi-oblate curve so it turns red, and Arc Rotate Selected to observe the relationship of the curve and points to the body of the whale. Hit Shift+Z to undo the view change.

6. Click the Create Fit Curve button in the NURBS Creation toolbox and create a curve through the first set of points and then another one through the second set.

T IP

You can press the Backspace key to undo a point selection while using Fit curve. You can also do that to undo a curve selection while working with U-loft.

7. Save the file for a later U-lofting exercise.

Converting and Importing Points

Although you can import a NURBS curve containing points, you have no direct access to them (obviously a feature), so it is always better to attach them. You also cannot import Helper Object points currently in MAX, but look for a script to show up soon that will enable you to do this.

You can only convert Dependent points into Independent points by selecting the points while in the Point Selection level and clicking Make Independent.

Now that you have learned about curves and points, you can proceed to using surfaces, the most commonly used aspect of NURBS.

Surfaces

The real meat of NURBS is Surfaces, which can be created either from scratch, using points, curves, and other surfaces to define them or by importing.

Because NURBS surfaces can contain all NURBS Sub-Object types, they are the most complex to navigate in. Many panels show up and disappear depending on what selection level you are in, what sub-object is selected, or what tool you're using.

A NURBS curve can be created and collapsed in the Edit panel to become a NURBS surface and then curves can be added to it to create different kinds of surfaces or be extruded/lathed into a surface. Surfaces, like curves, are either dependent, independent, or an import.

Independent Surfaces

Like Independent curves, Independent surfaces are sub-objects of a NURBS surface. They are what you see when creating a NURBS surface from scratch and are directly editable by their Control points or CVs.

The following are the six ways of creating Independent surfaces:

- Using the CV/Point Surf buttons in the NURBS Surfaces Command panel in the Geometry dropdown list.

- Using the CV/Point Surf buttons in the NURBS Creation toolbox floater while modifying a NURBS surface.

- Collapsing a NURBS curve to a NURBS surface through the Edit Stack button in the Modify panel.

- Collapsing a standard primitive to a NURBS surface through the Edit Stack button in the Modify panel, or attaching it to an existing NURBS surface using the Attach button in the Command panel.

- Collapsing a Patch surface to a NURBS surface through the Edit Stack button in the Modify panel or attaching it to an existing NURBS surface using the Attach button in the Command panel.

- Selecting a Dependent surface and clicking the Make Independent button while in the Surface Sub-Object Selection level.

The Point Surface and CV Surface tools create rectangular patches that can be used in much the same way MAX Patches are used. Because the current version of MAX NURBS surfaces (2.0) can't have holes in them, you patch surfaces together using Snap to line up the edges to keep the seams from showing. How you choose to compose one object or another using the different kinds of surfaces available is a matter of experience.

The most common ways to model using NURBS are to create a Main object by either patching together a number of surfaces, U-lofting a series of cross-sectional curves, or pushing and pulling CVs on a collapsed (NURBS) primitive. You can then join other surfaces to it using the technique covered in the following exercise.

The Independent CV and Point surfaces are each created with a default grid of 4 × 4 evenly spaced Control points (CVs). Creation time is the only time you can change the number of rows or columns of those Control points or CVs so that they are evenly spaced. If you want more later, you must use the Refine option while in the Surface CV or Point Sub-Object Selection level to add them.

The following exercise will take you through creating a CV NURBS surface first, then a Point surface as a sub-object, and then how to refine their Control grids. Note that you could create them both with their respective buttons in the NURBS Surface Command panel, but this is a better choice as it adds no significant overhead to calculation and saves time by not having to go in and out of Sub-Object to select the surfaces.

CREATING CV AND POINT SURFACES AND ADJUSTING THEIR CONTROL GRIDS

1. Reset MAX. Click the CV Surface button in the NURBS Surfaces Command panel.

2. Maximize the Perspective viewport and click somewhere to the left and drag out the surface.

Note that it is only at this time that you have the option to change the number of length and width CVs to give you evenly spaced rows and columns.

3. In the Modify panel, open the NURBS Creation toolbox, click the Point Surface button, and drag out a surface next to the other surface. It is again only at this time that you can change the number of evenly spaced rows and columns of points.

4. Click the Sub-Object button, choose the Surface CV Selection level, click Refine Row in the Refine area, and pass the cursor over the CV surface. Notice that all the CVs turn blue and an extra row of CVs appears adjusting the position of all the rows. At this point if you click, you will create the new row and another row shows up waiting to be placed.

5. Choose the Point Selection level, click Surf Row in the Refine area, and click anywhere in the Point surface. Notice that there is no adjustment of the other rows.

This is the only way you can add Points or CVs directly to a surface that controls it.

The previous exercise showed you how to create rectangular flat surfaces to demonstrate to you the basic nature of surfaces and how they are controlled. These rectangular surfaces are mostly used for landscape objects, though they can conceivably be manipulated into any shape. You will find, however, that starting with a 3D primitive shape converted to NURBS or a series of cross-sectional curves that are U-lofted better suits non-flat object creation.

Dependent Surfaces

Dependent surfaces are like Dependent curves in that they are dependent on curves and other surfaces for their definition. The following is a list of the different Dependent surfaces:

- **Transform surface:** Like Transform curve, the Dependent surface changes in shape and transform as the original surface does.

- **Blend surface:** Like Blend curve, a surface is created between the edges of two surfaces to create a smooth seamless continuity between those surfaces. If the surfaces are changed in shape or transform, the Dependent curve adjusts to maintain tangency.

- **Offset surface:** Like Offset curve, this creates a Dependent surface offset from the original surface. Unlike Transform surface, the Dependent surface does not remain precisely the same as the original surface because it is using the normals of the original surface to define it.

- **Mirror surface:** Like Mirror curve, this creates a Dependent mirrored surface that mirrors the original surface and any shape or transform changes.

- **Extrude surface:** This extrudes any curve any amount in the local X, Y, or Z directions of the NURBS surface (not the directions local of the curve).

- **Lathe surface:** This lathes a curve around an axis aligned with the X, Y, or Z directions of the NURBS surface local axes.

- **Ruled surface:** Creates a surface between any two curves. Note that everything you can do with the Ruled surface, you can do with the U-loft tool, but there is more overhead involved with U-loft, making it slower than Ruled surface.

- **U-loft surface:** Enables you to create a smooth surface using any number of curves as cross-sections. You can then later add more curves as necessary. This is one of the most often used Surface tools in NURBS.

- **Cap surface:** Creates a capped surface at the ends of a closed surface like an Extrude, Lathe, or U-loft surface or on a Closed curve.

These surfaces used in combination can create virtually any organic and smooth surface. It is important that you take the time to learn how each of these tools work in and of themselves before trying to combine them in a project because most of this work is like assembling a puzzle—putting the pieces together to get the bigger picture.

The Transform, Offset, and Mirror Surface tools are essentially the same in execution and result as their curve counterparts except that they create surfaces. The Blend Surface, however, is a little different, so an exercise to show how it works by connecting one landscape surface to another follows:

CREATING A BLEND SURFACE

1. Open Blend Surface.max from the CD, select the NURBS surface, and open the NURBS Creation toolbox in the Modify panel.

2. Click the Blend Surface button, hold the cursor over the edge of one of the surfaces until a blue line appears, then pick and drag to the edge of the other surface until a blue line appears and release. A new surface blending the other two is created.

3. Click Sub-Object, choose the Surface Selection level, and move the upper surface and observe how the dependent Blend curve adjusts to maintain smoothness at the joints. (You may want to hide the particle systems temporarily to speed up your display if response is slow).

If you are having difficulty selecting the edges when creating Blend surfaces, try clicking the surface a little away from the edge and you may find more success.

Blend curves are used extensively to connect between other surfaces when using the Patch method of constructing an object. You will do just that in the "Creating the Face of the Buddha" exercise later in the chapter.

The Extrude curve and Lathe curve perform exactly the same as their modifier counterparts. They are added in NURBS as tools because you can't use Shape modifiers to modify Sub-Object curves.

A Ruled surface can be used for objects, such as a path or road on a terrain where the edges were created using Fit curve through some Surface points on the terrain. It would also be good for something like ribbon where its edges are created with a Transform curve and it's original.

The following example will take you through creating a simple road on a terrain-shaped surface using a Ruled surface:

CREATING A ROAD USING A RULE SURFACE

1. Open Ruled Surface.max from the accompanying CD. Select the NURBS surface and open the NURBS Creation toolbox in the Modify panel.

2. Click the Create Ruled Surface button and drag from one Fit Curve to the other to create the Ruled Surface road.

3. Click the Sub-Object button, choose Surface, select the new Ruled Surface, and in the Material area set the Material ID to 2 and render (see Figure 13.10).

If you don't see the surface to select it, the normals are probably flipped. If that is the case, change your display to wire frame mode to see it. You can then either undo and pick the other line first, Flip Beginning and Flip End in the Ruled Surf panel at the bottom of the Command panel while the surface is selected, or go to the Surface Selection level and click the Flip Normals button.

The curves are created using Fit Curve and the Points are created using Surface Point with a Normal Offset of 1.

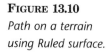

FIGURE 13.10

Path on a terrain using Ruled surface.

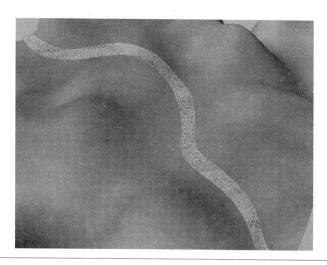

One of the most often used Surface tools is U-loft. It is used to create continuous smooth surfaces by connecting a series of curves arranged like spars in a wing or rafters in a house. How the surface arranges itself on the frame of curves is dependent on the position of the first vertex of each curve, so where you start your curve can save from having to adjust that first vertex. You of course can always adjust the position of the first vertex at any time.

Another issue is normals, in that they can be flipped when creating the U-loft surface. Although rules determine the results of the normals when choosing the curves' direction or the order to pick them, they are just complex enough to ignore, so you can use trial and error to get the results you want.

The following exercise will take you through creating a U-loft to complete connecting a fin to a whale:

PART TWO: ATTACHING A FIN TO A WHALE

1. Open the saved version of Whale Fin.max from the Points section or open Whale Fin2.max. Select the NURBS surface named Whale and open the NURBS Creation toolbox in the Modify panel.

2. Click Sub-Object, choose Curve Selection level, and click the Unhide All button. If necessary, Zoom Extents and arrange your view using Arc Rotate to make it easy to select all the curves for the fin.

3. Click the U-loft Surface button, pick the larger of the two curves you created, then the smaller one, and then all the curves that make up the fin (see Figure 13.11).

FIGURE 13.11

The U-lofted surface of the fin.

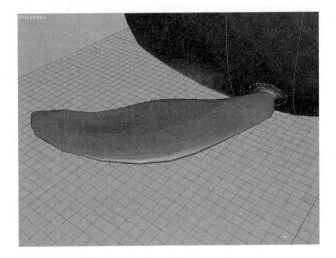

Don't be concerned if the fin looks twisted or strange. The normals may need to be flipped or the first vertex on the new curves may need to be set.

4. If the normals need to be flipped because it looks inside out, choose the Surface Selection level, select the fin surface and click the Flip Normals checkbox.

5. If the First Vertex needs to be set on the curves you created because the surface looks twisted, choose Curve Selection level, click the Make First button, and pick where you want the first vertex to be. You may need to click the Reverse button to get rid of any final twisting.

To compare the first vertices of all the curves, change the viewport display to wireframe. The green box on each curve is the first vertex and the other green vertex indicates the direction of the curve—clockwise or counterclockwise (see Figure 13.12).

6. Save this file for use in working with Materials later in the chapter.

FIGURE 13.12

The relationship between the smaller box and the larger (First vertex) determines the direction of the curve.

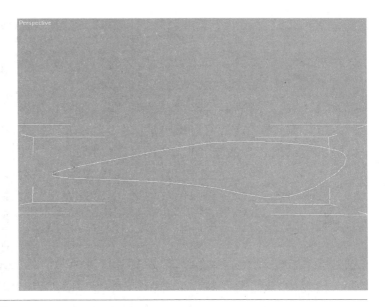

At this point you can fine-tune the shape of the Joined U-loft surface by adjusting the point positions on any of the curves or by moving the curves around. You could also make the fin surface a CV surface by clicking Make Independent, giving you a different level of adjustability.

You can add, remove, or edit the curves of a U-loft if later in the modeling session you find you need to. You can do this by choosing the Surface Selection level, selecting the surface, and scrolling to the bottom of the Command panel (see Figure 13.13). There you can change the order of the curves, pick where you want to insert a new one, or create a new curve by refining the surface in the same way you would use the U or V Iso Curve tools.

Besides the standard use of Cap surface, you can use it to create a non-rectangular surface by creating a Closed curve and capping it. That creates a CV surface that conforms to the shape of your curve. The lower surface in Blend Surface.max is created this way. Be aware that as of 2.0, this feature doesn't handle exaggerated concavity in the curve very well.

Working with Converted Primitives

All NURBS surfaces in MAX (as of 2.0) are essentially rectangular in that they all have a U and V direction that can be refined to create more CVs or Points. When converting Standard primitives to NURBS through the Edit

FIGURE 13.13

The U-loft roll-up lets you insert, delete, or rearrange the order of the curves used to define it.

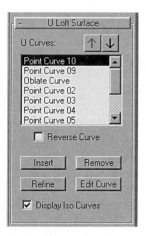

Stack, they are converted to CV surfaces. The number of vertices, faces, or segments doesn't matter as to how many CVs the converted NURBS object will have. Each primitive has built into them a default arrangement of CVs and surfaces used to define them whatever their basic parameters are when converted.

If you study each kind of primitive, you will get a small lesson in how objects can be constructed using NURBS. A good example is the teapot. The body and lid are lathed curves and the handle and spout are composed of four CV surfaces each. You might think that it would be better to create U-lofts for the spout and handle, but there is actually less calculation overhead when done this way. U-loft is a great tool, but it can be slow, as you will see when adjusting U-loft surfaces.

A problem with the Radial Primitive converts (as of 2.0) is that they come in with a seam. The following exercise will take you through repairing a converted sphere:

REPAIRING A CONVERTED SPHERE

1. Reset MAX, maximize the Perspective viewport, create a sphere, and convert it to a NURBS surface through the Edit Stack button in the Modify panel.

2. Choose the Surface CV Selection level in Sub-Object and Arc Rotate the view so you can see the group of columns of CVs in the back of the sphere.

3. Pick and move any of the CVs close to the center of the three rows of CVs (visually columns) that are close together and notice there is a seam.

4. Undo if necessary to return the sphere to its original shape, click the Rows of CV buttons, select the middle row and the row to the right of it, and delete them (see Figure 13.14).

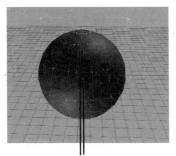  

Select these rows

FIGURE 13.14

The rows selected and deleted, and Columns closed to create a seamless NURBS converted sphere.

5. Choose the Surface Selection level, pick the sphere surface, scroll to the bottom of the Command panel, and click the Close Cols button. Now if you pull any of the CVs in that area, they will act like you expect.

You may want to Save Selected in the File pulldown as Seamless NURBS Sphere.max so you can later merge it into files where you need a seamless NURBS sphere surface.

Attaching and Importing Standard Primitives

Attached primitives create the same sub-objects as collapsing a primitive and are worked with in the same way.

If you import a primitive, you can modify it using its base parameters as well as using modifiers. The only editing process you have available for working with an import through the NURBS Command panel is to extract it out as a copy or instance, recreating it as a standard primitive.

Converting Surfaces

As with curves, there will be times when you want one kind of surface to be another, such as a Point surface to be a CV surface or a Dependent surface to be Independent. The following are the different conversions you can do and the steps to accomplish them:

- **Point surface to a CV surface**: Select the surface, choose the Surface selection level in Sub-Object, and click Make Independent.

- **CV surface to a Point surface**: Select the surface, choose the Surface Selection level in Sub-Object, click Make Loft, and select the number of curves you want and whether you want U or V direction curves. This actually creates a U-loft surface with CV Curves. You then choose the Curve Selection level, select each curve one at a time, and use Make Fit to convert them into point curves.

- **Dependent surface into an Independent surface**: Select the surface, choose the Surface selection level in Sub-Object, and click Make Independent.

Now that all the methods for creation have been covered, all the Command panels that haven't been covered will be explained in the following section.

NURBS Command Panels

A few buttons uses couldn't be avoided in previous sections in the interest of continuity and their use has already been explained, so only the significant buttons that haven't been explained will be covered here. To help with comparison of the Sub-Object panels an image file—Panels.pcx— is provided on the CD and can be printed out using any paint program.

NURBS Surface NURBS Curve Main Panel

In the Display area of the General rollup, you can toggle on and off the display of the toolbox, Lattices, curves, surfaces, and dependents. The following is a list of the keyboard shortcuts for each option when the Plug-in Keyboard Shortcut Toggle button is on:

- Ctrl+T to toggle NURBS Creation toolbox

- Ctrl+H to toggle Lattice display

- Ctrl+D to display Dependencies toggle

Turning off the display of sub-object types you aren't currently working with helps to speed up production. You can also use the Lattice and Dependents toggles to quickly see what sub-objects are dependent/independent or Point/CV in nature.

Surface Approximation

When working with a NURBS surface and the Sub-Object button is off, you have access to the Surface Approximation Rollup. When MAX renders a normal 3D object, it takes each face into account in the render solution, determining which faces are smoothed by smoothing groups. When it renders a NURBS object, it reduces each surface to faces that very closely approximate the way a true NURBS renderer would render the object. This is done using one of the Surface Approximation options under Mesh parameters (see Figure 13.15).

FIGURE 13.15

The different modes of Surface approximation.

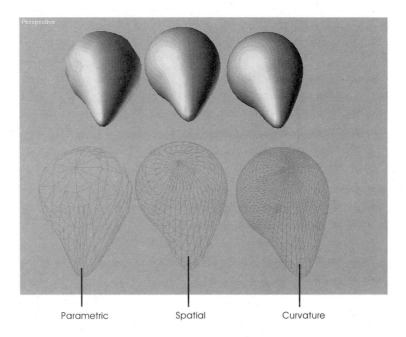

Parametric   Spatial   Curvature

The Default option is Curvature, which continually updates the number of faces and vertices on-the-fly as you edit a surface. You can observe this by being in Wireframe display with the Mesh Only radio button chosen in the Iso Parametric Lines area and moving the control points or CVs of a surface. This method endeavors to give the fewest number faces for any given shape of the surface.

The Parametric option keeps the same number of triangular faces for the approximation of a surface based on the number of steps set for the U and V direction. This option speeds up display while editing and keeps exact control of the number of faces an object has but risks creating non-smooth edges.

The Spatial option limits the maximum size of triangular faces used to approximate a surface and keeps them all the same size. This ensures smoothness on the edges of a surface but risks high numbers of faces.

As Display options, Iso And Mesh option radio buttons in Wireframe mode display Iso curves that represent the surface and a rendered surface in Smooth and Highlight mode. Mesh only displays faces to represent the surface in Wireframe and a rendered surface in Smooth and Highlight mode. Iso only displays Iso curves in either mode.

The Surface Approximation panel in the main NURBS control panel doesn't let you work with more than one surface at a time, so a utility has been created, called Surface Approximation, to allow that. It can be found under More in the Utility tab of the Command panel.

The last option in the Surface Approximation panel, Merge, is used to get rid of seams, if extreme conditions cause them to show up. Usually a small adjustment is all that's needed.

Point and CV Panels

The Curve point and CV panels are subsets of their surface versions. The CV panels contain two options that do not exist in the Point panels. You can toggle the display of the lattice for the selected surface or curve—and you can specify weight for selected CVs for determining how attractive they are to the part of the surface or curve that is local to them. A higher weight tends to make the curve or surface more pointed at that CV (see Figure 13.16).

Fuse enables you to lock CVs or Points together so that they act as one. They do not need to be in proximity to each other to be fused and can be unfused at anytime.

Refine enables you to add more CVs or points to a surface or curve. With curves, you can add them one at a time. With surfaces, they are added in rows or columns with the number added based on how many rows or columns already exist in the surface. When pushing and pulling points or CVs to model a surface, start with creating larger features and then add more rows and columns of points or CV's as you work with finer and finer detail.

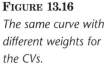

FIGURE 13.16

The same curve with different weights for the CVs.

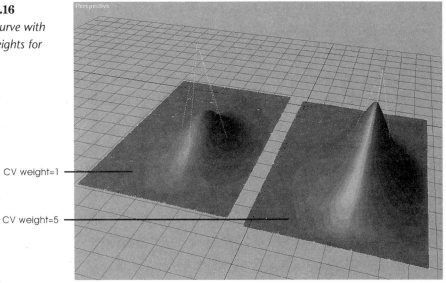

CV weight=1

CV weight=5

Extend will extend a Point curve by picking on the curve close to the end you want to extend to and dragging out to create a new point.

Affect Region works the same with Points and CVs as they do with Editable mesh's vertices. You set the shape and size of the region you want to influence with, using the Edit Curve button, and then move a CV or point. This influences surrounding CVs or Points, to move with diminished influence the further away they are from the CV or point being moved (see Figure 13.17).

Curve and Surface Panels

When in the Curve or Surface panel and a sub-object is selected, for most of the different curve and surface types, a rollup related to that sub-object displays at the bottom of the Command panel. If you edit with the Curve Common and Surface Common rollups open, you may not notice those sub-object specific rollups that can make learning where everything is in the beginning difficult. In Figures 13.18 and 13.19, those roll-ups are presented to familiarize you with them.

Now that you have been introduced to the tools needed to work with NURBS, this section will take you through the integration of their use by creating an organic object—a face—utilizing what you have learned.

FIGURE 13.17

Affect region influences the movement of CVs close to the CV moved.

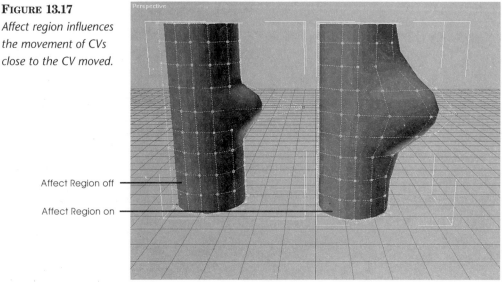

Affect Region off

Affect Region on

FIGURE 13.18

Panels found at the bottom of the NURBS curves Main Panel when the associated curve is selected.

FIGURE 13.19

Panels found at the bottom of the NURBS surfaces Main Panel when the associated surface is selected.

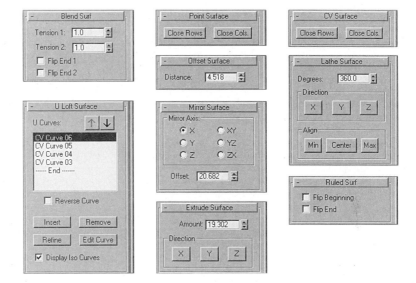

Creating a Face with NURBS

One way to create a face is to convert a sphere to a NURBS object and non-uniform scale it to the approximate shape of the head you want the face on. Then you refine the surface with enough rows and columns of CVs to let you create the positions of the eyes, nose, and mouth. You next pull the mouth hole into the center of the sphere, push in the eye cavities, pull out the eye brow ridges, the bridge of the nose, and shape the cheeks. Then using the method laid out in the exercise "Attaching a Fin to a Whale" you create the nose, lips, and eyelids as joined surfaces. This method works well for animating in that there are no seams but takes a lot of time to deal with materials to make the interface between the joined objects and the face look seamless.

Another method, some of which you will do in the following exercise, uses two 2D templates, one of the front view, and one of the side, to guide you in creating curves for U-lofting. You only do one side of the face, mirror it and then use Blend Surface to create a smooth transition from one side of the face to the other. You would then use the same process to add the back of the face to complete the head. What takes time in this method is adjusting the curves to get the look you want and matching up the seams to make the surface look seamless. It also requires a strong familiarity of how to use and manipulate curves with CVs, which can come through three or four hours of practice.

The curves for the face have been done here for you, but you can use them as a guide for creating your own face from scratch later.

CREATING THE FACE OF THE BUDDHA

1. Open Face.max, select the background NURBS curve, and hide it using the Display floater in the Tools pulldown. This outline is used as a guide for creating and adjusting curves that will be U-lofted next (see Figure 13.20).

FIGURE 13.20

A NURBS curve used as an outline to guide the creation of curves for U-lofting.

2. Select the NURBS surface, open the NURBS Creation toolbox in the Modify panel and click the U-loft Surface button.

3. Starting at the top, pick the first four curves to create the first surface. They are labeled 1 through 4 (see Figure 13.21).

4. Using the last curve you picked for the first surfaces as the first curve for the second surface, pick the next four curves. They are labeled 4 through 7.

5. Using curve 7 and 8 create the next surface.

6. Starting with 8, pick the next nine curves for the next surface. They are labeled 8 through 16.

FIGURE 13.21

Select curves 1 through 4 for the first U-loft surface.

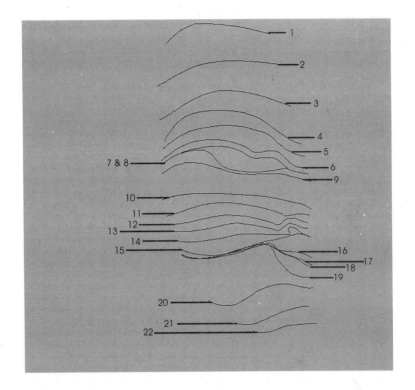

7. Using 16 and 17 make the next surface.

8. Using 18 and 19 make the next surface.

9. Starting with 19, pick the last four curves for the last U-loft surface. Your model should look like Figure 13.22

10. Click the Sub-Object button, choose the Surface Selection level, click the Mirror Surface tool, pick on the first U-loft surface and set the off-set to 47.1 in the Command panel.

11. Mirror each of the U-loft surfaces you created setting the offset to 47.1 for each mirrored surface.

12. Now with Blend surface, create a blend surface between each pair of original and mirrored surfaces. You will have to Flip End 2 for each blend surface you create (see Figure 13.23).

13. Using the Display Floater, unhide everything but the Outline NURBS curve, Zoom Extents, and Render.

FIGURE 13.22
All initial U-lofts created.

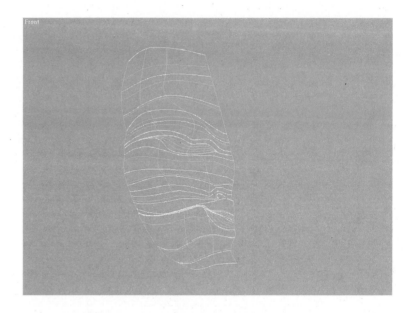

FIGURE 13.23
The Blend Surface rollup found at the bottom of the Command panel with Flip End 2 checked

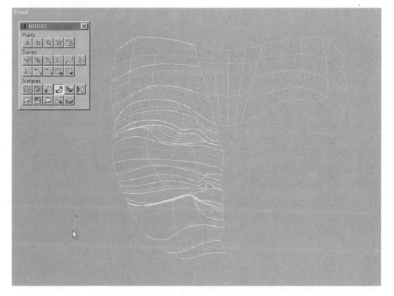

By stepping through the different Sub-Object levels of the head piece and ears, you can see that they are just more U-Lofts, mirrors, blends, and Cap surfaces. You will find that in your first attempts to try this method from scratch that it is easier than it looks to create the curves for the initial U-lofts.

The finished image, Figure 13.24, is in color on the CD called Buddha.tga.

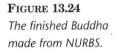

FIGURE 13.24

The finished Buddha made from NURBS.

Now that you have all these cool NURBS objects, it's time to learn how to animate them.

Animating NURBS

Animating with NURBS is much the same as animating anything else in MAX. You can animate all sub-objects including Control points and CVs, and most control panel spinners are animatable. Only those sub-objects that have been animated show up in Track View.

Any conversion, such as Make Fit, Make Independent, or Make Loft, removes any animation the converted sub-object may have had. If you fuse a CV to another, it takes on the animation of the one it's fused to.

Imports lose their transform animation when imported but keep any modifier animation provided MeshSelect is in the stack between the primitive and its modifiers.

Although you can do morph animation with NURBS objects using the Morph Compound object, there is a script that ships with MAX called Morpher.ms that contains weighted morph channels similar to some of the more popular weighted morphing programs. The following is an exercise to take you through using the Mopher.ms script to animate a very simple head because this script only works with a single CV NURBS surface:

ANIMATING YAMA WITH MORPHER

1. Open Morpher.ms from the MAX R2 CD. Click MAXScript in the Utilities Command panel, pick Run Script, and double-click Morpher.ms. This brings up the Morpher floater (see Figure 13.25).

FIGURE 13.25

The Morpher.ms floater lets you Morph single CV Surface Models.

2. Click the Select Object button in the floater and pick the Dude surface. This sets the primary state so that all changes snap back after assigning them to a slider.

3. Pick the Dude surface, choose the Surface CV Selection level, and choose the Mouth Corners Selection set of CVs from the toolbar. Then move them up in the Z direction and click the first Snap button on the floater.

Notice that the surface changes back to its original shape.

4. Now move the Mouth Corner CVs down in the Z direction and click the second Snap button.

5. Select the Left EyeBrow selection set of CVs, move them up in the Z direction, and click the third Snap button.

6. Repeat step five with the Right Eyebrow selection set.

7. Select the Upper Lip selection set, move it down towards the lower lip, and click the last Snap button.

At this point, you can adjust the sliders and see the effect that each slider has on the surface either by itself or in combination.

With slider combinations of your choice, you can now animate the Dude. Dude.avi on the CD is a simple example of such an animation. Although the script only has five slider channels, it is not complex and could be edited to contain many more channels.

As with any Mesh object, you can use bones along with Digimation's Bones Pro or Kinetix's Character Studio to animate your NURBS objects. The difference in effect is that the CVs or control points are controlled by the bones rather than the vertices of the mesh, which the NURBS object ultimately gets converted to before rendering.

In Track view, Animation Controller Reassignment for NURBS sub-objects has been turned off. This means that if the controller for a CV is a Bezier three point, it remains that way even though you can open the Assign Controller dialog and click a different controller. Transforms remain reassignable however.

The last issues with NURBS deal with a few rules about materials and a technique for creating smooth joints.

Materials and Mapping on NURBS

You can assign different material IDs to each surface in a NURBS surface object as well as activate the Generate Mapping Coords item for each. If you don't want to use the default mapping coordinates, you can assign separate UVW Map modifiers to each surface. If you assign UVW mapping to a NURBS surface and then assign a UVW map to a sub-object, the rest of the sub-objects automatically have their Generate Mapping Coords turned on and the overall UVW mapping is ignored.

An issue that comes up with Joined surfaces is how the material of the attached surface interfaces with the surface it's attached to. The following exercise will take you through creating a material that will visually join the fin of a whale to its body.

CREATING A MATERIAL FOR A JOINED SURFACE

1. Open a saved copy of Whale Fin 2.max from the exercise "Part Two of Attaching a Fin to a Whale" or Whale Fin 3.max from the CD and

Render. Notice the defined edge at the joint between the fin and the body (see Figure 13.26).

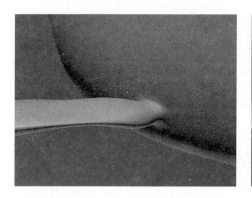
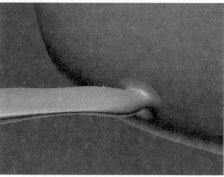

FIGURE 13.26

The Joined surface of a whale fin before and after material adjustment.

2. Open the Material Editor, click in the lower-right slot to select the dark yellow material, click the Type button, choose Multi/Sub-object, and choose Keep old material as submaterial.

3. Drag a copy of the color swatch for the first sub-material to the second sub-material swatch and click OK for Copy. Then click the Sub-Material button to take you to the basic parameters for it.

4. Click on the Map button next to the Opacity spinner and choose Gradient as a map.

5. Pick and drag the color swatch of Color 1 into Color 2's swatch and click OK to copy. Set the Color 2 Position to .05 and assign the material to the NURBS surface.

6. In the Modify panel, click the Sub-Object button, choose the Surface selection level, pick the fin surface and set its Material ID to 2.

7. Turn on Generate Mapping Coords and Render.

Notice that now the joint is a smooth continuous blending into the side of the whale.

In Practice: Modeling with NURBS

- The NURBS Surface and NURBS Curve objects are containers for holding Point, Curve, and Surface Sub-Objects. You create a NURBS object and then go to the Modify panel to add and edit components.

- Additional NURBS Sub-Objects are created using the NURBS Creation toolbox, which allows you to create Independent or Dependent sub-objects.

- Independent Sub-Objects are controlled using Control vertices, which indirectly influence their shape, or Control points, which rest directly on the sub-object being controlled.

- Dependent Sub-Objects are defined by their relationship to other Independent or Dependent Sub-Objects and are adjusted indirectly by adjusting the sub-objects they are dependent on.

- Generally, points are used to create curves, which are used to create surfaces. Surfaces can also be created by converting them from any of the Standard Primitives.

- The current version (2.0) does not allow holes in surfaces, but by applying Surf points on a surface, using them to create a Fit curve, and then using that curve with others to create a U-Loft surface, these "Joined Surfaces" can be added to any surface such as a face or torso.

- Face and vertex counts of NURBS surfaces continually update towards the optimum number needed to give a smooth result at rendering time. For this reason, modifying and animation are acting on the CVs or Control points rather than the resulting mesh.

- Only one material can be assigned to a NURBS object, but separate material IDs can be assigned to each surface as well as separate UVW Mapping Coordinates.

Part IV

MATERIALS AND MAPS

Chapter 14

MATERIALS AND TEXTURES

3D Studio MAX offers an unlimited capacity to create materials that transform your geometry models into living, breathing, realistic objects. The tools for constructing materials enable you to do so in a non-linear way, so that you are never at the mercy of your original ideas. A material can be adjusted throughout the entire design process; the options in working with materials are as powerful as your latest ideas.

Defining a material is nearly always an exploration with much experimentation. A common technique is to copy stages of your material into the adjacent sample slots so you can compare alternate approaches. Saving materials to the private experimentation libraries is also quite common (and highly advised).

Materials can be an end to themselves and many hours can be spent perfecting a scene's palette of textures. You will also nearly always be coordinating your efforts with a traditional paint package (such as Photoshop, Animator Studio, Fractal Design Painter, Ron Scott QFX, and so on), and possibly a 3D paint package as well. Often these are run concurrently with 3DS MAX, with artists switching between the two by using the Windows Alt+Tab key combination. Other studios prefer to have dedicated systems for paint and 3D, connecting their output through a network.

This chapter covers the Materials Editor interface and its navigation as well as fundamental material concepts including Material trees, library construction and techniques, and a look at the Basic parameters of a 3DS MAX Standard Material. The following two chapters examine the Standard Material Map Channels in depth and Mapping concepts as well. In particular, you'll be learning about the following concepts in this chapter:

- Understanding the Material tree concept

- Working with the Material Editor Interface

- Creating with the Standard Material

Paramount to digesting this information is a thorough understanding of how materials can branch to form hierarchies or material trees.

Understanding Material Tree Concepts

It's easy to think of materials in 3DS MAX as almost being "living" things. Each material is individual with incredible personality that can evolve over time. Materials begin with a somewhat simple base that can then be made more intricate by branching. As shown in Figure 14.1, the organization of various material properties and the source files referred to for each property of a Marble Green Tile material is clarified through indentation and graphical branch links. The material's base is shown at the top, and each material property is shown indented beneath it. In the same manner, source files for each property are shown indented beneath each property.

FIGURE 14.1

The Material tree concept.

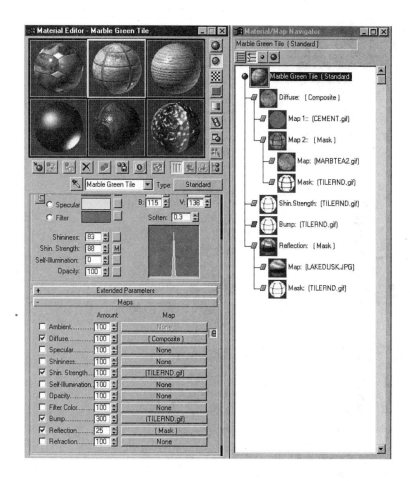

In this way, the Material Editor becomes a "tree," or an extremely visual version of Windows Explorer with the Base Material being the "tree trunk" or "root directory." Every long, thin button shown in the Maps rollout menu allowing a choice is a *map channel*, acting as a "branch" or subdirectory that is initially bare or empty. Clicking a Map Channel button enables you to choose a Map type, and thus "add leaves" or fill the directory. Most Map types then contain additional channels for yet deeper branches and more "branches" or subdirectories. The material shown in the sample window is the final result of all properties branched onto the material's tree trunk and the farther you branch, the more subtle the final result appears.

The base or "trunk" level of a material is the Material Map. The Material type contains all the initial map channels that can be branched from—a somewhat confusing concept because most programs (such as 3D Studio DOS) have the equivalent of just one Material "type." Using 3D Studio DOS as the example, its entire Materials Editor module is actually manipulating the equivalent of *one* material type. This one type has evolved into the Standard Material type in 3DS MAX.

Whenever you see a selection button titled Map, you're seeing a *Map channel*. A Map channel is essentially an Input point, or socket, for which you can choose a Map type, and so continue to build the material tree by adding branches. Map channels can exist within material or Map types. The Standard Material, for example, contains 11 Map channels for selecting up to 11 Map types. A *Map type* often feels like an entire material in itself, when actually it's just a branch from the Parent Material type or Map type. Bitmaps are an example of a Map type, where a single bitmap is used as primary input along with all its parameters and options. Other Map types, such as Checker, contain additional Map channels so the branching can continue by selecting yet more Map types.

In Figure 14.1, the Material/Map Navigator shows that the Map type for a Marble Green Tile material is Standard. Four Map channels have been branched off this tree trunk: Diffuse, Shininess Strength, Bump, and Reflection. Each of these channels points either to a raster file (.GIF or .JPG) or branches to further raster files using a Mask Map type.

Choices and controls that are not Map channels (that is, they aren't selection buttons) are either *parameters* or *options*. Parameters usually have ranges and edit fields with typical Material parameters including color, values, angles, and distances. Nearly every parameter has a track in Track View and thus can be animated. The remaining Material and Map controls are termed Material or Map *options*. These dictate how parameters are evaluated and are usually checkboxes or radio buttons. Examples of options include Soften, 2-Sided, and Bitmap Invert. Material options can rarely be animated and thus do not usually appear in Track View.

When a Material or Map type has parameters only and no Map channels, such as the Bitmap Map type, then that branch of the tree essentially stops. Of course, you can branch at that point by changing the Map type to one that has channels and choosing to keep the current Map type as a sub-map of the newly chosen Map type, as shown in Figure 14.2.

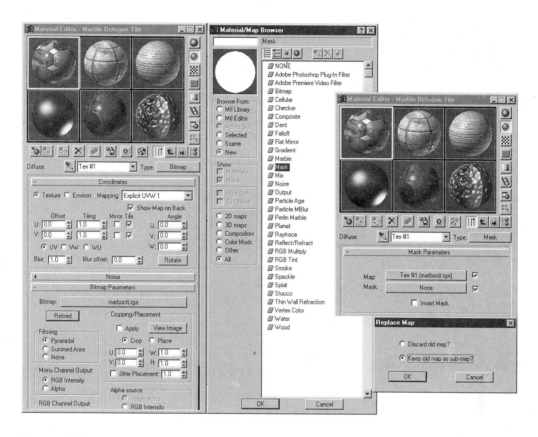

FIGURE 14.2

Making a Bitmap map type a sub-map by choosing another Map type.

Some Material types (such as Multi/Sub-Object, Top/Bottom, Double Sided, and Blend) contain *Material channels* rather than map channels. The status of being a Map or Material channel is signified by how the selection button is titled. When working at the base level of such materials, you are actually choosing other Material types to branch to and not Map types. While the Standard material has the most Map channels, it has no material channels. The Matte/Shadow material is the only real "dead end" by not providing any channels for branching.

As with most things in 3DS MAX, materials and maps are actually objects and thus can be instanced. Whenever you choose an existing map or material for a channel, you have the option to make it an instance of the original (meaning that any future edits you do to one are also made to the other). It is very common for a material to use the same map at numerous locations. For example, the same map might be used for the Opacity, Shininess Strength, Bump, and Reflection Mask. By making these instances, you need to adjust only one to adjust them all.

NOTE

Although you cannot instance parameters in the Material Editor, you instance them in Track View.

The next section describes numerous ways for selecting, navigating, and coordinating this tree of materials.

Working with the Material Editor Interface

The Material Editor is your alchemy lab for creating nearly any surface appearance you might imagine. As with other parts of 3DS MAX, the Material Editor is an extensible environment where all materials, maps, and bitmap types are actually plug-in components. The familiar rollup buttons for accessing areas are an indication that this framework contains plug-ins and, as such, its capabilities and interface change as different materials and maps are used.

One portion of the Material Editor interface remains rather constant in its appearance regardless of what type of material you're using or what kind of map you're working with. As seen in Figure 14.3, the border functions surrounding the sample slots and the sample slots area above the scrollable area in the interface remain fixed. The sample slots region (which is controlled through the Options button) can be configured in either a 3×2, a 5×3, or a 6×4 array. These functions are used commonly by all Map and Material types and are grayed out when not applicable. The following section describes how to navigate and use the Material Editor to its fullest.

Material Sample Slots

When activating the Material Editor, whether by its toolbar button, menu item, or a keyboard alternate, the Material Editor is presented according to its last state. The MAX scene file maintains the materials last edited in the scene as well as the Editor's options. When working in a new scene, the default set of material samples (in a 3×2, 5×3 or 6×4 configuration) is shown. These material windows, or slots, behave much like viewports. Clicking a Material window activates that window, making it current within the Editor, and changes the window border to white similar to the way viewports behave. If a sample window contains a material used in a scene, white triangles are placed at the corners of the window border. Your position in a material's tree is retained as you switch between sample windows.

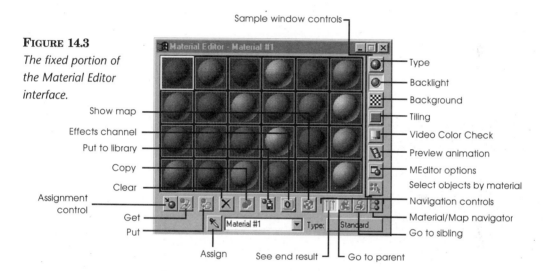

FIGURE 14.3

The fixed portion of the Material Editor interface.

Material Temperatures

Materials are said to have three "temperatures" (hot, warm, or cold) based upon their scene assignment. If the material is used in the scene, it's considered hot. If it's a copy of a material used in the scene, it's warm. If it's not used at all, it's cold. Hot materials are indicated in the material sample window by the four white corner triangles shown in the right-hand frame of Figure 14.4.

Hot materials are dynamic to their assignment in the scene. When you adjust any parameter within a hot material, you are affecting the scene's material definition at the same time—*not* just the definition in the Editor. As updates are made to the material sample, they are also updated in all shaded viewports. Although it's common to work this way, it can cause delays because shaded viewports are attempting to keep up with your edits.

TIP

For the fastest editing of hot (assigned) materials, it's best to make a copy of the material, make all changes to this warm version, and then put it back to the scene using Put Material to Scene as the new hot material.

FIGURE 14.4

The three material "temperatures."

Cold Material (Not Used in Scene)   Warm Material (In Scene, but not linked)   Hot Material (In Scene, and linked)

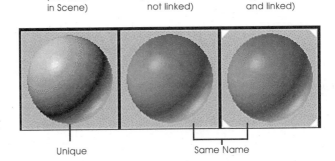

Unique   Same Name

Warm materials are formed when you copy a material by either using the Make Material Copy button or dragging a sample window onto another slot. As illustrated in Figure 14.4, the copied, warm material has the same name as the original but does not have the direct connection to the scene. Editing it does not impact what's currently in the scene. If you assign this copied, warm material to an object, you will be prompted to either rename the material or replace the like-named material's definition. Agreeing to replace the material is the same as using the Put function. Giving a warm material a unique name makes it cold.

Cold materials differ from warm materials only in that they do not share a name with a material that already exists in the current scene. Cold materials can be freely assigned without concern for them affecting any previous definitions. A cold material becomes warm if you change its name to one already in the scene.

Material Editor Display Controls

The Material Editor contains several controls for viewing your material samples and altering such qualities as shape, lighting, background pattern, and tiling. The intent is to enable you to make the Material Editor environment as close as possible to qualities of the scene in which you will be assigning them. These controls are located along the right-hand side of the material sample windows (refer to Figure 14.3).

The Sample Type button enables you to choose the geometry shown in the material sample slot. Choices are a sphere, a box, a cylinder and a custom sample object that can be set in the Material Editor Options dialog. Choosing the one that most closely represents your object's geometry enables you to better predict rendering qualities (see Figure 14.5).

FIGURE 14.5

Using primitives that most closely match scene objects.

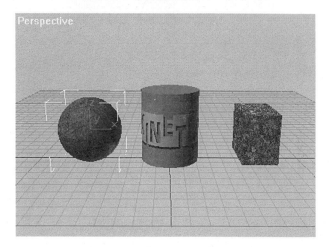

The Backlight button places a secondary light source below and behind the material sample to alert you of Material properties that can cause harsh highlights. While this option slows the rendering slightly, the information is critical when using Blinn or Phong materials without using Softening.

The Background button changes the sample window background from a solid shade of gray to a checker pattern containing the RGB primaries, black and white. This somewhat garish pattern is necessary to see the results of Opacity controls, especially those involving colored transparencies. The background can also be set to a bitmap that is configured in the Material Editor Options dialog.

The Sample UV Tiling button enables you to change the tiling repeat in the sample slot, as shown in Figure 14.6. This is convenient when you need to see how patterns repeat, but adjusting Map Tiling parameters just for that purpose is not practical. Changing the Tiling display has no impact on the material itself. Like the Sample Type button, the Sample UV Tiling button is a flyout button that may display one of four different modes, depending on the Tiling mode you have selected.

1×1   2×2   3×3   4×4

FIGURE 14.6
The result of viewing with different Tiling rates.

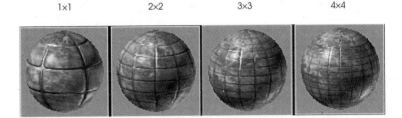

The Video Color Check button has the Editor check for colors that are illegal when put to videotape for display on NTSC or PAL monitors. Illegal colors (most notably bright reds) output very badly and catching such colors as early as material definition is often helpful. Figure 14.7 shows the Material Editor displaying illegal colors in a material. Note, however, that the colors are illegal only in respect to the sample's lighting and that your scene lighting will differ.

Illegal Area

FIGURE 14.7
A material showing illegal video colors.

The Make Preview button enables you to create an animated preview of the active sample sphere with control for size, timing, and duration. This is a quick alternative to rendering the scene for seeing the animated effects contained within material trees.

The Material Editor Options button accesses a dialog that contains the global options for the Material Editor as shown in Figure 14.8. This dialog is described in more detail in the following section.

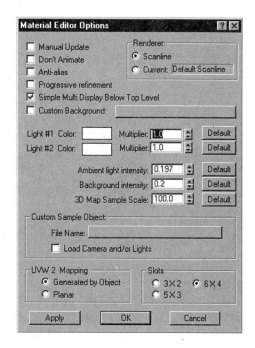

The Select by Material button brings up the Select By Name dialog and identifies which objects are assigned the current material. You can use this to select those objects, invert and select everything else, or create other selections. In practice, this is a very convenient method for selecting objects for many purposes and not just for assigning materials.

Inside the Material Editor Options Dialog

In this dialog, several controls, including toggles, are provided to control the following:

■ Whether sample slots update automatically or only after you click them.

■ Whether animated maps are updated in the sample slots while you play an animation or drag the time slider.

- Whether or not the sample slots use antialiasing.

- Whether Progressive Refinement is used for showing complex materials on slower machines. When Progressive Refinement is on, samples are rendered quickly, with large pixels, then rendered a second time in greater detail.

- Whether or not sample spheres for multi/sub-object materials display multiple patches only at the top level of the multi/sub-object.

A custom background to replace the default checkers background can also be specified in this dialog. You can also control the actual renderer used on the material samples. The Scanline Renderer listed in the Renderer rollout is the same as the 3DS MAX Production renderer. If you want to specify a different renderer, you can do so from the Rendering tab of the File/Preferences dialog and then select it from the Material Options dialog.

The Material Editor Options dialog is also where the background intensity, lighting, and map scale are defined. Light #1 is the top light and Light #2 is the backlight. Ambient Light Intensity (a value from 0 to 1) sets Ambient light in the sample slot. Background Intensity (a value from 0 to 1) also sets the background intensity of slots. The 3D Map Sample Scale globally sets the scale of the sample spheres to any size in order to make them consistent with the objects in the scene that have the texture on them.

T IP

The 3D Map Sample Scale also enables you to correctly preview the scale of 3D Procedural Maps, such as Noise, without having to render. If you have an object that is about 50 units across, set this parameter to 50 to see the Noise map correctly scaled on the sample sphere.

In addition to the sphere, box, or cylindrical Sample types, you can also use Custom Sample Objects for your sample slots. A filename button is provided for you to point to a 3DS MAX scene with a single unlinked object that fits inside an imaginary 100 unit cube. The object must be a primitive with a Generate Mapping Coords toggle or have a UVW modified applied to it. If the scene contains a camera and lights, their use can also be toggled in the sample slot.

Controls are also provided for affecting the way the second UVW Mapping channel appears in the sample slots. These controls have no effect on the way the mapping appears in the rendered scene. The second Mapping channel can either be governed by the sample window object, custom Sample Object Mapping coordinates, or a Planar mapping regardless of Mapping coordinates.

The number of sample slots shown can be configured for 3×2, 5×3, and 6×4 arrays.

Material Controls for Active Materials

The buttons located horizontally below the Material Sample windows provide functions that relate to the active Material sample and not the Material Editor as a whole. Functions on the left enable you to replace the current material in the Editor or the scene, assign the material, reset, copy, or put to the library. Buttons on the right control Material effects channels, texture display, result viewing, navigation, and browsing. Beneath this row and to the left of the editable Material (or map) Name field is the Pick Material from Object Eyedropper button. This tool enables you to select a material from an object in the scene. Upon moving the Eyedropper over an object in the scene and clicking, the object's material is placed in the active sample slot.

Creating New Materials and Maps

The Get Material button places you into the Material/Map Browser for the selection of a new material that replaces the *entire* active material. It's important to realize that the Get Material function is used to replace the current material and *not* to select a sub-material or map. To select maps or materials for use within the current material, you must access the Browser from the Type button.

If you use Get Material and are not at the active material's root level, a confirmation dialog appears, informing you that the entire material is about to be replaced. The assumption is that because you are not at the Root level, you may have used Get Material instead of Type. If you are at the Root level, no confirmation is requested and the material is replaced.

W ARNING

The Get Material action needs to be used with the knowledge that the active material will be discarded and if its definition does not exist within the scene, a library, or another slot, it is lost.

Replacing Materials with Put and Assign

The Put Material to Scene button is only available when you are editing a warm material. The Put function replaces the like-named material definition in the scene with the one you're editing. The previously hot material reverts to being warm. This is the same as performing a Replace when assigning a warm material to the scene, except there is no warning message to delay your update.

The Assign Material to Selection button assigns the current material to the selection of objects in the scene. This option is only active when you have a selection. Together, the Put and Assign functions supply the tools for changing material assignments, giving you the following options for changing an assigned material definition:

- Edit a hot material in the Material Editor and its definition is automatically updated in the scene.

- Assign a new material to the selected objects.

- Edit a warm material, assign it to any object in the scene, and choose to replace the like-named material.

- Edit a warm material and use the Put option to replace the scene definition.

The Make Material Copy button is only available when editing a hot material. Using this function changes the material from hot to warm. The newly warm material maintains the same definition and name but no longer has a direct link to the scene. If you plan on experimenting with a material, it's a good practice to use Copy to change a hot material to warm so that you do not immediately impact the scene's definition. Once satisfied with the material, use Put to redefine the scene's material. In the meantime, the scene's material definition acts as a backup that can be retrieved if needed.

Reset Map/Material to Default Settings

This button resets the values for the material in the active sample slot. When selected, the material colors are removed and set to shades of gray and other attributes, such as shininess, opacity, and so on, are reset to their default values. Maps assigned to the material are removed. If you are at a Map level, it resets the map to default values.

Saving Materials in Libraries

Materials' definitions are saved in the MAX scene file along with any object that is assigned to them. When you open or merge a scene, the materials assigned within can be retrieved from the Browser using the Browse From Scene or Selected option. In contrast, you can save just the material definitions themselves in a Material library.

A Material definition is actually no more than a "recipe" containing a list of ingredients and parameters for creating a material. The library is then analogous to a "recipe box" because it holds collections of Material definitions. In practice, it is often very convenient to store your favorite materials in assorted libraries.

TIP

Many artists find having separate libraries for specific needs (Brick, Stone, Marble, Flesh, Grit, Atmosphere, Backgrounds, and so on) speeds searching considerably and makes the materials more accessible to other artists.

The Put to Library button sends the active material definition to the currently loaded library. Although a hot material is automatically updated in your scene, it is *not* updated in the library from which it came. To add or update a material in a library, you must first use the Put to Library button. This updates the library entry in the currently loaded Material library. Even though the button image shows a diskette, the library is not saved to disk unless you specifically do so. To save a library, you must choose Save or Save As from within the Browser. As materials get perfected, their definitions become quite valuable. This two-step process ensures that you do not accidentally overwrite libraries and their contents.

Material Effects Channels

Every material in 3DS MAX can include a Material Effects channel that is used by Video Post filters to control the location of their post-process effects. Video Post can access the material effects channel when you are rendering a scene event or are using an RLA file that contains the Material Effects channel. Figure 14.9 shows a rendering with the Material channel being displayed as color codes rather than the typical rendered scene. This output is intended for use in post-processes and is not meant as an end in itself. The colors displayed are intended to be informational and not a finished result.

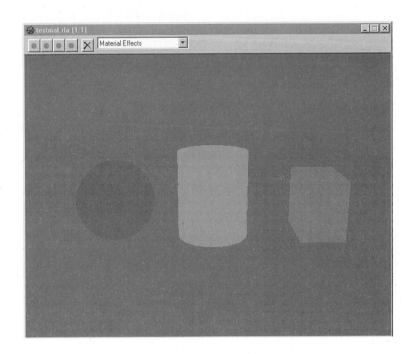

The most common use for the material effects channel is in conjunction with a Video Post image filter. Filter events such as Glow enable you to assign the glow to a material rather than an object (by using the RLA object channel) or a key-color in the image. In practice, the Object channel is used when affecting small numbers of objects and the material channel is used when you need to affect many objects with Video Post effects. The Object channel can also be used to apply a filter to a portion of an object when it has a Multi/Sub-Object material applied to it.

Displaying Textures

One of 3DS MAX's most useful features is the capability to display textures in the interactive viewports. Figure 14.10 shows a scene where textures exist throughout the viewports, and their display is critical for proper mapping alignment. One map per material can be shown in the viewports. The ability to do this is found within all the 2D Map types, using the Show Map in Viewport button.

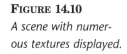

FIGURE 14.10

A scene with numerous textures displayed.

Because displaying maps requires additional RAM, 3DS MAX defaults to all maps not being shown. If you want to display a map in a viewport, you need to activate it yourself. This should be done with the knowledge that each displayed map requires RAM (although this is not a problem when using graphic accelerator boards with texture memory support). To aid in this RAM requirement, only a proxy image is actually displayed in the viewports. This allows even very large images to be displayed for the cost of much smaller ones.

Using Show End Result

By default, the Material Editor shows the entire material tree's result, regardless of which branch you are editing. Disabling the Show End Result option shows only the result at the current level in the material. As Figure 14.11 shows, disabling this option has a profound effect on Multi/Sub-Object materials.

Disabling this option is often helpful when you want to see the local effect and is especially useful when used to see the full material effect within Multi/Sub-Object materials. A disabled Show End Result state displays the material only from the last branch to your current position on the tree. This is similar to the Modifier Stack using its own Show End Result function for modifiers. If, for example, you're editing Material #4 on a Multi/Sub-Object material, turning off Show End Result displays only Material #4 in the sample slot. If you are editing the Diffuse map of a standard material, turning off Show End Result displays the bitmap without shading.

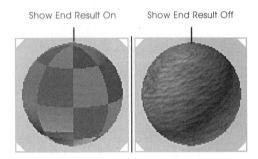

Show End Result On   Show End Result Off

FIGURE 14.11

The effect of Show End Result being on and off for a Multi/Sub-Object material.

Navigating the Material Editor

The Material Editor can appear quite complex, but with some practice it can prove to be a creative environment that is easily navigated. Navigating the material tree can be accomplished by navigating up the branches within the Editor or by selecting key levels with the Material/Map Navigator. The Material Editor interface is designed to show the current Map level at any one time.

The Need for Names

When browsing for Maps, usually as part of Standard material's Map channel, the Material trees can become deep. As numerous figures of the Browser have shown, the materials and map definition types are displayed differently, with materials being listed as Material Name (Material type) and maps as Map Channel: Map name (Map Type or File Name).

By default, maps are assigned the name Map #X, where X is an arbitrary number. Although a simple material may not require elaborate naming to keep track of map usages, it is always good practice to customize map and sub-material names immediately after they are selected for use in a channel. When maps are logically named, you can take full advantage of the browser and it is much easier to understand your intentions when you, or a fellow artist, return to the project at a later date. If you lapse into the habit of accepting default names, you will probably have a difficult time locating what you need in a detailed scene or a stored library.

Using the Material/Map Navigator

The Material/Map Navigator button provides a comprehensive overview of the materials shown in the sample slots currently within the Material Editor. This interface is accessed from the Material Editor's Material/Map Navigator button, whose icon is an abstract of the hierarchy tree.

TIP

While the Navigator enables you to traverse the Material tree similar to Track View, you cannot copy maps and their parameters as you can in Track View.

The Navigator is essentially a subset of Track View that is provided for examining the Material trees in the Editor and traversing them. Like Track View, the icons of blue sphere symbolize materials, and the green trapezoids are maps. Clicking on either symbol changes the Material Editor to that material or map at that level. This is a *very* useful technique for quickly navigating within or between complex materials.

Traversing Branches within the Material Editor

The Go to Parent and Go Forward to Sibling buttons are your primary navigation tools for traversing Material trees from within the Editor itself. The Go to Parent button moves you up one branch in the tree, while Go to Sibling moves you across branches stemming from the same parent.

Go to Sibling is often used when editing Multi/Sub-Object materials or Mask and Composite maps. These one-level steps can be used repeatedly to traverse the entire Material tree. The Name pulldown provides a listing of all parents from the current branch.

When deep in a Material tree, you can move several levels up at once by choosing an earlier parent. Note that if the material or map has not been named that the field is blank—yet another reason to develop a habit of naming materials and their maps.

Browsing Materials and Maps

The Material/Map Browser (see Figure 14.12) is used when you do any of the following :

- Get a material to replace the current sample slot.

- First access a map channel for selecting a map.

- First access a material channel for selecting a sub-material.

- Use the Type button to replace the current sub-material or map.

Once within the Browser, you can choose a material in a variety of ways: from a material in a Material library, from a material that is present in the scene, from a material that is currently within the Material Editor, from a material that is in the active slot of the Material Editor, or you can choose to define your own material from a new definition. The Browse From options control where your list of choices is presented from.

FIGURE 14.12

The Material/Map Browser showing both materials and maps.

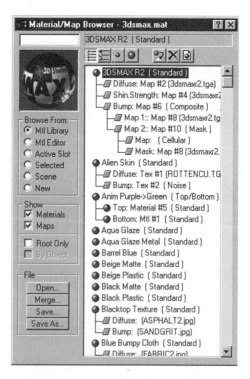

The default material library presented for browsing is the 3dsmax.mat file (see Figure 14.13) that shipped with the product and is located in the \3dsmax2\matlibs sub-directory. You can, of course, select any library you might have to browse from. By default, the Material Editor searches for the 3dsmax.mat file when the program begins.

FIGURE 14.13

The default
3dsmax.mat library.

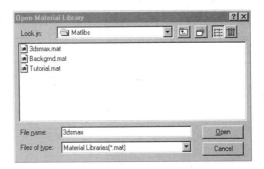

The Show options filter in the Material/Map browser indicates whether materials, maps, or both are displayed for selection.

The four buttons at the top-left corner of the Browser enable you to configure the display to show a View List, a View List with icons, small icons, or large icons. Although attractive in principle, this option can be slow for complex materials and uses RAM for all the bitmaps being processed. The reason for this is that the proxies are being generated at the moment and nothing is cached for future sessions. So while the sample spheres are useful for small libraries, they are not practical for large libraries. The buttons at the top-right corner of the Browser allow you to update Scene Materials from the Library (a very handy function), delete a Material from the library, or clear the Material Library.

When browsing materials by a View List method, materials are listed alphabetically and by case. Indented materials indicate they are children of one of the compound materials (Blend, Multi/Sub-Object, and so on).

Replacing Maps and Sub-Materials

You often have the need to replace a map that is currently assigned within a material. Adjusting the current map is not sufficient because you might need a different map type or the exact parameters currently used in another material. When you are at the map's Root level, clicking the Type button places you in the Material/Map Browser. From here you can choose a map from a library, the scene, the Material Editor, or start from scratch with New. Entering the Browser with the Type button is the same as the first time a Map Channel button is chosen, except that you are replacing an existing map.

When a material is used within another material, replacing it is very similar to replacing maps. While it might make sense to use the Get Material function, doing so replaces the entire Material definition and not just the sub-material at the current level. When you are at the sub-material's Root level, clicking the Type button places you in the Material/Map Browser. From here, you can select a material to replace the current sub-material.

Creating with the Standard Material

The Standard material has a modest name for all its capabilities. In practice, it usually is at least the starting point, and thus the "standard" material used for most creations. The Standard material is essentially the evolution of everything contained within the 3DS DOS Materials Editor. As Figure 14.14 shows, the Standard material type contains 11 map channels as the starting point for creating an extensive map tree.

Standard Material Color Components

The Standard material's shading characteristics are broken into three qualities: Ambient (the color shown in shade), Diffuse (the color shown in light), and Specular (the color of highlights). Figure 14.15 is an illustration that uses all three shading components: the teapot exhibits a medium blue Diffuse, a dark blue Ambient, and a bright blue Specular shading.

Choosing the correct colors for realistic effect can take a little practice. Begin by looking at real-world objects that share your material's qualities. Look deep into their color, shade, and highlights. Is the highlight's color similar to the light source's or is it tinting it? How is the shaded color affected by what it is placed on? Do the colors change as the light moves about them?

Specular highlights are seen on surfaces that have at least some shine and occurs when light striking the surface is angled back to your viewing position. The surface displays the material's Diffuse color when it is fully illuminated and is either dull or not within specular highlights. As illumination decreases, the Diffuse color mixes with that of the Ambient. Where no light occurs, only the Ambient color is rendered (and then only by the scene's Ambient light).

FIGURE 14.14

The interface for the Standard material including Basic Parameters, Extended Parameters, Maps, and Dynamic Properties.

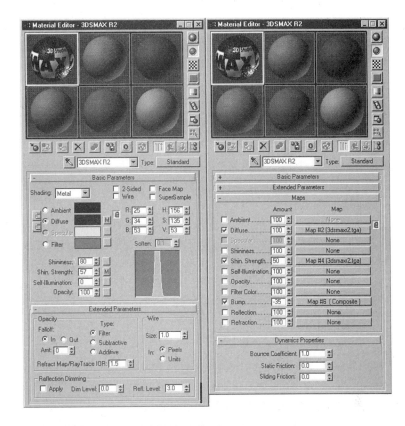

FIGURE 14.15

The three basic shading components.

Most materials relate their colors to one another, often being shades within the same color family. The Material Editor makes this easy by enabling you to copy color swatches by dragging them from one to another. You can then adjust the color properties, such as whiteness, blackness, or value, without disturbing the basic color relationships.

Diffuse Color Component

Of the three basic color qualities, Diffuse has the most impact on the material's appearance and is the easiest to determine. The Diffuse color is the one you refer to when you describe a material in real life. Refer as often as possible to the world around you and analyze its colors. You will probably notice that very few objects have fully saturated hues. Some exceptions might be signs (signage, packaging, advertisements), toys, and cartoons. Other objects tend to have much more complex blends. The Diffuse color is often replaced by or mixed with a bitmap, with the small button next to its color swatch giving you quick access to the Diffuse map channel.

TIP

When you analyze real-world colors, you need to flood at least an area of it with white light, eliminating any surface shading. This light is ideally quartz orxenon (the highest temperature lamps readily available), but halogen works well enough. You can isolate the diffuse color by holding a pocket halogen flashlight close to the surface and then viewing the object so you do not see a highlight.

Specular Color Component

The specular color mixes with the illuminating light's color. This mix varies between materials but is usually tinted to the Diffuse color or has no color (zero saturation). A good starting point for materials is to copy the diffuse color to the specular color and increase the Whiteness control towards white.

The influence that the specular component has on a material is directly related to its Shininess and Shininess Strength values. Materials that have no shine cannot form a specular highlight. If the material has shine and a highlight is formed on the material, the material's Diffuse color mixes with the specular in an *additive*, or light-like, manner.

A material's Specular color is not rendered unless a highlight is formed from a light source striking a surface and is reflected back to your viewing position. The angle from your viewing position to the surface needs to be less than the angle of incidence back to a given light for that light to create a highlight on the surface (see Figure 14.16).

FIGURE 14.16

Specular highlight locations being dictated by viewing and lighting angles.

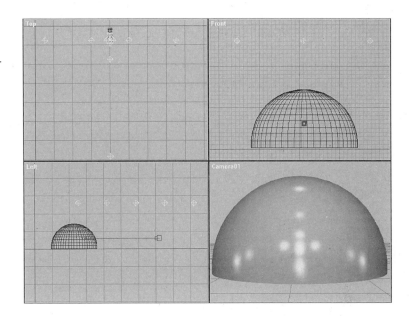

Ambient Color Component

Although the Ambient value represents a material's shaded portion, it affects a great deal of a surface because only a small portion of an object is usually in direct light at a given time. Most or at least parts of objects are illuminated with glancing light that is shaded across their surfaces. As surfaces are shaded, the Ambient color mixes with the diffuse in a *subtractive*, or pigment-like, manner. Once in complete shadow, the Ambient color is used exclusively. The resulting Ambient color seen without light is usually still quite dark because its only illumination is from your Ambient light value.

T IP

Darkening the Ambient value is often beneficial to achieve deep, rich material colors. You can do this easily by copying the Diffuse color swatch to the Ambient color swatch and lowering its value.

Theoretically, few materials have different Ambient and Diffuse values. (Some that do are those materials that glow or are naturally iridescent.) The shading that occurs across most surfaces is the simple reduction of illumination, which is why it is often suggested that you start by keeping the Ambient and Diffuse values constant.

In practice, however, most computer artists do *not* do this. The reason is that making the Ambient color darker than the Diffuse deepens the shading and tends to create richer renderings. This technique intensifies the shading and enables you to use more general lighting in your scene. Most artists make it standard practice to copy the Diffuse color swatch to the Ambient and then reduce the color's value by at least 50 percent. If you examine the Material libraries that ship with 3DS MAX, you will notice that nearly every material uses this technique.

T IP

You can simulate materials that have a very rich quality to them, such as lacquered woods, by bringing their ambient color to full saturation and value. A chestnut brown diffuse material given a bright red Ambient value forms a very warm, rich brown.

When a scene is illuminated solely with Ambient light, a surface's rendered appearance is controlled entirely by its material's Ambient color. The effect of color "switching" is important to realize when using a pure white Ambient light to illuminate the scene (a common situation when creating flat work for two-dimensional prints). When using white Ambient light, your interest focuses entirely on the Ambient color component and no other.

Locking Colors

To the left of the color swatches are Lock buttons, which lock the colors so that adjusting the color of one also sets the color value for the other. The use for locking is limited, considering the ease with which you can copy color swatches.

In general, locking is not encouraged unless you want an absolutely pure color. Materials that do benefit from locked color are those intended to look like bright plastic and for advertising art where you are creating two-dimensional objects for flat illumination.

The lock to the right of the color swatches controls the locking of the Diffuse and Ambient map channels. By default, it is always locked so that when a Diffuse map is chosen, it's used for both the Ambient and Diffuse colors.

If you disable the lock, the Ambient channel is ungrayed and a button appears next to the Diffuse color swatch—enabling you to tint a Texture map in the same way you darken or saturate the base color swatches.

Standard Material Basic Parameters

After defining the base color components for a material, several other controls complete the Basic parameters section of the Standard material. These control the Shininess, Self-Illumination, Opacity, and Soften Parameter values, and the Rendering mode, 2-Sided, Wire, Face Map, and SuperSample options. These base parameters are used as a starting point for these critical qualities. Most of these have corresponding Map channels that influence or replace the parameters.

Shading Modes

The most dominant option in the Standard material is the Shading mode. This option controls what rendering method (algorithm) is used to evaluate and shade the base colors and shine. The four shading modes (Constant, Phong, Blinn, and Metal) take approximately the same rendering time but change the overall characteristic of the material when rendered by the production renderer, as shown in Figure 14.17. The appearance of surfaces in the viewports is unchanged because the interactive renderer considers all materials to be Phong. Map channel capabilities, shadows, reflections, and atmospherics treat all shading models the same.

FIGURE 14.17

The Constant, Phong, Blinn, and Metal shading modes.

Phong

Constant

Blinn

Metal

The Constant, Phong, and Blinn shading modes all use the same Material properties but treat shading and smoothing differently. The Constant shading mode ignores smoothing groups and instead looks for coplanar surfaces. Each coplanar surface, or facet, is rendered with the same constant color with edges along facets being antialiased. This mode is of primary use for those who create games and flat art work.

TIP

When using Constant shading, you often want to ensure that your rendered output has pure colors per facet. To do so, you must uncheck Output Dithering for True Color in the Rendering Preferences settings.

The Constant, Phong, and Blinn shading modes can be influenced by a Soften value to reduce the striking highlight glare of glancing light, as shown in Figure 14.18. This value has a profound impact on the glossy appearance of materials such as glass, lacquers, gloss paint, or shiny plastic.

FIGURE 14.18

The impact of Soften on materials.

The Phong and Blinn shading modes appear very similar, but the Blinn mode highlights appear rounder. In general, you don't need to use as high a Soften value as you do with Phong shading. With Blinn shading, you can obtain highlights produced by light glancing off the surface at low angles; these highlights are lost when you increase the value of Soften using Phong shading.

The Metal shading mode (based upon the Cook/Torrance algorithm) does away with the Specular color swatch and value. Metal materials derive their highlight color directly from their Diffuse color component and the shape of their highlight curve. The shape of the highlight curve and the resulting Shine across the surface is very different between Phong/Blinn and Metal shading modes, even though the Shine values stay the same.

2-Sided Option

The 2-Sided option tells the renderer to ignore face normals for the surface and render both sides regardless of which way it is facing. This option is intended to be used for geometry or surfaces that you can see through, such as glass and wireframes (see Figure 14.19), in cases when modeling both sides of the object is not needed for realism. This is also used for opaque objects that are very thin and need to show both sides, such as playing cards or paper money.

Using 2-Sided materials on more substantial models can make them appear odd because their edges appear paper thin (which they really are). This option is also used when imported models have troublesome normals that may seem too time consuming to fix. In the last case, the option should be weighed against correcting the normals because this is a somewhat expensive option that causes the program to render many more faces than usual.

FIGURE 14.19

Single-sided versus the 2-Sided material option.

2-sided

NOTE

If a Refraction Map is in use, the 2-Sided option does not affect opacity or refraction. It has an impact only if the material is also a Wire material.

Wire Option

The Wire option eliminates the surface and replaces each visible mesh or patch edge with a line, or wire. This situation is one of the few where a surface's edge visibility impacts its rendered appearance. The rendered characteristic of wires is actually closer to being pieces of paper. The wire's surface is flat along the face whose edge it borders. If the edge is shared between faces, the wire appears like a creased piece of paper, as shown in Figure 14.20

FIGURE 14.20

The rendered effect of Wire materials.

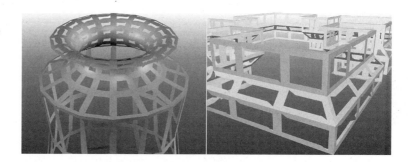

The size of the wire is controlled in the Extended Parameters rollout. The size can be controlled here by two methods: Pixels makes all edges the same width in the rendered image; Units gives real-world size unit widths to the wires. In either case, all wires have the same radius.

The impact of your choice of how to define the wire width comes when you view the surface in perspective. If defined in pixels, the wires do not diminish in perspective, much as if you trace a photograph with a single-width pen. If defined in units, they are essentially treated as geometry and diminish in perspective accordingly. When rendered in an Orthogonal or User view, the two methods produce the same effect, with all wires rendering with a constant width.

NOTE

Wire materials render as solid surfaces if antialiasing is not on. While you are in the Material Editor, the inside of the sample is always antialiased and you have no need to change the Material Editor option to antialias.

When defining Wire size in units, it's often worth the time to set the 3D Map Sample Scale parameter in the Material Editor Options dialog to a size that represents a typical scale for your scene. This gives you a better feel for the look of your material in relation to the surfaces that receive it. Your alternative is to make numerous test renderings.

TIP

The Renderer provides a Force Wireframe option that renders all surfaces in the scene as if they were Wire materials of one pixel width—more convenient than switching material properties for quick effects.

Face Map and SuperSample Options

The Face Map option applies the material to the faces of the geometry. The map is automatically applied to each facet of the object. If the material is a Mapped material, it requires no Mapping coordinates.

For making especially smooth specular highlights, use the SuperSample option. This creates an antialiasing pass on the material that can avoid scintillating or jagged bumps and smooth rendered results when using thin bump maps or rendering to high resolutions. When antialiasing is turned off in the production renderer, the SuperSample function is not used.

TIP

Use SuperSample only when you notice artifacts in the final renderings. This option does not require any additional RAM, but it does require considerably longer time to render.

Shininess Parameters

The amount of polish, gleam, or gloss a material has is determined by its Shininess and Shininess Strength values. These values combine to create the material's overall specular character, with the effect graphically shown in the Highlight curve (see Figure 14.21.)

FIGURE 14.21

Shine values for Phong without Softening, Phong with Softening, and Metal.

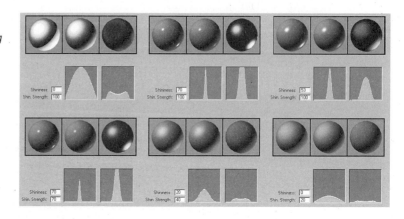

The Highlight curve, and not the numeric values, is your best gauge for how the Specular highlight will appear. The width of the curve dictates the width of the resulting highlight, with narrow curves being very small and wide ones being very broad. The height of the curve controls the color of the highlight. When the curve touches the top, the highlight color matches the Specular color, and as it lowers, it mixes proportionally with the Diffuse color. A tall, sharp curve creates a narrow point of Specular color while a low, broad curve creates a large, soft highlight that does not depart too much from the Diffuse. Many real-world materials (such as leather, oiled wood, or a matte balloon) have an even, low sheen that you can simulate by using zero shininess and increasing Shininess Strength levels.

As the width of the highlight curve increases, so does the angle from which a Specular highlight can be viewed. The higher the highlight curve, the more the highlight is composed of the Specular base color. The lower the curve, the more it mixes with that of the Diffuse base color.

The resulting Highlight curve varies greatly when you switch from Phong or Blinn to Metal shading. The meaning of the curve is the same, but the result is far different (see Figure 14.22). The Highlight curve has the greatest effect on metal materials because its mixture with the Diffuse base color determines the Specular color. The Highlight Curve display reacts differently with metal, creating a two-peaked curve at low settings and a tall, thick vertical line when high—the shinier a Metal material, the greater its contrast. It is in these dark areas that reflections are seen the most.

FIGURE 14.22

The difference in shine between Phong and Metal shading.

Opacity Parameters

By default, all materials begin 100 percent opaque. This percentage changes when you begin to adjust the various opacity controls of Opacity, Opacity Falloff, and possible Opacity Maps in the Basic Parameters and Extended Parameters rollouts. The characteristics of the opacity are further controlled by the Opacity type and possibly the Filter Color. The basic effects of these controls are shown in Figure 14.23. The Refract Map/Raytrace IOR parameter is for use with Refraction maps, Raytrace maps, and Thinwall refraction maps and impacts opacity when these map types are in use.

When a Refraction map is used at 100 percent strength, all Opacity controls are ignored except for the Opacity type. If the Refraction map is lower than 100 percent, the Opacity percentage (defined by either the Opacity map or Opacity parameter) effectively "tints" the Refraction map with the opaque surface color. When active, the Refraction map settings have complete control over what can be seen through the object.

FIGURE 14.23

The three types of Opacity.

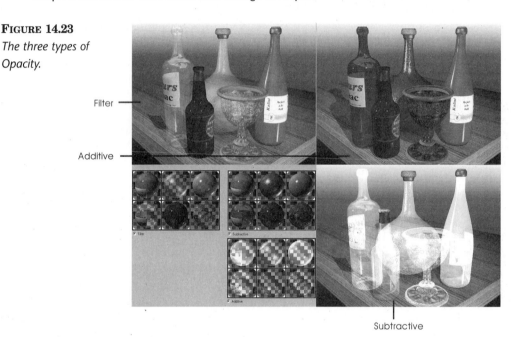

Three different types of transparency are in the Standard material: Filter, Subtractive, and Additive.

Filter Opacity

The (default) Filter Opacity type is the only one that also uses the Filter color (otherwise, the color swatch name is grayed out). The Filter color becomes the color in the transparent areas of the surface when the scene viewed through the material is bright.

Assuming the Filter color value is set to gray (128,128,128), and if a material's opacity is set to 50 percent and viewed against a white background, the Diffuse and Filter colors mix to create a brighter Diffuse. If the material's opacity is set higher than 50 percent, the Diffuse color grows more prevalent, and if it's set lower than 50 percent, the Background color grows more prevalent. When the same material is viewed against a black background, an opacity of 50 percent also results in the Diffuse and Background colors mixing. When the Filter Color value is set to black (0,0,0), however, the Diffuse and Filter colors mix to create a darker Diffuse against either a white or black background.

In practice, the Filter color acts as an extra gauge whose color value influences the overall opacity of the surface. If you do not want the Filter color to affect the transparency at all, leave the color at its default 128 gray value.

Subtractive Opacity

The Subtractive opacity type is simpler but different. As the material becomes transparent, it subtracts the Diffuse color from the background. This has the effect of removing color seen through the material inversely of the opacity. A magenta material of 0 opacity, for example, subtracts the blue and red channels of everything seen through it. The Subtractive material can produce deep, rich semi-transparencies but does become unnatural when used with low or zero opacities.

Additive Opacity

The Additive Opacity type adds the Diffuse color to what's seen through the surface, brightening it and making the surface look self-illuminated. Additive opacity is brightest when it is the most opaque, with moving from 100 to 99 being a huge jump. In reality, Additive opacity of 50 or less is the same as Filter opacity using a white Filter color. In practice, Additive opacity is often used for light bulbs, light beams, ghosts, and the like.

Opacity Falloff

It may be surprising to learn that the Opacity Falloff value always affects the material's opacity, regardless of whether the opacity is less than 100 or if an Opacity map is being used (see Figure 14.24). The Falloff value dictates the transparency of the surface's center with the In option or the surface's edges with the Out option. When a material is transparent, you can see through to its inside. Because of this, enabling the 2-Sided option is very common if the object was not modeled with an interior as well as an exterior.

FIGURE 14.24

The impact of Opacity Falloff values.

The apparent density of the material is the next transparent quality to consider. Most physical objects appear less transparent along their edges because more material is there to filter light. The edges of most transparent materials seem denser to your eye as you look through more material along the edges. If your model has an inside and an outside, you should try a zero Falloff value first and then adjust Inside Falloff upward until the desired effect is achieved. If your model only has an outside, then it will need Inside Falloff to not appear as an infinitely thin vessel (which it really is). The use of Outside Falloff is not as common because few surfaces are denser in their center than at their ends (some exceptions would be include translucent solids, light beams, and ghosts).

You can define the overall transparency of a material by using an assigned Opacity map. Whenever an Opacity map is active, the Map Percentage value specifies the percent of opacity to be provided by the map with the remainder specified by the Opacity value. Opacity falloff and type are still respected as before and work in conjunction with the Opacity Map definition, the settings, and the amount slider.

Self-Illumination Parameters

The Self-Illumination property produces the illusion of being self-illuminated by eliminating the Ambient shading component of the material. Increasing the value decreases the effect of the ambient calculation until shading is no longer occurring. If a material is fully self-illuminated with a value of 100, no shade is given to the surface and the diffuse color is used everywhere but at the highlights. Figure 14.25 shows how the ambient quality is replaced as Self-Illumination is increased.

FIGURE 14.25

The effect of Self-Illumination on the Ambient component.

NOTE

Because a fully self-illuminated material cannot be shaded, it appears to not receive a cast shadow.

A self-illuminated material does not cast any light of its own, giving the appearance that it is lit internally and refuses to be affected by shade and shadow—meaning that it has uses other than simulating a glowing object. Times will occur when you might want an object to appear cartoon-like, bold in color and unshaded (this works best if the object is coplanar).

Objects that are being used as background "billboards" are often assigned a self-illuminated material so that their image remains consistent throughout the scene. Other objects are self-illuminated, such as televisions, projection screens, signs, and lamps. Don't worry if a material is not casting light on its own because you can simulate and control this effect. Self-illumination is often combined with additive opacity for creating convincing lamps and light beams.

In Practice: Materials and Textures

- **Material representation:** What is the material to represent? This should be reflected in the material's name.

- **Material color:** What is the material's overall color? What color do you see in its highlights and shadows? These determine your choices for Diffuse, Specular, and Ambient colors.

- **Material surface:** Does it resemble a plastic or metallic surface? This type of question determines the shading you use, such as Phong or Metal.

- **Material shininess:** How shiny is it? How strong is the highlight? This question determines Shininess and Shininess Strength. It may also determine how much Softening is needed. Is the shine evenly cast across the surface or patterned? This may determine if Shininess and Shininess Strength map channels are needed.

- **Material transparency:** Is the material transparent? If so, how much? Is the edge thicker than the middle? Is the color weak or deep? Does it glow? These questions determine Opacity parameters, Opacity Falloff, and Type.

- **Material Illumination:** Does it cast a light or glow? If so, how much? This may determine whether Self-Illumination is required or not.

Chapter 15

MAP CHANNELS, MAP TYPES, AND MORE MATERIAL TYPES

All materials in 3D Studio MAX have the potential to use not only the images assigned to them, but the world around them as part of their appearance. Having a thorough understanding of the Map channels and Map types at your disposal, you are virtually unlimited in your capacity to imitate physical reality.

3D Studio MAX Release 2 introduces a vast array of new and exciting tools for material construction including the new Raytracer Material type. This chapter examines in detail:

- Working With Standard Material Map Channels
- Using Map types
- Animating Maps and their parameters
- Using Compound Material types
- Examining material pitfalls

As you may have gathered from the bulleted list, there are essentially three categories of Material types in 3D Studio: the Standard Material, the Compound Material, and the Raytracer Material. More than likely the majority of your materials in a scene will use the Standard Material type. In the last chapter, the Basic parameters of a Standard Material were explored. The Standard Material also has 11 Map channels, which can each point to over 30 different Map types.

Working with Standard Material Map Channels

The 11 Map channels at the bottom of the Standard Material are the starting points for perfecting your material's illusion. You can manipulate, combine, and branch maps in numerous ways to make even the simplest surface appear rich and complex. Careful use can make models extremely realistic yet efficient. Because of the impact of Map channels, having a strong working knowledge of their makeup and use is important.

Although a map channel can branch deeply, the way its result is interpreted varies according to the various channels. A channel's result is evaluated either in RGB *color* or as a grayscale *intensity* (see Figure 15.1).

The Ambient, Diffuse, Specular, Filter Color, Reflection, and Refraction Map channels all work with color. The Shininess, Shininess Strength, Self-Illumination, Opacity, and Bump Map channels only consider the intensity, treating the ending colors as if they were grayscale. Using Color maps for these channels can be confusing because the visual contrast between colors might not correspond to the contrast in luminance (for example, pure Red, Green, and Blue read as the same intensity values).

FIGURE 15.1

The Standard Material Map channels and their color usage: channels shown in green are controlled by RGB (color) while those shown in red are controlled by Intensity (grayscale).

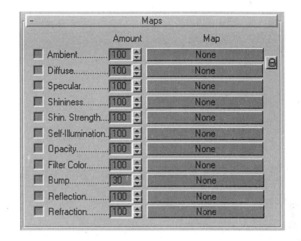

Using Bitmaps and RAM

Bitmaps are extremely common to use with all channels but can be costly in regards to RAM. You use 1 byte of RAM for every byte that map definition is deep. A 24-bit color map thus requires three bytes per pixel while a 256-indexed color or grayscale bitmap requires only 1 byte per pixel. If your bitmap uses filtering (which nearly all should), there is an additional cost of 1 byte per pixel if Pyramidal and a whopping 12 bytes per pixel if Summed Area.

Once a bitmap is referenced by a material or background, it can be used as often as you like without using additional RAM. Many artists devise several general use, tiling, random bitmaps as the starting point for nearly every material they create. These bitmaps give their materials some initial grit, spots, streaks, or texture that is essentially free of extra RAM consumption.

TIP

Using grayscale bitmaps for channels that read only intensity is very prudent. Not only do their shades relate directly to the map channel's effect, they use one-third the RAM of a 24-bit image.

When you define and use bitmaps, your goal should be to create and use the smallest image that does the job properly. The "right size" depends on your output image's size, the prominence of the object displaying the texture, and the speed at which it may be in motion. An often-used technique is to maintain several resolutions of the same image so the most appropriately sized one can be used for a given situation. A source image might begin from a Kodak CD-ROM with a resolution of 3072×2048 and using 25 MB. A series of smaller sized maps thus makes considerable sense, with 1200×800 using 3.8 MB, 600×400 using 1 MB, and 300×200 only 240K. Remember that reducing resolution is acceptable, but enlarging a bitmap merely blurs it.

T IP

A good rule for ensuring high-quality images is to not allow a bitmap pixel to be as large as a rendered pixel. Thus, all rendered bitmap pixels are sampled and the dreaded pixelated effect does not occur.

Working with Diffuse and Ambient Texture Maps

Of all the Map channels, Diffuse is probably the easiest to relate to. It applies the channel's result to the Material surface much like paint or wallpaper. Because of this function, Diffuse maps are often called *Texture* maps by many other programs. When active at full strength, the Diffuse channel replaces the Base Diffuse color. The Amount slider indicates the amount of the Map channel to be used. Levels of 0 to 100 mix with the Diffuse color component proportionally.

The Diffuse channel is unique in having a Lock icon to its right. When active (the default), the Ambient map is locked to the Diffuse. When locked, the Ambient Map channel is grayed-out and the Diffuse Map is used for both the Diffuse and Ambient shading components. Unlocking this option enables you to specify a different source for the Ambient component, as shown in Figure 15.2.

Separate Ambient and Diffuse Maps are used primarily to intensify a map's effect in the same way the Ambient Base color is often a darker or more saturated version of the Diffuse Base color. Copying the Diffuse Map as an Ambient Map enables you to control the intensity of the shade.

TIP

A saturated texture map can be made by adjusting an Ambient Map copy's output. Increasing the RGB Level while lowering the RGB Offset intensifies the colors of the light to midranges and deepens the dark areas. For example, the result can turn a flat wood grain into a lacquered one.

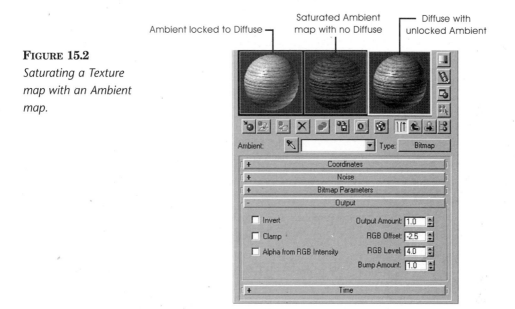

Ambient locked to Diffuse ⌐ Saturated Ambient map with no Diffuse ⌐ Diffuse with unlocked Ambient

FIGURE 15.2

Saturating a Texture map with an Ambient map.

Using an unlocked Ambient Map without a Diffuse Map creates a subtle pattern on the surface that disappears in full illumination. This effect can be used for patterns on metallic surfaces that represent etches, anodizing, or panels. Random patterns can give a subtle texture to a surface, making solid colors much more believable.

Specular Highlight Maps

The Specular channel is for the special purpose case when you want to control what is seen in the material's specular highlight. This effect may be a subtle reflection or just a variation that is seen as a light's highlight passes over the surface. When active at full strength, the Specular channel replaces the Base Specular color. The Amount slider indicates the amount of the Map channel to be used. Levels between 0 to 100 mix with the

Specular color component proportionally. This Map channel is the only one that impacts the color of the specular component. Metal shading does not have a specular component so the Specular channel is grayed out.

TIP

A light that has the object as its sole inclusion list entry can be very useful for controlling the placement and intensity of a highlight and thus the Specular Map image.

Specular Maps depend on several other variables within the material and the scene for their effect. While mapping coordinates dictate where the map is placed on the surface, the scene's lighting setup and your viewing position to the surface determine where a highlight will occur. The material's Shine properties then dictate how large and pure in color the highlight will be. As the Specular color blends with the Diffuse, so does the Specular map. Remember that the height of the Highlight curve indicates color purity, while its width indicates the highlight's size. Because you can always mix at least the edges, the Diffuse color or map has a significant impact on the coloring of the Specular image.

A common use for Specular Maps is to place an image of the scene's light source on the object. Because this image is simulating a reflection, the bitmap should be representative of what you want the area around the highlight-causing light source to be. A bare bulb, a patterned window with curtains, an ornate street lamp, or a blazing sun are just a few examples. This addition can add considerable realism and is often seen on curved, shiny objects in daily life.

When you see the shape of a window in the highlight on a balloon, you are seeing the equivalent of a Specular Map. Specular Maps are especially convincing when used in conjunction with Reflection Maps. The reflection enforces the illusion that the material is shiny. Seeing the Specular reflection of a nearby neon sign, for example, in the reflection bitmap's highlight can be a very realistic touch. Figure 15.3 shows how an "outside sunset" can be seen in the Specular reflection of an object. Another common use for Specular Maps is to place a texture that can only be seen when a highlight catches the surface. Water spots and stains are typical of this technique.

FIGURE 15.3

Using a Specular Map to show a "Specular reflection" of the light source, in this case, a sunset.

The effect of the Specular channel closely resembles that of the Shininess and Shininess Strength channels. This resembling effect is because the color of the Specular channel is combined with the diffuse in an additive, or light-based manner. If the Specular map is grayscale and has no saturation, the impact on the material's highlight is nearly identical to that of the Shine maps. In practice, the Specular channel is primarily for introducing color.

Bump Maps

Bump maps give a simulated texture to a surface by indicating areas to pull out, project, or "bump" out. The Renderer creates this illusion by altering the light values across the mapped surface in the way that edges or "bumps" would cast shadows and receive highlights. Bump maps do not affect geometry. What seem to be raised edges are just an illusion—it's a rendering effect that only simulates the effect of highlight and shade. The ability to actually deform a surface is often termed *displacement mapping* (in other programs) and is done in 3DS MAX with a Displacement modifier. If you need to change a surface's profile, use a Displacement modifier. Bumps are for more subtle illusions that occur across a surface and not its profile.

The Bump Map reads the intensity of the channel and treats black as having no effect, white as having full effect, and shades of gray as having a proportional effect. The Amount slider controls the strength or apparent "height" of the bump rather than the percentage of the channel. Unlike many of the other Map channel Amount sliders, the Bump channel Amount slider can contain values from -999 to 999. Positive and negative values control the effect of bright and dark colors in the channel's map. Using positive values, Bump Maps tend to be most effective when they begin at the lowest black values and work forward. In practice, you usually get a more controllable result if you have a black field and work toward mid-gray than if you start with mid-gray and work to white.

T IP

The Output Amount parameter is a valuable aid in making fine-tuned adjustments to your bitmap's effect or increasing the Bump effect far beyond what is capable with the map's Amount slider.

Behind the Scenes Workings of Bump Maps

Because a Bump Map's effect is so prominent, it's worth examining exactly what it is doing. Each pixel on a Bump Map projects forward in a square-like manner. Pixels that are of a different intensity project out from their neighbors like a terrace and do not slope toward one another. A good visualization for how Bump Maps work is to take a framing grid's square pegs (or pins) and push them against the surface you want to approximate. The elevations of the resulting pegs relate to the shades of gray that would be required to approximate the same surface with a Bump Map.

Although the preceding analogy is easy to relate to, it does lead you to believe that the bump is projecting or recessing the various areas. In actuality, the bump illusion is done by simulating the ridges and valleys. The prominence of the edge is derived from the difference in color between adjacent pixels. Bump maps do not affect the shading properties of the different "terraces," "levels," or "steps" that appear to be formed across the surface. These areas are all rendered as if they were one smooth surface—it's their bumped edges that give the illusion of depth. This illusion is shown most clearly when you use Mask maps with bitmaps, as shown in Figure 15.4.

FIGURE 15.4

Bump Maps create the illusion of ridges and valleys across the surface.

Creating the correct bitmap for a bump effect can be somewhat of an art. As with all mono-channel maps, you are always best off working in grayscale so you can easily determine contrast (and 8-bit bitmaps take one-third the RAM of 24-bit images). To simulate a dent, groove, or something else going into the surface, you might start by making the entire surface white, thus "out." The gray-to-black portions of the bitmap are then less projected, thus "in." To create a groove, you make the field white, the bottom line of the groove black, and the walls shades of gray. The "recipes" for common Bump Map types are listed as follows and are illustrated in Figure 15.5.

- Grooves for grout lines, ridges, and panels are all based on simple line work, where the contrast between the line and field determines the depth. Note that an additional adjacent line of gray gives a subtle bevel and reduces the possible scintillation common with thin lines.

- Slopes for siding, ramps, v-channels, and pyramids are defined by even linear gradations. Slopes can be done with a Gradient map type or with a bitmap given a gradient fill in a paint program.

- Cones for sharp points are actually a variation of slopes, except the even gradation happens radially. Creating cones can be done with the Gradient map type using a Radial Gradient type or with a bitmap given a radial gradient fill in a paint program.

■ Hemispheres for domes, rivets, and round grooves are formed by charting the sphere's shading. This process is a "weighted" gradation where it is whiter for a greater distance toward the center and falls away rapidly to black at the end. Reversing the coloration changes a dome into an ice cream scoop dent. Complicated gradations such as these are often most easily done by modeling the geometry and rendering them.

FIGURE 15.5

Common Bump Map effects and their bitmaps.

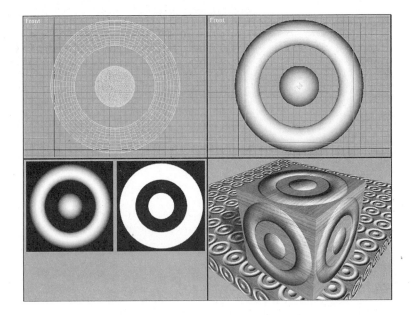

A convenient method for creating evenly shaded bump maps with anti-aliased edges is to model their basic geometry in 3DS MAX and use the rendered images as the basis for bitmaps (see Figure 15.6). A spherical Bump Map can be made by creating a sphere, assigning it a matte white material, and placing one spotlight dead center to it. Render the Spotlight viewport and you have a perfectly shaded and dithered image that is perfect for a Bump Map. If you use this technique, saving the alpha channel with the TGA file is very useful. This technique gives you a matching mask for the Bump effect and doubles the usefulness of your bitmap.

FIGURE 15.6

Using rendered geometry as a source for Bump Maps.

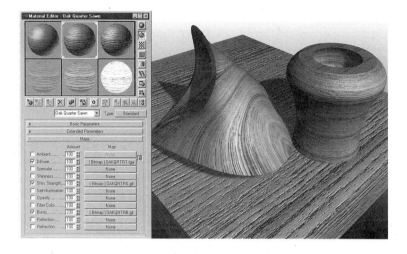

As with most maps in the Standard Material, Bump Maps are most convincing when they coordinate with other Map channels having appropriate maps. Figure 15.7 shows how separate Diffuse, Bump, and Shininess Strength Maps combine to form a realistic surface. You will find that when Bump Maps are used, they should often be copied as Shininess Strength Maps and possibly used as masks for other Map channels.

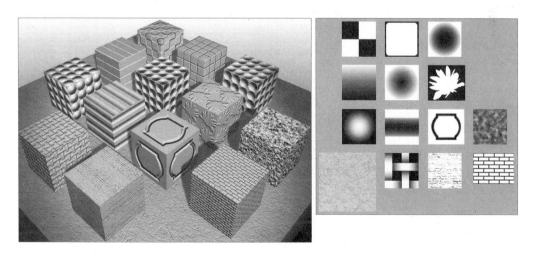

FIGURE 15.7

Coordinating Bump, Texture, and Shininess Strength Maps.

NOTE

A Bump Map's projection is unidirectional—it does not matter from what angle the mapping is projected. This is different from other programs (such as 3DS DOS) where the mapping projection pushes the bump in on one side and out on the other. In 3DS MAX, the material parameters control the bump's direction.

You can reverse the direction of a Bump Map three ways, summarized as follows:

■ Reverse the sign of the Amount spinner.

■ Reverse the sign of the Bump amount.

■ Use the Invert option.

Each has its advantages, although the first two can be animated while the Invert option cannot. There may be times when you need the bump to change direction on the same material. A bulge on one side of a surface might need to be a dent on the other side, for example. To accomplish this, you need to select the back side faces and assign them a duplicate material with a reversed bump setting.

Bump Maps are valuable because they can simulate far more geometry than is actually present. They are more susceptible to rendering with scintillation or "jaggies" if you are not careful. The following is an approximate order of steps to take in creating the best possible Bump effect:

1. Avoid using bitmaps with angled lines if the same result can be achieved by drawing rectilinear lines and adjusting the Angle parameter and/or rotating the mapping projection. An angled line has an inherent, fixed amount of anti-aliasing, whereas a rotated straight line is nearly resolution independent.

2. Ensure Filtering is used in the Map type and Filter Maps is active in the Render Scene options. Bump Maps render properly only if filtering is occurring.

3. Increase the Blur Offset parameter, with a value of 0.01 being a good starting point. Large values cause considerable blurring, so be careful with this setting.

4. Increase the Blur parameter. Balance this value with the Blur Offset to achieve the right effect.

5. Switch to Summed Area filtering if the Blur settings dull the effect too much. Remember that this option increases the overall RAM from four to 15 bytes per pixel. Note that less blur is usually required with Summed Area for a clean result.

6. Enlarge the size of the bitmap. Ensure no single-pixel-wide details occur. Remember the basic rule that no part of a bitmap should be rendered larger than the bitmap itself.

7. Add an intermediate gray border to edge details with sharp contrasts. A gray edge at a black to white transition eases the otherwise sharp transition considerably.

TIP

When you have an often-used Bump effect (a square tile for example), maintaining a suite of similar maps that are identical in proportion but vary in resolution is often prudent. This maintenance enables you to choose the most suitable bitmap for the surface's prominence in the scene and conserve RAM when large maps are not needed. In the case of a tile Bump Map, the lowest resolution might have the grout lines one pixel wide, the next three to five pixels, and the largest seven to perhaps 15 pixels.

Creating bumps within bumps is an often-needed effect. The Ceiling Tile Square material in the standard 3DS MAX library does this through the use of a Composite map that uses a Mask map (see Figure 15.8). The Output Amount parameter enables you to control the effect of each bitmap's bump strength independently.

Shininess and Shininess Strength Maps

Bump maps used in a material can appear to deform the geometry the material is applied to. Shininess and Shininess Strength maps used in a material can appear to make the object the material is applied to shiny or dull.

The Shininess and Shininess Strength channels (collectively referred to as "shine" maps) combine with the Shininess and Shininess Strength values set in Basic Parameters to control how broad and pure of color the resulting highlight is (see Figure 15.9).

FIGURE 15.8

Creating composite bump materials.

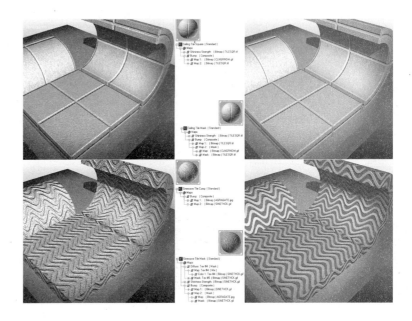

NEW TO R2

The behavior of the Shininess and Shininess Strength channels has changed in Release 2 from Release 1. The Highlight curve in Basic parameters reflects the values of the Shininess and Shininess Strength values in Basic parameters only and does not reflect any additional influence by the Shininess and Shininess Strength Map channels.

FIGURE 15.9

Patterns formed from using Shininess and Shininess Strength channels.

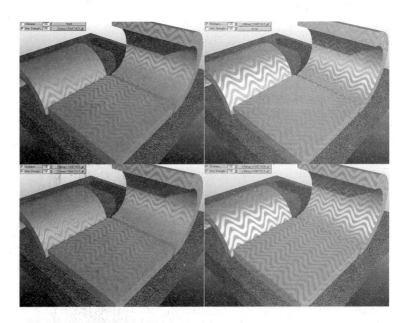

The Shininess and Shininess Strength channels affect the Shininess and Shininess Strength parameters independently—that is, the Shininess channel controls the size of the highlight while the Shininess Strength channel controls the amount the Specular color is mixed with the diffuse. You can control the purity of the highlight while maintaining its size, or you can define its extents while preserving the intensity. The Shine Maps are mono-channel in nature, working only with the intensity of the RGB color or the alpha channel (which by definition is grayscale).

WARNING

You should not use the Bitmap Output parameters or an RGB Tint map to increase the intensity of a Shininess or Shininess Strength map because it adversely affects the resulting Specular component. These methods only work if you wish to decrease the intensity. If you need to increase the intensity, and thus the highlight, you should use a Mix map type or adjust the bitmap in a paint program instead.

You should be cautious about using the two Shine channels in conjunction with one another because they control very different effects. The Shininess Strength channel controls the brightness of the highlight, dimming the highlight from full to none, and does not affect the highlight's size. In contrast, the Shininess channel increases the highlight size and does not directly affect the highlight's brightness. If you animate the strengths of matching Shininess and Shininess Strength channels, the highlight would be brightest at the beginning but largest during the end of the animation.

NOTE

Shine channels have a much greater impact on Metal shaded materials because the material's color is calculated from the Shininess properties. Because of this effect, Metal materials show the effects of a Shininess Map across their entire surface and not just in their highlights.

Shine Map Channels Alone

When used without any other map channels, the Shine map textures the highlights across the surface and you define Shine patterns for a perfectly smooth and consistently colored material. Situations that call for this include scraped, scratched, stained, and dusty areas on an otherwise shiny material, or burnished, polished, gilded, and wet areas on an otherwise matte surface.

Combining Shininess Channels with Other Channel Types

The Shininess channels are most often used in conjunction with other Map channel types to add critical realism to materials. As a material simulates different effects across its surface, you usually need to vary the highlights for the various regions. During the life of a surface, high spots are subject to daily abrasion. Surface roughness has different effects on different types of materials. Through age, the higher areas of polished surfaces grow duller, whereas those on rough surfaces start to wear smooth and become more polished. Rivets on rough metal, raised areas of old wood, and high points on a sculpture become shinier, whereas the treads of a tire, grips on a racquet, and ridges on glass become duller.

When combined with Bump Maps, the Shine channels can make raised areas more or less polished and recessed areas matte (see Figure 15.10). The shininess qualities of a material most often relate its recesses and projections. The grooves between metal panels, joints between glazed brick, and cracks in a pot all are matte in comparison to the rest of the material. A shimmer across these areas would spoil the illusion, and reusing the bump to control the highlight prevents this from happening. This is a common need so you should consider copying the Bump channel as a Shininess Strength channel (most often as an instance) as standard procedure.

FIGURE 15.10

Bumped materials with Shininess Strength maps on the left and without on the right.

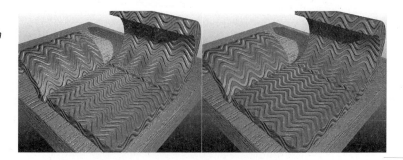

When using opacity to represent true holes, the Opacity channel needs to be copied (usually as an instance) to the Shininess Strength channel to prevent highlights where voids are supposed to be (see Figure 15.11). Otherwise, the 0 percent opaque areas are treated as if they were actually clear glass and highlights occur in "space," ruining the effect.

Figure 15.11

Transparent materials without a Shininess Strength Map on the left, and with a Shininess Strength Map on the right.

When combined with Diffuse maps, the Shininess maps make different areas of the "painted" surfaces more or less shiny and can differentiate areas that are actually smooth to the touch. The gloss paint on a wall, brass dividers in a wood parquet, gold leaf in a logo decal, burnished rivets on finished metal, polished dots on a watch face, or glass within a frame are all shinier than the rest of the material and would benefit from a Shininess Strength Map.

Shininess Maps can make reflective materials look especially real when combined with a reflection map. Varying shininess values can cause reflections to "dance" across the surface as the object is rotated. When representing materials in which everything is not perfectly smooth, such as with metal plating, Shininess maps can be used to chart the course of the irregularity and give play to a subtle, low-strength reflection.

Self-Illumination Maps

The Self-Illumination channel combines its effects with the Self-Illumination value in Basic parameters to isolate the simulation of light emission.

NEW TO R2

The behavior of the Self-Illumination Map channel has changed in Release 2 from Release 1. The channel value now mixes with the Self-Illumination parameter set in Basic parameters.

Remember that self-illumination is simulated in 3DS MAX by removing the Ambient shading. Full strength (white) areas of a Self-Illumination channel thus show the material's Diffuse component without any shade. A map that matches the Self-Illumination channel but contains a contrasting color is often used in the Diffuse channel to intensify the break between the field and the self-illuminated portions.

In Figure 15.12, a Self-Illumination Map has been applied to a teapot. Those areas of the channel's bitmap that are white appear as the Diffuse color without any shading.

FIGURE 15.12

The effects of using Self-Illumination Maps. When used without tiling, the Self-Illumination channel provides an excellent method for simulating signage, glow-in-the-dark paint, and etched patterns in a bright lamp.

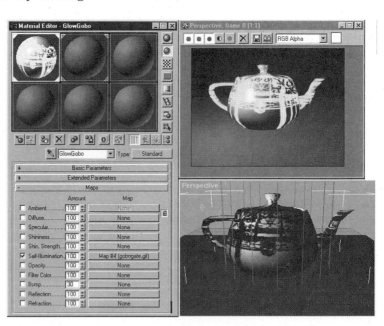

Self-illuminated Maps also prove quite useful in tailoring the effects of illuminated signage. Commonly, signs are painted on glass or pressed from plastic. The opacity of the paint and thickness of the plastic affects the amount of light emitted. You can reinforce this effect by using the material's texture or bump bitmap as a Self-Illuminated map and adjust its effects accordingly. Neon can be approximated with matching Bump and Shininess Strength channels and carefully placed Omni lights (if not viewed too closely).

Opacity Maps

The Opacity map channel is used for defining patterns in your surface that can be seen through, including such things as holes, patterned glass, or translucent panels, as shown in Figure 15.13. The Opacity channel combines with the base Opacity parameter to determine opacity. Pure white is opaque, while absolute black is fully transparent with shades of gray delivering proportional levels of opacity.

NEW TO R2

The behavior of the Opacity Map channel has changed in Release 2 from Release 1. The channel value now mixes with the Opacity parameter set in Basic parameters.

FIGURE 15.13

Using Opacity maps to define transparency and simulate holes.

WARNING

As with Shine maps, the same warning applies to using the Bitmap Output parameters or an RGB Tint map to increase the intensity of an Opacity Map; doing so adversely affects the resulting Diffuse component. If you need to increase the intensity, and thus the opacity, you should use a Mix Map type or adjust the bitmap in a paint program instead.

Opacity Maps only make a surface transparent—they do not eliminate the surface from existence, which means that the transparent areas are more like clear glass or plastic rather than holes. As with glass in real life, those transparent areas display highlights if the Shininess Strength is not zero. To realistically simulate voids with a material that has Shine, you must copy the Opacity Map (usually as an instance) to be a Shininess Strength Map as well.

Shadows only respect the transparency defined by Opacity Maps if they are Raytraced shadows. If you are using the default Filter Opacity type, the color of the shadow is tinted by the base filter color, or the Filter Map if one is defined. Lights using Shadow Maps for their shadows cast solid shadows, regardless of how the opacity is defined.

Filter Color Maps

Filter Color Maps usually work hand-in-hand with Opacity. When the Opacity type is Filter, a Filter Map tints the transparent areas of the surface with its map (note that other programs may call this transmissive color). If Raytraced shadows are used, the tinted areas will also be transmitted into the resulting shadow (see Figure 15.14).

FIGURE 15.14
Using a Filter map for a Stained Glass window.

In practice, Filter Color Maps are almost always color copies of a matching Opacity Map. This match is required to paint the correct color onto the cast shadow. Some opacity needs to be there for a Filter Map to have effect. Completely transparent surfaces are just that, so they cannot display or transmit any color. If the Opacity type is Subtractive or Additive, the Filter Map is ignored.

Reflection Maps

Although everything in a material is an illusion in the quest of simulation, nothing may seem more so than reflections. Reflections are fundamentally different from every other Map type because they are (or pretend to be) a result of the world around them. Because of this, they do not use and do not require Mapping coordinates. Although other maps are fixed to a surface, reflections are dependent on your viewing position to the object. If you rotate a Reflective object about its centroid, the reflection stays consistent. A chrome propeller blade hub is a perfect example; as the prop rotates, the reflection remains perfectly still.

Reflections can be used as an end in themselves, such as a mirror, or as a subtle touch to make a Shiny or Reflective object appear more realistic. Reflections can either use a reference image (bitmap or otherwise) or generate their own through the Reflect/Refract, Flat Mirror or Raytracer Map types. Flat Mirror Maps can simulate very realistic and accurate reflections on flat surfaces, Reflect/Refract Maps are usually used as the quickest way to create the illusion that a surface is shiny and reflective, and Raytracer Maps (although they take longer to calculate) create extremely accurate reflections. Using these Map types to automatically generate reflections is discussed later in this section.

Textures are fixed in location whereas reflections move across a stationary object as you move around it or stay constant as the object is revolved and your eye is stationary. The effect of reflections depends on your angle of view to them, and so they are calculated properly only when viewed in Camera viewports. Remember this when you make quick previews of your scene for material judgments.

Several rules govern the rendered appearance of a reflection, regardless of the reflected image's source. A reflection's color is primarily affected by the material's Diffuse component and to a smaller extent, its Ambient component. The Specular component remains unaffected by a reflection (remember that it's affected only by a Specular Map). Because of this effect, reflections cannot be seen in highlights. When you want to maximize a reflection and make it mirror-like, try the following steps (or do the reverse to minimize reflections):

- To minimize the impact of the Specular component, make the Highlight curve as thin as possible (increase the Shininess property).

- Untinted reflections require gray Ambient and Diffuse components. Making these reflections black allows the reflection to be seen at full effect.

- The Reflection Map's Amount slider dictates the percentage the reflection mixes with the Diffuse. Making this 100 replaces the Diffuse completely.

When using bitmaps as reflections, distorting or blurring the reflected image to at least some degree is common. Often this step is done because the "reflected" image has nothing to do with the actual environment and you only want to give the impression of being reflective. Other times the reflected image may not be large enough and the geometry not curvilinear enough to be convincing. Many materials are not mirror-like in appearance, but only have a gleam, and a crisp reflection is not appropriate.

NOTE

When using maps to represent a reflection, the result may at times appear to be "self-illuminated." This occurs because the Reflection Map replaces the material's diffuse and ambient components, and thus reacts minimally to shade—meaning the reflection can be seen independent of a light source.

The premise is that the Reflection Map represents a reflection, so there must be something in the scene that is illuminated and reflected back to the surface. Because you are defining what this surface is "seeing" in its reflection, you're responsible for adjusting this effect. This effect can be disturbing if the reflection's brightness is far different from the scene's light level. When the reflection is too bright, you have the following options:

- Decrease the Reflection Map's Amount slider.

- Increase the intensity of the Diffuse component.

- Decrease the Reflection Map's Output amount.

- Adjust the source image being used for the reflection.

- Switch to using a Reflect/Refract, Flat Mirror Map, or Raytracer Map type to create the Reflection Map.

To prevent a reflection from occurring at specific areas on a surface, you need to use a Mask Map type. When doing so, the surface requires Mapping coordinates to locate the mask. Figure 15.15 shows an example of using a Reflection Map with a mask. Using masks is very important when the material has areas that are shiny and dull. If you have defined a Shininess Strength or Shininess Map, you should probably reuse it as a Reflection mask as well. You can then modulate the amount of reflection that occurs in that area as well.

FIGURE 15.15

Using a Mask Map type as a Reflection Map.

Reflection masks also are good tools for blocking areas of a flat mirror. Reflection masks enable you to create a pattern on the surface of your mirror and alleviate some restrictions of not being able to extend a flat mirror beyond an element's extents. Some examples are picture frames, tiles, and etched mirror glass. Reusing the mirror mask as Bump, Texture, and Shininess masks and maps is natural.

Automatically Calculated Reflections

As mentioned, the Reflection Map can be calculated for you by using either a Refract/Reflect, a Raytracer, or Flat Mirror Map type. The choice depends entirely on the geometry of the reflecting object and the amount of time you want to spend in calculating accurate reflections. If the surface is curvilinear, such as a sphere, Refract/Reflect is the quickest choice whereas Raytracer is the most accurate choice. If the surface is coplanar, like a wall mirror, the Flat Mirror Map type should be used. If the object contains both conditions, such as chrome text, the Map types may need to be combined for a convincing reflection.

NOTE

Because Automatic Reflection maps are not created until rendering time, you cannot see their effects while within the Material editor—you must render the scene.

Figure 15.16 shows the controls for the Reflect/Refract and Flat Mirror Automatic Reflection Map types. The Blur parameters enable you to blur or smudge the resulting reflection (with Reflect/Refract also providing Blur Offset because heavier blurring is often required for that Map type). This effect is important for Reflective surfaces that are not polished to a perfect mirror-like quality (such as stainless steel).

The Render parameters for frames give you control over how often the Reflection Maps are created during an animation. If your viewing position is not changing and the Reflective objects are not moving, you may not need render the mirrors very often. The Use Environment Map option controls whether the Background Map is included in the rendering of the Reflection Map. If you are using a basic screen projection, the background may be reflected in an undesirable way (especially during animations) and you should disable it.

The Flat Mirror Map type can assign automatic reflection to individual object faces based on their material ID and apply distortions to the resulting reflections using either the material's Bump Map or Noise parameters. The Reflect/Refract Map type enables either automatic calculation of reflections or it can use premade maps generated by the object in a scene that renders much faster. Tools are also provided in this Map type to calculate atmospheric effects in a scene into the reflections (such as fog) either through ranges determined by the object the material is applied to and its location in the scene or through the ranges determined by a selected camera.

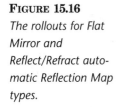

FIGURE 15.16

The rollouts for Flat Mirror and Reflect/Refract automatic Reflection Map types.

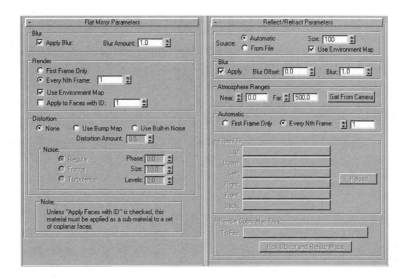

Figure 15.17 shows the controls for the Raytracer Automatic Reflection Map main rollout, its Global settings, and Exclude/Include dialogs. This Map type offers extremely accurate reflections, and although raytraced rendering takes longer than scan line rendering, the Raytracer Automatic Reflection Map type is packed with many options to increase rendering speed. Its Trace Mode can either be set to create reflections or refractions specifically on an object, or detect from the Map channel it is assigned to whether it should reflect or refract. It also has the capability to use global or local anti-aliasing settings and exclusion/inclusion lists of objects or selection sets to speed up rendering times. It can use the environment settings or override them with a specified color or specified map.

Like the other two automatic Reflection Map types, it too has Blurring capabilities, but it also offers a powerful defocusing feature that blurs according to distance from the object; closer objects remain focused while distant object appear out of focus.

The blur and defocusing can either be calculated from the scene or using premade maps. Through Attenuation settings, it is possible to set ranges, and beyond them objects are not considered in raytraced calculations. You can also specify the color that is returned by rays as they attenuate outward or by a custom falloff using ranges. The Basic Material extensions give you the ability to control how much raytracing is performed through a specified map and how much tinting is applied to reflected colors. The rollouts for the Raytracer Map type's Anti-aliasing, Attenuation, and Basic Material extensions are shown in Figure 15.18.

FIGURE 15.17

The rollout for the Raytracer Automatic Reflection Map type parameters and the Raytracer Map type options, Global settings, and Exclude/Include dialogs.

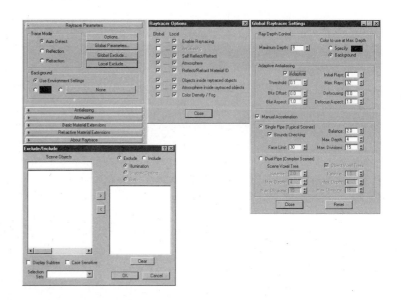

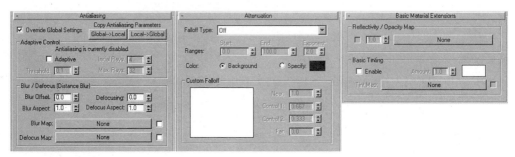

FIGURE 15.18

The Raytracer Automatic Reflection Map type Anti-aliasing, Attenuation and Basic Material Extension rollouts.

Although automatic reflections portray much of the scene, the object creating them cannot see itself unless Raytraced Reflection Maps are used. This is because the object's bounding box determines the mirror's clipping plane and its extents obviously lie within it. This occurs even if other elements within the object have different materials and can lead to unrealistic situations when an object is composed of separate elements that would normally be able to see one another (a text string being a classic example). The only way around this situation is to detach the distinct elements as separate objects so they are no longer clipped (see Figure 15.19).

FIGURE 15.19

A string of text made into separate objects so that each letter can be seen in reflections.

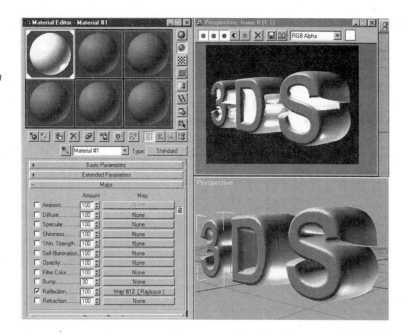

Automatic reflections are generated only for positive face normals. This situation is not normally a problem, but it may be if you are animating playing card-like mirrors. To render both sides of the same surface, you need to use a two-sided material with an automatic material on both sides.

An often forgotten fact regarding automatic reflections is that to be convincing, they must reflect something. Although this statement may seem obvious, many modelers forget that their isolated object has nothing to reflect and at first wonder why the surface is "black" rather than reflective. Reflections also base much of their effect on your angle of view and are calculated properly only when viewed in perspective viewports—something important to remember when making previews of your scene for material adjustments.

Generating Reflections with Refract/Reflect Maps

When the Source for the Refract/Reflect Map type is set to Automatic, it generates six maps at render time that enclose the object and are projected back on to the surface in a manner that is somewhat similar to box mapping. In concept, the renderer stands at the object's pivot point and takes a "snapshot" of the scene in each cardinal direction and assembles the six images into a reflection cube. These six images are then projected back onto the object. In computer graphic terms, this case is either termed a cubic environment map or a T-map (because the six images unfold from the box to form a "T").

TIP

You can control the placement of the cubic reflection by adjusting the location of the object's pivot point.

As the cubic reflection, maps are projected back onto the Reflective surface and each plane of the surface receives a specific portion. This occurrence explains why surfaces with curvilinear surfaces work best because the broad, flat sides of rectilinear objects have problems capturing enough of the projected scene to read as a reflection (see Figure 15.20).

The reflected scene is far more believable on a curved surface because every facet is catching its own portion of the scene and the scene wraps around the surface. A cube that sits on a textured floor reflects only a blurred portion because its face "sees" only a small piece of the reflection cube's image.

FIGURE 15.20
Reflect/Refract reflections on curvilinear and rectilinear surfaces.

Refract/Reflect is different from Flat Mirror in having a Size parameter to control the size of its calculated bitmaps. You are given control of this setting because it can become expensive; the cost can be calculated as:

Size × Size × 4 bytes × 6 maps or the Size^2 × 24 bytes

This cost is imposed for every object that uses the material because a new set must be made for every unique location. A good rule of thumb is that for an object that comprises half the rendered scene, the map size should be as large as the rendering output. If the rendered reflection is too blurred, rough, or pixelated, you need to increase this value.

Be careful, however, assigning large values used by numerous objects because even a 500-line map uses 6 MB per instance. If you have several objects sharing the same material but of different prominence in the scene, you will conserve the most RAM by creating duplicate materials with varying Size parameters and assigning them accordingly.

Generating Reflections with Flat Mirror Maps

The Flat Mirror map type also generates a reflection at render time, but the application and the result are much different than with Refract/Reflect. A Flat Mirror is just that—a single image of the scene is projected back onto the surface as the surface would see it. This effect is the one that most often comes to mind when people are asked to define a reflection. The operative word in this map type's title is *flat* because this mapping type works properly only with coplanar surfaces.

If the Apply To Faces with ID Flat Mirror parameter is not toggled on, the renderer analyzes the object that uses a Flat Mirror map by looking for the first face in the object definition that has the material ID# for that material. The first face found "wins" and defines the plane for the resulting reflection.

Because you rarely know which is the first face, assigning Flat Mirrors to a Face selection at the Sub-Object level or to perfectly coplanar surfaces is good practice if you're not assigning the Flat Mirror Map to an individual face or set of faces. This technique is not required, but by using it you are assured of what is defining the mirrored plane. If more than one plane is defined, the reflection may appear more like a spotlight projection because it does not turn at the edges.

TIP

The Box object is actually ideally designed for Flat Mirrors. The top face of a box contains the first face and is given Material ID #1. You can reliably assign the top face a Standard Material using a Flat Mirror Reflection map and always know the top will reflect correctly. This works best if the box height is zero because otherwise the sides will not correctly reflect.

Unlike Reflect/Refract maps, Flat Mirrors are always calculated with the appropriate resolution and do not have a Map Size parameter. Flat mirrors that cannot be seen from the rendered view are not calculated. This attribute does not cause additional problems because Flat Mirrors cannot be seen in reflections under any condition. The RAM required for a Flat Mirror varies with its size in the scene because only the slice of the scene that the surface can actually see is rendered.

Generating Reflections with Raytracer Maps

The Raytracer Map type also generates a reflection at render time, but the results take longer to calculate and appear far more accurate. It is generally good practice to really think about the parameters, settings, and options you should use with this Map type before applying it with the default settings. Doing this can save you a tremendous amount of rendering time. What follows is a general list of questions you should ask yourself whenever applying this Map type:

- Are atmospheric effects really necessary in the reflections?

- Do all objects in the scene (even if they're nearby) need to be shown in the reflection for it to be effective or believable or can they be excluded? Can objects that will never appear in the reflection be excluded?

- Can a simpler Environment Map be used instead of the scene's environment?

- What level of anti-aliasing is required for an effective reflection? Are the scene anti-aliasing settings overkill values for Raytraced reflections?

- What are effective ranges for attenuation of Raytraced reflections? Do distant objects seen in the reflection really make a difference in the reflections or can they be excluded?

- Is the reflection blurry enough to exclude further objects? When using blurry or unfocused settings, run a few test sample frames to see what objects get reflected effectively and do further object exclusions of the objects that are indiscernible if possible.

- Are the reflections as clear as the scene, or does the material tint the resulting reflections? As one example, think of a red Christmas tree bulb and how everything reflected in it is a red hue.

- More than any other danger, it is tempting to think that a reflective object *must* use the new Raytracer Map type to be completely believable. The Reflect/Refract Map type has been left in the program for good reason; it is still highly effective and quick. Before you jump to a Raytracer Map type, ask yourself what it is about the object that the Reflect/Refract Map type will not accomplish.

In some cases, you may have no option but to use Raytrace maps to produce believable results in a scene. An example of this might be a mirrored hallway with an object standing in it; two opposing mirrors create an infinite series of mirrored images in each other.

Raytracer maps would not only produce an extremely sharp series of reflected images in each mirror, but the impact of cumulative lighting effects with each deeper image. You can cut your Raytraced material rendering times down to a manageable size in three steps: by analyzing the scene in terms of which objects play a crucial roll in the reflections, by examining the resulting reflections of a few test frames to see which elements in the scene really count, and by taking advantage of existing environment maps rather than calculated environment maps. There are no magical settings within the Raytracer Map type that speed up its use; the sweet spot for the fastest and most effective reflections is dependent on your scenes and keyframing for each project.

T IP

One method to optimize Raytraced reflections, however, is to imagine the reflections themselves as an entirely separate resulting animation. Examine the necessity of every element in the reflections as you would every element in the resulting scene's animation. Then exclude those elements that are too far away, not "in front of the camera for long", not large enough to be considered, and so on.

Generating Reflections with Multiple Mirrors

Many surfaces contain more than one mirror condition. The text shown in Figure 15.21 is a typical example of this condition. The front faces are coplanar and have been assigned a Flat Mirror, whereas the bevel and sides share a common Refract/Reflect map. Making this distinction is straightforward but does require some planning. When the same Automatically Mapped material is applied to different objects, separate Reflection maps are generated. To create multiple mirrors within the same object if the Flat Mirror Map type is not being assigned to individual faces, each occurrence must have a different, Automatically Mapped material. So for multiple reflections within the same object, you must use a Multi/Sub-Object material with different material definitions for the different areas.

FIGURE 15.21

Mirrored text using both Reflect/Refract and Flat Mirror reflections.

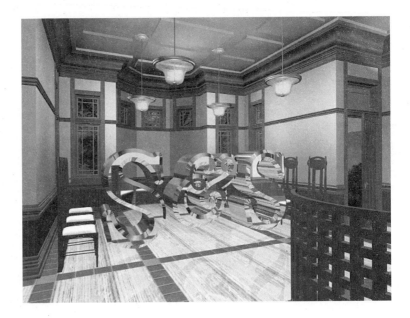

NOTE

Mirrored text is a good example of when the front faces should be detached as an object with a Flat Mirror map, and the remaining object assigned an Automatic Reflection.

When positioned appropriately, mirrored surfaces see each other's reflection and can bounce their reflections back and forth (an infinite number of times if they are actually perpendicular to one another). Because each iteration requires another rendering pass, the time can be excessive and you are given control over the number of bounces that occur.

For Reflect/Refract Maps, the number of times reflections are bounced is controlled by the Rendering Iterations parameter (under Auto Reflect/Refract Maps in the MAX Default Scanline A-Buffer rollout) in the Render Scene dialog. In practice, you will rarely need to increase this number beyond three unless the reflections are actually the focus of your composition.

Refraction Maps

When you look through a thick vase, a magnifying glass, or even a glass of water, the scene beyond the material looks bent, distorted, or warped. This effect is due to the light being bent, or refracted, through the surface. In computer graphics, this distortion is termed refraction and it is simulated with a Refraction Map. A Refraction Map is actually a variation on an Opacity Map. With it you are simulating the bending of light through a transparent, but thick, material, as shown in Figure 15.22.

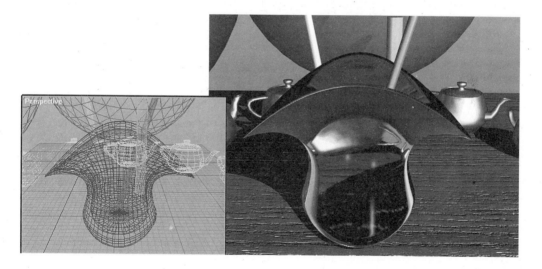

FIGURE 15.22

Using Refraction mapping for transparent distortion.

When you specify a Refraction Map, you are completely changing the method in which opacity is defined. As a result, the Opacity parameter, Opacity Falloff, and Opacity Map (if defined) are ignored whenever a

Refraction Map is active. As with Opacity Maps, a Refraction Map with an amount of 100 is fully transparent. So at full strength, Diffuse, Ambient, and Opacity Maps are ignored. The only Opacity parameter that is still respected is Opacity Type, which acts as it does with standard opacity.

The Refract Map/Raytracer IOR setting indicates the Index Of Refraction for the substance. The IOR value has no effect at 1.0, where it is the equivalent of air. The default IOR value is 1.5 (the equivalent of glass). The higher the value, the more like a solid glass sphere the object is (with very few "real" materials exceeding 2.0). Values below 1.0 cause the distortion to be from a concave lens instead of a convex one.

What may be difficult to grasp is that when you specify a Refraction Map, you cannot see through the object because the simulation of refraction makes the assumption that everything seen through it is bent. This difficulty occurs even if you lower the Refraction Amount to one and have the Opacity at zero. (All the Refraction Amount slider does is control the blend between it and the Diffuse component.)

Although you can define any Map type for a Refraction Map, it is meant to be used with the Refract/Reflect, Raytracer or Thin Wall Refraction Map types. If you do choose to use a bitmap, you have the greatest success using a cylindrical projection and then using the Tiling and Offset parameters to line up the map at a convincing location.

Automatically Calculated Refractions

The Refraction Map can also be calculated for you by using the Reflect/Refract, Raytracer or Thin Wall Refraction Map types. The Reflect/Refract Map type refracts when applied to the Refraction Map channel of a material and its settings for blurring. Its sensitivity to Environment Maps and atmospheres (as well as its ability to use and create Refraction Maps) govern its behavior in much the same manner as when the Map type is used for reflective purposes.

The Raytracer Map type, however, uses the Refractive Material Extensions rollout (see Figure 15.23) to control the color and color density of refraction within an object. Starting and Ending Distances govern the "perceived thickness" of the refracting material where the Starting Distance is the position in the object where the color density begins.

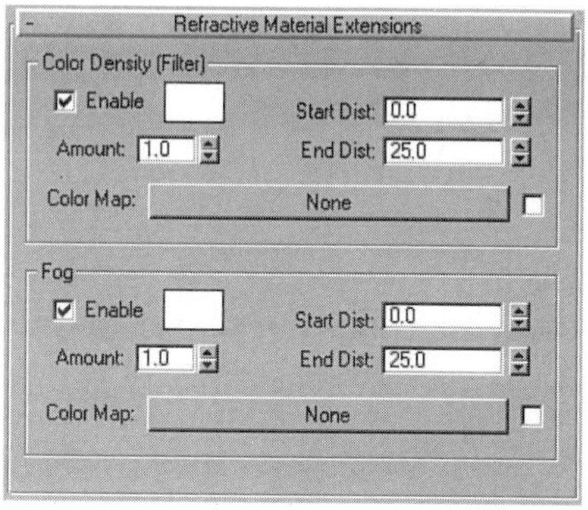

FIGURE 15.23

*The Refractive
Material Extensions
rollout.*

Figure 15.24 shows the rollout for a third Refractive Map type at your disposal for situations requiring a refracting offset or "jog" caused by thin objects. The Thin Wall Refraction Map type parameters include a Blur capability, a capability to use the environment map, and a render capability for the first or Nth frames. This Map type also has a Thickness Offset that controls the "jog" in the material and can range from a value of 0 to 10. If a Bump Map is present in the material, a Bump Map Effect value can be set to refract, according to the bumpiness of the material.

FIGURE 15.24

*The Thin Wall
Refraction Map type
and an example of its
"jogging" effect.*

Using Map Types

When you click a Map Channel button, you are automatically thrown into the Material/Map Browser shown in Figure 15.25. The Browse From options enable you to choose from among the following options:

- Select a previously defined map from the currently loaded Material library.

- Select from what is currently active in the 24 sample slots of the Material editor.

- Select from what is currently in the Active Slot.

- Select from what has been assigned to the objects currently selected.

- Select from anything assigned in the scene.

- Define a map from scratch by choosing the generic types.

FIGURE 15.25

Map type choices after clicking a Map channel button.

This process starts the layering of maps within a material tree. Figure 15.26 demonstrates this process by layering several different Map types within a single Standard material. Here, four maps use a Composite Map type to combine two bitmaps, while the Reflection Map uses a Mask Map type to perfect the illusion.

FIGURE 15.26

The bottle contains several maps including a Composite Map in the Diffuse channel for the large label and the label around the neck.

This next section discusses the various categories of map usage, including defining images, compositing, and modifying color.

Maps Types for Defining Images

The most commonly used maps are those that define an image. This may be procedural, being defined and calculated by the Map type itself, or a reference to a physically existing image, such as a bitmap. Often, Image maps enable you to define, yet others create combinations and overlays of patterns. Regardless of the options they present to you, each defines a bitmap that is passed through the map channel to be interpreted by the parent material.

2D Maps Types

The 2D Map category is what most people think of when one speaks of maps. Even the word "map" implies that it is flat. It also implies that it relates to something in a very specific manner, which is where mapping UV coordinates come into play. Of all the 2D maps, the Bitmap Map type is the easiest to relate to because it is a simple representation of a physical bitmap that could have come from a sample disk, paint program, or even a rendering in 3DS MAX. If someone is generically talking about a "map," they are most likely referring to a Bitmap Map type.

Most of the maps use similar Coordinate and Noise rollouts to control the offset, tiling, repeat, angle, blur, and distortion of the map (see Figure 15.27). The Output and Time rollouts are also common to several Map types. The most commonly adjusted parameters tend to be in the Coordinates rollout because this controls the size, placement, and rotation of the map. This rollout also controls the "fuzziness" of the map with the Blur and Blur Offset parameters.

FIGURE 15.27

Rollouts common to most Map types.

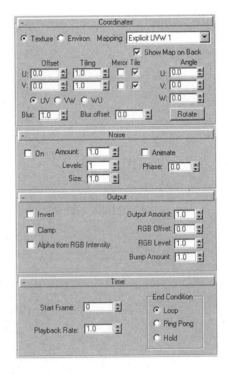

In general, common parameters affect the entire map, whereas unique parameters affect the inner characteristics of the map. The Gradient Map type, for example, has its own Noise parameters in addition to the common Noise rollout. The unique parameters create noise within the gradient itself, whereas the common ones affect the gradient as if it were one map.

Smoothing a 2D Map with Blur

By their very nature, bitmaps are not perfect. No matter how evenly shaded or complex in color depth, bitmaps are just an arrangement of colored squares, which are termed "pixels." These square pixels are fine when viewed straight on in 2D space, but they begin to be a liability when they are placed in perspective in 3D space. Contrasting pixels become more pronounced and visible when aliasing, scintillation, or stair-stepping sets in. This is also where Filter maps and Blur come into play. Filter maps do for 2D maps what anti-aliasing does for geometry, with Blur settings controlling their effect. Figure 15.28 shows the effects of no filtering, while Figure 15.29 shows the same scene with filtering enabled. Although filtering uses a bit more RAM, it's obvious to see why it's the default option.

FIGURE 15.28

The tile floor material rendered without Filter maps.

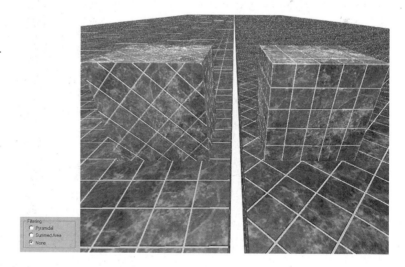

The preceding figures point out how Blur's primary effect is to eliminate scintillation, those extremely annoying lines of "dancing" pixels, and moiré patterns. Scintillation is especially noticeable as fine lines begin to converge in perspective (as in the distance) or come close together (as in the sides of the cubes).

FIGURE 15.29

The same scene rendered with Filter maps.

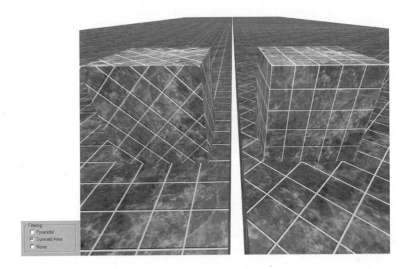

FIGURE 15.29

The same scene rendered with Filter maps.

Examine the left cube within both figures and you can also see how the diagonal lines appear "jagged" without blur but render smooth with it. Also notice that the appearance of the marble texture is nearly identical in both figures. In actuality, a slight but subtle difference is there, as the filtered marble is a bit "softer" in appearance. Of all the Map types, Blur has the most profound effect on Bump Maps, with bumps not rendering correctly at all unless Filter Maps are enabled.

Filter Map is a computer graphics term that may use various techniques. 3DS MAX provides two types of filtering for bitmaps: Pyramidal (also known as Mip mapping) and Summed Area (also known as Summed Area table). For other 2D maps, the default Pyramidal method is used. The Bitmap Map type enables you to choose which filtering type to use or to disable it completely.

NOTE

Blur cannot occur unless Filter Maps are enabled. When you disable filtering by either choosing None for a bitmap's filtering or turning off the Renderer's Filter Maps option, Blur settings for that bitmap or the entire scene are ignored.

The difference between the two filtering options is anti-aliasing quality and RAM requirements. Pyramidal filtering uses an extra byte per pixel, but the cost is minimal compared to its effectiveness. Summed Area filtering uses a superior but more expensive technique, and it uses an additional 12 bytes per pixel. Because of its cost, you may wish to remember it as "Summed Area" instead—choose it only when your bitmaps require it. For some bitmaps the switch to Summed Area filtering is critical, although for others it's barely noticeable. Summed Area filtering has the greatest effect on materials having closely spaced lines that diminish into perspective or those that use a heavy Blur setting to gain a "fuzzy" effect. Figure 15.30 illustrates the difference between the two filtering types.

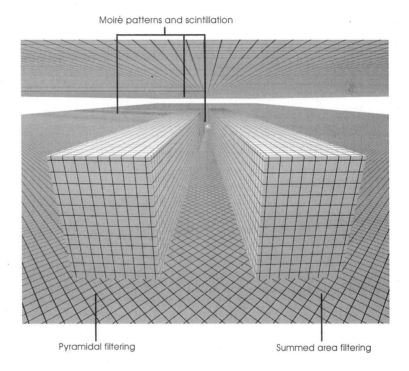

FIGURE 15.30

Comparing Pyramidal (left) to Summed Area filtering (right).

Moiré patterns and scintillation

Pyramidal filtering

Summed area filtering

As Figure 15.30 shows, Pyramidal filtering averages less of the image and causes moiré patterns to form in the distance. Summed Area does a larger averaging and avoids this condition. Up close, Pyramidal filtering tends to look fuzzier whereas Summed Area reads crisp. If you can afford the RAM, Summed Area will provide a better result for your bitmaps.

The Blur parameter can be thought of as a strength setting for the filter maps as it governs the distance-based blurring of the bitmap. The parameter provides its most basic effect at its default setting of 1.0 and a minimal effect at its 0.01 lower limit. Higher Blur settings predictably increase the Blur, which can be very desirable for subdued reflection maps.

The Blur Offset parameter is fundamentally different from Blur by filtering the 2D map before it is applied in perspective. The term "offset" is just like the Offset parameter; it shifts the bitmap by that amount, with 1.0 being a full bitmap offset. This explains why Blur Offset values as small as 0.01 have a significant effect because 0.01 means the source bitmap has been shifted by 1 percent. In most cases, use Blur Offset to adjust the softness or fuzz of the 2D map and Blur to control its anti-aliasing in perspective.

The common Noise rollout sends a distortion "wave" through the 2D map, as shown in Figure 15.31, when you enable the parameters by checking its On option. The Amount parameter controls the wave's height, Level controls the number of iterations, Size controls the distance of a phase repeat, and Phase controls the position of the repeat. The Phase parameter is not respected unless the Animate option is enabled. The other parameters animate with the Animate button as normal and do not require this option to be checked.

FIGURE 15.31
Noise parameters being applied to 2D maps.

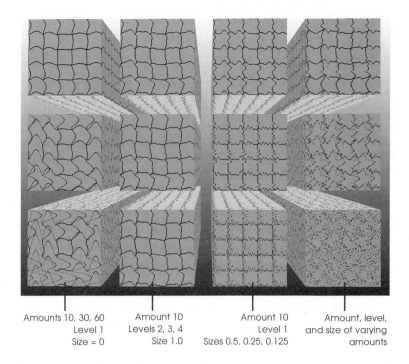

Amounts 10, 30, 60
Level 1
Size = 0

Amount 10
Levels 2, 3, 4
Size 1.0

Amount 10
Level 1
Sizes 0.5, 0.25, 0.125

Amount, level, and size of varying amounts

Unique 2D Map Controls

After you realize that controls such as Blur are common, those that are unique to the particular Map types aren't nearly as intimidating (see Figure 15.32). The use of the individual controls are described in depth in the standard 3DS

MAX documentation and, in the case of Photoshop and Premiere filters, in the Help file and associated Photoshop compatible plug-ins.

Although the Bitmap and Photoshop map types do not allow expansion, the Checker and Gradient Map types both provide Map channels that can be substituted for Color swatches, and so continue the Material tree even deeper.

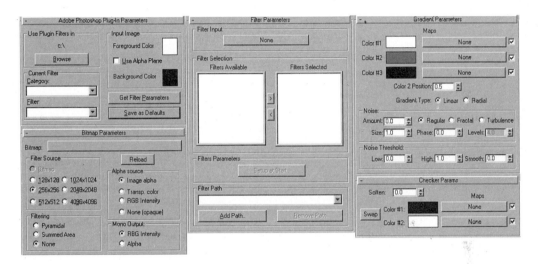

FIGURE 15.32
Controls unique to the various 2D Map types.

NOTE

The Photoshop Plug-In Filter Map type can load only Photoshop compatible, 32-bit plug-ins. These plug-ins come from such third parties as Metatools. The filters that ship with Photoshop are prevented from working in anything but the parent program.

3D Map Types

The 3D type is what most people in computer graphics think of when the term "procedural materials" (or shaders) is used. Because these maps are applied in three dimensions, they course though an object and do not normally streak the way a 2D map does when the projection becomes collinear, as shown in Figure 15.33.

Of all the procedurals provided, Noise is by far the most commonly used because it provides three variations that can be used to modulate many other map types and give realistic surface distortion, grit, and grime.

FIGURE 15.33
Using 3D Procedural maps to uniformly cover a surface.

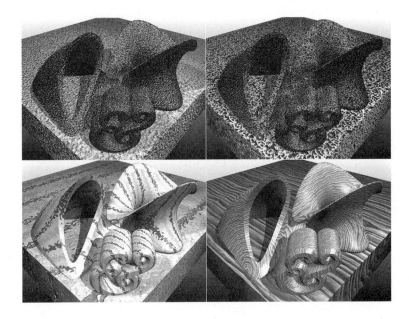

The Procedural 3D Maps (Cellular, Dent, Marble, Noise, Perlin Marble, Planet, Smoke, Speckle, Splat, Stucco, Water, and Wood) share a common set of parameters for locating their effects on the surface (see Figure 15.34). If XYZ mapping coordinates are chosen, the tiling is made according to the object's real-world size and no object mapping coordinates are required. The location of the map relates to the object's creation matrix, which cannot easily be changed. The Offset, Tiling, and Angle parameters are thus provided to give you control of the map and can be thought of as being analogous to position, scale, and rotation transforms.

This form of real-world XYZ scaling is the traditional method in computer graphics and works well as long as you only animate your objects with transforms. If, however, you animate the Modifier Stack, the mapping coordinates are still applied according to the original projection and the object moves through the mapping coordinates. Because this effect is not usually desirable, the UVW coordinate options are provided so you can use the assigned UVW mapping coordinates that translate with the vertices as the surfaces deform.

FIGURE 15.34

The common Coordinate rollout of XYZ, UVW1, and UVW2 coordinates for 3D Maps.

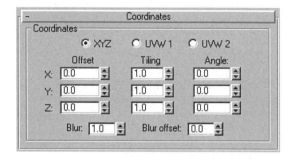

In practice, XYZ coordinates are best for static models. This statement is especially true when the same material is used between different objects because it ensures identical results. The result of these identical coordinates makes it appear as if the objects were punched or carved from the same solid block of material. When this effect is not desirable and you want the mapping to follow the lines of the object (or you are animating the object's Modifier Stack), UVW coordinates are the correct choice. When using UVW coordinates, you will most likely need to increase the Tiling considerably because a single repeat of a 3D map is usually intended to be quite small.

N OTE

This procedure is most easily done with the 3D map's Tiling parameter, rather than the UVW Mapping modifier tiling, because a change in the modifier's tiling also changes the tiling of 2D maps, which may not be desirable.

After the common Coordinate rollout, each 3D map type has its own characteristics. Coincidentally, several contain two color swatches to control the contrast and color of the particular effect. Each of these colors can be replaced by another Map type in the accompanying Map channel (and so continue the Material tree). The parameters for the different types each control the individual effects.

Falloff Map Type

The Falloff Map type (see Figure 15.35) creates a grayscale value derived from the face normals' angular falloff of the object's surface that the material is applied to. You can use it to create a more powerful Falloff effect than the Falloff capabilities found in the Extended Parameters rollout of a Standard Material.

FIGURE 15.35

The Falloff Map type parameters.

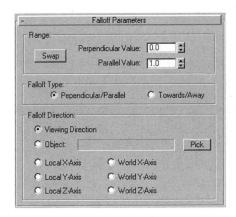

Depending on the Falloff Type mode selected, the Range spinners either control the Perpendicular/Parallel values or the Towards/Away value. The Swap button swaps the values of the two spinners, which inverts the effect. The Perpendicular/Parallel mode determines the angular falloff between face normals that are perpendicular to the Falloff direction and normals that are parallel to the Falloff direction. The Falloff range is based on a 90-degree change in Face Normal direction. The Towards/Away mode determines the angular falloff between face normals that face toward (parallel to) the falloff direction and normals that face away from the falloff direction. The falloff range is based on a 180-degree change in Face Normal direction.

The Falloff direction can be set to the viewing direction of the current viewport or the direction of a picked object. It can also be set to the Local XYZ axis of the object the map is applied to or the XYZ axis of the World Coordinate system.

Particle Age Map Type

The Particle Age Map type (see Figure 15.36) works with Particle systems and enables them to change color based on their life. It is generally applied as a Diffuse map. Particles begin in one color and at a specified age inter-polate to a secondary color, and interpolate to a third color before they die. This type of map might be applied to a Spray particle system to create a color-fading shower of metallic sparks, which upon emission are a fiery white-yellow and, after expansion, cool off to a deep molten red.

FIGURE 15.36

The Particle Age map type parameters.

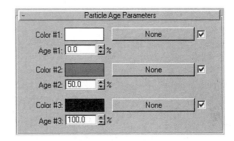

Particle MBlur Map Type

The Particle MBlur Map type also works with Particle systems and enables them to change color based on their speed. Color 1 is used at the particle's slowest speed and Color 2 at its fastest speed. The Sharpness variable con-trols the level of transparency based on the particle's speed. This Map type is usually applied as an Opacity Map but can also be applied as a Diffuse Map to create special effects.

Map Types for Compositing

The Compositors category maximizes your options and enables you to com-bine your library of material bitmaps in limitless ways. If you are joining the effects for two or more sources, you are doing a composite. In practice, using these map types appropriately is critical to complex, realistic materials.

Mask, Composite, Mix, and RGB Multiply Map Types

As Figure 15.37 shows, each Map type contains two or more channels for selecting yet other map types. Most often, these additional choices are bitmaps.

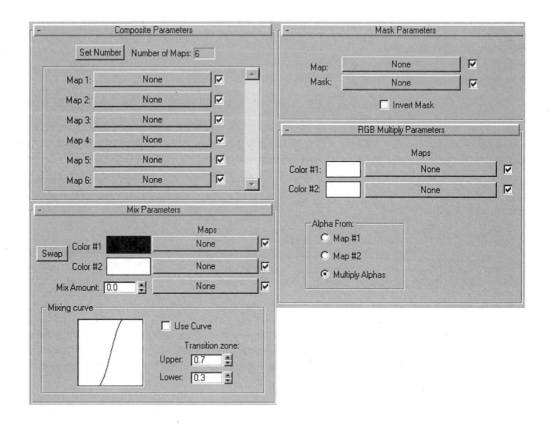

FIGURE 15.37

The Mask, Composite, Mix, and RGB Multiply Map type rollouts.

The Mask Map type contains a Map channel for supplying the source image and a Mask channel for suppressing the Source map. The mask can be thought of as a stencil, airbrush friskette, cookie pattern cutout, or patterned glass through which the source image is seen. The white areas of the mask map allow the source image to show through, black areas block the source, and gray areas allow proportional amounts through.

The Composite Map type combines any number of maps and defaults to a very manageable quantity of two. The maps are overlaid according to their number with Map 1 being the primary map and applied first. Map 2 is applied second over Map 1; Map 3 is applied third over Map 2, and so on.

In order to see the Primary Map, Map 2 must have at least some transparency. This could be by means of an alpha channel or using a Mask Map. As you layer more and more maps, the higher maps tend to need increasing amounts of transparency if the lower maps are going to be seen. This situation is similar to the way Video Post composites successive images with numerous Alpha Compositor events.

The Mix Map type blends two Map types and gives control over how the mixing occurs. The Mix Amount parameter indicates the percentage of Color 2 that is added to Color 1. Because the default Mix Amount is zero, you will not see Color 2's effect until you increase it. By default, this is a linear mixing. If you activate the Mixing Curve with the Use Curve option, you can weight the interpolation as shown in the accompanying Mixing Curve.

T IP

Mix maps are ideal for brightening or tinting other maps. You usually get far better, more predictable results using a Mix Map to adjust another map's effect rather using the map's own Output controls.

You can also specify a Map type for the Mix Amount. When you do so, the Mix Amount percentage is ignored, although the Mixing Curve works as before. The intensity of the Map controls the mix, with black being the same as a Mix Amount of zero and white a Mix Amount of 100. The Mix Amount Map thus becomes similar to a Mask Map type.

An important thing to note is that the Mixing Curve only modulates the Mix Amount. If the Mix Amount is 0 or 100 (black or white), you will not see any effect when adjusting the transition zone because there is nothing being mixed. To use the Mix Amount percentage after specifying a map, you need to choose a "None" Map to clear the channel and reactivate the Mix Amount parameter.

The RGB Multiply Map type multiplies the RGB and alpha channel values of two maps. Usually applied for Bump Maps, the red component of one map is multiplied by the red component of the second map and so forth. By setting one of the maps to a solid color, you can tint the other as well.

Map Types for Color Modification

The Color Modifying category is comprised of three Map types that adjust the image qualities of other Map types. The effects possible from this category are everything you might use a paint program for (brightness, contrast, gamma, color balance, posterization, and so on). It currently contains the Output, RGB Tint, and Vertex Color map types as shown in Figure 15.38.

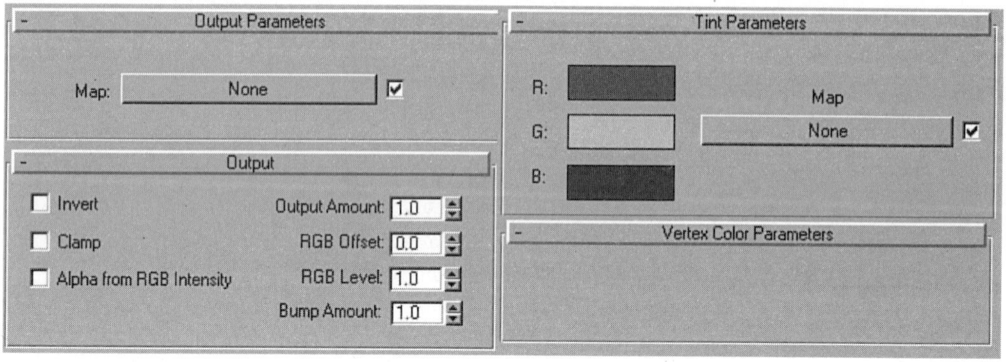

FIGURE 15.38

The Output, RGB Tint, and Vertex Color Map types.

The Output Map type enables procedural maps such as Marble and Checker to have Output settings. Once the Map button is selected to point to the Map type desired, the remaining parameters behave as they do for a regular bitmap. The RGB Tint Map tints the three color channels of a selected Map type.

The Vertex Color Map type can be confusing for a number of reasons, not the least of which is that it has no parameters! This Map type displays the effects of assigned vertex colors in the rendered scene. You assign vertex colors from the Editable mesh. If you make an object an Editable mesh and assign Vertex colors to it, then assign the Vertex Color map to the Diffuse Map channel of the object, you can create colorful surface effects.

NOTE

Once a Vertex Colors modifier has been applied to an object to assign colors to the vertices, manually changing vertex colors with the Assign Vertex Colors utility does not work. You must use the Editable mesh controls to do this.

Animating Maps and Their Parameters

As with most elements in 3DS MAX, map properties can be animated. As a general rule, if a parameter uses an Edit field for a value, then it is usually animatable. To confirm exactly what Map parameters can be animated, examine the Map Track View. Every animatable parameter is displayed with an Animation track, while non-animatable options are left out.

The most basic way to animate a bitmap is to specify an animated bitmap type. With 3DS MAX, the FLC, FLI, CEL, and AVI files can all contain animations that "play" across the material as the scene is rendered. When the end of the animation is reached, the animation loops. While easy to choose, it lacks control because it can be difficult to determine on what frame in the scene a given animation frame is presented.

For better control, you can specify a number of files that are either sequentially numbered or specifically listed in an IFL (image file list) file. For sequences, you specify the filename prefix that is common to the string of maps. For example, to use the 690 files in the blow0000.tga–blow0689.tga file sequence, you'd specify blow*.tga as the bitmap file name. When you do this, 3DS MAX automatically creates an IFL file with 690 file references. This IFL file resides in the directory that contained the file sequence and does not list any explicit path information.

After you get used to the idea of using an IFL file, you can expand on the concept and use more of its capabilities. An IFL file simply lists the files, in sequence, to be used. The bitmap references can contain explicit path names to any valid directory. Placing a number after the image name repeats the use of the image for that many frames. If the bitmap is an animated file, only the first frame is used. To use additional frames of an animated file, you need to split the animation to individual images and list them in the IFL file. In practice, most professional animators prefer using IFLs to other methods of animating bitmaps because of the control they afford.

Using Compound Material Types

Although the Standard material is unquestionably the most often used, several others are included with 3DS MAX that provide unique capabilities or ways of manipulating other material types as well. These materials are sometimes termed Compound materials and often begin elaborate Material trees. The most common situation is for Compound materials to branch to Standard materials, although they could be other compound materials as well. In this way, you can continue to branch Material definitions as you do with maps. Standard is the popular next step because these materials are primarily meant for combining the effects of other materials and have very few rendering properties of their own.

NOTE

Materials that rely on combining the effects of sub-materials (Top/Bottom, Blend, and Double Sided) need to maintain global characteristics. If the Face Map or Wire option is chosen within any sub-material, the others match that choice in the Compound material's result.

The Top/Bottom Material

The Top/Bottom material type enables you to assign two different materials to the top and bottom areas of an object. Which part of the object is considered "top" or "bottom" is dependent on either its orientation to the World coordinate's Z axis or the object's Local Coordinates.

NEW TO R2

A new option in Release 2 makes it possible to control whether World Coordinates or Local Coordinates are used for determining the top and bottom of a Top/Bottom material.

When the World Coordinates option is used, if a surface falls within the positive Z axis, it's assigned the Top material; and if a surface falls in the negative Z, it's assigned the Bottom material (see Figure 15.39). This means if the object assigned a Top/Bottom material changes its orientation relative to the World Z axis, the material assignments shift across the surface. Remember this situation when you're using Top/Bottom materials in an animation. If the object rotates, the location of the Top and Bottom assignments could shift across the object's surface.

When the Local Coordinates option is used, a Top/Bottom material behaves in the same way it does when World Coordinates are used except that the object's local positive Z axis overrides the World Coordinate's positive Z axis.

The definition of the top-to-bottom transition is further adjusted with the material's Position parameter. Position can be thought of as weight that pulls the definition down when set low and up when set high. In reality, the angle at which a face qualifies as facing up or down is being adjusted. The Blend parameter enables you to soften this transition.

The crocodile's mouth in Figure 15.40 is an example of where a Top/Bottom material works well. Normally, a mesh as complicated as a crocodile's mouth would make it difficult to select the separate areas within for separate Material IDs. Moreover, an obvious seam would occur between separate materials. With the Top/Bottom material, the top faces receive the inner flesh material and the lower faces get the scaly surface material. The transition between the materials is adjusted with a Blend value.

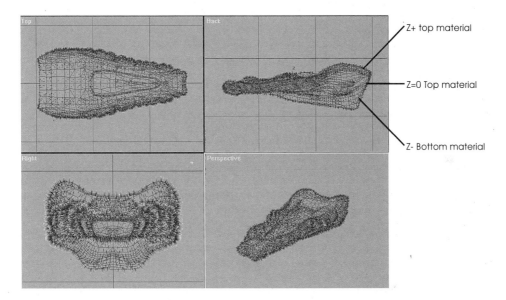

FIGURE 15.39

How the Top/Bottom material works. Based on the angle of the normal to the world Z, the face can receive either the top or bottom material.

FIGURE 15.40

Usage of the Top/Bottom material type. Notice how the two materials blend to produce a nice gum line transition.

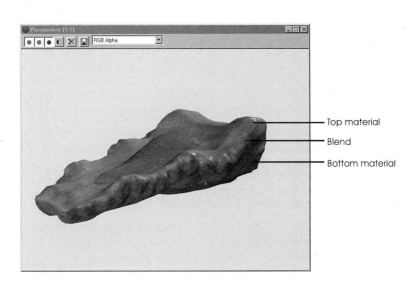

The Double Sided Material

A Double Sided material addresses the problem of wanting to assign a different material to either side of a surface. Normally, when you assign a material to an object, the material is applied to both sides of a surface. 3DS MAX renders the side with a positive face normal and ignores the backface unless 2-Sided is enabled. The Double Sided material enables you to assign one material to the surface having a positive face normal, and another material to the backface of the same surface. The material labels these directions as Facing and Back respectively. The Facing and Back materials channels can then branch to any other material type you want.

The Translucency value is used to blend the Facing and Back materials. If you have a Translucency setting of 0, the Double Sided material works as you might expect—one material on one side and the second material on the other side. Values between 0 and 50 mix one side with the other until they are the same at 50. Values greater than 50 mix the opposite side more and the effect is as if you switched the material assignments. This impression increases until a Translucency of 100 effectively flips the assignments.

Figure 15.41 demonstrates a simple example of a Double Sided material use. A line with several smoothed vertices is used with a Lathe modifier to construct a pot with a single surface. A red Diffuse material is used for the inside and a green Diffuse material is used for the outside. These could easily be substituted with more complicated materials, such as a bumpy baked glazed clay on the outside and a smooth pink painted inside.

The Blend Material

As its name implies, the Blend material allows you to blend two separate materials by a certain percentage. It also includes the capability to use a mask to control where the blend occurs and thus becomes a composite. The Blend material controls closely resemble those of the Mix Map type, and you should review that Map type's earlier description for more insight into Blend.

The Mix Amount value controls the percentage the two materials are blended. If a mask is referenced, the Mix Amount is grayed out and the blend is calculated by using the mask's intensity (as a mono-channel). The Mixing

Curve can be used to modulate the transition between the two materials (see the Mix Map type for more examples of these controls). A crocodile's skin in Figure 15.42 uses a Blend material to achieve its effect. The primary difference between the Blend material and the Mix Map is that Blend materials mix entire material definitions and not just map types. The Blend material mixes every parameter in the two material definitions whereas Mix affects only one channel within a material.

FIGURE 15.41

A Double Sided material type places two different materials on a lathed profile.

FIGURE 15.42

A crocodile's skin with two material types blended by a Noise Map type.

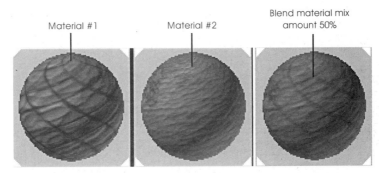

Material #1   Material #2   Blend material mix amount 50%

The Matte/Shadow Material

The Matte/Shadow material is 3DS MAX's most ironic and intriguing material type (see Figure 15.43). The irony is that the material doesn't render as a material; it essentially "cloaks" the surface it is assigned to. As the interface shows, there are no materials or maps to branch from. The Matte/Shadow material's sole purpose is its own special effect and is the only material from which you cannot branch. Within the Matte/Shadow is the capability to have the surface receive shadows and block other objects in the scene that might be behind it. The Matte/Shadow material becomes an essential technique for post-processing or compositing background images with scene objects.

FIGURE 15.43

The Matte/Shadow material type interface.

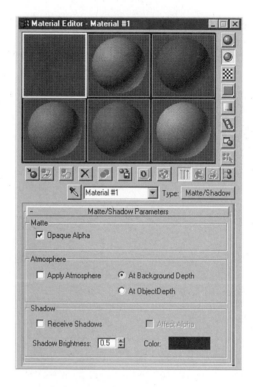

An object assigned a Matte/Shadow material becomes a "hole" in your scene that cuts out any geometry behind it and exposes the background beyond. This trait allows objects to be matched with elements of the background image.

The Opaque Alpha option controls whether the geometry assigned the Matte/Shadow material is included in the Renderer's alpha channel output. Leaving this box unchecked makes the objects invisible to the alpha channel, while enabling it includes the geometry's extents as being fully opaque. This option affects only the alpha channel; it has no impact on the rendered image itself.

The Atmosphere options integrate the matte object into atmospheric effects. If there is no atmosphere in the scene, these options have no effect. The At Background Depth option is used when rendering against background images and At Object Depth is used when rendering to files for future compositing.

The Matte/Shadow material gives considerable control for compositing, because shadows can be rendered without including the geometry that receives them. The Receive Shadows option enables this capability, and the accompanying Shadow Brightness controls the darkness of the cast shadow. Remember that control for casting shadows is an object property, and if you do not want your matte object to cast shadows, you must disable it from its Object Properties control. By turning off the Opaque Alpha toggle, the Affect Alpha is enabled. This toggle causes shadows cast on a matte material to be applied to the alpha channel. Higher values for Shadow Brightness make the resulting shadow more transparent. This can be helpful if you wish to render bitmaps with alpha channels, which can be composited at a later time.

The Multi/Sub-Object Material

The Multi/Sub-Object material type enables you to assign more than one material to the same object at the face level. In practice, a Multi/Sub-Object material is usually assigned to an entire object and contains as many materials as the object requires. The Multi/Sub-Object materials thus become fairly custom and are often unique for every object that requires them. Figure 15.44 demonstrates how a Multi/Sub-Object material works. Each part of a human body that might require a separate material can be given a separate ID corresponding to a separate sub-material.

FIGURE 15.44

The Multi/Sub-Object Basic Parameters roll-out.

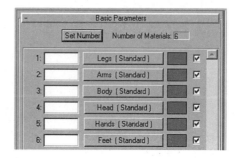

Editable Mesh is typically used to assign materials at the Sub-Object level, by selecting faces and assigning Material ID#s. The ID# corresponds to the Material # within the Multi/Sub-Object material. The multi-material begins with a default number of six materials but can be any number you want. An alternative method for assigning Material ID#s is to use a Volume Select modifier to select the faces and a Material modifier to assign the desired Material ID# to the selection. Because these are independent modifiers, the selection and even the assignment can be animated while the Mesh Select method is static.

Navigating a Multi/Sub-Object material can be challenging. To help in this regard, you are heavily encouraged to name every material so you know where you are in the Material tree. Because the small squares on the Material Editor samples are of little value in visualizing a given material's effect, turning off Show End Result is also recommended. This allows you to see the full material at each level.

Another option that can help you visualize a given material's effects is the Simple Multi-Display Below Top Level toggle in the Material Editor's Options dialog. Keeping the number of materials to a minimum makes navigation faster. If you only need two materials, use Set Number to change from the default number of six materials to two so you can make best use of the Go to Sibling option.

The Raytracer Material

The Raytracer material has several basic parameters that appear similar to the Standard material type, such as Ambient and Diffuse color swatches, the Shading model, 2-Sided, Wire, Face Map, and SuperSampling. It also has several different parameters such as Luminosity and Transparency; an

Index of Refraction; Shininess, Shininess Strength, and Specular color under Specular Highlights; and Map buttons for environment and bump as shown in Figure 15.45.

FIGURE 15.45

The Raytracer Material Type Basic Parameters rollout.

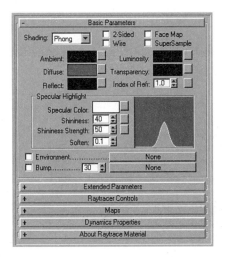

Special effects, dynamic properties, and a slew of new map channels all make it very obvious that a huge leap has been made from Release 1.2 to Release 2.0 of 3D Studio MAX. One of the most significant additions to the latest release is the Raytracer material and Raytracer Map type. Although using this material type usually requires far more additional rendering time, for those situations requiring highly accurate and realistic reflections and refractions, this material type can be well worth the additional waiting time.

To increase the speed of Raytraced materials, it is possible to exclude objects that are not essential in the resulting reflection or refraction of a material. The Raytracer map and Raytracer material have the same name because they use the same Raytracer and share global parameters.

Many of the controls in a Raytracer material create beautiful results using default settings, but in some cases, certain controls may behave differently (such as the appearance of colors deviating from the way they behave in Standard materials). The Raytracer material has a Reflect color swatch to control the amount of specular reflection of the material when its value and the value of the specular highlight are combined.

Similar to a Standard material, several of the color components have Map buttons to set their equivalent Map channels to Map types.

WARNING

Using SuperSampling with this material type can cause a significant increase in rendering time, so use it with caution.

Unlike a Standard material, the Ambient color swatch controls how much a material absorbs light. The Reflect color swatch controls how much diffuse can be seen. At a setting of 100 percent (pure white), the Diffuse color cannot be seen at all. The Material effects channels (which enable glow and other special effects) are treated by this Map type.

The Luminosity and Transparency swatches control the material's self-illumination capabilities and filter color. Unlike a Standard material though, the self-illumination is not dependent on the Diffuse color.

Index of Refraction Value

The Index of Refraction (IOR) setting regulates the refraction. Different substances in nature have different IOR values and using these values can help to create realistic refraction behaviors. Refraction caused by hot air appears very different than, say, refraction caused by water. Some examples of IOR values are summarized in Table 15.1.

TABLE 15.1

Index of Refraction Settings for Various Substances

Substance Causing Refraction	IOR Value
Air	1.0
Water	1.3
Glass	1.5 to 1.7
Diamond	2.5

These values stem from the manner in which light travels through materials and the way the human eye perceives them. Maps can be used to control this setting as well.

Raytracer Settings and Extended Parameters

The Specular highlights behave similarly to a Standard material, but the Shininess Strength value can be set extremely high for blindingly bright or tight highlights. The Soften value can also be set higher than 1.0 to achieve rubbery highlights. Also, you can set an Environment map to override the Global Environment map, which can reduce rendering times.

The Extended Parameters for Raytracer materials is shown in Figure 15.46. The Wireframe parameters behave the same as they do for a Standard material. Most of the special effects controls take some playtime to understand. The Extra Lighting swatch creates the effect of radiosity (ambient reflected light). Translucency enables you to create the illusion of backlit diffuse surfaces such as semi-transparent paper surfaces (such as vellum, rice paper, onionskin paper, and so on). Fluorescence and its bias slider can create the effect of materials under an ultraviolet lights or fluorescent paints using bias values higher than 0.5.

FIGURE 15.46

The Raytracer Material Type Extended Parameters rollout.

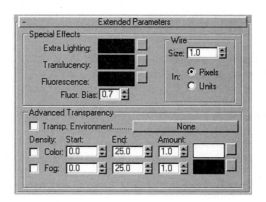

The Transparency Environment map enables Transparent objects to refract a specific environment map instead of the scene environment map. Density Color settings and Fog settings can create the effect of color and fog within a Transparent object. Like the Raytracer map's Attenuation Start and End controls, these densities are set in world units where Start is the center position of the object to which the material is applied.

Raytracer Controls

With the addition of two toggles to disable raytracing of reflections and refractions, and the addition of two Falloff sliders, the Raytracer controls operate much like the Raytracer Map. The Falloff sliders make it possible to dim out reflections or refractions to blackness at specified distances.

Much like the standard material, the Raytracer Material Maps rollout has Map buttons for mappable components of the Raytracer material.

The Raytracer Material versus Raytracer Map Type

There are some key differences between the Raytracer material and the Raytracer Map type.

- Raytracer Maps are used just as any other Map type. They can be added to any material.

- Raytracer Maps can be used in Map channels other than Reflections and Refraction (although these are the two Map channels they were designed for).

- Raytracer Maps have more extensive attenuation controls than Raytracer material.

- Raytracer Maps can render faster than Raytracer material.

Examining Material Pitfalls

Surfaces can be built correctly, illuminated well, follow all the rules of perspective, be rendered smoothly and flawlessly by 3DS MAX, and still look incorrect. You might see the effect yourself or it might be pointed out by a colleague—or worse—by a client. You can possibly work so much with a model and see its materials rendered so often that you become anesthetized to the effect the materials actually have. The reasons for a flawed effect are many; this section covers the most common and influential of them.

TIP

Artists often examine a work in progress by looking at it in a mirror (often a hand mirror over the shoulder). This trick of flipping the image can shock your visual senses and make you analyze the image with less bias.

Wrong Size—The Need for Scale

A very annoying effect is to have the incorrect scaling for a material that has a real-world size and proportion. Brick is a common example of this. Architects and builders know these proportions intuitively and base the size of details on the number of bricks required. If these sizes and proportions are off or are different for various areas of the model, the believability of the image or animation is shattered.

Wallpaper—The Need for Randomness

Because materials are used repeatedly throughout a model, their effects can be taken for granted and become ineffective. This result is the Wallpaper effect, in which the same pattern is repeated so often and so regularly that it reads as a tone instead of a texture. Most real-world materials that have a repeat to them do not do so with such regularity. Materials such as stone, tile, and brick have variation, and seeing a defined pattern destroys their believability. Applying them as basic tiled textures creates the effect of wallpaper and not, for example, brick.

To overcome the Wallpaper effect, materials need variation and require a bit of randomness. Traditionally, this has been done by using increasingly larger bitmaps, so the repeat isn't as often or not at all. The drawback for large bitmaps is the time taken to produce them and the RAM needed to use them. The capability to overlay maps to any depth, combine them at varying scales, and give them individual blur and (especially) noise is invaluable to giving surfaces the look of being individual and of having life. This can often be done with a small collection of good, tileable bitmaps.

Looking "Too" Good—The Need for Grime

If one quality appears in an image or animation that signals its computer-generated origins, it is that things tend to look too good to be real. Although somewhat humorous and possibly meant as a back-handed compliment, this criticism is very valid. Real-world objects have a life to them. They become scratched and stained, wear unevenly, or are not constructed perfectly to begin with. When materials meet, they tend to have a seam or gap and are rarely perfectly flush. Objects are rarely arranged in perfect order and doing so is viewed by many as obsessive. Yet these qualities are common to computer models and mapping.

If you are striving for true realism, you need to take the extra time to vary and give life to the materials. This extra effort is usually essential for high-resolution stills to be convincing. If you are rendering animations, you will often need to exaggerate these characteristics to make the same impact, just as they are exaggerated on stage and in film.

The key to simulating real-world materials is to represent their inconsistencies and faults. Objects are not perfectly smooth and completely clean in daily life. The best method for adding these elements of grit to your materials is to create a collection of tileable, random bitmaps that represent smears, streaks, dust, cracks, droplets, and stains. After these are created, use the same bitmaps throughout your "real-world" material library.

By designing effective maps, you can reuse them repeatedly in subtle ways without them seeming overused. When the same collection of randomizing maps is used for materials, the memory costs are not overly prohibitive because you pay in RAM for them only once. These random maps can be used to modulate nearly every Map type but are especially effective with Mask, Mix, and Composite Map types for textures, Shine, Bump, Opacity, and Reflection. Creating truly realistic materials is not easy, but then again, neither is painting them.

Jaggies—The Need for Blur

When does a material's bitmap need more Blur? This call is subjective and needs to be made by seeing the material's effect within the scene. If the bitmap is scintillating or showing irregular edges, increase its Blur. If it needs less definition, increase its Blur Offset. If it is creating moiré patterns, switch to summed area filtering.

Blur is not magical and cannot make an aliased source image anti-aliased. Blur can correct only the aliasing of the bitmap as it converges in perspective. If the bitmap is inherently jaggy, you need to smooth it with a paint program before assigning it. The quality of your map's effect improves as the bitmap's scale of detail, in pixel width, increases. Details that are six pixels wide create a much crisper Edge, and especially a Bump, effect than that created by one pixel-wide lines.

In Practice: Map Channels, Map Types, and More Material Types

- **Material Development:** How much time do you have to develop materials for the project as a percentage of the overtime time investment of the project?

- **Camera Time:** How much time will this material be seen in front of the camera and how close?

- **Material Types versus Map Types:** What kind of material type will create the effects you want with the least amount of maps? What types of maps will do the same?

- **Object Reflection and Refraction:** Does the object reflect or refract the scene around it? If so, is the entire scene required in that reflection or refraction or can certain objects be excluded from the materials' calculations?

- **Raytracer Maps:** If reflection or refraction is required, will the Reflect/Refract map type suffice or is the Raytracer Map type required? If raytracing is required, are certain objects far away from the reflecting object trivial?

- **Double Sided Materials:** Do you need to see both sides of a mesh, and if so, will the Double Sided material type be more effective than using the 2-Sided option of a material?

Chapter 16

MAPPING FOR MATERIALS

The believability of materials is always at the mercy of the geometry they are applied to and the effectiveness of the Mapping model used. Mapping is all about asking how a material should be "wrapped about" or "painted onto" geometry. If you were to apply a fantastically detailed jeans fabric material to a box, no one would believe they were real jeans.

The final effect of all Mapped materials is dependent on the Mapping coordinates assigned to the surface. Mapping coordinates can be assigned in a number of ways, through numerous projections, with the optimal choice depending on the object's geometry and desired surface effect. This chapter will cover the following topics related to mapping:

- UVW Mapping coordinate space and how it relates to maps
- Using the UVW Mapping modifier and material parameters to control mapping
- Techniques for Planar, Cylindrical, Spherical, Shrink Wrap, Box, and Face mapping
- Defining accurate mapping that is free of distortion and relates to real-world scale
- Mapping strategies for geometry

Mapping Coordinates

The challenge of predicting the placement and result of Mapping coordinates has essentially been eliminated in 3D Studio MAX because you can view the resulting bitmap in the interactive viewport.

When adjusting an assigned material that uses a bitmap or 2D procedural texture, you can display it within smooth shaded viewports by clicking the Show Map in Viewport button when in the Map type's controls. By showing the map in the viewport, you can accurately position exactly where your mapping is to occur. This chapter assumes you will be using this extremely valuable feature whenever you are adjusting mapping.

A few corners are cut to achieve the interactive speed of Viewport Mapping adjustment. When you view bitmaps in perspective viewports, the tiling of the map is distorted, as shown in Figure 16.1, because bitmap sampling and correction do not occur as they do with the production renderer. If viewing your textures in perspective is important, you can enable the viewport's Texture Correction option and take a decrease in performance. In practice, you may want to toggle this option on and off for a check because leaving it on slows down the viewport considerably.

NOTE

Texture correction is not an issue when using Glint-based graphics cards or other hardware accelerators that support texture correction in their HEIDI drivers. For these cards, texture correction is a property of the chip set and is provided without penalty at all times. Texture correction is not an option when using these HEIDI drivers; it's always active.

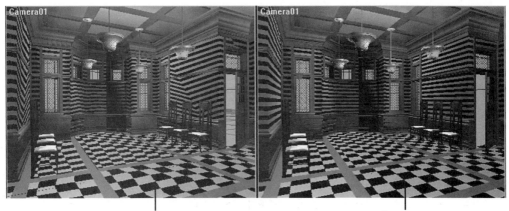

No texture correction | With texture correction

FIGURE 16.1

The same scene with and without texture correction enabled.

TIP

If you prefer to work with displayed textures, you will have the best performance using an accelerator board with texture support. Boards based on the new family of 3D-Labs Glint-TX and Permedia chips have proven to give extremely good performance value.

UVW Coordinate Space

Although the world and the objects within it are described in X, Y, and Z coordinates, bitmaps and mapping are described in U, V, and W coordinates to differentiate bitmap from geometric space, because the two are often very different. Geometric XYZ coordinates refer to exact locations in world or object space. Bitmap UVW coordinates represent proportions of the referenced bitmap. With UVW, you are always counting in increments of the bitmap, not referring to explicit sizes. Although the labeling may be a bit foreign, the concepts are simple (see Figure 16.2).

As Figure 16.2 shows, U and V represent a width or height unit in relation to the bitmap. The U and V axes cross in the bitmap's center to define the UV origin for the map. The origin is the point about which the map rotates when the Angle value of the Bitmap Map type is adjusted.

FIGURE 16.2

UV coordinate system for 2D bitmaps.

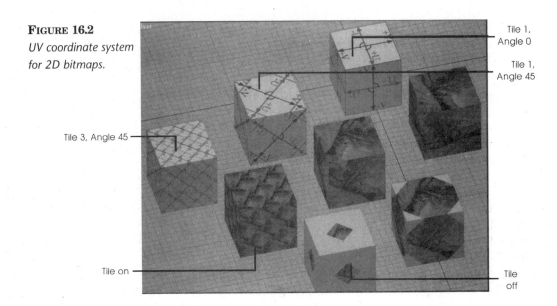

Tile 1, Angle 0

Tile 1, Angle 45

Tile 3, Angle 45

Tile on

Tile off

The W space changes the mapping projection 90 degrees to the side. As it switches, the side may be rotated 90 degrees from where you might expect it. The W space direction is used only if the material's Map type actually calls for it. Although intended primarily for the 3D Procedural maps (such as Wood and Marble), the W space can also affect the Bitmap Map type if you switch from UV projection (see Figure 16.3).

Parametric Mapping

Mapping coordinates can be applied either parametrically or in the Edit history pipeline with a UVW Mapping modifier. Parametric mapping is assigned as part of the object's creation parameters or the modifier that generated the faces and is usually enabled by a Generate Mapping Coordinates checkbox within the object definition or modifier. Parametric mapping can be found in the 3D primitives, loft objects, and with the Extrude, Lathe, and Bevel modifiers. None of these methods, except lofting, gives direct control over the resulting repeat of the rendered map (a characteristic known as tiling). Instead, the mapping usually has a tile of 1.0 in both directions.

FIGURE 16.3

The effects of changing from UV mapping to UW and WU.

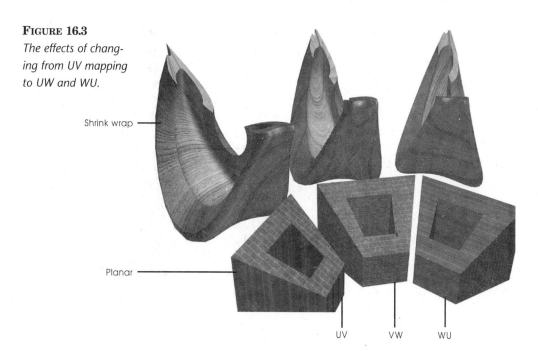

Shrink wrap

Planar

UV   VW   WU

NOTE

Mapping coordinates are not applied by default because they use extra RAM. Each face uses at least 12 bytes when it is mapped. Considering the fact that you can return in the Edit history and turn mapping on at a later date, you should leave it off unless you know the object is going to receive custom Mapping coordinates. You should also consider whether you want the Parametric mapping when collapsing a stack.

Because most Parametric mapping is applied with a 1×1 tile, you need to adjust the tiling for most materials you assign. Because you cannot adjust the Parametric coordinates (except for Loft objects), you need to do this with the Tiling controls present in the material. Figure 16.4 shows the result of Parametric mapping after the tiling is adjusted within the Material parameters.

When mapping is generated parametrically, you can adjust tiling and orientation only through the parameters of the material assigned to the surface. Alternatively, when you apply mapping with the UVW Mapping modifier, you have independent control over the mapping's projection, placement, orientation, and tiling. Mapping via a modifier, however, may not be as convenient as the Parametric mapping applied at creation.

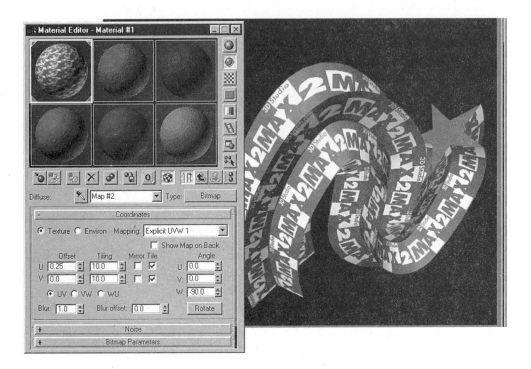

FIGURE 16.4

Adjusting the tiling of Parametric mapping with Material parameters.

NEW TO R2

New to R2 is the UVW Unwrap Modifier, which gives you better control over mapping on non-parametric surfaces. Unwrap lets you see the map and adjust the map vertices to change the way the texture is painted on the geometry.

The UVW Mapping Modifier

When Parametric mapping is not appropriate or no longer available, you need to assign Mapping coordinates manually with the UVW Mapping modifier (see Figure 16.5). UVW Mapping modifiers can be placed at any point in the stack, so the time when you apply the coordinates can be carefully controlled.

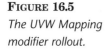

FIGURE 16.5

The UVW Mapping modifier rollout.

Like most 3DS MAX modifiers, the UVW Mapping modifier affects whatever is passed to it in the Edit History stack. If the active selection is Sub-Object faces or patches, mapping is assigned to only the Sub-Object selection of faces or patches. If the active selection is Sub-Object vertices or edges, the selection is ignored and the entire object is mapped instead.

This capability to map independent Sub-Object selections enables you to mix Mapping projection types and place mapping at numerous places within the same object, as shown in Figure 16.6. The stage for applying Mapping coordinates, however, is often at the end of modeling. If you model an object after applying mapping, the coordinates move with the vertices, stretch, and no longer produce even bitmaps. Mapping, therefore, is often one of the last things you do to a model.

One cylindrical UV projection   Five cylindrical UV projections

FIGURE 16.6

Sub-Object selections defining local Mapping coordinates.

When modeling is finished, you will often want to collapse the Modifier stack (unless you intend to animate the modeling operations, of course). The assignment of numerous Sub-Object Mapping coordinates usually works in conjunction with an equal number of EditMesh, MeshSelect, or EditPatch modifiers. These Edit modifiers define the face or patch selection that is being mapped by the subsequent UVW Map. Because of the expense associated with Edit modifiers, you may want to collapse the stack after applying several UVW modifiers as a way to eliminate their overhead.

Replacing EditMesh selections with Volume selections or MeshSelect modifiers is an alternative that requires very little overhead. Combining Volume Select modifiers with UVW Mapping provides an efficient mapping assignment that enables you to edit the selection and change what is mapped quite easily.

The capability to assign mapping at the Sub-Object level is very important in maintaining the surface properties of the object. Smoothing on faces and continuity on patches cannot occur if the surfaces are not part of the same, welded surface. Sub-Object selection mapping enables you to place mapping exactly where it needs to be without affecting the topology.

Adjusting Bitmap Size and Placement

The placement of a material's map is dependent on the surface's Mapping coordinates and the material's Mapping parameters. As it turns out, nearly everything you can adjust within the material can also be controlled within the UVW modifier. These general methods of adjustment, therefore, are discussed together. In short, you usually have the following options when changing the way a Mapped material appears on a surface:

- Adjust the Map type's Material parameters.

- Adjust the UVW modifier's Project type and parameters.

- Adjust the UVW modifier Gizmo's position, orientation, and scale.

- Adjust Creation parameters for Parametric mapping that allows for adjustment.

- Using Unwrap UVW modifier and positioning the UVW Map vertices.

The Bitmap Map type is the most commonly used of all Map types. It includes a wide range of options that most of the other map types (such as Checker) implement as well. Bitmap is the Map type this chapter uses as the example Map type for explaining mapping in general because it is so common and is easy to relate to.

For the sake of discussion, Planar mapping will also be used as the example UVW Modifier method for comparison to Bitmap Map type parameters (see Figure 16.7). When using Planar mapping and a tiling of one, the Mapping Gizmo essentially is your bitmap.

Gizmo Scale and Material Tiling Parameters

The Mapping Gizmo for the UVW modifier defines the extents to which a material's bitmap reaches. As you scale the Gizmo, the rendered bitmap uses those coordinates scales as well. As an alternative to scaling the Gizmo, you can control repeats through Material Tiling parameters. The Default tiling is one, which leaves the bitmap matching the extents of the Planar Gizmo. A tile means a single repeat, so increasing the value to three repeats the bitmap three times within the Planar Mapping Gizmo.

FIGURE 16.7

The Mapping controls present in the Material editor's Bitmap Map type.

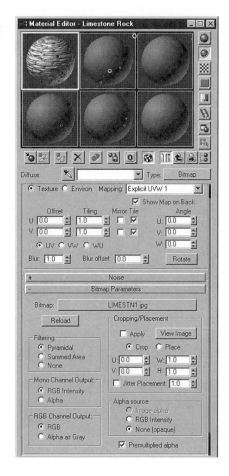

The Tiling values are analogous, in effect, to X and Y Scale parameters for a Planar Mapping Gizmo. This is because a tiling of two is the same as scaling the Gizmo by one-half.

TIP

To truly mirror a bitmap about either of its axes, enter a negative scale factor. For example, a V scale factor of –1.0 mirrors the map upside down.

When a material's Tile parameter is not checked, the bitmap does not tile along the given axis. Turning Tile off for both axes leaves a single imprint of the bitmap—what other programs refer to as a "decal." The location of the tile depends on where it is defined. As Figure 16.8 shows, materials always measure from the center of the bitmap, whereas the UVW Mapping modifier measures from the lower-left corner.

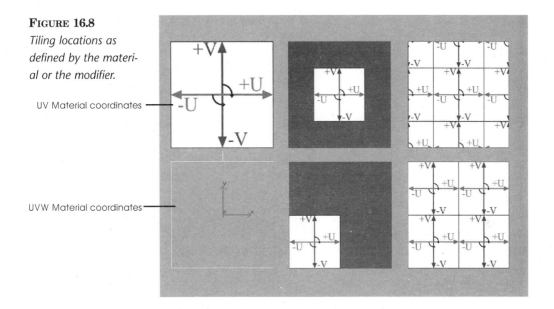

With tile off, and tiling greater than one, the resulting bitmap "shrinks" from the Gizmo's edges. If the tile is defined in the bitmap, it gets smaller about the Gizmo's center, with the bitmap's center always coincident with the Gizmo's center. If the tiling is defined by the UVW Mapping modifier, the bitmap gets smaller about the lower left-hand corner, with the bitmap's corner always matching the Gizmo's corner. Mixing the two methods produces a multiplied effect on the size, with the bitmap positioned closest to the origin giving the greatest tiling value.

Gizmo Position and Material Offset Parameters

The position of your material's bitmap is dictated primarily by the location of the UVW Map modifier's Mapping Gizmo. As an alternative to moving the Gizmo, the U and V Offset parameters of the material "move" the bitmap along the respective X and Y axes of the Gizmo (see Figure 16.9).

Keep in mind that Offset is *not* expressed in distance, but rather in units of the bitmap. The Offset value corresponds to the original bitmap size. When the Tiling value is 1.0, an Offset of 1.0 moves the bitmap a distance of one bitmap length to the side. When Tiling is 4.0 and the Offset is 1.0, the center of the moved bitmap remains where it was previously, but because the bitmap is smaller the map appears to have moved four times farther than when the tiling was 1.0. Although this Offset appears to be four times farther in relation to the current Map size, in actuality, the Offset is the same distance as measured before the map was scaled down with the Tiling parameter.

FIGURE 16.9

Placing bitmaps with Offset.

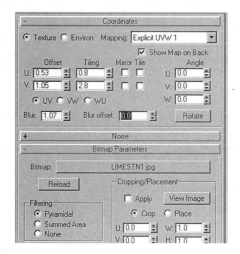

Offset parameters are primarily used when you need to position the bitmap but either do not want to move the Mapping Gizmo or do not have a Gizmo to move because the mapping is procedural. You may also find that you have far finer control in adjusting Offset parameters than you do in moving the Mapping Gizmo. It is also a good choice when you have to use a material on several different objects in the scene and do not want to adjust all their individual Mapping Coordinate Gizmos.

Gizmo Rotation and Material Angle Parameters

The angle of your material's bitmap is initially controlled by the angle of the Mapping Gizmo to the surface. The Angle parameter of the Bitmap Map type can also be used to rotate the mapping without affecting the Gizmo. Figure 16.10 shows how using the Rotation parameters can be very important for Projection methods where rotating the Gizmo dramatically changes the Project type and/or exposes points of singularity and swirling (such as cylindrical or spherical).

The Angle parameter rotates the bitmap about its center, with positive values rotating clockwise and negative values counterclockwise. The Angle parameter has limits at 360 degrees or –360 degrees, so animating beyond those limits must be done in coordination with the Gizmo.

FIGURE 16.10

Rotating Mapping projections with the Angle parameter.

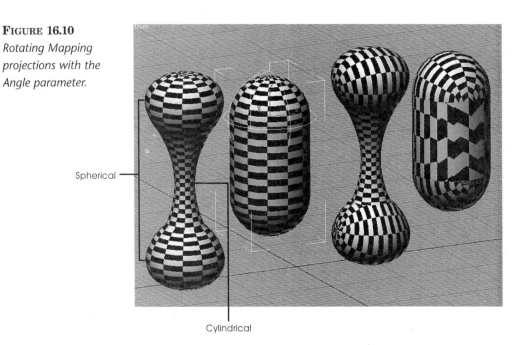

Spherical

Cylindrical

Mirror and Flip Options

Mirror and Flip are Scaling methods in the Material parameters and UVW modifier, respectively. The Mirror option found in Material Map types does not do what a Mirror transform does. For materials, mirroring is a combination of tiling and rotation. When mirroring is chosen, the map is scaled down by 50 percent and mirrored about the axes so that there are two bitmaps where there used to be one. If both the U and W axes are mirrored, there will be four bitmaps. The mirrored bitmap is scaled downward so that it fits the same Mapping Gizmo extents as a material not using the Mirror option. After being reduced in size, the bitmap tiles with this new bitmap image (see Figure 16.11).

If you want the material bitmap to mirror along only one axis, you will most likely want to double the tiling of the non-mirroring axis to compensate for the halved size. Mirroring is a method to make bitmaps appear to tile seamlessly when they do not. Some applications, such as Floor tile, Marble panels, and Wood veneer, make good use of a seamed, mirrored pattern.

The UVW modifier's Flip option is actually a negative scale in disguise and is somewhat similar to the material Mirror option. Performing a negative tile within the UVW Mapping modifier moves the resulting bitmap location because the origin for the modifier is in the corner. The Flip option performs a negative tile about the bitmap's center so the result is not displaced. Materials do not have a Flip option because the bitmap's center is the origin for materials, and a negative scale does not move the bitmap. For a material, a –1.0 Tile parameter is the equivalent to using the Flip option in the UVW Mapping modifier.

FIGURE 16.11

Using Mirror to tile bitmaps.

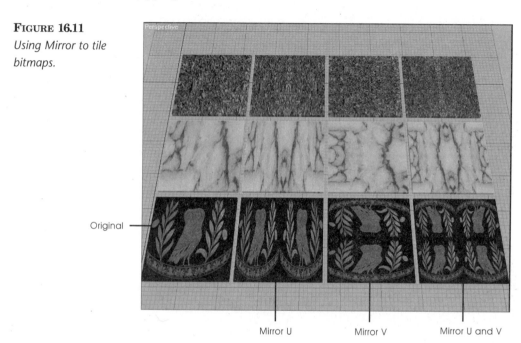

Original

Mirror U   Mirror V   Mirror U and V

To summarize, Table 16.1 relates the options available with the UVW Mapping modifier and their equivalents as Material parameters.

TABLE 16.1

Options Available for Adjusting Bitmap Size and Placement

Mapping Gizmo	Material Parameters
Move transform	Offset parameters
Rotation transform	Angle parameter
Scale transform	Tiling parameters
Tiling parameters (about lower-left Gizmo corner)	Tiling parameters (about Gizmo center)
Not applicable	Mirror option
Flip option	Tiling value of –1.0

Aligning Mapping Gizmos

The UVW Mapping modifier includes several functions to aid in aligning the Gizmo to the object quickly. These are all grouped in the Alignment section of the modifier, as shown in Figure 16.12. The various functions you see in the figure are discussed in the following sections.

FIGURE 16.12

The Alignment options for UVW Mapping.

Fit Function

The Fit function centers the Gizmo at the center of the Active selection and scales the Gizmo to match the selection's extents. The Gizmo is scaled to the extents seen by its Local coordinate system. You can orient your Gizmo as you wish and the Fit function scales the Gizmo appropriately. Fit should not be used when you have established a relationship to a bitmap's proportion (whether through Gizmo scale or tiling) because this action changes the tiling proportions. The Fit function can be undone so you can experiment with the results.

Center Function

The Center function preserves the Gizmo's orientation and scale and moves its center to that of the Active selection. The Center function is safe to use with precisely scaled Gizmos because it does not affect the resulting tiling.

Bitmap Fit Function

The Bitmap Fit function examines the proportions of a chosen bitmap and scales the Gizmo's horizontal dimension to match the bitmap's height-to-width ratio. This is important if you are using a company logo that should not be distorted as a bitmap.

Normal Align Function

The Normal Align function is extremely useful for aligning the Gizmo so that its Z axis is perpendicular to a selected face. The face or patch must be part of an object that is currently selected, although the specific face or patch does not need to be selected. The Normal Align function positions the Gizmo without affecting its scale, so it is safe to use with a Gizmo that matches a given bitmap's proportion. The following is one method of aligning the mapping Gizmo to a view, assuming that there is a face perpendicular to the view:

1. Click on Normal Align to place it in its (green) selection state.

2. Left-click and hold on the desired face or patch within the object.

3. While pressing the left mouse button, drag to move the Gizmo and align to other faces until the correct one is selected.

View Align Function

The View Align function reorients the Mapping icon to face the viewport without changing its size.

Region Fit Function

The Region Fit function enables you to define the region of the Mapping icon by dragging in the viewports without affecting the icon's orientation.

Reset Function

The Reset function is the same as deleting and reapplying the modifier. It centers the Gizmo on the selection with the Default orientation and scale. The Reset function should be used only if you want to start from scratch.

Acquiring Mapping Coordinates

The UVW modifier's Acquire function enables you to copy the mapping from an object that has already been assigned a UVW Map modifier or even a Displace modifier. The Acquire function works by taking the last UVW Mapping or Displace modifier it finds in the selected object's stack. You are then presented with the dialog. You can choose whether you want the mapping to be acquired absolutely or relatively.

Both options duplicate the Mapping type, Tiling and Flip options, and Gizmo scale. Choosing Absolute moves the Mapping Gizmo to the exact same location and orientation as the Target object, which is required when you need to match mapping between objects. Absolute should be chosen even if you intend to rotate the Mapping Gizmo because it ensures the alignment of the non-rotated axis. Choosing Relative keeps the target Gizmo exactly where it is, while copying the mapping Gizmo's orientation, scale, and offset. In reality, the transform from the chosen object's Gizmo is being copied to the selected object.

WARNING

Acquiring a Mapping Gizmo cannot be undone. It is prudent to save your file, perform a Hold, or clone the object as a backup before using the Acquire function.

Often you need to acquire the mapping from another UVW modifier applied within the same object. To do so, a few extra steps are needed because this operation is not directly possible with the Acquire function. The most straightforward method is to clone the object to the side and ensure the desired UVW Mapping modifier is the last UVW map in the stack. You can then use Acquire to match the Gizmos.

This cloning method, however, may not be practical if your object is extremely large because of the time it may take to perform the clone. As an alternative, enter Track View and copy the Position, Rotation, and Scale values from the desired Gizmo's tracks to the new Gizmo's tracks. This action is what happens when you acquire mapping absolutely (except Acquire copies all the parameters of the modifier and not just the transform).

TIP

A useful method for keeping mapping information in conjunction with the material is to assign the material and mapping to an object (for example, a box) and name it the material's name. Save the box in a separate file and merge it in when you want the particular material. The material can be taken from the scene by the Material editor and the mapping can be acquired by the UVW modifier. Other boxes representing other materials can be created and saved as well; you are on your way to creating an "acquirable Material library," which contains objects that can be merged into any model when needed.

Mapping Projection Types

The UVW modifier provides several methods to project Mapping coordinates onto the surface of your object. The best projection method and technique depend on both the object's geometry and tiling characteristics of the bitmaps. The six methods available for manually assigning the Mapping projection are

- Planar
- Cylindrical
- Spherical
- Shrink Wrap
- Box
- Face

The important concept to understand is that the Mapping Gizmo is the exact size and placement of your bitmap, regardless of its size or proportions. This is always the situation when both the UVW Map modifier and the assigned material have 1.0 Tiling and 0.0 Offset settings. Different settings for Tiling and Offset change this initial placement as described previously. Figure 16.13 shows how each of the first five different projection Gizmos contain visual cues to indicate which way is up and facing you.

FIGURE 16.13

The Gizmo representations of the first five projections.

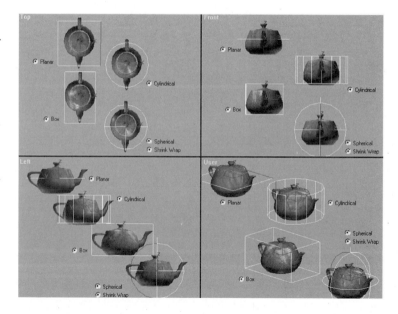

The Gizmo's small vertical line, or tick mark, indicates which way is up. The Planar Gizmo's green line is always the bitmap's right-hand side. The Cylindrical Gizmo's green vertical line indicates the seam at which the right and left sides of the bitmap label meet. Similarly, the Spherical Gizmo has a green arc that indicates the bitmap's seam edge. The Shrink Wrap Gizmo is identical to the Spherical Gizmo, but the green arc does not indicate a seam because the only seam is on the bottom, opposite the vertical line. The Box Gizmo has no indications because it is actually based on face normals that produce a seam at every abrupt surface transition. The Face option enables you to assign face mapping using the UVW Map modifier. This is identical to the Material Editor face mapping function that lets you assign face mapping to a selection of faces. The Unwrap UVW modifier (to be discussed later) makes it possible to edit this type of mapping.

Mapping coordinates project onto a surface as directed by their Mapping Gizmo. Mapping coordinates that strike the surface at 90 degrees produce bitmaps that are undistorted. As the angle of approach changes, the pixels become stretched. When this angle reaches 180 or 0 degrees, the surface is on edge to the projection and results in pixels streaking across the surface. To correct the streaking, the Gizmo must be oriented so it strikes the surface at an angle that is greater than 0 degrees.

The UVW modifier is infinite in its mapping projections, with Mapping coordinates being applied through whatever faces are currently selected in the stack.

Planar Mapping

Mapping is most easily understood with the Planar projection, usually the most commonly used Projection method. With Planar projection, the rectangular Gizmo represents the exact extents of your bitmap. As you change the shape of the Gizmo, you stretch the picture. Planar mapping is projected infinitely through the object, as shown in Figure 16.14. No matter how close the icon is to the mesh, only the icon's size and angle to the mesh matter.

Because the bitmap stretches to fit the Mapping coordinates, the Gizmo needs to be the same proportions as your bitmap if you want the result to be undistorted. The Bitmap Fit function shown in Figure 16.15 makes this task easy. Clicking Bitmap Fit enables you to select a bitmap to establish a new Gizmo width. The existing Gizmo height remains constant regardless of the bitmap's proportion.

FIGURE 16.14

Planar mapping projection.

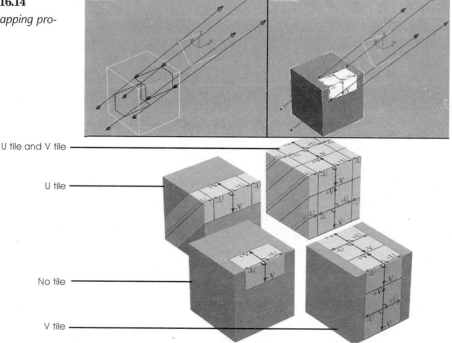

U tile and V tile

U tile

No tile

V tile

Often you know the exact size your bitmap represents and need to match the mapping Gizmo's size to it. For example, if you have a bitmap of an array of bricks and you know the actual size in real-world units of each brick, you can create an object that represents the real size of the brick array and use Bitmap Fit to scale the Gizmo to fit the object boundaries. Unfortunately, there is no clean way to make this match. You can match this size by creating a temporary object of that exact size first, as summarized in the following steps:

1. Establish the real-world size the bitmap represents.

2. Create a Rectangle spline of that size. Remember that keyboard entry can be fast if you don't mind the object appearing at the origin.

3. Assign the Rectangle a UVW modifier. The spline is automatically meshed by the applying the modifier.

4. Click Fit. The UVW Mapping Gizmo snaps to the rectangle's extents.

5. Return to the primary object having a UVW Map modifier and use the Acquire function to retrieve the properly scaled Gizmo. With the Gizmo properly scaled, you can position and rotate it as needed and even use the Center or Normal Align functions.

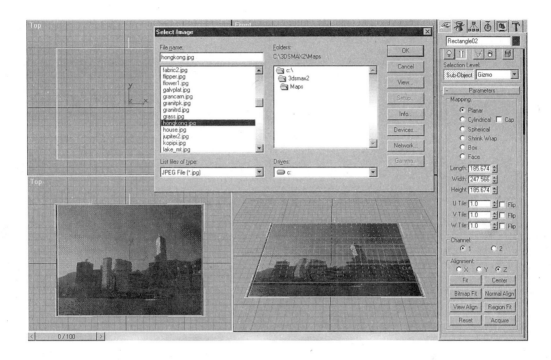

FIGURE 16.15

Using Bitmap Fit to scale the Gizmo's proportions to match a selected bitmap.

For the most accurate adjustment of Mapping coordinates, you need to use Track View because Transform Type-In reports only relative scale information, and when you are matching sizes, you need to control exact sizes. After adding a key for the UVW Mapping Gizmo scale, you can right-click the key to produce the Key Info, giving you an accurate report of the current Gizmo scale, with 100 percent equaling two inches. You can adjust the Scale value, divide by 50, and know the exact size (in inches) of your Mapping Gizmo.

NEW TO R2

Check out the new Map Scalar space warp in release 2. This tool enables you to scale an object without scaling its applied Mapping coordinates once the Mapping coordinates have been matched correctly in size.

When your object is based on a spline that is the result of an Extrude, Bevel, or Lathe, determining the correct scale becomes a bit trickier. All these Creation methods establish mapping, but they do so as a 1×1 repeat across the entire length and height. To be accurate in real-world units, you need to increase the material's tiling to be in accordance with the defining spline's perimeter. Unfortunately, a direct method does not exist to determine the perimeter length of a spline. You can perform the following steps to work around this and determine the perimeter length:

1. With the Perimeter object selected, turn off the Extrude, Bevel, or Lathe and subsequent modifiers leaving only the defining spline visible.

2. Create a loft from another spline shape.

3. With the Instance option active, click Get Path and select the Perimeter object. You now have a loft object using the Perimeter object as its path.

4. Type 100 for the Path percent and then switch from Percentage to Distance.

The perimeter distance of the path is given in the Path field. If you wish, you can delete this temporary Loft object or use it to trace where points lie on the path in distance or percentage of length. You can also modify the path spline and see the resulting length update. With the spline's perimeter distance known, you can divide this distance by the U axis length of the real-world bitmap to discover the tiling required, as shown in Figure 16.16.

Techniques for Planar Mapping

It is common to think of Planar mapping being applied square, or normal, to a surface. Although this application produces undistorted mapping, it is not often the most convenient approach. Few objects are coplanar and most turn corners that require matching coordinates on adjacent sides as well. For example, a brick wall that turns a corner needs perfectly aligned grout lines. For rectilinear geometry, which includes most structures, a few options exist:

- Select the faces with MeshSelect or EditMesh and assign them their own UVW Mapping modifier. Match the original mapping Gizmo's position, size, and orientation and then rotate it 90 degrees.

- Select the faces with EditMesh or EditableMesh and assign them separate Material IDs. Make the current material a multi-material, change the mapping from UV to VW and the angle to 90.

- Rotate the mapping Gizmo 45 degrees.

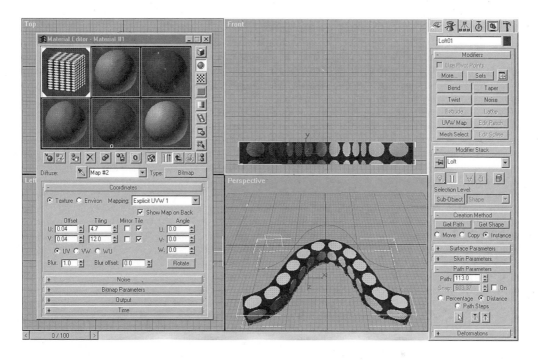

FIGURE 16.16

Using Map tiling to correct for an extruded length.

The problem with the first option is that keeping the different Gizmos in alignment with each other through future adjustments can be troublesome. You may, in fact, want to use expressions for such control. The second option is elegant but works only if the object is truly rectilinear. The last option is fast, has no overhead, and is applicable to the majority of situations. All three options assume that the Gizmo is of the correct proportions for the desired bitmap (that is, a Bitmap Fit operation has been performed).

The key to correctly angle Planar mapping is to ensure an equal angle of the Mapping icon to each side of the mesh. If the object has inconsistent corners, such as a hexagon or octagon, you need to apply separate coordinates to adjacent pairs of faces. In this case, you need to make Sub-Object face selections and apply separate UVW Mapping modifiers. A hexagon or octagon can be correctly mapped with two projections, while a 10- or 12-sided polygon would require three.

When applying mapping at an angle, you want the mapping projection to be even to each side receiving the mapping; the Gizmo's angle of approach must be similar to all faces. As the mapping Gizmo's angle alters from being 90 degrees, however, the projected image begins to stretch. The stretching can be corrected by adjusting the mapping along the stretched axis in one of three ways: scaling the mapping Gizmo, adjusting the UVW Mapping's tiling, or adjusting the materials' bitmap tiling. Whichever method you choose, you should use it consistently to make future editing an easier and clearer process.

Of all the methods, scaling the Gizmo is the least accurate and most difficult to adjust. The Material tiling is a good choice only if the material is always being applied at the angle it is being scaled to correct. In most cases, working with the UVW modifier's tiling makes the most sense because the modifier is relevant to the projection and can be acquired by other Mapping modifiers needing similar values. Figure 16.17 shows how this is accomplished with Tiling values.

FIGURE 16.17

Correcting for Planar distortion from angled projections.

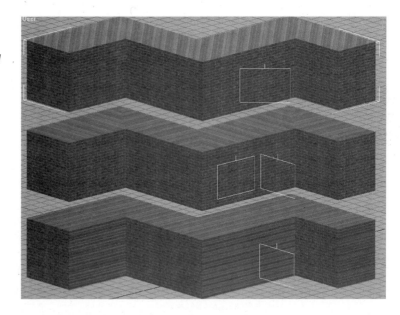

To correct for stretched mapping, you need to increase the Map tiling. The amount of the increase depends on the angle of the surface to the mapping Gizmo. For 90 degree (right) angles, the correction is a tiling of 1.414, the square root of two; this is a very good number to remember because correcting for square corners is so common. The correcting ratio can be gathered from either the approach or included angle:

Tiling Ratio=1 / Sine (Gizmo's angle of approach)

Or

Tiling Ratio=1 / Cosine (Gizmo's included angle of approach)

Figure 16.19 shows calculating this ratio in practice. Note that the Gizmo's angle of approach is half the corner's angle. If your Gizmo is at an even angle to the corner, the correcting ratio can be derived from the corner's angle, using the following formula:

Tiling Ratio = 1 / Sine (0.5×corner angle)

NOTE

Don't be scared by these formulas—they're *all* the same. It's just easier for some people to relate to one method over another. A little math goes a long way and the correcting ratio of 1.414 can be memorized to work for all rectilinear mappings.

Although an oblique planar projection can be corrected once for any surface, it cannot be corrected a second time. Figure 16.18 shows how rotating the mapping Gizmo a second time produces angled mapping on all surfaces. This application may be suitable if your bitmap is quite random and tileable, also shown in Figure 16.18. If you are after the latter effect, you may be better off with Box mapping.

FIGURE 16.18

Correcting for Planar distortion from angled projections.

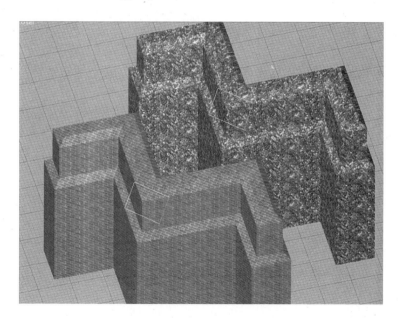

Cylindrical Mapping

Cylindrical mapping projects its coordinate from the Gizmo center outward to infinity, much like the ripples in a pond, as shown in Figure 16.19. The height of the Gizmo cylinder dictates the size of the bitmap's height or, rather, V dimension. Because of this situation, the Gizmo's radius is not important; only the location of its center matters. You can think of the cylinder as being a visual aid for determining the height, center, top, seam, and whether it has been non-uniformly scaled.

FIGURE 16.19

Cylindrical mapping projection.

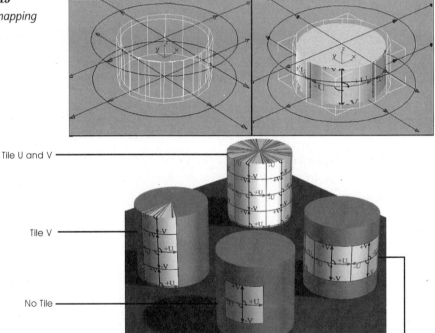

The icon's back, green edge indicates where the bitmap's edges meet; a seam appears when rendering if the material's bitmap is not tileable in its U direction. The back seam is also the initial tiling location. When working with tiled decals, the seam becomes the bitmap's lefthand side.

Traditionally, surfaces that are parallel to a cylindrical projection experience swirls or streaks, as shown in Figure 16.20. Because such streaks and swirls are rarely desirable, the production renderer treats such a situation as a special case and takes the first pixel found for the top as the cap's entire color. Because this correction is not shown in the interactive renderer, it can be confusing. Instead of accepting the correction, if you want to retain the spiraling effects shown in the viewport, you can either move one of the defining vertices a small increment or rotate the mapping Gizmo bay a small amount (0.03 degrees or more should do it).

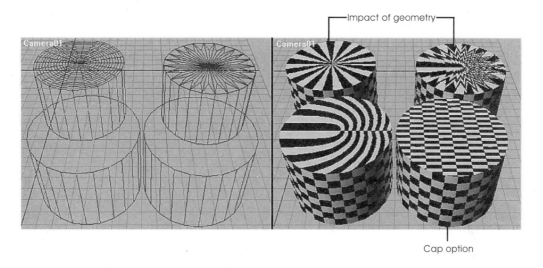

FIGURE 16.20

Cap conditions of Cylindrical mapping.

The Cylindrical Mapping Cap option applies Planar mapping to the top and bottom of the cylindrical projection. This application is similar to what Box mapping does. The qualifying angle for being a "cap," however, is much more shallow than the qualifying angle for being a Box mapping's side, with faces becoming planar mapped as they approach 20 to 25 degrees from the horizontal plane.

An interesting trait of the cylindrical Gizmo is that you can non-uniformly scale it so that you have an "elliptical" projection. Performing a non-uniform scale about the Gizmo's X,Y axis has no effect on the mapping, but scaling the X and Y axes non-uniformly from each other creates an ellipse. Figure 16.21 shows when such mapping may be appropriate.

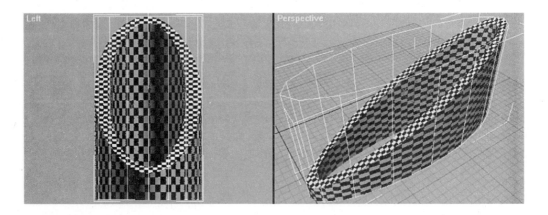

FIGURE 16.21

A non-uniformly scaled cylindrical Gizmo creating elliptical mapping.

TIP

Cylinder mapping takes its proportional clue from the Planar mapping. If you want a fit elliptical shape, fit the Planar mapping first and then switch to Cylindrical. If you want to reset the mapping, switch to Spherical and back again.

Techniques for Cylindrical Mapping

You often need a cylindrical projection to render the bitmap completely undistorted. This is especially true for items where distortion is easy to identify, such as text, labels, logos, portraits, or geometric patterns.

Consider the classic wine label as an analogy for discussion. There are several factors to determine: the radius of the bottle, the height of the label, the percentage of the bottle that is wrapped, and the proportions of the label. If you know three of these variables, you can reliably calculate the fourth. Thus, if you know the size of bottle and the label's proportion and height, you can determine how much it will wrap.

One method to ensure an undistorted map is to balance the bitmap's ratio with the model's radius to arrive at the required Gizmo height. Another approach is to use the geometric size and exact label placement to determine the proportions the material's bitmap needs to be. The fact is that for a given bitmap proportion, there is only one corresponding Gizmo height that works for a specific object's radius.

The material's bitmap is commonly the first thing to consider, with its width-to-height ratio determining the Gizmo's size. As the map wraps around the cylinder, its width is stretched to the length of the circumference. Multiplying this distance by the bitmap's ratio produces the required height of the Gizmo cylinder:

Gizmo Height=(Bitmap V / Bitmap U) × Object's Diameter × π

If you are creating a special bitmap for a specifically sized and proportioned object—for example, a can—you must proportion the bitmap to match the required label size:

(Bitmap V / Bitmap U)=Can's Diameter × π / Can's Height

Often your label is intended to wrap only a portion of the cylinder's circumference. Although you can establish the formulas, the easiest route is to define the Gizmo as if the label were to wrap the entire cylinder and then change the tiling to control its proportions. If the resulting label is too short or wraps the incorrect distance, your only recourse is to change the proportions of the label's bitmap.

When using the Bitmap Fit function, the Gizmo's height is maintained while the Gizmo's radius is scaled so that the bitmap wraps cleanly around the cylinder like a "soup can" label, producing a perfectly proportioned cylinder for that one bitmap. Once matched, you need to either uniformly scale the Gizmo to match the geometry's radius or scale the geometry so its radius matches the Gizmo's; the former approach is far more common.

Spherical Mapping

Spherical mapping projects its coordinates from a center point outward to infinity in all directions, much like an Omni light's illumination, as shown in Figure 16.22. The size of the icon has absolutely no effect on the resulting Mapping coordinates. If the icon is non-uniformly scaled, however, the Spherical mapping becomes ellipsoidal mapping, perfect for elongated, lozenge-shaped objects. Even in the case of non-uniform scaling, it is not the scale itself that affects the mapping, but rather the location of the Gizmo's center in relation to the object. The spherical Gizmo's primary purpose is to aid you in locating the center and indicating up, back, and uneven scaling.

FIGURE 16.22

Spherical mapping projection.

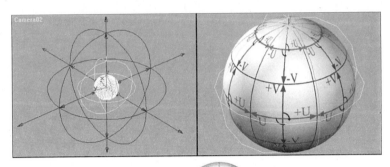

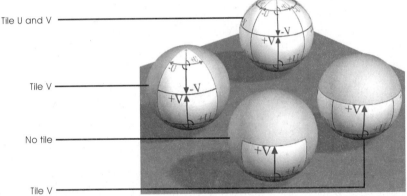

Tile U and V

Tile V

No tile

Tile V

The Spherical Mapping option can also be thought of as a "reset" for the other map types. Switching to Spherical from another type always resets the Gizmo to a pure sphere. Switching back to another type then sets that type to its defaults (a square for Planar and a cylinder with the sphere's height for Cylindrical).

The orientation of the Gizmo has the greatest effect on Spherical projections. The icon's poles are points of convergence for the bitmap and can cause pinching and swirls (also known as polar singularity). Much of the swirling has to do with the density of the mesh at that critical point—the denser the mesh is, the cleaner the resulting map.

The Gizmo's green arc indicates the seam at which a single tiling bitmap has its U axis edges meet. The seam can be very apparent if the bitmap is not tileable along this edge and can ruin many effects. Therefore, rotating the seam to the side where it cannot be readily seen is usually a good idea.

Techniques for Spherical Mapping

Spherical mapping begins by stretching the bitmap vertically from pole to pole and then wrapping it horizontally starting at the back meridian all the way around. The map is then projected back onto the surface. As any cartographer knows, there is no way to make a rectangular map fit on a sphere without distortion. The only area for which you do have some control of the distortion is the Mapping coordinate's equator, as shown in Figure 16.23. Here the bitmap has been wrapped the full circumference, whereas the height has been wrapped around only half the circumference. A bitmap, then, should have a width-to-height ratio of 2:1 in order for it to appear undistorted at the equator. Bitmaps that do not have an original 2:1 ratio should have their U or V tiling scaled to produce the same ratio.

FIGURE 16.23

Correcting for scale distortion at the equator.

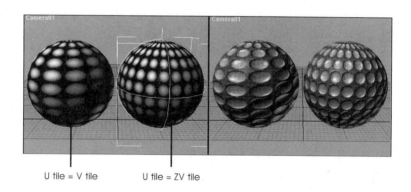

U tile = V tile   U tile = ZV tile

You can choose which axis to scale, although most bitmaps tend to be too narrow for their height. A square bitmap, for example, should have its U axis tile increased to two while the V axis remains the same. If the vertical dimension is to be full height, then the U tiling must be increased. A 640×480 bitmap requires its U value to be scaled by $640/(2\times480) = 0.6667$. If the horizontal dimension must be constant, the V value would need to be scaled up by $480/(640/2)=1.5$.

Shrink Wrap Mapping

Shrink Wrap mapping is an interesting alternative to Spherical mapping and is ideal for many applications. Whereas Spherical has singularity at both poles, Shrink Wrap has singularity only at its base—an area that is often easily hidden—making it ideal for heads, skies, trees, and spheres on a base, such as a finial.

Shrink Wrap works by considering only the central area of your bitmap. Shrink Wrap essentially treats the bitmap as a circular sheet of rubber, wrapping it around the object and tying the trimmed map up on the bottom, resulting in a nearly undistorted top half and fairly good sides. Figure 16.24 shows this treatment by wrapping a bitmap of a circle. Because Shrink Wrap trims away the corners, it appears as if only a white map was applied, rather than a white circle on a black field.

The Shrink Wrap Gizmo reacts in the same way as the Spherical Gizmo. Selecting it always results in a reset. The scale of the Gizmo does not matter, only its center does. Like Spherical, you can scale it non-uniformly to cover ellipsoidal shapes.

FIGURE 16.24

The circular trimming performed by Shrink Wrap mapping.

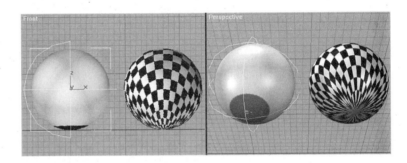

Techniques for Shrink Wrap Mapping

Shrink Wrap mapping is best used with bitmaps that can tile in both the U and V axes or with very high-resolution images. Shrink Wrap trimming leaves less of the image to project and smaller bitmaps may seem pixelated because they are viewed beyond their range. Those bitmaps that can tile are ideal for shrink wrapping. Tiling ranges of three or four in both the U and V directions produce amazingly convincing results as shown in Figure 16.25.

The next thing to consider with Shrink Wrap is that it often works well with VW and WU bitmap projections. When adjusting the Gizmo, especially those at angles and for organic models, the different projection axes can deliver surprisingly good results when using tiling maps as described previously.

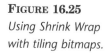

FIGURE 16.25

Using Shrink Wrap with tiling bitmaps.

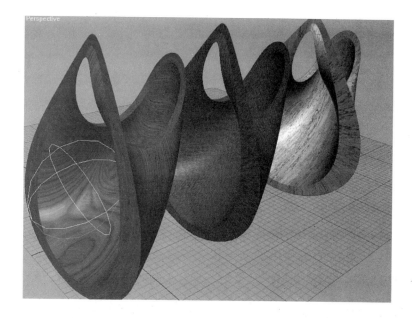

Box Mapping

Box mapping should be thought of as Planar mapping applied from six directions because that is exactly what it is. The proportions projected by each side correspond to the proportions of the referenced bitmap. Scaling the Gizmo scales the resulting mapping, just as it does with Planar mapping. Non-uniformly scaling the Gizmo means that sides have different mapping proportions from one another.

Bitmap maintains the height of the Gizmo and scales the X axis to match the bitmap's proportion. The Front, Back, Top, and Bottom projections have been fit, leaving a square left and right side. You can now rotate the Box Mapping Gizmo as needed, if a different facing is required. The reason it chooses the sides it does is inherent to the way it maps. The left and right sides (the Gizmo's X axis) are always considered "sides" whereas the others wrap around the Y axis, as shown in Figure 16.26.

FIGURE 16.26

Box mapping projection.

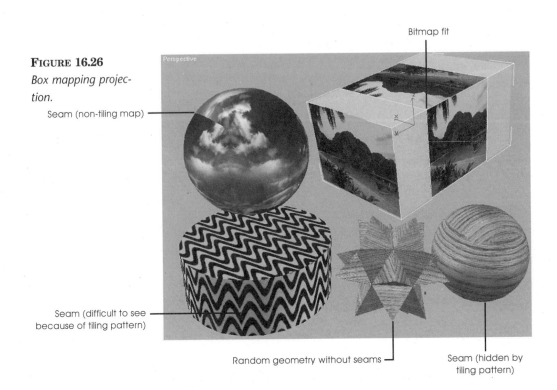

Box mapping assigns mapping according to the surface normal's orientation to the Gizmo. After a face crosses the 45-degree-angle threshold between projected planes of the mapping Gizmo, it receives mapping from the other side. Box mapping is thus a very fast way to assign mapping to otherwise difficult geometry.

Techniques for Box Mapping

More often than not, you want the mapping produced by Box mapping to be even for all sides of its projections. This occurs only when the Box Mapping Gizmo is a perfect cube. A perfectly cubical mapping Gizmo works fine for materials using square bitmaps, but it stretches or squashes bitmaps of different proportions. The Bitmap Fit function scales the Gizmo to match the bitmap but leaves two ends square and out of proportion with the other four. If you need all six sides to be in proportion with each other and the referenced bitmap, you need to adjust the map tiling instead, as shown in Figure 16.27. The following steps can be used to accomplish this:

1. Ensure the mapping Gizmo is a cube by switching to Spherical or Shrink Wrap and then back to Box.

2. Use the Info option in View File to identify the Resolution.

3. The bitmap's height-to-width ratio becomes the UTile-to-VTile ratio. This adjustment can be made either in the material or UVW Mapping modifier settings. Note that the U and V tiling is the reverse of the Height and Width.

4. The U/V ratio must now be maintained for all future adjustments. You can adjust the Tiling size by either uniformly scaling the mapping Gizmo or adjusting the tiling values.

One convenient method is to set the bitmap adjustment in the material, which is linked to the particular bitmap, and use the Modifier tiling to control the repeat. Either way, you have three methods to change the tiling that can be used individually or in conjunction with one another to produce the final tiling. For the sake of sanity, it is best to use only one method to adjust the bitmap's ratio and the others for overall tiling size.

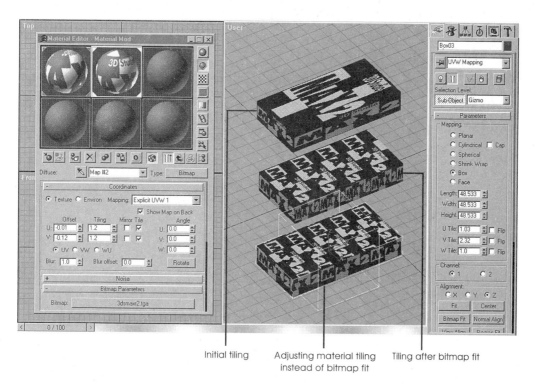

Initial tiling   Adjusting material tiling   Tiling after bitmap fit
                   instead of bitmap fit

FIGURE 16.27

Adjusting tiling to make even Box Map tiling.

When properly adjusted for bitmap size, Box mapping can be ideal for rectilinear geometry. Planar mapping may be preferable when you need localized control over specific areas to ensure critical alignments.

Face Mapping

Face mapping is a new mapping coordinate mode that behaves similarly to the face-mapping feature found in the Material Editor. It enables you to assign Face mapping to a selection of faces that can be edited by the Unwrap UVW modifier.

Unwrap UVW Modifier

The Unwrap UVW makes it possible to edit in UV space. When it is applied, one of three things happens:

- If the object has a UVW, it is stored in the modifier.
- If the object has no UVW, Planar mapping is applied to create a UVW and is stored in the modifier.
- If the object's incoming data on the stack is Face level Sub-Object selection, then the UVW of the selected faces is stored in the modifier.

When active, UVWs are reassigned to the object down the pipeline and modifications to UVWs up the pipeline have no effect beyond the modifier.

NOTE

If the modifier is applied to selected faces, upstream changes still apply to unselected faces beyond the modifier.

Before the Unwrap UVW modifier is applied, establish whether or not you will be applying it to the entire object or to selected faces. If you apply it to selected faces, use a Mesh Select modifier first to select the faces to be affected and then apply the Unwrap UVW modifier. Once applied, the Unwrap UVW Modifier brings up a dialog shown in Figure 16.28.

In the modifier's Parameters rollout are an Edit and Reset button and a Channel Area. The Edit button brings up the Edit UVW Dialog that gives you an interactive interface to position, scale, view, and apply the UVW. Reset reapplies the modifier without erasing maps assigned in the Edit UVW dialog.

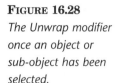

FIGURE 16.28

The Unwrap modifier once an object or sub-object has been selected.

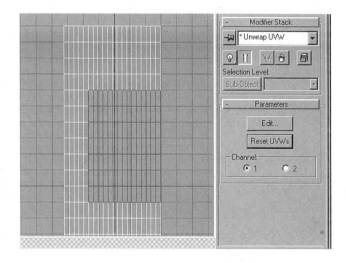

Mapping Coordinate Channels

Objects can have two UVW mapping coordinate channels. UVW1 is the Default channel and is set by the Generate Mapping Coordinates toggle. Coordinates can be sent to either channel (UVW1 or UVW2), which enables you to have two different coordinate sets on selected faces. This requires that you assign channels at the Map level of a material and for the UVW modifier. Access to these channels is available in the following places:

- In the Creation parameters of most objects, toggling Generate Mapping Cords sets UVW1.

- The UVW Map, the UVW XForm, and the Unwrap UVW modifier all enable you to assign both channels for any face (the mapping for a face is determined by the last two items in the stack that assign UVW1 and UVW2).

- In the Coordinates rollout of the Material editor, the channel to be used by a map can be specified according to the Map type (2D or 3D). For 2D maps in the Texture option, you can specify Explicit UVW1, Explicit UVW2, or Planar from Object XYZ (the map from the second channel is displayed as a Planar map). For 3D maps, radio button for XYZ, UVW1, and UVW2 are provided. The Options button in the Material Editor also gives you control over how UVW2 is to be displayed in the sample slots.

- NURBS Surface Objects and Sub-Objects also have toggles to specify between UVW1 and UVW2.

UVW XForm Modifier

 This modifier makes it possible to adjust the existing UVW coordinates of objects. This can be especially helpful when you are working with complex objects. Rather than having to depend on the self-generated coordinates of an object at the Material/Map level, you can apply this modifier to change them.

Mapping Strategies

Controlling how a material should traverse a surface depends on appropriately applied mapping. Deciding how to apply the mapping to gain the desired result becomes a planning issue: where to apply it, with what projection, at what orientation, and with what tiling. You must address these questions as you finalize your surfaces.

Although nearly every model requires slightly different techniques, the following strategies are useful guidelines to determine what mapping is best suited to your model's geometry. Examples of each type of geometry are given in parentheses:

- **Flat surface (paper):** Consider Planar mapping applied normal to the surface.

- **Rectilinear without caps (walls):** Consider Planar mapping applied at an angle that wraps around the corners.

- **Rectilinear with caps (a box):** Consider Box mapping, adjusting the ratio of the tiling or Gizmo to match the bitmap's proportion.

- **Symmetrical (a duck):** Consider Planar mapping a specially created bitmap that is allowed to project through the object and map both sides with the same image.

- **Cylindrical (a bottle):** Consider Cylindrical mapping, compensating for the bitmap's proportions with the Gizmo's height or tiling.

- **Spherical (a ball):** Consider Spherical or Shrink Wrap mapping, depending on the nature of the bitmap and how prominent the poles will be in the final renderings.

- **Irregular (a plant):** Ideally you want to assign the mapping at creation (loft, extrude, bevel, lathe). Alternatively, Shrink Wrap mapping can work with smooth-edged geometry, whereas Box mapping can work for sharp-edged geometry.

Another key with mapping is to assign the map while the object presents its most geometrically pure form. Before collapsing the modeling stack, analyze the progressing forms and identify points at which mapping is easiest. A leaf, for example, is best mapped when it is first extruded and is flat, rather than later when it has been curled and bent. It is not uncommon to deform an object to a more convenient shape for the sake of applying mapping and then reversing the deformation.

Irregular geometry can be most easily mapped by applying UVW Unwrap Modifiers to MeshSelect faces. Avoid putting UVW Unwrap on entire objects as you will get lost real quick.

The last thing to consider is the UVW modifier's placement in the stack, especially when the modeling is being animated. If deformations happen after the UVW modifier, the mapping coordinates "stick," and mapping stretches with the object's vertices. If the deformations happen before the UVW modifier, the object appears to move through the coordinates because that is exactly what is happening.

In Practice: Mapping for Materials

- **Applying mapping:** Mapping is usually applied at the end of the modeling sequence because further modeling threatens to distort previously defined mapping coordinates. The Modifier Stack allows you to traverse the modeling history and place the mapping when the object's form best conforms to the Mapping projection's shape.

- **MeshSelect and VolumeSelect modifiers:** These modifiers are superior to EditMesh modifiers in defining Sub-Object selections for mapping assignments because they use a minimum of RAM.

- **Unique mapping:** Each face on an object can have unique mapping, but only the last UVW mapping applied to a face is respected.

- **Infinite mapping**: Mapping projects infinitely through an object as determined by the projection method (planar, cylindrical, spherical, shrink wrap, or box).

- **Rectilinear geometry:** Rectilinear geometry can often be mapped with one planar projection applied at a 45-degree angle. The distortion of the angular projection is easily corrected with a 1.414 tiling or Gizmo scale along the angled axis.

- **UVW mapping Gizmo:** The UVW mapping Gizmo is your bitmap (when Tiling is 1.0 and Offset is zero). Bitmaps within materials are stretched to meet the corners of the Gizmo, so the Gizmo should have the same height-to-width proportion as the material bitmap to avoid distortion.

- **Real-world scale:** Many bitmaps relate to real-world scale. The size of such bitmaps should be determined and the mapping Gizmo should be made to match these dimensions so the rendered material will be in scale with the bitmap representation.

Part V

LIGHTING AND CAMERAS

LIGHTING IN **MAX**

Computer graphics follow the filmmaker's art and craft more than any other model, even though concepts from painting, sculpture, and the performing arts are at the core of successful modeling, texturing, and movement. Combining these elements in 3D space and managing dynamics in a pre-rendered animation, however, calls for skills best developed in the film and video disciplines. For real-time graphics, look to live and interactive theater. The good and bad news about CGI is that you get to play all the roles you see in the credits—from producer to caterer. This chapter covers the roles of gaffer, lighting designer, and technician through discussion of the following topics related to lighting and atmospheric environments:

- Setting up standard lighting

- Lights and their illumination

- Working with shadows

- Projecting images

- Setting up the environment

- Lighting with fixtures

Setting Up Standard Lighting

Lighting is something you naturally take for granted. Everywhere you go, you have a lit path already established. The sun illuminates our world simply and effectively. With 3D, however, it's a different story. In 3D environments, lighting is rarely set up for you. This section discusses MAX's default lighting, basic lighting styles, basic illumination styles (such as three-point lighting), and the concept of reflected light.

MAX Default Lighting

3DS MAX R2 features an interactive renderer. It is designed to provide you with immediate interactive feedback when you create and change objects in a viewport. If the viewport displays the object other than in wireframe mode, you see the effect of lighting on the scene. Lighting changes update interactively in the viewport just like modeling, animation, and material changes.

When no lights are present, 3DS MAX provides a default lighting setup so that the scene can be viewed effectively. This lighting works in both the interactive and the default scanline renderers. Think of this lighting as the "house lights" that provide enough illumination for you to work, but are not intended for your final rendered result. The default lighting provided is simply two omni lights placed at diagonal corners of your scene. Assuming your scene is centered at the origin, the lights are placed up in front at –X,–Y, +Z, and the other is down in back at +X, +Y, –Z.

When you first add a light to your scene, 3DS MAX removes the default lighting so that you can see the illumination of what you introduced. Your scene will become darker when you do this because two lights have been removed and replaced by one new light. You can now introduce additional lights as needed.

The default lighting is left off as long as light objects exist in the scene, regardless of whether they're on or off. When all lights are deleted from the scene, the default setup is returned automatically. You can, however, override the scene's illumination with the default lighting setup using a keyboard alternate (assigned to Ctl+L by default). This override affects only the interactive renderer on a viewport basis and is saved with the scene. It does not work with the scanline renderer. In practice, this is useful when the lighting you've created leaves objects or a portion of your scene in darkness and you don't want to disturb your lighting setup, but you need more light to work on an object or in that area.

Note

The interactive renderer can show a maximum of 32 lights using the HEIDI driver. For Open-GL, the limit is driver-specific with most implementations limiting you to eight lights. In a scene using more than 32 lights, the earliest 32 are used for the interactive illumination. This limitation has no impact on the production renderer's lighting.

Although the interactive renderer is useful, it is not a replacement for making test renderings with the production renderer. Because the interactive renderer uses Gouraud-based shading, the highlights you see are dependent on each surface's mesh density. A box having only 12 faces, for example, may have intense highlights, but none are shown in the viewports because the shading is being averaged across just two faces. Other subtleties, such as attenuation, atmosphere, and true material effects, can only be seen effectively in a full rendering.

Basic Illumination Styles

Lighting is always a stylistic issue, but two different illumination styles are often used to build upon: triangle lighting and zone lighting.

Triangle Lighting

Triangle lighting (also called three-point lighting) uses three lights to provide illumination. The primary light, called the key, is generally the brightest light and illuminates most of the scene (see Figure 17.1). The key is usually the light that casts a shadow in the scene.

Key light   Back light   Fill light

FIGURE 17.1
An object being lit with a key light, a key and back light, and a key, back, and fill light.

A second backlight is used to separate an object from its background and reveal more depth. This light is generally behind and above the object and of lesser or equal intensity than the key. The middle image in Figure 17.1 shows the backlight in tandem with the key light.

A third light, the fill, is generally left of the camera and fills dark areas missed by the key (see Figure 17.1). The fill light is used to control contrast between the brightest areas of the scene and the darkest. A bright fill creates even lighting whereas a dim fill increases the contrast and makes the scene more uneasy. Your selection of lighting intensities helps to create an overall mood. Just as happy cartoons are bright and well illuminated, spooky castles are dimly lit and full of contrast. Figure 17.2 shows the arrangement of the lights used in Figure 17.1.

Zone Lighting

Sometimes a large scene cannot use basic triangle lighting effectively, so a slightly different approach to lighting is needed. Zone lighting occurs when an area is broken down into zones, and each zone is illuminated individually. Zones can be chosen by areas of importance or similarity. After a zone is selected, basic triangle or three-point lighting can be applied. Sometimes, however, zone lighting doesn't create the proper mood so a freeform lighting scheme is used. When used carefully, accent lights—used to illuminate key objects or areas—can be used for drawing attention to something important.

FIGURE 17.2

Arrangement of key, backlight, and fill lights.

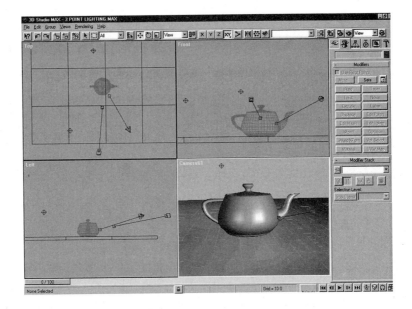

Each visual art has several styles of lighting, and all can be used in 3D space. In fact, 3D lighting isn't limited to available power or the brightness of a bulb. The lighting isn't limited by where it can be placed, what it illuminates, or where its shadow is cast. 3D lights can animate their brightness and color and move with complete freedom.

Illumination Principles

3DS MAX bases its illumination on the angle the light source is to the surface and not its distance to it. When a light source is square to a plane and far away, the angles of the light's rays that fall on the plane's surface are nearly parallel, and the resulting illumination is very even. If the same light is placed close, the angles of the light's rays that strike the surface vary considerably and produce a pronounced hotspot. It usually is desirable to shade objects gradually across their faces and not to create such hotspots. To do this, you must place the light sources at an angle to the object (to create gradations) and at a significant distance (to minimize hotspots). The resulting basic setup is composed of two omni lights placed at a diagonal to the model—the formula for the 3DS MAX default lighting setup.

The amount that a light illuminates a surface depends completely on the light's angle to the surface, not on the light's proximity. This is the light's angle of incidence to the surface. If the surface is at a right angle to the light, it is illuminated at full effect. As the surface tilts away from the light source, this angle is lowered, and the illumination received diminishes. This means that as a light is placed further away, it illuminates the scene more and more evenly; each mesh's angle to the light source slowly approaches 90 degrees.

NOTE

Lighting in 3DS MAX can literally redefine a material's color and texture. When you color or project images from a light, you may find you cannot tell whether you are seeing a light, texture map, or the effect of both in the final image. Sometimes you should project a texture onto an object with a projector light instead of texturing the object at all (as when working with brighter ambient settings). Conversely, the color and texture of a material can negate your intended lighting effect. At the design stage, work back and forth between lighting and material to develop your designs. The MAX R2 Material Editor permits using scene lighting in the Material Editor display slots.

Common Light Controls

All the different light objects in MAX share a common set of controls. They control a light's basic features, such as brightness and color. Clicking a light's color swatch brings up the General Parameters rollout (see Figure 17.3), which is divided into two sections: Color and Attenuation.

FIGURE 17.3
General light controls.

The color section of the General Parameters rollout is where you control whether the light is on or off in the scene, its color, and which objects are affected by the light. The available options are outlined in the following list:

■ **On/Off check box:** Controls whether a light affects the scene or not. The choice is explicit for the scene and cannot be animated.

■ **Exclude:** Brings up the Exclude/Include dialog (see Figure 17.4). The exclusion/inclusion lists enable you to place accent lights wherever necessary in the scene without worrying about how they may over-illuminate or cause undesirable highlights.

FIGURE 17.4

Objects can be included or excluded from illumination, shadow casting, or both.

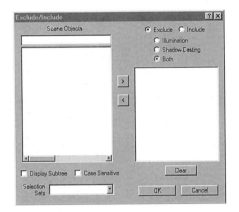

■ **RGB, HSV, Color Swatch:** Control the color and illumination of the light. Although the color can be animated by adjusting any of the values, the color is always animated according to RGB values and interpolates across RGB color space. The color of the light is significant, even at low levels.

TIP

To keep track of light colors in scenes containing many lights, drag-copy the color swatch from the light's Modify command panel to a Color Clipboard floater (Utilities/Color Clipboard/New Floater). Lighting color schemes can be saved as color clipboard files (*.ccb) for use throughout this or other scenes.

■ **Multiplier:** Multiplies the entered value against the color swatch's RGB values to define the light's actual output color. A value of less than one reduces the illumination, whereas values greater than one increase it. When the multiplier is given a negative value, the light actually removes illumination from the scene.

These "negative lights" are useful for simulating radiosity effects and otherwise perfecting interior lighting setups. A common use for a negative omni, for example, is to place them at interior corners to darken them in a way that is difficult to achieve with the positive lights in the scene.

You can use a light's multiplier setting to ensure the same color is being used across a series of lights. For example, give each light the same color, and vary their intensity with their multipliers. If the multiplier is small, the color swatch reads as a distinguishable color (this makes the light's color very dark).

Additionally, you can adjust the multiplier for all lights at once through the Global Lighting Levels multiplier. Located in the Global Lighting Section of the Environment dialog, this control acts as a master dimmer switch for all lights except ambient light, with the only difference being an inability to use negative values.

As multipliers are increased, each channel caps at 255. This means a red light that began as 255,10,10 is rose-pink with a multiplier of 10, very light pink with a multiplier of 20, and pure white with a multiplier of 26. When multipliers are this intense, the fact that the light is "red" is seen only at the falloff or with attenuation. Then the light progresses from white to bright red across the falloff halo. This characteristic is often useful for special effect lighting.

- **Contrast:** Adjusts the contrast between diffuse and ambient areas of a surface, useful for certain special effects, such as the harsh light in space.

- **Soften Diff(use) Edge:** Softens the edge between the diffuse and ambient portions of a surface. Softening the edge reduces the light amount, which you can offset by increasing the multiplier. This effect is subtle compared other lighting adjustments. Adjust the Soften Diffuse Edge and Contrast spinners after you've set the Attenuation, Decay and Hotspot/Falloff settings.

- **Affect Diffuse:** Permits the use of one light source to color an object. The default is on.

- **Affect Specular:** Permits you the use of one light source to place a specular highlight. The default is on.

You generally expect a light to affect the specular and diffuse colors the same because a highlight color is usually a variation of the diffuse. In some special effects lighting, you may want to split them—use one light source to affect color on the object and a second projector light to project a patterned highlight. The effect can be subtle, as in using a warm (yellow) color to illuminate the object (diffuse) with a cool blue highlight (specular).

Attenuation

Attenuation controls a light's falloff over distance. Without attenuation, lights illuminate according to their orientation to the surface. If the surface is at 90 degrees, the light gives its full effect. This means that the farther you place a light from a surface, the shallower the angle of incidence becomes and the brighter the surface is illuminated. In real life, however, light diminishes over distance. If you hold a flashlight directly over a table, it's quite bright. Aim it across the room and its illumination is much dimmer. Point it across the street and it barely has an influence on the neighboring home. This diminishing, decaying, or watering down of light is termed attenuation and is a simple result of physics. In R2, the controls are refined to permit optional attenuating near and far ends of spotlights, directional lights, and omni lights. The Near and Far points each contain Start and End spinners, so light can ramp from nothing to full power, similar to Hotspot and Falloff settings.

NOTE

Interiors tend to require numerous lights and if these are not attenuated, the scene rapidly becomes over-illuminated. When illuminating interiors, attenuation should be used on all lights except for the dimmest of fill lights. Setting Decay to Inverse or Inverse Square may diminish scene lighting too far, however, especially with volumetric lights or lights passing through transparent/translucent surfaces.

In the world around you, light attenuates at an inverse square ratio. For example, if a lamp had X illumination at 10 feet, it would have $1/4$X at 20 feet. Although physically correct, this amount of decay is usually considered too high for computer graphics. The reason for this is that light bounces off surfaces and illuminates the world from all angles, even though it is attenuating. Only radiosity rendering programs have the capability to reproduce this inherited light, and they are usually the only ones that adhere to the inverse square ratio. Most computer programs that include light attenuation, therefore, do so in a linear fashion—the same lamp that had X illumination at 10 feet would now have $1/2$X at 20 feet. 3DS MAX R1 provided a hybrid method of zero and linear falloff. This is how MAX R2 works.

NOTE

Attenuation is shown in the interactive viewports only if you enable the Attenuate Lights option in Viewport Preferences. Although useful, it does have a considerable impact on shaded view redraw times.

NEW TO R2

R2 adds Start and End range settings to both Near and Far light attenuation. This ramps attenuation at the Near and Far areas of the light, but how you set these options can affect how light fades in between the Near and Far ranges. For example, if you want a light to attenuate evenly, you need to reduce the Start range to zero. How these ranges are portrayed in the viewports (Near, Far, Start, and End ranges) can be color-coded in the Colors, Gizmos, and Apparatus section of User Preferences.

The Attenuation section of the General Parameters rollout contains the following options:

- **Use check box:** Indicates whether the selected light is currently using its assigned ranges. When activated, range circles appear around the lights indicating the extents of their Start and End ranges (see Figure 17.5).

FIGURE 17.5

Circles in the different viewports represent the lighting attenuation spheres.

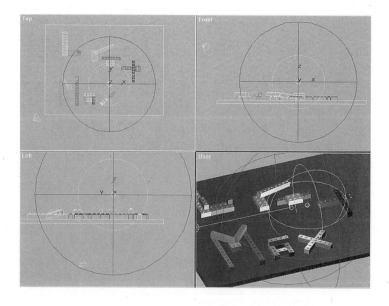

■ **Show check box:** Enables you to see the extents without their being active. These circles define the inner and outer extents for the light's illumination.

■ **Start Range (shown by the inner circle):** For Far, this is similar to a hotspot and defines a region where attenuation does not occur. The opposite is true for Near.

■ **End Range (the outer circle):** For Far, this is similar to a falloff and defines the distance at which the light stops illuminating. Light that falls between the Start and End range receives linear attenuation. The opposite is true for Near.

■ **Decay (None, Inverse, and Inverse Square):** The Decay settings can be used with or without activating the Near and Far attenuation options and, if used alone, appear always to be calculated from the Near range. Used alone, they are a quick way to attenuate lights. The default None setting creates no decay; the Inverse or Inverse Square options attempt to approximate how real-world lighting fades as you move away from the source. Use the Decay option when you have many lights in your scene as an alternative to laboriously setting each and every attenuation setting.

The Attenuation and Decay controls can operate independent of the other, so you can custom control attenuation range and ramping, or use Uniform Inverse or Inverse Square Decay. You may also use both settings together, which results in Inverse or Inverse Square Decay taking place within the attenuation range.

TIP

When lighting interiors pay special attention to the lights' ranges, all lights of an equal "wattage" placed in an area should have the same ranges. If ranges are different between lights, their perceived brightness is different because illumination distances will vary. This is especially noticeable in arrays of lights, where it's obvious that they should be the same. In such cases, it is usually best to make the lights instances of one another, so adjusting one affects them all.

Hotspot and Falloff

The hotspot and falloff are the most commonly adjusted aspects of spot lights and directional lights. (They are not available in the Omni or Ambient light settings). The difference between the hotspot and falloff, controls the crispness of the resulting light pool edge. The hotspot and falloff values have an effect similar to the inner and outer ranges of an attenuated Omni light.

The hotspot defines the extents of the light's full illumination; it does not increase illumination as the name might imply. Illumination within the hotspot is the light at full effect. The falloff defines the range at which the light ends its illumination. This fade, or decay, is not linear as with attenuation ranges but actually is a cubic spline interpolation; most of the transition occurs close to the falloff's outer edge.

The size difference between the hotspot and falloff define the softness or fuzziness of the light pool's edge. A narrow hotspot and broad falloff create a very soft edge, whereas a hotspot close to the same size as the falloff makes the light pool's edge very crisp. Adjust hotspot and falloff in conjunction with R2's other settings that control how light fades from the source: the Attenuation and Decay settings and the Contrast and Soften Diffuse Edge control.

When overshoot is active, the falloff still defines the range within which shadows are cast and images are projected. The falloff becomes an important mechanism to control the extent to which the light's shadow map is stretched. Larger falloffs require larger and more memory-intensive shadow maps to produce quality shadows. You can improve the quality of your shadows and reduce the RAM requirements by restricting the falloffs of shadow casting lights to their minimum size.

T IP

If a broad gradation over a spotlight's pool is needed, you can use attenuation to create the effect by setting the spotlight's inner range circle so that it just intersects the mesh's surface.

Overshoot

You can eliminate a directional or spotlight's light pool by activating the light's Overshoot option. (Note this option is not available with Omni and Ambient light settings.) Turning Overshoot on eliminates the falloff that normally occurs outside the hotspot area. If shadow casting is turned off and Overshoot is on, the light appears to pass through objects in its path. If shadows are turned on, the light is blocked by objects in its path, but otherwise extends outside the falloff constraint.

Overshoot basically turns a spotlight into an aimed omni light yet retains the rest of the light's capabilities. Because of these qualities, this capability is sometimes referred to as infinite overshoot. An overshot spotlight is not restricted to a cone of light; rather, it illuminates in all directions similar to an omni light and an overshot directional light casts light infinitely from side to side (see Figure 17.6). While ignoring hotspot constraints, lights using overshoot still respect their attenuation and decay settings.

FIGURE 17.6

Overshoot is checked on the right spot, resulting in the right-hand spot's falloff no longer constrained by the cone falloff.

Overshoot is useful when general illumination is needed, but you still need the spotlight's shadow or projector capabilities. These properties still observe the spotlight's falloff cone. A spotlight with overshoot should be thought of as an omni light with shadow casting and projector capabilities active and constrained to its falloff (see Figure 17.7).

FIGURE 17.7

An overshot, shadow casting spotlight creates shadows in its normal hotspot and falloff ranges, and acts like an omni outside them.

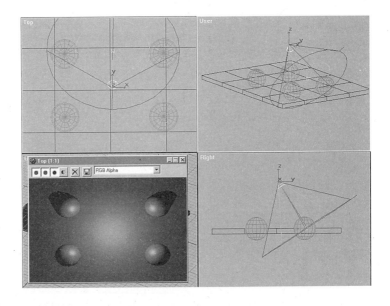

Using Overshoot with a directional light creates a strong, somewhat unusual light source. An overshot directional light, for example, illuminates all surfaces it strikes at a given angle evenly but has no impact on surfaces that are co-linear with the light's direction (see Figure 17.8).

FIGURE 17.8

This overshot directional light illuminates all the planes that the light shines upon, except for the faces at right angles to it.

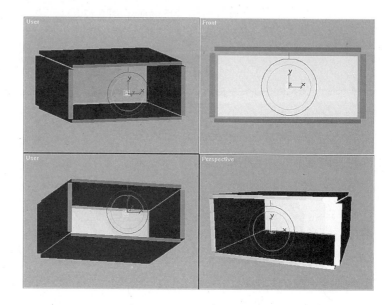

By adjusting a light's controls under the Modify command panel, you can localize and fade a light in 3D space, control shadow behaviors, and in the case of spot and directional light, project textures. In practice, however, these controls yield results according to the type of light implemented in the scene.

Lights and Their Illumination

The many built-in light types of 3DS MAX R2 can emulate nearly every light in nature, as well as add possibilities that can exist only in the virtual realm of computer graphics. 3DS MAX R2 contains several types of light objects—the targeted and free spotlights, the targeted and free directional lights, and the omni light. These are physical lights that can be placed and moved around in the 3D scene. These lights also contain common light controls that describe how a light behaves in the environment. There is also a Global Lighting Section in the Environment dialog that contains ambient light, global tint, and level features. These are not lights but are important to the general lighting in the scene. Lastly, there is a sunlight system that uses a directional light to emulate the sun's position based upon geography, date, and time.

Types of Lights

3DS MAX includes five different light objects: omni light, targeted directional light, free directional light, targeted spotlight, and free spotlight. Ambient light and Global Tint and Levels, which are not physical light objects, but are important factors in an overall lighting design.

All light within 3DS MAX respects the color laws of RGB additive illumination. The selection and assignment of light color is consistent with all forms of light. These colors can be mixed using any combination of Red, Green, Blue (RGB) and Hue, Luminance, Saturation (HLS) channels and values. Refer to Chapter 2, "Getting Oriented in 3D Space," for more information on color.

Omni Lights

Omni lights are point light sources very similar to a naked bulb hanging on a wire or a star in a solar system. An omni light traces its illumination from its position to all faces that are oriented toward it.

NEW TO R2

In R2, Omni lights have been redesigned to conform to the same feature set as Spot and Directional lights. Specifically, they now can cast shadows, support projectors, and except for the inability to show the lighting cone or overshoot, include the features and enhancements found in the other types of lights.

The primary purpose of Omni lights is to act as fill lights. It is quite common to have numerous omni lights at great distances, in varying colors, and with low levels to cast shades of light and mix them on the model. This technique is borrowed from theatrical lighting, but is quite applicable to 3DS MAX. However, with their added shadow casting and other capabilities in R2, you may opt to use one omni light in place of several spot or directional lights.

In being omni-directional, Omni lights are quite predictable in their resulting illumination. These lights have a variety of secondary uses as well. Placing Omni lights close to meshes creates bright specular highlights; placing Omni lights at strategic angles behind or below meshes can create subtle glows and give the effect of bounced color. Omni lights given negative multipliers are often placed in areas of the scene to create pools of shade.

A common mistake is to believe that placing an Omni light in a room creates a glow in the air about it as it would in real life. This cannot happen.

Lights in 3DS MAX can cast light only upon the faces that they strike. The street lamp outside your house creates a glow, or halo, because it strikes millions of airborne particles floating about it. To create this effect in MAX, use volume lights with an omni or other light, and have the omni light control shadows, attenuation, decay, and any projected image.

The following exercise begins the process of lighting an office environment. The first light you will place is an Omni light in the loft area.

ILLUMINATING THE LOFT WITH AN OMNI LIGHT

1. Open the file named lit_tut.max. The scene contains only default lighting with Ambient light set to default throughout. Notice how the office is set up. The office has an upstairs loft. The downstairs is a continuous space broken up with permanent dividers and a stairway. Large glass panes are on the southern wall, with a segmented glass roof. The space is sparsely furnished, but architecture and objects vary in their materials.

2. Set the lower-right viewport to camera04-upstairs and render the scene. You can see the environment bitmap, as tinted through the upper-right skylight and directly above the wall on the left.

3. Using the top and left viewports, create and position an omni light near the ceiling and center to the loft area. Render camera04-upstairs. The default lighting has been replaced, and the shine on the bookcase comes out.

4. Press the clone button at the top of the virtual frame buffer (VFB) to copy the render to the desktop.

5. Select the omni light (if not already selected), open the Modify panel and under Shadow Parameters, turn on Cast Shadows and Use Global Settings. Render camera04-upstairs again. Note soft shadows under and in the bookcase, and that the planter casts a shadow. Clone this render and leave it on the desktop.

6. Increase the multiplier to 10.0 and check Decay, Inverse, and press the Render Last button. The scene is slightly less bright, but you can see the floor lighting begin to fall off toward the corner. (If you use your original multiplier settings with Decay, the rendered image is almost black.)

7. Change the lower-left viewport to camera02-stairs and render the scene (keeping the omni settings the same as step 6). The scene is very

dark. Set Decay to None, leave shadows on, reduce the multiplier to 2.0 and re-render. Downstairs surfaces directly exposed to the omni light in the loft are illuminated. The rest is very dark. Clone the virtual frame buffer.

8. Uncheck Cast Shadows and render last. The entire downstairs is illuminated, even though much of it is physically blocked by the loft floor. You've now illuminated two stories with one omni light.

9. You have two ways of constraining the upstairs omni light without using shadows: Exclude and Attenuation. Here you use Attenuation. Turn Shadows on. Check the Use box under Attenuation, Far. Two spherical shapes appear around the omni light. Leave the Far, Start setting at the default 80 and increase the Far, End spinner and expand the attenuation range until it passes slightly through the loft floor (500). Render camera04-upstairs. The light is uniformly attenuated, going to 0 as it reaches the edge of the room, turning the scene almost black.

10. Double the Far range to 1000. Render camera04-upstairs and clone the VFB. Turn off shadows, and render camera02-stairs. The downstairs is dark because of the attenuation. The final scene is shown in Figure 17.9.

11. Save the scene to **lit_tut2.max**.

FIGURE 17.9

The upstairs loft illuminated by a single Omni light with Shadow Casting turned on.

Directional Light

A directional light is similar to the sun. As a light casts shadows, the angle of the shadow is the line traced from the light source to the subject. This effect is most visible when you have closely spaced objects with parallel surfaces, such as a picket fence, for example.

Placing a spotlight close to the fence produces highly flared shadows as each picket traces its own shadow line to the light source. As you move the light away from the fence, the angle between each picket's shadow becomes more and more shallow. When the light source is placed a considerable distance away, the angle between each shadow is so minimal that the shadows cast are effectively parallel to one another. This is what occurs with sunlight and in computer graphics this is termed parallel or directional light. This is the illumination produced by the 3DS MAX Directional Light object.

The Directional Light object in 3DS MAX is somewhat of a hybrid between a traditional parallel light and a spotlight. The Directional Light is similar to a spotlight in having a hotspot and falloff. These serve to control the extents to which shadows are calculated in the scene and the extent of falloff.

When the hotspot is minimized, the Directional Light is somewhat similar to a photographer's box light by casting a soft, area light. When the over-shoot option is enabled, the hotspot and falloff are ignored, and the illumination is similar to the sun. Attenuation should be used for soft area lights and should be off when simulating sunlight.

A Directional Light can be targeted or free. If free, it's similar to a Free Spot or Free camera in not having a target and being controlled entirely by its rotation. When overshoot is active, the distance a Directional Light is from the subject is of minimal importance. Unlike other light objects, it does not matter how far to one side the Directional Light is placed, only the angle it is to the subject. A Targeted Directional Light is the same as the Free Directional Light, except that it has a target to make it easier to adjust, and it doesn't have a Target Distance parameter.

Targeted Spotlight

The targeted spotlight is a directional light that casts light toward its target, which can be moved independently. A targeted spotlight is similar to tying a rope to the front of a spotlight, similar to those often used in concerts. Wherever the rope is pulled, the spot turns to aim in that direction.

The target is used only as an aid in aiming the spotlight. The distance of the target from the light has no influence on its brightness, decay, or attenuation.

TIP

Single left-clicking the line between a target light, camera, or tape measure helper object and its target selects the object and its target. Right-clicking the object gives the option to select/deselect the target.

The many capabilities of targeted and free spotlights make them the primary lighting tool within the 3DS MAX environment. Unlike Omni lights, the direction of their light can be controlled and they can be rectangular or circular in shape.

The following exercise continues lighting the office environment that you started in the previous exercise. In this instance, you will be placing a Target Spotlight to illuminate the painting in the corner.

ILLUMINATING THE PAINTING WITH A SPOT LIGHT

1. Continue from the previous exercise. In the Front viewport, create a Target Spot beginning just below the ceiling and at its center, extending toward the painting on the left wall (see Figure 17.10). Note the second light takes on the settings of the last one. Reduce the multiplier to 1.5.

2. Check Show Cone, Rectangle, Cast Shadows, Use Global Settings, and Use Shadow Maps. Change the lower-right viewport to Spot01 (right-click viewport name/Views/Spot01). This enables you to see where the light shines.

3. Adjust the Asp(ect) ratio spinner until the painting fits within the square (around 2.1). Then check to see that Decay is set to None and Attenuation is off. Change the viewport to camera03-painting and render the scene. The painting is illuminated, as well as the edges around it, but the rest of the scene is dark. Clone the VFB.

4. Check Overshoot and Render Last. Now the single spot illuminates the entire corner area and casts shadows. Render camera02-stairs. The entire room is illuminated by the one spotlight.

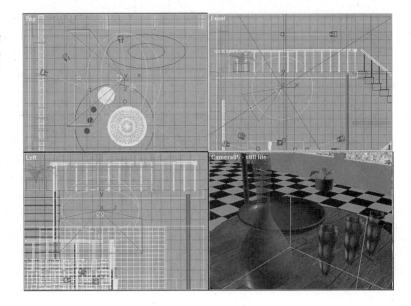

5. Add attenuation: Increase the Multiplier to 2.5. Under Attenuation, click Use and set Far/Start=200; Far/End=1000, and render camera03-painting. The light intensity falls off beginning at 200 and ending at 1000, with the effect that the corners and the area beneath the painting are darker.

6. Render camera03-painting. The attenuation settings override the Overshoot, creating a fade over distance. The still life in the foreground is illuminated while the background fades dark (see Figure 17.11). Note there is no light source outside the building. The apparent outside luminosity is from the environment map.

In order to reduce rendering time, no raytraced materials or map materials were included in this scene, even though some lights use raytraced shadows. R2's raytraced materials enable you to limit raytracing to the particular objects you are emphasizing, and to further limit what objects or background are reflected on them. Try selectively modifying the materials on individual objects in this tutorial and re-render the scene. Depending on camera angles and lighting, this noticeable difference can create the illusion that the entire scene is raytraced.

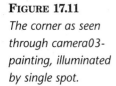

FIGURE 17.11

The corner as seen through camera03-painting, illuminated by single spot.

The lighting in this part of the scene still isn't complete. The still life on the table needs to be lit. The painting consists of three types of glass objects on a highly textured wood tabletop. For the purposes of this exercise, you don't care about shadows cast by the table or glass elsewhere in the scene, only how the glass affects and is affected by the table and the environment.

The glass bottle, drinking glasses, and fruit bowl, while having no raytraced materials, have highly reflective, transparent, and translucent texture mapping designed to show off reflections from outside, from the floor, and from the painting behind the camera. Also, you want the glass distortions to be visible as you look through each object. Finally, you want crisp shadows to set off the glasses, and to see the texture contrast between the glass and the wood tabletop.

In the following exercise, you use a three-light setup: a key light for highlight and raytraced shadows, a backlight to give minimum light to the back of the room, and attenuation toward the camera, and a fill light, caused by the spotlight on the painting, set to overshoot. Note, this is not the Triangle lighting discussed previously because the key and fill lights both come from the same side.

ILLUMINATING THE STILL LIFE WITH A THREE-LIGHT SETUP

1. Load lit_tut3.max. This should be identical to the final step of the previous exercise (see Figure 17.12).

FIGURE 17.12

Placement of the four lights in the scene: omni upstairs, spotlight on the painting, omni downstairs in front of room divider, and key spotlight illuminating still life. Note the placement and attenuation settings for the omni spotlight.

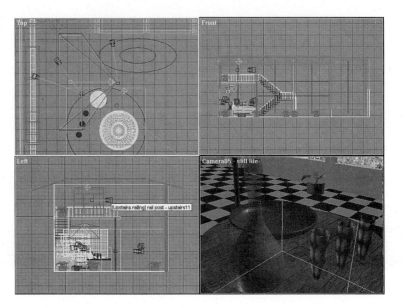

2. In the lower-left viewport, change to camera05-still life. Using the settings from the previous exercise, render the viewport. The still life gets a fill light effect from the spot on the painting, but the background is too dark.

3. In the Front viewport, create an Omni light downstairs, located at approximately X=1075, Y=300 View coordinates. Label it **Omni01 downstairs back**. Set multiplier=0.5, click cast shadows. Set Attenuation Near/End to 380, click Use, and position the light so that the attenuation circle touches the floor and the room partition. Set Far/Start=1500 and Far/End=2000 and click Use. (The Far/End attenuation should extend to the left wall.) The light ramps up from 0 to 1.0 intensity from attenuation ranges 0 to 380, it is at full strength at attenuation ranges 380 to 1500, and it fade down between 1500 and 2000.

4. Create a spotlight to the left of camera05-still life, pointing down toward the glassware on the table. You should see the area covered by the spot. This will be your "key" light. (Figure 17.13 shows placement in the top viewport.) Name it **Spot02-still life key**. Open the modify panel.

5. Set Hotspot=10 and Falloff=30. Set the multiplier at two times that for Omni01 downstairs back, in this case 1.0. Check Cast Shadows and Use Raytraced Shadows.

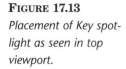

FIGURE 17.13

Placement of Key spot-light as seen in top viewport.

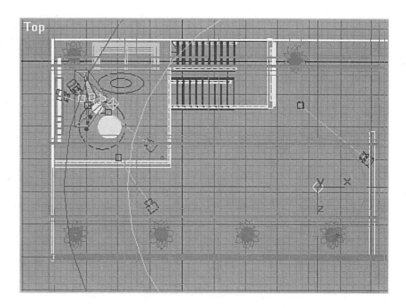

6. With the Spot02 still life key selected, go to the Modify panel, and click Exclude. In the Exclude, Include dialog, check Include and Both; choose the Table and still life group and click > to move it to the right column. Click OK. This assures that only the table and glasses are affected by the key spot. Render camera05-still life. Save the file.

   R2 includes selective raytracing, which is implemented through the Material Editor through the raytraced material and the raytraced map. (Do not confuse this with raytraced shadows which are implemented through lights, or a dedicated raytrace renderer such as Raymax). You can assign a raytraced map to a Reflection channel, or a Shininess channel for an extra sharpness in your render, which can create the illusion of having raytraced the entire scene. Step 7 is an optional step to do just that.

7. Open the Material Editor and locate the carafe material. Choose a raytraced map for the Reflection Map or a Shininess Map and re-render the scene (this will take quite some time). Compare the sharp reflections on the carafe with the fruit bowl. The final scene is shown in Figure 17.14.

FIGURE 17.14

The still life, using a key light with ray-traced shadows including only the table and glass, an attenuated omni light lighting the background, and the painting spot acting as additional fill.

Notice how the shadows change from object to object. The shadows are most pronounced on the bowl, lesser for the bottle and almost absent on the glasses, even though each object has its shadow casting/receiving properties turned on and reacts to the same light. The scene is a mix of natural and incandescent lighting in which shadows are present, but subtle and natural. With the previously described techniques, you can add drama by increasing contrast, by adding more lights to further illuminate the glasses or intensify their shadows. If you like, you can prevent any scene object from casting or receiving shadows altogether by right-clicking the object and choosing Properties (receiving and casting shadows are enabled by default). You also can *color* the shadows indirectly by adjusting the filter settings for the material on a transparent scene object.

Free Spotlight

A Free Spotlight contains all the capabilities of a Target Spotlight but without a target object. Instead of positioning a target to position the spotlight's cone, you rotate the Free Spot to aim its beam. The reason to choose a Free Spot over a Target Spot may be personal preference or the need to animate the light in conjunction with other geometries.

When animating lights, there are times when they need to remain stationary in relation to another object. Car headlights, spotlights, and a miner's cap are typical examples. These are situations for which a Free Spot is intended because they can be simply linked to the object and continue to aim their light as the object moves in the scene. This is especially important when the spotlight is rectangular or projecting an image. In such cases, the light needs to bank or roll with the parent object to produce the correct effect. Rotating the light and its resulting projection can only occur reliably with a Free Spot.

TIP

Lights are frequently animated by using different controllers types (the LookAt controller, Path controller, Expression controller). Understanding how the controller drives lighting motion usually determines whether or not you choose to use targets at all.

Ambient Light

If you were to eliminate all light objects in a scene, you would be left with ambient light. This is the ever-present light that seems to exist in the world when you cannot identify a specific light source. In actuality, light is bouncing off surfaces to illuminate surfaces that are not directly illuminated. Ambient light is a method in MAX to approximate this reflected light.

The color of the ambient light is applied to every surface in the scene before any other lighting is applied. The ambient light serves as the starting point from which all other lights add or subtract. Because ambient light is universally applied, increasing its level reduces contrast and "flattens" the scene. A scene illuminated solely by ambient light has no contrast or shading, with every side and facet being rendered with the same intensity. Only geometric silhouettes and material properties are definable.

NOTE

Because of its flat, uniform, brightening effect, ambient light is very limited in its ability to simulate indirect lighting. By illuminating light and shadow the same, it reduces the effect of bump maps as well as all contrast in the scene. Furthermore, ambient lighting washes out special effects you might include that simulate color reflection resulting from the proximity of neighboring objects (in the real world, if a red apple is placed against a white wall, the wall picks up a diffuse pink from the apple). Radiosity lighting and rendering technologies address these shortcomings. Radiosity solutions are not part of 3DS MAX R2 but are available as third-party plug-ins.

Ambient light is not an object, but rather is part of the Environment system and is adjusted in the Environment dialog accessed from the Rendering, Environment pull-down. Because ambient light is always present, its light and color are what you see in cast shadows. If you want to make the colors of your scene look especially deep, you should tint the ambient light's color slightly to be the complement of the dominant shadow-casting lights. If the light is the yellowish cast of the moon, an ambient light level of deep purple intensifies the moonlight's effect.

At times, a pure white ambient light is useful for rendering "flat" art such as text, logos, and illustrative designs where you do not want any shading to occur. Because the scene's total light level is white, no effects from any other light sources exist if the materials used have identical Ambient and Diffuse base colors (as in locked Diffuse and Ambient maps). If differences exist between the Ambient and Diffuse colors, the materials shift toward their diffuse values as illumination increases across their surfaces. Rather than adjusting material definitions, you can simply eliminate the other light sources. If you have no light objects in the scene, you will actually need to create one and turn it off to eliminate the influence of the default lighting setup.

NOTE

When only ambient light is used to illuminate the scene, the ambient base color of the assigned material is used. Illuminating a scene with pure white ambient light renders all materials according to their ambient color values. This may seem surprisingly dark, given the common technique of making the ambient color a darker version of the diffuse.

In practice, many artists prefer to use a dim ambient light or none at all. Instead they simulate the effect of indirect lighting by using several omni, directional, and spot lights, alone or in combination, as fill lights. This preserves color, contrast, and texture. One of the best examples of this is the initial shot of the Brachiasaurus in *Jurassic Park*, in which multiple spot lights are used as fill lights to match the dinosaur against the background live action plate.

A common mistake is to increase the ambient light considerably in an effort to reduce the need for other light sources. Rather than make things easier, this approach usually results in a dull scene without much contrast or mood.

Global Lighting

In 3DS MAX R2, you position and adjust fill lights in relation to the target geometry and each other, then adjust them globally with the Global Lighting settings in the Environment dialog.

Global Lighting was added in R2 Environment dialog box. The Tint and Level settings can be animated and affect all lights in the scene except Ambient light. A Tint color other than white tints all the colors in the scene; the Levelspinner acts as a multiplier. The default value for the Level Spinner is 1.0 and the minimum value is 0. At Level = 0, scene lights turn off. Ambient light and combustion objects are unaffected. This differs from other light objects that accept a negative multiplier (literally removing light from the scene).

One good use for these Tint and Level controls is matching fill lighting with live action footage; another is animating the change from afternoon to evening lighting for an interior scene illuminated by indirect outdoor light. This tool becomes increasingly useful as you add lights and their combined complexity increases—you now have a single animatable dimmer and color switch.

Transforming Lights

Light objects are positioned like any other object in the scene with the Move and Rotate transforms. Unlike other objects, the Scale transform only scales ranges and does not affect other attributes. Transform controls are often used to give finer control over the light's position and orientation. Path, Look At, and Expression controllers are often used to track a light on a path, follow key objects, or have them react to other events in the scene.

Spotlights and Directional Lights, like cameras, can be used to define a viewport. Spotlight or Directional Light viewports enable you to see where the light is aimed and are useful tools for locating shadows and projector maps. Spotlight viewports replace the navigation icons with those that relate specifically to spotlights. These controls correspond to their camera equivalents, with falloff equaling FOV. The hotspot control has no effect on the view unless it bumps into the falloff and forces the falloff to increase.

Lighting methods also rely on shadows and how to best use them in an overall lighting design. Specific control of shadows is of key importance when using lights. With too many or not enough shadows, a scene isn't as realistic and convincing.

Working with Shadows

In the world of 3DS MAX R2, light objects illuminate every face that is oriented toward them—that is, presents a normal to them—until they are stopped by their respective ranges or falloffs. This light transmits through the surfaces and is not blocked unless the light is told to cast shadows. Lights that do not cast shadows continue to penetrate the scene and devalue the darkness of any cast shadows.

3DS MAX R2's shadow casting ability is controlled for each light in that spot, direction, or omni light's Shadow Parameters in the command panel (see Figure 17.15). As discussed in the following section, this is where you control whether a light casts shadows at all, if it uses shadow maps or raytraced shadows, if it uses Global Settings for the shadow map, and how the Map Bias, Size, SMP Range, Raytrace Bias, and Absolute Map Bias settings apply.

FIGURE 17.15

The Shadow Parameter settings are available for spot, directional, and omni lights.

Casting shadows is an expensive option, but one that adds tremendous realism to the finished scene. Raytraced shadows consume rendering time, whereas shadow maps require memory resources in addition to some rendering time. Limiting the spotlight's falloff to just the area that requires shadows saves rendering time for both types. Excluding objects from shadows, either within the light or through the object's attribute, also aids in reducing rendering overhead.

Each light's shadow can be set individually or globally. Because each light affects a different area of the scene and has different requirements, you more than likely will be adjusting the shadow parameters of each light. Each directional, omni, and spot light contains a Local Shadow Control dialog that can be accessed with the light's parameters.

The global shadow values control the parameters of all shadow-casting lights that have the Use Global Settings check box turned on. The effects of these parameters are the same, but they are not tailored to each light's needs. Newly created lights are created with Use Global Settings turned off and use built-in system default values for the shadow parameters. If you turn on Use Global settings, the parameters are changed to the global settings if any other light has Use Global Setting on. If no other light has Use Global Settings on, the current values are used as the global setting values.

3DS MAX R2 supplies two forms of shadows with very different properties: raytraced and shadow maps. The choice of which to use comes down to the basic questions of "Should the shadow edge be crisp or soft?" and "Does the shadow need to respect the object's transparency?"

Using Raytraced Shadows

Raytraced shadows are accurate, have crisp edges, and nearly always engage, or touch the object that casts them. Any time a crisp edge is needed and an object's transparency values must be calculated, raytraced shadows are necessary. 3DS MAX R2 ships with a new raytrace material and raytrace map, which are configured and assigned through the Material Editor. You can use raytraced materials without using raytraced shadows and vice versa.

Raytraced shadows take into account any opacity information contained within a material. This can come in the form of an opacity map and its mask, the material's Transparency parameter sliders, and In/Out options. For non-raytraced materials, these are the only aspects that define transparency; the raytraced materials have additional parameters for luminosity, transparency, translucency, color density, and fog color that affect opacity information. Additional maps defining textures or bumps have no affect on the cast shadow. Simulation of these surface markings requires you to copy the appropriate bitmap to be an opacity map or mask for the material, or configure them within a raytraced material.

Spotlights that use raytraced shadows treat all opacity in terms of luminance or intensity. Material cutouts can be extremely convincing when illuminated by these lights. These materials have matching texture and opacity maps and often are used for entourage objects, such as trees, people, and cars, but also can be the individual leaves of a tree or the mullion bar pattern in a window.

NOTE

Raytraced shadows are ideal for simulating bright light sources, especially sunlight. The only drawback is that these shadows require extensive calculations during a rendering. Because the area calculated for each spotlight is based on its falloff, constraining their radii to smaller, specific areas can save considerable rendering time.

Raytrace Bias

The only parameter that controls the effects of raytraced shadows is the Raytrace Bias setting. This is not immediately obvious within the light's Shadow Parameters rollout because the three shadow map parameters remain editable when the Raytraced Shadows option is selected.

Unlike shadow map parameters, this value rarely needs to be adjusted. A value of 1.0 forms no bias, whereas large values begin to pull the shadow away from the casting object and lower values push it closer. This value needs to be adjusted if the objects casting shadows contain self-intersecting elements. Raytraced shadows that contain holes when they should be solid or do not engage the shadow-casting mesh have bias values that are too high and need to be reduced.

Using Shadow Maps

The primary capability of a shadow map is to create soft shadows. This is a more realistic effect than raytraced shadows, but can be difficult to achieve because its control is a critical balance of its map parameters. Casting shadows with shadow maps requires more memory but renders faster than raytraced shadows, especially within a complex model. The trade-off, however, is that shadow maps take preparation time and constant testing to ensure their accuracy and appropriateness.

In real life, the crispness of a shadow is a product of the object's proximity to the surface on which it is casting a shadow. A window that casts a shadow of its mullions across the room is very soft, whereas the chair that sits in the same light casts a very crisp shadow. Because of this duality, you might consider using multiple shadow-casting lights having different shadow effects for scenes that require extreme realism.

You may find that the realistic effect of soft shadows is lost on many people who view your work. To the majority of lay people, the definition of a shadow is a crisp, definite shape cast from the object. If you do not have the opportunity to examine the shadow, such as in an animation, the sophisticated effects gained from soft shadows are nearly always lost, so consider this as you are working.

Shadow Map Size and Shadow Quality

The shadow map's size is the most critical and expensive factor in getting a shadow "right." The Renderer creates a square bitmap to the size specified in the Map Size parameter. The memory cost for this map is four bytes per map pixel, so a 500-line shadow map costs 500×500×4 = 1 MB of RAM. This map is then stretched to the size of all shadow-casting objects with the light's falloff cone and projected back onto the receiving surfaces.

Because the shadow map is actually a bitmap, the shadow begins to pixelate and form jagged edges if it is not at least the size of the rendered area. The larger the shadow-casting object's extents, the more the shadow map is stretched and the higher its resolution needs to be to maintain an unaliased edge. You can limit the mapped areas size, and thus the size of the required shadow map, by constraining the spotlight's falloff. You can also decrease the shadow map's extents by turning off the cast shadows attribute of distant objects.

NOTE

Overshoot is extremely useful with shadow maps because their effect can be localized without creating distinct pools of light.

Map Bias and Engagement Accuracy

The Map Bias value is basically used to fix the inherent inaccuracy shadow maps have in engaging the objects that cast them. The lower the bias value, the more the shadow is pulled to the object. The Absolute Map Bias check box, on by default, determines whether the map bias is calculated absolute or relative to all the objects in the scene. Leave this box checked for most situations.

Map Bias values of 1.0 for architectural models and 3.0 for broadcast-design work are generally recommended. It is very important not to use these values without first experimenting with them in your scene. Each model's, and possibly each spotlight's, needs vary according to the light's angle, distance, and the final output resolution. In addition, the size of the scene casting shadows plays an important factor in the engagement accuracy of shadow maps.

Map Sample Range and Edge Softness

The Map Sample Range value controls the softness of the shadow's edge—the higher the value, the softer the shadow edge. The key word in this parameter is "sample" because the program actually samples more of the surrounding edge to blur the result together to create the soft edge. The quality and accuracy of this edge is a balance of the shadow map bias, size, and sample range.

As the sample values increase, so does the shadow's softness. The time it takes to render these soft shadows increases as well because the program is averaging more samples over a larger area of the shadow bitmap. These values are specific to the given resolution, bias map size, spotlight distance, and size of the scene; differing values vary proportionately.

Each object has shadow exclusion capabilities built into its attribute definitions. When these attributes are combined with the exclusion capabilities of lights, the capability to create special lighting effects is considerable.

As seen in Figure 17.15, you can control whether objects cast or receive shadows on a per light basis. Likewise, you can control this on a per object basis by right-clicking any object and accessing its Properties dialog. The use of these attributes is unique for every model, but remember that using them does save in rendering time. This is especially true for objects that take up a great deal of the scene, such as ground planes, walls, and ceilings. Most of the time, these objects do not need to cast shadows, and ceilings do not need to receive them. Turning off the appropriate attributes saves considerable rendering time and makes shadow maps much more accurate.

Shadows are very important, but too many shadows may be unnecessary or distracting. In this regard, careful selection of where shadows are cast both speeds up rendering time, as well as realism in a scene. In addition to casting shadows, lights have another useful function, and that is to project an image.

Because shadows in 3DS MAX are only an approximation of real-world shadows, scene realism comes from your artistry in controlling shadow parameters—the softness of the edges, and how close the shadow butts up against the object. In the following exercise, you will explore these controls and how the settings vary according to scene object characteristics.

EXPLORING SHADOW MAPS

1. Load the file bias_tut.max from the accompanying CD-ROM. Examine the spotlight in the scene. The Attenuation, Decay, Contrast, and

Soften Diff. Edges are set at 0 or are turned off. Hotspot equals 45 and Falloff equals 60. Cast Shadows and Use Global settings are off.

2. Render camera01 at 800×600. The objects are illuminated by the spot but cast no shadows. The edges of the spot light are softened.

3. Select Spot01. Under Shadow Parameters, check Cast Shadows, Use Global Settings, and Absolute Bias Map (checked on by default). Make sure Shadow Maps is checked. Render Last. All shadows have anti-aliased edges and the shadow "color" is the result of the backdrop material illuminated by the omni light (see Figure 17.16).

FIGURE 17.16

Shadows created with Cast Shadows, Global Settings, and Use Shadow Maps checked, and Map Bias equals 4.0, Size equals 256, and Smp Range equals 4.0.

The shadows for the small teapots show a good balance of definition and softness, while the shadows from the large objects appear course and hard.

4. Uncheck Absolute Map Bias and Render Last. The orange teapot's shadow is less defined. Check Absolute Map Bias.

5. Increase the Map Bias spinner from 4.0 to 20.0. Render Last. Note the shift in shadow placement away from the object; the small teapot is missing.

6. Reduce Map Bias to 0 and Render Last. The shadow maps are pulled in, so shadows on the object make them no longer appear smooth.

7. Set Map Bias = 4.0 (default) and increase size from default 256 to 1024. Render Last. The shadow edges are sharpened.

8. Increase Smp Range to 20 (the maximum value) and Render Last. The shadows on the torus and large teapot are antialiased over an area similar to that at the default settings, but the gradation is much finer. The small teapot's shadow is now out of focus and unnatural (see Figure 17.17).

FIGURE 17.17

Shadows created with Case Shadows, Global Settings, and Use Shadow Maps checked, with Map Bias equaling 4.0, Size equaling 1024, and Smp Range equaling 20.0.

The shadows from the large objects are smooth and clear, but the shadows from the small objects appear blurred.

Note the shadow errors in Figures 17.16 and 17.17 caused by checking Use Shadow Maps. The scene objects sit on a single, flat plane with a checkered texture map. The shadows should not "break" across the checkers. If you increase the Smp Range without increasing size, the error becomes more pronounced. Checking Use Raytraced Shadows cures this problem.

9. Check Use Raytraced Shadows. Render Last. The shadows take on a hard edge and flow accurately across the checkered surface (see Figure 17.18).

10. Return the spinners to their default value (Map Bias = 4.0; Size = 256; Smp Range = 4.0, check Absolute Bias). Render Last. The Map Bias, Size, and Smp Range settings have no effect on raytraced shadows.

11. Increase the Ray Trace Bias spinner from 0.2 to 2.0. Render Last. The shadow position and shape changes, and begins to break up at the edges. The distortion increases as you increase the spinner value.

Figure 17.18

Using raytraced shadows give shadows with crisp edges flowing evenly and accurately across the checker-mapped surface.

Projecting Images

Spot, Directional, and Omni lights can project images and animated materials in a film projector fashion. This opens up many special-effect possibilities. The colors of the projected image blend with the light's and reduce the amount of light according to the bitmap colors' luminance values. Black completely blocks light, whereas white does not stop any light.

Projector lights actually have a strong tradition of use in the theater and lighting design. One of the most traditional effects is when the image is opaque (black on white) and casts a shadow rather than an image. When used in this manner, a projector light is often called a gobo light. Implying cast shadows with this technique can create dramatic and memory efficient effects within 3DS MAX, as shown in Figures 17.19 and 17.20.

Figure 17.19

A gobo cutout for a projector's bitmap.

FIGURE 17.20
Textured light created
by casting "shadows"
with a projector light.

Projected Lights

Spot, directional, and omni lights can project an image when their Projector option is activated. Clicking the Map button brings up the Material Editor's Material/Map Browser (see Figure 17.21), from which you can choose an existing map that is defined in the Material Editor, or choose the scene, an active slot in the Material Editor, a selected object, a library, or define a new one. From here you assign the map to the projector; you can drag and drop the map to any slot in the Material Editor, which is useful if you need to modify the map or access the environment coordinates. The Environment Mapping Coordinates (Screen, Spherical) can only be adjusted from within the Material Editor, at the mapping level. Alternatively, you can bypass the Material Editor and drag the map directly from the Material/Map Browser and drop it on the projector Map button in the command panel.

Only maps, not materials, can be assigned to the projector button, but you can use multi-layered maps. You can also retrieve projected maps used in the scene from the Material Editor by using Get Material/from Scene or Material Editor.

NOTE

If an animated map type is chosen as the projector image, each frame is shown in sequence when a range of frames is rendered. The slide projector is thus turned into a movie projector. The animation may be an animated file type such as AVI, a sequence of files in a gobo, or the result of animated parameters in the chosen map channel.

FIGURE 17.21

The Material/Map Browser.

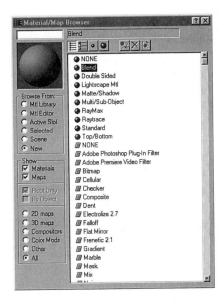

The projected bitmap is stretched to fit the limits of the spotlight's falloff. For a circular spotlight, the bitmap is stretched to the boundary square that encloses the circle, and the image is clipped by the circle. You can match the aspect ratio of rectangular lights to that of the projected image with the Bitmap Fit option.

NOTE

When the Projector option is used in conjunction with Overshoot, the image is still constrained to the size of the falloff. This edge, however, is aliased if the projected image's edge color (that is, background) blocks the spotlight's color. Because white never mixes additively, it should be the first choice for an image's background as long as the light has a positive multiplier.

TIP

Including a one-pixel-wide white perimeter on projected bitmaps eliminates the harsh aliasing that occurs when the projecting spotlight is employing overshoot.

Adjusting Light Projections

A projector light's falloff border should really be thought of as a Planar mapping icon because it acts in exactly the same way. The proportions and rotation of the bitmap are dictated by the placement of the border. The border has a small vertical line to indicate the top of a projection.

The Asp(ect) command under Spotlight Parameters in the command panel controls the aspect ratio of a spotlight when the cone is set to a rectangular shape. The proportions of a circular spotlight are obviously fixed, and consequently the Asp(ect) settings are disabled when you select the circular cone. In the tutorials, you used a rectangular spot light to illuminate a painting and it also works very well with projectors.

When projecting an image, the Bitmap Fit option should be your first choice because it is easiest, most accurate, and most relevant (see Figure 17.22). Select a rectangular spotlight and access the Bitmap Fit command. After selecting the desired bitmap, which more than likely is the projected image, the light's rectangular height and width is changed to match the image. Alternatively, you can use the Asp(ect) settings to adjust the rectangular proportions; this works well when you use patterned maps as projectors.

FIGURE 17.22
Bitmap Fit sizes a projection spotlight to fit the relative height and width of a bitmap.

NOTE

The projected image can be rotated, and its rotation can even be animated. This is done in the projector map's material settings, in the Material Editor.

In Practice: Lighting in MAX

- **Triangle lighting:** For many scenes, this lighting style may be the ticket to a well-lit scene. For larger scenes, move the lights out away from the objects. This helps to dissipate a light's intensity across the scene and help remove hotspots.

- **Attenuation:** This is a good place to start when lighting a scene. Very few lights illuminate objects far away, and the use of attenuation is essential in simulating this.

- **Shadows: raytraced versus shadow maps:** Both types of shadows have their strengths and limitations, and their use should be determined by assessing these factors. Raytraced shadows are easier to set up and cast the most accurate shadow, but take longer to render and generally have a crisp edge to them. Shadow maps offer a soft-edged shadow and require less rendering time, but take up more memory and have several settings that must be monitored in order to look realistic.

- **Projectors:** Omni, spot lights, and directional lights have the capability to project images, which are useful for a variety of things, such as simulating a movie projector and firelight, and projecting complex shadows.

Chapter 18

SETTING UP THE ENVIRONMENT

This chapter describes the many capabilities of 3DS MAX's environment features. The Environment dialog contains three types of controls: scene background color / map choice, Atmospheric Effects, and specific settings for each effect. Additionally, R2 contains a sun positioning system (Create / Systems / SunPos) to facilitate placing natural sunlight in the scene. With these features, you create effects and moods that heighten a scene's realism. Specifically, you can add volume lighting, standard, layered, and volume fog, and combustion. These objects offer a wide variety of effects, including fog, haze, fire, smoke, and dusty light rays.

Specifically this chapter covers the following topics:

- Setting up backgrounds
- Using Volume Lights
- Using Fog and Volume Fog
- Using Combustion
- The Sun System
- Establishing Moods
- Lighting with fixtures

NOTE

Note that all atmospheric effects work only in Perspective and Camera views, and some work only with Cameras.

Setting Up Backgrounds

A background can include either a solid color or a map material, which can be single or multi-leveled. Choosing the Background color swatch in the Rendering/Environment dialog brings up the 3DS MAX color selector, allowing precise control of the background color. Choosing a new color does not remove the possibility of saving the alpha channel information.

TIP

For times when you do not desire the rendered image to be aliased with the background, check Don't Antialias Against Background in the Preference settings. Removing aliasing is useful for rendering sprites against a solid background, or for creating borderless graphics for the web, by cutting out the extraneous background.

Selecting a background image is similar to using a projector map for lights. Select the Environment Map button to bring up the 3DS MAX Material/Map browser. From there, a custom map can be made or an existing map can be applied. Or simply drag any map from the Material Editor, Material Map Navigator, Asset Manager, or any other button in the interface that contains a map to the Environment Map button.

Using Volume Lights

Volume lights provide the ability to fill a light cone with particles so the beam or halo becomes evident in the rendering. In computer graphics, this is commonly known as volumetric lighting, and when shadows interrupt the cone, volumetric shadows. This effect is applied to existing light objects in the scene through the Atmosphere section of the Environment controls.

NEW TO R2

MAX R2 expanded the Atmosphere Effects dialog to include naming capability and the ability to Merge effects from other scenes. This opens the possibility of creating and saving modular, animated effects that can be recycled and combined. Volume lights, volume fogs, and combustion combinations become recyclable modules—with animations intact—to later be assigned to any number of lights or atmospheric gizmos.

A Volume light atmosphere can be assigned to numerous lights, and several Volume lights can be used throughout the scene to give local control. Volume lights have a wide variety of parameters that can alter the light's look considerably. A light's fog and attenuation colors, density, volume brightness and darkness, attenuation, filter shadows, and noise attributes are all easily controlled within 3DS MAX's Environment dialog. R2's Filter Shadows options include the ability to Use Light Smp Range. Increasing the light's Sample Range value blurs the shadow cast by the light, which makes the obstruction shadow a better match to the cast shadow and helps prevent aliasing in the fog shadows.

In order to use Volume lights, a light object must first exist. Then, after adding the Volume light to the Environment dialog, a light or series of lights can be assigned to the Volume light's settings. Although many lights can be assigned to one Volume light configuration, optimal results sometimes occur when all the lights don't have the same parameters.

It is important to note that the order in which Volume light effects are layered in the Environment dialog has an effect on how they are rendered (see Figure 18.1). Their order is controlled by the Move Up and Move Down buttons. Effects near the bottom of the list are layered in front of effects near the top of the list. Careful placement of atmospheric effects layers helps avoid any odd layering situations, where a Volume light in the background appears to be in front of another in the foreground.

FIGURE 18.1

*The order of
Atmospheric Effect
objects dramatically
effects the final image.
You can reorder them
or make any of them
inactive in the
Environment dialog.*

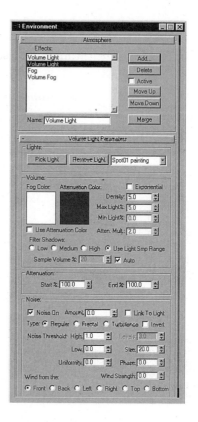

Fog Color and Attenuation Colors Parameters

Several☐REF Effects dialog:R2 expanded features" important parameters control the light's general look (see dialog in Figure 18.20). The Volume Light's fog and fog attenuation color affects everything else about the light. The attenuation color lets you ramp the color of your fog within the near and far attenuation ranges (not just between the Start and End values of either Near or Far). Note this controls near and far attenuation, and is different from the effect produced when the volume fog color is different from the light's color. The falloff color, for example, takes on the fog color, while the hotspot takes on the light's color.

The following exercise shows how colors are affected by the interaction between volume light attenuation settings, and the attenuation and hotspot/falloff changes for a spot light. You examine the effect when the spot is white, when it's a different color from both the fog color, and finally when the spot and fog attenuation values are the same.

USING ATTENUATION SETTINGS WITH VOLUME LIGHTS

1. Open the file vol_tut.max. This scene consists of a floor, one omni light, and one spot light.

2. Open the Environment dialog, under Atmospheric Effects click Add, and choose Volume Light.

3. Under Volume Light Parameters, click Pick Light and select Spot01.

4. Check Use Attenuation Color. Render the Perspective viewport. You should see a white fog light with white falloff. That the volume light's attenuation is enabled and set to blue has no effect.

5. Under the Spot01's command panel, check and Attenuation/Near/Use (This should be set to Start=0; End=40) and Attenuation/Far/Use (This should be set to Start=150; End=190). Render last. The white spot falls off and attenuates but remains white, notwithstanding the volume light's Attenuation Color setting. Uncheck the Spot01 Use boxes.

6. Under the Volume Light Parameters, click the Fog Color swatch and set this color to 100% red. Render Last. The fog is now red and falls off to white (a pink fade).

7. Check Spot01's Attenuation/Near and Far boxes. Render Last. The color result does not change, but the fog attenuates along the beam.

8. Uncheck both Use boxes. Click Spot01's color swatch and change it from gray to 100% green. Render Last. Now we see the full effect: The falloff edges of Spot01 are green, indicating how the light fades; the light cone is purple, a mixture of the red fog color with the blue attenuation color; the center is gray, a mixture of the green hotspot with red fog and blue fog attenuation.

9. Check Spot01's Use Near and Far Attenuation boxes. Render Last. The purple fog and attenuation remain, and some of the green falloff, but the red, green, blue mix at the hotspot disappears because Spot01's attenuation prevents the hotspot from reaching the surface.

10. At frame 0, turn on the Animate button. Under Volume Light Parameters, set Start% = 0 and End%=200. Advance to frame 30 and increase Start% to 200. Turn off the Animate button and render frames 0 to 30. The purple cone shows the effect of the fog attenuation setting.

11. Drag the Fog Color (red) color swatch to Spot01's color swatch in the command panel and choose copy. Make sure Spot01's Near and Far Attenuation settings are checked. Render the perspective view. With

> the fog color the same as the light color, you don't see much effect of the blue Attenuation Color. Change the Attenuation color to 100% green and Render Last. You should see only a slight change.

Fog attenuation requires that the light's Near and Far Attenuation settings be active. When the light and the fog color are both white, varying the Attenuation Start% and End% under the Volume Light Parameters attenuates the fog between the light's Near and Far Attenuation Settings (in the command panel). The fog's Attenuation Color has little impact. If the light's color, the Fog Color, and Attenuation Color are each different from the other, the three colors blend differently, depending on where you inspect the beam and fog Attenuation Start% and End% settings. The Start% and End% settings cannot be less than 0 but can be greater than 100%. (In the previous example, if you set End%=1000, the fog disappears altogether.)

White fog color and blue attenuation color are the defaults but not always the most appropriate. A Volume light's color should be considered as a part of an overall lighting design. Keep in mind that Volume light is additive and that the color of the light's glow changes an object's original color according to the intensity of the glow.

Other Volume Light Parameters

The Exponential checkbox affects the appearance of an object's opacity as it passes through a volume light or fog. Unchecked, objects may not blend properly in the atmosphere. The opacity maps on bitmaps used to map face particles may appear as squares rather than objects as they move through the atmosphere.

Density controls the light's volumetric density. The greater the value, the more opaque the entire light becomes. Looking around in nature, a really dense light is found only in dense atmospheric conditions, such as in fog. Unless you are creating a very dense atmosphere, therefore, keep the light density fairly low. The default value is 5, and a value between 2 and 6 is recommended.

After Density, the Max Light and Min Light parameters are used to control how the light dissipates. The Max Light controls the "whitest" glow of the light, and the Min Light controls the minimum glow. Note that the Min Light, if set greater than 0, creates a glow to the entire scene, similar to how Ambient light controls the entire scene. Also, a Max Light value of 100 is only as bright as is allowed by the Density parameter. To increase the brightness of the glow, increase the density.

Noise can also be added to the volumetric light, which gives the impression of a dustier environment. R2 expands the noise controls to make them consistent with settings in the Material Editor. When the Noise parameter is enabled, additional parameters become available, including Noise Type (Regular, Fractal, Turbulence, and Invert), Noise Threshold, Level, Amount, Uniformity, Size, Phase, Wind Strength, and Wind Direction. The Amount and Size parameters control the amount and size of the noise added; the threshold controls contrast between light and dark. Uniformity controls whether the noise is an even haze or a spotty turbulence. Checking the Link to Light setting makes the noise move with its light source, not suitable for most atmospheric solutions, but useful, for example, in creating a moving light source that is spinning off turbulence.

The remaining parameters, Phase, Wind Strength, and Wind Direction all control the look of the volumetric light as it is animated. Wind Direction is rather self-explanatory, but it is important to note that Phase and Wind Strength affect each other. Phase is the value that is to be animated, but the noise's movement is affected by Wind Strength. If there is no Wind Strength, Phase makes only the noise churn, but it does appear to go anywhere. With Wind Strength, a volumetric light appears to have particles that move through the scene following its Wind Direction.

N OTE

To animate noise in a volumetric light or fog you need only animate the Phase setting. Examine Envsmoke.max in 3D Studio MAX's SCENES directory (see Figure 18.2). All the scenes beginning with ENV are good files to explore for feature environment controls, in particular fogs and combustion. Experiment by animating the smoke in envsmoke.max from that directory.

FIGURE 18.2

Envsmoke.max—
Volumetric light noise.

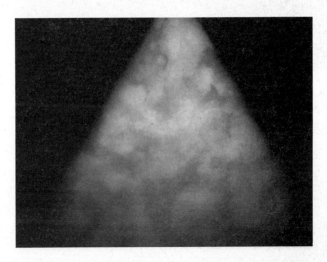

The following exercise adds atmospherics to the still life scene from the previous tutorial. Although using key, fill, and back lighting to illuminate overlapping objects varying in color, texture, and surface creates realism, you are accustomed to seeing some haze in the real world. Minimal fog effects work well to counter the overly pristine look of 3D graphics. R2 supports naming effects and merging effects from other scenes, encouraging you to accumulate a library of preset effects.

GENERATING VOLUME LIGHT

1. Open fog_tut.max. Open the Environment dialog. Under Atmosphere, Effects, click Add, and choose Volume Light. This opens the Volume Light dialog.

2. Select Pick Light and choose scene light Spot02-still life key. (The key light from the last tutorial.) In the Modify panel, make sure Use Shadow Maps is checked, which reduces rendering time.

3. Click the Environment dialog. If you render at the default settings, the area representing the Hotspot will be nearly opaque and will fade in the falloff area. Set Max. Light=10. Render camera02-stairs. With Min. Light=0, the fog is restricted to the light; with Max Light=10, you can see the beam of light as if it shines through dust, but the reflections and refractions of the glass remain visible. Clone the VFB.

4. Add a second volume light and pick Spot01-painting. Also, select spot01-painting in the main UI and access its settings in the Modify command panel. Because the Volume Light Parameters interact with the light's own settings, it's easiest to work back and forth between the two feature sets.

5. Set Max. Light=5.0, check Noise On and render last. Figure 18.3 shows the final scene.

Volume lights and R2's fog features share the capability of adding visible atmosphere to a scene. This atmosphere can be a uniform haze, as in the previous exercise, or it can evidence turbulence with the noise settings. Volume lights and fogs can be used together, can complement each other, and can overlap in their usage.

Three characteristics distinguish volume lights from fogs: volume lights cannot be active without a designated scene light (omni, directional, or spot); their size and location are defined by that light; and they can be used with projector lights for streaked-atmospheric effects. On the other hand, fogs either fill or layer the entire scene, or can be localized to a volume. The following section looks at the types of fog and their functions.

FIGURE 18.3

The still life with volume light added to create haze in the room. Notice how it affects the view of the entire room, and the outside, even though it is localized in the foreground.

Using Fog and Volume Fog

3DS MAX has three types of fog: standard, layered, and volume. They have similar but unique uses. You access them by first adding fog objects in the Environment, Atmosphere Effects dialog (see Figure 18.4):

- **Standard Fog:** 3DS MAX's standard fog is probably the simplest to set up and gives a general atmospheric wash to the scene. Requiring a camera, Standard Fog's depth is controlled by the camera's environment ranges. Standard Fog can use an Environment Color Map and an Environment Opacity Map for the fog's color, allowing a wide range of colored and textured fog.

NOTE

The Near and Far percent values affect the fog in an inverse manner of Volume Lights. With Fog, nothing is visible past 100%. This also means that, without any background geometry, the fog is rendered at 100% and comes out as a solid color. When Exponential is checked, the rate at which it goes from 0% to 100% is exponential, dramatically changing the look of the fog.

- **Layered Fog:** A layered fog atmosphere enables you to define a floating slab of fog that is fixed in place, independent of your camera placement. The slab is always parallel to your Top viewport, but you have

complete control over its vertical start and stop points with the Top
and Bottom parameters. These values refer to unit distances along the
vertical axis and position and are fixed for the scene.

FIGURE 18.4

*Standard/Layered Fog
settings.*

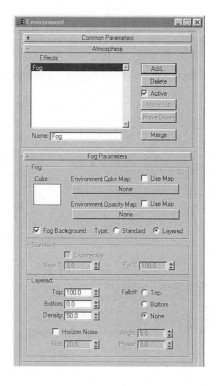

The layered fog's position is not fixed. You can animate the effect of
lifting fog by animating its Top and Bottom parameters. All other
parameters are animatable as well, by using the Animate button.

Varying a fog's density allows for a wide variety of fog, from a light
mist to a fully opaque wall of fog. Layered fog has a uniform density
of 50% of the fog color, and uneven density is achievable with the use
of an opacity map.

TIP

Layered fog has a clear, straight horizon. This effect is useful when the horizon is far away, but
sometimes looks unnatural. Noise can be added, blending the horizon, which is often useful
with scenes that do not offer a clear, distant horizon.

■ **Volume Fog:** This type of fog is useful in creating animated clouds that can blow or be flown through (see Figure 18.5). The effect is a true 3D effect and varies within space and time. Volume Fog is controlled similarly to other fog types, as well as volumetric noise. Wind Strength controls the speed of the wind and is used in conjunction with an animated phase parameter to create moving fog.

FIGURE 18.5

Volume fog, as constrained to each time of gizmo from env_vols.max, which ships with R2.

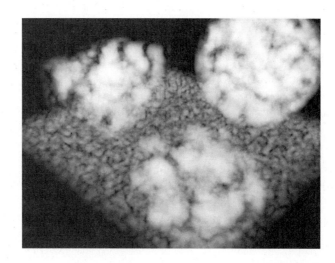

The following exercise adds fog to the outside environment. In this first example, you use Layered Fog. Because 3DS MAX's Standard and Layered Fogs objects fog the entire scene, you have a problem—how to make the fog appear outside but not inside the building? R2 introduced an Environment Opacity Map capability in the fog settings for this problem. You can use your completed tutorial file from the last exercise, or add fog_tut.max from the accompanying CD.

CREATING FOG

1. Change the lower left viewport to camera06-outside and set the viewport to Smooth + Highlights.

2. Open the Environment dialog and uncheck the Active box for any Volume Lights in the scene. Here you are looking out the window and have no interest in rendering volume lighting that doesn't show.

3. Display the background image in the viewport, and check Use Environment Background, Display Background, and Apply Source and Display to Active Only. Render the scene and clone the VFB.

4. Click the Save icon in the Virtual Frame Buffer. In the Browse Images for Output dialog, choose a targa type image file. Press Setup to open the Targa Image Control dialog. Set Bits per Pixel equal to 32 and check Alpha Split. Close the dialog, name the file **outside.tga**, and click OK. In the directory you saved the file to, you will see two new files, outside.tga and a_outside.tga. This second one is an alpha mask you will use to make the fog look as if it is outside but not inside. Your rendered file should match Figure 18.6.

FIGURES 18.6

Rendered View looking outside the window without fog and the alpha channel to be used as opacity map.

5. Open the Material Editor and choose an empty slot. Go to the Maps rollout and click Diffuse map button. Choose the Bitmap map from the Material/Map Browser. At the Bitmap level of the Material Editor, choose a_outside.tga. Set Coordinates, Environ Mapping=Screen. Under the Output rollout, check Invert. Then return to the parent level.

6. In the Environment dialog, click the Add button and choose Fog. Under Fog Parameters, make sure Fog Background is checked and choose Layered. Choose Top=-425, Bottom=-550, Density=50, and Falloff=Bottom. Check Horizon Noise, Size=30, Angle=10.

7. Drag the Diffuse Map button from the Material Editor to the Environment Opacity Map button in the Environment dialog and Use Map is automatically turned on.

8. Render the camera06-outside. You should see a morning view of the harbor outside as the sun begins to burn off the fog (see Figure 18.7).

FIGURE 18.7

View outside window with layered fog.

Layered fog has the advantage of allowing you to set a horizon line and specify noise along that horizon. The difficulty lies in the fact that you must use trial and error to locate the horizon line, set the fog thickness, and the angle of falloff. Also, you don't have as much control over fog (noise) consistency as you do elsewhere in MAX. There's an alternative—Volume Fog, which enables you to create an atmospheric apparatus, a specialized gizmo, which contains your volume fog (or combustion for that matter).

9. Return to the Environment dialog, select the fog object and uncheck Active. Click Add and select Volume Fog. Name it **Volume Fog1**. Note the first item under volume Fog Parameters is Pick Gizmo.

10. Go to Create command panel, Helpers. Click the drop-down menu and select Atmospheric Apparatus. You have three choices, BoxGizmo, SphereGizmo, and CylGizmo.

11. Select CylGizmo. In the Left viewport, create a cylinder, with its radius at 300 and height at 3000, and press New Seed.

12. Non-uniform scale the cylinder so that as seen from the end, it appears to be a flattened ellipse. Extend the longer elliptical axis until it is about the width of the building. Rotate the ellipse about 20 degrees, so the far end points up and away from the structure. The fog will fill this volume and will be slightly smaller than the apparatus. Your cylinder gizmo should resemble that in Figure 18.27.

13. Position it so that as you look through camera06 you see the cylinder laying parallel to the ground, about halfway up the window, with the upper edge even with the boat tops (see Figure 18.8). Name it **volume fog1**.

FIGURE 18.8

Setting up a Volume Fog gizmo.

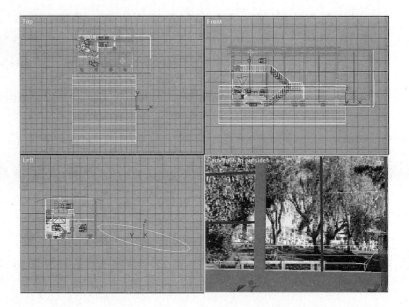

14. In the Environment dialog, select Pick Gizmo and click the cylinder in any viewport. Volume fog1 appears in the gizmo title box. Render camera06-outside. A granular fog shape appears outside the window.

15. Check Exponential and Fog Background and set Density to 1.0, Step Size to 5.0, Type equal to Turbulence. Check that Invert, Size equals 50, and Uniformity equals -0.67.

16. Change the fog color to the sky color in the background plate by right-clicking the last image you rendered in the VFB. An Eyedropper appears, and as you drag it around, you notice the color swatch on the VFB changes. When you see a sky color you like, drag the color swatch from the VFB to the fog color.

17. Render the camera06-outside. Your rendered image should resemble Figure 18.9.

Again, the fog is outside the window. By constraining it to a gizmo, however, you can animate the position, shape, and volume of the fog as well as fog settings. Remember each atmospheric effect is an object that can be assigned to multiple gizmos (or multiple effects assigned to one gizmo), and combined with any other combination of effects, such as layered fog, combustion, and volume lighting.

FIGURE 18.9

Volume fog in the environment as seen from within the building.

Using Combustion

Combustion is great for creating animated fire, smoke, and explosions. Because it is not a particle effect and does not generate geometry, it renders faster and uses less memory than other types of effects.

Combustion uses an atmospheric apparatus that can be a box, cylinder, sphere, or hemisphere. The apparatus contains the combustion effect, and its size, shape, and height can be non-uniformly transformed and animated over time, allowing a flame to flare up or die down, as well as move around the scene. The Stretch and Flame size parameters alter the effect within the apparatus. Multiple apparatus can use the same combustion effect, as well as different combust configurations. Combust uses a random number generator at each apparatus to create its randomness, but can also be reproduced exactly by using the same seed value.

The Atmospheric Apparatus are physical objects and are found in the Create, Helpers command panel, Atmosphere Apparatus sub-category (see Figure 18.10).

Like other atmospheric effects, the effect is easily animated by animating the phase value over time. Combustion contains a specific order in which its effects happen. The effect of the phase values differ, depending on whether Explosion is enabled. When enabled, phase values 0 to 100 are the start-up values of the effect, growing to full intensity when reaching 100. Phases 100 to 200 are when the explosion burns off and the fire turns into smoke. Phases 200 to 300 are when the smoke dissipates and Combustion is completed. When Explosion is not enabled, the phase controls the speed at which the flame churns (see Figure 18.11).

FIGURE 18.10

Creating an Atmospheric Apparatus.

FIGURE 18.11

Combustion settings.

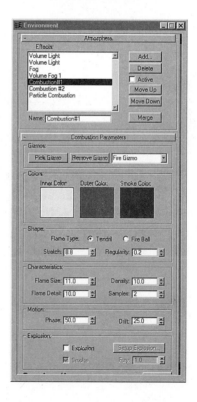

Combustion color is as critical as texture in a convincing effect. If the Explosion and Smoke options are turned on, the inner and outer colors animate to the smoke color during the final phase of the explosion.

If Explosion is off, the smoke color is not visible at all; the inner and outer colors define the entire effect. To add realism, use multiple combustion effects with different settings and with slight inner and outer color variations.

Animating a flame's phase values should be linear, meaning they do not accelerate over time but keep a steady rate. Explosions, however, should quickly rise to 100 and then gradually taper off until 300 is reached. Specific information on Combustion's many features can be found in the 3D Studio MAX R2 online help.

Combustion can either be set to be a Fire Ball, with no discernible top or bottom, or Tendril, which emulates a common flame. Fire Ball is a good choice for explosions and looks good joined with other hemisphere apparatus in a clump.

Combustion is most convincing when you combine multiple combustion effects, varying color, shape and characteristics. In the following exercise you build a fire in the fireplace.

BUILDING A FIRE WITH COMBUSTION

1. Load cmb_tut.max. Unhide [Fireplace group]. Change the lower right viewport to camera01-fireplace. (This scene is identical to that in the previous exercise, with the addition of the fireplace, grate, and log objects, and the Volume Fog object is no longer active).

2. Go to Create, Helpers, Atmospheric Apparatus and create a SphereGizmo inside the fireplace. Set the radius to 75, click New Seed, and check hemisphere. Name it **Fire Gizmo**.

3. Open the Environment dialog and verify that Active is unchecked for the four other atmospheric effects. Click Add and select Combustion. Name it **Combustion #1**. Click Pick Gizmo and select the Fire Gizmo.

4. Set the following parameters:
   Inner Color HSV: 42, 215, 252
   Outer Color HSV: 255, 238, 225
   Select Tendril:
   Stretch: 8.8
   Regularity: 0.2
   Flame Size: 11.0
   Flame Detail: 10.0
   Density: 10.0
   Samples: 2

Motion Phase: 50.0
Drift: 25.0

5. Go back to the Atmospheric Effects section, click Add, and select another combustion object. Name it **Combustion #2**. Pick the same Fire Gizmo.

6. Set the following parameters:
    Inner Color HSV: 34, 153, 253
    Outer Color HSV: 6, 238, 121
    Select Tendril:
    Stretch: 0.7
    Regularity: 0.25
    Flame Size: 15.0
    Flame Detail: 10.0
    Density: 13.0
    Samples: 3
    Motion Phase: 15.0
    Drift: 5.0

7. In the top viewport, create an omni light above Plant03 (the plant in the lower left), and in the viewport, make it level with the top of the fireplace. Label it **Omni-fireplace fill** and set its Multiplier to 0.5.

8. Render camera01-fireplace. Notice there is a multicolored flame in the fireplace, but no sparks and no light coming from the fire.

9. Go to Create, Geometry, and select Particle Systems from the drop-down list. Choose Spray. Create a Spray particle emitter on the log, facing upward. Move the frame slider to 30 to check the particles are spraying upward. Under Parameters, set Render Count to 500, Drop Size to 1.0, and leave other parameters at the default setting. Right-click Spray01 and select Properties. Set Object ID to 1.

10. Return to Atmosphere Effects in the Environment dialog, click Add and Select Particle Combustion. This is a free plug-in written by Peter Watje, included on the accompanying CD. This plug-in is based on the Combustion effect that ships with MAX. You will recognize the settings.

11. Click Pick Object and select the Spray emitter in the scene. Click Fire Ball Flame type, Stretch at 16, Regularity at 0.02, Flame Size at 35.0, Flame Detail at 3.0, Density at 25.0, Phase at 50.0, Particle Size at 2.0, particle Life at 30, and Seed at 50. Go to frame 30 and render camera01-fireplace. You should see sparks rising from the flame. Experiment with these settings to create a more natural turbulence.

12. Next add lighting out into the room. Create an omni light inside the fireplace immediately above the log, and inside the combustion gizmo. Set Multiplier to 5.0. Open the Modify Panel. Click Cast Shadows and Use Global Settings.

13. Choose an empty slot in the Material Editor and label it **Fire Light omni**. Press Get Material, New, and choose a Noise map.

14. Set Noise Type to Turbulence, Levels to 10, Phase to 25, Size to 20. Make Color #1 a dark brown and Color #2 a fire yellow.

15. Drag the Fire Light Omni map from the Material Editor to the Projector Button in the Modify Panel.

16. Return to the Environment dialog, turn on the Volume Light on the painting (used earlier in lighting the still life) and render camera01-fireplace. Save your scene to **mycmb_tut.max**.

17. As a final touch, add highlights to the sparks. This is best accomplished with the Lens Effects Hilight filter applied through Video Post. Load cmb_tut1.max from the accompanying CD. Make sure the camera01-fireplace viewport is active. Open the Video Post Dialog (Rendering/Video Post).

18. The Video Post queue has been set up for you. Select the Lens Effects Hilight filter event and double-click it. This opens the Edit Filter Event dialog box.

19. Click Setup. Lens Effects Hilight renders the image to its own interactive renderer (this may take some time). Once rendered, you can see updated images as you change the filter settings. The filter is preset to add highlights only to Object ID at 1, which in this case is the Spray01 particle system. You can alter the color, shape, and number of sparks and save your settings to a separate file for later use. When you are satisfied, click OK to close the filter. The current settings are also saved with your *.max file.

20. Click the Render button on the Video Post toolbar. In the render dialog, click Single and choose frame 30. Click Render. Video post first renders the image, and then applies the filter in a second pass. Your final render should resemble Figure 18.12.

FIGURE 18.12

The final combustion effect with Lens Effect Hilight applied through Video Post.

NOTE

Remember, Combust is not a light source and does not emit flickering light that would normally be seen in a real fire. Animated light sources are still needed to complete the effect. See env_burn.max, exprockt.max, and the other examples of combustion and explosion in your R2 Scenes directory.

Peter Watje known for his contributions to R1.2, has contributed three freeware plug-ins, Object Combustion, Particle Combustion, and Vertex combustion, included on the CD accompanying this volume, each based on the original Combustion plug-in. Particle Combustion is a volumetric effect similar to the Combustion effect except that Particle Combustion works with particle systems instead of Combustion Apparatus. It works with Snow, Rain, and Sand Blaster. Vertex Combust 1.0 is another combustion effect. It applies a combustion effect for each vertex and also enables you to apply a material to the effect. Further explanation and tutorials are available at his web site, http://www.blarg.com/~peterw/mtutor.html

The Sun System

The Sunlight System (Create, Systems, Sunlight) creates and animates a Free Directional Light that geographically follows the correct angle and movement of the sun over the earth at a given location. Figure 18.13 shows the Sunlight System command panel. You can choose location, date, time, and compass orientation, and can animate date and time, to the end of making a suitable shadow study for a proposed or existing structure. The system is managed by two special controllers, Solar Time, and Solar Date (linear float controllers). Once you create the directional Sunlight, with the light selected, you modify it in Motion Command Panel. The following exercise is the office scene with no atmospheric effects and the lighting turned off.

FIGURE 18.13

Sunlight System Command Panel.

CREATING SUNLIGHT

1. Open the file sun_tut.max from the accompanying CD-ROM. This is the building you've worked with in the previous exercise, but including all lights, atmosphere, and combustion effects with the fireplace removed. The only lighting in the scene is the default lighting. Notice building has a glass roof and wall. Render camera02-stairs, clone the virtual frame buffer (VFB), and leave the image on your desktop.

2. Open the Sunlight system by choosing Create, Systems, Sunlight. As seen from the top viewport, north is up. Click and drag in the top viewport to create a compass and to position the Sun object (a direct light).

3. Click the Get Location button to choose your geographical position. Here you use the default of San Francisco. Notice this sets Latitude and Longitude settings.

4. Set the compass position with the North Direction spinner. (If you cannot see the compass, you may have scaled it too large or small. If so, select Compass01 by name, open the modify panel, set Radius = 50.0 and make sure Show Compass Rose is checked. Then select Sun01 and return to the motion panel.)

5. Rotate the spinner and notice how both the compass and the spot rotate together. Adjust the Time and Date settings and notice how the light moves independently of the compass. In this example, the building has been position to get northern light, so North remains 0.0. Set the time to time to 11:00 AM PST, November 10. Although you can animate changes in the date and time of day, these don't effect the directional light's parameters in the Modify panel. To capture color changes at dawn or dusk, you need to animate the color changes as well.

6. To change the sun system settings after creation, select the Sun01 object and open the Motion panel; to change the sun directional light settings, use the modify panel. Here the Sun directional light default is too weak to illuminate the scene. Change the multiplier of 4.0. By default, Overshoot, Rectangle, and Cast Shadows, and Use Raytraced Shadows are checked. Render the scene from the Camera02 viewport.

7. The direct sunlight nicely illuminates the interior surfaces that are directly exposed, leaving the other surfaces dark or black. This would not be the case with a true radiosity renderer.

8. Place an omni light near the ceiling center in the upstairs loft. Set the multiplier at 1.0, check Cast Shadows and Use Shadow Maps, and leave the other settings at their default. Re-render the scene (see Figure 18.14).

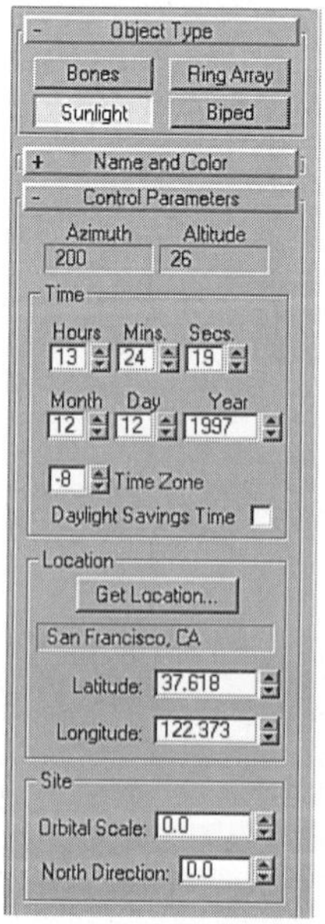

FIGURE 18.14

Sunlight illumination from exterior plus omni light from upstairs casting shadows (No fog or volume lighting; no fireplace or combustion effects).

Establishing Moods

Moods are challenging to create. Often, a moody environment is not registered and remembered for its specifics but rather registers as a feeling. This makes creating a mood even more difficult because it requires a considerable amount of deliberate observation to notice all the elements that make up a moody atmosphere.

Light Beams and Glow Lights

Beams of sunlight through a window and the hazy glow around a street light are just two examples of how a light's atmosphere affects the world. Without atmosphere, light would merely illuminate objects because there would be no atmosphere to reflect the light to begin with. For instance, in an atmospherically controlled room, light would be flat because of the lack of dust and humidity in the air. These things, although rather subtle, are important in creating a realistic, dusty world.

With 3DS MAX's volumetric lighting, light beams and glowing lights are quite simple to add to a scene. By turning down the density and keeping a wide attenuation span, a nice glowing street light can be created. Similarly, a spotlight or directional light can add a nice shaft of light, from which shadows can be cast.

R2 includes Digimation's Lens Effects plug-in. This set of video post filters quickly generates glows around selected objects, highlights, and lens-flare effects that can be difficult or impossible and time-consuming to create with scene lighting. The plug-in supports an interactive previews of your scene and allows great control over the color, attenuation, size, and animation of these effects. Lens Effects is a post-production tool and is designed for overlay on your scene at render time. In one sense, your lighting is complete when you invoke Lens Effects from the video post filters section. But if you intend to use it, you should design the scene lighting and materials in contemplation of that use.

Smoke, Haze, and Mist

Careful use of fog can add subtle touches of atmosphere that are otherwise difficult to achieve with lights and textures. Smoke, haze, and mist all soften the scene and tend to join the different elements. Animated volumetric fog can create realistic fog and clouds that can be used to give a scene depth and a sense of belonging to a larger world. Volumetric lighting and fog work well in an environment mapped with animated, multi-layered noise. Here the atmospheric elements can be applied minimally to emphasize areas and localize mood. Many artists will not compose a scene without fog elements— at least a fogged horizon line. Because transparent volumetric atmospheric and noise effects add substantially to render times, the issue becomes how to add the minimum amount of effects to achieving the same impression.

Radiosity Effects

When omni lights are used with exclusion, decay, softened edges and attenuation, they work well for simulating radiosity and inherited color. This approach slows the rendering process more than adjusting the material's ambient color value but creates a very realistic effect.

Implementing this technique takes some careful observation of a lit environment. Naturally, light often falls off in areas, such as under tables and chairs, as well as in corners of dimly lit rooms. Use of a negative multiplier and an attenuated omni light enables these areas to be carved out while retaining a brighter value and extended attenuation ranges to light brighter areas of a room.

Dedicated radiosity tools are the better choice if the scene contains many light sources or if accuracy is important, and you have additional rendering time. The radiosity tool calculates the total light energy in the scene, analyses the geometry surface by surface to determine the light distribution on and among surfaces, and assigns lighting properties. This results in a physically accurate rendering of indirect light, highlights, and shadows as they change across surfaces, as well as color reflections from surface to surface.

Because radiosity calculations are processor intensive and cannot take advantage of multiprocessors, you probably only want to do this rendering once. Radiosity is not cost-effective for moving elements where the solution must be calculated frame by frame. Therefore radiosity is ideal for architectural design, visualization, and walkthroughs. It's also good for creating photoreal environments in which you composite animated objects, lighting or shadows.

Two very good products for 3DS MAX R2 are Lightscape and RadioRay. Bear in mind both calculate based upon real-world physical information, and in that sense behave quite differently from other lights in MAX. They have a learning curve: you need to optimize geometry for radiosity (breaking surfaces down to enable calculations of light changes across an object), select surfaces to include and exclude, define or adjust materials, and use radiosity-specific Luminaire light together in a manner to balance accuracy against calculation time.

- **Lightscape 3.1:** A stand-alone radiosity and raytrace renderer, with plug-ins for importing and exporting their radiosity file format into MAX. The Lightscape importer for MAX R2 is included on the accompanying CD and is available, with sample files on the Lightscape web site (www.lightscape.com).

- **RadioRay:** Created by Lightwork and distributed by Kinetix, this is a combined radiosity and raytrace solution. It is not a standalone environment; instead, it is an alternative to MAX's scanline renderer and integrates entirely within the MAX interface. This integration is advantageous when combining radiosity and raytracing. At the time of this writing, RadioRay is being reworked to be compatible with 3DS MAX R2. The Kinetix web site has examples of work done with RadioRay.

Radiosity renderers generate an independent data set that is quantitatively accurate. Once you've rendered a space with a radiosity solution, you can view it from multiple angles or walk through it without re-rendering. By their nature, radiosity files add substantially to file size. If, for example, you are modeling a VRML scene, your best solution is to use prerendered bitmaps taken from a radiosity scene, remapped as texture maps on the VRML model.

Lighting with Fixtures

When you try to approximate real-life lighting situations, you should pay careful attention to how lamps actually cast light. Overdramatizing a lighting effect and casting harsh-edged light is a common mistake. Most light does not occur in this fashion and is much more diffused, soft, and without definite light pools. Lighting designers and architects go to great lengths to place and space fixtures so that they do not create hotspots, scallops, or solitary pools. Lighting manufacturers try to manufacture lights that distribute light evenly and without pattern. Both of these practices are difficult in the real world and you may find them equally difficult to simulate in 3DS MAX.

Interior Light Fixtures

There are often times, especially in architectural renderings, when simulation of interior lighting is essential. Although this may take additional time to ensure a realistic look, nice effects are certainly achievable.

Most lighting designers strive for even illumination in most areas and reserve dramatic lighting to call attention to architectural details or artwork or to act as a patterned light design on its own. Overemphasizing light sources and their impact is unfortunately all too common in computer renderings. Just because a light source is present does not mean that its effect is blatantly obvious.

Can lights are a typical example of this tendency. Many modelers feel that they must show the effects of each light; after all, they are there and they have been positioned and possibly even modeled. To make their presence clear, their light is often strong and their hotspots sharp. The result is pools of light—a characteristic that has its uses for highlighting certain objects—but that is generally considered poor lighting design. The correct way to illuminate the scene is to use broad soft lights that gently overlap and whose light pools are not particularly discernible.

Sconces and Light Scallops

Wall sconces are elements of lighting design that require emphasis of their effects. These indirect lights are often used to create scalloped light pools on the wall as they illuminate the ceiling, the intent being to light that area of the room indirectly by bouncing light off the ceiling. Because 3DS MAX's lights do not do this automatically (only a radiosity renderer can), their effect must be simulated, as shown in Figure 18.15.

The quality of the light scallop is controlled by the hotspot's size, not the spotlight's intensity. These effects did not require the use of shadows or even attenuation. A common misconception is that to get these effects requires the falloff to exceed the size of the fixture and cast a shadow to form the cutoff, producing a crisp edge and taking considerably longer to render. In actuality, you need to do this only when the lighting fixtures are transparent or translucent, and you need to cast the shadows of their enclosure. Because light cannot be reflected in 3DS MAX, simulating bounced light (radiosity) requires an additional light source.

Figure 18.15

Light scallops from spotlights with varying hotspots.

Linear Light Sources

Rectangularspot and directional lights provide a method to simulate the illumination of linear light sources, such as fluorescent lights. When made rectangular and carefully controlled with attenuation and falloff, these lights can simulate linear lights quite well. The directional light's illumination is quite strong as compared to the spotlight's, which is further adjusted by the fact that it is a point light source. The choice of which to use is dependent on the desired effect. For the most even light, the directional light is often the best choice.

Simulating Signage Illumination

Glowing signs are objects that users often need to simulate. But before modeling the mesh and placing the lights, take a good look at how the sign is really supposed to illuminate the scene.

Most signage is meant to be read, and the primary characteristic of making a sign readable is contrast. Contrast is created from color and illumination, which is why most signs do not illuminate the wall on which they are placed, but rather cast light forward. The edges or side walls of most signs are opaque and the backside of neon is painted black, preventing them from casting light onto their field and lowering, if not eliminating, their contrast.

Considering its needs, the self-illuminated material type works fairly well for signage. The object appears to glow because it has no ambient shading and does not cast light onto its surrounding area. For an added touch, the Glow filter included in Video Post adds a nice aura around a light source, revealing a slightly richer atmosphere. If the sign is freestanding or isolated on a wall's face, it is complete; there is no need for it to actually cast light if there is nothing to receive it. If the sign is close to another plane, it requires the creation of additional light sources to complete the illusion of self-illumination.

Self-Illuminated Signage

The most common form of lit signage is the self-illuminated sign. The self-illuminated sign usually takes the form of isolated letters with translucent faces that project colored light (see Figure 18.16), which is straightforward style to use.

FIGURE 18.16

A simulation of self-illuminated signage.

Starting with the desired text, use of self-illuminated materials (85% illuminated is a good starting point) as well as possibly using Glow creates a simple self-illumination without special lighting.

Backlit Signage

One form of signage that illuminates its mounting plane is backlit signage. Here light is cast from the back of the letters onto a plane, putting the text in a bright silhouette. Actually, you can easily create this effect by using the spotlight's exclude option, excluding the text, and illuminating the wall. Figure 18.17 shows such an effect.

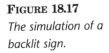

FIGURE 18.17

The simulation of a backlit sign.

Simulating Neon Signage

One of the most interesting lighting forms is neon. The curves and shapes that are possible and the intense colors that are emitted, make it a popular effect to simulate. It also is one that puzzles many modelers. Look closely at a neon sign and you notice that it casts little illumination of its own. The letters themselves are quite bright, but the light given off can only be described as a saturated glow, actually making it easier to simulate (see Figure 18.18).

The previous figure illustrates a technique that is adequate for closely spaced neon signage, but not very good for neon that is diverse in its form. Strip and free-form artistic neon are now simple tasks with the use of Glow. Figure 18.19 is an example of Glow used in freeform neon. By using a material effects channel and a lofted shape, creating freeform neon is a simple task.

In Practice: Setting up the Environment

- **Creating Backgrounds:** Use maps (bitmaps or procedural maps) to create backgrounds for your scenes. You can create or edit them and assign Environmental Mapping Coordinates in the Material Editor. You can display the background in a viewport for general reference, or to align the camera.

FIGURE 18.18

The simulation of neon signage.

FIGURE 18.19

Free-form neon signage, using Glow.

- **Volume Lights:** You can add atmosphere to your scene by creating volume lights in the Environment dialog and assigning them to any omni, directional, or spot light in the scene. Volume lights work well to simulate haze or fog, but require scene lights to be active. If you use volume lights with projector directional or spot lights, you create a streaked volume effect.

- **Using Fog:** Fog is a second way to create atmospheric effects. 3DS MAX R2 ships with two types of fog, Volume Fog, and regular Fog. The former works only with one of three specialized Atmospheric Apparatus, a BoxGizmo, SphereGizmo, or CylGizmo, which confine the fog to the shape of the apparatus. The latter fog type has two principal types, Standard Fog and Layered Fog, which fill the entire scene. You can use Environment Opacity Maps to mask your scene and create the illusion that fog is not present in part of the scene.

- **Using Combustion:** You can simulate pyrotechnic effects with Combustion. Like fogs, R2's standard combustion is an atmospheric effect accessed through the Environment dialog and requires an Atmospheric Apparatus to confine the effect. Photo-realistic fire is exceedingly difficult to simulate given the present state of computer graphics, but you can create a convincing portrayal by combining different-colored combustion objects with particles and video post filters, such as Glow or Hilight.

- **The Sunlight system:** This is a specialized directional light that uses geographical data to position a directional light, with default settings which mimic sunlight in a scene. Animating these settings can create the illusion of time passing. This light works best in conjunction with the rest of your scene lighting.

- **Lighting with fixtures:** For realistic worlds, fixtures should be used to physically place the lights in 3D space. Without such physical fixtures, light in a scene seems to come from out of nowhere, and oftentimes, the viewer is subtly aware that something is not quite right. Careful attention to realistic light fixtures aids in reproducing such fixtures.

Chapter 19

CAMERAS AND SETTING THE SHOT

While many recognize the importance of the camera, its degree of importance is often underestimated. The camera is one of the most powerful tools of the 3D artist. Using the camera effectively can dramatically affect the entire image or animation. Camera angle, focal length, and field of view, as well as camera movement itself, are important aspects of any animation. These concepts and some cinematic theory are discussed in detail within this chapter.

3D Studio MAX R2 provides an extensive tool set for control over camera attributes, including preset parameters to simulate cameras used in feature films. Once you control the camera effectively, you begin to control the mood of your imagery.

This chapter explores the following topics:

- Setting up camera objects
- Placing the camera objects
- Moving the camera
- Simulating camera techniques

To control the camera, you must first understand the fundamentals of setting up and using a camera. 3DS Max R2 cameras are designed to act very much like real-world cameras. If you understand the concepts of camera lenses and setup, you are well on your way to creating powerful and exceptional animations and scenes.

Setting Up Camera Objects

Two types of cameras are available in 3D Studio MAX R2: Target cameras and Free cameras. Each has its own strengths and weaknesses.

Target cameras comprise two objects: the camera and the camera target. The camera represents your eyes and the target indicates the point you are looking at. You can transform the camera and its target independently, but the camera is constrained to always look at its target. To create a Target camera, complete the following steps:

1. Click the Camera category in the Create panel.

2. Click Target in the Object Type rollout.

3. In a Top view, click the mouse where you want the camera placed, then drag and release where you want the target located.

By design, Target cameras try to keep their up vector (the camera's local Y axis) aligned with the world Z axis. Creating Target cameras in a top view sets the camera with the correct initial alignment and provides the most predictable results. Creating a Target camera in other views can cause unpredictable camera rotations.

Target cameras are your best choice for general-purpose camera work. The capability to transform both the camera and camera target provide you with the greatest flexibility for setting up and animating camera views. The Target camera's designed tendency to orient itself with the world Z axis also matches our natural expectations of real-world cameras.

A free camera is a single object, the camera. Because Free cameras have no target, they define their look-at point as being an arbitrary distance along their negative local Z axis. New to Release 2, you can adjust or define the target distance of a Free camera with the target distance spinner. To create a Free camera, complete the following steps:

1. Click the Camera category in the Create panel.

2. Click Free in the Object Type rollout.

3. Click in any viewport to create the Free camera.

The Free camera is placed in the scene with its Local coordinate system aligned with the coordinate system of the current construction plane. Because the Free camera's line of sight is along its negative local Z axis, the camera's default view is always looking into the construction plane. For example, a Free camera created in a top view is looking down, and a Free camera created in a left view is looking to the right.

Because Free cameras have no target to look at, they are more difficult to set up and aim than a Target camera. Free cameras have absolutely no sense of which direction is up, which is the Free camera's advantage. Free cameras are not limited by the rotational constraints caused by trying to maintain an up-vector as with Target cameras. Free cameras are best suited for complex animation, where the camera is used to fly through a scene with many banks and vertical orientations, such as when a camera is mounted on a roller coaster or a fighter plane.

Because the Free Camera has no target, it is easier to animate along a path than the Target camera.

TIP

You can turn Free Camera into a more versatile Target Camera by using the LookAt controller. The LookAt controller enables you to pick any object as the target. Using a Free camera in this fashion eliminates the Y vector problem associated with Target cameras, while creating a Free camera with a target.

You define how a camera views a scene by setting two interdependent camera parameters: field of view (FOV) and lens focal length. These two parameters describe a single camera property; so changing the FOV parameter also changes the Lens parameter and vice versa. Use FOV for framing the camera view and for cinematic effect.

Setting Field of View

Field of view (FOV) describes the area of the scene that is seen through the camera lens. The value of the FOV parameter is the horizontal angle of the camera's view cone.

3DS MAX uses an FOV definition that is different from a real-world camera FOV. 3DS MAX cameras use a horizontal FOV, defined as the angle between the left and right sides of the camera view cone. Real-world cameras use a diagonal FOV defined as the angle between the lower-left corner and the upper-right corner of the camera view cone. New to R2 is the ability to specify if the FOV is horizontal, diagonal, or vertical, which makes it much easier to match a real-world camera.

This difference between 3DS MAX FOV and real-world FOV is of consequence only if you are trying to match a shot taken by an actual 35mm camera. Fortunately, 3DS MAX compensates for this difference when calculating lens length and FOV angle. To correctly match a 35mm camera view, always specify the lens length by using the Lens parameter and let 3DS MAX calculate the horizontal FOV.

NEW TO R2

Alternatively, you may use the flyout button showing the horizontal arrow (see Figure 19.1), adjacent to the FOV parameter. By selecting any of the three choices—horizontal, vertical, or diagonal—you change the method of measurement of the FOV angle. Changing this affects only the method of measurement and has no effect on the view of the camera.

FIGURE 19.1

*FOV measurement
method flyout.*

Setting Focal Lengths

Focal length, which describes the size of a lens, is always measured in millimeters. The smaller the Lens parameter is, the wider the FOV and the farther away from the object the camera appears to be. The larger the Lens parameter is, or longer as it is most often described, the narrower the FOV and the closer to the object the camera appears to be. Lenses shorter than 50mm are referred to as wide-angle lenses, whereas those longer than 50mm are called telephoto lenses.

Wide-angle lenses are used for establishing shots or setting the scene in the first few frames of an animation. Telephoto lenses place the viewer directly in the picture. Because the wide-angle lens has a shorter focal length than the telephoto lens, it can include more information in the picture. A telephoto lens may also include fewer objects of the entire scene.

When compositing 3D with live action, or even a still image, it is necessary to match up the 3DSMax camera lens parameters to that of the real-world camera. This can be accomplished fairly easily through the camera Modify Command Panel. To set the Focal Length, choose any of the Stock Lenses or type in the Focal length of choice in the Lens parameter.

Figures 19.2 through 19.8 show how different lenses affect the look of a scene. The scene is exactly the same in each image, and the camera has not been moved—only the focal length of the camera lens has been changed.

FIGURE 19.2

Using various lens sizes on the same camera, same position. This camera uses a 15mm lens.

FIGURE 19.3

20mm lens.

FIGURE 19.4

35mm lens.

FIGURE 19.4

35mm lens.

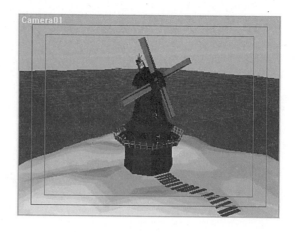

FIGURE 19.5
50mm lens.

FIGURE 19.6
85mm lens.

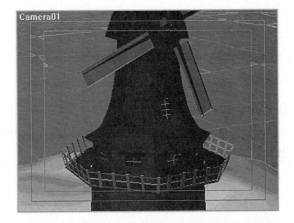

FIGURE 19.7
135mm lens.

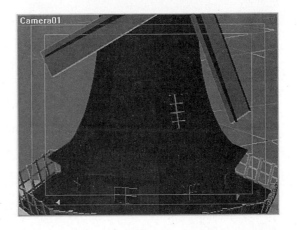

FIGURE 19.8

200mm lens.

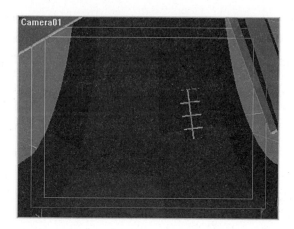

NEW TO R2

Cameras also can be set to an orthographic view, which is a view where there is no perspective. The standard Front, Top, and Side views are all orthographic views. The advantage of an orthographic view is that objects are viewed at their relational size in units, not in relation to distance. This is essential for object placement. Figure 19.9 compares a camera with orthographic projection on, as well as turned off.

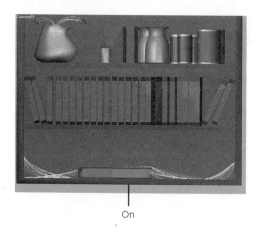

On

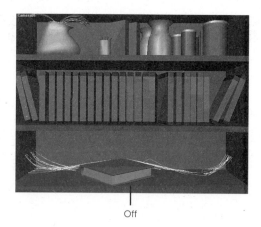

Off

FIGURE 19.9

The image on the left has Orthographic projection turned on, while the image on the right has it turned off.

To accommodate both budding filmmakers and experts in the field, 3DS Max R2 has enhanced the rendering options dialog in many ways. With respect to cameras and output, now you can easily match output with real-world cameras by selecting a preconfigured output size. Selecting any of the options from the pull-down menu also sets the aperture width, Image Aspect, and default render sizes. The preconfigured real-world cameras can be found in the Output Size section of the rendering dialog under the Rendering, Render Menu option.

Naming Camera Objects

More often than not, you will use multiple cameras within a scene. Whether for viewing a complex model at various angles, or for different perspectives of an animation, most animators find it beneficial to use multiple cameras. As scenes become more complex, it becomes increasingly difficult to remember which camera focuses on which shot. By naming your cameras something relevant (such as camground or camhigh), you can quickly select the exact camera you are looking for.

TIP

When naming cameras in scenes with many objects, it may be wise to use a common prefix (such as "cam") so that all cameras are listed together in the Select Objects dialog.

Placing the Camera

Often you will move the camera at some point after creating it. You can use transforms to position the camera, but in many cases it is easier to adjust the camera from within a Camera view. The following sections describe how to use the camera view navigation controls and how to transform cameras, but you should, however, be familiar with a couple of issues.

The camera and its target have independent transforms. You can select and move either object independently or move them together. To select both the camera and the target, you can simply click the line linking the camera and the target or select the camera and right-click and choose Select Target from the pop-up menu. When repeatedly moving the camera, locking the selection (space bar) helps because the target is typically located in an area crowded with objects.

When you activate the camera viewport, the camera object is not automatically selected. Any previously selected object in the scene remains selected.

New in R2 is a function that enables you to match a camera to an existing view. If you have a perspective view that you like, create any camera anywhere. Then with the camera selected, and the perspective view active, choose view, match camera to view.

Using Camera View Navigation Controls

The navigation controls for use within a camera view give you a great deal of control and flexibility. Although cameras and camera targets also can be transformed like any other 3DS Max object, using the camera controls from within the camera view is a more precise method of refining camera orientation.

The following exercise takes you through the steps necessary to set up a camera view.

SETTING UP THE CAMERA VIEW

1. Choose Create in the command panel and pick the Cameras Icon.

2. Create a Target camera in the top viewport by pressing the Target button under the Object Type rollout.

3. Click and drag in the Top view to create and place the camera and its target.

4. Repeat this method to create a few cameras of either type. Camera parameters and types are not important at this time. This exercise is primarily to illustrate how multiple camera views can be accessed.

5. Activate a viewport by clicking the mouse in any of the four view windows. A view is denoted as active by a thin white border around the window (when animating, an active window is denoted by a red border).

6. To make the current view a camera view, simply press C and select the camera you would like to use from the Select Camera dialog. The view is now that of the chosen camera.

If a camera is selected when pressing the hotkey C, that camera's view replaces that of the active view.

You could also right-click a viewport label and choose a camera from the Views item of the viewport properties pop-up menu. This is extremely helpful if cameras have been given useful names and have been hidden to unclutter the scene.

If you have only one camera in the scene, that camera is automatically selected and the Select Camera dialog does not appear.

To switch the viewport to another camera (in multiple camera scenes), press C on the keyboard. If a camera is selected, that camera view replaces the viewport; otherwise, the Select Camera dialog is presented.

The view navigation buttons for a camera view transform the active camera and change the camera parameters as follows:

- **Dolly:** Moves the camera away from or toward its target along the line of sight. Dolly is the same as moving a camera on its local Z axis. Dragging down dollies out away from the target; dragging up dollies in toward the target. The Dolly flyout has three options: Dolly Camera, Dolly Target, and Dolly Both, as seen in Figure 19.10. Select the appropriate choice for dollying each of the target camera components.

- **Perspective:** Dollies the camera, as described previously, and also changes the FOV. The result is that you maintain the same general view composition and either flatten or exaggerate the amount of perspective in the view. Dragging down dollies away from the target and narrows FOV; dragging up dollies in toward the target and widens the FOV.

- **Roll:** Rotates the camera about its own line of sight. Roll is the same as rotating a camera about its local Z axis. Drag left or right to change the roll angle.

- **FOV:** Changes the FOV for the camera. Drag down to widen the FOV, increasing the area viewed by the camera; drag up to narrow the FOV, decreasing the area viewed.

FIGURE 19.10

The camera dolly flyout.

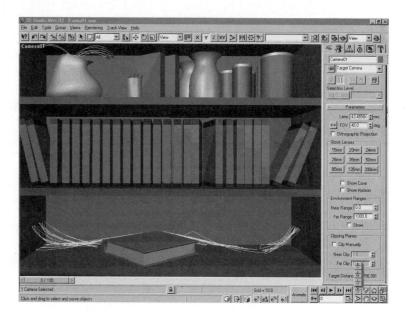

- **Truck:** Moves the camera and its target perpendicular to the line of sight. Truck is the same as moving the camera and its target on the camera's local XY plane.

- **Pan and Orbit:** These flyout buttons affect how the camera rotates around the scene. Pan rotates the target around the camera, much like swiveling the camera on a tripod. Orbit rotates the camera around the target, similar to a circular trucking shot. For Free cameras, the Target Distance sets the point about which the camera orbits. The Target Distance is in the Free camera's Parameters rollout.

  By holding down the Ctrl button while dragging in the viewport, you can constrain the pan and orbit to the vertical or horizontal axis, which is determined by the first direction you drag.

TIP

Although the Dolly flyout contains only one option for a Free camera, attaching a LookAt controller to the Free camera activates the Dolly Target and Dolly Both options (when a target has been chosen for the LookAt controller).

The use of the camera view navigation commands is essential in positioning the camera in the desired location in the scene, and for setting up the type of angles and effects you want for your animation. It may be necessary to move the camera in a viewport other than the camera's, but detail and fine adjusts are best left to the transforms that are performed in the camera viewport.

Transforming Cameras

All positional, rotational, or scale changes made to 3DS MAX objects (cameras, lights, geometry, and so on) are referred to as transforms. These transforms are used to calculate an object's relative position, rotation, and scale from its original values. Cameras and targets can be transformed much like any other object in your scene. As mentioned in the previous section, many of the camera view navigation commands can be duplicated by transforming a camera on its local axes.

Although the Camera Navigation Tools work very well for fine tuning camera parameters, using the standard transformation tools is often more suitable for overall positioning of the camera. By locking axes, you can also use the standard transform tools like the camera navigation tools. The key difference between the Camera Navigation Controls and the standard transform tools is that the standard transform tools can transform the camera on two axes at one time while the Camera Navigation Controls only allow for single axis change.

As well as transforming multiple axes, the standard transform tools can also use any coordinate system available, including that of another object's local coordinate systems. If the camera needs to follow an object along that object's local Z axis and the object is positioned (or animated) so that its local Z axis no long lies along a world or View coordinate plane, it is very difficult to transform the camera without the use of the standard transform tools.

Keep the following issues in mind when transforming camera objects:

- Do not scale cameras. The scale transforms cause the camera base parameters to display false values.

- Target cameras can rotate only about their local Z axes. Attempting to rotate Target cameras about their X or Y local axes has no effect.

- A useful technique is to rotate Target cameras using the Pick coordinate system and picking the camera target. This produces results similar to Orbit.

- Free cameras have none of the rotation restrictions of Target cameras.

TIP

If you create an animation with a Target camera and discover the camera rotates wildly at a certain frame, this is the time to use a Free camera. This phenomenon is called gimbel lock and Free cameras are used to avoid it.

Aligning Cameras

Times will occur when you need to align your camera to objects within the scene. More specifically, you may want to align your camera with a specific face on an object or with a current viewport. To accommodate this need, two features are now available to help with camera alignment: Match Camera to View and Align Camera (to Face Normal). Both are new features to R2. These features come in handy when the camera is animated and must focus on different objects through the life of the animation.

Match Camera To View

When a viewport has a desired angle, you may align a camera to that viewport. This is very helpful when a camera is animated and you do not want to create unnecessary key frames in your camera's transform track. You may also decide to save a particular view angle by adding a new camera and aligning it to that view.

The process of aligning a camera to a viewport is simple: select a camera, activate the desired viewport to align the camera with, and select Match Camera to View from the Views menu. One caveat: The viewport must be in perspective mode for the Match Camera to View menu item to be active.

NOTE

Aligning a camera to a view changes the FOV and Lens to match that of the view. You can use the Viewport Configuration dialog to check the FOV or set it prior to aligning a camera to that view.

Align Camera (to Face Normal)

Suppose your animation is shot with the perspective of looking through the eyes of one of your characters as it walks through a strange environment. As the scene progresses, you inevitably will want to look at different objects as you move through the scene. Instead of constantly repositioning a target, you can simply align the camera to face normals of different objects throughout the course of the animation. This also alleviates the problem of aligning to an object's center or pivot point as well.

To align a camera to an object's face normal, select the camera, then the Align Camera button (in the Align flyout), and drag the mouse over a targeted object. As you drag the mouse, the object's normals become visible (depicted by a blue arrow projecting from the face) as you move over individual faces. Release the mouse on the desired face and the camera becomes aligned to the object's selected face normal.

Aligning a camera to an object's face normal does not change the camera's FOV or Lens parameter. It merely changes the position and the line of site to match that of the view. When aligning a Target camera to a face normal, both the camera and the camera target may be repositioned, with the target being placed directly on the face with which it is aligned.

As you compose your shot looking through your camera you also need to see how the edges are being cropped. The camera viewport is always fixed, but the resolution of your output may vary. An animation may be used in television, film, or even print media, with each having very different resolution requirements. In the next section, you'll look at the Safe Frame option, which gives you this cropping information visually.

Safe Frame

Due to the nature of the cathode ray tube, all televisions do not have the same visible dimensions. Objects near the edges of the screen can be clipped or actually lost offscreen. To avoid losing important portions of a shot, concentric rectangles are used to determine where certain types of action could occur. In 3DS Max R2, the rectangles that make up the video safe area are called Safe Frame.

Safe Frame is an invaluable feature that shows how the final image will be cropped in your rendering. Three rectangles make up the Safe Frame: the

Live Area (outermost rectangle), Action Safe (middle), and Title Safe (inner). The Live Area shows the area that is actually rendered, regardless of the size or aspect ratio of the viewport. Action Safe shows the area in which it is safe to include your rendered action (the area not overshot or clipped on most TV screens). Title Safe shows the area in which it is safe to include titles or other information (low distortion in this area on most TVs). Because the Safe Frame rectangle is proportional, the output sizes of 600×400 and 3000×2000, for example, have the same Safe Frame (see Figure 19.11).

FIGURE 19.11

You can see the Safe Frame in the Perspective and Camera views. Safe Frame can be used in any viewport and can illustrate the areas where clipping may occur and where titles can be placed safely.

You can tailor the size of the inner border to your system's needs with the Safe Frame value located within Views, Viewport Configuration (see Figure 19.12). Within this dialog you can turn on Safe Frames, set which areas you want shown, and reduce the percentage of both the Action Safe and Title Safe areas.

FIGURE 19.12

Users can adjust the three Safe Frame rectangles. This dialog can be found by choosing Views, Viewport Configuration, Safe Frames.

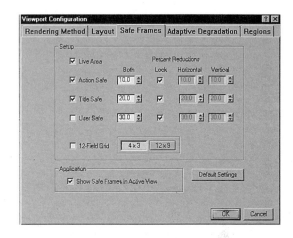

Using Safe Frames is essential when preparing for final render. If you do not use Safe Frames in your camera viewports, you may be cropping important elements that you want the audience to see, or you might find that elements fly into or out of the scene more quickly or slowly than you had planned. Using Safe Frame should become second nature during any animation project so that there aren't any surprises after a 24-hour rendering spree.

Moving the Camera

Camera movement is an integral part of adding realism to a scene. If you've ever seen a movie shot in IMAX or the immersion theater rides at theme parks, you may have felt the experience of how the camera can affect the viewers. While camera movement may be necessary, it should be done with great care because the camera represents the viewer's eyes.

Before getting into the theory behind camera movement within an animation, you must first understand the basics of camera movement within a scene. Target cameras have a fixed line of sight that is centered directly on their targets. The line of sight is depicted by a line connecting the camera and its target. If the target is moved, the camera rotates to follow the target. When the target is moved, the position of the camera does not change, just the direction in which it is pointing (always centered on the target). Moving the target toward the camera (along the camera's local Z axis) does not affect the field of view.

When cameras and their targets are moved, they keep a constant field of view. Moving the target does not change the camera lens size. Therefore, while the composition of the shot and displayed field of view cone may change, the field of view angle remains constant. To change the field of view and switch lenses, you can either change the camera's FOV or Lens parameters, or click the FOV view navigation button in a camera view.

Think about camera movement as if the audience is the camera and the target is where their eyes are focused. In other words, while the audience's body (the camera) can be moving in any direction, they are free to look in any direction (the target). Thereby, the slightest movement of either the camera or the target is noticeable. This fact works as both an advantage and an obstacle when animating a camera. A quick or sudden jerk in the camera motion is great if you want to simulate driving down a rocky road, but it does not work well when panning across a room. A good rule of thumb when moving the camera or its target is fluidity.

Panning a camera is the most common camera movement and present in most every scene. The camera moves slowly across the scene to the subject. Pans require plenty of frames for proper ease in and out, in addition to the smooth panning motion. The pan should slowly build to panning speed and slowly come to rest at the subject of the pan. When done properly, the audience does not notice the actual start or end of the pan.

To create a smooth pan, set key frames for the start and end of the pan and let 3DS Max R2 calculate the frames in between. A common mistake is to insert extra key frames during the pan to force the camera to point to specific objects. A correct pan does not force objects into the scene; it introduces them casually. If you are compelled to focus longer on a specific area of the scene, use the minimum number of key frames (typically one, two if you want to hold it there for a moment). Then be sure to lengthen the duration of the pan and adjust key frame tangents to smooth the interruption.

In addition to animated pans, you can animate rolls and dollies. Rolling gives viewers the sense of tilting their heads or spinning. You can use this device effectively if you are using a subjective viewpoint for your camera, such as in the cockpit of a fighter jet or on a roller coaster. When a camera rolls, it typically moves along a curved path and banks to one side, due to the physics of natural movement.

As well as panning, the camera can dolly or zoom. A camera can dolly in toward the subject or out (away from the subject). When creating a camera dolly, the same rules of a pan apply. For more information concerning the dolly motion, see the section, "Theory of Moving the Camera," later in this chapter.

Using the Trajectories section in the Motion command panel, you can view the path of a camera as a visible spline. Once a path has been created (or generated by 3DS Max R2), you can still go back and make finer adjustments. Using Track View, you can adjust or change the key frame tangent or controller type (use a Bézier position controller for finer adjustment). (For more details on controllers, see Chapter 25, "Using Controllers and Expressions.")

TIP

The basic rule for most camera or camera target animation is to keep the path smooth. Use plenty of frames and Ease In and Ease Out.

Creating Paths

In addition to paths being generated from transforms, even more control can be gained through the use of shapes as paths. By drawing a spline through a scene and assigning that as a camera's path, you gain greater control over the movement of a camera. For even more control, bind the camera or target to a dummy object and use the shape as the dummy's path.

Path shapes can be created any way that standard shapes are created, although using a line tool is great for drawing a precise path through the scene. Furthermore, using a NURBS curve tool automatically generates a smooth curve.

The following exercise takes you through the creation of a path for an office walk-through:

CREATING A CAMERA PATH

1. Open the 19office.max scene file from the accompanying CD-ROM.

2. Maximize the top viewport and click Zoom Extents All so that the entire scene is visible.

3. In the Create Panel, click Shapes, select NURBS Curve from the Splines drop-down menu, and click Point Curve in the Object Type roll-out. Using a Point Curve ensures that the path shape has a consistently smooth curve through the control points (and is more precise than a CV curve).

4. Draw a path through the scene from left to right, going between all objects within the scene. At the extreme right object, click a point so that the line goes around the object and heads into the middle of the group. Notice how the NURBS curves stay smooth. An example of the curve can be seen in Figure 19.13.

FIGURE 19.13

The easiest way to move a camera through a series of complex turns and movement is to draw a path and assign the path to the camera (and target if necessary) or to a Dummy object linked to the camera.

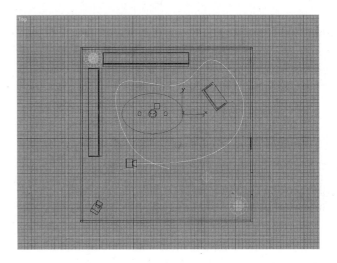

5. Though you can use either camera type, for this exercise, use a Free Camera. Free cameras work better during complex animation paths, though very complex camera movement can be accomplished for Target cameras by parenting them to dummy objects that use paths as their position controller.

6. Assign the path to the Free Camera by selecting the camera and clicking the Motion Command Panel. Select the Parameters button, click the Assign Controller rollout, and select the Position controller under the Transform list. Click the Assign Controller Type flyout and select Path as the Controller type. Click OK and click Pick Path under Path Parameters and choose the NURBS Curve as the Current Path Object.

While attaching a camera directly to a path works for this example, this setup would pose severe limitations in real-world animation. For complex camera movement, it is best to assign the camera to a dummy object or dummy chain. Dummy object chains can be used to control every aspect of camera movement. Dummy objects are discussed in greater detail in the section, "Using Dummy objects to Build a Virtual Studio," later in this chapter, but follow along the next few steps for an introduction to using dummy objects with cameras.

7. Unassign the path as the Free Camera's position controller. This can be done by following step 6, but you choose Bézier Controller as the Controller type instead of Path.

8. Create a dummy object of the approximate size of the camera icon. Follow step 6 to assign the path as the Dummy object's position controller.

9. After the Dummy object's controller type is changed to Path and the NURBS Curve is chosen as the path, the Dummy object is repositioned at the start of the NURBS Curve. Position the Free Camera so that it is centered to the Dummy object (use the Align Tool for quick alignment).

10. Create another Dummy object at the same position as the Free Camera and the first Dummy object. Parent this Dummy object to the first. This second Dummy object will be used for rotating the Free Camera. You may want to name this Dummy object "Camera Rotator."

11. Parent the Free Camera to the second Dummy object. You now have a Free Camera moving along a path, yet it's free to point in any direction.

Though this is a basic example of using a Dummy object to control a camera, it shows how transforms (such as rotation and position) cam be controlled by other objects. This is especially important for cameras because it smoothes out the camera movement. In a more sophisticated assembly, each axis of the camera is controlled by a separate Dummy object.

NOTE

When assigning a path controller as an object's position controller, 3DS Max R2 uses the length specified in Time Configuration as the time span of the path. You must go into Track View to adjust the keys for the exact start and finish times of the movement along the path.

Theory of Moving the Camera

Everyone has different goals when creating animation, but if you are going for good cinematic effects, camera movement should only be used when deemed necessary. Camera movement greatly influences the mood of the scene and camera movement should be choreographed accordingly. Although every scene is different, using the appropriate combination of dollying, panning, and tracking increases the quality of your animation and makes it a more engaging experience for your audience.

Dollying

You now know what dollying a camera does, but when and why would you use it? Typically, dolly-in is used to focus the audience on a very specific area within the scene, usually the subject. The dolly-in is used for dramatic effect and it works quite well, although overuse of dollying may appear awkward, amateur, and reminiscent of home movies. Discretion should be used when dollying so that the audience is not taken on a dolly-in and -out ride.

This is not to say that dollying should never be used. Many horror movies use dolly-in and -out extensively. There are no hard-and-fast rules, only guidelines. In animation or films where there is lots of action, dollying-in may be more prevalent and occur faster. In more dramatic scenes, the dolly-in may be slow and more subtle. Dollying the camera is a good technique for focusing the audience's attention.

When the director wants to focus on a subject, he may dolly the camera in closer for a tight shot. Just as often, the director may want to take the audience's attention off of the subject and turn to a new subject. To unfocus a subject, a dolly-out may be used. By doing so, the director is telling the audience that the subject is becoming less significant and a new subject or scene can be introduced.

Using the different dollying techniques can add dramatic impact to any animation and other techniques can also stimulate the way your audience sees your subjects. Many times, a dolly-in may be preceded by a pan toward the subject, which can draw the audience into the scene and be used to introduce new subjects.

Panning

In addition to dollying, the camera can pan. A pan generally occurs when the camera is locked-off (restricted to single-axis movement) and becomes the center of the scene. The camera can pan in a 360-degree arc. After the camera begins to move sideways, the movement is no longer called a pan, but instead becomes another form of tracking shot.

A 360-degree pan and the opposite 360-degree orbit (where a subject is the center of the world and the camera moves around it) are good techniques used to give the viewer a sense of omniscience. This technique reveals nearly everything about the subject and can be a very impressive camera technique.

Pans can be smooth and graceful or jerky and quick (referred to as quick, or flash pans). Quick pans can be effective when used with the subjective viewpoint, or first-person point of view (described in greater detail in "Theory of Frame Composition," later in this chapter).

Freezing

Sometimes you'll find it more effective to have no motion whatsoever—a freeze frame. This method can be effective to show death or conclusion in a scene. Abrupt changes in camera motion have a dramatic effect on the mood of the shot, whether the change is toward full motion or completely void of it.

To Move or Not to Move

Animation and filmmaking is an expression of art; therefore, there is no one correct way to shoot a scene. The successful director is the one who can engage the audience and draw them into the characters and the story. Some of that responsibility lies in the way the scene is shot. Some film directors do not like moving the camera, believing it draws attention away from the actors and action. Others believe the camera can become a character in its own right. As an animator, use your own creative inspiration to tell the story the way you would like it told. The main point is that camera movement is important, but not always necessary. As in music, the notes may be the same, just arranged differently. Use your own ideas to make your own music.

Camera movement is not a physical skill, it is an emotional one. If you can evoke emotions from your audience through your use of characters, action, lighting, and cinematic techniques, you've succeeded at your goal.

Using Dummy Objects to Build a Virtual Studio

If you have ever been on the set of a motion picture, you may remember being surrounded by all sorts of camera tripods, cranes, dolly tracks, Stedicams, and more. The director of photography uses all these mechanical devices to move the camera smoothly or keep it perfectly still. Unfortunately, in computer animation these types of devices do not exist. Or do they?

You can use Dummy objects to build some of the same camera equipment and make the process of animating a scene easier, giving yourself the ability to create smoother motion paths.

The simplest use of Dummy objects is to create a tripod for the camera.

1. Create a Target camera.

2. Create a Dummy object directly beneath the camera object.

3. Link both the camera and camera target to the dummy, with the dummy as the parent to both (see Figure 19.14).

FIGURE 19.14

By linking both the camera and target to a Dummy object, you can create a tripod that can make camera movements quick and simple.

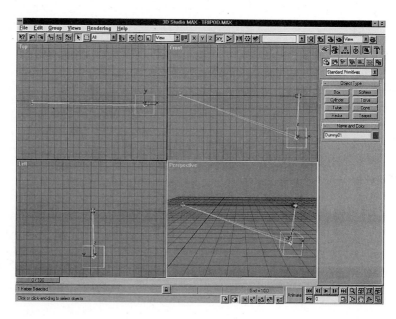

By creating this simple hierarchy you are able to move the dummy through complex motions and have the camera follow in a smooth manner.

More complex use of Dummy objects can be created to produce cranes. The following was developed by Angelo Guarino and posted to the 3D Studio forum of CompuServe (GO KINETIX):

1. Create a Target camera.

2. Create two Dummy objects at the camera position. You can call these cam-elevation and cam-azimuth.

3. Create three dummies at the camera target. You can call these trgt-elevation, trgt-azimuth, and cam-position.

4. Link all the dummies, the camera, and camera target in the following order:

   cam-position
   trgt-azimuth
   trgt-elevat
   cam-azimuth
   cam-elevat
   cam1
   cam1.target

By constructing this "crane" (see Figure 19.15), you should be able to achieve many complex motions by using only "endpoint" key frames in any one object's degree of freedom. Experiment with moving each of the Dummy objects separately, and then with combinations, to achieve the desired effects.

If, for example, you want to move into an object and then circle around it, move the cam-position dummy toward the desired object. When you have framed the object the way you want, rotate the trgt-azimuth dummy the desired amount. Concentrate on defining the motions by using endpoint key frames on each of the dummies, and you should find a greater amount of control in your camera movement.

Essentially you are creating a logistical way of producing smooth camera motion—because many factors of moving real-world cameras do not apply to computer cameras. If you lock off certain axes of motion on each Dummy object, so that it can move only in the direction that its name represents, and use these objects for all camera movement, it is easier to chart and correct unwanted jerkiness and jiggle. You know exactly how the camera has been moved and by what transform.

FIGURE 19.15

A more complex linking of the camera and target to multiple Dummy objects can create a camera crane.

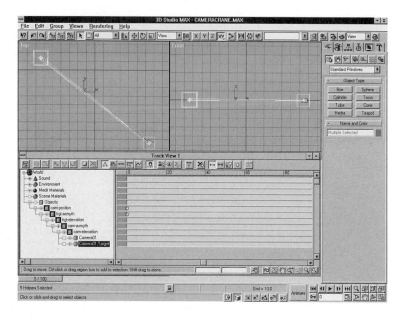

If you create a number of camera rigs, save them as separate 3DS MAX files and import them into scenes as needed. Now you have created a virtual studio facility in your computer.

Using the LookAt Controller

The LookAt controller is the default controller for targeted cameras, and points the negative local Z axis of the camera at the pivot of the Target object. Using the LookAt Controller is helpful when you want your camera to track a specific object throughout the course of an animation (see Figure 19.16). For instance, let's say a caterpillar is the central focus of the scene and is moving across a leaf. Assign the caterpillar as the target for the camera in the LookAt parameters rollout. Now you need only to animate the caterpillar, and the camera keeps the caterpillar in view. The camera target has been replaced by the caterpillar, saving you from having to animate both the camera target and the caterpillar. The result is a cleaner, smoother animation.

FIGURE 19.16

The LookAt rollout is found by selecting an object, clicking the Motion parameters rollouts, and then clicking Transform under Assign Controller.

Using Clipping Planes

Unlike real-world cameras, the cameras in 3DS MAX R2 are infinitely small. So small, in fact, the camera can squeeze through the eye of a needle with room to spare. While this allows animators to put 3D cameras virtually anywhere, it does cause problems when the camera angle extends through geometry. This phenomenon is called clipping and each camera has its own set of clipping planes.

Cameras have parameters to control the clipping plane, which enables you to exclude certain sections of the scene's geometry to view the inside of the geometry. The clipping plane is a handy tool when you want to create a cross section, or cut-away view, of a building, vehicle, person, and so on. Using clipping planes is an easy way to create architectural cross sections or create cool animated cut-away effects. The use of clipping planes can be effective as a purely logistical tool when rendering portions of a scene with a large amount of complex geometry.

Each camera has a near and a far clipping plane, which you can adjust and animate. The parameters for clipping planes are found in the creation parameters of the camera object. Both the near plane and the far plane are measured along the camera's local Z axis in current scene units.

In Figure 19.17, you see a scene as normally rendered with the clipping plane turned off. In Figure 19.18, you see how a clipping plane setting of 9750.0 and 20000.0 changes the scene. The clipping plane setting varies depending on the size of your models and the scene.

FIGURE 19.17

The clipping plane is a tool that cuts away from the model that the camera is focused on based on the settings in the Near and Far Clip spinners found under the Modify parameters rollout.

FIGURE 19.18

Using clipping planes is a quick and simple way to create great-looking cross-section views of architectural models.

Simulating Camera Techniques

Because cameras represent the observer's eye, it is important to relate what the camera sees to how the audience would perceive it. People have a strong sense of what speed looks like and will interpret your animation by relating what they see to their own experience. Additionally, people can be emotionally affected by certain camera angles and focal lengths.

When directing an animation, you decide what camera attributes and movement techniques to employ. Regardless of how good the models or textures are, if the camera isn't effective, the animation will suffer. As an artist, the director decides what the audience sees and how they see it. The director uses this power to evoke emotions that draw the audience into the story, allowing it to be believable. By learning and applying some basic techniques, your animation will become stronger and more interesting to the viewer.

NOTE

Being a great animator does not make great animations. To create great animation, you must study the art of motion picture cinematography. Like photography and motion pictures, animation is a collection of elements carefully selected for scene composition and then skillfully shot from camera angles that compliment the theme and mood of the story and characters. Too many animators drop a camera into a scene as the last step when, in fact, it should be one of the first elements considered when setting up an animation.

The first rule of good camera placement is composition. Composition is the art of filling the frame with the characters and objects that make up your scene. Whether your camera is locked-off (still) or animated, the frame can be filled in many different ways, each affecting how the scene is interpreted by the audience.

The two types of basic scene composition are symmetrical and random. With symmetrical composition, the camera's relation to the characters and objects in the scene is organized and symmetrical, giving your scene an artificial feel, detaching the audience from the scene. Random composition places characters and objects throughout the scene, giving the scene a more realistic feel while enticing the audience to relate to and become part of the scene.

The style of composition depends on the tone of the script and the type of animation you are producing. Is it to be stylized and artistic? If so, the symmetrical approach may work best. If the style is to be dramatic and intends to draw the viewer into the story, then a random style is preferable.

Theory of Frame Composition

Taking the art of scene composition one step further, one must consider frame composition. You may have a well-designed scene, but you must shoot the scene in a way that best delivers your intended message. Use the mood of the scene to suggest the type of frame composition required to properly convey that mood. Frame composition can be used to separate characters from the audience or to draw them in.

Frame composition is the art of giving the scene contents their respective hierarchy of importance. Using camera placement, you can dynamically change the importance of the objects within a scene, through the use of the camera movement techniques such as dolly, panning, and tracking.

By setting up the camera with foreground objects predominately placed between the main action and character, you are dislocating the viewer from the scene. The viewer may feel a lack of connection and a physical separation, but this technique works well if your character is in trouble or feeling a sense of separation within the context of the film.

When you want the audience to get a sense of the vastness of a scene or environment, use the long shot. John Ford, the famous director of classic western films, always used long, establishing shots throughout his films. This would set the tone of the grand spaciousness of the Wild West that the tiny, almost inconsequential, characters were up against. Setting this type of tone may tell the audience how fragile the character's existence is in the film.

Long shots can also establish the character's relation to the location. Does the character become lost in the background of a war-torn village in Vietnam? Maybe the larger story is the war, but the focus is on one story out of many. Using the long shot after a close up or medium shot can also draw the audience out of a subplot and back into the main plot of a story.

Conversely, close-ups draw the viewer into the scene and closer to the character. Again, because the camera is the audience's eyes, a close-up shot brings the audience face to face with the character. Using knowledge of different cultures' comfort zones can dramatically increase the effect of the

Another lens composition technique is the "deep focus." Because 3D cameras are simulated cameras, there is no depth of field, or loss of focus to objects which are farther away. You can actually use this "fault" to your advantage. In another scene from *Citizen Kane*, for example, the fact that the characters in the foreground, middle ground, and far background can all be seen equally well adds to the importance of a scene where a young, innocent Kane is playing in the background while his mother is signing over guardianship of her son. In the middle ground, Kane's father stands by helplessly. This composition shows the viewer the boy's innocence, while enabling the viewer to also witness the events that will forever deprive the boy of his childhood and freedom. By using this technique, the scene is more effective than if Welles had shot separate shots of each element.

NEW TO R2

In scenes where "deep focus" is not used, using the Lens Effect Focus Video Post filters can also create beautiful lens effects for dramatic cinematography, such as depth of field.

NOTE

There are two all-time classic films of cinematography that should be in the collection of any animator who desires to make "films" as opposed to animation. These are *An Occurrence at Owl Creek Bridge* (Robert Enrico, 1961) and *Citizen Kane* (Orson Welles, 1941). *An Occurrence at Owl Creek Bridge* was actually shown as a *Twilight Zone* episode.

Composition with Angles

While frame and scene composition accompanied by lens choice are needed to get a great shot, camera angle also plays a vital role in building a mood. There are four basic types of camera angles, each with its own variations:

- Eye-level
- High-angle
- Low-angle
- Subjective viewpoint

The eye-level camera setup is the standard setup for cameras. The view is basically neutral and objective to the scene. This shot is comfortable and can be seen in most mainstream films or love stories.

High-angle cameras point down toward the object or characters. Using this angle diminishes the character or object to the viewer because it is literally "being looked down on." This can make the character look small and vulnerable.

In *An Occurrence at Owl Creek Bridge*, the main character falls into a quick moving stream and is carried away in the rapids. The scene is shot from a high angle and the character appears small in the frame. This high-angle composition reinforces the fact that the character is vulnerable.

Conversely, a low-angle shot makes a character or object appear more powerful and have a greater stature. If you want a character to appear more heroic—a caricature of heroism—place your camera at his hip, looking up. This camera placement gives the character an appearance of confidence and strength. The low-angle shot makes objects appear more robust and monumental.

Low-angle setups can be used to achieve other types of effects as well. Steven Spielberg used a low-angle camera setup in *E.T.: The Extra-Terrestrial* to convey a child's point of view in many scenes. The camera was placed at a child's height, giving the audience a view from the child's perspective of the world, causing adults in the movie to seem more threatening.

With each of the previously mentioned angles, it is possible to mix and match them for even greater effect. For instance, composing a scene from a low angle with a slight roll in the FOV can achieve a disorienting effect or a heightened sense of drama. This technique is useful when filming the villain of an animation to make the character more ominous. The effect can also make the viewer feel off balance and vulnerable.

Citizen Kane used both high and low angles in numerous shots to give the Kane character a grander stature and to diminish the stature of Kane's wife in the film. This use of camera angles tells us something about each character subliminally. It may also show the audience how one character is perceived by another.

In every scene that Kane and his wife are in together, Kane is invariably shot from below waist-level, or low-angle, as if from the wife's perspective, thereby making him seem more dominating. In contrast, the wife is always shot from a high-angle, thereby revealing her weakness and subservience to Kane.

Using certain camera angles every time a character is on the screen establishes in the viewer's mind a strong feeling about that character. Later, when the character is shot from a neutral, eye-level angle, the feelings that were established earlier are felt subconsciously.

The subjective angle attempts to give the audience a first-person point of view of the scene. An effective shot when used sparingly, this effect can quickly become passé, ineffective, and actually distracts from the character-audience connection.

Examples of a subjective viewpoint can be seen in any horror film where the camera takes on the role of the killer stalking the terrified victim. Other examples can be more benign such as in *Downhill Racer*, where the camera takes on the role of the title character, a downhill skier.

To create subjective viewpoint cameras in 3DS MAX, it is best to use the Free camera because this camera is better set up for animating with banks, swoops, and skids. Refer to the section "Moving the Camera" earlier in this chapter.

Subjective viewpoint can also give the animator an opportunity for creative scene creation. A shot from a subjective viewpoint would be a perfect opportunity to show the world through an alien's eyes (or whatever your aliens see through) in some creative way. Films such as *Predator*, *Wolfen*, and other creature-oriented horror films do this to great effect. Viewing the scene through a character's eyes and with filter effects can also heighten the experience if the way the character sees the world is completely different from our own.

The use of subjective viewpoints can add excitement and tension to an animation. Or perhaps the audience is looking through the eyes of a psychotic killer or a character in an altered state of consciousness. You can see how a visceral effect can be achieved on your audience.

WARNING

These types of dramatic camera angles should be used wisely and sparingly. An animation that uses every trick in the book may be difficult to watch and enjoy.

Remember that too many tricks draw the viewer out of the story and into the art of film-making, which is typically not the experience the audience is looking for. Instead, these techniques should be used to further the story and better enhance the art of storytelling. As a rule of thumb, if the technique does not somehow advance the story, don't use it.

Animation is not just the art of moving a character in a realistic manner. Certainly, realistic motion of characters and objects is important, but no less important is the use of the camera in a scene. Think of the camera as another character. If you are attempting to create award-winning animations that are powerful and meaningful, learning the art of cinematography is essential.

In Practice: Cameras and Setting the Shot

- **Camera Types** 3D Studio MAX offers two camera types: Target cameras and Free cameras.

- **Real-world representation** A new equation used to calculate the field of view gives you a more accurate representation of real-world 35mm cameras if you specify cameras by lens length.

- **Camera adjustments** Cameras can be adjusted in multiple ways and many adjustments can be animated. This animation of the camera can be done in ways that enhance the animation and strengthen the storytelling process. With a good script, an animator will know when moving the camera is a good idea and when it will be overbearing for the scene.

- **Camera angles** Camera angles enhance the storytelling process as well. Choosing certain angles can tell the audience much about a character or location without having to actually verbalize this information through the dialogue.

- **Clipping planes** Use clipping planes to create great-looking, architectural, cut-away animation.

Part VI

ANIMATION

Chapter 20

ANIMATION CONTROL TOOLS

In 3D Studio MAX, virtually anything that can be made or modified can be animated. Turning on the Animate button enables 3DS MAX to record any changes that you make to the scene. A key is created and all the information for the modification is stored for that point in time.

Animation means taking your scenes and adding a fourth dimension to them—time. In MAX R2 you can work with many different time formats including frames, ticks, and SMPTE. You can easily change formats and rates of time without adversely affecting your timing.

Animators are rarely completely happy with an initial animation made to a scene. Fortunately MAX R2 has a complex set of tools for fine-tuning and manipulating animation keys to get the desired result. This chapter covers these animation controls and how to use them.

The topics covered in this chapter include the following:

- Configuring and moving through time
- The Track View
- Creating and manipulating keys
- Working with ranges
- Working with time
- Working with function curves
- Working with trajectories

The Animation Environment

MAX has many different object modifiers that can be used to animate objects in a scene, including modifiers, materials, and even Sub-Object selections. Animating is as easy as changing the parameter values of something at different key points in time.

Even though you can see most of your animation results in your viewports, you will often want to view the key information itself. You might, for example, want to change the point at which a certain action occurs or edit the data of a key. In 3DS MAX this is all possible using the Track View (see Figure 20.1). The Track View shows all the elements of your scene, as well as all aspects that have been animated, along with their associated keys. Keys can be moved in time or copied to other times, or the values associated with a key can be changed.

The use of keys to specify animation data at specific times reflects the practice of traditional cel animators. The master animators create keyframes showing the scene at critical points in the animation. Assistant animators then create the frames between those key frames, determining how the objects in the scene should change to reflect their start and end positions and appearances. With 3DS MAX, you specify the keys for your objects at specific frames, and 3DS MAX creates the positions or appearances of the objects.

FIGURE 20.1

Track View displays all other animation information in a scene and enables you to edit it.

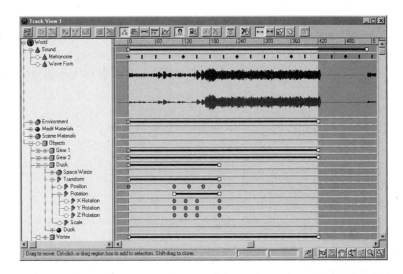

Configuring Time

Because of the variety of possible output formats for your animation (film, TV, and so on), 3DS MAX provides several options for displaying time and frame rates. These options are located in the Time Configuration dialog (see Figure 20.2). This dialog can be accessed by clicking the Time Configuration button or by right-clicking any of the playback buttons.

3DS MAX also enables you to choose between frame rates for different playback media. The default is 30 frames per second (fps) for NTSC (National Television Standards Committee), but you can also choose Film (24 fps) or PAL (Phase Alternating Line, 25 fps) or define your own rate. The way in which time is displayed in the MAX environment can also be changed between frames, SMPTE, Frames and Ticks, and Minutes, Seconds, and Ticks. Ticks are defined as 1/4800 of a second. The Time Slider and current frame field at the bottom of the 3DS MAX window show your animation in whatever time display format you choose.

3DS MAX enables you to change the frame rate and time display at any time without altering your animation. This can be useful if you have a project that is designed for film but later will be used for video. You can easily change the frame rate from 24 fps to 30 fps without altering the playback time. This is much more efficient than some other programs that require you to rescale the keys to fit the desired rate.

FIGURE 20.2

*The Time
Configuration dialog.*

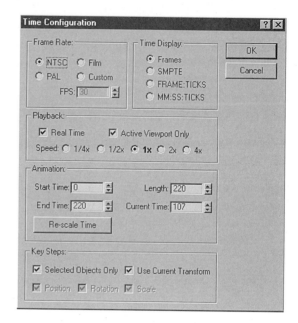

The start and end times of an animation are specified in the Time Configuration dialog, which actually only sets the active time segment. Setting the active time segment enables you to view only part of an animation in the viewport and show only the desired time range at the bottom of the screen. Changing the start and end times does not affect the time or values of any previously created keys.

By selecting the Re-scale Time button in the Time Configuration dialog, you can actually rescale the time associated with keys in your active time segment. In the Re-scale Time dialog (see Figure 20.3), you can change the start time, end time, and length of the new active time segment. The keys located within the current active time segment are rescaled to match the new active time segment. If the start frame is changed, any keys located before the start frame are moved back in time by the same amount that the start time is changed. The same applies to changing the end time.

Moving Through Time

3DS MAX offers several methods for moving through time and viewing your animation. The Playback section of the Time Configuration dialog enables you to change the playback parameters of a scene in the viewport. By unchecking Real Time, the animation plays every frame of the animation as fast as it can in your viewport. When Real Time is turned on, the frames are played back at a multiple of the specified frame rate. The multiple to be used is specified by the Speed option.

FIGURE 20.3

The Re-scale Time dialog.

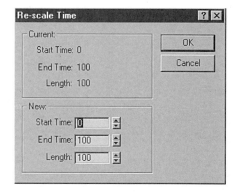

With complex scenes, playback often skips frames to maintain the proper play time. Active Viewport Only, when unchecked, plays back in all viewports instead of the default active viewport. This can be useful if trying to visualize the three-dimensional movement of an object in its environment. You can also set the playback to be slowed down or accelerated in the viewport by checking the speed buttons. The speed options are not available unless Real Time is checked.

You can disable a viewport by right-clicking the viewport title and selecting Disable View from the pop-up menu or by simply pressing D on your keyboard. Inactive viewports do not play animations during scene playback. You can still play an animation in a disabled viewport by selecting the viewport and pressing play. The viewport is temporarily reactivated until another one is selected.

You can also choose to play back only the selected objects in a scene. You can choose this method by clicking and holding the Play button and then selecting the Play Selected icon from the drop-down list. This method is very helpful for complex scenes with many objects being animated and when your display speed is affected. An example would be a scene with vehicles driving around and people walking on the sidewalks. Selection sets can be made for the cars and other sets for the people. When Play Selected is pressed, MAX temporarily hides all non-selected objects that are animated.

3DS MAX also has several options for stepping through time. By using the Frame Indexing buttons in the Play Control area, you can index to the beginning or the end of the Active Play segment, or move back and forth one frame at a time. You can also use the Next Frame and Previous Frame buttons located on the Time slider bar.

A powerful feature is the capability to step though an animation keyframe by keyframe, analyzing animation specified by Transform keys. To active Key Mode, select the Key Mode toggle button. Notice that when this mode is selected, the buttons change for Previous Frame and Next Frame. Clicking these keys takes you to the previous or next Transform key. By selecting the various Key Steps options in the Time Configuration dialog, you can control which transform keys are used to step through the animation. These options enable you to specify whether only Transform keys for the selected objects are to be used or whether the Transform keys for all objects are to be used. In addition, the Transform types to be used can be specified in this dialog.

Using the Track View

As mentioned earlier in the chapter, Track View shows the animatable parameters associated with each object. Track View can be shown by choosing Track View, Open Track View or by pressing the Open Track View button on the toolbar. You can also define custom Track Views that retain their characteristics by choosing New Track View.

In Track View, the hierarchy list of animatable items and their parameters is shown on the left, with animation ranges and keys on the right. The right side is referred to as the Edit Window. Keys are shown as dots, and ranges are shown as bars with squares for the start and end. The range bars stretch across the time that has keys assigned to it. You can view a key by clicking the plus sign located beside it to expand its animated parameters. You can continue to navigate through the hierarchy until the desired parameter keys are displayed. You can name your Track View by entering a name in the Name field on the right-hand side of the Track View. If you wish to delete a Track View, select Delete Track View from Track View menu.

In Figure 20.4, you see a sample Track View with several animated items displayed. Sphere 1 has been animated and has keys across the 0 to 100 range. The total animation extends beyond the current active selection of 95 frames.

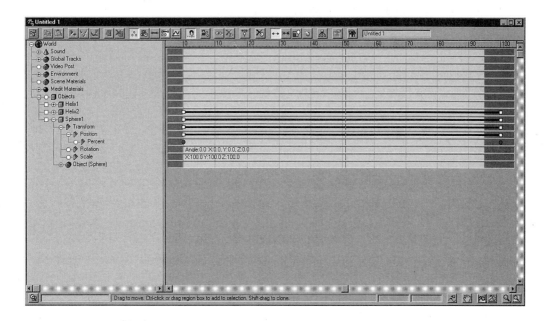

FIGURE 20.4

A sample Track View showing animated items.

Track View has five different animation edit modes:

- Edit Key

- Edit Time

- Edit Ranges

- Position Ranges

- Function Curves

The Track View in Figure 20.4 is in Edit Key mode. Each of these modes will be covered later in the chapter. The following section discusses the structure of the hierarchy list and the controls common to each of the edit modes.

The Hierarchy List

The hierarchy list presents a structured view of the elements in your scene. The highest levels of the hierarchy represent the main groupings in 3DS MAX of sound, environment, materials, and objects. Lower levels of the hierarchy progress through the details of the scene, such as individual objects, base objects, the modifiers applied to a base object, and the parameters associated with a base object and its modifiers. The lowest level of the hierarchy contains the animatable parameters associated with your scene. For any object that has more than one modifier applied, it is possible to switch between modifiers in the stack by simply clicking the orange diamond beside the desired modifier. If the Modify panel is active, the selected modifier is displayed for the selected object.

Each level of the hierarchy can be expanded or collapsed to show more or less detail. To edit a parameter's animation keys, you expand the branches of the tree to display that parameter. You can easily select all the items in a certain hierarchy level by pressing Alt and clicking an item. This selects all items on the current level of the hierarchy but does not select any subordinate items of the selection.

The root of the hierarchy list is World. The subordinate items of World are the following (see Figure 20.5):

- Sound

- Global Tracks

- Video Post

- Environment

- Medit Materials and Scene Materials

- Objects

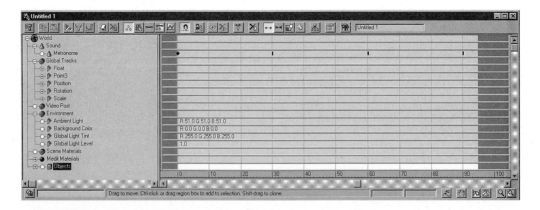

FIGURE 20.5

The Track View hierarchy list for World.

The World range bar reflects the animated range for all its subordinate items except Objects.

The Sound Branch

The Sound branch stores data related to sound. Two type of sound are available: the metronome and an audio sound file. You access the Sound options by right-clicking in the Sound track or by selecting an existing Sound item and selecting Properties in the toolbar. Either of these options displays the Sound Options dialog (see Figure 20.6).

FIGURE 20.6

The Sound Options dialog.

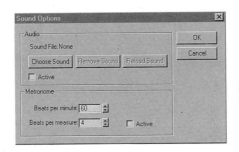

3DS MAX supports WAV files as the standard sound file type but can also read others, such as AU or AVI files. When rendering to an AVI file, your sound file is embedded into the AVI file. All sounds must be added in the Track View. If a background AVI is used with sound, the sound from it is ignored unless it is added to the sound channel.

To select a sound file, click Choose Sound and select a sound file from the browser window. Make sure you click the Active button for Audio. To delete a sound, simply click Remove Sound. In order to reload a sound after it has been edited, click Reload Sound. To maintain a link to a sound file but not play it during playback, click off Active. You can reactivate the sound before the final render by clicking the Active checkbox again. You will hear the sound file play after you render to an AVI file, during playback in a viewport with Real Time on, and when dragging the Time slider forward.

The Metronome produces a steady beat that uses two tones. The frequency of the beat is specified by the Beats per minute field. The second tone is heard every *n*th beat as specified in the Beats per measure field. To maintain the Metronome settings but not hear it, click off the Active button. You can hear the Metronome during playback in a viewport with Real Time on.

The Global Tracks Branch

Global Tracks is an area in which you can store controllers. By using expression controllers, for example, you can point to a controller in Global Tracks from several other tracks. By altering the expression in Global Tracks, all the other tracks are changed.

By pasting an instance of a controller in Global Tracks to a number of other tracks, you can change many tracks by altering the controller in Global Tracks.

The Video Post Branch

Animated parameters for Video Post plug-ins can be managed in the Video Post branch. These might include any of the built in Video Post filters or third-party filters.

The Environment Branch

The Environment branch shows the animatable items associated with the environment. This includes Ambient light, Background color, Global light tint, Global light level, and any environmental effects specified in the Rendering Environment dialog.

The Medit Materials and Scene Materials Branches

The Medit Materials branch shows the animatable parameters associated with materials currently defined in one of the 24 slots in the Material Editor. Only six materials can be visible in the Material Editor, but it is capable of containing up to 24 different materials at once. Using the Options button, you can display 6, 15, or all 24 slots. The Scene Materials branch shows all the materials currently assigned to objects in the scene. A single material may appear several times in the hierarchy—as a Medit material, a Scene material, or under the objects to which the material is assigned.

The Objects Branch

The Objects branch shows the animatable parameters associated with the objects defined in the scene. The hierarchy of objects shown is defined by which objects are linked to others and is similar to what you see in Select by Name with the Display Subtree option on.

Hierarchy List Commands

Several of the commands located in the Track View toolbar are used to control the hierarchy list display. They are shown in Figure 20.7 and are as follows:

- Filters

- Copy/Paste

- Assign Controller

- Make Controller Unique

- Parameter Out-of-Range Types

- Add/Delete Note Track

- Add/Delete Visibility Track

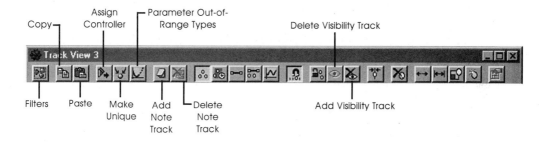

FIGURE 20.7

The Track View hierarchy list commands.

The Assign Controller command is used to assign a new controller to an item as covered in Chapter 25, "Using Controllers and Expressions."

The Parameter Out-of-Range Type command controls how a controller outputs values for time outside of its defined range. The effect of this command is best viewed in the Function Curve mode. This command is covered later in this chapter under the section "Function Curves."

Filtering the Hierarchy List

A fully expanded list for a scene can be very large. 3DS MAX provides you with many filters that help you narrow down what is displayed in

Track View. To set filters, click the Filters button on the toolbar to bring up the Filters dialog. The Show section lets you specify which tracks to display, most of which are self-explanatory.

The Hide by Controller Type section enables you to hide certain controllers from the hierarchy. You can select All, None, or multiple controllers by using the Ctrl key and selecting controllers.

The Show Only section is used to filter the Track View to show Animated Tracks, Selected Objects, Selected Tracks, and Visible Objects. Any combination of these can be chosen as filters.

Hide by Category can be used to narrow the field to certain types of objects in your scene. You can hide elements that are never animated in your scene, or that you don't wish to modify at the moment, in order to simplify the Track View. You can hide Geometry, Shapes, Lights, Cameras, Helpers, and Space Warps. This can be quite helpful in simplifying the hierarchy with complex animations.

The Function Curve Display section of the Filters dialog is used to control the color of the function curves shown in the Function Curve mode and is described in the section "Function Curves," later in the chapter.

Copying and Pasting Objects

By using the Copy and Paste buttons in the Track View toolbar, you can copy an item in the hierarchy list to one or more items of the same type. Most of the items in the hierarchy can be copied by this method. The easiest way to determine if an item can be copied is to select the item and see if the Copy button is grayed out. Click the Copy button to copy an item to the buffer.

To paste an item from the buffer, select the desired items of the same type to paste onto and click Paste. If one or more of the selected items is a different type, then the Paste button will be grayed out.

When you click Paste, the Paste dialog is displayed (see Figure 20.8). You can choose whether to paste as a copy or an instance. The same as any other copy function, a copy is independent of the original. An instance is dependent on the original, and making a change to one will change both of them.

The Replace all instances option tells 3DS MAX what to do if the item being pasted to is already an instance of something else. With this option checked, all the items that shared this instance continue to share the instance and all reference what is being pasted. If this option is not selected, the item(s) selected will be made unique before pasting.

FIGURE 20.8

The Paste dialog.

Making Unique

Use the Make Unique button to convert any selected instanced item(s) to unique status. These can be instanced controllers, instanced objects, or referenced objects. Select the desired items to be made unique and click Make Unique. All instanced items in the selection are made independent of all items, and any items that are already unique are not changed.

Note Tracks

It is possible in 3DS MAX to assign a note track to each track in Track View. To create a note track, select an item and click Add Note Track. A branch is created for the note track under the selected item. If more than one item is selected, a note track is created subordinate to each of the items.

To create a note, you must be in the Edit Key mode. Click Add Keys and then click the note track at the desired time. This creates a Note key. Right-clicking it brings up the Notes dialog (see Figure 20.9).

The note number is shown in the top left of the dialog. You can change between notes on that track by clicking the Left and Right arrows. The time of the current note is displayed on the top middle area and can be changed by typing in a new number. The Lock Key option sets the position of the note so that it is changed by the various key modifiers, such as Scale, Move, and Slide. Text can be entered into the field with the flashing cursor. The text field is a standard Windows Notepad style and the Cut and Paste commands will work. The first line of text is shown next to the note in the note track.

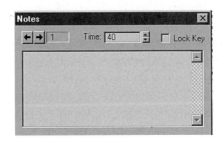

Visibility Tracks

Visibility tracks can be applied to individual objects. You must be in the Edit Key mode to create a Visibility track. Select the objects that you want to add a Visibility track for and click Add Visibility Track. A Visibility track enables you to have objects disappear and reappear in a scene at specified times.

In order to specify whether an object is visible or not at certain times, you must add keys to the track. The default controller used in a Visibility track is the On/Off controller, but other controller types can be used to have a partially visible object. The area shown as a blue bar is the visible time of the object. A non-visible object is displayed in the viewport as ghosted but does not render.

Keys and Ranges

In the edit window of Track View, keys are shown in the parameters' tracks as dots and the range bars are shown in the items' tracks. The range bars extend across the range of time for which keys are present on parameters subordinate to that item. The Edit Key mode of Track View is used to create and edit keys. Both the Edit Key and Edit Ranges modes are used to adjust the times associated with keys. The Position Ranges mode is used to adjust ranges without adjusting the key associated with the ranges.

Two Track View commands that act on the Edit window are available in all Track View edit modes. The commands are the Snap Frame and the Lock Selection command buttons (see Figure 20.10).

Usually it is desired that keys be placed exactly on frames. If you're working with detailed animations, it is possible to work at the sub-frame level. With Snap Frame selected, any keys created are placed at the nearest frame time. If Snap Frame is off, you can create and modify keys up to 1/4800 of a second accuracy or on the Tick level.

Lock Selection ─────┐   ┌─── Snap Frames

FIGURE 20.10

The Snap Frame and Lock Selection command buttons.

To avoid accidentally deselecting keys, you can click Lock Selection. The selection will be locked until you deselect the Lock Selection button.

In Track View there is also a button located on the toolbar called Track View Utilities. Clicking this button brings up the Track View Utilities menu, with several functions you can choose from (see Figure 20.11). These functions include Randomize Keys, Create Out of Range Keys, and Select Keys by Time.

FIGURE 20.11

The Track View Utilities menu.

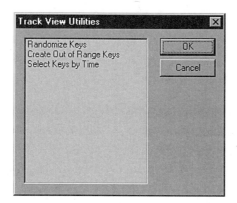

The previous section dealt with the main components of Track View. You will now begin to learn how to create and manipulate data in Track View.

Creating Keys

In order to create keys in Track View, you must be in Edit Key or Function Curves mode. To create a key, expand the hierarchy to display the parameter you want to create a key for. Click Add Keys and click in the Parameters track at the time you want the key created. Figure 20.12 shows the command buttons for Edit Key mode.

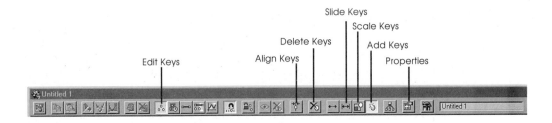

FIGURE 20.12

The command buttons for Edit Key mode.

Object transformation keys can also be created in the Parameters section of the Motion panel (see Figure 20.13). To create a key in the Motion Control panel, select an object and move the Time slider to the desired time. In the PRS Parameters rollout, click the desired button in the Create Key section. The animate button does not need to be on to create a key.

FIGURE 20.13

The Motion command panel enables you to create and modify object transform keys.

The following steps will go through how to add a key.

ADDING KEYS EXERCISE

1. Create a simple scene containing an object, a sphere, or a box.

2. Go to the last frame and click the Animate button. Move your object from its current position to another one.

3. Open Track View and expand the Position track. You will notice keys present at the beginning and the end of the track.

4. Add a key by clicking anywhere on the track in the Edit window. You can right-click the key and change its positional value in the scene. The current value of the scene will be set to that point in time specified by your animation.

5. Playback the animation to view your results.

It is important to be able to add keys to an object in a scene in order to control the object's behavior. It is equally important to be able to remove keys from Track View.

Deleting Keys

You must be in Edit Key or Function Curves mode to delete keys. Select the desire key and click Delete Keys or simply press Delete.

Object transformation keys can also be deleted in the Motion, Parameters command panel. Select the object and move the Time slider to the desired key time. Click the transformation key to be removed (Position, Rotation, or Scale) in the Delete Key section. You can easily move between keys by pressing the right and left arrows in the Key info rolldown while the appropriate transform is selected above. Pressing the arrows moves the Time slider to the next or previous location of a key for the selected transform.

Editing Key Values

To edit key values in Track View, select the key and click Properties or simply right-click the key. This brings up the Key Info dialog for that key. The format of the Key Info dialog changes, depending on the type of controller assigned and the number of values returned by the controller. The two basic types of controllers are the Tension/Continuity/Bias (TCB) controller and the Bézier controller. The difference between these two controllers is how they interpolate value between keys.

Controllers typically return one, three, or four values. Controllers that return one value are typically used for a creation parameter for an object, adjustment parameters for a modifier, and single field parameters for materials. Controllers that contain three values are typically used for position and scaling objects and for colors. Controllers that return four values are typically used for rotation of objects. Figure 20.14 shows the key info for a Bézier position controller returning three values and a TCB rotation controller returning four values.

FIGURE 20.14

Key Info dialogs for a Bézier and a TCB controller keys.

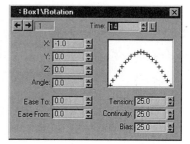

The key number is shown in the top left of the dialog. By clicking the arrows, you can move between keys on that track. The Time field shows the time at which that key is placed. The L button locks the key in place. If the key is locked, it is not affected by the various Move, Slide, and Scale commands in Track View.

The rest of the information in the Key Info dialog is the key values. You can adjust them by typing new values in the fields or by clicking the spinners.

These Key Info dialogs are duplicated in the Motion, Parameters command panel. They can be modified the same way, with the only difference being that current time must be equal to the key time. Simply select the transform key you wish to edit and adjust the key values.

Adjusting Key Timing

Although you can adjust the timing of keys in Track View and in the Motion panel by editing the key's Time value, you are limited to working with a single key at a time. It is often necessary to adjust multiple keys at one time.

In the Edit Key mode of Track View, you are supplied with several tools for adjusting key timing. They are the following:

- Align Keys

- Move Keys

- Slide Keys

- Scale Keys

Align Keys works for a single or selection of keys. When you click Align Keys, the first key in the selection is moved to the current location of the Time slider. Any other keys selected are moved relative to the first key and the times of non-selected keys are not changed.

Move Keys simply moves a selection of keys through time. Only the keys selected are affected by Move keys. You can clone a selection of keys by holding down Shift and dragging to the desired time. Move Keys is a button that remains on until another is selected.

Slide Keys moves a selected set of keys similar to Move Keys but also affects keys before or after them. If you move the selected keys to the left or back in time, the key before the selected one is moved back the same amount. The same occurs if you move the keys to the right; any keys forward of the selection are moved as well.

Scale Keys scales the time associated with the selected keys with respect to the current time. The selected keys are proportionally moved either away from or toward the current time (signified by a vertical line in the edit window) by dragging a selected key away from or toward the current time. The times associated with non-selected keys are not changed. You can clone and scale the set of keys by Shift-dragging the keys.

When Modify Subtree mode is on, the Items range bar is replaced by the keys of all items subordinate to the Items range bar as well as the keys of any linked objects.

Adjusting Key Timing via Range Bars

The next method for adjusting key timing is by adjusting range bars. The Edit Ranges toolbar is shown in Figure 20.15. When in Edit Ranges mode, all keys are replaced by a range bar that extends over the range of keys present. You can move the range bars, and all the keys included are moved.

If you move the end point of a range bar, the range bar and the keys of all items subordinate to that item are scaled down toward the opposite end point. If you drag the end point of the World range bar, all the animation in the scene is scaled.

FIGURE 20.15

The toolbar for Edit Ranges mode of Track View.

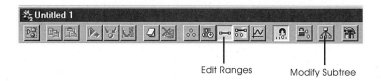

Edit Ranges   Modify Subtree

If you have objects that are linked, the Modify Subtree option is available that permits you to adjust the range of subordinate objects when you adjust the range of a parent object. If you turn on Modify Subtree by clicking it, the range bar for parent objects is extended to cover the animated region for that object and all subordinates. Moving or scaling the parent's range bar affects the keys of all subordinate objects.

This concludes the section on creating keys. As you learned, there are various ways to create and manipulate keys in MAX. The following section deals with the Edit Time mode in Track View.

Working with Time

This section deals with using the Edit Time mode of Track View. Although time is manipulated independently from animation keys, the Edit Time mode's primary purpose is to alter key timing. When in Edit Time mode, the edit window still shows range bars and keys, but they are grayed out and are for reference only. Figure 20.16 shows the toolbar for the Edit Time mode.

The first step when entering Edit Time mode is to select the tracks for which you want to edit time. Select one or more items in the hierarchy list by using the Standard Selection tools. All the tools in Edit Time—except Insert Time—require that a block of time be defined to perform the action. The time block can be specified by clicking Select Time or Scale Time and dragging in the edit windows. The selected time is shown as a dark line in the selected tracks. You can also specify the start and end times by entering the numbers in the fields at the bottom of the Track View window.

FIGURE 20.16

The toolbar for Edit Time mode of Track View.

Inserting Time

To insert time in the selected tracks, click Insert Time, and in any track, drag from the time point where you want to insert time. If you drag forward, time is inserted in the selected tracks. If you drag backward, time is deleted in the selected tracks. Yellow vertical lines are drawn showing the extents of the time being added or deleted. You can also see numerically the associated times in the fields at the bottom of Track View. Black lines are also shown in the selected tracks showing the time being added or deleted (see Figure 20.17). The keys to the right of the time associated with the initial click are moved to reflect the change in time.

FIGURE 20.17

Using Insert Time in Track View.

Scaling Time

To scale a block of time, select the desired tracks and click Scale Time. Then click and drag to select the time to be scaled. This is not necessary if you already have a time range selected with Select Time. You can then click anywhere in the selected time to scale it. Time is scaled from the left end of the time range. You can also scale in a negative direction by dragging the scale to the left of the beginning time.

Reversing Time

Reverse Time is used to reverse the order of keys in a selected block of time. Simply select the tracks and the time range to reverse and click Reverse Time.

Whether the keys at the end point of the range are reversed depends on the state of the Exclude Left End Point and Exclude Right End Point buttons. If the button is clicked on, then the end point on that side is not mirrored and is left where it is. Figure 20.18 shows the effect of Reverse Time.

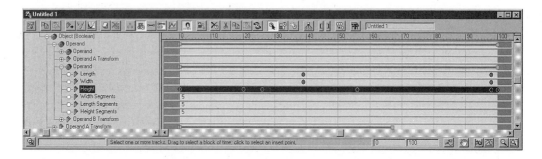

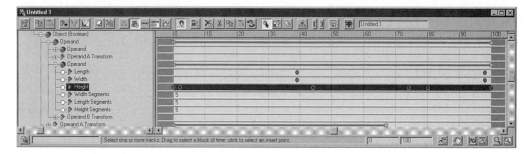

FIGURE 20.18

The effect of Reverse Time.

Deleting Time

Delete Time deletes the block of time and all the keys in it. The keys to the right of the end time are moved to the left by the amount of the time deleted. If Exclude Left End Point or Exclude Right End Point is on, a key occurring at the start or end time, respectively, is not deleted. If both are on and a key exists at each end, one of the keys is deleted. If neither key has been selected in Edit Key mode, the end key is deleted. If both keys have been selected, then the start key is deleted. Otherwise, the unselected key is deleted.

Using the Time Clipboard

The Time Clipboard is used to store a block of time and the keys associated with that block of time. The user can cut or copy blocks of time to, or can paste from, the Time Clipboard. Unlike copying keys in the Edit Key mode, you can paste the time block and its keys to other animatable tracks.

To copy a block of time to the Time Clipboard, mark the block of time and click Copy Track or Cut Track. If Copy Track is clicked, the original block of time and its keys are unaffected. If Cut Track is clicked, the block of time and its keys are deleted. The Exclude Left End Point and Exclude Right End Point options can be selected before performing the Cut Track. The same logic used for Delete Time is used with Cut Track if keys exist at both the start and end times.

To paste from the Time Clipboard, you need to select the target tracks to receive the paste. The simplest case is when you copy from and paste to single tracks. In this case, the controller type of the target track must match the controller type of the source.

To show controller types, click Filters and turn on Show Controller Types. This shows the controller type next to each item in the hierarchy list. Within the object hierarchy, you can safely assume that non-transform-related items can use the Bézier Float controller, even if no controller is shown for an item. Figure 20.19 shows a hierarchy with Show Controller Types turned on.

To assign a controller to an item that does not have a controller, click Assign Float Controller and select the controller that matches the source item's controller in the Assign Float Controller dialog (see Figure 20.20). If the Assign Float Controller dialog does not show the same controller type as the source item, you cannot paste from that source to that target.

If you paste from multiple items to multiple items or from a single item to multiple items, each target track must have the same controller type as the corresponding source track. If only the first one or more controller types match, 3DS MAX performs the paste operation up to the first controller mismatch.

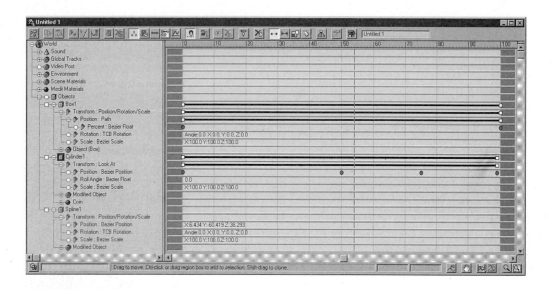

FIGURE 20.19

A Track View hierarchy with Show Controller Types on.

FIGURE 20.20

The Assign Float Controller dialog.

After selecting the target tracks to receive the paste, you need to specify where in time to perform the paste. You have two options: selecting a single point in time or dragging out a range of time. If you specify a single point in time, that time point is the insertion point. The block of time in the clipboard is inserted at this point and any original keys to the right of the insertion point are moved to the right by the length of time inserted.

If you specify a range of time for the paste, that range of time is deleted before the paste occurs. Any original keys to the right of the end time are moved to the right by the length of time inserted minus the length of the range of time specified.

After you select the items to receive the paste and the time to receive the paste, click Paste Track. The Paste Track dialog (see Figure 20.21) appears with an option to paste the time block absolute or relative. These options refer to the handling of the key values, as opposed to time.

FIGURE 20.21

The Paste Track dialog.

If the Paste Absolute option is checked, the values associated with the pasted keys have the exact same values as the source keys. If Paste Relative is checked, the value of the item at the paste insert time is subtracted from key values of all keys pasted. The keys after the insertion point are then adjusted by the difference in the values of the first and last key pasted.

Reducing Keys

The Reduce Keys command works with keys similar to how the Optimize modifier works with geometry—reducing the complexity while maintaining a specified level of detail. For each track selected, Reduce Keys calculates a smaller set of keys that closely match the original keys. Reduce Keys is handy for post-processing of Inverse Kinematic motions, as well as keyframes generated from motion capture devices.

To reduce the keys for a selected track, select a time range and click Reduce Keys. Figure 20.22 shows the Reduce Keys dialog. The Reduce Keys dialog prompts you to set a Threshold value. The Threshold value specifies how different from the original value at each frame the reduced set of keys is allowed to be. The unit of measure is your current unit setup for distances and degrees for angles. Each selected track is evaluated independently of all other selected tracks.

FIGURE 20.22

The Reduce Keys dia-log.

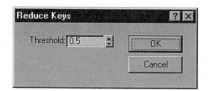

Working with Function Curves

The next editing mode in Track View is Function Curves mode. Function Curves mode visualizes both key position and actual animation values being used. You can change key values and watch the effect of that change over time. This mode enables you to fine-tune animations by adjusting the shape of function curves over time. Figure 20.23 shows the toolbar for Function Curves mode.

FIGURE 20.23

The Function Curves toolbar.

To display the Function Curve of an item, select the item and click Function Curves. The Edit window shows the shape of the controller's output over time. To show the keys for a curve, click the curve. Individual keys on the curve are shown as vertices, and the green triangles next to items in the hierarchy generating that curve are highlighted (see Figure 20.24). If that item outputs more than one value, the key vertices are displayed on all curves associated with that item.

In the Filters dialog, one section is devoted to function curve display options. These options can be set to specify which curves are displayed: X, Y, Z for Position, Rotation, and Scale Controllers and R, G, B for Color Controllers. Rotation is included in the event that a three-component Rotation Controller becomes available.

Editing Function Curves

You edit curves by manipulating vertices on the curve. You can select vertices the same way you select keys. You can click Lock Selection to prevent accidentally deselecting keys. If you are displaying curves from more than one item, you can select the curves that you want to work on and click Freeze Non-Selected Curves. Any non-selected curves will be grayed out.

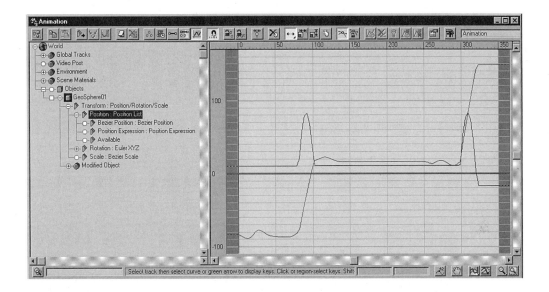

FIGURE 20.24

A Position Controller in Function Curves mode.

You can now edit the selected vertices in many ways. You can move them in time and value, scale them with respect to the current time or with respect to zero, or delete them. When using the Move or Scale Keys command, the output curves of the associated controller change to match. You can move or scale keys for value or time. To change which way to move keys, click and hold the Move button to choose between Move Keys horizontally, vertically, or both.

The Align Keys command can be used in the same way as in Edit Key mode. The selected key is moved to the current Time slider position. If more that one key is selected, then the leftmost key in each selected track is aligned with the current time and the others move in relation to it.

The values of individual vertices can be adjusted be right-clicking them, selecting a vertex, and clicking Properties, or by entering values in the fields at the bottom of Track View.

You can add keys to the curve by clicking Add Keys and clicking a point on the curve. The value assigned to the key will be the value of that point on the curve and can then be moved.

Ease and Multiplier Curves

Ease and Multiplier Curves can be applied to any animatable item. Ease Curves affects the timing of the keys for the controller it is applied to and Multiplier Curves affects the output value of the controller it is applied to. Click Apply Ease Curve after selecting one or many items to apply Ease Curve. The Multiplier command is in the drop-down menu of the Ease Curve button. Click and hold Apply Ease Curves to select Apply Multiplier Curve. Multiplier curves are assigned the same way as Ease Curves.

The following example shows the use of Ease Curves.

USING EASE CURVES

1. Load the file Easecrv.max, which is a scene containing two spheres moving from the left to the right of the top viewport. Sphere01 has an Ease Curve applied to it with the default values (see Figure 20.25).

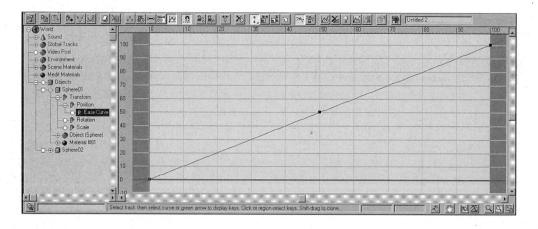

FIGURE 20.25

The default Ease Curve applied to the Position track of Sphere01.

2. Expand Sphere01 down to the Ease Curve level that has been applied to the Position track. Click Ease Curve and select Function Curves mode.

The default Ease Curve is a straight line with a slope of 1:1. This Ease Curve has no effect on the motion of the sphere, as you can see by playing the animation. The vertex in the middle of the line is at the same place as the sphere should be at that time.

3. Click the Position track and select the red curve to show the vertices. You will notice that there are more keys lying after the center point than before. This means that most of the object's motion occurs after the midpoint of the animation.

4. Click the curve and select the middle vertex. The current value is 50 at frame 50. Change the value to 30 and play the animation again.

You will notice that the top sphere (Sphere01) starts out slower than the bottom sphere but catches up at the end.

5. Select both the Position track and the Ease Curve track to display both, overlaid in the edit window. Select the Ease Curve located in the 0-100 value range and click Freeze Non-Selected Curves.

6. Drag the midpoint of the Ease Curve up and down. Notice the change that occurs in the position curve. Experiment and play back the animation to view the results (see Figure 20.26).

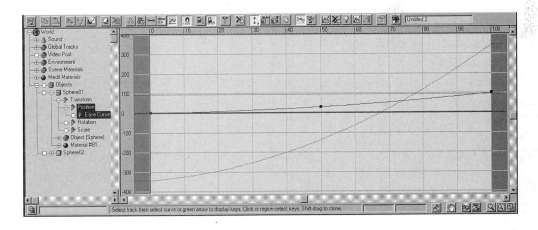

FIGURE 20.26

The new Ease Curve with a center vertex value of 30 overlapped with the Position curve.

Notice that when any part of the Ease Curve falls beyond the 0-100 range, the effect is a stop in motion of the sphere for that time.

The Multiplier Curve causes the value of the controller to which it is applied to be multiplied by the value specified by the Multiplier Curve. The default Multiplier Curve is a straight line with a value of 1.

Ease and Multiplier Curves can be deleted by selecting the name in the hierarchy and clicking the Delete Ease/Multiplier Curve. You can disable an Ease or Multiplier Curve by clicking the Ease/Multiplier Enable/Disable toggle.

Out-of-Range Types

The default output of a controller outside the range of its keys is to return the value of the nearest key. This is called a Constant Out-of-Range type, or ORT. Six ORTs can be to either side of the range. The ranges themselves can be decoupled from the underlying keys, enabling you to easily create looping or repeating cycles. The six ORTs are Constant, Cycle, Loop, Ping Pong, Linear, and Relative Repeat (see Figure 20.27).

FIGURE 20.27

The Parameter Curve Out-of-Range Types dialog.

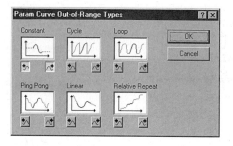

To change the ORT for an item, select the item in the hierarchy and click Parameter Curve Out-of-Range Types. The dialog enables you to apply any of the six types before or after the range. The solid portion of the sample graphs shows a function curve over its range. The dotted line shows the effect of each ORT on the item's range. The following example shows how to use ORTs to animate a rolling ball.

OUT-OF-RANGE TYPE EXERCISE

1. Load file Ballroll.max. The file shows a ball rolling along for a single rotation.

2. Expand the Transform track for the object Ball. The range bar for the Transform track is from 0 to 20. Select the Position track and click Function Curves.

3. Select the ball in the scene and go to the Trajectories section of the Motion panel. The ball's trajectory is shown in the viewport (see Figure 20.28).

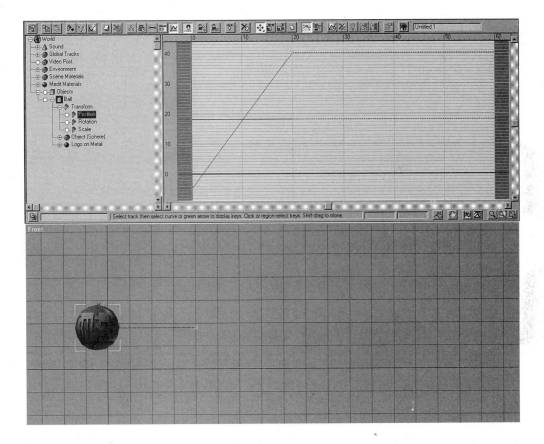

FIGURE 20.28

The scene with the trajectory of the ball shown in the viewport and in the Track View Function Curves mode.

4. Play the animation and leave it playing for the rest of the exercise.

The ball rolls for 30 frames and then stops. The ball is using the default ORT of Constant for both Position and Rotation.

5. Select the Position track and click Parameter Curve Out-of-Range Types. Click Cycle to select both in and out types. Now close the dialog. The ball rolls forward and then starts over at the beginning. Notice the rotation happens only once.

6. Select the Loop ORT and view the results.

The motion looks the same as for Cycle. The Loop ORT jumps from the value of the last key to the value of the first key. The Cycle ORT interpolates between the two values. In this case, the first and last keys are at the extreme edges of the range; therefore, there is no time to interpolate between the values.

7. Select the Ping Pong ORT. The ball moves back and forth between the two positions.

8. Select the Linear ORT. The ball continues its forward motion for the rest of the animation.

9. Select the Relative Repeat ORT.

Notice there is no difference from Linear or Loop. For more complex animations where more movement is involved, you can use Relative Repeat to ensure smooth motion.

10. Choose an ORT that works for the example and apply it to the Rotation track as well. For this example, Linear, Loop, and Relative Repeat all work for both Position and Rotation.

Position Ranges Mode

The range bars for an animation usually start at the first key and end at the last key. You can decouple the range for an item from its keys, which gives you added flexibility in creating loops and cycles. You can also recouple ranges in the same way.

When you choose Position Ranges, a new toolbar is shown (see Figure 20.29). To decouple a range bar for a track, select the track and click Position Ranges. The display changes to show range bars extending over the track's keys. You can move the range bar or adjust the length of the range bar by moving the end points.

FIGURE 20.29
The Position Ranges toolbar.

Working with Trajectories

You can use the Trajectories section of the Motion Control panel to display the trajectory of selected objects in the viewports. The trajectory is shown as a blue dashed line, with breaks where the frames are and white squares signifying key positions.

While in Trajectories, you can edit the keys of the trajectory curve, convert the trajectory to a spline, or convert a spline to a trajectory. To edit Trajectory keys, click Sub-Object in the Motion, Trajectory command panel (see Figure 20.30). You can edit individual keys by using the Move, Rotate, or Scale tool.

FIGURE 20.30

The Trajectories section of the Motion panel.

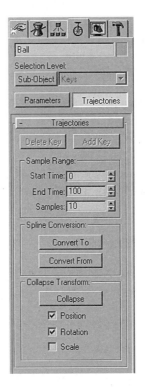

While in Sub-Object mode, you can add keys on the path by clicking Add Key and selecting a point on the path. To delete keys, select the keys to be deleted and press Delete or click the Delete Key button.

Sometimes it is easier to convert the motion path to a spline in order to modify it. You can then use any of the Shape modifiers to adjust the spline. The spline is created by sampling a specified region of time, where each vertex on the spline is one of the samples taken. The samples taken are evenly spaced according to time, as opposed to spaced evenly along the path. The region to be sampled can be specified in the Sample Range area. Set Samples to the number of samples to be taken across the region specified and select Convert To to convert the trajectory to an editable spline.

You can use the existing spline or a new spline to be used as the object's trajectory. Click Convert From and select the desired spline to be converted to Position keys. Any existing keys within the time range are replaced, and any keys lying outside of the time range selected are unaffected.

In Practice: Animation Control Tools

- **Time Configuration:** You can choose between different frame rates and display methods for time without adversely affecting the animation.

- **Animation Keys:** All aspects of animation keys can be created, modified, and deleted in Track View. The timing and value associated with Object Transform animation keys can also be set, edited, and deleted in the Motion Command panel.

- **Disabling Viewports:** For improved video speed in 3DS MAX, you can disable one or more viewports from playback. When working with parts of an animation, use Play Selected to temporarily hide other objects during playback.

- **Time Clipboard:** Animation keys can be copied between items of same controller types with the Time Clipboard. This enables you to copy animation from an object and apply it to another.

- **Animated Ranges:** The animated range for an object can be decoupled from the object's animation keys. This gives you extra flexibility in creating animation loops and cycles.

- **Function Curves:** Use Function Curves mode to view animation values between keys. This is a much easier way to visualize what is happening in an animation.

- **Out-of-Range Types:** Use ORTs to repeat a set of animation keys for an object. They simplify looped or repeated motions by not having to copy animation keys.

- **Position Over Time:** An object's motion can be viewed as a spline curve in the viewport. You can edit the spline path, convert it to a spline, or convert a spline to a trajectory.

Chapter 21

BUILDING AND ANIMATING HIERARCHIES

Most of the objects you create in 3D Studio MAX contain

many parts that can be held together with moveable joints

or links. These joints can be created in 3DS MAX by setting

up linked object hierarchies. After you build such a hierar-

chy, you can animate it easily by combining the techniques

of Forward and Inverse Kinematics. This chapter covers the

following topics about building and animating hierarchies:

- Creating object hierarchies

- Linking objects

- Working with pivots

- Using dummy objects

- Using inverse kinematics

- Defining IK joints

- Defining the kinematic chain

- Animating with inverse kinematics

Creating Object Hierarchies

The controls for creating hierarchical links can be found on the main toolbar. Pivot points and other link parameters can be found in the Hierarchy panel (see Figure 21.1).

With linked objects, Move, Rotate, and Scale are passed from a parent to all its children. Linking enables you to quickly and easily create complex hierarchical structures that become manageable. These structures can be several levels deep, with child objects whose parents are children of other parents. These structures can also be constrained in the ways they are allowed to move and whether they pass their constraints on down the chain. These constraints are defined in the Joint Parameters and Link Info rollouts.

Use the following steps to create a linked hierarchy:

1. Select the objects that you want to be the children.

2. Click the link icon from the toolbar and drag the selected objects to the desired parent object.

3. You can repeat steps 1 and 2 until all the desired child objects are linked.

4. Customize the location and orientation of the pivot point for the linked objects.

5. Specify link inheritance.

6. If you're planning to animate with Inverse Kinematics, define Joint Parameters.

FIGURE 21.1

The MAX R2 Linking controls are located on the toolbar.

Building linked hierarchies can be a very powerful technique that can save countless hours on complex scenes when used properly. The main functions of linking objects are the following:

- **Simulating the real world by linking objects together in a jointed assembly.** An example of this is a chain. If you move the ending link on a chain, you want the joining links to follow in relation to the first. Moving each of the links individually for an animation is nearly impossible and produces very artificial-looking results. Linking makes this task very easy.

■ **Assisting in the definition of complex motion.** Say you want to have an asteroid tumbling through space. This could be rather difficult by manually moving and rotating the asteroid. You can instead rotate it standing in place and link it to an invisible dummy object. Then move the dummy object and the asteroid follows it. Dummy objects can be used in this way to solve many complex animation problems.

Parent, Child, and Root Objects

Any object that has another object linked to it is called a parent object. A parent object can have any number of objects linked to it and these linked objects are called children. The children of any object can have children of its own and so on. Any object in this hierarchy down from the parent is called a descendant.

Parent objects can also be linked as a child to another object. Any transform done to a parent object also affects all the descendants of that object.

Although parent objects can have an unlimited amount of children, a child can have only one parent. If you attempt to link a child to a new parent, the previous link is destroyed and replaced by the new parent. New to MAX 2 is the capability to use a Link Controller that effectively lets you keyframe the linkage to various control objects.

As you trace the links of an object back up the tree, you will eventually reach the root of the hierarchy. All hierarchies contain only one root object. The root of a hierarchy is an object that has no ancestors (all objects above the child object) and a single object with no children is also a root object—it is its own root.

Hierarchies and the World

Technically speaking, the scene itself (called the World) is the root of all hierarchies. This means that every object in the scene is either linked to some other object as a child or is a child of the world.

This "hidden hierarchy" is evident in the following situations:

■ When you adjust a pivot point for a root object, you are adjusting the link between the object and the world.

- Choosing the Parent transform coordinate system for the root object returns the world coordinate system because the world is the parent of all root objects.

- When IK is active, you cannot transform root objects unless you release them from the world or define joint parameters between the root object and the world.

Viewing the Hierarchical Tree

When links are created between objects, they are arranged in a tree structure. This tree takes the form of a list in which the parent objects are at the top with its children below and to the right. This list can be viewed in either the Track View or by choosing the Display Subtree option in the Select Objects dialog box (see Figure 21.2).

FIGURE 21.2

Viewing object hierarchies.

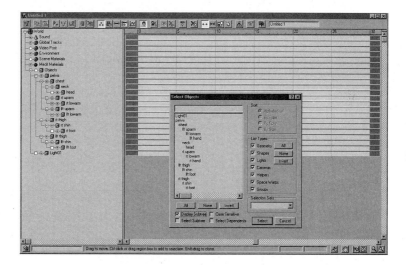

Linking Objects

The Link and Unlink buttons on the toolbar can be used to create and break links between objects. All other commands for modifying links are accessed in the command panels.

To link an object, you drag from a selection of child objects to a parent object as stated on the prompt at the bottom of the screen. You must always drag from the children to the parent object. It is easy to get this backwards and end up linking in the wrong direction.

TIP

If you are confused with the dragging process, you can always select by name and then link by name. The dialog box then changes to Select Parent and the confirmation button becomes Link rather than Select. This can drive you crazy, too, but you'll always know which way your hierarchy is going. Don't forget to turn the Select and Link Icon back to Select when you're done.

When you are making links, it is often difficult to get the correct parent object by simply dragging on top of it, especially with more complex scenes that have multiple objects overlapped in the viewport. After the link button has been pressed, you can easily select a parent by clicking the Select By Name button or by pressing H on your keyboard. This brings up a link selection dialog in which you can specify a parent. Figure 21.3 shows an example of using this method. You can see that left hand is selected as a parent, possibly for fingers. This dialog is the Select Parent objects dialog. After you have selected the desired parent object, simply press the Link button to complete the process.

TIP

When selecting by clicking an object in the viewport, pause and hold the cursor still for a second. In MAX 2, a new little label pops up showing you the name of the object you're about to select.

FIGURE 21.3

Selecting a parent object in the Select Parent dialog.

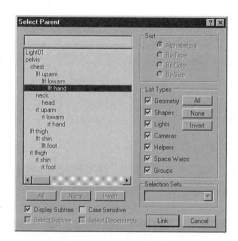

Press the Unlink Selection button in the toolbar to unlink the object from the chain above it. You can use the Select by Name command to select objects to be unlinked and then click Unlink. Because the command is named Unlink Selection, it requires that you select an object before using the command. This behavior is different from the Select and Link or other Select commands, so it takes some getting used to.

Setting Link Inheritance

You can set link inheritances in the Hierarchy panel to determine which transforms are passed from the parent to a child. You select the child object and then click the Link Info button in the Hierarchy panel. Change the desired options under the Inherit rollout.

In Figure 21.4, the Checked Link Inheritance options are active and the Unchecked are turned off. The Transform axes are represented by the Active options that pass Transform information from the parent to the selected child, causing the child to transform with the parent. Unchecked options disengage that transform of the parent from the selected child. This capability is rather useful when modeling mechanical-type systems. Quite often, an object is linked to its parent so that the object is constrained to a particular axis. Examples include the hands on a watch or the tray in your CD player. Both of these objects are constrained on a certain axis but are free to move or rotate on another axis defined by its pivot point.

Setting Object Transform Locks

You can use options in the Locks rollout of the Hierarchy panel to prevent an object from being transformed about any selected local axis. You can access the object locks by clicking the Link Info button of the Hierarchy panel and expanding the Locks rollout (see Figure 21.4). Although the Locks rollout is located in Link Info, locks have nothing to do with links between objects. Setting a lock affects only transforms applied directly to an object. Locks also only affect new keyframes created after the lock is turned on; they do not change existing keyframes.

FIGURE 21.4

Link Locks and Link Inheritance in the hierarchy panel.

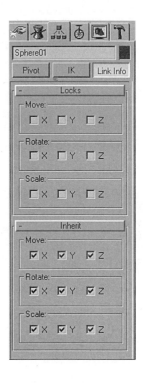

Viewing Links

With complex linked hierarchies it is often difficult to visualize which objects are linked to each other and where their pivot points lie. As covered earlier, you can use Track View or the Select Objects dialog to display the hierarchical tree structure, but there is a third way to display the links in a scene.

Under Display options, click the Link Display rollout to control the display properties of the selected objects (see Figure 21.5). The two display options work as described in the following list:

- **Display Links:** When checked, a small tetrahedron is placed at the pivot point of the selected object. When a parent and a child are selected, a three-sided cone is drawn from the parent, with its tip at the child (see Figure 21.5).

- **Link Replaces Object:** When checked, all the selected objects are replaced by tetrahedrons at the pivot points. When Link Replaces Object is checked, the Display Links option becomes checked as well.

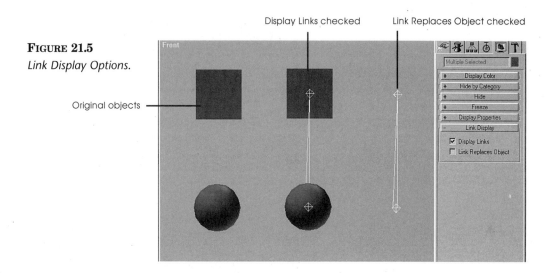

FIGURE 21.5

Link Display Options.

Display Links checked

Link Replaces Object checked

Original objects

Avoiding Nonuniform Scale with Hierarchies

Linking is designed as a way to pass transforms from one object to another. Transforming a parent object passes the transform information to any children of the object. This process works extremely well for Move, Rotate, and Uniform Scale transformations. Linking does not work well with objects that have been nonuniformly scaled.

A child object linked to a nonuniformly scaled parent will squash and skew as you rotate the child, which is probably not the result you want. As stated throughout this book, you should almost never apply nonuniform scale directly to an object. Always apply nonuniform scale to Sub-Object selections or use the XFORM modifier.

You can remove the nonuniform scale link effect from a parent object in many ways. Two of the easiest methods to remove the effect are as follows:

- Select the child of the nonuniform scaled object and uncheck the affected scale axis in the Link Inheritance rollout. You will need to do this for every child of the nonuniform scaled parent object.

- Reset the transform of the nonuniform scaled object after you unlink any children. After the transform is reset, you can relink the children to the object. Techniques for resetting an object's transform are presented later in this chapter, in the "Adjusting Transforms" section.

Working with Pivots

An object's pivot point defines where the link between a parent and a child occurs. Think of the tetrahedron that you see when Display Links is checked. Imagine that the cone is a rigid arm welded to the pivot point of the parent object and connects to the pivot point of the child with a joint. The joint enables the child to Move, Rotate, and Scale independent of the parent, but when you Transform the parent the cone moves and drags the child along with it.

An object does not have to be linked in order to modify its pivot point. In the instance of a single object, remember that it is still considered to be a child of the world. The pivot point defines the orientation of an object's Local coordinate system and is the point about which all object rotation and scaling is centered.

Adjusting Pivots

Tools for adjusting an object's pivot points are located in the Pivot panel of the menu. Click the Pivot button in the Hierarchy panel to display the Adjust Pivot rollout (see Figure 21.6).

FIGURE 21.6

Adjust Pivot options.

The top three buttons in this rollout are the most important. Use these buttons to decide whether you want to affect the pivot independent of the object or the object independent of its pivot, or even affect the children of a hierarchy without altering the parent. The following is a list describing the effects of the Affect Pivot Only, Affect Object Only, and Affect Hierarchy Only buttons:

■ When Affect Pivot Only is active, transforms and alignment are applied only to the pivot not affecting the object or its children. Use this to move an object's pivot point to a new location. You can't animate the pivot point over time.

■ When Affect Object Only is active, transforms and alignment are applied only to the selected objects leaving the pivots and any linked children where they are used. Use this button if a pivot is correctly placed, but you want to move the object.

■ When Affect Hierarchy Only is active, only the object's children are affected by the rotate and scale transforms leaving the selected object unchanged. If the object has no children, then no effect will be seen. Use this button if you want to alter the position or orientation of an object's children.

When any of these buttons is active, the pivot point is visible as a large three-axis icon (see Figure 21.7). When no button is active, transforms are applied normally to the object, pivot point, and any children. Clicking any button automatically deactivates any of the other buttons, and clicking a button that is already active deselects the button.

FIGURE 21.7

The Pivot Point icon.

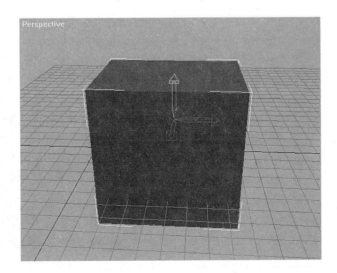

Aligning Pivots

The remaining four buttons in the Adjust Pivot rollout can be used to align either the object or the pivot point. The buttons change depending on whether Affect Object Only or Affect Pivot Only is active. When Affect Hierarchy Only or none is selected, the remaining four buttons are ghosted out. The effects of the buttons are as follows:

- **Center to:** If the button reads Center to Object, it moves the pivot to the geometric center of the object. The orientation of the object does not change. If the button is Center to Pivot, it moves the object so that its geometric center lies on the pivot. The orientation of the object does not change.

- **Align to:** If the button says Align to Object, it reorients the pivot to align to the original local coordinate system of the object. This is determined by how the object was created and the pivot's position is not affected. If the button says Align to Pivot, then the object is rotated to match its original coordinate system with the pivot. The object's position is not affected.

- **Align to World:** The object or the pivot is rotated to align with the World coordinate system. Its location does not change.

- **Reset Pivot:** The object's pivot is rotated and positioned at the location it would be at if it was not altered. The pivot will reflect and transform what has been done to the object since it was created.

Pivots can also be aligned using the Align command in the toolbar while the Affect Pivot Only button is active. Using this method you can align the pivot to any object in the scene with much more accuracy, or you can use the new 3D Snaps to snap the pivot point to a vertex, edge, or any of the other new snaps.

The following exercise deals with a linked planetary system utilizing the Pivot Alignment functions. You can follow along by loading the exercise file or examine the completed file included as planet.max.

A LINKED PLANET SYSTEM

1. Open planet-ex.max from the accompanying CD-ROM. The model begins with three spheres side by side representing the Sun, Earth, and Moon (see Figure 21.8).

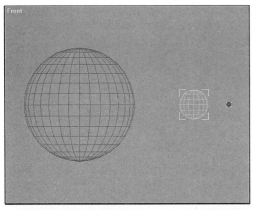
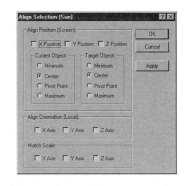
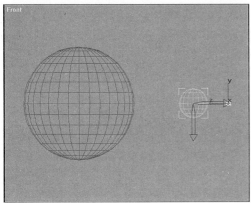
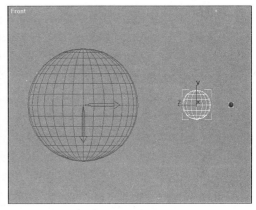

FIGURE 21.8

Various steps in planetary system.

2. Select the Moon.

3. Click the Link button on the toolbar.

4. Drag from the Moon to the Earth and release.

5. Under the Hierarchy panel, click Affect Pivot Only and then select the Align button from the toolbar.

6. Click the Earth to bring up the Align dialog.

7. Click the boxes for X, Y, and Z position and click OK. The Moon's pivot point is aligned with the center of the Earth.

8. Repeat steps 2-7 using the Earth and the Sun instead of the Moon and Earth. The Earth and the Moon now rotate around their respective gravitational partners.

9. Turn on the Animate button.

10. Drag the slider to the end time of the animation.

11. Rotate the Moon 1440 degrees or four full rotations and rotate the Earth 360 degrees.

12. Turn off the animate button and playback the animation.

You can view the final animation by loading planet.avi off the CD-ROM.

The preceding example shows how easy it is to set up a complex animation simply by moving pivot points. It would have been equally simple to set up the animation using dummy objects. Later in this chapter, you will repeat this exercise using the dummy object method.

If, however, you have textures on the planets that you want to rotate individually, you have to keep the textures' axes intact in their centers. You would be required to find a different means to move the planets around their respective gravitational parent.

Adjusting Transforms

You use the commands in the Adjust Transform rollout to transform and align a parent object (including its pivot) independent of any linked children. The buttons in the Adjust Transform rollout temporarily suspend link inheritance while you transform a parent object. Click the Pivot button in the Hierarchy panel to display the Adjust Transform rollout (see Figure 21.9).

Click the Affect Object Only button in the Adjust Transform rollout to Move, Rotate, or uniform Scale a parent object without affecting any of its children. (Do not use nonuniform scale with linked objects.) To align selected objects with the World or with the selected objects parents, click either of the alignment buttons in the rollout.

When the Affect Object Only button is active in the Adjust Transform rollout, you can use the Align command on the toolbar to align selected objects with any other object in the scene without affecting the selected objects' children.

FIGURE 21.9

The Adjust Transform rollout.

Resetting Transforms

The two buttons located in the reset area of the Adjust Transform rollout reset the rotation and scale so that the current condition is considered its original condition. These buttons generally pass the change on to all linked children. If you want to reset the transform of an object without affecting its children, you can click the Don't Affect Children button.

Reset Rotation is a better name for the Transform button because it rotates only the object's pivot to align to the World coordinate system. The difference between Reset Transform and Align to World is that Reset Transform affects the object's children and Align to World does not. If Don't Affect Children is active, then Reset Transform has the same effect as Align to World.

Scale changes the value of the object's current scale to 100 percent without actually changing the object's size. Reset Scale can have some strange effects in the way an object reports its size in the World. If you create a box with a width of 200 units and scale that axis to 150 percent, then you have a box with 300 units as its width. If you then reset the objects scale, you have a box that reports that it is 100 percent scaled with a width of 200 units, but it is actually 300 units in the scene.

Reset Scale can be used to fix a nonuniform scaled object to work properly in a hierarchy. Be sure to click Don't Affect Children before applying Reset Scale.

The Reset Transform Utility

You can use a utility in 3DS MAX to reset an object's transforms. Clicking Reset XFORM brings up the Reset Transform rollout. When you click Reset Selected, the object is returned to its initial orientation and scale, and any rotation and scale transforms are placed into an XFORM modifier.

FIGURE 21.10

Clicking the Reset XFORM utility brings up the Reset Transform rollout.

Using the Reset Transform utility has the benefit of separating the rotation and scale transform values from the object, while still having them accessible in the XFORM gizmo.

Setting Object Transform Locks

Sometimes it is necessary to lock certain transforms on an object, such as motion or rotation, in a certain way. Object locks can be used to constrain certain aspects of an object so that it can represent a real world system. Locking options can be found in the Hierarchy panel under Link Info and the Locks rolldown (see Figure 21.11). Even though locks are located in the hierarchy panel, they have nothing to do with object linking.

The Locks rollout contains three sets of X, Y, and Z check boxes—one set each for Move, Rotate, and Scale (see Figure 21.11). Checking a box locks that transformation along the specified axis. The locks set in Figure 21.11, for example, prevent the selected object from Moving along its X axis, Rotating around its Y and Z axes, and being Scaled about its Y axis.

FIGURE 21.11

The Transform Locks rollout.

The previous sections dealt primarily with building hierarchies and various ways to modify those parent/child relations. The remainder of the chapter discusses how to use dummy objects and Inverse Kinematics to animate those hierarchical structures.

Using Dummy Objects

Dummy Objects are invisible, non-rendering objects whose main reason for existence is to be linked to other objects. They can be used to aid in complex animations or simply as placeholders. You can create dummy objects from the Helper category of the Create panel (see Figure 21.12). Click the Dummy button and then you can click and drag anywhere in the scene to create a cube-shaped dummy object.

In this example, you repeat the previous tutorial, but instead of altering pivot points, you will utilize dummy objects for rotation. This method is much more versatile and easier to manipulate than the previous one.

FIGURE 21.12

*The Dummy button in
the Create panel.*

A LINKED PLANET SYSTEM 2

1. Open the file planet2-ex.max from the accompanying CD-ROM. The scene consists of three spheres with a dummy object in the middle of the Sun object and another in the Earth object (see Figure 21.13).

2. Select the Moon object.

3. Click link on the toolbar and press H to bring up the Select Object dialog.

4. Pick Earth Dummy and click link.

5. Select the Earth object and link it to the Earth Dummy object.

6. In the Hierarchy panel under Link Info, click the Inherit rolldown.

7. Remove the checks from Rotate X, Y, and Z.

8. Repeat steps 2 through7 using the Earth and the Sun instead of the Moon and the Earth.

The result of the previous steps should leave you with the Moon and the Earth linked to the Earth Dummy, and they do not inherit the dummy's rotation. This is necessary if you want to have planets rotate on their own axes at a later time or if they have textures that would be noticeable if they were to rotate.

9. Select the Earth Dummy Object.

10. Turn on the Animate button.

11. In the Top viewport, rotate the Earth Dummy object 1440 degrees on the Z axis. You can right-click the rotate button after selecting it to bring up a type in dialog.

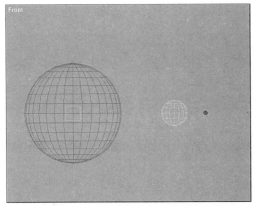

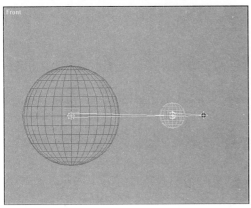
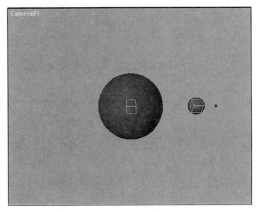

FIGURE 21.13

Steps for using dummy objects for the planet model.

12. Select the Sun Dummy object.

13. In the Top viewport, rotate it 360 on the X axis.

14. Turn off the animate button and play back the animation.

The preceding example demonstrates how easy it is to set up complex motion with a few dummy objects. This method produces a similar effect to the first tutorial but has far more control and versatility.

Using Inverse Kinematics

As pointed out in the previous sections, hierarchical linking is a one-way effect. Objects are linked from parent to child, and animation effects applied to a parent are passed along to its children. Effects applied to a child do not pass up the chain to parent objects.

This type of linking is useful, but it does not always simulate jointed objects in the real world. As you know, when real objects are linked together, moving one linked object affects all the linked objects based on their positions and the properties of the connecting joints. You simulate this behavior by using Inverse Kinematics (IK).

You use IK to manipulate an entire linked chain by moving or rotating a selected child object. When IK mode is active, such as moving or rotating an object in a hierarchy, the selected object is called the IK end effector. Descendants linked to the end effector inherit the transforms applied to the end effector in the normal way for hierarchies. Ancestors of the end effector define a kinematic chain back to the root of the hierarchy or back to a special terminator object. Moving or rotating the end effector moves and rotates all the ancestors in the kinematic chain based on their IK parameters.

The IK system in MAX R2 has been enhanced and improved to feature a new end-effector–only, real-time IK system. The old IK system has been left intact, but the new system has been added. To enable the original IK system, click the IK mode button on the toolbar. To set up IK parameters, click the IK button in the Hierarchy panel. To access the new IK system, go under Systems/Bones and use the Auto-Bone command on existing hierarchies. The old system enabled you to bounce back and forth between forward and inverse kinematics, while the new system gives you IK all the time with the advantage being that keyframes only appear for the end effector (see Figure 21.14).

The following sections present preliminary IK concepts that will help ensure successful animations with IK. Your first step in successfully using IK is to understand how IK interacts with the objects in your hierarchy.

Coordinate Systems

When using IK, an object's joint parameters are driven by a local coordinate system of that object's parent. The relationship between the orientation of an object's local coordinate system and the local coordinate system of that object's parent is important. The most predictable IK hierarchies occur when you set up the initial hierarchies with the local coordinate systems aligned with their objects and all the objects aligned with the World.

FIGURE 21.14

The IK controls.

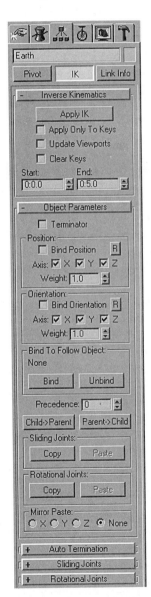

Figure 21.15 shows a figure properly laid out and ready for linking and an IK setup compared to a figure that will have problems with IK. The figure on the left is not laid out in any kind of alignment, and some local coordinate systems are obviously out of alignment with their objects. The figure on the right has all of its components laid out square to the World coordinate system, and the Local coordinate systems of each component are aligned with their objects. It would be difficult to set joint parameters for the figure on the left, and some joints may not work at all.

FIGURE 21.15

Improper and proper IK layout.

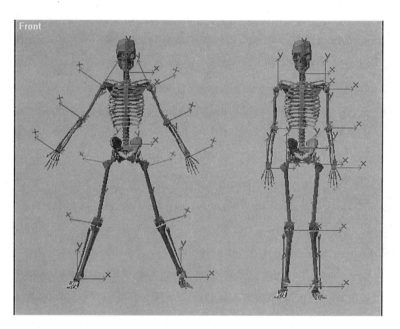

Well laid-out model   Poorly laid-out model

Because the relationship between an object's local coordinate system and its parent's local coordinate system is so important, you need to be aware of how various commands alter these systems and how to use this to plan for your animation. The following actions should be taken into consideration when using an IK chain:

- Rotating an object also rotates its local coordinate system. IK joint axis alignment is based on the relationship of an object to its parent when both the object and its parent are aligned to the World.

- Modifying objects at the Sub-Object level affects the Sub-Objects but does not change the local coordinate system.

- When attaching objects, the local coordinate system of the attached object is replaced by the selected object's.

- The various methods of resetting transforms always align an object's local coordinate system to the World.

- Any of the Adjust Pivot commands in the Hierarchy panel change the position and orientation of an object's local coordinate system.

Situations to Avoid with IK

IK works great for almost any situation, but a few instances are beyond its capabilities. Most of these situations arise from the use of non-standard controllers with IK or by applying the nonuniform scale transform to an object in the IK hierarchy.

Techniques to use when using IK include the following:

- Euler XYZ rotation controllers work best with IK. Other controllers, such as TCB or smooth rotation, will work but are not as accurate as Euler XYZ and sometimes can freeze when using joint limits.

- Do not disable Move or Rotate link inheritance for any object in an IK chain. IK is dependent on Move and Rotate transforms passed through the hierarchy.

- Do not use the Follow or Path controllers in the IK hierarchy. IK cannot function with these controllers. Use the Bind to Follow object and Apply IK buttons instead.

- Parametric controllers such as LookAt, Noise, Audio, or Expression controllers do not normally work with IK. You are allowed to select them, but you may get unusual results.

Defining IK Joints

After all your objects have been linked, you can begin to set up their IK joint behavior. The power of IK is in the definition of how the links between objects are constrained.

To define IK joint behavior, select an object in the hierarchy that you wish to animate and then adjust its IK controls in the Hierarchy panel. Click the Hierarchy panel and then on the IK button (refer back to Figure 21.13).

The following sections cover IK controls for joint behavior, known as Joint Parameters and Joint Precedence.

Setting Joint Parameters

When you set up a hierarchy, all joints are free to rotate in all directions but are prevented from sliding. In order to create a realistic effect in a joint, you must set up constraints on how that joint operates. In IK, there are two different types of joints, Rotational and Positional (Sliding and Path). Any joint can have freedom of motion for rotation, position, or both. You can also control the amount that a joint can move or rotate on each of its three axes.

Three of the rollouts in the Hierarchy panel control the joint parameters for a single selected object (see Figure 21.16). If you have more than one object selected, the joint rollout will not display. The joint parameter rollouts are the following:

- **Sliding Joints:** One of two standard positional joint types, Sliding Joints is the default type used for most Position controllers. It contains three sets of parameters, one for each of the three positional axes (X, Y, and Z).

- **Rotational Joints:** Always available for any type of rotating joint, they contain three sets of parameters for each of the rotational axes (X, Y, and Z).

- **Path Joints:** The second standard positional joint type, it is used whenever the selected object is assigned a Path position controller. It contains one set of parameters controlling the position of the object along the path.

All these joint types contain controls of the three basic joint properties: Joint Active status, Joint Limits, and Joint Friction (called Ease and Damping). Rotational and Positional Joints also have controls for spring back and spring tension. The following sections describe these joint properties.

Activating Joints

If you want the selected object to rotate or move on a certain axis, you must check the active check box for that axes. The default is for the entire Rotational axis to be active and all the Sliding axes to be inactive. Most real-world joints are active only on one axis but are occasionally active on two axes.

FIGURE 21.16

The standard joint parameter rollouts.

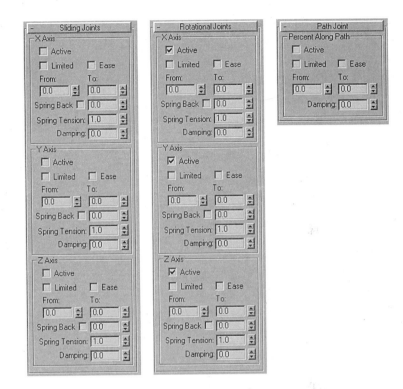

Some examples of real-world joints that you can create with 3DS MAX IK are doors, a drawer, a shoulder joint, and a bead on a ring. A door hinge would have one Rotational axis and no Sliding axes. A drawer would be active on one Sliding axis with limits and no Rotational axis. A shoulder joint would be active on all Rotational axes but no Sliding axes. A bead on a ring is active on one Rotational axis and active on a Path joint.

Limiting Joints

If a joint is active on a given axis, the joint is probably limited as well. If a Rotational joint is not limited, for example, the object spins freely. Certain joints may not have limits such as tires or gears but other joints, such as hinges or arms, have definite limits.

To set limits, you can do the following:

1. Check the Limit check box for each axis to be limited.

2. Enter value in the From and To fields to set the maximum range of motion for the object on that axis.

3. The selected objects move while a spinner is being dragged to give you a visual indication of the limit. You can also press the mouse button over the From or To title to cause the object to jump to that limit.

Joint limits are measured in different ways. Rotational joint limits are measured as the angle of the active axis of the parent's local coordinate system to the matching axis of the selected object's local coordinate system. Sliding joint limits are measured as the distance from the parent's pivot point to the pivot point of the selected object. Path joints are measured by the percentage of the path from the first vertex of the path.

The following example shows you how to use Inverse Kinematics to limit the motion of a door.

DOOR HINGE EXERCISE

1. Open door.max from the CD-ROM. The scene consists of a hinged door situated between two walls.

2. Go to the Pivot section of the Hierarchy panel and click Affect Pivot Only.

3. Move the pivot so that it is on top of the door hinge. The vertical positioning is not important for this example.

4. You may need to zoom in on the hinge to position the pivot.

5. In order to be able to set joint parameters, the door needs to be linked to the wall. Click the Select and Link button on the toolbar. Click and drag from the door to the left wall to link the door as a child of the wall.

6. Select the IK section of the Hierarchy panel to bring up the door's IK parameters. Go to the section titled Rotational Joints.

7. The only axis that you want the door to pivot on is the Y axis, so click Active in the Y Axis section. The door now only rotates at its hinge. Next, you set limits for the door.

8. Click the Limited button in the Y Axis section. Drag the spinner for From and watch the door rotate in the viewport. Select an appropriate value for the door's limit.

9. You can click the word From or To at any time to see the joints limit in the viewport.

10. Activate IK mode by clicking the IK button on the toolbar. Try rotating the door and see what happens. The door should act like a real hinged door. Figure 21.17 Shows the door at its limit in IK mode.

FIGURE 21.17

The door at its IK limit and its Y axis values.

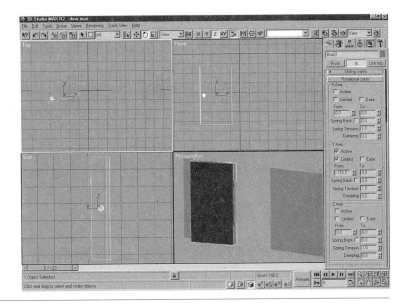

Easing and Damping Joints

The default for a joint in 3DS MAX is to have no friction or resistance to motion. This is not true in the real world. The only way to have no friction would be to have an object floating in space, but even then it would have inertia or resistance to change in motion. 3DS MAX simulates these effects using settings called Ease and Damping.

You can think of Ease as being similar to ease in and ease out with motion keys. A real-world example would be to extend your arm as far as you can. At first, the motion is easy and smooth, but as you reach the limit, the motion becomes more difficult. Checking the Ease box increases resistance to motion as the joint nears its limits. The more resistance there is in a joint, the more other joints in the IK hierarchy must contribute to the solution.

Damping can be thought of as tightness or a resistance to motion throughout the entire range of motion. Similar to a rusted hinge on a gate, Damped joints let other joints in the IK chain do most of the work. As all other joints begin to approach their limits, Damped joints begin to move. A Damping value of 0.0 applies no resistance, whereas a value of 1.0 stops all motion for that axis.

Spring Back and Spring Tension

With this option checked, joints work like a spring. Each joint has a rest position and, as the joint moves further from the rest position, an increasingly larger force pulls the joint back to its rest position.

Spring Back sets the rest position for the joint. For Rotational joints, this is the orientation of the joint in degrees; for Sliding joints, it's the position in units. Adjusting this is similar to adjusting the From/To spinners. While performing the adjustment, you see the orientation and position, but then the object returns to its previous state when you release the spinner.

Spring Tension sets the tension of the spring. Higher values cause the spring to pull harder as the joint moves further from its rest position. A setting of 0 turns off the spring. High settings can turn the joint into a limit because you can reach the point where the spring is too strong to enable the joint to move past a certain point.

Copying and Pasting Joints

Quite often you will want to use the same joint parameters for a series of joints. You can set up the desired parameters in one joint and then copy them for use on other joints. Rotational and Sliding joints each have an option to copy and paste joint parameters located in the object parameters rolldown (see Figure 21.18). Each of these joints has its own memory so you can copy one of each at a time.

Setting Joint Parameters for Root Objects

Even though a root object has no parent object, it still has a joint. Remember that an object is a child of the World. The joint parameters for a root object affect how it moves in relation to the World while IK mode is on.

When joint parameters for a root object are inactive, it cannot Move or Rotate. The root object acts like an anchor for the system, remaining unaffected by any IK movement. When joint parameters are active for a root object, it acts as any other joint and can only Move or Rotate as defined by the joint parameters.

FIGURE 21.18

*Joint parameter copy
and paste buttons.*

Sometimes you want the joint parameters of a root object to be inactive, so the root object acts as an anchor for any IK solution, but you may also want to be able to Move and Rotate the root object. You can do this in the Inverse Kinematics section of the Preferences by checking Transform Children of the World. When this option is checked, you can freely select and transform root objects, but when using IK, it acts in accordance of its joint parameters. When it is unchecked, root objects are constrained to its joint parameters.

Joint Precedence

Joint Precedence defines how motion is distributed throughout the joints. Having a high joint precedence means that the joint absorbs more of the overall motion than one with a lower precedence. The value of joint precedence has no effect if they are all the same; all that matters is the difference in numbers between joints.

Joint precedence is set in the Object Parameters rolldown. The default for all joints is zero. When all joints have the same precedence, joints closer to the end are affected more than joints further away.

You can manually set up joint precedence for each joint by selecting the object and entering a number for each joint. This method gives you the most control over the overall motion but can be very tedious. Two presets are built into 3DS MAX and should be adequate for most situations.

- **Child->Parent:** This preset is the most common and fits most situations. You select the parent and all its ancestors and click Child->Parent. You can select all ancestors by clicking the Select Subtree box in the Select Object dialog. Using Child->Parent assigns a decreasing value from child to parent. This setting causes objects closer to the transform to move more than objects further away.

- **Parent->Child:** Select a child object and its ancestors, and click Parent->Child to assign joint precedence that increases from child to parent. This preset causes child objects closer to the transform to move less than objects further away.

Defining the Kinematic Chain

As stated at the beginning of the IK sections, transforming an object with IK mode turned on affects all of the object's ancestors back to the root of the hierarchy. The chain of ancestors from the selected object back to its root is called the *Kinematic Chain*. Because each object can have only one parent, there is only one Kinematic Chain for any object to the root of the hierarchy.

It is often necessary to not have the Kinematic Chain go all the way back to the root of the hierarchy. An example would be if you were animating a leg and wanted the IK effect to end at the hip. You can stop the Kinematic Chain at a certain object by defining that object as an IK terminator. You can make an object an IK terminator by selecting the object and clicking Terminator in the Object Parameters rollout (see Figure 21.19). You can also set up Auto Termination after a certain number of objects on a Kinematic Chain. You can find the Auto Termination settings under the Auto Termination rolldown.

FIGURE 21.19

*The Terminator and
Auto Termination
check boxes.*

Animating with Inverse Kinematics

After you build a linked hierarchy, set joint parameters, and specify any terminator objects, you are ready to begin animating with IK. There are two main forms of animating with IK:

- **Interactive IK:** Manually transforming the end effect for specified keyframes.

- **Applied IK:** Binding an end effector to an animated object (dummy object) and having 3DS MAX calculate the IK solution for each frame.

Interactive IK

Use interactive IK when you want more control over the animation. To activate Interactive IK mode, click the IK button on the toolbar. You can then manually position end effectors while viewing the results in real-time. Turn on the Animate button, move to different frames, and Move or Rotate end effectors to create keyframes until you get the desired animation. Interactive IK can be quite slow on some machines while working on complex hierarchies.

Applied IK

Use applied IK when you want your hierarchy to match the motion of another object in the scene. 3DS MAX calculates all of the necessary motion for every frame of the animation, creating better accuracy than the Interactive method. Applied IK can be more flexible to use and much easier to change the animation by simply moving or selecting different follow objects.

To use Applied IK, you have to bind the selected end effectors to animated follow objects and then click Apply IK in the Hierarchy panel.

Binding Object Position

Check the Bind Position check box when you want an end effector to point at or even touch a selected follow object. To bind end-effector position to a follow object, complete the following steps:

1. Select an end effector from the hierarchy.

2. Check the Bind Position check box in the Object Parameters rollout.

3. Click the Bind button in the Bind to Follow Object area.

4. Drag from the end effector to an object in the scene. The cursor changes to a pin cursor when the cursor is over a valid follow object. You can also use the Select by Name dialog to select a follow object.

3DS MAX tries to match the pivot point of the end effector with the position of the pivot point of the follow object. If the pivot point of the end effector cannot reach the follow object due to joint constraints, then it will be placed as close as possible to the following object.

Clicking the R button to the right of the Bind Position check box causes the end effector to follow the motion of the follow object without moving to it. This option is useful for animating gestures and secondary motions.

If you check the bind position check box without selecting a follow object, the end effector is considered bound to the World. In this case, the bound object does not move; therefore, the bound object attempts to stay put until other transforms in the kinematic chain force it to move to complete an IK solution.

You can also specify which axes of the end effector are bound to a follow object. The default is to be bound on all axes but can be changed by unchecking the desired box. Below the axis boxes is a Weight value. Increasing the Weight value causes the end effector to try harder to reach the follow object. Decreasing the value has the opposite effect and a value of zero is the same as unchecking Bind Position.

Binding Object Orientation

Check the Bind Orientation check box when you want an end effector to match the orientation of a selected follow object. The steps for binding object orientation are the same as binding object position as well as the options.

Applying the IK Solution

After binding end effectors to animated follow objects, you must apply the IK solution. The controls are found in the Inverse Kinematics section of the Hierarchy panel.

To apply an IK solution, do the following:

1. Select any object in your IK hierarchy.

2. Set the Start and End time for the IK solution in the respective fields.

3. Click Apply IK.

While the IK solution is being calculated, a progress bar is displayed at the bottom of the MAX environment. Click Cancel at any time to end the IK process.

Three other options affect the applied IK solution:

- **Apply Only to Keys:** When checked, the IK solution only is calculated for existing keys. Use this if small changes are being made to speed up the calculation.

- **Update Viewports:** When checked, the viewports are updated as the IK solution is being calculated. Having this option checked slows down the IK calculation.

- **Clear Keys:** When checked, all position and rotation keys are deleted from the object in the IK hierarchy before beginning the IK calculations. If you are making only small changes to an existing IK solution, leaving Clear Keys unchecked can speed up the IK calculations. If you are making large changes, you should check clear keys to ensure the most accurate IK solution.

T<small>IP</small>

Using Applied IK can have the effect of putting a keyframe on every frame of your animation. You can manage these keys better by using the Reduce Keys control in Track View.

In Practice: Building and Animating Hierarchies

- **Building Hierarchies:** Use hierarchical linking to simulate complex systems of objects with moveable joints. Consider using Group or Attach for assemblies that are immobile.

- **Complex Motion:** If a complicated motion can be broken down into multiple simple motions, use a hierarchy of linked dummy objects. Each dummy object carries one of the simple motions and inherits the other motions from its ancestors.

- **Children of the World:** Remember that if an object is not linked to another object, it is considered to be linked to the World.

- **Never Scale Linked Objects:** Nonuniform scale produces undesirable side effects in the children of the scaled object. Any scale disrupts IK calculations. Always use XFORM modifiers to apply scale transformations to linked objects.

- **Pivot Points:** Adjust an object's pivot point to change the location and orientation of an object's local coordinate system and to define the location of the joint between an object and its parent.

- **Interactive IK:** Use Interactive IK mode to manually position and animate IK hierarchies. 3DS MAX uses simple interpolation to animate between your IK keyframes.

- **Applied IK:** Use animated follow objects with Applied IK to have 3DS MAX calculate an accurate IK solution for every frame of your animation.

Chapter 22

USING PARTICLE SYSTEMS

Have you ever wanted to simulate dust, smoke, or sparks flying around? Or how about a tire hitting a puddle, splattering the bystander on the curb? Or a flock of birds, a school of fish, or a crowd where everyone moves together, but each individual moves slightly different from the rest?

In the 3D world, such conditions are produced by Particle systems. A Particle system is a collection of particles that, when emitted, can produce a variety of animated effects. In 3D Studio MAX, Particle systems are objects and the particles emitted are actually sub-objects. You can animate a Particle system as a whole and you can adjust the Particle system's properties to control each particle's behavior over time.

The Particle systems included with MAX R2 represent a quantum leap from their predecessors by adding dynamic control over particle behavior—that is, control over the interaction between a Particle system and the scene through specialized Particle space warps. This control also includes the particles themselves with the new Spawning feature, which allows particles to mutate or multiply on collision or death.

This chapter focuses on Particle systems in R2. Release 1.0 shipped only with Spray and Snow, which remain useful for the simplest effects and for backward compatibility. Because R2's advanced Particle systems incorporate the principles underlying Spray and Snow, while expanding user control over their behavior, this chapter reviews the basic systems with exercises and examples. It then discusses the increased functionality in R2's new Particle systems, specifically on how to control their individual properties. Finally, the chapter looks at third party plug-in solutions and how they can complement this collection of tools. Specifically, this chapter explores the following topics:

- Examining 3D Studio MAX's Particle systems—Basic and Advanced
- Exploring the Spray Particle system
- Exploring the Snow Particle system
- Exploring Advanced Particle systems
- Exploring Third Party Particle systems
- MAX R2 Space Warps for Particle systems

The plug-in section of this chapter covers third party plug-in Particle systems for 3D Studio MAX R2—Sand Blaster and Shag; Hair from Digimation; Outburst from Animation Science; as well as Particles+, Deflector+, and charityware all by Peter Watje. The first topic at hand, however, is to understand how Particle systems work in 3DS MAX.

Examining 3D Studio MAX's Particle Systems

3D Studio MAX R2 ships with six Particle systems: Spray, Snow, Particle Array (PArray), Blizzard, SuperSpray, and Particle Cloud (PCloud). Spray and Snow, the basic systems, were included in Release 1 (R1) and are unchanged in R2. Particle Array (PArray), Blizzard, SuperSpray, and Particle Cloud (PCloud), the Advanced Systems, take these metaphors to the next level by permitting any object to become a particle (hence, an object inherits and can vary a particle's animation). These Advanced Particle systems can also combine particles, metaball modeling (MetaParticles), and several new, specialized materials designed to work with these systems. Other capabilities include adding particle "spawning" options.

Spray is used to simulate objects such as falling rain, whereby each particle falls in the same direction and is oriented the same way. Snow is used to animate objects that behave more like snow would—soft, falling, and usually tumbling. These two Particle systems share many of the same properties, but they also contain unique controls specific to the type of system used.

Particle Array (PArray), Blizzard, SuperSpray, and Particle Cloud (PCloud) likewise include many common features and similar rollouts, and here are discussed together. In approaching these systems, shift your thinking from any system's standalone feature set to how the Particle system works in conjunction with R2's specialized, particle-oriented space warps, materials, and dynamics. Figure 22.1 lists the Particle systems that ship with R2 and third party plug-ins available at the time of this writing. This figure diagrams their relationship with R2's space warps, Particle materials, dynamics, Material dynamics, and Atmospheric effects.

The possible combinations can be daunting, and like so much in MAX, there are many ways to accomplish a task. The goal, therefore, is how to accomplish this economically in terms of your creation and rendering times. Particle systems create geometry, which can multiply exponentially and bring a machine to a halt.

Sometimes the illusion of many particles substitutes for geometry, as in using a bitmap to texture map face-particles, using particle combustion on a small particle stream to create an illusion of volume, or using other atmospheric effects as an alternative to particles altogether.

NOTE

See R2's Online Reference, which contains a good description under the Particle systems entry, especially for the Advanced systems.

FIGURE 22.1

Particle systems are not used alone but together with materials and dynamics.

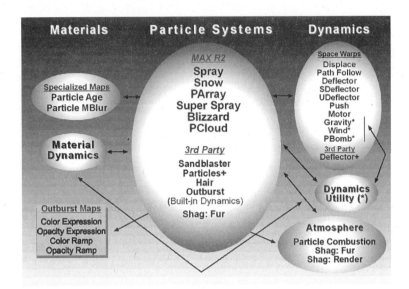

Creating Particle Systems

Particle systems are a form of geometry. You find the Particle system creation buttons in the Create panel in the Geometry category. From there, you choose Particle systems from the sub-category list. At that point, you find buttons for the six types. You may also see other third party systems that you've installed (see Figure 22.2).

FIGURE 22.2

The Particle System Creation interface.

When you click any system's button, all the editable parameters appear in the rollout (see Figure 22.3). Your cursor also changes in the viewport to reflect that you are in Create mode.

FIGURE 22.3

Access the MAX R2 particle system in the Create/Geometry/Parti cle Systems Command panel.

Create category

Create sub-category

PArray creation parameters rollouts

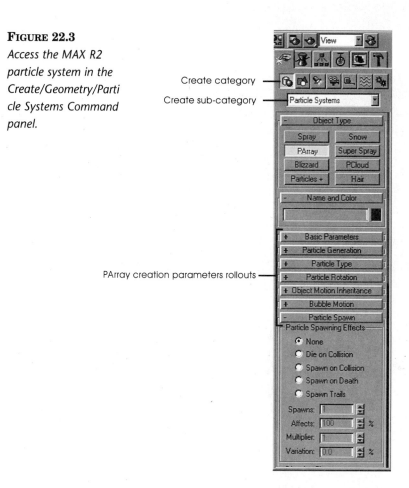

When you create a Particle system in 3D Studio MAX, you are defining where the particles originate from as well as the initial orientation. The point of origin is called the Emitter. The Emitter is a non-rendering representation in the viewports that is used to tell you where the particles are coming from and where they are going.

In the Advanced systems and certain third party plug-ins, any object can act as an Emitter, in which case the Emitter's icon orientation remains important while the geometry acts as the Emitter. This aside, to create one, you click in any viewport and drag out a rectangular shape. Notice that the Emitter is defined by a plane with a small line perpendicular to the plane's surface intersecting it in the center. The Emitter's size determines the "hole" from which the particles emanate. A small Emitter produces a concentrated area from which all particles originate, and a large Emitter spreads out the particle's distribution; the line indicates which direction the particles travel.

An Emitter's initial orientation depends on what viewport you create it in and whether you're using the Home plane or a Grid object. When using the Home grid as a Creation plane, the Emitter is always created parallel to the viewport with the Emitter's particle direction pointing away from you. The exception to this rule is in perspective-type views. In this case, the Emitter is created on the Home grid with the direction pointing down (see Figure 22.4).

The use of a Grid object results in the Emitter always being created on the grid's Infinite plane, regardless of what is displayed. The direction of the Emitter depends on the orientation of the Grid object itself, but the direction is always on the grid's Z axis.

FIGURE 22.4
The Emitter created on the Home grid (left) and on a Grid object (right).

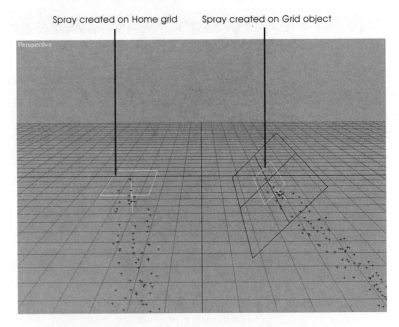

Spray created on Home grid   Spray created on Grid object

Perspective

T IP

When using Grid objects, it is best to create objects in a viewport that is not parallel to the grid's surface. Creating in a parallel viewport results in the object being created in "infinity" and makes it very difficult to navigate your viewports.

Depending on which frame you're on, you may or may not see particles with the Emitter. Because particles are time based, you see the default state of the Particle system on that frame. At frame 0, you usually don't see anything.

Spray and Snow Parameters

Spray and Snow are MAX R2's Particle systems at their most basic. The Advanced Particle systems, because of their larger feature set, are more calculation intensive and, hence, more prone to slowing your system. The Spray and Snow parameters remain valuable even with R2's Advanced systems for their speed and adaptability—they challenge you to see if the simplest solution can work. They have parameters common to each other and to the Advanced systems, and regardless of whether or not you'll use them, you must understand the basic features of Spray and Snow before moving on to use Advanced systems and third party plug-ins. The settings of both Spray and Snow react the same. This section describes the common settings and explores how to use them.

Particle Counts

Both Spray and Snow provide two parameters for specifying the number of particles. One method is through the Viewport Count parameter. This value only affects the number of particles displayed in your viewports. Valid ranges are from 0 to 1,000,000,000, although the latter is an extremely unrealistic number. Use it only if you want to bring your computer to its knees.

The primary purpose of the Viewport Count parameter is to optimize how well 3DS MAX redraws your viewports. A large number of particles in your viewports can slow down viewport updates dramatically. This slowdown is especially true when you're playing back an animation in the viewport. Keep this number as low as possible, but make sure that you are still able to see an accurate representation of your particles in your viewports.

The other parameter is Render Count. This value affects only the number of particles rendered and has no effect on the number of particles in your viewports. This value is usually higher because rendering quality is the key, not interactivity.

NOTE

You cannot animate Viewport or Render Count values.

In the Advanced systems, you control the particle's Render Count by setting either the number of particles emitted per frame or total particles. The viewport's Render Count is calculated as a percentage of these amounts.

Particle systems are geometric. They contain faces and vertices like any other object. Consequently, the higher that either the Viewport Count or Render Count get, the slower your scene becomes. You can often use small particle counts and still achieve outstanding results. Maintaining control over particle counts is key to having a rendering take one minute versus five.

Speed and Variation

Speed sets the initial velocity of each particle. The Speed value uses its own system of units to change a particle's position over time. With a speed of 1, a particle travels roughly 10 units in 25 frames. The Default value of 10 means that a particle travels 10 units in 2.5 frames. Any variation greater than 0 effectively negates this equation.

With Spray and Snow, variation controls size and direction. The Default value, 0, produces a steady stream of particles that go in the exact direction of the Emitter's directional vector. As you increase variation, two things happen. First, the speed of the particles increases; second, the particles begin to deviate from the Emitter's directional vector. Essentially, variation randomizes the direction and speed of each particle. When you increase the value, the randomization becomes more pronounced.

TIP

To have particles shoot in every direction, use Variation values greater than the value specified for speed.

SuperSpray provides substantially more control in this circumstance. Instead of pointing the Emitter and setting a variation number, you control the following together with phase and variation settings for these motions:

- Stream axis and spread

- Off-plane axis and spread

- Speed
- Particle rotation and spin
- Object motion inheritance
- Bubble motion of the stream

Viewport Representations

Particles can be displayed several ways: as Drops (with Spray) or Flakes (with Snow), as Dots, or as Ticks (see Figure 22.5). When you use Drops, particles are represented as lines that increase or decrease in size depending on the Drop Size value. When you use Flakes, particles are represented as 14-point stars that increase or decrease in size depending on the Size value. The Size settings most accurately represent the particle's rendering size.

FIGURE 22.5

A view of the three Particle system display methods for Snow. A zoomed-in area shows detail. Note that neither the Dots' nor the Ticks' Display methods appear to change in either view.

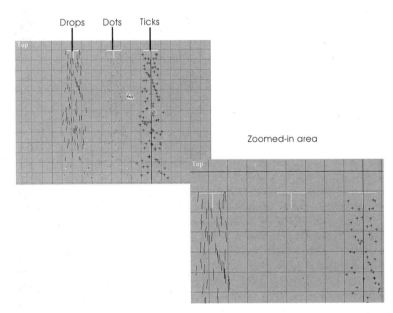

Dots appear as a single pixel in your viewport, regardless of drop size or zoom factor. Use Dots when you don't want to clutter your viewports with unnecessary geometry.

Ticks appear as small five-pixel-by-five-pixel crosshairs in the viewport. Like Dots, regardless of how far you're zoomed in, Ticks remain the same size. Ticks work well when you're zoomed in because you can easily see each particle. The farther you zoom out, however, the more cluttered the particles become. In that case, it is better to use Dots.

In addition to the foregoing, the Advanced systems support Particle display in the viewport as a Mesh or Bounding box around all particles. Figure 22.6 illustrates a rendered particle with a Gradient map applied.

FIGURE 22.6

A rendering of a Tetrahedron particle using a Gradient Opacity map to give the appearance of a fading raindrop.

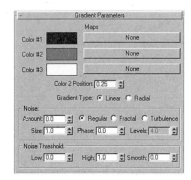

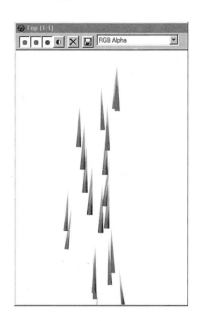

NOTE

All Particle Display methods redraw in the viewports at about the same rate. For faster playback of particles, lower the Viewport Count.

Material Assignment

Because particles are objects in 3D Studio MAX, Material assignment with Snow and Spray is always at the Object level. When you assign material to a Particle object (the Emitter), all particles use the same material. (The Advanced Particle Systems, discussed at length below, add the option of using instanced geometry as particles, with their Material assignments.)

If you want a Spray Particle object to emit particles with varying materials, you can assign a Multi/Sub-Object material to the Emitter. For instance, the fifth particle to be emitted receives Material #1 from a Multi/Sub-Object material comprised of five materials. Multi/Sub-Object material assignment works great when you're simulating objects such as multi-colored confetti.

NOTE

In Snow, six-point objects actually use two material IDs rather than one, which enables you to assign different materials to each side of a six-point particle.

The Advanced Particle systems provide an option to use the material applied to the Icon/Emitter from instanced geometry in the scene (if you use instanced geometry for the particles). With Particle Array, if your particles are object fragments, you can assign up to three Material IDs to these objects, and take them from either the Emitter material or from the fragmented object.

Controlling Particle Timing

3DS MAX gives you particle timing control based on frames as the measure of time. (With the Advanced Particle systems, discussed later, you have the capability to refine this with subframe sampling options). You can set the frames where the stream begins and ends. You can simulate a steady stream using a constant birth rate or short blasts simply by choosing a non-constant birth rate greater than the MAX Sustainable rate calculated by the Particle system. The next section explains how the values work and how to use them.

Start and Life

The Start value sets what frame the Emitter begins sending out particles. This can be any frame number, including negative frames. You use negative frames in cases where you want the particles to be on the screen at frame 0.

The Life value sets the life, in frames, of each particle and is assigned to each particle individually. With this value, you specify the length of time before a particle is destroyed. Set this value to the last frame in your animation if you want the particle to always be present in the scene.

The main control over how long a particle is displayed with a Basic Particle system is the Lifespan settings. These appear when a particle is born and remains onscreen until it dies. You can also limit the periods all particles are displayed in Track View by selecting the Particle system, adding a

Visibility track, and setting the key frames to turn the display off and on. Although this effectively hides the Particle system, if it reappears, it appears as if it had never been hidden at all. Note that the Advanced systems contain the previously mentioned display features, plus a Display Until frame setting, an alternative to a Visibility track so long as you don't need the Particle system to reappear or flash on and off.

Adjusting Defaults

You can change the default Start and Life values to adjust a steady stream of particles emanating from the Emitter. The Life value not only affects how long before a particle is destroyed, but also the distance it travels. The longer the life is, the farther the particle travels from the Emitter.

Constant and Varying Birth Rates

The Constant option provides a steady stream of particles at all times. By default, this option is selected. The Max Sustainable Rate right below the Constant checkbox takes the Particle Render Count and divides that by the particle lifetime to give the number of particles that can be born per frame while keeping the number of particles under the specified limit. This value changes when you alter the Life value for particles or the Render Count1. With the Default Life value of 30 and Render Count of 100, you get a sustainable rate of 3.3 particles born every frame. If you double the Life to 60, the Max Sustainable rate changes to nearly half, 1.7, because 3DS MAX now has more time to generate those 100 particles. Just by altering the Life, you can control how many particles are present in the scene at a specific frame.

NOTE

If you change the Render Count value, the Max Sustainable Rate does not change until you also change the Viewport Count value (even though the Viewport Count value is not used in the calculation).

TIP

If you want the total number of particles in your count fields to be present at frame 0, set the particle start frame to the negative of the Life value.

By unchecking the Constant option, you can now specify the maximum number of particles born per frame in the Birth Rate field (see Figure 22.7). However, you still use the Max Sustainable Rate value as a guide. Here's how it works:

- If you want a steady stream of particles, set the Birth rate to a value equal to or less than the Max Sustainable rate.

- If you want short bursts, set the Birth rate value higher than the Max Sustainable rate. A value of 50, for instance, emits 100 particles in two frames.

FIGURE 22.7

The Timing parameters for a Particle system. The current values cause the Particle system to emit short bursts of particles rather than a steady stream.

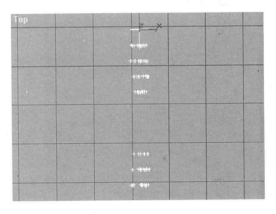

Because you can animate the Birth Rate value, you can utilize it as a Flow Control value for your particles. A value of 0 emits nothing and increasing the Birth Rate value produces more and more particles up to the Render Count, which is the upper limit.

TIP

Animating the Birth rate by using the Step In/Out option for keys in Track View produces controlled bursts versus using the Default curved assignment, which produces a gradual increase/decrease in particle Birth rates.

You can combine non-constant Birth rates with a Visibility track in Track View to create the illusion of your Particle system refiring from scratch at specified places in your animation.

With Advanced systems, you set Constant or Burst Particle streams under Particle Generation/Particle Quantity with Use Rate or Use Total, or by choosing Use Rate and animating the spinner to vary the number of particles emitted per frame. Like the Basic systems, you can vary the Lifespan, but you can build in random variations to that value and control the timing more accurately by sampling subframe timing.

Now that know when your particles appear, how many, and what size they will be, how they will disperse, you need to know where and over how large an area they will travel.

Emitter Size and Orientation

With Basic Particle systems Snow and Spray, the size of the Emitter controls the area from which the particles are emitted. A long, thin Emitter produces a narrow gap from which the particles emit. A larger Emitter spreads out the particles. Spray and Snow randomly emit particles from within the area of the emitter object. The distribution of where particles emit is controllable only through the Emitter size. This holds true for Blizzard and Particle Cloud, but not the other Advanced Particle systems. With Blizzard, the Advanced systems analogue to Snow, the size of the Emitter controls the distribution area. With Particle Cloud, a preset shape or external object is an Emitter, but particles are confined by it, not emitted from it. With SuperSpray, the analogue to Spray, Emitter size makes no difference; it is always a nozzle. With Particle Array, an object is your Emitter and the icon size is not relevant.

Because you can animate the Emitter's size, you can simulate effects such as a hose opening or sparks flying out from an increasingly growing area.

In Basic Particle systems and in Advanced systems where object geometry has not been substituted for the Emitter, the Emitter's orientation controls which direction the particles shoot. When using Spray or Snow, an emitted particle travels in a constant direction and orientation unless acted upon by another force, such as a space warp. You can use this fact to your advantage to control the direction of the Spray or Snow. Emitters work with normal Transform commands, so you can move and rotate them. If you need to scale the size of the Emitter, it is best to change the Length and Width values rather than using the Scale transform.

NOTE

Particles are created from the initial tip of the particle on the plane of the Emitter. As a result, portions of the particle can actually exist before the Emitter. This is especially visible when using large particle sizes.

Exploring the Spray Particle System

The Spray Particle system is useful for simulating falling water effects. Obvious uses are for effects such as rain or other liquid simulations. You can also use Spray to simulate things such as sparks on a bomb's fuse or glowing cinders from a fire.

Spray particles travel with a constant orientation—that is, a drop of water falling down always points down throughout its life cycle. You can, however, change the Emitter over time to simulate things such as an oscillating sprinkler system.

Drop Sizes

You use Drop Size to control the actual size, in units, of each particle. A Drop Size of 0 produces nothing, whereas a Drop Size of 20 produces a long streak. Depending on the effect you're looking for, the number varies.

Small sizes are useful for objects such as sugar or tiny granular-type objects. Sizes less than one produce extremely small particles. You usually have to set the Render Count relatively high to see small particles from a distance.

NOTE

You only see changes in the size of particles in your viewports if the particles are being displayed as drops. If you want to see the size of your particles reflected accurately in the viewports, make sure to use the Drops method of display.

Large sizes are great for creating streaks of light such as warp effects. In this case, you use smaller Count values because larger particles occupy much more space than smaller ones and "clump" if there are too many. This is true for both Viewport and Render Counts.

TIP

You can animate Drop Size to simulate the growth of streaking effects.

Particle size gets more sophisticated treatment in the Advanced systems. You not only set size, but you can set a percentage random variation on size, and you can specify that each particle grows or fades for a specific series of frames after birth and before death. With Particle Spawn, you can specify that particles be reborn on collision or death, and that they mutate size or form on that event.

Spray Render Types

Render types, chosen in the Spray particle's Parameter panel, enable you to specify the look of the particle when it's rendered. Spray enables you to render either Tetrahedrons or Square faces that can be mapped with any material. This section explores the two methods.

The Tetrahedron Spray particle looks much like a Hedra object using the Tetra type, except that the vertex at the lower pole is pulled further "south" to look more like a polygonal drop of water. When you're trying to simulate droplets, this is the best type of particle rendering to use. Usually, Tetrahedron renders faster than the facing particle.

Facing creates square faces that always face the camera, meaning that their rendering face always remains perpendicular to the camera. Their size is the Drop Size value for both width and height. Use facing Render types in conjunction with a specific material to render other types of particles.

NOTE

If you don't render the Camera view, the faces point in an arbitrary direction.

You can fly through Tetrahedrons and view them from different angles. Although you can also fly through facing particles, these particles are always "flat" to your point of view and can end up producing the wrong effect.

Materials and Spray Particles

Particle systems can use just about any Material type. More specifically, you can use Map types, such as Gradient and Noise, to generate special effects such as Smoke. This section explains the process of using mapping and materials with particles.

Mapping

Particles are fairly easy to assign materials to. They have Mapping coordinates assigned and they work well with Multi/Sub-Object material types. The following two paragraphs show how mapping breaks down.

Tetrahedrons are mapped with the Cylindrical Mapping type, with the V dimension of the UV mapping coordinates oriented along the length of the Tetrahedron. The origin of the mapping begins at the origin—the flat part—of the Tetrahedron. If you want to simulate a drop becoming more transparent with a Gradient Opacity map, the Gradient would start at black for color 1 and go to white for color 3; this is the opposite of the Default for Gradient maps.

Facing maps are fitted to their extents with planar mapping. If you look at a facing particle head-on in the viewport with the Emitter oriented in a top-down direction, the V is vertical to the viewport. The V, however, is actually the opposite orientation for facing rendering types. The previous example of a Gradient map would have to be reversed.

Mapping and materials options with the Advanced systems are more sophisticated. In general, if particles use Mapped materials applied (as opposed to Procedural materials), pieces of the map are applied sequentially to particles over a period of frames. The Advanced systems let you specify either the range of frames or a distance across which the map is applied. For example, you can apply a Gradient map to a Face-particle system that creates a gradient trail across the stream.

T IP

When you use Facing particles with Mapped materials, you have a choice. The bitmap can be mapped once over the entire Particle system, or it can appear on each Facing particle. The Spray and Snow Particle system assumes you prefer the complete bitmap on each particle (as in the Bubbles exercise below). Not so with the Advanced systems; to map the complete bitmap onto each Facing Particle, you must check Face Map under Basic parameters in the Material editor (see Figure 22.8). Otherwise, the single Mapped material is mapped once across the entire Particle system.

FIGURE 22.8

You must check Face map in the Basic parameters of the Material editor to place a Mapped material completely on each particle; otherwise, the single Mapped material is mapped once across the entire Particle system.

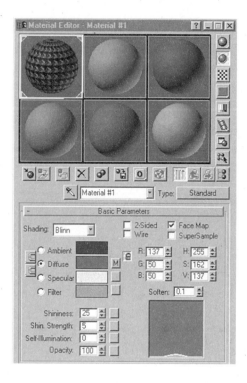

Spraying Sparks

One of Spray's best features is the capability to simulate all types of flying particle droplets, including sparks. When using Spray to create a Spark effect, it is best to increase the Variation value. That way particles travel in several directions from the emitter, including down. The following exercise shows that using a Spray system with the corresponding values produces the effect of sparks emitting along the fuse.

CREATING SPARKS USING SPRAY

1. Open 22spr01.max from the Chapter 22 folder on the accompanying CD.

2. Press H to select Spray01 by name.

3. Go to the Modify panel and note the spray's settings.

4. Play back the animation or create a preview.

5. Close the preview or stop playback.

Notice whether the spray is acting like you would normally expect. The Emitter simply sprays particles in one direction. By altering the variation to a large number, the particles shoot in many directions. You can also alter variables such as speed and particle size to create a great spark.

6. Change the variation to 3.

7. Set the speed to 1.

8. Change the Drop size to 8. Increase Render Count to 5000.

9. Assign the Sparks material in the Material editor to the Spray01 object. Move to frame 25 and render a single still from the Perspective view. You should see metallic sparks.

By default, particles are little Tetrahedrons. The sparks material takes advantage of Metal Type material, Self-Illumination, a gold foil bitmap, and Noise. It comes close to sparks.

To enhance the realism of the sparks, you can use Video Post to add a Lens Effects glow and Hilight filters to the particles. Video post is already set up to do this—the filters apply only to the Scene object assigned the spark2jra material. If you want, you can check out the parameters of the Glow filter to see what settings are used. Just click the Glow filter in the Video Post queue, press the Edit button on the toolbar, and then the Setup button in the Edit dialog.

 New with R2, Lens Effects Glow is very full-featured and appropriately enables you to save presets for later use. Here the glow is animated and the particles are highlighted, but the glow has been substantially toned down to prevent the aura from overpowering the sharp look of the sparks.

10. Choose Rendering/Video Post.

11. Double-click the image output event labeled sparks.avi (last entry in the queue). This brings up the Edit Output Image Event dialog. Click Files and point the sparks.avi output filename to a directory on your hard drive. Click OK twice.

12. Click the Execute button.

13. Click Render.

14. Open the Summary Info window (File/Summary Info). Notice the Spray01 has neither vertices nor faces. Because particles are

Sub-Object geometry, the statistic is not entirely accurate, but it illustrates the point that, if used appropriately, Particle systems can speed render time by reducing scene geometry. When the animation is finished rendering, play back the AVI from the View File option in the File menu.

Figure 22.9 shows a screenshot of how the sparks are represented in the viewports. Figure 22.10 shows a still frame from the animation. Note how the sparks fly in all directions. This is a result of a large variation value. See the final animation in sparks1.avi on the accompanying CD.

FIGURE 22.9

Sparks as seen in the viewport.

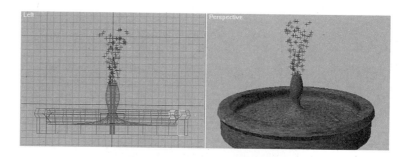

FIGURE 22.10

Still image from final animation.

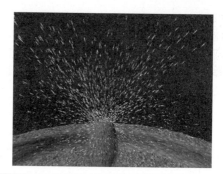

The Lens Effects filters are built into R2 and are available as a standalone product for R1. It looks like a standalone filter module, complete with its own interactive renderer, but it works interactively with the main interface as well, so you can animate Glow and other filter effects.

In order to apply the Glow effect to the Particle system and nothing else, you must assign the Particle system a unique designation. You can give the Particle system object a special Object ID by right-clicking the selected object in the scene, choosing properties, and choosing an Object Channel number. Alternatively, you can assign the material you're using for the

Particle system a Material Effects Channel from the toolbar within the Material Editor. Then within Lens Effects/Properties, check a source box and choose the Object ID or Material ID you assigned. Object and Material Channel ID numbers can be assigned to multiple objects.

Be careful: do not confuse this with assigning Material IDs as part of Sub-Object modeling, and using Multi/Sub-Object materials with those Material IDs. These functions play a very important but different roll in Particle systems.

T IP

Distinguish how to regulate Particle streams between Basic and Advanced systems. You can animate birth rate, but not the particle count with the Basic Particle systems. You achieve the same effect by animating the rate of particle generation with the Advanced Particle systems.

Using Spray with Gravity and Deflector Space Warps

As illustrated by the chart in Figure 22.1, Particle systems do not operate in a vacuum. Collision detection and movement is governed as much by space warp forces as by the Particle system itself, and these effects are further enhanced by applied maps and materials and effects filters applied in Video Post. In the following tutorial, you use Spray, a Basic Particle system, bound to Gravity, Wind, and Deflector space warps, to create a great fountain effect. Notice the interaction of the space warps to push and pull particles in various directions.

Adding Gravity to the Spray

The fountain object contains five iterations of Spray—one main spray and four accompanying sprays. Notice how the sprays are functioning just as you would expect—no real dynamics at all. It would be more natural to have the main fountain cascade down on itself and have the other four arc downward, which is most easily accomplished with the Gravity space warp. Gravity simulates real gravity by pushing or pulling particles to the icon. Its orientation and position in space can affect the particles significantly. To simulate gravity best for this scene, Planar Gravity should be used pointing downward. This is easily created by creating gravity in the Top or Perspective viewports.

USING SPACE WARPS WITH PARTICLE SYSTEMS

1. Open 22spr02.max from the Chapter 22 folder on the accompanying CD.

2. Go to the Create panel and click the Space Warps button.

3. Open the dropdown panel and choose Particles & Dynamics. Choose Gravity.

4. Click and drag gravity into the Top viewport. Its size doesn't matter, only its orientation.

5. Press H and select all iterations of Spray in the scene.

6. Click the Bind button in the toolbar and press H again and select the gravity you just created.

NOTE

Because the gravity is planar, its position in space is not relevant. Its orientation, how it is rotated, is important, however. Make sure it is pointing downward. Figure 22.11 shows the result of applying gravity to the fountain's Spray objects.

FIGURE 22.11

The effect of gravity on the fountain. Note how the particles are downward as a result of the gravity binding.

No gravity, particles continue upward

Gravity-created particles are bound

Adding Collision Using Deflector

The Deflector space warp adds planar collision detection to particles. In the next exercise, you create a single deflector to ensure that the particles don't go through the fountain on their trip downward.

ADDING THE DEFLECTOR

1. Continue from the previous exercise. Click the Deflector button in the Create panel.

2. Starting at the upper left-hand corner of the fountain, click and drag a deflector into the top viewport.

3. Use the Move command to move the deflector to the level of the inner base of the fountain.

4. Use the Bind command again to bind the sprays to the deflector. Figure 22.12 shows the effect of the deflector on the spray.

FIGURE 22.12

The fountain with the Deflector space warp created and bound to the spray.

No deflector, particles pass through

Deflector created and bound, particles now bounce

Using Wind to Add Turbulence

Wind acts like gravity; it has the capability to push and pull particles to the icon, but it also adds the capability to have turbulence distort the particles' travel. Have you ever noticed at the park how the wind often catches the spray of a fountain and sometimes blows it several feet in one direction (usually soaking some unsuspecting pedestrian)? To create the same effect with particles, you can use Wind. The following exercise shows you how.

ADDING TURBULENCE WITH WIND

1. Click the Wind button in the Create panel.

2. Click and drag a Wind space warp starting in the center of the left viewport. (The icon's size doesn't matter.)

3. Click the Bind button and bind only the center spray to the fountain (see Figure 22.13).

FIGURE 22.13

The completed fountain using the Gravity, Wind, and Deflector space warps to simulate real-life dynamics.

You can experiment with the Wind values to generate different styles of wind. Try animating the Wind value to gradually blow the fountain's spray.

The Spray Particle system is at once very adaptable and very limited—that is, you can use it to create the illusion of sparks, confetti, bubbles, or smoke. If you use face particles with Map materials, you can create the illusion of very complex streams or bursts with very little geometry, and very little drain on your system. Spray is very limited, however, as you shall see when you examine SuperSpray under the Advanced Particle systems section. Next you look at MAX's other Basic Particle system, Snow.

Exploring the Snow Particle System

Snow differs from Spray in the way particles behave after they have left the Emitter. Unlike Spray particles, which remain at a constant orientation and direction, Snow particles can *tumble* through space. You can use Snow to create any type of particle effect where soft particle movement is needed.

You can use the Tumble and Tumble Rate values to control how Snow particles rotate as they travel. Tumble values are valid from 0 through 1. A value of 0 produces no tumble at all, whereas a value of 1 completely tumbles the flake. The Tumble Rate specifies how many flakes actually rotate per frame. A higher tumbling rate produces wildly spinning flakes, whereas lower values produce more moderate rotation. A Tumbling Rate value of 0 effectively cancels any rotation regardless of the Tumble value set.

In the Advanced Particle systems in general, and particularly in Blizzard (the Advanced systems analog to snow), Tumble settings are replaced with the Particle rotation and Object Motion Inheritance rollouts (there is no Bubble Motion rollout as found in Particle Array, SuperSpray, and Particle Cloud). Blizzard's Particle Rotation rollout lets you set Spin Time and Phase (in degrees) and lets you set random variation percentages for each.

Flake Sizes

Use Snow's Flake size to control the actual size, in units, of each particle (see Figure 22.14). A Flake size of 0 produces nothing, whereas a size of 20 produces a large flake. Depending on the effect you're looking for, this number varies.

FIGURE 22.14

A viewport representation and rendering of two different Flake sizes for the Snow Particle system.

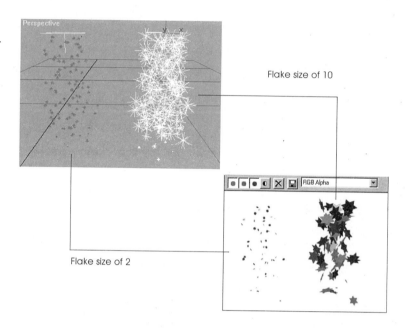

Flake size of 10

Flake size of 2

Small sizes are useful for effects such as tiny bubbles or dust particles. Sizes less than one produce extremely small particles. You usually have to set the Render Count relatively high to view particles from a distance.

NOTE

You see changes in the size of particles in your viewports only if the particles are displayed as flakes. Both Dots and Ticks display at a fixed resolution. The Flakes Display method is the only method that displays the size.

Large sizes can be used to create real Snow particles or Confetti effects. In either case, you want to use smaller count values because larger particles occupy more space than smaller ones and "clump" if there are too many. This is true for both Viewport and Render Counts.

Snow Render Types

Render types, chosen in the particle's Parameter panel, enable you to specify the look of the particle when it's rendered. You can use the Render types to generate many effects from Confetti to Smoke. This section describes the three Render types for the Snow Particle system.

Six-point snow flakes produce flat six-point stars that emit at varying orientations. Six-point stars can use any type of material, including Multi/Sub-Object materials. Six-point flakes can also have two different materials assigned to them, one for each side. Depending on your needs, six-point stars may produce the best rendering results when used in combination with the proper materials. The six-point flake is available as a standard Particle type in the Advanced Particle systems. Unlike Snow, these six-point Flake implementations do not scale in the viewports when you adjust their size settings.

Triangle produces triangular faces emitting at varying orientations. Triangular faces work much like the Six-point option with respect to materials, except that only the front faces render, and only one material can be assigned. You can randomize the material assigned to each particle by using a Multi/Sub-Object material.

Facing creates square faces that always face the camera, meaning that the rendering face always remains perpendicular to the camera. Their size is the Flake Size value for both width and height. Use facing Render types in conjunction with a specific material to render other types of particles.

You can fly through Six-point and Triangle and view them from different angles. Although you can also fly-through facing particles, the particles always remain "flat" to your point of view and may end up producing the wrong effect.

Materials and Mapping

Six-point particles are automatically mapped with Planar mapping to the extents of the particle. The mapping is assigned as if the Six-point were actually a square with a six-point star cut out of it.

Triangle maps are also assigned Planar mapping, much like Six-point, except that a triangular shape is cut out of the map rather than a six-point star.

Facing maps are fitted to their extents with Planar mapping. If you look at a facing particle head-on in the viewport with the Emitter oriented in a top-down direction, the V component of the UV coordinates is vertical to the viewport; however, the V is actually the opposite orientation for facing Rendering types. Figure 22.15 demonstrates how mapping works on the Snow particles.

FIGURE 22.15

The Snow Particle System Rendering types. The same map is used for all three examples, but the application is different depending on the rendered object.

Material
(Using Daisy.tif)

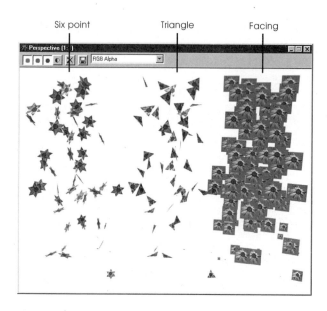

Using Snow to Generate Bubbles

The Snow Particle system is well suited to create gently rolling bubbles for several reasons. The primary reason is that the particles get smaller as they get farther from the Emitter. In this exercise, you see how to create bubbles just by altering a few settings in the Snow Particle system.

CREATING BUBBLES USING SNOW

1. Open 22snw01.max from the Chapter 22 folder found on the accompanying CD.

2. Go to the Create panel Geometry/Particles Systems and click Snow.

3. Click H to examine the Particle systems in the scene. Select them one at a time and examine their settings in the Modify panel. They are slightly different from each other to give naturalistic variation among the bubble particles.

4. With the Perspective view active, click the Mirror button. Choose the Z mirror axis and then click OK.

5. Drag the frame slider to frame 100 and then click Zoom Extents All.

Currently, 3D Studio MAX is using the Snow's Default parameters. This includes the Size and Render type, both of which you need to alter to produce bubbles.

6. Change the Flake size to 8 for Snow01, to 6 for Snow02, and to 5 for Snow03.

7. Change the Render type on each Particle system to Facing.

You're just about finished, except that you need to assign a material to the Snow. A material called Bubble material is already stored with this scene. You can simply choose the material from the Material editor and apply it to the Snow.

8. Open the Material editor.

9. Choose the second sample slot labeled Bubble material (top middle) and click the Assign Material to Selection button.

10. Render frame 100 (see Figure 22.16).

FIGURE 22.16

The bubbles you created with the Snow Particle system.

If you're satisfied with the material and background, render the scene as an animation. From this point, you can add effects such as Tumble and Variation to randomize the bubbles a bit more. You can also clone the snow to two or more objects and vary the clone's Variation and Speed parameters to further add depth to the scene.

Notice how the Bubble material is created—by first making a sphere. In the Material editor, create a transparent material and apply it to the sphere (look at the Sphere material settings as a good source). Zoom in until the sphere fills the viewport and render a single 32-bit targa file. Use the resulting bitmap in the Diffuse Map and an Opacity Map channels to make the Bubble material. Apply this material to the Snow Particle system and choose a large Facing particle. This technique effectively substitutes a single texture map on one particle for the entire bubble geometry—an enormous savings in resource and rendering time.

The foregoing discussion of the Basic Particle systems gives the sense of how easily particles can be introduced into your scene, and how basic particles and a little imagination can save a lot of geometry. MAX R2 introduces several new Particle systems, (collectively, the Advanced Particle systems), which expand the Basic Particle systems to give you more control over particle/Particle System behavior, and specialized systems that offer capabilities not available with the Basic systems. Particle Array (PArray) embodies the same rollouts and most of the features found in the other advanced systems. For this reason, the chapter examines PArray in some detail. The discussion of the remaining Advanced Systems cover how they differ from PArray, and when to take advantage of their unique features.

Exploring Advanced Particle Systems

The discussion of Advanced systems begins with Particle Array (PArray) because, except for the Basic Parameters rollout, all the Advanced Particle systems use the same set of rollouts and Particle Array (PArray) contains most of the features found in all the Advanced Particle systems. With this foundation, you can compare and contrast all other Advanced systems to PArray. As you compare the Advanced Particle systems to each other, you will find the controls and settings differ according to the specific purpose of the system.

The many features and controls contained in the Advanced systems can drastically slow system performance. Work around this by temporarily reducing Particle Quantity (Use Rate or Use Total under the Particle Generation rollout), and then increasing the percentage of particles displayed in the viewport (Basic Parameters/Viewport Display/Percentage of Particles).

Use the Particle Array (PArray) Particle system when you want a piece of geometry to serve as your Emitter (called a Distribution Object), and when you want to explode an object into fragments. PArray has a very large feature set, but take heart; all of it is well-documented in R2's Online Help system under the Particle Systems entry. In this instance, the Help file incorporates the original specification nearly word for word with examples. Once you understand it, R2's other Advanced systems are quickly mastered (the features largely repeat themselves).

If you've had experience with Sisyphus Software's All Purpose Particles plug-in for R1, or Digimation's Sand Blaster, you'll find the many rollouts for R2's Advanced Particle systems very familiar (see Figure 22.17). The Advanced systems rollouts are available in the Command panel at time of creation (Create/Geometry/Particle Systems), and thereafter in the Modify panel. R2's Advanced systems have their roots in Spray and Snow but are tailored to specialized usage and each offer great control over the Emitter, particle generation, type and rotation, and object motion inheritance— except that R2's particles add Bubble motion, Particle Spawn, and with PArray, they add MetaParticles.

FIGURE 22.17

The Particle Array roll-outs are a blueprint for features common to all the Advanced Particles systems.

Creating the PArray

PArray requires that you pick a geometric object called the Distribution object to be the Emitter. This must be an object, not a Sub-Object selection, a vertex, face, or edge. The Distribution object restricts where particles are formed on the object to the following five choices:

- Over the entire surface

- Along visible edges

- At all vertices

- At distinct points

- At face centers

To view how each of these settings affects particle distribution, set the Particles Speed setting to 0 to prevent movement. If you want particle emissions limited to a specific object on the geometry, you must first make a Sub-Object selection of faces or some such and detach it as a separate element. Once your selection is a separate object, you can designate it as the Distribution object, and then further limit where particles can form on your selection. After you prepare the Distribution object, then you create the PArray icon in any viewport. Its size and orientation make no difference. You can achieve the effect of scaling, moving, or orienting an emitter by animating a transform on the Distribution object.

Next, click the Pick Object button and select the object you intend to be the Distribution object. Icon Size has no effect with PArray, because particles emit from the Distribution object, not the icon. The Viewport display in the Advanced systems also differs from that in Snow, Spray, and some third party Particle systems; the Basic systems distinguish between Render and Viewport Display Counts. The Advanced systems determine quantity with Use Rate or Use Total settings, and they regulate display with the Viewport Display/Percentage of Particles spinner.

NOTE

Although there is obvious logic to how controls in Advanced Particle systems are organized by categorical rollouts, this can be confusing because the settings from one section control settings in another. For example, the Lifespan setting under Particle Generation controls the frequency of Particle Spawn. Likewise, the Particle Motion settings are influenced by settings in the Particle Rotation, Object Motion Inheritance, and Bubble Motion rollouts. Furthermore, these motions are influenced by how you apply specialized space warps and Particle materials. Although there's no way around the learning curve, you can save and reuse settings.

Particle Generation and Motion Parameters

The Particle Generation rollout contains the main settings regulating particle movement. You can set particle quantity for measurement as particles per frame or total particles. As with Spray and Snow, you can't animate the Use Total setting. You can animate the Use Rate setting; this is how you regulate particles into a stream or bursts.

The Particle Motion section regulates speed, random variations in speed, and, in PArray, divergence. The Particle Timing section is similar to that for Snow and Spray, except you can add randomness to the lifespan with the Variation setting and have a non-animatable Display Until setting with which to make the entire system disappear. (If you need it to reappear later, do not rely on this setting; instead add a Visibility track in Track View and animate the Use Rate setting.)

You set or animate particle speed, variation, and divergence settings in the Particle Motion section. Variation adds a percent of randomness to particle velocity. Divergence controls how the particle stream spreads as it moves along the face normal away from the Distribution object. For example, if you use a box Distribution Object and a Divergence setting of 0, the particles emit six streams, each perpendicular to a side. Increasing the setting to 90 degrees makes particles emit uniformly, as if emanating from a sphere.

Motion occurs along the face normal of the Distribution object, and the normal value varies depending on whether you choose surface, edge, or vertex distribution in Basic parameters. The speed setting can create very diverse results, depending on the scale you work at. In the tutorial below, speed is kept to 0.1 in order to keep the bugs within Camera view. Particle Motion settings also play an important role in fragmentation particles, where the fragment is composed of a cluster of faces. The fragment direction is based on the normal for the seed face, not surface, edge, or vertex.

Particle Timing controls when emission starts and stops, how long the particles live, random variation on the lifespan, and when the entire system is no longer visible onscreen. The Life and Variation spinners (in the Particle Timing section) are animatable; Emit Start, Emit Stop, and Display Until are not. The Life setting is critical to using the Particle Spawn function. Particle Spawning, discussed at length below, controls the PArray capability to generate or mutate new particles, or new multiples of particles on the occurrence of an event, such as particle death. By default, Particle Spawn looks for particle life to define the spawning event.

The Emitter start and stop settings are the same as with Spray and Snow. Display Until is new with Advanced systems, permitting the Particle display to become invisible even if new particles are being generated in successive frames—an effective alternative to using a Visibility track with a Particle system so long as you don't require the Particle system to reappear. The Subframe Sampling checkboxes provide fine control when the Distribution object's motion creates an uneven particle flow. These boxes are listed in order of increasing calculation requirements.

Under the Particle Size section, in addition to setting particle size and variation, you can set beginning and ending Particle Fade settings. While useful to portray the effect of particles moving through space and trailing off, or bubbles underwater, consider how these settings work with specialized Particle materials: Particle MBlur and Particle Age. These materials help to portray the particles changing color or disappearing over time; if scaled down with the Grow For or Fade For settings, much of this effect can be lost.

Particle Types

The Particle Type rollout offers four particle choices: Standard, MetaParticles, Object Fragments, and Instanced Geometry. Most options are new with the Advanced Particle systems. Only PArray offers Object Fragment options.

Using the Standard Particles Type

The eight types of Standard particles include both 2D and 3D options, vary in their geometric complexity, and for the most part derive or extend the Type options from Spray and Snow. Triangle, Tetra, Face, and Six-Point particles carry-over from the Basic systems. Cube and Sphere are geometric primitives. Constant generates face particles that maintain uniform screen size regardless of their distance the camera. Special is similar to a Face particle, except in 3D, when it is made up of three perpendicular intersecting planes, with no one plane always facing the camera.

Facing particles can be very useful. Available in both Spray and Snow, they are the most "inexpensive" Standard particle because they always face the camera. They can be used with Texture maps to provide a low-geometry alternative for creating the illusion of complex particle effects.

For example, first render a bitmap and alpha map of what you will use as a particle. It can be a single object, or a picture of many objects. Then make a material from the bitmap by placing the image in the Diffuse Map channel and the alpha mask in the Opacity channel. (This makes the square edge border and space between particle images disappear.) Then create a PArray Particle system, select the Facing type, and make the size large (15 or 20). Then assign this material to the Particle system. Depending on the complexity of the bitmap image, the illusion can be anything from moving galaxies to smoke trails.

R2 includes a "special" Standard particle, which is similar to the Face particle, but is made of three perpendicular intersecting planes. This enables the same mapping possibilities as with Face particles but with rotational control as well.

TIP

Facing and special particles can create a problem because the alpha mask doesn't always hide the bitmap's edges, in which case you see a slew of floating translucent squares with pictures on them. This occurs when face particles pass through an atmospheric effect such as fog or a volume light. There are two workarounds that may or may not be 100 percent effective: first, check the Exponential box in the settings for the Atmospheric effect. Second, in the material's Opacity channel, create one or more layers of Noise maps over the alpha mask. Remember the purpose of this technique is economic: to reduce rendering overhead. R2 has many alternative solutions that are more elaborate, spectacular, and physically accurate.

PArray and PCloud are the only Advanced systems to support any object as an Emitter. PArray is the only one to use Object fragments as particles. The other Advanced systems, Blizzard, SuperSpray, and PCloud, have their own Emitter and each support Standard particles, MetaParticles, and Instanced Geometry.

Using the Object Fragments Particle Type

Use Object Fragment controls with the PBomb space warp to explode objects into fragments made from the object. In R1, objects could explode into 2D triangular faces that appeared unnatural and they generally forced the creation of debris objects with a visibility track(s) in Track View. You still have this option in PArray if you choose All Faces under the Object Fragment Controls, but you also can create 3D fragments by using the

Thickness setting and irregular fragments with the Number of Chunks option. No treatment of this part of 3D graphics is complete without a demolition exercise.

PArray and Fragmented Distribution Object

1. Open the file bmb_tut.max. This file contains a single object, Jet Plane, mapped with a three-part Multi/Sub-Object material. It moves along a path, accomplished by making the plane a child of a dummy object, assigning a Path controller to the dummy, and assigning the Path controller to the flight path. Scrub the slider to see the plane move and bank along the path. Return to frame 0.

2. In the Top viewport near the nose of the plane, create a PArray object (Create, Geometry, Particle Systems, PArray). The actual position of the icon has no effect.

3. Under Basic Parameters, click Pick Object and select the Jet Plane object. (The name should appear below the Pick Object button). Click Mesh under Viewport Display.

4. Under Particle Generation, set Speed and Divergence to 0. Under Particle Timing, set Emit Start at 85 (the explosion occurs at frame 85).

5. Open the Particle Type rollout, select Particle Types/Object Fragments. Under Object Fragment Controls, set Thickness at 5.0, click Number of Chunks and set Minimum to 200. (Increase this later as desired.)

6. Under Material Mapping and Source, check Picked Emitter.

7. Under Fragment Materials, set Outside ID at 1, Edge ID at 3, and Backside ID at 1. This gives the metal look to the front and back sides and a black edge to each fragment.

8. Under the Particle Rotation rollout, set Spin Time to 5 and Variation at 25%. Check Random in Spin Axis Controls, if not already checked.

9. Under the Object Motion Inheritance rollout, set Influence at 80, Multiplier at 2.0, and Variation at 50%.

10. Open the Material editor and assign the Jet Fighter Material to PArray01.

11. At frame 0 near the cockpit, create the PBomb space warp (Create, Space warps, Particles & Dynamics sub-type, PBomb). Move the PBomb space warp to within the plane. Link it as a child to the Plane

object. In the Modify panel, under Explosion parameters, set Start Time to 85, Duration to 10, and Linear and Range to 500.

12. Select the PArray icon and click the Bind to Space Warp button on the toolbar. Press H or click the Select by Name icon, select PBomb01, and click Bind.

13. Open Track View, and under Objects, find and highlight Jet Plane. Create a Visibility track for the Jet Plane (press the Eye icon on the Track View toolbar). Create a new key on the Visibility track at frame 84. This assures the Jet Plane mesh disappears at the moment the explosion occurs and fragments appear.

14. Now that you have the bomb and fragments, you need an explosion. At frame 0, create a SphereGizmo Atmospheric apparatus located at same area as the PBomb space warp. Link this to the PBomb object. In the Modify panel, set Radius at 300 and click New Seed.

15. Open the Environment Dialog, click Add under Atmosphere Effects and Choose Combustion. Under Combustion parameters, click Pick Gizmo and choose SphereGizmo01.

16. Set Flame Size at 50.0, Flame Detail at 10.0, and Samples at 5. Check Explosion and Smoke. Under Setup Explosion, set Start Time at 84 and End Time at 95.

Now render the scene. When the plane reaches frame 84, the original mesh disappears; at frame 85, a substituted Distribution object appears. PArray, PBomb, and Combustion combine to create the explosive effect. You can embellish the scene by adding additional combustion effects, another Particle system, volume fog to create smoke and sparks, or by creating more elaborate Mapping materials for the back faces of object fragments. See the completed file bmb_tut1.max on the accompanying CD.

Using the MetaParticles Particle Type

R2 introduces MetaParticles, which, as the name implies, uses metaballs as particles primarily to simulate fluid effects. Metaball-based models were available as plug-ins for R1, the two most powerful being Clay Studio from Digimation and Meta Reyes 3.0 from Rem Infographica. Metaballs are specialized spheres that exert influence and tension on each other. Metaball modeling tools include a capability to create a single mesh "skin" around a group of metaballs that is defined by the number of balls, their proximity to each other, and the tension or influence settings. In the earliest incarnations, metaball shapes were restricted to spheres. In these commercial plug-ins, they can be spheres, ellipsoidal, cubical, or any combination of these connected by spline "tendons."

The strength of metaball tools lies in their capability to create naturalistic organic shapes; by moving the underlying metaballs and splines, you can move organic forms or fluid dynamics. By using MetaParticles in MAX R2, together with such space warps as Wind, Gravity, or UDeflector, you can simulate the movement of fluids and of several fluid objects combining into a single fluid object. This can also be done using dynamics.

Tension and Variation Settings

MetaParticles are an optional Particle type in PArray, SuperSpray, Blizzard, and PCloud. Choosing this type activates Tension and Variation spinners. The Tension setting controls the tendency of the particles to blend together—the higher the tension, the harder the blobs and the less likely they are to merge. The Variation spinner adds and controls the percentage of randomness attributable to the Tension settings. The Evaluation Coarseness settings control how much calculation goes into smoothing out the particles in the rendered scene.

The following exercise illustrates how to use MetaParticles to simulate fluid, specifically molten metal, moving along a path. This time you use the SuperSpray Particle system instead of PArray, because you do not need an object Emitter. You use the Path Follow space warp to direct the flow along a helix.

MAKING MOLTEN METAL FOLLOW A PATH

1. Open the file named meta_tut.max. In this tutorial, we will spray MetaParticles down a helix path onto a floor surface, using the UDeflector space warp to create collision detection and the Path Follow space warp to make the particles follow the helix.

2. In the Top viewport, create a SuperSpray Particle system. Center and place it about 600 units above the Ground Object plane.

3. Under Basic parameters, set Off Axis Spread and Off Plane Spread each to 10.0, Icon Size to 35.0, and Viewport Display Percentage of Particles to 100%.

4. Under Particle Generation, set the following parameters:

Use Rate = 2
Animate the speed range from frame 0 = 1.0, to frame 100 = 0.5
Emit Start = - 10
Emit Stop = 90
Display Until = 100
Life = 70
Variation = 50

5. Animate Particle Size from frame 0 Size = 60 and Variation = 10.0 to frame 100 Size = 85.0 and Variation = 50.0.

6. Under Particle Type, select MetaParticles and set Tension to 1.0, Turn off Automatic Courseness and set Evaluation Coarseness-Render to 10.0. Set Material Mapping and Source equal to Icon.

7. Under Particle Rotation, set Phase at 10.0 degrees and Variation at 50.0%.

8. Under Object Motion Inheritance, set Influence to 100.0%, Multiplier to 1.0, Variation to 25%.

9. In the Top viewport, create a Helix shape (Create, Shape, Helix) that runs from SuperSpray01 to below the Ground plane. Name it "particle path" and set Radius 1 to 100.0, Radius 2 to 200.0, Height to -500.0, Turns to 4.0, Bias to 0, and with CW checked.

10. Create a UDeflector space warp. Select SuperSpray01 and bind it to UDeflector01. Pick Ground as the Deflector object. Set the UDeflector Particle Bounce settings as follows: Bounce at 0.67, Variation at 10.0, Chaos at 10.0, Friction at 10.0, and Inherit Vel. at 50.0.

11. Create a Path Follow space warp above the Particle path. Click Pick Shape Object and select the Particle path as the shape. Uncheck Unlimited Range and set Range to 200. Check Along Parallel Splines, Stream Taper to 50%, Variation to 10%. Check Both (converge and diverge). Set Stream Swirl to 0.14, Variation to 0, Clockwise. Set Motion Timing Start Frame to -10, Travel Time to 90, Variation to 10%, Last Frame to 100, and Icon Size to 100.0 (see Figure 22.18).

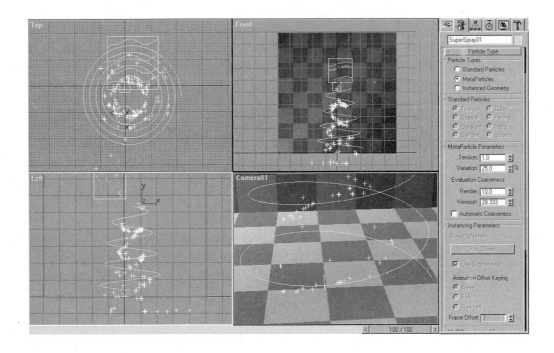

FIGURE 22.18

Final MetaParticles setup. See the final animation file meta.avi on the accompanying CD.

12. Select SuperSpray01 and bind it to the Path Follow space warp.

NOTE

The Path Follow space warp has many and broad applications (see Figure 22.19). Fortunately R2's online documentation clearly describes its many settings.

You can send particles along a spline path, or along an Offset path, and if you move the spline, you get very different results. Perhaps the best way to visualize the difference is to imagine going down a spiral slide, holding a six-foot pole perpendicular to the slide surface. Now imagine the path traced by each end of the pole and you have a sense of how the Offset path works. Additionally, you have animatable control over Range. Stream Taper, Swirl amount and direction, and random variations controls for each cannot be animated. Path Follow has its own Motion Timing controls, distinct from those belonging to the bound Particle system, allowing you to limit the time particles following the path before proceeding on, or allowing multiple paths to effect the particle stream at different times.

FIGURE 22.19

The Path Follow space warp interface.

13. Render the sequence or view meta.avi on the accompanying CD.

By animating particle size and variation, the blobby forms combine, shift, separate, and recombine as the MetaParticles move down the spiral path. Also note the interaction between the Path Follow and UDeflector with MetaParticles; the UDeflector does not prevent path particles from passing through the floor, regardless of where the particle path ends. However, varying the setting and changing the order of the space warp binding on SuperSpray effects the behavior particle stream. This comes from a peculiarity in the Path Follow space warp—it overrides, although not entirely, the effect of other space warps bound to the same Particle systems. This may change in future releases. Try altering the path shape and motion timing to make the particles pool at the bottom.

TIP

How you set Tension under any of the Advanced Particle systems' MetaParticle parameters has a dramatic effect on rendering times. As you lower Tension, MetaParticles become more elastic and rendering times increase. This has a dramatic effect where animating Tension settings from 1.0 to 0.2 can increase final frame render from a few minutes to several hours. This is magnified as particle quantity increases. In the previous example, SuperSpray only emits particles at the rate of two per frame; changing Tension from 1.0 to 0.5 doubles render time. Likewise, as you reduce the Render value under the Evaluation Coarseness setting, you increase rendering time.

In R1, you could achieve MetaParticle-like effects with third party plug-ins—by using metaball objects from Clay Studio together with Digimation's Atomizer and Sand Blaster plug-ins. This third party alternative is available to you in R2 and is a more flexible solution provided you have the third party plug-ins available to you. Clay Studio, Clay Studio Pro, and Meta Reyes support non-spherical metaballs and allow for more sophisticated mapping, and the latter two support spline "Metamuscle" shapes as well. These products work well with either Digimation's Sand Blaster or Outburst by Animation Science.

Using the Instancing Geometry Particle Type

Another option under PArray, SuperSpray, Blizzard, and PCloud Particle Types rollout is the Instanced Geometry type, which lets you use any geometry as a particle. The following tutorial uses PArray to generate a flow of animated insects emanating from a houseplant. You will use a continuous flow of bugs to explore how to use mapped, instanced geometry as particles, and varying motion of the particles.

The following exercise demonstrates the fact that because particles are geometry, and the more complex the particle, the more their proliferation drains system resources. To use animated objects as particles, you should use optimized, low polymesh geometry, use the lowest level of detail necessary to create your effect, and make minimal use of complex transparent materials.

USING ANIMATED GEOMETRY AS PARTICLES

1. Open the file pary_tut.max. For convenience, the face selection for the leaves is detached and linked back as a child of the planter. Note this has no effect on the original Multi/Sub-Object material used for the plant.

2. In any viewport, create the PArray icon. Click Modify and, under the PArray Basic Parameters rollout, click Pick Object and select Leaves01. The leaves become the Emitter — the Distribution object.

3. Under the Particle Generation rollout, set the following

   Set Speed = 0.1
   Variation = 0.05%
   Divergence = 5 deg
   Use Rate = 10 (default setting)
   Set Particle Timing Emit Start = 0
   Emit Stop = 100
   Display Until = 100
   Life = 80
   Variation = 10
   Set particle Size = 1.0
   Variation = 15.0
   Grow For = 0
   Fade For = 0

4. Open the Particle Type rollout. Select Instanced Geometry. Unhide bug. Under Instancing Parameters, click Pick Object, press H (or click the Select By Name icon), and select the bug geometry. Under Animation Offset Keying, check Random and set Frame Offset equal to 2.

5. Under Mat'l Mapping and Source, make sure Instanced Geometry is checked.

6. Next, animate the motion of the leaves. Select Leaves01. Apply a Bend modifier to Leaves01 and make sure the Bend Axis equals Z. Animate the Bend modifier by turning on the Animate button and right-clicking the Front viewport. At frame 0, set Angle to 39.0; move to frame 100 and set Angle to 45.0. Scrub the slider and the leaves should sway back and forth.

7. Examine the bug. Select the Bug object and scrub the slider. The wings flap and are children of the bug body.

8. Now make the bug a particle. Select the PArray icon and open the Particle Type rollout under the Modify panel. Click Pick Object under Instancing parameters, check Use Subtree Also, and select the Bug Body object (the top of the hierarchical chain). Also under Particle type, check Random Animation Offset Keying, set Frame Offset to 10, and check Instanced Geometry under Mat'l Mapping and Source.

9. Open Track View and examine the bugs; there is only one entry for the instanced geometry and one for the controlling Particle system. This is an easy-to-manage alternative to utilities such as Scatter, which create Track View entries for each instance.

10. Open the Particle Rotation rollout and set the following parameters:

    Set Spin Time = 30
    Variation = 25%
    Phase = 45 deg
    (Phase) Variation = 25%
    Check User Defined in the Spin Axis Controls
    X axis = 0
    Y axis = 45
    Z axis = 0
    Variation = 15 deg

This produces insects that rotate across a 90 degree span, with random variations of up to 30 degrees.

11. Open the Object Motion Inheritance rollout. You want the bug motion to be influenced by the plant's movement, but not determined entirely by it. Set Influence to 50.0%, Multiplier to 1.0, and Variation to 25.0%.

12. Render frames 0 to 100. The bugs emerge as an infestation to the plant (see Figure 22.20).

13. Create a UDeflector space warp. In the Basic parameters, click Pick Object, press H (select by name and pick Leaves01).

14. Select PArray01, click the Bind to Space Warp icon, press H, and select UDeflector01.

FIGURE 22.20

Plant emitter and animated bug used as particle. See the finished MAX file, parry_tut01.max, and the animation file, bugs.avi, on the accompanying CD.

15. Open the Particle Spawn rollout. Click Spawn on Collision in the Particle Spawning Effects section and set the following parameters:

    Spawns = 3
    Affects = 50%
    Multiplier = 3
    Variation = 50.0
    (Direction) Chaos = 33.0
    Speed Chaos Factor = 25.0% Both
    Check Inherit Parent Velocity
    Scale Chaos Factor = 10% and check Both.

Spawn on Collisions results in a Spawn effect when a particle collides with a Deflector space warp, not when particles collide with each other.

16. Renderer frames 0 to 100. The spawn effect occurs on a percentage of the bugs that collide with the plant leaves.

To make the effect more realistic, introduce additional Particle systems to the scene that use the same geometry but include less particles per system and different motion paths and spawning rhythms.

Refining Particle Motion

Although simple particle motions are set in the Particle Generation rollout in the Particle Motion and Particle Timing sections, you can refine their motion substantially in the Particle Rotation, Object Motion Inheritance, and Bubble motion rollouts.

Particle Rotation

The Spin Speed Controls address the timing and amount of particle rotation. The Spin Time setting controls the number of frames for one rotation of a particle; if set to 0, there is no rotation. The Phase spinner sets the initial particle rotation amount in degrees. Each has a Variation spinner for adding a percentage of randomness to each setting.

The Spin Axis Controls permit you to constrain the spin axis. No doubt you will usually use the default Random setting, but for animated instanced geometry, such as in the preceding bug-particles exercise, you must constrain movement to the Y axis and limit the variation in degrees to achieve any believability.

Object Motion Inheritance

Object Motion Inheritance determines to what extent the particles motion is influenced by the motion of the particle Emitter. Set at the maximum of 100 percent, the particles take on the Emitter motion. The Multiplier setting positively or negatively multiplies that effect. For example, you might have influence set to 100 percent but have a multiplier of 0.5. Assuming Speed equals 0, the particles inherit the Emitter movement entirely but won't keep up with it as it moves.

Bubble Motion

Bubble Motion is a specialized effect included with the Advanced Particle systems to create the wobbling effect seen when bubbles rise underwater. It operates and is adjusted much like a wave form, allowing control over

Amplitude, Period of oscillation, and Phase with variation spinners for each control. Bubble Motion is not affected by space warps, which enables you to apply or animate this effect independently to the Particle system, or even as an afterthought.

Using Particle Spawn

Particle Spawn probably has the greatest potential of all the features in Advanced systems because it adds both collision detection to the systems and possibilities of pre-planned particle mutation and regeneration. It looks to what occurs when particles die or collide with a deflector, not between particles. (The only Particle system to support inter-particle collision at this writing is the third party plug-in, Outburst.)

Particle Spawn has five settings: Die on Collision, Spawn on Collision, Spawn on Death, Spawn Trails, and None, which is the default. Except for MetaParticles, these options are available for all Particle types (only None and Die on Collision are available for use with MetaParticles).

Die On Collision makes the particle disappear when it hits a deflector to which it's bound; Spawn on Collision enables the Spawn effect on collision with a Deflector space warp.

If you choose Spawn on Collision, you can choose the number of Spawns, Affects (the percentage of colliding particles that Spawn), a Multiplier (how many particles are created on each spawn event), and Variation (randomness measured as a percentage). The Affects and Variation Settings can be animated. Experiment by setting Use Rate to 1 under Particle Generation, and setting the multiplier to 2 or 4. If you set the Multiplier greater than 1, you must set at least one of the Chaos factors greater than 0 or the new particles superimpose over each other.

The Spawn Trails option makes new particles spawn from existing particles at each frame of the particle's life. The Multiplier spinner specifies the number of new particles created from each "parent" particle, and the Spawn's spinner determines how many times regeneration occurs. This exponential effect can quickly stop your computer.

The three chaos settings control how spawned particles vary from source particles. Setting Direction Chaos to 0 produces no variation, 100 results in a random direction, and 50 results in deviance from the source up to 90 degrees. The Speed Chaos settings control the movement of the spawned particle relative to the parent, which can be slower, faster, or both. The Inherit Parent Velocity checkbox ties the slower, faster, or both settings to the parent particle, and if necessary you can prevent any speed variation by spawned particles with the Use Fixed Value checkbox. The Scale Chaos option operates analogous to Speed Chaos.

The spawned particles use the Particle Life setting by Default. You can override this in the Lifespan Value Queue, which enables you to specify a list of alternative, different lifespans for each Spawn event. Use the Lifespan spinner to set a value, and then click Add to put the value in the Queue. In this way, you can orchestrate a sequence of Spawn events and mutate between objects at each Spawn event.

Mutating between particles only works with instanced geometry, chosen under the Particle Type rollout. Note that when by using instanced geometry as particles, you have control both over mutating the geometry, and by implication, the materials as well (you can use two identical meshes mapped with different materials.) However, to mutate between materials, you must use Get Material From Instanced Geometry, not the Icon under Particle type.

The following exercise demonstrates how to use Instanced Geometry Particles with Gravity and UDeflector space warps. Because you do not need a Distribution Object Emitter and will not use object fragments, you use the SuperSpray Particle system.

USING INSTANCED GEOMETRY, PARTICLE SPAWN, AND GRAVITY AND UDEFLECTOR SPACE WARPS

1. Open the file spwn_tut.max. In this scene, you have a ground plane, sphere, teapot, torus, lights, and camera.

2. Create a SuperSpray icon of about 35 units centered about 125 units above the Ground plane, with the icon arrow pointing toward the plane. Scrub the slider to make sure the particles move toward the plane. Open the Material Editor and assign the Confetti material to the icon.

3. Create a UDeflector space warp. Pick the Ground object as the Deflector object.

4. Set the following parameters:

   UDeflector Bounce = 1.0
   Variation = 50.0
   Chaos = 10.0
   Friction = 50.0

5. Create a Gravity space warp above SuperSpray01 that has an icon size about 400 with the directional arrow pointing perpendicular to the Ground plane. Set Strength to 1.91, Decay to 0, and check Planer. Select and bind SuperSpray01 to Gravity01.

6. Select SuperSpray01 and bind it to the UDeflector space warp. Notice the deflector uses the Ground plane but can be bound only to the Particle system. Now bind SuperSpray01 to the Gravity01 space warp.

7. Under Basic parameters for SuperSpray01, set Off Axis Spread, and Off Plane Spread each to 22.0 degrees.

8. Under Particle Generation, set the following parameters:

   Check Use Rate = 20
   Speed = 20
   Variation = 25.0%
   Emit Start =0
   Emit Stop = 100
   Display Until = 100
   Life = 50
   Variation = 50
   Size = 0.5
   Variation = 100%
   Grow For = 10
   Fade For =10.

9. Under Particle Type, select Instanced Geometry. Under Instancing Parameters, click Pick Object and select Teapot01. Under Mat'l Mapping and Source, check Instanced Geometry.

10. Under Particle Rotation, set the following parameters:

    Spin Time = 30.0
    Variation = 10.0
    Phase = 10.0
    Variation = 50%
    Check Random under Spin Axis Control

11. Under Particle Spawn, set the following parameters:

    Check Spawn on Death
    Spawns = 2
    Affects = 80%
    Multiplier = 4
    Variation = 50%
    Direction Chaos = 20%
    Speed Chaos Factor = 20, Both
    Inherit Parent Velocity
    leave Scale Chaos = 0.

12. Under Object Mutation Queue, click Pick and select Torus01. The name should appear in the Queue.

13. Render frame 100. You should see two types of geometry because the teapot mutates to the torus when it collides with the ground.

14. Return to the Particle Type rollout. Under the Mat'l Mapping and Source section, you can choose between the Particle system icon and the Instanced Geometry particle. Check Instanced Geometry and click Get Material From. The Icon checkbox becomes grayed out because choosing the material from the Instanced Geometry *overwrites* the previous assigned material selection.

15. Open the Material Editor and assign the Confetti material to SuperSpray01. The Icon checkbox becomes enabled. With the Icon material chosen, Render frame 100. The Confetti material results in colors cycling through the objects and that material is retained even though the geometry mutates on collision.

See the final MAX file, spn_tut1.max, and the final animation, mutate1.avi, on the accompanying CD. For further study, experiment with multiple spawning events using Spawn on Death, entering different Lifespan values in the Lifespan Queue and mutating between geometries at each Spawn event. (A Sphere object is included in the scene for this purpose.)

Save and Load Presets

The Load/Save Presets rollout lets you name and save any Particle system settings for later use. The next time you open that type of Particle system, the set name can be loaded from the preset window. This is useful for a single scene, as well as across files. Having a preset also assures accuracy as well as time savings.

Presets are saved independent of the source *.max file; they are available if you reload or reset MAX. For example, suppose you've spent substantial time developing a convincing particle-based smoke effect, and the only variation you anticipate is adjustment to the Emit Start and Stop settings. The preset is convenient. The presets, however, do not save animated settings beyond frame 0 and cannot be transferred from one Advanced Particle system to another—SuperSpray settings can't be transferred to Particle Array. If you need to reproduce a Particle system containing animated settings, copy the Particle system. Do not use presets.

Using Materials with Advanced Particle Systems

With Snow, Spray, and R2's Advanced Particle systems, the materials are mapped on particles by assigning the material to the emitter. With Advanced systems, the material source can also be from instanced geometry, and in the case of PArray, the material can come from the Distribution Object. (You make your choice in the Particle Type rollout).

Multi/Sub-Object materials have special rules. At creation, each particle is assigned the next successive submaterial, continuously cycling through the sub-materials in numerical order. There are two exceptions: MetaParticles and Object Fragments use only the first submaterial. With Object Fragments, however, you have the option of assigning material IDs to the front, side, and back of the fragments.

Mapped materials (those requiring mapping coordinates) behave different from Procedural materials; they add another level of analysis. Up to this point, you have looked at the material source and if a Multi-Sub-Object material has materials assigned to the particles. With Mapped materials, you must also consider how they are applied to particles.

Planar mapping coordinates are applied across the icon's vertical axis, from bottom to top. The material is mapped on a particle, beginning with the bottom at birth and progressing to the top portion at death. The Time or Distance spinners determine how many frames or how much distance it takes to complete this sequence.

This is not the case with Triangle, Six-Point, and Facing particles, which are automatically mapped with planar mapping to the extents of the particle.

(Six-point particle mapping is assigned actually as a square with a six-point star cut out of it; likewise with Triangle particles, only a triangle shape is cut out.) Facing maps are fitted to their extents with planar mapping.

Tetra particles have the entire map on each particle and are mapped with the Cylindrical mapping type, with the V dimension of the UV mapping coordinates oriented along the length of the Tetrahedron. The origin of the mapping begins at the origin—the flat part—of the Tetrahedron.

Object Fragments are another exception: if Object Fragment Thickness is set to 0, the fragment is mapped with the same part of the object's surface. When Thickness is greater than 0, the particle's outer surface derives from the Distribution Object's surface, but the edges and back side can accept other material IDs. Multi/Sub-Object materials can be very useful with Object Fragment particles.

There are two specialized Particle materials, the Particle MBlur map and the Particle Age map. These are covered in the following sections.

Particle MBlur Map

You can achieve Particle Motion Blur by assigning the Particle MBlur map as an Opacity map to the Particle system and adjusting speed and other system settings. This only works with PArray, PCloud, SuperSpray, and Spray. You cannot use Multi/Sub-Object materials. You must check Direction of Travel under Particle rotation/Spin Axis Controls, and the Stretch spinner must be greater than 1. Lastly, MBlur won't work on certain Particle types, including SixPoint, Triangle, Constant, Facing, MetaParticles, and Object Fragments.

The MBlur map contains two color swatches and a Sharpness Spinner. The colors pertain to the particle's speed. It takes on Color #1 as it reaches it's slowest speed (default equals white) and Color #2 as it reaches its fastest speed (default equals black). Because the map is intended for use as an Opacity map, these colors translate to visible and invisible depending on particle speed and stretch settings.

Particle Age Map

The Particle Age Map alters the particle color over the particle's life. It must be part of a Standard material, preferably a Diffuse map, and works well with the Particle MBlur map used as an Opacity map. It will not work with the Blizzard Particle system. Three color swatches pertain to different particle ages. The documentation recommends using a Particle Age map in the Mask channel of a Blend material. You can then assign a Material Effects channel to one of the two Blend materials, together with a Glow filter in Video Post.

SuperSpray, Blizzard, and Particle Cloud

Once you understand the interface and capabilities of PArray, understanding the other Advanced Particle systems comes down to understanding their specialized uses. Blizzard and SuperSpray are advanced versions of Snow and Spray. They include the features of PArray but do not use a Distribution Object as an Emitter and do not support Object Fragments as particles. With their addition, no advantage remains to using Snow or Spray; you have greater choices over particle types and materials (such as eight Standard Particle types, Instanced Geometry and MetaParticles, and different material sources), and greater control over particle behavior than with the originals.

In PArray, particle formation is concerned with how particles are distributed across the Emitter object; in SuperSpray, particle formation concerns how you direct the particle stream under the Basic parameters rollout and how particles diverge. Generally, the speed settings refer to particle velocity in general, not their movement away from a Distribution object. That said, however, this is modified by the settings in the Object Motion Inheritance rollout that controls the extent to which particles pick up the relative movement of the Distribution object.

With Blizzard, icon size makes a difference. The Emitter icon determines the area from which particles emanate and these dimensions can be animated. The Blizzard controls differ from those in PArray in how the particles move. Tumble settings are in the Particle Motion section of the Particle Generation rollout—and there is an Emitter Fit Planer option in the Mat'l Mapping and Source section of the Particle Type rollout, which, if chosen, results in particles mapped based upon their place of emission on the Blizzard Emitter icon. (Remember, when mapped, materials are placed on particles; mapping is progressive from bottom to top across a range of particles). Lastly, there are no Bubble Motion settings for Blizzard.

The Particle Cloud (PCloud) system places particles within a defined volume. It's useful for creating a flock of birds, a starfield, a troop of soldiers, or, as in the Jet Plane tutorial, creating an Atmospheric effect when you want more control over the movement of the atmosphere than can be afforded by using volume fog. For example, use PCloud with a UDeflector space warp to animate a spaceship passing through a cloud nebulae, pushing the cloud aside as it goes.

In the following exercise, you return to the exercise in which the aircraft is breaking into object fragments, to add a sequence where the jet passes through the cloud. If particles are in motion, they can escape the confines of the cloud emitter.

USING PCLOUD AND THE DEFLECTOR SPACE WARP TO SIMULATE AN AIRPLANE PASSING THROUGH A CLOUD

1. Load the file named pclod_tut.max. (This is the prior scene with the Jet Plane exploding.) Click PCloud and use a sphere emitter to create a PCloud Particle system in the top viewport, upper-right corner.

2. Set the following parameters:

   Set Rad/Len = 2000.0
   Percentage of Particles = 10.0%

3. Turn on the Animate button and as you move from frame 0 to frame 100, move the cloud toward the lower left so it intersects the jet in at least one place. Return to frame 0. Turn off the Animate button.

4. In the Modify panel, under Particle Generation, set the following parameters:

   Use Rate = 1
   Speed = 0.5
   Variation = 10.0
   Random direction
   Emit Start = -5
   Emit Stop = 150
   Display Until = 170
   Life = 150
   Variation = 30
   Particle Size = 200.0
   Variation = 22.0%
   Grow For = 20
   Fade For = 22.

5. Under Particle Type, select Standard Particles and the Standard Particles type to Sphere.

6. Under Particle Rotation, set Spin Axis Controls to Random.

7. Under Object Motion Inheritance, set the following parameters:

Influence = 100.0
Multiplier = 1.0
Variation = 0
Particle Spawn is set to None.

8. Create a UDeflector object. To help your visual organization, you can place it around and link it to the plane, although this is not necessary for the plane to function as a deflector.

9. Open the Modify panel, click Pick Object and select the Jet Plane (Jet Plane should appear above the button). Set the following parameters for Particle Bounce:

Bounce = 1.0
Variation = 25%
Chaos = 25%
Friction = 0
Inherit Vel. = 100.0%

10. Select PCloud01 and bind UDeflector01 to PCloud01.

11. Open the Material editor and assign the cloud material (PCloud atmosphere) to PCloud01. Return to PCloud01's Particle Generation rollout and increase the Use Rate value from 1 to 100.

12. Advance to a frame that shows a close-up of the jet within the cloud, around frame 55 (see Figure 22.21).

FIGURE 22.21

The finished scene at frame 55.

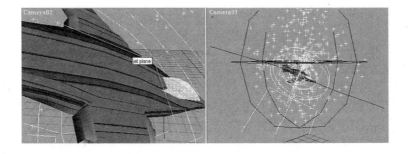

13. Render Camera02 at that frame. Note the particles pass around the jet in Figure 22.22.

View the final animation on the CD, pcloud3.avi. Note the Cloud effect appears a little thin and granular. This results from lowering the PCloud particle count for this exercise. In practice, you would increase the particle count and hide the Particle system altogether when it's off-camera. Increasing particle size to simulate density makes interaction with the plane-deflector appear unnatural. One promising solution is the UltraShock plug-in from Digimation, which creates density by adding a volumetric effect around particles.

The addition of the second Particle system with large transparent particles as an Atmospheric effect increases render time substantially. It's useful in the few situations where you show deflector effects. Normally you can achieve nearly the same results more economically with Noise added to fogs, volume fog, and volume lights. See the final file pcl_tut01.max on the accompanying CD.

The PCloud Emitter object can be a sphere, cylinder, box, or any other 3D geometry. Although PCloud particles conform in overall shape to the shape of a deformed Emitter object and follow its animated change in position, the particles won't adapt to animated rotations, scales, space warps, or animated modifiers. You can fill the volume with particles by setting particle speed to 0. Alternatively, you can control particle behavior within the Emitter object by using animatable XYZ spinners to create a directional vector, or you can use the Z axis of any geometric reference object.

TIP

Changing settings on Particle systems containing a large number of particles can slow your machine substantially. Instead, set the Particle Generation/Use Rate to 1, adjust all other settings, and, as the final step, correct the quantity in Use Rate or Use Total box.

Exploring Third Party Particle Systems

This section focuses on the major third party plug-ins that you will find useful while working with Particle systems. The following plug-ins are covered:

- Sand Blaster
- Outburst
- Shag;Fur
- Particles+
- Ultrashock

Sand Blaster

Sand Blaster is a Particle system plug-in designed to literally blow apart objects into small particles. You can have these particles blow into space or even reform into other objects. Sand Blaster also gives you the option to explode an object into tiny particles that can actually be other objects. As a matter of fact, you can have up to 999 interim objects to alternate among before you reform to the target object. Objects can blow apart in different directions, follow a path, or fly around randomly and reform the exact same way.

With the enhancements in the Advanced systems, Digimation's Sand Blaster remains valuable for its unique capability to use targets (single or grouped) as interim or final particle destinations. It supports grouped emitters as a single source emission object (see Figures 22.23 for an example of the Sand Blaster Interface).

Particles form on the Emitter object and propagate outward or toward a Target object, which can be the final destination, or an interim stop until the next successive target. Since the targets vary in geometry and materials, Sand Blaster provides a competing solution to the Particle Spawning features in R2's Advanced Particle systems. In other words, instead of setting up alternative lifespans and mutation sequences, you can establish a series of targets, adjust the movement and time between targets, and animate the targets themselves. R2's Particles and Dynamics space warps work with Sand Blaster. Also, Sand Blaster works well with Digimation' Clay Studio/Pro, making it an attractive competing alternative to R2's MetaParticles implementation.

FIGURE 22.23

The Sand Blaster Particle System Interface.

Although the interface for Sand Blaster differs from the Advanced Particle systems in this chapter, the similar concepts translate well once you realize Sand Blaster works by assembling particles in one place, disassembling and moving them over time, and reassembling them at the (next) target. Sand

Blaster and Clay Studio demo versions are included on the accompanying CD. To familiarize yourself with this operation, repeat the Particle Array tutorials in this chapter using Sand Blaster.

If you feel adventurous, repeat the SuperSpray-MetaParticle tutorial using Sand Blaster and Clay Studio with the R2 space warps. The combination of these products provides a more sophisticated, flexible, and manageable approach to using metaballs as particles. Clay Studio/Pro supports a wide variety of spherical, ellipsoid and spline-based shapes as metaballs that Sand Blaster can use as particles. Sand Blaster's "target" approach to particle mutation is also preferred over the current state of Particle Spawn implementation in R2. This preference is not to denigrate R2's advanced particle systems, but it is rather an acknowledgment of how well Sand Blaster has developed since it was introduced shortly after R1's release.

Outburst

Outburst is a true physically-based Particle system, which underwent development and extensive refinement as the Particle system implemented in SoftImage. In September 1997, Animation Science released Outburst as a plug-in for R1, and at this writing is undergoing beta testing for the R2 version. There will be no difference in the initial R2 feature set.

Although particle effects in 3DS MAX R2 are designed to be the combined result of the Particle system, space warps, and materials, Outburst provides a fully *self-contained* solution. It ships with dedicated Outburst materials. The plug-in interface combines the Particle system with the forces that act on it, such as Wind, Gravity, and so on. The R2 version is identical to its R1 counterpart. How well Outburst works with native MAX space warps and materials is an open question and beyond the scope of this chapter.

To create the Outburst Particle system, click the Create/Geometry/Outburst dropdown and create an icon in the top viewport (a sphere with an arrow). Open the Modify panel and you find a self-contained interface. Global and local forces are applied within this interface, in contrast to R2 where forces are applied through space warps.

Outburst ships with specialized materials. You access Outburst color expression, color ramp, opacity expression, and opacity ramp maps through the Material editor. The expression maps support scripting through MAX's expression interface. The ramping maps are gradients with Noise settings.

Animation Science indicates their Outburst materials are compatible with other R2 materials. If so, you can build layered maps for Outburst particles.

The interface includes six tabs: System, Source, Particle, Custom, Local, and Obstacle (see Figure 22.24). Each tab brings up its own set of rollouts. Simulations can be built interactively. For example, to create a simple fountain, you create an Outburst system by clicking the Source tab and adding a Source, which can be their preset geometry or any geometric object in the scene. You then adjust rate, speed, and spread. Then you click the System tab to add a global force, which can be Gravity, Wind, Electric, or Magnetic (similar to space warps). Next, you create an obstacle, which has its own deflector settings. Finally, you assign a material to the particles.

As with MAX's particle systems, you can add custom and local forces, path assignments, particle decay, Noise, Turbulence and Collision between Particle systems. Outburst works with Clay Studio and should work with other metaball tools to create an alternative approach to R2's MetaParticles.

FIGURE 22.24

The Outburst Particle System Interface.

Because Outburst has not made its final release for R2 at the time of this writing, it's not possible at this moment to discuss any limitations concerning its interaction with R2's space warps, non-Outburst materials and maps, and MAX's Dynamic utility. In its present form, however, Outburst has a unique smooth flow and visual elegance that makes it distinct. And it is a true physical-based Particle system with a special capability to represent inter-particle collision. Further information can be found at the Animation Science Web site, www.anisci.com.

Shag; Fur

Digimation's Shag; Fur is the first of two Hair plug-ins for MAX R2 (see Figure 22.25). Shag;Hair, to be released in the first quarter of 1998, is optimized for longer strands and curls. It uses particle technology but is implemented as an Atmospheric effect.

The Shag; Fur atmospheric apparatus is accessed through Create/Helpers/Shag;Fur dropdown and created in any viewport as an atmospheric gizmo. You then create the geometry you want to add fur to, open the Environment dialog, and under Atmospheric Effects, click Add, and add both Shag Fur and Shag Hair objects. In the Shag;Fur Object rollout, you select the geometry and set length, thickness, density, leaning, color, bending, and render quality. Finally, you add hair-enabled lights (create/lights/Hair Enabled Lights) that parallel R2's other lights but are needed to render the fur, or you have the option to convert existing lights to hair enabled.

Hair is memory-intensive, but it renders quickly to provide a particle-like effect that is difficult, if not impossible to duplicate. Below is a test render of fur on a simple cone. A demo version is included on the accompanying CD. Further information about Shag;Fur, Sand Blaster, and Clay Studio/Pro is available on the Digimation web site, www.digimation.com.

Particles+

Peter Watje released his Particles+ particle system as charityware and it is included on the accompanying CD. It first made its appearance with R1 and is useful in allowing you to change Material IDs on collision with a deflector. It also supports loopable particles, regularized Emitters, and radial angle controls, but it contains acknowledged bugs and may not be updated in the future. See the part+.txt file that accompanies this plug-in.

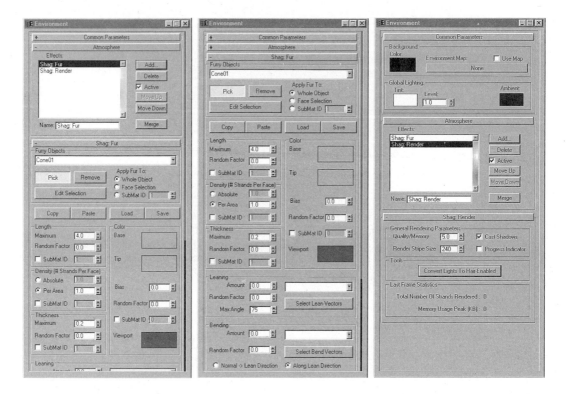

FIGURE 22.25
The Shag;Fur Interface.

Ultrashock

Although not a particle system, Digimation's Ultrashock is a volumetric shading routine designed to add volumetric effects to any Particle system, which in effect function like another type of Particle system.

Ultrashock is useful for making Smoke, Flame, and Fog effects. It has the advantage of doing so with very few particles—200 particles can yield very full, dense fog plumage. UltraShock works well with all MAX-compatible Particle systems. For example, it would be useful to enhance the Particle Cloud exercise earlier in this chapter. In that tutorial, an aircraft flies through a cloud, acting as a deflector to the particles as it passes through. To achieve proper deflection, the particle size needs to be small. To save rendering times in the tutorial, the particle count in the cloud is low, with the result that deflector action appears proper, but the "cloud" form is less than natural. In practice, this scene would be rendered with a high particle count that would make the particles appear to be one object. UltraShock provides an alternative solution, because its volumetric capabilities can create the illusion of density without increasing particle count or render time.

UltraShock consists of a helper object, UltraShock Lights, three Video Post filters, UltraShock Motion Blur, UltraShock Shader, and UltraShock Shadow. UltraShock lights are required if you want particles to cast shadows in the scene. You create the helper object and pick a Particle system in the scene to apply it. Each UltraShock helper creates a single effect; you can create multiple effects with multiple objects applied to the same Particle system, and conversely, you can apply a single effect to multiple Particle systems with a single helper object. UltraShock can replace the Particle system over the entire sequence, or you can set the UltraShock lifespan to be different from that of the underlying Particle system, resulting in an effect that has the underlying particles visible over some frames and UltraShock visible over the balance.

You work with UltraShock by selecting the Helper object and setting parameters in the Modify Command panel. Conveniently, this panel contains a Preview window, much like that in the Lens Effects Video Post filter, so you can interactively tune the effect in the scene without setting up the Video Post queue.

MAX R2 Space Warps for Particle Systems

In 3DS MAX R2, you find three types of space warps: Geometric/Deformable, Modifier Based, and Particles and Dynamics. Of the Particles and Dynamics space warps, Deflector, Wind, Gravity, and Displace shipped with R1. R2 expands the selection with PBomb, UDeflector, SDeflector, Path Follow, Push, and Motor—all optimized for particles and/or dynamics.

The foregoing tutorials made use of the UDeflector, Path Follow, PBomb, and Gravity space warps to create collision detection and influence particle motion. Space warps are designed to be used in combination bound to single or multiple Particle systems. The combined effects may not always be obvious and the binding order on the Particle system can make a difference.

PBomb

PBomb pertains only to Particle systems, not to be confused with Bomb in the Geometric/Deformable category that blows up geometry. You have the option of shaping the blast area as a sphere, cylinder, or planer. The Chaos spinner adds motion to the blast, but only when the Duration setting is 0. Normally you set Duration between 0 and 3. The Unlimited Range, Linear, and Exponential affect if and how the blast force decays. The Strength spinner affects the change in velocity of bomb particles as they move along the vector away from the blast.

PBomb works with Particle systems and dynamics (found in the Utility Panel). If you are using it with particles, PArray is the best choice. In the Jet tutorial, the explosion results from the interaction between PArray and PBomb, with flames caused by Combustion. Return to the tutorial and try making the explosion using only PArray, or only PBomb with the PArray motion settings turned off (you'll still need it to create object fragments).

SDeflector and UDeflector

SDeflector is a spherical deflector for Particle systems. The Bounce setting controls the particle velocity setting after collision, compared to the pre-collision velocity. The Variation spinner allows variation in the velocity. The Chaos Spinner controls the perfect angle of reflection, with 100 percent inducing up to 90 degree variation. The Inherit Velocity spinner controls how the deflector affects the particles. Use this when you have a deflector moving through slow moving particles and you want the particles to move off the deflector. (This is implemented in the Jet tutorial but is only visible in close up from certain angles.) You can scale SDeflector both uniformly and non-uniformly. The icon size had direct bearing on the other settings and the overall effect.

UDeflector is a universal deflector, which enables any 3D geometric shape to be the particle deflector. Its settings are identical to SDeflector, except for friction settings. In the Particle Spawn and MetaParticles tutorials, UDeflector is used to create collision detection with the floor.

Deflector is the oldest and simplest deflector, permitting you to vary only its size and bounce settings. Peter Watje has released his charityware version of Deflector, called Deflector+, which includes Friction settings, and an Energy Trns spinner that determines how much energy is transferred when a particle is resting on a moving deflector that slopes. A version is included on the CD.

Path Follow

Path Follow forces particles to follow a spline path. You can use any spline as a path; the Range settings allow you to control the influence of the path on the Particle system; the position of the path follow icon is ignored. You can choose Particle Motion along Offset Splines or Along Parallel Splines. Where the Particle system is not on the path, the former combines the offset distance with the spline and creates a motion path from this combination; the latter makes particles flow from the system in the exact shape as the spline, only at the location.

Eric Peterson provided an excellent explanation of this difference with a water slide example. To paraphrase him, the Parallel offset is like having identical parallel slides. Whatever path is followed on the first is recapped in the second. Offset is the case of only one slide with the rider holding a ladder as he goes down the slide. The rider's path down the slide is different from the path of a rider on top of the ladder. Path Follow's Stream Taper and Path Swirl settings control the shape of the particle stream alone the path and are not animatable.

Push

Push applies a force to either a Particle system or a Dynamics System, with slight differences in each case. With a Particle system, Push applies a uniform unidirectional force in a positive or negative direction—in other words, in the direction of the pad on the hydraulic jack icon. With a dynamic simulation, it is a positive or negative point force, moving toward or away from the hydraulic jack pad. All settings can be animated except for the Timing (the frames over which the force is active) and Icon Size.

Push has both a Basic Force and Feedback/Reversible force. The latter dampen/increase the Basic Force as the object approaches the Target Speed setting. You can also introduce wave-type variation as Noise while the force is applied. The Period 1 spinner sets the entire time of the Noise cycle.

Amplitude 1 sets the magnitude of the Noise, Phase 1 offsets the variation pattern. Period 2, Amplitude 2, and Phase 2 each provide additional noise variation on top of this. The Particle Effect Range settings give the option of having all bound particles in the scene effected by the Push, or limiting the range.

Motor

Motor works similar to Push but applies rotational torque instead of direction force to Particle systems or objects. When Motor is applied to a Particle system, both the position and orientation of the Motor icon affects the particles. When applied to a Dynamic simulation, the icon position has no effect on the object(s), although the orientation of the icon does. While the units of measure differ for Motor, they otherwise are similar to the Push controls.

The key to successful, artistic particle effects lies in combination—designing economical layers or combinations of Particle systems, and further combining these with materials, space warps, Atmospheric effects, and dynamics. Just as great painting does not result from a single, very complex stroke, you'll likely find it easier and more naturalistic to build a several particle systems with few particles that isolate specific movements and paths, and to use them together as if they were a single system. Having them share materials and space warps provides unity.

Also consider the relationship between instanced geometry, Particle systems, and Atmospherics. There are times Atmosphere works better than particles. It's generally "cheaper" to render and a simple Particle system adds accents or creates the illusion of a much larger Particle system. In the same way, a Particle system can be cheaper than duplicating geometry with the Scatter utility, especially if you want to globally manipulate the instanced geometry. Conversely, you cannot control or manipulate individual particles, in which case Scatter is useful.

In Practice: Using Particle Systems

- **Similar controls in MAX R2's Basic and Advanced Particle Systems:** Remember that the Basic Particle systems are the predecessors to R2's Advanced Particle systems and remain useful for their simplicity and economical use of resources. The same principles apply to both Basic and Advanced Particle systems. Advanced Particle systems approach, but Advanced Particle systems are extended to give you more control over particle creation, type, path movement, materials, and regeneration behavior. Advanced systems features are best showcased in PArray. Once you master that Particle system, your understanding easily transfers to the others, as well as to most third party plug-in systems, which are truly variations on a theme.

- **Spray Versus Snow:** Both Spray and Snow have unique characteristics that make one more suitable for a particular effect over the other. Use Spray to create effects where the particles need to remain a constant direction and orientation. Snow works better for particles where soft and tumbling effects are required.

- **SuperSpray and Blizzard:** Advanced versions of Snow and Spray, which add extensive control over particle generation, motion, and lifecycle, with the capability of saving presets.

- **Particle Array (PArray):** Allows you to use object fragments as particles. You can combine this with the PBomb space warp, Combustion, and a Visibility track to create a convincing explosion.

- **Particle Cloud (PCloud):** Allows you to confine a Particle system to a volume by setting Speed to 0. This can be used with deflectors to create the turbulence effect of an object passing through the particles.

- **Advanced Particle Systems:** support standard particles (eight choices), instanced geometry as particles, and MetaParticles (metaballs used as particles)

- **The Emitter:** All Particle systems must originate from one point. This point is referred to as the Emitter. You can animate the Emitter's orientation, position, and size to create several effects. Because the Emitter is an object, you can also use MAX's animation controllers, such as noise, to affect its behavior as well. Only PArray lets you choose any geometric object as an Emitter. The third party plug-ins Sand Blaster and Outburst also have this capability.

- **Materials and particles:** MAX enables you to assign any type of material to a particle. Remember to combine several Mapping types to create the illusion of different shaped particles. For example, use Facing particles with a Gradient Opacity map to create the effect of round objects, like bubbles, floating along. Using bitmaps on Facing particles have limitations when used in conjunction with Atmospheric effects.

- **Particle MBlur and Particle Age Map:** R2 introduces Particle MBlur and Particle Age Map materials for Motion effects and to simulate particle decay.

- **Hair and fur generation:** Available with third party plug-ins based on particle technology.

- **Material mapping and source choices:** Expanded in the Advanced Particle systems. Multi/Sub-Object materials can be used to cycle different materials on particles or, in the case of PArray, to employ different Material IDs on each particle.

- **Mapped materials behave differently from General materials:** They are mapped from bottom to top across many particles. Alternatively, they can be assigned in their entirety to face particles.

- **Particles and post effects:** Through the usage of Video Post effects, in particular Lens effects, you can give particles the appearance of being tiny sparks or glowing snowflakes and change the Filter effect over time. Any Video Post effect that utilizes the material channel ID or object ID parameter will work with a Particle system.

- **Particles with space warps:** For more realistic particle behavior, MAX R2 introduces seven new space warps in addition to Gravity, Deflector, and Wind. Combining the space warps has an additive effect on the Particle systems. Space warps work with all R2's Particle systems and with most third party plug-in systems as well to add collision detection and affect particle movement. Some space warps have been designed to work with both Particle systems and R2's Dynamics utility.

- **Particle systems overlap in use with approaches like Scatter and Atmospheric effects:** Use Scatter when you want multiplied instanced geometry over which you keep control. Use Particle systems when you want control over the whole system, but no particular particle, and use atmospherics when you need volumes but don't need particle control or collision effects. Use materials with Particle systems to minimize geometry and speed rendering.

Chapter 23

ANIMATING WITH SPACE WARPS

When creating animation, and specifically special effects, often the animator will need to affect many objects within the scene. If you were to animate a breeze blowing through a field of grain, a rock skipping across a pond, or heat rising from hot pavement in 3D Studio MAX, you would use a space warp. Simply put, space warps are nothing more than locations in space that deform objects that pass through them.

A primary use of space warps is with particle systems. Creating realistic smoke effects or swarming object motion, such as a school of fish or a swarm of bees, can be tedious without space warps. Space warps enable you to affect any number of objects within a scene uniformly with a single space warp.

In this chapter, you learn how space warps work and how to use them. Specifically, this chapter explains the following:

- Space warp basics
- Different types of space warps
- Using space warps on objects and particles

Space Warp Basics

Space warps are created very much the same way as geometric primitives. Select the Space Warps type from the Create panel, choose from the class of Space Warp (Geometric/Deformable, Particles & Dynamics, or Modifier-Based), select the Space Warp from the Object Type rollout, then click and drag to set initial Space Warp parameters.

The various classifications of space warps are due to the differences in characteristics of objects and particles. Not all space warps work with all objects. Because particles do not react the same as geometric objects, they each have their own set of space warps. To create real world physics simulation on geometric objects, some of the Particle space warps can also be applied to non-particle objects using the Dynamics utility. For more information regarding the Dynamics utility, see Chapter 24, "Animation Utilities." Figure 23.1 shows the various space warps and their classifications.

FIGURE 23.1

The three space warp classifications.

The Difference Between Space Warps and Modifiers

Many of the space warps available are also available as modifiers. So why would you choose one over the other? The choice depends on the effect you want to achieve. Modifiers are carried by the object and apply deformation in the object's local space. Space warps exist as independent objects and apply deformations to bound objects based on the object's world space location. For example, applying a Ripple modifier to a selection of spheres has quite a different effect than binding the spheres to a Ripple space warp (see Figure 23.2).

FIGURE 23.2

Objects with the Ripple modifier applied versus the Ripple space warp binding.

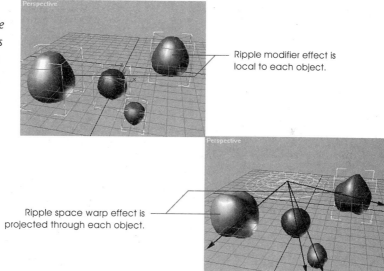

Ripple modifier effect is local to each object.

Ripple space warp effect is projected through each object.

When you apply a ripple as a modifier, the ripple is applied as a gizmo to the object. The effect of the ripple depends on the relative position of the gizmo with respect to the object. Moving the object does not affect how the ripple modifies it, but a ripple as a space warp has quite a different effect. As seen in Figure 23.2, the ripple is projected from its center outward to all objects bound to it—in this case, the spheres. The ripple's position in space, as well as its orientation, directly affect the objects bound to it. If you transform the Ripple space warp, its effect on the bound objects changes. If you move one or several of the bound objects, the relation of their position and orientation in 3D space to the space warp affects the object's appearance.

By design, space warps make simulating object interaction easier to animate. If you are going to animate a snowman melting as it gets closer to a heat lamp, the space warp can be located in the exact position where the melting is to occur and the snowman need only walk into the space warp for the effect to take place. Although the same effect can be done with modifiers, it can become more difficult to make changes to the animation at a later time.

With the exception of the space warps used for Dynamic Simulation, the application of all space warps is nearly identical. The only difference between one space warp and another is the parameters and the effect of the space warp itself. While each space warp has its own characteristics and deformation properties, all must be bound to objects to have any effect.

Space Warps and the Stack

Objects are bound to a space warp using the Bind to Space Warp button located in the toolbar (see Figure 23.3). Any number of objects can be bound to a single space warp. To bind objects to a space warp, click the Bind to Space Warp button, select the objects you want to bind, and then drag from the objects to the space warp you need.

FIGURE 23.3

The Bind button located in the toolbar.

Bind

Space warps are last to be evaluated in the object history stack. It's easy to forget this, but 3DS MAX has a way of telling you that the space warp is evaluated last. Figure 23.4 shows how space warp bindings are displayed in the stack. All bindings are listed after all modifiers and are further separated by double dotted lines. Sub-object bindings are displayed with an asterisk before the binding name. This occurs only if the last modifier in the stack is sending sub-object selections out of the pipeline.

FIGURE 23.4

Space warp bindings as displayed in the modifier stack. The sub-object binding is indicated by an asterisk.

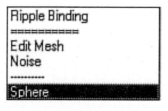

Space warp binding separator

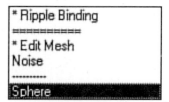

Sub-object binding

Different Space Warp Types

Space warps have been reorganized in 3D Studio MAX R2. They are now classified under the Space Warps rollout in the categories Geometric/Deformable, Particles & Dynamics, and Modifier-Based (refer to Figure 23.1).

Because objects of different types have different characteristics, it is important to realize that not all space warps can be applied to all objects. Physical characteristics such as gravity, however, work great for particles systems and also work equally well as physical properties for geometric objects. The Dynamics utility enables you to attach some Particle space warps (such as Gravity and Wind) to geometric objects formally for use with particles only. For more information regarding the Dynamics properties, see the section on the Dynamics utility in Chapter 24.

Geometric/Deformable

3DS MAX R2 ships with a variety of space warps that offer many different types of control over object deformation. This section explores the space warps that affect geometric objects. In short, all objects other than Particle systems can use space warps of the Geometric/Deformable class, including lights and cameras. The Geometric/Deformable space warps include the following:

- FFD (Box)
- FFD (Cyl)
- Ripple
- Wave
- Displace
- Conform
- Bomb

FFD (Box) and FFD (Cyl)

One of the most versatile space warps is the Free Form Deformation (FFD). The FFD Box and FFD Cylinder provide you with a lattice that you can manipulate to create any shape deformation you desire. Using the FFD (Box or Cylinder) space warp, you can animate exaggerated special effects as in cartoons or films, such as *The Mask* and *Men in Black*. Effects, such as an eyeball squeezing through a keyhole as it peers into a room or an overexcited heart pounding wildly, can be achieved using FFD space warps. Figure 23.5 shows an example of the FFD (Box) being used on a curious eyeball.

FIGURE 23.5

Imagine animating something more complex than this to squeeze through the keyhole. It's possible with FFD space warps.

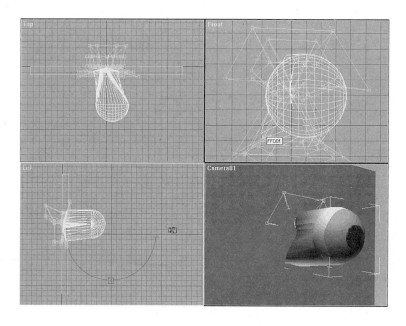

The FFD (Box) and FFD (Cyl) are created very much the same as their geometric counterparts, the Box and Cylinder primitives. The difference is that instead of creating geometry, the FFD space warps create a control lattice. A control lattice is represented by a framework of points that can be manipulated and animated. The control points are used to control vertices on bound objects. When a control point on a lattice is transformed, the transformation properties are passed to the corresponding geometry. Control lattice points do not need to have a one-to-one correspondence to the vertices on the object they are deforming. The control points are used for approximation and influence, very much like the CVs on NURBS curves.

Do not let the fact that the FFD space warps have only a few parameters lead you to believe they are not powerful. Although the parameters are sparse, these space warps are powerful. Using either FFD (Box) or FFD

(Cyl), animated objects can quickly be made to look like animated putty, as in Figure 23.6. The real power lies in the capability to create complex shapes through the use of the FFD control lattice.

FIGURE 23.6

Using the FFD space warps on text can also lead to logo animation that's more exciting than Beveled text.

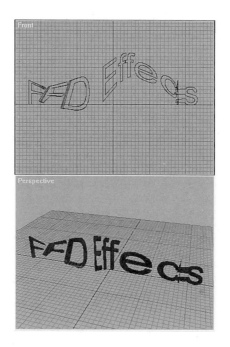

Dimensions

The first set of parameters in the FFD Parameters rollout is the dimensions, which are used to set up the size of the FFD space warp and are measured in standard units. This size corresponds to the size of the area in which bound objects are affected. Thought should be given to the size of the FFD prior to adjusting or animating the control points. Adjusting the size after modifying the control points results in the lattice changing in size as well (thereby affecting the animated object, possibly negatively).

TIP

If you intend for the FFD space warp to affect the entire object, be sure the size of the FFD encompasses the bound object prior to its deformation or select the All Vertices option in the Deform parameters.

Set Number of Points

Because all deformations are not created equal, you can change the number of control points of each dimension. The default is a 4×4×4 matrix of control points, although you can change this number to match your deformation needs. Changing the number of control points enables more complex deformations but also increases the number of calculations involved, thereby increasing rendering time. For all FFD space warps, use the least number of control points necessary to create the desired effect.

NOTE

Any changes to control points, whether animated or static, are lost when Number of Points parameters are changed. Changing the number of points used in the deformation lattice resets the control point' position. This can be used to reset the lattice by typing in the same values, or it can inadvertently reset all control point information. Be sure of the number of control points prior to making Control Point transforms.

Display

Depending on how the FFD space warp is used, it may be beneficial to turn on or off the display of either the lattice or the source volume. The display options are for display purposes only and do not alter the effects of the space warp. They do, however, help when using the FFD space warps in various situations.

The lattice is the framework that deforms the bound object, while the Source volume is the area of deformation. Although the two are similar, their actions are quite different. The lattice defines the deformation shape, and the Source volume defines the deformation boundaries. When defining the shape through the control points sub-object, it is important to see the lattice. If the warp is based on Only in Volume, it is important to see the Source volume. In many cases, both options are used intermittently during the course of animating the FFD space warp itself or the objects it affects (see Figure 23.7).

Deform

The FFD space warps can be applied to objects in two ways, either by geometry intersecting the Source volume or by affecting the entire object. These options can be set through the Deform section in the Parameters rollout.

When the Only in Volume option is used, objects are only affected when they intersect the Source volume. If a soap bubble slowly wafts into the airflow of a slow moving fan as it enters the wind path, for example, the deformation takes place (see Figure 23.8). If the bubble is just being blown around the room, it might be more appropriate to use the All Vertices option because it affects the bound object regardless of whether it is within the Source volume or not.

FIGURE 23.7

Both of the torus objects and space warps in this shot are identical. The space warp on the left uses the All Vertices option, while the one on the right is set to Only in Volume.

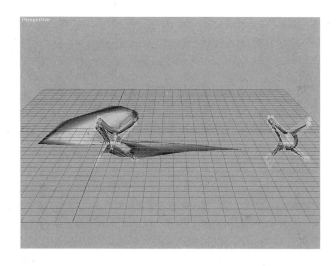

FIGURE 23.8

As the bubbles move into the FFD (Box) space warp, they become distorted.

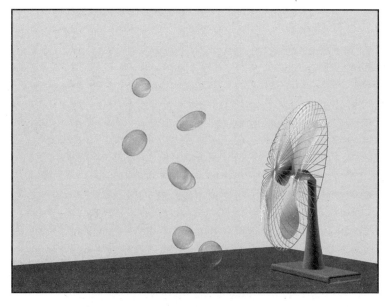

When using the All Vertices option, the Falloff parameter also becomes active. The Falloff parameter enables you to set an amount (relative to source volume size) at which the effect on the bound object is zero. In other words, a Falloff value of two means that the effect goes to zero at a distance of twice the size (width, height, and depth) of the source volume.

The Tension and Continuity controls are available through either Deform option and are used to change the effect the lattice has on bound objects. By changing the values in the Tension and Continuity spinners, you are effectively changing the tension on the splines that create the deformation.

Though you cannot see the tension and continuity of the splines in an FFD space warp, you can definitely see their effects. Tension can be described as how tight a curve enters and exits a control point. The higher the Tension value is, the tighter the curve. The Continuity level describes curvature, and changing its value changes the amount of continuous curve through the control point. Smaller Continuity values equate with less curvature or tighter curves, while more Continuity makes for a wider, sweeping curve.

Selection

When in the Sub-Object selection level, three controls make it easier to move groups of control points with a single move. By choosing All X, All Y, or All Z, you can easily select all the control points along that axis by clicking one of the control points, as shown in Figure 23.9. This is extremely useful after control points have been transformed and no longer lie on a single plane. These selection controls (of which one or more may be toggled at a time) use the original order of control points when selecting along an axis.

Using the FFD Space Warps

To use the FFD (Box), simply click the FFD (Box) object type button under the Geometric/Deformable space warp tab on the Create tab. Clicking and dragging in any viewport creates a 4×4×4 lattice in very much the same way you would create a box primitive. Selecting the Modify tab, you can then adjust or animate the lattice control points using the Sub-Object selection method.

The FFD (Cyl) works exactly the same as the FFD (Box) except that its creation parameters are cylindrical. Each FFD Cylinder contains height and radius parameters for determining its physical size, and within the Set Number of Points dialog, the Side, Radial, and Height parameters for determining the number of control points used to describe the lattice itself.

FIGURE 23.9

Though the control points do not lie on a single plane, they are easily selected using either the All X, All Y, or All Z selection option.

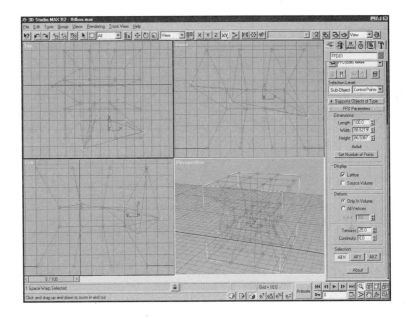

The following exercise shows the basic principles of using an FFD space warp in animation. The ball falls into the tube and stretches the tube as it falls through. You may open the scene file ffddone.max or run 23maxffd.avi to see what the finished deformation should look like.

SQUEEZING THROUGH A TUBE

1. Open 23maxffd.max from the accompanying CD-ROM.

2. Click Space Warps in the Create panel. Select FFD (Cyl) from the Object Type rollout under the Geometric/Deformable space warp types.

3. From a Top view, click and drag out a FFD (Cyl) space warp with an approximate radius of 75 and a height of 300, centered over the tube. The FFD should be a 4×8×4 control point configuration. Use the Align tool to center the FFD (Cyl) with the sphere on all axes.

4. From a Front view, select the FFD (Cyl) and click Sub-Object selection level in the Modify panel. You can now select and transform individual or groups of control points of the lattice.

5. In the Selection parameters, click All X and All Y. Select a point on the second row vertically. All the Control points of that horizontal row are selected because they all lie on the local X and Y planes.

6. Using the Ctrl key, select a control point on the second middle row. You should now have the two middle rows of control points selected.

Figure 23.10 shows the correct selection of control points.

FIGURE 23.10

The two middle rows of the FFD (Cyl) are selected.

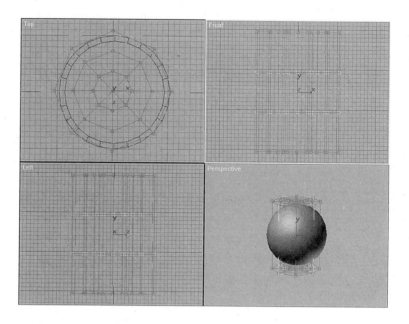

7. Now that the two middle rows of control points have been selected, lock the selection by pressing the space bar or clicking the Lock icon.

8. Using the Select and Uniform Scale tool, click and drag up to scale the control points until they are slightly larger than the sphere. Lock the X axis only so that the Control points are scaled horizontally only. Unlock the selection and deselect Sub-Object selection. See Figure 23.11 for comparison.

9. Click the Bind to Space Warp tool in the toolbar. Bind the Tube to the FFD (Cyl) by clicking the Tube icon and dragging it to the FFD (Cyl) space warp. The FFD (Cyl) flashes briefly to show that the tube has been bound to it.

10. Using the Align tool, center all objects to the Tube object. Once centered, drag all objects so that they are slightly above the tube. If you lock the transform to Y only and drag the FFD (Cyl) space warp, you will see how it deforms the Tube object.

FIGURE 23.11

The two middle rows of control points have been scaled up to create the bulge.

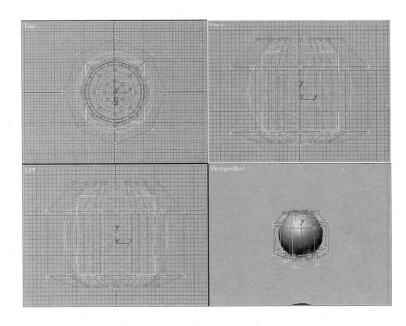

11. For greater control, link the FFD (Cyl) and the GeoSphere to a Dummy object (also centered). Animate the Dummy moving through the tube and the ball, and the FFD (Cyl) space warp will follow.

Figure 23.12 depicts a frame from the completed animation, or you can view 21maxffd.avi from the accompanying CD-ROM for the completed animation.

FIGURE 23.12

A still image from the deformation of the tube. Note how the tube deforms as the ball moves through it.

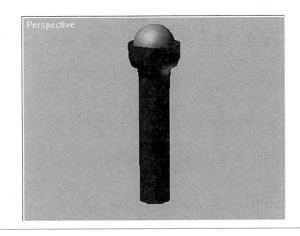

The FFD space warps are great for a variety of deformation types. While they are versatile and used extensively, there are some deformation types that they are not well suited for, in particular, simulating explosions and undulating wave patterns. When you need to give an object a gelatinous or putty appearance, use the FFD space warps. For wave patterns, use the Ripple or Wave space warps.

Ripple

The ☐Ripple space warp sends concentric waves from its center out to infinity. Use Ripple to create undulating effects in geometry or effects such as ripples on a pond.

Any geometric object can be bound to a Ripple space warp. What's more, you can also bind lights, cameras, and helpers to a Ripple space warp. Lights, cameras, and helpers are not deformed the way geometric objects are but are instead transformed to move with the ripple effect. You can simulate such effects as a camera on a ship at sea by binding a Free camera to a Ripple space warp.

You can also deform part of an object by binding Sub-Object selections to a space warp by using an Edit modifier or the Volume Select modifier. The key to this technique is placing the Edit or Volume Select modifier at the top of the Modifier stack after any other selection modifiers.

If you have ever been outside on a hot day, you've seen how the heat coming off hot pavement distorts your view. This effect is used often in films when a low shot is used. In the following exercise, you will use a Ripple space warp to distort the entire scene, indirectly.

CREATING A HEAT WAVE

1. Open 23maxhw.max from the accompanying CD-ROM. All the required objects except for the space warp have already been created.

2. In the Front view, create a Ripple space warp by clicking Ripple in the Geometric/Deformable class of space warps in the Create panel.

3. Click and drag to create the Ripple space warp. Link the Ripple space warp to the Box object named Heatbox. This is done by selecting the Bind to Space Warp tool and clicking the heatbox, then dragging to the

Ripple space warp. The Ripple space warp flashes briefly to signal it has been linked to the selected object.

4. After the Ripple space warp and the heatbox have been bound, adjust the parameters of the Ripple space warp. For this exercise, both the amplitude parameters should be set around 1 and the wave length set to .5. These values are arbitrary and any adjustments should be made to suit the situation. Play with the Decay value by starting with it set to .05. This will lessen the effect as it reaches the top of the scene.

5. To make the ripples animate, move the Selection slider to the last frame and click the Animate button. The view border should become red. Change the Phase parameter to 4.0. Turn off the Animate button by clicking it again. The red view border should disappear.

When rendered, you'll notice a warping of the scene (or you can view 23maxhw.avi). The camera is placed behind a box object (heatbox) which is bound to a Ripple space warp. The Ripple space warp is used to cause distortion in heatbox object, which has a Thin Wall Refraction material attached to it. As the camera moves up away from the heatbox object, the distortion is no longer there, because the effect is intended to simulate heat rising from the desert floor.

Wave

Wave is much like Ripple in the sense that it distorts geometry in a wave-like pattern. Rather than its distortion being concentric such as Ripple, Wave is linear. The waves travel in only one direction at any given time.

N OTE

Remember that all space warps are based on 3DS MAX units, so their scale and detail affect variously sized objects in different ways.

Both Ripple and Wave contain parameters called Amplitudes 1 and 2. The primary purpose of having these two amplitudes is to enable you to specify different amplitudes for the X and Y axes of a space warp (Amplitude 1 is X; Amplitude 2 is Y). For instance, if you wanted to make a crease through the center of a wave, set one of the amplitude values to 0. By default, when you're creating a Ripple or Wave space warp, both parameters are created with the same value. Manually edit one value or the other either immediately after creation or later in the Modifier panel.

NOTE

Both Wave and Ripple have a Display section, which is purely for controlling the display of the space warps in the viewports. The Display section has no effect on the space warp or the objects bound to it.

You can use Wave to create multiple types of scenes. In the following exercise, you learn how to distort geometry for both modeling and animation purposes. You have a scene that contains a yacht traveling on the high seas. Unfortunately, the scene has come upon some nasty weather, and the waves have become increasingly choppy. To simulate this weather, you need to use Wave for two effects: modeling the waves on the seas and the boat riding the waves.

MODELING AND ANIMATING WITH WAVE

1. Open imx17wav.max from the accompanying CD-ROM. When you load the scene, the first objects you see are the boat, a box, a spline, and a Wave space warp.

2. Click the Bind button, choose the box, and then drag to bind the box to the Wave space warp.

3. Select the Wave space warp and go to the Modify panel.

4. Alter the wave's parameters so that Amplitude 1 reads 5, Amplitude 2 reads 7, and the Wavelength reads 120. Phase and Decay should be set to 0.

   Notice that moving the wave up and down in the Top viewport has no effect on the box, but moving it side to side does. This movement is a result of the linear distortion that the wave provides. Both Wave and Ripple have no effect on the objects bound to them if you move them along the axis of amplitude.

   Both Wave and Ripple work on all types of geometry, including 2D splines. In this part of the exercise, you bind the spline to the wave, and have it deform just like the Box object. The yacht is using the spline as a path controller with the Follow option on.

5. Scroll the Frames slider back and forth to see the animation.

6. Click the Bind button, and then choose the Spline object.

7. Drag to the Wave space warp.

The spline deforms to the wave and, consequently, so does the ship's movement (see Figure 23.13).

Wave space warp bound to 2D spline (path)

FIGURE 23.13

The yacht traveling along both the ocean and spline path bound to the Wave space warp.

Wave space warp bound to ocean

NOTE

The spline must have a sufficient number of vertices to properly deform to the wave. If not, the result is a much less smooth deformation and animation.

Suppose you wanted the yacht to gradually enter the rough seas. That's what the Decay parameter is most useful for. Here's how it works for wave.

8. Go to the Modify panel and select the Wave space warp.

9. Change the Decay parameter to .005.

The wave tapers off as it gets farther away from the Space Warp icon because, for both Wave and Ripple, Decay causes the effect to gradually decrease as you get farther away from the center of the space warp. The size of the space warp has a direct effect on the Decay parameter.

Figure 23.14 shows two of the possible Decay settings for this scene.

FIGURE 23.14

The Decay values at two different settings.

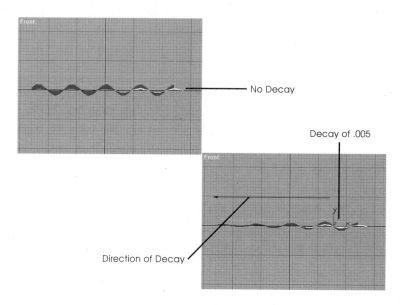

Decay is based on scale. As the objects to which that wave is bound get larger, larger Decay parameters are needed to see an effect.

Flexibility

A common parameter between Ripple and Wave is Flexibility. As a matter of fact, Flexibility is used only with Ripple and Wave. It is a binding-specific parameter; Flexibility doesn't apply to the space warp, but rather specifies how much effect the space warp has on each object. The Flexibility parameter is located in the Modify panel.

In this exercise, you see how to use a regular sphere to create lava for a lava lamp. Through a combination of multiple space warps with varying orientations, you can easily create lava snaking upward in the lamp. Ready to return to the sixties?

MAKING A LAVA LAMP

1. Open imx23rp1.max from the accompanying CD-ROM.

2. Click the Lava object or select it by using Select By Name.

3. Click the Bind to Space Warp button in the toolbar.

4. Use Hit By Name to bind the sphere to Ripple01 and Ripple02. Figure 23.15 shows the Select Space Warp dialog that is used to select the valid space warps in your scene.

5. With the object selected, go to the Modify panel.

6. Alter the Flexibility value.

7. Notice that increasing the value magnifies the effect of the ripple on the sphere, whereas decreasing it has the opposite effect.

Figure 23.16 shows two values of the Flexibility parameter and how the value is displayed in the Modify panel.

Flexibility is entirely animatable. This means that a space warp's values can remain constant, and you can animate the amount of effect the space warp has on a single object by changing the Flexibility value. That way, other objects bound to the same space warp can be affected differently as well. If you want to change the effect globally, adjust the space warp's values.

8. Set Flexibility to 0. Click Ripple Binding in the Modifier stack, and select the first Ripple Binding.

9. Set Flexibility to 0.

10. Go to frame 20, and turn on the Animate button.

FIGURE 23.16

The Modifier panel with the Ripple Binding chosen from the stack. The Flexibility parameter is the only editable and animatable value.

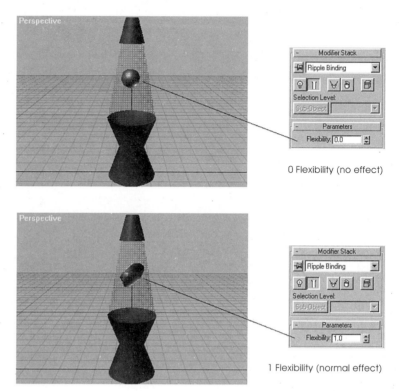

0 Flexibility (no effect)

1 Flexibility (normal effect)

11. Set Flexibility to 1.

12. Repeat this process for the second Ripple Binding.

13. Make a preview of the animation.

    With Flexibility, you can specify when and how much the space warp affects the object. In this example, the lava starts out as a squashed sphere and changes into an undulating lava shape as it travels up the lamp.

NOTE

The 3D Studio MAX User's Guide specifies that changing Flexibility is like adding or removing vertices, when actually this is not the case. Changing Flexibility is more like changing the multiplier value on a light. At 1, the values for Amplitude, for instance, are 1 to 1. At 2, the effect is twice as great, and so on.

Phase

The Phase parameter tracks the change in amplitude from the highest point in the ripple to the lowest point and back again. Changing the phase has the effect of moving the ripples along the local XY plane of the Ripple space warp. Both the Ripple and Wave space warps use a Phase parameter to position and animate their effect.

To make a ripple or wave appear to move, animate the Phase parameter. A whole number change, from 0 to 1 for example, represents a complete cycle in the wave. With that in mind, remember to keep the changes in Phase small if you're looking for subtle movement. For more radical movements, change the parameter more radically. The values you use depend on the size of the objects you are working with. Large phase changes, for example, have a great effect on small objects but have a much more reduced effect on a larger object.

T IP

To make Ripple or Wave appear to animate in the opposite direction, animate the phase from zero to a negative value.

Displace

The Displace space warp is a universal space warp, in that it works on geometry as well as particles. Displace uses the Luminance value from a grayscale image to displace (or change) an object's geometry. It works very much like a bump map except that the displace map actually changes the geometry of an object whereas a bump map only simulates changes through rendering by affecting surface normals. The Displace space warp is great for creating customized effects that work on a single axis. Where a Wave or Ripple effect is great for a general purpose wave, you may be better off using a Displace map if a boat is traveling over a smooth lake. Figure 23.17 shows a Displace space warp for a simple boat and the small ripple forming off the bow.

The intensity of the grayscale values dictates how far the object or particle is displaced. Much like a Bump map, the lighter or more toward white the image is, the further the displacement. You can use Displace to create multiple types of effects—from cookie-cutter modeling to animated geometric distortion. Figure 23.18 demonstrates what a simple image of a white ring can do to simple geometry in 3DS MAX to create a rather intricate object. Figure 23.19 demonstrates another use of the Displace space warp on two objects.

FIGURE 23.17

The Displace space warp can be used for exact placement of deformations. In this example, the small ripples caused by the boat are due to the Displace space warp.

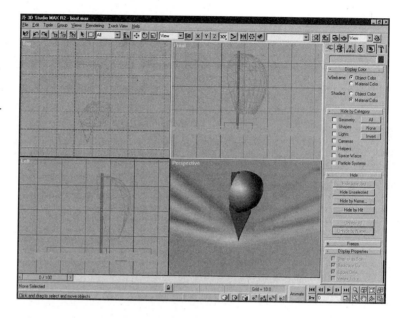

FIGURE 23.18

The Displace space warp bound to a torus. The Displace map used is projected using planar mapping in this example.

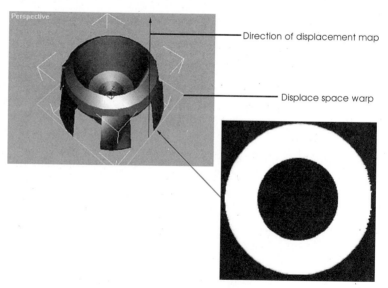

Direction of displacement map

Displace space warp

Displace map

FIGURE 23.19

Use Displace space warp to displace a terrain object and a road. The effect of using one space warp on two objects creates a road that twists and turns as it adheres to the contour of the terrain.

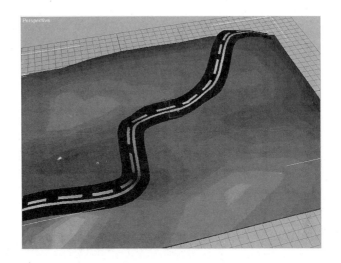

Using Displace on a particle system has a different effect. Rather than displacing geometry, the Displace space warp actually distorts the particle system's path. You can use multiple Displace space warps to alter a particle system's direction several times. Unlike Deflector, which can do the same thing, Displace can enable some particles to pass through or even deflect unevenly based on the grayscale of the image (see Figure 23.20). As you can see, Displace space warps act much like forces on a particle. Using the Displace space warp can actually cause a particle to accelerate based on the strength of the warp.

FIGURE 23.20

The Displace space warp displacing the particle's trajectory.

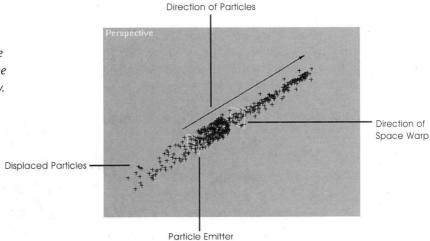

Conform

The Conform space warp is very unique in that a bound object's vertices are pushed toward the surface of the target object specified by the Conform space warp. This a great space warp for creating flowing water effects.

The basic premise of this space warp is simple: project the vertices of one object onto the surface of another based on the orientation of the Conform space warp. Bound objects use this orientation to search for the surface of the Wrap To object. If the Wrap To object is not found, the bound object is not affected. Also see the Conform Compound object, which can be used to morph two objects with differing numbers of vertices, in Chapter 10, "Compound Objects."

The Conform space warp has minimal parameters because it is the target object's geometry that defines the look of the deformation. The main parameter is the Wrap To object. By clicking the Pick Object button, you can select a target object onto which the space warp's bound object's vertices are projected.

After the object has been selected, the Move Vertices parameters should be set, if desired. There are three parameters in this category: Default Projection Distance, Standoff Distance, and Use Selected Vertices. The projection distance is the distance that vertices of a bound object will move when not intersecting with the target object. This can be considered the rest state of bound objects. If the Default Projection Distance is set to 10, then all vertices of bound objects move 10 units when not intersecting with the target object.

The Standoff Distance is the distance between the vertices and the target object. The smaller the number is, the closer the vertices are projected toward the actual surface of the target object. Vertices are not pushed closer than the Standoff Distance toward the target. If the object is a hovercraft flying over rocky terrain, the standoff distance may be greater than that of water trickling down a cascading stairway waterfall.

When Use Selected Vertices is checked, only the vertices selected in a Sub-Object selection are used. This is useful in situations where portions of an object are meant to conform while the rest of the object remains somewhat undeformed. An example of this is the underwater scene's bubbles in Figure 23.21. As the bubbles rise to the surface from inside a cave, the tops of the bubbles need to conform to the geometry of the cave wall, while the bottoms of the bubbles are somewhat flat.

FIGURE 23.21

Bubbles rising to the surface move along the bottom of the rocks and conform to the rock's geometry when bound to the Conform space warp.

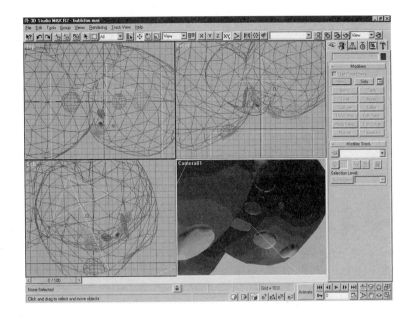

Bomb

Bomb produces an "egg shell" type explosion; it explodes an object into tiny faces. The result is that you're exploding what appears to be an object with no volume—a shell. The pieces of the "shell" are expelled in all directions (as seen in Figure 23.22), based on the parameters set in the Bomb space warp.

FIGURE 23.22

The Bomb space warp causes an object to be blown up in a shell-like fashion.

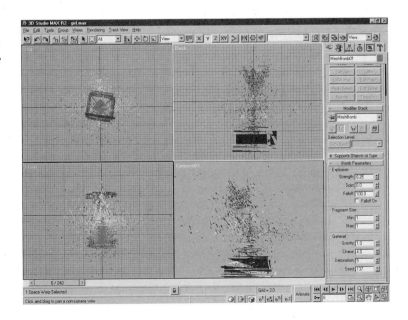

Bomb's real usefulness lies in its parameters. Through manipulation of the Bomb space warp's settings, you can use Bomb to create many types of effects. Several of the values associated with Bomb can be negative, such as strength. You can implode objects rather than explode them. You can also give the appearance of little, none, or reverse gravity through effective use of the Gravity parameter.

Most people think bombs are used to blow objects up; however, 3DS MAX has the capability to put things back together by using Bomb. In this exercise, a soda can starts out in hundreds of tiny little pieces.

USING BOMB TO PUT THINGS BACK TOGETHER

1. Open 23maxbmb.max from the accompanying CD-ROM.

2. Go to the Create panel and create a Bomb space warp and center it to the statuette on all axes.

3. Bind the statuette to the space warp.

4. Move the Frames slider back and forth to see the animation.

As you can see, the bomb's force is causing the statuette to break apart starting at frame 5. The reason the explosion occurs is the Strength parameter. If you set the strength to −.25, you see a different result. With a negative strength, the bomb actually pulls the objects bound to it toward the bomb center and then forces them outward, much like a jet engine.

5. Select Bomb, and go to the Modify panel.

6. Change the Strength to −.25.

Notice how the statuette implodes rather uniformly. There is an obvious pattern to the explosion. The Chaos variable works well to diminish the uniformity of the bomb's force. For this example, set Chaos to 3, which randomizes the explosion pattern.

7. Set the Chaos value to 3.

8. Scroll the Frames slider to see the result of the animation.

9. Now make some changes to the gravity to alter how the statuette comes together. Gravity affects the motion of the exploded geometry after the detonation frame (discussed next). For now, set the gravity to 0.

10. The detonation frame specifies when Bomb affects the geometry with the Strength variable set. The default is frame 5, which means that the

object will implode starting at frame 5. This is the opposite effect from what you want, which is for the object to explode at frame 0, and reform by frame 120. In order for this to happen, the detonation frame needs to happen before frame 0, so set the detonation parameter to −100.

The last step is to animate the Strength parameter. To have an object start exploded or imploded and reform to the original object, animate the Strength, going from whatever Strength you specify at frame 0 to zero Strength by the frame you want.

11. Go to frame 120, and click the Animate button.

12. Set the Strength value to 0.

13. Make a preview of the animation.

14. Notice how the statuette comes together by frame 100. You can further tweak this animation by going into Track View and editing the function curves for the Strength parameter. Figure 23.23 shows the result of using Bomb with the preceding steps.

FIGURE 23.23

Four frames from the completed statuette animation showing the various Bomb space warp parameters.

Particles & Dynamics Space Warps

This chapter has discussed space warps for geometry, but what about creating effects with particles? In the Create panel, under the Space Warps tab, is the Particles & Dynamics class of space warps. The Particles & Dynamics class of space warps is used for just that, Particles and Dynamics simulation. This section will describe this class of space warps on particles. For information on using these space warps in Dynamics Simulation, refer to Chapter 24 and the section on the Dynamics Utility.

Particles in and of themselves are just a stream of particles. In fact, a Particle system without some type of influential force on it can quickly become quite boring. Particles do, however, have some wonderful personality traits.

Particles are unique in that they have flocking characteristics. Although some Particle systems are rendered as dots or ticks, in 3DS MAX R2 they can also be instanced geometry (for more information on particles, see Chapter 22, "Using Particle Systems"). Regardless of which type of particles are used, the characteristics are similar. Groups of particles are typically moving in generally the same direction with some degree of variance between individual particles.

Using space warps on Particle systems is necessary to create effects where similar objects react to environmental factors. Effects such as a school of angel fish, light air currents through a rising column of smoke, or the orderly confusion of a tornado as it rips through a trailer park are all made possible and easier through the use of space warps for Particle systems.

Quite a number of space warps of the Particles & Dynamics class ship with 3DS MAX R2. They include all of the following:

- Gravity
- Wind
- Path Follow
- Displace
- PBomb
- Deflector, SDeflector, UDeflector
- Push
- Motor

Gravity

Probably the most used space warp for Particle systems is Gravity. The Gravity space warp can be used to simulate natural or unnatural gravity. Since Gravity is a simulation, this force of gravity can come from any angle. Particles that move in the direction of the force of gravity accelerate, while particles moving away from the force decelerate.

The Gravity space warp has only three force parameters: Strength, Decay, and Shape. The Shape parameter is that of either a planar effect or a spherical effect. Using the planar effect causes the gravitational force to be distributed along the plane perpendicular to the Gravity space warp object. Using a spherical shape on the Gravity space warp causes the particles to be drawn toward the center point of the space warp object and continue out into a slight spiral effect. The spherical shape option works very well with fountain effects. Figure 23.24 shows how the two affect identical Particle systems differently.

FIGURE 23.24

Identical Spray particles and space warps. The Gravity space warp on the right has a spherical influence.

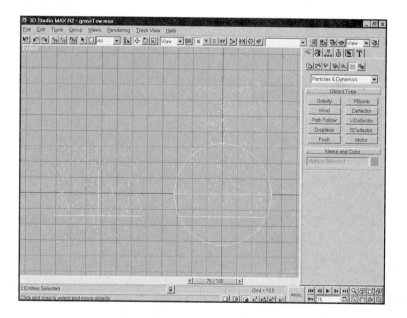

To enhance the effect of Gravity, there are Strength and Decay spinners. By increasing the Strength value, you can increase the amount of gravity placed on particles. If you are animating a scene in which sparks float out

Because this is a space warp, the range of its effect on bound Particle systems can be controlled via the three Range parameters. Using Unlimited Range, all bound particles are affected, while the Linear and Exponential options use the Range spinner to decay the blast force toward zero either linearly or exponentially.

To create geometric explosion effects, (blowing up a space ship, planet, or watermelon), the PBomb can be used with more control than the standard Bomb space warp. Unlike the standard Bomb space warp, the PBomb space warp can be used to explode outward in all directions on a planar, spherical, or cylindrical basis. Figure 23.25 shows the same object using each of the three Blast Symmetry options.

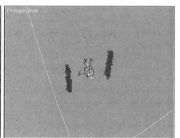

FIGURE 23.25

The same PBomb explosion using Spherical, Cylindrical, and Planar Blast Symmetry options.

Wind

Even on the calmest days, there is always some movement in the air. Using the Wind space warp, you can create disturbances in the atmosphere to give particle streams a more realistic look, from a rising column of smoke to a Level 5 tornado. Study how smoke rises from a match in a very still room and you can learn how subtly wind can affect smoke, steam, or fog. The Wind space warp can be used to create these subtle yet striking effects, and it works on the same principles as the Gravity space warp with the added parameter of turbulence. Both space warps are used to divert particles from their path.

To use the Wind space warp, create the initial space warp icon by selecting Wind from the Particles & Dynamics class of space warps in the Create panel. Bind the Particle system to the Wind space warp using the Bind to

Space Warp button on the toolbar. The Wind space warp parameters can be very sensitive. While you may want your particles to fly around wildly, for many effects, the values are adjusted in small increments to get just the right effect.

When creating a Wind space warp, the initial direction of the wind is in the direction the view's Z axis. In other words, for wind to blow up, create the Wind space warp from a bottom viewport. To blow right, create it from a left viewport, and so on.

The Force parameters in the Wind space warp are the Strength and Decay parameters. Increasing the Strength value increases the effect of the wind. Using a negative value causes the force of the Wind space warp to be in the negative local Z axis of the Wind space warp. By increasing the Decay value, the influence becomes less as the distance between the space warp and the bound object increases.

Primarily, the parameters within the Wind space warp cause subtle effects. By animating the strength (even between positive and negative numbers), a realistic smoke effect can be achieved, as is seen in Figure 23.26.

FIGURE 23.26

Using the Wind space warp with particles can make for interesting smoke effects (with a little help from Video Post).

To further enhance the realism of your wind effect, add some turbulence. The Turbulence, Frequency, and Scale parameters are what give the Wind space warp character. The Turbulence parameter causes a random directional change on the particles, while the Frequency and Scale parameters adjust the behavior of the Turbulence itself. By changing the Frequency value, you can vary the turbulence over time. The Scale factor causes the turbulence effect to be more erratic and irregular as its value increases.

Deflector

Simply put, Deflector space warps act as collision objects. When a Particle system is bound to a deflector, particles that encounter it during their path bounce off or stick to the deflector, depending on the value in the Bounce parameter. Without deflectors, particles continue on their path until either their lifespan expires or they encounter a bound space warp. With a Deflector space warp, you can make rain hit an awning without passing through or water from a fountain flow over a series of obstacles.

Deflector space warps are probably the simplest of space warps to use. They consist of three parameters; Bounce, Width, and Length. The Width and Length are used to size the icon, which is representative of the size of the space warp. The Bounce value is a comparative effect to define the speed of the particles after they hit the Deflector surface. At a value of 1.0, particles leave the Deflector at the same speed at which they hit. Values less than 1.0 cause particles to leave slower, while a value greater than 1.0 causes the particles to increase their speed as they leave the surface of the deflector.

To use the Deflector space warp, click the Deflector space warp button in the Particles & Dynamics class of space warps in the Create panel and drag a 2D rectangle in the desired viewport. Position the Deflector space warp so that it intercepts the particle stream. Bind the Particle system to the Deflector space warp and adjust the parameters as needed. Though the Deflector space warp is two-dimensional, the effect is not one sided. Regardless of which side the particles hit the Deflector, they bounce off according to the Deflector's parameters. Figure 23.27 shows two Deflector space warps in action.

FIGURE 23.27

Two Deflector space warps interrupt the flow of particles to create a small cascade.

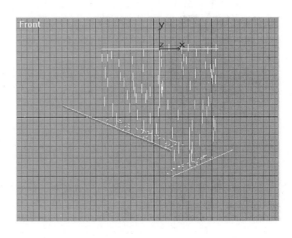

SDeflector

The SDeflector space warp is one variation of the Deflector space warp. While the standard Deflector space warp is planar, the SDeflector is spherical. There are some similar parameters, although the SDeflector also has Variation, Chaos, and Inherit Velocity as additional parameters.

The Bounce parameter works the same as in the Deflector space warp, in that the Bounce value is like a multiplier of the speed at which the particles hit the SDeflector. Values less than 1 cause the particles to move slower after they hit the SDeflector, while values greater than 1 cause the particles to move faster after they leave the surface of the SDeflector.

The Variation and Chaos parameters directly affect the way that particles react when they hit the surface of the SDeflector. The Variation parameter is a percentage parameter that sets the variance limit of the Bounce setting. The variance parameter must be a non-zero positive number. A positive non-zero variation value is the percentage of change in the Bounce setting within particles. The Variance parameter actually creates a range of values for the Bounce setting. If the Bounce was set to 10 and the variance was set to 50 percent, then the actual Bounce value used can be anywhere from 7.5 to 12.5.

The Chaos parameter is also a percentage parameter that sets the variance of the ricochet angle. As particles hit the SDeflector, the angle they bounce off is determined by a number of factors. By setting the Chaos factor to a non-zero positive number, the angle at which the particle normally leaves the surface of the SDeflector is varied by up to 90 percent (if a Chaos value of 100 percent is used).

The Inherit Velocity parameter is used when the SDeflector has motion. It signifies the percentage of the SDeflector's velocity inherited by the colliding particles. If the SDeflector is in motion when it passes through a particle stream, the Inherit Velocity parameter is used when calculating the speed and trajectory of colliding particles' Bounce. If this parameter is set to 0.0, only the other SDeflector parameters have any effect on colliding particles.

Use of the SDeflector is similar to the standard Deflector space warp. Click the SDeflector button in the Particles & Dynamics class of space warps in the Create panel, and click and drag in a viewport to create the spherical SDeflector icon. Bind particle systems to the SDeflector and set the Space Warp parameters. The SDeflector's parameters can be animated to create varying effects.

UDeflector

The most powerful of the deflector space warps is the UDeflector. This space warp enables any renderable object to be used as a deflector object. This is a handy device when the object with which the particles are supposed to collide has a more complex surface than that of a plane or sphere. Using the UDeflector works very much the same as the other deflector type space warps, with some additional parameters, such as Pick Object, Friction, and Inherit Velocity.

The Pick Object parameter is the same as is seen in many other aspects of 3DS MAX R2. Click the Pick Object button and select an object from the scene or from the Select By Name object list. Any renderable mesh object may be used as a deflector object for the UDeflector space warp. The object you choose now becomes the deflector, and particles bounce off of the selected object's surface.

While the Bounce, Variation, Chaos, and Inherit Vel parameters work exactly as they do in the SDeflector space warp, the Friction parameter is used only in the UDeflector space warp. The Friction parameter determines how "tacky" the surface of the deflector is. For particles bouncing off of a concrete fountain, for example, the Friction parameter is higher than if the particles were snowflakes hitting ice. This field is subjective and requires fine-tuning when all other parameters are in place.

To use a UDeflector space warp, click and drag an icon in a view port. Click the Pick Object button in the Object-Based Deflector rollout and select a geometric object. The object which is used as a collision object must interrupt the stream of particles. The selected object will now act as a deflector as particles strike its surface. As seen in Figure 23.28, any geometric object can be used as a deflector object.

FIGURE 23.28

The UDeflector space warp utilizes any object as a deflector of particles.

Path Follow

If you would like particles to travel in a very specific path, the Path Follow space warp is just the thing for you. This space warp uses a Shape object as a path for the particles to travel along. Any shape or NURBS curve can be used, although if a shape with multiple splines is used, only one of the splines is followed.

To use a Path Follow space warp, click the Path Follow button in the Particles & Dynamics class of space warps in the Create panel. Click and drag in any view to create a Path Follow space warp icon, represented by a cube with wavy lines.

Using the Path Follow space warp can really offer increased control over how your particles react. By animating the shape of a NURBS curve Path Follow object, interesting effects can be achieved with greater control and ease.

The Path Follow space warp has an extensive parameter list. Primarily, it is necessary to pick a Shape object as the Current Path. Picking a path utilizes the standard Pick Object functionality. Click Pick Shape Object in the Current Path parameter, then click a Shape object or select from the Select By Name button on the toolbar.

Checking the Unlimited Range button means that, regardless of where the Path object is located, its effect on bound particles is the same. When unchecked, the influence the Path object has on bound particles is limited to the value in the Range spinner. This influence is based on the distance between the first vertex in the path shape and the particle emitter location.

NOTE

If the life span of the particles is longer than the time it takes for the particles to travel the length of the Path Follow Path shape, different results occur, based on the Range spinner value. If the Range is Unlimited or large enough to more than cover the distance of the Path Follow Path shape, the path is repeated and particles continue along on another instance of the path. If the Path Follow Range spinner value is longer than the distance covered by the path and less than the life span of the particles, the bound particles repeat the Path shape pattern until the Path Follow Range spinner value has been exceeded.

In the following exercise, you will create a tornado effect using the Path Follow Space Warp.

CREATING A TORNADO USING THE PATH FOLLOW SPACE WARP

1. Open file 23maxtrn.max. This file contains a camera, dummy, helical spline, and a spray Particle system.

2. Create a Path Follow space warp by selecting Path Follow from the Particles & Dynamics class of space warps, found under the Space Warps button in the Create panel, and dragging out a PathFollow space warp icon.

3. With the Path Follow space warp selected, select the Modify panel and click on the Pick Shape Object button to choose the path to follow. Select the helical spline (linked to the Dummy object).

4. In the Particle Motion parameters, choose Along Offset Splines for the Path Follow space warp.

5. To expedite the process, much of the work for the Spray Particle system has been done. Select the spray Particle system and bind it to the Path Follow space warp using the Bind To Space Warp button located on the toolbar.

6. Because the tornado is a mass of organized chaos, the Particle Motion parameters should use some degree of variance. Select the Path Follow space warp, then go to the Modify panel and set both the Stream Taper and Variance parameters to 85 percent. Select Both for the Converge/Diverge characteristics. Stream Swirl can be set to 5 with an 88 percent Variance setting. Also, set the Swirl characteristics to Bi-directional.

7. The key to this effect is in the Motion Timing parameters. The Travel Time is the length of time in frames it takes for particles to travel the length of the spline. In effect, this is the speed of the particles. For this exercise, set the Travel Time parameter to 50. Set the Variance to 13.31 percent.

8. For the particles to continue throughout the animation, set the Last Frame parameter to 250.

To really have fun with this exercise, you may want to add a few trailer parks and cattle to get swallowed up in the storm. By using different Particle systems, you can achieve other exciting effects. In particular, a PArray Particle system can be used with instanced geometry to pick up innocent passersby as the storm moves through unassuming communities.

Particle Motion

The actual motion of the particles is determined by the Particle Motion parameters. These parameters determine the speed, path, taper, convergence, and swirling effects that can be applied to bound particles.

The first choice to make is whether to choose Along Offset or Parallel Splines. When using Along Offset Splines, the distance between the Particle system and the Path object affects the motion of the particles. The particles follow the path using the first vertex of the path as a guide, but if the path is moved away from the emitter, the particles take into account this offset during their motion. When using Along Parallel Splines, a copy of the spline path is aligned to the center of the bound Particle system regardless of the distance of the original spline. Although distance is irrelevant when using Along Parallel Splines, orientation of the spline does matter.

If you select the Along Parallel Splines option, the particles follow a copy of the selected spline projected through the particle emitter. When a rotational transform is applied to the path spline, the particles of the bound Particle system inherit that transformation as well. Particles are also still emitted in the direction used by the Particle system but immediately follow the path along its transformed vertices. Figure 23.29 shows the same Particle system bound to duplicate splines, although one has a 90 degree rotation.

FIGURE 23.29

All duplicate objects in this scene are identical. The only difference is that the spline on the right has been given a 90 degree rotation.

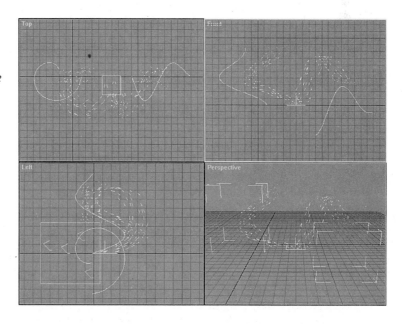

To add a little variation to the particles traveling along the path, you can set Stream Taper parameters to Converge, Diverge, or both. This option causes the particles to move toward or away from the path (or both) over time. Setting Variation causes a variation of that amount in Stream Taper when Stream Taper is set to a non-zero number. When Stream Taper is set to zero, the Variation amount has no effect.

To add a swirling effect to the particles as they travel along the path, set the Stream Swirl parameter. Although this adds additional variance to the particle stream, when used with the Stream Taper effect, you can actually change the diameter of the swirling particle stream as it moves along the path.

Motion Timing

In addition to controlling how the particles are affected by the path, the Path Follow space warp also controls how long the path influences the particle stream. Within the Motion Timing parameters, the Start and Last Frame parameters specify the first and last frame in which the specified path influences the particle stream. Use the Travel Time parameter to control how long (in frames) it takes for a particle to travel the length of the path. By changing the Variation parameter, you can effectively add random slowing and speeding up of particles within the stream. The Uniqueness parameter is used to seed the effect, and each number affects the space warp slightly, so that the effect is varied and won't look canned.

By changing the Start Frame and Last Frame parameters, multiple Path Follow space warps can be applied to a Particle system, with each spline influencing the particle stream during the frames specified in the Start Frame and Last Frame parameters. Particles will move about unaffected by the space warp until the specified range of frames is encountered. This is a nice feature when using multiple Path Follow space warps to create complex smoke effects. Making realistic smoke takes patience and practice (and sometimes many space warps) to create an effect that looks convincing.

Push

The Push space warp is used to exert a unidirectional force onto a particle stream for a given period of time. This is unique because, unlike Wind, the Push space warp applies steady pressure to the particle stream for a specified time only. The Push space warp can also be used in Dynamic

Simulation using the Dynamics Utility. For more information regarding the Dynamics Utility, see Chapter 24.

Push has Timing and Strength control parameters as well as a Periodic Variation parameter set. Use the Periodic Variation parameter to randomly add variation waves to the Force parameter. This gives the push a kind of pulsing effect.

The Timing parameters determine the time range in which the Push space warp is in effect. Setting the On Time parameter to zero and the Off Time parameter to the end of the animation causes Push to continue through the course of the animation. The Push space warp works well if there is a sudden change in environment that would cause the particle stream to bend. An example of this might be when a door is opened and a light breeze blows in to slightly push a rising column of smoke from a cigar. It's a periodic interruption to the regular flow of particles.

The Strength parameters have a Basic Strength parameter that can be based on newtons or pounds. When using the Push space warp on particles, the Basic Strength parameter appears not to be very accurate, but that is simply due to the many factors involved with the Particle system itself. There is no cut and dry formula when using the Push space warp on particles. To create the appropriate Push effect, you must play with the values until the desired effect is achieved.

For additional control over the particle stream, use the Feedback On parameter. This parameter uses the speed of the bound particle stream to control the Push effect. As the particles approach the target speed, the force applied to the particle stream decreases. The Target Speed parameter is calculated in the number of units per frame particles move. The Gain parameter is used in conjunction with the Target Speed to control how immediate the effect is adjusted. With a Gain of 100 percent, the change is immediate, with values less than 100 percent slowing the reactionary time of the Push effect. Overall, the Feedback On feature is a more subtle effect but works well if multiple particle streams are attached to the same Push space warp as each are affected individually, based on the speed of their particles.

To enable a bit of randomness to your Push effect, enable the Periodic Variation. You can select two variation periods and the percentage of effect they have on the Push space warp. When Enable is checked, you can enter a value in Period 1 and Period 2. These values are the frame counts it takes to complete a variation cycle. Setting Period 1 to 15 and Period 2 to 20 means that the first cycle lasts 15 frames and the second cycle lasts 20 frames. The Amplitude settings control the strength of the variation. This is a percentage of the Basic Strength parameter and can be set to any positive value.

The Phase parameter works like the standard Phase parameter in other space warps. It is used to offset the variation of the cycles. There is an Amplitude and a Phase parameter for each of the two periods.

When the Particle Effect Range is enabled, the effect on particles becomes less as the particles move closer toward the boundaries of the Range sphere. Figure 23.30 shows the Push space warp effect.

FIGURE 23.30

The Push space warp and its effect on a particle stream.

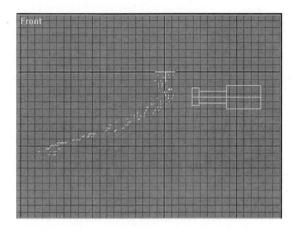

Motor

A cousin to Push, the Motor space warp adds a little twist to the equation. Particles can fly off like sparks on a fiery pinwheel when bound to Motor (see Figure 23.31). Both the Motor and Push space warps share some common parameters, but there are some slightly different applications.

Like the Push space warp, the Motor space warp has Timing, Strength, Periodic Variation, and Particle Effect Range parameters. As in the Push space warp, the Timing parameters are used to determine at what time the effect is to take place. The Strength parameters are based on real-world torque ratings, being calculated either in newton-meters, pound-feet, or pound-inches.

When Feedback On is enabled, the force exerted onto the particles decays as the particles reach the Target Speed value. This limits the effect the

Motor space warp has on particles as they get closer to a predetermined revolution speed. Speed can be measured in rotations per hour (RPH), per minute (RPM), and per second (RPS).

FIGURE 23.31

The Motor space warp flinging bound particles.

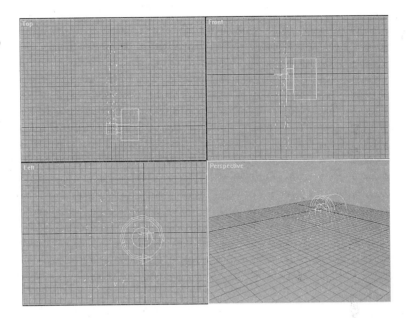

To get the Motor space warp a little variance (similar to a noise effect), use the Periodic Variation parameters. As described in the Push space warp, varying degrees of influence can be implemented by enabling the Periodic Variation and setting cyclical parameters of influence.

Modifier-Based Space Warps

The Modifier-Based space warps are nearly identical to the Object Modifiers of the same name (accessible through the Modify panel). The major differences between Modifier space warps and their Object-Modifier counterparts is that these can affect many objects and they have no Sub-Object selection parameters. Being able to affect many objects is quite a benefit. If you wanted to achieve the same effect with modifiers, you would need to reapply the same modifier with the same parameters to every affected object. That could become a tedious exercise.

The parameters in the Modifier-Based space warps may be very similar to the Object Modifier version, but there are some very important differences. The first difference is the Decay parameter present in the Modifier space warps, which is used to lessen the effect through distance. The effect of a Modifier-Based space warp is based on the relative distance between the space warp and bound objects. What this means is that as the distance between a space warp and a bound object becomes less, the effect is more localized. Notice how in Figure 23.32 the Twist effect changes as the Twist space warp changes proximity to the bound objects.

FIGURE 23.32

The amount of Twist exerted on bound objects depends on their relation to the Twist space warp.

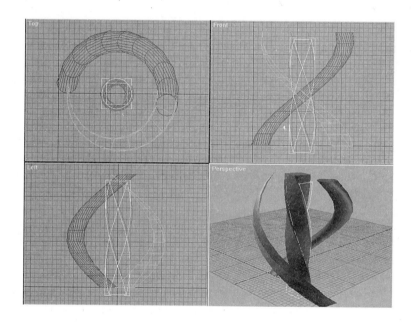

There are six standard Modifier-Based space warps that ship with 3DS MAX R2. They are listed as follows and have the same parameters as their object-based counterparts:

- Bend
- Twist
- Taper
- Skew
- Noise
- Stretch

NOTE

When using Modifier-Based space warps, the relational distance between the space warp and each bound object acts as the center offset. Therefore, the location of the space warp dramatically affects the deformation effect it has on bound objects. Moving it closer to bound objects increases or localizes the effect, making the space warp more pronounced as the distance between the bound object and the space warp gets smaller.

The Modifier-Based space warps are nice in that they can apply a modifier to multiple objects based on relative distance from the space warp. In the following exercise, you will add a Twist space warp to a group of primitives.

USING THE TWIST MODIFIER SPACE WARP

1. Open file 23maxmod.max. There are three primitives and a camera object in this scene.

2. Select the Twist Modifier space warp from the Modifier class of space warps in the Space Warps Create panel. In the Top view, click and drag a Twist space warp icon with a Height and Width of 40 and a Height of 250. This creates a box about the size of the box in the center of the scene.

3. Using the Align tool on the toolbar, align the Twist space warp with the box in the center of the scene. Align on all axes.

4. With the Twist space warp selected, go to the Modify panel and set the Twist Angle parameter to 180 degrees.

5. From the Select By Name tool in the toolbar, select Box01, Cylinder01, and Pyramid01 and click the Select button. With these three objects selected, click the Bind to Space Warp button on the toolbar.

6. Click the Select By Name button again and select the Twist space warp. As you can see, all three objects have now been deformed by the Twist space warp (as can be seen in Figure 23.32).

The important note to realize here is that each object is affected differently by the Twist space warp. If each was applied an individual Twist modifier, the effect would be completely different. This is because the Modifier-Based space warps use world space, while the Object Modifiers use object space.

Modeling with Space Warps

Space warps not only work well for animated objects and special effects, but they work equally well for modeling. This can be done by using Geometric/Deformable space warps on sub-object selections, or using the World Space Modifiers described later.

If space warps are going to be used for modeling, decide whether the bound object or the effect will be animated. Space warp effects are based on the World Coordinate System and cause the effect to appear animated if bound objects are transformed. For this reason, it may be wise to link both the space warp and the bound object to a Dummy if the effect is not to be animated, yet the bound object must be transformed.

TIP

When using a space warp for modeling purposes only, link both the space warp and the bound object to the Dummy. Instead of transforming the bound object, transform the Dummy so that the space warp and the bound object remain at a constant offset from each other.

As well as considering whether an object will be transformed when using space warps for modeling, you must also consider the Modifier Stack. Unlike modifiers applied to an object, space warps cannot be collapsed into the stack and are evaluated last. This may be a consideration when modeling, because complex models can have very long Modifier Stacks.

The versatility of space warps continues in that not only can they be used in modeling, but they can also be applied to sub-object selections. As you can see in Figure 23.33, a Wave space warp has been applied to only half of the box object.

FIGURE 23.33

Using sub-object selection, a space warp can be applied to only selected faces of an object's geometry.

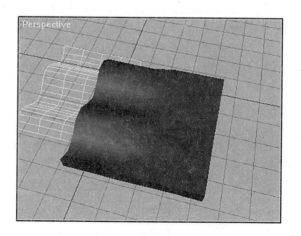

To add a space warp to only a portion of an object, use the MeshSelect modifier, select the desired faces, then bind the faces to the space warp.

ADDING A SPACE WARP TO A SUB-OBJECT SELECTION

1. Open file 23maxsom.max. This file contains a box primitive and a Wave space warp.

2. Select the box object and from the Modify panel apply a MeshSelect Object Modifier.

3. With a MeshSelect modifier applied, you can now select by Vertex Face or Edge. Click the Sub-Object selection level button and choose Face.

4. With the Sub-Object Selection button pressed and Face Selection turned on, you can now select faces. In a Top view, drag to select the left two rows of faces. The selected faces can be seen in darker gray in Figure 23.34.

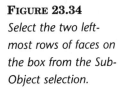

FIGURE 23.34

Select the two left-most rows of faces on the box from the Sub-Object selection.

The selected faces ———

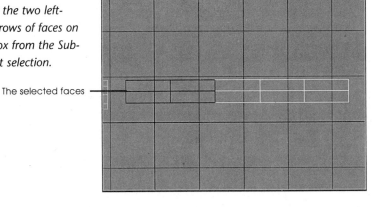

5. With the faces selected, choose the Bind to Space Warp button and click and drag from the selected faces to the Wave space warp. The individual faces are now bound to the Wave space warp (as can be seen in Figure 23.35).

FIGURE 23.35

*The Wave space warp
has been applied to a
Sub-Object selection of
faces.*

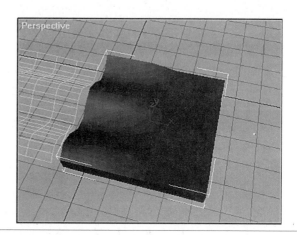

NOTE

When using the MeshSelect modifier and space warps, you must leave the Sub-Object selection button engaged. This appears in the Modifier stack as a MeshSelect modifier with an asterisk preceding it. If the Sub-Object selection is disengaged, the entire mesh is selected, causing the space warp to affect the entire mesh.

NOTE

When working with Sub-Object selection and space warps, remember that the space warps work with world space, not object space. Forgetting this can lead to incorrect results or undesirable effects.

World Space Modifiers

Some Space Warps can only be applied as modifiers and are called World Space modifiers. Like Object modifiers, they must be applied at the object level. Their influence, however, works in World Space. The main reason for this is that these modifiers are based on a link to a geometric object located within the scene. As their name implies, the Path Deform, Patch Deform, and Surf Deform world space modifiers all use geometric objects as the Space Warp gizmo.

Path Deform

Of the World Space modifiers, Path Deform is probably the most straight-forward. You can use Path Deform to twist and turn objects based on a 2D spline. Nice logo effects can be created using the Path Deform space warp because of its ability to deform an object along any single spline. For objects that need to bend and twist along a specific path, the Path Deform space warp is the perfect choice.

The World Space modifiers act a bit differently from other space warps. As a matter of fact, after you create the Path Deform space warp, you really never work with it. The space warp serves only as the deforming catalyst and not as an interactive object. All changeable parameters are accessible through the binding options in the Modifier stack. This is true with all World Space modifiers.

Understanding how Path Deform works can be a bit tricky. First of all, the object deforms in its local space about its pivot point. It does not immediately snap to the path as you might expect. Furthermore, the path deformation takes place in local space by using the space warp as a reference.

The best way to understand Path Deform is to use it. A common example is deforming text along a path.

USING PATH DEFORM TO MODIFY TEXT

1. Open 23maxpat.max from the accompanying CD-ROM.

2. Select the object Text01 and apply the Path Deform modifier from the Modifier List. The default configuration has the Path Deform modifier listed under the World Space modifiers in the More dialog.

3. In the Path Deform parameters, click Pick Path and choose the helical spline object.

You have just created a Path Deform World Space modifier. Because the Path Deform space warp is applied as a modifier, the object does not need additional binding.

As you can see in Figure 23.36, the object re-orients itself. What's happening at this point is that the object is using the Path Deform World Space modifier's Pick shape to deform the bound object, but the deformation takes place in the Pick shape's local space.

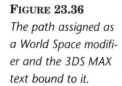

FIGURE 23.36

The path assigned as a World Space modifier and the 3DS MAX text bound to it.

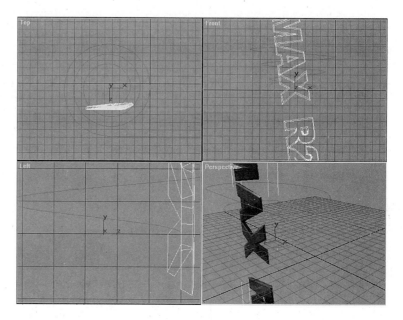

By default, the object deforms along its Z axis. The X axis runs along the length of the text, so you need to change the axis of deformation. All controls for the object using the space warp are located in the Modify panel.

4. In the Modify panel, change the PathDeform axis to X.

5. Check on the Move to Path option.

6. Set the Rotation value to -110.

At this point, the object is on the path and deforming on the proper axis. To animate the object traveling along the path or any other option, you need to change the values by using the Animate button.

7. Click the Animate button or press the N key on your keyboard.

8. Move the Time slider to frame 0 and change the Percent value to -27.5.

9. Click the Animate button, or press the N key on your keyboard. Move the Time slider to frame 150. Change the Rotation value to -50.

10. With the Animate button still on, change the Percent parameter to 101.

11. Make a preview and then play it back to see the results.

Figure 23.37 shows four frames from the final animation.

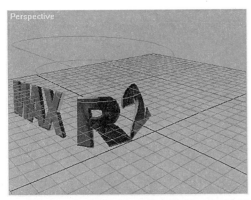 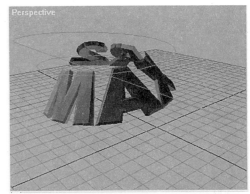
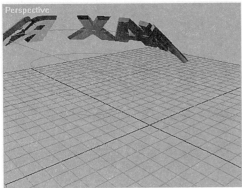 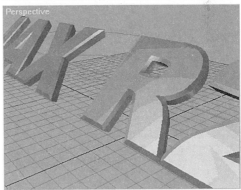

FIGURE 23.37
Four frames from an animation of text using a PathDeform World Space modifier.

Other values include Stretch and Twist. You can use these values to alter the shape of the deforming object on the path. Use Stretch when you want to give the object the appearance of shrinking or growing along the path. The Twist value actually twists the object the number of degrees set in its value over the length of the path. If you had a straight line path and a twist value of 360, the object would twist along the path 360 degrees from one end to the other.

WARNING

The Move To Path option is animatable. Use caution when toggling this option on or off while the Animate button is on.

Patch Deform and Surf Deform

The Patch Deform and Surf Deform World Space modifiers are very similar in that the only difference between the two is that the Patch Deform uses Patch objects, and the Surf Deform uses NURBS surfaces. Like the Path Deform World Space modifier, these space warps use other objects within a scene as a Reference Gizmo for influencing bound objects.

What is really exciting about these space warps is that, in effect, they are customizable space warps. By creating surfaces through patch or NURBS modeling, you can use those surfaces to deform bound objects. Patch Deform and Surf Deform use the control points of the patch or NURBS surface to deform the bound object.

Both the Patch Deform and Surf Deform space warps have two parameter sets: Deform and Deform Plane. The Deform parameters are used for selecting a patch or surface and for positioning and scaling the bound object. The Deform Plane parameters are used to assign an alignment plane for the bound object.

To use a Patch Deform or Surf Deform World Space modifier, it must first be applied to an object through the Modify panel like a standard modifier. Once applied, all access to the space warp is done through the space warp binding in the Object Modifier Stack. Before any other adjustments can be made to the modifier, a reference object must be selected. This is done through the standard Pick Object button in the Deform parameter set.

PatchDeform only allows for quad patches, while the Surf Deform only allows for NURBS Point and CV surface objects. Once the reference object has been picked, you can position the bound object on the reference object. The offset position of the object's pivot point against that of the patch or NURBS surface when the modifier is applied influences at which position the object is placed on the Deform modifier's gizmo. The UPercent and VPercent parameters are used to position the object along the horizontal and vertical axis of the Reference Gizmo, respectively, when using the Move To button. Positioning is based on percentage of the overall distance for each parameter. The default of 50 percent centers the object with the Reference Gizmo. Values other than 50 percent move the object closer to one side or the other, with 0 and 100 being at either end (depending on the view used for creation).

The Stretch parameters scale the bound object along the gizmo object by the value of the UStretch and VStretch spinners. This value works as a multiplier, in that a value of 1 is 100 percent, while a value of .5 is one half the scale of the original object.

The Rotation parameter is used to rotate the bound object in relation to the Reference Gizmo. This can be set to any value and can also be animated (along with the other Deform parameters).

WARNING

The Move To option is animatable. Use caution when toggling this option on or off while the Animate button is on.

Using the Move To button, an object can be moved to an absolute position on a Patch or Surface object based on the spinner values. When using the Move To button to move an object, the actual movement is based on the relative position of the object's Pivot point and the Patch or Surface object.

The Deform Plane parameters are used to specify which plane (XY, YZ, ZX) of the bound object is to be made parallel to the XY plane of the Gizmo patch. When the Flip option is checked, the gizmo path is flipped 180 degrees.

With the Patch Deform and Surf Deform World Space modifiers, you can create your own space warp shapes, instead of using the standard Ripple and Wave types. Since NURBS are inherently smooth curves, using the SurfDeform modifier can really lead to some very interesting animated effects. In the following exercise, you can see how the Surf Deform space warp can be used.

USING THE SURF DEFORM WORLD SPACE MODIFIER

1. Open file 23surfdf.max from the accompanying CD-ROM. This file contains two objects: a teapot primitive and a NURBS surface.

2. Select the teapot primitive. Apply a Surf Deform World Space modifier by clicking the More button in the Modify panel and selecting Surf Deform from the World Space modifiers.

3. Under the Surface Deform parameters, click the Pick Surface button and select the NURBS surface object located next to the teapot.

4. Notice that the teapot immediately becomes re-oriented based on the NURBS surface parameters. Lock the X axis (View mode) and move the teapot along the view's X axis.

As you move the teapot along the X axis, you can see that the deformation of the teapot coincides with the shape of the NURBS surface.

5. Select the NURBS surface and make a sub-object selection on the Surface CVs. Select one of the interior surface CVs and move it around. Notice how the teapot changes shape.

Although this example is a very preliminary example of how to use the Surf Deform World Space modifier, the possibilities are endless. By using very complex NURBS surfaces or quad patches, you can create many exciting things. If you want teardrops to roll down the face of a statue, for instance, you can use a NURBS surface of the statue's face to deform the tear as it rolls down an alabaster cheek.

In Practice: Using Space Warps

- **Space warps work in world space:** Unlike modifiers, space warps affect objects in world space. Both the object's and the space warp's position in space are important. The effects of a space warp change as a bound object moves through a scene.

- **Space warps are evaluated last in the stack:** When you bind a space warp to an object, remember that the binding is evaluated after all modifiers are applied. If you want to bind a space warp to a sub-object selection, make sure the selection modifier is the last modifier in the stack.

- **Displace space warp:** The Displace space warp can be found under both the Geometric/Deformable and the Particles & Dynamics space warp categories. Though the Displace space warp is identical for particles and for geometry, it affects particles somewhat like a Deflector, while it affects geometry by distorting the vertices. In either case, the Displace space warp uses a grayscale image's luminance values to determine the effect.

- **Geometric/Deformable space warps:** The Geometric/Deformable space warps work on any deformable object. This includes lights, cameras, standard geometry, 2D splines, and NURBS objects. Applying a space warp to a spline used as an animation path deforms the path according to the type of space warp.

- **Space warps on NURBS surfaces:** When using a space warp on a NURBS surface, the effect must be calibrated to influence the points or CV on the surface. If the points or CV of the NURBS surface are greater than the parameter values in the space warp, the effect may not move the control points enough to make the space warp's effect visible.

- **Particles & Dynamics:** The Particles & Dynamics space warps can be used on Particle systems for many effects, including collision, turbulence, and explosions. Some of the Particles & Dynamics space warps may also be used for Dynamic Simulations.

- **Modifier-Based space warps:** The Modifier-Based space warps are identical to their named modifier counterparts, although they work in world space instead of object space. These are extremely useful when applying the same modifier to a selection of objects.

- **World Space modifiers (WSM):** The World Space modifiers are space warps that are applied at the object level, but their effect is based on world space, as opposed to object space.

Chapter 24

ANIMATION UTILITIES

When you open the Utilities Command panel, you'll notice many newly added tools to aid in the creation of your scenes and animations. In the previous versions of MAX, the utilities did not show up in the panel itself until selected from the dropdown list and were limited to several small moderately helpful tools. This Command panel has been greatly expanded to include many more useful tools, which are now accessed by buttons on the panel. Two of these utilities are specific to animation. This chapter covers the following animation utility topics:

- Working with Motion Capture
- Dynamics

Working with Motion Capture

 The addition of the Motion Capture capability for MAX R2 has greatly broadened the power of the animator. With this controller you can now use several common computer devices to gain control over any of the properties for objects, cameras, lights, and materials. From your desktop you can orchestrate an entire scene with your mouse, keyboard, joystick, or even a MIDI keyboard. This section will go over the types of Motion Capture devices, their properties, and using Motion Capture to set up character animation.

The Motion Capture Controller

Before you begin to use Motion Capture, you should become familiar with how to set up the controller and assign a device to the properties of an object. The Motion Capture utility is linked through a controller that is assigned to an object's property from inside the Track View window. When you open the Track View, the list in the left window contains the objects, materials, lights, and everything else that makes up the world you have created. Anything in this list has properties that are editable directly with keys or through controllers. The controller that allows your property to be used with the Motion Capture utility is the Motion Capture controller, which is assigned with the Assign Controller button on the Track View toolbar.

Once the controller is assigned to the desired property of an object, the Properties button on the toolbar becomes activated. By accessing the properties of the controller, you can now assign the type of Motion Capture device to that object property.

Types of Motion Capture Devices and Their Properties

In MAX R2, four types of devices can currently be used for a Motion Capture session: the keyboard, mouse, joystick, and a MIDI input. You might think a Motion Capture device includes a bulky suit worn by a participant with sensors inside to measure the movement of the participant. This traditional approach is not very user-friendly and the cost is too high for all but the largest of facilities. For the average user, however, the Motion Capture tools in MAX R2 will do very nicely because the cost is already built into your existing setup. The Motion Capture utility is included with MAX, and the keyboard and mouse are standard equipment included with your computer.

The Keyboard

The keyboard, the most common computer component, takes your keystrokes and transforms the keypresses into your desired motion. After you have made the proper link to your object's desired property, you assign a key to that property by pressing the Assign Key button. Once assigned, the motion of your object is governed by the settings in the Envelope Parameters and Parameter Scaling areas of the Motion Capture Properties dialog (see Figure 24.1).

FIGURE 24.1

The Keyboard Motion Capture dialog.

The Envelope Parameters area contains the following settings:

- **Envelope Graph:** Graphically depicts the settings found in the groups below it.

- **Attack:** Measures how long after the keypress the full range of motion takes place. The greater the number is, the longer it takes to reach the full range of motion. The full range is the number of units set in the Parameter Scaling area of the dialog. The default value is 10 units.

- **Decay:** Determines how long it takes to fall back down to the level specified in the Sustain spinner after the object has reached the maximum value of motion.

- **Sustain:** The fraction of the full range of motion that you decay to. A Sustain level of 1.0 means that the motion does not fall back; the object remains at the maximum motion level. A Sustain level of .5 means the motion falls back to half the original forward motion at the rate set in the decay.

- **Release:** Governs the rate of going back to the original at-rest position after you release the key.

The Parameters Scaling section contains the following parameters:

- **Time:** Measured in seconds and sets the scale of the Attack, Decay, and Release settings. An Attack setting of .25 with a Time setting of 1.0 means the Attack will be one-quarter of a second.

- **Range:** The range of motion for the object measured in units. A Z position motion with a range of 20 moves the object 20 units up in the Z axis.

The Mouse

When used as a Motion Control device for a position, rotation, or scale of an object, the mouse offers a wide range of motion. A mouse has two directions of travel: horizontal and vertical. The motion of your object is taken from the horizontal or vertical movement of your mouse or a combination of both. (see Figure 24.2).

FIGURE 24.2

The Mouse Motion
Capture dialog.

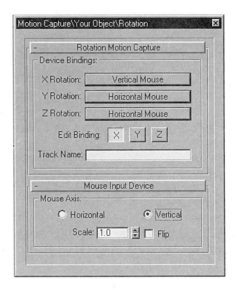

The Mouse Axis option in the Mouse Motion Capture dialog enables you to choose a direction for an object's movement based on the choice of mouse movement selected. Here you select either the horizontal or vertical choice.

- **Scale:** With a low scale value, it takes more mouse movement to affect the object. A higher number moves the object a great amount with very little movement of the mouse.

- **Flip:** Flip reverses the direction of movement. If you set the X position of an object to be a horizontal mouse movement, moving the mouse to the right produces a positive X movement of the object. If you select Flip, a right movement of the mouse produces a negative X movement.

The Joystick

The Joystick device driver is designed to take advantage of the many controls on the Microsoft Sidewinder joystick. It works with a standard joystick as well (see Figure 24.3).

FIGURE 24.3

The Joystick Motion Capture dialog.

The Joystick Motion Capture dialog contains the Joystick Axis area on its panel. This choice enables you to choose the joystick direction that will cause object action, either in the X, Y, or Z axis. On the Sidewinder you have the additional Z direction not found on standard joysticks. Twisting the joystick handle activates the Z axis on the sidewinder.

- **Throttle:** This slider control on the Sidewinder is found next to the joystick handle.

- **Scale:** This is equivalent to the Mouse Scale parameters.

- **Flip:** This the same as the Mouse Flip.

- **Accumulate:** When left unchecked, the motion of the object is an absolute movement based on your joystick moves. When checked, a small movement of the joystick starts the object in motion and continues to move until the stick is returned to the rest position.

The Joystick Buttons area in the Joystick Motion Capture dialog is specific to the Sidewinder. Some joysticks may or may not support these button settings. These buttons are as follows:

- **Point of View Hat:** This is for the Minor Joystick control on the tip of the joystick handle and sets the direction indicated by your choice on the panel, either Left-Right or Up-Down.

- **1,2,3,4:** The numbers are for one of the four buttons on the Sidewinder. When the control is set and the button is pressed, the output value for the object is only active for the time the button is pressed. Releasing the button returns the value to zero.

- **Inc/Dec:** When one of the numbers above is chosen, the Inc/Dec choice increments the output value while the corresponding button is pressed and decrements it when let go.

- **Inc:** When a selected button is pressed, the output value assigns increments only, leaving the object where you sent it even after letting go of the button.

- **Absolute:** If Absolute is selected, the output value instantly changes to the value specified by Speed when the joystick button is pressed. When the button is released, the output value instantly returns to zero.

- **Speed:** This is a rate of change for motion assigned to either the Point of View Hat, or the numbered buttons options.

The MIDI Device

The MIDI Motion Capture contains 16 channels that allow you to set up a MIDI event from a MIDI keyboard or other MIDI device as the Motion controller. Select a channel and set the parameters from the areas in the MIDI Device rollout.

Using the Motion Capture Utility

A typical Motion Capture session consists of the creation of the objects in the scene, assigning the Motion Capture controller to a property of the object, testing the range of values of the capture device, and finally recording the animation using the capture device. The recording will typically be done in stages so you do not have to perfect the motion in one sitting. For instance, in a facial animation you may decide to record all the eye movements first. When you are satisfied, you'll work on other facial movements until the entire face has been animated to your specifications.

In the following exercise, you will create a teapot and assign the Motion Capture controller to several of its properties. You will then test several values for the device. After the values for the device have been tested and you are satisfied with the motion, you record the animation in stages. You will rotate the teapot and make it squash. The lid will also pop up and down.

USING MOTION CAPTURE TO ANIMATE A TEAPOT

1. After starting MAX, open the file named TBouncer.max found on the accompanying CD. The file consists of a moving and bouncing teapot that has been tilted.

2. Open the Track View and expand all the objects. Look for the teapot, select the Rotation transform and assign it a Rotation Motion Capture controller using the Assign Controller button on the toolbar.

3. Select the Properties button on the toolbar or right-click the Rotation transform. Go to the Properties window and in the Device Bindings area, select the X Rotation button, and assign a Keyboard Input Device.

4. Click the Assign button and press the X key. In the Track Name window type: **X Rotation/X-Key**. Close the dialog.

5. Select the Scale transform and assign it a Scale Motion Capture controller. In its Properties window, select the X, Y, and Z scale and assign the Keyboard Input device to each. To assign a key to each, select the appropriate axis next to the Edit Binding label, and assign the S key for all of them using the Assign Key button. Name this **Squash/S-Key**.

6. In the X scale and the Z scale, scroll to the bottom of the panel and make the range -10.0. This squashes the object when the S key is pressed. Close the dialog.

7. Find the Lid object and in its Position transform assign the Position Motion Capture controller. In the Z Position, assign a Keyboard Input Device and assign the L key. Name it **Lid Pop/L-Key**. Close the dialog.

You now have a basic setup and are ready to test the initial values.

8. Open the Utilities panel and select the Motion Capture button. This opens the Motion Capture rollout. The large window in the Tracks area contains the names you typed in for the various transforms. The names aid in testing so you don't forget which key or device you have assigned.

9. Close the Track View window and begin testing by selecting the small white square next to the X Rotation/X-Key label in the Tracks window of the panel. The square fills in red and is now active for either testing or animation.

10. Click the Test button and press the X key. The teapot rotates on the X axis, but its motion does not go far enough. Right-click to exit the Test mode.

WARNING

When you press your key and hold it, MAX plays a sound and keeps playing it until you release the key.

11. Open the Track View and go to the Properties window for the rotation of the teapot. Expand the window to its full length and at the bottom of the panel there is the Parameter Scaling area. Set the Range to -30 and retest the rotation. This is much better.

12. To get a better idea of how this rotation looks with the already prepared animation, click the Play During Test checkbox and retest your X key rotation. This is where you can perfect your timing before actually committing to the animation. Try to get the rotation timed so that the teapot rotates at each dip in the path.

13. When you are ready to capture the sequence, scroll to the bottom of the utility and set the Record Range Out value to match the animation length of 200 frames.

14. Press the Start button in the Record Controls area at the top of the utility. The rotation is recorded in real time as the animation plays.

As the animation plays you may notice that the timing does not quite work. The teapot rotates, but the action is completed before the teapot gets to the bottom of the bounce. You can fix this time lag by adjusting the attack and release values for the rotation.

15. In the Motion Capture utility panel, double-click the X Rotation/X-Key entry. This is an alternative method of getting to the Motion Controller window.

16. Expand the window by dragging the bottom downward. In the Envelope Parameters area, change both the attack and release values to .5. This value allows the rotation to take its time before settling at the maximum rotation value you set.

17. Recapture the sequence. If you're not satisfied with your results, you can simply record over the last capture setting. New keyframe info is written over the last. Continue until you are satisfied with the motion, then save your file. A file with the completed action is on the CD and is named T_Rot.max.

This stage of the Motion Capture is now complete. By building an animation in stages, it is much easier to tweak and perfect individual motions without becoming confused by trying to capture too many actions at once.

In the following exercise, you will add a squash at the appropriate moments and make the lid bounce up and down. You will use the two remaining entries in the Motion Control Utility window, the Squash and Lid Pop entries.

SQUASHING THE TEAPOT

1. Open the file from the previous exercise and go to the Motion control utility. Uncheck the X Rotation/X-Key entry and check the Squash/S-Key entry.

2. Click the Test button and press the S key several times. The squash seems minimal. To get a better cartoon effect, make the squash a little more noticeable. Double-click the entry and expand the Controller window. For the X, Y, and Z axes change the value from 10 to 15, keeping the negative value for the X and Z axes. Retest the squash.

3. Using the same method from the previous exercise, record the squash sequence and time the squash to happen at the bottom of the bounce curve. A file with the finished motion is on the CD and is called T_Squash.max.

4. Uncheck the Squash entry from the utility and check the Lid Pop entry and press the Test button to examine the motion. The attack and release are not good enough to create the desired action, so double-click the Lid Pop entry and change the attack value to 1.5 and the release value to 0. Retest your actions, then record them. A finished file with these actions completed is on the CD and is named T_Bounce.max.

Setting Up Motion Capture for Character Animation

In the previous section, you have seen that the Motion Capture Controller can be used on all of the basic Track View entries for an object, such as its position, rotation, and scale. A further look into the Track View reveals many more possibilities. Just about any object property that shows up in the Track View can be assigned this controller and works as long as the values for that property are adjustable. A bend angle, the position of FFD control points, Taper amounts—these types of adjustments work well with Motion Capture and can be exploited for character animation with relative ease.

In the following exercise, you'll take a static figure and add several modifiers to various parts of his face. You'll next add the Motion Controller to the animatable portions of the Modifier properties and set up the devices you'll use to control these properties. This exercise assumes you have completed the previous exercise and are familiar with the basics of the Motion Capture Controller and its properties.

WOBERT WABBIT EXERCISE

1. Open the file on the CD called Wobert.max. Wobert the Wabbit needs some character, so begin by examining what he is made of. His head is a hierarchy beginning with a dummy object placed at his head's center. The eyes, nose, whiskers, and teeth are all linked to the head (see Figure 24.4).

2. Select the dummy01 object and open the Track View. Go to the dummy01 entry in the Track View and select the Rotation transform.

FIGURE 24.4

Wobert's Hierarchy.

TIP

When you have selected an object onscreen, the fastest way of finding it in the Track View is to press the Zoom Selected Object button on the lower-left corner of the Track View window.

3. Assign the Rotation Motion Capture controller to the Rotation transform of the dummy01 object.

4. In the properties window for the Rotation, assign a Vertical Mouse input device to the X and a Horizontal Mouse to the Y and Z rotation. Name the track **Head Turn/Mouse**.

5. Minimize the Track View window and open the Motion Capture utility. Select the Head Turn/Mouse entry and test the motion. The head turns too much with a small movement of the mouse and the movement does not follow the rotation of the mouse.

6. Maximize the Track View or double-click the Head Turn/Mouse entry and change the scale for each of the rotation axes to 0.2. Click the Flip checkbox for the X Vertical axis. Retest the motion.

The Flip parameter makes the motion you select happen in the opposite direction of the axis for which it is selected. This corrects the motion for Wobert so that a circular mouse movement translates to a corresponding motion on our character.

7. In the MAX toolbar, click the Select by Name button and select the RightEye. In the Track View, click the Zoom Selected Object button. Select the Rotation property for the Right and Left Eyes and assign the Motion Capture controller to them.

8. In the properties for each Rotation entry, select a Mouse Input for all axes. Make the X axis for both eyes a Vertical Mouse movement. Retest the motion for all the entries so far.

Wobert now moves his head around and his eyes move with the mouse as well. You can now add some more interesting motions for Wobert. Now get one of his ears to bend at the touch of a key.

9. In the Front viewport, select Wobert's head. Maximize the viewport and in the Modify panel select the Vertex Sub-Object level. Marquee-select at least half the vertices on Wobert's right ear, the ear facing your left.

10. Add a Bend modifier at this level of the stack. This adds the bend to the Vertex level for the vertices you have selected.

If you change the bend angle at this point, you'll notice the bend happens toward the right. If you wish to have the ear bend forward, you need to change the direction to reflect the forward bend.

11. Select the Sub-Object Gizmo level of the bend and in the Top viewport rotate it 90 degrees clockwise. Now rotate the Gizmo in the Front viewport so it lines up with the ear, as in Figure 24.5.

FIGURE 24.5

The Gizmo placement as seen in the Front viewport.

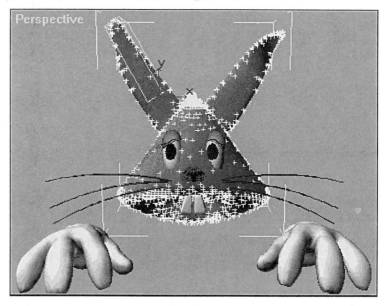

The pivot for the bend is still at the center of the bend rectangle and does not make a convincing movement. You need to move the pivot to the bottom of the bend rectangle.

12. Select the Sub-Object Center level of the bend and move the pivot to the bottom of the rectangle in the middle of the ear. Change the Bend angle and you now have a correct motion.

Now you need to add the Motion Capture controller to the angle property of the Bend modifier and assign it to a key.

13. With the Bend modifier still selected, go to the Track View and click the Zoom Selected Object button. Select the Angle property of the Bend modifier and assign it a Float Motion Capture controller. Go to its properties and in the Device Bindings, select a Keyboard Input Device. Assign the E key and name the track Ear Bend/E-Key. Change the Range to 80 so the ear bends more than the default 10 units and test the motion.

Wobert's ear now bends with the press of the E key. Next, get his whiskers to twitch as well. You'll assign a key for the rotation of the whiskers.

14. Select the RWhiskers and in the Track View, assign a Motion Capture Controller to the rotation transform. Assign a vertical Mouse Input Device to the Y rotation. Do the same for the LWhiskers. The LWhiskers were created using the Mirror tool, so their rotation is in the opposite direction. Select the Flip checkbox for the LWhiskers. When you are finished, test all the separate components.

At this point, you have a selected set of vertices for the Bend modifier. If you wish to give Wobert more motion capabilities, you have to add another Edit Mesh modifier and make the proper vertex selection. Next, get a twitch on his nose assigned to a Motion Capture device.

15. Select Wobert's Head and add a Mesh Select modifier to the stack. Click in the viewport to deselect the ear's vertex selection. In the Left viewport, zoom into the area for Wobert's nose. Select the vertices for the nose area (see Figure 24.6).

FIGURE 24.6
Wobert's nose area showing correct vertex selection.

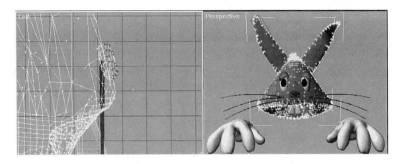

The vertices that are selected are not directly animatable, so you have to add another tool that has an animatable object.

16. Add an XForm modifier to the selected vertices. The XForm has an animatable Gizmo. This is the object you add your Motion controller to. In the Track View, click the Zoom Selected Object button and expand the XForm's hierarchy.

17. Assign the Motion Capture Controller to the Rotation of the Gizmo. In the properties window, add a Horizontal Mouse Input Device to the Y rotation and give it a name like Twitch/H-Mouse. Test the motion.

You can now record some motions for Wobert. Create a final animation using the animation in the stages method you explored in the previous exercise. There is a finished version of Wobert on the CD called Wobert01.max.

The possibilities for assigning Motion Control devices are as limited as the properties you encounter in the Track View window. All the changeable properties for each object, light, or camera can accept the Motion Capture controller, including properties for Object materials. If there is static value data in the Track View edit window, then the corresponding property accepts the controller.

Working with the Dynamics Utility

One of the hardest tasks an animator faces is creating a realistic collision scene. When faced with trying to make pool balls react to the hit of a cue ball, or making an object bounce inside a curved surface, an animator has a formidable and time-consuming task ahead of him. There are just too many variables for consideration to get the effect to look real. 3D Studio MAX R2 now ships with a Dynamics utility that injects all the necessary physics for your dynamic simulation to look very convincing. New dynamic properties for materials and physical objects give you incredible power in determining the action for your scene objects. In this section, you will explore the following concepts and simulations:

- Setting up a dynamic simulation

- Properties of simulation elements

- Pool table simulation

- Reducing keyframe information

Setting Up for Dynamic Simulations

The process of creating great effects with the Dynamics utility is fairly straightforward, as outlined in the following text. Objects are created and forces are added to your scene. You open the Dynamics utility and set up any collisions that may occur, and test the simulation to make sure all is going according to plan. Adjustments are made and retested until the effect is perfected.

You create your scene as you would normally by adding geometry and placing it where you want. After your scene has been completed, you next set the simulation up for static and collision objects. This is accomplished by using the Dynamics utility. You open the Dynamics utility, in the Utility Command panel, and you are presented with a rollout that contains a panel of groups, all of which are ghosted out (see Figure 24.7).

You must first create a new simulation with either a custom name or the name the Utility assigns. This is accomplished by pressing the New button just under the Dynamics Utility rollout. The objects in your scene are added by pressing the Edit Object list and adding all the objects you want in the simulation (see Figure 24.8).

After the Scene objects are added, you now must tell the simulation which forces to apply to which objects, and whether the objects collide or not. Other settings are determined and assigned by pressing the Edit Object button. On the top left of the Edit Object window (see Figure 24.9) is the word OBJECT with a dropdown list underneath. The objects you added with the Edit Object List button will show up here.

FIGURE 24.7
The MAX Dynamics utility.

FIGURE 24.8
Adding objects using the Edit Object List window.

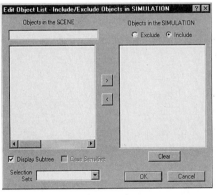

FIGURE 24.9

The Edit Object window.

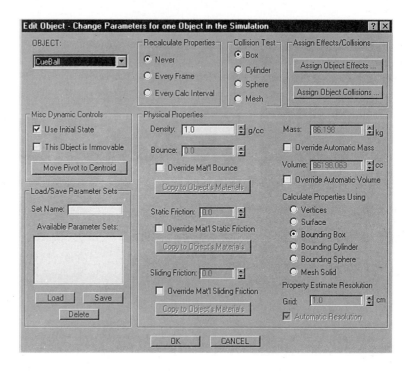

The following sections cover the various groups of the Edit Object window in detail.

Misc. Dynamic Controls

The Misc. Dynamic Controls group below the Object dropdown list tells the utility that you want the object either as a Stationary object or to use its initial state. If an object needs to remain at rest, check the This Object Is Immovable checkbox. The Move Pivot to Centroid button moves the pivot point of the object to its center of mass. You'll only need to select this if you've done some transforming to the pivot point of your object and want to calculate its movement considering where the center of mass may have changed to. Your change to the pivot takes place after you select another object in OBJECT, or when you choose the OK button to exit the Edit Object dialog.

WARNING

Be careful of objects that are part of a hierarchy and the pivot has been carefully arranged. Checking this button alters your linkage.

If you use the initial state of an object in motion, this allows you to give your object a push start. For instance, if an object has a Gravity effect assigned to it, the object drops straight down if its initial state is standing still. If you create a small 5-10 frame animation of the object moving to the right, you can tell the Dynamics utility to start the calculations at frame 10. This allows the Motion vector of the object to be used as its initial state, giving your object a push start in a direction that the simulation then continues to its conclusion. If your object is to start without any preset animation, the Use Initial State checkbox is ignored and you can leave it in its Default state (checked) or you can uncheck it.

Load/Save Parameter Sets

The next group you encounter is the Load/Save Parameter Sets group. Here you can save a particular group of settings and later retrieve them for another simulation. If you want to test many variations of settings for the same group of objects in subsequent MAX sessions, a saved set can eliminate having to retype the information.

Recalculate Properties

The Recalculate Properties group gives you a choice of whether to recalculate the center of mass of an object or not. This recalculation can take place every frame or for every calculation interval. For an object that remains in its initial shape over the course of the animation, the Default of Never will suffice. For an object that changes its shape over time, you may want to explore the Every Frame or Every Calc Interval choices. The Calc Interval refers to the Calc Intervals Per Frame setting in the Timing and Simulation rollout on the main panel of the Dynamics Utility. When the calculation interval is greater than one, there are that many calculations per frame, which leads to a more precise simulation.

Collision Test

Next is the Collision Test group. It is here that you choose how accurately the simulation calculates any collisions that may occur. Think of these test types as a container for the calculation. A box test uses the bounding box of an object and is good for square objects. This test is the least calculation-intensive. The cylinder choice places a cylindrical container around the object in question and restricts its test to the outer edges of the cylinder. The cylinder test calculates the collision from the local Z axis of the cylinder outward to its edges. The sphere test takes a bit longer to calculate and works well for round-to-near-round objects. The last choice takes the longest to calculate and uses the whole mesh surface to figure collisions. Visualize where your objects hit each other to determine the type of collision test to perform. Mesh tests on all objects in your scene take the longest to calculate so be careful with large scenes.

T IP

When testing a large simulation, you should use box, cylindrical, or spherical collision tests. When you are satisfied with the results of this test, apply the mesh test only to the objects for which the animation benefits. Calculation times increase greatly when using the mesh test—remember that you can tweak the placement of objects after the simulation has been calculated. All object motion calculated by the utility is keyframed so you have great control after the fact. Use the Dynamic utility to "rough out" the action and use the Track View to finish up.

Assign Effects/Collisions

The Assign Effects/Collisions group is where forces such as Wind and Gravity are assigned to the object you are working on. If this object must collide with another, this is where you do your setup. Click the Assign Object Collision button to make your object aware of others in the scene.

N OTE

It is not necessary to cross-list all object collisions in a scene. If, for instance, you have two spheres that you want to collide, you only need to assign the collision to one of the spheres.

In the following simple exercise, you will cause one sphere to bounce off of two other spheres. You add the Gravity space warp and complete the effect using the appropriate tools in the Dynamics utility. It is not necessary to bind the space warp forces to the objects they affect. In the Dynamics utility, the forces are taken into account when the scene is calculated.

Scene Elements and Forces

1. Load file ch24_1.max from the accompanying CD.

2. Create a Gravity space warp in the Top viewport, anywhere onscreen.

3. In the Front viewport, rotate the gravity in the Z axis three degrees.

If you rotate a Gravity, the object or objects assigned to it move in the direction of the gravitational arrow. Gravity does not necessarily have to face downward.

4. Click the Utilities tab and click the Dynamics button.

5. Click the New button to create a new dynamics simulation. You can accept the Default name or name the simulation whatever you wish.

6. In the Objects in Simulation group, click the Edit Object List button and select all the spheres. Click the arrow pointing to the right, found in the middle of the Object List window, to add the spheres to the simulation. Click OK.

7. Click the Edit Object button in the same group. For all the spheres, select the Mesh Collision test. Use the dropdown list under the word OBJECT: to select each sphere, and in the Collision Test group, select Mesh.

8. For sphere02 and sphere03, click the checkbox labeled This Object Is Immovable found in the Misc. Dynamic Controls group.

These two spheres remain at rest and sphere01 bounces off them.

9. Select sphere01 from the dropdown and click the Assign Object Effects button in the Assign Effects/Collisions group. Choose the gravity and pass it over to the right window. Click OK.

10. Click the Assign Object Collisions button in the same group. Then choose sphere02 and sphere03, and click OK.

11. Click the OK button on the Edit Object window. You are now ready to have the utility calculate the simulation. Scroll the panel up to reveal the Solve group and click the Solve button. After the simulation has been calculated, play the animation.

With few variations, this exercise has all the elements of a typical Dynamics Simulation. More complex scenes obviously take longer to calculate and as the list of objects grows you should take steps to organize your simulation outside of the MAX environment, with some type of list to help you keep track of what is going on in your scene.

Properties of Simulation Elements

MAX R2 has some new space warps that are linkable to dynamic simulations. The following list of forces can be found in the Space Warps category of the Create Panel. Click the dropdown list and select the Particles and Dynamics choice.

- **Gravity:** Assigning Gravity to a Scene object gives it a constant acceleration. Gravity can be planar, which pulls the object in the direction the icon is pointed; it can also be spherical, which pulls objects with a radial force. Gravity does not take into account an object's size or mass (see Figure 24.10).

FIGURE 24.10

Planar and Radial gravitational forces.

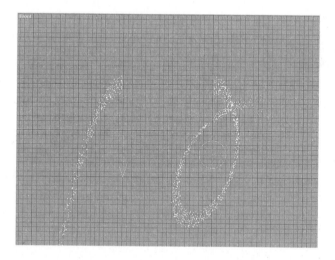

- **Wind:** Wind gives your objects the effect produced by the natural earth force. Wind can be planar, which is like the force that blows leaves all over your lawn, or spherical, which is like the force produced by a fan (see Figure 24.11).

FIGURE 24.11
*Planar and spherical
wind.*

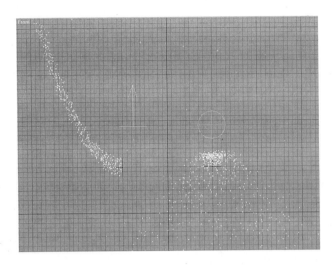

- **Push:** A Push is a force that is affected by an object's size and mass. As in the real world, a heavier object needs more force to move it. The center of mass of an object is taken into account when a Push is applied. If you place a Push on the edge of a box, the box spins about its center of mass. The pushing force must be great enough to overcome the mass and friction for the objects set up in the simulation (see Figure 24.12).

FIGURE 24.12
*A Push applied in this
manner causes the
box to spin.*

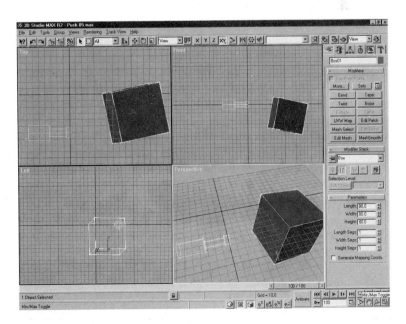

- **Motor:** Motor is an interesting force that creates a torque force for your simulation. This effect can reproduce the forces found in the carnival rides that have chairs on chains propelling the occupants' outward. The object for the Motor effect is rotated about its center of mass and, like the Push, the Motor force must be great enough to overcome any friction and mass forces.

- **Particle Bomb:** Particle Bomb works best with Particle systems for creating explosive shockwaves. In a dynamics simulation, the Pbomb offers an impulse push to an object.

Material Properties

 MAX R2 has a new rollout in the Material Editor that assigns dynamic properties to the material you create for an object. Here you set the Bounce Coefficient, Static Friction, and the Sliding Friction for the material. These settings are then used in a simulation for the object in question. You have the option of overriding the material properties in the Edit Object dialog of the Dynamics utility. This enables you to control the object's behavior entirely from the Edit Object dialog if you are not satisfied with the initial results of your simulation based on the Material properties (see Figure 24.13).

Bounce Coefficient

When an object hits another, the amount of kinetic energy it loses determines how far it bounces. An object that has almost no loss of energy bounces high with a bounce coefficient of near 1.0. A massive object made of lead won't bounce and has a bounce coefficient of near 0 (see Figure 24.14). This spinner has a range of 0 to 1.0.

Static Friction

An object at rest tends to stay at rest. You've heard Newton's gravitational observances. Static friction is how hard it is to get an object into motion on a surface. An oily surface has a static friction value of near 0 while a rough cement surface is more like .6 to .8. This spinner has a range of 0 to 1.0.

FIGURE 24.13

The Material Editor's Dynamic properties rollout.

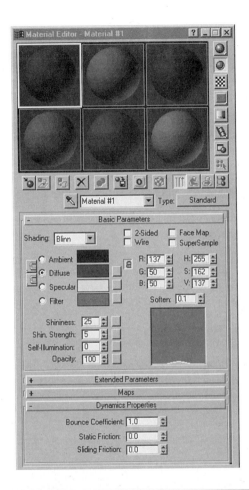

FIGURE 24.14

Objects with differing bounce coefficients at the point of impact. The surface has a coefficient value of 0.0.

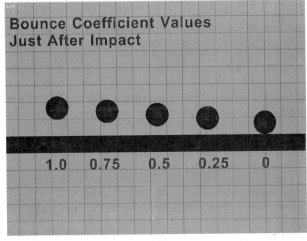

Sliding Friction

An object in motion tends to stay in motion, so goes the rest of Newton's observance. The values for sliding friction allow a surface to keep an object sliding over it or reducing this ability. If an object is in motion and is sliding on a surface with a sliding friction value of 0, it tends to keep on going, and a value of 1 tries to resist it. This spinner has a range of 0 to 1.0.

Physical Properties

In the Edit Object window of the Dynamics utility, there is a large area set aside to assign or override the Material properties you may have set in the Material editor. All objects are given an initial value for their density of 1 gram per cubic centimeter. This value is sufficient for most things like wood or plastic. MAX calculates the mass of an object by multiplying the density by the volume. Volume is measured in cubic centimeters and the mass is given in kilograms. There are several choices you have to make about how dynamics figure the volume of your object; they are listed in the Physical Properties group on the Edit Object window (see Figure 24.15).

FIGURE 24.15

The Physical Properties group.

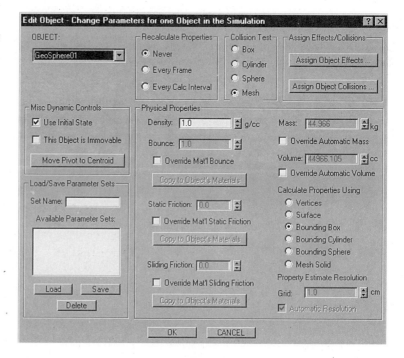

- **Vertices:** An assignment of 1.0 cubic centimeter for each vertex on the object. For objects with an uneven distribution of vertices, the center of mass is closest to the area with the most vertices. This is best used with objects having an even distribution of vertices, such as a sphere.

- **Surface:** This method gives your object a thickness of 1.0 centimeter and if the surface has been deformed, the area with the most deformation is where the center of mass is drawn to. This method is best used for evenly irregular surfaces.

- **Bounding Box/Cylinder/Sphere:** The object is surrounded by the type of bounding container you select and the mass is based on the overall size of the bounding container. This works well for objects that match the shape of the type of container you choose.

- **Mesh Solid:** This method is the most accurate of the selections and calculates the volume based on the geometry of the object itself. This should be your choice if you are trying to depict motion and forces accurately. The Physical Properties group contains spinners and checkboxes that allow you to override the automatically assigned mass and volume. This enables you to give your object properties for a wider range of materials and substances.

In the following exercise, you will create a pool table simulation and attempt to get two balls to go into the pockets. The table and the cue stick have already been created. You will create and place the cue ball and the other two balls.

POOL TABLE SIMULATION

1. Load file ch24_2.max from the accompanying CD. The file consists of a pool table with a cue stick. A Push space warp has been aligned with the cue stick.

2. Create a Geosphere in the top viewport and name it CueBall. Edit it to be 5.5 units in diameter. Check the Base to Pivot checkbox to move the ball up to the level of the table surface.

3. Create two more copies of this ball.

4. Create a Gravity Space Warp anywhere in the top viewport.

5. In the top viewport, move the CueBall so it's in front of the cue stick and place the other balls as in Figure 24.16.

FIGURE 24.16

Pool ball placement.

6. Open the Dynamics utility and create a new simulation. Press the Edit Object List button and add all the objects. Because you are using all the objects for the scene, an easier way to select all the objects is to simply click the Exclude radio button. This works because in effect you are excluding everything in the blank inclusion window.

7. Click the Edit Object button and begin the setup by clicking the drop-down list underneath the word OBJECT. Choose the Table object and make it immovable with a Mesh Collision test.

8. Select each of the balls and make their collision tests a mesh. Then assign each the gravity effect in the Assign Effects/Collisions group.

9. Select the cue stick and assign it the Push effect.

10. Select the Cue Ball and in the Assign Effects/Collisions group, assign collisions with the cue stick, the table, and the other two balls. Close the Edit Object window by choosing OK.

11. Select the other balls and assign them a collision with the table and the other balls in the scene.

12. In the rollout for the Timing and Simulation, set the start time to 0. You are now ready to solve the simulation. Press the Solve button and let the simulation conclude. Time for the calculation is dependent on the speed of your machine.

When your simulation is finished, you may find some of your objects falling through the table surface. To remedy this, increase the Calc Intervals Per Frame and try again. If your balls don't go in the pockets, move them and retry again. A finished version of this simulation with the balls going into the pockets is included on the CD and is called TrckShot.max. There is also an AVI file of the same simulation called TrckShot.avi.

Key Reduction

After creating any dynamic simulation, the objects have many keys associated with their motion. In the Keys Every N Frames option of the Timing and Simulation rollout, the Default value for the amount of keys per frame is one. In a 200-frame animation with several objects, there are invariably more keys than you need. The Track View window contains a feature that allows you to reduce the unneeded keys. In the next exercise, you will open a file with key info already in place and minimize this Track View information.

KEY REDUCTION EXERCISE

1. Load the file TrckShot.max from the accompanying CD. This is a finished working version of the exercise created earlier.

2. Open the Track View window and look at the Motion keys for the three balls in the simulation.

3. On the menu bar, click the Edit Time button. Click the light gray time segment area at the start of the keys at frame zero and drag the yellow line to frame 200. This selects all 200 frames of your animation. The selected time segment length is reported in the boxes at the bottom of the Track View and should read 0 in the first and 200 in the second (see Figure 24.17).

FIGURE 24.17

*Track View Key Info
before reduction.*

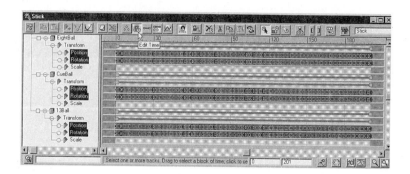

4. In the hierarchy window, select the position and rotation tracks for each of the balls. When these tracks are selected, the Reduce Keys button becomes active.

5. Click the Reduce Keys Button and accept the default threshold. Your keyframe information has now been significantly reduced (see Figure 24.18).

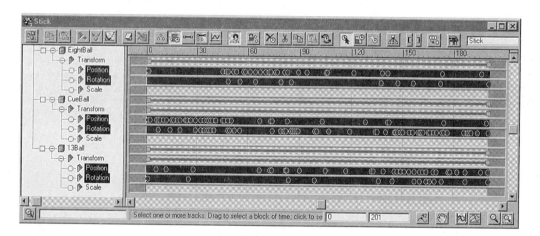

FIGURE 24.18

Track View Key Info after reduction.

Play the animation (or view trakshot.avi from the accompanying CD) and you can see that the motion of the balls has not been adversely affected. Keep this exercise in mind whenever you have created an animation that appears to have too many keys. All Dynamics, Inverse Kinematics (IK), and complex manual animations can benefit by this method.

In Practice: Animation Utilities

■ **When using Motion Capture with complex objects, create the hierarchy needed to get the parts to follow each other.** If the whole object needs to rotate, use a dummy object as the Base object and apply the Motion Capture Controller to it.

■ **Test your motions as you build your capture session.** Work out all the values for the Motion Capture device and then move on to the next task.

■ **When animating, set up in single tasks such as head movement first, eye movement second, and so on until the animation is complete.** If the captured session does not look right, do it over. Redoing it overwrites the last keyframes created.

■ **Test your Dynamics simulations:** If your simulation contains more than a few objects, test it with either a Box or Cylinder Collision test, and use a setting of one for the Calc Intervals Per Frame. After you tweak the simulation, you can then increase the level of collision to a mesh and then increase the Calc Intervals.

■ **Object Collisions:** It's not necessary to cross-reference colliding objects. If Object A hits Object B, you do not have to set up A hits B and B hits A. Keep it as simple as possible.

■ **Object Placement:** If your objects start off on a surface, make sure their geometry does not intersect. Use your Region Zoom tool to get a close look at the Contact point and move the objects close but not actually touching. Objects fall through each other if an intersecting condition exists.

■ **Finalize With Track View:** Remember that the simulation makes keyframe info for all the objects in your scene. Use the Track View to reduce the keys and perhaps change the calculated placement of scene elements.

Chapter 25

USING CONTROLLERS AND EXPRESSIONS

Every time an object is animated in the scene, 3D Studio

MAX saves the data necessary to reproduce the animation.

Usually only keyframes are specified by the animator and

3DS MAX needs to calculate (or interpolate) the animation

data for all frames in between. The object-oriented concept

of 3DS MAX facilitates the usage of various interpolation

types, the superposition of animation data, and the creation

of completely parametric animations.

All animation data in 3DS MAX is handled by items called controllers, which store animation values and manage the interpolation from one value to the next. 3DS MAX ships with a variety of controllers. Understanding the differences between the controllers, how the controllers operate, which controller to use in which circumstances, and how to adjust controller behavior is essential for achieving the exact animation you desire.

To that end, this chapter explains the use of controllers by covering the following topics:

- Understanding controllers
- Choosing controller types
- Classifying controllers
- Single parameter versus compound controllers
- Parametric versus key-based controllers
- Controller data types
- Basic key-based controllers
- Advanced key-based controllers
- Parametric controllers (including expressions)
- Compound controllers
- Copying and pasting controllers
- Global tracks and Global variables
- Converting parametric controller output to key-based animation

Understanding Controllers

When an object is created in 3DS MAX, the core component plug-in associated with that object specifies a list of parameters that can be animated. To conserve memory, these parameters are typically not assigned a controller. If the user animates the parameter, a default controller is assigned to the parameter.

One exception to this is the transform controller, which is always assigned to every new object at creation time. The transform controller keeps track of where the object is located in world space, any rotation data associated with the object, and the scaling factors to be applied to the object. Default controllers are assigned to the transform controller and its input (or subordinate) controllers when the object is created.

Figure 25.1 shows the parameters and default controllers associated with a box that has not been animated but has a material assigned to it. Animatable parameters are signified by a green triangle. For each parameter, the parameter name is shown, and if a controller has been assigned, the controller type follows the parameter name.

FIGURE 25.1

The parameters and default controllers associated with a box with basic material assigned.

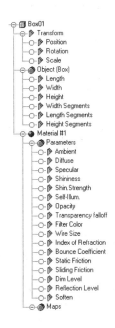

Choosing Different Controller Types

Although default controller types are assigned by 3DS MAX, a parameter's controller can be changed, as well as the default controller types that are assigned to parameters. The controller types for all parameters can be changed in Track View. Transform level controller types at the object level can also be changed in the Motion panel.

To change an object parameter's controller in Track View, complete the following steps:

1. Open Track View and expand the object's tracks to the level of the parameter.

2. Select the parameter and then click Assign Controller.

3. Select the desired controller in the Assign Controller dialog and then click OK (see Figure 25.2).

FIGURE 25.2

The Assign Position Controller dialog in Track View.

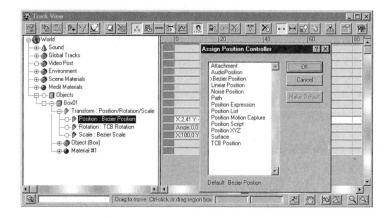

To change an object parameter's controller in the Motion panel, complete the following steps:

1. Select the object and open the Motion panel.

2. Click Parameters and open the Assign Controller rollout (see Figure 25.3).

3. Select the parameter and click Assign Controller.

4. Select the desired controller in the Assign Controller dialog and then click OK.

FIGURE 25.3

The Assign Controller rollout in the Motion panel.

After a controller is selected in the Assign Controller dialog, the Make Default button becomes active. By clicking this button, the selected controller is defined as the default controller for all parameters with the same data type. Now, any time 3DS MAX assigns a controller to a parameter with this data type, the selected controller is used.

WARNING

If a parametric controller (such as the Noise or Waveform controller) is selected as the default controller for a data type, the values for the parameters that use that data type cannot be set interactively. For example, if the Position Expression controller is set as the default position controller, all new objects are created at world origin and cannot be interactively moved.

When a controller type is changed for a parameter, 3DS MAX converts any existing animation data to the format required by the new controller when possible. The animation data will be preserved when changes are performed within this subset of controller types. These include Linear, Smooth, Bézier, TCB, Euler XYZ, Point3 XYZ, Color, and Motion Capture; by changing from one of these to the List controller; or from the On/Off controller to a type of this subset, they are perserved. Otherwise, the animation data is lost.

Classifying Controllers

3DS MAX comes with a multitude of different controllers. Table 25.1 lists all controllers available, sorted by their data types. Most of the controllers support multiple data types and therefore are listed more than once.

TABLE 25.1

Overview of All Controllers Available in 3DS MAX R2

Controller Data Type	Controller Type
Transform	PRS, Look At, Link Control
Position	Linear, Bézier, TCB, XYZ, List, Audio, Path, Noise, Expression, Attachment, Surface, Motion Capture, Script
Rotation	Linear, Smooth, TCB, Euler XYZ, List, Audio, Noise, Motion Capture, Script
Scale	Linear, Bézier, TCB, List, Audio, Noise, Expression, Motion Capture, Script
Float	Linear, Bézier, TCB, On/Off, List, Audio, Noise, Expression, Motion Capture, Waveform, Script
Point3	Bézier, Bézier Color, TCB, XYZ, Color RGB, List, Audio, Noise, Expression, Motion Capture, Script
Morph	Cubic Morph, Barycentric Morph
IK used by Bones Systems	IK-Controller (see Chapter 21, "Building and Animating Hierarchies," for details)
Visibility/Level of Detail	LOD Controller

Controllers can be classified in several ways: by single parameter versus compound, by parametric versus key-based, and by controller data type.

Single Parameter versus Compound Controllers

Single parameter controllers are located at the lowest level of the controller hierarchy (though they can have animatable parameters themselves). These controllers store the animation values specified by the user for an object's parameter and output values over time. The values returned can have either a single component (such as the height of a box) or multiple components (such as the X, Y, and Z position of the object). A single parameter controller can be either parametric or key-based.

Compound controllers take as their inputs the output of other controllers. They then combine this data with any parameter data associated with the compound controller, manipulate the data, and output the results (see Figure 25.4). The compound controllers are the Position/Rotation/Scale (PRS), the Look At and Link Control transform controllers, the Euler XYZ rotation, Position XYZ, Point3 XYZ, Color RGB, and the List controllers. Each of these compound controllers is described in more detail later in this chapter.

FIGURE 25.4

An example of multiple nested compound controllers.

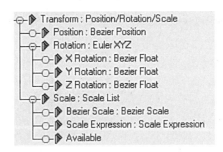

Parametric versus Key-based Controllers

Single parameter controllers can be classified by whether the controller is parametric or key-based. A parametric controller takes as input user-specified data values and then provides as output values based on the equation the controller implements and the input data values. A key-based controller takes as input user-specified data values at specific time points and then provides as output interpolated values for any time point.

An example of a parametric controller is the Noise Position controller. The input for this controller is specified in the controller's properties dialog and includes the frequency and strength of the noise (see Figure 25.5).

Normally this data is specified once and does not change during the length of the animation; no keys are associated with a parametric controller, although some of the parameters of a parametric controller may be animatable by keys, like the strength of the noise in this example. The presence of the controller is represented by a range bar in the parameter's track in Track View. The output of the controller at a given time is based on the parameters (the input data), the time, and the equation implementing the noise function.

FIGURE 25.5

The Noise Position controller properties dialog.

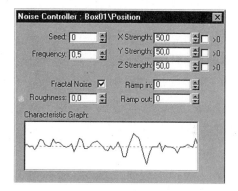

An example of a key-based controller is the Tension/Continuity/Bias (TCB) Rotation controller. The input to this controller is the rotation of the object at specific time points. This data is typically provided by setting the animation frame, turning on the Animation button, and rotating the object. Each time an object is rotated at a different frame, a new data point is generated. These data points are referred to as *keys* and the data specifying the amount of rotation are referred to as the *key values*. The presence of a key is represented by a dot in the parameter's track in Track View.

The output of a key-based controller is based on the key values, the time, and the equation used to interpolate between keys. For some of the controllers, the equation used to interpolate between keys can accept additional user input. With the TCB controller, for example, the user can adjust tension, continuity, bias, and Ease From/Ease To parameters at each key (see Figure 25.6). Other controllers, such as the Linear controller, always interpolate the same way and cannot be adjusted.

FIGURE 25.6
The TCB Position controller Key Info dialog.

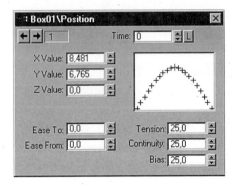

Controller Data Types

Controllers can also be classified by the data type the controller returns. The data type of the controller must match the data type of an object's parameter for the controller to be used with that parameter. A Scale data type controller, for example, cannot be used for an object's position parameter because the two are of different data types. Table 25.2 shows the available data types and examples of the parameters with which they can be used.

TABLE 25.2

Data Types Associated with Parameters

Controller Data Type	Valid Parameters
Position	Object or modifier gizmo position, gizmo center position
Rotation	Object or modifier gizmo rotation
Scale	Object or modifier gizmo scale
Float	Any parameter with a single component value (height, number of segments, roll angle, opacity)
Point3/Color	Any parameter with three component values other than Position and Scale
Morph	Used only for morph parameter
IK (Inverse Kinematics)	Used only for IK of Bones systems
Level of Detail	Used only for visibility/LOD tracks

The Position and Scale data types are dedicated versions of the Point3 data type and can be considered the same data type except when assigning controllers. The only apparent difference between these controllers is that a dedicated Linear interpolation type is available for the Position and Scale data types, but not for the Point3.

3DS MAX internally uses quaternion math to control rotation. Quaternion math, which is used by almost every animation system for things like camera and object rotations, is polar-based (using a three-component vector and an angle/scalar). Quaternion math results in smooth interpolated rotations, whereas matrix solutions (separate X, Y, and Z rotations) result in areas that are not very smooth.

The Rotation data type consists of four component values required for quaternion math: the X, Y, and Z values of a unit vector, and the rotation angle about the unit vector.

T IP

Because the Rotation data type returns four values, it is not possible to display the function curves for a rotation controller in Track View. To work with rotation function curves, use a Euler XYZ compound controller. The input to a Euler XYZ controller is three float data type controllers specifying the X, Y, and Z rotation values. The function curves for each of these float data type controllers can be displayed.

The Color data type is a special case of the Point3 data type. The output from Point3 controllers can have any range of values. The output from Color controllers is limited to a range of 0 to 255.

Now that you're familiar with the differences between classes of controllers, the following sections explore the controller types in more detail.

Basic Key-based Controllers

In this context, basic means that these controller types are fundamental and represent the traditional class of key-based animation controllers, as described previously. They differ by the type of interpolation the controller uses to determine the value(s) to return between keys. For all controllers, the function curve always passes through the key values at the time associated with the key. The different controllers only affect the interpolation of values between keys, not the keys themselves.

Table 25.3 lists the data types for each interpolation type of the basic key-based controllers.

TABLE 25.3

Data Types Available for Each Interpolation Type

Interpolation Type	Valid Data Types
Linear	Position, Rotation, Scale, Float
Smooth	Rotation
Bézier	Position, Scale, Float, Point3, Color
TCB	Position, Rotation, Scale, Float, Point3, Morph (based on TCB)

Each combination of interpolation type and data type is implemented by a unique controller. The method for varying the key values and interpolation parameter values for keys is the same within a group of controllers of a given interpolation type.

For all controllers, key values can be set or adjusted by turning on the Animate button, setting the appropriate time, and then setting the new value for the parameter being varied. Alternatively, the key edit and function curve tools provided in Track View—for transform-related controllers—and the tools in the Motion panel can be used to create and change key values (see Chapter 20, "Animation Control Tools").

For the Bézier and TCB controller types, the values of keys can also be adjusted by right-clicking a key while in the Edit Key or Function Curve modes in Track View. This displays the Key Info dialog, where the values can be changed. Figure 25.7 shows examples of Key Info dialogs for Bézier and TCB controllers. As these dialogs indicate, within an interpolation type, the only change is the number of key value fields; the controls are otherwise the same. The exception to this is the Bézier Color controller. This controller is for use with color parameters only, and the dialog is customized to reflect this. In this controller's Key Info dialog, the user may specify colors by using either the RGB or HSV color models. A color swatch that displays the color specified by the color values is provided. When clicked on the color swatch, the standard Color Selector dialog is displayed.

For transform-related controllers at the object level, the key values and other controller-related parameters (if available) can also be adjusted in the Key Info rollout in the Motion command panel.

FIGURE 25.7

Left side: The Bézier Float, Scale, and Color Controller Key Info dialogs; right side: The TCB Float, Scale, and Rotation Controller Key Info dialogs.

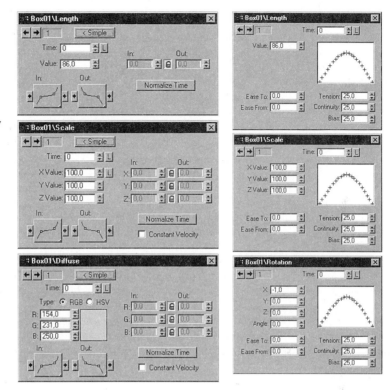

Linear Controller

Controllers using the Linear interpolation type evenly divide the change in key values between one key and the next by the amount of time between the keys. The values returned from the controller follow a straight line between the keys, and the values are evenly spaced over time; that is, the values change at a constant velocity between keys. No adjustments can be made as to how the values are interpolated.

Smooth Controller

Controllers using the Smooth interpolation type adjust the tangent of the curve passing through a key value to provide a smooth interpolation through the key. No adjustments can be made as to how the values are interpolated.

Bézier Controller

Controllers using the Bézier interpolation type use an adjustable Bézier spline curve fitted through the keys to calculate values between keys. The shape of the spline curve is based on the key and tangent values at the keys. Right-clicking a key while in the Edit Key or Function Curve modes in Track View displays the Key Info dialog, where the tangent values can be adjusted.

3DS MAX provides five predefined tangent types and one custom tangent type, which is selected by using the Key Tangent flyout in the Key Info dialog. Figure 25.8 shows a Key Info dialog with the Key Tangent flyout expanded.

FIGURE 25.8

The expanded Key Tangent flyout in the Bézier Key Info dialog.

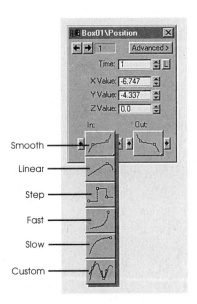

In the following example, you look at the effect of each of the key tangent types on the motion of an object. The scene consists of a sphere that travels in a circular path. Two spline shapes show what the path would be if the path followed was circular or linear. Note that throughout this example, the location of the sphere at a key is always the location specified by the key, and that the time associated with a key never changes.

THE EFFECTS OF BÉZIER TANGENT TYPES ON OBJECT MOTION

1. Load file ch25_1.max from the Chapter 25 folder on the accompanying CD-ROM.

2. Select the sphere and click Trajectory in the Display command panel. A blue line displays the trajectory of the sphere, with white dots signifying frame increments and white squares signifying keys.

3. In Track View, expand the tracks to display the position track for Sphere01. Click Function Curves and then click a curve to display the keys.

4. Perform a region select to select all the keys. Right-click a key to display the Key Info dialog (see Figure 25.9). Reposition the Key Info dialog so that you can see the function curves in Track View and the trajectory for Sphere01 in the Top viewport.

FIGURE 25.9

Accessing the Key Info dialog from Track View.

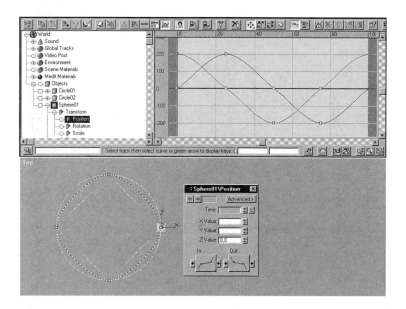

The Key Info dialog shows that all the keys are using the smooth tangent type. The trajectory shown in the viewport and the function curves shown in Track View are representative of smooth interpolation.

5. Click the Y (green curve) key dot at frame 25 in Track View. The Key Info dialog now shows just the parameters for that key.

6. Click and hold the Out Key Tangent flyout, and select the Linear tangent type. The trajectory between the second and third key still curves but is straighter as it exits the second key.

7. Click the right arrow next to the out tangent flyout to set the In tangent of the next key to the Linear tangent type.

As seen in Figure 25.10, the trajectory between the second and third key is straight. The interpolated value 3DS MAX calculated between two keys is based on both the Out tangent of the first key and the In tangent of the second key. The effect of the tangent for a key drops off as you move closer to the other key.

FIGURE 25.10

The sphere trajectory with a Linear tangent type.

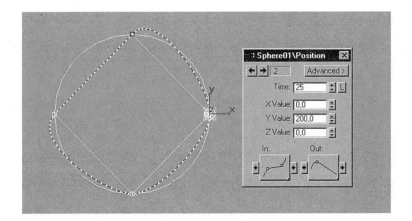

8. Set the Out tangent to the Step tangent type. Drag the time slider through the range of 25 to 50.

9. If the Out tangent for one key is a Step tangent type, the In tangent on the next key is automatically changed to a Step tangent type. The Step tangent type holds the output value constant until the time of the next key. At that time, the value jumps to that key's value.

10. Set the Out tangent to the Fast tangent type. Click the right arrow next to the Out tangent flyout to set the In tangent of the next key to the Fast tangent type. Drag the time slider through the range of 25 to 50.

As seen in Figure 25.11, the sphere moves quickly as it leaves key number 2, slows down, and then speeds up again as it approaches key number 3. The frame increments on the trajectory curve are widely spaced near the two keys and closely spaced in the middle.

FIGURE 25.11

The sphere trajectory with a Fast tangent type.

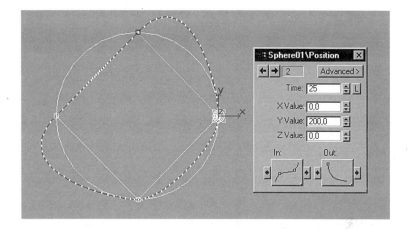

11. Set the Out tangent to the Slow tangent type. Click the right arrow next to the Out tangent flyout to set the In tangent of the next key to the Slow tangent type. Drag the time slider through the range of 25 to 50.

As seen in Figure 25.12, the sphere moves slowly as it leaves key number 2, speeds up, and then slows down again as it approaches key number 3. The frame increments on the trajectory curve are closely spaced near the two keys and widely spaced in the middle.

FIGURE 25.12

The sphere trajectory with a Slow tangent type.

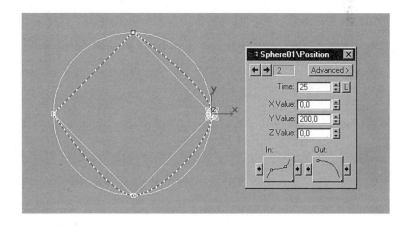

12. Set the Out tangent to the Custom tangent type. The In tangent is automatically changed to a Custom tangent type. In Track View, select all the key dots for this key (frame 25).

13. On each key dot the In and Out tangent handles are shown. The tangents for this key can be adjusted by moving the tangent handles up and down, or by adjusting their values in the Advanced section of the Key Info dialog.

14. Click and drag a tangent handle. As you move the handle, the handle on the other side of the key moves in the opposite direction. The shape of the curve through the key changes as you adjust the handle. An example of a tangent handle adjustment and the resulting trajectory is shown in Figure 25.13.

FIGURE 25.13

The sphere trajectory with a Custom tangent type.

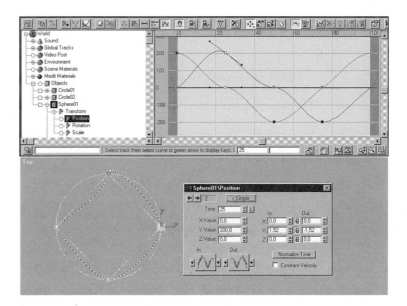

15. Click Advanced in the Key Info dialog, and adjust an In or Out value. Again, both handles change.

16. Unlock the handles by clicking the Lock icon between the In and Out fields for a value. Adjust the In or Out value. Only one handle moves.

The handles can also be unlocked by doing a Shift+click and dragging a handle. After they are unlocked, adjusting one handle does not cause the other to move. You can relock the handles by clicking the Lock icon between the In and Out fields for the value. You can also temporarily lock the handles by clicking Lock Tangents in the Track View toolbar before dragging the handles to adjust them.

TCB Controller

Controllers using the TCB interpolation type interpolate between keys based on five interpolation parameters: tension, continuity, bias, ease to, and ease from. The shape of the function curve is based on the key and parameter values at the keys.

The following list and figures look at the effects of varying each of the TCB parameters on the motion of an object.

- **All keys using the default TCB parameters.** As seen in Figure 25.14, the frame increments on the trajectory curve are a bit closer as you approach or leave a key than they are when you are in the middle between the keys. The sphere moves more slowly around the keys.

FIGURE 25.14

The sphere trajectory with default TCB parameters.

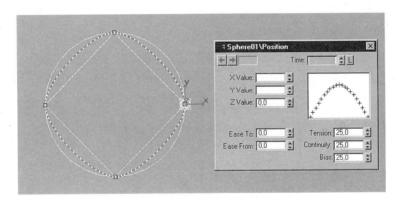

- **Gradually increase the value of Ease To.** As seen in Figure 25.15, as the value increases, the frame increments on the trajectory curve become closer as you enter a key, and further apart as you leave a key. The sphere moves quickly as it leaves a key and slows down as it approaches a key.

- **Set the Ease To value to 0 and gradually increase the value of Ease From.** The effect is the exact opposite of increasing the Ease To value.

- **Set both Ease To and Ease From to 50.** As seen in Figure 25.16, the frame increments on the trajectory curve become closer as you approach or leave a key than they are when you are in the middle between keys. The sphere moves more slowly around the keys.

FIGURE 25.15

The sphere trajectory with an Ease To value of 50.

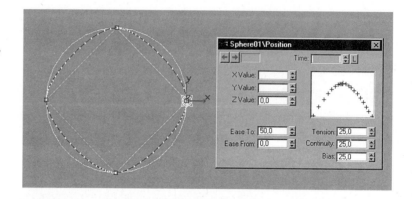

FIGURE 25.16

The sphere trajectory with Ease To and Ease From values of 50.

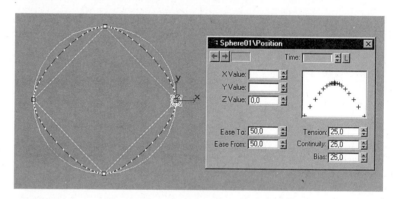

■ **Set both Ease To and Ease From to 0 and gradually increase the Tension value.** As seen in Figure 25.17, the curvature of the trajectory is decreased until it is a straight line between keys. The frame increments are closer around the keys and farther between them.

FIGURE 25.17

The sphere trajectory with a Tension value of 50.

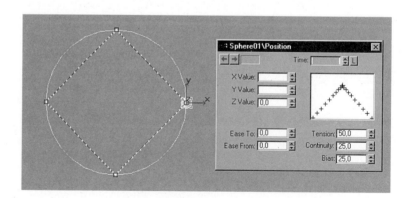

■ **Gradually decrease the Tension value.** The curvature of the trajectory is increased between keys (see Figure 25.18). The frame increments are evenly spaced on the trajectory curve.

FIGURE 25.18

The sphere trajectory with a Tension value of 0.

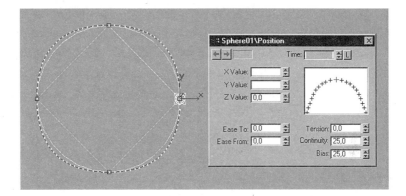

■ **Set the Tension value to 25 and gradually increase the Continuity value.** The angle between the In and Out tangents of the trajectory and function curves increases, causing the interpolated values to overshoot the key values on both sides of the keys (see Figure 25.19).

FIGURE 25.19

The sphere trajectory with a Continuity value of 50.

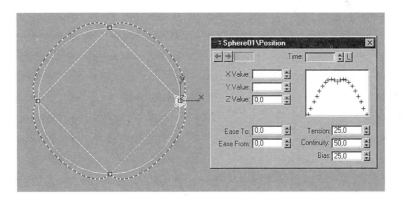

■ **Gradually decrease the Continuity value.** As seen in Figure 25.20, the angle between the In and Out tangents of the trajectory and function curves decreases, causing the curvature of the trajectory and function curves to approach a straight line between keys. The frame increments are evenly spaced on the trajectory curve.

FIGURE 25.20

*The sphere trajectory
with a Continuity
value of 0.*

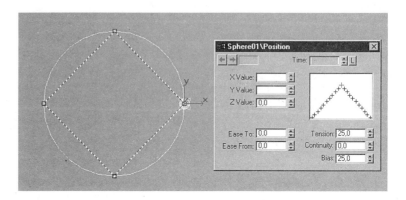

- **Set the Continuity value to 25. Gradually increase the Bias value.** As seen in Figure 25.21, the In and Out tangents of the trajectory and function curves rotate, causing the interpolated values to overshoot the key values as you leave the keys.

FIGURE 25.21

*The sphere trajectory
with a Bias value
of 50.*

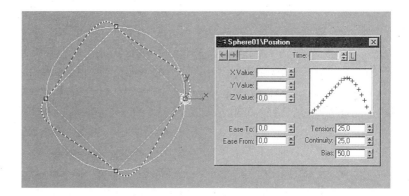

- **Gradually decrease the Bias value.** As seen in Figure 25.22, the In and Out tangents of the trajectory and function curves rotate, causing the interpolated values to overshoot the key values as you enter the keys.

Animators often prefer using the Bézier controller over the TCB controller, especially for complex animations that require a considerable amount of tweaking. The ability to fine-tune function curves by adjusting the tangent values of the keys directly in the function curve display gives better control over the animation. Additionally, it is not possible to adjust the TCB-parameters for one axis of a key without affecting the others (such as when it's used as TCB Position controller). In fact, the TCB controller is a leftover back from the days of 3DS DOS.

FIGURE 25.22

The sphere trajectory with a Bias value of 0.

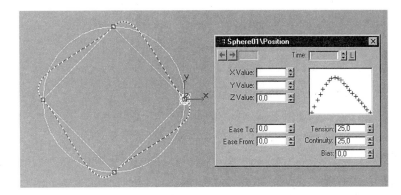

TIP

Position controller keys can be moved, added, and deleted directly in the viewports. Enable Trajectory in the Display Properties of the Display panel for the desired object, then go to the Motion/Trajectories panel and activate Sub-Object Keys.

Advanced Key-based Controllers

The controllers in this section have a more specialized feature set. They provide solutions for certain situations that otherwise would be difficult or impossible to accomplish with the basic key-based controllers.

Table 25.4 lists all the data types for the advanced key-based controllers.

TABLE 25.4

Data Types Available for Each Advanced Key-based Controller Type

Controller	Valid Data Types
On/Off	Float
Attachment	Position
Path Controller	Position
Surface	Position
Motion Capture	Position, Rotation, Scale, Float, Point3
Cubic Morph	Morph
Barycentric Morph	Morph

The complete parameter set for the Attachment, Path, and Surface Position controllers can only be accessed in the Motion panel, not in Track View.

On/Off Controller

This controller, new to R2, provides binary -1/1 output, which can be useful when animating checkbox settings or the visibility of an object by using a visibility track. Every time a new key is set, the output value is toggled. A blue line indicates On status in Track View.

TIP

Gradual visibility can be achieved by changing the controller type of the visibility track to Bézier.

Attachment Controller

The Attachment controller, new to R2, attaches an object (source) to a face on another object (target). The effect is like sticking one object onto the other object's surface. Figure 25.23 shows the Motion panel parameter rollout for this controller.

This controller is applicable especially for situations where objects need to be glued to animated surfaces like an ocean or on top of objects with Bend or Twist modifiers applied.

WARNING

Although it is possible to use this controller with NURBS target objects, the source object position is based on the current viewport surface approximation settings for that target object. Changes of these surface approximation parameters are causing the attached object to jump (same with patch target objects).

TIP

For NURBS target objects, the Surface controller is preferable to the Attachment controller.

The following exercise shows how to animate a buoy floating on a wavy water surface by utilizing the Attachment controller.

FIGURE 25.23

Attachment Controller properties in the Motion panel.

ANIMATING A BUOY ON A WATER SURFACE

1. Load file ch25_3.max from the Chapter 25 folder on the accompanying CD-ROM and play the animation. The buoy does not move yet (see Figure 25.24).

2. Select the buoy object, open the Motion Panel, and assign the Attachment Position controller.

3. Click the Pick Object button and click the water surface in one of the viewports to assign this object as a target.

4. Now the exact face of the target object needs to be specified: Click the Set Position button and drag the mouse over the top of the water surface and release the left mouse button where you want the buoy to be placed. Notice that the buoy already follows the surface of the target object while doing this.

5. Play the animation again: The buoy is floating on the water surface (see Figure 25.25).

FIGURE 25.24
Wireframe view of the scene.

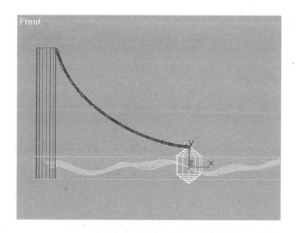

FIGURE 25.25
The buoy, attached to the water surface.

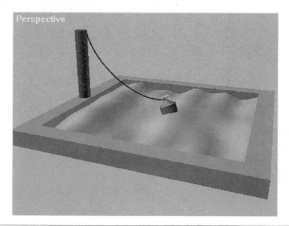

The Attachment controller provides controls to animate the source object moving over the target surface as well. To animate the attach-position, go to a different frame, activate Set Position and drag the source object to the new position.

WARNING

Because animation of the source object is done in the Motion panel, changing the source position causes new keyframes to be created, regardless of the state of the Animate button.

Because animation of the source object is handled by normal TCB interpolation for all frames in between keyframes, its attachment to the target is only fixed at the keyframes. Therefore, it can be difficult to animate the source object moving along the surface of the target object, especially when the target object is animated as well.

TIP

A more precise way to set up animated source objects moving along the surface of animated mesh target objects is to use a Script controller instead of the Attachment controller. An example for such a setup can be found on the MAX2 CD: /Samples/Scenes/MS_tpot.max.

Path Controller

The Path controller positions an object so that the object's pivot point is located on a spline. A parameter subordinate to the Path controller called Percent is also created. The Percent parameter specifies the location on the spline to use at a particular time point. The value of Percent is automatically set to 0 at the beginning of the active time range and to 100 at the end of the active time range.

The spline to be used as a path is specified as a parameter of the Path controller. The Path controller's path spline can only be set and displayed in the Parameters section of the Motion panel. The Path Parameters rollout in the Motion panel is shown in Figure 25.26. If the selected shape contains more than one spline, the first spline created in the shape is used as the path spline.

FIGURE 25.26

Path controller properties in the Motion panel.

Specify which axis of the object is aligned

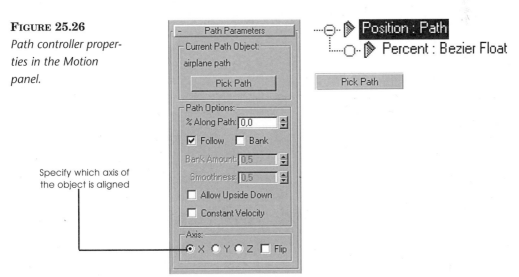

The following exercises show how to use the Path controller to animate an airplane and explains the meaning of the Path controller parameters available in the Motion panel.

USING A PATH CONTROLLER TO ANIMATE AN AIRPLANE

1. Load file ch25_4.max from the Chapter 25 folder on the accompanying CD-ROM.

2. Select the airplane, open the Motion panel, and assign a Path controller to the position parameter for the airplane.

3. Ensure that Follow is off in Path Options, click Pick Path, and select the spline path. The airplane is repositioned so that its pivot point (located at its bottom center) is located at the first vertex of the ellipse. Note that the orientation of the airplane is not changed (see Figure 25.27).

FIGURE 25.27

The position and orientation of the airplane on the path.

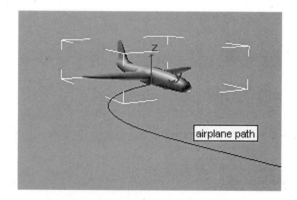

4. Play the animation. The airplane travels the length of the spline over the active time segment.

5. Choose Edit, Hold. You continue from this point in the next exercise.

Although the Path controller is classified as a position data type, it can also change the rotation of the object to which it is applied. The Follow and Bank options cause the object to rotate based on the curvature of the path spline. The rotation applied by the Path controller is in addition to any rotation defined by the user.

When the Follow option is off, the orientation of the object is not changed. When the Follow option is on, the object is rotated such that the "front" of the object is always pointing along the forward tangent of the spline.

NEW TO R2

The "front" of the object is defined by choosing one of the object's local axes in the axis section of the Path Parameters rollout.

The Bank option specifies where the top of the object points ("top" being defined as the direction perpendicular to the "front" of the object, pointing along the positive World Z axis). If Bank is off or if the Bank Amount is zero, the top of the object tries to point in the direction of the positive World Z axis. (Two degrees of freedom are used by the Follow option, so only one degree of freedom is left for the Bank option. Therefore, the top only points in the direction of the positive World Z axis as much as it can.)

If Bank is on, the object is rotated based on the local curvature of the spline. Bank Amount specifies by how much the direction of the top of the object is to be affected by the curvature. For low and moderate values, the top of the object tends to point toward the inside of the spline. For high values, the top of the object rotates wildly about the spline.

Smoothness specifies how fast the rotation resulting from banking is allowed to change. Higher values dampen the resulting rotation. The effects of the Bank Amount and Smoothness parameters interact with each other, so some interactive tweaking of values is usually required to achieve the desired motion. Typically, you want to use the lowest values possible for these parameters to achieve smooth motion.

THE EFFECT OF BANK AMOUNT AND SMOOTHNESS VALUES WITH PATH CONTROLLERS

1. Choose Edit, Fetch to retrieve the scene from the previous exercise.

2. Select the airplane.

3. Right-click in the Camera01 viewport, click Play Animation, and continue playing the animation through the rest of this exercise.

4. In Motion panel, turn on Follow. The airplane rotates so that its top points forward on the spline (see Figure 25.28).

5. Turn on Bank. The airplane banks as it moves along the ellipse. The amount of banking varies with the curvature of the spline.

6. Set Bank Amount to 5. The airplane banks much more now (see Figure 25.29).

FIGURE 25.28

The position and orientation of the airplane with Follow on, Bank off.

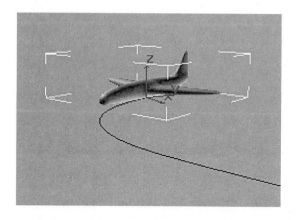

FIGURE 25.29

The position and orientation of the airplane with Follow on, Bank on.

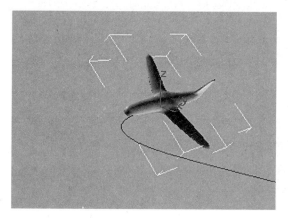

7.   Set Smoothness to 2. The banking is more natural.

As you played the previous animation, you may have noticed that the airplane moved faster at the middle of the spline path than it did on the beginning and end. An important consideration when using the Path controller is the relationship between the location of vertices in the spline used as the path and time. By default, 3DS MAX positions the object on the spline over time, based on the number of spline vertices—not on the length of the spline or on the distance between the vertices. Each vertex is converted to a position key evenly spaced over time. For example, if a line with 11 vertices is used as an object path, 11 position keys are created. If the active time range is 0 to 100 frames, the object is located at vertex 0 at frame 0, vertex 1 at frame 10, and vertex 2 at frame 20. Depending on the distance between these vertices, the velocity of the object can change greatly over time.

NEW TO R2

To change the animation to constant velocity, activate the Constant Velocity checkbox in the Motion panel. The Allow Upside Down option is to avoid possible flipping problems that can occur when objects follow a vertically oriented path like a roller-coaster loop.

Surface Controller

NEW TO R2

The purpose of the Surface controller, new to R2, is similar to the Attachment controller. It can be used to stick or move a source object along the surface of a target object. Unlike the Attachment controller, however, which is used for mesh target objects, the Surface controller is specialized to work with the following parametric target objects: Sphere, Cone, Cylinder, Torus, single Quad Patch, Loft, and NURBS objects (see Figure 25.30).

FIGURE 25.30

Surface controller properties in the Motion panel.

Adjusts the position of the object along the U and V coordinates of the parametric target surface

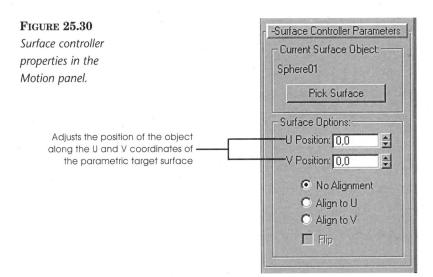

A great advantage over the Attachment controller is that the Surface controller interpolates the animation between keyframes based on the parametric data of the target object in a way that the source object follows the surface of the target object exactly.

WARNING

When a modifier is applied to the target object that converts the parametric object to a mesh (for example, Edit Mesh), the Surface controller no longer works.

Motion Capture Controller

The motion capture controller, new to R2, allows for real-time recording of animation via peripheral devices such as the mouse, MIDI keyboards/mixer, and joysticks. The device assignment is specified in the properties menu pertinent to this controller. For a detailed description of this Controller see Chapter 22, "Using Particle Systems."

Barycentric and Cubic Morph Controller

The Barycentric Morph controller, new to R2, is applied automatically to Morph Compound objects at creation time (see Chapter 10, "Compound Objects"). In the single target Cubic Morph controller already known from previous releases of 3DS MAX, it is now possible to assign multiple weighted morph targets at the same time. The weight of each target is controlled within the controller's properties window (see Figure 25.31). It is not possible to display function curves for the target weights.

FIGURE 25.31

The Barycentric Morph Controller Key Info dialog.

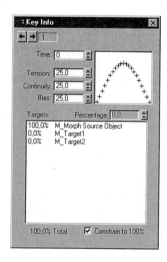

Due to a very special implementation of this controller, it is a bit tricky to use it for situations where you want to set the overall weight of all targets to more than 100 percent (for facial animation), because this causes the Morph Compound object to change scale.

The following exercise provides instructions on how to work around this scaling problem of the Morph Compound object by adjusting the source target weight for every key to counteract this.

AVOIDING UNWANTED SCALING OF THE MORPH COMPOUND OBJECT

1. Load file ch25_5.max from the Chapter 25 folder on the accompanying CD-ROM.

2. Play the animation. The Morph Compound object has two morph targets assigned: Target1 and Target2. Notice the unwanted scaling at frame 40 because both Targets have a weight of 100 percent here (see Figure 25.32).

FIGURE 25.32

The scaling of the Morph Compound object at frame 40 is not intended.

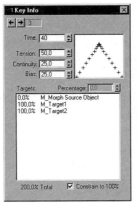
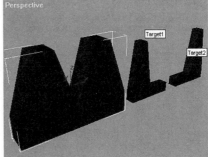

3. Open Track View, select the Barycentric Morph controller of the Morph Source object and open its Properties window.

4. To fix this scaling problem, the weight of the source object has to be adjusted according to the sum of the weights of all other targets, in a way to get an overall weight of 100 percent. In this example, you need to adjust the weight of Morph Source object at frame 40 to -100 percent to achieve an overall percentage of 100 (-100+100+100=100). This technique works best with a Tension value of 50.

5. Play back the animation again. The scaling problem is fixed now (see Figure 25.33).

FIGURE 25.33

The scaling problem is fixed by adjusting the weight of the source object.

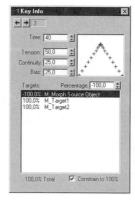

TIP

To improve the user interface of Barycentric morphing, use the Morph-Manager script utility morphmgr.zip supplied in the Chapter 25 folder on the accompanying CD-ROM.

The Attachment, Surface, and Motion Capture controllers are especially valuable additions to the toolset of 3DS MAX. Due to the lack of function curve support of the Barycentric Morph controller and the extra work to fix unwanted scaling, third-party plug-ins like Mix, MorphMagic and Smirk—all focusing on weighted morphing—may be useful add-ons to accomplish more complex facial animation tasks.

Parametric Controllers

A Parametric controller provides output values based on user-specified input data (the parameters) and the equation the controller implements. From all the parametric controllers available in 3DS MAX, the Script controller is the most versatile, followed by the Expression controller. For both, the input data, as well as the equation, can be defined in a very flexible way. Table 25.5 lists the data types available for each Parametric controller type.

TABLE 25.5

Data Types Available for Each Parametric Controller Type

Controller	Valid Data Types
Audio Controller	Position, Rotation, Scale, Float, Point3
Noise Controller	Position, Rotation, Scale, Float, Point3
Waveform Controller	Float
Expression Controller	Position, Scale, Float, Point3
Script Controller	Position, Rotation, Scale, Float, Point3

Each combination of parametric type and data type is implemented by a unique controller. Within the group of controllers of a given parametric type, the manner in which the parameters for the controllers are specified is the same.

For all data types, the Properties dialog in Track View can be accessed by selecting the parameter to which the controller is assigned, clicking in a free area of the edit window to ensure that no keys are selected, and then doing one of the following: right-clicking the parameter name, right-clicking the range bar in the parameter's track, or clicking Properties in Track Views toolbar.

For transform-related controllers at the object level, the controller's parameters can also be adjusted in the Motion command panel by selecting the parameter in the Assign Controller rollout, right-clicking the parameter, and choosing Properties from the pop-up menu.

Audio Controller

The Audio Controller can be used to control the value of a animatable parameter either by the amplitude of audio files or by real-time audio input. The Audio controller dialog (see Figure 25.34) provides a file selector and a configuration section for Real Time Control. The Min and Max spinners in the Controller Range section are used to define parameter values corresponding to the minimum and maximum amplitude of the audio source. According to the audio input, the parameter is animated within this interval. For example, this controller is applicable for doing simple lip synching, or to trigger actions within MAX by external audio events.

FIGURE 25.34

The Audio Controller
Properties dialog.

Noise Controller

The parameters for the noise controller are specified by accessing the controller's Properties dialog.

Figure 25.35 shows examples of Property dialogs for Noise Float and Position controllers. As can be seen from these dialogs, the only change is the number of strength fields. The controls are otherwise the same.

FIGURE 25.35

The Noise Float and
Noise Position
Controller Properties
dialogs.

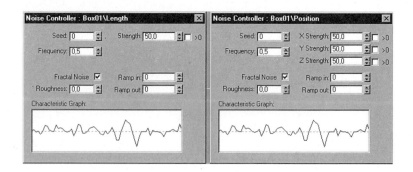

NEW TO R2

The noise strength parameter is now animatable.

The Characteristic Graph in the Noise Properties dialog shows roughly the effect that changes in the noise parameters have on the output. In many cases, it is better to see the exact effect of these changes by clicking Function Curves in the Track View toolbar to show the function curve of the parameter. This curve changes as the noise parameters change.

TIP

Because rotation controllers do not display function curves, the effect of changes in noise parameters with these controllers cannot be seen. Instead, use the Euler XYZ compound controller and apply a noise controller to each axis. The values in each noise controller would typically be the same except for the seed value, which should be different in each (see Figure 25.36).

FIGURE 25.36

The hierarchy branch before and after the modification.

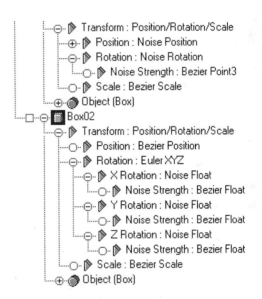

The Strength fields specify the range of output values from the noise controller. The range is from Strength/2 to –Strength/2 if the >0 option is off, or 0 to Strength if it is on. There are two exceptions to this. First, for the scale data type, a value of 100 is automatically added to each of the noise output values. This means that noise is applied to a 100 percent scale factor. Second, if fractal noise is on, the output range is increased, but the center point is not. Therefore, the values can be less than 0 even if the >0 option is on. For a roughness of 0.0, the range is increased by approximately 10 percent; for a roughness of 1.0, the range is increased by approximately 100 percent.

T IP

To control the center point, use a List controller with a Noise controller and a key-based controller as inputs. Turn off the >0 options in Noise and then create a key for the key-based controller whose value is the desired center point.

The Ramp In and Ramp Out fields dampen the amount of noise at the start and end of the range. This dampening is not linear; it is equivalent to a Bézier curve. For a Ramp In, the curve is defined by Bézier vertices located at time 0 and at the time specified in the Ramp In field with the vertices having zero interpolation velocity. Figure 25.37 shows the curve for a Ramp In value of 10. The shape of this curve is not adjustable.

FIGURE 25.37

The shape of a Noise Controller Ramp in Curve.

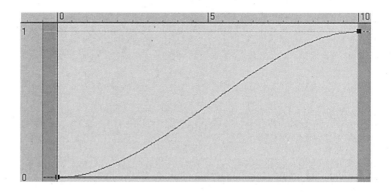

The Ramp In and Ramp Out fields behave similarly to a Multiplier Curve applied to the Noise controller. An interesting consequence of this is that if the >0 option is on and a Ramp In value is specified, the output value of the controller goes to zero at time zero, rather than the midpoint of Strength/2.

T IP

To ramp to the midpoint value, use Ramp In or Ramp Out and turn off the >0 option, put the Noise controller under a List controller, and add a key-based controller to the List controller. Create a key for the key-based controller and set its value to Strength/2.

Waveform Controller

This controller provides periodic waveforms like sine, square, triangle, and half sine. Additionally, it is possible to stack numerous waveforms to produce more complex waves. For every waveform, parameters control the amplitude, offset (vertical bias and phase), and whether the waveform is added, multiplied, or clamped to the former (see Figure 25.38).

FIGURE 25.38

The Waveform Controller Properties dialog.

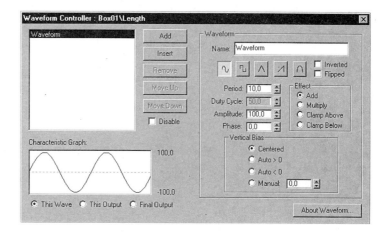

A basic application for this controller is creating blinking lights, or periodic motion of parts in technical visualizations.

T IP

If the final output of a complex waveform needs to be scaled, just multiply one further waveform with Amplitude=0, and use the Manual Vertical Bias spinner to adjust the scaling of the output.

Expression Controller

Expression controllers evaluate user-defined mathematical expressions to determine their output values. They can be applied to nearly all animatable parameters in 3DS MAX. An Expression controller can access the outputs of other controllers, and those values can be used in the expression. The time point for which the expression is evaluated also is available in several forms. A variety of intrinsic functions are provided for use in expressions.

Expression Controller Data Types

Figure 25.39 shows a sample Expression controller dialog. When an Expression controller is first assigned to a parameter that already has a controller, the equation box shows the value for that parameter at frame 0.

If the parameter does not have a controller, the value is set to 0. The value shown is in one of two formats. If the parameter to which the Expression controller is assigned has a Position, Scale, or Point3 data type, the controller returns a three-component vector. The format of the expression is [eqn1, eqn2, eqn3]. If the parameter to which the Expression controller is assigned has a Float data type, the controller returns a floating-point scalar value. The format of the expression is eqn1. If the format of the expression is incorrect or if an error occurs while evaluating the expression, an error message is displayed.

FIGURE 25.39

A sample Expression Controller dialog.

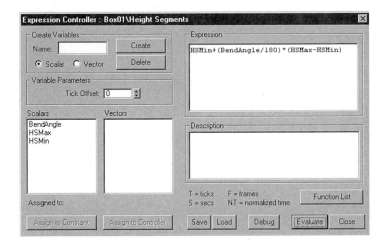

Expression Controller Variables

Two types of variables can be used in an equation. The first, Scalar, is used to reference single-value float data. The second, Vector, is used to reference three-component vectors. To create a variable, type the name of the variable into the name field in the Create Variables box, select whether the variable is supposed to be a scalar or vector variable, and click Create. The variable is created and its name appears in the Scalars or Vectors columns.

When a variable is created, it is assigned a constant value of 0 if it is scalar or [0,0,0] if it is vector. Variables either can be assigned a constant value over the animation or the output of another controller can be assigned to the variable. To assign a constant value to a variable, select the variable name in the Scalars or Vectors columns, click Assign to Constant, and assign the value to use.

To assign a controller output to a variable, select the variable name, click Assign to Controller, and select the controller from the Track View Pick dialog that appears (see Figure 25.40).

FIGURE 25.40

The Track View Pick dialog.

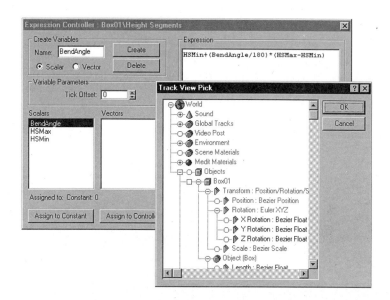

If a variable is assigned to a Position controller, the position value the variable receives is the position of the object with this Position controller relative to the position of that object's parent (remember: by default, every object is a child of the world). But when the variable is assigned to the object (by selecting the object name in the Track View Pick dialog instead of the object's Position controller), the returned value is the absolute position value of the object (position data, relative to the world).

In the Track View Pick dialog, controllers and objects that can be chosen are displayed in boldface. A controller can be chosen if the controller data type matches the variable type and if a controller has been assigned to a parameter. Objects only can be chosen for vector variables.

In some cases, 3DS MAX enables the user to select a controller and then gives a Can't Assign Control Circular Dependency error message. This error message is generated if the parameter selected and the parameter to which the expression controller is applied are both subordinate to the same controller. For example, an expression for the Length parameter of a box cannot reference the box's width parameter. It can, however, reference the box's transform parameters and the parameters for any modifiers applied to the box.

Tick Offset Values

The value returned from a controller assigned to a variable is normally the output value of the controller at the same time point that is being evaluated. In some cases, the value desired is the controller's output at a different time point. 3D Studio MAX enables the user to specify a fixed offset for a variable. 3DS MAX adds this offset value to the time point being evaluated and evaluates the assigned controller at that time point. This offset value is specified in the Tick Offset field in the Variable Parameters box. It is set when the variable is created and can be changed by selecting the variable name and setting the new Tick Offset value, which can be either positive or negative. As its name implies, the Tick Offset value specifies the offset time in ticks. There are 4,800 ticks to a second. If the frame rate is 30 frames per second, then there are 160 ticks per frames.

Reserved Variable Names

Several variable names cannot or should not be used when creating a variable. Four of these (T, S, F, and NT) are predefined variable names with special values, and a variable cannot be created with one of these names. In addition, the names e, pi, or TPS should not be used. These variable names are also predefined with special values; however, 3DS MAX enables the user to override these values. The following are the values associated with each of these variables:

T	The time point being evaluated in ticks
S	The time point being evaluated in seconds
F	The time point being evaluated in frames
NT	The normalized time. This value linearly increases from 0 at the beginning of the active time segment to 1 at the end of the segment.
e	The constant e (2.71828...)
pi	The constant pi (3.14159...)
TPS	The number of ticks per second (4800)

Data Value Ranges Associated with Parameters/Debug Window

Frequently, the data values specified to 3DS MAX and the data values shown by 3DS MAX are not the actual data values stored in the controllers.

An Expression controller applied to a parameter must output values in the actual range of values that the parameter expects. If it does not, the animated effect may be off by orders of magnitude.

When an object is created in 3DS MAX, the core-component plug-in associated with that object specifies a list of parameters that can be animated. In this case, an object can refer to a material, a geometric object, or a modifier. For the sake of discussion, call the core-component the parent. For each animatable parameter, there is a controller that is subordinate to the parent.

The parent decides how to handle the data values returned from a subordinate controller. The parent also specifies how the data values are to appear in the command panels, Track View, and other dialogs where data values can be viewed or set. Frequently, the data values seen are not the true data values passed from the controller to the parent, but they are data values that are "massaged" by the parent. One example of this is with parameters that deal with angles. In all cases, the data values the user sets and see are in degrees. Internally, most of these angles are handled in radians.

Expression controllers are directly accessing and setting the raw data values stored in the key. If the Expression controller is applied to a parameter dealing with angles, the output should most likely be in radians. If the expression has a variable assigned to a controller that is dealing with angles, expect to get the results in radians.

In some cases, the way the parent handles the data from a subordinate controller varies. Although most angles are internally handled as radians, in some cases they are handled in degrees. An example of this is Bend Angle in the Bend and Twist modifiers.

The position of a modifier gizmo is specified relative to the pivot point of the object to which the modifier is applied. That is, a modifier located at the pivot point of the object returns the position value [0,0,0] when assigned to a vector variable. When an Attachment, Path, or Surface controller is applied to an object or gizmo, the position values returned to the vector variable are relative to world center.

The following are general rules of thumb for actual controller output values:

- If a parameter is time-based, the controller output is typically in ticks. Examples of this are the Ease Curve and the Phase parameter of the Noise modifier.

- If a parameter is a percentage, or the viewable range of values is 0 to 100, the actual controller output range is typically 0 to 1. Examples of this are the material opacity parameter and the Percent parameter of the Path controller.

- If the parameter is angle-based, the controller output is typically in radians. Examples of this are camera FOV and rotation controllers subordinate to a Euler XYZ controller.

- If the parameter is a color, the controller output range is always 0 to 1.

- For parameters displayed as integers, the controller output is rounded to the nearest integer. An example of this is the Material ID parameter in the Material modifier.

- If the parameter is displayed as an option, the option is typically turned on when the controller output is greater than 0.5. Examples of this are the Fractal option in the Noise modifier and the Symmetry option in the Taper modifier.

- For other values that can be freely adjusted, the controller output is typically the value seen in the command panel and in Track View.

As with all rules of thumb, there are always exceptions.

NEW TO R2

The actual output of a controller or object assigned to a variable, as well as the expression value itself, can be monitored with the new Debug window, which can be accessed through the Expression Controller Properties menu (see Figure 25.41).

FIGURE 25.41

The Expression Controller Debug window.

An additional point to be aware of is that the limits 3DS MAX places on some parameters are applied only during data entry. Because Expression controllers bypass the data entry, these limits are not always enforced. An example of this is a camera's FOV. The FOV is limited to 175 degrees during data entry, but an Expression controller can supply any value it desires. Although rarely fatal, Expression controllers returning out-of-range values can result in unexpected behavior. It is best to determine the limits present on a parameter and remain within those limits.

In the following exercise, you rotate a billboard so that the front of the billboard always faces the camera; however, you also want the billboard to remain perpendicular to the ground—you only want to rotate the billboard about a single axis. To accomplish this, use an expression controller that rotates Billboard about its Z axis based on the position of the camera relative to Billboard.

The scene contains the camera, a box that acts as the ground (Ground), and a texture-mapped box (Billboard). The pivot point for Billboard has been adjusted so that its +Z axis is perpendicular to Ground.

The rotation expression controller to be applied to Billboard needs to access the position of Billboard. Because a rotation expression for an object is not allowed to access the same object's position controller, a dummy object is created at the same position as Billboard, and Billboard is set as a child of the dummy object.

AN EXPRESSION CONTROLLER IMPLEMENTING A LOOK AT CONTROLLER ABOUT A SINGLE AXIS

1. Load file ch25_6.max from the Chapter 25 folder on the accompanying CD and play the animation.

2. Press Esc to end the playback and click Min/Max to display all view ports.

3. Create a dummy object.

4. Choose Align and select Billboard as the Align Target Object. Choose X Position, Y Position, and Z Position, and choose Pivot Point for both Current Object and Target Object. Choose X, Y, and Z axes in Align Orientation. Click OK to exit.

5. Choose Select and Link, and link Billboard to the dummy object.

6. Open Track View and select the rotation controller for Billboard.

7. Choose Assign Controller and choose the Euler XYZ controller.

8. Expand the rotation controller track and assign a Float Expression Controller to the Z Rotation track. Figure 25.42 shows the screen at this point.

FIGURE 25.42

Track View and two views of the scene.

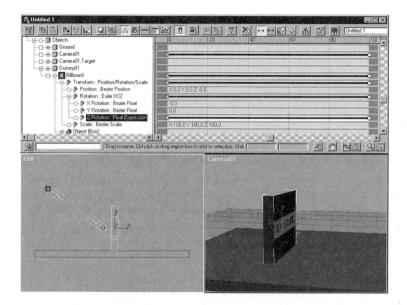

9. Right-click the Z Rotation controller and choose Properties.

10. Click Load and load Lookat_z.xpr from the Chapter 25 folder on the accompanying CD. Figure 25.43 shows the Expression controller dialog containing the Lookat_Z equation.

11. Select MyPos in the Vector column, click Assign to Controller, and choose the position track for the dummy object.

12. Select TargetPos in the Vector column, click Assign to Controller, and choose the position track for the camera.

13. Click Close, activate the camera view port, and play the animation.

An additional expression controller has been provided as file Lookat_x.xpr. Figure 25.44 shows the Lookat_X equation. By using this equation to control the X Rotation track of an object and the Lookat_Z equation to control the Z Rotation track, the –Z axis of the object always points at the target object. An example scene, ch25_7.max, found on the accompanying CD, shows two objects—one using the Look At controller and the other using the previous expressions.

FIGURE 25.43

The Lookat_Z Expression controller equation.

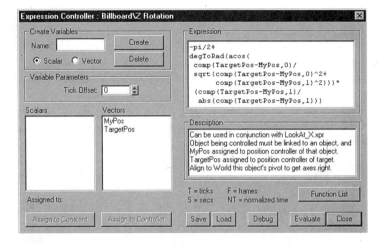

FIGURE 25.44

The Lookat_X Expression controller equation.

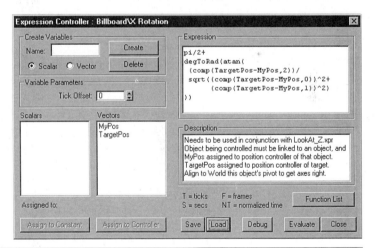

Script Controller

Parametric controllers can help to facilitate complex animation tasks by automating certain parts of an animation, taking the burden to keyframe every little action. Scripts and Expressions especially can help to save a lot of time when used intelligently (such as setting up macro controls when working with complex hierarchies). Obviously, a decent knowledge of mathematics is beneficial for working extensively with parametric controllers.

Compound Controllers

As previously described, compound controllers take as their inputs the output of subordinate controllers and then they combine this data with any parameter data associated with the controller, manipulate the data, and output the results. 3DS MAX ships with three transform-level compound controllers (the Position/Rotation/Scale, LookAt, and Link Control controllers); several controllers that combine the float data of three single tracks to form rotation, position, point3, or color data (the Euler XYZ, Position XYZ, Point3 XYZ, and Color RGB controllers); and a controller that adds the results of its input controllers (the List controller).

Table 25.6 shows the data types available for the compound controller types.

TABLE 25.6

Data Types Available for Each Compound Controller Type

Controller	Valid Data Types
PRS Controller	Transform Level
LookAt Controller	Transform Level
Link Control Controller	Transform Level
Euler XYZ Controller	Rotation
Position XYZ Controller	Position
Point3 XYZ	Point3
Color RGB	Point3
List Controller	Position, Rotation, Scale, Float, Point3

The way the values returned from the subordinate controllers are used by a transform-level controller depends on whether the controller is assigned to an object, a modifier gizmo, or a modifier center. For a transform controller at the object level, the position value returned is the object's pivot-point location relative to the world origin. The rotation and scale values returned are relative to the object's pivot-point location.

For a transform controller at a modifier gizmo or center level, the position value returned is relative to the pivot point of the object; that is, a modifier center positioned at [0,0,0] is located at the pivot point of the object. If the pivot point of the object is changed after the modifier is applied, the modifier gizmo and center remain at their original location relative to the pivot point. The rotation and scale values returned are relative to the gizmo's center point location.

PRS Controller

The Position/Rotation/Scale (PRS) transform controller combines the output from position, rotation, and scale controllers (see Figure 25.45). The output of the PRS controller is the transformation matrix used internally by 3DS MAX. The PRS controller can only be used in the transform tracks of objects and modifier gizmos.

No user-adjustable property data are associated with the PRS controller.

FIGURE 25.45

Example Position/Rotation/Scale Transform controllers and their input controllers.

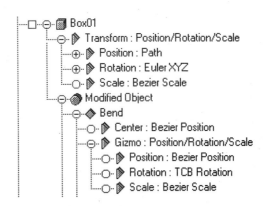

Look At Controller

The Look At transform controller combines the output from position, roll (a float data type), and scale controllers. It can be used only as the transform controller for objects, not modifiers.

The controller rotates an object so that one axis of the object always points at the pivot point of another object.

NEW TO R2

The axis can be defined in the axis section of the Look At Parameters rollout in the Motion panel.

The roll parameter specifies the roll angle of the object around its local Z axis. The Look At controller's target object can be set and displayed only in the Parameters section of the Motion panel, which is shown in Figure 25.46.

FIGURE 25.46

The Look At Controller Properties in the Motion panel.

USING A LOOK AT CONTROLLER ON AN OBJECT

1. Create two cones in the Top view. Drag up while specifying the cone height.

2. Choose Local from the Transform Coordinate System drop-down list in the toolbar. This shows the local axes for selected objects.

3. In Motion, Parameters assign a Look At controller to the transform parameter for Cone02, which rotates so that its negative Z axis points to the World origin.

4. Click Pick Target and select Cone01. Cone02 rotates so that its negative Z axis points at Cone01. The pivot point for a cone is located at its bottom center; as a result, that is the point at which Cone02 points.

5. Move either cone in the Top view. As you move a cone, the base of Cone02 always points at Cone01. Remember to change the Transform Coordinate System or the axis constraints before trying to move a cone in another view.

6. Rotate Cone02. The cone always rotates about its local Z axis.

When working with characters, use Look At controllers to focus the character's pupils to a dummy object that can be placed much more comfortably than animating the pupils directly.

The Look At controller is the controller used by Target cameras and Target Spotlights. When one of these objects is created, a Look At controller is assigned to the object, a dummy object is created to act as the target, and the Look At target is defined as the dummy object.

Link Control Controller

This controller is used for transferring hierarchical links from one object to another. Position links no longer have to be static in 3DS MAX (see Figure 25.47).

FIGURE 25.47
The Link Control Controller properties in the Motion panel.

The following exercise shows how to use this controller to couple a wagon to an engine. The engine moves back to couple on the wagon at frame 20. Then you want the wagon to be pulled to the right by activating a temporary position link at frame 20.

COUPLING A WAGON TO AN ENGINE

1. Load file ch25_8.max from the Chapter 25 folder on the accompanying CD-ROM.

2. Play the animation. The wagon does not follow the engine yet.

3. Select the wagon, open the Motion Command panel, and assign the Link Control Transform Controller.

4. Go to frame 20, click the Add Link button in the Link Parameter rollout and select the engine in one of the viewports. Notice that the Link Start Time spinner is set automatically to frame 20.

5. Play the animation. The wagon follows the engine from frame 0 to 100.

This happened because the first link, which is defined in the Link Controller rollout, is always active for all frames (like a static link), regardless of the Start Time spinner setting (that is correctly set to frame 20 here). To fix this problem, it is necessary to add another temporary link for the frames 0 to 19.

6. Click Undo Pick Link.

7. Go to frame 0, click the Add Link button again (if it is not still active) and select the dummy object below the wagon.

8. Go to frame 20 and select the engine.

9. Play the animation again. Now the wagon is coupled on the engine at frame 20 correctly (see Figure 25.48).

FIGURE 25.48

The Link Control Controller parameters in the Motion panel at the end of this exercise.

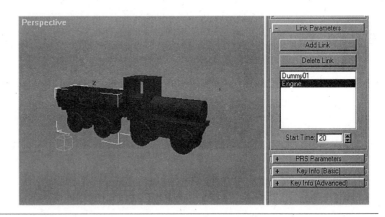

Euler XYZ Controller

The TCB Rotation controller is the default controller used for rotation tracks. Although this controller provides smooth rotation, the function curves associated with this controller are not available in Track View because the TCB controller uses quaternion math to control the rotation. Quaternion math has four values—the X, Y, and Z values of a unit vector, and the rotation angle about the unit vector. Additional rotation controllers that use quaternion math are the Linear and Smooth controllers.

Besides being unable to display the rotation function curves for these controllers, more control over rotation than can be provided with these controllers is sometimes desired. 3DS MAX ships with an additional rotation controller, the Euler XYZ controller, which offers function curve display capabilities and individual control of rotations about each of the object's local axes. Figure 25.49 shows the Euler Parameters rollout in the Motion panel.

FIGURE 25.49

The Euler XYZ Controller properties in the Motion panel.

Consider a case where you are rotating an object about its X and Y axes, and you want to adjust the interpolation at one of the keys for the X axis rotation. You can adjust the TCB controller values for that key in either the Motion panel or in Track View, but you are also adjusting the interpolation of the Y axis rotation at that key. When using the TCB controller, it is not possible to adjust interpolation values for one axis without also adjusting them for all axes. If a Euler XYZ controller is used, the interpolation for keys associated with the X axis rotation can be adjusted without affecting the Y axis rotation.

ADJUSTING THE INTERPOLATION PARAMETERS FOR INDIVIDUAL ROTATION AXES

1. Load file ch25_9.max from the Chapter 25 folder on the accompanying CD and play the animation.

The box is animated to rotate 180 degrees about its local Z axis over frames 0 to 100. The box is also animated to rotate 45 degrees about its Y axis over frames 25 to 75. As can be seen in the view ports, there is rotation about the Y axis prior to frame 25 and after frame 75. You could try adjusting the TCB parameters for the keys at frames 25 and 75, but that would also affect the rotation of the box about its Z axis at these frames.

2. Open Track View and expand the tracks to display the rotation parameter for Box01.

3. Select the rotation parameter and assign a Euler XYZ controller to the parameter.

4. Expand the tracks for the rotation parameter.

5. Select the Y Rotation parameter and click Function Curves. Click the curve to display the keys.

The function curves are shown in Figure 25.50. The function curves show that the Y rotation value varies between the first and second keys, and between the third and fourth keys.

FIGURE 25.50

The rotation function curves for object Box01.

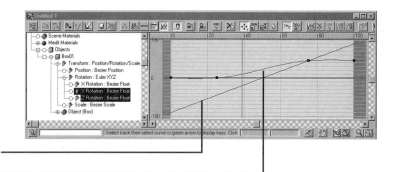

Z rotation function curve ————

Y rotation function curve ————

6. Right-click the first key to display the Key Info dialog.

7. Set the Out tangent to a Step tangent type for the first key.

8. Set the In tangent to a Step tangent type for the fourth key.

9. Play the animation.

There is no rotation about the Y axis prior to frame 25 or after frame 75. The rotation about the Z axis is still smooth.

NEW TO R2

A new pop-up list lets the user change the axis order of the Euler rotation (see Figure 25.51). The axis order is important any time an object or gizmo is rotated about more than one axis at the same time. In previous versions of 3DS MAX, the Euler XYZ controller always calculated the axes in a XYZ order.

The following example shows the connection between a given motion and the Euler axis order needed to reproduce this motion correctly:

FIGURE 25.51

The axis order
pop-up list.

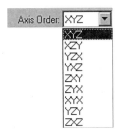

Take a pen, put its tip on a desk, and rapidly spin it about its vertical Z axis. Shortly after letting the pen go, it falls over (for this example, assume the pen falls by rotating about its X axis), so overall the Z axis rotation is itself rotated about the X axis: first Z, then X.

To reproduce this movement with an Euler controller, you need to choose either the ZXY, ZYX, or YZX axis order. File ch25_10.max shows the effect of Euler controllers with different axis orders on two objects with the exact same rotation keyframes applied.

Additional benefits of using the Euler XYZ rotation controller are that expression controllers can be used for each rotation axis and other expression controllers can reference the rotation of the object.

Position XYZ, Point3 XYZ, and Color RGB Controllers

These controllers split the X, Y, and Z components into three separate tracks, similar to the way the Euler XYZ Controller does for rotations. This can be used to apply different subordinate controllers or to set up specific references from Expression Controllers.

List Controller

List controllers are used to combine the results of multiple controllers. It is possible, for example, to add noise to a predefined motion by assigning a List controller to the desired parameter, and adding a Noise controller as an input to the List controller. Another use of the List controller is to interactively add additional motion to a parameter controlled by a parametric controller, such as the Noise controller. The Set Active button in the List controller properties dialog is used to determine which subordinate controller is assigned to interactive user input (see Figure 25.52).

FIGURE 25.52

The List controller properties dialog.

In the following exercise, you use a Path controller for a portion of the animation and then switch over to a Bézier curve controller to complete the animation. The scene consists of a ball whose motion is controlled by a path controller. The path being followed is a circle. What you want to do in this animation is have the ball motionless at the beginning of the animation, accelerate three times around the circle, and then fly off to the location shown by the dummy object.

COMBINING PATH, BÉZIER, AND LIST CONTROLLERS TO RESTRICT THE PATH CONTROLLER TO A TIME RANGE

1. Load file ch25_11.max from the Chapter 25 folder on the accompanying CD-ROM.

2. Open Track View, click Filters, and turn on Show Controller Types.

3. Expand the tracks for Sphere01 to show the Percent controller under the Position: Path controller.

4. Right-click the position key at frame 100 to bring up the Key Info dialog.

5. Change the value for the keyframe to 300 and exit the dialog.

6. Play the animation. The ball moves at a constant velocity three times around the circle.

7. In Track View, click Function Curves, and then click Add Keys.

8. Add three keys to the Path Percent function curve and then click Move Keys.

9. Adjust the three keys to obtain a curve similar to the one shown in Figure 25.53.

FIGURE 25.53

*The Location of keys
on the Path Percent
Function Curve.*

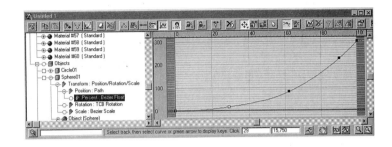

Note that you can play the animation as you are adjusting the curves
and see the corresponding motion in real time. The ball now starts from
a rest position and accelerates three times around the circle over 100
frames.

Now you want to perform this motion over 80 frames and then fly off to
the position of the dummy object.

10. Click Edit Keys and select the Position: Path controller.

11. Click and drag the end of range marker for the Position controller to
    frame 80.

12. Select the Position track, click Assign controller, and choose Position
    List.

13. Expand the tracks for Position List, select Available, and assign a
    Bézier Position controller to the track.

14. Click Add Keys, click at frame 80 in the Bézier Position track to create
    a key, and click Move Keys.

15. Click in a free area of Track View to deselect the key you just created.

16. Click the Position List controller to select it, right-click it, and choose
    Properties from the pop-up dialog. The List Controller dialog that
    appears shows the Path controller as the active controller. You want the
    Bézier Position controller to be active so that you can interactively
    adjust the position of the ball.

17. Select Bézier Position, click Set Active, and exit the List Controller
    dialog.

18. Turn on Animate and move to frame 100.

19. In the Top view, move Sphere01 to the location of the dummy object.

20. Turn off Animate and play the animation.

The ball now accelerates around the circle three times over 80 frames and then flies off to a new position. Note that there is a small variation in the velocity of the ball as it passes through frame 80.

21. To get a smooth transition of velocity, move the end of the range marker on the Path controller to frame 87. Select the key at frame 80 for the Bézier Position controller and move it to frame 87.

The List controller can be used to combine a Path controller and a Bézier, and also used to cause a camera to follow an object along a path. One restriction to keep in mind is that if a Path controller is a subordinate controller to a List controller, it must be the first controller in the list; if it is not, any values from controllers prior to it in the list are ignored.

Copying and Pasting Controllers (R2 Updated)

Most controllers can be copied and pasted in Track View. With some restrictions, as long as a parameter has a controller attached to it, that controller can be copied; a controller can be pasted to a parameter as long as the parameter can accept the controller's data type.

If an Ease or Multiplier channel is assigned to a Waveform, Expression, Script, or Audio controller, the Ease and Multiplier channels are not retained in the copy. It is, however, retained when instanced.

TIP

In the previous Look At Expression example, the Billboard is linked to a dummy object because the rotation Expression Controller needed the Billboard's position but is not allowed access to the object's position track. Instead of linking the objects, you could have copied the Billboard's Position Controller to the dummy object's Position Controller as an instance. Then, if either object is moved, the other object is also automatically moved.

TIP

Controller types can be specified for any animatable value in Track View. This includes the transform controllers for gizmos of modifiers applied to an object. Although Path controller can be specified for the position of a gizmo, there is no direct way of specifying the path to follow. This limitation can be circumvented by applying a Path controller to another object, specifying the path to follow in the Motion panel, and then cutting and pasting the Path controller to the position controller of the gizmo.

Global Tracks and Global Variables

Global tracks are used to store controllers and to define global variables. These tracks provide a List controller for every controller data type. By instancing controllers from a Global track, these controllers can operate as master controllers for all instanced tracks. Global variables are defined by assigning an Expression controller to a Global track, which can be referenced from other Expression controllers.

Converting Parametric Controller Output to Key-based Animation

By using the controllers supplied with 3DS MAX, the resulting object motions can get very complex. For example, imagine an object with a Path controller, List controllers, a Look At controller, and parametric controllers, such as the Noise controller, or the object could be part of an animated hierarchy.

In some cases, you may want to collapse the motion for an object to simple position, rotation, and scale keys. You may want to do this to use an expression controller that needs to reference the position or rotation tracks of such an object, or to create a path for another object to follow. The motion is collapsed to transformation keys with the help of the Collapse tool in the Motion Trajectories panel (see Figure 25.54).

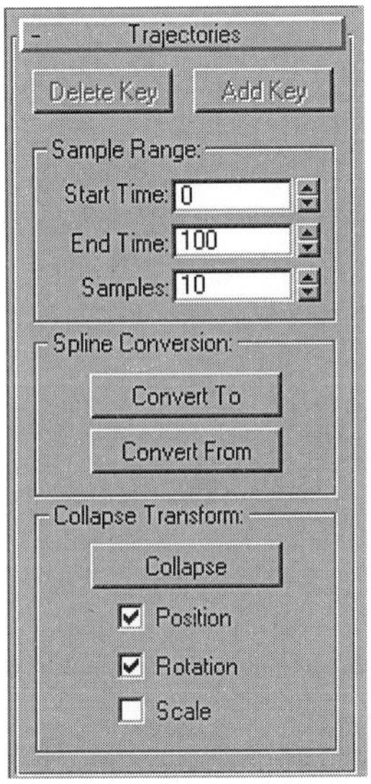

FIGURE 25.54

*The Motion panel
Trajectories rollout.*

However, this tool does not work for objects within an animated hierarchy. The motion transferred through hierarchical links is not taken into account when calculating the transform keys. The motion of objects that are part of an animated hierarchy can be collapsed to transformation keys by linking an object to the object from which you want to capture the motion and then applying Inverse Kinematics/Bind.

In the following exercise, Box01 is linked to Sphere03, which is linked to Sphere02, which in turn is linked to Sphere01. Each of the spheres is rotated 360 degrees about the Z axis over the length of the animation. The diffuse color of the material mapped to Box01 is controlled by an expression controller. This controller changes the diffuse color of the box based on the X, Y, and Z velocity of the box at the current frame. This velocity is determined by vector variables assigned to Box01's position track. As you play the animation, you see that the diffuse color never changes because there has been no motion defined for Box01 other than that provided through the hierarchy. Thus, the values returned from the position track are constant.

USING IK/BIND TO CREATE ANIMATION KEYS FROM A PROCEDURAL CONTROLLER

1. Load file ch25_12.max from the Chapter 25 folder on the accompanying CD and play the animation.

2. Create a dummy object and open the IK portion of the Hierarchy command panel. Click Bind and bind the dummy object to Box01. Turn on Bind Position and Bind Orientation, and in Sliding Joints rollout, set the X, Y, and Z axes active. Click Apply IK.

3. Open Track View, expand the tracks and select the Diffuse parameter for Material #1 under Box01. Right-click Diffuse and choose Properties. The expression controller dialog shown in Figure 25.55 is displayed.

4. Select variable PosLast in the Vector column and click Assign to Controller. Select the position track of Dummy01 in the Track View Pick dialog that appears. Repeat for PosNow and close the expression controller dialog.

5. Leaving Track View open, activate the camera view and play the animation. The color of the box changes as the box's velocity changes. The box's color at frame 0 is very different from the color at frame 1 and frame 100.

FIGURE 25.55

The Expression controller dialog and equation for the box's diffuse color.

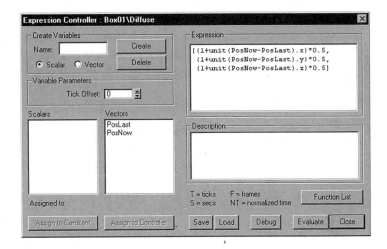

6. In Track View, with Diffuse still selected, click Function Curves. Note the discontinuity at frame 0. Select the position track for Dummy01.

Also note that constant values are being used outside the active time range. Because the PosLast variable in the expression is accessing the position one tick back from the current frame, there is no change in velocity at frame 0.

7. Click Parameter Curve Out-Of-Range Types. Click the two buttons below Cycle and exit the dialog.

8. Close Track View and play the animation. The color at frame 0 is now correct.

This last exercise is a good example how to manage a problem by using a combination of already known tools in a new and creative way. Often, it is not the pure availability of features, but the intelligent usage of them what makes your work outstanding.

In Practice: Using Controllers and Expressions

- **Rotation controllers:** When frequent modifications of key-framed rotations need to be done, a Euler XYZ rotation controller is better suited than a TCB rotation controller. The Euler XYZ controller displays function curves in Track View and allows modifications to the rotation for each of the object's axes.

- **List controllers:** List controllers are used to combine the results of multiple controllers. A hierarchy of object motions can be built, similar to a hierarchy of object modifiers.

- **Surface and Attachment Controllers:** Surface and Attachment Controllers are used to stick objects onto another object's surface.

- **Expression controllers:** The range of values returned from an expression must match the range expected for the parameter the controller is applied to.

- **Instanced controllers:** With instanced controllers, the output of a single controller can be used as input to multiple parameters. Changing the value for one parameter results in the remaining parameters using the new value. By combining instanced controllers with List controllers, complex interacting controllers can be constructed.

- **Global tracks:** Global tracks can be used to store controllers and to define global variables referenced by Expression controllers.

Chapter 26

Using MAXScript

MAXScript has its roots in the script extensions plug-in for 3D Studio for DOS. The idea behind this is to allow for the easy manipulation of commands with a user-defined interface, which, in other words, is an easy method of writing plug-ins. Object creation can be scripted into a single button and full-featured applications can be written. These special programs can be used for internal company use or third-party developers can write applications. With included encryption technology, the scripts can be encrypted and offered for sale. This chapter explores the following topics:

- Working with MAXScript

- Programming a simple user interface

- Creating a Cloud Generator with a sample renderer

Working with MAXScript

Before you can work with the scripting utility, you'll need to become familiar with its interface. This section will familiarize you with the MAXScript interface and its rollout options. To access the MAXScript utility, go to the Utility command panel and click the MAXScript button. The MAXScript rollout appears (see Figure 26.1).

FIGURE 26.1

The MAXScript utility.

The MAXScript rollout contains several buttons: Open Listener, New Script, Open Script, Run Script, and the Close button. The following list describes the functions of these buttons in detail:

- **Open Listener:** Starts a window, which is a text editor with command line functionality. Commands may be entered in the window and executed by pressing Enter. This window is a good way to instantly test a command you may place in a program you are working on.

- **New Script:** Opening a new script with this button enables you to start the creation of a new scripting program. The text editor presented enables you to type in a program and, if you want, test the various commands as you type. While typing, the keyboard Enter key adds a new line and the Number Pad Enter key tests the command on the current line.

- **Open Script:** This button calls a file selection window, allowing you to open a previously constructed script for you to edit. You can also use this window to copy code from an opened script to paste into a new script.

- **Run Script:** Pressing the Run Script button bypasses the editor window and executes the chosen script as written.

- **Close:** When a script is opened, the title appears in the drop-down list and the functions become loaded into the panel after selecting the listed script. If more than one script is opened, then the panel is populated with more than you might want to scroll through. The Close button depopulates the script panel and closes the MAXScript utility.

In the following exercise, you'll explore the Listener by creating and placing a camera in 3D space. You'll create a simple object and instruct MAXScript to render the scene. After typing each line in the Listener, you press Enter to evaluate the line you have typed.

CREATING AND PLACING A CAMERA USING THE LISTENER

1. Start MAX. Go to the Utilities panel and click the MAXScript button. Next, click the Open Listener button. A text editor window opens welcoming you to MAXScript.

2. Type **cam=freecamera()** and press Enter. Here you have created a variable named *cam* and included the correct syntax for calling for the creation of a non-target Freecamera. The Listener creates the camera and places it at a default location in 3D-space and reports information about the camera in blue text.

3. Rename the camera to MyCamera by typing **cam.name="MyCamera"**.

The camera's default positioning has it pointing downward. The following steps rotate the camera in the X axis so that it is pointing into the screen in the Front Viewport.

4. The MAX user interface uses the right-hand rule for rotations, which mean positive angles are in the counter-clockwise direction. Rotations in MAX are called out using the *quat* Constructor. You want to rotate the camera 80 degrees in the X axis. To do this, type **cam.rotation=quat 80 x_axis**.

5. Next, position the camera so it looks at the 0,0,0 point in 3D space from -100 units in the Y direction and up 20 units in the Z direction. Add **cam.position=[0,-100,20]** to the Listener.

6. Create a teapot for the camera to look at and give it a radius of 20 units by typing the line **teapot radius:20**.

7. Now change the current viewport to the camera view by typing `max vpt camera` (max commands are covered in "The max Command" section below).

8. Type **render vpt** to render the viewport.

The max Command

max commands are an extensive set of calls to the toolbar and menu system. There are over 170 commands, allowing you complete control from the scripter. In your scripts, the syntax for invoking a MAX menu or toolbar command is:

```
max <command name>
```

for example:

```
max file open
max select all
max render scene
max quick render
```

With these commands you can automate a complete process, from opening a file to playing the animation. You can get a partial list of commands by typing the command name after the word "max" in the listener window. To get the list of selection commands, open the listener window and type **max select ?**, which yields the following list:

```
max select ?
  cycle select
  freeze selection
```

```
     hide selection
     select
     select all
     select by color
     select child
     select invert
     select none
     select parent
     shade selected
```

If you need a list of commands that contain the letters "se" for instance, you can also use a partial word after the word "max."

max se ? yields the following:

```
     max se ?
        cycle select
        freeze selection
        group close
        hide selection
        reset file
        select
        select all
        select by color
        select child
        select invert
        select none
        select parent
        shade selected
        subobject sel
        unitsetup
        vpt iso user
        vpt persp user
        zoomext sel
        zoomext sel all
```

To get the complete list of max commands available, type **max ?**.

Programming a Simple User Interface

The simple commands you wrote have been carried out as if you pressed the right buttons in the command panels in the MAX user interface. The real power behind the MAXScript utility is being able to preprogram these commands into a simpler interface of your own design.

While you are working in MAX, the first thing you encounter is a panel populated with buttons, spinners, drop-down lists, and rollouts, all of which control MAX's program functionality.

Interface items, such as buttons, are pressed to cause action in the viewports, spinners change values for objects, rollouts can host a new set of tools, and you encounter floating windows that can pop up on the screen, such as the Material Editor or the Track View.

Throughout this section, you will complete exercises that build a simple user interface with the same type of functionality. The first exercise establishes the user interface, while the second and third exercises add the functionality to the script.

The following exercise will introduce the New Script button and show how to get a few of the most common interface elements onto a panel of your own design. You'll first create a simple Utility Rollout and a Group, both with customized text.

CREATING THE BASIC UTILITY PANEL

1. Start by opening MAX. Go to the Utility Panel and click the MAXScript utility button.

2. Press the New Script button. A modeless window appears, which is your text editor. This is the workspace where you enter the commands that MAXScript evaluates into your application. After all your commands have been typed in, you complete the evaluation by choosing the File, Evaluate All menu choice.

TIP

A handy shortcut for evaluation is the Ctrl+E keys pressed simultaneously. During a programming session, your changes appear on the panel after you evaluate your code. If you are trying to line up text or buttons, this shortcut comes in handy.

3. The most basic of the interface items is the Utility Panel. The utility command creates an initial rollout, which contains your interface items. The following code creates this panel:

```
utility MyUtil "My First Utility"
(
)-end utility
```

All your scripts will begin with the previous statement and must follow the syntax given. The components you can personalize are the name you give the utility, in this case MyUtil, the text in quotes, and the comment after the last parentheses. The —end utility comment helps you keep track of your parentheses count. Comments are two dashes followed by your descriptive note.

4. Press Ctrl+E to evaluate the expression. Notice the title appears in the drop-down list of the MAXScript panel. Your code has been evaluated and the functioning program now lies in the panel.

5. Click the drop-down list on the MAXScript Utility and select My First Utility from the list.

Your first utility has been created. The following steps will take you through creating a rollout, which is a common MAX interface item. It usually has a bar on the panel with a + or − sign, and a title.

6. Your rollout needs to be nested in-between the parentheses you created for the utility. Type the following code to generate the rollout:

```
utility MyUtil "My First Utility"
(

    rollout bout "About My Utility"
        (
        )

    on MyUtil open do
        (
            addRollout bout rolledup;true
        )

) —end utility
```

The previous code is the basic method for creating a rollout on the panel. The rollout statement is the call for the rollout panel item; the word bout is the variable name that you reference when you need to work with the rollout. About My Utility is the title that appears in the rollout's bar. on Myutil open do executes the addRollout event that causes the rollout defined by the variable about to open in a rolled-up state.

Thus far, the utility you created doesn't do much. You need to add a few simple items that extend its capabilities. MAXScript gives you access to the creation of all objects and their properties, so if you want to create an object and change some or all of its settings, you would need to create spinners and sliders for values and buttons for creation.

In the following exercise, which builds upon the previous one, you'll create a button that creates a teapot when pressed. You'll also create two spinners and a slider. The spinner will be used to change the value for the teapot's size and the slider will change the value for the segments of the teapot. You'll set the range of values in the spinners so the user can only change a parameter the way you want.

ADDING FUNCTIONALITY TO THE BASIC UTILITY PANEL

1. Continue from the previous exercise. Create a button called aboutMU. The text on the button will read About. The size of the button will be 45 pixels wide and 20 high. In the definition for the rollout, you placed two parentheses for including more items. Type the following code inside these parentheses:

```
button aboutMU "About" width:45 height:20
on aboutMU pressed do
(
    messagebox "My First Utility\nby ME\nVersion .1" title:"About
My Utility"
)
```

The commands create a button that, when pressed, will pop up a message box with the words in the quotes formatted as in Figure 26.2. When placing text in quotes for messages, a \n will place the text, following it on a new line.

FIGURE 26.2

What your message-box will look like when you press the About button you created.

Next you'll create another panel item called a group, which will help to organize several tools you'll need to add. A group is a bordered area on the panel that can contain the interface items a user will manipulate.

2. Add the following code just above the on MyUtil open command to make the button that creates the teapot, a spinner, and a slider that enables the user to change the radius, and another spinner to change the segments. Text in quotes is typed as a description appearing on the panel. The range is defined as the start value, end value, and current value. The type: parameter line specifies the types of numbers in the control, and the scale;parameter specifies the value for each mouse click in the spinner.

```
Group "Object Creator"
(
button tea "Teapot"
spinner rad "Spin Radius" range:[10,50,20] type:#integer
spinner seg "Segments" range:[4,32,12] type:#integer scale:1
slider  slrad "Slide Radius" range:[10,50,20] type:#integer
)
```

The last value in the square brackets is the number that shows up in the spinner at the time the utility is started, the default value. You'll use this value when you create your teapot.

3. Press Ctrl+E, or in the File menu, choose Evaluate All to reevaluate the script. Press your About button to call the message box.

4. Save your script using the File, Save menu choice.

The buttons and slider have been created, but you need to add functionality to them (see Figure 26.3).

5. Add the following code to get the teapot button to start the creation process. Just above the on MyUtil open command, type the following:

```
on tea pressed do
(
    pot=teapot radius;rad.value
    pot.name="TestPot"
    pot.segs=seg.value
)
```

This statement says when the button you named tea is pressed, the action in the parentheses will take place. The first action creates a teapot and stores a reference to the teapot in the variable name *pot*. The initial radius of the teapot is set at the creation level to the value of the spinner created earlier named *rad*. Properties that have default values inherent at the time of their creation, such as an object's name and an amount of segments, are given their default values if they are not specified by your code. These properties can be changed as shown in the previous statements where the name and number of segments are set after the object is created.

FIGURE 26.3

Your basic panel to this point.

6. Evaluate and rerun the script. Press the teapot button. Select the teapot on the screen, and go to the Modify panel to verify that the settings and teapot name are correct.

In order to link the spinner values to the teapot you created, it's necessary to make the name *pot* visible to the rest of the script. You'll do this by declaring a local variable in the beginning of the script.

7. Add the following line in the beginning of the script just above the roll-out commands:

```
local pot
```

Then add these lines under the on tea pressed section of code:

```
on rad changed value do
    (
      pot.radius=rad.value
      slrad.value=value
    )
on seg changed value do
    (
      pot.segs=seg.value
    )
on slrad changed value do
    (
      pot.radius=value
      rad.value=value
    )
```

The on rad changed value do statement indicates that when the value in the spinner named rad is changed, the radius of the teapot you named pot is updated to the new value in rad.

8. Evaluate the code and rerun your script. Press the teapot button and spin your spinners to change the values for your teapot. Save the file as **MyUtil.ms**. The finished script is found on the CD and is named MyUtil.ms.

T IP

Good programming conventions will make your scripts easy to read and understand. Notice that the parentheses are vertically aligned. This aids in your analysis of the code after the program becomes larger.

One of the types of panels that is prevalent in MAX is modeless floating panels, full of buttons, checkboxes, spinners, and other useful informational windows. MAXScript enables you access to these. The following exercise will change your introductory script to add one of these floating panels.

ADDING A FLOATING PANEL TO THE INTERFACE

1. Open MAXScript and open your MyUtil.ms script file.

2. Just above the group Object Creator add the following line:

```
rollout creator "Wow I'm Floating!"
    (
```

3. Just above the on MyUtil open do code, place the closing parentheses for the rollout and add a comment to remind you that this is the closing parentheses.

4. Add the following code to the on MyUtil open do section:

```
nr=NewRolloutFloater "Wow I'm Floating!" 200 250
addRollout creator nr
```

Your new rollout code should now read like the following:

```
rollout creator "Wow I'm Floating!"
(
group "Object Creator"
  (
    button tea "Teapot"
    spinner rad "Radius" range:[10,50,20]
    spinner seg "Segments" range:[4,32,12] type:#integer scale:1
    slider  slrad "Slide Radius" range:[10,50,20] type:#integer

  )

on tea pressed do
    (
        pot=teapot radius;rad.value
        pot.name="TestPot"
        pot.segs=seg.value
```

```
            )

on rad changed value do
    (
            pot.radius=value
    )
on slrad changed value do
  (
        pot.radius=value
    )

on seg changed value do
    (
            pot.segs=seg.value
    )
) — end rollout creator

on MyUtil open do
    (
            addrollout bout rolledup;true                 —adds
the about rollout
            nr=NewRolloutFloater "Wow I'm Floating!" 200 250   —
sets up the floater
            addRollout creator nr                         —adds
the float rollout
    )
```

5. Evaluate your code and your Object Creator is now a floating window.

The finished code can be found on the CD and is called MyUtil2.ms. Some text has been added to the slider area for instructions to the user.

Creating a Cloud Generator with a Sample Renderer

The simple example explored earlier will provide the background for the creation of your next tutorial. In this lesson, you create a new MAX 2 object called a Boxgizmo, and you'll set it up to be the cloud container. You'll also create a test renderer so you can see the effect of your setting changes before committing to a full render.

This section will explore these topics:

- Creating the panels
- Creating scene objects and cameras
- Making a test renderer
- Changing scene element settings with spinners
- Simple error trapping
- Resetting original values
- Encrypting your script

Creating the Panels

When designing an application, good planning will help you to avoid going back and trying to fix up a mess in your code. Define what it is you want to do, create logical and balanced areas for your interface items, and set the code up accordingly.

Your first task, then, is to define the panel layout. Starting with the main group, you need a group that will contain a button for the Cloud Generator creation using a boxgizmo and three spinners for the size of the boxgizmo. The content of the group and the syntax for their creation is as follows.

Buttons `button button_name "Description" additional_parameters`

Spinners `spinner spinner_name "Description" additional_parameters`

Sliders `slider slider_name "Description" additional_parameters`

One of the additional parameters you will add to your spinners and sliders is a range. The range has a minimum, maximum, and default value and is written at the end of the spinner or slider.

For example, `Slider slides "Slide Me" range:[-100,100,0]`

Some descriptive text on the panel will aid the potential user in the use of the program. This text is in the form of a label and can be aligned right, center, or left as an additional parameter.

Label `Label label_name "Description" additional_parameters`

For example, `Label first "Just Some Text" align:#center`

CREATING YOUR INTERFACE PANELS

1. Type the first of the code as follows:

```
utility Cgen "Cloud Generator"
(
  rollout bout "About"
    (
     button aboutCG "About" width:45 height:20 —WxH of the button
     on aboutCG pressed do
        (
          messagebox "Cloud Generator\nBy: ME"title:"About Cloud
Generator"
        )
    ) —end rollout bout
) —end utility
```

2. Add a group for the boxgizmo interface items described at the beginning of this section. You'll call the group Cloud Creation and place the three spinners and four lines of descriptive text, called labels, inside the group. In-between the end rollout and end utility, type the code for the new group:

```
group "Cloud Creation"
(
  label a "First Create Scene W/Gizmo" align:#center
  label b "Gizmo Size is:" align:#left
  label c "-1000 to 1000" align:#right
  spinner hi "Height " range:[-1000,1000,200]
  spinner wide "Width " range:[-1000,1000,200]
  spinner len "Length " range:[-1000,1000,200]
  label blank0 —a blank line to separate lines of text
  button create "Create Clouds"
)
on Cgen open do
  (
    addrollout bout rolledUp;true
  )
```

3. Evaluate the script to make sure all is working (see Figure 26.4). Save your script as **Cloud1.ms**.

The finished code can be found on the CD and is called Cloud1.ms. This completes the first of your groups. The next addition to the panel is the test renderer group.

FIGURE 26.4

Group 1, the scene
creator

Now, you'll create another group for the renderer with a bitmap window, bitmap sizing spinners, and a button to start the render process.

4. Open your Cloud1.ms file if it isn't still open.

5. Place the following code right under the cloud creation group:

```
group "Test Renderer"
  (
      label d "Next Test Render Your Scene" align:#center
      bitmap testrend Width:120 Height:120 align:#center
      button renview "Render Viewport"
      label ss "Change Render Window Size" align:#center
      spinner Xsizer "X-Size: " range:[20,120,120] type:#integer
```

```
scale:10
  spinner Ysizer "Y-Size: " range:[20,120,120] type:#integer
scale:10
  )
```

6. Evaluate the script and take a look at the panel (see Figure 26.5).

FIGURE 26.5

The Cloud Generator is taking shape.

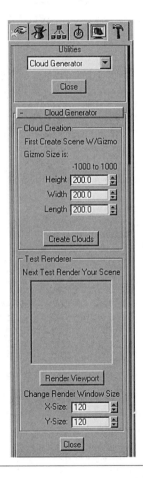

Examine your code. Note the scale factor added to the spinners, which determines how many numbers each click of the spinner will produce, or the snap value. This completes the second of your groups. Save your file as Cloud2.ms. The finished code can be found on the CD and is called Cloud2.ms.

The empty bitmap window created using the bitmap command is the place where the test rendering will go. You can put any picture file in a bitmap window. Render a scene at the size of the window you created (120 × 120) and save it as a .bmp file, or use a scanned photo sized to your bitmap, and add the line: `filname:"my_pic.bmp"` to the end of the line of your *bitmap*. My_pic is your own file name. Make sure my_pic.bmp is in your MAX/Images subdirectory. MAX will look for the file there first, then in the startup script subdirectory, and then in the PATHS environment variable. This feature is great for placing custom pictures on buttons that may have special functionality.

The last group you will add is the group that holds the utilities for changing the cloud parameters from the default values of the program. The following exercise takes you through the steps to create this group.

CREATING THE FINAL GROUP

1. Open your Cloud2.ms file.

2. Add the following group code after the group "Test Renderer" code:

```
group "Change Initial Settings"
  (
    label e "Next Change Your Settings" align:#left
    label f "And Re-Render" align:#left
    label Blank1
    spinner dens "Cloud Density" align:#left range:[10,50,30]
    colorpicker pik "Cloud Color: " color:[255,255,255]
    label np "Noise Parameters"
    spinner nsize "Size" align:#right range:[5,50,10]
    spinner nlthr "Low Threshold"align:#right range:[0,1,.1]
    spinner nuni "Uniformity" align:#right range:[0,.9,0.02]
  )
```

3. Evaluate the code to see the finished interface, Then save your file as cloud3.ms (see Figure 26.6). The finished script can be found on the CD and is named Cloud3.ms.

The fifth line enables a colorpicker to the interface panel. The colorpicker is a common window found in MAX that enables the user to change an object or light's default color.

FIGURE 26.6

The Renderer and Settings Changer groups.

All the groups have now been created. The next task is to add the functionality to the buttons, spinners, and the rest of the items you created. You will begin in the following section by creating the scene objects and cameras.

Creating Scene Objects and Cameras

The first functionality you should add to the program is the creation of the components necessary to contain and view the cloud environment. MAX 2.0 has three new helpers in its toolbox called Gizmos. The Atmospheric Apparatus you'll use is the Boxgizmo, and in it you'll create your fog and your camera. You'll name both and also set up an environmental fog atmosphere to give the background some color. The button, *Create*, will do all the necessary work when pressed.

CREATING THE CAMERA AND GIZMO

1. Open your Cloud3.ms file.

2. Just above the on Cgen open do code, type the following:

```
on create pressed do

(
 CloudBox=boxgizmo height;hi.value length;len.value
width;wide.value
 cam=freecamera rotation:(quat 90 x_axis) pos:[0,(-
len.value/2),(hi.value/3)] name:"Sky & Clouds"


 max vpt camera
)—end on create
```

Before you continue adding more functionality to this button, examine the code to see what you have so far. The first line is the command to create a boxgizmo called CloudBox with the current height, length, and width values taken from the spinners named hi, len, and wide. Because the position is not specified, the gizmobox is created at world [0,0,0]. Next is the Freecamera statement, creating a non-target Freecamera, rotating it, and positioning it at X=0, Y=(-len.value/2), and Z=(hi.value/3). The Y and Z values are small formulas to get the value property from your length and height spinners and divide them by another value, so that no matter what length and height the boxgizmo, the camera will always be inside it. Properties for objects can be specified on one line as in the above example, or on separate lines as in the fog code in the next step. The last command typed takes the active viewport and makes it the camera view.

3. Continuing the example, type the following lines right underneath the code in step 2, with the atmospheric content code.

```
Foggy=Fog fog_color:[0,0,255]
Foggy.name="SAfog"
Foggy.Fog_type=1
Foggy.falloff=1
VFatmos=Volume_Fog density;dens.value
Addatmospheric Foggy
Addatmospheric VFatmos
```

```
Appendgizmo VFatmos CloudBox
VFatmos.name="SAclouds"
VFatmos.Soften_Gizmo_Edges=.5
VFatmos.Noise_Type=1
VFatmos.Low_Threshold=nlthr.value
VFatmos.Uniformity=nuni.value
VFatmos.size=nsize.value
```

4. The creation of the various items in the previous step have been listed in a sort of enclosed environment inside the on create pressed do section. You named these variables *VFatmos* and *Foggy*, but they are not visible to the program outside this statement. In order to allow any changes to the objects assigned to these local variables, you need to make them local to the whole program. In the area above the code for the rollout but inside the first bracket for the main utility, add 2 variables for the fog. When declaring variables separate each with a comma. Type the following:

```
local  VFatmos,
       Foggy
```

5. Save the file as Cloud4.ms and evaluate it. Run the program and press the Create Clouds button. When pressed, the button creates the boxgizmo you named *CloudBox*, the camera called *cam*, and the two atmospheres declared as local variables in the beginning of the program. You also attached the volume fog to the boxgizmo named CloudBox. The finished script can be found on the CD and is named Cloud4.ms.

The Create Clouds button has done a lot of work for you. Open the menu for Rendering/Environment and examine the entries for the newly added items. The first line added the fog parameters through the variable name Foggy you added in the beginning of the program. The fog color is blue with the name SAfog and the fog type is a layered fog with a bottom falloff. The next code is for the VFatmos variable, which is given a volume fog with a density value taken from the dens spinner. The atmospheres were next added to the environment and the boxgizmo was attached to the variable for the volume fog. The name was changed to SAclouds. The last of the lines changed several of the volume fog parameters.

To get information about any of the properties, known as MAX Classes, of the objects you create on the screen, open the Listener and type **showclass** **"class_name"**. For example, to find what properties of the Volume_Fog can be added to the code you created, type **showclass "Volume_Fog*.*"** and then press Enter.

FIGURE 26.7

Showclass for
Volume_Fog.

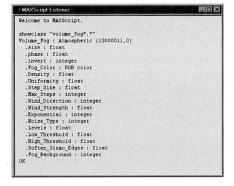

The previous exercise introduced you to the methods for creating several common MAX interface items, objects, and effects. Many times when testing effects you would like to see a preview before committing to a full render. You created the necessary panel for the renderer but need to add functionality to this set of panel items.

Making a Test Renderer

The next focus of your attention will be on the panel for the preview renderer. You'll add the necessary code to fill the render window with a small adjustable sample picture rendered by the MAX renderer.

Adding Functions to the Renderer Exercise

1. Open your Cloud4.ms.

2. In the code for the renderer group, you created a bitmap window, a button for rendering, and two spinners for changing the render window size. In order to get the window to receive the rendered bitmap, add the following code just above the on Cgen open do lines:

```
on renview pressed do
(
 view=render outputwidth;Xsizer.value OutputHeight;Ysizer.value
vfb;off
 testrend.bitmap=view
)
```

Here a variable, view, is assigned to the resulting output image from a MAXScript command that renders a viewport. The rendered image size is taken from the values in the spinners you added to the group. The vfb;off refers to the Virtual Frame Buffer in MAX. You are shutting this off so that the render takes place only in the test render space. The .bitmap property of the testrend variable is then given the parameters in the view variable, and the result is that the rendered viewport shows up in your window (see Figure 26.8).

3. Save the file as Cloud5.ms and evaluate it. Press the Create Clouds button, and then the Render Viewport button to see the results. The default values have given the clouds a natural look. Because the clouds were created with a volume fog, the effect takes place three-dimensionally inside the boxgizmo. The finished code can be found on the CD and is called Cloud5.ms.

To complete the last group you created, the spinners must be linked to the proper property values for the volume fog. The proper method to code these links has already been discussed in previous exercises. You can find the updated section on the CD and is called Cloud6.ms. Before you peek at the program, try to finish the section yourself.

The only thing that remains for the completion of this program is some small additions, which are not absolutely necessary if you are the only person who will use this program. Some additional code should be added to bulletproof some areas and make some small additions to enhance functions.

FIGURE 26.8

The test renderer showing the Sky & Clouds Viewport.

Simple Error Trapping: Disabling and Enabling User Input

This script is now functionally complete and will work well if you first create the clouds and then change the values for them. If you try to change the values first before creating the clouds, however, an error is generated. You can eliminate a potential user from making a mistake by shutting some of the spinners and the colorpicker off temporarily. These objects can then be turned back on after an event allowing for their designed purpose. In this case you'll turn off the items that change the as-yet-uncreated atmospheres, and when the Cloud Creator button is pressed the items will be turned back on.

DISABLING AND ENABLING INTERFACE CONTROLS

1. Reset MAX and start MAXScript with the Cloud Generator. Change one of the settings for the Cloud Generator in the Change Initial

Settings panel. An error reporting an "Unknown property in unde-fined" is generated. This is because the Volume Fog hasn't been creat-ed yet and the program cannot change what doesn't exist.

Because this Cloud Generator produces an initial state of settings that are preprogrammed to look good at the press of the Create button, you need to somehow deactivate the spinners and colorpicker in the Change Initial Settings panel.

2. In the group called Change Initial Settings, add the following code to the spinners and the colorpicker, at the end of each line:

```
enabled;false
```

The group should read:

```
group "Change Initial Settings"
(

label e "Next Change Your Settings" align:#left
label f "And Re-Render" align:#left
label Blank1
spinner dens "Cloud Density" align:#left range:[10,50,30]
enabled;false
colorpicker pik "Cloud Color:   " color:[255,255,255] enabled;false
label np "Cloud Noise Parameters" align:#left
spinner nsize "Size" align:#right range:[5,50,10] enabled;false
spinner nlthr "Low Threshold"align:#right range:[0,1,.1]
enabled;false
spinner nuni "Uniformity" align:#right range:[0,.9,0.02]
enabled;false
label blank2

) — end
```

This shuts down the spinners and colorpicker when the program starts up.

3. Evaluate the code and try to change a value in the spinners in the Change Initial Settings group. Press the Create Clouds button to cre-ate the scene and render with the preview renderer. The scene is cre-ated and can be rendered, but if you try to change your settings, the spinners are still grayed out and nonfunctional (see Figure 26.9).

FIGURE 26.9

The nonfunctional spinners and color-picker.

4. When the user presses the Create Button, you want the grayed out entities to become active. To enable the functionality of the various buttons, spinners, and colorpicker, add the following code into the `on create pressed do` section:

```
create.enabled=false
nsize.enabled=true
nlthr.enabled=true
nuni.enabled=true
pik.enabled=true
dens.enabled=true
```

Your new `on create pressed do` section should now read as follows:

```
on create pressed do
   (
```

```
create.enabled=false
nsize.enabled=true
nlthr.enabled=true
nuni.enabled=true
pik.enabled=true
dens.enabled=true
boxgizmo height;hi.value length;len.value width;wide.value
cam=freecamera()
cam.rotation=quat 90 x_axis
cam.pos=[0,(-len.value/2),(hi.value/3)]
cam.name="Sky & Clouds"
max vpt camera
Foggy=Fog Fog_Color: [0,0,255]
VFatmos=Volume_Fog Density;dens.value
Addatmospheric Foggy
Addatmospheric VFatmos
appendgizmo VFatmos $BoxGizmo01
VFatmos.name="SAclouds"
Foggy.name="SAfog"
Foggy.Fog_Type=1
Foggy.falloff=1
VFatmos.Soften_Gizmo_Edges=.5
VFatmos.Noise_Type=1
VFatmos.Low_Threshold=0.1
VFatmos.Uniformity=0.02
VFatmos.size=10

)
```

The first line deactivates the Create button on the Create clouds panel
so the user can't create another set of clouds over the ones you created.
The next lines turn on the spinners and colorpicker in the Change
Initial Settings group.

5. A nice addition to this program would be another colorpicker to change
    the color of the Fog environment. Add this line under the first color-
    picker in the Change Initial Settings group:

```
colorpicker pik2 "Fog Color:   " color:[0,0,255] enabled;false
```

6. Now you must add the code to enable the second colorpicker. In the on
    create pressed do section, add the following:

```
pik2.enabled=true
```

7. There now has to be a link from the second colorpicker to the fog environment you named Foggy. Under the on pik changed color do code, add the following:

```
on pik2 changed color do
        (
                Foggy.Fog_Color = color
        )
```

8. Save this file as Cloud7.ms. The finished example is on the CD and is named Cloud7.ms.

This added code will not allow the user to set values for nonexisting objects, eliminating the possibility of generating an error. If you plan on distributing your scripts, including error-trapping code will be a wise addition.

Resetting Original Values

While playing around with the values in the program, you may have forgotten what the original settings were and you might want to reset the values to start over. This kind of functionality is found in many programs. In this next exercise, you'll add a Reset button and the necessary code to reinitialize the spinners and colorpickers to their original values.

GOING BACK TO THE BEGINNING

1. Open the script called Cloud7.ms, and add a new button in the Change Initial Settings group. Then place the line of code at the bottom of the group. Name the button re_set, and make sure it's not enabled:

```
button re_set "Reset Settings" enabled;false
```

2. Now add the code to get the button working. In the on create pressed do section, type the following:

```
re_set.enabled=true
```

3. Make a new section for the re_set button pressed event by adding the following lines:

```
on re_set pressed do
        (
```

```
            create.enabled=true
            hi.value=200
            wide.value=200
            len.value=200
            Xsizer.value=120
            Ysizer.value=120
            nsize.value=10
            nlthr.value=0.1
            nuni.value=0.02
            pik.color=[255,255,255]
            dens.value=30
            nsize.enabled=false
            nlthr.enabled=false
            nuni.enabled=false
            pik.enabled=false
    pik2.enabled=false
            dens.enabled=false
    re_set.enabled=false
            max reset file
        )
```

4. Save the file as **Clouds.ms**.

All the original values will be set back to the original settings. The last command is a call to MAX for a reset.

T IP

An alternate method of resetting MAX is to use the command resetMAXFile #noPrompt. This does not generate the prompt for the user to save the file, or for the "Are you sure" message box. The finished script with this alternate is on the CD and is called CloudGen.ms.

5. Evaluate this new code. Create the environment and change all the default settings. Next use the Reset button to test its functionality. The completed code can be found on the CD and is named Clouds.ms.

The more you work with the MAXScript Utility, the more you will see that the scope of it is vast. Without knowing a full-featured programming language, you can tap into the deepest regions of MAX's functioning core. You can certainly never end your tweaking and adding given the robust nature of this scripting utility! Experiment with more additions and start gathering ideas for programs of your own design.

Encrypting Your Scripts

One of the best features of the MAXScript Utility is the ability for the creator of the script to hide the actual code used to create it, and still be able to give it away or sell it. This opens the door for the casual user and the professional to market their ideas for scripts. If the proliferation of plug-ins for MAX is any indication, there will certainly be many more scripts available for people to play with.

Encrypting a script you have created is not very difficult, as shown in the following exercise.

ENCRYPTING THE SCRIPT

1. Start MAX and go to the Utility Tab. Start the MAXScript utility and open the Clouds.ms script.

2. Make sure that the full script name including the file extension of .ms is typed inside the quotes after the encrypt command. Open the Listener window and type the following:

   ```
   EncryptScript "Clouds.ms"
   ```

3. Press either Enter key and you receive an OK prompt. The script is encrypted and renamed to Clouds.mse.

The encrypted scripts run in the same manner as an unencrypted script, but you will not be able to edit the text. The encryption process will not delete your original file, so if you need to change something, you can use the original unencrypted script and then reencrypt the newly changed file.

In Practice: Scripting with MAXScript

- **Readable Code.** Always make sure your code is logical in its organization. Place opening and closing parentheses lined up vertically so you know what major and minor blocks of code belong together. Make use of comments in your code as reminders about what a particular piece of code is for.

- **Group Like Items Together**. When designing your interfaces, keep your groups organized so the end user can understand what does what in the program. Use descriptive text as instructions on the panels of the various groups.

- **Save Incremented Versions of Your Programs**. If you are creating a fairly large application, save as prog1, prog2, and so on. If you totally mess up, you can always go back to a previous version you know is good. This is also a good strategy for the saving of scene files.

- **Don't try to reinvent the wheel**. Look over scripts from other writers and learn from their examples; this is the best way to learn. If a scripting concept looks foreign at first, try to rewrite it in your own style in a short test program so you can get a grasp on how the logic of a section of code can benefit your program.

Part VII

RENDERING AND COMPOSITING

Chapter 27

RENDERING STILL IMAGES

As with any technique, 3D graphics start as an idea and evolve into a finished work of art. One difference between computer-generated graphics and traditional techniques, such as photography and painting, is the amount of control you have over every aspect of your image. The benefits of computer graphics are many, including the vast array of special effects you may use. To achieve the look you want in your final composition, you must master many techniques, including rendering your final output.

Rendering often seems simple enough at first glance, but it isn't as simple as clicking Render and hoping for the best.

You must consider the type of output for your images. Will you render still images for print, or will it be output to videotape? You may plan to output to a digital format, such as Video for Windows, for playback from a hard drive. Regardless of which output your project requires, a successful rendering requires output-specific settings. This chapter is focused on still images and covers the following topics:

- 3D Studio MAX rendering basics

- Understanding color depth

- Determining output resolution and selecting media

- Examining model complexity and accuracy

3D Studio MAX Rendering Basics

You might think of the Render button in 3DS MAX as the equivalent of the Print button in any other application. Rendering is the process of generating the still image, or a series of still images, you've created in MAX. There are many decisions to be made when you reach for the Render button. Fortunately□3DS MAX gives you a wide range of control over what objects and areas of the viewport are rendered. It has many settings that reduce repetition usually necessary to initiate a render in other programs.

To set up a render, use the Render Scene option. You can choose the icon or select Render from the pull-down menu, which is the render command center, with all the most commonly used settings in its window (see Figure 27.1).

NOTE

3D Studio MAX includes a high-quality, fast scanline production renderer, and additional renderers are available as plug-ins. This capability adds a tremendous flexibility to the 3D Studio MAX environment, allowing unlimited different rendering types within one seamless package. Choose File, Preferences and select the Rendering tab to use plug-in renderers for raytracing or radiosity.

The Time Output area of the Render Control dialog selects the frames to render. The render could be a still frame, the active time segment, a specific range, or a string of specific frames. When using the active time segment, or a specific range, it is possible to render every Nth frame. Every tenth frame out of a specific range can be rendered, for example. This is often useful for rendering a progression of frames that represent what takes place in the animation.

FIGURE 27.1

3D Studio MAX common render parameters.

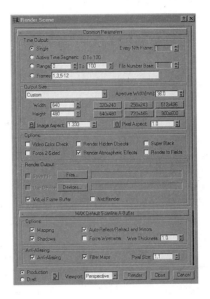

A wide variety of settings also are available in the Render Control dialog, including Video Color Check, Atmospheric Effects, Super Black, Fields, and Force 2-Sided. Only two of these are particularly useful for still images: Force 2-Sided and Atmospheric Effects.

Force 2-Sided is used to force all objects to render as two-sided objects. Although this can sometimes be helpful, especially with objects that have inverted normals or are missing back faces, it is generally not recommended for regular use because two-sided materials allow specific control-saving render time. Atmospheric Effects enables you to render such things as fire, fog, and volume lighting. Also in this dialog are video and animation settings, which are covered in Chapter 28, "Rendering Animation."

Rendering Control

3D Studio MAX's render controls can be broken down into two sections: initiating the render and controlling what's being rendered. These sections work together to produce an image. 3DS MAX provides several ways to initiate the render, or draw it to the screen. It also offers several ways to control exactly what is rendered by the use of render types.

Initiating a Render

3DS MAX can initiate a render by selecting Rendering, Render from the menu bar, or more commonly, by pressing one of three icons related to rendering: Render Scene, Quick Render, or Render Last (see Figure 27.2).

FIGURE 27.2

A view's render icons and render types.

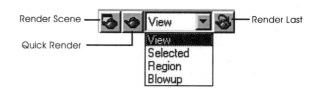

- **Render Scene:** Clicking the first, Render Scene (Shift+R), brings up the Render Scene dialog, enabling you to configure the resolution, output filename, and so on (refer to Figure 27.1). Use this option when you need to change settings or are ready to output to a file.

- **Quick Render:** For quick test renders, the second icon, Quick Render, (Shift+Q) is an even more useful selection. This offers a one-click way to render any viewport.

- **Render Last:** Use Render Last (Shift+E), the icon furthest to the right, to render the viewport and render type last rendered. Therefore, this method is most useful when working in one viewport, and adjusting lighting, or textures.

Render Types

3D Studio MAX provides several options for controlling how much of a scene to render. These options are available as a cluster of render types at the top-right portion of the interface. These include the capability to render View, Region, Blowup, and Selected (shown in Figure 27.2).

- **View Render:** View is the most common render type because it renders the entire viewport. For final renders, this type is the one to choose.

- **Region:** The Render Region option enables you to render just a section of the scene. It comes in handy when you fine-tune one area of your view. Objects that cast shadows or reflections in another object's surface within your render region are still calculated, even though the shadow or reflection-casting object itself is not within the region.

- **Blowup:** Blowing up a view enables an area to be enlarged during the rendering process.

- **Selective:** The capability to render only selected objects is primarily an aid to see the effects of material or mesh modifications for that object. The drawback is for any material that contains a reflection or objects that have shadows cast across them. Neither of these effects can be shown using Render Selected because only the selected objects are being considered.

NEW TO R2

3DS MAX R2 now includes the ability to set two different rendering modes, one as draft renderer, the other as production renderer. Two radial buttons labeled Draft and Production are located at the bottom of the Renderer dialog box. You define each rendering mode by selecting one of the radial buttons, then adjusting the appropriate settings. You can switch between the two different settings with the flyout menu located by holding down the Render Scene button.

Selective Raytracing

A long-awaited addition to the rendering capabilities of 3DS MAX is raytracing. Raytracing, in the most simplified definition, enables you to render reflections and refractions in your scene with incredible realism. 3D Studio MAX has always been able to produce accurate raytraced shadows, but not for raytracing reflection and refraction for the objects in your scene until now.

There are two ways of assigning raytracing: raytracing material and the raytracing map. By assigning the new raytracing material or raytracing map to the objects in your scene that can benefit from raytracing, MAX renders raytracing effects only for those objects. Controlling which objects are included saves valuable rendering time. Figure 27.3 shows the new ray-tracing material type, and the new raytracing map, as assigned in the Materials Editor. Subtle differences exist between the two. Essentially, the raytracing material is a new material, just like the Standard material. The raytracing map enables you to assign a raytracing map to any type of material, just as you would any other diffuse, bump, or reflection map. When you select raytracing as your map type, the Raytracer Parameters menu, seen in Figure 27.4, is displayed.

FIGURE 27.3

Shown on the left is the new raytracing material. On the right is the new raytracing map applied just as any other type of bump, diffuse, or reflection map.

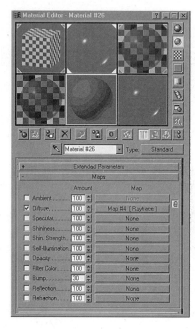
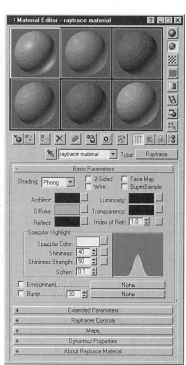

Raytracing dramatically increases rendering time, so it's worth taking the time to experiment with all the settings available to help speed up rendering on your particular scene.

FIGURE 27.4

Shown here are the options associated with the raytracing map type.

Understanding Color Depth

Color depth (also called bit depth) refers to the number of colors a computer-generated image contains. Computers must convert information of any kind into numeric sequences, so naturally, they must number and store colors.

Several common bit depths are used in computer-generated imagery, including an 8-bit adjustable palette, 15- and 16-bit fixed palettes, and 24-bit and 64-bit color depths. The more bits, the more colors. The actual mathematics of each color depth isn't as important to know for the average user as is knowing the number of colors each color depth contains, and their strengths and weaknesses. Chapter 2, "Mixing Color and Light," has in-depth discussions about each bit depth. The following is a brief description of each bit depth.

- **8-bit adjustable palette:** Images contain only 256 colors out of the entire spectrum. The exact colors can differ between different images as well because the palette is adjustable on an image-by-image basis. The low number of colors is not sufficient to realistically display the entire color spectrum, but this palette type is quick to load and display, and has a small file size.

- **15- and 16-bit fixed palette:** Images contain 32,768 and 65,536 colors, respectively. These bit depths are less common than 8-bit and 24-bit bit-depths, but they are a good trade-off between large file size and color realism. Containing a fixed palette also ensures that many images in either 15- or 16-bit color will not conflict in the colors they use, which is useful in games, as well as in multimedia production.

- **24-bit color:** Images are the most common true color image types. At 16.7 million colors, these images contain sufficient color to faithfully reproduce any image viewable to the naked eye. Animation, whether going to film or video, is almost always rendered in 24-bit color.

- **64-bit color:** Images are pretty uncommon, although this color depth is an important one for 3D Studio MAX users because 3D Studio MAX renders internally to 64-bit color, and then dithers down to lower color depths from there. While 64-bit color is not displayable on common computer screens, this color depth is used in 3D Studio MAX's superior analytical antialiasing. This color depth, especially when used with other render information (such as G-buffer), can be saved into the RLA file format and used at a later time by any 3D Studio MAX Video Post plug-in or composite.

Working with 8-Bit Still Images

Much of the focus in magazines and in Kinetix's marketing of 3D Studio MAX is on 24-bit images and high-end output devices. Many people are intimidated by this emphasis and fail to realize that 3D Studio MAX is an excellent tool for creating 8-bit images and Animator Pro-style FLIC files.

You're not going to get your work on a major television network using 8-bit technology, but most computer games, Web sites, multimedia projects, disk-based presentations, and informational kiosks rely primarily on 8-bit technology.

Many markets exist for 8-bit images and animation. Using 8-bit color doesn't mean that your images are inferior or nonprofessional. It just means you've chosen to use this file format, for one reason or another. The 8-bit file format also has some advantages that justify its use, such as the following:

- **Small file size:** Small files are a necessity for WWW-based sites or for presentations that must run on limited hardware or from a floppy disk.

- **Fast loading and display:** The small file size helps speed up the time it takes to load 8-bit images into memory and display 8-bit images onscreen, essential for today's high-speed games.

- **Wide software compatibility:** Many paint and presentation programs support 8-bit file formats, such as BMP, PCX, and PNG.

- **Low video hardware requirements:** The low-end VGA standard that supports 8-bit color at 320×200 resolution still is used on many systems. SVGA support of 8-bit color at a resolution of 640×480 also is very popular.

If you're creating images to display on the World Wide Web, PC-based games, a client's system, portable presentations, or disk-based marketing, you may need to work with 8-bit images.

Working in 8-bit color imposes some restrictions on what you can do, but these restrictions are not as onerous as they might at first seem. The limit of 256 colors requires that you exercise care when you plan the use of color in your images. You also must compromise between minimizing file size or minimizing the side effects of the color restrictions.

Banding

Banding refers to what happens when too few colors are available to represent a smooth transition from one color to the next. These transitions are called color ramps or gradients, and are used for shading geometry or when you choose a gradient background material in 3D Studio MAX. Because not enough colors exist to represent the gradient smoothly, it is divided into a few broad bands of color that approximate the gradient. Figure 27.5 shows a sphere rendered against a gradient background. Both the sphere and the background exhibit severe banding.

The two main techniques for avoiding banding are careful color selection and the avoidance of gradients. Color selection focuses on the fact that you have only 256 colors with which to work. If you choose colors for your scene that are widely different, such as multiple primaries or fully saturated hues, each color receives only a few palette slots for its shading colors, and banding is inevitable. If, instead, you choose most of your colors from one color family with a complementary color thrown in for contrast, the colors can share many of the same shades and you reduce banding.

FIGURE 27.5

*Color banding in an
8-bit image.*

Avoiding gradients requires breaking up the surface of your geometry. Smooth, solid-color objects suffer the most from banding effects. The only way to represent shading on the surface of a smooth object is to use a gradient as the color changes from light to dark. One way to break up the surface and avoid banding is to use mapped materials. Look at the objects around you right now. How many have smooth, solid-color surfaces? Painted metal usually has a smooth, solid surface, but almost everything else has bumps, grooves, and patterns. Not only do bump maps, texture maps, and reflections add to the realism of your scene, but they also break up the surface to reduce banding.

Figure 27.6 shows a rendering using solid colors of widely different hues. The vase is green, the sphere is blue, the table top is brown, and the whole scene is banded. Figure 27.7 is the same scene with only the materials changed. The vase is now a tan marble, the sphere is shiny copper, and the table has a wood grain texture. Banding is hardly noticeable. The key to this rendering is that the textures break up the surfaces and the materials share a similar color range.

Dithering

Sometimes banding is unavoidable. For example, say you need to model smooth-painted surfaces when textures and bumps aren't acceptable. In such a case, 3D Studio MAX provides a setting in the Rendering

Preferences called Dither Palette. The default for this setting is on, but you might want to change it or at least consider whether you want to use dithering when you prepare to render. Dithering blurs the edges between bands, which helps your eye ignore the edges and accept the illusion of a smooth color gradient.

FIGURE 27.6

A scene with banding caused by poor material selection.

FIGURE 27.7

The same scene using mapped materials to avoid banding.

The drawback to dithering is that it can greatly increase file size. Most 8-bit image formats use a compression technique that identifies and compresses areas of contiguous color. A side effect of dithering is that it eliminates many areas of contiguous color, causing file size to increase. For example, the image in Figure 27.7 increased in size by 30 percent with dithering turned on, even though dithering provided almost no improvement in the quality of the image. In general, you should try to use mapping techniques with Dither Palette turned off to achieve your goals for image quality. You then must decide whether you need dithering for the image quality that you want and balance that decision against the need for smaller file sizes.

Understanding Model Complexity

Another issue concerning 8-bit imaging is rendering resolution and model complexity. Typically, 8-bit images are rendered for display on a standard computer screen, often at a rendering resolution of 640×480. Compare that to typical 24-bit resolutions for video at 756×512 or for film printing at 2048×1536. You quickly realize that the detail necessary for high-color, high-resolution rendering is overkill for 8-bit rendering. Save yourself rendering time and build your models knowing that low color and low resolution don't require as much detail.

24-Bit High-Resolution Imaging

True color, 24-bit rendering, isn't nearly so demanding. It always produces the top-quality image and enables you to spend your time compositing materials and lighting the model to the highest possible degree.

Determining Output Resolution and Selecting Media

Determining the project's ultimate goals as early as possible in the modeling process is critical—preferably before you begin to model. You should ask several questions at this point, and use the answers to determine the direction to go with the modeling. These questions are important for all models and animations, but are especially important for high-resolution work because they dictate model complexity and detail, memory requirements, and file-exchange issues. Answer the following questions before you begin to model:

- What size will the printed image be?

- What media will the final image use?

- How crisp does the image need to appear?

- What resolution will be used for printing?

- Where is the visual focus within the model?

- How close will the viewer get to the various parts of the model?

You should discuss these questions during conception and planning of the project, and you should ask them even if the project is for in-house use, has no client, or is an independent venture. The answers furnish vital direction for what otherwise could end up being an overly large model that isn't accurate enough or that can't be rendered or printed.

The resolution of the output image depends on the print media, the crispness of the printed image, and the printed size. You need to make decisions on all of these issues before you can determine what you need for your final output image.

Impact of Media Selection

The most important issue when selecting the type of output media is deciding whether you want to produce a continuous tone or screened print. The choice you make has a significant impact on the required resolution. In general, a screened print is one produced by dithering the image, and a continuous tone print resembles a photograph.

Continuous Tone Prints

When you print a bitmap image, the pixels that form the composition must be translated to a format the printing device can understand. A continuous tone process places the pixels immediately next to one another without any space between them to allow the white of the paper to show through. The tones of the print are thus blended together, and no isolated dots exist, making it the easiest print type to understand because it produces an image that looks a lot like what you see onscreen. A continuous tone print also is the easiest to print because the sole determining factor of the image's quality is the resolution you supply in the image.

Standard Photographic Print

The most common type of continuous tone print is the standard photographic print. Outputting to photographic film involves using a film recorder to expose the image on conventional 35mm film or 4"×5" large format film. You can use any standard 100 ASA photographic print or transparency film (although transparency is recommended to ensure proper color reproduction). Film recorders usually are capable of 4,000 to 8,000 lines of resolution.

NOTE ─────────────────────────────────

A film recorder's lines of resolution refers to the number of scanlines through which an image is interpreted. Because each pixel must have at least one scanline, a 4,000-pixel-wide image is the maximum size for a 4,000-line recorder. Even though film recorders have this high capability, the image you supply doesn't have to be that large. All images are shot to fill the frame, regardless of their original resolution. Convincing images are quite possible with resolutions of 1200×800, and images with resolutions as low as 600×400 can be worth presenting.

Dye Sublimation Prints

Dye sublimation printers are another common form of continuous tone printing available for computer images. These can be desktop or E-size production printers and typically range from 100 to 400 dots per inch (dpi) of resolution. The look of a dye sublimation print resembles a color glossy print—both cover the entire paper and perform no dithering of their own. The dye sublimation printers deliver an explosion of molecules so that the dots run into each other, giving the appearance of continuous tone from a dot process.

Quality of the Final Image

The quality of the final continuous tone image is determined by the density of pixels per printed inch. This is subjective and varies from one image to the next. Images that contain text and fine detail require more pixels per printed inch, whereas abstract images can get by with fewer pixels per printed inch.

If you output to 35mm film, you should consider the size of the prints rather than the size of the film. For photo-retouching or high-end reproduction, you should use the lowest pixel-to-scanline ratio possible. The standard resolution for photographic reproduction is 3072×2048 because of the introduction of Kodak's Photo CD. This translates to approximately 2,200 pixels per inch on 35mm film. File sizes for an image of this resolution are 18.69MB each and require large storage and transfer considerations.

Screened Prints

A screened print is one that takes the original image and dithers it to achieve true color. Screens are essential for many processes because the inks would bleed and blend together in pools of mottled color. The screens place the color components (cyan, yellow, magenta, and usually black) onto separate areas of the printed page. The pattern of the dispersed color dots is created by the screen. If you examine most printed material closely, you can see the individual dots that appear to be true color at a distance.

Screened images are commonly used for mass production purposes, such as magazines, marketing brochures, or advertisements. Screened images also are used with noncontinuous tone printers. The latter includes most varieties of laser, inkjet, electrostatic plotters, thermal wax, and thermal dye transfer printers. All of these devices require that you screen the image for printing.

When you print to any of these devices, the image first is dithered by a halftone screen. Screens come in many shapes and sizes, including dot, line, and diffusion. The size of the halftone screen is expressed in lines per inch (lpi) and often is referred to as its screen frequency. This is an expression of how many screen lines per printed inch are on the final document—the larger the lpi, the finer the screen. Printing houses vary their standard lpi use depending on the application. Coarse printing, such as for newspapers, might use an 85-line screen, whereas magazines typically use a 133- or 150-line screen for images. The size of the screen used determines how many pixels per printed inch are required in your images.

NOTE

It's easy to confuse the terms dots per inch (dpi) and pixels per inch (ppi). Pixels per inch refers to the number of pixels displayed per inch on your monitor, whereas dots per inch refers to the number of ink dots that the printer can print per inch. When creating computer images, you are interested in a third ratio: the number of pixels in the final printed inch. This often is termed pixels per printed inch and governs the size of your final image.

Many desktop publishing applications and some printers enable you to specify the type of screen used for printing images. (Often a default screen is applied to an image by the printer itself.) Converting images to screens takes time and can demand an enormous amount of memory for large images. It is not uncommon to wait hours for a high-resolution image to process on an average desktop printer, whereas commercial machines and film recorders can process in minutes. Image quality is determined by the sophistication and alignment of a screen. In general, the screens in desktop printers aren't as high quality as those typically found in commercial, high-quality printing.

The shape, density, and angle of screens used by commercial printers often are considered proprietary information. Because of this, each printer has individual rules of thumb for the best dpi-to-lpi ratio. You should discuss image-clarity requirements with your printer early on. Most printers prefer to work with images that have between 200 and 400 pixels per printed inch. The number of pixels per printed inch makes a dramatic impact on your file sizes and memory requirements. Increasing your image from 200 to 400 pixels per printed inch requires four times more processing memory and file disk space.

Issues Surrounding Image Clarity

As images are reproduced beyond their optimum resolution, they begin to blur, fuzz, or pixelate. The extent and distraction of these effects vary according to the print media.

Pixelation

The larger an image is, the more obvious are the square pixels from which it is composed. This is generally known as pixelation and is usually something you should avoid. Pixelation destroys the photorealistic illusion of computer-rendered images. Making an image pixelate is the easy part. Making it appear photorealistic takes more effort and considerably more memory. You reduce pixelation by rendering an image at a higher resolution.

> **NOTE**
>
> Sometimes pixelation is exactly what you want. Some dramatic images have been produced by pixelating the foreground to lead the viewer into a high-resolution center focus—actually an overlay of two or more images or an entire image created at high resolution, but employing an undersized bitmap to cause the close-up pixelation. You also can use pixelation to disguise an area or reinforce the fact that the image is computer-generated.

Crispness of Screened Images

The crispness and clarity of a screened image is determined by the number of image pixels per screen line (or the pixels per printed inch to screen lines per printed inch). This is discussed in terms of the ratio of pixels per screen line and often is termed the screen ruling ratio. To avoid poor-quality images, never use a ratio less than 1:1. For optimum quality, use a ratio of 2:1. Increasing the number of pixels beyond 2:1 has diminishing, if not imperceptible, returns of image quality. Avoid creating images larger than 2:1 because they require substantially more memory to render, disk space to store, and time to print; all without returning a higher quality print.

If your printer uses a 150-line screen, then you provide an image that has between 150 and 300 pixels per printed inch. The needs of various screens, presses, and printers vary, so discussing this ratio with your printer before determining the final output resolution for the project is important.

Printed Size and Output Resolution

The print size of the image has the biggest impact on the required image resolution and what your model needs as far as the detail necessary to make it convincing. After selecting the media and determining the pixels-per-inch ratio for desired clarity, the image's resolution is simply a matter of arithmetic:

$(ppi) \times (Print\ Width) = Width\ Resolution(ppi) \times (Print\ Height) = Height\ Resolution$

The memory required to store an image on disk and a printer to process in RAM is as follows:

$(ppi)2 \times (printed\ width\ in\ inches) \times (printed\ height\ in\ inches) \times (3\ bytes\ per\ pixel) = memory\ required\ in\ bytes$

The data size of a 24-bit color pixel (8 bits of color per channel × 3 channels) is 3 bytes. The size of the print multiplies its impact against the needs of crispness and the resulting dpi. Every printed inch requires more memory.

The media often dictates the size, or at least the maximum size, of your output. Desktop printers typically are limited to 4×5-inch or 8×10-inch prints, whereas dye sublimation printers are available in E-size (36×48-inch). As an example, a 4×5-inch print using a 150-line screen prints best if the supplied image is sized to print as follows:

(150 lpi)×(2.0 pixels per line) = 300 ppi

N OTE

E-size is a paper type, like letter or legal size. It is basically a bigger paper size, commonly used in CAD/architectural work.

This in turn means that the image's resolution needs to be 4"×300 ppi = 1,200×5"×300 ppi = 1,500 or 1,550×1,200. Such an image will require 1,500×1,200×3 = 5.4MB of printer processing RAM.

Printing with Less Than True Color

You may be forced to print with equipment that can't print in 24-bit, true color. Most plotters and many desktop printers commonly have a maximum capability of 15- or 16-bit color.

When you send a 24-bit image directly to an output device, you are relying on its programming to interpolate the differences in the color depths. This usually doesn't produce the best results because most drivers rely on basic algorithms that average the differences. Typical results are banding, streaking, and moiré patterns. You can avoid much of this by having 3D Studio MAX write a 16-bit color TGA file with dither true color on.

Calculating Screens for Existing Images

Many times you will have an image that you need your printer to print the best it can. Doing so is quite easy if you know the following information:

- Resolution in pixels
- Screen lines per inch
- Printed dots per printed inch

The optimum screen size (lpi) to print an image is half the image's pixel-per-printed-inch resolution. If you have a 1024×768 image to print and the finest screen available is 150-line, the image should be printed at 300 pixels per printed inch, which results in a final image of 3.41"×2.56". If you want to use the same image to fill a 4×3-inch space on the page, you need a 256- pixel-per-printed-inch ratio and a 128-line screen. Although coarser line screens enable you to use smaller resolutions, they also minimize the amount of detail printable in any given inch.

Examining Model Complexity and Accuracy

You need to balance the accuracy and detail of the model against the accuracy and detail of the intended final output. Determining an object's detail is twofold:

■ How close will the observer get to any particular object?

■ What will be the final output resolution?

NOTE

When producing animations, the speed at which an object passes across the screen creates a third accuracy factor you need to take into account.

You need this information when you build a model so that you can include the proper amount of detail at the critical locations. An object that looks acceptable at a video resolution of 512×486 could easily fall apart or look foolish when you print it as a color glossy photo with a resolution of 3072×2048.

Many times, an object created in 3D Studio MAX has parameters that can be increased and decreased at will. This is great for adding detail to objects that are being used for both print and animation because the detail can be increased for print, and then decreased for animation, thus improving render times.

You can adjust the parameters of parametric objects to achieve this. On polygonal models, you can add an Optimize Modifier and then adjust its parameters. Add the Optimize Modifier only to the faces that need to be adjusted by first using a Mesh Select or an Edit Mesh.

Model Focus Detail Hierarchy

Most scenes have a focus, be it a specific object, a group of objects, or an area. As your model begins to take shape, you should have a rough idea of the final composition and how prominent you want the focus objects to be in the final images. This object or area obviously requires the most detail and attention. For an efficient and manageable model, you should consider sketching out a list of areas as they fit into a "detail hierarchy."

NOTE

Such an organization can be traced to traditional illustration as well. Architectural and design drawings often use rough sketches and loose brush or pen strokes to achieve the illusion of detail, without overwhelming the rendering's focus. Artists call this vignetting and frequently use it on entourage, backgrounds, and even extension foreground materials.

A detail hierarchy clarifies which objects will be made detailed and which will be minimized. Detail comes in two forms—geometry and mapping. As the object occupies more pixels in the final output, modeling techniques that worked at one resolution might become coarse or cartoon-like at higher resolutions.

Geometry Detail

Arcs and curves need special attention as they begin to occupy more pixels in the final output. Distant arcs might be capable of getting by with as little as 15-degree arc steps, whereas objects that arc through the entire scene might require 0.1-degree steps. Seeing the segmented outlines of round and curved objects is the best way to destroy their believability. Your model is most efficient if you concentrate high arc steps at the focus of the scene and reduce them in distant or less-focused areas. Just because the foreground spheres have 80 segments doesn't mean the background spheres cannot use 10.

Maps that are convincing as modeled textures can be much less convincing if you enlarge them, especially bump maps. The dents or grooves that were once faked might now need to be modeled. Close-ups, seams, and grooves are much more convincing if you take the time to model them. Taking the time often is much less trouble than making larger bitmaps and adjusting their blur until they appear acceptable. You cannot truly antialias bump maps, whereas you can automatically do the modeled joints using the Renderer's antialiasing engine, and with much less memory overhead at that.

3DS MAX 2 also has the capability to create and use NURBS models, which have a characteristic called view-dependent tessellation. The faceting is automatically calculated based on the distance from the camera, so that curves maintain their smoothness as you zoom in on them. This is an alternate way to deal with geometry and rendering.

T IP

Don't be afraid to add faces for detail when the alternative is to use larger bitmaps. Adding appropriate geometry detail requires more modeling time than it does rendering resources. You can add 8,000 faces, for example, for less than the cost of rendering one 640×480 bitmap.

Bitmap Detail

You generally need to use bitmaps in renderings. Follow these two rules of thumb:

- Use a bitmap with as high a level of color detail as possible.

- Try not to exceed the original bitmap's size in the rendering.

N OTE

Materials that use procedural textures don't need nearly as much adjustment because their effects are based on algorithms and are independent of resolution.

The size of the bitmap can become a problem as its presence in the scene increases. When you render bitmaps in excess of their original size, they begin to show signs of pixelation and square patching. The ability to notice this effect depends on the image's subject. Bitmaps that portray square, block, and rectilinear images don't show much, if any, degradation as you increase them beyond their original bitmap size. You could enlarge a bitmap of a checker pattern, for example, to 10 times its size and it would look fine as long as you didn't use it as a bump map. If the same bitmap was an image of a hummingbird, however, the pixelation would be obvious.

Background Image Issues

Unlike bitmaps, you have little leeway in the selection of a background image for high-resolution output. Background bitmaps should always be 24-bit color (without JPEG compression) and should not be stretched much beyond their original dimensions.

NOTE

Antialiasing against the background sometimes is undesirable, especially when creating artwork to be cut out of the background. Sprite artwork for games and buttons for multimedia projects are two such uses. You can turn off antialiasing by checking the Don't Antialias Against Background checkbox in the Rendering section of the Preferences window.

NOTE

Don't forget to set your background up in the Materials Editor and then apply it under Rendering, Environment. Seeing your background using Views, Background Image does not add that background to your rendering.

If you enlarge a background, it appears in the rendered image that the foreground has been pasted on the background. The discrepancies between the two resolutions are apparent, although a layman might not be able to identify why it looks wrong. When you enlarge images, they inevitably blur. Enlarging a black square on a white field doesn't produce just a larger black square—a soft gray gradation also forms at the square's edges.

You should always try to use images that don't need to be enlarged. Ideally, you should use images that require reducing. Images in Kodak CD-ROM format are convenient for this purpose because they have a 3072×2048 resolution.

If you must use an existing, smaller bitmap as a background image, you should bring it into a true-color paint program for conversion, which enables you to enlarge the image to exact dimensions and use soften or sharpen tools to disguise the effects of the enlargement.

$\mathbf{T}_{\text{IP}}$

Some images lend themselves to enlargement much better than others. Images of skies, smoke, water, and other freeform objects don't suffer as much as street scenes, forests, and interiors. If your smaller bitmap contains such elements, you might consider concentrating its enlargement specifically to those areas.

Using Background Objects

Several more opportunities present themselves when the background is made a backdrop object with a texture map material. Used in this way, if other materials use the same bitmap, they can access the bitmap without having to load it again.

The object that contains the background image acts as a billboard. You position the backdrop object as you want, making it larger or smaller by using placement, mapping coordinates, or mapping parameters. This method of adding a background image eliminates the memory overhead of resizing a background image. It is also the best, and fastest, way to align the objects in your scene with your background.

Background image objects in a scene are rendered in perspective along with everything else. Because the object is placed parallel to the viewing plane, there are no horizontal perspective effects. The elements that are vertical are affected by perspective. This can be especially important for backgrounds that contain architecture, tall straight trees, flag poles, or any objects with definite vertical lines.

The recipe for such an image is simple. You don't want lighting conditions in the scene to affect it, so it should be 100 percent self-illuminating and dead flat with a black specular color. In addition, you should have the billboard object's shadow casting and receiving attributes turned off.

Using the Show Background Image Preview

The Show Background option (accessible by right-clicking a viewport name) can help position objects in the scene in relationship to a background image.

Background preview isn't an ideal choice for large images. As a workaround, you should reduce your background image proportionally and use it as a thumbnail of your true image. You gain no advantage by using an image that has a resolution greater than the viewable size of the viewport.

The background images can also be frames from an animation (such as an AVI, or sequence of bitmaps), or captured media from film or video. The frame number of such an animation is locked to the frame number of the scene and is extremely useful for rotoscoping and compositing. Several digital disk recorders include sophisticated plug-ins that enable direct composition of video and 3D graphics, all within 3D Studio MAX.

New to MAX R2 are the capabilities to load a different bitmap into each viewport as a background, to zoom and pan on those backgrounds, and to play an AVI frame-by-frame in the background of the viewport. These capabilities do not translate over to the environment map, which is the background used during rendering.

NOTE

Safe Frame is often used to show how the background fits within the view. It is easy to forget that a viewport is a different aspect ratio than most renderings and reveals more than is actually rendered. Right-click the viewport name, and select View Safe Frame from the revealed menu list to enable this feature.

Incorporating Text Overlay

A common need is to position text on top of a final image; perhaps in the form of a logo, title, signature, or diagrammatic text. All paint programs provide some capability to create text for overlay; some even have the capability to create antialiased text. No paint programs, however, have the antialiasing capability built into 3D Studio MAX. 3D Studio MAX actually is the best text compositor available on the desktop. If you want to have complete control over final text placement, you should composite it before you send it to the printer.

Issues Concerning Text Objects

Text is acutely sensitive to the effects of resolution. The resolution of the final image must be large enough to render the text sharply, with full definition and no fuzzy edges. Bold sans serif fonts are the most tolerant of lower resolutions but might not be appropriate. Curves and fine lines of light serif fonts require the highest resolution to preserve their edges' fine detail. The text can be created quite easily using TrueType fonts. Examine these fonts carefully because large curves may require more detail given by extra steps.

After creating the text, you can compose it against the background image and render it against the background bitmap for final output. You should render in an orthogonal viewport for non-distorted text. You can render in either a Perspective or Camera viewport for three-dimensional text.

NOTE

Adjusting a views perspective is useful for controlling the perspective flare of 3D text.

The Video Post Option for Compositing Images

Video Post suite provides options for queuing bitmaps for overlay and underlay. Video Post can create multilayer effects by accessing alpha channels and overlapping images. Video Post also provides control over a bitmap's placement, alignment, and scale. If the bitmap is smaller than the output size, it doesn't tile but rather floats against a black or colored bitmap image background.

If you need to compose the scene's geometry with more than one image, Video Post is the way to go. If you're just overlaying the geometry onto a single image, Video Post requires much more memory than the background image method. You also can't align the text with a background proxy image.

Using Video Post for compositing is critical for large architectural projects. Rather than bringing in a huge model which drags the system down, try bringing in pieces, rendering them, and then compositing in Video Post. Alternately, these renderings can be texture-mapped to backdrop objects with alpha channel transparency.

Compositing with Alpha Channels

It is common to have a "signature" credit text or logo inserted at the bottom of an image. You would do this most easily by modeling your logo text in 3D Studio MAX and rendering it to a 32-bit file. After you like the final appearance and resolution of the text or logo, you can use perfected 32-bit image to stamp or sign many images. Video Post can perform this application quite well and has no problem overlaying multiple images.

Image Output Parameters

Several factors are important to your final output decisions. The first is the size and proportions of the image. These should be the true proportions of the final print and should never need to use anything but a 1.0 Aspect Ratio. The Aspect Ratio is intended for converting images between different display devices and resolutions. Doing so for hard copy only stretches the image.

Using output gamma should be carefully considered. Many output devices, such as film recorders, don't need gamma to produce a correct image. Many of these devices work best with a gamma of 1.0 (that is, off) and deliver exactly what you see on your preview monitor. Coordinating your output with your printer's requirements is important, and you always should run a series of tests with and without gamma to ensure the proper color interpretation. If Aspect Ratios are in doubt, renderings of true circles provide a good test for image distortion. Run this test early in the process to avoid wasting time.

Final Image Considerations

Early on in the production process, and certainly before you make final renderings, you should consider who will use them and what is needed or preferred in the way of formats. If the printing facilities are in-house, you should know these requirements and count yourself lucky. The majority of 3D Studio MAX users require the use of service bureaus and printers. You should contact these bureaus and printers so that the correct form of data storage medium and the preferred image format (TGA/TIF/BMP/PNG, compressed/uncompressed, gamma, and so on) are used. Making incorrect assumptions can cost both time and money. These businesses also should be contacted before making substantial storage device purchases because local device compatibility is highly desirable.

Although 3D Studio MAX was designed as an animation program, it can produce superb high-resolution still images. The animation capabilities it has enable you to explore changing lighting options and capture multiple-camera compositions at the same time. Creating high-resolution images usually involves pushing your system's resources to the max and demands a full understanding of the requirements and how best to utilize available resources.

In Practice: Rendering Still Images

- **Render control:** 3D Studio MAX offers a wide range of control when rendering, including resolution and file type as well as which objects and areas in the viewport are rendered.

- **Selective raytracing:** This new feature in R2 enables realistic rendering of reflections and refractions. Carefully weigh the benefits with the excessive rendering time raytracing requires. Assigning raytracing effects only to selected objects helps keep those rendering times under control. Take time to work through all the raytracing settings to help optimize your scene.

- **Using 8-bit images:** While 8-bit isn't good for print, it can be very useful when rendering still images for computer-based multimedia productions due to small file size, fast loading and display, wide software compatibility, and low graphics display requirements.

- **Dithering:** Sometimes banding is unavoidable in 8-bit images, and dithering often helps blur the edges between bands. This, however, can increase file sizes. If file size is important, some experimentation might be necessary to determine if the visual improvement is worthy of the larger file.

- **Model complexity:** When modeling, it is important to know how the object is going to be rendered. For print, film, or slide resolutions, careful attention to detail is important. Game production, or WWW-based graphics, often require lower resolutions, decreasing the necessary detail required for the object.

- **Working with a service bureau:** Early on in the production process, you'll want to get with your service bureau and talk with them about file types, compression, removable storage devices, turnaround times, and other vital areas of importance for your project. Doing some test prints and working out problems ahead of time will often save you money and headaches when deadlines loom.

Chapter 28

RENDERING ANIMATION

3D Studio MAX has been, and always will be, a great choice for creating 3D animations for video and film. As technology has evolved, however, so have the output choices for animators. Chapter 27 concentrated on rendering still images and this chapter looks at the issues involved in rendering animation for recording and playback with digital, videotape, and film media. Methods for recording animation to various equipment will be discussed, as well as methods for creating digital MPEG files. Some of the topics you will read about include the following:

- Rendering animation overview
- Planning for playback
- Understanding digital playback
- Using 3D animation for online content
- Rendering output for videotape and film playback
- Rendering frames versus fields
- Understanding rotoscoping

Rendering Animation Overview

As the basic and fundamental document of their effort, professional 3D artists and animators render an animated scene to a sequence of high-resolution, color digital image files. Although the 3D Studio MAX platform provides very powerful processing, with snappy real-time rendering in its viewports and a useful window to the virtual frame buffer, in 3D work you do not always "get what you see." This same processing power, combined with graphics acceleration and digital video editing systems, now affords you the opportunity to quickly and reflexively view the rendering. Your preview and testing may in fact simultaneously provide the final product in the form of collateral material, online marketing, and interactive content. In this chapter, you will examine tools and techniques for rendering 3DS MAX animation for the three basic forms of playback media: digital (disk-based and online), videotape, and film.

3D Studio MAX is a workstation-class, professional-quality modeling and animation program that internally manages 64 bits of information—that is, 16 bits per channel of RGBA. 3DS MAX can produce the highest quality digital animation for commercial motion picture production. It is important, however, to realize that professional work now includes a spectrum of output from 8-bit color to the highest resolution and color depths. Creating animation for video or film is very different from creating 3D animation intended for digital playback.

You should know both the editing and playback formats for your project long before you create your preliminary storyboards. The differences among formats has a bearing on almost every decision you make during the course of your project, both creative and technical. The diverse need for 3D animation demands a playback-media-targeted approach to the rendering of your 3DS MAX scenes. You can deliver efficient multidimensional animation for the new, content-hungry digital formats (CD-ROM and online) as well as rich, complex scenes and effects to be presented on video and film.

Planning for Playback

Because animation is composed of individual images, the design process is frame-centric. The playback medium's method of displaying frames dictates the approach you must take to both creating and rendering your 3D animation. Consideration for output is best made during the planning, setup, and production process. 3D Studio MAX's default preferences are generally set for PC display and the rendering of sequential, individual files to a bitmap format. If your animation is going to be played back exclusively as a digital video on a computer, or from videotape or film, you can plan for that eventuality by adjusting the appropriate settings in the Preferences feature.

As an example, 3D Studio MAX manages Gamma correction globally (for display, input, and output). You can also override the system settings, such as when you composite input images with your scenes in Video Post or render to a device such as a Digital Disk Recorder. You can implement serial numbering of files in step-sequenced renderings (common for character animation in CD-ROM title development) by turning on the Output File Sequencing setting.

When rendering in consideration of your target media playback, be sure to check and record your current Preference settings under the Rendering tab. You should also be aware of other medium relevant settings that are saved with the each individual scene. Such settings include Views and Time Configuration.

Ideally, you want to create "platform-independent" content, but the timeline and specifications of a project often demand focused, media-specific output. To cope with this, you should become familiar with 3DS MAX's preference settings. Create template MAX files and 3dsmax.ini files from your projects that correspond specifically to playback configurations.

You can understand how untitled 3D Studio MAX files configure from the configuration settings in the maxstart.max file. You can save MAX files from projects to a different name, reduce or eliminate geometry, materials, and so on. When you begin a similar project, rename your project file maxstart.max and place it in the appropriate directory (default=Scenes) to load a specific set of file configurations for your new project.

Likewise, you can template overall 3D Studio MAX settings, such as the viewport configuration, time configuration, and default directory locations by saving the 3dsmax.ini file as project-specific filenames, renaming them to 3dsmax.ini, and loading them into your root MAX sub-directory before launching 3DS MAX.

Understanding Digital Playback

Most multimedia applications now include support for creating and playing digital "movies" in the AVI (AVI), MPEG (MPG), and FLIC (FLC or FLI) file formats. A growing number of applications, especially online browsers, also provide support for three-dimensional objects and animation. Special ASCII text files containing Virtual Reality Modeling Language (VRML) provide standardized methods for representing 3D objects and animation within a Web page. These files also carry the extension WRL (for world).

3D Studio MAX fully supports reading and writing AVI and FLIC formats, including support for several AVI codecs (compression-decompression algorithms). Through the use of plug-ins, you can also render directly to QuickTime or MPEG formats. MAX R2 has also added a plug-in for exporting scenes as VRML files. To create digital video or VRML animation successfully, you must understand and manage the limitations inherent in their formats and with their playback environments.

When you create animation for digital playback, you are faced with a wide variety of constraints. Some of the issues that you must address include the following:

- Normalizing the color palette over multiple frames.
- Choosing and configuring the appropriate codec.
- Avoiding playback anomalies, such as video tearing.
- Smaller file sizes and polygon counts for efficient playback and responsive interactivity.
- Optimizing your presentation to fit the chosen delivery method.
- Planning break points and using transitions.

Palette Control

An important problem that you must address when producing CD-ROMs and online animation is the issue of working with 256-color palettes (8-bit). Some CD-ROM titles require display in 256 colors or they offer 8-bit and higher color depth configuration options. The typical target customer's graphics display card may only support 256 colors, so in this case, you must define a standard palette for the low-end option. The two most important issues to be aware of are the color scheme's design and the avoidance of dithering. Although 256 color graphics cards are increasingly becoming a thing of the past, this is still a consideration for many multimedia applications.

You must plan the colors and materials selection of your 8-bit images carefully. With only 256 colors available, you need to get as much as you can out of each color selection. You can do this by keeping most of your color and material selections within the same family of colors. This restriction is not as limiting as you might think, especially when you're talking in terms of warm earth tones, cool blue-greens, and subtle grays. Indeed, you might find that working with these limitations improves your eye for color. Most good color designs work with a limited palette.

Not only do you have to manage color limitations within a single image, you also must be aware of how color is expressed over time, between scenes, and in conjunction with interactive choice. What objects move in and out of view? Does the position or color of the lights change? Does your animation move to a different scene, or is it embedded within a web page that contains its own color requirements? These questions complicate the selection of a good color palette.

You can manage color change requirements by using 3D Studio MAX to help you build a color palette. Scene and location matching is best handled by creating multiple scenes with separate palettes and designing a transition between them. Embedded animation should be coordinated with the color schemes of the web site.

Creating an 8-Bit Color Palette

To render a custom palette from your 3DS MAX animation or from a sequential file in Video Post, choose the FLC (FLC or FLI) file format as your output file type in the Render Scene or the Video Post Execute Sequence dialog, as shown in Figure 28.1.

FIGURE 28.1

Using a custom palette to render a file in the FLC format. Make sure the location of this file is available for rendering, especially when rendering over a network.

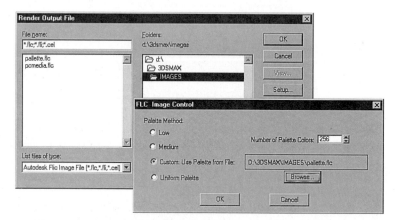

FLC output presents four palette choices: Low, Medium, Custom, and Uniform. Additionally, you have the choice to identify the number of colors that 3DS MAX uses from the designated palette choice. When you choose less than 256 colors, a Windows optimized palette is constructed and the remaining colors are filled with black. Windows reserves 20 colors overall, so therefore you should use a palette size of 236 (or less) for animations played in Windows.

The following list describes these output options in more detail:

- **Low:** Calculates the colors for the first frame of the animation and then uses that fixed set of colors for all subsequent frames. The low setting is very fast but leads to few problems. First and foremost, if any objects are out of the scene on the first frame, their color requirements are not taken into account. For example, imagine animating a backyard scene. You have bright green grass, dark green trees and bushes, brown tree trunks, and a blazing blue sky. After a few frames, a child's red ball bounces into view. Where do the red colors come from? If you render using the Low palette setting, you have no reds. A few warm tones may be associated with the colors for the tree trunks, but the ball will most likely be anything but red.

- **Medium:** Renders each frame with its own 256-color palette. After you finish rendering the animation, 3D Studio MAX looks at all the individual color palettes and builds a single palette to serve all the frames. This option works extremely well and provides you with almost the best possible palette for the animation. The main draw-back is that it's slow. After 3D Studio MAX renders the FLC file with a separate palette for each frame, it must rewrite each frame using the new color palette that it has created. This process can take a considerable amount of time.

- **Custom:** Requires that you provide 3D Studio MAX with a predefined color palette from either a GIF, FLC, or BMP file. Fortunately, 3D Studio MAX provides you with the tools to easily create this color palette. The trick involves rendering a sample set of frames at Medium mode and then having 3D Studio MAX render the whole animation with a custom palette taken from the sample frames. The Custom palette option is the most commonly used option.

- **Uniform:** Also renders each frame using one palette, but in this case the render uses a generic optional color cube. The palette is a system-generated, uniformly distributed table of colors. A uniform palette ensures that every frame uses the same Windows-supported colors.

You identify the sample set of frames for creating a custom palette by using the Every Nth Frame field in the Render Scene or Execute Video Post dialogs (see Figure 28.2). The value that you enter in this field should be sufficient to render anywhere from 10 percent to 25 percent of the total frames in your animation. The more frames your animation has, the larger the number you'll enter in the Every Nth Frame field.

FIGURE 28.2

Rendering a representative portion of a file using the Every Nth Frame setting.

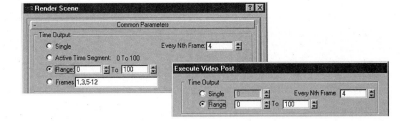

NOTE

Be sure to save your sample FLC file to disk and note the location. The reason for this is that when you render the final animation, you choose Custom palette and assign the sample FLIC as the Custom palette files. If the FLC is not in the directory from which you loaded the MAX file or not in a Map path directory, the FLC can't be found during rendering and 3D Studio MAX displays a warning dialog, halting the rendering process.

To create an AVI file that uses the custom palette, output the scene as a FLIC file using the custom palette. Then use Video Post to convert the FLIC file to an AVI file. Make sure to uncheck the Dithering options in the Rendering tab of the Preferences dialog. Add the FLC file as an Image Input event and the AVI file as an Output event. Choose the Full Frame (Uncompressed) codec and execute the sequence. You now have an AVI file with a controlled 8-bit color palette.

Using Multiple Palettes

Sometimes your animation has scenes that change drastically in both lighting and color. An example might be a walk-through animation in which you move from the warm and neutral tones of a living room to a bright and colorful patio. When this happens, you should render each part as a separate segment with its own color palette. Trying to fit the wide ranges of colors from both scenes into a single palette leaves neither scene with sufficient colors to produce acceptable results. Likewise, if your animation occupies several environments through web page embedding or multiple composites and rotoscoping, custom palettes should be used for each condition.

Avoiding Dithering

As mentioned previously, when rendering to a digital video format, you are generally better off not dithering color. To prevent 3D Studio MAX from dithering, uncheck the Paletted (256-color) check box in the Output Dithering section of the Rendering tab in the Preferences dialog. By default, 3D Studio MAX dithers images bound for an 8-bit file format. This may be fine for individual bitmaps, but dithering does not translate well in a digital video file where compression routines are searching for commonalities in files, including redundant color. Dithering reduces banding in solid color objects but does little else to improve the realism of digital video images, and it greatly increases the file size. As an alternative, you can use various mapping techniques to add realism to the scene because maps generally prevent banding better than dithering, and without creating large files.

Another reason to avoid dithering when you render digital video files is that it is very difficult to make the dither patterns stand still. As objects move around the scene and lighting patterns change, the dithering pattern also changes. Sometimes the changes in the dither pattern are harmonious with the animation and are hardly noticeable, but other times the dither patterns seem to take on a life of their own on the surface of your objects. The Custom palette technique described previously helps to minimize this effect but does not completely eliminate it. Your best results come from using a Custom palette in conjunction with using realistically mapped materials and avoiding dithering altogether.

Understanding Digital Video Compression

Compression is the process of removing or restructuring data to decrease file size. When 3DS MAX renders to an AVI file type, it compresses each frame's image information based on your selection from a list of software-driven codecs.

Codecs are categorized in three fundamental ways. First, they are lossless or lossy. Lossless compression retains all the image data, usually employing a technique called run length encoding (RLE). RLE discards continuous regions of duplicate color, marking the file with a code that recalls the duplicate color at decompression time. RLE is very effective for computer-generated graphics with large areas of similar pixels, but it is not very effective with digitized analog video and photographs because these images usually contain few areas of continuous color.

Lossy codecs are designed to recognize and permanently remove image information that is not likely to be noticed by the viewer. The algorithm is sensitive to dithering and diffusion over a range of frames. Lossy codecs have a quality setting that controls the degree of loss (and consequently the resulting file size). These codecs are effective when compressing animated 3D geometry composited with analog video.

The second important codec category has to do with how the compression approaches the whole frame, spatially or temporally. Spatial compression examines one frame at a time, recognizing and removing detail within the frame. Temporal compression compares frames over time to strategically and gradually remove data. An important kind of temporal compression (frame differencing) stores only the changed pixel information from sequential frames.

Finally, codecs support certain pixel depths and are platform-specific. Some codecs compress only to 8 bits; others support 16-bit and 24-bit compression. Some only play back on Video for Windows. Decompression (and recompression) takes place as the movie plays back. 3D Studio MAX's View File feature launches the MS Windows (NT or WIN95) Media Player for this purpose.

Codecs are critical if your animation is to play from a CD-ROM drive or play at full size from a hard drive. The codec you choose in rendering file output from 3D Studio MAX affects the visual quality and the playback speed of your digital animation. As shown in Figure 28.3, codecs are reached by entering your output filename with the AVI extension and pressing the activated Setup button in the File browsing dialog.

FIGURE 28.3

Setting up an AVI codec.

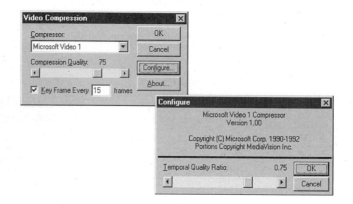

You can compress AVI files by using any of the software codecs that come with Video For Windows. At least one codec is probably installed with your operating system, and more often are installed with multimedia titles and Internet browsers. You also can add third-party codecs to your system for a variety of compression formats. Apply your understanding about how a codec works, along with a healthy amount of experimentation, to achieve the results you need for your project.

Common Codecs and 3DS MAX

The following are some codecs that are likely to be present on your system, including the codec that Kinetix ships with 3D Studio MAX:

- **Microsoft Video 1:** Use this 8-bit, lossy codec to compress analog video, for example, compositing a 3DS MAX scene with uncompressed digital or frame-controlled analog video capture. Although this is not the most highly configurable codec, improved quality is available through its temporal quality slider, as well as the overall compression quality adjustment in the main Video Compression dialog.

- **Radius Cinepak:** This lossy codec is used primarily for compression to 24-bit video for eventual playback from CD-ROM discs. (Sprite animation is one example.) This codec attains higher compression ratios, better image quality, and faster playback speeds than Microsoft Video 1, but you should not use it for data that contains previous lossy compressed images (such as an AVI used as a material or background). You can configure this codec to compress to black and white or color. Adjust its compression quality in the 3D Studio MAX Video Compression dialog.

- **Intel Indeo Video R3.2:** This lossy, 24-bit codec is comparable to the Radius Cinepak codec.

- **Autodesk RLE:** This Kinetix-supplied codec compresses a lossless, run-length encoded, 24-bit video that can also be viewed with Autodesk's Animator Studio software. Use this codec to compress larger but higher quality 24-bit video when you want to ensure no RGB information loss. Because this codec does not remove information, you can effectively use it for objects mapped with AVI or FLIC animation.

- **Full Frames (Uncompressed):** This is the high-quality, universally accessible method for storing animation information in a data stream. This codec requires large amounts of disk space for the finished AVI file but provides the convenience of a single sequential file for your animation. Because it is compatible across machine types and desktop video applications, it is quite effective for interactive multimedia production.

If you choose to use a video playback card, such as those offered by Truevision or DPS, you'll have the added option of formats native to their specific hardware (DVM or Targa AVI from Truevision, and the PVD file from DPS). These digital formats play back broadcast-quality video direct from A/V hard drives, in conjunction with the playback card required. Most digital editing software, including Adobe Premiere, AVID, and In-Sync's Speed Razor, all recognize these proprietary formats.

A digital video format that has been gaining in popularity is MPEG. It has a distinct advantage over other digital movie formats when it comes to final file size. A typical MPEG may be up to 1/10th the size of an identical AVI file. MPEG has been developing so quickly, it now has more than one specification. With regards to animation, you should become familiar with the pros and cons of both MPEG 1 and MPEG 2.

MPEG 1 only supports rendered file sizes of 352×240 and the actual video tends to look better than computer-generated images. Although an MPEG 1 movie can be scaled to any size, you do lose considerable quality as you approach 640×480 or larger playback. MPEG 2 is a step above MPEG 1, increasing the rendered file size to broadcast quality 720×480. To play back MPEG 2, you'll need a hardware decoder, but the image quality is superb.

NOTE

DARVISION (www.darvision.com) offers a Win95/WinNT program called DVMPEG that works within any program that can render to an AVI format. Within MAX, you would select AVI as your output type and select the DVMPEG Video codec in your setup. The program writes a dummy AVI file and, when all frames are rendered, prompts you to name your final MPEG movie. You then delete the dummy AVI file. The program also ships with a standalone program that can batch process sequential files or convert AVIs to MPEGs. The utility also lets you add or remove audio from MPEG files, called multiplexing and demultiplexing. A sample MPEG and identical AVI are on the accompanying CD-ROM. Load mpegtest.mpg and avitest.avi to see the quality of each and compare the file sizes.

Video Tearing

Video tearing refers to the inability of your display hardware to keep up with the playback speed of an animation. Figure 28.4 shows a frame of an animation captured during playback that exhibits video tearing. The phenomenon occurs when your system cannot pump information through your graphics card fast enough to keep up with the motion of objects in the animation. What you see is the display of two frames at the same time. The top part of the screen shows the next incoming frame, whereas the bottom part of the screen shows the previous outgoing frame.

This effect is more common in AVI files. Due to their 24-bit color depth and file size, they tend to put more demand on a typical display card. At resolutions of 640×480 or higher, the effects become quite noticeable as the AVI file literally skips frames when it can't keep up with demand. By skipping frames, the file's audio and video can stay in sync, but you see noticeable skips and jumps in the video. FLC files, in contrast, don't skip frames to keep up. Rather, they actually slow down the frame rate, playing every single frame, but not at the speed you intended. Coupled with the fact that FLC files are only 8-bit color, you tend to get better results with FLC files at resolutions of 640×480. The downside to FLC files is they do not have the ability to embed sound with the video as AVIs do. Experimenting with each format will help you decide which best fits your needs.

FIGURE 28.4

This animation demonstrates video tearing. Note the off-set in the robot's legs and the scene's vertical posts.

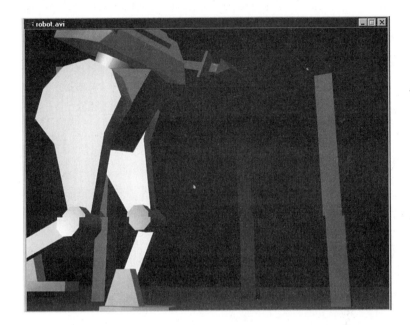

Hard-and-fast rules, which tell you under exactly what circumstances video tearing occurs, don't exist. The best you can do is plan for the lowest typical system on which your animation will be played and design according to the playback quality.

A few rules of thumb exist that you can observe to help reduce the likelihood of video tearing. The degree to which the rules are effective depends highly upon understanding the hardware on which the animation is played.

- **Avoid fast-moving objects:** Video tearing is a direct result of the speed at which the computer displays a single image. The faster an object moves, the more likely it is to tear apart.

- **Avoid motion of vertical edges:** The mechanics of video information transmission (left to right, then top to bottom) means that large vertical edges that move horizontally across the screen represent the worst-case scenario for video tearing. If moving vertical edges are unavoidable, such as in architectural walk-throughs, try to detract from the area that may exhibit tearing.

- **Use the smallest acceptable screen size for the project:** The more pixels in the image, the more data to send, and thus, the more likely the system can't keep up. In other words, if 320×200 satisfies the client, don't push for 1024×768.

- **Experiment with motion blur effects:** A little bit of motion blur can enhance the realism of the motion and help mask video tearing. See Chapter 29, "Compositing Effects," for more information on motion blur.

File Size

You waste all your efforts to produce realistic images and avoid video tearing if you force the playback system to play the animation from disk rather than memory. Disk access slows everything down so much that you may as well be viewing an old-fashioned slide show. You must know the system on which you plan to play the animation and then you have to size your animated segments to fit within the memory limitations of that system.

If you render for playback on another system, you must decide what the minimum memory requirements for running your presentation are. The typical home and small business PC probably has no more than 16 MB of RAM and some systems have a measly 8 MB. How much memory is actually available for holding your digital video file depends on the player program and how memory is configured and managed by the playback operating system. The only way you can make an educated guess is by experimenting with a system configured the same as your target audience machine.

The goal is to design your animation so that you can break it up into segments that fit the available memory. This enables each segment to run as smooth and as fast as possible without the typical frequent pauses when you play animation from a hard drive. The key word here is design. You don't just slice up an animation to make it fit. If you want your animation to be successful, you must plan where the segment breaks occur, and then stage those breaks around a sequence in the animation where a break makes sense.

NOTE

Using dedicated hardware to play back digital movies, in particular MPEG 1 and 2, eliminates the concerns of having large movie files and reducing playback speed. Many of the newer video cards have some form of MPEG decoder built in them. Video cards, such as Sigma Designs RealMagic, exist only to playback MPEG movies, taking all of the burden off your system processor and memory. By using such a card you can play an MPEG video file that may be 30 MB (or even larger) and still maintain 30 frames per second, even if the computer only has 8 MB of RAM memory.

Determining Playback Speeds

Before you can plan your transitions and break points for your animation, you must determine the final playback speed. Typically, video files are not played at 30 frames per second (fps). The hardware to play digital movies that fast is not widely available yet. A more typical playback speed is 15 to 20 fps. By default, 3D Studio MAX renders AVI and FLIC files at 30 fps. Use the Time Configuration feature to adjust your animation's frame rate. The dialog is reached by double-clicking the Time Configuration icon in the lower-right section of the main program window, just to the right of the frame entry field among the VCR controls.

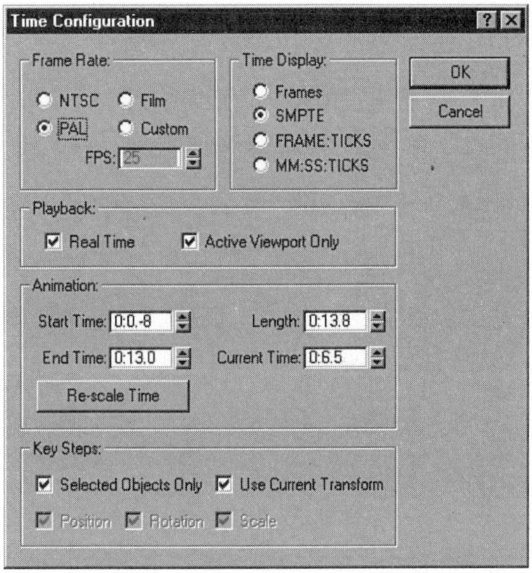

FIGURE 28.5

The Time Configuration dialog enables you to control frame rates for specific playback media.

NOTE

Remember that changing the frame rate does not change the overall length (in frames) of the animation. It DOES affect the amount of *time* it will take to play back the same number of frames. So if you change the frame rate and still need the animation to occupy a certain amount of time, you will also need to change the length of the animation. You may think you can accomplish this by changing the length setting in the main Time Configuration dialog, but changing that setting simply truncates to the start and end frame, or extends the last frame of the animation. You must select the Rescale Time button and change the Start, End, and Length settings to have 3DS MAX actually shrink or stretch the animation by adding or subtracting in-between frames to accommodate your time length (again, NOT frame length) requirements. Be forewarned, however: If you are using Character Studio, do not use the Rescale Time button. Stretch out time in the Track View instead.

Planning for Break Points

In today's fast-paced world, it is hard to hold someone's attention for more than five seconds. If you watch television, track how often a scene changes. You will notice that a change occurs every three to five seconds. If you watch music videos, the scene changes occur even faster. It's not uncommon for a music video or commercial to have a scene change every one to two seconds. Surfing the Net is much like changing television channels. At any time, you can interrupt what you are viewing and introduce completely new images.

Although consideration of scene changes and the length of a shot are important for all well-designed animation, they are absolutely critical for animation you intend to use for real-time recording and playback. Every time you change a scene in your animation, you have the opportunity to break the animation into separate segments. Carefully manage these scene changes, or transitions, by using cuts, fades, and interactive pauses to accommodate limited playback resources.

Using Transitions

The term transition refers to any change from one scene to another. Many different types of transitions are common in film and video, but two are important for digital video playback: cuts and fades. Cuts, in the simplest sense, are the abutted end frame and start frame from two animations.

They may be composed of the same scene elements (including objects and materials) or completely different scenes and images. Fades offer a gradual image introduction (fade-in), a change from one sequence to another (cross-fade), or completion (fade-out).

Both of these techniques are useful for maintaining interest in your animation and for identifying break points to separate the digital video files into segments. Cuts are not as useful as fades, however, because the rapid change from one scene to the next defies the capabilities of most systems. In general, for a cut to work properly during video playback, both segments must be in memory and both must use the same color palette.

Cuts and fades are one way you join animated segments together, but a pause is where you sneak the segments in and out of memory. Unless you are animating a music video or a fast-paced commercial, you need to plan for various pauses in your animation. The pause enables your viewer to read text on the screen, examine a scene more closely, or just catch up and digest the last segment of animation before moving on to the next.

The hidden benefit of a pause is that it gives you a chance to release previous animation segments from memory and load the next segments. The number of pauses required for loading and unloading animation has a direct relationship to the amount of memory available on the playback system. The less memory available, the more pauses are required to move segments in and out of RAM, which is why you need to know what type of system your animation plays on before you start keyframing and rendering the digital video.

Using 3D Animation for Online Content

One of the most exciting aspects of 3D animation today is its inclusion within web pages. This technology is now making its way into the Kinetix core products, including 3D Studio MAX (see Figure 28.6). The VRML export utility opens an entirely new and differentiating creative channel and you must engage in a specific strategy when rendering animation for this specialized digital medium. This section will cover some of the optimization techniques you can employ in this endeavor.

FIGURE 28.6

3D Studio MAX R2 enables you to export VRML files for use in web pages.

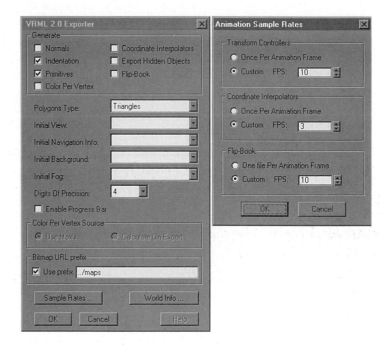

Several technologies are converging in the World Wide Web environment, including telephony, video-conferencing, interactive agents, vast client-server applications, and multimedia database management. From an animation perspective, producing imagery for the web is much like production for video games; the interactive environment trades off image detail in favor of performance. As bandwidth improves, so will the content on the web and, likewise, as the browsing applications incorporate VRML extensions, 3D content will populate web pages, creating an expectation for the virtual experience. You can immediately use 3D Studio MAX to produce fantastic, optimized animation for this experience.

Using the 3D Studio MAX VRML Exporter

Virtual Reality Modeling Language (VRML) is a specification for including and manipulating three-dimensional objects in a program. VRML is used specifically in conjunction with web pages, themselves specified in

Hypertext Markup Language (HTML). The 3D Studio MAX VRML Exporter was introduced in conjunction with the release of several World Wide Web products from Kinetix. Hyperwire, the core web product, is a powerful object-based multimedia authoring application that creates Java applets—highly portable, Internet-savvy programs.

The 3D Studio MAX VRML Exporter produces files (WRL) that can be viewed in any VRML Aware application and, most importantly, web browsers when they include a VRML browser. VRML browsers are generally plug-in components to web browsers, such as Netscape Navigator. The 3D Studio MAX VRML Exporter also has additional features designed to work specifically with Topper, the VRML browser from Kinetix. VRML Exporter includes interactive triggers, for example, that can launch activities based on whether an object is within the line of sight.

Optimizing for 3D Worlds

The 3DS file format, originating from 3D Studio and now supported by 3D Studio MAX through import and export features, is a standard for conveying 3D object information. Some virtual reality software toolkits work with raw 3DS MAX files that have been optimized for 3D world building. Due to bandwidth limitations, three-dimensional object manipulation cannot occur unless you constrain the total number of polygons (faces) in a scene. At this time, that constraint is around 1,000 polygons.

Whether you export to 3DS MAX files or export VRML, you need to understand and utilize the optimization capabilities in 3D Studio MAX. This entails placing the Optimize modifier on objects in your scene and adjusting the Level of Detail parameters. Figure 28.7 shows you where to add the modifier for optimization.

If you export to VRML, you can gain an amazing level of control over geometry simplification by using the 3D Studio MAX Optimize modifier in conjunction with the Level of Detail feature in the VRML Exporter. This Level of Detail feature substitutes cloned objects of various face counts as they are needed based on the original object's proximity to the viewer (see Figure 28.8). You'll find the Level of Detail feature under VRML Helpers.

FIGURE 28.7

Use the Level of Detail parameters in the 3D Studio MAX Optimize modifier to create optimized versions of objects for strategic placement in 3D worlds.

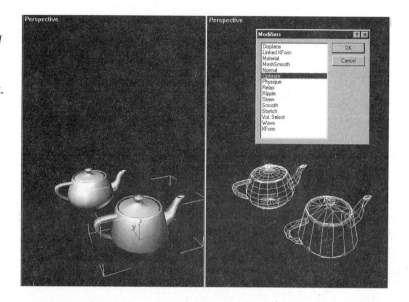

FIGURE 28.8

As the ship moves relative to the planet and the viewer's point of view, you can substitute more efficient geometry by using the Level of Detail parameters in the 3D Studio MAX VRML Exporter plug-in.

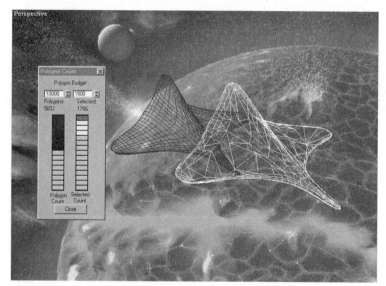

Rendering Output for Videotape

Creating animation for playback from analog videotape or film is very different from creating animation intended for computer playback. As stated in the beginning of this chapter, you should know the final format for your project long before you create preliminary storyboards because the differences between computer and video playback affect every aspect of 3D animation.

This section covers the details of animation for eventual videotape recording and offers a brief discussion of hardware technologies in real-time recording, such as record and playback cards from DPS and Truevision, and digital disk recorders (DDRs).

Understanding Real-time Recording of Computer-Based Animations

The best animation quality is achieved when high-resolution images are played back as fast as or slightly faster than your eye/brain combination can distinguish individual images in full color. When the frame rate drops below 20 frames per second, the typical viewer will begin to notice "chunkyness." Completely smooth motion is the goal, but certain physical factors make this difficult to achieve in playing back digital video from disk.

A single frame of 24-bit color (16.7 million colors) at video resolution is almost one full megabyte uncompressed and compressed images are approximately half a megabyte in size. Playing back these images at the speed of videotape, 30 frames per second, means reading 15 MB of data from your hard disk and transferring that data onto your graphics card every second. Keeping a sustained transfer rate of that magnitude is not possible with today's standard PC technology, but many hardware solutions now exist that enable real-time recording and playback of full-frame, compressed (or even uncompressed) video and animation.

Any animation that requires extremely accurate playback speed should not depend on standard computer playback. The differences in computers, graphics boards, and even the amount of memory available affect the speed of playback.

There are two ways to overcome potential playback problems. Traditional frame-by-frame recording of the animation to videotape might be a good option if you already own the analog recording equipment needed. The second, and better, option is to use new systems from companies such as DPS and Truevision that guarantee smooth, 30-frame-per-second playback from their specialized boards. With each method, every frame of the animation is stored separately on the computer hard drive or on newer, specialized

SCSI-streaming audio-video drives. All 16.7 million colors are available at high resolution. When copied to videotape one frame at a time, or when played back on the computer via the specialized hardware, you can depend on your animation playing back smoothly at exactly 30 frames per second. If your project must play back smoothly, with accurate timing, plan on using one of these methods.

When rendering for playback from a video signal (broadcast or tape), you have the option of field rendering. This type of rendering, discussed later in the "Rendering Frames versus Fields" section of this chapter, plays back on your video system at 60 fields per second, for the absolute smoothest animation possible.

Rendering to Disk

With the move towards digital output, 3D Studio MAX R2 does not offer the option to render directly to a videotape deck (as 3D Studio DOS used to support). If you plan on recording your animation to tape frame by frame, you'll need 3D Studio MAX controller software and hardware to do so. Without the software and hardware to control a videotape deck, you must render to disk or to a Digital Disk Recorder first and then lay the images to tape from that device. Carefully consider your decision to render directly to videotape, even if you already have the necessary software and hardware.

Although rendering directly to tape means you never have to worry about running out of disk storage space, if a problem occurs, the entire project has to be rendered again. With direct frame-by-frame taping, you also wear down the VTR recording head mechanism with repeated and frequent placement for each frame. Professional, workstation-class, PC-based video recorders, such as the Perception from DPS, the Targa boards from Truevision, and standalone Digital Disk Recorders, have become the preferred method for accurate frame control and recording of digital 3D to videotape.

Professional 3D Studio MAX renderings bound for analog video can first be rendered as files on a standard hard disk, a dedicated high-speed SCSI AV drive, a RAID system, or a disk array within DDR, and then recorded to the analog video medium. The most common file format for this rendering is a compressed Targa file. If space is at a premium, you can render to other bitmap file types—a JPEG file, for example, which has a user-definable compression ratio. As in our discussion of AVI codecs earlier in this chapter, the main difference to remember is that a compressed Targa file uses lossless compression, meaning that what you get out is exactly what you put into the file. JPEG is a lossy compression scheme and the results of its compression ratio can be noticeable. Targa, therefore, is recommended for higher-quality results.

If you have the Targa 2000 card or one of the DPS cards, you can render to DVM, Targa AVI, or PVD files as opposed to individual sequential still frames. Most of these digital recording solutions are priced under, or around, $2,000 for a basic setup. These basic systems are suitable for industrial use. True Broadcast quality setups can cost substantially more.

3D Studio MAX outputs files directly to devices as well as drive locations. One driver for such a device is included with the product. The Accom Work Station Disk (WSD) is a professional DDR. The WSD stores up to eight minutes of uncompressed digital video in a proprietary format. WSD offers an uncompromising, independent mechanism for storing and moving your animation to other professional media. Look for information about using the Accom WSD in your 3D Studio MAX Plug-In Help.

Most manufacturers of the real-time playback cards provide plug-ins that enable 3D Studio MAX to record directly to their boards' proprietary format. DPS provides Lockstep, for example, a plug-in that allows you to select their boards as a device for rendering. The plug-in also enables you to access animations you have recorded to your dedicated A/V drive and play them back within 3D Studio MAX.

Advantage of Rendering to Disk

Rendering to files on disk provides much more control over the final output than rendering directly to tape. If the images are too dark or too light, you can run them through Video Post to change them. If an object has an error, you can rerender just that object and composite it back into your scene with Video Post. Also, if there is a problem while recording the animation on your VTR—such as a dropped frame, drop-out, or random glitch—you need only to lay the frames to tape again, which is much faster than rerendering the entire project.

The new boards, such as those from DPS and Truevision, enable the user to render directly to their digital format, and still have the ability to insert edits when sections of the animation need to be rerendered.

Sequential Files

3D Studio MAX saves each frame as a consecutively numbered file. Up to four of the characters you give it are used as the first four characters of the filename and the next four characters are numbers (for example, TEST0000.TGA, TEST0001.TGA, and so on). Be careful in naming your output because the second group of four characters of a filename is overwritten. A filename of SEASHORE.TGA, for example, overwrites SEASHELL.TGA, giving you SEAS0000.TGA in both cases.

It is also recommended that the fourth character of the filename be a letter rather than a number. If you use the name GP14, 3D Studio MAX adds its number sequence to it. Suddenly, instead of starting at 0000, your animation numbering sequence starts at 140,000!

Disk Space Considerations

Each file can be between 500 KB and 1 MB. These file sizes can add up quickly, especially if you are rendering on a network. Rotoscoped maps and textures used in the project add further to disk space requirements.

Different file formats have different disk space requirements. BMP files have only 8 bits per pixel, or 256 colors; the file size is much smaller than a 24-bit (16.7 million color) Targa. A compromise is to render to a 16-bit (64,000 color) Targa file. When dithered from 24 bits to 16 bits, you may notice little or no difference in the final output and the disk space required is reduced drastically.

N OTE

If you are rendering the alpha channel, either as Alpha-Split or as a 32-bit Targa file (the resulting disk space is identical), remember that this takes twice as much disk space as a 16-bit Targa.

Time Code

Even if you are not rendering directly to videotape, a brief understanding of time code is helpful. Time code (also referred to as SMPTE time code for the Society of Motion Picture and Television Engineers) is a system whereby a separate track is recorded on the tape that holds the frame information in an hours;minutes;seconds;frames format, such as 01:22:35:03, for example. The format is stored on the tape similar to the way audio information is stored on tape and, in fact, some tape decks that do not have a separate time code track work very well by storing the time code information on an audio track.

The two types of time codes are Longitudinal Time Code (LTC) and Vertical Interval Time Code (VITC). No practical difference exists between the two; each stores the same information, just in a different way. LTC is stored on a third audio track, whereas VITC is super-imposed onto the vertical blanking interval. With LTC, the time code information is recorded along with the signal on a video or audio track. It cannot be read when the tape deck is paused. VITC stores the time code statically between frames, making it accessible regardless of the status of the tape motion. For this reason, it is generally preferred over LTC.

Drop Frame versus Non-Drop Frame Time Code

The National Television Standards Committee (NTSC) video, the standard in the United States, is not exactly 30 frames per second; it is actually 29.97 frames per second due to the carrier wave frequency and field interlacing of the video signal. For very short-length television segments 15 to 30 seconds long, this does not present a problem. Over a longer period, however, enough of a discrepancy exists to cause a problem in a time-critical application, such as a network television broadcast show or a 60-second commercial. If you lose .03 frames per second, you will lose 1.8 frames per minute.

To alleviate the timing issues, a system called Drop Frame (DF) time code is used. In this method, one frame for every 1,000 or so is dropped to make up for the time differential. This is not a problem in continuous video editing because the editor can factor in the dropped frame. With computerized single-frame animation, however, the system cannot account for the lost frame. 3D Studio MAX cannot provide output with the correct frame number "missing." If you need your final output to be on DF time code, you must first record your animation on a Non-Drop Frame (NDF) tape and then only rerecord the time code track with a DF time code, or dub it onto a tape with a DF time code.

NOTE

A tape must be prepared to accept data before it is first used in single-frame animation. This process is analogous to formatting a floppy disk before using it in a computer and is sometimes referred to as *blacking* or *striping* a tape.

VTR Formats

If your final output is targeted at videotape, you'll need to consider a professional-level VTR, even if you don't plan on frame-by-frame rendering direct to tape. If you use a DPS, Truevision, or similar card, you'll still want to output your digital signal to a quality machine. Do not expect a $3,000 SVHS deck to compare with a $15,000 BetaSP deck in mechanical quality, performance, or image quality, but if you don't need frame, accurate editing capabilities, don't invest too much on VTR.

The four major categories of video equipment are consumer, prosumer, industrial, and professional (sometimes referred to as broadcast). Consumer decks are not capable of frame-accurate work. Prosumer decks are the next level up and include both SVHS and Hi-8 decks. Prosumer decks are the least expensive decks that can be used for frame-accurate animation and recording-quality SVHS images.

The industrial category offers better quality images, in addition to a higher-quality deck. Into this area fall the 3/4" decks—both 3/4" and 3/4" SP (Superior Performance).

The professional decks include Beta and BetaSP, recordable laser disc, M-II, 1-inch, and the digital formats D1, D2, and D3. Professional-level decks keep the video signal separated into its component parts for higher-quality images. These formats can be edited numerous times without the signal degradation that accompanies copying one tape onto another. If, for example, you lay your animation onto one tape, edit it into a video, and then make dubs of the copy to distribute, you take your master down two generations. Each generation degrades the quality of the video. Professional-level decks minimize or eliminate generational loss of quality.

Rendering Frames versus Fields

Knowing the difference between frame rendering and field rendering, and when to use each, can make the difference between a good animation and a great one. The increased smoothness of a field-rendered animation over one rendered by frames is like night and day.

If all video is shown at 30 frames per second, what can you do to make it smoother? The answer to this lies surprisingly in a technology, which the industry strives to avoid in computer monitors, called interlacing. This feature is used in recording to video. A computer monitor displays every scan line in succession, starting with the top one and working down in a method called non-interlaced, or progressive scan.

A television set, on the other hand, starts with the top line but displays every other line to the bottom, and then comes back to pick up the lines it missed. This is called an interlaced display. Each separate set of scan lines is called a field. As shown in Figure 28.9, a video camera records images in the same manner using two fields.

FIGURE 28.9

If you labeled frames as if they were on a film strip, you would see the relationship between fields and frames.

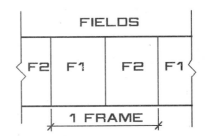

If you use a video camera to record an image of a basketball moving quickly, and then play it back and pause on a single frame with a high-quality deck, you will see that the basketball moves between the time the camera records the first field and the second one. The basketball actually appears to be in two places at once; the image appears to be jittering back and forth. This is a demonstration of field recording.

To demonstrate this effect in 3D Studio, create a sphere approximately one-third the size of your camera view and aim a light at it. Now, in the Time Configuration dialog, set the total number of frames to two and place the sphere at the left edge of the camera view in frame 0 and at the right edge of the viewport in frame 2 (see Figure 28.10). Render frame 1 and observe that the sphere is in the center of your viewport (see Figure 28.11).

Prepare to render the same scene, but before starting the Renderer, change the Render To Fields option in the Render Scene dialog. Now render the sphere again. The Renderer now renders the scene twice, but only renders every other line each time, calculates the location of the sphere based on fields instead of frames, and renders both fields on the same file (see Figure 28.12).

FIGURE 28.10

Looking at a camera view of the image you will be rendering in fields and frames. Note the use of Safe Frames when rendering for playback on videotape.

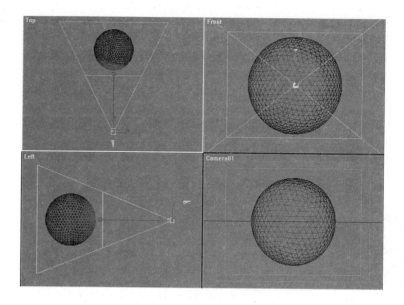

FIGURE 28.11

The rendered image without fields provides a single image per frame.

FIGURE 28.12

The rendered image with fields provides sub-frame samples of the object, which smoothes the motion upon playback.

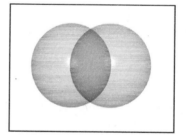

Depending on the animation, field rendering can take almost no more time than frame rendering. This is because only half the image is rendered in each pass. The time to render fields increases if shadows or automatic reflections are used. Both of these must be recalculated for each field and this can be the most time-consuming portion of rendering.

When to Render Frames

In certain situations, frame rendering should be used, such as when you render still images. Field rendering is not a substitute for motion blur. Never use fields if you will utilize computer playback of your animation because fields are not used in progressive scan devices. The same holds true if you are rendering to film. Film projectors play back one frame at a time.

Another use for frame rendering is when you anticipate many holds, or when your animation is to be used for slow playback, such as courtroom animations. If you want the viewer to be able to pause on any frame to review the video, render to frames.

When to Render Fields

Render to fields whenever smooth motion is required and the project will be output to videotape or for television broadcast. If the first or last frame is held on the tape, it is a good idea not to render these two frames with fields so that no jitter occurs during the hold.

If you hold the first or last frame when recording to videotape, it is especially important to have an "ease from" or an "ease to" on these frames for a smooth start and end to your animation. If not, your animation has a noticeable jump when the action starts or stops.

Setting Up Fields

Preparing for field rendering is a very simple procedure. Check the configuration settings for devices that play back your animation, such as Digital Disk Recorders and real-time playback cards for specific field order requirements. Confirm the correct specification when working with a service bureau. Verify that your Field Order parameter in Preferences on the Rendering tab is checked to either Odd or Even, in accordance with your devices specifications.

Now load your animation and access the Render Scene dialog. Check the Render to Fields option (see Figure 28.13). Any renderings you do after these preparations are properly field-rendered.

FIGURE 28.13

The Render to Fields
check box is set in the
Render Scene dialog.
Note appropriate set-
tings for rendering for
videotape playback,
such as Video Color
Check and Super
Black.

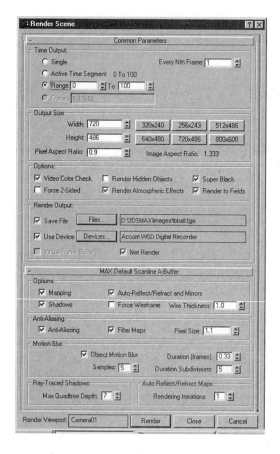

Understanding Rotoscoping

Rotoscoping, a term that comes from a traditional film technique, is applied in computer animation for the process of using video, one frame at a time, as a background or texture map. The older film definition refers to using a frame of film to trace cel animation and special effects.

3D Studio MAX provides a new facility for rotoscoping. There are three main ways you can provide reference and composite images (see Figure 28.14). You can use the Views menu, Display Background feature to build your scenes over captured or recorded video frames from a device (the Accom DDR, for example), or from audio-visual streaming, SCSI drives controlled by the Perception Video Recorder, or Truevision Targa 1000 and 2000 cards. After you complete the animation, you can composite it with the same background as a Layer event in Video Post. You can also use the very powerful Environment feature in conjunction with the Material Editor to map the video as a screen (traditional background), plane, sphere, or shrink wrap relative to your scene.

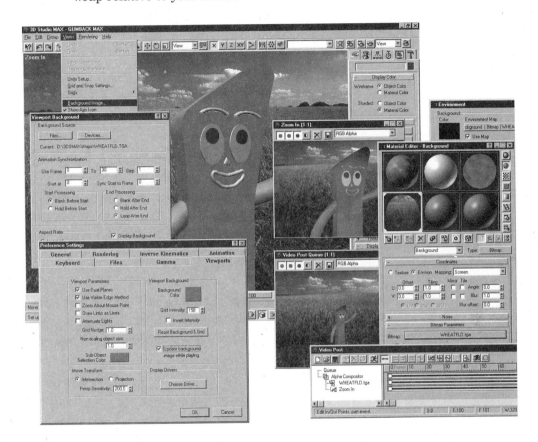

FIGURE 28.14

There are three methods to using your scene objects in conjunction with bitmaps and environments to produce backgrounds. The simplest method for traditional screen backgrounds is to composite using Video Post.

Disk Space Considerations

Files rotoscoped from tape are extremely large because they do not compress well. This is because every pixel has a different color value. Compression schemes depend on adjacent pixels being identical and this does not happen often with live video capture.

If you are not using a specialized RAID system, a Digital Disk Recorder, or a PC-based dedicated controller and drive, plan on keeping a large amount of hard disk space available for rotoscoped files. If you plan as if you had uncompressed files, you will not be very far off when predicting the amount of free disk space required to store the files. A 720×486, 24-bit file is just over 1.1 MB in size.

Capture Methods

As mentioned earlier, 3D Studio MAX includes a device controller for the Accom WSD DDR, which captures frames directly to a hard disk in its own proprietary uncompressed format. Models are available that can hold up to eight minutes (14,400 frames) of uncompressed digital video. New Windows NT-specific, PC-based digital video recorders are now available from Truevision, DPS, and other companies. Some require a dedicated storage drive, whereas others can use shared drives. In any case, video is captured and subjected to very minimal, or no, compression. The result is that you can achieve high-grade professional video capture (recording) and output (playback) from digital storage. Use the software that comes with the PC add-in board or standalone device to access frames or transfer the files to a series of standard bitmap files.

Another method of rotoscoping and outputting files quickly is the recordable laser disc or CD-ROM. The video to be rotoscoped is simply dubbed onto the disc and each frame is brought into the computer. Like digital storage, the laser disc needs no preroll and transfer occurs very quickly. Again, 3D Studio MAX does not include drivers for directly accessing these devices. Consult the latest third-party products catalog from Kinetix for driver and device availability.

When to Remove Fields

Files rotoscoped from live video are usually captured with fields. This is not a problem if the images are to be used as a background because the animation actually appears smoother due to the extra sub-frame motion. If you are mapping the images onto an object, however, the field containing images may not align correctly or could clash with other material effects. The way to solve this problem is to remove fields, which is accomplished in two ways. The simplest way is to have a program copy every other scan line down one line. This removes all field effects and is a relatively quick procedure, cutting the vertical resolution of your bitmap in half. If the object onto which the material is mapped takes up a small portion of the screen, this may be all that is needed.

If the object is prominent in your animation, however, you might want to clean up the rotoscoped map. This can be accomplished by running the files through a program that not only copies each line of pixels down but also interpolates between the two lines that remain to have a smooth image. When done properly, the image looks much better than if the fields are just copied down. Some of the PC-based digital recorders include utilities for this purpose.

Using Frame Control Features and IFLs

You can use the Animation Synchronization feature in the Viewport Background dialog to control when each image is presented relative to the scene's frame position. Likewise, you can use similar controls in the Material Editor Time rollout and Video Post Image Input event Options dialog to control which frame of a source digital video file or animation sequence is in position relative to your scene animation. You can gain very precise control by creating an IFL from video frames you've captured with a device such as a DDR or a PC-based capture card. You can transfer or convert the files to sequential bitmap files and let MAX generate an IFL (Image File Loader) in the directory with the files. Then load the IFL into the File section of the View Background Image dialog.

 A new utility in R2, called the IFL Manager, lets you create and edit IFL Files. It has options to create IFLs with every Nth frame, among other tools. Although 3D Studio can automatically make IFLs for you without this utility, the IFL Manager gives you more control.

Rendering for Film

The presence of digital special effects and animation in film has now been established as a legitimate mechanism for conveying realistic effects as well as creating cinematically beautiful images. This is a function of better, cheaper, and faster technology as well as a growing awareness and appreciation for the unique images that can be created with products such as 3D Studio MAX.

As stated in the very beginning of the chapter, the playback mechanism for frames determines significant elements in the 3D modeling and rendering production planning process.

Controlling Frames and Animation Length for Film Playback

Film is played back at 24 fps, so it is important to set your frame rate to that setting and rescale your animation in the Time Configuration dialog to maintain the same animation length in time. As more commercial films are made with consideration for collateral properties on CD-ROM, for the web, and for the video cassette marketplace, you should become familiar with creating multiple rendering schemes for this eventuality.

T IP

If you are using Character Studio, do not Rescale Time. Increase or decrease the time segment and then use Track View to change the timing of your animation.

Working with High Resolution Files

You may be supplied with very high-resolution sequential files from another system, such as Abekas, to rotoscope with. Be careful to match the sequential filenames with your automatic numbering feature in 3D Studio MAX. Make a low-resolution copy of the files by running the files through Video Post or by using a batch file conversion utility such as Image Alchemy. Use your low-resolution copies for most of your work. Run several high-resolution output tests with single files to measure your system's current memory capabilities. You may need to reset virtual memory to accommodate disk paging.

Using Object Motion Blur for Cinematographic Effect

You can simulate film blur effects with this feature, but be aware of the iterative time penalty when applying object motion blur. Experiment with applying this effect discretely in small movement circumstances to great effect.

In Practice: Rendering Animation

- **Planning for Playback:** With new forms of media distribution including the web, CD-ROM titles, and the growth of digital editing technology, plan for rendering by strategically establishing media-specific configuration settings. Create template configuration (3dsmax.ini) and startup (maxstart.max) files.

- **Digital Video Formats:** When rendering Digital Video file formats, avoid dithering and optimize the geometry of your scene to create smaller file sizes. Take advantage of the integrated VRML and Java tools available from Kinetix to explore the creation of 3D content for the web and disc-based animation. Use the custom FLC rendering feature to control color palettes. Experiment with codec settings to achieve optimal quality versus compression in AVI files.

- **Digital Recording:** 3D Studio MAX is designed to take advantage of the power of Windows NT. New desktop video controllers and software that offer real-time playback of sequentially rendered files are available. Although you cannot render directly to tape, the quality of these devices complies with professional video signal standards. Engage the client/server network rendering capabilities within 3DS MAX in combination with NT and these devices to gain productivity and strategically target your rendering output. When videotape is the target playback medium, use Field Rendering to smooth motion. Coordinate Field Order and Gamma settings for devices with which you or your associates will edit and play back animation.

- **Backgrounds and Rotoscoping:** For straightforward screens—that is, flat backgrounds—use the Video Post feature to composite your Scene with an Image Input event. Coordinate the output of Video Post with your Viewport Background for rotoscoping scene images with the Image Input event. For unique, procedurally controlled backgrounds (Environments), you must understand the relationship between the environment maps in the Material Editor and the Environmnent feature. Create template configuration and maxstart.max files to accommodate project requirements.

Chapter 29

COMPOSITING EFFECTS

3DS MAX gives you tremendous animation control and the ability to create and animate almost anything you can imagine. This includes setting up complete animated sequences with multiple camera views, transitions, and titles. You can even composite your animated objects over recorded video or other animated sequences layer upon layer. If you're familiar with the layer concept used in Photoshop, you'll find the same basic concept used in 3D Studio MAX. The powerhouse tool that makes this possible is found in Video Post. This chapter will explore what Video Post offers and how best to put it to use. You'll discover it's like having a complete post-production house within 3DS MAX. The following is a list of topics covered in this chapter:

- Understanding Video Post
- Using scene events
- Using image input events
- Using filter and layer events
- Understanding and using alpha
- Using loop and external events
- Controlling composite output

Compositing Effects Overview

Compositing effects in 3DS MAX are used when creating still images, as well as animations. Perhaps you need to place your 3D character in front of a live shot of your office building for a print ad. Maybe you need to have that character stand on the street corner and wave to cars driving by in a recorded video sequence. In almost every animation, you'll need some way of transitioning between scenes or camera views. Regardless of your needs, you can use the Video Post tool within 3DS MAX to do all of the following and more:

- Merge objects from your still or animated scene with other still images, animations, or recorded video.

- Add titling or credits to your scene. You can even add running time clocks when you need to demonstrate duration in technical applications.

- Create transitions between scenes including simple cross-fades to complex wipes.

- Add special effects such as lens flares, glows, or any of the endless number of plug-in effects available. You can even use most Adobe Premiere and Photoshop plug-ins within 3DS MAX.

An understanding of what you can create using compositing effects will help you plan for production. Once your animation is storyboarded, you should make plans for how each element will be created and animated, then turn your attention to how all the elements will be brought together. With proper planning, your use of Video Post for compositing effects and adding transitions will increase your productivity and allow even greater creative freedom.

TIP

Plan for the viewer's playback medium and use techniques of composition that will be revealed in that specific medium relative to the width of the overall 3DS MAX window by editing the 3dsmax.ini file. Change the [Window State] Size values (width and height) appropriately. Your viewports then correspondingly change their aspect ratio. Coordinating the custom background safe frame and the viewport aspect ratio will help you produce effects bound for a specific format (see Figure 29.1).

FIGURE 29.1

A letterbox composite using bitmap sized background, Render Output size, and Safe Frames.

Understanding Video Post

Video Post is derived from the term post-production, the final stage of film-making. Post-production occurs after the shooting of the film and the actual production work is complete. In this final stage, each of the elements are edited into a finished form. This includes adding transitions and special effects. Usually, the transition is a cut, which switches to the new scene on the very next frame without any effect. In some situations, however, a more dramatic transition is called for, such as slowly fading in one image while fading out another, or revealing an image with a wipe from left to right across the screen. Many of these tasks can be completed without ever leaving 3D Studio MAX by using Video Post.

3D Studio MAX's Video Post feature enables you to rapidly produce a wide variety of useful images and animation. These might include set design visualization, on-the-fly virtual backgrounds to composite with a video feed of live actors, or dazzling post-production special effects and transitions.

Rather than a complete desktop video editing application, Video Post is a utility application used to composite 3DS MAX scenes with other animation or video images. Depending on your project and its destination (film, video, digital movie, and so on), you may use Video Post to prepare an image or animation for a professional compositing or editing platform, or to visualize and prototype a larger comprehensive animation effort. For some projects, however, you may be able to complete most or all of your compositing for final output completely within MAX using Video Post.

Additionally, the Video Post feature in 3DS MAX assists you in automating image processing for content inclusion in such products as video games, CD-ROM titles, and interactive online animation.

Elements of Video Post

Video Post works elements in terms of events. There are three general categories of events:

- **Inputs**: scenes and images
- **Effects**: filters, layers, loop and external
- **Outputs**: files and devices

Input Events

Video Post performs as if it is a standalone compositing and video editing software program, so it really doesn't matter where the input events come from. You don't even need to include any frames from a 3D Studio MAX scene; you can use Video Post with input events from virtually any source. The two types of input events are the following:

- **Scene Events:** these add sequences of frames from your MAX scene to Video Post to be rendered and manipulated by another Video Post event. For example, you may add different scene events for each camera view in your scene, designating frame ranges for each different event. You might have an event for Camera 1 from frame 1 to 100 and a second event for Camera 2 from frame 101 to 200.

- **Image Events:** these add prerendered images, or sequences of images or video, to Video Post. Image events can be animations, scanned photographs, digitized video, or a series of still images you want to combine into your Video Post rendering.

Effects Events

Effects events come in two varieties; layer and filter. Each performs some action on other events in Video Post. For example, MAX ships with 13 standard filters for layering and special effects. These include effects such as Fade, Contrast, Alpha Composite, and many variations of Lens Effects.

Any 32-bit filter from Adobe Premiere or Photoshop can also be added as a filter in Video Post. This makes a tremendous amount of effects available that you can create without ever leaving 3D Studio MAX.

Output Events

The final event in your Video Post sequence is an image output event. This event designates how your final image(s) are saved. Your choices are to save individual bitmaps, series of sequential bitmaps, any number of popular digital video formats, or proprietary real-time formats for users of Truevision, DPS, or similar playback cards.

All the events you add are collectively referred to as the queue. Figure 29.2 shows the two main areas of the Video Post dialog: identifying the Queue window on the left and the Edit window on the right. The queue displays the actual events and the Edit window displays the frames over which each event occurs.

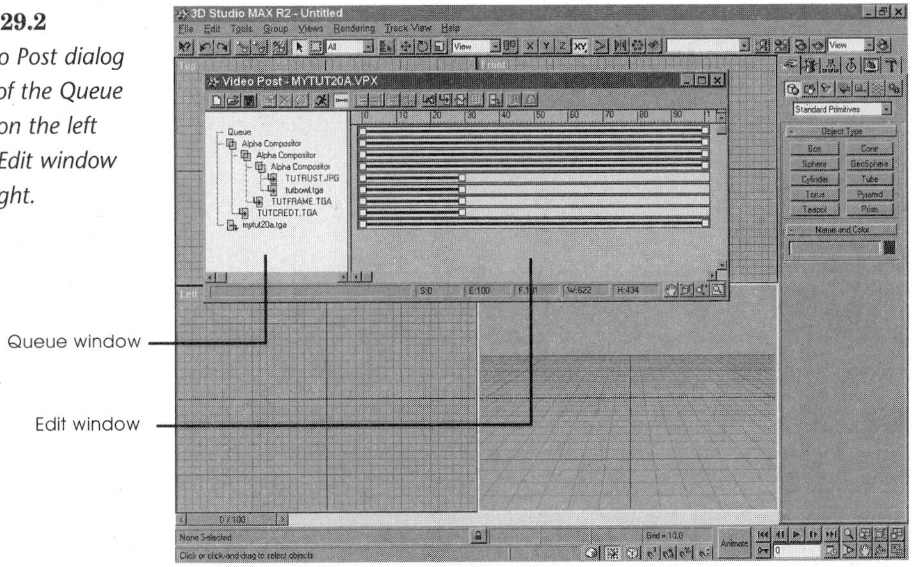

FIGURE 29.2

The Video Post dialog consists of the Queue window on the left and the Edit window on the right.

Queue window

Edit window

Working with Video Post

To visualize what happens when you execute a Video Post sequence—that is, render the events listed in the Queue window—consider the following: Video Post renders each event in the queue from the top down, drawing layer over layer, but what you see in the final image is best visualized from the bottom up. Figure 29.3 shows how this analogy works.

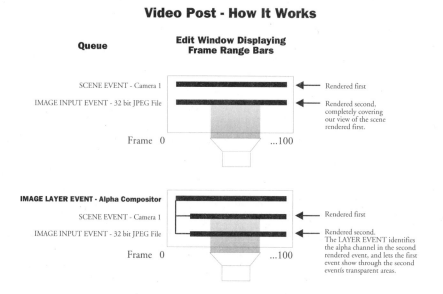

FIGURE 29.3

The layering concept of Video Post can best be understood by imagining a camera looking through each queue event from the bottom up.

Imagine a camera filming the events in the queue from the bottom, looking up. In this example, the first scene event in the queue is the camera view from your MAX scene. The second event is an image input event which might be a title slide or other image you want to layer (composite) over the first scene. Simply adding the second event to the queue causes it to render over the first event, completely obscuring the first event (in this example, blocking the camera's view of the first event). You must instruct Video Post how to create the composite image by adding what is called a layer event. In this example, the second event is a 32-bit JPEG file, meaning the file contains an additional 8 bits of alpha channel information defining areas in the image that are transparent.

By adding a layer event called an Alpha Compositor, you're instructing Video Post to composite the second event over the first event, respecting the alpha channel information in the second event. This enables you to see a composite image that reveals the first event through the transparent areas of the second event. Each event you add to Video Post has a fixed hierarchical and relative position represented in the queue (the left side of the Video Post window) by a label, and in the Edit window (the right side) by a horizontal line (the range bar) indicating its appearance over time. If you change the contents of the queue by adding, removing, repositioning or altering them, the final rendered image will obviously change.

The 3DS MAX renderer evaluates each scene event in the queue and determines the order in which each is executed by reading the Event labels (see Figure 29.4). The final image is viewed in the Virtual Frame Buffer window while rendering and can be recorded to a file or device.

FIGURE 29.4

The Video Post Queue in tut20_2.max (from the MAX R2 CD-ROM) with the actual rendering order indicated for frame 550.

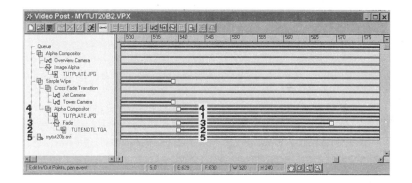

The Renderer does not simply make its way through the queue in a top-to-bottom fashion. A given event may be standalone in the queue or it may have a hierarchical relationship to another event—that is, the event may be a parent, child, or sibling to other events.

In Figure 29.4, note the column of numbers both to the left of the Video Post queue event labels and in the Edit window over the range bars. The numbers represent the actual event rendering sequence for frame 550. By repeatedly rendering a single frame (such as 550) to the Virtual Frame buffer, you can observe the Current Task section of the progress dialog and follow the actual rendering sequence in the order shown in the columns. Familiarity with the actual rendering order will help you construct queues according the renderer's logic. The order in which you place the events in the queue is very important.

The Edit Window is a timeline. Starting with zero, the timeline represents a range of frames that extend infinitely to the right in a positive direction. Each event has a corresponding range bar that enables you to manage how and when a given event appears. The "how" is accomplished by adding Scene or Image Input events to the queue and applying modifying effects, such as Filters and Layers. "When" is accomplished by arranging the specific start and end parameters of range bars.

Other than its launching command in the Render menu, Video Post has no pull-down menus. The tools across the top of the Video Post window provide the methods for placing new entries in the queue. Depending on the type and number of selected events in the queue, various tools become enabled for application to the selection.

T IP

It is essential that you construct your Video Post sequences carefully and conservatively. You should save Video Post (VPX) files for each major stage in constructing the sequence by clicking the Save Sequence tool and confirming the overwrite of an existing file or by naming a new one. Save your 3DS MAX file regularly, too. This part of 3DS MAX contains no Undo or Redo function, and you cannot right-click to snap your range bars back to their original positions.

Generally, you select events for editing by double-clicking their labels, not their range bars. By doing the latter, you can inadvertently shift the Video Post Start Time and End Time parameters. It can become tedious and cumbersome to adjust single frame mismatches between adjacent events or beginning and ending points, especially when you are anxious to see your composite effects and a full render is required to preview your work.

Using Scene Events

The Scene event is a defined range of frames that may represent all, or a portion of, the overall 3DS MAX scene. When you add a Scene event to the Video Post queue, you specify which view and what frames to render.

When you add a Scene event, a viewport or camera name displays at the top of the View list in the dialog. The View list is sorted alphabetically by viewport or camera name.

To place a rendering of a scene viewport in the queue, click Add Scene Event (see Figure 29.5). To change the viewport you want to render, select the desired viewport from the View drop-down list. You can add Scene events with different views or use the same view multiple times in the queue to generate special effects, such as staggered motion. You can animate the same ant walking across the screen, for example, and make it look like a parade of ants continuously walking across the screen one behind the other.

To create this animation, use Video Post to add several Scene entries to the queue, specifying the same viewport and same frame ranges. You then stagger, or overlap, the point at which each Scene begins by adjusting the range bars in the Edit window. If the ant walks across the screen from frame 1 to 10, for example, add three scene events of frame 1 to 10. Set the first range bar for frames 1 to 10, the second for a range of 5 to 15, and the third event from 20 to 30. The result is a parade of ants marching across the screen. To do this, you'll need to be familiar with the difference between the Scene Range and the Video Post Range. Both are discussed in the next section.

FIGURE 29.5

The Add Scene Event dialog is where you define viewports and frame ranges to render.

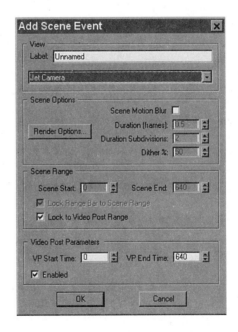

If you want to use different 3DS MAX files in the same Video Post queue, render one 3DS MAX file to disk and then add it to the queue as an Image Input event. If no Scene event is listed in the Queue, the current scene is ignored by Video Post.

Managing The Scene Range Relative to the Video Post Range

By default, 3DS MAX uses the scene's active time segment for the Video Post Start Time and End Time parameters. You may assume that Video

Post time and 3DS MAX scene time are the same, but that is not the case. 3DS MAX scene time extends infinitely back (negative) or forward (positive) in time, whereas Video Post defines a range of positive frames. This difference becomes evident when you compare the way time is represented in the Track View and Video Post windows.

Figure 29.6 illustrates this difference. This scene has an active time segment ranging from -10 to 10. The figure shows both the Track View and Video Post windows. In the Track View, notice that the range bars expand in both a positive and negative direction. In the Video Post window, notice the range bars are fixed at frame zero and expand toward the right side of the window. Video Post is only representing the length of the segment, whether or not it is a negative frame number is not displayed.

FIGURE 29.6

The Video Post window does not represent negative frame ranges.

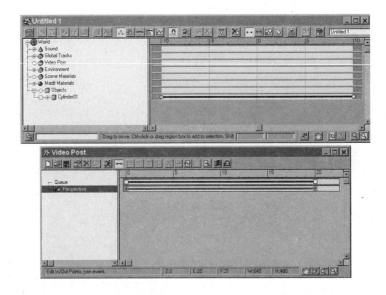

The Scene Range settings in the Add and Edit Scene Event dialog enable you to separately and relatively position Scene time in the context of Video Post time. By default, the Scene Range is locked to the Video Post range. By unchecking the Lock to Video Post Range and then, if desired, the Lock Range Bar to Scene Range box in the Add or Edit Scene Event dialog, you can indicate whether the defined Video Post range contains frames other than ones that directly correspond to the VP Start Time and End Time parameters.

Unchecking the Lock Range Bar to Scene Range box provides an interesting way to create slow and fast motion effects. If the overall range defined in the Scene range is less than the range specified in the Video Post Start and End Time parameters, Video Post adds frames to fit the Scene range into the larger Video Post range. This process stretches the motion over playback time, creating a slow-motion effect. If the overall number of frames in the Scene range is greater than the Video Post range, Video Post skips frames to fit the overall sequence into the smaller Video Post range. More motion in less time creates a fast-motion, or sped-up, effect.

In one Scene event, for example, you could move a spaceship slowly across the screen. You could abut a second Scene event that contains the same view and Scene range, but over fewer Video Post frames. When rendered and played back, the spaceship would appear to suddenly speed up. Engage!

Render Options

The Render Scene dialog contains two sections separated by the characteristic 3D Studio MAX rollups: Common Parameters and the default Scanline A-Buffer. Within these sections are options for anti-aliasing, mapping, rendering to fields, and others. These two sections are accessible from the Render Scene dialog, as well as the Add or Edit Scene Event dialogs from within Video Post (see Figure 29.7).

FIGURE 29.7

These are the render options as seen in the Add or Edit Scene Event dialog within Video Post. These option settings are also located in the Render Scene dialog and may be set from either location.

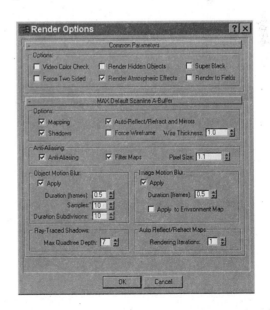

You have the option of which dialog you want to use to configure these settings. Regardless of where you make your choices for these settings, you only need to set them in one location. Turning on anti-aliasing from the

Render Options dialog, for example, also selects the anti-aliasing option from within the Add or Edit Scene Event dialog. The other sections of the Render Options dialog are not shared with Video Post. These options, which include Time Output, Output Size, and Render Output settings, exist separately in each location. In Video Post, these settings are in the Execute Sequence dialog. (See the section "Controlling Composite Output" later in this chapter for more information.)

Although you can set Common Parameters and the Scanline-A buffer options from Render Options in an individual Scene event, remember that these settings are not unique to the specific Scene event. The Render Options sub-dialog simply provides access to the global rendering settings for convenience in setting up the Scene event.

If you have a Scene event in the queue and add a second, any changes you make in the Render Options dialog affect the previously added Scene event as well. This means that you cannot separately set Anti-Aliasing, Object Motion Blur, Raytrace Shadows, Atmospheric effects, or any other overall render setting for each Scene event in the queue. The only way to composite and edit same scene segments with different render effects settings is to render the segment individually and add it as an Image Input event to the queue with other segments from the scene.

Using Image Input Events

An Image Input event can contain any image file or device supported by 3DS MAX including AVI, FLC files, IFL files, sequentially numbered or single-bitmap files, and files residing on devices, such as a Digital Disk Recorder (DDR). The name, format settings, and location of the images are saved with the 3DS MAX file and with the independent VPX file if appropriate.

To create a file that includes a series of numbered-image files, use global characters to identify and generate an Image File List (IFL) file. For example, enter the first few letters of the name of the file series, followed by an asterisk. 3DS MAX creates a file that begins with the designated letters, appends a sequence number after the letters that matches the sequence number of the first file in the list, and adds IFL as a file name extension. The IFL file is automatically placed in the same directory as the files it lists. The IFL file name is loaded into the Event dialog as your input file and the Event's label in the queue reflects its name too. If you have an animation or list file, such as IFL, AVI, or FLC files, the number of frames in the animation appears in three places: the Video Post parameters Start Time and End Time fields, the status fields at the bottom of the Video Post window, and the range bar for that Event where they are graphically represented.

If you want to set a specific gamma value for the inbound bitmap image, choose the Gamma button in the Browse Images for Input dialog. The Preference dialog's Gamma tab enables you to globally correct Input Images. For composition with Video Post, select the Enable Gamma correction check box in 3DS MAX Preferences, set your display gamma appropriately, and plan strategically for the correction of gamma in Image Input and Output events. This is especially relevant when using images associated with devices such as a DDR.

T IP _____

When you edit an Image Input event by changing information in Browse Images for Input sub-dialog (location, format, or Gamma setting, for example), 3DS MAX resets the Video Post Start and End Time parameters to default settings. You can lose some very exacting range parameters in the process because the default parameters not only change the overall range length, they will likely remove the event from its relative location in time by placing the event at the beginning of the animation. The most conservative practice is to separately keep a list of all parameters in the sequence, particularly the Video Post Start Time and End Time parameters. One strategy is to create an entirely new standalone event in the queue, referring to the parameter settings from the one you need to edit. Use the Swap tool to replace the original and the Delete tool to delete it following the Swap.

You can align and resize input images during rendering. If these images are animation files or sequences, you can specify which frames to include. To do this, enter values in the Add or Edit Image Input Event dialog, Options sub-dialog (see the User's Guide). Composite effects, such as embedded 2D offset animation in the scene, accurately placed masks, and Stretch and Squash techniques can all be achieved with this feature.

When Image Input events that contain a sequence of images or animation are added to the Video Post queue, their length and range are determined by settings in the Options sub-dialog of the Add or Edit Image Input Event dialog. Should the frame range differ from the Video Post range, Video Post simply locks the Image Input Start frame to VP Start Time, cuts off or holds the last image at the VP End Time, and loops the entire sequence depending on your settings.

Working with Backgrounds

Video Post does not directly access the Background image, which may be positioned in the Viewport and used for Rotoscoping. This is useful for constructing the scene against a background image. There are several ways to include that image in your Video Post rendering. You can use the Environment feature to map the same image to a Screen Environment map. It then is included with the Scene event in Video Post and rendered accordingly. If you wanted to use that image (or animation) as a composite element in Video Post, however, it must be added separately as an Image Input event. If it is an animation, its synchronization with the queue is managed in the Input Image Event/Options dialog.

Generally speaking, if you won't be applying an effect to the background image by using the Material Editor or Environment feature (matte/shadow materials, for example), you would simply add the background as an Image Input event in Video Post by using the Alpha Compositer in the Layer event to position the image as a background. The bitmap processing of that image as a Video Post event is very straightforward and takes less time to render. If the background is static, you can cache the image during render and save even more rendering time. Typically, you construct a Layer event for this purpose, composed of your background Image Input event followed by a Scene event or another Input Image with an alpha channel.

Using Filter and Layer Events

As stated earlier, Filter and Layer events fall into the broader category of Effects events. These effects generally act on and behave relative to other events (Input events—Scene and Image). It is somewhat confusing as to how the queue is processing these effects, particularly the order in which they are processed and the way in which transparency is used in images that contain an alpha channel. Again, remember to render single frames of complex queues to the Virtual Frame buffer, observing the progress dialog's Current Task field. This facilitates an understanding of the order in which filters, masks, and composites are rendered.

TIP

If you delete a child of a Layer event, the parent is also deleted. If you have several nested events, the ancestral line all the way through the root or topmost level is deleted. You can copy root sections of a queue by using the Ctrl key and dragging the root parent to an insertion point in the queue. Make sure that no events are highlighted before you depress the Ctrl Key. Press the key and then click the root parent. Drag the selection to an insertion point. All children of the parent are copied to the queue. If you just need to substitute a different child, add your new child event as a standalone event in the queue, then swap it (using the Swap tool) with the unwanted event. You can then delete the remaining standalone event without losing the hierarchy.

Strategies for Using Filter Events

Filter events are used in Video Post to produce specialized photographic effects, such as lens distortion, posterization (reducing the number of colors in an image), glows, and other overall image manipulation. Generally, particularly with Adobe Photoshop plug-in filters, these events render the effects to a temporary image, enabling it to process each pixel according to the parameters you set.

With Photoshop plug-in filters, you have a limited opportunity to preview the effect, either with a Video Post-supplied stand-in image or user-defined file. In any case, the ability to preview the exact result of the filter on the events in the queue is not available during setup. Remember to coordinate your stand-in image or user-defined image with the Output Size of the Video Post queue. This value is visible in the last two Status fields at the bottom of the Video Post window.

3DS MAX R2 now incorporates a series of lens effects filter events. The following exercise sets up a very simple lens flare.

THE LENS FLARE FILTER EVENT

1. Load lensflare.max from the accompanying CD-ROM.

2. This very simple scene contains a few objects and an Omni light set up to render a single frame still image. We'll quickly add the lens flare event in video post and assign the Omni light as the seed for the lens flare effect.

3. Click Rendering and select Video Post.

4. Click Add Scene Event and click OK in the dialog.

5. Click Add Image Filter Event and select Lens Effects Flare. Click OK.

6. Double-click the Lens Effects event you just added and open the Edit Filter Event dialog. Click Setup to launch the Lens Effects Flare dialog (see Figure 29.8).

FIGURE 29.8

The Lens Effects Flare event lets you preview your settings from within it settings dialog.

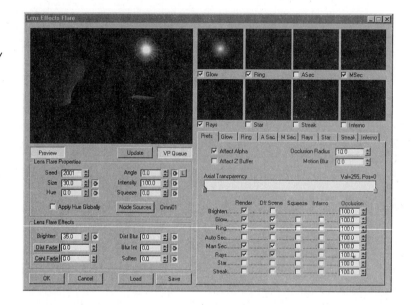

7. The Lens Effects dialog provides a preview window with which you'll be able to monitor all your settings. Click the VP Queue and then the Preview buttons to see your current scene in the Preview window.

8. In the Lens Flare Properties section, click Node Sources.

9. The Select Flare Objects dialog is similar to the Select Objects By Name dialog. Click the Omni light as the object you want to accept the flare settings and click OK.

10. Click the Update button to see the rendered scene with the default flare settings the Preview window.

11. Click OK to return to the Video Post window. When your scene is complete, along with any other effects or scenes you desire, add an Image Output Event and Execute the Sequence to save your rendered image.

Using Layer Events

Layer events enable you to composite two events relative to one another. The Alpha Compositor Layer event, for example, recognizes the transparency values of the second child so that values from the first child show through. Because only two images can be layered at a time, it is easy to construct a very deeply nested hierarchy of Layer events. This can be a very difficult process to manage, particularly when events take place "later" in Video Post time but reside "before" other events in the queue from a hierarchical point of view. At first, it seems illogical, for example, that an event such as the Simple Wipe Layer event for the animation in Tutorial 20 (MAX R2 CD-ROM) is a root level parent to two other Layer events that precede it in Video Post time.

This brings us back to the camera metaphor described earlier in the chapter. In the preceding circumstance, the Simple Wipe Layer event acts on two child Layer events. It might be tempting instead to place a Simple Wipe Filter event on the second child, which is the Alpha Compositor Layer event that contains the end title and plate. The slide projector lamp, however, would not be able to pass light through the non-transparent portion of the Simple Wipe Filter event because this filter cannot recognize any alpha or transparency in its children. The filter does not create a transparent window because it "paints" the wipe from its child image. The filter paints a combination of black pixels from the empty end title image track and the pixels from the non-transparent composite as it wipes across. When rendered, the Plate would wipe into view, but the Tower Scene would be obscured. The Simple Wipe Layer event, however, has the property of translating the empty track as transparent and "paints" the end title pixels as they wipe in. The lamp shines through to the Tower Scene until the non-transparent wipe is complete.

Managing Alpha

Color bitmap image files, such as Targa (TGA) files, come in a variety of bit depths, such as 8, 16, 24, and 32 bits per pixel. In a 32-bit true-color file, each pixel in the image has four channels that describe it—RGBA, Red-Green-Blue-Alpha. Three of the channels—Red, Green, and Blue—comprise the source for creating the full spectrum of color hues. The Red, Green, and Blue channels use 8 bits of memory each to describe the color of every pixel in the image ($3 \times 8 = 24$ bits per pixel). A pure green pixel, for example, has RGB values of 0,255,0. Each 8-bit channel is represented by the numbers 0 to 255 because 256 possible combinations of zeros and ones exist in a string of eight characters, or bits ($2\times2\times2\times2\times2\times2\times2\times2$).

Alpha, in its simplest form, can be thought of as another channel. It represents the level of transparency by using another 8 bits of memory for every pixel in the image. Suppose that you render a flat, white circle over a black background by using a material on the circle that is 50 percent transparent. When the Renderer encounters a pixel that falls inside the circle, it writes the values [128,128,128,128] to a 32-bit image file for that pixel, or 8 bits for each channel. MAX uses pre-multiplied alpha, which means that the effect of the transparency is included in the RBG values. This enables any image beneath that pixel to be 50 percent visible—that is, the black background showing through the white circle, thereby producing gray. The benefit of this is that you can now composite the 50 percent transparent circle over any image in Video Post, such as a cloud-filled sky, and you see the clouds through the circle.

TIP ───

3D Studio MAX creates images in TGA, RLA, and PNG file formats. Whenever you output a bitmap image with 3DS MAX for the first time, the Setup dialog appears automatically. In this dialog, you have the ability to designate whether an alpha channel is included with the file. 3DS MAX remembers the last settings you entered for a particular file format.

When in the Browsing Image for Input dialog, you can select any file and choose the Info button to view details about the file. Here you can quickly discern whether the file contains an alpha channel. By choosing View, you bring the file into a frame buffer and examine the alpha channel as well.

In Video Post, you can take advantage of the alpha channel within bitmap files by specifying parameters from within the Filter and Layer events. The Alpha Composite Layer event enables you to composite two currently selected events, for example, by recognizing the alpha channel of the second of the two images. If you recall the slides, think of alpha as the opacity of the images on the slide. Some images are opaque; others are translucent or transparent.

Not all images have alpha information—only 32-bit, true-color files have this capability. For this reason, you are given a variety of methods to create and use alpha information for your Video Post effects. For example, the Pseudo Alpha Filter event takes the upper left-hand pixel of an RGB, non-alpha file and converts all identical pixels in the image to fully transparent alpha.

In addition to the capability of some Layer and Filter events to recognize and use the alpha channel in the files they act on directly, some also provide a Mask feature that enables you to use the alpha channel of a different file to fashion a custom area of transparency (see Figure 29.9). Here you can specify how the Mask effect is to be applied with the others in the queue. You have the ability to invert the Mask and use other channels in the Graphics buffer (G-buffer) to control the Mask effect.

FIGURE 29.9

The mask settings in Video Post event dialogs.

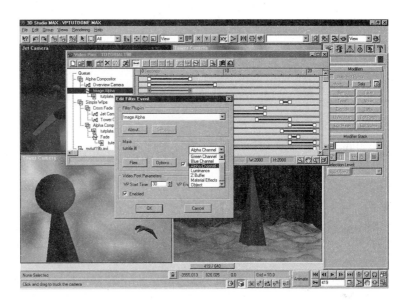

When you click in the box to the right of the Mask section in the dialog, you are presented with a list of bitmap channels, one or all of which may be contained within a source image. These are the channels that 3DS MAX currently supports for the purpose of creating the mask. 3DS MAX can output files with 16-bit RGBA channels as well as unique 3D channels like Z-buffer and object or material identification channels. The mask feature uses some of these unique channels to create its effects. The most common mask is an Alpha Channel mask. It creates a mask from the alpha channel of the source bitmap image.

If the Red, Green, or Blue channel is chosen as the source for the mask, the binary value (0–255) of each pixel in that channel is used for the mask with 0 being completely transparent and 255 completely opaque.

Using Loop and External Events

Loop events provide repeated frames and reverse direction (ping-pong) for individual tracks and whole sequences. Although limited looping is available in Image Input events, you can use the Loop event to loop composites, thereby creating unusual images and motion.

Assume, for example, you add a Scene event to the queue, which has 100 frames and you want the event to repeat three times. If you change the VP End Time to 299, your animation simply stops at frame 99 and Video Post renders frame 99 for the rest of the range bar's length. Recall that when you change the Scene Range to a different value than the Video Post Start and End Times, Video Post adds or skips frames, thereby creating slow- and fast-motion effects. So the only way to repeat a Scene event, other than adding the scene multiple times in the queue and abutting the Event tracks, is to use the Loop event. You can use this event to control the Start and End of the repeated frames by dragging the range bar relative to its child event. Experiment with this feature to achieve interesting loops and ping-pong effects.

As mentioned earlier, Input Image events will loop if the Options dialog Loop check box is selected. Otherwise, it behaves like a Scene event, repeating the last frame for the duration of the Video Post range bar.

With the External event, you can insert other applications or your own batch files into the Video Post queue. Typically, this is how you would batch process Output events using a conversion application that can accept a command-lines parameter, such as Image Alchemy or PKZIP. You can also embed processes that write out files used in subsequent events. Make sure to create PIF files for DOS applications, such as PKZIP, and use those as your External event file.

Examining Motion

Motion blur is an effect that now exists in three variations in 3DS MAX. The first version is Object motion blur (the same type used in 3DS MAX R1), configured in the Render Scene and Video Post's Scene Event, Render Options dialogs. It enables you to specify a motion blur effect for the absolute change in position of individual objects. Object motion blur occurs during rendering. The second version is Image motion blur (new in 3DS MAX R2). Similar to Object motion blur, it occurs after rendering and adds the ability to blur the environment as well as the object. The third version is Scene motion blur in Video Post's Scene event (the same type used in 3DS MAX R1). Scene motion blur applies the blur effect to the entire scene, acting on the absolute and relative (camera) motion of all objects in the scene. The technique you use for motion blur, or how you combine multiple techniques, depends on the effect you're trying to achieve.

The 3D Studio MAX User's Guide describes Object and Image motion blur as forms of smoothing an object's motion over time and describes Scene motion blur as an applied special effect. The manual indicates that you can combine the different types to get the best result. More than likely, you will have to combine and manipulate the different types to apply the actual motion blur you want. This section describes each type of motion blur and how they work separately, together, and relative to field rendering, which uses a similar method to effect "smooth" lines and motion.

Motion Blur Concepts

Most people think of motion blur in conjunction with photography. If an object is moving fast enough when a picture is taken, it appears blurred on the film. This is the result of the object being in one position when the camera shutter opens and in another position when the camera shutter closes. The blur effect is the result of an infinite number of copies of the object, each exposed for an infinitely small fraction of the total exposure time. The copies are exposed as the object moves from one position at the start of the exposure to a second position by the end of the exposure.

3DS MAX divides time into discrete segments and renders one motion blur copy of an appropriate object for each specified time segment. Settings control the size of the time segments and the number of motion blur samples.

Perhaps Object and Image motion blur should have been named Object and Image motion smoothing. Kinetix suggests you use the effects to smooth motion, as mentioned earlier, similar to rendering to fields, which is where you get the most benefit from these settings. To add motion blur trails as a special effect requires you to start combining the effects and using Scene motion blur in Video Post. The Object and Image motion blur technique that 3DS MAX employs is mathematically and technically correct. Unfortunately, it is not what viewer's might expect to see for motion blur. The top left ball in Figure 29.10 shows the way 3DS MAX renders Object motion blur. The bottom left ball shows Image motion blur. The balls on the right show the same blur effects as those on the right, with a lead ball composited over them to create the special effects motion blur trails people expect to see.

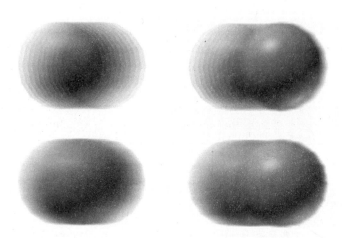

The multiple copies created with Object motion blur appear to have greater density in the middle than at the ends. Most observers would consider this to be an image of something vibrating rapidly rather than moving forward. Your natural perception of moving objects sets an expectation that the leading edges of the object will be sharply focused, whereas the trailing edges blur back along the line of motion. That's why you draw "speed lines" behind objects in motion and why traditional animators are taught to draw motion blur by blurring the trailing edges only. Image motion blur comes closer to a true motion blur effect, but it still looks more like a distorted original object over time. As shown in Figure 29.10, simulating a special effect motion blur technique in Video Post generates the best results.

Creating the effect shown for the bottom ball in Figure 29.10 requires that you use Video Post to composite a less-blurred version of the object in front of the more-blurred object. The trick involved here is to get the less-blurred object to lead the more-blurred object. The amount of lead required depends on the type of motion blur and the settings for each type. The following exercise shows how to create the Video Post blur, including how to:

- Create the blur and lead objects to create realistic motion blur.

- Render the series of images of the lead objects that are composited over the blurred objects.

MOTION BLUR WITH VIDEO POST

1. Load blurtest.max from the accompanying CD-ROM.

2. Four spheres make up the scene. The two spheres to the right in the Front view are the lead objects that receive a slight blur. The other spheres are the blur objects that receive more blur. The first step is to render the lead objects we need to composite in Video Post. Click the Display tab and the Hide By Name button. Select the two spheres named "object blur 2" and "image blur 2" and click the Hide button.

3. To assign the slight blur to the lead objects, you have to access their object properties. Select and right-click on the top sphere to open its pop-up menu. Select Properties.

4. In the Motion Blur section at the bottom of the Object Properties dialog select Object, then click OK.

5. Repeat the same steps to the bottom sphere. This time select Image in the Motion Blur section, then click OK.

6. Activate the Camera viewport and click Render Scene.

7. Accept the settings making these changes. Choose Save File in the Render Output section and choose a directory and file name for your images. Save the files as Targa (.tga) files with the name lead.tga. You will create a series of targa files named lead0000.tga, lead0001.tga, and so on. Click Setup and make sure 32 bit is checked so an alpha channel is saved with the images.

8. Click the Common Parameters header bar to zip up that section of the window. In the MAX Default Scanline A Buffer section, click the Apply button for both Object Motion Blur and Image Motion Blur.

9. Change the durations setting for both Object and Image Motion Blur to 1.0.

10. Click Render. The 51 images are rendered to the directory you specified.

11. We are finished with the two lead spheres. Click the Display tab and the Unhide All button to unhide the two other spheres.

12. Click the Hide By Name button and select the two spheres named Object Blur lead and Image Blur lead and click the hide button.

13. Click the Rendering drop-down menu and select Video Post.

14. In the Video Post window, click the Add Scene Event button.

15. In the Add Scene Event dialog, click Render Options.

16. Change the durations setting for both Object and Image Motion Blur to 6.0. Click OK to close all dialogs and return to the Video Post window. You may wish to click the Zoom Extents button to see the full range bars for the events you're adding.

17. Click the Add Image Input button and click the Files button in its dialog.

18. Open the directory where you rendered you targa files and click the lead0000.tga filename.

19. In the File Name section at the top of the dialog, change the four zeros to an asterisk. Inserting this wildcard (*) informs 3DS MAX to create an image file list (IFL) of all the Targa files in that directory that start with lead. The IFL file is saved in the same directory and will be inserted into Video Post as the image event.

20. Select both the Camera01 Scene Event and the lead0000.ifl Image Event. Click the Add Image Layer Event button.

21. Select Alpha Compositor and click OK. This uses the alpha channel information in the Targa images to composite the files over the rendered scene.

22. Deselect all queue events and click the Add Image Output Event and click Files.

23. Save as an .AVI file and choose a directory for your file. Your Video Post Queue should now look like Figure 29.11.

FIGURE 29.11

The rendering queue for the video post motion blur exercise should look like this.

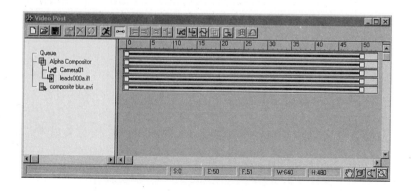

24. Click the Execute Sequence button and set the Range from 0 to 50 and the size to 320 × 240. Click Render.

25. Your composited .AVI file will be saved where you specified. You can see the rendered composite blurs in the blurs.avi file on the accompanying CD-ROM. The file will show the differences between using Object and Image Motion Blur.

Object and Image Motion Blur

You can use Object and the new Image motion blur to reproduce an analog-like blur and "smoothness" for moving objects and characters (machine parts or character appendages, for example). Recall the discussion in the rendering to "Frames Versus Fields" section of Chapter 28, "Rendering Animation." The Render to Fields setting is also used to enhance the smoothness of animated objects, specifically when rendering for video playback. The effect from field rendering is similar but not the same as the one employed by Image motion blur.

Field rendering divides a given frame into two scanline images. Each half is combined with half of a preceding or following frame's scanlines. The resulting frames contain two half-images offset in time. When the frames are played by a field-savvy device, the animation is "smoother," resulting from the two-fields-per-frame video playback, which provides more moving image representations over time.

TIP

Unlike Object motion blur, field rendering does have the capability to smooth the motion in an Environment map. Rendering to Fields actually works with buffer information, not the geometry to create its sub-frame samples, by dividing and reconstituting the scanline output over a series of frames. Scene motion blur and the new Image motion blur settings also work with buffer information and offer the option of affecting the environment map.

Object or Image motion blur can certainly enhance, and sometimes entirely substitute, for field rendering. Object and Image motion blur provide discrete control over individual objects in the scene, dithering between object copies and the number of sub-frame images over a range of motion. If you are rendering animation to digital video, such as AVI or FLC formats, and you want to simultaneously provide a smoother animation for playback on video tape without rendering to fields (inappropriate for digital video), it

will be worth the extra planning and rendering time to employ Object or
Image motion blur.

To apply Object or Image motion blur to individual objects, you must select
the object in the viewport and right-click to reveal the object's pull-down
menu. When you select Properties, the Object Properties dialog appears (see
Figure 29.12). Use this dialog to enable motion blur by clicking the appropriate check box. You must specify Object or Image motion blur parameters
in the Render Scene or Add/Edit Scene event dialog (refer to Figure 29.7).
When you start the render, those objects that have their properties set for
this effect are blurred.

FIGURE 29.12

*You set Object or
Image motion blur by
right-clicking an object
and editing its object
properties.*

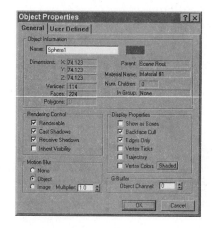

Object motion blur works by creating multiple copies of the objects to which
it is applied. In doing so, the object's modifier stack is evaluated for each
copy created for the blur. This causes animated translation, rotation, scale,
and modifier parameters to be evaluated for the time point of each copy. So,
for example, if you translate, rotate, and scale an animated bent cylinder,
all these transformations are reflected in the object motion copies.
Animated materials are not reflected in the object copies. If an animated
space warp is bound to the object, the animation of the space warp is not
reflected in the copies. If the binding flexibility is animated, it is reflected
(because it is on the object's stack).

Image motion blur is actually applied after the scene is rendered, so the
object's modifier stack is irrelevant. Instead of making copies of the individual objects, it creates a smearing effect behind each object. Generally,
Image motion blur gives a smoother appearance blur than Object motion
blur.

Duration Subdivisions

The value in the Duration Subdivisions field represents the number of copies to be rendered for each frame. The number you enter in this field is critical to the production of a successful effect. If the number is too small, the copies are completely separate—an effect called strobing. If the number is too large, the copies pile up on top of each other and the result looks more like a solid smudge than a motion blur. Also, rendering motion blur copies takes time. Rendering more copies than you need can waste a considerable amount of time for a long animation.

3DS MAX imposes a maximum value of sixteen copies. You can calculate a good starting number by using the following formula:

Duration Subdivisions >= (distance/size)/overlap

The following list describes the formula's variables:

- **Distance:** The distance the object travels over the Duration setting. In general, if duration is set to 1.0, distance equals the distance traveled over one frame. If duration is set to 0.5, distance equals the distance traveled over half a frame.

- **Size:** The length of the object along the line of motion.

- **Overlap:** A value between 0 and 1 that controls how much the copies overlap each other. The smaller the overlap value, the more the copies overlap one another. The overlap value should usually be less than 0.5; anything greater causes the objects to appear to separate.

Figure 29.13 shows a motion-blurred ball that exhibits strobing as a result of too small a value being entered in the Duration Subdivisions field.

FIGURE 29.13

Strobing from too few Duration Subdivisions.

Samples

Samples controls the amount of dithering that occurs between the copies. As this value decreases, the samples are selected randomly from the Duration Subdivisions. The lower the value, the fewer samples are selected, corresponding to fewer, differentiated objects (looks grainy or dithered).

The lowest valid value of 1 results in maximum dithering; the maximum valid value is equal to the Duration Subdivisions value and produces more copies that appear semi-transparent.

Dithering is not generally recommended for digital video because the compression algorithms employed by codecs can produce color banding. So, in the preceding ball example, if you were rendering to a digital video format, you would want to carefully adjust the Samples setting, which controls dithering in Object motion blur (see the "Samples" section later in this chapter). Also make sure dithering (color averaging as opposed to transparency blending) is not checked in the Rendering section of Preferences. In the Render Scene dialog, set the Samples value to the highest possible setting (least amount of dither), equal to the number of Duration Subdivisions. Also remember that apparent object movement caused by camera motion is not taken into account by Object or Image motion blur, although it is taken into account by Scene motion blur.

Duration

Duration controls the amount of motion applied to the rendering on each frame. The 3D Studio MAX User's Guide describes this as similar to the amount of time the camera's shutter is open. Refer to the previous "Duration Subdivisions" section for the description of calculating distance traveled under the Duration Subdivision field. The number of copies specified by the Duration Subdivisions field is spread over the distance covered in the number of frames specified in the Duration field. The Duration value can be less than one, which means that the copies are compressed into a distance less than what is covered by one frame.

An interesting point about Object motion blur concerns where the copies are placed. The copies are spread over the distance specified by the Duration value and then the copies are centered on the position of the object on that frame. This means that when you look at a blurred image that is produced with Object motion blur, the true position of the object is in the center of the blur effect. Figure 29.14 shows a non-blurred ball composited over its motion-blurred image.

The results you get from Object and Image motion blur are very similar with low duration settings (1 frame or under). The effect at that duration level can produce a subtle smoothing to your object's motion. Above that setting, the blur becomes very apparent and takes on an entirely different use. At duration settings above 1 frame, Object motion blur looks like a jittering object and Image motion blur tends to make your object look distorted.

Image motion blur differs another way from Object motion blur in that it has the option of affecting the environment map as well as the geometry in the scene. By selecting this option in the object's Properties pop-up menu, you force the renderer to evaluate the bitmap you apply to the environment.

FIGURE 29.14

A non-blurred ball composited over its motion-blurred image.

Scene Motion Blur

Scene motion blur is best at emphasizing rapid motion and is more of a special effect than an aide in smoothing motion (which Object motion blur is best at). The effects of Scene motion blur are applied to the entire scene after it is rendered. It does consider camera movements as well. You may find you get the best overall results by combining Object or Image motion blur with Scene motion blur. Use Scene motion blur to provide the general blur effect and Object or Image motion blur to provide extra dithering between the Scene motion blur copies.

Scene Motion Blur Settings

Scene motion blur is applied in Video Post. You control it with entries in the Add or Edit Scene Event dialog in the Scene Options area (see Figure 29.15). Unlike Object motion blur, multiple copies of individual objects are not being generated. Rather, multiple renderings based on the durations setting your specify are being rendered and composited with each other to create a single image.

A check box enables the Scene motion blur effect. When enabled, all objects in the Scene event view are subject to the blur effect—including materials and Environment maps, but excluding parent events acting on the Scene, such as layer composites or filters. The Duration Subdivisions field specifies the number of copies to render. The Duration value works the same for Scene motion blur as it does for Object motion blur. The default for Scene motion blur duration is set at 0.5, or half the default value of Object motion blur. This assumes that Scene motion blur is strategically employed to convey movement inclusive of apparent camera motion, which would take place within the frame's duration. (See the next section.)

FIGURE 29.15

Entries in the Video Post Edit Scene Event dialog for applying Scene motion blur.

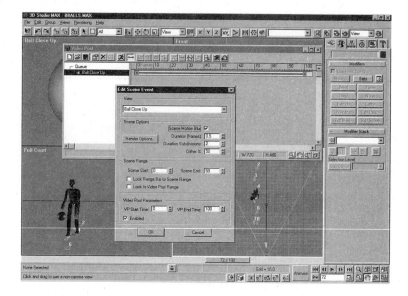

You have the option to dither in conjunction with applying Scene motion blur. Dithering of this type is a method of smoothing the edges between the overlapping redundant color regions in the frame. The pixels are mixed so that the edges of objects appear to blend together. The Dither Percent field sets the percentage of dither applied to the copies created by Scene motion blur. A value of 0 produces distinct edges, whereas a value of 100 fully dithers the copies, producing semi-transparent edges within the blur.

Controlling Composite Output

Output events are generally standalone events in the queue and are usually the last event. Multiple output events can be used to simultaneously produce sequential files and digital animation, such as AVI files. Unlike the Input and Effects event types, which act on other events, the Output event becomes a child of the event it acts upon. As such, it writes a file composed of the information that has been processed up to the point in the queue where the parent resides, which may, for example, represent an incomplete alpha composite. Adding Output events in the Queue is like inserting the lamp in the slide projector at a point in the middle of the stack of slides. The slides (events) that fall behind it never "see the light."

In Practice: Compositing Effects

- **Creative Principles:** Basic aesthetic techniques, some unique to 3D graphics as an artistic medium, should be practiced in an effort to compose and animate the scene. Identify a center of interest. Use asymmetry to suggest movement and control balance. Position objects strategically. Plan ahead for the playback medium.

- **Utilitarian and Collaborative use of Video Post:** Understand and use Video Post for practical workgroup purposes. Prepare images and animation for professional compositing or editing. Use it to visualize and prototype for a larger comprehensive animation effort.

- **Video Post—the Magic Lantern:** The Video Post queue is analogous to a very special slide projector. The lamp's beam navigates through transparency, opacity, and other effects as it moves through time. Effects are determined by the object between the light source and the surface upon which the light falls, as well as by the speed and direction the light travels. Use single frame renderings to view the progress dialog's Current Task readout. This gives you a practiced understanding of the rendering process.

- **Create sequences carefully and conservatively:** Save your Video Post file (VPX) and MAX file (MAX) frequently and systematically (there is no Undo or Redo in Video Post). Select events and highlight range bars by clicking the Queue event label, not the range bar (to avoid moving the start and end points).

- **Video Post time versus Scene Time:** Uncheck the Lock to Video Post Range and Lock Range Bar to Scene Range boxes in the Scene event to add multiple ranges from the scene and manipulate the direction and speed of animation. It is here that you can reverse the direction of animation without actually affecting the keyframes.

- **Blurring the lines:** Use Object or Image motion blur and Scene motion blur together to create realistic animation of quick motions and smooth out jerkiness in moving objects and characters. Understand the differences between Object, Image, and Scene motion blur as well as the smoothing effect of field rendering. Develop strategies for motion based on playback media. For example, avoid dithering when your playback medium is digital video.

- **Smart events, effective effects:** Start and end parameters are easily lost when you change settings during the event edit. Keep a record of all parameters in the sequence. Make copies or create substitute events and use the Swap tool to replace events rather than edit them.

NETWORK RENDERING

The animator's credo should read, "Be creative, plan ahead, and beg, borrow, or steal time on every machine available for rendering." The latest processors on the market have accelerated rendering, but when you deal with hundreds and thousands of images including Video Post effects and complex geometry, it still takes a long time.

Thankfully, 3D Studio MAX has the capability to use any size networks to render animations. You can use one copy of 3DS MAX to render on up to 10,000 computers with no extra software or fee. Best of all, 3DS MAX integrates with the NT networking and security systems to give you a fault tolerant solution. If the power goes down in the middle of a job, 3DS MAX can pick up rendering right where it left off as soon as power is restored.

Regardless of your needs and current network configuration, users with one to hundreds of computers can benefit from network rendering. Many companies dedicate a group of computers to only rendering purposes, known as a "rendering farm." Smaller companies, without the luxury of having dedicated rendering computers, can set up all available networked computers to render overnight. If you have just one computer, you can still use network rendering for batch processing multiple projects.

If you already have a network setup, network rendering is fairly easy. If not, you have a little more work ahead. Network rendering requires Windows NT with network drivers installed and a minimum installation of 3DS MAX to work properly; however, there is no need to be logged on to the computer for network rendering to take place.

In this chapter, you will see how to set up network rendering for various types of network topologies and explore the various components of 3DS MAX's network rendering capabilities. This chapter examines the following topics:

- Networking basics
- Components of 3DS MAX's network rendering
- Setting up 3DS MAX for network rendering
- Rendering a job
- Using the Queue Manager

With the 3DS MAX network rendering system, if two rendering jobs are assigned to the same computer (referred to as a server), that server starts the second job after it has completed the first. With multiple servers involved, however, any one job doesn't need to be completed before another job is started by another server on the network. If a user submits a one-frame job, for example, it is assigned to the first available server. Because the job only has one frame, requiring only one server to render, the other servers start any new jobs that are submitted. In this particular one-frame job scenario, the currently rendering computer joins the rendering of the new job(s) when it has finished its current job.

The following section covers other fundamentals you need to be familiar with before you begin working with 3DS MAX's networking features.

Networking Basics

You must have administrator privileges on the computers you're planning to use for network rendering. Without administrator privileges, you probably won't be able to install network drivers for NT, much less get them running. For step-by-step instructions on setting up a network in Windows NT, refer to your NT documentation or the 3DS MAX online help on network rendering accessible within MAX. If you are currently part of a network, work with your network administrator when setting up MAX's network rendering. Following is a brief overview of networking basics.

The TCP/IP Protocol

TCP/IP stands for Transmission Control Protocol/Internet Protocol. A network protocol is a "language" that enables two or more computers to talk to each other. TCP/IP is one of many types of protocols used by networks. Protocols are languages computers can use to communicate with each other. Computers can use many protocols simultaneously. For instance, an NT-based computer could access Novell NetWare, Microsoft Windows, and UNIX servers all at the same time by using completely different protocols. This way, you have access to all types of computers from your PC, not just IBM-compatible computers. You can't use multiple instances of a protocol at the same time, however, mainly because there is no need.

After a protocol is initialized by a computer, it can communicate with as many computers as possible. You don't need the same protocol for each computer with which you communicate. Because of its universal acceptance as a networking standard, especially across the Internet, TCP/IP has been chosen as the protocol for 3DS MAX's network rendering system.

TCP/IP uses an IP address to talk to any computer. An IP address is a series of numbers that represents a computer on a TCP/IP network. For instance, your computer's TCP/IP address might look like the following:

192.144.92.143

All TCP/IP addresses use a four-number combination to designate a computer on the network and each computer must have a unique address to communicate correctly. Each of the four sets of numbers, when combined, represents a specific address. Think of it as a house number, city, state, and zip code for your computer. Windows NT is capable of detecting other computers on the network that use the same address and alerts you that the protocol hasn't been loaded, as a result. To remedy this, you need to get a unique address. Most networks use one of two TCP/IP address systems: DHCP (Dynamic Host Configuration Protocol) or a fixed address.

DHCP dynamically assigns a new TCP/IP address to your computer each time you log on the network. This way, a company can have a pool of IP addresses that it can swap in and out of computer systems on the network. DHCP is useful when you have a company with multiple subnets all using the same address. A user can move to any subnet and always have a valid TCP/IP address.

When using DHCP, there is no need to configure the address manually. DHCP is not recommended for 3DS MAX network rendering, however, because 3DS MAX needs to know a rendering computer's address and use that address all the time. The address cannot be changed automatically. You should avoid using DHCP if you want consistent performance from your network rendering setup. If your existing setup uses DHCP, ask your administrator for a fixed range of addresses to use.

Fixed addresses are the preferred method for network rendering in 3DS MAX. A fixed address remains assigned to that computer regardless of who is logged on or when.

The ideal environment for network rendering is a closed network. This consists of a group of computers that is not part of a company-wide network. Setting up a rendering farm on a company-wide network is a bit more challenging. Besides extra configuration headaches, there is the potential for a considerable increase in network traffic, thereby slowing overall throughput. Consult with your network administrator throughout the setup process to avoid any conflicts.

The Components of 3DS MAX Network Rendering

The major components of network rendering in 3DS MAX include 3DS MAX itself, the network rendering Manager and Server, and the Queue Manager. All these components come with 3DS MAX and are installed as part of a default installation.

NOTE

All computers that take part in network rendering must have at least a minimal installation of 3D Studio MAX installed and authorized.

Understanding the Manager and Server

New in 3DS MAX release 2, the Manager and Server programs are now accessible from your Kinetix program group. In release 1.x, these programs ran in DOS windows. Now, each opens as a modeless Windows dialog, so there is no longer any need to open DOS windows and enter command-line commands (see Figure 30.1).

FIGURE 30.1

The Manager and Server programs now open as Windows dialogs. No more DOS commands necessary!

The Manager program is run on only one computer on the network. It sets up that one computer as the ultimate manager of network rendering, which identifies and tracks activity on all servers on the network. The Manager's main role is to coordinate the delegation of frames to each server. The Manager also maintains a list of jobs submitted and pending, and acts on those jobs as current ones are completed. Manager runs only on an NT-based computer and must have a fixed TCP/IP address.

The Server program enables a computer to act as a server (referred to as a "rendering slave" in previous releases). The Server receives frame rendering jobs from the Manager. When a job is received from the Manager, Server launches 3D Studio MAX in a special server mode. By default, you only see the rendering scene dialog open onscreen. You do have the option of having the virtual frame buffer image display on each server. This option is designated at the time of job submission.

Every computer on the network can be a server, including the same computer designated as the manager. Therefore, every computer on your network will be rendering frames.

NEW TO R2

3DS MAX release 2 is now a true multitasking application. This means you can actually open two or more instances of MAX on the same computer at the same time and have them rendering two different jobs. You could also have one instance rendering while you work on another project in the other, but don't get carried away. It's a good idea to only open one instance for each processor in your system (for example, dual pentium equals open two instances).

Thanks to multitasking capabilities, the network rendering manager can submit and accept rendering job assignments simultaneously. In previous releases, you had to open 3DS MAX on the manager, submit the job, exit 3DS MAX, then start the Server program on that computer to start rendering.

Understanding the Queue Manager

The most interactive portion of network rendering lies in the Queue Manager program (see Figure 30.2). Inside Queue Manager, you have complete control of your network rendering process—including viewing and reordering every job sent to the Manager. Queue Manager doesn't have to be run on any computer taking part in network rendering; it simply needs to be on the network somehow. It could even be located at a remote site. Imagine leaving the office for the evening and being able to check up and manage your network rendering off-site. If you have a remote access account, it's possible.

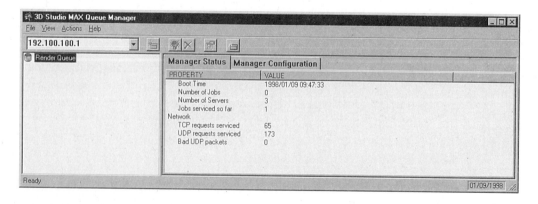

FIGURE 30.2

The Queue Manager provides status on submitted jobs and can be run from any computer on the network.

Setting Up 3DS MAX for Network Rendering

After your computer is properly configured for a network, you're ready to set up 3DS MAX's network rendering system. The following sections describe the simple setup process and identify some of the important files involved. You will also learn how to perform a minimal install on machines that will function as network rendering servers but won't be used as 3DS MAX workstations.

Installing Necessary Files

New in 3DS MAX release 2, all elements needed for network rendering are installed as part of the default setup. As previously mentioned, you don't need to own a separate copy of 3DS MAX for each rendering server on your network. You can install the same copy of the program on all servers using the Custom Setup option. What you're doing is installing the minimum files necessary to run 3DS MAX. Servers set up this way do not require a hardware lock and cannot be used as a workstation; they will only be able to network render.

The main elements you don't need on your servers are the maps that come with 3DS MAX, as well as the tutorial files. This reduces the amount of disk space you'll need on each server from 140 MB for a full install, to 37 MB for a minimal install. Simply run the setup program on the 3DS MAX 2 CD-ROM and choose Custom for the setup type. On the Select Components screen, clear all the checkboxes except for Program Files, 3DS MAX R2, and Support Files. Figure 30.3 shows the steps involved in setting up a computer as a server with the minimal components necessary.

TIP

Make sure to have your 3DS MAX serial number and authorization code handy during the installation process. You'll need the serial number during installation from the CD-ROM. You'll need the authorization code when you run the Authorize program from the Kinetix program group.

FIGURE 30.3

The installation dialogs for 3DS MAX. Choose Custom Setup and only check the boxes for Program Files, 3DS MAX R2, and Support Files.

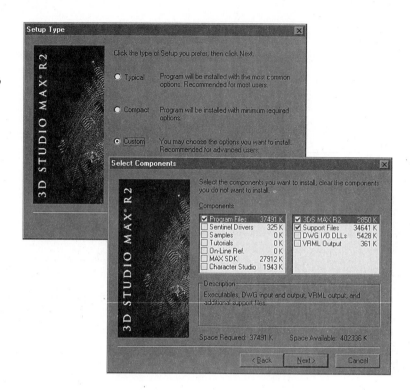

Installing Third Party Plug-Ins for Network Rendering

Because 3D Studio MAX is component-oriented, there are times when you will install a third party plug-in on your production computer and not on the rendering farm itself. 3DS MAX does not know which plug-ins you intend to use for network rendering, so you must make sure a copy of each third party plug-in is installed on every network rendering system.

Many commercial plug-ins for 3DS MAX use an authorization protection scheme. With this setup, you may have to call the developer and authorize the plug-in for each machine you intend to use it on for a fee. Some plug-in developers, however, enable you to install an unauthorized copy of their plug-in for every computer on your network. In this case, the plug-in does not allow you to use it within MAX, but it can be accessed for rendering purposes.

Configuring the Manager and Server Programs

In order for network rendering to occur, the Manager and Servers must be connected. Figure 30.4 shows the messages each program's dialog would report for a two computer network that is connected and ready for rendering. In previous releases of 3DS MAX, you had to manually edit manager.ini and server.ini files with the appropriate TCP/IP addresses. Release 2 has made changes to each program that takes your input and edits the .ini files for you. It makes setup a breeze. The first time you launch the Network Rendering Manager or Server you are prompted to configure the service (see Figure 30.4). When you click OK, you see the properties dialog for that particular service.

FIGURE 30.4

When you run the Server and Manager programs for the first time, you receive this dialog prompting you to configure each service.

Setting Manager Properties

Figure 30.5 shows the properties of the Manager. In most cases, you may simply accept the defaults and click OK. The only thing to be aware of is the Port settings, which must match for the manager and server. By default, the settings do match and you shouldn't have to change them. The only reason you may need to change Port settings is if you know another program on the network uses the 3DS MAX defaults. Consult your network administrator for that information.

Setting Server Properties

Figure 30.6 shows the properties of the server. Once again, the defaults should work fine. The critical entry in this dialog is the field for Manager Name or IP Address. Only two values can be expressed here: a TCP/IP address or a computer name. This value must be the name or address of your Network Rendering Manager. Without the proper information, the computer is not able to take part in network rendering. Enter the name or number in the space labeled Manager Name or IP Address. Figure 30.5 shows the manager properties with an IP address entered.

FIGURE 30.5

The Properties dialog for the Network Manager. 3DS MAX takes the information you enter here and creates the manager.ini file it needs to run the program in the future.

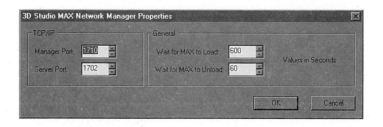

FIGURE 30.6

The Manager's IP address must be added to the properties dialog for each server. The IP address 192.100.100.1 has been entered in this example.

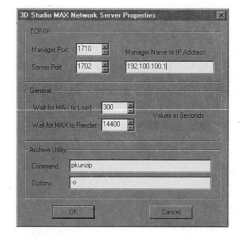

Rendering a Job

Try a test run before embarking on a major rendering job. If you can get two computers to talk to each other, you can get a whole room talking as well, provided that the computers are configured similarly. In the following section, you'll see how to assign a job from the 3DS MAX rendering dialog. As well, there is a discussion on setting up maps and map paths.

The Job Assignment Dialog

When you're ready to Network render, check the Net Render option in the Render Scene dialog or the Video Post Execute dialog from within 3DS MAX. At that point, the Job Assignment dialog appears as seen in Figure 30.7. The Job Assignment window enables you to specify a manager to send the job to, as well as the servers you wish to use. The options available in the Job Assignment dialog are discussed in the following sections.

NOTE

For any of the steps in this section to work properly, you first have to run the manager program from the manager computer and the server program on all servers involved in the rendering for that job.

FIGURE 30.7

The name Swamp Scene (100-200) is the job's name, The IP address of the manager computer shows up in the Network Manager field (192.100.100.1 in this example).

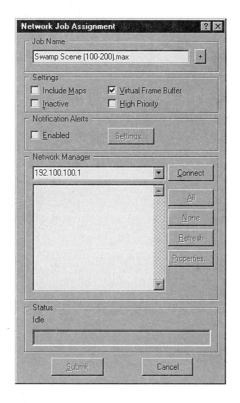

The Job Name

The Job Name field enables you to specify a name for the job that is displayed in the Queue Manager. Pick a name that is representative of what you're rendering. If you are rendering a swamp scene from frames 100 to 200, for instance, the name may be

Swamp Scene (100–200)

With this type of naming, anyone who looks at the job list instantly knows what the scene is and how many frames of that scene are being rendered. If a job exists with the current name you have selected, you are warned and you must choose another name before continuing.

WARNING

When naming jobs, note that you cannot use ";", "\", or "/" as part of the name. 3DS MAX reports an error if you try to do so.

NOTE

All current jobs are given their own directories, based on the job name, in the Manager's 3dsmax2/Network/Jobs directory.

The Include Maps Option

Configuring this option incorrectly could cause your entire job to fail. So what does it do? When this box is checked, 3D Studio MAX archives the scene and all its associated maps into one file and distributes that file to each server. When the file reaches the server, it is unarchived and the rendering process begins, ensuring that every computer has exactly the same maps, and as a result, almost no rendering using this method fails. But what are the caveats?

- Each server must have the same archiving program installed as the computer issuing the rendering job using the Include Maps option.

- Each server must have access, through path settings, to the archiving program specified in the server.ini file.

- Only one archiving program can be used for a rendering farm.

- If the proper options aren't specified in the server.ini file, a server may fail. This usually happens when the archiving program requests user input, such as a confirmation.

WARNING

Both PKZIP and PKUNZIP are limited to the DOS naming convention (eight-character name and three-character extension). All operations that use the Include Maps option (job names, map files, and scene files) must adhere to this format.

A better option than using the Include Maps button is to locate all maps in a common map directory on the network. For example, on the Manager computer, create a map directory that is shared on the network and have all servers log on to this directory. This technique is discussed in detail in the "Maps Central" section later in this chapter.

Job Assignment Options

The following are new job assignment options in Release 2:

- **Virtual Frame Buffer:** This option lets you have the virtual frame buffer image display on each server. This way you can see the frames being rendered by each server. This might be a good way to assure things are going well.

- **High Priority:** This option moves the current job to the top of the rendering queue, above any previously submitted jobs.

Picking a Manager

Because it is possible to have multiple managers present on a network, you need to choose one to use for your rendering job. The manager you specify can be either by name or TCP/IP address. 3D Studio MAX remembers the last four managers entered in the Manager drop-down list.

After you choose the manager you want to use, click the Connect button. If everything is set up properly, 3DS MAX connects and a list of the servers registered with that manager appears (see Figure 30.8). If nothing appears or you receive a connection refused message, you have several problems to check out.

1. Make sure the Manager program is running on the computer you want to use as a manager. If it is not running, select the Manager program from the Kinetix program group.

2. If Manager is running, check to see whether you typed the right computer name or IP address in the Job Assignment dialog.

3. If 3DS MAX appears to connect but no servers are listed, make sure the Server program is running on each computer you intend to render on.

4. Last, check to see whether each computer is physically connected to the network. You can usually do this by going to the File Manager (or Network Neighborhood in NT 4.0) and connecting to each computer.

FIGURE 30.8

Three servers are listed in this example. The arrows next to Houndpuppy and P200 indicate they have been selected for rendering on this job. Topdog will not be included (although it is available).

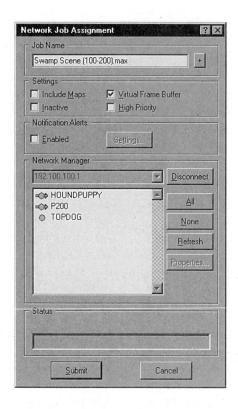

The colored dots that appear next to their name indicate the server's current status. See the next section to understand and manage servers and the various states in which they may be.

Server States

Servers can be in four potential states: Ready (green), Busy (yellow), Absent from the network (gray), and Error (red). You typically see yellow while other jobs are currently rendering on that server. A Red dot signifies some kind of problem, which usually happens when a previous job fails on that server, and the server is in a holding pattern until the job is either canceled or the situation that caused the error is resolved.

No matter what state the server is in, you can assign your job to it. The only purpose of the colored dots is to make you aware of what the current status of the server is. Assigning your job to that server ensures that as soon as that server is available, it will pick up your job and begin rendering. If a computer is in an error state, however, you first have to remove it from that job using the Queue Manager. Otherwise, the server can never pick up your job.

Map Paths, Shared Drives, and UNC

Perhaps the most challenging part of getting network rendering right is the use of Texture maps across the network. Computers can access multiple directories on multiple computers and pull down multiple versions of the same file. This can result in mass confusion not only while working on the project, but it also can be a nightmare when it comes to rendering the scene across the network. In this section, you learn the best way to organize your network rendering farm to load maps and save files.

Map Central

When several people are working on a scene, access to maps at a central location is necessary. Thus, everyone involved always has access to the most recent version of textures on which the 2D artists have worked. In Windows NT, this type of setup is common. Computers can mount drives on other computers, known as shared drives, and utilize the drives just as if they were local to their computer. Having a central location for maps is key to organizing network rendering.

WARNING

Novell-based network servers understand only the DOS naming structure: eight characters with a three-character extension (see Figure 8.3).

You can use the following organizational steps to make sure your maps are loaded by every rendering server during a net render:

1. At the beginning of a project, set up a location on your network where everyone on the project has access. Then make directories for maps and scenes. Be sure to give the directories a meaningful name.

2. Next, have every person on the project connect to the central computer by using the same path and drive letter. For instance, have everyone access the maps as drive letter M. You can do this in File Manager or by using Network Neighborhood in NT 4.0. Make sure you specify to reconnect to this drive at logon. This way, a user is always connected to that drive by using the same drive letter each time he or she logs on.

    If possible, place maps and scenes in the same directory. 3DS MAX looks for maps for a scene in the same directory where it loaded the scene the first time. From there, it looks in the map paths directories.

3. If you have a rendering farm or other computers that aren't used in the production except for rendering, set up the drive letter assignment the exact same way as the other computers. If you are using the previous example, for instance, every server would be connected to the maps directory also using the drive letter M.

4. If you cannot use the same drive letter, connect to the computer using any drive letter. The key here is to make sure the computers are connected.

When the file is sent to be network rendered, it looks first in the same directory as the MAX file and then it searches out the maps in the directories specified in the MAX file itself. Finally, it looks in the map paths configured in the Configure Paths option in the File menu.

NOTE

Map paths are stored in the 3dsmax.ini file for a particular computer.

If you use the steps previously mentioned, all the maps should be picked up by the second step. This is because 3DS MAX uses what is known as UNC (Universal Naming Convention) for map path storage. This means that a map named weave1.tga stored on a computer named Mapserver in the Carpets directory would be stored in the .max file as

\\MAPSERVER\CARPETS\WEAVE1.TGA.

WARNING

3DS MAX will "hardwire" the directory of a locally stored map file. As a result, even if the file is available on a network somewhere, the server attempts to find the file in the same directory on the server's hard drive. To avoid having this problem, make sure all maps are stored and accessed in the material editor from a common location on some networked map server.

Notice that no drive letter is stored in the path information. UNC doesn't rely on letters; it only relies on computer names. That's why you can be connected to the computer by using any drive letter. As long as you're connected, 3DS MAX will find the map. Note that if you want to have the UNC information for a file that is stored locally, you can connect to your computer through File Manager.

Output Paths

Much of the same information for setting up map paths for a network rendering farm applies to output directories. After the file is rendered, where does it go?

Once again, setting up a common location for output is critical for rendering farms. If 3D Studio MAX cannot write the rendered file, the rendering server fails on that particular job. You can use much of the same logic to specify where files go after they're rendered. The following organizational steps outline how to best configure paths in a net rendering setup.

1. Set up a directory on a central computer where all the output from a rendering is stored. Make sure everyone has access to the directory.

2. Have all users connect to the drive. For convenience, use a drive letter that makes sense, such as O. Make sure that all other computers taking place in network rendering are also connected to that computer and directory.

3. Once a job is rendered using network rendering, instruct every user to send output in the Rendering dialog to that computer and directory. Because 3DS MAX uses UNC, as long as the computer's connected, it is able to output to the location specified.

Single Computers and Maps

Much of what you have read applies to a multiple computer setup. If you're using a single computer to do batch rendering, your job for setting up map paths and output directories is much simpler.

The easiest way to make sure that a job finds all maps is to use the Configure Paths option in the File menu and add as many map paths as you need. If you're loading maps from another computer somewhere on the network, you have two options. The easiest and fastest method is to copy the files local to your computer. If you can't copy the files because of space constraints, create a map path to that computer. You first have to connect to the computer, however, using File Manager or Network Neighborhood.

NOTE

For faster map loading, reorganize the map paths so that the directories where maps are located are at the top of the list. 3D Studio MAX searches for maps by using this list in descending order.

Output is even easier. Specify a location on your hard drive or on the network to store the files.

The only caveat to loading maps from the network or sending output to the network is that if the network goes down for any reason, your rendering job fails. If space on your hard drive is a concern, it's best to clear off noncritical data by storing it somewhere on the network and moving the maps onto your hard drive. Remember that 3DS MAX fails if it can't find even one map or it can't store the rendered image in the location you specified. With respect to output, there is no contingency for looking for other hard drives or directories to store images in other places as a backup.

Network Rendering to FLCs and AVIs

Network rendering is primarily intended to render out still frames, but you may want to use it to render AVI or FLC files. The problem with AVI or FLC files is that they need to be assembled linearly. Frames must be submitted one after another. With network rendering, frames can finish rendering totally out of sequence.

Because of this limitation, when you choose FLC or AVI as the output file format, you are limited to network rendering on only one server. 3DS MAX does not enable you to choose more than one server. So how would you distribute a rendering across several computers using AVI or FLC as output? Easy. Use Video Post. The following sections describe how to use multiple computers to render out an AVI or FLC file, all using 3DS MAX.

Rendering from the Render Dialog

You can render AVIs or FLCs from the Rendering dialog by using network rendering as you normally would to render a sequence of still images. Then you can use Video Post to assemble them into an AVI or FLC. The following steps describe this process:

1. Choose the resolution to which you want to render. Remember that FLC and AVI files usually should be a lower resolution image than still frames.

2. Choose a still file format to which to render—TGA, TIF, JPG, and so on.

3. Next, choose the Net Render option.

4. Choose the Manager and servers as you normally would and then click Submit.

5. The frames are rendered as sequential still frames, distributed across the network.

Skip to the section "Putting It All Together" to see how to assemble all the frames into an AVI or FLC.

Rendering from Video Post

Video Post does enable you to render FLC or AVI files, but you are not be able to directly render to any digital format via network rendering. You can render to the network, however, using Video Post via still frame output. Then you can reuse Video Post to assemble your still frames into an FLC or AVI. See the next section, "Putting It All Together," for instructions. To render out still frames from Video Post, complete the following steps:

1. Set up your Video Post queue with all the transitions, filters, and compositing effects you need.

2. Add an Image Output event at the end of your Video Post queue and choose the output to be a still frame file format such as TGA, TIF, JPG, and so on.

3. Click the Execute Sequence button. Select the frames you want to render and the desired resolution.

4. Choose the Net Render option and then submit the job to the Manager using the servers you want.

Your animation is rendered to a sequence of still frames. From here, you're ready to go on to the next section.

Putting It All Together

Now that you have the entire sequence of frames rendered, you can use Video Post to assemble them into an FLC or AVI. Video Post enables you to take sequentially numbered frames via an Image Input Event and save the result using an Image Output event to an FLC or AVI. Use the following steps to accomplish this:

1. Go to Video Post and Add an Image Input event.

2. Choose the Files button in the dialog.

3. Select the First frame from your sequence, delete the number from it and add an asterisk in its place followed by the file extension. Click OK.

4. 3D Studio MAX automatically creates an IFL file (Image File List) that contains all the names of all of the images that are part of your sequence.

5. Add an Image Output event.

6. Choose the Files button and type a name for your file. Your file name should include an FLC or AVI extension.

7. Execute the sequence and choose Render.

3D Studio MAX and Video Post load each file from your sequential list and output it to an AVI or FLC file as seen in Figure 30.9. This file must be rendered locally. Unfortunately, you cannot render this part to the network, but this method is a sufficient workaround if you need to render output from either the Rendering dialog or Video Post that used net rendering to an AVI or FLC.

Image Input (Sequential Files)

FIGURE 30.9

Video Post with an IFL sequence assigned and set to render to an AVI file.

Image Output —
(Animation File Type)

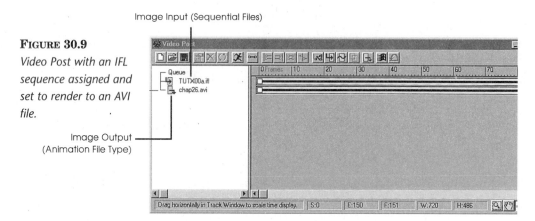

Using Queue Manager

You have your computer talking to the network and rendering away. Now how do you control this thing? All control elements for network rendering exist in the Queue Manager. The Queue Manager icon is located in the Kinetix program group with the rest of the 3DS MAX-related icons.

You can use Queue Manager to control all network rendering functions—from activating jobs to specifying what times a computer is available for rendering. You can run Queue Manager on any 32-bit Windows operating system and control the queue as long as the computer is hooked to the network. See Figure 30.10 for a breakdown of the Queue Manager Interface.

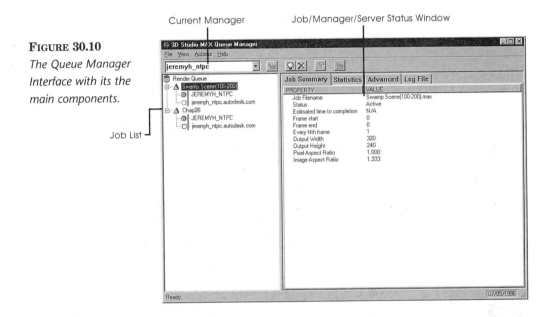

FIGURE 30.10

The Queue Manager Interface with its the main components.

Job Status and Control

The manager, server, and queue manager programs all report status of currently rendering jobs. Figure 30.11 shows the messages each program displays during a typical rendering.

Sometimes you need to escalate a job's priority in the rendering process or delegate when a server is available for rendering. All of this functionality is available through the Queue Manager. This section outlines key components in the Queue Manager that help you control the network rendering process.

Job and Server Priority

A job's priorities are ordered in descending priority. The jobs at the top of the queue receive priority over the later jobs—a job is rendered in the order it was received. Sometimes you want to reorder a job, however, so that it is completed before current jobs. With 3D Studio MAX 1.1, reordering a job is a trivial process. Just click the job name you want to reorder and drag it to the place you want in the queue. 3D Studio MAX automatically stops any jobs that now appear after your newly positioned job (if they were running) and begins rendering yours.

FIGURE 30.11

You receive real-time status on rendered frames, errors, and other important happenings from each of the manager, server, and queue manager programs.

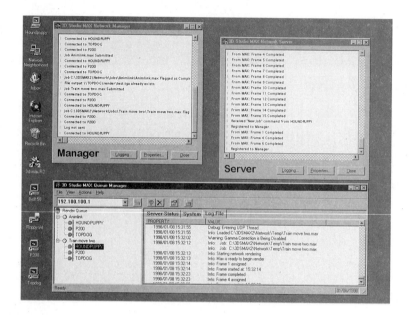

Scheduling Servers

Rendering servers are often used during the day as workstations for other tasks. Even if a computer is being used for another task, it can be used for network rendering purposes—as long as it is not running 3DS MAX. A job could be assigned to someone's computer while they're working in, for example, a 2D paint program. Needless to say, running 3D Studio MAX's rendering system and a sophisticated 2D paint program at the same time slows the computer to a crawl and potentially makes the user irate. To avoid this, you can specify through the Queue Manager interface when rendering servers are available for network rendering (see Figure 30.12).

Right-click any server and choose Properties. From there, you can select which hours the server is available or unavailable. The primary purpose of this window is to disable servers during certain times. By default, all servers are active all hours. Within this dialog, you can click and drag over the hours or a specific day(s) to disable a server. To do the same for a group of servers, use the Apply To button.

FIGURE 30.12

The Server Scheduling dialog. Through this window, you can block off one-hour increments for server availability.

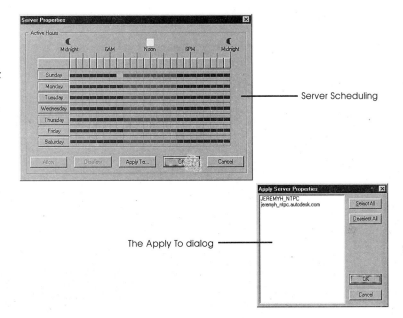

Server Scheduling

The Apply To dialog

NOTE

After you set availability for a server, that availability remains in place until you change it. The only way to change the times that server can be rendered to is by creating a fake, inactive job. From there, you can go into the Queue Manager and change the scheduling of the server.

In Practice: Network Rendering

- **Desktop mode:** The best way to get a handle on networking is to run services in the Desktop mode, which was described in this chapter. That way, you'll see all communication between the manager and its servers when you need to troubleshoot your net rendering setup. Once you feel comfortable with your setup, you can run both the Manager and Server programs as Windows NT services, eliminating the need to run them each time a network rendering is started. Refer to the 3DS MAX Online Help for instructions on setting up the Manager and Server programs as NT services.

- **Map organization:** When you're working with a large network, it's always a good idea to have all users place maps at a central storage location. All rendering servers should have access to that location. With this method, you'll never have to worry about a failed rendering due to missing map files.

- **Animation file output:** Because rendering an animation file, such as a FLC or AVI, across a network from MAX is impossible, you can use Video Post as a workaround. Render your animation to a sequence of still frames, much like a flip book, and use Video Post to compile the sequence into an animation format on one computer.

Index

S